ECONOMIC ORGANIZATION, INDUSTRIAL DYNAMICS AND DEVELOPMENT

Wherever possible, the articles in these volumes have been reproduced as originally published using facsimile reproduction, inclusive of footnotes and pagination to facilitate ease of reference.

For a list of all Edward Elgar published titles visit our website at www.e-elgar.com

Economic Organization, Industrial Dynamics and Development: Selected Essays

Giovanni Dosi

Professor of Economics
Sant'Anna School of Advanced Studies, Pisa, Italy

Edward Elgar
Cheltenham, UK • Northampton, MA, USA

Published by
Edward Elgar Publishing Limited
The Lypiatts
15 Lansdown Road
Cheltenham
Glos GL50 2JA
UK

Edward Elgar Publishing, Inc.
William Pratt House
9 Dewey Court
Northampton
Massachusetts 01060
USA

A catalogue record for this book is available from the British Library

Library of Congress Control Number: 2012946660

ISBN 978 1 84720 913 9 (cased)

Printed and bound by MPG Books Group, UK

Contents

Acknowledgements   viii
Preface   xi
Introduction   Giovanni Dosi   xiii

PART I   KNOWLEDGE, PROBLEM SOLVING AND THE ORGANIZATION OF ECONOMIC ACTIVITIES

1   Giovanni Dosi, Luigi Marengo and Giorgio Fagiolo (2005), 'Learning in
    Evolutionary Environments', in K. Dopfer (ed.), *The Evolutionary Foundations
    of Economics*, Chapter 9, Cambridge, UK: Cambridge University Press, 255–338   3
2   Giovanni Dosi, Marco Faillo and Luigi Marengo (2008), 'Organizational
    Capabilities, Patterns of Knowledge Accumulation and Governance Structures in
    Business Firms: An Introduction', *Organization Studies*, **29** (8 and 9), 1165–85   87
3   Luigi Marengo and Giovanni Dosi (2005), 'Division of Labor, Organizational
    Coordination and Market Mechanisms in Collective Problem-Solving', *Journal
    of Economic Behavior and Organization*, **58** (2), October, 303–26   108
4   Giovanni Dosi, Mike Hobday and Luigi Marengo (2003), 'Problem-Solving
    Behaviors, Organizational Forms, and the Complexity of Tasks', in Constance E.
    Helfat (ed.), *The SMS Blackwell Handbook of Organizational Capabilities:
    Emergence, Development, and Change*, Chapter 11, Malden, MA and Oxford,
    UK: Blackwell Publishing, 167–92   132
5   Giovanni Dosi, Daniel A. Levinthal and Luigi Marengo (2003), 'Bridging
    Contested Terrain: Linking Incentive-Based and Learning Perspectives on
    Organizational Evolution', *Industrial and Corporate Change*, **12** (2), 413–36   158
6   Giovanni Dosi and Marco Grazzi (2006), 'Technologies as Problem-Solving
    Procedures and Technologies as Input–Output Relations: Some Perspectives on
    the Theory of Production', *Industrial and Corporate Change*, **15** (1), 173–202   182

PART II   DEMAND AND MARKET DYNAMICS

7   Roberta Aversi, Giovanni Dosi, Giorgio Fagiolo, Mara Meacci and Claudia
    Olivetti (1999), 'Demand Dynamics with Socially Evolving Preferences',
    Industrial and Corporate Change, **8** (2), 353–408   215
8   G. Bottazzi, G. Devetag and G. Dosi (2002), 'Adaptive Learning and Emergent
    Coordination in Minority Games', *Simulation Modelling Practice and Theory*, **10**
    (5–7), December, 321–47   271
9   Giulio Bottazzi, Giovanni Dosi and Igor Rebesco (2005), 'Institutional
    Architectures and Behavioral Ecologies in the Dynamics of Financial Markets',
    Journal of Mathematical Economics, **41** (1–2), February, 197–228   298

PART III PATTERNS OF INDUSTRIAL EVOLUTION AND THEIR SPATIAL EMBEDDEDNESS

10 Giovanni Dosi (2007), 'Statistical Regularities in the Evolution of Industries: A Guide through some Evidence and Challenges for the Theory', in F. Malerba and S. Brusoni (eds), *Perspectives on Innovation*, Chapter 5, Cambridge, UK: Cambridge University Press, 153–86   333

11 Giulio Bottazzi, Giovanni Dosi, Marco Lippi, Fabio Pammolli and Massimo Riccaboni (2001), 'Innovation and Corporate Growth in the Evolution of the Drug Industry', *International Journal of Industrial Organization*, **19** (7), July, 1161–87   367

12 Giulio Bottazzi, Giovanni Dosi, Nadia Jacoby, Angelo Secchi and Federico Tamagni (2010), 'Corporate Performances and Market Selection: Some Comparative Evidence', *Industrial and Corporate Change*, **19** (6), 1953–96   394

13 Giulio Bottazzi, Giovanni Dosi and Gaia Rocchetti (2001), 'Modes of Knowledge Accumulation, Entry Regimes and Patterns of Industrial Evolution', *Industrial and Corporate Change*, **10** (3), 609–38   438

14 Giulio Bottazzi, Giovanni Dosi, Giorgio Fagiolo and Angelo Secchi (2007), 'Modeling Industrial Evolution in Geographical Space', *Journal of Economic Geography*, **7** (5), 651–72   468

15 Giulio Bottazzi, Giovanni Dosi, Giorgio Fagiolo and Angelo Secchi (2008), 'Sectoral and Geographical Specificities in the Spatial Structure of Economic Activities', *Structural Change and Economic Dynamics*, **19** (3), September, 189–202   490

PART IV ECONOMIC EVOLUTION AND THE ROLE OF HISTORY

16 Carolina Castaldi and Giovanni Dosi (2006), 'The Grip of History and the Scope for Novelty: Some Results and Open Questions on Path Dependence in Economic Processes', in A. Wimmer and R. Kössler (eds), *Understanding Change: Models, Methodologies, and Metaphors*, Chapter 8, London, UK: Palgrave Macmillan, 99–128   507

17 Andrea P. Bassanini and Giovanni Dosi (2006), 'Competing Technologies, Technological Monopolies and the Rate of Convergence to a Stable Market Structure', in Cristiano Antonelli, Dominique Foray, Bronwyn H. Hall and W. Edward Steinmueller (eds), *New Frontiers in the Economics of Innovation and New Technology: Essays in Honor of Paul A. David*, Chapter 2, Cheltenham, UK and Northampton, MA: Edward Elgar Publishing, 23–50   537

PART V MACROECONOMIC DYNAMICS AND DEVELOPMENT

18 Giovanni Dosi, Christopher Freeman and Silvia Fabiani (1994), 'The Process of Economic Development: Introducing Some Stylized Facts and Theories on Technologies, Firms and Institutions', *Industrial and Corporate Change*, **3** (1), 1–45   567

19 Carolina Castaldi and Giovanni Dosi (2009), 'The Patterns of Output Growth of Firms and Countries: Scale Invariances and Scale Specificities', *Empirical Economics*, **37**, 475–95   612
20 Giovanni Amendola, Giovanni Dosi and Erasmo Papagni (1993), 'The Dynamics of International Competitiveness', *Review of World Economics*, **129**, 451–71   633
21 Mario Cimoli and Giovanni Dosi (1995), 'Technological Paradigms, Patterns of Learning and Development: An Introductory Roadmap', *Journal of Evolutionary Economics*, **5**, 243–68   654
22 Giovanni Dosi and Bruce Kogut (1993), 'National Specificities and the Context of Change: The Coevolution of Organization and Technology', in B. Kogut (ed.), *Country Competitiveness – Technology and Re-organization of Work*, Chapter 13, Oxford, UK: Oxford University Press, 249–62   680
23 Mario Cimoli, Giovanni Dosi, Richard Nelson and Joseph E. Stiglitz (2009), 'Institutions and Policies Shaping Industrial Development: An Introductory Note', in *Industrial Policies and Development: The Political Economy of Capabilities Accumulation*, Chapter 2, Oxford, UK and New York, NY: Oxford University Press, 19–38   694
24 G. Fagiolo, G. Dosi and R. Gabriele (2004), 'Matching, Bargaining, and Wage Setting in an Evolutionary Model of Labor Market and Output Dynamics', *Advances in Complex Systems*, **7** (2), 157–86   714
25 Giovanni Dosi, Giorgio Fagiolo and Andrea Roventini (2010), 'Schumpeter Meeting Keynes: A Policy-Friendly Model of Endogenous Growth and Business Cycles', *Journal of Economic Dynamics and Control*, **34** (9), 1748–67   744

Acknowledgements

The editor and publishers wish to thank the authors and the following publishers who have kindly given permission for the use of copyright material.

Andrea P. Bassanini and Giovanni Dosi for their own excerpt: (2006), 'Competing Technologies, Technological Monopolies and the Rate of Convergence to a Stable Market Structure', in Cristiano Antonelli, Dominique Foray, Bronwyn H. Hall and W. Edward Steinmueller (eds), *New Frontiers in the Economics of Innovation and New Technology: Essays in Honor of Paul A. David*, Chapter 2, 23–50.

Blackwell Publishing Ltd for excerpt: Giovanni Dosi, Mike Hobday and Luigi Marengo (2003), 'Problem-solving Behaviors, Organizational Forms, and the Complexity of Tasks', in Constance E. Helfat (ed.), *The SMS Blackwell Handbook of Organizational Capabilities: Emergence, Development, and Change*, Chapter 11, 167–92.

Cambridge University Press for excerpts: Giovanni Dosi, Luigi Marengo and Giorgio Fagiolo (2005), 'Learning in Evolutionary Environments', in K. Dopfer (ed.), *The Evolutionary Foundations of Economics*, Chapter 9, 255–338; Giovanni Dosi (2007), 'Statistical Regularities in the Evolution of Industries: A Guide through some Evidence and Challenges for the Theory', in F. Malerba and S. Brusoni (eds), *Perspectives on Innovation*, Chapter 5, 153–86.

Elsevier for article: Giulio Bottazzi, Giovanni Dosi, Marco Lippi, Fabio Pammolli and Massimo Riccaboni (2001), 'Innovation and Corporate Growth in the Evolution of the Drug Industry', *International Journal of Industrial Organization*, **19** (7), July, 1161–87.

Elsevier via Copyright Clearance Center's Rightslink Service for articles: G. Bottazzi, G. Devetag and G. Dosi (2002), 'Adaptive Learning and Emergent Coordination in Minority Games', *Simulation Modelling Practice and Theory*, **10** (5–7), December, 321–47; Giulio Bottazzi, Giovanni Dosi and Igor Rebesco (2005), 'Institutional Architectures and Behavioral Ecologies in the Dynamics of Financial Markets', *Journal of Mathematical Economics*, **41** (1–2), February, 197–228; Luigi Marengo and Giovanni Dosi (2005), 'Division of Labor, Organizational Coordination and Market Mechanisms in Collective Problem-Solving', *Journal of Economic Behavior and Organization*, **58** (2), October, 303–26; Giulio Bottazzi, Giovanni Dosi, Giorgio Fagiolo and Angelo Secchi (2008), 'Sectoral and Geographical Specificities in the Spatial Structure of Economic Activities', *Structural Change and Economic Dynamics*, **19** (3), September, 189–202; Giovanni Dosi, Giorgio Fagiolo and Andrea Roventini (2010), 'Schumpeter Meeting Keynes: A Policy-Friendly Model of Endogenous Growth and Business Cycles', *Journal of Economic Dynamics and Control*, **34** (9), 1748–67.

Preface

Most works in this second volume of selected articles have been produced in the new millennium, even if a few of them had been already written in the 1990s but had been reluctantly left out from the previous collection for the sake of thematic coherence.

Just the list of co-authors strikingly illustrates both the collective nature of the research enterprise which led to the works in this collection, and the crucial role in it of many graduate and doctoral students, post-doc, research fellows, with their skills, originality and analytical sharpness. And also, yes, with their intellectual integrity because working from a broadly defined evolutionary perspective does not increase the probabilities of publishing in the *Journal of Political Economy* or *Econometrica*.

This young band (or at least they were young when we started working together!) first primarily from the faculty of Statistics at the University of Rome 'La Sapienza' and later from the Sant'Anna School of Advanced Studies, includes Giovanni Amendola, Roberta Aversi, Andrea Bassanini, Giulio Bottazzi, Carolina Castaldi, Giovanna Devetag, Silvia Fabiani, Giorgio Fagiolo, Marco Faillo, Roberto Gabriele, Marco Grazzi, Nadia Jacoby, Mara Meacci, Erasmo Papagni, Igor Rebesco, Massimo Riccaboni, Gaia Rocchetti, Andrea Roventini, Angelo Secchi and Federico Tamagni (I am only mentioning those co-authoring below). Of course in the meantime all have become older and by now some of them are known professors or senior researchers spread all over Europe. [Some other (ex-)young boys and (ex-)young girls ended up also in the US, South America and Australia.]

The authorship pattern also reveals the long-lasting research intimacy with Luigi Marengo and Mario Cimoli.

The overwhelming presence of 'Rome and Pisa boys and girls' should not induce an underestimation of my continuing deep links with the international 'evolutionary' research community (of which a few, albeit prominent, members feature below as co-authors). However, it does reveal, in my view, a worrying scarcity in such a community of 'hubs', trying – as the philosopher of science Imre Lakatos would put it – to *harden the paradigm*, both empirically and from a formal perspective. Too often one finds repeated attempts to reinvent the wheel, or yet another discussion on methodology, or yet another critique of neoclassical economics. Rather, it has long been time to get down to business and refine Copernicus instead of prominently criticizing Ptolemy. And the worry becomes a fearful sentiment, when noticing that very few Ph.D. programmes (and all in Europe) teach both Ptolemy *and* Copernicus reasonably well.

Conversely, on the brighter side the research body presented below has lived within rich international networks including the EU-sponsored Dynamics of Institutions and Markets in Europe (DIME) 'Network of Excellence'; the Initiative for Policy dialogue (IPD), based at Columbia University, New York, coordinated by Joe Stiglitz; and, more recently, the Institute for New Economic Thinking (INET), centred again in New York.

In a more personal vein, over most of the last decade Marianna V. has been uniquely near, supportive, with limitless and sometimes undeserved love. And repeatedly offered challenging intellectual hints. This book is dedicated to Marianna.

xii   *Economic Organization, Industrial Dynamics and Development*

Last but not least, it is impossible to overpraise the importance of my assistant Laura F., who has organized and supervised – with iron hand, deep friendliness and dedication – all my professional life, crucial in preventing it from being more of a mess than it already is. Without her, some of the contributions below might not have reached light.

Introduction

Giovanni Dosi

This volume of selected articles follows the first one published around 10 years ago (Dosi, 2000).[1]

The introduction to the previous volume presents a relatively detailed discussion of several interpretative questions which has been shaping my scientific production, together with abundant indulgence into several autobiographical details. There is no reason to repeat the latter here. However it might be useful to spell out some major building blocks of the research programme underlying the perspective which moulds the articles that follow.

While in the dominant paradigm, 'the combined assumptions of maximizing behavior, market equilibrium and stable preferences, used relentlessly and consistently, form the heart of the [*that is, their*] economic approach' (Becker, 1976), an alternative one – which I shall call *evolutionary*, in line with many like-minded colleagues, but the name is not so important – is based on largely opposite building blocks.

Telegraphically, such a perspective attempts to understand a wide set of economic phenomena – ranging from microeconomic behaviours to the features of industrial structures and dynamics, all the way to the properties of aggregate growth and development – as outcomes of far-from-equilibrium interactions among heterogeneous agents, characterized by endogenous preferences, most often 'boundedly rational' but always capable of learning, adapting and innovating with respect to their understandings of the world in which they operate, the technologies they master, their organizational forms and their behavioural repertoires.

And on methodological grounds, far from disdaining formal modelling and statistical analysis, the research programme is largely *inductive*, taking very seriously indeed empirical regularities at all levels of observation as discipline for the modelling assumptions.

I present below a few more detailed observations that might also help you to see the thread across the contributions to this second volume. Let me start, however, by placing such an interpretative perspective against some fundamental questions addressed by the economic discipline in general and against the answers to such questions that contemporary theory has to offer.

Coordination and change, or, where Walras, Schumpeter and Samuelson got it at least partly wrong and Adam Smith, Marx and Keynes got it fundamentally right

As mentioned, one way to look at the evolutionary research programme (or for that matter any research programme in economics) is by reference to the basic questions it addresses and the way it does it.

In my view *the* two basic questions at the core of the whole economic discipline since its inception regard, first, *the drivers and patterns of change of the capitalistic machine of production and innovation* and, second, the *mechanisms of coordination among a multitude of self-seeking economic agents* often characterized by conflicting interests.[2] Of course, of crucial importance are the answers which diverse theories offer to the two questions, but equally important are the relations purported by each theory between the two.

Interestingly, Adam Smith begins his *Wealth of Nations* with a detailed analysis of the drivers of change, in particular the positive feedback between division of labour, mechanization, productivity growth and demand growth. Conversely, issues of coordination are discussed much later, building on such a dynamic background: in fact, apologists of unbridled free market, eager to recruit Adam Smith among their supporters, are not generally aware of the fact that he talks of the (in)famous 'invisible hand' much later, *only once*, in his whole work (Book IV, chapter 2, of the *Wealth of Nations*).

Somewhat similarly, Karl Marx builds upon a long discussion on the relationships between a theory of production and labour relations – centred around the theory of value, capital accumulation and technological progress. 'Coordination', if we can call it that (or, more rudimentary, a theory of sectoral relative prices and their dynamics) comes much later, taking of course for granted the intrinsic dynamic nature of capitalists' interactions.

From a quite different angle, Keynes too never dreamt of separating 'what keeps the system together' from 'what keeps it going': in fact, the properties of shorter-term coordination – as revealed prominently by involuntary unemployment – were derived from the properties of capital accumulation and the 'animal spirits' driving it.

The current dominant theoretical creed is very much on the analytical opposite. It builds on the separation between 'coordination' and 'dynamics'. Notwithstanding the fundamental Schumpeterian contribution to the understanding of technological innovation as the driver of long-term change, even Schumpeter turned out to subscribe to this 'separation epistemology', building as a point of departure not on Adam Smith and other classics but upon the Walrasian approach to coordination.

Many readers are well aware of the basic Schumpeterian story, at least of 'Schumpeter Mark I', vintage 1912.

One starts with a *Walrasian* state of (equilibrium) *circular flow*. Nowadays we would say that one begins with a *general equilibrium (GE)*, grounded of course on well-specified *fundamentals* in terms of technologies, endowment and preferences. Then comes a 'shock': in the Schumpeterian story, the entrepreneurial innovator introduces an *unexpected* innovation, in turn yielding disequilibrium profits for the innovator himself (yes, most likely for Schumpeter, *him*self!), changing relative prices, 'creative destruction', etc. Thereafter, the economic system adapts via technological imitation and diffusion of the innovations. This is the 'transient', until the system converges to a new (equilibrium) *circular flow* characterized by a new ensemble of fundamentals of the economy. In the original work of Schumpeter there are of course many important historical qualifications and nuances. However, the story is in principle in tune with the young Samuelson's formalization of the idea in terms of the 'correspondence principle' (in fact Paul Samuelson was a Ph.D. student of his).

If S(0) is the vector of *equilibrium* state variables of the system at time zero and S(1) stands for the values of the same variable in the new equilibrium state of the 'circular flow', why not comparing S(1) and S(0) as the most elegant and parsimonious way of doing 'dynamics'? Naturally, one may think of a whole sequence of such equilibrium states. And, here we are, we have an *equilibrium theory of growth nested upon a narrative of (transient) creative destructions*, temporary disequilibria, etc.[3]

Indeed, this is more or less one of the three pillars of the intellectual edifice on which the economic discipline has run for long time after the Second World War, with a rough division of labour between (i) 'microfounded' (GE) models; (ii) 'short run' macroeconomics; and (iii) growth theories.

The 'coordination research programme', as it is known, soon culminated into the Arrow–Debreu–McKenzie *General Equilibrium* model; indeed, an elegant and institutionally very parsimonious demonstration of the *possibility* of equilibrium coordination among decentralized agents. In fact, subsequent, basically *negative*, results have shown the general impossibility of moving from *existence theorems* to that sort of 'implicit dynamics' captured by proofs of global or local stability – loosely speaking, the property of the system, when 'scrambled', to get back to its equilibrium state. Quite the contrary, even empirically far-fetched processes such as *tâtonnements* (with the omniscient Walrasian auctioneer proclaiming equilibrium transaction when he sees them) in general do not converge.

Even more powerfully, some of the founding fathers of GE themselves have shown that 'existence' does not bear any implication in terms of the shape of excess demand functions (this is what the Sonnenschein–Mantel–Debreu theorem implies). Putting it briefly, in general, *forget even local stability*!

Conversely, any careful look at the tall requirements which *sheer existence* entails – in terms of information and rationality – highlights the extent to which GE is a beautiful but extremely fragile creature, certainly unable to withhold the weight of any account of the dynamics of the economy as a whole and even less so to offer any serious microfoundation to transforming economies undergoing various forms of innovation. In fact, even forgetting search, innovation, etc., it is quite ill-founded to claim that standard GE models can be an account, no matter how utterly stylized, paraphrasing Adam Smith, of 'why the butcher offers meat day after day more or less at the same price' mainly motivated by self-interest. If the conditions – in term of rationality, characteristics of the exchange, etc. – required in reality were even vaguely as stringent as those required in GE models, probably no one would ever offer meat or whatever else!

Concerning all the foregoing points, my friend Alan Kirman has insightfully discussed in various works the achievements, limitations and dead ends of GE analysis. Kirman (2010) offers an overall assessment together with alternative proposals on how to tackle economic coordination. See also Stiglitz (2011) and below.

In any case, that was the 'micro'. Then there were basically two 'macros'. One was (equilibrium) growth theories which largely lived until the end of the 1970s a life of their own. While it is the case that, for example models *à la* Solow invoked maximizing behaviours in order to establish equilibrium input intensities, no claim was made that such allocations were the work of any 'representative agent' in turn taken to be the 'synthetic' (?) version of some underlying GE.[4]

By the same token, the distinction between *positive* (that is, purportedly descriptive) and *normative* models before Lucas and companions was clear to the practitioners.

Finally, in the good and in the bad, technological change was kept separate from the mechanisms of resource allocation: the famous 'Solow residual' was, as well known, the statistical counterpart of the drift in growth models with an exogenous technological change.

Together, in some land between purported GE 'microfoundations' and equilibrium growth theories, lived for at least three decades a macroeconomics sufficiently 'Keynesian' in spirit and quite neoclassical in terms of tools. It was the early 'neo-Keynesianism' – pioneered by Hicks, and shortly thereafter by Modigliani, Patinkin and a few other American 'Keynesians' – which Joan Robinson contemptuously defined as 'bastard Keynesians'. It is the *short-term* macro which students used to learn up to the 1980s, with IS–LM curves – meant to capture the aggregate relations between money supply and money demand, interest rates, savings and investments – Phillips curves on the labour market and a few other curves. In fact, the 'curves' were (are) a precarious compromise between the notion that the economy is supposed to be some sort of equilibrium – albeit of a short-term nature – and the notion of a more 'fundamental' equilibrium or equilibrium path to which the economy is bound to tend in the longer run. Needless to say, forget any formal demonstration of the proposition, for example, in terms of 'slow' and 'fast' variables: hand-waving in economics is one the most robust conventions!

IS–LM curves and the like, I straightforwardly admit, were a major pain in my early studies and still are. The quick 'Keynesian synthesis' presented by Hicks (1937) and Modigliani (1944) had been offered as a seemingly sensible and parsimonious account of Keynes' *General Theory* – cutting out all the detours and qualifications. In fact they were the most rudimentary 'GE' translations with an implicit representative agent and various sorts of 'frictions' added up. (However it took almost half a century for the American macro mainstream to further sterilize, reformulate, refine it and baptize the monster 'Stochastic Dynamic General Equilibrium', DSGE, see below).

'New Classic (?)' Talibanism and beyond
What happened next? Well, in my view, everything which could get worse got worse and more. (For a much more detailed reconstruction, which I largely share, of what happened to the theory, intertwined with the reconstruction of the actual policy dynamics which led to the 2008 crisis, see Cassidy, 2009.)

First, 'new classic economics' (even if the reference to the classics cannot be more far away from the truth) fully abolished the distinction between the normative and positive (i.e. descriptive) domains – in other words, between models *à la* Ramsey *vs.* models *à la* Harrod, Domar, Solow, etc. (notwithstanding the differences among the latter ones). In fact, the striking paradox for theorists who are in good part market talibans is that one starts with a model which is essentially of a benign, forward-looking, *central planner*, and only at the end, by way, again, of an abundant dose of hand-waving, one claims that the solution of whatever intertemporal optimization problem is in fact supported by a decentralized market equilibrium. I have already mentioned it: things could be much easier for this approach if one could legitimately 'summarize' a genuine 'GE' (that is, with many agents, heterogeneous at least in their endowments and preferences) into some 'representative agent'. But the fact is that *one cannot*. By doing that nonetheless, one simply *assumes away as solved by construction the coordination problem*. Notwithstanding the name, there is very little of 'GE' in the DSGE models, and earlier antecedents (all that irrespectively of the trust in the ability of GE to capture the essentials of the coordination hurdle in market economies, which in my case is very low indeed).

Second, but relatedly, the last three decades has seen the disappearance of the distinction between 'long term' and 'short term', with the latter as the locus where 'frictions', 'liquidity traps', Phillips curves, some (temporary!) real effects of fiscal and monetary policies, etc. would all hazardously survive. Why would a representative agent able to solve sophisticated intertemporal optimization problems from here to infinity display frictions and distortions in the short run? We all know the outrageously silly propositions, sold as major discoveries, associated with infamous 'rational expectation revolution' concerning the ineffectiveness of fiscal and monetary policies and the general properties of markets to yield Pareto first-best allocations (in this respect, of course, it is easier for that to happen if 'the market' is the representative agent: coordination failures and allocation failures would involve serious episodes of schizophrenia by that agent itself!).[5]

Personally, I believe that in other times, nearly the entire profession would have reacted to such a 'revolution' as Bob Solow once did when asked why he did not take the 'new classics' seriously. Let me extensively quote him – one of the great few, with a great mind and a great intellectually integrity. When interviewed early on about the supposed 'new classics', Bob replied:

> Suppose someone sits down where you are sitting right now and announces to me he is Napoleon Bonaparte. The last thing I want to do with him is to get involved in a technical discussion of cavalry tactics at the battle of Austerlitz. If I do that, I am tacitly drawn in the game that he is Napoleon. Now, Bob Lucas and Tom Sargent like nothing better than to get drawn in technical discussions, because then you have tacitly gone along with their fundamental assumptions; your attention is attracted away from the basic weakness of the whole story. Since I find that fundamental framework ludicrous, I respond by treating it as ludicrous – that is, by laughing at it – so as not to fall in the trap of taking it seriously and passing on matters of technique (Solow in Klamer, 1984, p. 146).

The reasons why the profession, and even worse, the world at large took these 'Napoleons' seriously, I think, have basically to do with a *Zeitgeist* where the hegemonic politics was that epitomized by Ronald Reagan and Margaret Thatcher, and their system of beliefs in the 'magic of the market place' *et similia*. And, crucially, it was a *Zeitgeist* which was largely politically bipartisan. Compare the subsequent Blair and Clinton administration who sometimes did things which even the former would not dare, including, among many reckless measures, the abolition of the Glass–Steagall Act, a measure which contributed to fuel the greatest crisis over the last 80 years. Or think of the disasters produced for decades around the world by the International Monetary Fund (IMF), inspired by the so-called *Washington Consensus* – as such another creed on the magic of markets, the evil of governments and the miraculous effects of blood, sweat and tears.

The point I want to make is that the changes in the hegemonic (macro) theory should be primarily interpreted in terms of the political economy of power relations among social and political groups, with little to write home about 'advancements' in the theory itself ... On the contrary!

I must end this sub-section with a cautionary *caveat*. I often hear the objection to the foregoing telegraphic, inevitably rough, account, that new macro theory, in the form of the newest generation of DSGE models, takes on board various forms of 'imperfections', 'frictions', 'inertias' (cf. Blanchard, 2009, and Woodford, 2009 for bold claims on the DSGE – 'New Keynesian Synthesis'). True, we are now in the late-Ptolemaic phase of the theory: add epicycles at full steam without any empirical discipline and you will get some greater possibilities of *calibration* of the model ('calibration' is the new game in town, often not too short of voodoo: see also below).[6] Of course, in the epicycles frenzy one is never touched by the sense of ridiculous in assuming that the mythical representative agent at the same time is extremely sophisticated when thinking about future allocations but falls into backward-looking habits when deciding about consumption or, when having to change prices is tangled by 'menu costs'! (Caballero, 2010 offers a thorough picture of this surreal state of affairs.)

What about innovation dynamics?

I have argued that even the coordination issue has been written out of the agenda by *assuming* it as basically solved by construction. But what about change? What about the *Unbound Prometheus*[7] of capitalist search, discovery and indeed destruction? Very simply, in the DSGE workhorse, there is no Prometheus: 'innovations' come as exogenous shocks upon the aggregate production function, with the same mythical agent (or in recent more sophisticated versions the representative household (?!)) optimally adjusting its consumption and investment plans. End of story.

However, the last 30 years have seen also the emergence of *new growth theories*, bringing – as compared to the original Solow model – some significant advancements and, in my view, equally significant drawbacks. The big plus is the endogenization of technological change: innovation is endogenized into economic dynamics as either a learning externality or as the outcome of purposeful expensive efforts by profit-maximizing agents. However, in the latter case the endogenization comes at what I consider the major price (although many others would deem it as a major achievement) of reducing innovative activities to an *equilibrium* outcome of optimal intertemporal allocation of resources. Hence by doing that, one loses also the genuine Schumpeterian notion of innovation as a disequilibrium phenomenon – *at least as a transient*. In fact, putting it another way, innovative activities undertaken by private actors are ultimately reduced to yet another instance of optimal intertemporal resource allocation, with or without (probabilizable) uncertainty. Let me be a bit hard on my friend Philippe Aghion and colleagues: certainly they masterly endogenized innovation, but was it necessary to do that by squeezing Mandeville, Smith, Marx, Schumpeter – that is dynamics – into Lionel Robbins ('... economics as the science of allocation of scarce resources to alternative uses ...')? If anything, innovation and knowledge accumulation are precisely the domains where the dismal principles of scarcity and conservation are massively violated: one can systematically get more out of less, while dynamic increasing returns are the general rule.

... And, incidentally, there was, and is, a major crisis ...

All the foregoing discussion takes the bird's-eye view of the theory. But, as someone might remember, there has been a major financial and real crisis, and that crisis continues to be largely there at the time of the writing of this introduction and will remain there for quite a while after the publication of this volume. Indeed, its very arrival and its sheer size are as near as one can get in social sciences to a falsifying 'crucial experiment': as the 'Dahlem Manifesto' puts it the crisis highlights a *systemic failure of the economic profession* (Colander et al., 2009).[8] Of course, one cannot demand economists to predict precise dates or modes of occurrence of any crisis, but what is astonishing is that the mainstream paradigm briefly outlined above is unable to allow the *very possibility* of a crisis. I cite again from the 'Manifesto':

> The implicit view behind standard models is that markets and economies are inherently stable and that they only temporarily get off track. The majority of economists thus failed to warn policy makers about the threatening system crisis and ignored the work of those who did ... The confinement of macroeconomics to models of stable states that are perturbed by limited external shocks and that neglect the intrinsic recurrent boom-and-bust dynamics of our economic system is remarkable ... The

failure [of the economic discipline] has deep methodological roots. The often heard definition of economics – that it concerned with the 'allocation of resources' – is short-sighted and misleading. It reduces economics to the study of optimal decisions in well-specified choice problems. Such research generally loses track of the inherent dynamics of economic systems and the instability that accompanies its complex dynamics (Colander et al., 2009, pp. 2–3).

Can the mainstream paradigm be saved by appropriate modifications? I do not think it can, precisely because its massive interpretative failure is connected to its core building blocks (forward-looking rationality, equilibrium, etc.) I take indeed some pride in having worked at an alternative well before the crisis itself; witness also the articles that follow.

The alternative interpretative venue: the economy as a complex evolving system

The research project that I have been pursuing throughout my academic life (cf. also the introduction to Dosi, 2000, the previous volume of selected articles) and which I share with the broad community of evolutionary economists – at least I hope we do! – stand in most respects *at the opposite* to the state-of-the-art outlined above. Indeed it starts acknowledging that the object of study is the *economy as a complex evolving system* (this is also the name of a series of conferences and books sponsored by the Santa Fe Institute, rich of interesting insights, even if what was subsequently delivered was somewhat less than the promises: cf. Anderson et al., 1988 and Arthur et al., 1997).

I want to start here with the most minimalist notion of 'complexity', standing at the very least for the fact that the economy is composed by multiple interacting actors – hence the illegitimacy of its 'antropomorphization'. (On 'complex dynamics', see Kirman, 2010, near the spirit of these notes; indeed, an important source of inspiration, and Rosser, 2011.)

Moreover, 'evolution' entails that any assumption of 'given the fundamentals' (including technologies and preferences) in most circumstances implies a significant rape to the object of study. Of course, in analysing a complex evolving economy, one has to go well beyond the Schumpeter/Samuelson separation between coordination and change. The (imperfect) coordinating features of the system are fundamentally shaped by its evolving nature. This is what I jokingly call the 'bicycle theorem'. It is easier to stand up on a bicycle when you cycle, while only a few *virtuosos* are able not to fall while standing still. That is, out of the metaphor, the relatively orderly properties (which are there often but not always!) of capitalist economies derive from its being in motion. This is the relative order of 'restless capitalism', as Stan Metcalfe put it (cf. Metcalfe, 1998 and Metcalfe and Ramlogan, 2006).

So, for example, prices move roughly in line with the average costs of production which in turn depend on the underlying (technology-specific and sector-specific) rates of process innovation.

Demand patterns are shaped by the ensuing prices and, possibly even more importantly by the 'trajectories' in product innovation.

Gross and net labour demand are affected by the double nature of technical progress as a 'labour saver' and as a 'demand creator'.

Among many others, these are all features of *imperfect coordination* and *relative order* in the distributional properties of whatever statistics on economic variables – stemming precisely from the fact that the system is changing all the time in its process and product technologies, consumption patterns and organizational forms. In fact, the evolutionary paradigm, at least the way I see it, precisely addresses the properties of such endogenously changing multi-agent systems. A few general features of such interpretations follow, partly drawing upon Dosi and Winter (2002).

Methodology

Dynamics first!

The emphasis on dynamics and change is indeed quite in tune with a more general methodological prescription common to the whole evolutionary research programme, which my friend and mentor Sid Winter sums up in the imperative 'dynamics first!'. Such methodological imperative demands that the explanation for why something exists, or why a variable takes the value it does, ought to rest on a process account of how it became what it is. Loosely speaking, that amounts to the theoretical imperative: provide the process story either by formally writing down some dynamical system, or telling a good qualitative historical reconstruction (or, when possible, *both*).

Putting it in terms of negative prescriptions, be extremely wary of any interpretation of what is observed that runs just in terms of ex-post equilibrium rationalizations ('it has to be like that, given rationality'). Together, notwithstanding a very widespread practice in the economic profession, never take as a good 'explanation' either an existence theorem or a purely functionalist claim (entity x exists because it performs function y ...). Moreover, note, in this perspective, Milton Friedman's old 'as ... if' interpretation of the properties of equilibrium behaviours (Friedman, 1953) should be taken as a (daring, and indeed most often wrong!) conjecture on the limit properties of some unspecified dynamics; and so should be notions such as those of evolutionary stable strategies (ESS) as originally put forward in biology by John Maynard Smith (1976), (although the dynamical intuitions are more understandable in the biological rather than in the social case).

In fact, only under very special circumstances observed phenomena can be interpreted as the outcome of behaviours 'as ... if' the latter were maximizing ones, on the assumption that those which were not had been driven away by some selective process. Indeed, in any serious scientific discipline, the reading of Winter (1964) critique would have put an end to any 'as ... if' claim. However, our poor quasi-theological discipline is deaf to both theoretical argumentation and empirical evidence when it comes to defend its epistemological core.

Realism

Realism is a virtue and in certain respects a necessity. Although theories are necessarily abstract and admit less of reality than they omit: indeed 'the map is never the territory' as Kay (2011) puts it. At the same time, there are some broad features of reality that the are omitted at the theorist's peril – in the sense that the conclusions are unreliable guides to the interpretation of reality, though perhaps instructive regarding important mechanisms or otherwise useful. [The broadest point that I cannot pursue here as much as I would like to is that, in a word, the 'prediction-centred' justification of running modelling practices – 'it does not matter the assumption you make, what counts is the quality of your prediction' – is basically epistemological trash ...].

Some substantive building blocks

Given these general epistemological prescriptions (admittedly not obvious ones or even generally accepted among economists), the following substantive building blocks give shape to a full-fledged evolutionary research programme (much more on the substantive part of evolutionary research programme is in Nelson and Winter, 1982; Dosi et al., 1988; Metcalfe, 1998; Dopfer, 2005; Dosi and Nelson, 1994; Coriat and Dosi, 1998; Dosi and Winter, 2002 and, as mentioned, the introduction to Dosi, 2000).

Microfoundations

Theories ought to be *micro-founded*, in the sense that they ought to be grounded explicitly (though perhaps indirectly) in a plausible account of what agents do and why they do it.[9] (Note that the proposition does *not* imply, however, that agents' objectives are in general achieved or their expectations fulfilled. In other words, only a massive misunderstanding has 'microfoundations' equivalent to rational expectations.)

'Bounded rationality', broadest sense

Among the fundamental micro features is the fact that agents have at best imperfect understanding of the environment they live in, and, even more so, of what the future will deliver. I must say in this respect that I rather dislike the word 'bounded rationality' as it seems to hint at a full 'Olympic' rationality whose distance from actual behaviours measures also how much 'bounded' is 'bounded'. On the contrary, it happens that in changing complex environments, such an Olympic 'perfect' rationality might not be definable even in principle; we discuss this issue at length in Chapter 1 of this volume (Dosi et al., 2005). Come as it may, we (meaning also the co-authors of the chapter, Giorgio Fagiolo and Luigi Marengo) adopt a very expansive notion of 'bounded rationality', related most obviously to limitations in (i) access to information; (ii) memory; and (iii) computational abilities; but also more fundamentally to (i) intrinsically imperfect *representations* of the environment in which agents operate; (v) abilities to master physical and 'social' technologies;[10] and (vi) the very perception of one's own preferences.

Heterogeneity

Straightforwardly, imperfect understanding and imperfect, path-dependent, learning entails persistent heterogeneity among agents. Of course agents are heterogeneous in (i) their preferences and endowments – a property well acknowledged also by standard models in their full GE version (but hardly so by most current macro models!). However, they are heterogeneous also with respect to (ii) the *models-of-the-world* they hold, even when facing identical information; (iii) their technological repertoires; and (iv) (possibly) their learning processes (in fact we still know very little on learning patterns, both at the levels of individuals and, even more so, organizations).

Capturing heterogeneity is crucial to the representation of aggregate dynamics: to repeat, the lack of it contributes significantly to the pitiful state of contemporary macroeconomics.

Persistent innovative opportunities

The knowledge margin is always active: agents are always capable of discovering new technologies, new ways of organizing and new behavioural patterns. Allowing for the *immanent possibility of novelty* in the system is a major theoretical and modelling challenge that cannot safely be ignored. In this respect, evolutionary-inspired students of technological and organizational change have contributed to open up a whole new field of analysis addressing the structure and dynamics of technological knowledge: we review the state-of-the-art in Dosi and Nelson (2010). (In this volume on organizational knowledge and change, see Chapters 2–6.)

Interactions, coordination and selection
While (imperfect) adaptation and persistent discovery generate variety, collective interactions within and outside markets operate, first, as mechanisms of *information exchange and coordination*, and second, as *selection mechanisms*, generating differential growth (and possibly also differential survival probabilities) of different entities that are the 'carriers' of diverse technologies, routines, strategies, etc. Indeed, crucial issues here regard (i) the coordinating power of whatever 'invisible (or visible) hand' of decentralized interactions; (ii) the drivers, powers and efficiency of selection mechanisms and (iii) the interactions between the foregoing two processes. [Obviously, under a 'dynamic first' rule, demonstrations of existence of a purported equilibrium followed again by some 'hand-waving theorem' based on pub-like anecdotes arguments and assertions such as 'the system must get there after all' do not count as serious points …]

Aggregate regularities as emergent properties
As a result of all this, collective aggregate phenomena (e.g. regularities at different levels of aggregation, in the growth processes, in industrial structures and dynamics, etc.) ought to be generally captured theoretically as *emergent properties* – i.e as the collective and largely unintentional outcome of *far-from-equilibrium micro interactions* and heterogeneous learning.

Putting it another way, they are the relatively orderly properties of processes of *self-organization* (what Stan Metcalfe calls 'self-transforming market order') without however any equilibrium connotation attached to it, neither in terms of market clearing of all markets, nor in terms of fulfilment of the underlying expectations of the individual agents. In addition, such properties often have a *metastable* nature, in the sense that while persisting on a time scale longer than the processes generating them, might ultimately disappear with probability one.[11]

Organizational forms
A similar style of representation and interpretation should apply to the emergence and self-maintenance of *organizational forms* and institutions: they are partly the result of directed (purposeful) actions by the agents but also, partly, the unintentional outcome of collective interactions and the interplay of agents learning. I return to the organization domain shortly.

Co-evolutionary dynamics
The relation of the 'higher level' regularities manifested in institutions, rules and organizational forms to 'lower level' evolutionary processes in technologies, production patterns etc. is a complex one of co-evolution across *levels of analysis* and *time scales* – and ought to be properly understood and possibly modelled as such. While on some (longer) time scales also the former are emergent phenomena, on shorter time scales they may be considered as relatively invariant structures which constrain and shape the latter.

This is the 'grand programme', as Sid Winter – with whom I wrote down the foregoing list of paradigmatic building blocks – and I see it. It is impossible to review in this introduction the rapidly growing literature that share some or all them. Some discussions and a quick review of the achievements up to a decade ago are in Dosi and Winter (2002), and a much more detailed one addressing specifically technological change and industrial dynamics in Dosi and Nelson (2010). Here let me just highlight how the works in this collection link with the 'grand programme', and, hopefully, contribute to its advancement.

Microfoundations: cognition, behaviours and learning in complex evolving environments

'Microfoundations' of course stand also for the account of actual behaviours of agents, be they individuals or organizations.

I have repeatedly discussed stories of the type '... let us start with assuming that agents max (something) and build some theory from there ... ', with all the paraphernalia of very dubious epistemological claims such as 'this is just a useful yardstick', 'this is the outcome of an 'as ... if' process even if I am unable to formally write it down', etc. One of such discussions of mine is indeed in the introduction to Dosi (2000). And of course major rebuttals are in Winter (1964), Nelson and Winter (1982), and many works in Herbert Simon (1957) and (1983). The defence of 'start from max (...)' in fact in my view is too pathetically near the old story of the drunkard looking for his keys under a street lamp because that was the only lit-up place even if he remembered that he lost the keys somewhere else.

Incidentally, this was not originally the case. Savage (1954) in his classic *Foundations of Statistics* was extremely cautious: any reasonable representation of behaviours in terms of max (something) had to be limited to *small worlds* (and even that was an *upper bound*). (*Note*: The notion did not have to do with the current network-related meaning but rather to a much more down-to-earth restriction that the *possible states-of-the-world* upon which agents were taking decisions had to finite, well-known to everyone, and everyone could somehow come up with probability distributions over them. On that, Savage was extremely clear and utterly humble).

We know what happened since then: the wide spreading of the description of behaviours in terms of increasingly sophisticated maximizing assumptions without any empirical or theoretical discipline, the only constraint being 'how much math I can learn and sell on intertemporal maximization'. On the contrary, in most economic circumstances, featuring change and innovation, maximizing rationality cannot be characterized *even in principle*, let alone being an attribute of actual behaviours.

But then what do people and organization do? We try to address the question from several angles in the articles in Part I of this volume.

Chapter 1 discusses a few rather complementary research paths on behaviours and learning, heavily borrowing from cognitive and social psychology. Indeed, I fully share Kahneman's view that:

> Psychological theories [...] cannot match the elegance and precision of formal normative models of belief and choice, but this is another way of saying that rational models are psychologically unrealistic [...] Psychology offers integrative concepts and mid-level generalizations, which gain credibility from their ability to explain ostensibly different phenomena in diverse domains (Kahneman, 2003, p. 1449).

Since we wrote that article, a lot of progress has been made in several directions. Let me just mention two.

One is neuroeconomics. The way I see it as a fruitful venue of research is not related to the reductionist flavour that some of the exercises convey (… 'map greediness in this part of the brain and generosity in that other part …'). Rather, because some such *proximate* mapping does appear indeed to be possible, neuroeconomics helps in identifying and taxonomizing multiple drivers and processes underlying evaluations and decisions (for thorough reviews of the field, see Rangel et al., 2008 and Camerer, 2007).

A second venue of progress has been the exploration and refinement of the conjecture that humans operate on the grounds of two distinct systems of cognition (and as a consequence also of action elicitation). Kahneman (2003) calls them *System 1* (driven by intuition – fast, parallel, automatic, effortless, associative, slow-learning, emotional) and *System 2* (driven by reasoning – slow, serial, controlled, effortful, rule-governed, flexible, neutral). (See Kahneman, 2003 and 2011; see also the early Schneider and Shriffin, 1977a and 1977b.)

Loosely speaking, most contemporary developments are somewhat *Simonesque* in spirit, although they move much further away from any notion of rationality (even of the *procedural* kind) than Herb Simon would have been ready to go. In fact, the variegated body of research bordering economics, psychology and cognitive studies are increasingly filling in a 'model of man' which, as we are advocating in Chapter 1, shall ultimately include also (i) cognitive foundations of both 'System 1' and 'System 2' based on imperfect and evolving *categorizations* and *mental models*; (ii) ubiquitous valuation and decision *heuristics;* (ii) *context-dependence* and *social-embeddedness* of both interpretative models and decision rules; and (iv) evolving (and possibly inconsistent) goals and preferences. [We attempt to formalize such dynamics with respect to demand patterns and explore their economic implications in Chapter 7 by Aversi et al., 1999.]

The 'transparency of the world' and the assumption that 'there cannot be money left on the table': a digression
I keep repeating it on every possible occasion and I have already mentioned it above. Economics is the only discipline which assumes that the economic world is *structurally transparent* to the agents who populate it. They might have imperfect information – in the sense of some noise on the signals they receive form the environment – and also incomplete information – basically meaning that I might not precisely know whether the agent in front of me is Saint Therese of Calcutta or Al Capone – but for the rest everyone knows the *true* structure of the world, what causes what, how it works and will always work. While the very existence of all scientific disciplines is motivated by the search for *causes* and processes – from the movements of the planets, the drivers of biological evolution, the causes of particular diseases, all the way to the working of our brain … And even all of us in everyday life operate as 'naïve scientists' asking, say, what causes the firm where I work to give a pay rise or not, or asking whether the changed attitude of my wife is because she has got a lover …

All this does not happen in economics. Indeed, the dominant theorizing mode implies that 'the map *is* the territory' in some ontological sense: it is a bit as if one started from the assumption that physical bodies know Newton laws, particles know the Boltzmann equation and bees know the dynamics governing the beehive.

What is the 'true' model then? Needless to say, it looks very much like the model that any particular economist developed in his Ph.D.! And the majority of the profession is so convinced by this utterly naïve (one could say outrageous) ontology that an inordinate amount of scientific energies has gone (with the usual confusion between the descriptive and normative domains) into the thread of instruments by which agents try to channel and control the stochasticity of the relevant variables of an otherwise perfectly understood world: witness the bulimic amount of work on options, Black and Scholes, derivatives, etc. [In that, not even 'stochasticity' in general, but most often the Gaussian one which they could more or less master!] It should come as no surprise, then, that many economists were so surprised by the arrival of the big financial crisis. *At last* (!) they noticed that the variables of interests generally are not normally distributed, but fatter-tailed: there are a lot of 'big events' and 'black swans' are relatively frequent. In all that what is actually striking is that there was and still is whole community religiously believing in statistical normality! However the acknowledged of fat-tailedness – as welcome as it is – just scratches the surface of the foregoing, much deeper, issue: as the world is everything but transparent, agents operate on the grounds of different, sometimes wildly different, models of the same world while, ultimately, the observed variables are the outcomes of their very interactions.

All this has a lot to do also with the 'no money left on the table' assumption. This is yet another *mantra* that all graduate students in respectable US universities soon have to learn. It is a sort of non-arbitrage hand-waving theorem stating the presumption that if there is an opportunity, someone sooner or later will grab it (Chari's witness to the US House of Representatives *after the crisis* says it all with moving faith (Chari, 2010)). The 'no money left' creed however withers away as soon as one acknowledges the intrinsic opaqueness of causes and processes, so that opportunities if they are there, they are hard to see, and can be detected with some spectacles and not with others.

Was the financial crisis due to the fact that out there there was an outrageous number of exploitable idiots and not enough clever exploiters? Not at all. On the contrary, a major driver has been an endogenous evolution of cognitive models and behavioural patterns fostering the 'survival of the reckless', as Jacobides and Winter (2010) put it, ultimately driving the system towards the abyss (see also Bottazzi et al., 2012).

Organizations: behaviours and learning patterns

Isomorphic questions concern *organizations*. What do they actually do? And how do they change their behaviours and their internal functioning? [That is how do they learn, if they do it at all?]

Again, one familiar answer is that firms max (something) – plausibly profits – subject to a technological constraint (their 'production function') and conditional on the information they access. In this case, as Herb Simon argued long ago, one does not have any need to open up the 'organizational blackbox'. It is sufficient to know what the firm maximizes, the production function and the information set in order to be able to account for what the firm will do, without, so to speak, looking into its belly.

To be fair, also mainstream theory has moved a long way away from such a blackboxing. The acknowledgement of the trivial fact that organizations are made up by more than one person, possibly with interests not perfectly aligned, calls for the opening-up of the box because what the organization does and ultimately its performance does depend on the intra-organizational relations among its members. This is what *agency theories* have been basically doing, in fact much more than Transaction Cost Economics (TCE), whose primary and most natural focus has been the Coasian question of the boundaries between organizations and markets.

However, the agency-inspired opening-up of the box had very little to do with any inquiry of how organizations *actually behave*, and even less so of their *actual internal set-ups*. Rather, the intellectual industry has been to offer a rapidly expanding menu of models of firms as microcosms composed by asymmetrically informed, self-seeking, sophisticatedly rational individuals linked up by equilibrium contracts. What the members of the organization do and ultimately its overall performance depend on the characteristics of such contracts together with conditions that are partly *lato sensu* 'technological' and partly 'social' – including the distribution of information, the degrees of observability of efforts and outputs, etc.

In essence, the *virtuoso* exercise is to substitute the maximizing 'organizational blackbox' with an ensemble of many, even more sophisticated, contractually linked, *individual blackboxes* And here and throughout the magic word is *incentives*.

Contracts – whether of the formal, legally enforceable kind or of the 'relational', informal one – entail an incentive structure, and, given the contract, these mini boxes will fire out the optimal response (optimal for each of them of course, even if generally not first-best for the organization as a whole). Incentives, as crisply reviewed by my friend Bob Gibbons (see Gibbons, 2010), one of the best in the trade, may be directly *economic* ('have a price attached') or *political* (in terms of lobbying, influence, collusion, etc.). Indeed, the prescription 'find the incentive structure able to account for behaviour *x*' is as core to mainstream Ph.D. teaching in microeconomics as it is to 'find the DSGE model and the appropriate calibrations to account for statistics *y*' in macroeconomics. Well, not surprisingly, my intellectual efforts have gone in the *opposite* direction.

This is not to underplay the role of incentives as drivers of economic behaviours. As Evita Paraskevopoulou pointed out in her comments on a previous draft, they are likely to exert a powerful influence whenever there is a straightforward link between elicitation of particular actions and rewards ('if you publish on the AER or Econometrica you will fast get tenured', or even more directly, think of piece-dependent wages). Note, however, that even in these circumstances capability-related constraints are generally active (so, for example, only a small subset of the young economists who will go through the appropriate ideological rituals at the end actually succeed in getting on the top mainstream journals).

In any case, in most circumstances one hardly finds such direct links action/reward. Rather, most often, rewards are the (generally significantly lagged) outcomes of long chains of cognitive and behavioural acts of each individual, and their relationship with the acts of other members of the organization. The issue is isomorphic to the 'no money on the table' discussion above: with opaque and complex causal structures, disentangling the incentive patterns boils down to disentangling the mapping between all the 'ifs' (the cognitive frames) and all the 'thens' (the operational repertoires) into the pay-off structures (see also Dosi et al., 2012).

As Luigi Marengo and I argue in Chapter 3 and elsewhere (cf. also the chapters on organization in Dosi, 2000), we may clear the way by just assuming, to begin with, that a *weak incentive compatibility* is there, simply standing for the assumption that – at least in economic organizations – no one will be required to heroically undertake actions which benefit the organization while massively damaging the person undertaking them. Full stop.

Granted that, our perspective offers, as *first-order* account, a view of organizations as *complex problem-solving institutional arrangements* – where, as we have repeated endless times, 'problem-solving' stands for production problems (e.g. how to build a car) and search problems (e.g. finding the vaccine for malaria) which are typically *complex* also in the technical sense that (i) they might not be perfectly decomposable (so that whatever 'solution' to a sub-problem thereof influences other sub-problems as well), and, (ii) several instances of such problems might be computationally 'hard', so that the full exploration of the problem-solving tree might take a time more than polynomial (indeed exponential) in the problem's arguments. (On problem-solving in general, see the classic Simon, 1969 and 1983; a germane discussion of ours is in Dosi and Egidi, 1991.)

Note that problem-complexity, decomposability (or not) and their mapping into different *intra-* (and *inter-*) organizational division of labour in principle has nothing to do with issues of incentive governance (even if it influences the latter), but rather impinges on the characteristics of organizational knowledge and its distribution. In turn, that has a lot to do with the characteristics of *organizational routines* (on the notion, growing out of the seminal Nelson and Winter, 1982, see also Cohen et al., 1996; Becker et al., 2005; Becker, 2005, and the literature reviewed there) and, relatedly, of *organizational memory* (indeed, we are currently working on its formalization: cf. Dosi et al., 2012).

In Chapters 2, 3 and 4 we develop such a *procedural* view of distributed organizational knowledge, explore its implications in terms of intra-organizational architectures and inter-organizational boundaries, and formally investigate the properties of different learning mechanisms – nested into different patterns of cognitive and physical labour.[12] All this fits well into an emerging *knowledge-based, capability-based*, theory of the firm, whose contours we outline in Chapter 2.

I admit that there is the risk of being taken as too much of a 'technological determinist', in the sense that such capability-centred theories derive crucial characteristics of organizational set-ups from stringent knowledge-related requirements. I am ready to run that risk: I have spent a good deal of my academic life, at least since Dosi (1982), investigating the nature and dynamics of technical knowledge, and I do stand comfortable by the notion that such knowledge entails quite hard constraints either to the fine-tuning of incentives – as the smartest agency theorists currently address – or to various sorts of 'political negotiations' and 'social constructions' – as a few post-modernist streams of thought vocally argue. My never forgotten friend and mentor, Keith Pavitt, used to ironically reply to the latter that 'no one wants to fly the Atlantic in a socially constructed aeroplane'! By the same token I would never fly either on an aeroplane that is the outcome of a bundle of optimal contracts!

In the *capability view* of the firm, capabilities are large chunks of interrelated routines and 'other quasi-genetic traits of the firm ...' (Winter in Cohen et al., 1996) – inertial, path-dependent, quite opaque to environmental feedbacks: in the short term, *organizational state variables* as opposed to *control variables* as Winter (1988) put it. And they are resilient, primarily because they are learned, knowledge-rich, responses to external or intra-organizational signals grounded on cognitive and habit-related factors. Their nature is indeed far from being a decision either derived from some argmax (...) subject to some constraints. By the same token, I do not believe for a second that 'routines are equilibria' in some game-theoretic space (indeed, I do not believe that Bob Gibbons, suggesting it in Gibbons (2006; 2010), is too hot about it either!). Granted that, broadly defined motivations and rewards are indeed important in shaping behaviours.

This is what we try to start formally exploring in Chapter 5.[13] There, we present a general model of organizational problem-solving in which we explore the relationship between problem complexity, decentralization of tasks and reward schemes. When facing complex problems which require the coordination of large numbers of interdependent elements, organizations face a decomposition problem which has both cognitive dimensions and reward dimensions. The former relate to the decomposition and allocation of the process of generation of new solutions: since the search space is too vast to be searched extensively, organizations employ heuristics for reducing it. The decomposition heuristics take the form of divisions of cognitive labour and determine which solutions are generated and become candidates for selection. The reward dimensions basically shape the selection environment which chooses alternative solutions.

Consider this just as an initial inroad within a broader agenda whereby one begins to bring also *power*, yes, *incentives* and *conflict over the distribution of net output* into a story that so far – for good reasons, as I have argued above – begins with knowledge, its distribution within and across organizations and its patterns of accumulation.

Problem-solving procedures and the theory of production
As I emphasized above and we detail in Chapters 2–5, I believe that the 'primitive' levels of description of technologies are in terms of, first, the nature of problem-solving knowledge, and, second, the actual production and search *procedures* implemented by organizations (business firms, but also other non-profit organizations). This is 'where the action is'. And the characterization of these procedures is also where ultimately the *theory of production* rests (like-minded arguments are in Winter, 1982, 2005 and 2006). However, procedures are obviously linked with several sorts of material and immaterial inputs (ranging from raw materials to machines all the way to software and services) and finally yield some outputs which, again, can be goods or services. But, how do procedures map into this lower dimensional space of inputs and outputs? This is a question which we begin to explore in Chapter 6.

Certainly, there are candidates to any empirically founded theory of production which have to be ruled out. They prominently include standard production functions in their familiar version on the continuum (and, even more unlikely, homogeneous, degree one, etc.), but also in the discrete version of activity analysis – coming together with the axiomatics of divisibility, additivity, convexity, topological closure of the production possibility set, etc. Indeed, many of these assumptions are far from innocent – and a few are far from plausible: Winter's works on the production theory bear many precious hints (in addition to those cited above, cf. Winter, 2008, and on replication of techniques Winter and Szulanski, 2001). Also in this domain I believe that one should be very cautious about any form of axiomatics. [One day some historians of economic thought will document the damages that the related, French and non-French, topological formalism brought to economics, one of the early monuments to it being Debreu's *Theory of Value*.]

On a much more phenomenological ground, it seems to me more reasonable to characterize firms with the same 'industry' – no matter how precisely defined in terms of output – as distributions of fixed ('Leontief') coefficients in the short term, with longer term dynamics shaped by both idiosyncratic learning and environmental selection (see below).[14]

Demand patterns
Part I of this collection basically concerns what goes on in the head of individual economic agents and the somewhat more metaphorical head of organizations. In a sense, all articles (except the first one, more general and agnostic) address the microeconomics of the supply side. But what about demand and market interaction?

We tackle demand patterns in Chapter 7. It is an attempt to formalize the demand profiles of multiple socially adaptive, but possibly innovative, agents – characterized by lexicographic (that is hierachically ordered) preferences, obviously a budget constraint, and some inclination to reduce cognitive dissonance ('… how much I would like to get good z, but I cannot afford it, therefore let me convince myself that I do not like it that much after all …': … the fox and the grapes …).

The topics are near one of the cores of economic analysis. In fact most economists even undergraduate trainees, when asked what economics is about, would put very high on the list the answer: 'it has to do with supply and demand … if prices increase demand falls, and symmetrically if prices increase supply augments …'.

Let me leave supply for the moment, as it has to do with the foregoing issues concerning the theory of production. Rather let me focus on demand. After second thoughts, what is the *demand curve* about? It could be two things.

First, it could be a 'psychological proposition' about agent-specific *notional* but indeed, by assumption, clear and coherent preferences. After all this is what in many models agents deliver to the mythical 'Walrasian auctioneer' (as you will see, we do that too in Chapter 9, but the purpose is precisely to show that some market dynamics properties hold *even if* one makes such a far-fetched and admittedly absurd assumption, and *even more* so otherwise …). To the same effect in the GE perspective no one explains its preferences to anyone else but still behind the existence of an equilibrium there are well-behaved individual demand functions. [That notwithstanding, I have already mentioned the dramatic pitfalls of aggregation: well-behaved (downward-sloping) individual demand do not translate into isomorphic aggregate excess demand functions]. In any case this first interpretation of 'demand' involves an ensemble of *counterfactual thought experiments* (one for each individual) while of course at each time one just observes an ensemble of points (i.e. particular combinations of prices/demanded quantities). Alternatively, *second*, demand functions could be understood as representing a *notional aggregate* relation in any one market, given *distributions* of micro preferences, not necessarily well behaved or even coherent (in this perspective, Hildebrand, 1994 investigates the statistical conditions under which such aggregate relations themselves are 'well behaved').

In Chapter 7 we try to identify a few 'stylized facts' on consumption behaviours and demand patterns: none of them lend any support to the first view. Conversely in that chapter we explore the second one, building on a microfoundation made of multiple heterogeneous agents which evolve their preferences over time, both through 'innovations' in their tastes and by social imitation.

Market dynamics

The actual relations prices/quantities in any one market depend on (i) the way markets are organized and on (ii) the different 'ecologies' of decision rules and behaviours. Both determine *how markets work*. But what do we know about it?

In a striking paradox, relatively little: economists, who tend to use the word 'market' in every other sentence, have mostly kept away from investigating their actual working, maybe fearful that by looking at them some of the 'magic' would disappear! Notable exceptions here are the works of Alan Kirman and colleagues on the fish and other markets: see among other Kirman and Vignes (1991) and the *Journal of Economic Behavior and Organization (JEBO)* Special Issue (Sapio et al., 2011).

All these studies reveal, first, robust behavioural patterns quite at odds with optimizing behaviours (at least in their most naïve versions).

Second, they vividly illustrate the already mentioned lack of isomorphism between individual behaviours – including the price/quantity profiles of individual buyers – and the aggregate price/quantity patterns of the market. The latter have to be properly understood, to repeat, as emergent outcomes of the interaction of multiple, heterogeneous, rule-governed, budget-constrained agents.

Third, all studies abundantly support the proposition that the institutional architectures of the markets (e.g. whether based on pair-wise interactions vs. auctions of different types) influence the revealed outcomes – in terms of price levels and changes, dispersion, volatility, etc. – even when holding unchanged the characteristics of the object traded and the *ecology of behavioural rules* of market participants.

Chapters 8 and 9 broadly fit into this *how-markets-work* field of investigation.

In Chapter 8 we study the properties of a stylized market in which agents repeatedly compete to be in the population *minority* (itself a metaphor for market arbitrage strategies). Two results which I consider quite important are, first, that efficient coordination turns out robustly to be, again, an emergent property resting on an ecology of *diverse* agents who do *not* play Nash equilibrium strategies. Second, we show that collective efficiency is not monotonic either in the rational sophistication of the players or in the information they are able to access. Rather, again, it crucially depends on the ecology of behaviours over the population of agents.

In Chapter 9 we address the impact of different market architectures and compare the properties of market dynamics under different trading protocols. At the empirical level, we present some evidence stemming from the comparison between different intra-daily trade regimes within the world largest stock exchanges: the distributions of returns are indeed remarkably different. Such evidence motivates also our exploration of the properties of an agent-based model for three alternative market mechanisms, namely (a) a 'Walrasian auction'; (b) a batch auction; and (c) an 'order book' trade protocol. The results not only support the importance of specific institutional arrangements – *holding constant the characteristcs of the traded assets and the ecology of behavioural rules of market participants* – but also generate statistical time series displaying distributions of returns whose differences under different architectures qualitatively match the empirical ones.

Industrial evolution
Part III of this volume is devoted to the analysis of several aspects of industrial structures, the patterns of industrial evolution and their geographical embeddedness.

The empirics of industrial structures and dynamics: heterogeneity everywhere
Contemporary economic analysis is largely subject to a rather bizarre schizophrenic syndrome.

On the one hand, as already discussed above, over the last 30 years or so, macro theories have tried to squeeze the interpretation of aggregate dynamics down to some sort of decision-theoretic framework in which the mythical "representative agent" was doing all the action. Whatever the statistical properties of the time series, be it productivity and GDP growth, fluctuations, employment, investment, etc., it had to be explained as the equilibrium outcome of some sophisticated intertemporal maximization exercise by such an agent. Conversely, on the micro side the evidence largely pushed towards the opposite side. Empirical analyses drawing upon an increasing ensemble of micro longitudinal data–sets have powerfully highlighted the ubiquitous, large and persistent heterogeneity in all dimensions of business firms' characteristics and dynamics one cared to look at.

Thanks to massive infusions of micro-data (at plant and firm level levels) into economic investigation over the last 20 years, one has begun to identify a few robust statistical properties characterizing industrial structures, their changes, and performance indicators such as corporate growth and profitability. This is what we analyse in Chapter 10 see also Dosi and Nelson, 2010 and Dosi, Lechevalier and Secchi, 2010). In brief, the 'stylized facts' include:

i.   Highly right-skewed firm *size* distributions (which at the level of the whole manufacturing industry are unimodal and closely resembling a Power Law[15] but significantly depart from it at higher degrees of sectoral disaggregation).
ii. Phenomenological descriptions of firms growth as a multiplicative stochastic process independent from size ('Gibrat Law') as a fairly good first-order description of the observed dynamics. However, significant deviations from the simplest benchmark process concern (a) small firms; (b) the general (negative) dependence of growth rates upon age; and (c) the (negative) scaling of growth *variances* with size itself.
iii. The fat-tailed distributions of *growth rates* themselves, as such a sign of some underlying correlating mechanism which would not have been there if growth events were small and independent.
iv. At any level of disaggregation widespread *differences in productivity* (no matter whether measured as labour- or 'total factor' productivity, whatever that means) across firms and across plants. Note also that such differences are highly persistent over time.
v.   Equally widespread *differences in profitability*, again at all available levels of disaggregation. And, again, profitability differentials are persistent in time.
vi. Finally, the number of innovators within each industrial sector is a small fraction of the whole population of firms, even in technologically leading countries.

Given this evidence, one is bound to ask what drives persistent asymmetries in performances and heterogeneity in corporate characteristics.

In brief, as we argue at length in Chapter 2 and in Dosi and Nelson (2010), the single most important factor in accounting for persistently heterogeneous performances rests upon equally heterogeneous organizational capabilities – idiosyncratic, difficult to imitate, often only incrementally changing over time.[16] Granted that, a set of tricky and difficult questions concerns the relationships between corporate characteristics, performances and their dynamics.

There are here both empirical challenges and tangled theoretical issues. For example, can one rationalize such relationships in terms of some underlying GE, albeit of a rather weird kind? What would that add to our interpretation of the evidence? Or, conversely, should one understand it as far-from-equilibrium evolutionary dynamics? In any case, what drives such processes? What is the balance in it between idiosyncratic and mistake-ridden innovation, learning, adaptation, on the one hand, and environmental selection among competing firms, but also among products, technologies, organizational patterns, behavioural rules, on the other? We explore some of these issues empirically in Chapter 11, Chapter 12 and with a formal model in Chapter 13.

An archetypical evolutionary story about the relationship between firm-specific characteristics and performances runs roughly like the following.

Different productivities, organizational set-ups, propensities to innovate and corporate strategies make up the distinct corporate identities which in turn should influence firms' performances. More productive firms are able to charge lower prices for the same quality goods and thus increase their market shares; more innovative firms are able to sell products which are 'better' in some dimensions, likewise increasing their shares in differentiated industries; and, finally, more efficient and more profitable firms are able to grow more because they are able to invest more given far less than perfect capital markets.

On the theory ground, the formal account of the same story is either in terms of some explicit Fisher – Price or whatever *replicator dynamics*, such as in Silverberg et al. (1988) and Metcalfe (1998) among many others, or in terms of some implicit efficiency-related replication as implied by a Nelson–Winter type investment dynamics.[17] But how does this story fares against the evidence?

Let me consider first the impact of different productivities upon profitability, growth, and survival probabilities. Mainly North American evidence, mostly at plant level, does suggest increasing output shares in high-productivity plants and decreasing shares of output in low-productivity ones as drivers in the growth of average sectoral productivities, even if the process of displacement of lower efficiency plants is rather slow (extensive references are in Dosi et al., 2010).

In complementary efforts, a growing number of scholars has indeed began doing precisely what we could call evolutionary accounting, even if most do not call it that way (for an early example of the genre, however, cf. Nelson and Winter, 1982; an application is in Chapter 10). The fundamental evolutionary idea is that productivity distributions change as a result of (i) learning by incumbent entities; (ii) differential growth (i.e. a form of selection) of incumbent entities themselves; (iii) death (indeed, a different and more radical form of selection); (iv) and entry of new entities.

Favoured by the availability of micro longitudinal data, an emerging line of research (cf. Olley and Pakes, 1996; Foster et al., 2001; Chapter 10, this volume; and the discussion in Bartelsman and Doms, 2000), investigates the properties of such decompositions, identifying the contribution to productivity growth of (1) firm-specific changes holding shares constant (sometimes called the *within* component); (2) the changes in the shares themselves, holding initial firm productivity levels constant (also known as the *between* component); (3) some interaction term; plus, to repeat, (4) exit; and (5) entry. Of course, there is a considerable variation in the evidence depending on countries, industries, and methods of analysis. However, some patterns emerge.

First, the *within* component generally is significantly larger than the *between* one: putting it another way, improvements in productivity by existing firms dominates upon selection across firms as a mode of industry advancement, at least concerning productivity (both labour and total factor productivities). This emerges both from the foregoing evolutionary accounting exercises and from estimates of the relationship between efficiency and subsequent growth, allowing for firm fixed effects. The latter is what we explore in Chapter 12. Based on data for France and Italy we show that in both countries firms identified as more productive tend also to be more profitable than other firms. The impact on growth is, instead, much less clear-cut. Both Italian and French data only show a weak relationship between relative (labour) productivities and growth (even if with the 'correct' sign): more efficient firms do *not* grow much more. Further, when some positive relation between efficiency and growth appears, this is almost exclusively due to the impact of few outliers (the very best and the very worst). And, this holds in both the short and the medium term. So, in the analyses of Chapter 12 firm-specific factors generally account for almost an order of magnitude more than selection in the explained part of the variance in firm growth rates.

Second, relative efficiencies do influence survival probabilities, and it may well turn out that selective mechanisms across the population of firms operate much more effectively in the medium/long term at this level rather than in terms of varying shares over the total industry output. (Here the challenge is primarily empirical/statistical, as it is relatively hard to find reliable data on genuine 'death' of firms, linkable with their past performances).

Third, the statistical evidence on the relations between innovation and growth – at least that regarding indeed an innovation-driven sector, pharmaceutical, studied in Chapter 11 – suggests that differential innovativeness does *not* spur differential growth. Rather, what emerges looks like a relatively stable ecology of different 'types' of firms, ranging from the innovative-only to the imitative-only firms.

In any case, the foregoing patterns hint at a sort of a puzzle, awaiting further research, in that such statistical evidence appears to be somewhat at odds with more qualitative reconstructions of industrial evolution whereby improvements in productivity (and in product characteristics), as induced by technological and organizational advances, appear to be at the centre of competitive advantages and ultimately a crucial driver towards corporate leadership: see among many others, Dosi (1984) on semiconductors and Murmann (2003) on chemicals.

I have focused so far upon the linkages between admittedly rough proxies for productivity and innovativeness, on the one hand, and corporate growth on the other. What about the relationships between profitability and the latter?

The evidence we are familiar with strikingly shows little or no link between profitability and firm growth of incumbents (cf. again Chapter 12 on Italian and French longitudinal data). However, other pieces of evidence suggest also systematic effects of profitability upon survival probabilities (cf. Bartelsman and Doms, 2000 and Foster et al., 2008).

The implications of all the foregoing empirical regularities identified so far are far-reaching. Certainly, the recurrent evidence at all levels of observation of inter-firm heterogeneity and its persistence over time is well in tune with an evolutionary notion of idiosyncratic learning, innovation (or lack of it), and adaptation. Heterogeneous firms compete with each other and, given (possibly firm-specific or location-specific) input and output prices, obtain different returns. Putting it in a different language, they obtain different quasi-rents or, conversely, losses above/below the notional 'pure competition' profit rates. Many firms enter, a roughly equivalent number of firms exit: a lot of churning always occurs. Together, the evidence increasingly reveals a rich structure in the processes of learning, competition and growth.

As already mentioned, various mechanisms of correlation, together with the sunkness and indivisibilities of many technological events and investment decisions, yield a rather structured process of change in most variables of interest – including size, productivity, profitability – also revealed by the fat-tailedness of the respective growth rates. At the same time, market selection among firms – the other central mechanism at work together with firm-specific learning in evolutionary interpretations of economic change – does not seem to be particularly powerful, at least on the yearly or multi-yearly time scale at which statistics are reported. Diverse degrees of efficiencies seem to yield primarily relatively persistent profitability differentials. That is, contemporary markets do not appear to be too effective selectors delivering rewards and punishments in terms of relative sizes or shares, no matter how measured, according to differential efficiencies. Moreover, the absence of any strong relationship between profitability and growth militates against the naïvely Schumpeterian notion that profits feed growth (by plausibly feeding investments).

Selection among different variants of a technology, different vintages of equipment, different lines of production does occur and is a major driver of industrial dynamics. However, empirically, it seems to occur to a good extent *within* firms, driven by the implementation of better processes of production and better performing products, and the abandonment of less productive, older ones.

Chapter 13 does indeed formally study the coupled effects of knowledge accumulation and market selection upon the properties of industrial evolution, trying to disentangle those features that are sort of *evolutionary invariances* holding across different *learning entry and selection regimes*, and those that are not regime-specific. I do believe that our results have some significant interest and interpretative importance. However, they, too, are subject to the foregoing 'selection caveat'. In turn the apparent 'selection weakness' might be rooted into multiple reasons – from sheer statistical to genuinely interpretative ones.

First, one measures productivity – supposedly an underlying driver of differential selection – very imperfectly: one ought to disentangle the price component of value added (and thus the price effects upon competitiveness) from physical efficiency to which productivity strictly speaking refers. However, only very rarely one is able to do it. This applies to homogeneous products and even more so when products differ in their characteristics and performances. As in modern industries most often product innovation and product differentiation are a fundamental competitive dimension that one should explicitly account for in their impact of the latter on revealed selection processes.

Second, but relatedly, the notion of sharp boundaries between industries and generalized competition within them is too heroic to hold. It is more fruitful in many industries to think of different sub-markets of different sizes as the locus of competition (see Sutton, 1998). The characteristics and size of such submarkets offer also different constraints and opportunities for corporate growth. Ferrari and Fiat operate in different sub-markets, face different growth opportunities, and do not compete with each other. However, the example is interesting also in another respect: Fiat can grow, as it actually happened, by acquiring Ferrari.

Third, a growing microevidence highlights the intertwining between technological and organizational factors as determinants of Schumpeterian competition: Bresnahan et al. (2012) illustrate the point in the case of IBM and Microsoft facing the introduction of the PC and the browser, respectively. Both firms, the work shows, faced organizational *diseconomies* precisely in the corporate activities where they were stronger, due to the mismatching between trajectories of technological change, internal organizational set-ups and market requirements.

Fourth, the links between efficiency and innovation, on the one hand, and corporate growth, on the other, are in any case mediated by large degrees of behaviour freedom, in terms, for example, of propensities to invest, to export, to expand abroad; of pricing strategies; and of patterns of diversification.

Come as it may, the evidence on the apparent weakness of selection processes requires that evolutionary theories rethink their account of the *selection landscapes* – that is the space over which competitive interactions are represented – certainly increasing the number of arguments (e.g. not only production efficiencies and prices but also product characteristics) and maybe allowing for non-linear effects (so that for example competitive forces might bite hard just in favour of the very 'best' and against the very 'worst'). Indeed, important challenges ahead for the theory.

The geography of industrial evolution
Until recently, the models of industrial evolution have been developed without much attention to their spatial dimension. Only recently evolutionary analyses have begun to meet economic geography (see Boschma and Frenken, 2006 and 2011; and the Special Issue on the topic of the *Journal of Economic Geography*, 2007). Chapter 14 and Chapter 15 are part of this drive to embed industrial dynamics in a geographical space.

Chapter 14 is a sort of 'reduced form' evolutionary model based on a stochastic Markov dynamics of firm location aimed to distinguish location-specific from sector-specific drivers of spatial agglomeration. The former act, so to speak, 'horizontally' (i.e. across all industrial sectors) while the latter unfolds in the form of dynamic increasing returns to the the stock of installed business units in a particular sector. The model is tested on Italian data in Chapter 15.

Our results suggest that different locations do exert different structural influences on the distribution of both variables. A significant horizontal power of 'urbanization', which makes some locations, especially metropolitan areas, more attractive irrespectively of the sector, emerges. However, after controlling for the latter, one is still left with very significant sector-specific forms of dynamic increasing returns to agglomeration, which vary a lot across different manufacturing activities and which plausibly have to do with technology-specific and localized forms of knowledge accumulation and spin-offs, or simply, by chance, reinforced by local path-dependence. (Indeed such statistical evidence is qualitatively well consistent with the historically much more detailed analyses of agglomeration over the life cycles of industries by Steve Klepper and colleagues; cf . Klepper, 1997 and 2010, among others.)

History and evolution
The evolution of technologies, firms, industries, institutions and whole economics unfold as a historical process entailing varying degrees of *path-dependence* and *irreversibility*. Path-dependence stands for the influence that initial conditions and subsequent events along the historical process bear on long-term outcomes. And the (related) notion of 'irreversibility' stands for the varying measures of *lock-in* of the process itself and the difficulties in, so to speak, 'run it backward'. As Davidson (2011) emphasizes in the 'Kay dabate' over the INET website, *non-ergodicity* is the general rule in economic processes.

Indeed, while sheer intuition would suggest that *history matters* at all domains of socio-economic change, it is sad to acknowledge that history does *not* matter for most contemporary economic theory and econometric practice, and when it does it is via initial, possibly persistent, but exogenous conditions of otherwise invariant processes (the hunt for 'instruments' in current econometrics of 'comparative political economy' is a good case to the point).

Part IV of this volume is focused on various aspects of the historicity of technological and economic evolution.

Chapter 16 takes the reader through a long tour in the field of path dependence.[18] First, we discuss the levels at which it might occur (e.g. individual vs. system level): indeed one could observe systems composed of path-dependent agents which are however collectively *ergodic* (that is, history-free) at least in the long term, or alternatively systems composed of agents with history-free behaviours displaying nonetheless aggregate path dependence.

[With respect to that, my priors are that in many circumstances one is going to find some path dependence at both levels. My friend Paul David has done an excellent job in showing the emergence of path-dependent phenomena even under microeconomic assumptions of rational and 'flexible' agents (i.e. sophisticated agents fine-tuning their responses to changes in the environmental signals): see for example David (1988, 1993, 2005).]

Second, we analyse some of the sources of path-dependence – including the dynamic increasing returns associated with the accumulation of technological knowledge, network externalities, complementarities in the adoption of innovation and agglomeration economies. Moreover, we fully agree with David (1994): corporate organization and institutions – largely rule-governed entities – are as such *carriers of history*.

Third, path dependency is going to appear whenever the 'selection landscapes' (see also the brief discussion above) – over which technologies, organizational traits, behaviours, etc. evolve – are *rugged*, with multiple peaks. In this case, the process is likely to get stuck in one of the multiple local maxima.

Fourth, we discuss the formalisms through which path-dependent processes are represented. In a strange paradox, to which we shall return below, fully fledged evolutionary models have so far paid relatively little attention to the path dependent features of techno-economic evolution. Conversely, different streams of 'reduced form' models suppress the inter-firm competition dynamics trying to offer succinct accounts of diffusion and social contagion, nested into heterogeneous populations and driven by dynamic increasing returns, network effects and endogenous preferences.

One of such modelling *genres* is based on Markov fields with multiple absorbing states. Another one builds upon *generalized Polya urns* (cf. Arthur, Ermoliev and Kaniovski, 1983; Dosi and Kaniovski, 1994; Bassanini and Dosi, 2001; and Chapter 16, this volume). Indeed, such machinery is well apt to account for (a) the influences of stochastic events along the evolutionary dynamics upon the long-term outcomes (and thus the related path-dependence of e.g. technology selection); (b) the widespread importance of dynamics increasing returns within 'badly behaved' dynamics: cf. Dosi and Kaniovski (1994); and, (c) the possibility that technological evolution 'gets it wrong' – in the sense that convergence is to the dominance of a technology which is 'inferior' to other ones available in some form from the start, which however the collective dynamics of adoption did not reinforce.

The common story is that unbounded increasing returns are the cause of the path-dependent emergence of monopolies of particular technologies, organizational forms, etc. In fact as we show in Chapter 17 the story is a bit more subtle than that. Indeed, we prove, unbounded increasing returns are neither necessary nor sufficient to lead to technological monopolies. Rather, asymptotic patterns depend on the relative impact of increasing returns and the degrees of heterogeneity in the population of potential adopters.

But why then does the diffusion of competing technologies display most often either 'lock in' to a quasi-monopoly or apparent turbulence but rarely stable market sharing? The answer is in terms of rates of convergence. We show that convergence to market sharing is slower than to monopoly: thus, in the former case, the environment often changes before the market-share trajectory becomes stable.[19] Just to repeat myself also in these areas, I consider our work, as well as other works by Brian Arthur, Paul David, Yuri Kaniovski, Robin Cowan – among others – as just scratching the surface of some grand interpretative questions.

The first – paraphrasing Stephen Jay Gould – concerns what 'would be conserved if the tape of history could be run twice', that is, what are the aspects of socio-economic evolution which can be thought of as relatively invariant and those that are specific to a particular sample path, to a particular history.

A second grand question regards what one could call the permanent *tension between freedom and necessity* in human affairs, i.e. the degrees of tightness of the 'grip of history' on what people and organizations can and/or 'choose' to do.

And, relatedly, third, what are the factors which are able to *delock* from particular technologies, organizational set-ups and institutional arrangements?

Again, it is sad to observe that not much research has gone into all this: in my view, this is another lethal consequence of the trivialized 'Vision of Man' (and the isomorphic 'Vision of Society') in which forward-looking agents, living in a causally transparent world maximize statistical expectations of something. In the world I have in mind, on the contrary, there is much less transparency, much less 'shadow of the future upon the present', as Gibbons (2010) puts it, and much more 'shadow of the past upon the future': even when behaviours are actually grounded upon expectations, the latter bear the mark of the evolution of collective beliefs, and also of collective illusions and sheer self-propelling madness, as the current financial crisis vividly illustrates.

To repeat, I strongly believe that path-dependency is ubiquitous in human affairs (and not only there), from the very micro of individuals to the levels of institutions and macroeconomics. In turn, this is intimately related to what economists – mostly with some uneasiness – acknowledge as instances of potential *multiple equilibria* (if equilibria are more than one, historical circumstances are the likely candidates to explain which one is chosen) and *hysteresis* – as path-dependence has been called for a while in macroeconomics by a brave minority largely reduced to publication silence since. (An insightful example is Cooper and John, 1988, unfortunately with not much follow-up.)

If 'history matters', however, economists should then give up the ritual of the last section of their articles; namely, 'welfare and policy implications' of whatever analysis, since different possible historical paths may lead to different outcomes also in terms of rates of growth, income distributions, etc. Should one care, at least in term of the common Paretian arguments? Most emphatically *not*. Just think of how pathetic an ending would be of Darwin's *Origin of the Species* in terms of 'welfare implications'! Certainly, the ambition of many analyses may and should legitimately involve the identification of the few or many *achievable worlds*, conditional on whatever initial conditions (and of course 'initial' means at any time of the evolutionary process). This is indeed a tall but fundamental challange. But 'Paretian' comparisons ? Let us please leave them to science fiction.

Indeed multiplicity of growth paths is one of the topics of the last part of these collected works.

Development and growth as institutionally embedded evolutionary processes
The articles in Part IV deal with several aspects of the development process, the patterns of aggregate growth and their microfoundations. In its essence, development has to do with the *great transformation* – borrowing a Karl Polanyi (1944) expression – leading from traditional,

mostly rural, economies to economies driven by industrial activities (and nowadays also advanced services), able to systematically learn how to implement and how to generate new ways of doing things (i.e. new techniques of production), new products and new organizational modes – typically under conditions of dynamic increasing returns.

Such a *great transformation* entails a major process of *accumulation of knowledge and capabilities*, both at the levels of *individuals* and *organizations*. Certainly, part of such capabilities builds on education and formally acquired skills (what in the economists' jargon often goes under the heading of 'human capital'). However, at least equally important, capabilities have to do with the problem-solving knowledge embodied in organizations discussed in the articles in Part I – concerning e.g. production technologies, governance of labour relations, marketing, etc., as well as 'dynamic capabilities' of search and learning.

As we argue at greater length in Cimoli et al. (2009), the patterns of accumulation of knowledge are at the core of the development processes: the 'unbound Prometheus' systematically improving technological and organizational knowledge was a crucial *deus ex machina* of early industrialization almost three centuries ago, and is also of subsequent episodes of development (Landes, 1969 and Cipolla, 1965; cf. also Landes, 1998; Freeman, 1982; Reinert, 2007; Rosenberg, 1976; Mokyr, 1990; Nelson, 2005). However this is far from being the identification of some 'magic bullet'. In fact, economic historians investigating the 'European exceptionalism' (cf. Landes, 1998) leading to the industrial revolution do point at the advances of technical knowledge as a crucial factor in the industrial take-off. However, the European industrialization precisely illustrates that not even technological advances are such a 'magic bullet'. Many of the technological advances upon which the industrial revolution drew were originally developed, or at least equally known, in other regions, *in primis* China. 'European exceptionalism' was made possible by a conjunction of complementary conditions ranging from the 'scientific attitude' of inquiry about nature which fostered knowledge accumulation and its codification and diffusion, all the way to the characteristics of the political structure and the relations between rulers and subjects. In this vein, C. Freeman (2008) – in his Selected Essays which puts together an ensemble of his classic contributions – suggests that *national systems of innovation and production* develop and advance (or do not) on the grounds of the co-evolutionary dynamics among five sub-domains, and related institutions, governing

i.   the generation of *scientific knowledge* (he is talking primarily of 'frontier' countries);
ii.   the development, improvement, adoption of new artefacts and new techniques of production (that is the domain of *technology*);
iii. the *economic machine* which organizes the production and distribution of goods, services and incomes, and *together, information flows and governance modes*;
iv.   the *political and legal structure*;
and, finally
v.   the *cultural domain*, shaping values, norms and customs.

Several scholars are indeed adding substance (implicitly or explicitly) to this 'grand political economy' programme: we have already mentioned a few contributors to the technology-focused literature, but the 'ground view' takes on board the complementary importance of the political economy of labour relations, income claims, property rights and, indeed, of culture (working our way backwards, from Mokyr, 2009, North, 2005, Greif, 2006 and Boyer, 1990, all the way to Karl Marx and Adam Smith).

This is not the place to discuss in any detail the long history of industrialization. Suffice to say that if there is some truth in this co-evolutionary story, such a story does not apply only to the Low Countries four centuries ago or England three centuries back. It does apply equally well to all the later episodes of industrialization and subsequent self-sustained growth. The point is indirectly revealed by the overall shaky results stemming from the quest for overarching *institutional preconditions* for growth or invariant policy recipes for it.[20] On the contrary, the co-evolutionary account rests on some sorts of *congruence conditions* between *ingredients* (including state variables which influence the subsequent dynamics) and *processes* where the matchings or mismatchings feature prominently between capabilities accumulation and the institutional set-ups of any one economy feature prominently.

[Incidentally, note that if this view is correct, the outcomes of different *combinatorics* among such institutional set-ups and learning dynamics are not likely to be statistically captured by heroic 'reduced form' estimations in search of general preconditions, or driving factors of differential growth – supposedly shielded from endogeneity – invariant in their effects across countries.]

The identification of feasible combinatorics between technological, organizational and institutional arrangements is indeed a major promise of the *National* (and *Sectoral*) *Systems of Innovation* research programme, to which Chapter 22 in this volume attempts to contribute (major references in the field are Lundvall, 1992, Nelson, 1993, Malerba, 2004 and Amable, 2003).

In this area, I must confess that while I share the spirit and also the appreciation of the importance of the whole scientific enterprise, I hold mixed feelings on the results so far, in that I find myself uneasy with exercises that a bit too often end up just with descriptions of individual instances, which, as interesting as they might be, fall short of any attempt of taxonomization. However, taxonomies are crucial. After all a fundamental contribution of Linnaeus, well before Darwin's theory of the *processes of evolution* was the tentative classification of species, families, etc. If one had only the morphology of individual plants or animals or even their inner workings, that would not have been any adequate match for any theory of *variation, selection, retention*. Anyhow, Chapter 18 (with the never forgotten Chris Freeman and Silvia Fabiani) and Chapter 19 attempt to map a few 'stylized facts' – that is the statistical and 'qualitative' invariances – in the processes of development and growth.[21]

A first set of stylized facts concern the secular trends since the Industrial Revolution. Here the dominant tendency is towards differentiation and increasing divergence in per capita incomes and technological capabilities, intertwined by episodes of catching-up, forging ahead and falling behind.

A second ensemble of regularities concerns the structure and the inner working of industrialized economies (of which a few had been already identified by Kaldor, 1961) – including the exponential growth of labour productivities, and the *rough* long-term constancy of distributive shares between wages and profits and of capital/output ratios.[22]

Finally, a third ensemble has to do with microeconomic regularities – some already discussed when addressing the contributions from Part III – featuring prominently the persistent heterogeneity among business firms on every performance dimension, even within the same line of business.

In Chapter 19, we take a closer look at the international distribution of incomes and their dynamics, and compare the properties of the latter with the micro properties of firm growth rates. Concerning (per capita) income distribution we refine on the properties discussed by Durlauf and Quah (1999) and Temple (1999) finding further evidence on an *increasing* multimodality of the distribution, supporting the notion of *groups* of countries – distinct in terms of income levels – with only a limited mobility across them. Conversely, regarding growth rates, the evidence presented in Chapter 19 suggests striking invariances in the processes of growth which hold at different levels of observation, from firms to whole countries. The common exponential properties of growth rates which they share mark widespread correlating mechanisms which aggregation does not dilute. That is precisely the *mark of complex evolving systems*.

A puzzling question regards precisely the nature of each mechanisms which might well be different across levels. So, as mentioned above, one may conjecture that at micro level 'lumpy' technological events, idiosyncratic increasing returns, together with the interdependences induced by the the the very competitive process, may account for the 'tent-shape' distribution of growth shocks. Conversely, at country level, it might well be due to, again, some forms of increasing returns together with the inter-sectoral propagation of technological and (*Keynesian*) demand impulses.

Of course the understanding of the evolutionary dynamics of economic system is far from confined to the understanding of its statistical properties. The thread of such a story crucially builds upon an account of the *nature and dynamics of technological knowledge*, its sources, modes of access and mechanisms of economic exploitation. We discuss all this at length in Dosi and Nelson (2010), and in earlier works of mine (Dosi, 1982, 1988), as well as in a few other works included in the Dosi (2000) collection.

In this volume, Chapter 21 analyses in particular the implications for the understanding of the process of development, seen – to repeat – as painstaking processes of accumulation of individual and organizational capabilities. Such processes are fostered (or hindered) by a rich ensemble of institutions and public policies. We analyse their *institutional embeddedness* in Chapter 23.

Note that the perspective has indeed very little to do with any *market failure* argument. In fact, were one to judge the occurrence of 'market failures' in terms of the discrepancies between empirically observed markets and the theoretical no-market failure archetype, it is easy to come to the conclusion that the 'world is a huge market failure' as Joe Stiglitz once put it! And in fact it is, if judged on the far-fetched requirements of orthodox theory (in terms of information distribution, completeness of markets, indeed, *absence of innovation*, etc.) Rather, it is much more useful – from both interpretative and normative points of view – to see markets themselves as institutions, coupled with other non-market ones shaping (i) the nature and distribution of knowledge in any one economy, and dynamically its learning patterns; (ii) the very nature of the economic agents and their boundaries; (iii) the economic signals and incentive profiles they face; and (iv) the organization of their interactions in product, financial and labour markets (what my friends Robert Boyer and Benjamin Coriat and colleagues would call *modes of socio-economic regulation* specific of different *varieties of capitalism*).

[Chapter 22 was originally prepared within the research which led to the book on *Industrial Policies and Development: The Political Economy of Capabilities Accumulation* (cf. Cimoli et al., 2009) studying comparatively across different historical experiences the co-evolutionary processes between technological capabilities, organizational forms and assessing the role of public policies and various measures of *institutional engineering* in all that. I warmly suggest it to the reader!]

I have emphasized repeatedly that at all domains of observation, *heterogeneity* is ubiquitous *even within* the same country; *a fortiori* this applies to the comparison across different countries characterized by different technological capabilities and per capita incomes. Indeed the general conjecture that we have explored at greater length in Castaldi et al. (2009), and earlier – on the grounds of admittedly pathetic statistics (but sound hypotheses, I continue to believe) – in Dosi et al. (1990) is that in fact the former are a fundamental determinant of the latter (see also Fagerberg, 1994).

Another major implication concerns the interpretation of trade patterns. Trade theory as such stands out as an exception in economic analysis for its empirical testability. In most areas one finds a long list of ludicrous propositions in fact shielded from refutation, as they basically involve purported exercises of maximization over an *unobservable* function whose choice of the arguments and functional form is left to the analyst, subject to some *unobservable* 'production function' constraint, left, again, to the analyst's arbitrariness.

Not so in trade theories, which historically attempted to predict trade flows on the grounds of country-wide and product-specific technologies of production. It was so for the Ricardian theory of comparative advantage and also, later, for the Heckscher–Ohlin–Samuelson theorem, predicting – as known – that countries will export commodities whose production is intensive in the factors of which the country is relatively more endowed. And the other way around for the imports. Being a testable proposition, Leontief did test it (Leontief, 1954). The results were as sound a falsification as it can come in the socio-economic domain: the US – a capital-rich country – were exporting more labour-intensive goods and importing more capital-intensive ones!

Did economists abandon the theory as falsified? Not at all. On the contrary they called it the *Leontief paradox*, a bit as if physicists would have called the results of the Michelson– Morley experiment on the speed of light as the 'Michelson–Morley paradox' rather than taking it, as they correctly did, as a falsification of the ether theory.[23]

Keith Pavitt, Luc Soete and myself did attempt to put forward an alternative, accounting for the observed export patterns in terms of *technology gaps and leads*. It is a theory based on *absolute* advantages/disadvantages, in that it does *not* compare sectors within the same country (with some GE or at least some notion of opportunity cost lurking in the background) but rather it compares *countries within the same sector*. Indeed, on the grounds of admittedly very poor data (they were the only available at the time) we find a good corroboration of the model, and since then further explored (but still far from enough) both theoretically and empirically in Cimoli and Soete (1992), Fagerberg (2002), Laursen and Meliciani (2010), Verspagen and Wakelin (1997), Guerrieri and Meliciani (2005). [Conversely, theoretical and empirical ancestors are Posner (1961), Freeman et al. (1963) and Hufbauer (1966).]

Since the basic model is as far as one can get away from any assumption of the 'world as a GE', one is also entitled to analyse the dynamics of the overall shares of countries in world exports, again, as a function of overall technology gaps and leads across countries themselves. This is what we do in Chapter 20 showing how the long-term share of dynamics is fundamentally affected by the relative innovative capabilities (proxied by international patenting) and by fixed investments (as such capturing also capital embodied technical change), while changes in unit labour costs and exchange rates exhaust their effects in the shorter term.

There are straightforward venues ahead for this whole research enterprise. One regards the refinement of the analysis of *sectoral* dynamics, in that better understanding the (most likely sector-specific) balances between technological, organizational, and cost-related factors as determinants of the changing shares in world trade.

A second venue concerns the *microeconomics* of such processes, trying to identify the evolving features of exporting firms and their changing competitive success on the international markets.[24]

Towards a soundly micro-founded evolutionary macroeconomics: some contributions to the Grand Project, and a few challenges ahead

Chapter 24 and Chapter 25 try to address, so to speak 'head on', the interpretation of macroeconomic dynamics. In both works the microfoundation explicitly rests on multiplicity of heterogeneous interacting agents.

Macroeconomic dynamics is generated in the models via aggregation of individual behaviours. Typically, non-linearities in system dynamics induced by heterogeneity and far-from-equilibrium interactions are the rule. And the statistical properties exhibited by dynamically coupled aggregate variables (employment, output, etc.) ought be properly interpreted as emergent properties grounded on persistent micro disequilibria. The observed stable relations among those same aggregate variables indeed emerge out of turbulent, disequilibrium, microeconomic interactions.

In Chapter 24, making use of a model built on such premises, we address two types of questions.

First, we ask whether the model is able to reproduce robustly over a large set of behavioural and institutional settings the main aggregate regularities that we observe in real-world labour market data. For instance: does our model generate jointly Beveridge, Wage (or Phillips), and Okun curves for a sufficiently large region of system parameters?

Second, we try to map different behavioural and institutional settings into statistically distinct patterns of labour market dynamics. For example: are there institutional and technological settings wherein the economy is unable to display robustly a downward-sloping relation between vacancy and unemployment rate? Under which conditions can one observe shifts of the Beveridge curve? And, similarly, under which technological regimes does the Okun curve display an absolute elasticity greater than one (as such revealing a form of aggregate increasing returns)?

Simulations show that the model is able robustly to reproduce Beveridge, Wage and Okun curves under quite broad behavioural and institutional set-ups. Moreover, the system generates endogenously an Okun coefficient greater than one even if individual firms employ techniques exhibiting constant returns to labour use. Monte Carlo simulations also indicate that statistically detectable shifts in Okun and Beveridge curves emerge as the result of changes in institutional, behavioural and technological parameters. Finally, the model generates quite sharp predictions about how system parameters affect aggregate performance (i.e. average GDP growth) and its volatility.

In Chapter 25 we further study an agent-based model that bridges Keynesian theories of demand generation and Schumpeterian theories of technology-fuelled economic growth. Agents always face opportunities of innovations and imitation, which they they try to tap with expensive search efforts, under conditions of genuine uncertainty (so they are unable to form any accurate expectations on the relation between search investment and probabilities of successful outcomes). Hence (*endogenous*) technological shocks (the innovations themselves) are unpredictable and idiosyncratic.

The model builds on evolutionary roots, and is also in tune with 'good New Keynesian' insights (cf., e.g., Stiglitz, 1994a). It tries to explore the feedbacks between the factors influencing aggregate demand and those driving technological change. By doing that it begins to offer a unified framework jointly accounting for long-term dynamics and higher frequencies' fluctuations.

The model is certainly well in tune with the growing literature on agent-based computational economics (see Tesfatsion and Judd, 2006; LeBaron and Tesfatsion, 2008), clearly meeting evolutionary but also Solow's (2008) pleads for microheterogeneity: a multiplicity of agents interact without any ex ante commitment to the reciprocal consistency of their actions.[25]

Furthermore, the model – like most evolutionary ABMs – is "structural" in the sense that it explicitly builds on a representation of what agents do, how they adjust, etc. In that, our commitment is to "phenomenologically" describe microbehaviours as close as one can get to available microevidence. Akerlof's (2002) advocacy of a "behavioural microeconomics", we believe, builds on that notion. In fact, this is our first fundamental disciplining device. A second, complementary discipline involves the ability of the model to jointly account for an ensemble of stylized facts regarding both "micro/meso" phenomena with genuinely macro 'stylized facts'. In the case of the mentioned model they include (i) endogenous growth; (ii) persistent fluctuations; (iii) recurrent involuntary unemployment; (iv) pro-cyclical consumption, investment, productivity, employment and changes in inventories; (v) fat-tailed distributions of aggregate growth rates; together with (vi) persistent asymmetries in productivity across firms; (vii) 'spiky' investment patterns; and (viii) skewed firm size distributions; (ix) fat-tailed firm growth rates.

We employ the model to investigate the properties of macroeconomic dynamics and the impact of public polices on supply, demand and the 'fundamentals' of the economy. We find that the complementarities between factors influencing aggregate demand and drivers of technological change affect both 'short-run' fluctuations and long-term growth patterns. From a normative point of view, simulations show a corresponding complementarity between 'Keynesian' and 'Schumpeterian' policies. I consider this a major result, with far-reaching implications in terms of theory and policies.

Both types of policies seem to be necessary to put the economy into a long-run sustained growth path. Schumpeterian policies *potentially* foster economic path, but they do not appear to be able alone to actually yield such sustained long-run growth. In a broad parameter region, 'fundamental' (indeed, endogenously generated) changes in technology are unable to fully propagate in terms of demand generation and ultimately output growth. By the same token, demand shocks (in the simplest case, induced by government fiscal policies) bear persistent effects upon output levels, rates of growth and rates of innovations. Hence, Keynesian policies not only have a strong impact on output volatility and unemployment but seem to be also a necessary condition for long-run economic growth.

In fact, our results suggest that the matching or mismatching between innovative exploration of new technologies and the conditions of demand generation appear to yield two distinct 'regimes' or 'phases' of growth (or absence thereof), also characterized by different short-run fluctuations and unemployment levels. Even when Keynesian policies allow for a sustained growth, their tuning affects the amplitude of fluctuations and the long-term levels of unemployment and output. Symmetrically, fluctuations and unemployment rates are also affected by 'Schumpeterian policies', holding constant macro demand management rules.

As I see it, the model is a very encouraging template to be modified and refined in order to explore further domains of economic analysis. As such, however, it represents already in my view an important advancement vis-à-vis a whole first generation of evolutionary models pioneered by Nelson and Winter, which – I keep repeating to often less than enthusiastic evolutionary audiences – contain far too much Schumpeter and far too little Keynes.

Take the Nelson–Winter model(s). Together with their path-breaking merits in formalizing endogenous uncertainty-ridden technological search, they are, from the macroeconomic point of view, *equilibrium models*: the labour market clears and so does the product market. A central reference of them is Solow's growth model and the related quest is for much more reasonable (indeed, evolutionary!) foundations to the macro patterns of growth Solow identified. In that, however, they fall short of Keynesian economics, which – as Paul Krugman puts it, and I fully agree – is 'essentially about the refutation of Say's Law, about the possibility of a general shortfall in demand'. And in that view one finds 'it easiest to think about demand failures in terms of quasi-equilibria models in which some things, including wages and the state of long-term expectations in Keynes' sense, are held fixed, while other adjust toward a conditional equilibrium of sorts' (Krugman, 2011, p. 3).

Indeed, as Kaldor (1983) sharply points out in his 50-year assessment of the *General Theory*, generic multiplicity of *non-Say quasi-equilibria* is the rule. Let me refine this a bit, citing again Kaldor:

> The originality in Keynes's conception of effective demand lies in the division of demand into two components, an endogenous component and an exogenous component. It is the endogenous component which reflects production, for much the same reasons as those given by Ricardo, Mill or Say – the difference is only that in a money economy (i.e. in an economy where things are not directly exchanged, but only through the intermediation of money) aggregate demand can be a function of aggregate supply (both measured in money terms) without being equal to it – the one can be some fraction of the other.
>
> To make the two equal requires the addition of the exogenous component (which could be one of a number of things, of which capital expenditure – 'investment' – is only one) the value of which is extraneously determined. Given the relationship between aggregate output and the endogenous demand generated by it (where the latter can be assumed to be a monotonic function of the former), there is only one level of output at which output (or employment) is in 'equilibrium' – that particular level at which the amount of exogenous demand is just equal to the difference between the value of output and the value of the endogenous demand generated by it. If the relationship between output and endogenous demand (which Keynes called 'the propensity to consume') is taken as given, it is the value of exogenous demand which determines what total production and employment will be. A rise in exogenous demand, for whatever reasons, will cause an increase in production which will be some multiple of the former, since the increase in production thus caused will cause a consequential increase in endogenous demand, by a 'multiplier' process. How large this secondary increase will be will depend on a lot of things such as the retribution of the additional output between wages and profits, and the change in productivity (or in costs per unit of output) associated with the increase in production, etc. [...] A capitalist economy ... is not 'self-adjusting' in the sense that an increase in potential output will automatically induce a corresponding growth of actual output. This will only be the case if exogenous demand expands at the same time to the required degree; and as this cannot be taken for granted, the maintenance of full employment in a growing economy requires a deliberate policy of demand management.
> [...]

Keynes was no student of Walras. However, there was enough in Marshall (particularly in Book v, the short period theory of value) to raise the same kind of qualms – why don't all markets behave in such a way to compel the full utilization of resources? Marshall's own theory suggested that saving provide the supply of 'loanable funds' which, given an efficient capital market which equates supply and demand, governs the amount of capital expenditure incurred. This amounts to a denial of the whole idea of an exogenous source of demand – the latter notion presupposes that the supply and demand for savings are brought into equality by changes in income and employment and not by the 'price' of savings in the capital market, which is the rate of interest. In order to explain why the market for loans is not 'market-clearing' in the same sense as other markets, Keynes introduced the liquidity-preference theory of interest – which, as is evident from his own later writings, was added more or less as an afterthought (Kaldor, 1983, 172–175).

And, if I may, it was a bad, empirically far-fetched, and theoretically misleading idea. The one which allowed the Patinkin, Modigliani, etc. of this world to step in and show that Keynes' model was after all a DSGE with frictions ... (the paradox being that the neoclassical Vatican took so long to realize!). In fact, to repeat, in Chapter 25 we take the opposite route and analyse, together, the properties of *endogenous fluctuations* and *multiple non-Say growth paths*, conditional on different mechanisms of demand formation.

There are several further challenges for analysis broadly within an 'evolutionary/Keynesian' perspective.

Financial dynamics and transmission mechanisms with the real economy
Finance is not a 'veil' just rapping up real dynamics. At last, after the latest crisis, a rapidly growing ensemble of models takes seriously the fact that financial dynamics might systematically depart from some 'fundamental process' (whatever that means ...)

I think that major advances have been made in the understanding of correlating mechanisms of whatever origin on financial markets – with network theories helping a lot on the formal side – together with the acknowledgement of cognitive and behavioural correlations. But also in this domain there is a long way to go.

There are obviously theories that one should rule out: at this point I think that sheer decency should prevent any respectable scholar to talk about 'market efficiency' *et similia*. Granted that, among decent candidates to the interpretation of financial market dynamics, I see a divide demanding to be fruitfully bridged.

On the one side, a set of investigations – going under the heading of 'evolutionary finance' – seriously takes on board some form of inter-agent heterogeneity (at very least in term of risk aversions) and focuses on the properties of markets as *selection environments*. In that wealth variations play the role of a 'replicator process' (cf. above): see among others Levy et al. (2000), Blume and Easley (1992, 2010), Anufriev and Bottazzi (2010) and Anufriev and Dindo (2010).

Almost symmetrically, a variegated ensemble of analyses addresses primarily *expectation variety* and *expectation dynamics*, in ways disjointed to varying degrees from 'fundamentals'. This ensemble includes, first, a good deal of behavioural finance.

It includes also more radical departures from any 'fundamentalist' anchor, correspondingly accounting for phenomena such as imperfect, heterogeneous learning; imitation; herd behaviour; 'beauty contests' and 'market reflexivity'; and changing knowledge frames. In addition, it includes Frydman and Goldberg (2011), building their interpretation on cognitively rather sophisticated agents but fully taking on board an assumption of *lack of transparency* similar to the one discussed above. Although coming from a quite different tradition they happen to share with most scholars of the economics of innovation and organizational studies the ideas that knowledge is *not* sheer information and cognitive maps are *not* isomorphic to the territory they try to represent.

To the opposite end, within the same ensemble, one finds much simpler 'strip down' models of social imitation, mimetism, herd or contrarian behaviours, etc. sometimes amenable to formal treatment. The models outlined in Kirman (2010) are a good example.[26] Note that I am not advocating here any sort of meta model unifying the two foregoing ensembles. However, more systematic links between the two would help a lot in understanding the *irresistible evolutionary drive towards the financial abyss*, as we call it in Bottazzi et al. (2011).

A second related major challenge concerns the coupling of financial markets with the real economy. Putting it another way, we are still relatively far from a coherent merging between Minsky-type financial processes (Minsky, 1982, 1986), on the one hand, and explicit accounts of decentralized evolving economies, on the other. But evolutionary agent-based models are promising candidates for the task (and indeed we have a project along these lines involving Giorgio Fagiolo, Mauro Napoletano, Andrea Roventini and Tania Treibich).

Towards a classic/evolutionary theory of value?
A third grand challenge facing evolutionary theory is nothing short of a theory of value and distribution. Again, here as elsewhere, I might not find full consensus even amongst my fellow travellers. Basically in the canonical evolutionary theory so far – as Benjamin Coriat has kept *rightly* voicing – there are no workers, no capitalists, no rentiers, no financial sharks ...

It could well be that there is no need to have them because all of them are here to offer 'the services' of their stock of whatever – labour, capital, sharkness ... – and there are appropriate markets for them, plausibly accounting for expectations on future (alternative) returns. I happen to think nearly the opposite, in the good company of A. Smith, Ricardo and Marx, but very far away from Debreu and like-minded.

We need a theory of value in which (a) claims are made in worlds in which bygones are bygones, and therefore in a historical economy also the expected returns at the time of investment have very little to do with the actual revenues at any subsequent time (unless one invokes the epistemological horror of 'rational expectation'); and (b) socially and functionally differentiated groups have vastly different powers of 'voting with their orders and their feet'.

Relatedly, all the above bears crucial links with macroeconomic dynamics and in particular unemployment rates. To quote Keynes (1943) as cited in Kaldor (1985):

> ... unemployment is not a mere accidental blemish in a private enterprise economy. On the contrary, it is a part of the essential mechanism of the system and has a definite function to fulfil. The first function of unemployment [...] is that it maintains the authority of masters over men. The master has usually been in a position to say: 'If you do not want the job, there are plenty of others who do'. When the men say 'If you do not want to employ me there are plenty of others who will' the situation is radically changed.

Policy experiments
A fourth domain focuses on the refinement of the 'policy experiments', including those regarding monetary and fiscal policy prescriptions. For example, were one to trust that our model (Chapter 25) captures something important of the real world, what happens if on the top of it one puts a Central Banker applying some sort of Taylor's Rule – linking purportedly,

money supply, interest rates and inflation rates? Needless to say, there is nothing in our artificially created world that implies any such relation. Want my guess: if you do not build it in, you do not get it out – at par with mythical properties like the so-called 'Ricardian equivalence'[27] or in the the the Middle Ages, the Unicorn, the miraculous properties *Mandragora roots*, etc.

Are we doomed to live forever with unbridled globalization? Some policy-related conclusions
We live an international economy which is – fortunately or unfortunately – 'globalized'.

On the formal side, agent-based, evolutionary, models ought to offer at least some pale images of it. Bad luck that most of models are closed economy ones. Of course the latter are bound to be a necessary first approximation. But we urgently need to go beyond them.

To be fair, quite a few works within the 'institutionalist/evolutionary family' address diverse features of our 'globalized world'. Frankly I think that most of the 'family' takes myopically globalization as inevitable as geological movements, while in fact it has been the outcomes of very purposeful dynamics in politics and academia. By the same token, there seems to be little urgency within such a family to offer also reasonable *formal* accounts of interacting, technologically and organizationally asymmetric, economies.

Symmetrically, on the policy front, yes, there are a lot of insightful hints, but I think the whole evolutionary community is committing a major intellectual and political crime not to forcefully link up with the admirable policy battles by Paul Krugman (and unfortunately very few others, including however Joe Stiglitz and Gerry Silverberg) on the whole macro side, and with the point put forward by the usually cautious Dan Rodrik on the inner incompatibility between globalization, national sovereignty and democracy (Rodrik, 2011).

I have emphasized a lot in the foregoing comments on *formal* theories. This is not because I consider other forms of analysis less important. On the contrary, other approaches – from history grounded 'appreciative' (qualitative) theorizing, to bottom-up statistical analyses all the way to case studies – are at least equally important complements, and sometimes more compelling indeed. The point is however that a good deal of the interpretation of economic phenomena and an overwhelming part of the policy debate is informed by *theory* – indeed, as the reader who got so far in this introduction well understands – in my view a *very bad theory*. And with very *pernicious policy* implications. Take the diagnosis of the current crisis.

Let me leave aside the *pasdarans* who believe that it was just the outcome of some aggregate supply shock (and therefore presumably there is no voluntary unemployment or if there is, it is just due to 'adjustment frictions'?!) They belong to Bob Solow's Napoleons' cited earlier.

Even neglecting them, a great number of scholars in the profession, after the initial surprise, are rapidly converging back to the propositions and policy advocacies derived from their old theoretical spectacles. And so one gets also the rosary of too familiar advices: 'in order to increase employment, labour market in general and wage setting in particular have to be made more flexible ...' (as if unemployment were not a consequence of a worldwide aggregate demand); 'the priority now is to balance the budget because only then growth will start again ...' (as if there were the slightest evidence of a crowding out between private investment and public expenditure, even after all the econometric cooking); 'one should stop pumping liquidity into the economy because this will fuel a hike in long-term interest rates and inflation ...' (when in fact, net of imported inflation of primary commodities,

Organization for Economic Co-operation and Development (OECD) countries are in the middle of a price *deflation*); etc.

Indeed, establishing a sound *theoretical* alternative is probably a necessary, even if not sufficient, condition for an alternative menu of policies. In shorthand I would call it a programme of *innovation-centred, environment-friendly, heavily redistributive, Keynesianism.*

The works that follow – even when at face value many of them are very far from the policy domain – have been driven also by the ambition to 'better understand the world in order to contribute to make it better'. Needless to say, they witness the enormous gap between elements of an alternative understanding of how the economic system works (or doesn't) and a coherent ensemble of policy prescriptions. Of course, filling this gap is bound to be a huge collective enterprise. Let me just end this introduction by flagging its urgency, in a historical moment when the scourge of misleading orthodoxies – much like the early 1930s – carries its sinister impact on the management of a crisis that they contributed to generate in the first place.

Endnotes

1. Comments on previous versions of this introduction by Pietro Dindo, Bill Janeway, Francisco Louça, Stan Metcalfe, Dick Nelson, Alessandro Nuvolari, Evita Paraskevopoulou, Andrea Roventini and Sid Winter, really helped a lot towards this draft. I gratefully acknowledge support to the whole enterprise by the Institute for New Economic Thinking (INET), grant no. IN01100022, and by FINNOV – Finance, Innovation & Growth – FP7/2007-2013, European Union, grant agreement no. 217466; with Scuola Superiore Sant'Anna.
2. We have already raised this issue in Dosi and Orsenigo (1988) to which we still refer for more details.
3. To be fair, Schumpeter, especially from the 1930s onwards, grew increasingly unhappy of such separation between 'shocks' and subsequent adjustments to equilibrium: witness his reluctance to accept the related distinction in the emerging econometrics field between (exogenous) impulses and subsequent propagation, suggested by his friend Ragnar Frisch. (Thanks to Francisco Louça for pointing it out to me: much more on the point in Louça, 2001.)
4. For a devastating critique of the notion of 'representative agent', cf. Kirman (1989, 1992).
5. To be precise, 'rational expectations' alone are not sufficient to guarantee 'neutrality' of monetary and fiscal policies, but one loses the straightforward Keynesian relations such as those implied by IS–LM curves and the like.
6. Strictly speaking, DSGE are typically estimated through a Bayesian procedure, which actually boils down to a calibration of the parameters over intervals
7. I borrow the term from Landes (1969).
8. Partly overlapping considerations about the current state of macroeconomics are in Stiglitz (2011).
9. Note, however, that quite a few 'aggregate' (i.e. non-microfounded) dynamic models are nonetheless consistent with an evolutionary interpretations (some of them are surveyed in Silverberg and Verspagen, 2005 and Coriat and Dosi, 1998) The point is also discussed in the introduction to Dosi (2000).
10. On the latter notion related to nature of institutions and behaviours therein cf. Nelson and Sampat (2001).
11. On the notions of the 'emergence' and 'metastability', cf. the suggestive discussion in Lane (1993); see also below.
12. For a more detailed review of the whole *genre* of formal models trying to grasp procedural knowledge, routines and their dynamics, cf. Dosi et al. (2011). Important contributions in this domain include Levinthal (1997), Gavetti and Levinthal (2000), Ethiraj and Levinthal (2004) and Siggelkow and Rivkin (2005).
13. See also Dosi et al. (2003, Chapter 4, this volume).
14. I easily admit that this stand on 'axiomatics' is quite radical and even Sid Winter is unwilling to go that far. So, in a comment on a previous draft of this Introduction, Sid wrote to me stating that he 'would argue that the familiar axioms have a reasonable claim to being a good approximation to some parts of economic reality …[depending] strongly on the scale of the phenomena [one] is talking about, e.g. whether [one is] talking about capacity utilization levels of an industry or in a single plant', while of course acknowledging that the 'key shortcoming of the traditional apparatus is its built-in distancing from technological change'. Of course I fully share the last part of the comment. Concerning the former part, I do think that a theory of production is *in primis* a *micro* theory, but it is there where the distance between the standard axiomatics and the empirical evidence is particularly high (I trust Sid agrees on that). And, in my view, taking on board the standard axiomatics is also misleading in that it tends to induce an appreciation of, say, 'industry level production technology' as an allocative problem across micro techniques. Yes, most often at this level it is easy to describe

an industry *ex post* in terms of convex, divisible, etc. sets of microtechniques even when one abhors any choice-theoretic description of what goes on behind them (an example is in Hildenbrand, 1981, which I find very insightful). These sets, however, are very interesting objects in their own right for the description and analysis of the moving distributions of industries techniques (indeed I use them with my collaborators), but in my view, they do not offer foundations to any theory of production – *except under central planning* – if by the latter we mean a theory interpreting why the micro coefficients are what they empirically are. Let the discussion unfold. In any case, as the reader has certainly noticed, I hold a sort of methodological prescription which even my mentor and co-author Sid possibly shares to a lower degree: *build the least decision-theoretic, or worse, game-theoretic, model possible.*

15. A Power Law is a relationship of the type $Pr(X > x) = a-bx$, accounting for the probability that a random variable X is greater than x, with a and b as constant, and b often empirically found to be near one.

16. Here a crucial challenge for the research ahead is the identification of non-tautological proxies for capabilities themselves (for an attempt in this direction, cf. Argote and Darr, 2000, Henderson and Cockburn, 2000, Pisano, 2000 and Baldwin and Johnson, 2001). Conversely obvious tautological measures are of course those performance measures that one tries to explain by means of organizational capabilities themselves.

17. A replicator dynamics relates the variation of the frequency of traits (or individual entities carrying such traits), in a whatever population, to the relative 'fitness' of the traits themselves. In biology, the classic formalization is from Fisher (1930), which several works by Stan Metcalfe build upon and refine. Gerry Silverberg and a few others (including several works of mine and collaborators) broadly follow the same formalization pattern allowing for a dynamics in the 'fitness' and their distributions across micro entities. In Nelson–Winter style modelling, no explicit 'replicator equation' is there but in their models the relation from *relative production efficiency to relative profitabilities to relative investment possibilities* plays the same role.

18. An overlapping work is Bassanini and Dosi (2000) while several of the ideas resonate with those put forward in Arthur (1994), David (1988, 2001, 2005), Freeman and Louçã (2001) and Hodgson (2001).

19. In Bassanini and Dosi (2000) we use a similar type of formalism to account for the observation that sometimes different countries converge to the quasi-monopoly of different, competing technologies and we formally show that convergence to a 'world dominant' technology or to a multiple local monopolies depend on the relative weight and strength of international spillovers as compared to nation-wide (or regional) dynamic increasing returns.

20. Sachs and Warner (1997) is a known short example of the *genre*; more specifically on the role of institutions and policies within the 'new political economy' style of interpretation, cf. the somewhat diverging views of Acemoglu et al. (2001), Easterly and Levine (2003) and Rodrik (2006). For a sharp critique of a mono-causal explanation of underdevelopment, see Adelman (2001), together with a few other contributions to Meier and Stiglitz (2001).

21. The remote origin of Chapter 18 is in itself a revealing episode of the epistemology of our discipline. During one of the 'Economy as a Complex Evolving System' meetings at Santa Fe jointly held by economists and physicists – including Nobel laureates Ken Arrow, Phil Anderson and Murray Gell-Mann – the physicists grew increasingly impatient: 'if you do not tell us what the phenomena you want to explain are, we cannot understand what you are talking about', they started saying. Most of the economists found their remark quite awkward (are there phenomena in economics to explain, after all?!) Only Ken Arrow and myself went to the blackboard and for a half a day wrote down an ensemble of regularities, which were later developed with Chris and Silvia.

22. Especially concerning distributive shares the regularity is quite rough indeed and the absence of any clear secular trend goes together with major long-term swings. Just to take an example, over the last three decades income distribution has systematically worsened in all advanced countries against wages and now it is approximately back to what it was before the 1929 Great Depression.

23. Together, economists tried to explain away the 'paradox' by trying to show that American labour was different from foreign labour, being more skilled, and, as one would say nowadays more 'human capital intensive', but with relatively little success. At the end, the profession simply chose to forget the 'paradox' and proceed with business as usual (witness the low number of young economists who know about its very existence).

24. This venue has obvious overlappings with the stream of research heralded by Melitz (2003) bringing inter-firm heterogeneity to bear on to their propensities to export. However, abandoning any attempt to rationalize all that via some underlying 'structural model' with heterogeneous but rational maximizing firms, as we are obviously urged to do, may allow us to go further into the understanding of the microeconomics of international competition.

25. For germane ABMs, see Delli Gatti et al. (2005, 2010, 2011), Russo et al. (2007), Dawid et al. (2008, 2011), Ashraf et al., (2011), and with both some Keynesian and Schumpeterian elements, see Verspagen (2002), Saviotti and Pyka (2008), Ciarli et al. (2010). See also the discussion in Silverberg and Verspagen (2005).

26. Here I want, however, to mention an old model by Marengo and Tordjman (1996) with ecologies of forex trading strategies evolving over endogenous landscapes in absence of any fundamental.

27. In fact, I think that the famous 'intertemporal inconsistency of policies' belongs to the same *genre*. Indeed, one is led to think, and worse teaches students in textbooks, that maybe up to the 1970s people were so stupid to adapt to fiscal and monetary policies, but thereafter, possibly rationally anticipating the 'rational expectation

revolution' of Lucas, Sargent et al., they stopped doing it. A sudden outburst of forward-looking intelligence by the general people? Or an outburst of novel cleverer (and more 'perverse') cooking of the data? You have my guess.

Bibliography

Acemoglu, D., Johnson, S. and Robinson, J. (2001), 'The colonial origins of economic development: an empirical investigation', *American Economic Review*, **91**, 1369–1401.

Adelman, I. (2001), 'Fallacies in development theory and their implications for policies', in Meier and Stiglitz (2001).

Akerlof, G.A. (2002), 'Behavioral macroeconomics and macroeconomic behavior', *American Economic Review*, American Economic Association, **92**, 411–433.

Amable, B. (2003), *The Diversity of Modern Capitalism*, Oxford: Oxford University Press.

Anderson P.W., K.J. Arrow and D. Pines (eds) (1988), *The Economy as an Evolving Complex System I*, Redwood City, CA: Addison-Wesley.

Anufriev, M. and G. Bottazzi (2010), 'Market equilibria under procedural rationality', *Journal of Mathematical Economics*, **46**, 1140–1172.

Anufriev, M. and P. Dindo (2010), 'Wealth-driven selection in a financial market with hetero-geneous agents', *Journal of Economic Behavior and Organization*, **73**, 327–358.

Argote, L. and E. Darr (2000), 'Repositories of knowledge in franchise organizations: individual, structural and technological', in Dosi, Nelson and Winter (2000).

Arthur, W.B. (1988), 'Competing technologies: an overview', in G. Dosi, C. Freeman, R. Nelson, G. Silverberg and L. Soete, (eds), *Technical Change and Economic Theory*, London: Pinter Publisher.

Arthur, W.B. (1994), *Increasing Returns and Path Dependence in the Economy*, Ann Arbor, MI: University of Michigan Press.

Arthur, W.B., Y.M. Ermoliev and Y. Kaniovski (1983), 'A generalized Urn problem and its applications', *Kibernetika*, **19**, 49–56 (republished in Arthur, 1994).

Arthur, W.B. and D.A. Lane (1993), 'Information contagion, structural change and economic dynamics', **4**, 81–104 (republished in Arthur, 1994).

Arthur, W.B., S. Durlauf and D. Lane (eds) (1997) *The Economy as an Evolving Complex System II*, Redwood City, CA: Addison-Wesley.

Ashraf, Q.B., B. Gershman and P. Howitt (2011), Banks, market organization, and macroeconomic performance: an agent-based computational analysis. NBER Working Paper No. 17102.

Augier, M. and J. March (eds) (2002), *The Economics of Choice, Change and Organizations: Essays in Memory of Richard M. Cyert*, Cheltenham, UK and Northampton, MA: Edward Elgar.

Baldwin, J.R. and J. Johnson (2001), 'Business strategies in innovative and non innovative firms in Canada', Analytical Studies Branch Research Paper 73, Statistics Canada, Technical Report.

Bartelsman, E.J. and M. Doms (2000), 'Understanding productivity, lessons from longitudinal microdata', *Journal of Economic Literature*, **38**, 569–594.

Bassanini, A. and G. Dosi (2000), 'When and how chance and human will can twist the arm of Clio', in R. Garud and P. Karnoe (eds), *Path Creation and Path Dependencies*, Nahwah, NY: Lawrence Erlbaum Publishers.

Bassanini, A. and G. Dosi (2001), 'Heterogenous agents, complementarities and diffusion: do increasing returns imply convergence to international technological monopolies?', in D. Delli Gatti, M. Gallegati and A. Kirman (eds), *Market Structure, Aggregation and Heterogeneity*, Cambridge: Cambridge University Press.

Becker, G.S. (1976), *The Economic Approach to Human Behavior*, Chicago, IL: University of Chicago Press.

Becker, M.C. (2005), 'A framework for applying organizational routines in empirical research: linking antecedents, characteristics and performance outcomes of recurrent interaction patterns', *Industrial and Corporate Change*, **14** (5), 817–846.

Becker, M.C., N. Lazaric, R.R. Nelson and S.G. Winter (2005), 'Applying organizational routines in understanding organizational change', *Industrial and Corporate Change*, **14** (5), 775–791.

Blanchard, O. (2009), 'The state of macro', *Annual Review of Economics*, **1**, 209–228.

Blume, L. and D. Easley (1992), 'Evolution and market behavior', *The Journal of Economic Theory*, **58**, 9–40.

Blume, L. and D. Easley (2010), 'Heterogeneity, selection, and wealth dynamics', *Annual Review of Economics*, **2**, 425–450.

Boschma, R. and K. Frenken (2006), 'Why is economic geography not an evolutionary science? Towards an evolutionary economic geography', *Journal of Economic Geography*, **6**, 273–302.

Boschma, R. and K. Frenken (2011), 'The emerging empirics of evolutionary economic geography', *Journal of Economic Geography*, **11**, 295–307.

Boschma, R. and R. Martin (eds) (2007), 'Evolutionary economic geography', *Journal of Economic Geography*, Special Issue, 7.

Bottazzi, G., G. Dosi and L. Marengo (2011), 'The irresistible evolutionary drive toward the abyss: a baseline model of bubbles, risk aggregation and bursts', LEM Working Paper in progress.

Bresnahan, T., S. Greenstein and R. Henderson (2011), 'Schumpeterian competition and diseconomies of scope: illustrations from the histories of Microsoft and IBM', in J. Lerner and S. Stern (eds), *The Rate and Direction of Inventive Activity Revisted*, Chicago: University of Chicago Press.

Caballero, R.J. (2010), 'Macroeconomics after the crisis: time to deal with the pretense-of-knowledge syndrome', NBER Working Paper No. 16429.

Camerer, C.F. (2007), 'Neuroeconomics: using neuroscience to make economic predictions', *The Economic Journal*, **117**, C26–C42.

Cassidy, J. (2009), *How Markets Fail*, London and New York: Allen Lane.

Castaldi, C., M. Cimoli, N. Correa and G. Dosi (2009), 'Technological learning, policy regimes, and growth: the long-term patterns and some specificities of a "globalized" economy' in Cimoli, Dosi and Stiglitz (2009).

Chandler, A. (1990), *Scale and Scope: The Dynamics of Industrial Competition*, Cambridge, MA: Harvard University Press.

Chandler, A. (1992), 'Organizational capabilities and the economic history of the industrial enterprise', *Journal of Economic Perspectives*, **6** (3), 79–100.

Chari, V.V. (2010), 'Testimony before the committee on Science and Technology', Subcommittee on Investigations and Oversight, US House of Representatives, 20 July 2010.

Ciarli, T., A. Lorentz, M. Savona and M. Valente (2010), 'The effect of consumption and production structure on growth and distribution. A micro to macro model', *Metronomica*, **61**, 180–218.

Cimoli, M., G. Dosi and J.E. Stiglitz (eds) (2009), *Industrial Policy and Development: The Political Economy of Capabilities Accumulation*, Oxford and New York: Oxford University Press.

Cimoli, M. and L. Soete (1992), 'A generalized technology gap trade model', *Economie Appliquée*, **3**, 33–54.

Cipolla, C.M. (1965), *Guns, Sails, & Empires: Technological Innovation and the Early Phases of European Expansion, 1400–1700*, New York: Pantheon Books.

Cohen, M., R. Burkhart, G. Dosi, M. Egidi, L. Marengo, M. Warglien and S. Winter (1996), 'Routines and other recurring action patterns of organizations: contemporary research issues', *Industrial and Corporate Change*, **5**, 653–699.

Colander, D., H. Foellmer, A. Haas, M. Goldberg, K. Juselius, A. Kirman, T. Lux and B. Sloth (2009), 'The financial crisis and the systemic failure of academic economics', Kiel Institute for the World Economy, Working Papers No. 1489.

Cooper, R. and John, A. (1988), 'Coordinating coordination failures in Keynesian models', *Quarterly Journal of Economics*, **103**, 441–463.

Coriat, B. and G. Dosi (1998), 'The institutional embeddedness of economic change: an appraisal of the "evolutionary" and the "regulationist" research programme', in K. Nielsen and B. Johnson (eds), *Institutions and Economic Change*, Cheltenham, UK and Northampton, MA: Edward Elgar (republished in Dosi, 2000).

David, P.A. (1975), *Technical Choice, Innovation and Economic Growth: Essays on American and British Experience in the Nineteenth Century*, Cambridge: Cambridge University Press.

David, P.A. (1985), 'Clio and the economics of QWERTY ', *American Economic Review*, **75**, 332–337.

David, P.A. (1988), 'Path dependence: putting the past into the future of economics', Stanford University, Institute for Mathematical Studies in the Social Science, Technical Report No. 533.

David, P.A. (1992), 'Heroes, herds and hysteresis in technological history: Thomas Edison and "The Battle of the Systems" reconsidered', *Industrial and Corporate Change*, **1**, 129–181.

David, P.A. (1993), 'Path dependence and predictability in dynamic systems with local network externalities: a paradigm for historical economics', in D. Foray and C. Freeman (eds), *Technology and the Wealth of Nations*, London: Pinter Publishers.

David, P.A. (1994), 'Why are institutions the "carriers of history"? Path dependence and the evolution of conventions, organizations and institutions', *Structural Change and Economic Dynamics*, **5**, 205–220.

David, P.A. (2001), 'Path dependence, its critics and the quest for "Historical Economics"', in P. Garrouste and S. Loannides (eds), *Evolution and Path Dependence in Economic Ideas: Past and Present*, Cheltenham, UK and Northampton, MA: Edward Elgar.

David, P.A. (2005), 'Path dependence in economic processes: implications for policy analysis in dynamical system contexts', in Dopfer (2005), pp. 151–194.

Davidson, P. (2011), 'Paul Davidson: a response to John Kay', accessed 5 October 2011 at http://ineteconomics.org/blog/inet/.

Dawid, H., S. Gemkow, P. Harting, K. Kabus, K. Wersching and M. Neugart (2008), 'Skills, innovation, and growth: an agent-based policy analysis', *Journal of Economics and Statistics*, **228** (2 and 3), 251–275.

Dawid, H., S. Gemkow, P. Harting, S. van der Hoog and M. Neugart (2011), 'The Eurace@ Unibi model: an agent-based macroeconomic model for economic policy analysis', accessed at http://www.wiwi.uni-bielefeld.de/vpl1/research/eurace-unibi.html.

Delli Gatti, D., C. Di Guilmi, E. Gaffeo, G. Giulioni, M. Gallegati and A. Palestrini (2005), 'A new approach to business fluctuations: heterogeneous interacting agents, scaling laws and financial fragility', *Journal of Economic Behavior and Organization*, **56** (4), 489–512.

Delli Gatti, D., S. Desiderio, E. Gaffeo, P. Cirillo and M. Gallegati (2011), *Macroeconomics from the Bottom-up*, Milan: Springer.

Delli Gatti, D., M. Gallegati, B. Greenwald, A. Russo and J.E. Stiglitz (2010), 'The financial accelerator in an evolving credit network', *Journal of Economic Dynamics and Control*, **34** (9), 1627–1650.

Dopfer, K. (ed.) (2005), *The Evolutionary Foundations of Economics*, Cambridge: Cambridge University Press.

Dosi, G. (1982), 'Technical paradigms and technological trajectories: a suggested interpretation of the determinants and directions of technical change', *Research Policy*, **11**, 147–162 (republished in Dosi, 2000).

Dosi, G. (1984), *Technical Change and Industrial Transformation – The Theory and an Application to the Semiconductor Industry*, London, Macmillan; American Edition: New York, St. Martin Press.

Dosi, G. (1988), Sources, procedures and microeconomic effects of innovation, *Journal of Economic Literature* (republished in Dosi, 2000).

Dosi, G. (2000), *Innovation, Organization and Economic Dynamics: Selected Essays.* Cheltenham, UK and Northampton, MA: Edward Elgar.

Dosi, G. (2008), 'Technological innovation, institutions and human purposefulness in socioeconomic evolution: a preface', in Freeman (2008).

Dosi, G. and M. Egidi (1991), 'Substantive and procedural uncertainty: an exploration of economic behaviours in changing environments', *Journal of Evolutionary Economics*, **1**, 145–168 (republished in Dosi, 2000).

Dosi, G., C. Freeman, R. Nelson, G. Silverberg and L. Soete (eds) (1988), *Technical Change and Economic Theory*, London: Francis Pinter and New York: Columbia University Press; available online at http://www.lem.sssup.it/books.html.

Dosi, G. and Y. Kaniovski (1994), 'On "badly behaved" dynamics: some applications of generalized Urn schemes to technological and economic change', *Journal of Evolutionary Economics*, **4** (2), 93–123.

Dosi, G., S. Lechevalier and A. Secchi (2010), 'Introduction: interfirm heterogeneity – nature, sources and consequences for industrial dynamics', *Industrial and Corporate Change*, **19**, 6, 1867–890.

Dosi, G., L. Marengo, E. Paraskevopoulou and M. Valente (2012), *The value and dangers of remembrance in changing worlds: a model of cognitive and operational memory of organizations*, LEM Working Paper, forthcoming.

Dosi, G. and R.R. Nelson (1994), 'An introduction to evolutionary theories in economics', *Journal of Evolutionary Economics*, **4**, 153–172 (republished in Dosi, 2000).

Dosi, G. and R.R. Nelson (2010), 'Technical change and industrial dynamics as evolutionary Processes', in Hall and Rosenberg (2010), vol. I, 51–128.

Dosi, G., R.R. Nelson and S. Winter (eds) (2000), *The Nature and Dynamics of Organizational Capabilities*, Oxford: Oxford University Press.

Dosi, G. and L. Orsenigo (1988), 'Coordination and transformation: an overview of structures, behaviours and change in evolutionary environments', in G. Dosi, C. Freeman, R. Nelson, G. Silverberg and L. Soete (eds.) *Technical Change and Economic Theory*, London: Francis Pinter and New York: Columbia University Press.

Dosi, G., K. Pavitt and L. Soete (1990), *The Economics of Technical Change and International Trade*, Brighton, Wheatsheaf and New York: New York University Press

Dosi, G. and S.G. Winter (2002), 'Interpreting economic change: evolution, structures and games', in Augier and March (2002).

Durlauf, S.N. and D. Quah (1999), 'The new empirics of economic growth', in J.B. Taylor and M. Woodford (eds), *Handbook of Macroeconomics*, vol. 1A, Amersterdam, Oxford: Elsevier.

Easterly, W. and R. Levine (2003), 'Tropics, germs, and crops: how endowments influence economic development', *Journal of Monetary Economics*, **50** (1), 3–39.

Ethiraj, S. and D. Levinthal (2004), 'Bounded rationality and the search for organizational architecture: an evolutionary perspective on the design of organizations and their evolvability', *Administrative Science Quarterly*, **49** (3), 404–437.

Fagerberg, J. (1994), 'Technology and international differences in growth rates', *Journal of Economic Literature*, **32**, 1147–1175.

Fagerberg, J. (2002), 'International competitiveness', in J. Fagerberg (ed.), *Technology, Growth and Competitiveness*, Cheltenham, UK and Northampton, MA: Edward Elgar, pp. 201–220.

Fisher R.A (1930), *The Genetical Theory of Natural Selection*, Oxford: Oxford University Press.

Foster, L., J.C. Haltiwanger and C.J. Krizan (2001), 'Aggregate productivity growth, lessons from microeconomic evidence', in C.R. Hulten, E.R. Dean and M.J. Harper (eds), *New Developments in Productivity Analysis*, Chicago, IL: University of Chicago Press, pp. 303–372.

Foster, L., J.C. Haltiwanger and C. Syverson (2008), 'Reallocation, firm turnover and efficiency, selection on productivity or profitability?', *American Economic Review*, **98**, 394–425.

Freeman, C. (1982), *The Economics of Industrial Innovation*, London: Frances Pinter.

Freeman, C. (2008), *Systems of Innovation: Selected Essays in Evolutionary Economics*, Cheltenham, UK and Northampton, MA: Edward Elgar.

Freeman, C., J.K. Fuller and A. Young (1963), 'The plastics industry: a comparative study of research and innovation', *National Institute Economic Review*, **26**, 26–62.

Freeman, C. and F. Louçã (2001), *As Time Goes By: The Information Revolution and the Industrial Revolutions in Historical Perspective*, Oxford: Oxford University Press.

Friedman, M. (1953), 'The methodology of positive economics', in *Essays in Positive Economics*, Chicago, London: University of Chicago Press.

Frydman, R. and M.D. Goldberg (2011), *Beyond Mechanical Markets: Asset Price Swings, Risk, and the Role of the State*, Princeton, NJ and Oxford: Princeton University Press.

Gavetti, G., and D. Levinthal (2000), 'Looking forward and looking backward: cognitive and experimental search', *Administrative Science Quarterly*, **45** (1), 113–137.

Gibbons, R. (2006), 'What the folk theorem does not tell us', *Industrial and Corporate Change*, **15**, 381–386.

Gibbons, R. (2010), 'Inside organizations: pricing, policies and path dependence', *Annual Review of Economics*, **2**, 337–365.

Gode, D.K., Sunder, S. (1997), 'What makes markets allocationally efficient', *Quarterly Journal of Economics*, **112**, 603–630.

Greif, A. (2006), *Institutions and the Path to the Modern Economy: Lessons from Medieval Trade*, Cambridge: Cambridge University Press

Guerrieri, P. and V. Meliciani (2005), 'Technology and international competitiveness: the interdependence between manufacturing and producer services', *Structural Change and Economic Dynamics*, **16**, 489–502.

Hall, B.H. and N. Rosenberg (eds) (2010), *Handbook of the Economics of Innovation*, Burlington, MA: Academic Press.

Henderson, R. and I. Cockburn (2000), 'Measuring competence? Exploring firm effects in drug discovery', in Dosi et al. (2000).

Hicks, J.R. (1937), 'Mr. Keynes and the "Classics": a suggested interpretation', *Econometrica*, **5**, 147–159.

Hildenbrand W. (1981), 'Short-run production functions based on microdata', *Econometrica*, **49**, 1095–1125.

Hildenbrand, W. (1994), *Market Demand: Theory and Empirical Evidence*, Princeton, NJ: Princeton University Press.

Hodgson, G. (2001), *How Economics Forgot History: The Problem of Historical Specificity in Social Science*, London: Routledge.

Hufbauer, G.C. (1966), *Synthetic Materials and the Theory on International Trade*, London: Duckworth.

Jacobides, M.G. and S.G. Winter (2010), 'The survival of the reckless: feedback, foresight and the evolutionary roots of the financial crisis', London Business School Working Paper.

Kahneman, D. (2003), 'Maps of bounded rationality: psychology for behavioural economics', *American Economic Review*, **93**, 1449–1475.

Kahneman, D. (2011), *Thinking, Fast and Slow*, New York: Farrar Straus and Giroux.

Kaldor, N (1961), 'Capital accumulation and economic growth', in F.A. Lutz (ed.) *Theory of Capital*, London: Palgrave Macmillan.

Kaldor, N. (1981), 'The role of increasing returns, technical progress and cumulative causation in the theory of international trade and economic growth', *Economie Appliquée*, Reprinted in F. Targetti and A.P. Thirlwall (eds) (1989), *The Essential Kaldor*, New York: Holmes & Meier.

Kaldor, N. (1983), 'Keynesian economics after fifty years', in J. Trevithick and D. Worswick (eds), *Keynes and the Modern World*, Cambridge: Cambridge University Press.

Kaldor, N. (1985), *Economics without Equilibrium*, New York: M.E. Sharpe Inc.

Kay, J. (2011), 'The map is not the territory: an essay on the state of economics', accessed 4 October 2011 at http://ineteconomics.org/blog/inet .

Keynes, J.M. (1936), *The General Theory of Employment Interest and Money*, New York: Kessinger Publishing, LLC.

Keynes, J.M. (1943), 'Planning full employment: alternative solutions to a dilemma', *The Times*, 23 January 1943.

Kirman, A. (1989), 'The intrinsic limits of modern economic theory: the emperor has no clothes', *Economic Journal*, Supplement to 99, 126–139.

Kirman, A. (1992), 'What or whom does the representative individual represent?', *Journal of Economic Perspectives*, **6**, 2, 117–136.

Kirman, A. (2010), *Complex Economics: Individual and Collective Rationality*, London: Routledge.

Kirman, A. and A. Vignes (1991), 'Price dispersion: theoretical considerations and empirical evidence from the Marseille fish market', in K.G. Arrow (ed.) *Issues in Contemporary Economics*, London: Macmillan, 160–185.

Klamer, A. (1984), *The New Classical Macroeconomics: Conversations with the New Classical Economists and their Opponents*, Brighton: Wheatsheaf Books.

Klepper, S. (1997), 'Industry life cycles', *Industrial and Corporate Change*, **6**, 145–182.

Klepper, S. (2010), 'The origin and growth of industry clusters: the making of Silicon Valley and Detroit', *Journal of Urban Economics*, **67**, 15–32.

Krugman, P. (2011), 'Mr Keynes and the Moderns', Paper presented at the Cambridge conference commemorating the 75th anniversary of the publication of Keynes' *General Theory of Employment, Interest, and Money.*

Landes, D.S. (1969), *The Unbound Prometheus*, Cambridge: Cambridge University Press.

Landes, D.S. (1998), *The Wealth and Poverty of Nations: Why Are Some So Rich and Others So Poor?*, New York: W.W. Norton.

Lane, D. (1993), 'Artificial worlds and economics, Parts I and II', *Journal of Evolutionary Economics*, **3**, 89–107, 177–197.

Laursen, K. and V. Meliciani (2010), 'The role of ICT knowledge flows for international market share dynamics', *Research Policy*, **39**, 687–697.

LeBaron, B. and L. Tesfatsion (2008), 'Modeling macroeconomies as open-ended dynamic systems of interacting agents', *The American Economic Review*, **98** (2). Papers and Proceedings of the One Hundred Twentieth Annual Meeting of the American Economic Association, 246–250.

Leontief, W. (1954), 'Domestic production and foreign trade: the American capital position re-examined', *Economia Internazionale*, **7**, 9–38. Reprinted in R.E. Caves and H.G. Johnson (eds) (1968), *Readings in International Economics*, Homewood, Ill: Irwin (for American Economic Association).

Lerner, J. and S. Stern (eds) (2012), *The Rate and Direction of Inventive Activity Revisited*, Chicago: University of Chicago Press.

Levinthal, D. (1997), 'Adaptation on rugged landscapes', *Management Science*, **43** (7), 934–950.

Levy, M., H. Levy and S. Solomon (2000), *Microscopic Simulation of Financial Markets*, London: Academic Press.

Louçã, F. (2001), 'Intriguing pendula: founding metaphors in the analysis of economic fluctuations', *Cambridge Journal of Economics*, **25**, 25–55.

Lundvall, B-A. (ed.) (1992), *National Systems of Innovation – Towards a Theory of Innovation and Interactive Learning*, London: Pinter Publishers.

Malerba, F. (ed.) (2004), *Sectoral Systems of Innovation*, Cambridge: Cambridge University Press.

Marengo, L., G. Dosi, P. Legrenzi, and C. Pasquali (2000), 'The structure of problem-solving knowledge and the structure of organizations', *Industrial and Corporate Change*, **9** (4), 757–88.

Marengo L. and H. Tordjman (1996), 'Speculation, heterogeneity and learning: a model of exchange rate dynamics', *KYKLOS*, **49**, 407–438.

Maynard Smith, J. (1976), 'Evolution and the theory of games', *American Scientist*, **64**, 46–61.

Meier, G.M. and Stiglitz J.E. (eds) (2001), *Frontiers of Development Economics*, New York and Oxford: Oxford University Press.

Melitz, M. (2003), 'The impact of trade on aggregate industry productivity and intra-industry reallocations', *Econometrica*, **71** (6), 1695–1725.

Metcalfe, J.S. (1998), *Evolutionary Economics and Creative Destruction*, London: Routledge.

Metcalfe, J.S. and R. Ramlogan (2006), 'Restless capitalism: a complexity perspective on modern capitalist economies', in E. Garnsey and J. McGlade (eds), *Complexity and Evolution*, Cheltenham, UK and Northampton, MA: Edward Elgar.

Minsky, H.P. (1982), *Can "It" Happen Again? Essays on Instability and Finance*, Armonk, NY: M.E. Sharpe Inc.

Minsky, H.P. (1986), *Stabilizing an Unstable Economy*, New Haven, CO: Yale University Press.

Modigliani, F. (1944), 'Liquidity preference and the theory of interest and money', *Econometrica*, **12**, 45–88.

Mokyr, J. (1990), *The Lever of Riches: Technological Creativity and Economic Progress*, Oxford: Oxford University Press.

Mokyr, J. (2009), *The Enlightened Economy: An Economic History of Britain 1700–1850*, New Haven, CO: Yale University Press.

Murmann, J.P. (2003), *Knowledge and Competitive Advantage: The Coevolution of Firms, Technology, and National Institutions*, Cambridge: Cambridge University Press

Nelson, R.R. (1981), 'Research on productivity growth and productivity differences: dead ends and new departures', *Journal of Economic Literature*, **19**, 1029–1064.

Nelson, R.R. (1991), 'Why do firms differ and how does it matter?', *Strategic Management Journal*, **12**, 61–74.

Nelson, R.R. (ed.) (1993), *National Innovation Systems: A Comparative Analysis*, New York and Oxford: Oxford University Press.

Nelson, R.R. (2005), *Technology, Institutions, and Economic Growth*, Cambridge, MA: Harvard University Press.

Nelson, R.R. (2008), 'Why do firms differ and how does it matter? A revisitation', *Seoul Journal of Economics*, **21**, 607–619.

Nelson, R.R. and B. Sampat (2001), 'Making sense of institutions as a factor shaping economic performance', *Journal of Economic Behaviour and Organization*, **44**, 31–54.

Nelson, R.R. and S.G. Winter (1982), *An Evolutionary Theory of Economic Change*, Cambridge, MA: The Belknap Press of Harvard University Press.

North, D.C. (2005), *Understanding the Process of Economic Change*. Princeton, NJ: Princeton University Press

Olley, G.S. and A. Pakes (1996), 'The dynamics of productivity in the telecommunications equipment industry', *Econometrica*, **64**, 1263–1297.

Patinkin, D. (1950), 'A reconsideration of the general equilibrium theory of money', *The Review of Economic Studies*, **18**, 42–61.

Pisano, G. (2000), 'In search of dynamic capabilities', in Dosi et al. (2000).

Polanyi, K. (1944), *The Great Transformation: The Political and Economic Origins of Our Time*, Boston, MA: Beacon Press.

Posner, M. (1961), 'International trade and technical change', *Oxford Economic Papers*, **13**.

Rangel, A., C. Camerer and P. Read Montague (2008), 'A framework for studying the neurobiology of value-based decision making', *Nature – Neuroscience*, **9**, 545–559.

Reinert, E.S. (2007), *How Rich Countries Got Rich ... and Why Poor Countries Stay Poor*, London: Constable.

Rodrik, D. (2006), 'Goodbye Washington Consensus, Hello Washington Confusion?', *Journal of Economic Literature*, **44**, 969–983.

Rodrik, D. (2008), *One Economics, Many Recipes: Globalization, Institutions, and Economic Growth*, Princeton, NJ: Princeton University Press

Rodrik, D. (2011), *The Globalization Paradox: Democracy and the Future of the World Economy*, New York and London: W.W. Norton.

Rosenberg, N. (1976), *Perspectives on Technology*, Cambridge: Cambridge University Press.

Rosenberg N. (1982), *Inside the Blackbox: Technology and Economics*, Cambridge: Cambridge University Press.

Rosser, B.J. (2011), *Complex Evolutionary Dynamics in Urban–Regional and Ecologic–Economic Systems: From Catastrophe to Chaos and Beyond*, New York: Springer.

Russo, A., M. Catalano, E. Gaffeo, M. Gallegati and M. Napoletano (2007), 'Industrial dynamics, fiscal policy and R&D: evidence from a computational experiment', *Journal of Economic Behavior & Organization*, **64** (3 and 4), 426–447.

Sachs, J.D., and A.M. Warner (1997), 'Fundamental sources of long-term growth', *American Economic Review*, Papers and Proceedings, **87**, 184–188.

Sapio, A., A. Kirman and G. Dosi (eds) (2011), 'Special issue on the emergence and impact of market institutions: the wholesale market for fish and other perishable commodities', *Journal of Economic Behaviour and Organization*, **80**, 1–264.

Savage, L. J. (1954), *The Foundations of Statistics*, New York: John Wiley and Son.

Saviotti, P.P. and A. Pyka (2008), 'Micro and macro dynamics: industry life cycles, inter-sector coordination and aggregate growth', *Journal of Evolutionary Economics*, **18** (2), 167–182.

Schneider, W. and R.M. Shiffrin (1977a), Controlled and automatic human information processing: I. Detection, search, and attention, *Psychological Review*, **84** (1), 1–66.

Schneider, W. and R.M. Shiffrin (1977b), 'Controlled and automatic human information processing: II. Perceptual learning, automatic attending and a general theory', *Psychological Review*, **84** (2), 127–190.

Schumpeter, J.A. (1912), *The Theory of Economic Development*. Leipzig: Duncker and Humblot, trans R. Opie (1934), Cambridge: Harvard University Press, reprinted (1961), New York: Oxford University Press.

Schumpeter, J.A. (1939), *Business Cycles*, 2 vols., New York: McGraw-Hill.

Schumpeter, J.A. (1942), *Capitalism, Socialism and Democracy*, New York: Harper and Brothers. 5th ed., 1976, London: George Allen and Unwin.

Siggelkow, N., and J.W. Rivkin (2005), 'Speed and search: designing organizations for turbulence and complexity', *Organization Science*, **16** (2), 101–122.

Silverberg, G., G. Dosi and L. Orsenigo (1988), 'Innovation, diversity and diffusion: a self-organising model', *The Economic Journal*, **98**, 1032–1054 (reprinted in Dosi, 2000).

Silverberg, G. and B. Verspagen (2005), 'Evolutionary theorizing on economic growth', in Dopfer (2005).

Simon, H.A. (1957), *Models of Man: Social and Rational*, New York: John Wiley and Sons.

Simon, H.A. (1969), *The Sciences of the Artificial*, Cambridge: MIT Press.

Simon, H.A. (1983), *Reason in Human Affairs*, Palo Alto, CA: Stanford University Press.

Solow, R.M. (2008), 'The state of macroeconomics', *Journal of Economic Perspectives*, **22**, 243–246.

Soros, G. (1994), *The Alchemy of Finance: Reading the Mind of the Marke*, New York: John Wiley and Son.

Stiglitz, J.E. (1994a), Endogenous growth and cycles, in Y. Shionoya and M. Perlman (eds), *Innovation in Technology, Industries, and Institutions: Studies In Schumpeterian Perspectives*, Ann Arbor, MI: University of Michigan Press, 121–256.

Stiglitz, J.E. (1994b), *Whither Socialism?*, Cambridge: MIT Press.

Stiglitz, J.E. (2011), 'Rethinking macroeconomics: what failed, and how to repair it', *Journal of the European Economic Association*, **9**, 591–645.

Sutton, J. (1998), *Technology and Market Structure: Theory and Evidence*, Cambridge, MA: MIT Press.

Temple, J. (1999), 'The new growth evidence', *Journal of Economic Literature*, **37**, 112–156.

Tesfatsion, L. and K.L. Judd (2006), *Handbook of Computational Economics: Agent-based Computational Economics*, Oxford: Elsevier.

Verspagen, B. (2002), 'Evolutionary macroeconomics: a synthesis between neo-Schumpeterian and post-Keynesian lines of thought', *Electronic Journal of Evolutionary Modeling and Economic Dynamics*, IFReDE – Université Montesquieu Bordeaux IV.

Verspagen, B. and K. Wakelin (1997), 'Trade and technology from a Schumpeterian perspective', *International Review of Applied Economics*, **11**, 181–194.

Winter, S.G. (1964), 'Economic "natural selection" and the theory of the firm', *Yale Economic Essays*, **4**, 1; accessed at http://www.lem.sssup.it/books.html.

Winter, S.G. (1982), 'An essay on the theory of production', in S.H. Hymans (ed.), *Economics and the World Around it*, Ann Arbor, MI: University of Michigan Press, pp.55–93.

Winter, S.G. (1987), 'Knowledge and competence as strategic assets', in D. Teece (ed.), *The Competitive Challenge*, Cambridge, MA: Ballinger.

Winter, S.G. (1988), 'On Coase, competence, and the corporation', *Journal of Law, Economics, & Organization*, **4** (1), 163–180.

Winter, S.G. (2005), 'Toward an evolutionary theory of production', in Dopfer (2005).

Winter, S.G. (2006), 'Toward a neo-Schumpeterian theory of the firm', *Industrial and Corporate Change*, **15**, 125–141.

Winter, S.G. (2008), 'Scaling heuristics shape technology! Should economic theory take notice?', *Industrial and Corporate Change*, **17**, 513–531.

Winter, S.G. and G. Szulanski (2001), 'Replication as strategy', *Organization Science*, **12** (6), 730–743.

Woodford, M. (2009), 'Convergence in macroeconomics: elements of the new synthesis', *American Economic Journal: Macroeconomics*, **1**, 267–279.

PART I

KNOWLEDGE, PROBLEM SOLVING AND THE ORGANIZATION OF ECONOMIC ACTIVITIES

[1]

Learning in evolutionary environments[1]

Giovanni Dosi
Luigi Marengo
Giorgio Fagiolo

1   Introduction

In the most generic terms, learning may occur in all circumstances when agents have an imperfect understanding of the world in which they operate – either due to lack of information about it, or, more fundamentally, because of an imprecise knowledge of its structure; or when they master only a limited repertoire of actions in order to cope with whatever problem they face – as compared to the set of actions that an omniscient observer would be able to conceive of; or, finally, when they have only a blurred and changing understanding of what their goals and preferences are.

It is straightforward that learning, so defined, is a ubiquitous characteristic of most economic and – generally – social environments, with the remarkable exception of those postulated by the most extreme forms of economic modelling, such as those assuming rational expectations (RE) or canonical game-theoretic equilibria. But, even in the latter cases (and neglecting any issues about the empirical realism of the underlying assumptions), it is natural to ask how agents learned in the first place about – for example – the 'true model' of the world in an RE set-up, or the extensive form of a particular game. And, moreover, in the widespread case of multiple equilibria, how do agents select among them (i.e. how do they learn how to converge onto one of them)?

Of course, learning acquires even greater importance in explicitly *evolutionary* environments (which we believe are indeed the general case), where a) heterogeneous agents systematically display various forms of 'bounded rationality'; b) there is a repeated appearance of novelties, both as exogenous shocks and, more importantly, as the result of technological,

[1] Support for this research from the International Institute of Applied Systems Analysis (IIASA – Laxenburg, Austria), the Italian National Research Council (CNR) and the Italian Ministry of Research ('MURST, Progetti 40%') is gratefully acknowledged. The authors benefited from comments on earlier drafts by Giovanna Devetag, Daniel Friedman, Luigi Orsenigo, Oliver Williamson and the participants in the Schumpeter Society conference, Stockholm, 2–5 June 1996, and from the lectures given by one of them at the University of Paris I in May 1996.

behavioural and organizational innovations by the agents themselves; c) markets (and other interaction arrangements) perform as selection mechanisms; d) aggregate regularities are primarily emergent properties stemming from out-of-equilibrium interactions (more detailed discussions are in Dosi and Nelson, 1994, Nelson, 1995, and Coriat and Dosi, 1998).

The purpose of this chapter is to present a sort of selective guide to an enormous and diverse literature on learning processes in economics insofar as they capture at least some of the foregoing evolutionary aspects. Clearly, this cannot be a thorough survey. Rather, we shall just refer to some examples of each *genre*, trying to show their links and differences, setting them against a hypothetical ideal framework of 'what one would like to understand about learning'. This will also permit easier mapping of a wide and largely unexplored research agenda. A significant emphasis will be put on learning *models*, in their bare-bone formal structure, but we shall always refer to the (generally richer) non-formal theorizing about the same objects.

Needless to say, we are exclusively concerned here with *positive* (i.e. descriptive) theories of learning: standard 'rational choice' models might well go a longer way as *normative* tools.

In section 2 we set the scene for the discussion that follows by reference to the usual decision-theoretic archetype, briefly outlining many compelling reasons why one needs to go well beyond it in order to account for most learning processes. Once we do that, however, a pertinent and unified – albeit probably irrelevant – paradigm is lost. Learning happens in different cognitive and behavioural domains, has different objects, and most likely occurs through somewhat different processes. Relatedly, we propose that a few basic empirical regularities on cognition, decision making and learning stemming from disciplines outside economics – ranging from cognitive psychology to sociology – should be among the 'building blocks' of an emerging theory of agency (section 3). Some taxonomic exercises are a useful introductory device; these we present in section 4. A taxonomy of learning dynamics, and the restrictions on its domain, helps in grouping and assessing various classes of learning models. In particular, a useful distinction appears to be whether one retains some elements of Savage's original 'small world assumption' (Savage, 1954) – in essence, the idea of a finite list of objects exhaustively present from the start in the 'heads' of learning agents. This is the case of learning representations through 'evolutionary games' and other mechanisms of adaptation via environmental reinforcement. Conversely, lower restrictions on the domain of learning and on the dimensionality of the state space may well entail *open-ended* evolutionary dynamics involving not only adaptation but also the discovery and emergence of novelty; in section 5 we compare different formal approaches in these various veins.

The general thrust of the argument, there and throughout this work, is that learning crucially entails cognitive activities of construction and the modification of mental models and behavioural patterns hardly reducible to well-defined problems of choice under imperfect information and probabilizable risk.

Some achievements and limitations of current learning models within this perspective and a few other broad topics of investigation – such as the relationship between learning and selection in evolutionary models, the possible tension between individual and collective learning, and the specificity of organizational learning – are outlined in section 6.

2 Beyond 'rational choice' and Bayesian learning: some preliminaries

As is well known, the standard decision-theoretic model depicts agency (and, *in primis*, economic agency) as a problem of choice where rational actors select, among a set of alternative courses of action, the one that will produce (in their expectation) the maximum outcome as measured against some utility yardstick. In that, agents are postulated to know the entire set of possible events of 'nature', all possible actions that are open to them, and all notional outcomes of the mapping between actions and events – or, at least, come to know them after some learning process. Clearly, these are quite demanding assumptions on knowledge embodied in or accessible to the agents – which hardly apply to complex and changing environments. In fact, they *cannot* apply, almost by definition, in all environments where innovations of some kind are allowed to occur – irrespective of whether they relate to technologies, behavioural repertoires or organizational arrangements; as Kenneth Arrow has been reminding us for some time, if an innovation is truly an innovation it could not have been in the set of events that all agents were able to contemplate before the innovation actually occurred . . .

Moreover, equally demanding are the implicit assumptions concerning the *procedural rationality* involved in the decision process. As a paradigmatic illustration, take the usual decision-theoretic sequence leading from 1) representation/'understanding' of the environment (conditional on whatever 'information' is available) to 2) evaluation/judgement, 3) choice, 4) actions and – ultimately – 5) consequences – determined, for example, by the stochastic pairing of actions and 'events of nature' and/or actions by other agents.

We argue at some greater length elsewhere (Dosi et al., 1999) that, in order for this 'rationalist' view to hold, at least two assumptions are crucial.

First, the linearity of that sequence must strictly hold. That is, one must rule out the possibility of reversing, so to speak, the procedural sequence. For example, one cannot have preferences and representations that adapt to an action that has already been undertaken, and, likewise, one must assume that consequences do not influence preferences (i.e. preferences are not endogenous).

Second, at each step of the process agents must be endowed with, or be able to build, the appropriate algorithm in order to tackle the task at hand – be it representing the environment, evaluating alternatives, choosing courses of action, or whatever.

There are some rather compelling reasons why these assumptions may, in fact, be a misleading starting point for any *positive* theory of learning and choice.

2.1   Complexity and procedural rationality

On purely theoretical grounds, computability theory provides some sort of dividing line between problems that are solvable by means of general recursive procedures in non-exponential times and problems that are not (for discussions and some results, see Lewis, 1985a, 1985b, Casti, 1992, Andersen, 1994, Dosi and Egidi, 1991, and Dosi et al., 1999). It is plausible to use such criteria to establish the *upper bound* of the complexity of the problems, for which the theory is allowed to assume that the agents 'naturally' possess the appropriate problem-solving algorithm (or are able to access it in finite time). It happens, however, that many decision tasks within and outside the economic domain fall outside this category (Lewis, 1986, Dosi et al., 1999).

We do not mean to overemphasize this point. After all, human agents tackle every day, with varying degrees of success, highly complex and 'hard' problems (in the sense of computability theory). However, we do claim that the understanding of how and when they happen to do it is a major challenge for any theory of cognition and learning, which cannot be written out by assuming that agents embody from the start a notionally unbounded procedural rationality[2]. Note that all this equally applies to the 'procedural rationality' of both decision processes and of

---

[2] In this respect, the reader might notice that the view suggested here tends to imply a somewhat more radical departure from fully 'rational' theories of decision than Herbert Simon's ground-breaking works on 'bounded rationality' (Simon, 1976, 1981, 1988), in that it does not only demand a constructive theory of the procedures themselves by

learning. The 'rationality' of the latter implies the availability of some inferential machinery able to extract the 'correct' information from environmental signals (Bayes' rule being one of them, and possibly also the most demanding, in terms of what the agents must know from the start about alternative hypotheses on what the world 'really is'). But, again, our foregoing argument implies that such an inferential machinery cannot be postulated innocently. Indeed, outside the rather special domain of 'small worlds' the structure of which is known *ex ante* to the agents, a few impossibility theorems from computation theory tell us that a generic inferential procedure does not and cannot exit (more on this point in Dosi and Egidi, 1991, Dosi et al., 1999, and Binmore, 1990).

What has been said so far mainly implies restrictions on the applicability of the canonical 'rational' account of learning and decision making. The bottom line is that the demands it makes in terms of the a priori knowledge of the environment and 'algorithmic endowments' of the agents cannot be met, *even in principle*, except for the simplest decision problems.

But, then, how do we theoretically depict agency and learning?

2.2   'As . . . if' interpretations of rational behaviour

One possible strategy basically involves a continuing commitment to 'rational' micro-foundations of economic interactions, together with a radical redefinition of the status of rationality assumptions themselves.

'Rationality' (however defined), rather than being an approximation to the empirical behaviour of purposeful and cognitively quite sophisticated agents, is assumed to be – so to speak – an 'objective' property of behaviours in equilibrium. Add the presumption that (most) observed behaviours are indeed *equilibrium* ones. And, finally, postulate some dynamics of individual adaptation or intra-population selection leading there. What one gets is some version of the famous 'as . . . if' hypothesis, suggested by Milton Friedman (1953) and rejuvenated in different fashions by more recent efforts to formalize learning/adaptation processes the outcome of which is precisely the 'rationality' assumed from the start (archetypical examples of this faith can be found in Sargent, 1993, and Marimon, 1997).

A thorough and critical discussion of the 'as . . . if' epistemology has been put forward by Sidney Winter in various essays (e.g. Winter, 1971), to which we refer the interested reader (see also Silverberg, 1988, Andersen, 1994, and Hodgson, 1988).

---

which agents develop their representations and action rules but it allows the possibility of persistently incoherent procedures. There is more on this later.

For our purposes here let us just note the following.

(i) Any 'as . . . if' hypothesis on rationality, taken seriously, is bound to involve quite a few restrictions similar to those briefly overviewed earlier with reference to more 'constructive' notions of rational behaviours, simply transposed into a more 'ecological' dimension – be it the 'ecology' of minds, ideas, organizations, populations, or whatever. That is, canonical rationality, *stricto sensu*, postulates that one decides and acts by purposefully using the appropriate procedures, or by learning them in purposeful, procedurally coherent ways. 'As . . . if' hypotheses of any kind apparently relax the demands on what agents must consciously know about the environment, their goals and the process of achieving them, but at the same time must assume some background mechanism that generates the available alternatives – *which must include the 'correct' ones*. However, without any further knowledge of the specific mechanisms, such a possibility remains a very dubious short cut, and it is utterly unlikely when there are infinite alternatives that ought to be scanned.

(ii) While 'realistic' interpretations of rationality put most of the burden of explanation upon the power of inbuilt cognition, 'as . . . if' accounts shift it to selection dynamics – no matter whether driven by behavioural reinforcements, like salivating Pavlovian dogs, or by differential reproduction of traits within populations[3]. But, then, supporters of the view ought to show, at the very least, that robust convergence properties are demonstrated by some *empirically justifiable* selection dynamics. In our view, as it stands, nothing like that is in sight. On the contrary, except for very special set-ups, negative results are abundant in, for example, evolutionary games or other forms of decentralized interactions. No matter whether applied to biology or economics, path dependency cannot easily be disposed of; cyclical limit behaviours might occur (see Posch, 1994, and Kaniovski et al., 1996), etc. And all this appears even before accounting for environments that are genuinely evolutionary in the sense that novelties can emerge over time.

---

[3] Note incidentally that the outcomes of purely 'Pavlovian' – i.e. reinforcement-driven, consciously blind – and 'Bayesian' – apparently sophisticated and rational – dynamics can be shown to be sometimes asymptotically equivalent (the reviews in Suppes, 1995a and 1995b, develop much older intuitions from behaviourist psychology – e.g. Bush and Mosteller, 1955). However, in order for that equivalence to hold, reinforcements must operate in the same direction as the Bayesian inferential machinery – which is a hard demand to make indeed. The so-called condition of 'weak monotonicity' in the dynamics of adjustment that one generally finds in evolutionary games is a necessary, albeit not sufficient, condition to this effect. Moreover, it is a subtle question with regard to the interpretative value that one should attribute to asymptotic results: what do they tell us about finite time properties of empirical observations? We come back briefly to this issue later.

Of course, the 'as . . . if' theoretical enterprise in its wildest formulation does not set any falsification challenge for itself. Any kind of observation-based discipline on behavioural assumptions tends to be contemptuously dismissed as 'ad hoc'. Thus, the question 'what do people do and how do they learn' is generally transformed into another one, namely 'given whatever behaviour, and knowing that, *of course* (?!), such a behaviour is an equilibrium one, how can I – the theorist – rationalize it as the outcome of some adaptive process?' (Dr Pangloss, theologians and Marxist-Leninists would not have any problem with such an exercise . . .)

2.3 Bounded rationality

Another major perspective maintains that cognitive and behavioural assumptions have to keep some empirical foundations, and thus, when needed, account for constraints on memory, on the maximum levels of complexity of problem-solving algorithms and on computational time. It is, in a broad sense, the *bounded rationality* approach, pioneered by the work of Simon (best encapsulated, perhaps, in Simon, 1986) and developed in quite different fashions in, for example, organizational studies (starting with March and Simon, 1958, and Cyert and March, 1992); evolutionary theories (building on Nelson and Winter, 1982; see also Dosi et al., 1988, Andersen, 1994, and Hodgson, 1993); and 'evolutionary games' (for a rather technical overview, see Weibull, 1995). For insightful remarks on bounded rationality and games in general, see Kreps (1996), and also in otherwise quite orthodox macroeconomics see, for example, Sargent (1993)[4]. Again, this is not the place to undertake any review of this vast literature. However, a few comments are required.

Necessarily, the very idea of 'bounds' on rationality implies that, at least in finite time, agents so represented fall short of full *substantively rational* behaviour, the latter involving – among other things – a) a full knowledge of all possible contingencies; b) an exhaustive exploration of the entire decision tree; and c) a correct appreciation of the utility evaluations of all mappings between actions, events and outcomes (Simon, 1986, 1988).

Given that, a first issue concerns the characterization of the origins and nature of the 'boundedness' itself. It is not at all irrelevant whether it relates mainly to limitations on the memory that agents carry over from the past, or to algorithmic complexity, or to a limited ability of defining preferences over (expected) outcomes, or whatever. Alternatively, and

---

[4] Note, however, that in some interpretations – including Sargent's and others discussed in section 4 – boundedly rational behaviours are considered mainly insofar as they entail convergence to some pre-defined equilibrium outcomes. Hence, they turn out in the end to be primarily instrumental building blocks of some dynamics vindicating, in the intentions of the proponents, an 'as . . . if' story.

more radically, couldn't it be due to the fact that agents get it basically wrong (in terms of representation of the environment, etc.)?

Here the theory faces a subtle but crucial crossroads. One alternative (unfortunately found all too often in economic models, and especially – but not only – in game theory) is to select the bounded rationality assumptions with extreme casualness, suspiciously well fitted both to the mathematics the author knows and to the results he wants to obtain. We have no problem in aligning ourselves with those who denounce the 'ad-hockery' of this procedure. The other alternative entails the acknowledgement of an *empirical discipline* on the restrictions one puts upon the purported rationality of the agents. No doubt we want to advocate here the scientific soundness of this procedure, notwithstanding the inevitable 'phenomenological' diversity of cognitive and behavioural representations that one is likely to get. That is, whether and how 'rationality is bounded' is likely to depend on the nature of the decision problem at hand, the context in which the decision maker is placed, the pre-existing learning skills of the agents, etc. Taxonomical exercises are inevitable, with their seemingly clumsy reputation. But, in a metaphor inspired by Keith Pavitt, this is a bit like the comparison of Greek to modern chemistry. The former, based on the symmetry of just four elements, was very elegant, but grounded in underlying philosophical principles that were utterly irrelevant and, from what we know nowadays, essentially wrong. The latter is clumsy, taxonomic and for a long time (until the advent of quantum mechanics) lacking in underlying foundations, but it is undeniably descriptively and operationally more robust.

A second major issue is with regard to *procedural* rationality. Granted the bounds on 'substantive' rational agency, as defined above, when and to what extent should one maintain any assumption of coherent purposefulness and logical algorithmic consistency on the part of the agents[5]? In a first approximation, Simon's approach suggests such a theoretical commitment (associated as it is with major contributions to the identification of *constructive* procedures for learning and problem solving in this vein; see Newell and Simon, 1972, and Simon, 1976). However, even procedural consistency might not be a generic property of empirical agents at all (including, of course, us!). A lot of evidence from most social disciplines also seems to point in this direction (this discussion is picked up again later).

---

[5] Note that procedural rationality requires all the 'linearity assumptions' mentioned above (ruling out, for example, state-dependent preferences) and also consistent search heuristics (allowing, for example, assessment rules along any decision tree that, at least in probability, lead in the 'right' direction).

Third, and relatedly, the very notion of 'bounded rationality' commits from the start to an implicit idea that 'full rationality' is the underlying yardstick for comparison. In turn, this implies the possibility of identifying some metrics upon which 'boundedness' and, dynamically, learning efforts can be measured and assessed. In quite a few circumstances this can be achieved fruitfully[6], but in others it might not be possible either in practice or even in principle. In particular, this applies to search and learning in complex functional spaces (as many problems within and outside the economic arena commonly do)[7]. And, of course, this is also the case of most problems involving the discovery of and/or adaptation to novelty.

Since these features are highly typical of evolutionary environments, an implication is that one might need to go well beyond a restricted notion of 'bounded rationality', characterized simply as an imperfect approximation to a supposedly 'full' one – which, in these circumstances, one is even unable to define precisely.

But then, again, how *does* one represent learning agents in these circumstances?

3   'Stylized facts' from cognitive and social sciences as building blocks of evolutionary theories of learning

Our somewhat radical suggestion is that evolutionary theories ought to make a much greater and more systematic use of the evidence from other cognitive and social sciences as sort of 'building blocks' for the hypotheses on cognition, learning and behaviours that one adopts. We fully realize that such a perspective almost inevitably entails the abandonment of any invariant axiomatics of decision and choice. But, to paraphrase R. Thaler (1992), this boils down again to the alternative between being 'vaguely right' or 'precisely wrong': we certainly advocate the former (however, compare Marimon, 1997, for a sophisticated contrary view).

In this respect, the discussion of *routines* as foundational behavioural assumptions of evolutionary models in Nelson and Winter (1982) is an excellent example of the methodology we have in mind, unfortunately not pursued enough in subsequent evolutionary studies (for a discussion of the state of the art in this field, see Cohen et al., 1996).

---

[6] Promising results stem from a better understanding of the formal structure of problem-solving heuristics (see, for example, Pearl, 1984, and Vassilakis, 1995, and – in a suggestive, experimentally based instance – Cohen and Bacdayan, 1994, and Egidi, 1996). See also below.

[7] For example, in Dosi et al., 1994, we consider quantity and price setting as cases in point.

There are, however, many other fields that a positive theory of learning in economics can draw on, ranging from cognitive and social psychology all the way to anthropology and the sociology of knowledge.

3.1   Cognitive categories and problem solving

A crucial aspect of learning is with regard to *cognition* – that is, the process by which decision makers form and modify representations in order to make some sense of a reality that is generally too complex and uncertain to be fully understood. Hence the necessity to acknowledge the existence (and persistence) of a systematic gap between the agent's cognitive abilities and 'reality' (were there an omniscient observer able to grasp it fully). Such a gap can take at least two, often interrelated, forms[8]: first, a *knowledge gap*, involving incomplete, fuzzy or simply wrong representations of the environment; and, second, a *problem-solving* gap between the complexity of the tasks agents face and their capabilities with respect to accomplishing them.

Regarding both, evolutionary theories of learning might significantly benefit from that branch of cognitive studies concerned with the nature and changes of *categories and mental models* (for different perspectives, see Johnson-Laird, 1983, 1993, Lakoff, 1987, Holland et al., 1986, and Margolis, 1987, and for the presentation of a few alternative theories see Mayer, 1992). It is crucial to notice that, if one accepts any 'mental model' view, learning cannot be reduced to information acquisition (possibly including Bayesian processing of it) but rather is centred around the construction of new cognitive categories and 'models of the world'. Few studies in economics have explicitly taken this road: one of them is the promising attempt in Tordjman (1996) to interpret the dynamics of financial markets in this framework (see also Marengo and Tordjman, 1996, and Palmer et al., 1994).

In turn, robust evidence shows that cognitive categories are not clear-cut constructions with sharp boundaries, put together in fully consistent interpretative models. Rather, they seem to display (in all our minds!) blurred contours, shaded by an intrinsic fuzziness, held around some cognitively guiding 'prototypes', and organized together in ill-structured systems kept operational only via a lot of default hierarchies (on all those points, see Lakoff, 1987, Holland et al., 1986, Tversky and

---

[8] Heiner (1983) introduces a similar concept, which he calls the 'C-D (competence-difficulty) gap'. In his definition, such a gap reflects the agent's imperfect ability to process correctly the available information and act reliably. Heiner's C-D gap does not properly belong to the realm of cognitive gaps, but, rather, it captures their behavioural consequences.

Kahneman, 1982, Kahneman and Tversky, 1986, Griffin and Tversky, 1992, Marengo, 1996, Margolis, 1987, Marengo and Tordjman, 1996, and Einhorn and Hogarth, 1985)[9].

3.2   *Framing and social embeddedness*

Cognitive categories, it has been repeatedly shown, go together with various mechanisms of *framing*, by which information is interpreted and also rendered operationally meaningful to the decision makers (see Kahneman et al., 1982, Borcherding et al., 1990, and March, 1994).

Indeed, frames appear to be a ubiquitous feature of both decision making and learning. What one understands is filtered by the cognitive categories that one holds, and the repertoires of elicited problem-solving skills depend on the ways the problem itself is framed. That is, framing effects occur along all stages of the decision-making process – affecting representations, judgements and the selection of behaviours (see Kahneman et al., 1982, and, concerning the patterns of activation of experts' skills, Ericsson and Smith, 1991).

As James March (1994, p. 14) puts it,

[d]ecisions are framed by beliefs that define the problem to be addressed, the information that must be collected, and the dimensions that must be evaluated. Decision makers adopt paradigms to tell themselves what perspective to take on a problem, what questions should be asked, and what technologies should be used to ask the questions. Such frames focus attention and simplify analysis. They direct attention to different options and different preferences. A decision will be made in one way if it is framed as a problem of maintaining profits and in a different way if it is framed as a problem of maintaining market share. A situation will lead to different decisions if it is seen as being about 'the value of innovation' rather than 'the importance of not losing face'.

Note that, in this view, 'frames' include a set of (not necessarily consistent) beliefs over 'what the problem is' and the goals that should be achieved in that case; cognitive categories deemed to be appropriate to the problem; and a related menu of behavioural repertoires.

Moreover, framing mechanisms appear at different levels of cognitive and behavioural observation: they do so in rather elementary acts of judgement and choice, but are also a general organizing principle of

---

[9] 'Prototypization' is easy to understand intuitively: you would give a sparrow rather than a penguin as an example of what a bird is . . . But, with that, it is also easier to understand the basic ambiguity of borderlines, fuzziness and categorical attributions by default. How should one treat a duck-billed platypus? As a mammal? Or should one create a separate category – that of ovoviviparous? A discussion of these issues bearing on economic judgements and behaviours is in Tordjman (1996).

social experience and collective interactions (Bateson, 1972, Goffman, 1974).

One can also intuitively appreciate the links between framing processes and the *social embeddedness* of both cognition and action[10].

Frames – in the broad definition given above – have long been recognized in the sociological and anthropological literature (whatever name is used to refer to them) as being grounded in the collective experience of the actors and in the history of the institutions in which the agency is nested[11].

Indeed, embeddedness seems to go a strikingly long way and affect even the understanding and use of cognitively basic categories, such as that of causality and the very processes by which humans undertake basic operations such as inferences, generalizations, deductions, etc. (Lakoff, 1987, Luria, 1976).

3.3   *Heuristics in judgement and learning*

We mentioned above the issue of *procedural coherence* in decision making and learning (which, to repeat, is a quite separate one from the sophistication – in terms of memory and computing power – of the procedures themselves). An overwhelming body of evidence points to the widespread use by empirical agents of *heuristics*, which may well lead to systematic biases in judgements and action choices compared to the predictions of 'rational' decision-theoretic models (see Kahneman et al., 1982, and also Kahneman and Tversky, 1986, Slovic et al., 1989, Borcherding et al., 1990, Thaler, 1992, and Shafir and Tversky, 1992).

Broadly defined, heuristics are methods, rules or criteria guiding – for example – representation, judgement or action, and they include simple rules of thumb but also much more sophisticated methods explicitly evoking the use of mental categories.

It is impossible to provide here any thorough account of the findings in this area (the classic reference is Kahneman et al., 1982). Let us just recall heuristics such as *representativeness* (i.e. evaluating whatever observation in terms of distance from some prototype or modal case)[12], *availability*

---

[10] On the notion of 'social embeddedness' from contemporary economic sociology, see Granovetter (1985) and several contributions in Smelser and Swedberg (1994). There is also a discussion quite germane to the argument developed here in Tordjman (1996).
[11] Within an enormous volume of literature, a good deal of the sociological tradition has been influenced by the works of Talcott Parson or of the classic Pierre Bourdieu (1977); in anthropology, among others, see the discussions of 'embeddedness' by Karl Polanyi (1944, 1957) and Clifford Geertz (1963); see also Robert Edgerton (1985).
[12] Tordjman (1996) discusses speculative expectations in this light.

Learning in evolutionary environments   267

(i.e. 'what is primarily in your mind is what is in your sight'), and *anchoring* (the initial conditions, related either to the way the problem is posed or to how the experience of the agent influences the final judgement). Other observed phenomena – touching, togetherness, representations, choices and the perceived utility of the latter – include *status quo biases* (entailing, for choice under risk, risk aversion for gains and risk seeking for losses – as formalized by Kahneman and Tversky through 'prospect theory'); *overconfidence* and the *illusion of control* (associated with the overestimation of one's own capabilities and the neglect of potentially relevant outside information[13]); and, more generally, systematic 'incoherence' vis-à-vis any canonical model of utility-based decision under uncertainty.

Note that all these cognitive and behavioural regularities apply both to decisions (taken once and for all) *and learning processes* (for example, representativeness heuristics leads to learning patterns at odds with Bayesian predictions; and illusion of control is likely to entail information censuring and escalating commitments in the face of unfavourable outcomes).

It is straightforward that those cognitive and behavioural patterns openly conflict with 'procedural rationality' – which, as mentioned earlier, is a fundamental and necessary condition for a standard decision-theoretic account of agency.

It is also remarkable that the foregoing evidence has been drawn to a considerable extent from experiments that are simple enough to provide a corresponding 'correct' decision-theoretic answer (i.e. procedurally coherent, making the best use of the available information and in accordance with some supposedly basic preference axioms)[14]. And, in fact, much emphasis has been placed on the *biases* that all this entails, as measured against the canonical normative yardstick. However, together with such (crucial) exercises of empirical falsification, our impression is that not enough has been done in terms of the development of *alternative theories of cognition and action* (Kahneman and Tversky's 'prospect theory'

---

[13] See Kahneman and Lovallo (1993) and Dosi and Lovallo (1997).

[14] Incidentally, an issue that is seldom raised, and that – unfortunately – we shall not be able to discuss here either, is whether the 'rationality' of decision and learning is assessed *procedurally* at each elicited step of the process or whether it is 'black-boxed' and just evaluated in terms of the coherence of final (expected utilities/revealed preferences) outcomes. It is a matter bearing some resemblance both to the 'as . . . if' discussion and also to entrenched debates in psychology between 'behaviourist' and 'cognitivist' views (whether 'strong', *à la* Chomsky, or much weaker ones, *à la* Johnson-Laird or Lakoff). We do not profess the arrogant casualness by which some practitioners of economics switch from one to the other. However, just note that the experimental results on heuristics etc. are equally damaging for the defences of standard rationality in *both* views. So, for example, one finds that not only 'cognitive incoherence' but also revealed behaviours might well display the 'pessimization' (!) as opposed to the 'maximization' of utility (Herrnstein and Prelec, 1991).

being one of the few exceptions in the wider picture). More than that: it might well be that so-called 'biases' emerging in relatively simple decision set-ups could be revealing clues about cognition and behaviour in all other genuinely evolutionary circumstances that are common to human decision makers (whether individuals or organizations). After all, pushing it to the extreme, the collective evolution of human cultures has not been drawn from repeated trials on lotteries but on quite diverse experiences that have in common, nonetheless, *uniqueness* features, out of which our cognition and beliefs had to make some precarious sense – ranging from the various threats in the forest to the deaths of the relatives, from unexpected violence by kinsfolk to the discovery of fire[15].

3.4   *Endogenous preferences*

The separation here from the previous point is somewhat arbitrary; indeed, the aforementioned heuristics and behavioural patterns often entail preferences that are state-dependent. *Status quo* biases are a case to the point: the reference is not some invariant utility – however defined – but '. . . where I was, what I had, etc., at time t minus one . . .'[16]. Moreover, as has been shown, the framing of the problem shapes revealed preferences (a vast amount of literature in the field of marketing points in this direction, but particularly relevant experiments are to be found in Kahneman et al. (1990) and, in connection with authority relations, in Milgram (1974).

Endogenous preference may often be driven by attempts to reduce regret and cognitive dissonance (see Festinger, 1957): that is, as it is put jokingly in Dosi and Metcalfe (1991), citing a pop song from the 1960s, 'if you can't be with the one you love, love the one you're with!' Finally, of course, endogeneity of preference is likely to stem from social imitation and other forms of social interactions (such as Veblenian 'conspicuous consumption' and 'snob effects', etc.; an early discussion is in Leibenstein, 1950)[17].

---

[15] To the best of our (limited) knowledge, one of the few exploratory attempts to account positively for 'rational biases' as crucial clues to cognitive patterns is to be found in Margolis, 1987. Sharing the idea that they should not simply be dismissed as pathologies (see Tordjman, 1996), in another work (Dosi and Lovallo, 1997) it is suggested that they could indeed provide a crucial *collective* evolutionary role, at least with regard to a particular bias – i.e. overconfidence and illusion of control. See also below.

[16] Which, of course, is in open violation of any standard, utility-based decision-theoretic approach, whereby preferences are supposed to be defined on levels and not history-dependent variations and, moreover, are supposed to change on a time scale that is significantly longer than the decisions and random occurrences of 'nature'.

[17] In economics, empirical studies of preference formation were a lively field of investigation in the 1950s and 1960s (see Katona, 1951, 1968), but they were pushed aside

3.5   *Collective beliefs, behaviours and learning*

What has been said so far about cognition, judgement, etc. applies in principle also to all set-ups where individual agents may be assumed, in a first
approximation, to act as insulated entities (notwithstanding, of course,
the whole experience of socialization that they carry with them). Other
circumstances, however, are explicitly and immediately social; decision
making by multiple actors, such as that required by 'teams', economic
organizations and other institutions, belong to this group (for a thorough
discussion, see March, 1988a, 1988b and 1994).

Once more, it would be futile to try to review the enormous quantity
of publications in the field. Let us just offer a few comments.

First, the evidence suggests that, if anything, collective decision making
rather than curbing the judgemental 'biases' mentioned earlier (say, via
some equivalent of a 'law of large numbers') tends, on the contrary, to
reinforce them (Lovallo, 1996; March, 1994).

Second, the 'opaqueness' of the relationship between beliefs,
behaviours and outcomes undermines the usefulness of representing
multi-actor choice in terms of the canonical, linear, sequence outlined
at the beginning of section 2. Rather, the general case seems to fit
quite well the observation of Purkitt and Dyson (1990, p. 363), who –
describing the decision process during the Cuban missile crisis – note
the general lack of 'explicit linkages between information, a sense of the
problem and problem responses' (!). On the contrary, the archetypical
decision process – and, dynamically, the archetypical learning process –
might fit quite well the *garbage can* model (Cohen et al., 1972). That is
(p. 200),

in a garbage can process, it is assumed that there are no exogenous, time-
dependent arrivals of choice opportunities, problems, solutions, and decision-
makers. Problems and solutions are attached to choices, and thus to each other,
not because of any means-ends linkage but because of their temporal proximity.
At the limit, for example, almost any solution can be associated to almost any
problem – provided they are evoked at the same time.

Third, multiple (and possibly conflicting) beliefs, goals and identities are likely to entail systematic decision inconsistencies, while learning and adaptation in these circumstances may well 'path-dependently'
strengthen these inconsistencies themselves (March, 1988a, 1994).

by a new generation of believers in expected utility theory. Among the few contemporary discussions and formal models dealing with these issues in economics see March
(1988a, 1988b), Akerlof and Dickens (1982), Kuran (1991) and Brock and Durlauf
(1995).

270   *Giovanni Dosi, Luigi Marengo and Giorgio Fagiolo*

All this applies, only even more so, in the presence of multiple objectives of individual organizational members and of the organization as a whole. (A related and more detailed discussion is in Dosi, 1995a.)

3.6   *Rules, organizational routines and competencies*

More generally, the issue of *organizational learning* involves the understanding of the processes by which organizational *rules* and *action patterns*[18] change over time. Here, the relevant evidence coming from organizational studies – albeit far from 'clean' and unequivocal – points to organizations as being rather inertial behavioural entities, which are, nonetheless, able to change (path-dependently), either under the pressures of external adversities or internal conflicts (see, from an immense range of published material, March and Simon, 1958, March, 1988a, Nelson and Winter, 1982, and Levinthal, 1996b, 1996a). A particularly important analytical task, in this respect, concerns the identification of the nature of *organizational routines* (i.e. recurring, often complex, rather automatic action patterns, set in an organizational context) and their changes; in our view, the discovery, establishment and modification of routines are indeed an essential part of organizational learning (on all these issues, see Cohen et al., 1996). Routines, in this perspective, store and reproduce a good deal of the problem-solving competencies of the organization and, together, its acquired patterns of governance of potentially conflicting interests among its members (Nelson and Winter, 1982; Coriat and Dosi, 1995).

3.7   *Towards an 'evolutionary' view of agency and learning?*

There are deep linkages among the findings, conjectures and 'stylized facts' that we have telegraphically mentioned so far. In fact, we would dare to suggest that eventually they may fit well together into an 'evolutionary' view of agency and learning, still to come. Some basic features, however, can be appreciated already[19].

---

[18] Note that the two might not correspond at all, if by 'rules' one means the explicitly stated operating procedures of organization, and 'action patterns' are what members of the organization actually do in practice.

[19] We call it an 'evolutionary view' because it is consistent with the evolutionary research programme as it is emerging in economics. Similar views, defined from the perspective of other disciplines, might well take different labels. For example, what we label here as 'evolutionary' has considerable overlap with the research programmes on 'adaptive learning' and 'mental models' in cognitive psychology and artificial sciences. See also below.

Learning in evolutionary environments 271

As we see it, such a view is going to embody the following 'building blocks':

- Cognitive foundations focused on the dynamics of *categories* and *mental models*;
- *Heuristics* as quite general processes for decision and learning;
- *Context dependence*, and, relatedly, *social embeddedness* with regard both to interpretative models and decision rules;
- *Endogeneity* with respect to (possibly inconsistent) *goals* and *preferences*;
- *Organizations as behavioural entities* in their own right (the persistence and learning patterns of which undoubtedly also depend on what the members of the organization do and learn, but cannot at all be reduced to the latter)[20]; and
- Processes of *learning, adaptation* and *discovery* apt to guide representations and behaviours (imperfectly), including (or primarily?) in *ever-changing environments* (so that, even if one 'cannot bathe twice in the same river', one still tries to develop some robust representations of the river itself and some swimming heuristics).

It is easy to understand the radical divergence that this view entails vis-à-vis the canonical decision-theoretic one.

First, it abandons any 'small world' assumption; in fact, it is centred on a sort of *open world* postulate (one tries to make sense and survive in a world where there are many more things between heaven and earth than in anybody's philosophy – and, thus, one always has to face surprises). The clear downside of this perspective is that, *in practice and in principle,* neither the agents we want to describe nor the theorist (if not a god with an *infinitely* accurate knowledge of all possible histories[21]) might be able even to define what a 'rational' decision procedure is. The experimental evidence recalled above suggests, in fact, that most of us also depart from it when such procedures exist and are rather simple. To reiterate, however, these 'biases' might be precious symptoms of the ways we develop tentatively robust cognitive categories, search heuristics and decision rules in environments intrinsically characterized by knowledge gaps and problem-solving gaps. The upside is that one is also able to recombine cognitive categories in unlikely, highly conjectural *thought*

---

[20] In fact, in Dosi (1995a) we push the argument further and suggest that, for many purposes, *institutions rather than individual 'rationality' and preferences* ought to be considered as the *fundamentals* of the analysis.

[21] Note that this condition on infinitely perfect knowledge does not apply only to the case of genuinely evolutionary worlds; it holds also in all environments where the basic laws of motion are given and understood but exhibit non-linearities and sensitive dependence on initial conditions – such as chaotic dynamics (a few further remarks are in Dosi and Metcalfe, 1991, and the references therein).

experiments and, paraphrasing March et al. (1991), 'learn from samples of one or fewer'!

Second, the evolutionary view, as we see it, is not committed to any procedural consistency; rather than black-boxing the algorithms for cognition and action, it considers the understanding of their mistake-ridden development as a crucial analytical task.

Third, it implicitly acknowledges the failure – as a general *descriptive* theory – of the axiomatic route and undertakes the less elegant path of a *constructive theory*, almost inevitably tinted by phenomenological specifications and restrictions.

The challenges and enormous difficulties involved in this research programme on the 'evolutionary micro-foundations' of socio-economic change should be quite obvious to every reader. And these difficulties are compounded by the too frequent lack of robust taxonomies, models and generalizable 'process stories' from the social disciplines where one should find them (e.g. psychology, sociology, etc.). In fact, in an ideal perspective, an economist with evolutionary/institutionalist inclinations ought to be able to get there some 'level zero' first-approximation properties – concerning, for example, cognition, social adaptation, collective learning, etc. – in order to build his microeconomic assumptions[22]. Unfortunately, this too is rarely the case. Worse still, one has witnessed significant inroads by the canonical decision-theoretic axiomatics into the soft underbelly of many other social sciences (with the result that one finds childbearing, voting behaviour, drug addiction and – coming soon, no doubt – infibulation as the equilibrium results of forward-looking rational choices . . .)[23].

---

[22] A bit like, say, the relationship between physics and chemistry, whereby quantum physics provides – so to speak – the 'micro-foundations' of chemical laws; or, probably more pertinently, the relationship between chemistry and biology. While it is impossible to derive the notion of what a cow is just from the laws of chemistry, at the very least the description of a cow should be consistent with the latter, and, at best, the laws ought to provide 'level zero' bricks in a constructive theory of cows' development. For a fascinating discussion of the generative processes of different levels of biological organization, with some possible bearings on the issues of concern here, see Fontana and Buss (1994).

[23] It is impossible to discuss here the reasons for this phenomenon, which have to do, jointly, with the incumbent epistemological looseness of those disciplines; the apparent rigour, parsimoniousness on assumptions and generality of 'economic imperialism' (going back again to the strength of being rigorously wrong); and, last but not least, a social Zeitgeist that makes today 'intuitively obvious' an account of behaviours in terms of utility maximization in the way that it was grace/temptation/Divine Providence up to three centuries ago. (On the latter, Hirschman, 1965, presents a broad fresco on modern cultural history, which helps in putting Gary Becker and disciples into perspective; nearer to the disciplinary topics of this paper is Hodgson, 1988; more specifically, on the current interchanges between economic and sociology, see Barron and Hannan, 1994; a less concise outline of the views on these themes of one of the authors is in Dosi, 1995a.)

However it may be arrived at, the evolutionary research programme on agency and learning in economics cannot remain just as a user of 'stylized facts' and workable generalizations from other disciplines. Rather, it seems to us, it has become an urgent matter to put to the practitioners of other disciplines the backlog of puzzling questions that one faces when dealing with the micro-foundations of evolutionary processes, and possibly also acquire some of their investigative skills[24].

Rather than developing any comprehensive synthesis, it is useful to start, more modestly, from some basic taxonomical exercises.

4　Learning processes: some taxonomies and appreciative theories

It is tautological to say that learning has the precondition of knowing less than one notionally could. And, of course, the simplest representation of a learning process – familiar from anyone's economic training – is in terms of refinements of information partitions, or the updating of probability distributions, or estimations of parameters of some model, or statistically coherent comparisons among competing models, etc.

However, if one accepts the view of cognition and problem solving sketched above, one needs also to open up the 'procedural black box' and map different learning procedures into diverse types of problems and learning contexts. Let us consider them from a few, complementary, perspectives.

4.1　Substantive and procedural uncertainty

One angle from which to look at learning processes focuses on the levels of *cognitive* and *problem-solving complexity*, and the causes of this complexity.

It is useful to distinguish between two different, albeit interrelated, sets of causes that make problems 'hard' and that match our earlier distinction between knowledge gaps and problem-solving gaps. In general, knowledge gaps arise from the lack of isomorphism between the environment and the agent's model of it. This is what is called – in Dosi and Egidi (1991), paraphrasing Herbert Simon – *substantive uncertainty*. In turn, one may further distinguish between *weak* uncertainty (i.e. probabilizable

---

[24] The list of such questions is, obviously, very long: it includes, for example, possible invariance in individual and organizational learning processes, the nature and evolution of 'rules' for both cognition and action, and better specifications of the social embeddedness of individual behaviours. Regarding the interdisciplinary efforts we have in mind, the works by Cohen and Bacdayan (1994) and Egidi (1996) on routines and learning are good examples.

risk) and *strong* uncertainty, involving genuine ignorance and the intrinsic inadequacy of the mental models of the agents to capture fully the structure of the environment.

Conversely, problem-solving gaps entail different degrees of *procedural uncertainty*, with or without substantive uncertainty (an impressionistic taxonomy is presented in figure 9.1). The distinction is clear, for example, with reference to puzzles such as the Rubik cube. Here the structure of the problem is rather simple, the rules are known, and there is no substantive uncertainty: rather, solving the problem itself is the difficult task, involving relatively complex skills of sub-problem decomposition and sophisticated logical skills (Dosi and Egidi, 1991). Similar considerations apply to activities such as theorem proving, and – nearer to the economist's concerns – to many tasks associated with technological innovation, such as the design and implementation of new products and processes.

The distinction also helps to illuminate the somewhat different nature of the related learning processes. In the case of procedural uncertainty they concern primarily the development of problem-solving skills and heuristics.

Conversely, when the latter can be reduced to rather simple and well-understood algorithms, but uncertainty is primarily substantive, learning essentially concerns the representation and framing of the problem[25].

4.2   Learning and the 'logic of appropriateness'

We have already mentioned that, in most circumstances, knowledge gaps and problem-solving gaps are related.

First of all, they are likely to appear together in evolutionary environments; it is a logical assumption that the possibility that innovations will arrive continually implies 'strong' substantive uncertainty, but, relatedly, this implies a symmetric procedural uncertainty. (How can I cope with a changed environment? How can I, myself, innovate?)

Moreover, the psychological evidence shows that knowledge of the 'structure' of the problem and our problem-solving capabilities strongly influence each other: the way we perceive the structure of the problem depends largely on the kind of problem-solving skills we possess, and, conversely, the problem-solving skills we develop are shaped by the ways we frame the problem. (A germane discussion of the intertwining between a particular representation and a particular expertise is in Lane et al., 1996.)

---

[25] Note incidentally that the standard decision-theoretic tool kit handles essentially substantive uncertainty (in its 'weak' form) but is much less appropriate for dealing with learning in the case of problem-solving procedures.

Substantive uncertainty / Procedural uncertainty		Certainty	'Weak' uncertainty (risk)	'Strong' uncertainty
Certainty		Trivial maximization problems (e.g. choosing between winning or losing $1 with certainty!)	Lotteries and most other set-ups considered by standard theory of decision under uncertainty	
Procedural uncertainty	With finite decision trees	Puzzles such as the Rubik cube	Quite a few game-theoretic problems; relatively simple economic decisions in stationary environments	
	With infinite decision trees	Proving theorems; developing technological innovations on the grounds of known physical/chemical principles, etc.	Non-recursively computable games	Adaptation and innovation in an evolutionary environment

Figure 9.1 Substantive and procedural uncertainty: a taxonomy of problems

The phenomenon hints at a more general property of decision making and learning, which March has named the *logic of appropriateness*. As opposed to the archetypical decision process, based on the evaluation of alternatives in terms of the consequences for utilities (i.e. the 'logic of consequences'), in the appropriateness logic (March, 1994, pp. 57–58)

individuals and organizations fulfill identities, they follow rules or procedures that they see as appropriate to the situation . . . [while] neither preferences as they are normally conceived nor expectations of future consequences enter directly into the calculus . . .

Decision makers are imagined to ask (explicitly or implicitly) three questions:

1 – The question of *recognition:* what kind of situation is this?
2 – The question of *identity:* what kind of person am I? Or what kind of organization is this?
3 – The question of *rules:* what does a person such as I, or an organization such as this, do in a situation such as this?

Note that under the logic of appropriateness, so defined, an important part of learning is about the understanding and implementation of the appropriate rules, and – in a broader perspective – entails the coevolution of identities, representations and rules.

It is our belief that the logic of appropriateness does indeed inform a good deal of individual and organizational behaviour, and, to anticipate one of our conclusions, an urgent task ahead is to incorporate it formally into evolutionary theorizing.

4.3   Information, knowledge and learning[26]

Many contributors to contemporary evolutionary theory have drawn a fundamental distinction between *information* and *knowledge*. The former entails *well-stated and codified* propositions about a) the state of the world (e.g. 'it is raining'), b) properties of nature (e.g. 'A causes B'); c) the identities of the other agents ('I know Mr X and he is a crook') and d) explicit algorithms on how to do things[27]. Conversely, knowledge, in the definition we propose here, includes a) cognitive categories; b) the codes of interpretation of the information itself; c) tacit skills; and d) search and problem-solving heuristics that are irreducible to well-defined algorithms.

So, for example, the few hundred pages of demonstration for Fermat's last theorem would come under the heading of 'information'. Having said that, only some dozen mathematicians in the world have adequate *knowledge* to understand and evaluate it. On the other hand, a chimpanzee,

---

[26] This section is drawn largely from Dosi, 1995b.
[27] These four sets correspond quite closely to the codified aspects of Lundvall's taxonomy, distinguishing *know-what, know-why, know-who* and *know-how* (Lundvall, 1995).

Learning in evolutionary environments   277

facing those same pages of information, might just feel like eating them; and the vast majority of human beings would fall somewhere in between these two extremes[28]. . . . Similarly, a manual on 'how to produce microprocessors' is 'information', while knowledge concerns the pre-existing ability of the reader to understand and implement the instructions contained therein. Moreover, in this definition knowledge includes tacit and rather automatic skills, such as operating a particular machine or correctly driving a car to overtake another one (without stopping first in order to solve the appropriate system of differential equations!).

Finally, it also includes 'visions' and ill-defined rules of search, such as those involved in most activities of scientific discovery, and in technological and organizational innovation (e.g. proving a *new* theorem, designing a *new* kind of car or figuring out the behavioural patterns of a *new* kind of crook who has appeared on the financial markets).

In this definition, knowledge is to varying degrees tacit, at the very least in the sense that the agent itself, and even a very sophisticated observer, would find it very hard to state explicitly the sequence of procedures by which information is coded, behavioural patterns are formed, problems are solved, etc.

In fact, as Winter (1987) suggests, varying degrees of tacitness together with other dimensions (see figure 9.2) provide a sort of interpretative grid by which to classify different types of knowledge.

In this perspective, learning has three interrelated meanings.

First, rather obviously, it might involve – as in the conventional view – the acquisition of more information (conditional on the ability of correctly interpreting it).

Second, it entails various forms of augmentation of knowledge *stricto sensu* (which might well be independent of any arrival of new pieces of information).

Third, it might concern the articulation and codification of previously tacit knowledge (learning here involves, so to speak, 'knowing better what you know').

---

[28] This argument largely overlaps with the so-called (post-Keynesian) Shackle-Vickers view, for which ignorance is a fact of economic life and is determined by the inability to know and fully understand the past and the present as well as the impossibility of foreseeing the future (see Shackle, 1955, 1969, and Vickers, 1986). The unexpected can – and most often does – occur, if anything because some aspects of the future are created by human action today (Davidson, 1996). This idea is at the core of Shackle's crucial experiment analysis: a crucial decision is one that changes the economic environment for ever so that identical conditions are never repeated. Such 'uniqueness' of a course of action is also stressed by Katzner (1990) with reference to firms' behaviour, and is strictly related to the notion of the irreversibility of decisions (see Lesourne, 1991).

Tacit ---------- Articulable	
Not teachable ---------- Teachable	
Not articulated ---------- Articulated	

Not observable in use ---------- Observable in use

Complex ---------- Simple

An element of a system ---------- Independent

Figure 9.2 Taxonomic dimensions of knowledge assets
Source: Winter, 1987, p. 170.

In particular, this third aspect has recently sparked a lively debate about whether new information technologies accelerate the pace of codification and fundamentally upset the relative importance in contemporary economies between 'information' and 'tacit knowledge' (for different views on this point, see, for example, Foray and Lundvall, 1996, and several contributions therein, and Hicks, 1936).

4.4   *Appreciative theories of knowledge accumulation and innovation*

The levels of generality of most of what has been said so far – on decisions, knowledge, learning processes, etc. – place the argument very near major foundational issues on cognition and agency in evolutionary environments. However, a good deal of (highly complementary) efforts by evolution-inclined scholars has recently been devoted to empirically grounded 'appreciative' theories (to use the definition of Nelson and Winter, 1982), in particular in the fields of technological and organizational learning. As a result, within the broad field of the 'economics of innovation', one knows much more than, say, thirty years ago about the variety of processes by which knowledge is augmented and diffused in the economy; major contributions in this area include those of Christopher Freeman (1982, 1994), Nathan Rosenberg (1976, 1982, 1994), Keith Pavitt (1984), Richard Nelson (1987, 1993) and Paul David (1975, 1985).

A first broad property (which is probably not surprising for non-economists, though it has far-reaching analytical implications) is the diversity of learning modes and sources of knowledge across technologies and across sectors. For example, in some activities knowledge is accumulated primarily via informal mechanisms of 'learning by doing' and 'learning by interacting' with customers, suppliers, etc. In others it involves much more formalized search activities (such as those undertaken in

R&D laboratories). In some fields knowledge is mostly generated internally and is specific to particular applications. In others it draws much
more directly upon academic research and scientific advances. Recent
research suggests that this diversity of learning modes may be a major
determinant of the diverse patterns of evolution in industrial structures
(e.g. in terms of the distribution of firm sizes, the natality and mortality
of firms, and corporate diversification).

An important step in the understanding of the 'anatomy' of contemporary systems of production and knowledge accumulation has involved
taxonomic exercises (e.g. Pavitt, 1984) trying to map families of technologies and sectors according to their sources of innovative knowledge
and their typical innovative procedures. At the same time, one has tried
to identify possible invariance that holds across technologies, in the patterns of learning (notions such as 'technological paradigms', 'regimes'
and 'technological trajectories' belong to this domain of analysis), and
descriptive indicators for these same patterns (e.g. Dosi, 1984). Relatedly, variables such as the levels of 'innovative opportunity' associated
with each technological paradigm, the degrees of 'cumulativeness' displayed by technical advances, etc. have turned out to be quite useful in
interpreting the determinants of the particular 'trajectories' of innovation
that one observes (Malerba and Orsenigo, 1996).

Second, in modern economies firms are major, albeit by no means
unique, *repositories of knowledge.* Individual organizations embody specific ways of solving problems that are often very difficult to replicate
in other organizations or even within the organization itself. In turn,
organizational knowledge – as mentioned earlier – is stored to a considerable extent within the operating procedures ('the routines') and the
higher-level rules (concerning, for example, 'what to do when something
goes wrong', or 'how to change lower-level routines') that firms enact
while handling their problem-solving tasks in the domains of production,
research, marketing, etc.

Dynamically, technological knowledge is modified and augmented
partly within individual firms and partly through the interaction with
other firms (competitors, users, suppliers, etc.) and other institutions
(universities, technical societies, etc.). In these domains, a growing body
of literature on organizational capabilities and competencies has begun to
explore the links between specific ensembles of organizational routines,
types of organizational knowledge and corporate strategies (see Teece
and Pisano, 1994, introducing a special issue of *Industrial and Corporate Change* on these topics; Lundvall, 1996; Winter, 1987, 1988; Montgomery, 1995; and also the somewhat more theoretical considerations in
Dosi and Marengo, 1994).

Third, building upon the foregoing properties of the nature of technological learning and of the ways that organizations incorporate knowledge, a few scholars have started to explore an explicit coevolutionary view, whereby the accumulation of technological knowledge is shaped and constrained by the nature of the organizations and institutions where this knowledge demand originates, possibly triggering changes in corporate organizations and broader institutions (Nelson, 1994, Kogut, 1993, and Coriat and Dosi, 1995).

4.5   From appreciative theories to formal models

To what extent have formal theories been able to capture the foregoing 'stylized facts', taxonomies and historically grounded generalizations on collective learning?

In order to offer some answers, let us rephrase the earlier taxonomic intuitions into a language nearer to possible modelling translations.

Recall the canonical steps of decision processes mentioned at the beginning of this work (i.e. representation; judgement; choice; action; consequences). When accounting for learning, each of these steps defines some *state-space* of exploration. Accordingly, different classes of learning models can be distinguished with respect to the dimensions of the state-space in which learning occurs.

4.6   Objects and state-spaces of learning processes

What is learning about?

There are basically four classes of *objects of learning*: a) the 'state of the world' (as in games against nature); b) other agents' behaviours (as in strategic games); c) how to solve problems (where the object of learning is not forecasting but designing algorithms); and d) one's own preferences (i.e. agents learn, so to speak, about their own characteristics and identity).

Note, first, that a full-fledged evolutionary model (yet to come) ought to be able to account for all four classes, and – even better – generate empirically testable conjectures on the coupled dynamics among the different learning processes.

Second, it may well be that different objects of learning may also imply *different mechanisms of search and learning* (as far as we know, no robust generalization appears to be available on this issue; this is yet another question that needs to be sorted out with cognitive psychologists, sociologists, etc.).

This categorization of learning objects partially maps into a different formal representation of the dimensions of the state-space in which learning is generally assumed to occur, namely a) the space of representations or models of the world, b) the space of parameters within a given model, c) the space of actions, and d) the space of realized performance outcomes[29].

In the former case, learning is modelled as a search for *better* representations of the environment in which the agent is operating. Agents are supposed to hold models of the environment either explicitly (as, within psychology and artificial sciences, in rule-based models) or implicitly (as in connectionist models), and learning is defined as a structural modification (and not just the tuning of parameters) of the models themselves. Note that, in the expression 'better representation', *better* can have two very different meanings: it can either indicate better performing models – that is, yielding more effective action – or more knowledgeable models – that is, producing better predictions of the state of the environment. In the case where 'better' means 'better performing', the agent is assumed to adjust behaviours according only to the pay-offs he receives, and a completely wrong representation that by chance produces effective action in relation to the actually experienced states of the world has to be preferred to an 'almost' correct representation that, though being 'close' to the real model, produces less effective actions in some of the same states of the world. But a similar question also arises when 'better' means 'better predicting', both because – in a similar fashion – bad representations that produce good predictions are preferred to good representations that produce worse predictions, and also because the very perception of what a good prediction is depends on the model itself. For instance, a change in the state of the world form s_i to s_j might not be perceived as such by the agent whose information partition has s_i and s_j in the same equivalence class, and thus the agent is led to think that his model has not decreased his predictive power (see also below).

Learning in the space of parameters assumes that the model of the world is given in its functional structure and is equal or at least isomorphic to the 'real' one, and learning is just a refinement of the estimation of some unknown parameters. A typical example is Bayesian learning, where the learning agent updates his probability estimates within a given and immutable set of categories that constitute a partition of the real world.

Learning in the space of actions assumes, instead, that either the representation is constant or that it does not exist at all. As we shall see, this

---

[29] Mapping with the above classification is imprecise also in the sense that one leaves out – as most of the formal literature does – endogenous changes in goals and preferences.

is typically the case with simple stimulus-response models of learning and most of the evolutionary games models, where the learning is simply modelled as a selection process in the space of alternative actions.

Finally, learning can be modelled as a dynamic process in the space of realized performance outcomes, whereby the actual process of learning is not modelled at all but the model considers only its results in terms of dynamics in the space of some performance parameters. Typical examples can be found in models of technological learning, where learning is a stochastic process in the space of productivity coefficients.

It is clear that a) implies b) implies c) implies d): learning in the space of representations involves also the possibility of parameter estimates within a given structural form and a selection process among possible actions[30], and – of course – results in some movement in the space of performance outcome. Thus, modelling strategies that remain at the higher level of description and do not explicitly address the 'deeper' cognitive search and behavioural adaptation either assume that the latter has been 'solved' (for instance, the 'right' information partition has been found) or – acknowledging the relevance of these lower levels – only model, more parsimoniously, a 'reduced form'.

4.7   *Domains and constraints of learning processes*

Given the underlying object of learning, or, more formally, the dimensions of state-space of learning dynamics, what constraints does one assume on the domains of learning processes themselves?

Here the most important distinction is between search/adaptation over a *fixed menu* of possibilities that are all accessible from the start to all agents and an *open-ended dynamics* where the discovery of genuine novelties is always possible. As we shall illustrate below, this distinction marks an important cleavage between alternative modelling frameworks.

If all the notional elements of the learning set are known from the start, agents might be assumed to attach probabilities to each of them and to their consequences, thus possibly using some inferential procedure to adjust their behaviours (here the basic paradigm is the Bayesian model). Or, often with the same effect, the sheer availability of all possible behaviours in a population, given a stationary environment, establishes an environmental landscape in which it might be too difficult to define the adaptation drive at work and the related equilibria (the philosophy of 'evolutionary games' is near to this spirit). Conversely, whenever novelties

---

[30] Note that actions might be considered part of the representation, as is the case, for instance, when representations are modelled as condition-action rules.

happen to appear persistently, probability updating is likely to turn out to be a rather clumsy learning procedure, since the state-space can no longer be usefully partitioned due to the emergence of surprises and unforeseen (indeed, unforeseeable) events[31].

Rather symmetrically, in population-based adaptive frameworks the systematic appearance of novelties also implies an ever-expanding pay-off matrix, continuously deformed by the interaction with new events and strategies[32].

4.8   Mechanisms of learning

The very notion of 'learning', as in common usage, implies a sort of reference yardstick, measuring some 'improvement' – however defined – in terms of, for example, cognition, forecasting abilities, collectively assessed performances, inwardly evaluated utilities, etc.

Assume, in a first approximation, that those same criteria are what drive the learning process. Even then, one may well find quite different mechanisms at work (and correspondingly different formal 'laws of motion'). For example, 'learning' could be simply a shorthand characterization of a population-level selection mechanism involving the differential reproduction of entities (e.g., in economics, business firms) carrying different behavioural, organizational or technological traits. Or, it may mean an adaptation process driven by stimulus-response adjustments, without any explicit underlying cognitive process. Or, again, it could be based on agent-specific mechanisms involving expectations, the internal involvement of credit, etc. While in the simplest specifications of the object of learning the three types of dynamics may well turn out to be (asymptotically) equivalent, they may also make a major difference in terms of *finite-time* properties even for simple learning processes, and, *a fortiori*, in terms of the long-term outcomes of discovery and adaptation in more complex evolutionary environments.

With respect to the modelling frameworks, at one extreme stimulus-response adaptation (with or without environmental selection) implies

---

[31] It is true that probabilistic decision making allows for the introduction of a 'complement to the universe' category (i.e. 'all other events') in the information partition in order to close it, but in the presence of genuine novelty (that is, 'strong' substantive uncertainty, as defined above) it is unreasonably far-fetched to assume that a probability could be attached to an unbounded set of events not even conceivable to the decision maker. On the debate between the advocates of non-probabilistic approaches to uncertainty and supporters of the probability paradigm, see also Dubois and Prade (1988) and the references therein.

[32] In biological models, this corresponds to endogenous landscapes with no *ex ante* definable fitness maxima.

Learning spaces

		Action/strategies	Representation/ 'models of the world'	Realized performances	Preferences
Domains and constraints on learning processes	'Fixed menus'	■ Learning in game-theoretic set-ups ■ 'Evolutionary' games ■ Adaptive learning in multi-arm bandit problems (e.g. Arthur, 1993) ■ Self-organization models *à la* Lesourne (1991) ■ Urn models and other types of innovation adoption models (see Arthur et al., 1987, Arthur and Lane, 1993, Kirman, 1992, etc.) ■ Special cases of evolutionary models (see Winter, 1971) (Implicitly) adaptive models in stationary environments (e.g. Arifovic, 1994, Marimon et al., 1990)	■ Bayesian reduction of information incompleteness in games	■ Learning by doing and by using for given best-practice technologies (e.g. Silverberg et al., 1988, Eliasson, 1985)	■ Socially shaped preferences (e.g. Kuran, 1987, Brock and Durlauf, 1995, Akerlof and Dickens, 1982)
	'Open-ended' sets of learning objects	Behavioural search, in Lindgren, 1991, Silverberg and Verspagen, 1995b, Andersen, 1994 ■ Marengo and Tordjman (1996) and Dosi et al. (1999)	Marengo and Tordjman (1996) and Dosi et al. (1999)	■ Open-ended technological search, such as in Nelson and Winter, 1982, Silverberg and Verspagen, 1994, Chiaromonte et al., 1993, Dosi et al., 1995	

Figure 9.3 Dimensions of learning and constraints on the learning process: a guide to the (modelling) literature

agents without any explicit 'reasoning', memory or inferential algorithms leading from the outcomes of their actions to the revision of their future decision rules. At another extreme agents may be modelled as forward-looking users of the best available information (at least in terms of what their bounded competencies allow).

In some peculiarly simple circumstances, the two apparently opposite mechanisms of learning can be shown to lead to identical limit outcomes (which all too often look like those cases whereby electrical shocks to rats lead them to converge to those equilibrium behaviours predicted by 'rational expectation' rats facing the same environment)[33].

However, in most other set-ups the specification of the mechanisms of learning does make a difference: this is an area where, unfortunately, to our knowledge, one does not yet have empirically robust generalizations that can be translated easily into formal modelling assumptions.

On the basis of the foregoing distinctions, figure 9.3 presents an impressionistic classification of examples of each *genre* in the current modelling literature. These differences in learning processes can also be formally accounted as variations and restrictions on the basis of a unified basic representation. This is what we attempt to do in the next section.

5   A basic model and various specifications

Let us consider a standard decision problem whereby an agent faces an environment that can have one out of an enumerable set of elementary outcomes:

$$S = \{s_1, s_2, \ldots, s_i, \ldots\}$$

In most relevant economic problems, the agent will not know the whole set of states of the world S (and even less so their causal links), but he will possess only an imprecise and partial representation thereof:

$$\Theta^t = \{\vartheta_1^t, \vartheta_2^t, \ldots, \vartheta_j^t, \ldots\}$$

where $\vartheta_j^t \subseteq S$ and $\Theta^t \subseteq 2^S$.

Each ϑ_j includes all the states of the world that the agent considers to be possible, or cannot discriminate, when one or more elementary outcomes contained in ϑ_j occur. (Note that in most economic models it is assumed that $\Theta^t = S$, meaning that the agent 'knows' the structure of the world; or, at least, Θ^t is assumed to be a partition of S.) Assuming

---

[33] This is precisely the amusing behavioural support that Lucas (1986) proposes for the rational expectation hypothesis.

instead that, more generally, $\Theta^t \subseteq 2^S$, we have a representation that can account for

1. complete ignorance:

$$\vartheta_i^t = S$$

   for every $i = 1, 2 \ldots n$;

2. partial ignorance of some states of the world, if

$$U_i \vartheta_i^t \subset S$$

(i.e. the agent may be 'surprised' by some events that he did not even think of);

3. hierarchies of hypotheses and/or partially overlapping hypotheses:

$$\vartheta_i \subset \vartheta_j$$

or, more generally,

$$\vartheta_i \cap \vartheta_j \neq \emptyset \quad \text{and} \quad \vartheta_i \neq \vartheta_j;$$

4. systematic mistakes, when an outcome is believed to occur when it does not, and is not thought to be possible when it actually does occur.

Let us, then, assume that the agent is notionally endowed with an innumerable set of possible actions:

$$A = \{a_1, a_2, \ldots a_j, \ldots\}$$

At any point in time the agent holds a finite behavioural repertoire constructed from the basic 'atomic' actions contained in A, subject to revision, modification and recombination. Note that, in general, one ought to allow the agent to know only a subset of the complete notional repertoire derivable from A. Let us call the known repertoire at time t

$$\Xi^t = \{\xi_1^t, \xi_2^t, \ldots\ldots, \xi_j^t, \ldots\}$$

where $\xi_j^t \subseteq A$ and $\Xi^t \subseteq 2^A$.

It must be pointed out that Θ^t and Ξ^t not only reflect the agent's sharpness at interpreting the information coming from the environment, by defining how sharp or coarse his categories are ('information-processing capabilities', in the standard decision-theoretic jargon), but also embed much of the 'cognitive order' that the agent imposes on the world. Θ^t, in particular, contains the variables and categories that the agent perceives as relevant to the representation problem in the undifferentiated flow of signals coming from the environment.

Hence, beyond very simple and special cases, Θ^t and Ξ^t entail some sort of *grammar* determining the legal cognitive and behavioural structures that can be notionally generated. Genuinely constructive models of cognition and problem solving ought to tackle the processes of search in some functional space of which some ϑ's are themselves the outcome. So, for example, the proposition 'we are in the state ϑ_i' is generated through cognitive operations attributing a semantic value to the signals received in the environmental state interpreted by the agent under ϑ_i. As we shall see, we are, unfortunately, still very far from the fulfilment of this research task (see, however, Fontana and Buss, 1996, for a fascinating framework that may possibly also be applicable to these problems).

The set of 'perceived' histories at time t contains some finite-length histories of perceived states of the world and perceived actions that have occurred up to time t:

$$H^t = \{h_k^t\}, \quad k = 1, 2, \ldots, t$$

where $h_k^t \in \Theta^k \times \Theta^{k+1} \ldots \times \Theta^t \times \Xi^k \times \Xi^{k+1} \ldots \times \Xi^t$.

We have repeatedly emphasized that a satisfactory understanding of learning processes entails an account of cognitive categories and 'mental models' that attribute a causal structure (an 'interpretation') to perceived histories. In this formal setting, an interpretation or model can be seen as an algorithm that attributes a causal sense to perceived histories or a subset of them. Call such 'models'

$$\Phi^t = \{\varphi^t(h), h \in H\}$$

There are three points to note. First, particular cases include those whereby agents retain only a dissipating memory of their representations and actions. Second, a single agent may well hold multiple (and contradictory) models at each t. Third, in terms of most current models, a sort of naive 'transparency assumption' rules out an interpretation stage ('everyone knows what really happened').

A decision rule is a mapping between interpretations, so defined, and action repertoires:

$$r_i^t \colon \Phi^t \to \Xi^t$$

A special case, which is commonly considered in the models discussed below, is when the mappings r_i^t define a probability distribution over the set of action repertoires.

An agent's decision-making capabilities at time t can, therefore, be represented by the (finite) set of decision rules it holds:

$$\Re^t = \{r_1^t, r_2^t, \ldots, r_q^t\}$$

When the agent acts upon the environment, it receives a 'response' (or an outcome) out of a set P of possible responses:

$$p^t: S \times A \to P$$

However, in general, the agent will know only an imprecise and partial representation of such outcomes. Moreover, over time it might well change its evaluation criteria (i.e., in standard language, its 'preferences'). Call such evaluations *pay-offs* in terms of some desirability criterion (be it utility, peace of mind, a problem-solving achievement, morality, pleasure and pain, minimum regret, etc.):

$$U^t = \Psi^t (p^t)$$

Hence, let us define a pay-off function as:

$$\pi^t: \Theta^t \times \Xi^t \to U^t$$

On the strength of this very general sketch of a decision-making model, we can re-examine the different *loci* of learning discussed earlier in a more qualitative fashion. However, it might be useful to begin with some extreme examples in order to flag some basic points of this exercise.

First, note that the most familiar economic models of decision making assume that:

a) Θ's are strictly partitions of S;
b) there is a known and often trivial set of action repertoires Ξ and, hence, the distinction between Ξ and A is redundant (witness the fact that economists and decision theorists are generally more comfortable in dealing with metaphors such as lotteries, where the very action – putting a finger on the object of the set – could be performed by any chimpanzee, rather than building computers, proving theorems, etc.);
c) 'interpretations' are always identical to 'true' stories, and, again, the Φ algorithm is redundant;
d) evaluation criteria on outcomes are time invariant, so that one can also innocently assume invariant pay-off functions that drive learning.

All in all, under this scenario it turns out that some well-specified dynamics on learning about the mapping $S \times A \to R$ include everything one needs to know.

Second, at the opposite extreme, a caricatural 'sociological' individual might well claim that:

a) as a first approximation, Ξ's are invariant in t (i.e. 'you do what you are supposed to do');
b) outcomes are always 'good' (Dr Pangloss' rule: we live in the best of all possible worlds; for simplicity, U^t is always in the neighbourhood

of some $\overline{U}$, irrespectively of p^t – 'like what you get no matter what');

c) learning is basically about the endogenous development of representations, interpretations and 'utilities' that fulfil the invariance in the Ξ's and U's.

No doubt, the former caricatural model has been taken formally more seriously than the latter. However, as a first *descriptive* approximation, we tend to bet on the worth of the latter.

5.1 Learning about the states of the world[34]

This obviously implies changing the representation Θ^t. Moreover, these changing representations can simply involve a search in the parameter space or, more fundamentally, the very structure of the model of the world itself.

Suppose, for instance, that S is governed by a stochastic process. The agent might know which kind of stochastic process generates the sequence of states of the world (e.g., for sake of illustration, a Markov process) and have only to 'learn' the correct estimate of the parameters (e.g. Markov transition probabilities). Or he might ignore the nature of the stochastic process itself, or even deny that there is a stochastic process at all[35].

Note also that the possibility for the decision maker to learn about the stochastic process in S depends on the representation Θ^t he holds: only if the latter discriminates among the states in the sequence $s_1, s_2, \ldots ,$ $s_t, \ldots$ in separate categories will the agent have a chance of correctly learning the underlying stochastic process. But the converse might also be true: having chunks of states held together might make it easier to find deterministic patterns out of what might look like a random sequence.

The nature and degree of uncertainty about the stochastic process depends also on the general causal structure of the environment. In particular, we can distinguish among:

- interactions with nature without feedback;
- interactions with nature with feedback;
- multi-agent strategic interactions (including standard game-theoretic ones)[36].

---

[34] Here and throughout we shall hint at some basic and proximate structure of a few models, with inevitable gross approximations on both the detailed formalisms and the assumption refinements. Apologies to misinterpreted authors are due.

[35] There exists ample experimental evidence that probability matching, which amounts to ignoring that data are generated by a stochastic process, is a typical judgemental bias that appears even in the behaviour of expert decision makers.

[36] A similar distinction is made in Marimon (1997).

A fundamental case for our purposes arises when the actions of the agent himself generate new states of the world that did not exist in the original notional set S. Innovative behaviours are a typical case in point: new environmental opportunities are endogenously created, thus also making any sharp distinction between exploration over S and exploration over A only a first-cut approximation[37]. As argued in Dosi and Egidi (1991), it may well be the case that in such an innovative environment a) the set S loses the enumerability property and b) even an agent who has a perfect knowledge of S to start with will be bound to revise his representation.

5.2   *Learning about the actions space (changing the repertoires Ξ^t)*

The set of action repertoires Ξ^t can be modified through time, reflecting the 'technology' of the agent. New actions can be discovered that were not in the agent's repertoire beforehand, or existing actions can be combined in new ways: both circumstances are isomorphic to the search in the problem-solving space (and the related procedural uncertainty) discussed earlier.

5.3   *Learning about the pay-off function (changing the mapping π^t)*

If the agent does not know S and A but holds only imprecise and partial representations thereof, *a fortiori* he will have an imprecise and partial knowledge of how the pay-off function – as earlier defined – maps into 'objective' outcomes. It is worth pointing out that most learning algorithms model learning as a modification of representation of the world, and action repertoires where the learning agent adaptively develops *quasi-pay-off-equivalent* categories of events and actions – i.e. categories that tend to reflect the regularities of the pay-off function rather than the regularities of the underlying sets of states and actions. Thus, under some conditions, adaptive learning algorithms tend to produce better knowledge of the pay-off function than of the sets S and A.

Note also that endogenous preferences *and* a reduction of cognitive dissonance etc. (see above) involve a dynamics in both π^t and Θ^t conditional

---

[37] Notwithstanding this, we maintain that it is a useful first approximation, and in this we take issue with the radical proponents of 'social constructivism' (which, in the formal framework presented here, would also mean collapsing representations into actions). Putting it in a rather caricatural way, while we claim that a world with the atomic bomb entails a set of events different from (and greater than) a world without it, we also maintain that any exploration in the problem-solving space, no matter how well 'socially constructed', will hardly allow violation of the law of gravitation or the time reversibility of actions. Several issues concerning the 'social construction' of technological knowledge are discussed in Rip et al. (1995). From a different angle, collective learning processes are discussed in Lane et al. (1996).

on past realizations – something that one hardly finds in any current model, evolutionary or not.

5.4 Learning about the decision rules (changing the set of rules $\mathfrak{R}^t$)

A basic (and again largely unresolved) issue concerns the dimension of the state-space of rule search. In the spirit of the foregoing discussion, it ought to concern some (metaphoric) representation, internal to the agent, of the mappings on $\Theta^t \times \Xi^t \times \pi^t$. However, the general run of existing models is stuck to a much simpler view (a reduced form – or, rather, a trivialization?) with a fixed menu of rules to begin with and three, possibly overlapping, learning mechanisms. These are, first, some selection mechanism that modifies the weights attributed to each rule, and therefore its probability of being selected for action; second, mechanisms for modifying the domain of applicability of a rule – that is, the subset of the set of perceived histories that fires the rule; and, third (often not easily distinguishable from the above), a process for generating new rules that did not exist previously, possibly by modifying or recombining in some way already existing ones.

What kind of formal modelling and results does one currently find? In the rest of this section we will discuss briefly some of the main classes of models. Departing from a sketch of the classical Bayesian learning models, we will then consider a class of models that is evolutionary in the sense that they explicitly take on board learning and adjustment dynamics of some kind, although they primarily tackle adaptation rather than evolution *stricto sensu*. In other words, they still keep some 'small world' assumption on S, A, etc., and, moreover, they generally tend to rule out (with some noticeable exceptions) any endogeneity of the environmental (or cognitive) landscapes over which representations, actions and decision rules are selected. (Most of the work in this field comes under the heading of 'evolutionary games'.)

5.4.1 Bayesian learning: single- and multi-agent situations without feedback

As a starting point, consider Bayesian learning in the single- and multi-agent situations without feedback from the environment. A typical case is based on the assumptions that the state of the world is determined by some stochastic process and the agent has to select at each time t a proper action. Hence, the agent has to produce an estimate of the stochastic process and compute the expected utility of a course of action. A 'subjectively rational' agent holds a prior distribution μ, which he updates through a Bayesian rule by computing a posterior distribution after observing the realizations of the stochastic process and the pay-off received.

In the multi-agent case (Kalai and Lehrer, 1993), the prior distribution concerns the actions of the other players (their 'types'). Contrary to the hypotheses that are made in the literature on, for example, rationalizable strategies, such a prior distribution does not require knowledge of the other agents' pay-off matrices, but only of one's own; however, S and A must be common knowledge.

Bayesian updating processes in this case strongly converge ('strongly merge') if the sequence of posterior distributions converge, in the limit, to the real distribution on S (Blackwell and Dubins, 1962). But this can happen only if prior distributions attach positive probability to all, and only the subsets of S that have positive probability for the underlying stochastic process. This amounts to postulating perfect *ex ante* knowledge of all possible events. Kalai and Lehrer (1993) show this result in an $n \times n$ game without feedback, in which they assume that agents do not have complete knowledge of the space or strategies of the other players, and that they do not have to share homogeneous priors, but their prior must be 'compatible with the truth' – that is, they have to attach positive probability to all, and only the events that can occur with positive probability (the so-called 'grain of truth' condition).

Moreover, Feldman (1991) has shown that, if the set A is non-enumerable, convergence of posterior distributions to the true one cannot be guaranteed.

5.4.2   Stochastic learning models

Of course, Bayesian learning is highly demanding on the prior knowledge agents are assumed to have from the start (a point also acknowledged nowadays by scholars otherwise inclined to some 'rationalist' axiomatics of learning processes).

A much less demanding way to introduce learning, common in the contemporary literature, is to suppose some form of selection process among a finite set of possible actions. Two modelling strategies are possible in this respect. On the one hand, models might assume the existence of a population of agents, each identified with one action[38], and consider the learning/selection process taking place entirely at the population level. On the other hand, each agent could be modelled by a set of actions, with the selection process being a metaphor of its search capabilities (see Fudenberg and Kreps, 1993, and Kaniovski and Young, 1994). This distinction goes beyond the interpretation of the metaphor itself, but – as will shall see – has some substantial consequences on the modelling strategy.

---

[38] Coherently with the terminology introduced in the basic model, we use the term 'action' rather than the more common 'strategy' for this kind of model.

First, consider a face-value interpretation of standard evolutionary games. Indeed, evolutionary games assume away any problem of representation, both on states of the world and on actions, and – so to speak – collapse the learning of decision rules into selecting among a set of given behavioural repertoires (further assuming that such a selection process is exogenously driven by the environment). Agents carry no cognitive capability, but have basically two roles: that of carrying the 'memory' of the system (e.g. that of being 'replicators' of some kind), and that of introducing some exploration (via random mutation).

In one standard formulation, evolutionary game models (see the pioneering work of Maynard Smith, 1982, and later, with regard to economics, examples such as the work by Friedman, 1991, Kandori et al., 1993, Young, 1993, and Weibull, 1995) assume that there exists a population of N agents and a finite set of actions $a_1, a_2, \ldots, a_k$. If we denote by $n_i(t)$ the number of agents adopting strategy a_i, the basic selection principle states that

$$\frac{n_i(t+1) - n_i(t)}{n_i(t)} > \frac{n_j(t+1) - n_j(t)}{n_j(t)}$$

$$\text{if and only if } \pi^t(a_i, s_t) > \pi^t(a_j, s_t) \tag{1}$$

The fundamental selection principle therefore implies that actions that have a higher pay-off are increasingly sampled in the population. It is often (though not always) the case that this selection principle takes the special form of replicator dynamics equation, originally suggested by biological arguments (see Maynard Smith, 1982, and – earlier – Fisher, 1930) but also widely used in economic models – though with less convincing arguments[39]

$$n_i(t+1) = g\left(\pi^t(a_i, s_t) - \overline{\pi}^t\right) n_i(t) \tag{2}$$

where $\overline{\pi}^t$ is the average pay-off across the population.

Learning is driven by the joint action of a selection principle and a variation mechanism – i.e. the constant introduction of search by means of random mutation, whereby some agents mutate their strategy with some given (small) probability.

Originally, mutation was conceived as a pointedly and isolated phenomenon (Maynard Smith, 1982), introduced as a device for studying the evolutionary stability of equilibria. An equilibrium was said to be

---

[39] Many recent models have worked with a more general setting, where broader classes of selection rules are considered, rather than strict replicator dynamics (see, for instance, Kandori et al., 1993, and Kaniovski and Young, 1994).

evolutionarily stable if, once achieved, it could not be disrupted if a small proportion of mutants appeared in the population. More recent developments (see, for instance, Kandori et al., 1993, Foster and Young, 1990, and Fudenberg and Harris, 1992) of stochastic evolutionary games have incorporated mutation as a continuous process; hence, the equilibria generally emerge as limit distributions of some dynamic process (in some cases, however, ergodicity is lost – as in Fudenberg and Harris, 1992, and Kaniovski and Young, 1994).

Further developments concern the nature of the selection process in (2). The dynamics can, in fact, be made dependent upon the past history of interactions, as summarized by the relative frequencies of actions within the population and/or by some sample of past pay-offs. Along these lines, Young (1993) considers a stochastic version of a replication mechanism whereby an action diffuses across the population according to a sample of the pay-off obtained in the last few periods. Along similar lines, a class of models (see especially Milgrom and Roberts, 1991, Fudenberg and Kreps, 1993, and Kaniovski and Young, 1994) considers more sophisticated agents by endowing them with some form of memory that keeps track of the consequences of actions and of the other players' replies in the past. Learning becomes a process of selection of a sequence of actions that constitute the best reply to sampled strategies (Kaniovski and Young, 1994) and might induce the emergence of 'conventions' – i.e. stable patterns of behaviour (which are, at least, locally stable Nash equilibria; Young, 1993, shows this in the cases of very simple memory endowments).

5.4.3   Stochastic models with self-reinforcement

In evolutionary games it is customary to assume that actions that have performed better in the past tend to diffuse more rapidly across the population of players, while the selection mechanism itself is either a replicator equation or is constructed via adaptation driven by infinitely frequent interactions among agents at each iteration (as in Kandori et al., 1993). Other kinds of models consider different mechanisms of diffusion, where agents choose an action according to some simple algorithm, such as a majority rule – that is, choosing the action that is adopted by the majority of some observed sample of the population.

First, if one considers a finite population of players, the number of agents who select action a_k at time t defines a Markov chain where transition probabilities depend on actual frequencies of actions in the population. For instance, assume a population of N individuals and $A = \{a_1, a_2\}$. Agent i, who has selected action a_1 at time $t-1$, switches at time t to action

Learning in evolutionary environments   295

a_2 with probability

$$P_i^t(a_1 \rightarrow a_2) = \alpha \frac{n_2(t)}{N} + \varepsilon \qquad (3)$$

where $n_2(t) = N - n_1(t)$ is the number of agents selecting action a_2. The α parameter measures the weight of the self-reinforcing component of the selection process, while ε captures components that are independent from the choice of the other agents[40]. It is possible to show the existence of a limit distribution: see Kirman, 1992, 1993, Orléan, 1992, and Topol, 1991. Depending on the values of α, the population may oscillate between the two states, with the limit distribution itself determining the average frequencies at which the system is observed in each state in the limit.

A second modelling strategy considers infinitely growing populations, where at each time step t a new agent makes a 'once and for all' choice of action a_k, with probability depending on the relative frequencies of past choices. In these models (see, among others, Arthur et al., 1987, Dosi and Kaniovski, 1994, Kaniovski and Young, 1994, and Fudenberg and Kreps, 1993) learning takes place primarily at the population level (agents cannot change their decision), and this occurs in a typical 'incremental' fashion.

The population dynamics can be described by an equation of the type

$$x_k(t+1) = x_k(t) + \frac{1}{N_t}\{[f_k(x_k(t+1)) - x_k(t)] + \varepsilon(x(t), t)\} \qquad (4)$$

where N_t is the size of the population after t arrivals of 'new agents', $x_k(t)$ is the share of the population that has chosen action a_k, and $\varepsilon(x(t), t)$ is a stochastic term with zero mean, independent in t.

The function f_k embeds possible self-reinforcing mechanisms, and its functional form determines the number and the stability properties of fixed points. In case of multiple equilibria, the process is generally non-ergodic (i.e. it displays path dependency), and convergence to one or other equilibrium depends on the initial conditions and sequences of 'early' choices (see Arthur et al., 1987, and Glaziev and Kaniovski, 1991).

It is worth pointing out that in the former class of models with finite population, in the limit the population might also keep oscillating between states and spend some fraction of time on each of them. Models can predict only the limit distribution and – possibly – the average time the population spends on each of the states that have, in the limit, positive

---

[40] As mentioned above, we skip any technical details here – such as, for example, the not so minor difficulty of keeping such dynamics as those represented in (3) consistently on the unit simplex.

probability measure[41]. In the latter class of models with infinitely increasing population, the size of the population instead goes to infinity in the limit and the system will almost surely be found in one of the absorbing states. But, if such absorbing states are multiple, which one is selected depends on the initial conditions and on the path followed by the system in finite time[42].

Moreover, in both classes of models it is assumed that agents base their decisions on observed frequencies. Thus, if these models are to be taken as representations of distributed, agent-based learning, such information must somehow be available to them. For example, a plausible interpretation of Arthur et al., 1987, is that frequencies are free public information (possibly with noisy disturbance), while Dosi, Ermoliev et al., 1994, assume that agents estimate frequencies by observing a sample of the population.

Finally, note that in the models with infinite population no learning takes place at the level of a single agent, as the latter cannot modify its once and for all decision, while in finite population models some primitive form of individual learning does occur, as agents modify their actions in line with some observation of the behaviour of other agents.

In fact, all this hints at a more general issue, namely the interaction between – so to speak – the 'weight of history' and agents' abilities to extract information from it. For example, Arthur and Lane, 1993, consider a model of choice between two technologies A and B, with a feedback between past adoptions and choice criteria. The states of the world represent the properties of such technologies $S = \{s_A, s_B\}$; these

---

[41] It is true that, after determining the limit distribution as $t \to \infty$, one might collapse it to a measure-one mass corresponding to one of the equilibria by further assuming that $\varepsilon \to 0$ (i.e. that the 'error' or 'search' term vanishes). However, it seems to us that this is primarily a display of technical *virtuosity*, with not much interpretative value added. Note also, in this respect, that if one takes the assumption of $\varepsilon \to 0$ as realistic one must, symmetrically, allow a speed of convergence to the 'good' equilibrium that goes to zero.

[42] Note also that the infinite population case, most often formalized through generalized Polya urns (for a survey and applications, see Dosi and Kaniovski, 1994), allows a much easier account of dynamic increasing returns. Formally, the latter imply some equivalent to a possibly unboundedly increasing *potential function*. Conversely, all the finite population cases we are aware of are driven by some equivalent to an invariant *conservation principle*. As we see it, learning most often does imply dynamic increasing returns; for example, even in the most trivial cases, efforts in search, when successful, yield relatively easy replication (and thus near-zero marginal costs). A straightforward implication is that history matters, and increasingly so as the process goes on. The fact that, so far, in the finite population cases one must rely formally upon time-invariant Markov processes most often leads – due to the formal properties of the model itself – to the conclusion that the system may also fluctuate in the limit across action patterns (or systems of collective representations). We do not have any problem with accepting the heuristic value of the conclusion under bounded increasing returns (such as those stemming from informational interdependencies on, for example, financial markets), but we have great reservations in the cases where returns to knowledge are in principle unbounded.

are unknown to agents, who only hold prior distributions $N(\mu_A, \sigma_A)$ and $N(\mu_B, \sigma_B)$. At each time t one agent adopts one of the two technologies by maximizing his expected utility:

$$E[U(c_i)] = \int U(c_i)\pi(c_i|X)dc_i \tag{5}$$

where U is the utility function (with constant risk aversion) and $\pi(c_i|X)$ is the posterior distribution computed as follows. When an agent makes its choice, it samples τ agents among those who have already chosen. X is thus a vector of dimension τ, the components of which are each a single observation in the sample, which is supposed to be drawn from a normal distribution with finite variance

$$x_j = c_i + \varepsilon \quad \varepsilon \approx N(0, \sigma^2)$$

By applying Bayesian updating, agents can compute posterior distributions and choose the technology with higher expected utility.

Interestingly, it can be shown that in these circumstances, notwithstanding the procedural 'rationality' of the agents, the dynamics might lead to collective lock-in into the 'inferior' option (but, remarkably, in Lane and Vescovini, 1996, it appears that less 'rational' decision rules turn out to be dynamically more efficient from a collective point of view).

Note that this model is equivalent to a learning model with single agent and environmental feedback: at each time t the agent observes τ realizations of the states of the world, where the probability that each observation is generated by A or B is initially identical and is then modified through Bayesian updating. But this very learning process will change the distribution from which the agent samples the following time step by producing feedback on the states of the world. (In this respect, notice incidentally that, empirically, agents tend to display much less procedural rationality than that postulated here, leading to systematic misperception even in simple deterministic environments: see Sterman, 1989a, 1989b).

5.4.4 *Models with local learning*
The class of models illustrated above assumes that agents base their actions on some global observation of (or feedback with) the population or a sample thereof. Another perspective describes instead set-ups where agents respond to some *local* observation of the characteristic of a given subset of the population. Agents observe only their 'neighbours' (see, for instance, Kirman, 1997, David, 1992, and Dalle, 1993, 1994a, 1994b), defined according to some spatial or socio-economic measure of distance. Let $d(i, j)$ be the distance between agents i and j and d^* be a given threshold; the set of agents who are neighbours of agent i is defined as

$$V_i = \{j \in I : d(i, j) \le d^*\}$$

If the set V_i is not mutually disjoint, it is possible that local phenomena of learning and adaptation (i.e. inside a given neighbourhood) spread to the entire population.

One way of modelling this kind of process is based on Markov fields (see, for example, Allen, 1982a, 1982b, An and Kiefer, 1995, Dalle, 1994a, 1994b, Durlauf, 1994, and Orléan, 1990), assuming that agents stochastically select their actions depending on the actions or 'states' of their neighbours. Suppose, for instance, that pay-offs increase in the degrees of coordination with neighbours. Collective outcomes will depend upon the strength of the incentives (as compared to some 'internal' motivation of each agent): when incentives are not strong enough, high levels of heterogeneity will persist; conversely, if the premium on coordination is high enough, the system will spend most of its time in states of maximal coordination (though it might keep oscillating between them – see Kirman, 1993)[43].

Another class of models assumes that agents choose their action deterministically (see Blume, 1993, 1995, Berninghaus and Schwalbe, 1992, 1996, Anderlini and Ianni, 1996, Herz, 1994, and Nowak and May, 1992, 1993), in ways that are basically isomorphic to simple cellular automata, whereby the state of each agent depends – according to some deterministic rule – on the states of its neighbours.

Certainly, having some space that specifies learning mechanisms, conditional (in principle) on 'where a particular agent belongs', is a fruitful development in accounting for heterogeneity and path dependency in processes of adaptive learning[44]. However, note also that, in terms of how learning occurs, a fixed 'spatial' structure implies in fact a 'structure' – be it on metaphorically geographical, technological or cultural spaces – that ought to be phenomenologically justified; on the contrary, it is lamentable to find very often a two-dimensional lattice, or a torus, or something else being introduced with careless casualness.

In the perspective discussed so far, both stochastic and deterministic models of local learning consider learning as a selection over a fixed menu of *actions*. However, an alternative interpretation suggests that they could somehow also model processes of learning in the (fixed) space of *representations*.

Consider N agents on a bidimensional graph who select among k possible actions, and assume further that:

---

[43] Such results do not seem to show much robustness, however, with respect to both the algorithm that agents use to choose actions and the size of the population; see Föllmer (1974) and Hors and Lordon (1997).

[44] An important limitation of these models is the rigidity with which the structure of the neighbourhood is defined. However, Kirman et al. (1986), Ioannides (1990) and Bala and Goyal (1998) have given a more general formulation, in which the very structure of the graph is modified stochastically.

- the set of states of the world is given by all the Nk possible configurations of the graph (assuming that the action taken by the corresponding agent characterizes the state of a node); and
- agents hold a partial representation of such a set *S*, so that they observe only a part of the state of the world – i.e. that given by the state of their neighbours.

An agent's neighbourhood represent a sort of window through which it can observe only a part of the world; thus the agents try to infer adaptively the state of the entire graph from such window observation.

But, given this interpretation, we should expect that learning would involve a progressive 'enlargement of the window', so that agents can achieve an ever more complete picture of the world. Some results show that, above a threshold of interconnection in the graph, all agents globally converge to a state where they implicitly have access to all the information available in the system (see Bala and Goyal, 1998, Hammersley and Welsh, 1980, and Grimmett, 1989). However, there seems to be no monotonicity in the relation between the 'width of the window' and the asymptotic quality of the learning process (holding the nature of interconnections constant, between agents and between the past and the present).

5.4.5   Population-level versus agent-level learning

We have already remarked that one way of interpreting standard evolutionary games is in terms of agents who are simple replicators and who, individually, do not actually learn anything: only the population does. More sophisticated models (see, for instance, the already mentioned contribution by Young, 1993) take a different route, and are also meant to explore some (boundedly rational) cognitive capability of agents, such as some memory of previous events and some simple decision-making algorithms[45].

But it is clear that, with some modification, these kinds of selection-based models also have an immediate appeal as models of individual learning, once the population of individuals – each characterized by a single action – has been replaced by a single individual who adaptively learns to select among a set of possible actions at his disposal. Stochastic approximation models of adaptive beliefs try to move in this direction. The basic idea behind these models can be cast in the following way. Suppose that the learning agent has a set of actions $A = \{a_1, a_2, \ldots, a_n\}$; he does not know the realization of the state of the world s^t, but perceives only a realized pay-off π^t. In this case, a rational Bayesian decision maker

---

[45] A further step towards models of agent-level learning could be introduced by labelling agents (see the models with local learning presented below).

should form prior beliefs on all the possible pay-off matrices. An adaptive learner, instead, randomly chooses among actions according to some strength that he attaches to actions. Let us call F_k^t the strength assigned to action a_k at time t. The strength is updated according, say, to the rule

$$F_k^{t+1} = F_k^t \frac{f^k(\pi^t(s^t, a_k))}{\sum_h f^h(\pi^t(s^t, a_h))} \tag{6}$$

Actions are randomly selected at t with probabilities given by

$$P^t(a_k) = \frac{F_k^t}{\sum_i F_i^t} \tag{7}$$

This selection mechanism induces a stochastic process on the strengths assigned to competing rules, the asymptotic behaviour of which can be studied.

   This and similar selection mechanisms can be found, for instance, in Arthur (1993), Posch (1994), Easley and Rustichini (1995), Fudenberg and Levine (1995) and Marimon et al. (1990). Easley and Rustichini's model, in particular, provides a neat connection between population-level and individual-level evolutionary arguments. In their model, Easley and Rustichini consider an individual decision maker facing an unknown environment, represented by a stochastic variable. Instead of forming beliefs on the set of possible processes and updating them according to the Bayesian approach, he adaptively selects among a set of behavioural rules $\Re$ (of the same kind as our basic model) according to a strength-updating rule of the kind of expression (6) and a random selection rule of the kind of expression (7). This enables them to study the stochastic process induced on the strengths of rule r_i, which is given by the expression

$$F_k^{t+1} = \prod_{z=0}^{t} F_k^z \frac{f^k(\pi^z(s^t, a_k^t))}{\sum_h f^h(\pi^z(s^t, a_h^t))} \tag{8}$$

   With some further assumptions on the characteristics of the underlying stochastic process on the states of the world (stationarity and ergodicity) and on the selection dynamics (monotonicity, symmetry and independence), they are able to prove that an individual who uses this kind of adaptive selection dynamics eventually acts as if it were an objective expected utility maximizer, and, moreover, that the set of rules selected by such dynamics corresponds to the set of rules that would be selected by a replicator dynamics.

Some considerations on the importance and limitations of these kinds of model are in order. First of all, note that these approaches end up being pure adaptation/selection models. It is an encouraging result indeed that such simple selection mechanisms are sometimes (but not always) able to select behavioural rules that mimic the optimizing behaviour prescribed by normative theories, but, of course, a necessary (and highly demanding) condition for such behaviour to be selected is that it is there in the first place. Populations must contain optimizing individuals in order to have them selected by replication mechanisms of selection. By the same token, rules that mimic the expected utility-maximizing behaviour must be in the decision maker's endowment of behavioural rules in order to have them asymptotically selected by the strength-updating process. One could say that, by moving from standard models of optimizing behaviour to stochastic models of adaptive learning, one moves from a world where agents are assumed to be naturally endowed with the correct model of the world to a world where agents are endowed with the correct behavioural rules (which define an implicit model of the world), but that these are mixed together with incorrect ones and have to emerge adaptively. It is clear that the latter assumption amounts to assuming away the cognitive problem of how such rules are formed and modified. In complex and changing environments in particular, it seems a rather far-fetched assumption to start with. In fact, stationarity in the underlying selection environment is a fair approximation whenever one can reasonably assume that the speed of convergence to given fundamentals is an order of magnitude faster than the rate of change in the fundamentals themselves. Ergodicity comes here as a handy auxiliary property: if it does not hold, much more detail is needed on initial conditions and adjustment processes.

Relatedly, an important question concerns how long the selection process takes to select good rules[46].

Second, and again related to the previous points (as in Easley and Rustichini, 1995), suppose that, at each stage of the adaptive learning process, the strength of all rules is updated according to the pay-off they would have received in the realized state of the world. This assumption is justified if, and only if, the learning agent's actions do not determine any feedback on the environment and if, and only if, the agent knows it. When this is not the case, only the strength of the rule actually employed can be updated, and therefore lock-in phenomena and non-ergodicity may well

---

[46] Some considerations on this problem can be found in Arthur (1993), who argues that the speed of convergence is highly sensitive to the variance of the pay-offs associated with different actions. Of course, the longer the convergence process the more implausible appears the assumption of the stationarity of the environment.

emerge: exploitation versus exploration and 'multi armed bandit'-type dilemmas are unavoidable.

These quite fundamental questions in fact hints at some general issues, *a fortiori* emerging in fully-fledged evolutionary environments. And, indeed, a theoretical in order to explore them is based on so-called 'artificially adaptive agents' (AAAs), which are briefly examined in the next section.

5.4.6   *Artificially adaptive agents*

If we drop the assumption that agents are naturally endowed with the correct model of the environment in which they operate, the fundamental topic of inquiry shifts to how models and representations of the world are generated, stored and modified by economic agents. On the one hand, as we have already argued, this consideration carries the requirement for some form of cognitive and psychological grounding. On the other hand, it opens new possibilities for applications to the economics of families of models developed in artificial intelligence (AI), and especially in that branch of AI that considers selection and variation mechanisms as a basic driving force for learning.

The main point of interest in these kinds of model is that the dynamics involved is essentially open-ended, both when the object of the modelling exercise is the dynamics of multi-agent interactions and when, instead, modelling concerns individual learning[47]. For a general overview on the AAA perspective in economics, see, for instance, Arthur (1993) and Lane (1993a, 1993b).

Open-ended dynamics is a consequence of two strong theoretical commitments of the AAA perspective. First, AAA models are not restricted to pure selection dynamics, but consider the introduction of novelty, innovation and the generation of new patterns of behaviour as a basic force for learning and adaptation. Thus, the dynamics never really settles into equilibrium states.

Second, the AAA perspective considers heterogeneity among agents and the complexity of interaction patterns (among agents in models of collective interaction and among behavioural rules in models of individual learning) as crucial aspects of the modelling exercise. In fact, in the

---

[47] All this notwithstanding the spreading practice of using AAA models to show adaptive convergence to conventional equilibria (often characterized by seemingly 'rational' forward-looking behaviours at the equilibrium itself). Of course, we do not deny that adaptive AAA learning might lead there sometimes. However, we consider the epistemological commitment to the search for those adaptive processes displaying such limit properties (often also at the cost of ad hoc rigging of the learning assumptions) as a somewhat perverse use of AAA modelling techniques.

AAA approach heterogeneity among agents (in terms of representations, expectations and learning paths) is the norm and homogeneity the exception; therefore, seemingly persistent equilibria tend in fact to be transient states of temporary 'ecological' stability, where small variations can trigger non-linear self-reinforcing effects.

An interesting prototypical example of AAAs can be found in Lindgren (1991). He considers a classical repeated prisoner's dilemma played by a given population of players. Each agent is defined by a strategy, which deterministically maps finite-length histories of the game (here represented by sequences of 'defeat' or 'cooperate' actions performed by the player itself and his opponent) into an action (defeat or cooperate). This population is then processed via an extended genetic algorithm that allows for variable-length genomes. Simply allowing for strategies based on variable-length histories makes the number of possible species in the population practically infinite and the search space unlimited. Hence, evolution is no longer a selection path in a finite and closed space of alternatives, but 'can then be viewed as a transient phenomenon in a potentially infinite-dimensional dynamical system. If the transients continue for ever, we have *open-ended evolution*' (Lindgren, 1991, p. 296; emphasis in original).

The dimension and complexity of strategies themselves become two of the elements subject to evolutionary selection and variation. This perspective enriches the concept of strategy implicit in the standard evolutionary game framework. While, in the latter, 'strategy' is most often squeezed down to an action taken from a given set of possibilities, in AAA models it is easy to account for evolving 'strategies' made up by changing combinations of a set of basic operators, categories and variables. (However, what is still missing in AAA models is the possibility of modelling learning as a modification of this set of basic operators, variables and detectors of environmental states, unless they originate from some combination of the elementary ones with which the system is initially endowed.) In terms of our earlier basic model, this difference amounts to an explicit search process regarding the algorithm mapping 'internal' representations to action patterns (in the case of AAA models), as compared to its 'black-boxing' into the adaptive selection of actions themselves (in the case of most evolutionary games).

This distinction is even clearer in more explicitly rule-based AAA models. Rule-based AAA models differ from the stochastic models outlined in the previous section in at least two fundamental respects. First, they consider learning as the joint outcome of the processes of the generation, replication, selection and modification of behavioural rules. As the space of behavioural rules is potentially unlimited – even in relatively simple problems – and the search space itself is ill-defined and subject to change, the generation of new rules, new representations and new actions is an essential mechanism for learning and adaptation.

The second aspect, related to the previous one, is that – except in very simple problems nested in stationary environments – the outcome of the learning process cannot be constrained to be a single behavioural rule but may be a whole 'ecological' system of rules, which together form a representation of the environment (on the so-called 'computational ecologies', see also Huberman and Hogg, 1995). Behavioural patterns that emerge in AAA models may, therefore, be much richer than those predicted by pure selection models. Here, learning takes place explicitly in both spaces of representations/models of the world and action repertoires[48].

A prototypical example of rule-based learning models is represented by the so-called 'classifier systems' (see Holland et al., 1986; for an overview of actual and possible applications to economics, see Arthur, 1991, 1993, and Lane, 1993b; for some specific applications, see Marimon et al., 1990, Marengo, 1992, and Marengo and Tordjman, 1996; for a survey, see also Hoffmeister and Bäck, 1991).

Learning in classifier systems presents the following general features.

(i) Learning takes place in the space of *representations*. In a complex and ever-changing world, agents must define sets of states that they consider to be equivalent for the purpose of action. In other words, they have to build representations of the world in order to discover regularities that can be exploited by their actions. These representations have a pragmatic nature and are contingent upon the particular purpose the routine is serving.

(ii) Learning must be driven by the search for better performance. Learning agents must therefore use some system of *performance assessment*.

(iii) If rules of behaviour have to be selected, added, modified and discarded, there must exist a procedure for the *evaluation of the usefulness* of rules. This problem may not have a clear solution when the performance of the system is assessed only as a result of a long and complex sequence of interdependent rules (such as in the game of chess, for instance).

---

[48] In this respect, a particularly interesting question concerns the circumstances under which simple behavioural patterns do emerge notwithstanding the potential cognitive complexity that these models entail. In Dosi et al. (1995) it is shown that this is often the case in the presence of competence gaps of the agent vis-à-vis the complexity of the changing environment (see also below).

Let us consider again the basic model of decision making introduced above and suppose that it is faced repeatedly by the same agent. The decision maker, by using his/her experience of the previous stages of the game, makes a forecast of the state of the world that will occur next and chooses an action that he/she considers as appropriate. At the outset the player has no knowledge either of the pay-off matrix or of the 'laws' that determine the changes in the environment. The decision process consists therefore of two elements: the state of knowledge about the environment, represented by the agent's forecasting capabilities; and the rules for choosing an action, given this forecast.

In its most basic formulation, a classifier system is a set of condition-action rules that are processed in parallel. Each rules makes the execution of a certain action conditional upon the agent's perception of a certain state of the world.

A first element that characterizes a classifier system is the message (signal) the learning agent receives from the environment. Such a message has to be interpreted and connected to a consequent action according to a model of the world that is subject to revisions. The signal is usually encoded as a binary string of given length:

$$m_1 \, m_2 \ldots m_n \quad \text{with } m_i \in \{0,1\}$$

Learning is modelled as a set of condition-action rules that are processed in a parallel fashion. Each rule makes a particular action conditional upon the fulfilment of a condition concerning the present state of the world. The condition part is, therefore, actually made up of a string of the same length as the message's, which encodes a subset of the states of nature and is activated when the last detected state of the world falls into such a subset:

$$c_1 \, c_2 \ldots c_n \quad \text{with } c_i \in \{0,1,\#\}$$

The condition is satisfied when either $c_i = m_i$ or $c_i = \#$. That is, the symbol # acts as a 'don't care' symbol that does not pose any constraint on the corresponding part of the environmental message.

Thus, consistently with the framework discussed in the previous section, a set of conditions defines a subset of the power set of S. It is important to notice that each condition defines one subjective state of the world, as perceived by the agent, and defines its relationship with the objective states of the world. This relationship always remains unknown to the decision maker, who 'knows' only the subjective states.

The action part is, instead, a string of length p (the number of the agent's possible actions) over some alphabet (usually a binary one) that encodes possible actions:

$$a_1\ a_2\ \ldots\ a_p \quad \text{with } a_i \in \{0,1\}$$

The decision maker can therefore be represented by a set of such condition-action rules

$$R = \{R_1, R_2, \ldots, R_q\}$$

where

$$R_i : c_1\ c_2\ \ldots\ c_n \rightarrow a_1\ a_2\ \ldots\ a_p \quad \text{with } c_i \in \{0,1,\#\}$$

$$\text{and } a_i \in \{0,1\}$$

In addition, each rule is assigned a 'strength' and a 'specificity' (or its reciprocal 'generality') measure. The *strength* basically measures the past usefulness of the rule – that is, the pay-offs cumulated every time the rule has been applied (minus other quantities, which will be specified later). The *specificity* measures the strictness of the condition; the highest specificity (or lowest generality) value is given to a rule where the condition does not have any symbol '#' and is therefore satisfied only when that particular state of the world occurs, whereas the lowest specificity (or the highest generality) is given to a rule where the condition is formed entirely by '#'s' and is therefore always satisfied by the occurrence of any state of the world.

At the beginning of each simulation the decision maker is usually supposed to be absolutely ignorant about the characteristics of the environment; initially, therefore, all the rules are randomly generated. The decision maker is also assumed to have limited computational capabilities; as a result, the number of rules stored in the system at each moment is kept constant and relatively 'small' in comparison to the complexity of the problem that is being tackled.

This set of rules is processed in the following steps throughout the simulation process.

(i) *Condition matching*: a message is received from the environment that informs the system about the last state of the world. The message is compared with the condition of all the rules, and the rules that are matched – i.e. those that apply to such a state of the world – enter the following step.

(ii) *Competition among matched rules*: all the rules where the condition is satisfied compete in order to designate the one that is allowed to execute its action. To enter this competition each rule makes a bid based on its strength and on its specificity. In other words, the bid of each matched rule is proportional to its past usefulness (strength) and its relevance to the present situation (specificity).

$$\text{Bid}(R_i,t) = k_1(k_2 + k_3 \text{ Specificity}(R_i)) \text{ Strength}(R_i,t)$$

where k_1, k_2 and k_3 are constant coefficients. The winning rule is chosen randomly, with probabilities proportional to such bids.

(iii) *Action and strength updating*: the winning rule executes the action indicated by its action part and has its own strength reduced by the amount of the bid and increased by the pay-off that the action receives, given the occurrence of the 'real' state of the world. If the j-th rule is the winner of the competition, we have

$$\text{Strength}(R_j,t+1) = \text{Strength}(R_j,t) + \text{Payoff}(t) - \text{Bid}(R_j,t)$$

(iv) *The generation of new rules*: the system must be able not only to select the most successful rules but also to discover new ones. This is ensured by applying 'genetic operators', which, by recombining and mutating elements of the already existing and most successful rules, introduce new ones that may improve the performance of the system. In this way new rules are constantly injected into the system, and scope for new search is continually made available.

Genetic operators generate new rules that both recombine the 'building blocks' of and explore other possibilities in the proximity of the currently most successful ones, in order to discover the elements determining their success and exploit them more thoroughly; the search is not completely random but influenced by the system's past history. New rules so generated substitute the weakest ones, so that the total number of rules is kept constant.

Three types of genetic operators are normally employed. The first two types are forms of simple mutation that operate in opposite directions:

a) *specification*: a new condition is created that increases the specificity of the parent one; wherever the parent condition presents a '#', this is mutated into a '0' or a '1' (randomly chosen) with a given (small) probability;

b) *generalization*: the new condition decreases the specificity of the parent one; wherever the latter presents a '0' or a '1', this is mutated into a '#' with a given (small) probability.

The third operator is a standard *crossover*, which reflects the idea of generating new conditions by recombining the useful elements ('building blocks') of the conditions of successful rules. Two parent rules are probabilistically selected among the ones with higher strength, then a random crossover point is selected for each condition part and strings are exchanged across such crossover points.

If, for instance, the conditions of the two parent rules are

aaaaaa

AAAAAA

with a, A ∈ {0,1,#}, if 2 is randomly drawn as the crossover point the two following offspring are generated

aaAAAA

AAaaaa

The above-mentioned economic models, which employ classifier systems for the analysis of multi-agent interaction problem, basically study the emergence of 'ecologies of representations'. Heterogeneous agents adaptively modify their models of the world in order to achieve better performance, and stationary environments tend to generate relatively stable ecological equilibria, but – in general – agents will not converge to homogeneous models, but only to models that are somehow 'compatible' for the particular states of the world that actually occur. The same environment can in fact support very diverse non-partitional representations: stochastic elements in the learning process, combined with the high degree of path dependency of the systems, will very likely produce a high degree of diversity of representations even when we begin with perfectly homogeneous agents. Moreover, learning never actually stops, and the application of the genetic algorithm always introduces an element of exploring new possibilities, which might disrupt the temporary ecological equilibrium.

Marengo (1992, 1996), applies this model to the emergence of a commonly shared knowledge basis in team decision-making processes, and shows that different types of environment can generate very different balances between the homogeneity and heterogeneity of knowledge. Palmer et al. (1994), Vriend (1995) and Marengo and Tordjman (1996) examine a population of rule-based AAAs operating in an artificial market and show that the market can sustain a persistently high degree of diversity between agents' models of the world and, at the same time, generate a price dynamics that has many features in common with real speculation market phenomena.

A slightly different modelling strategy, albeit very much in the same spirit, employs 'genetic programming' (Koza, 1993); unlike standard genetic algorithms and classifier systems, search does not take place in the space of fixed-length binary string representations but in the space of all variable-length *functions* that can be generated with a given, primitive set of operators and operands. Representations here are no longer mere sets of subsets of subjective states of the world but are more complex functional relationships, linking variables to actions by means of mathematical and logical operators. Dosi et al. (1994) show an application of this methodology to pricing decisions by firms in oligopolistic markets[49].

In general, these models produce simulations of 'artificial economies', in parallel with the 'artificial life' approach; see Langton (1989) and Langton et al. (1991), in which the analysis is no longer based on equilibrium concepts and on the search for convergence and stability conditions but on the investigation of collective emergent properties – i.e. aggregate regularities that are relatively robust and persistent (see also Lane, 1993a, 1993b).

An interesting family of 'artificial economy' models analyses local learning phenomena. For instance, Epstein and Axtell (1996) consider a population of agents located on a bidimensional space where some resources (e.g. food) are also (unevenly) distributed. Agents are endowed with a set of simple algorithms that control their movements, their use of available resources and their behaviour towards other agents they can meet. Adaptation takes place at two different levels: a) with respect to the environment, agents move towards sites where they more easily fulfil their objectives; b) with respect to their neighbours, they generate a local organization of exchange (i.e. markets where they can exchange goods and achieve a Pareto superior distribution of resources). Take all this as a preliminary metaphor of a set of models – still to come – where propositions of economic theory (e.g. downward-sloping demand curves, laws of one price, etc.) can be derived as emergent properties of decentralized interaction processes.

5.5   Learning as dynamics in the space of outcomes

The typologies of learning models reviewed so far attempt, to different degrees, to provide some account of the dynamics of, for example, what agents know about the world, or the ways people select among different actions.

Alternative modelling strategies involve, on the contrary, an explicit 'black-boxing' of the learning/decision processes, folding them together into some dynamics on the possible states in which the agents might happen to be. In turn, this 'black-boxing' in some approaches has to be considered as just a *reduced form* of an underlying richer dynamics on

---

[49] In particular, what was demonstrated was the endogenous emergence of pricing routines as an evolutionary robust form of adaptation to non-stationary environments.

cognition, problem solving, etc., while in others almost all that can be said about learning tends to be considered.

The latter perspective certainly applies to a long tradition of formal models in psychology building on stimulus-response processes, dating back at least to Estes (1950), and Bush and Mosteller (1955). (Note that, insofar as the 'states' – through which the agents are driven by reinforcement – are behavioural responses, this modelling philosophy largely overlaps with that of 'evolutionary games', briefly discussed earlier.)

A good summary of the basic ideas is from Suppes (1995a, p. 5).

> The organism is presented with a sequence of trials, on each of which he makes a response, that is one of several possible choices. In any particular experiment it is assumed that there is a set of stimuli from which the organism draws a sample at the beginning of each trial. It is also assumed that on each trial each stimulus is conditioned to at most one response. The probability of making a given response on any trial is postulated to be simply the proportion of sampled stimuli conditioned on that response, unless there is no conditioned stimuli in the sample, in which case there is a 'guessing' probability for each response. Learning takes place in the following way. At the end of the trial a reinforcement event occurs that identifies which one of the possible responses was correct. With some fixed probabilities the sample stimuli become conditioned to this response, if they are not already, and the organism begins another trial in a new state of conditioning . . .

Notice that here all the dynamics on Θ, Ξ, R, and π that one was trying to disentangle above are black-boxed into the distribution of stimuli and the conditional probabilities of transition across responses.

A simple illustration (Suppes, 1995a) with two states, one conditioned to the correct response (C) and the other unconditioned (U), is a Markov process of the type

	C	U
C	1	0
U	C	1–C

with the elements of the matrix being the transition probabilities. Not too surprisingly, 'learning is the convergence to the absorbing state'.

Moreover, notice that the basic methodology requires an underlying 'small'/stationary world assumption (all states must have from the start a positive probability measure) and is essentially looking for asymptotic properties of the models[50].

---

[50] It is true that, in some simple experimental set-ups, stimulus-response models also generate predictions on the convergence paths. But this is not the case in general, especially outside the domains where stimulus sampling and conditioning can be given a straightforward psychological interpretation (representation building and problem solving are

5.6   *Technological learning*

Nearer to the spirit of a good deal of contemporary evolutionary theories, a quite different type of 'black-boxing' is common to a lot of models of growth and industrial change driven by technological advances. Here the learning dynamics is typically represented in terms of changes in the space of some technological coefficients.

Possibly the simplest formalization is the early account by Arrow (1962), of learning by doing, subsequently corroborated by a few empirical studies, showing a 'quasi-law' of falling costs (or increasing productivity) as a function of cumulated production[51].

In Silverberg et al. (1988), learning how to use a new capital-embodied technology efficiently (i.e. a new 'paradigm'; see above) is formalized via a logistic-type dynamics on firm-specific skills (s_i), dependent on current and cumulated production using the new technology (x_i and X_i, respectively).

$$s_i' = B_1 \frac{x_i}{X_i + C} s_i(1 - s_i) \quad \text{if } s_i \geq s_p$$

$$s_i = s_p \qquad\qquad\qquad\qquad \text{otherwise}$$

where s_i' is the time derivative, C is a constant proportional to the capital stock and s_p is the level of skills generally available in the industry, which is a sort of dynamic, industry-wide externality changing as

$$s_p' = B_2(\bar{s} - s_p)$$

with $\bar{s}$ a weighted average of firm-specific skills[52].

Further, many evolutionary models, starting with the seminal work of Nelson and Winter (1982), account explicitly for the uncertainty associated with technical search, and often also for the dependence of future discoveries upon the knowledge already achieved in the past. In the last

---

two cases in point). So, for example, one is left to wonder what the empirical content is of the 'main theorem' from Suppes, 1969 (see also Suppes, 1995a), according to which 'given any finite automaton, there is a stimulus-response model that under appropriate learning conditions asymptotically becomes isomorphic to the finite automaton'. One is very far indeed from any constructive, empirically disciplined notion of learning . . .

[51] Something like $c_t = c_0 X_t^\beta$, where X_t is cumulated production, $-1 < \beta < 0$, and c_0 is unit production costs.

[52] Of course, $\bar{s}$ and s_p are bound to be less than or equal to one (i.e. the 'perfect' ability to exploit fully the technical specifications of use on any one given vintage of capital). Somewhat more complicated learning patterns, modelled in a similar spirit, are in Eliasson (1985). A 'Verdoorn-Kaldor' law, with learning driven by learning by doing and economies of scale, underpins the model by Verspagen (1993). And system-level deterministic learning dynamics is presented in Granstrand (1994).

resort, modelling learning in the technology space comes down to specification of the stochastic process driving agents from one technique to the next.

For example, in one of the models presented in Nelson and Winter (1982) learning occurs in the space of two variable input coefficients a_1 and a_2. After some renormalization[53], assume that the technique of each firm at time t is the random pair U_t, V_t, and the search outcome is represented by the random pair (G_t, H_t), which captures the number of steps that the firm takes in the U and V dimensions[54], with (G_t, H_t) – in the simplest formulation, independent of $(U_{t,1}, V_{t,1})$ – distributed on a finite support (Nelson and Winter, 1982, pp. 177–79). The time-independent random process, together with a selection criterion simply comparing $(U_{t,1}, V_{t,1})$ and (U_t, V_t) at prevailing input prices, implies that the sequence of techniques is a Markov chain[55]. The distribution of innovative outcomes is centred on the prevailing productivity of a firm, and, in the more general formulation, there is no exogenous constraint on technological possibilities (Nelson and Winter, 1982, p. 285), although there is one related to internal capabilities: what one knows limits what one can achieve within a given number of search periods.

Other representations in a similar spirit include Silverberg and Lehnert, (1994), whereby innovations arrive according to a Poisson distribution, adding to the productivity of new technological vintages of equipment; Chiaromonte and Dosi (1993) and Chiaromonte et al. (1993), which have the support of the probability distributions on (labour) coefficients for 'machine' production and machine use dependent on time T realizations for each firm; Dosi et al. (1994) and Dosi et al. (1995), who model the dynamics of (proportional) increments in firm 'competitiveness' drawn from different variants of a Poisson process; and Kwasnicki (1996), who presents more complex dynamics of search driving as well as recombination and mutation on incumbent knowledge bases (see also below).

In other versions of evolutionary models, one assumes an exogenously determined drift in learning opportunities (a metaphor for scientific advances, etc.). For example, in another model presented in Nelson and

---

[53] So that the refined dimensions are $U = \log (a_2/a_1)$ and $V = \log (a_1 a_2)$.

[54] Subject to the constraint that $u_1 \leq U \leq u_n$. Conversely, V, itself a proxy for input productivity (in the spirit of evolutionary models), is allowed to range on $-\infty < V < +\infty$.

[55] See Nelson and Winter, 1982, pp. 179–92. Note also that in this Nelson–Winter model, while in terms of relative input intensities the process defines a finite, time-invariant Markov process, in the V-dimension the number of states is notionally infinite and the system is allowed, so to speak, to climb to ever greater levels of productivity (although only finite levels of them are accessible from a given state).

Learning in evolutionary environments   313

Winter (1982), firms sample from a log-normal distribution of values of capital productivities the increasing mean of which follows a time-dependent trend. And, somewhat similarly, Conlisk (1989) postulates productivity growth driven by draws from a normal distribution (with positive mean).

Finally, a few evolutionary models also account for learning via *imitation* – that is, by the stochastic access of each firm to the best practice available at each time or to the set of combinations between best practice and the technique currently known by any generic incumbent (see Nelson and Winter, 1982, Chiaromonte et al., 1993, Silverberg and Verspagen, 1994, 1995b, and Kwasnicki, 1996, among others).

The first point to note is that the spirit of most formalizations of learning processes in a technology space, however defined, has an essentially 'phenomenological' flavour; formal representations are meant to capture stylized facts, basic dynamic regularities, etc. generally placed at a much 'higher' (and more aggregate) level of description than the 'foundational' processes of cognition, problem solving, etc. discussed earlier (we shall come back in a moment to the relationships between the two levels). Given this more phenomenological level, however, a requirement far from fulfilled in the current state of the art concerns the *empirical robustness* of the purported dynamics[56]: for example, on what empirical grounds does one justify the assumption of Poisson arrival processes? Why not another random process? On what criteria does one choose the specification of the Markov processes driving search? The questions could go on . . .

This is an area where evolutionary modellers would certainly benefit from more precise insights coming from 'inductive' statistical exercises concerning, for example, microeconomic processes of innovation, productivity growth, etc.

The second point is that, even when considering learning over an upper-bounded set of 'knowledge states' (such as in Silverberg et al., 1988), and – obviously so – in open-ended knowledge dynamics, the analytical focus is upon *transient* rather than limit properties.

An example in the set-up concerning innovation diffusion and learning by using on two technologies is presented in Silverberg et al., 1988. The properties of limit states could, in principle, be found – given the initial conditions, etc. However, the attention is mainly devoted to the *finite-time* properties of the system and the finite-time learning profile of individual agents.

---

[56] Indeed, this should be a self-criticism of all of us who have worked on evolutionary modelling . . .

A fortiori, all this applies to learning dynamics that is *open-ended* in the sense that there is an infinite number of states that agents can take as time goes to infinity, even if, most likely (conditional on the given knowledge level), only a finite number of states can be reached with positive probability in a finite time[57].

The third point is that it seems to us rather obvious that any representation of learning as a dynamics across technological (or, for that matter, 'organizational') states in low-dimensional spaces is just an inevitable (indeed, very useful) *reduced form* of underlying learning process in spaces of explosively high dimensionality (like those entailed in the earlier, more 'constructive' discussion of exploration on cognitive and problem-solving categories)[58]. But then the question of the compatibility and mappings across different levels of description becomes crucial (let alone a direct derivation of 'higher' from 'lower' levels, which might well turn out to be an impossible task without a lot of further phenomenological details and constraints).

5.7   *Behavioural and cognitive foundations of technological learning*

Of course, the easiest way to provide cognitive/behavioural foundations to learning in the technology space is by assuming that it is the direct outcome of the choices of fully rational (and forward-looking) agents. This is, indeed, the path followed by 'new growth' theories – if their microfoundations are to be taken at face value (see Romer, 1990, Grossman and Helpman, 1991, or – in a stochastic version – Aghion and Howitt, 1992)[59].

However, if one accepts the foregoing argument, fully 'rational' decision models fall well short of applicability to technological search and innovation: on the contrary, this is the domain where one is most likely to find strong substantive and procedural uncertainty, surprises, delusions

---

[57] A major analytical challenge ahead regards the possibility of characterizing in the limit some expected (average) properties of these open-ended processes (an ongoing research involving Sidney Winter, Yuri Kaniovski and the authors at the International Institute of Applied Systems Analysis, Austria, is currently beginning to address the problem painstakingly).

[58] Collective learning entities such as 'firms' further explore the space of search/adaptation.

[59] This applies equally to, for example, game-theoretic models of innovation and diffusion, 'patent races', etc. (thorough surveys are in Stoneman, 1995). Whether such microfoundations ought to be taken seriously is a debatable question. The more sophisticated view suggests that they should not, forward-looking representative agents etc. being only a sort of theoretical short cut in order to get to some some aggregate dynamic properties that *a fortiori* hold under less restrictive behavioural assumptions; a lot of contributions by, for example, Paul Romer and, in other perspectives, Joseph Stiglitz (among others) are interpretable in this way. On the contrary, the conclusions of too many other models seem to be sensitively dependent upon the fine specifications of 'rational behaviours' themselves.

Learning in evolutionary environments   315

and unexpected successes (for a review of the empirical evidence in this area, see Dosi, 1988). But then one is back to the relationships between a phenomenological account of learning processes and the underlying cognitive and behavioural procedures . . .

In this respect, Nelson and Winter (1982) suggest a promising appreciative theory, nesting technological learning (and some of its properties, such as the possible cumulativeness of technological advances, the 'locality' of search, etc.) into a theory of organizational learning based – in good part – on the establishment, reproduction and change of organizational routines.

Moreover, Nelson and Winter – as well as, earlier, the inspiring work of Cyert and March (1992, but first published in 1963), and later, many models in this evolutionary tradition – formally model the 'access' to change as being triggered or driven by some stylized decision rule.

A way of capturing this bridge between the behavioural domain and an apparently 'agent-free' learning dynamics is by assuming some sort of rather simple 'allocation to search' rule (such as 'invest X per cent of turnover in R&D') – which is indeed robustly corroborated by the managerial evidence – and then formalize a probability of access to innovative (or imitative) learning dependent on these search efforts.

A binomial distribution of the kind

$$P(\text{inn} = 1) = a \cdot \exp(b \cdot \text{R\&D})$$

is a first approximation to the general idea (with a and b being parameters that implicitly account for both 'objective' opportunities and firm-specific competencies; see, for example, Nelson and Winter, 1982, and Chiaromonte et al., 1993)[60].

Hence, the learning dynamics is modelled as the outcome of a two-stage stochastic process, separating a first ('behavioural') process depending, in principle, on beliefs, expectations and action patterns (that is, the ϑ and ξ variables in our earlier formulation) from a second one trying to capture some modal properties of the learning process itself[61].

Other formalizations of the interactions between behaviours and learning modes stylize 'triggering effects', so that, for example, change and search is undertaken only if actual performance falls below a certain threshold level[62].

---

[60] The same goes for imitation as well.

[61] Which, putting it into our earlier formalization, would be a synthetic account of externally evaluated (or 'market-evaluated') performances of the combinations between menus of actions and 'states of the world'. It is also important to notice that the general assumption here is that agents do not and cannot know that mapping algorithm.

[62] See Nelson and Winter (1982) and also, outside the technological domain, Cyert and March (1992).

316   *Giovanni Dosi, Luigi Marengo and Giorgio Fagiolo*

For many analytical purposes, the assumption that behavioural rules (such as R&D rules) are given and invariant throughout the history of each agent is a perfectly legitimate approximation (which also captures the relative inertia of organizational routines). And this is what one finds in many evolutionary models up to now.

In fact, invariant search rules (or invariant 'meta-rules' for change) can be understood in two ways, namely a) as empirically grounded 'stylized facts', or b) as useful first-approximation assumptions the precise status of which has also to be understood in terms of complementary processes of behavioural learning. They certainly capture a bit of both; in order to move further at the former level, though, it is vital to achieve more robust micro-behavioural evidence[63], and, at the latter level, it is essential to show if and how endogenous processes of adaptation lead to relatively persistent (meta-stable) search rules. This latter analysis is what Silverberg and Verspagen (1995a) have begun to do, assuming rules that are invariant as such but with parameters that may adaptively change via a stochastic search process (with different modelling tools based on genetic algorithms, Kwasnicki, 1996, explores a similar path).

Alternatively, one might want to take a more constructive route to behavioural search and adaptation, but, so far, only at the cost of further simplifying the environment in which agents operate (an example is Dosi et al., 1994, where 'routines' such as mark-up pricing are indeed shown – as already mentioned – to be endogenous emergent properties but one totally neglects learning in the technology/problem-solving domain).

More generally, technological learning is possibly one of the most revealing points of observation in order to assess the state of the art in theories of learning in evolutionary environments. Hopefully, there should be little doubt that technologies (together with organizational forms and institutions) are major domains of economic evolution. Technical change is also one of the few fields where explicitly inspired evolutionary thinking has a widely acknowledged lead in the methodology of empirical reseach and appreciative theories, not to mention formal models. And it also continues to be a major challenge for all those scholars who want to take micro-foundations seriously. As it stands now, it is probably a crucial test for any foundations of cognition, decision and learning (at least in economics) that are robust enough to account for what people and organizations do when they inevitably know little about what the future might

---

[63] The collection of this evidence, interestingly enough, has nearly stopped since the 1960s, partly as a result of the conflict between what researchers were finding and the axiomatic boldness of the theory (see, for example, the neglect on mark-up findings with regard to pricing behaviours; a short but pertinent discussion is in Winter, 1975).

deliver to them. In this respect, 'rational' formalizations sometimes sound hopelessly silly (suppose, for example, that Stone Age men had rational expectations about helicopters, or that IBM's first senior executives knew what a PC was and had some prior probability distribution on its impact . . .). But competing interpretations face the equally formidable challenge of developing 'level zero' theories consistent with 'higher-level' models of the empirical patterns of learning in, for example, companies, industries, communities or whole countries.

For the purposes of this work, let us just notice that a major step forward would result from constructive theories of entities that, at higher levels of observation, one calls 'knowledge bases', 'organizational competencies', 'heuristics', etc. – that is, theories showing how elementary 'pieces of knowledge', or routines or elementary actions, coherently combine in higher-level entities that self-maintain over time. But, in turn, as convincingly argued by Fontana and Buss (1994, 1996) in the domain of biology, this demands a constructive theory of organizations, the existence of which, on the contrary, is usually postulated rather than explained[64].

6   Many open questions by way of a conclusion

It was one of the purposes of this chapter to provide a broad map of diverse lines of enquiry that, in different ways, take the analysis of cognition, action and learning beyond the boundaries of the canonical model of rational decision and rational learning. The underlying perspective – as we have tried to argue – is that a positive theory of agency in evolutionary environment will have to rely upon quite different building blocks compared to the standard model.

Notwithstanding the length of this essay, we have been obliged to leave out a few pertinent issues. Let us conclude by flagging them, and by suggesting some further research questions that we consider to be very high on the evolutionary research agenda.

---

[64] In economics, principal/agent models as well as transaction cost theories, of course, try to do that. In the former case, though, they do it by reducing them to a sort of epiphenomenological 'veil', which is just a collective name for an ensemble of contracts among rational agents. Conversely, transaction cost models do fully acknowledge organizations as entities in their own right, but, in our view, they still fall short of providing a 'physiology' of organizations themselves, whereby governance procedures and problem-solving knowledge are reproduced and modified over time. For remarks in a similar spirit, see Padgett (1997), who also presents a simple 'hypercycle model' of the emergence of an 'ecology' of mutually consistent skills. See also Warglien (1995) on the evolution of organizational learning as a hierarchically nested process of selection among 'projects'.

6.1   Learning and selection

Coupled with learning, the other major tenet of evolutionary theory is, of course, selection; that is, some collective mechanism providing differential rewards and penalties (also involving differential diffusion and survival probabilities) for different traits (be they behaviours, routines, technologies or whatever), of which the agents are – so to speak – 'carriers'[65].

More generally, we suggest that almost all dynamics of socio-economic change fall somewhere in between the two extreme archetypes of 'pure learning' and 'pure selection'. The former corresponds to the extremist decision-theoretic or game-theoretic models: all agents make the best use of the available information, are endowed with identical information-processing algorithms, etc. (representative-agent rational expectation models are the most striking example). Clearly, selection plays no role here since every agent has the same access to the available opportunities (i.e., in some loose sense, has the same 'environmental fitness'). Conversely, in the opposing 'Darwinian' archetype, nobody learns, and system dynamics is driven by selection operating upon blindly generated variants of, for example, behaviours, technologies, etc. (taken literally, this is also the 'as . . . if' interpretation of rational behaviour). As briefly discussed earlier, the outcomes of the two dynamics, for whatever given environment, are equivalent only in some rather special cases. In general, the balance and interaction between learning and selection matters in terms of both the finite-time properties of the process and the long-term outcomes.

An implication of this is that the nature and intensity of selective mechanisms are not orthogonal to learning patterns. There might be subtle trade-offs here. Weak selective pressures most likely allow the persistence of 'slack' and 'inefficient' behaviours (no matter how 'efficiency' is defined in a particular context). On the other hand, excessively strong selective pressure might hinder learning insofar as the latter involves trial-and-error processes that are probably destined to be, on average, failures. It is a dilemma that March has phrased in terms of 'exploitation versus exploration' (March, 1991).

It can also be seen as a timescale issue: learning and selection may well proceed at different paces. So, for example, even the tightest selection environment can leave room for individual learning provided that

---

[65] General discussions about selection processes in socio-economic evolution can be found in Nelson and Winter (1982), Hodgson (1988), Dosi and Nelson (1994), Witt (1992), Metcalfe (1994), Nelson (1995), Silverberg (1988) and Winter (1988), among others.

selection is a low-frequency event compared to the rates of search/ learning. In biology, selection takes place at a generational time scale. Hence the trade-off is very clear: individual learning is favoured by having long-living organisms, while collective evolution takes advantage of short-living organisms and frequent generational renewal. Conversely, in the social domain the picture is more complicated: environments such as markets are not only fundamental selection mechanisms but also an essential source for feedback that stimulates learning processes.

Low-frequency feedback can slow down and render 'opaque' individual learning, but a frequent and tight application of selective forces might leave little room for experimentation and innovation. Moreover, note that the cultural reproduction of knowledge and behaviours within economic institutions introduces strong 'Lamarckian' features into the relationships between learning and selection.

Another, related, issue concerns the possible tension between individual and collective learning; for example, it might well happen that persistent individual mistakes (e.g. decision biases) turn out to have a positive collective role (an interpretation along these lines of the process of entry of business firms is in Dosi and Lovallo, 1997, but a lot more needs to be done in order to explore the value of this conjecture).

6.2   Learning, path dependency and coevolution

A quite general property of learning processes is often their path-dependent nature. This sometimes holds even under quite conventional learning mechanisms[66], and even more so in evolutionary environments. Of course, path dependency implies that initial conditions and/or early fluctuations along the learning path shape long-term outcomes. Furthermore, if learning entails the development of rather inertial cognitive frames and routinized action rules, one should indeed expect inertia and 'lock-in' to be one of the corollaries of the very fact that 'agents have learned'.

Above, we have surveyed a few models of, for example, technological learning that do generate path dependency, lock-in, etc. even in rather simple environments, driven by some form of dynamic increasing returns or social adaptation. A more complicated and fascinating question

---

[66] For example, this is true for Bayesian learning if the set of events upon which agents form their priors is different, and also in finite time if agents hold the same priors but are exposed to different sample paths. It also appears as a limit property of environments where Bayesian agents sample across other Bayesian agents in order to decide among alternative options (see Arthur and Lane, 1993).

concerns those path-dependent outcomes that are driven by the correlation across cognitive, behavioural or organizational traits, which in biology comes under the heading of *epistatic correlation* (see Levinthal, 1996a, for a suggestive exploratory application to the analysis of organizational 'inertia')[67]. The basic intuition is simple. Suppose that, say, cognitive and behavioural repertoires come as rather folded packages – due either to some proximate internal coherence or simply to the fact that originally they randomly happened to come together. For example, in the above formal framework, suppose that the set of representations/actions that turned out to be 'learned' involves the rule r_p mapping an 'understanding' of the world in terms of $(\vartheta_1, \vartheta_2, \ldots)$ into procedures $(\xi_1, \xi_2, \ldots)$. Suppose also that that rule happened to 'win' because, in an environment with 'true' states that are cognitively coded under ϑ_i, procedure ξ_i was reinforced by the obtained pay-offs. However, under some other states (which, say, are coded in ϑ_j, triggering ξ_j), the decision rule is strikingly bad. Of course, with no trait correlation, agents would hold on to that part of the original rule that links ϑ_i to ξ_i and change the rest of the repertoire by merging it with, for example, representation ϑ_k and intended action ξ_k. However, suppose that the first 'package' can hardly be unbundled, and that the same applies to the other one, where, say, ϑ_k and also ξ_k come correlated within another 'model', yielding 'bad' responses under the states coded under ϑ_i. One can intuitively see here how some system interrelatedness can easily produce inertia and lock-in (see David, 1992, who also discusses the appealing analogy between technological and institutional systems).

It is important to note that interrelatedness and trait correlation are far from being theoretical *curiosa*. Rather, it is almost as if they are intrinsic properties of all entities embodying relatively coherent inner structures. This applies to knowledge systems, as well as business organizations and all other institutions. (A deeper understanding of this correlation leads back to the challenge of developing constructive theories of these entities themselves, as mentioned earlier.)

The ramifications of this point are even broader, linking with the idea of *learning as a coevolutionary process*. It is a straightforward conclusion from our earlier discussion that the general view of learning that we propose rests on coevolution between cognitive representations, behavioural repertoires and preferences. In a nutshell, this implies a notion of mutual adaptation not only, of course, along the canonical sequence from what one believes to know to what one does (judged according to what one

---

[67] Kauffman's model of biological evolution is an acknowledged source of inspiration (Kauffman, 1993).

deems to be better for himself) but also the other way round, from what one does to what one has to believe in order to justify what has been done, and from what one gets to what one likes.

6.3   Preference and expectation

We have presented above some tentative insights towards the formalization of coevolution between mental models and action repertoires. Two other domains, however, have been largely neglected so far, namely expectation formation and endogenous preferences. With regard to expectations, the rather unfortunate state of the art is that one is largely stuck between a rational expectation paradigm (which basically assumes agents who already know what they are supposed to learn) and various extrapolative expectation mechanisms. Between the two, evolutionary modellers tend – and rightly so – to choose the latter as a first approximation (see, for example, Chiaromonte et al., 1993), but sooner or later one should try to model agents that elaborate conjectures about the 'structure of the world' and its parametrization and test them against experience. More precisely, this is indeed what adaptive learning models do (e.g. Holland et al., 1986, and Marengo and Tordjman, 1996), but the drawback is that one either has 'pure forecast' models (whereby the triggered 'action' is the forecast itself) or models where forecast and action selection (concerning, for example, price levels, selling or buying, etc.) are folded together. A major step forward, in our view, would be the development of models whereby search in the space of expectations on the states of the world and search in the space of actions is partly decoupled[68]. One consequence would be the possibility of handling the coexistence of partly conflicting systems of belief and action patterns[69], and it would also allow an explicit account of phenomena such as cognitive dissonance (see Festinger, 1957, Hirschman, 1965, and Akerlof and Dickens, 1982, for some economic applications)[70].

This leads directly to the issue of endogenous preferences. Some progress has recently been made towards modelling preferences as

---

[68] See a preliminary attempt in Riolo (1990).

[69] Think, for example, of action patterns that continue to be implemented because they 'work' even if they conflict with agent-held theories. Speculative behaviour involving both a rule ('buy as long as the market is bullish') and an expectation ('the market is going to collapse') belongs to this class (we owe this observation to Tordjman).

[70] The fact that the belief system and the action system remain partly coupled generally entails imperfect attempts to reduce cognitive dissonance by modifying the system of beliefs in order to accommodate the action patterns. Every smoker, for example, is familiar with such exercises! In a similar vein, we plan to call a model of this kind (which we are beginning to build) 'the spirit is strong, but the flesh is weak . . .'(!?).

influenced by social interactions (see, for example, Kuran, 1987, and Brock and Durlauf, 1995). The time is perhaps ripe to take the issue further, right into the foundational model of agency, and account for the endogeneity of the criteria by which representations, actions and 'pay-offs' are evaluated, certainly as a result of social imitation but also driven by attempts to adjust 'desires' to realized outcomes. (A probably apocryphal saying attributed to Joseph Stalin mentions his definition of 'pure happiness as the perfect correspondence between expectations and reality' [!]; certainly, he was trying hard to work on the former . . .) So far, these phenomena have been neglected by adaptive learning models; indeed, an aspect that we consider rather unsatisfactory is the general assumption of an invariant pay-off function, which also drives the learning process by providing the yardstick against which the outcomes of cognition/action are judged. Our proposal, on the contrary, in our earlier language, is to render the π function endogenous – some implications being that one disposes of any notion of 'utility' as one of the primitives of the theory and operationalizes an idea of the adaptive identities of agents much nearer a lot of sociological intuitions.

6.4   Coevolutionary determinants of routines and other organizational traits

Isomorphic issues appear also at higher levels of description. Consider, for example, the coevolution of technologies, business organizations and related institutions, raised in an appreciative and theorizing mode by Nelson, 1994); or the multiple nature of routines as procedures for both problem solving and the governance of conflict (Coriat and Dosi, 1995). In both these cases organizational learning is driven by multiple, and possibly contradictory, selection mechanisms (for example, success in innovative search but also control over the possibility of opportunistic or conflictual behaviours, and the political 'coherence' of the organization, etc.)[71]. There is a wealth of empirical evidence supporting all this, and one starts forming some appreciative theories; it might be worth also beginning to explore some simple formal models whereby organizational learning concerns the development of collectively shared cognitive models and action repertoires that, so to speak, 'make sense' according to multiple dimensions (suggesting also that what members of the organization 'know', do and believe to be their interests all coevolve).

A major implication of all this is that evolutionary theories of learning might head towards the hierarchically nested levels of description

---

[71] A few more comments are in Dosi (1995a).

of learning processes[72], possibly related to different learning entities. At one extreme, one is only beginning to explore the dynamics of, so to speak, 'agentless' organizations where learning is driven by evolution under some selective pressure upon bundles of routines, skills, etc. (preliminary efforts are to be found in Marengo, 1996, and Padgett, 1997). At the other extreme, it seems equally promising to explore explicitly agent-based models where collective knowledge emerges from endogenous networking among entities embodying diverse pieces of knowledge[73].

Somewhere in between, as discussed at greater length in Coriat and Dosi (1995) a major challenge ahead is modelling agents that imperfectly learn how to adapt (in terms of skills, behaviours and goals) to existing institutions while the imperfection of adaptation is itself a fundamental source of institutional change[74].

There is much food for thought here. It seems to us that one faces nowadays the possibility of an interdisciplinary construction of a positive theory of agency and learning the scope of which goes well beyond the limits of applicability of the usual (rational) decision-theoretic model. And, for the first time, one is beginning to develop the instruments to make it 'harder' – able also to generate formal 'toy models' that, moreover, have a positive interaction with models based on more orthodox notions of rationality. (In our view, though, it will never be able to present the axiomatic 'hardness' of the latter, notwithstanding its measure-zero empirical content, whenever stripped of any phenomenological restrictions.)

As economists, we are tempted to mark this emerging approach with the label of 'evolutionary' or 'institutionalist'. But, in other disciplines similar approaches come under quite different headings. Moreover, even within the economists' arena, a few 'revisionist' developments building on 'bounded rationality', 'far-from-equilibrium learning', etc. promise challenging dialogues. At the present moment it is certainly far too early to know whether it will turn out to be scientifically more fruitful to pursue some equivalent of a 'new Ptolemaic synthesis' or, conversely, some more radical views, still largely to be developed. Where our inclinations are should be clear from this chapter. In any case, whether one

---

[72] An exploratory attempt is in Warglien (1995).

[73] This would certainly put on a more rigorous footing the Hayekian proposition about capitalist institutions (including markets) as mechanisms for the coordination of distributed knowledge (see also Egidi, 1996, and Lane et al., 1996).

[74] One can easily see how this could also represent a major bridge between evolutionary theories and institutionalist analyses of the mechanism holding together and changing the social fabric (a thorough discussion of many related issues is to be found in Hodgson, 1988). Enormously difficult but fascinating issues such as, for example, the dynamic coupling between institutions and economic behaviours, and the role of trust and power, come under this broad heading.

succeeds or not, it remains important to establish some sort of equivalence classes, partly mapping problems and formal instruments across different approaches. This kind of bridge is also part of what we have tried to achieve in this chapter.

7   A post-scriptum (October 2001)

Even though the bulk of this chapter was written in 1996, we have decided to keep it – with the exception of some bibliographical updating – largely unaltered. It has, hopefully, its own internal consistence and, conversely, it would be futile to try to follow up on the fast-expanding literature of the last few years; a brand new article would be required.

Here, let us just flag for the convenience of the reader some promising directions of enquiry that overlap, complement or improve upon those discussed so far.

First, growing attention has been focused on learning processes in general and experimental games in particular; see, among others, Erev and Roth (1998, 1999), Camerer (1997) and Camerer and Ho (1998, 1999).

Second, empirical regularities in decisions and behaviour – concerning systematic deviations from the predictions of canonical 'rational' theories in particular – are at least adding up into an emerging 'behavioural' perspective concerning, for example, intertemporal choices, financial investments and consumption; after the early contributions in Loewenstein and Elster (1992), see the discussions in Browning and Lusardi (1996) and Rabin (1998), among many others.

A big and controversial issue, of course, concerns how the observed patterns of decision and behaviour ought to be interpreted. One way involves the 're-axiomatization' of choice, twisting it just enough so as to make theoretical postulates not conflict too much with the evidence (for example, rationalization of the evidence on intertemporal choice just in terms of hyperbolic rather than exponential discounts is a paramount illustration of this genre).

An alternative way of tackling observed 'biases' is by arguing that, in fact, they are not biases after all, but rather relatively smart forms of evolutionary adaptation (e.g. Gigerenzer et al., 1999, and Gigerenzer, 2000, and some of the contributions to Gigerenzer and Selten, 2001).

Third, yet another approach, in tune with some of the conjectures discussed in the preceding section, painstakingly proceeds with the exploration of the very foundations of reasoning and 'mental models' underlying cognition, motivations and behaviours; see Girotto et al. (2000), Goldvarg and Johnson-Laird (2000), Johnson-Laird (2000) and Johnson-Laird and Byrne (2000).

The alternative interpretation of purported 'biases', as well as of seemingly 'unbiased' behaviours, hints in fact at deeper conjectures on 'human nature' itself (whatever that means). Being unable to discuss here the many controversies concerning the tangled relations between learning and environmental selection, let us just mention three critical issues.

(i) What is the extent of the 'hard-wiring' of human cognition and behaviours into some underlying 'genetic' predisposition?

(ii) Does such evidence, if any, regard primarily syntactic and inferential rules (such as our relative ability of performing syllogism, *modus ponens* versus *modus tollens*, deduction versus induction, etc.)? Or does it impinge on the very content of behavioural patterns (such as our deepest inclinations to selfishness, obedience, altruism, etc.)?

(iii) Can one impute some optimality properties to whatever 'mankind-invariant' regularities these may be, if any?

Given the preceding section, our deep scepticism about 'strong hard-wiring' *à la* Dawkins (1986) should come as no surprise. And, even more so, it comes together with deeply rooted presumptions on the evolutionary optimality of the revealed outcomes (the arguments in Cosmides and Tooby, 1994, 1996, being an appealing but, in our view, also misleading template).

Instead, our discussion above is quite agnostic as to 'hard-wired' inclinations, leaving the possibility of this existence very much open, but, all in all, we conjecture: a) a very long leash between genes and utterly diverse cultural expressions; and b) the general lack of evidence supporting Panglossian attitudes ('whatever exists, it must be optimal, at least in a local sense, otherwise it would not exist').

Indeed we are rather worried about the increasingly frequent encounters between Dr Pangloss and rudimentary versions of evolutionary theories, yielding rather unfounded but often sinister apologies for a status quo the optimality of which is supposedly grounded in our very genes.

One way of supporting such a theoretical perspective has been through what we consider an improper use of *evolutionary games*. As hinted above and argued at some length in Dosi and Winter (2002) in the socio-economic domain such games are important instruments to explore 'reduced form' evolutionary processes essentially driven by collective adaptation. We are adamant, though, in considering rather far-fetched any application grounded on daring equivalencies between 'genes' and 'cultural memes', and on doubtful simplifications of the selection landscapes over which socio-economic adaptation occurs.

Fourth, today, compared to just a few years ago, one finds a much richer discussion about *endogenous preferences*. They can indeed be studied from many different angles. In some quarters, tentative beginnings to

326   *Giovanni Dosi, Luigi Marengo and Giorgio Fagiolo*

the exploration of the coupled dynamics of preferences, behaviours and mental models are being made (see, for example, Aversi et al., 1999, and the critical discussion of the evidence in Devetag, 1999). Along different lines of research, others ingeniously attempt to unveil the 'rationality' hidden behind preference dynamics (see Elster, 1998).

Fifth, over the last few years a lot of work has gone into the understanding of *organizational* capabilities and learning; see, among others, Dosi et al. (2000). At the same time, a few researchers have attempted to formalize the problem-solving dynamics of organizations themselves, in ways certainly rooted in the pioneering lessons of Herbert Simon but possibly further relaxing even the Simonesque requirements of procedural rationality and the quasi-decomposability of problems; see Levinthal (1996), Levinthal and Warglien (1999) and Marengo and Lazaric (2000).

Nonetheless, it remains the case that many of the issues raised in this chapter concerning a would-be positive theory of agency are obviously still far from settled. However, the comparison between the state of the art even half a decade ago and nowadays highlights a genuinely encouraging picture. To be sure, there are still many neoclassical 'Talibans' at large, and there is still a lot of fuzziness regarding alternative perspectives on cognition, behaviours and learning. But, encouragingly, there are also many and various signs of progress towards the micro-foundations of economic behaviours that do less and less violence to the increasingly rich micro-evidence.

REFERENCES

Aghion, P., and P. Howitt (1992), 'A model of growth through creative destruction', *Econometrica* **60**(2): 323–51.
Akerlof, G. A., and W. T. Dickens (1982), 'The economic consequences of cognitive dissonance', *American Economic Review* **72**(3): 307–19.
Allen, B. (1982a), 'A stochastic interactive model for the diffusion of information', *Journal of Mathematical Sociology* **8**: 265–81.
   (1982b), 'Some stochastic processes of interdependent demand and technological diffusion of an innovation exhibiting externalities among adopters', *International Economic Review* **23**: 595–608.
An, M., and N. Kiefer (1995), 'Local externalities and societal adoption of technologies', *Journal of Evolutionary Economics* **5**(2): 103–17.
Anderlini, L., and A. Ianni (1996), 'Path dependence and learning from neighbours', *Games and Economic Behavior* **13**: 141–78.
Andersen, E. S (1994), *Evolutionary Economics: Post-Schumpeterian Contributions*, London: Pinter.
Arifovic, J. (1994), 'Genetic algorithm learning and the cobweb model', *Journal of Economic Dynamics and Control* **18**: 3–28.

Arrow, K. J. (1962), 'The economic implications of learning by doing', *Review of Economic Studies* **29**: 155–73.

Arthur, W. B. (1991), 'On designing economic agents that behave like human agents: a behavioural approach to bounded rationality', *American Economic Review* **81**: 353–70.

(1993), 'On designing artificial agents that behave like human agents', *Journal of Evolutionary Economics* **3**(1): 1–22.

Arthur, W. B., Y. M. Ermoliev and Y. M. Kaniovski (1987), 'Strong laws for a class of path-dependent urn processes', in V. Arkin, A. Shiryayev and R. Wets (eds.), *Proceedings of the International Conference on Stochastic Optimization*, Kiev, 1984, Lecture Notes in Control and Information Sciences no. 81, Berlin: Springer-Verlag, 287–300.

Arthur, W. B., and D. Lane (1993), 'Information contagion', *Structural Change and Economic Dynamics* **4**: 81–104.

Aversi, R., G. Dosi, G. Fagiolo, M. Meacci and C. Olivetti (1999), 'Demand dynamics with socially evolving preferences', *Industrial and Corporate Change* **8**: 353–408.

Bala, V., and S. Goyal (1998), 'Learning from neighbors', *Review of Economic Studies* **65**: 595–621.

Barron, J. N., and M. T. Hannan (1994), 'The impact of economics on contemporary sociology', *Journal of Economic Literature* **32**: 1111–46.

Bateson, G. (1972), *Steps to an Ecology of Mind*, New York: Ballantine Books.

Berninghaus, S. K., and U. G. Schwalbe (1992), *Learning and Adaptation Processes in Games with a Local Interaction Structure*, Mimeo, University of Bonn.

(1996), 'Evolution, interaction and Nash equilibria', *Journal of Economic Behavior and Organization* **29**: 57–85.

Binmore, K. (1990), *Essays on the Foundations of Game Theory*, Oxford: Blackwell.

Blackwell, D., and L. Dubins (1962), 'Merging of opinions with increasing information', *Annals of Mathematical Statistics* **33**: 882–86.

Blume, L. E. (1993), 'The statistical mechanics of strategic interaction', *Games and Economic Behaviour* **5**: 387–424.

(1995), 'The statistical mechanics of best-response strategy revision', *Games and Economic Behavior* **11**: 111–45.

Borcherding, K., D. L. Larichev and D. M. Messick (eds.) (1990), *Contemporary Issues in Decision Making*, New York: North-Holland.

Bourdieu, P. (1977), *Outline of a Theory of Practice*, Cambridge: Cambridge University Press.

Brock, W. A., and S. N. Durlauf (1995), *Discrete Choice with Social Interactions I: Theory*, Working Paper 9521, Social Systems Research Institute, University of Wisconsin, Madison.

Browning, M., and A. M. Lusardi (1996), 'Household saving: micro theories and micro facts', *Journal of Economic Literature* **34**: 1797–855.

Bush, R. R., and F. Mosteller (1955), *Stochastic Models for Learning*, New York: Wiley.

Camerer, C. F. (1997), 'Progress in behavioral game theory', *Journal of Economic Perspectives* **11**: 167–88.

328   *Giovanni Dosi, Luigi Marengo and Giorgio Fagiolo*

Camerer, C. F., and T. H. Ho (1999), 'Experience-weighted attraction in games', *Econometrica* **67**(4): 827–74.

    (2004), 'Learning in games', in C. R. Plott and V. L. Smith (eds.), *Handbook of Experimental Economics Results*, Amsterdam and New York: North-Holland.

Casti, J. L. (1992), *Reality Rules*, New York: Wiley.

Chiaromonte, F., and G. Dosi (1993), 'Heterogeneity, competition and macroeconomic dynamics', *Structural Change and Economic Dynamics* **4**: 39–63.

Chiaromonte, F., G. Dosi and L. Orsenigo (1993), 'Innovative learning and institutions in the process of development: on the microfoundations of growth regimes', in R. Thomson (ed.), *Learning and Technological Change*, London: Macmillan, 117–49.

Cohen, M. D., and P. Bacdayan (1994), 'Organizational routines are stored as procedural memory: evidence from a laboratory study', *Organizational Science* **5**: 554–68.

Cohen, M. D., R. Burkhart, G. Dosi, M. Egidi, L. Marengo, M. Warglien, S. G. Winter and B. Coriat (1996), 'Routines and other recurring action patterns of organisations: contemporary research issues', *Industrial and Corporate Change* **5**: 653–98.

Cohen, M. D., J. G. March and J. P. Olsen (1972), 'A garbage can model of organizational choice', *Administrative Sciences Quarterly* **17**: 1–25.

Conlisk, J. (1989), 'An aggregate model of technical change', *Quarterly Journal of Economics* **104**: 787–821.

Coriat, B., and G. Dosi (1995), *Learning How to Govern and Learning How to Solve Problems: On the Co-evolution of Competences, Conflicts and Organizational Routines*, Working Paper WP 95-06, International Institute of Applied Systems Analysis, Laxenburg, Austria.

    (1998), 'The institutional embeddedness of economic change: An appraisal of the "evolutionary" and "regulationist" research programmes', in K. Nielsen and E. J. Johnson (eds.), *Institutions and Economic Change*, Cheltenham: Edward Elgar, 3–32.

Cosmides, L., and J. Tooby (1994), 'Better than rational: evolutionary psychology and the invisible hand', *American Economic Review* **84**(2): 327–32.

    (1996), 'Are humans good intuitive statisticians after all? Rethinking some conclusions from the literature on judgment and uncertainty', *Cognition* **58**: 187–276.

Cyert, R. M., and J. G. March (1992), *A Behavioral Theory of the Firm*, 2nd edn., Cambridge: Basil Blackwell.

Dalle, J. M. (1993), *Dynamiques d'Adoption, Coordination et Diversité: Le Cas des Standards Technologiques*, Strasbourg: Beta.

    (1994a), *Decisions Autonomes et Coexistence des Technologies*, Working Paper 9401, Institut d'Economie et de Politique de l'Energie, Grenoble, France.

    (1994b), *Technological Competition, Micro-decisions and Diversity*, paper presented at the EUNETIC conference on evolutionary economics of technological change: assessment of results and new frontiers, 6–8 October, Strasbourg.

David, P. A. (1975), *Technical Choice, Innovation and Economic Growth: Essays on American and British Experience in the Nineteenth Century*, Cambridge: Cambridge University Press.

(1985), 'Clio and the economics of QWERTY', *American Economic Review* 75(2): 332–37.

(1992), 'Path dependence and predictability in dynamic systems with local externalities: a paradigm for historical economics', in D. Foray and C. Freeman (eds.), *Technology and the Wealth of Nations*, London: Pinter, 208–31.

Davidson, P. (1996), 'Reality and economic theory', *Journal of Post-Keynesian Economics*, **18**: 479–508.

Dawkins, R. (1986), *The Blind Watchmaker: Why the Evidence of Evolution Reveals a Universe Without Design*, New York: Norton.

Devetag, M. G. (1999), 'From utilities to mental models: a critical survey on decision rules and cognition in consumer choice', *Industrial and Corporate Change* **8**: 289–351.

Dosi, G. (1984), *Technical Change and Industrial Transformation: The Theory and an Application to the Semiconductor Industry*, London: Macmillan.

(1988), 'Sources, procedures and microeconomic effects of innovation', *Journal of Economic Literature* **26**: 1120–71.

(1995a), 'Hierarchies, markets and power: some foundational issues on the nature of contemporary economic organisations', *Industrial and Corporate Change* **4**: 1–19.

(1995b), *The Contribution of Economic Theory to the Understanding of a Knowledge-based Economy*, Working Paper WP 95-56, International Institute of Applied Systems Analysis, Laxenburg, Austria.

Dosi, G., and M. Egidi (1991), 'Substantive and procedural uncertainty: an exploration of economic behaviours in changing environments', *Journal of Evolutionary Economics* **1**(2): 145–68.

Dosi, G., Y. M. Ermoliev and Y. M. Kaniovski (1994), 'Generalized urn schemes and technological dynamics', *Journal of Mathematical Economics* **23**: 1–19.

Dosi, G., S. Fabiani, R. Aversi and M. Meacci (1994), 'The dynamics of international differentiation: a multi-country evolutionary model', *Industrial and Corporate Change* **3**: 225–41.

Dosi, G., C. Freeman, R. R. Nelson, G. Silverberg and L. Soete (eds.) (1988), *Technical Change and Economic Theory*, London: Pinter.

Dosi, G., and Y. M. Kaniovski (1994), 'On "badly behaved" dynamics', *Journal of Evolutionary Economics* **4**(2): 93–123.

Dosi, G., and D. Lovallo (1997), 'Rational entrepreneurs or optimistic martyrs? Some considerations on technological regimes, corporate entries, and the evolutionary role of decision biases', in R. Garud, P. R. Nayyar and Z. B. Shapira (eds.), *Technological Innovation: Oversights and Foresights*, Cambridge: Cambridge University Press, 41–70.

Dosi, G., and L. Marengo (1994), 'Toward a theory of organizational competencies', in R. W. England (ed.), *Evolutionary Concepts in Contemporary Economics*, Ann Arbor, MI: University of Michigan Press, 157–78.

330   *Giovanni Dosi, Luigi Marengo and Giorgio Fagiolo*

Dosi, G., L. Marengo, A. Bassanini and M. Valente (1999), 'Norms as emergent properties of adaptive learning: the case of economic routines', *Journal of Evolutionary Economics* **9**: 5–26.

Dosi, G., O. Marsili, L. Orsenigo and R. Salvatore (1995), 'Learning, market selection and the evolution of industrial structure', *Small Business Economics* **7**: 411–36.

Dosi, G., and J. S. Metcalfe (1991), 'On some notions of irreversibility in economics', in P. Saviotti and J. S. Metcalfe (eds.), *Evolutionary Theories of Economic and Technological Change: Present Status and Future Prospects*, Chur, Switzerland: Harwood Academic, 133–59.

Dosi, G., and R. R. Nelson (1994), 'An introduction to evolutionary theories in economics', *Journal of Evolutionary Economics* **4**(3): 153–72.

Dosi, G., R. R. Nelson and S. G. Winter (eds.) (2000), *The Nature and Dynamics of Organizational Capabilities*, Oxford: Oxford University Press.

Dosi, G., and S. G. Winter (2002), 'Interpreting economic change: evolution, structures and games', in M. Augier and J. G. March (eds.), *The Economics of Choice, Change, and Organizations*, Cheltenham/Northampton: Edward Elgar, 337–53.

Dubois, D., and H. Prade (1988), 'Modelling uncertainty and inductive inference: a survey of recent non-additive probability systems', *Acta Psychologica* **68**: 53–78.

Durlauf, S. N. (1994), 'Path dependence in aggregate output', *Industrial and Corporate Change* **3**: 149–71.

Easley, D., and A. Rustichini (1995), *Choice without Beliefs*, working paper, Center for Operations Research and Economics, Catholic University of Louvain, Louvain-la-Neuve, Belgium.

Edgerton, R. B. (1985), *Rules, Exceptions and Social Order*, Berkeley and Los Angeles: University of California Press.

Egidi, M. (1996), 'Routines, hierarchies of problems, procedural behaviour: some evidence from experiments', in K. J. Arrow, E. Colombatto, M. Perlman and C. Schmidt (eds.), *The Rational Foundations of Economic Behaviour*, London: Macmillan, 303–33.

Einhorn, H. J., and R. M. Hogarth (1985), 'Ambiguity and uncertainty in probabilistic inference', *Psychological Review* **86**: 433–61.

Eliasson, G. (1985), *The Firm and Financial Markets in the Swedish Micro-to-Macro Model*, working paper, Research Unit of Industrial Economics (IUI), Stockholm.

Elster, J. (1998), 'Emotions and economic theory', *Journal of Economic Literature* **36**: 47–74.

Epstein, J. M., and R. Axtell (1996), *Growing Artificial Societies: Social Science from the Bottom Up*, Washington, DC: Brookings Institution.

Erev, I., and A. E. Roth (1998), 'Predicting how people play games: reinforcement learning in experimental games with unique, mixed strategy equilibria', *American Economic Review* **88**(4): 848–81.

(1999), 'On the role of reinforcement learning in experimental games: the cognitive game theory approach', in D. Bodescu, I. Erev and R. Zwick (eds.), *Games and Human Behavior: Essays in Honor of Amnon Rapoport*, Mahwah, NJ: Lawrence Erlbaum Associates, 53–77.

Ericsson, K. A., and J. Smith (eds.) (1991), *Toward a General Theory of Expertise*, Cambridge: Cambridge University Press.

Estes, W. K. (1950), 'Toward a statistical theory of learning', *Psychological Review* 57: 94–107.

Feldman, M. (1991), 'On the generic nonconvergence of Bayesian actions and beliefs', *Economic Theory* 1: 301–21.

Festinger, L. (1957), *A Theory of Cognitive Dissonance*, Stanford, CA: Stanford University Press.

Fisher, R. A. (1930), *The Genetical Theory of Natural Selection*, Oxford: Clarendon Press.

Föllmer, H. (1974), 'Random economies with many interacting agents', *Journal of Mathematical Economics* 24: 51–62.

Fontana, W., and L. W. Buss (1994), 'What would be conserved if "the tape were played twice"?', *Proceedings of the National Academy of Sciences USA* 91: 757–61.

   (1996), *The Barrier of Objects: From Dynamical Systems to Bounded Organizations*, Working Paper WP 96-27, International Institute for Applied Systems Analysis, Laxenburg, Austria.

Foray, D., and B.-Å. Lundvall (1996), *The Knowledge-based Economy*, Paris: Organisation for Economic Co-operation and Development.

Foster, D., and P. Young (1990), 'Stochastic evolutionary game dynamics', *Theoretical Population Biology* 38: 219–32.

Freeman, C. (1982), *The Economics of Industrial Innovation*, London: Pinter.

   (1994), 'The economics of technical change', *Cambridge Journal of Economics* 18: 463–514.

Friedman, D. (1991), 'Evolutionary games in economics', *Econometrica* 59(3): 637–66.

Friedman, M. (1953), *Essays in Positive Economics*, Chicago: University of Chicago Press.

Fudenberg, D., and C. Harris (1992), 'Evolutionary dynamics with aggregate shocks', *Journal of Economic Theory* 57: 420–41.

Fudenberg, D., and D. M. Kreps (1993), 'Learning mixed equilibria', *Games and Economic Behaviour* 5: 320–67.

Fudenberg, D., and D. K. Levine (1995), 'Consistency and cautious fictitious play', *Journal of Economic Dynamics and Control* 19: 1065–89.

Geertz, C. (1963), *Peddlers and Princes*, Chicago: University of Chicago Press.

Gigerenzer, G. (2000), *Adaptive Thinking: Rationality in the Real World*, Oxford: Oxford University Press.

Gigerenzer, G., and R. Selten (eds.) (2001), *Bounded Rationality: The Adaptive Toolbox*, Cambridge, MA: MIT Press.

Gigerenzer, G., P. M. Todd and the ABC Research Group (1999), *Simple Heuristics that Make us Smart*, Oxford: Oxford University Press.

Girotto, V., P. N. Johnson-Laird, P. Legrenzi and M. Sonino (2000), 'Reasoning to consistency: how people resolve logical inconsistencies', in L. Garcia-Madruga, M. Carriedo and M. J. Gonzalez-Labra (eds.), *Mental Models in Reasoning*, Madrid: Universidad Nacional de Educación a Distancia, 83–97.

Glaziev, S. Y., and Y. M. Kaniovski (1991), 'Diffusion of innovations under conditions of uncertainty: a stochastic approach', in N. Nakicenovic and

332   *Giovanni Dosi, Luigi Marengo and Giorgio Fagiolo*

A. Grubler (eds.), *Diffusion of Technologies and Social Behaviour*, Berlin: Springer-Verlag, 231–46.

Goffman, E. (1974), *Frame Analysis: An Essay on the Organisation of Experience*, Harmondsworth: Penguin.

Goldvarg, Y., and P. N. Johnson-Laird (2000), 'Illusions in modal reasoning', *Memory & Cognition* **28**: 282–94.

Granovetter, M. S. (1985), 'Economic action and social structure: the problem of embeddedness', *American Journal of Sociology* **51**: 481–510.

Granstrand, O. (ed.) (1994), *The Economics of Technology*, Amsterdam: North-Holland.

Griffin, D., and A. Tversky (1992), 'The weight of evidence and the determinants of confidence', *Cognitive Psychology* **24**: 411–35.

Grimmett, G. (1989), *Percolation*, New York: Springer-Verlag.

Grossman, G. M., and E. Helpman (1991), *Innovation and Growth in the Global Economy*, Cambridge, MA: MIT Press.

Hammersley, J. M., and D. J. A. Welsh (1980), 'Percolation theory and its ramifications', *Contemporary Physics* **21**: 593–605.

Heiner, R. A. (1983), 'The origin of predictable behavior', *American Economic Review* **73**(4): 560–95.

Herrnstein, R. J., and D. Prelec (1991), 'Melioration: a theory of distributed choice', *Journal of Economic Perspectives*, **5**: 137–56.

Herz, A. V. M. (1994), 'Collective phenomena in spatially extended evolutionary games', *Journal of Theoretical Biology* **169**: 65–87.

Hicks, J. R. (1936), *Value and Capital*, Oxford: Oxford University Press.

Hirschman, A. (1965), 'Obstacles to development: a classification and a quasi-vanishing act', *Economic Development and Cultural Change*, **13**: 385–93.

Hodgson, G. M. (1988), *Economics and Institutions: A Manifesto for a Modern Institutional Economics*, Cambridge: Polity Press.

(1993), *Economics and Evolution: Bringing Life Back into Economics*, Cambridge: Polity Press.

Hoffmeister, F., and M. Bäck (1991), *Genetic Algorithms and Evolution Strategies – Similarities and Differences*, Paper on Economics and Evolution no. 9103, European Study Group for Evolutionary Economics.

Holland, J. H., K. J. Holyoak, R. E. Nisbett and P. R. Thagard (eds.) (1986), *Induction: Processes of Inference, Learning and Discovery*, Cambridge, MA: MIT Press.

Hors, I., and F. Lordon (1997), 'About some formalisms of interaction: phase transition models in economics?', *Journal of Evolutionary Economics* **7**(4): 355–73.

Huberman, B., and T. Hogg (1995), 'Distributed computation as an economic system', *Journal of Economic Perspectives* **9**: 141–52.

Ioannides, Y. M. (1990), 'Trading uncertainty and market form', *International Economic Review* **31**: 619–38.

Johnson-Laird, P. N. (1983), *Mental Models*, Cambridge, MA: Harvard University Press.

(1993), *The Computer and the Mind*, London: Fontana Press.

(2000), 'The current state of the mental model theory', in J. Garcia-Madruga, M.Carriedo and M. J. Gonzalez-Labra (eds.), *Mental Models in Reasoning*, Madrid: Universidad Nacional de Educación a Distancia, 17–40.

Johnson-Laird, P. N., and R. M. J. Byrne (2000), 'Mental models and pragmatics', *Behavioral and Brain Sciences* **23**: 284–86.

Kahneman, D., J. L. Knetsch and R. H. Thaler (1990), 'Experiment tests of the endowment effect and the Coase theorem', *Journal of Political Economy* **98**(6): 1325–48.

Kahneman, D., and D. Lovallo (1993), 'Timid choice and bold forecast: a cognitive perspective on risktaking', *Management Science* **39**: 17–31.

Kahneman, D., P. Slovic, and A. Tversky (eds.) (1982), *Judgment under Uncertainty: Heuristics and Biases*, Cambridge: Cambridge University Press.

Kahneman, D., and A. Tversky (1986), 'Rational choice and the framing of decision', *Journal of Business* **59**: 251–78.

Kalai, E., and E. Lehrer (1994), 'Weak and strong merging of opinions', *Journal of Mathematical Economics* **23**: 73–86.

Kandori, M., G. J. Mailath and R. Rob (1993), 'Learning, mutations, and long-run equilibrium in games', *Econometrica* **61**(1): 29–56.

Kaniovski, Y. M., A. V. Kryazhimskii and H. P. Young (1996), *On the Robustness of Stochastic Best-Reply Dynamics in Repeated Games*, Working Paper WP 96-45, International Institute of Applied Systems Analysis, Laxenburg, Austria.

Kaniovski, Y. M., and H. P. Young (1994), 'Learning dynamics in games with stochastic perturbations', *Games and Economic Behavior* **11**: 330–63.

Katona, G. (1951), *Psychological Analysis of Economic Behavior*, New York: McGraw-Hill.

(1968), 'Behavioral and ecological economics, consumer behaviour: theory and findings on expectations and aspirations', *American Economic Review* **58**(2): 19–30.

Katzner, D. W. (1990), 'The firm under conditions of ignorance and historical time', *Journal of Post-Keynesian Economics* **13**: 124–56.

Kauffman, S. A. (1993), *The Origins of Order*, Oxford: Oxford University Press.

Kirman, A. P. (1992), 'Variety: the coexistence of techniques', *Revue d'Economie Industrielle* **59**: 62–74.

(1993), 'Ants, rationality and recruitment', *Quarterly Journal of Economics*, **108**: 137–56.

(1997), 'The economy as an interactive system', in W. B. Arthur, S. N. Durlauf and D. Lane (eds.), *The Economy as an Evolving Complex System II*, Santa Fe Institute Studies in the Sciences of Complexity, Reading, MA: Addison-Wesley, 491–531.

Kirman, A. P., C. Oddou and S. Weber (1986), 'Stochastic communication and coalition formation', *Econometrica* **54**(1): 129–38.

Kogut, B. (ed.) (1993), *Country Competitiveness: Technology and the Organizing of Work*, Oxford: Oxford University Press.

Koza, J. R. (1993), *Genetic Programming*, Cambridge, MA: MIT Press.

Kreps, D. M. (1996), 'Market, hierarchies and mathematical economic theory', *Industrial and Corporate Change* **5**: 561–95.

334   *Giovanni Dosi, Luigi Marengo and Giorgio Fagiolo*

Kuran, T. (1987), 'Preference falsification, policy continuity and collective con-
    servatism', *Economic Journal* **387**: 642–55.
    (1991), 'Cognitive limitations and preference evolution', *Journal of Institutional
    and Theoretical Economics* **146**: 241–73.
Kwasnicki, W. (1996), *Knowledge, Innovation and Economy*, Cheltenham: Edward
    Elgar.
Lakoff, G. (1987), *Women, Fire and Dangerous Things: What Categories Reveal
    about the Mind*, Chicago: University of Chicago Press.
Lane, D. (1993a), 'Artificial worlds in economics: part 1', *Journal of Evolutionary
    Economics* **3**(2): 89–107.
    (1993b), 'Artificial worlds in economics: part 2', *Journal of Evolutionary Eco-
    nomics* **3**(3): 177–97.
Lane, D., F. Malerba, R. Maxfield and L. Orsenigo (1996), 'Choice and action',
    Journal of Evolutionary Economics **6**(1): 43–75.
Lane, D., and R. Vescovini (1996), 'Decision rules and market share: aggregation
    in an information contagion model', *Industrial and Corporate Change* **5**: 127–
    46.
Langton, C. G. (ed.) (1989), *Artificial Life*, Reading, MA: Addison-Wesley.
Langton, C. G., C. Taylor, J. D. Farmer and S. Rasmussen (eds.) (1991), *Artificial
    Life II*, Reading, MA: Addison-Wesley.
Leibenstein, H. (1950), 'Bandwagon, snob and Veblen effects in the theory of
    consumer demand', *Quarterly Journal of Economics* **64**: 183–207.
Lesourne, J. (1991), *Economie de l'Ordre et du Désordre*, Paris: Economica.
Levinthal, D. (1996), 'Surviving in Schumpeterian environments', in G. Dosi and
    F. Malerba (eds.), *Organization and Strategy in the Evolution of the Enterprise*,
    London: Macmillan, 27–42.
Levinthal, D., and M. Warglien (1999), 'Landscape design: designing for local
    action in complex worlds', *Organizational Science* **10**: 342–57.
Lewis, A. (1985a), 'On effectively computable realization of choice functions',
    Mathematical Social Sciences **10**: 43–80.
    (1985b), 'The minimum degree of recursively representable choice funtions',
    Mathematical Social Sciences **10**: 179–88.
    (1986), *Structure and Complexity: The Use of Recursion Theory in the Founda-
    tions of Neoclassical Mathematical Economics and the Theory of Games*, mimeo,
    Department of Mathematics, Cornell University, Ithaca, NY.
Lindgren, K. (1991), 'Evolutionary phenomena in simple dynamics', in C. G.
    Langton, C. Taylor, J. D. Farmer and S. Rasmussen (eds.), *Artificial Life II*,
    Reading, MA: Addison-Wesley, 57–92.
Loewenstein, G., and J. Elster (eds.) (1992), *Choice Over Time*, New York: Russell
    Sage Foundation.
Lovallo, D. (1996), 'From individual biases to organizational errors', in G. Dosi
    and F. Malerba (eds.), *Organization and Strategy in the Evolution of Enterprise*,
    London: Macmillan, 103–24.
Lucas, R. E. (1986), 'Adaptive behavior and economic theory', *Journal of Business*
    59: S401–S426.
Lundvall, B. Å. (ed.) (1995), *National Systems of Innovation: Towards a Theory of
    Innovation and Interactive Learning*, London: Pinter.

Learning in evolutionary environments 335

(1996), *The Social Dimension of the Learning Economy*, Working Paper 96-01, Danish Research Unit for Industrial Dynamics, Aalborg, Denmark.

Luria, A. R. (1976), *Cognitive Development: Its Cultural and Social Foundations*, Cambridge, MA: Harvard University Press.

Malerba, F., and L. Orsenigo (1996), 'The dynamics and evolution of industries', *Industrial and Corporate Change* 5: 51–87.

March, J. G. (1988a), 'Variable risk preference and adaptive aspirations', *Journal of Economic Behavior and Organization* 9: 5–24.

(1988b), *Decision and Organizations*, Oxford: Basil Blackwell.

(1994), *A Primer on Decision Making: How Decisions Happen*, New York: Free Press.

March, J. G., and H. A. Simon (1958), *Organizations*, New York: Basil Blackwell.

March, J. G., L. S. Sproull and M. Tamuz (1991), 'Learning from samples of one or fewer', *Organization Science* 2: 1–13.

Marengo, L. (1992), 'Coordination and organizational learning in the firm', *Journal of Evolutionary Economics* 2: 313–26.

(1996), 'Structure, competences and learning in an adaptive model of the firm', in G. Dosi and F. Malerba (eds.), *Organization and Strategy in the Evolution of the Enterprise*, London: Macmillan, 199–216.

Marengo, L., and N. Lazaric (2000), 'Towards a characterization of assets and knowledge created in technological agreements: some evidence from the automobile-robotics sector', *Industrial and Corporate Change* 9: 53–86.

Marengo, L., and H. Tordjman (1996), 'Speculation, heterogeneity and learning: a model of exchange rate dynamics', *Kyklos* 47: 407–38.

Margolis, H. (1987), *Patterns, Thinking and Cognition*, Chicago: University of Chicago Press.

Marimon, R. (1997), 'Learning from learning in economics: towards a theory of the learnable in economics', in D. M. Kreps and K. F. Wallis (eds.), *Advances in Economics and Econometrics: Theory and Applications*, vol. 1, 278–315.

Marimon, R., E. McGrattan and T. J. Sargent (1990), 'Money as a medium of exchange in an economy with artificially intelligent agents', *Journal of Economic Dynamics and Control* 14: 329–73.

Mayer, R. E. (1992), *Thinking, Problem Solving and Cognition*, New York: W. H. Freeman.

Maynard Smith, J. (1982), *Evolution and the Theory of Games*, Cambridge: Cambridge University Press.

Metcalfe, J. S. (1994), 'Evolutionary economics and technology policy', *Economic Journal* 425: 931–44.

Milgram, S. (1974), *Obedience to Authority: An Experimental View*, London: Tavistock Institute.

Milgrom, P., and J. Roberts (1991), 'Adaptive and sophisticated learning in normal form games', *Games and Economic Behaviour* 3: 82–100.

Montgomery, C. A. (ed.) (1995), *Resource-based and Evolutionary Theories of the Firm*, Dordrecht: Kluwer Academic.

Nelson, R. R. (1987), *Understanding Technical Change as an Evolutionary Process*, Professor Dr F. de Vries Lectures in Economics no. 8 – Theory, Institutions, Policy, Amsterdam: North-Holland.

336   *Giovanni Dosi, Luigi Marengo and Giorgio Fagiolo*

(ed.) (1993), *National Innovation Systems: A Comparative Study*, Oxford: Oxford University Press.

(1994), 'The coevolution of technology, industrial structure and supporting institutions', *Industrial and Corporate Change* **3**: 47–63.

(1995), 'Recent evolutionary theorizing about economic change', *Journal of Economic Literature* **33**: 48–90.

Nelson, R. R., and S. G. Winter (1982), *An Evolutionary Theory of Economic Change*, Cambridge, MA: Harvard University Press.

Newell, A., and H. A. Simon (1972), *Human Problem Solving*, Englewood Cliffs, NJ: Prentice Hall.

Nowak, M. A., and R. M. May (1992), 'Evolutionary games and spatial chaos', *Nature* **359**: 826–29.

(1993), 'The spatial dilemmas of evolution', *International Journal of Bifurcation and Chaos* **3**: 35–78.

Orléan, A. (1990), 'Le rôle des influences interpersonnelles dans la détermination des cours boursiers', *Revue Economiques*, **41**: 839–68.

(1992), 'Contagion des opinions et fonctionnement des marchés financiers', *Revue Economiques* **43**: 685–97.

Padgett, J. F. (1997), 'The emergence of simple ecologies of skills: a hypercycle approach to economic organization', in W. B. Arthur, S. N. Durlauf, and D. Lane (eds.), *The Economy as an Evolving Complex System II*, Santa Fe Institute Studies in the Science of Complexity, Reading, MA: Addison-Wesley, 199–216.

Palmer, R. G., W. B. Arthur, J. H. Holland, B. LeBaron and P. Tayler (1994), 'Artificial economic life: a simple model of a stockmarket', *Physica D* **75**: 264–74.

Pavitt, K. (1984), 'Sectoral patterns of technical change: towards a taxonomy and a theory', *Research Policy* **13**: 343–73.

Pearl, J. (1984), *Heuristics*, Reading, MA: Addison-Wesley.

Polanyi, K. (1944), *The Great Transformation*, Boston: Beacon Press.

(ed.) (1957), *Trade and Market in the Early Empires*, Glencoe, MN: Free Press.

Posch, M. (1994), *Cycling with a Generalized Urn Scheme and a Learning Algorithm for 2 X 2 Games*, Working Paper WP 94-76, International Institute of Applied Systems Analysis, Laxenburg, Austria.

Purkitt, H. E., and J. W. Dyson (1990), 'Decision making under varying situational constraints', in K. Borcherding, D. L. Larichev and D. M. Messick (eds.), *Contemporary Issues in Decision Making*, New York: North-Holland, 353–65.

Rabin, M. (1998), 'Psychology and economics', *Journal of Economic Literature* **36**: 11–46.

Riolo, R. L. (1990), *Lookahead Planning and Latent Learning in a Classifier System*, mimeo, University of Michigan.

Rip, A., T. J. Misa and J. Schot (eds) (1995), *Managing Technology in Society*, London: Pinter.

Romer, P. M. (1990), 'Endogenous technological change', *Journal of Political Economy* **98**(5, part 2): S71–S102.

Rosenberg, N. (1976), *Perspectives on Technology*, Cambridge: Cambridge University Press.

(1982), *Inside the Black Box*, Cambridge: Cambridge University Press.

(1994), *Exploring the Black Box: Technology, Economics and History*, Cambridge: Cambridge University Press.

Sargent, T. J. (1993), *Bounded Rationality in Economics*, Oxford: Clarendon Press.

Savage, L. (1954), *The Foundations of Statistics*, New York: Wiley.

Shackle, G. L. S. (1955), *Uncertainty in Economics*, Cambridge: Cambridge University Press.

(1969), *Decision, Order and Time in Human Affairs*, Cambridge: Cambridge University Press.

Shafir, E. B., and A. Tversky (1992), 'Thinking through uncertainty: inconsequential reasoning and choice', *Cognitive Psychology* **24**: 449–74.

Silverberg, G. (1988), 'Modelling economic dynamics and technical change', in G. Dosi, C. Freeman, R. R. Nelson, G. Silverberg and L. Soete (eds.), *Technical Change and Economic Theory*, London, Pinter, 531–59.

Silverberg, G., G. Dosi and L. Orsenigo (1988), 'Innovation, diversity and diffusion: a self-organisation model', *Economic Journal* **393**: 1032–54.

Silverberg, G., and D. Lehnert (1994), 'Growth fluctuations in an evolutionary model of creative destruction', in G. Silverberg and L. Soete (eds.), *The Economics of Growth and Technical Change*, Cheltenham: Edward Elgar, 74–108.

Silverberg, G., and B. Verspagen (1994), 'Learning, innovation and economic growth: a long-run model of industrial dynamics', *Industrial and Corporate Change* **3**: 199–223.

(1995a), *From the Artificial to the Endogenous: Modeling Evolutionary Adaptation and Economic Growth*, Working Paper WP 95-08, International Institute for Applied Systems Analysis, Laxenburg, Austria.

(1995b), *Evolutionary Theorizing on Economic Growth*, Working Paper WP 95-78, International Institute for Applied Systems Analysis, Laxenburg, Austria.

Simon, H. A. (1976), 'From substantive to procedural rationality', in S. J. Latsis (ed.), *Method and Appraisal in Economics*, Cambridge: Cambridge University Press, 129–48.

(1981), *The Sciences of the Artificial*, Cambridge, MA: MIT Press.

(1986), 'Rationality in psychology and economics', in R. M. Hogart and N. W. Reder (eds.), *Rational Choice*, Chicago: University of Chicago Press, 25–40.

(1988), *Models of Thought*, New Haven, CT: Yale University Press.

Slovic, P., S. Lichtenstein and B. Fischerhof (1989), 'Decision making', in R. J. Herrnstein, G. Lindrey and R. D. Luce (eds.), *Steven's Handbook of Experimental Psychology*, Chichester: Wiley, 673–738.

Smelser, N. J., and R. Swedberg (eds.) (1994), *The Handbook of Economic Sociology*, Princeton, NJ: Princeton University Press.

Sterman, J. D. (1989a), 'Deterministic chaos in an experimental economic system', *Journal of Economic Behavior and Organization* **12**: 1–28.

(1989b), 'Modeling managerial behavior: misperceptions of feedback in a dynamic decision making experiment', *Management Science* **35**: 321–38.

338   *Giovanni Dosi, Luigi Marengo and Giorgio Fagiolo*

Stoneman, P. (ed.) (1995), *Handbook of the Economics of Innovation and Techno-logical Change*, Oxford: Basil Blackwell.

Suppes, P. (1969), 'Stimulus-response theory of finite automata', *Journal of Mathematical Psychology* **6**: 327–55.

(1995a), *A Survey of Mathematical Learning Theory 1950–1995*, mimeo, Stanford University.

(1995b), *Learning by Doing, or Practice Makes Perfect*, mimeo, Stanford University.

Teece, D. J., and G. Pisano (1994), 'The dynamic capabilities of firms: an introduction', *Industrial and Corporate Change* **3**: 537–55.

Thaler, R. H. (1992), *The Winner's Curse: Paradoxes and Anomalies of Economic Life*, New York: Free Press.

Topol, R. (1991), 'Bubbles and volatility of stock prices: effects of mimetic contagion', *Economic Journal* **407**: 786–800.

Tordjman, H. (1996), *The Formation of Beliefs on Financial Markets: Representativeness and Prototypes*, Working Paper WP 96-87, International Institute of Applied Systems Analysis, Laxenburg, Austria.

Tversky, A., and D. Kahneman (1982), 'Judgments of and by representativeness', in D. Kahneman, P. Slovic and A. Tversky (eds.), *Judgment under Uncertainty: Heuristics and Biases*, Cambridge: Cambridge University Press, 84–98.

Vassilakis, S. (1995), *Accelerating New Product Development by Overcoming Complexity Constraints*, working paper, European University Institute.

Verspagen, B. (1993), *Uneven Growth between Interdependent Economies: An Evolutionary View on Technology Gaps, Trade and Growth*, Aldershot: Avebury.

Vickers, D. (1986), 'Time, ignorance, surprise, and economic decisions', *Journal of Post-Keynesian Economics* **9**: 48–57.

Vriend, N. J. (1995), 'Self-organization of markets: an example of a computational approach', *Computational Economics* **8**: 205–31.

Warglien, M. (1995), 'Hierarchical selection and organizational adaptation', *Industrial and Corporate Change* **4**: 161–85.

Weibull, J. W. (1995), *Evolutionary Game Theory*, Cambridge, MA: MIT Press.

Winter, S. G. (1971), 'Satisficing, selection and the innovative remnant', *Quarterly Journal of Economics* **85**: 237–61.

(1975), 'Optimization and evolution in the theory of the firm', in R. H. Day and T. Groves (eds.), *Adaptive Economic Models*, New York: Academic Press, 73–118.

(1987), 'Knowledge and competence of strategic assets', in D. J. Teece (ed.), *The Competitive Challenge*, Cambridge, MA: Ballinger, 159–84.

(1988), 'Economic natural selection and the theory of the firm', in P. E. Earl (ed.), *Behavioural Economics*, vol. 1, Aldershot: Edward Elgar.

Witt, U. (ed.) (1992), *Explaining Process and Change: Approaches to Evolutionary Economics*, Ann Arbor, MI: University of Michigan Press.

Young, H. P. (1993), 'The evolution of conventions', *Econometrica* **61**(1): 57–84.

[2]

Organizational Capabilities, Patterns of Knowledge Accumulation and Governance Structures in Business Firms: An Introduction

Giovanni Dosi, Marco Faillo and Luigi Marengo

Giovanni Dosi
LEM, Sant'Anna
School of Advanced
Studies, Pisa, Italy

Marco Faillo
University of Trento,
Italy

Luigi Marengo
LEM, Sant'Anna
School of Advanced
Studies, Pisa, Italy

Abstract

The capability-based view of the firm is based on the assumption that firms know how to do things. Assuming the existence of a thing called 'organizational knowledge', in the first part of the paper we identify its main building blocks and we provide a description of its inner structure. This results in an analysis of the relationships among key concepts like organizational routines, organizational competencies and skills. In the second part, we consider some empirical implications of the adoption of a capability-based view of the firm in dealing with issues like horizontal and vertical boundaries of the firm, innovation and corporate performance. Some implications for strategic management are also discussed.

Keywords: capabilities, routines, organizational knowledge, problem solving

Introduction: Nature and Dynamics of Firms' Competencies and Capabilities[1]

It is familiar enough that business firms and other organizations 'know how to do things' — things like building automobiles or computers, or flying people from one continent to another. On second thoughts, what does this mean? Is there not a sense in which only a human mind can possess knowledge? If so, can this proposition somehow be squared with the idea that organizations know how to do things? And if organizational knowledge is a real phenomenon, what are the principles that govern how it is acquired, maintained, extended and sometimes lost?

Our focus here is on the particular forms of organizational knowledge that account for an organization's ability to perform and extend its characteristic 'output' actions — particularly the creation of a tangible product or the provision of a service, and the development of new products and services.

Pending a more thorough discussion of terminology, we identify the term 'organizational competencies or capabilities' with the know-how that enables organizations to perform these sorts of activities.

In a first instance, let us just build on the idea that organizational knowledge is a fundamental link between some collective pool of knowledge, skills, incentives

Organization
Studies
29(08&09):
1165–1185
ISSN 0170–8406
Copyright © 2008
SAGE Publications
(Los Angeles,
London, New Delhi
and Singapore)

DOI: 10.1177/0170840608094775

and opportunities, on the one hand, and the rates, directions and economic effectiveness of this exploration, development and exploitation, on the other.

In turn, distinctive organizational competencs/capabilities bear their importance insofar as they can be shown to shape persistently the destiny of individual firms — in terms of, for example, profitability, growth, probability of survival and, at least equally important, the patterns of change of broader aggregates such as particular sectors and whole countries.

Organizational Competencies, Routines and Capabilities

A general equivalence between 'competencs' and 'capabilities' is often assumed within the literature.

As discussed in Dosi et al. (2000), it should be clear that we think of 'capability' as a fairly large-scale unit of analysis, one that has a recognizable purpose expressed in terms of the significant outcomes it is supposed to enable, and that is shaped significantly by conscious decision both in its development and deployment. Intentions and conscious purposes, however, may be remote from the instances of capability, such as observed activities and outcomes, which are often automatic and habitual.

These features distinguish 'capability' from 'organizational routines', as the latter term is used in organizational theory and evolutionary economics.[2] In this literature, however, some organizational routines might equally well be called capabilities. In general, however, the notion of a routine involves no commitment regarding size (large routines are typically structured sets of medium-sized ones, and so on). It involves no presumption regarding evident purpose: one of the interesting things about routines is indeed that they are often found in contexts where nobody can explain what they are, except in the vague terms of 'the way things are done around here'. Moreover, there is no presumption of deliberation or conscious choice; a flight crew probably does not choose its response to unexpected turbulence any more than a football player 'deliberates' on how to take a penalty.

In a very broad sense, the concept of routines refers to simple decision rules that require low levels of information processing (rules of thumb), but also to complex, automatic behaviours that involve high levels of repetitive information processing (Cohen et al. 1996).

Cohen et al. (1996) suggest a synthesis of different points of view, defining an organizational routine as 'an executable capability for repeated performance in some context that has been learned by an organization in response to selective pressure'. Thus, the capacity to generate a specific action (the capability) is conceived as possible only in some context, which is seen as a kind of 'external memory' and as a source of inputs to actions. The fact that routines are learned implies the possibility of the tacitness and automaticity stressed so far. The concept of selective pressure represents a broad term that indicates a wide variety of forces that operate on action sequences.

Routines and other organizational practices do not only represent problem-solving and coordination procedures, but represent at the same time specific control and governance devices. The suggestion that organizational routines also entail a 'truce' among potentially conflicting interests goes back to Nelson and Winter (1982). It is also true, however, that, until recently, the 'governance' side of organizational practices was largely neglected within knowledge-centred views of the firm (needless to say, exactly the opposite applies to 'incentive-centred' perspectives, including agency theories, and, to a large extent, also to transaction cost economics, with its neglect of most knowledge issues).

Coriat and Dosi (1998) attempt to investigate the emergence of specific organizational forms as a co-evolutionary outcome of organizational innovation affecting both the problem-solving and governance/control roles of corporate practices and structures. In order to do that, they analyse the origins and the properties of some sets of routines from two organizational archetypes, namely, the US 'Tayloristic' firm and the Japanese 'Toyotist' firm.

Let us consider the Tayloristic example. The time and motion studies, at the core of the Tayloristic revolution, have been the prerequisite for the codification of previously tacit productive knowledge in a set of elementary procedures. At the same time, however, this codification was a precondition for a new design of control mechanisms for effort elicitation (new pay and control systems). In fact, one of the major obstacles to productivity growth in the 19th century was skilled workers' ability to bargain on the condition of the use of the knowledge embodied in their experience due to employer ignorance about 'the way to do things'. Rather than attempting to refine the incentive structure, the general Tayloristic programme involved a major redefinition of the nature of productive knowledge. With that, came a major reshuffling of the distribution of knowledge within the organization (from the shop floor up to the departments of planning, design and so on) and the inclusion of broader changes in the general structure of the labour market (including new rules for labour mobility, hiring and firing). At the same time, such an organizational revolution opened the way to the development of new organizational capabilities conducive to efficient manufacturing of high-volume, standardized, low-cost products.

Indeed, the investigation of the 'governance side' of problem-solving procedures, while still at an early stage, promised finally to take on board issues of incentives, control and power distribution as co-determinants of organizational arrangements and behaviours.

To conclude, capabilities involve organized activity, and the exercise of capability is typically repetitious in many cases. Routines, as defined above, are the building blocks of capabilities with a repetitive and context-dependent nature, although they are not the only building blocks of capabilities. A marketing capability, for instance, might require a customer database, for example, which neither is a routine itself nor does it resemble a routine in the way that the working of complex equipment sometimes does. The database is instead a contextual requisite of some of the organizational routines supporting the capability.

Individual skills, in turn, are among the building blocks of organizational routines. What we commonly think of as individual skills are quasi-modular components of routines; their names are useful in expressing, for example, the idea that the role played by one skilled machine operator might well be played by another. 'Knowing the job', however, involves knowing things that are relational — involving other participants — and organization-specific (Nelson and Winter 1982). That is why the skilled operator still needs to learn the job of operating a familiar machine when joining an unfamiliar organization, and why someone who is a perfectly adequate machine operator might nevertheless fail to learn the job. Some of the non-modular knowledge required is skill-like, regardless of what it is called, but these are skills that can be learned only through experience in the specific organization.

Following Dosi et al. (2000), the term 'skills' will be reserved for the individual level and the term 'routines' for the organizational level.

Turning to the concept of competency, some research has addressed similar ideas, but by making use of some notion of competency. An influential article by Prahalad and Hamel (1990) popularized the term 'core competence'. A brief reading of the article brings to light the following four points: (1) large corporations have multiple core competencys (five or six maximum, they suggest, not 20 or 30 — but not one, either); (2) competencs are fundamental to the dynamics of the firm's competitive strength, lending strategic coherence to a string of new and improved products appearing over an extended period; (3) the competencs referred to are all areas of 'hard technology'; (4) while the relationship of competencs to large-scale structural features of the organization is highlighted, the organizational aspects of the competencs themselves do not capture the authors' attention.

As discussed in Dosi et al. (2000), the last two points are greatly at odds with the concept of organizational capabilities, which need not be related to technology, and which certainly have a significant organizational aspect. The first two, however, could be considered compatible with the concept of capabilities.

We thus arrive at the idea that a successful large corporation derives competitive strength from its excellence in a small number of capability clusters where it can sustain a leadership position over time. This comes very close to the concept of 'dynamic capabilities' advanced by Teece et al. (1997), wherein dynamic capabilities are defined as the 'firm's ability to integrate, build, and reconfigure internal and external competencs to address rapidly changing environments' (see also below). In areas of 'hard' technology, the dynamic capabilities of a firm depend heavily on its R&D resources. Nevertheless, they cannot be built simply by spending on R&D or making analogous investments. On the contrary — and to an increasing extent, as the competitive pace quickens — coordination between R&D and other functions, and often with suppliers or alliance partners, is essential. Such coordination is needed, among other things, for effective identification and linking of technological options and market opportunities, and for identifying the strengths and weaknesses of existing resources relative to the requirements of a new product or process.

Thus, the concepts of 'core competency' and 'dynamic capabilities' point in the same direction: both are broadly concerned with the firm's ability to carry off the balancing act between continuity and change in its capabilities, and to do so in a competitively effective fashion.

Another important idea in this general area is referred to as 'combinative capabilities' by Kogut and Zander (1992). Here, again, the emphasis is on the firm's availability to handle change by transforming old capabilities into new ones. Two points about the nature of this transformation are emphasized: (1) firms produce new capabilities by recombining existing capabilities and other knowledge; (2) the ability of the firm to do this is affected by the organizing principles guiding its operation principles, which include matters of formal structure, but, more importantly, internal social relations that are shaped in part by differences in the knowledge bases of individuals and groups within the firm. Pursuing these ideas, the authors develop a view of the firm and the make-or-buy decision that is quite different from that put forward in transaction cost economics.

The character of decision making in this realm, and in contexts in which both competency (or vision) and capabilities play an important role, has been explored by Fransman (1994a,b). The question of the value that top management competency brings to the firm and its relation to managerial compensation has also been studied by Castanias and Helfat (1991), although both the orientation and terminology are different.

Evidently, the concept of capabilities relates to Edith Penrose's (1959) notion that the profitability and the growth of a firm should be understood in terms of its possession and development of unique and idiosyncratic resources, which is nowadays shared, albeit with a different interpretation, by the 'resource-based' view of the firm (Barney 1991, 2001).[3] Scholars who identify themselves with the 'resource-based view' examine the question of what sorts of resources confer lasting competitive advantages, how these advantages can be extended 'leveraged', and what considerations prevent the elimination of the gap between the cost of the resources and the market value of the output. Many discussions in this vein seem to imply that firm resources are 'idiosyncratic' in only a weak sense; they are relatively discrete and separable from the context of the firm and are the sorts of things that would naturally carry a market price. On this interpretation, the resource rubric does not subsume capabilities. Some authors, notably Dierickx and Cool (1989), offer a sharply contrasting view, suggesting that competitively significant resources are gradually accumulated and shaped within the firm, and are generally non-tradable. Unique, difficult-to-imitate capabilities acquired in a protracted process of organizational learning are example of the sorts of resources they see as sources of competitive advantage.

This discussion of terminology would certainly be incomplete without making reference to what was (at least to our knowledge) the original use of the term 'capabilities', in a sense closely akin, if not identical, to our own. George B. Richardson, in his article 'The Organization of Industry' (Richardson 1972), made the fundamental point that organizations do tend to specialize in activities for which their capabilities offer some comparative advantage, and that the pursuit of activities that are similar in the sense of drawing upon the same capabilities may lead a firm into a (coherent) variety of markets and a (coherent) variety of product lines.

After all this definitional tour de force, let us also propose, for the time being, a narrower interpretation of the notion of competencs, which gives the latter a distinct meaning confined to a scale of observation: intermediate between single routines and overall firm-wide capabilities (as defined above), capturing 'chunks' of organizational abilities identified in terms of the tasks performed and knowledge bases upon which they draw.

Thus, one might talk of mechanical competencs to capture, together, ensembles of skills of individual members of the organization and, at the same time, to capture directly organization-embodied elements of knowledge, routines and so on, all aimed at the design of production improvement of, say, machine tools. Note that, in this example, mechanical competencs are not likely to fulfil the overall organizational capability of producing and effectively selling the machine tools themselves. Other complementary competencs will be required to that effect, concerning, for example, electronic technologies, marketing activities, and so on.

If one accepts this interpretation of competencs *stricto sensu*, some important consequences follow. First, in line with Patel and Pavitt (2000), one may begin to distinguish different, but complementary, types of competencs concurring to determine the overall capabilities of an organization. Patel and Pavitt, in this respect, single out some distinctive functional features, discriminating between background, core and niche competencs of an organization, while at the same time emphasizing their interdependencies. Second, in this context, one is always referring to organizational competencs, bearing in mind that the 'competence of company *x* in technology *y*' is something different from 'the ensemble of the individual skills in technology *y* of all the members of company *x*'.

That said, it is useful to distinguish between what we shall call technological and organizational competencs (similar distinctions are made in Dosi and Teece 1998; Coriat and Weinstein 2002). The two types of competencs are clearly overlapping in the empirical world. The distinction, however, rests in that technological competencs refer to shared pieces of scientific and technological knowledge concerning essentially 'the structure of the (physical) world' and routines concerning 'how to handle it'.

Conversely, we shall call organizational competencs those shared pieces of knowledge and routines concerning the governance of coordination and social interactions within the organization and with outside entities (customers, suppliers and so on), in other words, 'how to handle people'.

Thus, while it is straightforward that technological competency requires some organizational arrangements in order to be put to work, it is also true that fundamentally similar bodies of technological knowledge might be nested in and exploited by diverse organizational arrangements and coordination modes.

Indeed, a number of works have addressed (a) the exploration of the patterns in such diversities (even when strictly holding knowledge bases constant); (b) the impact of organizational competency upon corporate performances; (c) the role of organizational innovations; and d) the co-evolutionary dynamics between organizational and technological competencies.[4]

Individual Skills and Collective Competencs/Capabilities

Fundamental questions in the interpretation of the nature of organizational competencs/capabilities concern, as already mentioned, first, the loci where they reside, and, second, the extent to which they are additive in the skills and knowledge of organizational members.

In order to highlight some major underlying issues, let us present two alternative views. The first archetype, which we shall call the modular view, holds that 'organizational knowledge' is primarily a shorthand for the knowledge of the individuals belonging to the organization. By the same token, in this perspective, strong warnings come — as H. Simon puts it — against 'reifying the organization and talking about it as "knowing" something or "learning" something. [Rather], it is usually important to specify where in the organization particular knowledge is stored and who has learned it' (Simon 1991: 126).

Here, one is, of course, far from denying the importance of individual skills as constituents of the broader organizational competencs/capabilities. However, largely in tune with an alternative collective view of organizational knowledge, let us suggest that competencs have a dimension that is not easily reducible to an organization's individual members: 'it is firms, not people that work in firms, that know how to make gasoline, automobiles and computers' (Winter 1982). Furthermore, dynamically, organizational learning is a social phenomenon and cannot be reduced to the individual learning processes of the members of the organization (more in Marengo 1996).

Let us suggest, here, that organizational knowledge is not only incorporated into the minds of organizational members, but also into (a) a set of routines, other organizational practices and shared representations; and (b) a set of material artefacts that shape intra-organizational relations and individual behaviours (a germane discussion is found in Cohen et al. 1996).

Organizational Problem solving and Task Complexity

Let us consider again, as a sort of extreme reference point, the Taylorist/Fordist organizational archetype, whereby the decomposition of the overall design/production/distribution problem is, so to speak, solved 'top-down' and 'once-and-for-all', involving a first 'cut' of broad sub-problems (for example, production) attributed to the various divisions and a much finer decomposition at the operational level into minute tasks to be tackled in a highly routine way.

At the opposite extreme, however, a much less studied archetype is the one whereby organizational design problems cannot be solved once-and-for-all, and, in a related way, the distribution of problem-solving knowledge is bound to be much more fluid.

Indeed, Dosi et al. (2003) consider six ideal types of organizational forms, ranging from the pure functional form, with separated functional departments, to the project-based form, where the entire organization is dedicated to one or more complex projects and where there are no clear-cut functional boundaries.

Within such a taxonomy, they present an analysis of the co-evolution of problem-solving knowledge and organizational design in complex, non-routine and non-stable tasks. In particular, they focus on the so-called *complex product systems* (CoPs), broadly including complex capital goods. These CoPs consist of many interconnected and customized elements, which sometimes exhibit emergent properties during their production, that is, unpredictable properties that reveal themselves only at the stage of system engineering and integration, or later during their actual use.

CoPs include relatively traditional goods, such as railway engines, but also mobile communication systems, military systems, corporate information technology networks, aircrafts, air traffic control systems, tailored software packages and many others. Their complexity is also due to the number of components and inputs required, the presence of many design choices, the degree of customization and the breadth and depth of knowledge involved in design and production.

The project-based form, it is argued, seems to be well suited to the complexity of the problem and the fuzzy decomposition tasks characteristic of CoPs. A good illustration of how the nature of technical/organizational problems and the related knowledge bases shape organizational arrangements stems from the comparison of the role of the project manager under 'project-based' form, on the one hand, and under traditional 'functional' patterns of division of labour, on the other. In the former mode, 'decompositions' tend to be rather loose and 'credit assignments'/incentive schemes rather ill-defined. This, however, demands a core role for the project manager, who represents the main channel of communication and is pivotal in the coordination and integration of specialist functions and would-be solutions to sub-problems. Indeed, the evidence discussed in Dosi et al. (2002) suggests that the overall project management be undertaken by distinct firms which act as *system integrators* (see Brusoni et al. 2001).

At the other end of the spectrum are integrated organizations that may well produce complex products, but which do so under rather precisely defined decompositions, lines of command and incentive schemes (think of the 'classic' Fordist automobile industry). Under these circumstances 'project management' is nothing but one of the many functions within the firm.[5]

The Horizontal and Vertical Boundaries of the Firm

Another promising domain to which the 'capability' view can be fruitfully applied concerns the proximate 'boundaries' of the firm. It is well known that almost all large firms and a good deal of small ones are multi-product, both in a 'vertical' sense — that is, firms produce some of their own inputs — and in a 'horizontal' sense — meaning firms produce more than one output. Moreover, as Rumelt (1974, 1982) has shown, after World War II, at least in the United States, the largest corporations increasingly diversified their production. Between 1949 and 1974 the proportion of the largest 500 industrial firms that were substantially diversified more than doubled, rising from 30% to 63% (Rumelt 1982). Using a sample of 100 firms and the definition of categories of firms ranging from single business to unrelated business (based on Rumelt 1974), Rumelt observes a steady decline in the number of single-product firms and rapid growth in diversified ones. A similar pattern is described by Montgomery (1994) for the period 1985–1992. She also cites evidence about other countries (Japan and the UK) that are in line with this conclusion.

There are, of course, different theoretical candidates for the explanation of such empirical patterns, including those broadly deriving from 'agency' theories (see the discussion in Holmstrom and Roberts 1998); transaction cost considerations, limited to *vertical* integration (Williamson 1975, 1985, 1999; Holmstrom and Roberts 1998); and the (partly overlapping) 'resource' and 'capabilities' views. Here, let us focus on the achievement of the latter (see Montgomery 1994; Rumelt 1982; Markides and Williamson 1994; Bettis 1981; Palepu 1985; Zollo and Reuer 2001; Teece et al. 1994).

In particular, Teece et al. (1994) stress three fundamental characteristics of modern corporations, namely: (a) their multi-product scope; (b) the non-random distribution of their product portfolios conditional on their principal activities; and (c) the stability in the composition of their portfolios over time.

The work suggests that firms are 'coherent' in their portfolios in so far as they diversify by adding activities which share some market or technological characteristics with the existing ones — in other words, they build on the capabilities that they already have.

Teece et al.(1994) make use of two measures of 'coherence'. The first one indicates the degree to which an activity *i* is related to all the other activities of the firm. Relatedness is defined by the comparison between the observed number of corporations that are active in any combination of industries and the number of corporations that one would expect under the hypothesis that diversification is random. The second measure of coherence refers to the strength of association between activity *i* and its closest neighbours.

The empirical analysis, based on the 1987 TRINET database, largely corroborates the notion of 'coherent diversification'. The suggested interpretation is that the boundaries of the firm, and thus the predicted degrees of diversification and coherence, can be understood in terms of characteristics of (a) learning, (b) path dependencies, (c) technological opportunities, (d) selection environments, and (e) firms' endowments of complementary assets (p. 274). Thus, for example, rapid learning, rich technological opportunities and tight path dependencies will correspond to (almost) single-product, fast-growing, firms. Conversely, within a context of rapid learning, converging technological trajectories and tight selection, one can expect to see coherent diversifiers. Moreover, the interpretation suggests that unrelated diversification is likely to be viable only under conditions of weak market selection.

Chang (1996) gives a complementary analysis by studying both diversification and divestment decisions through examining the entry–exit patterns triggered by 'satisfying' criteria of performance and driven by the human resource profiles embodied by the different organizations. The evidence, from the TRINET and COMPUSTAT databases, with some caveats, supports the behavioural, knowledge-driven model of diversification.

So far we have discussed the capability-centred views with an emphasis on the determinants of the *horizontal* boundaries of the firm. Let us now focus on the *vertical* ones.

A well-known interpretation of the vertical boundaries of the firm is given in terms of the relative costs of governing market-mediated as opposed to hierarchically governed transactions (Williamson 1975, 1985, 1999). However, while not denying the importance of transaction cost considerations, a few studies have begun to explore resource/capability-based explanations of the choices between market and other forms of governance of input/output flows (see, among others,

Argyres 1996; Jacobides 2000; Jacobides and Hitts 2001; Delmas 1999). The central conjecture here — as well as in the earlier discussion of the governance of CoPs — is that the degrees of vertical integration and the selection of governance forms are shaped by the nature and distribution of problem-solving knowledge. Consider, for example, Delmas's study (1999) on the waste industry, characterized by high technological and regulatory uncertainty. Her evidence corroborates the idea that a major determinant of the vertical boundaries of the firm rests on the distribution of capabilities across segments of activities and across firms: 'firms will rely on alliances for tacit technologies in highly uncertain environments. Although incurring high transaction costs, collaborations are perceived as possessing the flexibility and the adaptability necessary to build competencs and to gain a competitive advantage' (Delmas 1999: 664).

Technology and Organization

Following the foregoing interpretation, mapping knowledge dynamics into organizational and industrial dynamics has become a priority research task. For the sake of illustration, consider the response of an industry to the appearance of a technology that provides a new way of performing functions of central importance to the industry's activities. Such episodes can be identified on a very large scale — such as the replacement of mechanical and electro-mechanical devices by electronic devices in a wide range of types of equipment — and on a quite smaller scale — such as the successive generations of the displacement of larger disk drives by smaller ones in computers (Christensen and Rosenblom 1995; Christensen and Bower 1996; Christensen 1997; Rosenblom 2000).

A common pattern in such episodes is that the leading firms in an industry often seem to react slowly to the challenge, with the result that leadership passes to some of the pioneers of the new technology. Sometimes a previously leading firm even fails to survive or has a very close call.

One problem is to understand why this happens. Another problem is to understand why it does not happen: the pattern described is not universal, and the intuitive expectation that a 'bigger' technological change ought to make it more likely is not always confirmed. Among a number of explanations that are complementary and, hence, difficult to untangle, considerations related to the nature of the adjustment of firms' capabilities needed to cope with the challenge have received increasing attention. (For different perspectives, see Tushman and Anderson 1986; Henderson and Clark 1990; Pavitt 1999).

Certainly, technology-specific modes of knowledge accumulation are likely to shape and constrain the ways 'particular firms do particular things'. In a related way, the 'combinatorics' among different competencs are likely to be product-specific and possibly sector-specific.[6]

An important dimension concerns the nature of technological opportunities. Are they cumulative, meaning that new knowledge builds upon already existing industry capabilities, or are they, on the contrary, characterized by discontinuities in the knowledge base? In the former case, large incumbent firms are better placed to exploit technological opportunities.

Determinants of Corporate Performances

Some of the most robust, stylized facts emerging from industry studies are that firms persistently differ, even within the same lines of activities, in their innovativeness, productivity and profitability.

Concerning the patterns of innovation, plenty of evidence confirms (a) systematic differences in the propensity to introduce and adopt innovation (Dosi 1988; Freeman and Soete 1997; Freeman 1994). Moreover, (b) probabilities of success and failures in innovative activities appear to be influenced by underlying differences in organizational arrangements and behaviours, such as circumstantial evidence of different 'capabilities'. (The SAPPHO project from the 1970s is a pioneering study, described in Freeman and Soete (1997), which attempts to identify systematic differences between successful and failing innovators.)

With regards to various indicators of efficiency (*in primis*, labour productivity), as Jensen and McGuckin (1997) note, an increasing number of studies highlights a pervasive heterogeneity in firms' and plants' characteristics, both cross-sectionally and over time.[7]

The crucial question here is whether one can identify robust relations between (non-tautological) proxies of capabilities, on the one hand, and the various dimensions of performances, on the other.

We have no difficulty in admitting that the quest for the foregoing proxies is far from over. Nevertheless, in addition to counts of discrete innovations and patents (that is, measures of innovative output), researchers are painstakingly identifying an increasing number of (often sector-specific) proxies for capabilities: see, for example, Baldwin and Johnson (1995), Argote and Darr (2000), Pisano (2000) and Henderson and Cockburn (2000).

All in all, the ultimate test of validity for any capability theory of industrial performances resides in its capability to account for inter-firm differences in profitability and growth patterns.

Consider, first, the relationship between innovativeness and profitability. In this vein, Geroski et al. (1993), in the case of a sample of large UK firms, identify a positive relationship between innovativeness and profitability. Next, they ask whether the correlation reflects transitory (innovation-specific) effects or, conversely, long-term differences between innovating and non-innovating firms. The conclusion is that *both* phenomena are present. In particular, we would argue that permanent differences reflect more general underlying differences in corporate capabilities. Furthermore, the analysis shows that profit margins of innovating firms seem to be less sensitive to cyclical downturns than those of non-innovating firms.

Cefis (1999) uses data on UK firms from the period 1978–1991 and investigates the persistence in firms' profits as a function of the persistence in innovation (patent applications). First, the separate analysis of the distribution of profit and innovation shows a significant persistence in both variables. Second, a similar pattern emerges from the analysis of the joint distributions of profits and innovations: 'firms which are systematic innovators and earn profits above the average have a high probability to keep innovating and earning profits above the average, as well as firms which are occasional innovators and earn profit below the average have a high probability to remain in the initial situation' (Cefis 1999: 4). It is also worth noting that changes in the relative position of a firm with respect to the average profitability are not correlated with the relative position in the innovation dimension in the short run, but are correlated with it in the long run.

The evidence on the relationships between capabilities and corporate growth is much more controversial. On the pessimistic side, Geroski (2000) concludes his discussion of the statistical evidence by saying that 'corporate growth rates ... differ between firms in temporary and unpredictable ways, and it is hard to reconcile the inimitability and durability of organizational capabilities with these data' (2000: 181). Since that survey, however, some investigations have detected much more structure in the growth process. In particular, the findings of Bottazzi et al. (2001), in the case of the international pharmaceutical industry, include a significant autocorrelation in growth dynamics and a 'fat-tailed' distribution of growth shocks, which may correspond quantitatively to the arrival of major innovations.[8]

As we see it, this remains indeed a priority area of research and boils down to the two related questions: (1) what are the statistical properties of the growth profiles of different firms in the markets where they compete with each other (that is, by line of business); and (2) what are the statistical properties of the growth profiles of whole corporate entities, when, in both cases, properly conditioning for 'capabilities' by proxies?

Conclusion: Some Implications for Strategic Management

So far, we have mentioned some of the interpretative implications of a 'knowledge-centred' theory of the firm and the related empirical predictions. What, however, are the implications of such a theory for strategic management? That is, if the theory holds, what does it predict managers do? Moreover, which variables and processes should they look at in order to improve organizational performance? Let us conclude with some remarks on these issues.

Indeed, an important theme in the recent strategy literature is the idea that the most distinctive role of business firms, in general, and of strategic management, in particular, is the way they bring knowledge to bear on productive effort. This and related ideas have been discussed under the heading of the 'knowledge-based' theory of the firm (Grant 1996; Kogut and Zander 1992; Dosi and Marengo 1994). As with the notion of resources, this discussion converges with the capabilities discussion, as knowledge is conceived as know-how embedded in the organization's activities, as opposed to passive, library-like stocks that are stored in the heads of participants.[9]

In this perspective, as forcefully argued by Teece et al. (2000), strategic management has a key role in shaping:

(1) *organizational processes*, by the establishment of specific organizational structures and, equally important, by introducing and by *breaking* particular organizational routines (cf. Rumelt 1995);

(2) the *position* of the firm (broadly defined to cover their specific assets, their locations along the value chain and their relationship with suppliers and customers);

(3) *paths*, that is, the patterns of change in the former two sets of characteristics.

These activities are indeed at the core of what Teece et al. (2000) call the *dynamic capabilities* of the firm. Moreover, managerial tasks involve:

(4) presiding over the *replication* within the organization of well-performing bundles of routines (Szulanski 2000; Winter 2003);

(5) defining the *cognitive frames* and the *aspiration levels* of the organization (this includes the shared 'representations' and perceived 'fitness landscapes' discussed earlier);[10]

(6) mastering the persistent and tricky dilemmas between *exploitation* and *exploration*, or as March (1991) puts it, between the improvement of what the organization 'is already good at', on the one hand, and the search for more radical innovative opportunities, on the other.

These tasks, in turn, involve the rethinking of traditional management tools — such as team staffing and mobility, incentive policies and information storage and retrieval — and conceptualizing them as tools for setting the parameters of intra-firm exploitation/exploration dynamics (Warglien 1999).

In such a context, the management of a *variety of exploration trajectories* implies a view of an organization as an 'artificial ecology' (Levinthal 2000) wherein managers look somewhat like contemporary bioengineers trying to 'fine tune' ex ante the discovery of new traits/biochemical properties, and so on, and to test and select ex post among them (indeed, the analogy would be chilling were one to extrapolate the rate of managerial success to the biological domain!).

It is important to notice that this perspective on organization, organizational learning and their management clearly shifts the focus of analysis from 'clever strategizing' against market rivals to the process of problem-solving, organizational governance and, dynamically, capability-enhancing strategies (Tidd et al. 1997 is an insightful and thorough management text in this perspective). It also sets the relationship between capabilities and (managerial) decision making in a different light.

As a useful contrast, notice how in economics and other disciplines that employ the theoretical tools of decision theory, key assumptions about skills and capabilities often remain implicit. Consider, for example, the simple and basic tool called the 'pay-off matrix': an array with choice alternatives on one side, 'states of the world' (or opponent choices) on the other, and the outcome utility values in the cells. Typically, the choices are actions or entail actions. While in some cases the choices listed are everyday actions that are familiar and perhaps available to the typical reader of the analysis (for example, 'carry an umbrella'), in other cases they emphatically are not (such as, 'conduct seismic tests' or 'shut down nuclear reactor').

In these latter cases, the availability of the actions is apparently presumed to be inherent in the identity of the decision maker, and this presumption goes unnoticed. Arguably, the development of the menu of future choices would be a candidate for the first exercise introducing the topic of sequential decision analysis, but, in fact, the question of where the menu comes from is generally ignored.

In addition, choices available to the decision maker are, in decision theory, feasible by definition: any uncertainty attached to the consequences of *trying* to take specific action (the sort of choice that is, in fact, readily available) is subsumed in the uncertainty attached to states of the world. This is, in principle, an inconsequential formal convention, but, in practice, significant questions of feasibility tend to get swept under the rug in the process of abstracting an analysable problem from a real situation. The rich sequences of unfolding events that often follow a failed attempt — sequences that may involve wholly unanticipated outcomes and learning, among other things — could be represented in a sufficiently elaborate decision-theoretic formalism, but generally are not.

These habits of decision-theoretic thought contribute to the obscurity in which capabilities issues have long resided in economic analysis. The entries in the menu of choices are specified and promptly taken for granted, one situation at a time, even when choices involve complex actions. Little is seen of the costly and protracted learning process that places alternatives on the menu. The consequences for future menus of the choices made today — for example, the likely strengthening of the capabilities that are exercised and the likely withering of those that are not — generally are abstracted away. These practices may well represent largely tacit, sound judgment about the domain in which decision theory is useful. They nevertheless leave a major gap in the understanding of behaviour, a gap best filled, perhaps, by the use of other tools.

Just as the market system accomplishes remarkable feats of coordination without the aid of a central plan, organizational learning produces the coordinated performances of organizational capabilities without the aid of a recipe — or, alternatively, without the aid of a comprehensive plan, optimized or not. According to the mainstream tradition in economics, economic actors do not have to understand the price system for it to work. Similarly, an organization produces coordinated activity without anyone knowing how it works, even though participants may be well aware of managerial intentions to achieve coordination. There are far more of these details than any amount of observation could possibly uncover or any imaginable set of manuals could ever record. Tentative choices that are actually incompatible with or substantially subversive to the overall performance get rooted out in the course of learning, not in response to the imperative 'follow the recipe', but in response to 'try something different!' Choices compatible with the overall performance are allowed to stabilize and become habitual, without either the choices or the habits necessarily being recognized as such along the way. Finally, in a well-established capability, the activity in progress is its own best (and only) operating manual.

In all that, one role of strategic management is painstakingly to steer the process at the level discussed above, while both recognizing the weight of the path dependencies in knowledge and organizational practices inherited from the past and trying to detect the 'windows of opportunity' ahead.

Certainly, there is no general recipe for managerial success (and there *cannot* be). Simply consider the foregoing remarks as pointing towards *managerial heuristics* and *diagnostic tools*, which, in our view, are at the core of the dynamic capabilities of business organizations.

Notes

We acknowledge financial support from the European Commission 6th FP(Contract CIT3-CT-2005-513396), Project: DIME (Dynamics of Institutions and Markets in Europe).

Comments by the participants at the Saint-Gobain Centre for Economic Studies Conference on 'Organizational innovation within firms' (Paris, 7–8 November 2002), and, in particular, by Masahiko Aoki, Jean-Luis Beffa, Xavier Ragot and Keith Pavitt, are gratefully acknowledged.
We would like to dedicate this work to the memory of our friend and mentor, Keith Pavitt, whom we met for the last time at that conference.
This work draws upon Dosi et al. (2000), the introduction to Dosi et al.(2000) and Dosi et al. (2003).

1   This section largely builds on the introduction to Dosi et al.(2000).
2   For a review of the literature on organizational routines, see Becker (2004); a few contributions to the analysis of routines can be found in the Special Section on this topic in *Industrial and Corporate Change* 14/5, 2005.
3   With regard to the contribution of Penrose's work to the resource-based view of strategic management, see Kor and Mahoney (2004) and Pitelis (2002).
    The capability/competency-based view of the firm overlaps greatly with the resource-based view: see Barney (1991, 2001); a few of the contributions in Montgomery (1995), and Foss and Mahnke (2000). Part of the difference rests in the terminology. However, terminology as such is not void of importance: a 'resource-centred' language risks conveying a 'reified' view of capabilities as 'object-like' entities, while — we hope — the explicit capability/competency language makes it easier to conserve the underlying process story. Capabilities are not 'things' but 'ways of doing', collective fuzzy algorithms, properties of collective knowledge essentially revealed through its implementation.

    A critique of Barney's (1991) version of the resource-based view and a comparison with the evolutionary (and capability/competency-based) approach are provided by Bromiley and Fleming (2002).

    For an inquiry into the behavioural roots of the two approaches, see also Pierce et al. (2002) and Rumelt (1995).
4   See, for example, Coriat (2000) and Florida and Kenney (2000).
5   In the literature, some exploratory attempts have been made to identify 'bottom-up' the seemingly viable combinatorics among multiple, interrelated organizational traits: on automobile manufacturing, see McCarthy et al. (1997).
6   The paper by Padgett et al. (2003) contributes to the analysis of the co-evolution of products and firms, that is, how a firm's skills are influenced by the flow of products. Using a chemistry analogy, the authors conceive of the firm as an organism that contains products, which, like chemicals, are transformed by skills, which, like reactions, are rules that transform products into other products. Trade, like food, allows for the passage of transformed products among firms. The composition of a firm's skills evolves through learning by doing; thus, the more a skill is used, the more it is reinforced. The question the paper seeks to answer is how a coherent and self-organized transformation network can emerge from randomly distributed skills across firms. The models developed are based on the chemistry concept of hyper-cycles.
7   See, among others, Rumelt 1991; Davis et al. 1996; Baldwin 1995; Haltiwanger 2000; Nelson 1991; Dosi 1988; Bartelsman and Doms 2000; Foster et al. 2001; Noda and Collis 2001.
8   The latter 'fat-tailedness' property is confirmed also by different pieces of evidence from the Italian industry: the autocorrelation in growth dynamics is not, however (Bottazzi et al. 2002; Bottazzi and Secchi 2003.).
9   For a broader discussion of the recent emphasis on capabilities in the strategic management literature, see Rumelt et al. (1991), Teece et al. (1997) and Stalk et al. (1992). The discussion in Robert Grant's excellent textbook illustrates the appearance of these ideas in the business school curriculum (Grant 1996, Ch 5).
10 On organizational aspiration levels, see Massini et al. (2002).

1180   Organization Studies 29(08&09)

References

Argote, L., and E. Darr
2000 'Repositories of knowledge in
        franchise organizations' in G. Dosi,
        R. R. Nelson and S. G. Winter (eds).
        *The nature and dynamics of
        organizational capabilities.*
        Oxford: Oxford University
        Press.

Argyres, N. S.
1996 'Evidence on the role of firm
        capabilities in vertical integration
        decisions'. *Strategic Management
        Journal* 17/2: 129–150.

Baldwin, J. R.
1995 *The dynamics of industrial
        competition.* Cambridge: Cambridge
        University Press.

Baldwin, J. R., and J. Johnson
1995 'Business strategies in innovative
        and non-innovative firms in Canada',
        Analytical Studies Branch
        Research Paper, No. 73,
        Ottawa: Statistics Canada.

Barney, J. B.
1991 'Firm resources and sustained
        competitive advantage'. *Journal
        of Management* 17: 99–120.

Barney, J. B.
2001 'Is the resource-based "view" a
        useful perspective for strategic
        management research? Yes'.
        Academy of Management Review
        26: 41–46.

Bartelsman, E. J., and M. Doms
2000 'Understanding productivity: Lessons
        from longitudinal microdata'. *Journal
        of Economic Literature*
        38/3: 569–594.

Becker, M.
2004 'Organizational routines: A review of
        the literature'. *Industrial and
        Corporate Change* 13/4: 643–678.

Bettis, R. A.
1981 'Performance differences in related
        and unrelated diversified firms'.
        Strategic Management Journal
        2/4: 379–393.

Bottazzi, G., and A. Secchi
2003 'A stochastic model of firm growth'.
        Physica A, 324: 213–219.

Bottazzi, G., E. Cefis, and G. Dosi
2002 'Corporate growth and industrial
        structures: Some evidence from the
        Italian manufacturing industry'.
        Industrial and Corporate Change
        11: 705–723.

Bottazzi, G., G. Dosi, M. Lippi, F. Pammolli,
and M. Riccaboni
2001 'Innovation and corporate growth in
        the evolution of the drug industry'.
        *International Journal of Industrial
        Organization* 19/7: 1161–1187.

Bromiley, P., and L. Fleming
2002 'The resource-based view of strategy:
        A behaviorist critique' in *The
        economics of choice, change and
        organization: Essays in memory of
        Richard M. Cyert.* M. Augier and
        J. G. March (eds). Cheltenham, UK,
        and Northampton, MA: Edward
        Elgar.

Brusoni, S., A. Prencipe, and K. Pavitt
2001 'Knowledge specialization and the
        boundaries of the firm: Why firms
        know more than they make?'
        Administrative Science Quarterly
        46: 597–621.

Castanias, R. P., and C. E. Helfat
1991 'Managerial resources and rents'.
        Journal of Management 17:
        155–171.

Cefis, E.
1999 'Persistence in profitability and in
        innovative activities'. *Quaderni del
        dipartimento di Scienze Economiche,*
        N.6. University of Bergamo, Italy.

Chang, S. J.
1996 'An evolutionary perspective on
        diversification and corporate
        restructuring. entry, exit, and
        economic performance during
        1981–1989'. *Strategic Management
        Journal* 17/8: 587–611.

Christensen, C. M.
1997 *The innovator's dilemma: When new
        technologies cause great firms to fail.*
        Boston, MA.: Harvard Business
        School Press.

Christensen, C. M., and J. L. Bower
1996 'Customer power, strategic
        investment and the failure of leading
        firms'. *Strategic Management
        Journal* 17: 197–218.

Christensen, C. M., and R. Rosenblom
1995 'Explaining the attacker's advantage:
        Technological paradigms,
        organizational dynamics, and the
        value network'. *Research Policy*
        23: 233–257.

Cohen, M., R. Burkhart, G. Dosi, M. Egidi,
L. Marengo, M. Warglien, and S. Winter
1996 'Routines and other recurring action

patterns of organizations:
Contemporary research issue'.
Industrial and Corporate Change
5/3: 653–699.

Coriat, B.
2000 'Organisational innovation in
European firms: A critical
overview of the survey evidence'.
Sant'Anna School of Advanced
Studies LEM, Pisa, Italy,
Dynacom working paper
series.

Coriat, B., and G. Dosi
1998 'Learning how to govern and learning
how to solve problems: On the co-
evolution of competences, conflicts
and organizational routines' in *The
dynamic firm*. A. Chandler, P.
Hagström, and Ö. Sölvell (eds).
Oxford/New York: Oxford University
Press.

Coriat, B., and O. Weinstein
2002 'Organization and institution in the
generation of innovations'. *Research
Policy* 31/2: 273–290.

Davis, S. J., J. C. Haltiwanger, and S. Schuh
1996 *Job creation and destruction*.
Cambridge, MA: MIT Press.

Delmas, M.
1999 'Exposing strategic assets to create
new competencs: The case of
technological acquisition in the
waste management industry in
Europe and North America'.
Industrial and Corporate Change
8: 635–671.

Dierickx, I., and K. Cool
1989 'Asset stock accumulation and
sustainability of competitive
advantage'. *Management Science*
35: 1504–1511.

Dosi, G.
1988 'Source, procedures and
microeconomic effects of
innovation'. *Journal of
Economic Literature*
26: 1120–1171.

Dosi, G., and L. Marengo
1994 'Some elements of an evolutionary
theory of organizational
competences' in *Evolutionary
concepts in contemporary economics*.
R. W. England, (ed.). Michigan
University Press,

Dosi, G., and D. J. Teece
1998 'Organizational competences and the

boundaries of the firms' in *Markets
and organizations*. R. Arena and C.
Longhi (eds). Berlin/Heidelberg,
New York: Springer-Verlag.

Dosi, G., B. Coriat, and K. Pavitt
2000 'Competence, capabilities and
corporate performances'. Sant'Anna
School of Advanced Studies, LEM,
Pisa, Italy, Dynacom working paper
series.

Dosi, G., M. Hobday, and L. Marengo
2003 'Problem-solving behaviors,
organizational forms and the
complexity of tasks' in *The
Blackwell/Strategic Management
Society handbook of organizational
capabilities: Emergence, development
and change*. C. E. Helfat (ed.).
Oxford: Blackwell.

Dosi, G., D. Levinthal, and L. Marengo
2003 'Bridging contested terrain. Linking
incentive-based and learning
perspectives on organizational
evolution'. *Industrial and Corporate
Change*, vol. 12, 2003, 413–436.

Dosi, G., R. Nelson, and S. G. Winter, (eds)
2000 *The nature and dynamic of
organizational capabilities*.
Oxford/New York: Oxford University
Press.

Dosi, G., M. Hobday, L. Marengo, and
A. Principe
2002 'The economics of system
integrators: Toward an evolutionary
approach', Sant'Anna School of
Advanced Studies, Pisa, Italy, LEM
Working Papers.

Florida, R., and M. Kenney
2000 'Transfer and replication of
organizational capabilities' in *The
nature and dynamic of organizational
capabilities*. G. Dosi, R. Nelson and
S. G. Winter (eds)' Oxford/New York:
Oxford University Press.

Foss, N., and V. Mahnke, (eds)
2000 *Competence, governance and
entrepreneurship*. Oxford: Oxford
University Press.

Foster, L., J. C. Haltiwanger, and C. J.
Krizan
2001 'Aggregate productivity growth:
Lessons from microeconomics
evidence' in *New developments in
productivity analysis*. C. R. Hulten,
E. Dean and M. J. Harper (eds).
Chicago, Ill.: University of Chicago
Press.

(continued overleaf)

Fransman, M.
1994a 'Information, knowledge, vision and theory of the firm'. *Industrial and Corporate Change*, 3/3: 713–758.

Fransman, Martin
1994b 'Economics and innovation: The knowledge-based approach to Japanese firms and the relevance of economic thought' in *Economics of technology*. O. Granstrand (ed.). Elsevier: Amsterdam.

Freeman, C.
1994 'Technological revolutions and catching-up: ICT and the NICs' in *The dynamics of technology, trade and growth*. J. Fagerberg, B. Verspagen and N. Von Tunzelman (eds). Cheltenham: Edward Elgar.

Freeman, C., and L. Soete
1997 *The economics of industrial innovation*, 3rd edn. London: Pinter.

Geroski, P. A.
2000 'The growth of firms in theory and practice' in *Competence, governance and entrepreneurship*. N. Foss and V. Mahnke (eds). Oxford: Oxford University Press.

Geroski, P., S. Machin, and J. van Reenen
1993 'The profitability of innovating firms'. *RAND Journal of Economics* 24/2: 198–211.

Grant, R. M.
1996 'Toward a knowledge-based theory of the firm'. *Strategic Management Journal* 17 (Winter special issue): 109–122.

Haltiwanger, J. C.
2000 'Aggregate growth: What we have learned from microeconomic evidence'. OECD Economic Department Working Paper No. 267.

Henderson, R., and K. Clark
1990 'Architectural innovation: The reconfiguration of existing product technologies and the failure of established firms'. *Administrative Science Quarterly* 35: 9–30.

Henderson, R., and I. Cockburn
2000 'Measuring competence? Exploring firm effect in drug discovery' in *The nature and dynamics of organizational capabilities*. G. Dosi, R. Nelson and S. G. Winter (eds). Oxford/New York: Oxford University Press.

Holstrom, B., and J. Roberts
1998 'The boundaries of the firm revisited'. *Journal of Economic Perspectives* 12/4: 73–94.

Jacobides, M. G.
2000 'Capabilities, transaction costs and limits to growth: A formal model of scope and profitability in mortgage banking'. Working Paper, Wharton Financial Institutions Center, The Wharton School.

Jacobides, M. G., and L. M. Hitt
2001 *Vertical scope revised: Transaction costs vs capabilities and profit opportunities in mortgage banking*. Working Paper, Wharton Financial Institutions Center, The Wharton School.

Jensen, J. B., and R. H. McGuckin
1997 'Firm performance and evolution: Empirical regularities in the US microdata'. *Industrial and Corporate Change* 6/1: 25–47.

Kogut, B., and U. Zander
1992 'Knowledge of the firm, combinative capabilities, and the replication of technology'. *Organization Science* 3: 383–397.

Kor, Y., and J. Mahoney
2004 'Edith Penrose's (1959) contribution to the resource-based view of strategic management'. *Journal of Management Studies* 41/1: 183–191.

Levinthal, D.
2000 'Organizational capabilities in complex worlds' in *The nature and dynamics of organizational capabilities*. G. Dosi, R. Nelson and S. G. Winter (eds). Oxford/New York: Oxford University Press.

McCarthy, I., M. Leseure, K. Ridgeway, and N. Fielles
1997 'Building a manufacturing cladogram'. *International Journal of Technology Management* 13: 2269–2296.

March, J. G.
1991 'Exploration and exploitation in organizational learning'. *Organization Science* 2: 71–87.

Marengo, L.
1996 'Structure, competence and learning in an adaptive model of the firm', in *Organization and strategy in the evolution of the enterprise*. G. Dosi and F. Malerba (eds). London: Macmillan.

Markides, C. C., and P. J. Williamson
1994   'Related diversification, core
       competencs and corporate
       performance'. *Strategic Management
       Journal* 15: 149–165.

Massini S., A. Lewin, T. Numagami, and
A. M. Pettigrew
2002   'The evolution of organizational
       routines among large western and
       Japanese firms'. *Research Policy*
       31/8–9: 1333–1348.

Montgomery, C. A.
1994   'Corporate diversification'. *The
       Journal of Economic Perspectives*
       8/3: 163–178.

Montgomery, C. A., (ed.)
1995   *Resource-based and evolutionary
       theories of the firm: Towards a
       synthesis.* Boston: Kluwer Academic
       Publishers.

Nelson, R. R.
1991   'Why do firms differ, and how does it
       matter?' *Strategic Management
       Journal* 12: 61–74.

Nelson, R. R., and S. G. Winter
1982   *An evolutionary theory of economic
       change.* Cambridge, MA.: Harvard
       University Press.

Noda, T., and D. J. Collis
2001   'The evolution of intraindustry firm
       heterogeneity: Insights from a
       process study'. *Academy of
       Management Journal* 44/4: 897–925.

Padgett, J. F., L. Doowan, and N. Collier
2003   'Economic production as chemistry'.
       Industrial and Corporate Change
       12/4: 843–877.

Palepu, K.
1985   'Diversification strategy,
       profit performance and the entropy
       measure'. *Strategic
       Management Journal*
       6/3: 239–255.

Patel, P., and K. Pavitt
2000   'How technological competencs
       help define the core of the firm' in
       *The nature and dynamic of
       organizational capabilities.* G. Dosi,
       R. Nelson and S. G. Winter (eds).
       Oxford/New York: Oxford University
       Press.

Pavitt, K.
1999   *Technology, management and systems
       of innovation.* Cheltenham: Edward
       Elgar.

Penrose, E.
1959   *The theory of the growth of the firm.*
       New York: Wiley.

Pierce, J. L., S. Boerner, and D. J. Teece
2002   'Dynamic capabilities, competence
       and the behavioral theory of the
       firm' in *The economics of choice,
       change and organization:
       Essays in memory of Richard
       M. Cyert.* M. Augier and J.G.
       March (eds). Cheltenham:
       Elgar.

Pisano, G. P.
2000   'In search of dynamic capabilities' in
       *The nature and dynamic of
       organizational capabilities.* G. Dosi,
       R. Nelson and S. G. Winter (eds).
       Oxford/New York: Oxford University
       Press.

Pitelis, C. (ed.)
2002   *The growth of the firm: The legacy of
       Edith Penrose,* 1–15. New York:
       Oxford University Press.

Prahalad, C. K., and G. Hamel
1990   'The core competence of the
       corporation'. *Harvard Business
       Review,* May–June, 79–91.

Richardson, G. B.
1972   'The organization of industry'.
       Economic Journal 82: 883–896.
       Reprinted in G. B. Richardson (1998)
       *The economics of imperfect
       knowledge.* Cheltenham: Edward
       Elgar.

Rosenbloom, R. S.
2000   'Leadership, capabilities, and
       technological change: The
       transformation of NCR in the
       electronic era'. *Strategic
       Management Journal* 21: 1083–1103.

Rumelt, R. P.
1974   *Strategy, structure and economic
       performance.* Division of Research,
       Harvard Business School, Boston.

Rumelt, R. P.
1982   'Diversification strategy and
       profitability'. *Strategic Management
       Journal* 3: 359–369.

Rumelt, R. P.
1991   'How much does industry matter?'
       Strategic Management Journal
       12/3: 167–185.

Rumelt, R. P.
1995   'Inertia and transformation' in
       *Resource-based and evolutionary
       theories of the firm: Towards a*

(*continued overleaf*)

synthesis. C. A. Montgomery (ed.). Boston: Kluwer Academic Publishers.

Rumelt, R., D. Schendel, and D. Teece
1991   'Strategic management and economics'. *Strategic Management Journal* 12: 5–29.

Simon, H. A.
1991   'Bounded rationality and organization learning'. *Organization Science* 2: 125–134.

Stalk, G., P. Evans, and L. E. Shulman
1992   'Competing on capabilities: The new rules of corporate strategy'. *Harvard Business Review,* March–April, 57–69.

Szulanski, G.
2000   'The process of knowledge transfer: Adiachronic analysis of stickiness'. *Organizational Behavior and Human Decision Processes* 82/1: 9–27.

Teece, D. J., G. Pisano, and A. Shuen
1997   'Dynamic capabilities and strategic management'. *Strategic Management Journal* 18: 509–533. Revised version in *The nature and dynamic of organizational capabilities* (2000). G. Dosi, R. Nelson and S. G. Winter (eds). Oxford/New York: Oxford University Press.

Teece, D. J., G. Pisano, and A. Shuen
2000   'Dynamic capabilities and strategic management' in *The nature and dynamics of organizational capabilities*. G. Dosi, R. Nelson and S. G. Winter (eds). Oxford/New York: Oxford University Press.

Teece, D. J., R. Rumelt, G. Dosi, and S. Winter
1994   'Understanding corporate coherence. Theory and Evidence'. *Journal of Economic Behavior and Organization* 23: 1–30.

Tidd, J., J. Bessant, and K. Pavitt
1997   *Managing innovation.* New York: Wiley.

Tushman, M., and P. Anderson
1986   'Technological discontinuities and organization environments'. *Administrative Science Quarterly* 31: 439–465.

Warglien, M.
1999   'The evolution of competencs in a population of projects: A case study'. Sant'Anna School of Advanced Studies, LEM, Pisa, Italy, Dynacom working paper series.

Williamson, O. E.
1975   *Markets and hierarchies: Analysis and antitrust implications*. New York: Free Press.

Williamson, O. E.
1985   *Economic institutions of capitalism*. New York: The Free Press.

Williamson, O. E.
1999   'Strategy research: Governance and competence perspective'. *Strategic Management Journal* 20: 1087–1108; also in *Competence, governance and entrepreneurship* (2000). N. Foss and V. Mahnke (eds). Oxford: Oxford University Press.

Winter, S. G.
1982   'An essay on the theory of production' in *Economics and the world around it*. H. Hymans (ed.), 55–93. Ann Arbor, MI.: University of Michigan Press.

Winter, S. G.
2003   'Toward an evolutionary theory of production' in *Principles of evolutionary economics*. K. Dopfer (ed.). Cambridge: Cambridge University Press.

Zollo, M., and J. J. Reuer
2001   'Experience spillovers across corporate development activities'. Wharton School Center for Financial Institutions, University of Pennsylvania, Center for Financial Institutions Working Papers.

Giovanni Dosi   Giovanni Dosi (PhD, University of Sussex) is Professor of Economics at the Sant'Anna School of Advanced Studies in Pisa, where he also coordinates the Laboratory of Economics and Management (LEM). His major research areas include economics of innovation and technological change, industrial organization and industrial dynamics, theory of the firm and corporate governance, economic growth and development. He is Co-Director of the task forces 'Industrial Policy', and 'Intellectual Property Rights', within the Initiative for Policy Dialogue, founded and chaired by Joseph Stiglitz, at Columbia University (New York); editor for Continental Europe of Industrial and Corporate Change; and visiting professor at the University of Manchester (UK). He is author and editor of several works in the areas of economics of innovation, industrial economics, evolutionary theory and organizational studies. A selection of his works has been published in (2000) *Innovation, Organization and Economic Dynamics. Selected Essays*. Cheltenham: Edward Elgar.
Address: LEM, Scuola Superiore S. Anna, Piazza dei Martiri della Libertà 33, 56127 Pisa, Italy.
Email: g.dosi@sssup.it

Marco Faillo   Marco Faillo (PhD, Sant' Anna School Pisa) is Research Fellow at the Department of Economics of the University of Trento. His main research interests include economic theory of organizations and institutions, evolutionary theory of the firm and behavioural economics.
Address: Department of Economics, University of Trento, Via Inama 5, 38100 Trento, Italy.
Email: mfaillo@economia.unitn.it

Luigi Marengo   Luigi Marengo (PhD, University of Sussex) is Professor of Economics at the Laboratory of Economics and Management (LEM) of the Sant' Anna School of Advanced Studies in Pisa. He has published articles in organizational economics, evolutionary economics, decision theory and economics of technological change in, among the others, *Journal of Economic Behavior and Organization, Organization Science, Journal of Economic Dynamics and Control, Journal of Evolutionary Economics, Research Policy*.
Address: LEM, Scuola Superiore S. Anna, Piazza dei Martiri della Libertà 33, 56127 Pisa, Italy.
Email: l.marengo@sssup.it

[3]

ELSEVIER

Journal of Economic Behavior & Organization
Vol. 58 (2005) 303–326

JOURNAL OF
Economic Behavior
& Organization

www.elsevier.com/locate/econbase

Division of labor, organizational coordination and market mechanisms in collective problem-solving

Luigi Marengo [a,*], Giovanni Dosi [b,1]

[a] *DSGSS, Università di Teramo, Loc. Colleparco, 64100 Teramo, Italy*
[b] *Scuola Superiore S. Anna, P.za Martiri della Libertà 33, 56127 Pisa, Italy*

Received 16 March 2003; accepted 10 March 2004
Available online 25 August 2005

Abstract

This paper builds upon a view of economic organizations as problem-solving arrangements and presents a simple model of adaptive problem-solving driven by trial-and-error learning and collective selection. Institutional structures and, in particular, their degree of decentralization, determine which solutions are tried out and undergo selection. It is shown that if the design problem at hand is "complex" (in terms of interdependencies between the elements of the system), then a decentralized institutional structure is unlikely ever to generate optimal solutions and, therefore, no selection process can ever select them. We also show that nearly-decomposable structures have, in general, a selective advantage in terms of speed in reaching (good) locally optimal solutions.
© 2005 Elsevier B.V. All rights reserved.

JEL classification: C63; D21; D23; L22; O30

Keywords: Theory of the firm; Vertical and horizontal integration; Computational complexity

1. Introduction

One way to describe any economy or, for that matter, any economic organization, is as a huge ensemble of partially interrelated tasks and processes that, combined in certain ways,

---

* Corresponding author. Tel.: +39 050883343; fax: +39 050883344.
  E-mail addresses: marengo@unite.it (L. Marengo), gdosi@sssup.it (G. Dosi).
[1] Tel.: +39 0861266661; fax: +39 0861266665.

0167-2681/$ – see front matter © 2005 Elsevier B.V. All rights reserved.
doi:10.1016/j.jebo.2004.03.020

304   *L. Marengo, G. Dosi / J. of Economic Behavior & Org. 58 (2005) 303–326*

produce "well-constructed" goods and services. It is a perspective that dates at least back to Adam Smith who identified a major driver of productivity growth in the progressive division of tasks themselves and the associated specialization among workers. More recently, several of Herbert Simon's seminal works have explored the general structure of problem-solving activities of which technological search and economic production activities are just subsets (Simon, 1969). From different angles, several investigations from the team theory perspective have addressed the symmetric problem concerning coordination amongst multiple interrelated tasks (Marschak and Radner, 1972; Radner, 2000; Becker and Murphy, 1992). Finally, a flourishing literature has focussed on the "cognitive" characteristics of organizations (Richardson, 1972; Langlois and Robertson, 1995; Loasby, 1998; Teece et al., 1994; Dosi et al., 2000).

The contribution which follows has its roots in the foregoing perspectives and focuses on the comparative properties of different decomposition schemes (i.e., intuitively, different patterns of division of labor within and across organizations).

Since a good deal of current interpretations of at least the vertical boundaries of economic organizations is grounded on transaction cost considerations, this is also a good place to start. Indeed, as we shall argue in Section 2, the latter do tell part of the story but fail to account for those powerful drivers of intra- and inter-organizational division of labor that concern the nature of problem-solving knowledge, addressed by more "cognitive" approaches to organizational analysis (Section 3). Next, by building on the discussion of some fundamental features of problem-solving (Section 4), a rather novel formalization of the decomposition of problems and tasks is presented in Section 5 (perfect decompositions) and Section 6 (near decompositions). Section 7 discusses some analytical and simulation-based properties of the model regarding the relative efficiency and speed of adaptation of diverse set-ups characterized by different boundaries between organizations and markets. Finally, we draw some conclusions in Section 8.

2. Problem-solving tasks versus transactions

Think of an industry or the whole economy as a sequence of tasks leading from, say, raw materials to final products. How does one "cut" such sequences within single organizations and across them?

As known, transaction costs economics (henceforth, TCE), albeit rather silent on the intra-organizational division of tasks, focuses on the latter issue, the *vertical* boundaries of organizations.

In a nutshell, TCE (Williamson, 1975, 1985; Riordan and Williamson, 1985), and the seminal argument first developed by Coase (1937)) starts from a hypothetical "state of nature" (a logical, if not a historical one) in which all coordination of transactions across technological separable units takes place within markets[1] and predicts that whenever the working of the market price mechanism incurs costs that are higher than the corresponding costs of bureaucratic governance, then the latter can prevail on the grounds of higher allocative efficiency.

---

[1] "... in the beginning there were markets"(Williamson, 1975, p. 20).

L. Marengo, G. Dosi / J. of Economic Behavior & Org. 58 (2005) 303–326   305

In our view, however, this explanation does not tell the whole story, although it does indeed capture some determinants of the governance structure. Let us just mention three major difficulties of the theory that are crucial for the argument that follows.[2]

First, the logical process traced by Coase and Williamson often conflicts with actual historical records. With some remarkable exceptions, most technologies and industries are born with a highly vertically-integrated structure, undergo a disintegration process as the industry grows in the expansion phase, and then re-integrate in the maturity phase, but often along integration profiles that differ significantly from those of the original infant industry. Thus, the degree of vertical integration of an industry undergoes major changes along its life cycle (Klepper, 1997), and historical evidence seems to turn the transaction costs argument the other way around. One could say that "at the beginning" there were hierarchies and then they partially disintegrated, giving rise to markets. Actually, it is the very process of division of labor, usually taking place within hierarchical organizations, that creates the opportunity for markets to exist: thus Williamson's story on markets as original state of nature presents clear limitations even as a logical instrument. Transaction cost views of vertical integration and, for that matter, all standard vertical integration models based on information and agency problems (Perry, 1989), appear relatively more appropriate in describing the processes of growing vertical integration that take place in mature industries where the division of labor is relatively stable and allocative efficiency requirements tend to prevail. On the contrary, these models seem to have limited explanatory power when the early stages of the industry life-cycle are considered and whenever the firm main activity is the design of effective solutions to new technological and organizational problems.

Second, and relatedly, the transaction costs perspective deals with the efficiency of different governance structures in managing transactions across given technologically-separable interfaces; technology and the division of labor are taken as given, and organizational structures are derived. But the story could be very different if one assumed that technology and the division of labor were themselves at least partly determined by the organizational structure. For example, one would easily obtain multiple organizational/technological equilibria (Pagano, 1992; Aoki, 2001) and a strong institutional path-dependency (David, 1994). This point has as well been repeatedly emphasized by scholars of the so-called "'radical school" (Bowles, 1985; Marglin, 1974) who had in mind an opposite view of the world in which it is primarily the governance structure that determines the technology, not the other way around. Even without taking a position in this old debate, it seems hardly questionable that most of the division of labor processes take place within organizations. Therefore, the latter cannot be taken as irrelevant with respect to where the technologically separable interfaces are placed and what their economic characteristics are. Moreover, a technologically separable interface requires well-defined sets of codified standards for compatibility, especially if it has to be managed by transactions in a competitive market. As is well known from the literature on technological standards (David and Greenstein, 1990), they emerge either as unplanned conventions or as outcomes of deliberative processes (or as combinations of the two) and in turn have a relevant influence on the directions of further technological change and division of labor. Again, markets cannot be original and spontaneous "states of nature",

---

[2] For a broader critical appraisal of transaction costs theory see, for instance, Granovetter (1985) and Dow (1987).

306   *L. Marengo, G. Dosi / J. of Economic Behavior & Org. 58 (2005) 303–326*

but require all sorts of institutional and technological conditions, some of which are put in place by explicit organizational planning. Moreover, once established, standards shape specific technological trajectories, limiting the directions of innovation.

Finally, a third weakness of the transaction costs approach resides in its account (or, better, the lack of it) of the processes through which superior governance structures do emerge. Proving that a given governance structure is more efficient than another one is not an explanation of its emergence through "spontaneous" processes driven by market selection: a selection mechanism can indeed, under certain conditions, select for the fittest structures, but only if the latter exist in the first place.[3] Selection can account for the convergence of a population toward some given form, not for the emergence of such a form. The variational mechanisms through which new structures are generated and thus tested by the selection process are essential in determining the outcome of the selection itself. If the set of possible structures is "large", only a small subset of it can ever be generated by any computationally feasible mechanism; thus we have to specify what the likelihood is that such a subset also includes the optimal structure.

3. "Cognitive" perspectives on organizations: some roots in the literature

As already mentioned in Section 1, a respectable tradition, dating at least back to Adam Smith, attempts to identify the efficiency properties of different organizational forms by looking at the patterns of division of labor and at the learning opportunities which they entail *quite independently from any issue of incentive compatibility and transaction governance*. Smith's famous example of the pin factory vividly illustrates the relationship between division of tasks, improvements in operational skills and opportunities for production mechanization, as argued in, e.g., Leijonhufvud (1986) and Langlois and Robertson (1995).

It is true, however, that what we could call a "procedural", knowledge-centered approach to production and coordination patterns has been dormant for a long time. Rather, in mainstream economics, the prevailing style of analysis has rested upon a thorough "blackboxing", summarized into production functions of various sorts.

With such a view, the procedural aspects of production processes and, dynamically, of learning processes are explicitly censured. This also includes the removal of any investigation of the sequences of operations that are "legal", in the sense of being able ultimately to yield the desired output, and of their relative efficiencies. Of course, one may always claim that these are issues for engineers and not for economists, but then the economists' analysis of the patterns of production and coordination also loses any reference to the underlying patterns of knowledge distribution and learning.

Certainly, Smith's seminal insights have been followed by some other major contributions to the "procedural" analysis of the links between division of labor, production patterns and organizational forms. In the 19th century, Karl Marx's investigation of the capitalist factory system is an outstanding one, and Babbage's is another; in the 20th century, the work

---

[3] "... in a relative sense, the *fitter* survive, but there is no reason to suppose that they are *fittest* in any absolute sense" (Simon, 1983, emphasis in original). On this point see also Winter (1975).

of Georgescu–Roegen comes to mind; while across the two centuries several authors of the Austrian school have kept the interest in the importance of the links between forms of economic organization and the patterns of knowledge distribution within society alive (Langlois, 1986; Morroni, 1992).

All this notwithstanding, it is fair to say that a new impetus to a procedural, knowledge-centered analysis of production and economic organization has occurred mostly over the last four decades. This has come together with the development and partial convergence of four interpretative perspectives, namely (i) the investigations by Herbert Simon and colleagues of the properties of problem-solving procedures in their relation to some measure of complexity of the problems themselves,[4] (ii) behavioral theories of organizations in general and firms in particular,[5] (iii) evolutionary theories of economic change, with their emphasis on the process features of organizational knowledge and its partial embeddedness into organizational routines[6] and (iv) capabilities and competencies-based views of firms.[7]

As the intersection between these perspectives, the work which follows will try to offer a "constructive" (that is, explicitly process-based) formal account of, first, the links between problem-solving knowledge and division of labor within and across organizations and, second, the characteristics of diverse processes of selection amongst diverse organizational arrangements entailing distinctly different problem-solving repertoires.

The initial angle of investigation is clearly "Simonian". We put forward a notion of problem complexity which builds upon and refines Simon's ideas of decomposability and near-decomposability of complex problems (Simon, 1969). An advantage of our notion is that it also allows straightforward mappings into selection dynamics where problem-solving entities are nested.[8]

As we shall see, our notions of decomposability and the related one of problem complexity bear upon the presence or absence of interrelations among the elementary activities that make up the overall problem-solving process.

It seems quite natural indeed to assume that business firms and other economic organizations fully belong to this category of complex entities made up of many non-linearly interacting elements.

One of the conjectures we shall investigate concerns, in fact, the evolution of vertical integration in terms of the characteristics of problem-solving tasks. The main argument can be stated as follows: the division of problem-solving labor into decentralized decision units coordinated by markets determines which solutions (i.e. technological and organizational designs) can be generated and then tested by the selection process. On one hand, this division

---

[4] See for instance Simon (1969, 1983).

[5] To mention just the seminal works, see March and Simon (1958) and Cyert and March (1963).

[6] See Nelson and Winter (1982) as well as Nelson (1981) and Winter (2004) more specifically on production theory, and Cohen et al. (1996) on routines.

[7] See, among others, Teece et al. (1997), Dosi et al. (2000). Inspiring antecedents of this view are in the works of Penrose (1959) and Richardson (1972).

[8] Our model is also strictly related to the growing literature on modularity in technologies and organizations (Langlois and Robertson, 1995; Baldwin and Clark, 2000) and represents a formalization of a problem-solving approach to modularity. Problem decompositions define the modules on which selection applies. As we shall see, this problem-solving approach may bring a different perspective and different conclusions from the one based upon option value proposed by Baldwin and Clark.

is necessary for boundedly rational organizations in order to reduce the dimensions of the search space, but on the other hand, it might well happen that the division of physical and cognitive labor is such that the best designs will never be generated and therefore never selected by any selection mechanism whatsoever. In particular, we show that everything else being equal, the higher the degree of decentralization, the smaller the portion of the search space that is explored and therefore the lower the probability that the optimal solutions are included in such a portion of space. Finally, one can easily prove that computing the optimal division of problem-solving activities is more difficult than solving the problem itself; thus we cannot assume that boundedly rational agents in search of solutions to a given problem do possess the right decomposition of the problem itself.[9]

In particular, if the entities under selection are made up of many components that interact in a complex way, the resulting selection landscape will present many local optima (Kauffman, 1993), and selection forces will be unlikely to drive such entities to the global optima: sub-optimality and diversity of organizational structures can persistently survive in spite of strong selection forces (Levinthal, 1997). Sub-optimality is due to the persistence of inferior features that cannot be selected out because of their tight connections with other favorable features; this indeed is the rule in strongly interconnected systems. In other words, whenever the entities under selection have some complex internal structure, the power of selective pressure is limited by the laws governing internal structures. In fact, one of the purposes of the present work is to provide a measure of these trade-offs and establish under which conditions either force prevails.

4. Problem-solving: some special features

Problem-solving activities (which include, we repeat, most production and innovation activities) present some distinctive features that make them difficult to analyze with standard economic tools. First of all, they involve or are the outcome of a search in large combinatorial spaces of components, which must be closely coordinated. Interdependencies among such components are only partly understood and can only be locally explored through, for example, trial-and-error processes, rules of thumb or the application of expert tacit knowledge. Consider the following cases:

- The *design of complex artifacts* (e.g. an aircraft). It requires the coordination of many different design elements (engine type and power, wing size and shape, materials used, and so on, each of them, in turn, composed of many elements) whose interactions can only partly be expressed by general models and they have to be tested through simulation, prototype building and trial-and-error exercises, where tacit knowledge plays a key role.

---

[9] One important caveat must be considered here: this paper assumes that there is a set of atomic components that cannot be further decomposed. This necessary analytical assumption does not allow us to capture another important advantage of division of labor, the possibility of further divisions: once a task has been specified, a new process of subdivision can be autonomously carried out on it. Contrary to what is assumed, for simplicity's sake, in the model that follows, there is in general no given lower bound to the process of in-depth hierarchical decomposition.

L. Marengo, G. Dosi / J. of Economic Behavior & Org. 58 (2005) 303–326   309

- The *solution to a difficult game* (e.g. solving a Rubik's cube or playing chess). An effective solution is a long sequence of moves, each of which is chosen out of a set of possibilities that is large enough to make the exploration of the entire tree of the game computationally impossible for boundedly rational agents. The relations among such moves in a sequence (e.g. what changes we get in the overall performance of the solution if we change, say, the *i*th move) are only partly understood. Actually, understanding it fully would imply the knowledge of the entire game tree.[10]
- *Managing organizations* such as business firms. The latter are complex multi-dimensional bundles of routines, decision rules, procedures, incentive schemes and so on, whose interplay is largely unknown also to those who manage the organization itself — witness all the problems and unforeseen consequences whenever managers try to promote changes in the organization.

Moreover, since components within a problem most often present strong inter dependencies, the search space of a problem typically presents many local optima. Marginal contributions of components can rapidly switch from negative to positive values, depending on which value is assumed by the other components.[11] For instance, adding a more powerful engine could lower the performance and the reliability of an aircraft (Vincenti, 1990) if other components are not simultaneously adapted. In a chess game, a notionally optimal strategy could involve, for example, castling at a given moment in the development of the game but the same castling as a part of some sub-optimal (but effective) strategy could turn out to be a losing move. Finally, introducing some routines, practices or incentive schemes that have proven superior in a given organizational context could prove harmful in a context where other elements are not appropriately co-adapted.

As a consequence, in the presence of strong inter dependencies, one cannot optimize a system by separately optimizing each element it is made of. Consider a problem that is made up of N elements and whose optimal solution is $x_1^* x_2^* \ldots x_N^*$ while the current state is $x_1 x_2 \ldots x_N$. In the presence of strong inter dependencies, it might well be the case that some or even all of the solutions of the $x_1 x_2 \ldots x_i^* \ldots x_N$ kind show a worse performance than the current one.[12]

However, as pointed out by Simon (1969), problem-solving by boundedly rational agents must necessarily proceed by decomposing any large, complex and intractable problem into smaller sub-problems that can be solved independently, by promoting what could be called the division of problem-solving labor. At the same time, note that the extent of the division of problem-solving labor is limited by the existence of interdependencies. If sub-problem decomposition separates interdependent elements, then solving each sub-problem independently does not allow overall optimization.

---

[10] In fact, one of the fundamental problems faced by human and artificial players is to build effective heuristics to evaluate the positions during the game without the knowledge of the entire tree.

[11] Similar aspects are present even in the simplest production technologies. Consider, for instance, team production as explored by Alchian and Demsetz (1972): two workers lifting a heavy load. Additional individual effort generally raises team production, but when the levels of effort applied by the two are disproportionate this might result in turning over the load, thus sharply decreasing team production.

[12] Note that this notion of interdependency differs from the notion of complementarity as sub-modularity as in Milgrom and Roberts (1990). Here, in fact, we allow for the possibility that positive variations in one component can decrease the system's performance value.

It is important to remark that the introduction of any decentralized interaction mechanism, such as a competitive market for each component does not solve the problem. For instance, if we assume that in our previous example each component x_i is traded in a competitive market, superior components x_i^* will never be selected. Thus, interdependencies undermine the effectiveness of the selection process as a device for adaptive optimization and they introduce forms of path-dependency with lock-in into sub-optimal states that do not originate from the frictions and costs connected to the selection mechanism, but from the internal structure of the entities undergoing selection.

As Simon (1969) pointed out, since an optimal decomposition (i.e. a decomposition that divides into separate sub-problems all and only the elements that are independent from each other) can only be designed by someone who has a perfect knowledge of the problem (including its optimal solution), boundedly rational agents will normally be bound to design near-decompositions, that is decompositions that try to put together, within the same sub-problem, only those components whose interdependencies are (or, we shall add, agents believe to be) more important for the overall system performance. However, near-decompositions involve a fundamental trade-off: on one hand, finer decompositions exploit the advantages of decentralized local adaptation, that is, the use of a selection mechanism for achieving coordination "for free" together with parallelism and adaptation speed. However, on the other hand, finer decompositions imply a higher probability that interdependent components are separated into different sub-problems and therefore cannot, in general, be optimally adjusted together. One of the purposes of this paper is to provide a precise measure of this trade-off and show that, in the presence of widespread interdependencies, finer than optimal decompositions have an evolutionary advantage (in terms of adaptation speed), although they inevitably involve lock-in into sub-optimal solutions.

One way of expressing the limits that interdependencies pose to the division of problem-solving labor is that global performance signals are not able to effectively drive decentralized search in the problem space. Local moves in the "right direction" might well decrease the overall performance if some other elements are not properly tuned. As Simon puts it, since an entity (e.g. an organism in biology or an organization in economics) only receives feedback from the environment concerning the fitness of the whole entity, only under conditions of near independence can the usual selection processes work successfully for complex systems (Simon, 2002, p. 593).

A further aspect concerns the property that, in general, the search space of a problem is not given exogenously, but is constructed by individuals and organizations as a subjective representation of the problem itself. If the division of problem-solving labor is limited by interdependencies, the structure of interdependencies itself depends on how the problem is framed by problem-solvers. Sometimes problem-solvers make major leaps forward by reframing the same problem in a novel way. As shown by many case studies, major innovations often appear when various elements that were well known are re-combined and put together under a different perspective.[13] Indeed, one can go as far as to say that it is the representation of a problem that determines its purported difficulty and that one of the fundamental functions of organizations is precisely to implement collective representations of the

---

[13] An example is provided by Levinthal (1998), in his detailed account of the development of wireless communication technologies.

L. Marengo, G. Dosi / J. of Economic Behavior & Org. 58 (2005) 303–326   311

problems they face (Loasby, 2001). In the simple model of problem-solving presented in this paper finding the "correct" representation of interdependencies is more complex than solving the problem itself. However, by changing the representation, lock-ins into suboptimal solutions can be avoided and better solutions can be discovered. Division of problem-solving labor is therefore very much a question of how the problem is represented.[14] Needless to say, boundedly rational individuals cannot be innocently assumed to hold optimal representations.

Having given the foregoing qualitative intuitions, let us next develop a formal model that provides a precise measure of the above-mentioned tradeoffs.

5. Decomposition and coordination

5.1. Definitions

We assume that solving a given problem requires the coordination of N atomic "elements" or "actions" or "pieces of knowledge" that we generically call **components**, each of which can assume some number of alternative states. For the sake of simplicity, we assume that each component can assume only two alternative states, labelled 0 and 1. Note that all the properties presented below for the two-states case can very easily be extended to the case of any finite number of states.

More precisely, we characterize a problem by the following elements:

The set of **components**: $C = \{c_1, c_2, \ldots, c_N\}$ with $c_i \in \{0, 1\}$

A **configuration** (that is, a possible solution to the problem) is a string $x^i = c_1^i c_2^i \ldots c_N^i$

The **set of configurations**: $X = \{x^1, x^2, \ldots, x^{2^N}\}$

An **ordering** over the set of possible configurations: we write $x^i \succeq x^j$ (or $x^i \succ x^j$) whenever x^i is weakly (or strictly) preferred to x^j.

In order to avoid technical complications, we assume, for the time being, that there exists only one configuration that is strictly preferred over all the other configurations (i.e. a unique global optimum). This simplifying assumption will be dropped in Section 6 below.

A **problem** is defined by the pair $(X, \succeq)$.

As the size of the set of configurations is exponential in the number of components, whenever the latter is large, the state space of the problem becomes much too vast to be extensively searched by agents with bounded computational capabilities. One way of reducing its size is to decompose[15] it into sub-spaces.

Let $I = \{1, 2, \ldots, N\}$ be the set of indexes and let a **block**[16] $d_i \subseteq I$ be a non-empty subset of it; we call the **size of block** d_i, its cardinality $|d_i|$. We define a **decomposition scheme**

---

[14] A formal treatment of the properties of different representations in a particular class of problems can be found in Marengo (2003).

[15] A decomposition can be considered as a particular case of search heuristics; search heuristics are, in fact, ways of reducing the number of configurations to be considered in a search process.

[16] Blocks in our model can be considered as a formalization of the notion of modules used by the flourishing literature on modularity in technologies and organizations (Baldwin and Clark, 2000) and decomposition schemes are a formalization of the notion of system architecture that defines the set of modules into which a technological system or an organization are decomposed.

(or simply **decomposition**) of the problem $(X, \succeq)$ a set of blocks:

$$D = \{d_1, d_2, \ldots, d_k\}.$$

such that $\bigcup_{i=1}^{k} d_i = I.$

Note that a decomposition does not necessarily have to be a partition.

Given a configuration x^i and a block d_j, we call block-configuration $x^i(d_j)$ the substring of length $|d_j|$ containing the components of configuration x^i belonging to block d_j:

$$x^i(d_j) = x^i_{j1} x^i_{j2} \ldots x^i_{j|d_j|}.$$

for all $j_h \in d_j$.

We also use the notation $x^i(d_{-j})$ to indicate the substring of length $N - |d_j|$ containing the components of configuration x^i not belonging to block d_j.

Two block-configurations can be united into a larger block-configuration by means of the $\vee$ operator so defined:

$$x(d_j) \vee y(d_h) = z(d_j \cup d_h) \text{ where } z_v = \begin{cases} x_v \text{ if } v \in d_j \\ y_v \text{ otherwise} \end{cases}$$

We can therefore write $x^i = x^i(d_j) \vee x^i(d_{-j})$ for any d_j.

Moreover, we define the **size of a decomposition scheme** as the size of its largest defining block:

$$|D| = \max\{|d_1|, |d_2|, \ldots, |d_k|\}.$$

Coordination among blocks in a decomposition scheme may either take place through market-like mechanisms or via other organizational arrangements (e.g. hierarchies). Dynamically, when a new configuration appears, it is tested against the existing one according to its relative performance. The two configurations are compared in terms of their ranks, and the superior one is selected, while the other one is discarded.[17]

More precisely, let us assume that the current configuration is x^i and take block d_h with its current block-configuration $x^i(d_h)$. Let us now consider a new configuration $x^j(d_h)$ for the same block. If

$$x^j(d_h) \vee x^i(d_{-h}) x^i(d_h) \vee x^i(d_{-h}),$$

then $x^j(d_h)$ is selected and the new configuration $x^j(d_h) \vee x^i(d_{-h})$ is kept in place of x^i; otherwise $x^j(d_h)$ is discarded and x^i is kept.

It might help to think in terms of a given division of labor structure (the decomposition scheme) within firms whereby individual workers and organizational sub-units specialize in various segments of the production process (a single block). Decompositions, however, sometimes determine also the boundaries across independent organizations specialized in different segments of the whole production sequence.

---

[17] As a first approximation, we assume that this sorting and selection mechanism is errorless and operates at no cost and without any friction.

Note that, dynamically, different *inter*-organizational decompositions entail different degrees of decentralization of the search process. The finer the inter-organizational decompositions, the smaller the portion of the search space that is being explored by local variational mechanisms and tested by market selection. Thus, there is inevitably a trade-off; finer decompositions and more decentralization make search and adaptation faster (if the decomposition is the finest, search time is linear in N), but on the other hand, they explore smaller and smaller portions of the search space, thus decreasing the likelihood that optimal (or even good) solutions are ever generated and tested. In the following we try to provide a precise characterization of this trade-off and its consequences.

5.2. Selection and search paths

A decomposition scheme is a sort of template that determines how new configurations are generated and can be tested afterward by the selection mechanism. In large search spaces in which only a very small subset of all possible configurations can be generated and undergo testing, the procedure employed to generate such new configurations plays a key role in defining the set of attainable final configurations.

We will assume that boundedly rational agents can only search locally in directions that are given by the decomposition scheme; new configurations are generated and tested in the neighborhood of the given one, where neighbors are new configurations obtained by changing some (possibly all) components within a given block.

Given a decomposition scheme $D = \{d_1, d_2, \ldots, d_k\}$, we say that a configuration x^i is a preferred neighbor or simply a **neighbor** of configuration x^j with respect to a block $d_h \in D$ if the following three conditions hold:

1. $x^i \succeq x^j$,
2. $x^i_v = x^j_v \forall v \notin d_h$,
3. $x^i \neq x^j$.

Conditions 2 and 3 require that the two configurations differ only by components that belong to block d_h. According to the definition, a neighbor can be reached from a given configuration through the operation of a single decentralized coordination mechanism.

We call $H_i(x, d_i)$ the set of neighbors of a configuration x for block d_i.

The set of **best neighbors** $B_i(x,d_i) \subseteq H_i(x,d_i)$ of a configuration x for block d_i is the set of the most preferred configurations in the set of neighbors:

$$B_i(x, d_i) = \{y \in H_i(x, d_i) \text{ such that } y z \forall z \in H_i(x, d_i)\}.$$

By extension from single blocks to entire decomposition schemes, we can give the following definition of the set of neighbors for a decomposition scheme as,

$$H(x, D) = \bigcup_{i=1}^{k} H_i(x, d_i).$$

A configuration is a local optimum for the decomposition scheme D if there does not exist a configuration y such that $y \in H(x,D)$ and $y \succ x$.

A search path or, in short, a **path** $P(x^i, D)$ from a configuration x^i and for a decomposition D is a sequence, starting from x^i, of neighbors:

$$P(x^i, D) = x^i, x^{i+1}, x^{i+2}, \ldots \text{ with } x^{i+m+1} \in H(x^{i+m}, D).$$

A configuration x^j is **reachable** from another configuration x^i and for decomposition D if there exists a path $P(x^i, D)$ such that $x^j \in P(x^i, D)$.

Suppose configuration x^j is a local optimum for decomposition D; we call the basin of attraction of x^j for decomposition D the set of all configurations from which x^j is reachable:

$$\Psi(x^j, D) = \{y, \text{ such that } \exists P(y, D) \text{ with } x^j \in P(y, D)\}.$$

Now let x^0 be the global optimum[18] and let $Z \subseteq X$ with $x^0 \in Z$. We say that the problem $(X, \succeq)$ is locally decomposable in Z by scheme D if $Z \subseteq \Psi(x^0, D)$. If $Z = X$, we say that the problem is globally decomposable by scheme D.[19]

Among all the decomposition schemes of a given problem, benchmark cases are those for which the global optimum becomes reachable from any starting configuration. One such decomposition always exists and it is the degenerate decomposition $D = \{\{1, 2, 3, \ldots, N\}\}$ for which, of course, there exists only one local optimum and it coincides with the global one. But, obviously, we are interested in smaller decompositions (if they exist) and in particular in those of minimum size. The latter decompositions represent the maximum extent to which problem-solving can be subdivided into independent sub-problems coordinated by decentralized selection, with the property that such selection processes can eventually lead to optimality irrespectively of the starting condition. On the contrary, finer decompositions will not, in general, allow decentralized selection processes to optimize (unless the starting configuration is "by chance" within the basin of attraction of the global optimum).

Proposition 1. *There exist problems that are globally decomposable only by the degenerate decomposition* $D = \{\{1, 2, 3, \ldots, N\}\}$

Proof. we prove the statement by providing an example. Consider a problem whose unique global optimum is configuration $x^0 = x_1^0 x_2^0 \ldots x_N^0$ and whose second best configuration is $x^1 = x_1^1 x_2^1 \ldots x_N^1$, where $x_i^1 = |1 - x_1^0| \forall i = 1, 2, \ldots, N$. It is obvious that the global optimum can be reached from the second best only by mutating all of the N components together. $\square$

The next proposition establishes a rather obvious but important property of decomposition schemes. As one climbs into the basin of attraction of a local optimum for a decomposition D that is not the finest one, then finer decomposition schemes can usually be introduced that can reach the same local optimum more quickly.

---

[18] We recall the assumption of uniqueness of the global optimum.

[19] A special case of decomposability, which is generalized here, is presented in Page (1996) and is called dominance. In our terminology, a block configuration $x^j(d_h)$ is dominant when $x^j(d_h) \vee x^i(d_{-h}) \succeq x^i$ for every configuration $x^i \in X$.

For this proposition we need an additional definition: given a decomposition scheme D, we say that two configurations x^i and x^j totally differ with respect to block $d_h \in D$ if the corresponding block configurations $x^i(d_h)$ and $x^j(d_h)$ differ in every component: $x^i_k(d_h) \neq x^j_k(d_h) \forall k = 1, 2, \ldots, |d_h|$.

Proposition 2. *Let $\Psi(x^\alpha, D) = \{x^\alpha, x^{\alpha+1}, \ldots, x^{\alpha+m}\}$ be the ordered basin of attraction of a local optimum x^α (with $x^{\alpha+j} \succeq x^{\alpha+j+1} \forall j = 0, \ldots, m-1$). Define $\Psi^i(x^\alpha, D) = \Psi(x^\alpha, D)/\{x^{\alpha+i+1}, x^{\alpha+i+2}, \ldots, x^{\alpha+m}\}$ for $0 \leq i \leq m$. Let $d_{vi} \in D$ be the maximum size block(s) in D. Then, unless x^α and $x^{\alpha+1}$ totally differ for some maximum size block d_{vi}, there exists a $0 < i \leq m$ such that the set $\Psi^i(x^\alpha, D)$ admits a decomposition D^i with $|D^i| < |D|$.*

Proof.   Suppose, for simplicity, that D contains a unique maximum size block $d_v \in D$ with $|D| = |d_v|$. If the local optimum x^α and the second best of its basin of attraction (with respect to D) $x^{\alpha+1}$ do not totally differ with respect to d_v, then there exists a smaller decomposition D^i that is identical to D except that its largest block d_v can be split into two sub-blocks containing respectively the components for which $x^\alpha(d_v)$ and $x^{\alpha+1}(d_v)$ differ and those for which they do not. By construction x^α is reachable from $x^{\alpha+1}$ for D^i and $|D^i| < |D|$ and, therefore, $i = 1$ satisfies the proposition. If there are multiple maximum size blocks $d_{vi} \in D$, it necessarily follows that x^α and $x^{\alpha+1}$ cannot totally differ for any of them. $\square$

Among all the possible global decompositions of a problem, those of minimum size are especially interesting; in fact, they set a lower bound to the degree of decentralization that preserves optimality with certainty. Conversely, note that for decompositions which are finer than those of minimum size, whether or not the optimal solution will ever be generated and thus selected depends on the initial condition.

Minimum size decomposition schemes can be found recursively with the procedure informally described in the following.[20]

Let us rearrange all the configurations in X by descending rank $X = \{x^0, x^1, \ldots, x^{2^N-1}\}$ where $x^i \succeq x^{i+1}$.

The minimum size decomposition can be computed as follows:

1. start with the finest decomposition $D^0 = \{\{1\}, \{2\}, \ldots, \{N\}\}$,
2. check whether or not $x^0 \in P\{x^i, D\} \forall x^i \ i = 1, 2, \ldots, 2^N - 1$. If there is a path leading to the global optimum from every other configuration for decomposition D; STOP,
3. if not, build a new decomposition D^1 by union of the smallest blocks for which condition 2 was violated and go back to 2.

Let us illustrate it with an example.

Example.   A hypothetical ranking (where 1 is the rank of the most preferred) of configurations for $N = 3$

---

[20] The complete algorithm is quite lengthy to describe in exhaustive and precise terms. Its Pascal and C++ implementations are available from the authors upon request.

Configurations	Ranking
100	1
010	2
110	3
011	4
001	5
000	6
111	7
101	8

If search proceeds according to the decomposition scheme $D = \{\{1\}, \{2\}, \{3\}\}$, there exist two local optima: 100 (which is also the global optimum) and 010. The basins of attraction of the two local optima are, respectively

$$\Psi(100) = \{100, 110, 000, 111, 101\} \text{ and}$$

$$\Psi(010) = \{010, 110, 011, 001, 000, 111, 101\}.$$

Note that the worst local optimum has a larger basin of attraction[21] because it covers all configurations except the global optimum itself. Thus, only a search that starts at the global optimum will (trivially) stop at the global optimum with certainty, while for the other initial configurations, a search might end up in either local optima (depending on the sequence of mutations) or even (in three cases) in the worst local optimum with certainty.

By using the notion of dominance (see footnote 19 above) it is possible to establish that the only dominant block-configuration is actually the globally optimum string itself, corresponding to the degenerate decomposition scheme $D = \{\{1, 2, 3\}\}$. Thus, apparently no decentralized search structure can always locate the global optimum from every starting configuration.

Granted that, can one find some alternative decompositions allowing for partly decentralized search processes yielding global optima? In our example, one such case occurs with the decomposition scheme $D = \{\{1, 2\}, \{3\}\}$. For instance, if one starts from configuration 111, one can first locate 011 (using block $\{1, 2\}$) then 010 (using block 3) and finally 100 (again with block $\{1, 2\}$); or, alternatively, one can locate 110 (using block 3) and 100 (with block 1, 2). It can be easily verified that the same blocks do actually "work" for all other starting configurations. The algorithm just presented will find this decomposition.

6. Near decomposability

When building a decomposition scheme for a problem, we have that far looked for perfect decomposability, in the sense that we require that all blocks be optimized in a way

---

[21] Kauffman provides some general properties of one-bit-mutation search algorithms (equivalent to our bit-wise decomposition schemes) on string fitness functions with varying degrees of interdependencies between components. In particular, he finds that as the span of interdependencies increases, the number of local optima also increases while the size of the basin of attraction of the global optimum shrinks.

L. Marengo, G. Dosi / J. of Economic Behavior & Org. 58 (2005) 303–326   317

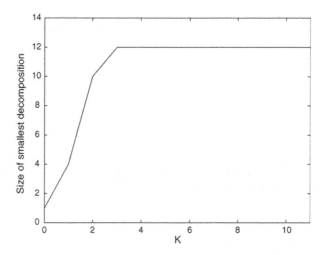

Fig. 1. Size of minimum decomposition schemes for random NK problems ($N = 12$).

totally independent from the others. In this way, we are sure to decompose the problem into perfectly isolated components that can be independently solved. This is, however, a very stringent requirement; even when interdependencies are rather weak but diffused across all components, one easily tends to observe problems for which no perfect decomposition of size smaller than N exists. For instance, Fig. 1 shows that in Kauffman's NK random landscapes[22] the above-described algorithm finds only decomposition schemes of size N or just below N even for very small values of K (that is, for highly correlated landscapes). In other words, a little bit of interdependence spread across the set of components immediately makes a system practically indecomposable.

We can soften the perfect decomposability requirement into one of near-decomposability; we no longer require the problem to be decomposed into completely separated sub-problems (i.e. sub-problems that fully contain all interdependencies) but we might be content to find sub-problems that contain the most "relevant" interdependencies, while less relevant ones can persist across sub-problems. In this way, optimizing each sub-problem independently will not necessarily lead to the global optimum, but to a "good" solution.[23] In other words, we construct **near-decompositions** that give a precise measure of the trade-off between

---

[22] An NK random fitness landscape is similar to our definition of "problem" except that, instead of a preference relation, a real valued fitness function $F : X \mapsto \mathbb{R}$ is defined as an average of each component's fitness contribution. The latter is a random realization of a random variable uniformly distributed over the interval $[0,1]$ for each possible configuration of the K-size block of the other components with which each component interacts (Kauffman, 1993). Note, however, that Kauffman's K is not a good ex-post complexity measure (in terms of its decomposability) of the optimization problem on the resulting fitness landscape; small values of K usually generate landscapes that are not decomposable, but on the other hand, it is always possible that, even with very high values of K, the resulting landscape is highly decomposable.

[23] This procedure can also deal with the case of multiple global optima and thus we can now also drop the assumption of a unique global optimum.

318   *L. Marengo, G. Dosi / J. of Economic Behavior & Org. 58 (2005) 303–326*

decentralization and optimality: higher degrees of decentralization, while generally displaying a higher adaptation speed, are likely to be obtained at the expense of the asymptotic optimality of the solutions which can be reached.

Let us rearrange all the configurations in X by descending rank $X = \{x^0, x^1 \ldots, x^{2^N-1}\}$ where $x^i \succeq x^{i+1}$, and let $X_\mu = \{x^0, x^1, \ldots, x^{\mu-1}\}$ with $0 \leq \mu \leq 2^N - 1$ be the ordered set of the best μ configurations.

We say that X_μ is reachable from a configuration $y \notin X_\mu$ and for decomposition D if there exists a configuration $x^i \in X_\mu$ such that $x^i \in P(y, D)$.

We call the basin of attraction $\Psi(X_\mu, D)$ of X_μ for decomposition D the set of all configurations from which X_μ is reachable. If $\Psi(X_\mu, D) = X$ we say that D is a μ-**decomposition** for the problem.

μ-Decompositions of minimum size can be found algorithmically with a straightforward generalization of the above algorithm, which computes minimum size decomposition schemes for optimal decompositions.

The following proposition gives the most important property of minimum size μ-decompositions:

Proposition 3. *Let D_μ be a minimum size μ-decomposition for problem $(X, \succeq)$; then $|D_\mu|$ is monotonically weakly decreasing in μ.*

Proof. If $\mu = 2^N - 1$, the set X_μ includes all configurations, and it is trivially reachable for all decompositions, including the finest with $|D_\mu| = 1$. If $\mu = 1$, then X_μ includes only the global optimum, and therefore the size of the minimum size decomposition is $1 \leq |D_\mu| \leq N$. We still have to show that $D_{\mu+1} > |D_\mu|$ cannot happen: if this were the case, X_μ could not be reached from $X_{\mu+1}$ for decomposition D_μ, but this contradicts the assumption that X_μ is reachable from any configuration in X for decomposition D_μ. □

The latter proposition shows that higher degrees of decomposition and decentralization can be attained by giving up optimality and it provides a precise measure for this trade-off. As an example, we generated 100 random problems of size $N = 12$, all characterized by not being decomposable[24] (i.e. $|D| = 12$ for all of them). Fig. 2 displays the average size of the minimum size decomposition schemes for the 100 random problems as we vary the number μ of acceptable configurations. Fig. 2 shows that second-best solutions can be reached by search processes based upon finer decompositions (that is with more decentralized processes) that can find such solutions more quickly by exploiting coordination "for free" provided by the selection mechanism. In fact, when the size of the decomposition scheme decreases by one unit, the expected search time decreases by half.

---

[24] Random problems are generated in a straightforward way: we generate random rankings of all the binary strings of size $N = 12$ and then compute (using the algorithm presented above) their minimum size decomposition schemes. Only those problems for which the size of the smallest decomposition schemes was 12 were used in these simulations. An alternative (and equivalent) method is to generate random NK landscapes *à la* Kauffman with $N = 12$ and a high K and then check that the resulting landscape is not decomposable, as it may happen that landscapes with a very high K may also be highly decomposable.

L. Marengo, G. Dosi / J. of Economic Behavior & Org. 58 (2005) 303–326   319

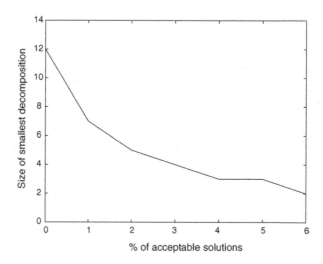

Fig. 2. Near decomposability.

7. Search speed and optimality: some consequences for organizational structures

The trade-offs outlined in the previous sections between decomposability, complexity reduction and search speed on one hand and asymptotic optimality on the other enable us to discuss some interesting evolutionary properties of various organizational structures competing in a given problem-solving environment.

Let us consider the properties of near-decompositions. As illustrated in Fig. 2 for randomly generated problems,[25] if second-best solutions are accepted we can reduce considerably the size of the decomposition schemes and the expected search time. This shows that the organizational structure sets a balance in the trade-off between search and adaptation speed and optimality. It is easy to argue that in complex problem environments, characterized by strong and diffused interdependencies, such a trade-off will tend to produce organizational structures that are more decomposed and decentralized than what would be optimal given the interdependencies of the problem space. This property is shown in Figs. 3 and 4, that present the typical search paths on a non-decomposable problem of two search processes driven, respectively, by decompositions:

$$D1 = \{1, 2, \ldots, 12\}$$
$$D12 = \{\{1\}, \{2\}, \ldots, \{12\}\}$$

Fig. 3 shows the first 180 iterations in which the more decentralized structure (D12) quickly climbs the problem space and outperforms a search based on a coarser decomposition. If there were a tight selection environment, a more-than-optimally-decentralized

---

[25] In this figure and the following (with the exception of Fig. 5), we indicate on the vertical axis the rank of configurations re-parametrized between 0 (worst) and 1 (best).

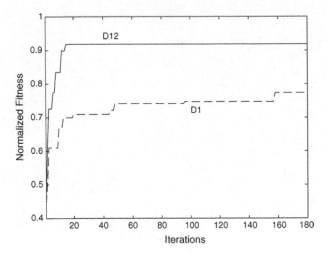

Fig. 3. Fitness values for search processes with finest (D12) and coarsest (D1) decompositions ($N = 12$). First 180 iterations. . . .

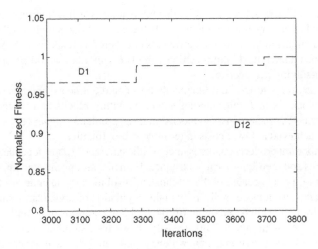

Fig. 4. . . . After 3000 iterations.

organizational structure would quickly displace structure D1 that reflects the "true" decomposition of the underlying problem space.

However, the search process based on the finest decomposition quickly reaches a local optimum from where no further improvement can occur, while the process based on the coarser decomposition keeps searching and climbing slowly.[26] Fig. 4 shows iterations

---

[26] If we imagine that each iteration corresponds to a day, then the decentralized organization achieves a good fit with its environment within 2 or 3 weeks, while the centralized structure requires some years.

L. Marengo, G. Dosi / J. of Economic Behavior & Org. 58 (2005) 303–326   321

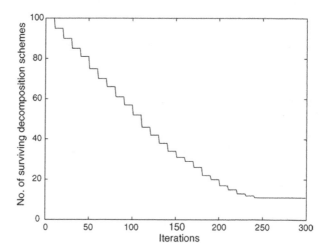

Fig. 5. Diversity of surviving decomposition schemes.

between 3000 and 3800, where the finest decomposition is still locked-into the local optimum it reached after very few iterations, while the coarsest one slowly reaches the global optimum (normalized to 1). Strong selective pressure therefore tends to favor organizational structures whose degree of decentralization is higher than what would be optimal from a mere problem-solving perspective.

This result is even stronger in problems that we could define as "modular", those characterized by blocks with strong interdependencies within blocks and much weaker (but non-zero) interdependencies between blocks; in these problems, higher levels of decompositions can be achieved at lower costs in terms of sub-optimality.

Another important property concerns micro ("idiosyncratic") path-dependencies of organizational forms and their long-term persistence. If finer-than-optimal decompositions tend to emerge and to spread because of their "transient" evolutionary advantages, then one will generally observe also long-term diversity in the population of organizations in terms of (i) the decomposition they are based upon, (ii) the problem solutions they implement and (iii) the local peaks they settle into.[27] This is easily shown by a simulation exercise where we model a simple selection environment in which we generate 100 organizations characterized by a randomly generated decomposition and a random initial string and let them search a randomly generated indecomposable problem. The 10 worst performing organizations are selected out every 10 iterations and replaced by 10 new organizations where 5 are randomly generated and 5 have the same decomposition scheme of the best performing ones but are placed on a randomly chosen configuration.

Fig. 5 plots the number of diverse organizational forms at every iteration. Initially, diversity does indeed sharply decrease because of selective pressure but then it stabilizes on numbers consistently and persistently higher than 1.

---

[27] On this latter point, a similar result is obtained by Levinthal (1997).

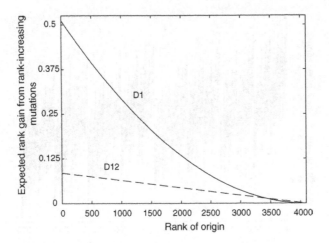

Fig. 6. Expected gain from rank-improving mutations for the finest (D12) and coarsest (D1) decompositions in a fully decomposable problem ($N = 12$).

A very similar trend describes the number of different surviving configurations, reflecting the fact that the population of organizations settles onto several local peaks of similar value.

We have also run other simulations where, at given intervals, we have changed the current problem with one having exactly the same structure in terms of decomposability but different randomly generated orderings of configurations. This can be taken as a metaphorical proxy for environment volatility. For instance, consumers might have changing preferences for a given set of characteristics or, on the production side, relative input prices may change. Interestingly enough, it turns out that, even with totally decomposable problems, as the change ranks becomes more frequent, the population is entirely invaded by organizations characterized by coarser and coarser decompositions and, at the limit, by organizations that do not decompose at all. This robustly suggests that growing volatility has stronger consequences than does growing interdependence. The reason that this happens is shown in Figs. 6 and 7 that present, respectively, the expected improvements and the probability of improvement for searches based on the finest (D12) and coarsest (D1) decomposition schemes in a fully decomposable problem.[28] It is shown that, when starting from low rank configurations, a search based upon coarser decomposition has a higher probability of finding a better configuration and, when such a better configuration is found, its expected rank is higher for coarser decompositions. This is because finer decompositions search only locally, and this, on average, cannot produce large improvements in fully-decomposable problems. When the problem space is highly volatile (though always fully decomposable) sooner or later every organization will fall into an area of very "bad" configurations from which coarser decompositions have a higher chance to recover promptly.

---

[28] Figs. 6 and 7 refer to the fully decomposable search space given by the binary numbers between 0 and $2^N - 1$, but the same qualitative results are obtained for any kind of fully decomposable search space.

L. Marengo, G. Dosi / J. of Economic Behavior & Org. 58 (2005) 303–326   323

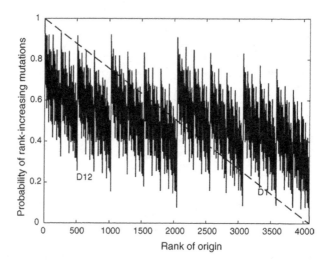

Fig. 7. Probability of rank-improving mutations for the finest (D12) and coarsest (D1) decompositions in a fully decomposable problem ($N = 12$).

8. Conclusions

In this paper, we have presented a novel model of 'Simonian' ascendancy concerning the properties of the division of problem-solving labor and we have accounted for the properties of different institutional arrangements and in particular for different boundaries between un-decomposed (in principle, organization-embodied) tasks and decomposed tasks (possibly coordinated via market-like mechanisms but also via mechanisms based on the interaction of quasi-independent units within simple organizations).

The issue is basically one of organizational (and technological) design: can optimal organizational structures (or optimal technological designs) emerge out of decentralized local interactions? This paper, in fact, shows that this is only possible under some special and rather implausible conditions and that, on the contrary, the advantages of decentralization usually bear a cost in terms of sub-optimality.

The results are largely consistent with Simon's general proposition suggesting that "near decomposability is an exceedingly powerful architecture for effective organization . . . [that] appear with regularity also in human social organizations — e.g. business firms and govern-ment agencies — with their many-layered hierarchies of divisions, departments and sections" (Simon, 2002, pp. 598–599). However, our model also highlights the subtle trade-offs between decomposition levels, degrees of suboptimality of the achievable outcomes, and adaptation speed. Together, it casts strong doubts on the general validity of any "optimality-through-selection" argument in the sphere of organizational and technological designs and, more in general, of any "optimistic" view of market selection processes that can be found, for instance, in Alchian (1950) and Friedman (1953), as forces that substitute individual optimization with evolutionary optimization.

On more empirical grounds, the analysis of the foregoing trade-offs can provide a plausible mechanism that is compatible with the observed changing depth and profile of the integration of organizations along technology and industry life cycles. The results of our model are fully consistent with vast empirical evidence suggesting that new technologies develop in highly integrated organizations because of the need to control the strong interdependencies that characterize difficult problems. Market-like decentralized mechanisms, it has been argued, do not provide appropriate signals in this early "problem-solving" phase, because they do not (except in very simple problems) allow for the coordination of interdependent elements. As search proceeds and a local peak (a set of standards in the techno-organizational design problem) is selected, the degree of decentralization can be greatly increased in order to allow for fast climbing of this peak (and indeed transaction cost factors can very well be responsible at this stage for variations in the degree of integration), but the more that decentralization is pushed forward, the more unlikely it will be that new and better local optima can be discovered. There is an inevitable trade-off between decentralization and optimality that can hardly be avoided.

Finally, we suggested that organizations could actually play the even more fundamental role of building collective representations of the problems to be solved, and that such representations could act as frames within which the division of labor takes place inside and across organizations. Consider such a proposition as the beginning of a promising line of inquiry concerning the crucial role of organization in the construction of collectively shared representations—fundamental ingredients of coordination in the presence of any form of division of cognitive and productive labor.

Acknowledgements

We are greatly indebted to Marco Valente for his comments on the subject and for his help in building and running the simulations reported in Section 7. We also thank Esben Andersen, Massimo Egidi, Koen Frenken, Yuri Kaniovski, Thorbjørn Knudsen, Scott Page, Corrado Pasquali, the late Herbert Simon and two anonymous referees for their useful remarks and suggestions. G.D. thanks the St. Anna School of Advanced Studies (project no. E6099GD) and the Italian Ministry of University and Research (project no. 2002.132415). L.M. gratefully acknowledges financial contributions from the NORMEC project (SERD-2000-00316), funded by the European Commission, Research Directorate, 5th Framework Programme. The authors are solely responsible for the opinions expressed in this paper, which are not necessarily those of the European Union or the European Commission.

References

Alchian, A., 1950. Uncertainty, evolution and economic theory. Journal of Political Economy 58, 211–222.
Alchian, A., Demsetz, H., 1972. Production, information costs and economic organization. American Economic Review 62, 777–795.
Aoki, M., 2001. Towards a Comparative Institutional Analysis. MIT Press, Cambridge, Mass.
Baldwin, C.Y., Clark, K.B., 2000. Design Rules. The Power of Modularity. MIT Press, Cambridge Mass.

Becker, G.S., Murphy, K.M., 1992. The division of labour, coordination costs and knowledge. Quarterly Journal of Economics 107, 1138–1140.

Bowles, S., 1985. The production process in a competitive economy: Neo-hobbesian and Marxian models. American Economic Review 75, 16–36.

Coase, R.H., 1937. The nature of the firm. Economica 4, 386–405.

Cohen, M.D., Burkhart, R., Dosi, G., Egidi, M., Marengo, L., Warglien, M., Winter, S.G., 1996. Routines and other recurring action patterns of organizations: contemporary research issues. Industrial and Corporate Change 5, 653–699.

Cyert, R.M., March, J.G., 1963. A Behavioral Theory of the Firm. Prentice Hall, Englewood Cliff, NJ.

David, P.A., 1994. Why are institutions the 'carriers of history'? Path dependence and the evolution of conventions, organizations and institutions. Structural Change and Economic Dynamics 5, 205–220.

David, P.A., Greenstein, S., 1990. The economics of compatibility standards: an introduction to recent research. Economics of Innovation and New Technology 1, 3–41.

Dosi, G., Nelson, R.R., Winter, S.G., 2000. The Nature and Dynamics of Organizational Capabilities. Oxford University Press, Oxford.

Dow, G.K., 1987. The function of authority in transaction-cost economics. Journal of Economic Behavior and Organization 8, 13–38.

Friedman, M., 1953. Essays in Positive Economics. University of Chicago Press, Chicago.

Granovetter, M., 1985. Economic action and social structure: the problem of embeddedness. American Journal of Sociology 91, 481–510.

Kauffman, S.A., 1993. The Origins of Order. Oxford University Press, Oxford.

Klepper, S.J., 1997. Industry life cycles. Industrial and Corporate Change 6, 145–181.

Langlois, R.N., 1986. Economics as a Process: Essays in the New Institutional Economics. Cambridge University Press, Cambridge.

Langlois, R.N., Robertson, P.L., 1995. Firms, Markets and Economic Change. Routledge, London/New York.

Leijonhufvud, A., 1986. Capitalism and the factory system, in economics as a process: essays in the new institutional economics (Langlois 1986), 203–223.

Levinthal, D., 1997. Adaptation on rugged landscapes. Management Science 43, 934–950.

Levinthal, D., 1998. The slow pace of rapid technological change: Gradualism and punctuation in technological change. Industrial and Corporate Change 7, 217–247.

Loasby, B.J., 1998. The organization of capabilities. Journal of Economic Behavior and Organization 25, 139–160.

Loasby, B.J., 2001. Organizations as interpretative systems. Revue d'Économie Industrielle 97, 17–34.

March, J.G., Simon, H.A., 1958. Organizations. Wiley, New York.

Marengo, L., 2003. Problem-complexity and problem-representation: some implications for the theory of economic institutions. In: Rizzello, S. (Ed.), Cognitive Developments in Economics. Routledge, Dordrecht, pp. 371–388.

Marglin, S.A., 1974. What do bosses do? The origins and function of hierarchy in capitalist production. Review of Radical Political Economics 6, 33–60.

Marschak, J., Radner, R., 1972. Economic Theory of Teams. Yale University Press, New Haven.

Milgrom, P., Roberts, J., 1990. The economics of modern manufacturing. American Economic Review 80, 511–528.

Morroni, M., 1992. Production Process and Technical Change. Cambridge University Press, Cambridge.

Nelson, R.R., 1981. Research on productivity differences. Journal of Economic Literature 19, 1029–1064.

Nelson, R.R., Winter, S.G., 1982. An Evolutionary Theory of Economic Change. The Belknap Press of Harvard University Press, Cambridge, MA.

Pagano, U., 1992. Organizational equilibria and production efficiency. Metroe-conomica 43, 227–246.

Page, S.E., 1996. Two measures of difficulty. Economic Theory 8, 321–346.

Penrose, E., 1959. The Theory of the Growth of the Firm. Wiley, New York.

Perry, M.K., 1989. Vertical integration: determinants and effects. In: Schmalensee, R., Willig, R. (Eds.), Handbook of Industrial Organization, vol. I. North Holland, Amsterdam, pp. 185–255.

Radner, R., 2000. Costly and bounded rationality in individual and team decision making. Industrial and Corporate Change 9, 623–658.

Richardson, G.B., 1972. The organization of industry. Economic Journal 82, 883–896.

Riordan, M., Williamson, O.E., 1985. Asset specificity and economic organization. International Journal of Industrial Organization 3, 365–378.

Simon, H.A., 1969. The Sciences of the Artificial. MIT Press, Cambridge, MA.

Simon, H.A., 1983. Reason in Human Affairs. Stanford University Press, Stanford.

Simon, H.A., 2002. Near decomposability and the speed of evolution. Industrial and Corporate Change 11, 587–599.

Teece, D.J., Pisano, G., Shuen, A., 1997. Dynamic capabilities and strategic management. Strategic Management Journal 18, 509–533.

Teece, D.J., Rumelt, R., Dosi, G., Winter, S.G., 1994. Understanding corporate coherence: theory and evidence. Journal of Economic Behavior and Organization 23, 1–30.

Vincenti, W., 1990. What Engineers Know and How They Know It: Analytical Study from Aeronautical History. The John Hopkins University Press, Baltimore.

Williamson, O.E., 1975. Markets and Hierarchies: Analysis and Antitrust Implications. Free Press, New York.

Williamson, O.E., 1985. The Economic Institutions of Capitalism: Firms, Markets, Relational Contracting. MacMillan, London.

Winter, S.G., 1975. Optimization and evolution in the theory of the firm. In: Day, R.H., Groves, T. (Eds.), Adaptive Economic Models. Academic Press, New York, pp. 73–118.

Winter, S.G., 2004. Toward and evolutionary theory of production. In: Dopfer, K. (Ed.), Principles of Evolutionary Economics. Cambridge University Press, Cambridge, pp. 223–254.

[4]

Problem-solving Behaviors, Organizational Forms, and the Complexity of Tasks

Giovanni Dosi, Mike Hobday, and Luigi Marengo

Introduction

The dominant form of analysis of organizational behaviors and structures, closely drawing from mainstream economics, takes a rather extreme agency approach, seeking to identify the most efficient incentive mechanisms for the coordination of decisions. However, such an incentive-based approach adopts the highly dubious assumption that both the structures for problem-solving and the necessary search heuristics (e.g. "rules of thumb" for decision-making) exist, unproblematically, from the outset. Here and throughout the chapter, the term "problem-solving" includes all the acts undertaken by individuals and groups within economic organizations (firms) to resolve organizational and technological problems and to conceptualize, design, test, and build products and processes.

In the case of most firms – new and incumbent ones – facing market and technological uncertainty, what one could call the "problem-free" assumption is profoundly unrealistic and assumes away the difficulty of constructing a theory to explain the co-evolution of problem-solving knowledge and organizational arrangements in firms. In turn, this demands some basic analytical tools to examine how firms deploy and match problem-solving activities with governance arrangements.[1] This is especially important where tasks are inherently complex and non-routine in nature and where many possible problem-solving and organizational solutions are possible.

The first purpose of this chapter is to outline an evolutionary framework for analyzing how problem-solving knowledge in firms co-evolves with organizational forms in complex task environments. These characteristics apply to most activities performed by new high technology firms and to the many functions in larger established corporations which are non-routine and non-codifiable by nature, including strategy formulation, R&D, marketing, distribution channel management, new product design, process engineering, human resource development and supply chain management.[2]

The second and complementary aim is to operationalize the evolutionary view of how firms as knowledge repositories cope with complex, non-routine tasks by evolving appropriate structures to deal with them. The practical application of the approach considers one important class of economic activity, which represents an extreme case of product and task complexity, namely the production of complex products and systems (or "CoPS"), including high cost, tailored capital goods, systems constructs, and services.[3] Because each new product tends to be different and because production involves feedback loops from later to early stages (and other unpredictable, "emerging" properties), highly innovative non-functional organizational structures are required to co-ordinate production, particularly in the commonly found case of unclear and uncertain user requirements.

The chapter is structured as follows. We describe the basic principles underlying an evolutionary approach to problem-solving behavior (PSB) in firms, contrasting these with the dominant (incentive-centred) formulation of agency in organizations. Next we present the building blocks of an evolutionary theory of PSB and firm organization, representing PSB as a form of complex design activity. The model – spelled out in more detail in Marengo (1999) and Marengo et al. (1999) – expands upon a "Simonian" representation of PSB grounded on the notions of combination of elementary physical and cognitive acts, and de-composability of firm behavior and structure in relation to particular product or process outcomes (Simon, 1981, 1991).

We apply the conceptual framework to CoPS found in sectors such as aerospace, information systems, many utilities, engineering construction, military systems, transportation, and telecommunications. Then we compare some properties of different organizational set-ups within multi-firm CoPS projects and their implications for innovative PSBs. Next we draw upon the organizational behavior literature to provide a practical set of heuristics for gathering "benchmark" data for complex non-routine projects: in the language we shall introduce below, such heuristics entail procedures for re-shaping "problem representations" and "problem decompositions". Some examples of the application of these concepts for the purposes of business improvement in CoPS are touched upon.[4]

An Evolutionary Approach to Problem-solving Behavior in Firms

Before presenting the basic building blocks of an evolutionary theory of PSB it is useful to briefly recall the governing principles behind the dominant agency approach. As known, agency theory identifies efficient incentive mechanisms for the coordination of decisions (see e.g. Tirole, 1986; Grossman and Hart, 1986; Laffont and Tirole, 1986), while implicitly assuming that PSB structures and search heuristics exist from the outset. Within firms, people are postulated to play extremely sophisticated games according to rules designed to prevent them from doing much harm to others (and indirectly to themselves). Neither the complexity of the task itself, nor the product of the firm or the production technology have much, or any, bearing on the subject at hand. The main aim is to generate admissible incentive-compatible procedures based, when taken at face value, on hyper-rational agents.[5]

Relatedly, individuals within organizations are assumed to hold the entire plan of what to do, possibly akin to a well-functioning computer model. The issue of firm competence and its relationship with performance does not arise, except for problems of the misrepresentation of "intrinsic" individual abilities and adverse selection, or incentive misalignment in eliciting effort from individuals. Within the firm, as a first approximation, the social division of tasks is irrelevant to practice and performance. In the extreme, according to the mainstream approach, given the "right" incentives, any firm can make any product as well as any other firm (e.g. microprocessors as well as Intel or bioengineering products as well as Genetech).[6]

By contrast, at its most general level, the evolutionary approach sees economic organizations as problem-solving arrangements, viewing the different observed institutional set-ups in the real world as reflecting the complexity of the tasks and objectives faced by the firm (March and Simon, 1958; Nelson and Winter, 1982; Dosi and Marengo, 1994). In the world of non-trivial, complex, and uncertain tasks, governance arrangements and search heuristics play a central part in determining which eventual solutions are considered as possibilities, tested, and ultimately selected. Relatedly, a key evolutionary proposition is that in making decisions, firms and individuals and groups within them, confront extremely large, computationally intractable search "spaces" to choose from. Therefore the particular organizational arrangements and approaches, skill and experience in proceeding, shape and define the distinctive competence of individual firms.[7]

As can be formally demonstrated, the design of suitable organizational arrangements tends to be even more computationally complex than finding an optimal solution to the problem itself (Marengo et al., 1999). To the extent that this is a correct representation of real world decision-making, this implies that it is not sensible to assume that problem-solvers operate within ex ante established organizational structures, governance arrangements, and PSB routines. Indeed, organizational form has to be established as part of, and alongside, the problem-solving activity. Within this co-evolution of PSBs and organizational arrangements, individuals, groups and entire firms are far from having perfect knowledge or foresight, but "bounded rationality," broadly defined, is the rule (Simon, 1981; Dosi and Egidi, 1991; Dosi et al. 1996).[8]

To resolve highly complex dynamic problems, boundedly rational individuals and groups within firms (as with the firm itself) are highly likely to adopt problem decomposition procedures, (for a thorough illustration, see among others, the example of aeronautical engineering in Vincenti, 1990). Here and throughout this work, largely in tune with Herbert Simon's perspective on problem-solving, by "decomposition" we mean the identification of ensembles of tasks or "sub-problems" whose solution is meant to yield also to the solution of the overall problem. So, for example, if the general problem is the development and construction of an airplane with certain technical characteristics, "decompositions" might involve the identification of "sub-problems" concerning e.g. engine thrust, wing loads, aerodynamic shapes of the body, and so on. Over time, decomposition heuristics and routines are likely to evolve differently in different firms as they learn to reduce the dimensions of search space through experience. As a result, not all decomposition strategies are necessarily successful (or equally successful), and no selection mechanism or process of choice (e.g. incentives) necessarily exists to ensure an optimum solution to product, process, or organizational problems.

Consequently it is reasonable to assume that the problem-solving abilities of firms are nested within a "ubiquitous sub-optimality." Intra-firm learning patterns and inter-organizational selection processes need initially to be considered as evolutionary processes, even neglecting, in a first approximation, the diverse incentive-driven behaviors which different organizational forms elicit.[9]

These propositions are naturally consistent with an emerging evolutionary approach to "what business firms are and do" (e.g. Nelson and Winter, 1982; Winter, 1982, 1988; Dosi, 1988, Teece et al., 1994; Dosi and Marengo 1994; Marengo, 1996) and are largely overlapping and complementary with the view expressed by Simon (1991), March and Simon (1958) and Radner (1992) among others.

In this approach, the product in question clearly matters (e.g. steel, computers, or polypropylene) as does the great diversity in processes and organizational arrangements deployed to make a particular product. No single individual knows the entire production plan and, within both the management of business-as-usual and in the search for new product designs and efficient processes, organisations display an ensemble of routine procedures, through which organizations often manage to coordinate their tasks well enough to deliver a coherent set of processes and products. In contrast to the "optimal machine" analogy, the firm can be viewed as an intelligent but fallible "organism" trying to adapt imperfectly and path-dependently to a changing environment shaped also by other organisms (including competitors, suppliers, and buyers).

In the evolutionary view, the basic units of analysis for PSBs are, on the one hand, elementary physical acts (such as moving a drawing from one office to another) and elementary cognitive acts (such as a simple calculation) on the other. Problem-solving can then be defined as a combination of elementary acts within a procedure, leading eventually to a feasible outcome (e.g. an aircraft engine or a chemical compound). Or, seen the other way round, given the possibly infinite set of procedures leading to a given outcome or product, it is possible to decompose these procedures into diverse series of elementary cognitive and physical acts of varying lengths which may be executed according to various possible execution architectures (e.g. sequential, parallel, or hierarchical).

PBSs straightforwardly link with the notion of organizational competencies and capabilities. First, a firm displays the operational competencies associated with its actual problem-solving procedures (in line with the routines discussed by Nelson and Winter, 1982 and Cohen et al., 1996). Second, the formal and informal organizational structure of the firm determines the way in which cognitive and physical acts are distributed and the decomposition rules which govern what is and what is not admissible within a particular firm (providing a route into the analysis of incentive structures and processes). Third, the organization shapes the search heuristics for, as yet, unresolved problems, thereby governing creative processes within the firm.

This theoretical approach to PSB within the firm also corresponds closely to empirical accounts of firm behaviour from the economics of innovation (Freeman, 1982; Dosi, 1988; Pavitt, 1999). Moreover, it has the benefit of being applicable both to the analysis of intra-firm structures and to the analysis of the boundaries between firms and the market. Indeed, such boundaries can be seen as particular patterns of decomposition of an overall problem-solving task. In other words, the boundary of the firm is shaped, in part, by the problem to be solved, often corresponding to the product to be created (e.g. a car or a piece of steel). Particular decomposition strategies will range from the totally centralized and autarkic types (with no decomposition at all) to the equivalent of a pure market, where one person acts on each task with market-like transactions linking each elementary act.

From an empirical perspective, it then becomes important to ask whether and under which circumstances "markets" (i.e. complete decentralized distributions of knowledge) have problem-solving advantages over more centralized, "hierarchical" forms of decomposition. The next section presents some simple conceptual building blocks for analyzing this type of question.

Products, Tasks, and Organizations as Problems of Design

It is helpful to think of complex problem-solving activities as problems of design: the design of elaborate artefacts and the design of the processes and organizational structures required to produce them. In turn, these processes require the design of complex sequences of moves, rules, behaviors and search heuristics involving one or many different actors to solve problems, create new "representations" of problems themselves and ultimately to achieve the techno-economic goals at hand. Common to all these design activities is that they involve search in large combinatorial spaces of "components" (as defined above in terms of elementary physical and cognitive acts) which have to be closely coordinated. To complicate matters still further, the functional relations among these elements are only partly understood and can only be locally explored through a process of trial-and-error learning, often involving also the application of expert, partly tacit knowledge.

For example, the design of a complex artefact such as an aircraft or a flight simulator requires the co-ordination of many different design elements, including engine type and power, wing size, and shape and other materials. The interaction between each of the sub-systems and components is only partly understood and each comprises many smaller components and sub-systems (Miller et al., 1995; Prencipe, 1997). The interactions between the elements of the system can only be partly expressed by general models and have to be tested through simulation, prototype building, and trial-and-error moves where learning and tacit knowledge play an important part. Producing an effective solution, such as a new aircraft, involves a long sequence of moves, each of which is chosen out of an enormous set of possibilities. In turn, the relations among the moves in the sequence can only be partly known as a full understanding would (impossibly) require the knowledge of the entire set of possibilities. The likelihood of combinatorial explosion within the search space presents a computationally intractable task for boundedly rational agents. As Metcalfe and de Liso (1995) argue, the beliefs and routines of the firm act as a focusing device, indicating where to search in order to produce functioning artefacts: "Paradoxical though it may seem, to make progress it is necessary to limit progress" (p. 21). In that, also the "culture" of the firm acts as an interpretative system grounded in the community of practice of the firm, which allows progress and learning under conditions of extreme uncertainty and vast opportunities for design choice.

Business firms as well as collaborative ventures among them can therefore be seen as complex, multi-dimensional bundles of routines, decision rules, procedures and incentive schemes, whose interplay is often largely unknown both to the managers of the organization and also to managers, designers, and engineers responsible for single projects. Of course, over time many repeated technical and business activities become routinized and codified, allowing for stable, formal structures and established codified routines as, for example, in the volume production activities of automobiles or commodity chemicals. In these circumstances, some sort of "steady state" problem decomposition becomes institutionalized, also allowing the establishment of neat organizational structures, and, together, the exploitation of economies of scale and scope. The "Fordist" and "Chandlerian" archetypes of organization are the classic examples. This is also the organizational arrangement which most forcefully highlights potential advantages (and also the in-built rigidities) of division of labor and specialization. However, even in this stable case there remain many non-routine, complex activities within the firm, including new product design, research and development, new marketing programmes, and so on. In these areas the foregoing properties of search for new PSBs continue to apply and organizational forms take a variety of shapes in relation to these tasks. In addition, under conditions of rapid market and technological change even stable ("Fordist") organizations are often forced to re-assess and re-constitute their structures in order to respond to new market demands and to exploit new technical opportunities (see, for example, the related discussions by Coriat and by Fujimoto in Dosi et al., (2000), on Japanese – "Toyotist" – organizational arrangements and routines).

During the multi-stage product design task, the basic elements to be co-ordinated are characterised by strong interdependencies which create many local optima within the search space. For instance, adding a more powerful engine could lead to a reduction in the performance of an aircraft or prevent it from flying altogether if the other sub-systems and components are not simultaneously adapted. Similarly, at the organizational level, the introduction of new routines, practices, or incentive schemes which have proven superiority in another context, could also prove counter-productive if other elements of the organization are not appropriately adapted to suit the new inputs (Dosi et al., 2000).

A helpful "reduced form" metaphor of the complex task problem is presented in Kauffman's (1993) model of selection dynamics in the biological domain with heterogeneous interdependent traits. Kauffman considers a model of the selection mechanisms whereby the units of selection are complex entities made of several non-linearly interacting components. Units of selection are combinations of N elementary components (genes or morphological or behavioral traits) which can assume one of an finite number of states and a fitness value is exogeneously assigned to each "gene" producing a fitness landscape on the space of combinations, reflecting the interdependencies among the constituent elements. His model shows that as the number of interdependent elements increases the fitness landscape presents an exponentially increasing number of local optima. In the presence of strong interdependencies (as occurs in many complex products, see part III) the system cannot be optimized by separately optimizing each element it is made of. Indeed, in the case of strong interdependencies it might well be the case that some, or even all, solutions obtained by tuning "in the right direction" each component yield a worse performance than the current one.

In the presence of strong interdependencies the problem cannot therefore be decomposed into separate sub-problems which could be optimized separately from the others (Marengo, 1999). However, as argued by Simon (1981) problem-solving by boundedly rational agents must necessarily proceed by decomposing a large, complex and intractable problem into smaller sub-problems which can be solved independently. Within the firm this is equivalent to a division of problem-solving labor. However, the extent of the division of problem-solving labor is limited by the existence of interdependencies. If, in the process of sub-problem decomposition, interdependent elements are separated, then solving each sub-problem interdependently does not allow overall optimization. As Simon (1981) also points out, since a perfect decomposition, which isolates in separate sub-problems all and only the elements which are interdependent to each other, can only be designed by someone who has perfect knowledge of the problem, boundedly rational agents will normally try to design "near-decompositions". The latter are decompositions which try to isolate the most performance relevant interdependencies into separate sub-problems.

Unlike the biological analogy above, the design space of a problem faced by an engineer or a firm is not given exogenously but, rather, is constructed by them as a subjective representation of the problem itself where, in practice, much of the search takes place. If the division of problem-solving labor is limited by interdependencies, the structure of the latter, in turn, depends on how the problem is framed by the problem-solvers. Sometimes with major innovations, problem-solvers are able to make important leaps forward by re-framing the problem itself in a novel way. For example, in the accounts of wireless communications development provided by Levinthal (1998) and the Polaris missile system by Sapolsky (1972) various known system elements were combined and re-combined in creative new ways.

In short, the representation of the problem itself plays a crucial part in determining its complexity. By acting on its representation, decision-makers can make a problem more or less decomposable. The division of problem-solving labor is therefore very much a question of how the problem is represented and its elements encoded.

Given the limits that interdependencies pose to the division of problem-solving labor, an important part of the representation is how agents evaluate the "goodness" of solutions. As already mentioned, the problem of interdependencies amount to a problem of misalignment of local vs. global performance signals: local moves in the "right direction" may well decrease overall performance if particular elements are not properly adjusted to the moves. Thus there is room for the design of many alternative methods of performance assessment. In the formal model presented elsewhere (Marengo et al., 1999), for every problem of a given class there can be different performance assessment schemes, providing a set of payoffs to variations of components of the solution which allow for maximum decomposition. This form of performance assessment makes local adaptation and decentralized trial-and-error search effective as strategies.

During the design of PSBs and in the long-term building of the distinctive competence of firms, the architecture of the firm co-evolves with its decomposition schemes. Indeed, any organizational hierarchy may be seen, from a problem-solving perspective, as entailing particular decompositions into blocks of elements (sub-problems and organizationally admissible behaviors and tasks assigned to them) which, together make the overall configuration of the PSBs and organizational governance of the firm. In complex tasks, firms continue to go through step-by-step experiments with groups of elements in order to improve the performance of the overall system. In some cases, activities are more or less decomposable (e.g. finance and manufacturing, or a mechanical and electrical system). Here the firm is able to rapidly find an appropriate "robust" decomposition.

However, in many cases (e.g. product design and systems integration) notwithstanding the ubiquitous search for "modularity," tasks are highly interdependent, leading to indeterminacy in PSBs and governance arrangements and many different solutions to chose from. When building a decomposition scheme, firms might ideally search for perfect decomposability, so that all groups of elements can be optimized in a totally independent way from the others. However, near-decomposability is more common as many problems cannot be divided into neatly isolated groups of components which can all be solved independently.

Problem-solving design does not only involve search within a given space but also, and very importantly, a re-framing of the problem itself by the agents within the firm. Changing the frame or representation of the particular problem is a powerful form of PSB. Indeed, as argued in Marengo (1996), the establishment of collectively shared representations and problem-solving frames is one of the fundamental roles of top management. Equally important, when the organizational architecture allows it, groups within the firm, by experimentation, are able to collectively evolve new representations, possibly yielding more effective decompositions. In the formal model presented by Marengo et al. (1999) the construction of shared representations allows for the simplification of complex problems, offering a more powerful strategy than attempting to optimize any particular given representation. Experience and learning provide the agents with knowledge of probable viable decompositions as well as probably "well-behaved representations."

In the real world of decision-making, agents rarely hold a full representation of the overall problem and can only control a limited number of elements involved. Firms have to proceed by roughly defining an architecture for various blocks of elements to be integrated (e.g. electronic hardware and software systems), assigning the blocks to individuals and groups, co-ordinated by a project manager or equivalent. This way they try to achieve decomposability and, where not possible, effective communications and interactions between agents across the various blocks of sub-tasks. Note that top-down assignments of sub-problems and formal tasks rarely match perfectly the actual decompositions achieved via "horizontal" self-organizing adjustments (for a fascinating longitudinal story of these dynamics throughout the establishment of a major telecom company see Narduzzo, et al. 2000). Indeed, the mismatches between "formal" representations and decompositions and actual (emergent) ones, are at the same time a major drawback on organizational performances but also a potential source of organizational learning. These processes are endemic to most activities involved in the production of CoPS, as discussed in the following sections.

PSBs in Complex Products and Systems

Complex product systems (CoPS) are high value artefacts, systems, sub-systems, software packages, control units, networks and high technology constructs.[10] As high technology customized capital goods, they tend to be made in one-off projects or small batches. The emphasis of production is on design, project management, systems engineering and systems integration. Examples include telecommunications exchanges, flight simulators, aircraft engines, avionics systems, train engines, air traffic control units, systems for electricity grids, offshore oil equipment, baggage handling systems, R&D equipment, bio-informatics systems, intelligent buildings and cellular phone network equipment.

There are many different categories of CoPS, ranging from relatively traditional goods (e.g. train engines) to new IT networks (e.g. internet super-servers) to established goods which have been radically transformed by IT (e.g. integrated mail processing systems and printing press machinery). They can be categorized according to sector (e.g. aerospace, military and transportation), function (e.g. control systems, communications and R&D), and degree of complexity (e.g. as measured by the number of tailored components and sub-systems, design options and amount of new knowledge required).

The physical composition and production processes of most CoPS have changed due to the diffusion of IT and embedded software. As software becomes a core technology, many CoPS are becoming more complex and difficult to produce, partly as a result of the human, craft design element involved in software development.[11] Technical progress, combined with new industrial demands have greatly enhanced the functional scope, performance and complexity of CoPS throughout, from jet engines to nuclear power simulation systems.

CoPS have at least three defining characteristics which distinguish them from mass produced goods. First, as high cost, capital goods they consist of many interconnected, often customized elements (including control units, sub-systems and components), usually organized in a hierarchical manner and tailored for specific customers and/or markets. Often their sub-systems (e.g. the avionics systems for aircraft) are themselves complex, customized and high cost. Second, they tend to exhibit emergent properties during production, as unpredictable and unexpected events occur during design and systems engineering and integration (Boardman, 1990; Shenhar, 1994). Emerging properties also occur from generation to generation, as small changes in one part of a system's design often call for large alterations in other parts, requiring the addition of more sophisticated control systems and, sometimes, new materials (e.g. in jet engines). Third, because they are high value capital goods, CoPS tend to be produced in projects or in small batches which allow for a high degree of direct user involvement, enabling business users to engage directly into the innovation process, rather than through arm's length market transactions, as normally the case in commodity goods.

There are many different dimensions of product complexity, each of which can confer task complexity and non-routine behavior to production and innovation tasks. These dimensions include the numbers of components, the degree of customization of both system and components, multiple design choices, elaborate systems architectures, breadth and depth of knowledge and skill required, and the variety of materials and information inputs. Users frequently change their requirements during production, leading to unclear goals, uncertainty in production and unpredictable, unquantifiable risks. Managers and engineers often have to proceed from one production stage to the next with incomplete information, relying on inputs from other suppliers who may be

competitors in other multi-firm projects. Project management often involves negotiat-
ing between the competing interests, goals and cultures of the various organizations
involved in production.

Many CoPS are produced within projects which incorporate prime contractors, systems integrators, users, buyers, other suppliers, small and medium sized enterprises
and sometimes government agencies and regulators. Often, these agents collaborate
together, taking innovation (e.g. new design) decisions in advance of and during production, as in the case of flight simulators (Miller et al., 1995). Projects consist of
temporary multi-firm alliances where systems integration and project management
competencies are critical to production. The project represents a sort of focusing device which enables the problems of design and production to be addressed. It is also
responsible for realizing the market, coordinating decisions across firms, enabling buyer
involvement, and matching technical and financial resources through time. Because
production is oriented to meet the needs of large business users, the project management task is fundamentally different from the mass production task. As Joan Woodward (1958:23) already put it in her research into UK project-based companies in the
1950s:

> Those responsible for marketing had to sell, not a product, but the idea that their firm was
> able to produce what the customer required. The product was developed after the order
> had been secured, the design being, in many cases, modified to suit the requirements of
> the customer. In mass production firms, the sequence is quite different: product develop-
> ment came first, then production, and finally marketing.

Designing Organizational Forms for CoPS

Although vast and diverse bodies of literature exist on organizational forms, there are
not many studies which examine in any depth the project-based organization or forms
suited to CoPS.[12] Certainly, the relation between organizational form and the problem solving nature of the firm is at the heart of "competence-based" and, largely overlapping, evolutionary perspectives (e.g. Dosi et al., 2000; Dosi and Marengo, 1994;
Kogut and Zander, 1992, 1996; Nelson and Winter, 1982; Nelson, 1991; Teece,
Pisano and Schuen, 1994; Teece et al, 1994; Conner and Prahalad, 1996; Leonard-
Barton, 1995; Winter, 1988). The competence view in fact focuses on organizations
as repositories of problem-solving knowledge and analyzes some salient properties of
knowledge accumulation and the ways the latter co-evolve with organizational structures and practices (including, of course, routines but also managerial heuristics and
strategies).

Organizational specificities and persistently different revealed performances, are thus
interpreted also on the grounds of path-dependence in knowledge accumulation and
inertial persistence of organizational traits. Bounded rationality, in its broadest meaning, is the norm. Its general sources include the "complexity" and procedural uncertainty associated with problem-solving procedures and the intrinsic "opaqueness" of
the relationship between actions and environmental feed-backs, so that it is seldom
obvious, even ex post, to state how well one did and why (March, 1994).

Taking all that as a (quite sound, in our view) point of departure, one must acknowledge, however, that one is still far from having comprehensive taxonomies mapping discrete *organizational types* into diverse forms of knowledge distributions and problem-solving behaviours, even if one finds suggestive exercises in this direction. So, for example, Mintzberg (1979), partly building on the work of Burns and Stalker (1961) attempts to derive a classification contingent on the nature of markets, tasks and technologies. (A somewhat extreme notion of "contingency" of organizational forms upon environmental characteristics is, of course, in Lawrence and Lorsch, 1971.

Mintzberg describes five basic organizational forms: (1) the "machine bureaucracy" with highly centralized control systems, suited to a stable environment; (2) the divisional form suited to mass production efficiency; (3) the professional bureaucracy made up of flat organizational structures, useful for delegating complex, professional tasks (e.g. in universities); (4) the simple or entrepreneurial structure, valuable for its informality and flexibility; and (5) the "adhocracy," which is a temporary project-based design, suited to complex tasks and turbulent and uncertain markets. Somewhat similarly largely building upon a competence-based view of organisations, Teece (1996) proposes six categories of firm: (1) stand-alone entrepreneur inventor; (2) multiproduct integrated hierarchy; (3) high flex, Silicon Valley type; (4) "virtual" corporation; (5) conglomerate; and (6) alliance enterprise.[13] Other observers of organization form (e.g. Galbraith 1971, 1973; Larson and Gobeli, 1987, 1989) describe a range of alternatives from pure functional form through to pure "product form," where management structures are centered upon each product.

A general conjecture lurking through many such taxonomic efforts is the positive relation between some form of organizational flexibility, on the one hand, and complexity and variability of tasks, on the other. In that vein, Burns and Stalker (1961) make the famous distinction between "organic" and "mechanistic" organizational types. They argue that the latter is more suited to stable environments and routine PSB, taking advantage of, for example, clearly defined job description, stable operational boundaries and tayloristic work methods. Conversely, they suggest, under rapidly changing technological and market conditions, open and flexibile ("organic") styles of organization make for easier coordination between different organizational functions – such as R&D and marketing, etc.

The spirit of most of the foregoing studies tend to be either *prescriptive* (that is, focused on how to design suitable organizations) or *cross-sectionally* descriptive (comparing different sectors, technologies, etc.). That makes an interesting contrast with long-term historical studies, *in primis* the path-breaking investigations by Chandler (1962), highlighting a secular trend from the rather simple owner/manager firms of the eighteenth century, all the way to the twentieth-century divisionalized/matrix form. This is not to say that the two views are necessarily at odds with each other. For example, it could well be that profound inter-sectoral variations (nested into different problem-soling tasks, as mentioned) happened to go together with an overall average increase in organizational complexity.[14] We cannot tackle the issue here. Let us just mention that such "cross-sectional" and "historical" patterns are all nested into diverse forms of division of cognitive and manual labour which in turn is reflected in diverse PSB and learning patterns. In the perspective of the interpretation outlined above in this work, diverse organizational forms map into diverse

1   problem *representations;*
2   problem *decompositions;*
3   task *assignments;*
4   *heuristics for* and *boundaries to exploration and learning.*
5   *mechanisms for conflict resolution over interests,* and, equally important, over *alternative cognitive frames* and *problem interpretations.*

With respect to these dimensions, to repeat a telegraphic caricature we are rather fond of, one might think, at one extreme, of an archetype involving complete, hierarchical, ex ante representations, precise task assignments according to well defined functions/tasks, quite tight boundaries to exploration – "learning" being itself a specialized function – and, if all that works, no need for ex post conflict resolution.

The opposite extreme archetype might be somewhat akin to university departments, with a number of representations at least as high as the number of department members, fuzzy decompositions, little task assignments, and loose boundaries to exploration, fuzzy conflict resolution rules, and so on. clearly, Taylorist/Fordist organizational forms tend to be nearer the former archetype, which, to repeat, are not appropriate for CoPS, for all the reasons mentioned above. However, they do display a quite large variety of arrangements, and with that equally diverse PSB.

Figure 11.1 provides a description of six ideal-type organizational forms ranging from the pure functional form (type A) to pure product/project form (type F).[15] The various functional departments of the organization (e.g. marketing, finance, human resources, engineering, R&D, and manufacturing) are represented by F1 to F5, while notional CoPS projects are represented by P1 to P5. Type B is a functionally oriented matrix, with weak project coordination. Type C is a balanced matrix with stronger project management authority. Type D is a project matrix, where project managers are of equal status to functional managers. Type E, is a "project-led organization," in which the needs of projects outweigh the functional influence on decision-making and representation to senior management, but weak coordination across project lines occurs. Finally, type F is the pure project-based form where there is no formal functional coordination across project lines and the entire organization is dedicated to one or more CoPS projects.

The positioning diagram helps to contrast many of the various forms of organization available for dealing with complex tasks, accepting that a mixed organizational structure is possible even within a single business unit. Forms A to C tend to be unsuitable for CoPS, because they are inappropriate for performing non-routine, complex project tasks in an uncertain and changing environment. CoPS projects typically require "super-heavyweight" professional project managers (or directors), capable of integrating both commercial and technical business functions within the project and building strong lines of external communication both with the client (often the source of the innovation idea) and other collaborating companies. The collaborators may well have different goals, structures and cultures and the task of the project director is to skilfully negotiate a path towards successful completion.

The pure project form (F) appears to be well suited for large innovative projects and single project firms, where resources have to be combined and shared with other firms in the project (i.e. a large multi-firm project such as the English–French Channel Tunnel). The project form is suitable for responding to uncertainty and changing client requirements, coping with emerging properties and learning in real time. By contrast, the project form is weak where the functional and matrix structures are strong: in coordinating resources and capabilities across projects, in executing routine production and engineering tasks and achieving economies of scale for mass markets.

To illustrate the problem-solving advantages of the project-based form for CoPS,

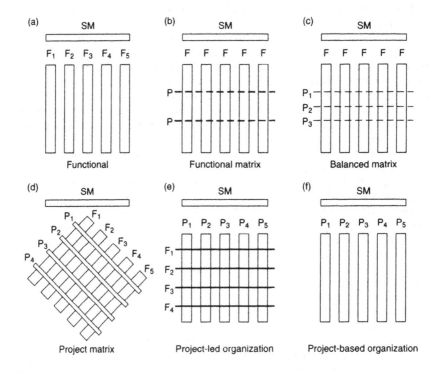

Key

* F_1-F_5 = various functional departmentss of the organization (e.g. marketing, finance, human resources, engineering, manufacturing, R&D)

* P_1-P_5 = major projects within the organization (e.g. CoPS projects)

* SM = senior management

Figure 11.1: Positioning the project-based organization

figure 11.2 contrasts the project management task within a functional matrix (type B) with that of a pure project form (type F). Figure 11.2(a) shows the position of the "weak" project manager within the functional matrix, involving multiple lines of communication, control and command, and the sub ordination to various department managers. Here project coordination embodies a linear or sequential model of project management, in which the project passes through various stages and departments in turn. Client and suppliers are external to the project and the project manager has to perform a highly complex internal task of balancing various internal interests and meeting different demands (e.g. in terms of reporting and quality control) of the departments. There are many lines of communication with project team members (TM 1 to TM 6) who also report to functional or departmental managers (FM 1 to FM 6) to whom they owe their career allegiance.

Throughout the problem-solving process, project managers in the functional and matrix forms also face many difficulties in external co-ordination. To reply to customer requests they often have to gain information and commitments from engineering, purchasing, and planning departments. The larger and more complex the project, the more difficult the task of keeping the client informed and responding to requests for changes.

By contrast, figure 11.2(b) shows the position of the project managers in a project-based organization in relation to the specialist functions within the project. The project manger is the main channel of communication and can exercise control to coordinate and integrate specialist functions, focusing on the needs of each project. Because there are few internal lines of command and communication to interfere with project objectives, the internal coordination task becomes simpler and the ability to react to emerging properties is enhanced.

Similarly on the external front, clear strong lines of command and communications can be built up with the client (figure 11.2(c)). In principle, the project manager is able to quickly assess and react to changes in client needs and learn from feedback from the client and major component suppliers (S 1 to S 5). The project manager has both the responsibility and power to react to unexpected events, negotiate changes with the client and, if necessary, put suppliers of sub-systems together with the customer to resolve difficult problems.

The project-based organization embodies a concurrent model of project management in which tasks are integrated as required by the project. In principle, the project-based form boasts several advantages over the functional and matrix forms for CoPS. Producing a CoPS is often a creative task, requiring innovation at both the product and organizational levels. Production typically involves many knowledge-intensive, non-routine tasks and decision-taking under conditions of uncertainty. These uncertain processes cannot easily be codified within routine procedures as learning during production is required to complete the task. Because the project-based form is able to create and re-create organizational structures and processes around the needs of each product (and customer) it contrasts sharply with the anti-innovation bias which are likely to be displayed by large functional organizations with their semi-permanent departments and rigid processes. The challenge of managing CoPS is one of ensuring responsiveness to the changing needs of customers, and dealing with the emerging properties which arise in production. It is

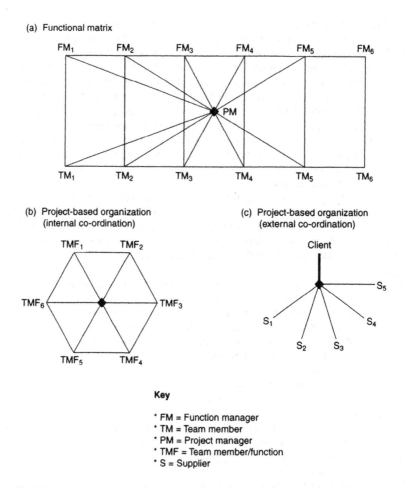

(a) Functional matrix

(b) Project-based organization
(internal co-ordination)

(c) Project-based organization
(external co-ordination)

Key

* FM = Function manager
* TM = Team member
* PM = Project manager
* TMF = Team member/function
* S = Supplier

Figure 11.2: Comparing the project-management function in functional and project-based organizations

also a challenge of anticipating future client needs and convincing buyers of the firm's competence to deliver new systems in the future. On the other hand, the looser the structure is, the more difficult it is also to codify past learning achievements into some organizational memory; the informal mobility of employees is usually the chief method of building organizational capabilities and performances. There are indeed subtle trade-offs in all the foregoing organizational arrangements – and unexploited learning opportunities – of which most often the actors involved are only partly aware. Symmetrically, "diagnostic" techniques and heuristics for organizational design might be surprisingly effective in the improvement of decision-making processes and PSB.

Heuristics for Organizational Design and Collective Action in Complex Task Environments

In this respect, let us briefly report on how the foregoing framework on problem-solving can be combined with work from the organization development field to produce a method to assist in the real world of problem-solving, at least in the case of the design and the production of complex products and systems. We have been discussing above, from a theoretical point of view, the crucial step of *decomposition* of complex problems into nearly independent sub-problems and the difficulties thereupon. Indeed, a first operational task in a practical, diagnostic, exercise is to help identify alternative representations and, relatedly, decompositions of the problem at hand. Second, the exercise ought to be aimed to elicit the differences between formal vs. informal processes (and structures) for each project. Third, and relatedly, it provides mechanisms for a sort of *endogenous benchmarking*. This technique avoids the need for conventional benchmarking which, in any case, cannot be applied to one-off, non-routine tasks, but rather tries to elicit the very representation of such a benchmark and feeds back this data to the "actors" in a structured manner in order to help them design and develop the complex product and ensure an appropriate organizational structure. The outcome tends to be a re-combination of tasks and structures in the companies in which the intervention was made and, in general, a reduction of the difficulties inherent in complex one-off tasks, through a narrowing of the gap between formal and actual practices and processes.

To operationalize the theory, an experimental attempt was made to develop and apply an action research technique to collective decision-making in six large multi-project CoPS suppliers in Europe.[16] The approach is partly based on intervention techniques developed within the field of organization development (a sub-field of organizational behavior), which spans both management strategy and implementation (Schein, 1990; Mullins, 1994; Handy, 1993; French and Bell, 1973; Tyson and Jackson, 1992), and tends to treat strategy, management, learning and innovation as iterative processes rooted in working practices, which are "crafted", informal and sensitive to organizational forms (Mintzberg, 1989; Seeley Brown and Duguid, 1996). Using research data, selective outside interventions can sometimes be helpful in surfacing issues, identifying problems, and stimulating new working practices (French and Bell, 1973).

The method was initially developed for the analysis and improvement of PSBs in complex software projects in collaboration with process analysts in a large French corporation. The purpose of the method (or "tool") is to assist collective decision-making in order to arrive at effective PSBs and appropriate organizational forms for projects and specific tasks within projects (e.g. design, bidding, and sub-contractor management), in the common situation where each product and project is different and processes are, to a large extent, uncodifiable.[17] The method involves generating benchmark data on behaviors, routines, and structures and feeding this back to company teams in real time in order to assist problem-solving under conditions of bounded rationality and task complexity, by promoting more effective collective action by "shining a mirror" on the organization.

A distinctive feature of the method is that it focuses on the tacit, informal side of the PSB and informal organizations, comparing these systematically with formal processes and organizational structures. In other words it compares "what should be and what should happen" with real, actual practices ("what actually happens"), in order to identify variance (for explanation and discussion) problems, their causes and strategies for improvement. The tool complements other formal procedures which exist in most large firms by delivering a "bottom up" practitioner view of real processes in action.

The method is applied by decomposing the CoPS project roughly into tasks, which include not only the main technical activities, but other functions such as finance, manufacturing, and scheduling. To carry out a minimalist intervention in a large firm, typically two projects are identified, to allow for comparability and contrast. Within (and above) the projects, twelve or so individuals at three or four levels of seniority are selected across the project tasks. The researchers then carry out the intervention with the members of the "slice group" for each project, according to five standard steps, each with more detailed sub-processes and outputs (Hobday and Brady, 1998).

Step 1 involves agreeing with management and practitioners the scope, aims, outputs and timing of the exercise, and identifying the slice group of interviewees (this focuses especially on practitioners who understand best the informal project processes). In step 2 data is collected on formal codified practices as usually contained in toolkits, manuals, flow charts, formal procedures (and a few interviews with senior managers), on how the process "should" proceed. If the firm does not have formal codified procedures for the project, then senior management views or any "best practice" model of project management can be used.[18] Using a standard questionnaire, qualitative data is gathered from practitioners on how processes actually proceed in the two projects and in the wider organization (inputs, activities, and outputs are described and informal flow charts are drawn). Step 3 involves comparing the formal ("should be") practices with informal, uncodified activities to generate key differences (e.g. by comparing formal and informal flow charts). This represents a rapid form of real-time benchmarking (comparing actual with codified practices) for complex tasks.[19]

Variances tend to fall into two categories: major problem areas and best practices (or solutions to problems). Often solutions consist of engineers resolving problems caused by the formal processes! In step 4 the findings are presented back to practitioners for verification, which involves feedback on the accuracy of the data collected, omissions, the extent and depth of problems identified and the nature of the solutions. At this stage, quantitative data can be gathered if needed (using Likert scales, for example, on the extent of particular problems in the organization). Step 4 also includes an analysis of the causes of problems, a discussion of possible solutions and proposals for implementation, as applied both to project processes (including PSBs) and organizational structures. Step 5 involves reporting back to senior management (who have agreed to act on the findings) and the agreement of a plan for improvement. The actual format depends on the culture of the company. In some, the practitioners are happy to have senior managers involved closely in all steps. In others practitioners are inhibited in the presence of functional and project managers. The five basic steps of the process analysis and improvement method are as follows:

1   *Set up programme*; identify structured group for interviews and workshops;
2   *Data collection*: codified processes (management) *vs* actual informal processes (prac-
     titioners);
3   *Benchmark analysis*: identify key variances (a) problem areas (b) best practices –
     prepare workshop 1;
4   *Workshop 1*: (a) verification, (b) establish causes of problems, (c) identify solutions,
     (d) proposals on implementation;
5   *Workshop 2*: report back to senior management – agree actions/support for imple-
     mentation.

Although the method was initially developed for complex software projects, it has
subsequently been modified and applied to other domains and other non-routine,
complex processes. However, the approach remains the same – the application of an
outside intervention to benchmark codified against actual processes in order to provide data to question, assess and sometime re-compose organizational structures and
processes. The following six examples give some idea of the scope of the intervention
technique.

Company A is a producer of complex embedded software for flight simulators. Here,
the purpose was to improve software processes within a new change programme. The
group discussions led to the questioning of (redundant) software tools and a
reconfiguration of parts of the software process, contributing to an upgrading of the
latter according to the official international quality standard "CMM." The intervention enabled software practitioners to shape work processes by contributing new more
appropriate tools and training programmes aligned with real, rather than formal work
processes, with the consequence of reducing also variances between initial software
estimates and actual outcomes in terms of budget and costs. In the language introduced above, the objective was achieved by the identification of a closer alignment
between formal problem decompositions/task assignments and actual, "informally
learned," ones.

Company B is a supplier of components for naval equipment organized along lines
established in the 1960s. The task was the improvement of product development processes for a new generation of nuclear submarine cores. The two main technical groups
involved – design engineering and manufacturing engineering – organized separately
along traditional lines, were brought together during the intervention, enabling them
to analyze, question, and reconfigure the "normal" linear sequence of design and
production. By introducing more concurrency into the design-build cycle, re-work
was reduced as a result of closer engineering-manufacturing integration: more "fuzzy"
decompositions, broader "spans of exploration" and faster information exchange cycles have been key organizational modifications.

Company C is a producer of synchrotron particle accelerators and large-scale mag-
netic equipment for scientific research. This intervention focused on the assessment of
the relative merits of two different organizational structures (one project based and
one functionally based) in the company. The data gathered from practitioners during
the interviews showed that the functionally based structure was generally unsuitable
for large one-off projects, although it operated well for batch production and standard
product lines with little new technology. By contrast, the project-based structure re-

vealed a close matching between formal and informal processes and an ability to cope with emerging properties in design and production, by virtue of project team coherence and strong leadership. The data were used to design and implement a new project-based structure for all major projects as an alternative to the functionally based system. Some functional coordination was also introduced to promote learning and technical leadership along the lines of the project-led organization (see figure 11.1).

Company D is a producer of base stations for mobile phone systems. The intervention focused on the installation and extension of new turnkey systems for a mobile telecommunications network. The work, which compared formal project management processes with what actually occurred during the first implementation phase, captured major problems in the formal project management procedures and revealed many differences between formal and actual practices – some of which hindered the project, others which helped. The data were used by the company to develop a "best practice" "Turnkey Project Start-up Guide" which formally embodied many of the informal practices and excluded unnecessary procedures. This was placed on the company intranet to be updated with new experiences as learning occurred in new projects.

Company E is a large telecommunications service provider introducing a new business line of "integrated system and service solutions," involving several areas of network technology new to the company. The intervention helped practitioners decide which new processes and routines would be needed in bidding for new business contracts and which were only appropriate for traditional business lines. Eventually, this led to the setting up of, first, a consultancy wing of the company and, then, a new projects division, largely independent of the main organization. This recomposition of the organization turned out to be a valuable way of capturing and accelerating learning and rapidly expanding the new business.

Company F is a supplier of high value equipment for monitoring and measuring large-scale (rolling mill) steel production. The intervention, which focused on both research and the development of prototypes for in-house use and for sale to external users, revealed that the main total quality program (TQP) in place was suited to routine manufacturing activities, but unsuitable for the needs of R&D. In this case, the intervention was a rare opportunity for R&D staff to review internal procedures and external relations with university and sub-contractor partners. Eventually, the TQP was modified to recognize the uncertainties involved in R&D and the emerging properties expected in prototype development. Some modifications were made to the formal systems to bring them closer in line with real practices especially where sub-contractors and universities needed to be more closely integrated into the project teams.

To sum up, the diagnostic and benchmarking technique helped to analyze and recombine processes and structures for one-off, non-routine activities. In terms of scope, as the above cases indicate, the method has been applied to various complex tasks, cutting across sectors, technologies and different stages of the project life cycle, contributing to project processes and wider organizational structures. The above examples cover R&D, prototype development, design, engineering, production, and installation of CoPS, as well as bid phase and new business development activities. In describing impacts and benefits, it is important to emphasize that the cases above represent experimental, small-scale interventions and that much depended on management follow-through and, in some cases, on the success of the wider change programmes in which the interventions were embedded. It is also difficult to disentangle the effects of the interventions from the impact of other changes taking place (for example, three companies underwent mergers and restructuring during our work). However, each of the firms claimed that the decomposition and questioning of processes and structures, based on the foregoing heuristics had a significant impact on organizational learning and performances.

Conclusion

In this work, we have proposed and tried to make operational an evolutionary perspective for understanding firms as imperfect, collective problem-solving entities, suggesting an interpretative framework for the patterns by which firms deploy and match problem-solving activities with organizational structures. The chapter applied these concepts to a broad class of high value capital goods (or "complex product systems") which are inherently complex and non-routine in nature, conferring extreme task complexity throughout many stages of production and innovation.

The chapter focuses on the processes through which problem-solving and creative knowledge co-evolve with organizational form in complex, non-stable, non-routine and complex task environments. Following Simon (1981), problem-solving and organizational structure are viewed as a type of design activity, where elementary physical and cognitive acts (or "elements") are tested, combined, and recombined to arrive at solutions. Because of bounded rationality, firms de-compose problems into manageable, but interdependent, and most likely "sub-optimal" blocks of elements. Within the firm, this is equivalent to a division of problem-solving labour, where the extent of the division of problem-solving labour is limited by the existence of interdependencies. If, in the process of sub-problem decomposition, interdependent elements are separated, then solving each block interdependently does not allow overall optimization. Since perfect decompositions with perfectly independent sub-problems rarely exist, boundedly rational agents normally try to design "near-decompositions" which try to isolate the most performance relevant interdependencies into separate sub-problems. Problem-solving design does not only involve search within a given space but also, and very importantly, a re-framing of the problem itself by agents within the firm. By such re-framing the organization and groups within it arrive at more powerful representations, which often (but not always) allows also greater decentralization and decomposability.

While the approach was applied to non-routine complex tasks and environment, the "spirit" of the model also applies to routine, decomposable tasks. Here, however, the decomposition problem is, so to speak, resolved "once-and-for-all," as for example in the Fordist/Taylorist archetype where the organization is thoroughly designed and tasks are unequivocally assigned. Notice however that, even here, many activities remain by nature non-routine and complex, including strategy formulation, R&D, marketing, and new product design and the decomposition approach to PSB and organizational governance is likely to apply. Furthermore, even the Fordist archetype eventually confronts technological and market changes which force organizational and task re-composition.

The application of the approach to complex products and systems showed how the various dimensions of product complexity can confer extreme task complexity and difficult problems of organisational design. For CoPS, one highly innovative form is the project-based organization. While traditional functional and matrix structures embody a linear or sequential model of project management, the project form provides a concurrent model for integrating various complex technical and marketing functions under conditions of high uncertainty, emerging properties, and changing user requirements.

To operationalize these ideas, an experimental attempt was made to facilitate collective decision-making for the purposes of process and structure analysis and re-composition in six large multi-project firms supplying CoPS in Europe. The method used is partly based on intervention techniques from the field of organization development, which tends to treat problem-solving as iterative processes rooted in both formal and informal working practices and structures. The intervention method was designed to assist firms re-frame problems using research data which compares formal, codified processes with "real"/informal ones. The aim was to re-compose PSBs and structures to arrive at more appropriate organizational forms at the levels of projects and specific sub-tasks within projects (e.g. design, engineering, production, bidding, sub-contractor management, etc.), and wider organizational arrangements.

The apparent success of such heuristics – notwithstanding their simplicity and subject to the caveats mentioned above – is in our view an encouraging evidence of the rich *operational* implications of an evolutionary view of organizations centered on their changing problem-solving capabilities. Adding more explicitly incentive – and power – related dimensions will certainly refine the analysis. However, as we tried to show, disentangling the processes of knowledge generation within firms is an activity of paramount importance in its own right – at both levels of theory and managerial practices. And one is only at the beginning of such an enterprise.

Acknowledgement

Paper prepared for Dynacom Project (European Union, TSER, DGXII) in collaboration with the UK Complex Product Systems Innovation Centre (ESRC funded). Comments by Connie Helfat and Keith Pavitt helped in improving various drafts of the work.

Notes

1   The terms organizational form, structure, and governance arrangements are used interchangeably in this chapter.
2   The chapter builds on previous works by Marengo (1999) and Marengo, et al. (1999), which provide a formal mathematical treatment of the approach presented here.
3   Many CoPS confront extreme task complexity because they embody a wide variety of distinctive skills and types of knowledge, and involve large numbers of firms or organizational units in their production. In the past 20 years or so, CoPS have been transformed by software and information technology (IT), leading to new levels of risk and uncertainty in

design and production. See Hobday (1998) for definition and discussion of CoPS as an analytical category, and also Miller et al. (1995) for an application to the flight simulation industry.

4 For more details see Hobday and Brady (2000).

5 Curiously, in the field of software engineering a vaguely similar approach (actually called "rational") dominates and is defended as a practical way of producing complex software systems (Parnas and Clements, 1986). See Hobday and Brady (1998) for a critique.

6 Although, as presented here, this "rational" incentive-based view is a caricature, it does help convey the nature of the major difference between the latter view of economic behaviour in organizations and the problem-solving evolutionary perspective suggested in the following.

7 With roots in the earlier contributions of Penrose (1958), Chandler (1962) and Richardson (1972), a growing literature is exploring the nature of organizations in terms of "competencies" and "capabilities": see, among others, Teece, Pisano, and Schuen (1994), Teece et al. (1994), Barney (1991) and the contributions in Dosi et al. (2000).

8 Problem-solvers in firms most likely include engineers, designers, or project managers, but also, in different ways, most other employees. This applies in particular to CoPS projects, wherein each worker or "practitioner" (e.g. a software writer or draftsperson) is an "intelligent agent" responsible for managing his or her task and interfacing with other individuals and groups working on different aspects of the same product or problem (Hobday and Brady, 1998).

9 A comprehensive account of economic behavior of firms should, of course, account for incentives as well as the co-evolution of PSBs and governance arrangements, as argued by Coriat and Dosi (1998) and Dosi and Marengo (1994). However, a second point of departure is given by the understanding of the diverse PSBs of firms, and then proceeding to assess the ways in which incentive structures co-evolve with PSBs.

10 This section draws from Hobday (1998). The term CoPS is used, as "capital goods" fails to capture the diversity and range of systems involved. CoPS are, in fact, a subset of capital goods (and might eventually include sophisticated consumer goods). Somewhat similar issues, related to the variety and complexity of knowledge emerge in connection with products which are relatively simple as such but require complex search procedures to be discovered. Pharmaceutical are an archetypical example: cf. Orsenigo et al. (1999).

11 The effect of software can be interpreted as shifting the emphasis of production from a relatively predictable "engineering" task to a much more imprecise design-intensive "development" process, increasing the degree of uncertainty and learning involved in the production of each system.

12 Works germane to our analysis include Gann and Salter (1998) who provide a rare account of how project processes relate to wider organizational activities within a project-based organization, and Middleton (1967) on the establishment of projects within functionally based organizations. See also Miller et al. (1995). Research on new product development and project success factors also illustrates the importance of the project form (Clark and Wheelwight, 1992; Pinto and Prescott, 1988; Shenhar, 1993).

13 On this see also Miles and Snow (1986), whose formulation of network brokers and partners is similar to Teece's virtual firm and alliance enterprise respectively.

14 And some scholars further speculate that the future "archetypical" firm might be somewhat different from the classic "M-form": cf. among others, Miles et al. (1997) on the prediction of "cell-based" organizational structures.

15 This section draws heavily on Hobday (2000).

16 This work is carried out by one of us (M. H.) within the CoPS Innovation Centre at SPRU. Hobday and Brady, (1998, 2000) provide full details of the method, one in-depth case

study, and the results of the six applications mentioned briefly below.

17   In such cases, firms cannot apply normal benchmarking or improvement techniques (e.g. total quality management, continuous improvement, statistical process control or business process re-engineering) as these presume routine codifiable procedures, determinate tasks and established forms (usually departments), rather than temporary project forms.

18   Formal procedural models are presented in many project management and software engineering texts (including Boehm, 1988, 1989; Kellner, 1996), most of which are rationalist in that they do not recognize or deal with informal processes, structures or emerging properties.

19   The aim is not to gather comprehensive data, but sufficient information to run the verification and improvement workshops.

References

Argyris, C. and Schön, D. A. (1996) *Organisational Learning*. Reading, MA: Addison-Wesley.

Barnard, C. I. (1938) *The Functions of the Executive*. Cambridge, MA: Harvard University Press.

Barney, J. (1991) Firm resources and sustained competitive advantage, *Journal of Management*, 17(1), 99–120.

Bennis, W. G. (1966) *Changing Organizations: Essays on the Development and Evolution of Human Organizations*. New York: McGraw-Hill.

Boardman, J. (1990) *Systems Engineering: An Introduction*. New York: Prentice Hall.

Boehm, B. W. (1988) A spiral model of software development and enhancement; *IEEE Computer*, May, 61–72.

Boehm, B. W. (1989) *Software Risk Management*. Washington, DC: IEEE Computer Society Press.

Burns, T. and Stalker, G. M. (1961) *The Management of Innovation*. London: Tavistock.

Chandler, A. D. Jr. (1962) *Strategy and Structure: Chapters in the History of Industrial Enterprise*. Cambridge, MA: MIT Press.

Clark, K. B. and Wheelwright, S. C. (1992) Organizing and leading "Heavyweight" Development Teams, *Californian Management Review*, 34(3), 9–28.

Cohen M. D., Burkhart, R., Dosi, G., Egidi, M., Marengo, L., Warglien M. and Winter S. (1996) Routines and other recurring action patterns of organizations: contempory research issues, *Industrial and Corporate Change*, 5, 653–98.

Conner, K. R. and Prahalad, C. K. (1996) A resource-based theory of the firm: knowledge vs. opportunism, *Organization Science*, 7, 477–501.

Coriat, B. and Dosi, G. (1998) Learning how to govern and learning how to solve problems. In A. D. Chandler, P. Hagstrom and O. Solvell (eds). *The Dynamic Firm: the Role of Technology, Strategy, Organization and Regions*. Oxford: Oxford University Press.

Davis, S. M. and Lawrence, P. R. (1977) *Matrix*. Reading, MA: Addison-Wesley.

Dosi, G. (1988) Sources, procedures and microeconomic effects of innovation, *Journal of Economic Literature*, 26, 1120–71.

Dosi, G. and Egidi, M. (1991) Substantive and procedural uncertainty: an exploration of economic behaviours in complex and changing environments, *Journal of Evolutionary Economics*, 1, 145–68.

Dosi, G. and Marengo, L. (1994) towards a theory of organisational competencies. In R. W. England (ed.), *Evolutionary Concepts in Contemporary Economics*. Ann Arbor, MI: Michigan University Press.

Dosi, G., Marengo, L. and Fagiolo, G. (1996) Learning in evolutionary environments, University of Trento, CEEL working paper.

Dosi, G., Nelson, R., and Winter, S. G. (eds) (2000) *The Nature and Dynamics of Organisational Capabilities*. Oxford: Oxford University Press.

Freeman, C. (1982) *The Economics of Industrial Innovation*. London: Frances Printer, 2nd edn.

French, W. L. and Bell, C. H. (1973) *Organization Development: Behavioural Science Interventions for Organization Improvement*. New York: Prentice Hall, 2nd edn

Galbraith, J. (1971) Matrix organizational designs: how to combine functional and project forms, *Business Horizons*, February, 29–40.

Galbraith, J. R. (1973) *Designing Complex Organizations*. Reading, MA: Addison-Wesley.

Gann, D. and Salter, A. (1998) Learning and innovation management in project-based, service-enhanced firms, *International Journal of Innovation Management*, 2(4), 431–54.

Grossman, S. and Hart, O. (1986) The costs and benefits of ownership: a theory of vertical and lateral integration, *Journal of Political Economy*, 94, 691–719.

Handy, C. (1993) *Understanding Organizations*. London: Penguin Books, 4th edn.

Hobday, M. (1998) product complexity, innovation and industrial organisation, *Research Policy*, 26, 689–710.

Hobday, M. (2000) The project based organizations: an idial form for managing complex problems and systems *Research Policy*, 29, 871–93.

Hobday, M. and Brady, T. (1998) Rational *vs* soft management in complex software: lessons from flight simulation, *International Journal of Innovation Management*, 2(1), 1–43.

Hobday, M. and Brady, T. (2000) A fast method for analysing and improving complex software processes, *R&D Management* 3, 1–21.

Kauffman, S. A. (1993) *The Origins of Order*. Oxford: Oxford University Press.

Kellner, M. I. (1996) *Business Process Modeling: Lessons and Tools from the Software World*. Software Engineering Institute, Carnegie Mellon University.

Kogut, B. and Zander, U. (1992) Knowledge of the firm, combinative capabilities and the replication of technology, *Organization Science*, 3, 383–96.

Kogut, B. and Zander, U. (1996) What do firms do? Coordination, identity and learning, *Organization Science*, 7, 502–17.

Laffont, J. J. and Tirole, J. (1986) the dynamics of incentive contracts: *Econometrica*, 94, 1153–75.

Larson, E. W. and Gobeli, D. H. (1987) Matrix management: contradictions and insights: *Californian Management Review*, 29(4), 126–38.

Larson E. W. and Gobeli, D. H. (1989) Significance of project management structure on development success, *IEEE Transactions on Engineering Management*, 36(2), 119–25.

Lawrence, P. and Lorsch, J. (1971) *Organization and Environment*. Cambridge, MA: Harvard University Press.

Leonard-Barton, D. (1995) *Wellsprings of Knowledge: Building and Sustaining the Sources of Innovation*, Boston, MA: Harvard Business School Press.

Levinthal, D. (1998) The slow pace of rapid technological change: gradualism and punctuation in technological change, *Industrial and Corporate Change*, 7, 217–47.

March, J. G. (1994) *A Primer on Decision Making: How Decisions Happen*, New York: Free Press.

March, J. G. and Simon, H. A. (1958) *Organizations*, New York: Wiley.

Marengo, L. (1996) Structure, competencies and learning in an adaptive model of the firm. In G. Dosi and F. Malerba (eds), *Organisation and Strategy in the Evolution of the Enterprise*. London: Macmillan.

Marengo, L. (1999) *Decentralisation and market mechanisms in collective problem-solving*. Mimeo, University of Teram.

Marengo, L., Dosi, G. Legrenzi, P. and Pasquali, G. (1999) The structure of problem-solving knowledge and the structure of organizations. Paper prepared for the conference "The

Roots and Branches of Organizational Economics," SCANCOR, Stanford University, September.

McKelvey, B. (1982) *Organisational Systematics*, Berkeley CA: University of California Press.

Metcalfe, J. S. and de Liso, N. (1995) Innovation, capabilities and knowledge: the epistemic connection. Mimeo, University of Manchester, England.

Middleton, C. J. (1967) How to set up a project organization, *Harvard Business Review*, March–April, 73–82.

Miles, R. E. and Snow, C. C. (1986) Organizations: new concepts for new forms, *Californian Management Review*, 28(3).

Miles, R. E., Snow, C. C., Mathews, J. A., Miles, G. and Coleman, H. J. (1997) Organizing in the knowledge age: anticipating the cellular form, *Academy of Management Executive*, 11, (4), 7–24.

Miller, R., Hobday, M., Leroux-Demers, and Olleros, X. (1995) innovation in complex systems industries: the case of flight simulation, *Industrial and Corporate Change*, 4(2), 363–400.

Mintzberg, H. (1979) *The Structuring of Organizations*. Englewood Cliffs New Jersey: Prentice Hall.

Mintzberg, H. (1989) *Mintzberg on Management: Inside Our Strange World of Organisation*, New York: The Free Press.

Morgan, G. (1986). *Images of Organization*. London: Sage.

Mullins, L. J. (1994) *Management and Organisational Behaviour*. London: Pitman Publishing, 3rd ed.

Narduzzo, A., Rocco, E., and Warglien, M. (2000) Talking about routines in the field: the emergence of organizational capabilities in a new cellular phone network company, in Dosi, G., Nelson, R. R. and Winter S. G. (2000).

Nelson, R. R. (1991) How do firms differ, and how does it matter? *Strategic Management Journal*, 12, 61–74.

Nelson, R. and Winter, S. (1982) *An Evolutionary Theory of Economic Change*. Cambridge, MA: Harvard University Press.

Orsenigo, L., Pammolli, F., and Riccaboni, M. (1999) Learning, market selection and the evolution of industrial structures. S. Anna School, Pisa, Italy, working paper.

Parnas, D. L. and Clements, P. C. (1986) A rational design process: how and why to fake it, *IEEE Transactions on Software Engineering*, Vol. SE-12, February, 251–7.

Pavitt, K. (1999) *Technology, Management and Systems of Innovation*. Cheltenham: Edward Elgar.

Penrose, E. T. (1958) *The Theory of the Growth of the Firm*. New York: Wiley.

Pinto. J. K. and Prescott, J. E. (1988) Variations in critical success factors over the stages in the project life cycle, *Journal of Management* 14(1), 5–18.

Prencipe, A. (1997) Technological competencies and product's evolutionary dynamics: a case study from the aero-engine industry, *Research Policy*, 25(8), 1261–76.

Radner, R. (1992) Hierarchy: the economics of managing, *Journal of Economic Literature*, 30, 1382–15.

Richardson, G. B. (1972) The organization of industry, *Economic Journal*, 82, 883–96.

Sapolsky, H. M. (1972) *The Polaris System Development: Bureaucratic and Programmatic Success in Government*. Cambridge, MA: Harvard University Press.

Sayles, L. R. (1976) Matrix management: the structure with a future, *Organization Dynamics*, autumn, 2–17.

Schein, E. H. (1990) Organizational culture, *American Psychologist*, 45(2), 109–19.

Seeley Brown, J. and Duguid, P. (1996) Organizational learning and communities of practice: towards a unified view of working, learning, and innovation. In M. D. Cohen and L. S. Sproull (eds), *Organizational Learning*, Thousand Oaks, CA: Sage Publications, Chapter 3.

Shenhar, A. J. (1993) From low- to high-tech project management, *R&D Management*, 23(3), 199–214.

Shenhar, A. (1994) Systems engineering management: A framework for the development of a multidisciplinary discipline, *IEEE Transactions on Systems, Man, and Cybernetics*, 24(2), 327–32.

Simon, H. A. (1981) *The Sciences of the Artificial*. Cambridge, MA: MIT Press.

Simon, H. A. (1991) Organizations and markets, *Journal of Economic Perspectives*, 5, 25–44.

Teece, D. J. (1996) Firm organization, industrial structure, and technological innovation, *Journal of Economic Behaviour & Organization*, 31, 193–224.

Teece, D. J., Pisano, G. and Shuen, A. (1994) Dynamic capabilities and strategic management. CCC Working Paper 94–9, Berkeley, University of California.

Teece, D. J., Rumelt, R. Dosi, G and Winter, S. G. (1994) Understanding corporate coherence: theory and evidence. *Journal of Economic Behaviour & Organization*, 23, 1–30.

Tirole, J. (1986) Hierarchies and bureaucracies: on the role of collusion in organizations, *Journal of Law, Economics and Organisations*, 2, 181–214.

Tyson, S. and Jackson, T. (1992) *The Essence of Organizational Behaviour*. New York: Prentice Hall.

Vincenti, W. G. (1990) *What Engineers Know and How They Know It. Analytical Studies from Aeronautical History*. Baltimore, MD: Johns Hopkins University Press.

Winter, S. G. (1982) An essay on the theory of production. In H. Hymans (ed.), *Economics and the World around It*, Ann Arbor: University of Michigan Press, 55–93.

Winter, S. G. (1988) On Coase, competence and the corporation, *Journal of Law, Economics and Organisation*, 4, 181–97.

Woodward, J. (1958) *Management and Technology*. London: Her Majesty's Stationery Office, London.

[5]

Industrial and Corporate Change, Volume 12, Number 2, pp. 413–436

Bridging contested terrain: linking incentive-based and learning perspectives on organizational evolution

Giovanni Dosi, Daniel A. Levinthal and Luigi Marengo

In this paper we present a general model of organizational problem-solving in which we explore the relationship between problem complexity, decentralization of tasks and reward schemes. When facing complex problems that require the co-ordination of large numbers of interdependent elements, organizations face a decomposition problem that has both cognitive dimensions and reward and incentive dimensions. The former relate to the decomposition and allocation of the process of generation of new solutions: since the search space is too vast to be searched extensively, organizations employ heuristics for reducing it. The decomposition heuristic takes the form of division of cognitive labour and determines which solutions are generated and become candidates for selection. The reward and incentive dimensions fundamentally shape the selection environment which chooses over alternative solutions. The model we present begins to study the interrelationships between these two domains of analysis: in particular, we compare the problem-solving performance of organizations characterized by various decompositions (of coarser or finer grain) and various reward schemes (at the level of the entire organization, team and individual). Moreover we investigate extensions of our model in order to account for (admittedly rudimentary) power and authority relationships (giving some parts of the organization the power to stop changes in other parts), and discuss the interaction of problem represent-entations and incentive mechanisms.

1. Introduction

Social organizations—in their impressive variety over history, across societies and across domains of human activities—generally display also very diverse forms of division of operational and 'cognitive' labour, and, at the same time, equally diverse hierarchical arrangements, distributions of power and mechanisms of elicitation of efforts by individual agents. While it is easy to see that this is generally the case, it is much more difficult to disentangle the different domains of analysis which tend to correspond to multiple, coexisting, levels of interactions among organizational members. These levels of interaction are also likely to map onto different forms of 'social embeddedness' of individual actions. In many respects, the understanding of these processes is one of the fundamental tasks of social sciences since their origins.

The task is obviously enormous. It may clearly begin from different angles. It happens that the dominant strand of contemporary analyses start with 'primitives' of the interpretation of the nature of organizations based on sophisticated, self-seeking, agents. Together, the behaviours of these self-interested actors are viewed as typically directed by market forces. Only in those settings in which, due to failures of information and contract incompleteness, markets are less effective in this task, are organizations called for to surrogate such imperfections. It is a story too familiar to be repeated here.[1]

Conversely, a small—but not negligible and growing—minority of the economic profession has classed the (first approximation) *'primitives'* of the analysis of the nature of economic organizations as *problem-solving features*, in turn nested in ubiquitous forms of human 'bounded rationality', grossly imperfect processes of learning and diverse mechanisms of the social distribution of 'cognitive labour'. Needless to say, it is a perspective that finds seminal roots in the works of Herbert Simon, James March and indeed Richard Nelson and Sidney Winter.

Let us offer the following caricature to illustrate the differences between the two interpretative philosophies. Suppose that two delegations of intelligent but totally uninformed beings from Mars are sent to Earth with the mandate of reporting 'what business firms are'. The delegations are not allowed to visit the firms themselves. Rather, the first one is given to read, out of an enormous literature, say, Holmstrom and Tirole (1989), Grossman and Hart (1986), and Laffont and Tirole (1993), while the second is given March and Simon (1958), Cyert and March (1963), Nelson and Winter (1982), and Dosi *et al.* (2000). What would they report back to Mars? (We reasonably assume that these entities, given their empirical naïveté, are unable to catch all the caveats from footnotes, side remarks, etc.).

Well, the first delegation would probably convey the idea that earthly firms are places where one confines vicious and cunning people who are made to play extremely sophisticated games according to rules designed in order to prevent them from doing much harm to themselves and to others. Only casual mention would be made—if at all—to conventional labels by which the outcomes are denominated ('steel', 'shoes', 'computers', and so on), while lengthy accounts would be devoted to the details of the admissible rules and the mathematical equipment humans utilize in order to figure out how to behave.

The second delegation is likely to return with a strikingly different story. It would probably begin with a rather long description of the impressive variety of 'things' that each day come out of earthly firms—i.e. precisely, steel, computers, polypropylene, etc.—and the equally impressive diversity in the processes leading to them. Moreover, these Martians would almost certainly remark that no one has the entire plan of what to

---

[1] A few more detailed epistemological remarks are provided in Dosi (1995) and Coriat and Dosi (1998).

do in their heads. Most of the members of each organization repeatedly undertake recognizably few operations, yet nevertheless organizations co-ordinate their tasks in ways generally yielding coherent artefacts at the end of the day. Indeed, this second delegation is likely to suggest the analogy of a 'firm' with a messy but most often reliable computer program, with little mention of possible conflict of interests among the individual carriers of various 'subroutines.'

Notwithstanding its being a caricature, the foregoing story does convey the spirit of an actual major divide cutting across current theorizing about organizations, having at the two extremes *a pure incentive-governance view versus a pure problem-solving view.* Clearly, there are elements of truth in both perspectives (Coriat and Dosi, 1998): an ambitious research programme ahead entails indeed connecting the two.

The starting point for such a bridge building has important consequences for the sort of bridge that one creates. The starting point embodies a commitment to some assumptions on first-order versus second-order effects. Forced to such a choice, we would pick the second *Weltanschaung* as a provisional point of departure (which also happens to be the least explored one). We do need to assume a *weak incentive compatibility* to begin with (see Dosi and Marengo, 1995) in the loosest sense that there exists some selection pressure which, in turn, generates some connection between performance and rewards. However, having that, one precisely focuses (as a first theoretical approximation) on the diverse problem-solving characteristics of different organizations, and only in the second instance one tackles the ways in which incentive structures interact with problem-solving knowledge.

Putting it in another way, the archetype 'incentive view' fully censors any competence issue associated with what organizations do and how well they do it—except for issues of misrepresentations of 'intrinsic' individual abilities and adverse selection, or incentive misalignment in effort elicitation. As an extreme characterization, given the 'right' incentives, any firm can make microprocessors as well as Intel, or bioengineer as well as Genetech.

The second, 'problem-solving', archetype, on the contrary, censors precisely the incentive-alignment issue. In a sense, all agents are 'angels' as their motives are concerned. Conversely, it focuses on the problem-solving efficacy of what they do, especially in so far as what they do does not stem from any differential 'ontological' ability but rather from the social division of tasks and their combinatorics.

So, in the first approximation of this latter view, the basic units of analysis are elementary physical acts, such as moving a piece of iron from one place to another, and elementary cognitive acts, such as applying inference rules. Problem solving can be straightforwardly understood as combinations of elementary acts, within a procedure, leading to a feasible outcome (an engine, a chemical compound, etc.).[2]

One can also describe it the other way round. Given all the problem-solving procedures leading to a given 'outcome' (e.g. an engine, etc., and, for that matter, a theorem,

---

[2]See Marengo *et al.* (2000) for further discussion of this point.

a statement about the purported structure of the observed world)—which might well be an infinite set—one may decompose them in subsequences of elementary acts of varying length that may be eventually performed according to various execution architectures (sequential, parallel, hierarchical, etc.)

At this level of analysis, an organization embodies problem solving in at least three senses.

First, it displays the operational competencies associated with its actual problem-solving procedures [much in accordance with the routines discussed in Nelson and Winter (1982); see also Cohen *et al.* (1996)]. Secondly, the organizational structure—both the formal and informal ones—determines the distribution of informational inputs of the processing tasks and of the 'allowable acts' (i.e. 'who can do what to whom') and, as such, it determines all the decompositions of problem-solving procedures that are, so to speak, 'legal'. Thirdly, it shapes the search heuristics for yet-unsolved problems—e.g. a new engine, a new chemical compound—that is, broadly speaking, the heuristics of innovative search.

Note that, although a bit more abstract, this characterization of problem-solving knowledge is well in tune with the evidence stemming both from the economics of innovation (for a survey, see Dosi, 1988) and capability-based views of organizations (Dosi *et al.*, 2000, among others). Further, it has the advantage of being directly applicable to both the analysis of intra-organizational structures and of the boundaries between organizations and markets.[3] Indeed, such boundaries may be straight-forwardly seen as a particular decomposition of an overall problem-solving task, say the one leading from raw iron oxide to auto engines. Relatedly, one might enquire about the problem-solving properties of particular decompositions, ranging from the totally centralized and autarkic one (no decomposition at all), to the analogue of a 'pure market', one person–one task, with market transactions linking each elementary act. Note that here one is facing a sort of 'anti-Coasian' question asking whether, and under what circumstances, markets, i.e. highly decentralized decompositions of knowledge, bear some differential problem-solving advantages, if any, when neglecting the more familiar arguments concerning the high-powered incentives of markets. An analysis along these lines is presented in Marengo *et al.* (2000). Marengo *et al.* explore the effect of different decompositions of the same 'true' environments on adaptive performance. We build on this analytical framework by incorporating *cognitive and political conflict* into the analysis, together with (admittedly rudimentary) issues of inventive-compatibility and effort elicitation. Or, putting it again as a sort of caricature, we begin to explore what happens in our stylized organizational models when adaptive, but not omniscient 'angels' start (i) clashing on diverse 'visions of the world'; (ii) facing some hierarchical filtering and/or veto powers on their adaptive search; or, worse, (iii) they stop being 'angels' but react to incentives and orders.

The following section presents the basics of our model. We then engage in some

---

[3]In the latter respect, it bears at least the same generality as the representation in terms of elementary transactions advocated by Oliver Williamson.

basic analysis of the effect of alternative problem decompositions and reward structures of the adaptive process. Global reward structures, while manifestly the desired payoff scheme for a population of omniscient and compliant actors, are not so clearly desirable in the face of not so omniscient, though still compliant, problem-solvers. We find that there is an important interaction between issues of knowledge and issues of incentives. In particular, 'wrong', excessively local, reward structures, may help compensate for the problem of incorrect cognitive representations.

Narrow, group-wide incentives create conflict of interests among problem-solving teams. These conflicts, however, may help prevent organizations from locking into modest local peaks. Together, these conflicts have the dysfunctional property that they may be unending and result in the continual perturbation of the problem space of one subunit, or actor, by another. We find that there is a further complement, a complement not from the world of incentives or cognitively limited automatons but from the world of politics—i.e. *power*. Power may be horizontal, in that one subunit is privileged above others, or, as more traditionally viewed, vertical. In either form, the presence of an asymmetrical power distribution within the organization helps to stem the potentially endless cycling of self-perturbing changes that result from incorrect decompositions of the actors' problem environment. More specifically, we explore how the ability of one subunit, or a hierarchically superior, to veto proposed policy changes may enhance the performance of the system.

Finally, we explore the more direct costs of problem decompositions and change efforts. Decompositions have costs not only as a result of the fact that they may incorrectly capture the 'true' structure of the problem space, but more refined structures in and of themselves are difficult to sustain. Similarly, change efforts not only run the risk of yielding an inferior policy choice, they are also effortful. Maintaining an established routine surely requires less effort than initiating a new action pattern. We revisit the interaction among cognitive patterns (in the form of problem decompositions) and reward structures, while incorporating these features of the cost of more refined problem decompositions and the direct costs of organizational change. 'Correct' decompositions may suffer not only because of the cost of sustaining refined problem decomposition but also because they may induce actors to engage in excessive search.

2. Model structure

We explore complex, though structured, problem surfaces. That is, following on recent work on *rugged landscapes* (Kauffman, 1993; Levinthal, 1997), we highlight the role of interactions among elementary organizational behaviours and policy choices. However, we try to link to this line of modelling, with Simon's argument regarding the interpretative importance of (quasi-)decomposable systems (Simon, 1969) and recent modelling work by Page (1996), Marengo (2000), Marengo *et al.* (2000), Ethiraj and Levinthal (2002), and Rivkin and Siggelkow (2002). Interactions are certainly present among behaviours of organizational members and among organizational policy choices. However, these interactions are not dispersed randomly among the set of possible combinations. Rather, they are tightly clustered within decompositions of the broader system. In keeping with the tradition of bounded rationality (Simon, 1955) and in contrast to many recent examinations of modular systems (e.g. Baldwin and Clark, 2000), we do not presume that this interaction structure is known to the actors. The partitioning of the decision problem may or may not correspond to the 'true' decomposition structure. A critical element of our analysis is indeed how the appropriate reward structure depends on the degree to which the task partitioning corresponds to the actual structure.

In tune with Kauffman (1993), let us define 'landscapes' as some (highly 'reduced form') mappings between some combinations of organizational traits/cognitive patterns/behavioural rules, one the one hand, and 'performances'—no matter how defined, for the time being—organizations themselves, on the other. In this formal representation, whenever individual traits, behaviours, etc., have totally distinct effects upon performances, it is easy to reproduce a familiar (*probably too familiar!*) conjecture according to which even 'local', piecewise, ameliorations generally lead to global optima. Conversely, this might not be generally the case whenever the contributions of 'traits' to 'performances' are correlated, so that, say, the contribution of trait *a* depends on the presence and value of trait *b*, etc.—which in biology come under the heading of *epistastic correlations*.

A fitness landscape is a simple model of complex systems in which the elements (policy choices in our model of organization) function interdependently. Kauffman (1993) developed the *NK*-model primarily to simulate the evolution of populations of organisms over a complex fitness landscape that are described by a string of genes, but the model's formal structure allows for various applications in other domains (e.g. Levinthal, 1997).

A system is described by a string of loci which refers to the set of elements (policy choices) that make up the system. The variable N refers to the number of elements (genes in biology, organizational policy choices in our model), for each element $i = 1, \ldots, N$ there exist a finite number A_i of possible states (choices). The set of all possible strings that can be formed by combining different choices for each element is called the possibility space S and is given by the Cartesian product:

$$S = A_1 \times A_2 \times A_3 \times \ldots \times A_N$$

A fitness landscape is a function $F : S \rightarrow R^+$ which assigns a performance (fitness) measure to every possible configuration.

The K-value of a system describes the system's inner structure and refers to the number of 'epistatic' relations among elements, i.e. the scope of interdependencies among elements. The epistatic relations between elements imply that the contribution of one element to the overall fitness of the system is dependent both upon its own state and upon the state of K other elements: in our case it indicates that the contribution to the overall performance of the organization of each single policy choice depends upon K other choices.

We stick to Kauffman's rather extreme hypothesis that interdependencies and interactions among elements are so highly non-linear, badly understood and difficult to control that we can assume that fitness contributions are basically random numbers (drawn from a uniform distribution). If $K = 0$, i.e. there are no interdependencies, each element gives a different randomly drawn contribution for each of its possible states A_i; the overall fitness value of a string will simply be the average of each component's fitness contribution.

This can be more easily understood by means of the example described in Table 1, which contains the individual fitness contributions of a landscape with $N = 6$ binary elements which are not interdependent (i.e. $K = 0$). We read that, for instance, if element 4 takes value 0, its fitness contribution is 0.99, whereas if it takes value 1, its contribution is 0.45. The fitness value of every string in the possibility space can simply be computed as average of the corresponding individual fitness contributions. For instance string 011010 has the following fitness value:

$$F = (0.29 + 0.54 + 0.11 + 0.99 + 0.22 + 0.35)/6 = 0.417$$

It is very easy to check that the globally optimum string is 100000 has fitness value 0.698 and can be reached from every other string with at most six fitness-increasing mutations. In fact, if a mutation increases the individual fitness f_i, it always increases also the global fitness F; therefore each component can be optimized independently of the other, and individual and global fitness signals are perfectly aligned.

Suppose now that every one of the same six elements interacts with two other elements (i.e. $K = 2$); this means that the individual fitness contribution of each element is a function of the state of the element itself and also of the state of two other elements. Suppose for instance that element 1 interacts with 2 and 3, 2 with 3 and 4, and so on until element 6, which interacts with 1 and 2; we can then generate the landscape starting from the random individual fitness contributions shown in Table 2.

In Table 2 we read that, for instance, if element 4 takes value 0, its fitness contribution is 0.99 when elements 5 and 6 are both set to 0, 0.24 if element 5 takes state 0 and 6 takes state 1, 0.33 if they both in state 1, and so on.

Table 1 Example of individual fitness contributions with $K = 0$

Bit	f_1	f_2	f_3	f_4	f_5	f_6
0	0.29	0.73	0.64	0.99	0.83	0.35
1	0.65	0.54	0.11	0.45	0.22	0.07

Table 2 Example of individual fitness contributions with $K = 2$

Bit	Block	f_1	f_2	f_3	f_4	f_5	f_6
0	00	0.29	0.73	0.64	0.99	0.83	0.35
0	01	0.67	0.68	0.28	0.24	0.75	0.03
0	10	0.74	0.33	0.18	0.34	0.55	0.69
0	11	0.63	0.63	0.57	0.33	0.54	0.46
1	00	0.41	0.19	0.47	0.76	0.58	0.48
1	01	0.25	0.58	0.67	0.74	0.89	0.58
1	10	0.55	0.64	0.44	0.56	0.34	0.73
1	11	0.85	0.67	0.39	0.08	0.55	0.47

The global fitness of a string is again computed as the average of individual fitness contributions, thus, for instance, string 011010 has the following fitness value:

$$F = (0.63 + 0.64 + 0.67 + 0.34 + 0.58 + 0.03)/6 = 0.482$$

It is easy to show that the landscape is now much more complex than in the case $K = 0$: there are numerous local optima and one-bit mutation searches are path-dependent and can easily get stuck in a local optimum. More precisely, Kauffman (1993) analyses the statistical properties of random fitness landscapes for different K and N; among such properties the most important are the following:

1. The number of local optima increases exponentially as K increases from 0 to its maximum value $K = N - 1$.
2. The locations of local optima in the possibility space are *correlated* for low K values. Put another way, the local optima of systems with low K have many states of elements in common.
3. The fitness values of local optima of systems with low K are higher on average. Thus, the interdependencies between a system's elements are strongest if the number of epistatic relations is small.
4. The basins of attraction of local optima of systems with low K are larger on average, and, generally, the higher their fitness, the larger their basin of attraction. As a consequence, a population tends to evolve towards strings of local optima with higher fitness.

In the model that follows, landscapes are generated according to the following procedure. Let N be the number of bits or policy choices ($N = 20$ in the simulations below). We will typically suppose that the structure of interdependencies forms a partition of the set of elements: all elements of the partition interact with all other elements within the partition, while policy choices are assumed to have no interdependence with choices outside the partition. In this sense, we are assuming the problem corresponds to a fully decomposable system. We use the following decomposition scheme as a baseline characterization of the problem space:

$$D = \{\{1,2,3,4,5\},\{6,7,8,9,10\},\{11,12,13,14,15\},\{16,17,18,19,20\}\}$$

This structure implies that the 20 dimensions of the landscape can be decomposed (cf. Marengo, 2000; Marengo *et al.*, 2000) into four separate blocks of five dimensions each, and each of these blocks can be optimized independently of the others. However, given that actors may adopt an incorrect partition, the false representation may induce lasting interaction effects across the perceived decompositions.

Individual 'fitness' (i.e. plainly, actual performances) contributions for each bit, or policy choice, are generated by assigning a random number from a uniform distribution between 0 and 1. Each bit has 2^k individual fitness values, where k is the size of the block to which it belongs.

In addition to considering the fitness contribution of an individual policy choice, possibly contingent on other choices, let us consider the value of broader aggregations of policy strings. In line with Kauffman (1993) we assign 'fitness values' to broader systems by merely averaging the fitness contributions of the individual elements; however, in contrast to this earlier tradition, we are sensitive to the possibility of different levels of aggregation. Performance, and in turn rewards, may be based on the fitness value of the entire policy string, or some partition of this broader string. In particular, a special case of more refined partitions is the set of partitions consisting of singletons, or individual policy choices.

Consider a landscape with the following structure of interaction:

$$D = \{\{1,2,3\},\{4,5,6\}\}$$

Using the illustrative fitness table provided in Table 2 above,[4] let us evaluate performance at different levels of aggregation. Consider the string 101110. We can define three notions of 'fitness':

1. *Individual* fitnesses, which are respectively:

$$f_1 = 0.25, f_2 = 0.63, f_3 = 0.44, f_4 = 0.56, f_5 = 0.34, f_6 = 0.46$$

2. *Block* fitness, defined for each of the two blocks of the decomposition scheme:

---

[4]Note that we are again using Table 2 but we generate from that a different landscape than the one in the above example. Here in fact we have again $K = 3$ but interdependencies form a partition, whereas in the example above (which followed Kauffman's *NK*-model) interdependencies were overlapping. The reason of this difference is that we want decomposable environments, which would not be the case with overlapping interdependencies.

$$F_{1,2,3} = (f_1 + f_2 + f_3)/3 = (0.25 + 0.63 + 0.44)/3 = 0.44$$
$$F_{4,5,6} = (f_4 + f_5 + f_6)/3 = (0.56 + 0.34 + 0.46)/3 = 0.453$$

3. *Global* fitness (of the entire string):

$$F = (F_{1,2,3} + F_{4,5,6})/2 = (f_1 + f_2 + f_3 + f_4 + f_5 + f_6)/6 = 0.4465$$

These same three levels—individual, block and global—can not only be the basis for evaluating actual performance at different levels of aggregation, but can also define the search space by which alternatives are generated and evaluated. The nature of alternative generation mechanisms is, in fact, determined by ways the choice problem is decomposed. The organization explores the landscape according to its own decomposition scheme Δ, which may or may not coincide with the 'real' decomposition scheme D (i.e. the one that generates the landscape). Different actors, or subunits within the organization, may explore each of decomposition sets.

Consider, for instance, the illustrative 6-bit landscape provided above. Suppose that this landscape is explored by an organization characterized by the following *incorrect* decomposition scheme: $\Delta = \{\{1,2\},\{3,4\},\{5,6\}\}$. Search within a block of the decomposition Δ (in our example either $\{1,2\}$ or $\{3,4,5,6\}$) involves mutating at least one and at most all the bits of the selected block.[5] We explore settings in which we restrict the mutation to be a change in a single bit within the decomposition (corresponding to ideas of local search: Levinthal, 1997), as well as settings (following Marengo, 2000), in which one of the full set of possibilities is drawn at random.

Independent of the problem decomposition, the reward structure faced by the actors may be more or less aggregate. For instance, the imposed decomposition of the problem space may be quite narrow; however, each subunit could still be evaluated on the basis of the global fitness of the overall system. As a result, in such a setting, action would be 'local', while thinking would be 'global'. The benefit of having a reward structure that maps more or less closely to the task partition depends, in turn, on the degree to which the task partition itself reflects the actual problem decomposition.

Thus, under a global reward structure, a new policy alternative is adopted if it enhances the fitness of the overall system. Depending on the problem decomposition, this policy initiative could consist of a single, one-bit mutation or, under more aggregate problem decompositions, it could consists also of more radical changes in the set of actions or policies. Under a block, or team reward structure, proposed alternatives are viewed favourably if they enhance the fitness level of the set of policies corresponding to the overall partition of the problem decomposition. Note that this reward scheme is equivalent to the global one if the 'conjectural' decomposition Δ and the 'real' one D are identical. With individual level rewards, a proposal is viewed favourably if the fitness contributed by the particular policy choice being changed increases.

---

[5]In our example, if block $\{1,2\}$ is selected, mutation could produce one of the following three strings: 100000,010000,110000.

Let us clarify how the three schemes actually work by referring again to the above example.

Suppose that fitness values are those of Table 1, that the real decomposition is $D = \{\{1,2,3\},\{4,5,6\}\}$, the conjectural one is $\Delta = \{\{1,2\},\{3,4,5,6\}\}$, and the current string is 000000. Suppose now that the block $\{1,2\}$ is selected and the current string gets randomly mutated into 110000. Let us examine the rewards computed by the three different schemes in this case:

1. Global reward: 000000 has global fitness 0.638, 110000 has global fitness 0.667. Thus 110000 is retained.
2. Team reward: for block $\{1,2\}$ the configuration 00 has fitness 0.51 [i.e. $(0.29 + 0.73)/2$], while 11 has reward 0.595]i.e. $(0.55 + 0.64)/2$]. Thus 11 is retained.
3. Individual reward: (i) for the first bit, choice 0 within string 000000 has fitness 0.29, while choice 1 within string 110000 has fitness 0.55. Thus choice 1 is retained. (ii) For the second bit, choice 0 within string 000000 has fitness 0.73, while choice 1 within string 110000 has fitness 0.64. Thus choice 0 is retained.

All in all, both global and team reward schemes select string 110000, while the individual scheme selects string 100000.

In the following, at each period of the simulation, the 'behavioural'/'policy' configuration of any single block of the perceived decomposition of the problem structure is chosen at random. In some of our analyses, we restrict this random draw to consist of a one-bit mutation from the existing policy choice; in other settings, the random draw is not restricted and, as a result, potentially all elements of the partition could be changed in the proposal. The former setting corresponds to ideas of incremental search. In contrast, the latter structure assumes that search is only limited by the problem decomposition. The new alternative is evaluated on the basis of the reward structure (global, team or individual) and adopted if it enhances performance from the perspective of the relevant reward structure.

When we explore the role of power on the process of adaptation, an additional criterion is added to the evaluation of a proposal. Proposals must look attractive from the perspective of the initiating subunit, but must also be attractive (i.e. 'fitness improving') from the perspective of the 'powerful' subunit. Thus, proposals may be subject to vetoes.

3. Analysis

The following simulations consider a problem of size $N = 20$, generated by the following 'true' decomposition: $D = \{\{1,2,3,4,5\},\{6,7,8,9,10\},\{11,12,13,14,15\},\{16,17,18,19,20\}\}$. The following figures present results, respectively, for one typical simulation run and for averages and standard deviations over 200 different simulations. Each of the 200 replications uses the same structure in terms of the partitioning of the problem, but the seeding of the landscape is independently drawn in terms of fitness values.

3.1 *Alternative problem decompositions and local search*

The 'conjectural' decomposition on which organizational search is based has a double role, which is typical of any division of labour. On the one hand, it defines a 'cognitive' structure under which the problem is considered. This cognitive structure translates into a decomposition of the problem into subproblems, which are treated as if they were independent and, in turn, constrain the portion of the search space that can undergo examination. The perceived decomposition also influences the potential reward structure. In particular, the team, (or block) reward is a function of what the organization conceives of as a block. We are interested in exploring this double role, but in the initial simulations we isolate the reward structure definition role by supposing that search always proceeds by a one-bit mutation only.

Figure 2 illustrates the average performance over 200 replications for a process of local search (one-bit mutations) for a conjectured problem decomposition consisting of the minimum partitions of single choice variables, i.e. $\Delta = \{\{1\},\{2\},\{3\}, \ldots,\{N\}\}$, while Figure 1 illustrates a particular run among this set of 200. Given this task

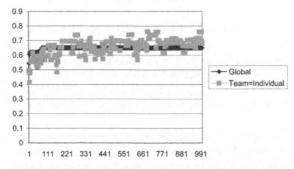

Figure 1   One-bit mutation on minimal decomposition (single run).

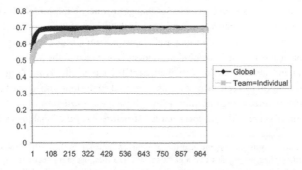

Figure 2   One-bit mutation on minimal decomposition (average over 200 repetitions).

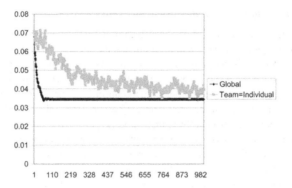

Figure 3 One-bit mutation on minimal decomposition (standard deviation over 200 repetitions).

partitioning, the individual and team-based evaluation scheme result in the same evaluation.

Consider now that the same kind of landscape is explored by an organization whose conjectural decomposition are almost correct. In particular, suppose that the conjectural decomposition catches most of the epistatic interactions but misses some of them, as in the following conjectural decomposition:

$$\Delta = \{\{1,2,3,4,5\},\{6,7,8,9,10\},\{11,12,13,14,15\},\{16,17,18,19,20\}\}$$

Under the global reward structure, the organizations rapidly reach a local optimum in the fitness landscape.[6] This fact is not surprising. A global reward structure by design only accepts proposed changes that enhance overall system performance.

More interesting is the behaviour of less aggregate reward structures. Such a reward structure provides, in some sense, a *false* signal of the value of a proposed alternative. A subunit may accept an initiative (i.e. a change in one of the policy choices) that enhances its own performance, but may degrade the fitness of the overall organization. As a result, such an organization may walk 'downhill' on a fitness landscape. Indeed, evidence of such occasional downhill movement is provided in the depiction of an individual run in Figure 1. Despite such 'inefficient' behaviours, this type of organization, on average, tends to increase its performance. Indeed, in the long-run, it reaches similar levels of performance as organizations with a global reward structure.

The conflict generated by a local reward structure has functional, as well as dys-

---

[6]A local optimum consists of a point such that any one-bit mutation of the vector of policy choices decreases fitness. However, the fact that a point constitutes a local optimum does not imply that the simultaneous shift in multiple policies could not lead to improved fitness. In general, fitness landscapes with interaction effects among policy choices have multiple local peaks (Kauffman, 1993).

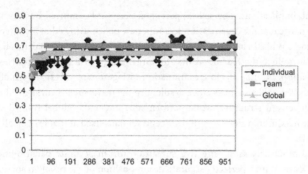

Figure 4 One-bit mutation on 'almost right' decomposition (single run).

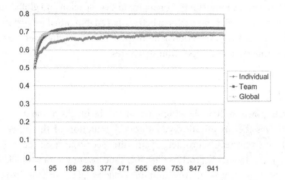

Figure 5 One-bit mutation on 'almost right' decomposition (average fitness over 200 repetitions).

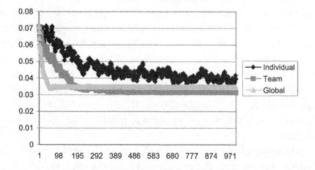

Figure 6 One-bit mutation on 'almost right' decomposition (standard deviation across 200 repetitions).

functional, implications. The selfish, parochial perspective induced by a local reward structure may cause the organization to adopt new policy strings that are inferior to its prior actions. While in an immediate sense such action is dysfunctional, this behaviour also acts to reduce the likelihood that the organization will remain absorbed on an inferior local peak. Indeed, close examination of Figure 2 reveals that even after 1000 periods, there is still a slight positive gradient to the performance curve for the team = individual reward structure, while performance under the global reward structure reaches its maximum value by period 100 and remains fixed at that level in all remaining periods.

Goal conflict acts as an effective substitute for an accurate partitioning of the problem space. With a perfectly accurate decomposition of the problem space, there is no conflict between the team (or block) evaluation of a proposed initiative and a global perspective. As a result, with an accurate partitioning of the problem, one sees no distinction between the long-run performance under the team and global reward: both these more aggregate structures perform better than an individual reward structure that fails to capture the actual interactions among policy choices. However, this property is not robust to 'imperfect' decomposition structures.

3.2 *Veto power*

We model veto power in the following way: one of the blocks of the decomposition Δ that characterizes the organization can stop any mutation of the other blocks that decreases its own fitness. Consider, again, the decomposition: $\Delta = \{\{1,2,3,4,5\}, \{6,7,8,9,10\}, \{11,12,13,14,15\}, \{16,17,18,19,20\}\}$ and assume that block $\{1,2,3,4,5\}$ is endowed with veto power. Any mutation taking place in, for instance, block $\{11,12,13,14,15\}$ will be retained if and only if it increases the team-fitness of block $\{11,12,13,14,15\}$ *and* it does not decrease the team-fitness of block $\{1,2,3,4,5\}$. When the second condition is not satisfied, the mutation is vetoed. Note that veto power is meaningless when the reward scheme is global.

As seen in Figure 7, which indicates fitness level over time for a single run of the model, and Figure 9, which provides the standard deviation over a set of 200 iterations of the model, the introduction of veto power has in general a stabilizing effect with respect to variability of the corresponding reward scheme. This analysis was done assuming, as before, that the 'real' decomposition is $D = \{\{1,2,3,4,5\}, \{6,7,8,9,10\}, \{11,12,13,14,15\}, \{16,17,18,19,20\}\}$, while the organization searches the landscape according to: $\Delta = \{\{1,2\}, \{3,4\}, \{5,6\}, \{7,8\}, \{9,10\}, \{11,12\}, \{13,14\}, \{15,16\}, \{17,18\}, \{19,20\}\}$. Thus, the perceived partitioning of the problem space is more fine-grained than the actual partition.

Team and individual reward schemes with veto power are effective in stabilizing good solutions when attained. These results appear to be linked to the following factors: (i) the subjective decomposition on which organizational search is based must be finer than the 'real' decomposition which originates the landscape; and (ii) the latter must

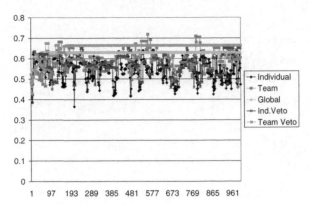

Figure 7 Veto power with partitions of two (single run).

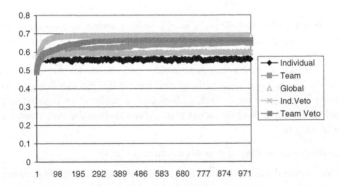

Figure 8 Veto power with partitions of two (average fitness across 200 repetitions).

not be too complex. In fact, the result is stronger if we consider a 'real world' generated by the following simpler decomposition structure:

$$D = \{\{1,2\},\{3,4\},\{5,6\},\{7,8\},\{9,10\},\{11,12\},\{13,14\},\{15,16\},\{17,18\},\{19,20\}\}$$

and the organizational decomposition is the finest possible: $\Delta = \{\{1\},\{2\},\{3\}, \ldots, \{18\},\{19\},\{20\}\}$. In this case, we see that team rewards, in conjunction with veto power, can actually lead to a superior performance than a global reward structure.

In the face of an incorrect decomposition, the conflict that stems from team rewards induces more search than that which results from a global reward structure. This greater search effort may identify a superior solution than that identified under global search; however, a team-based reward structure is ineffective in 'holding on' to the strong

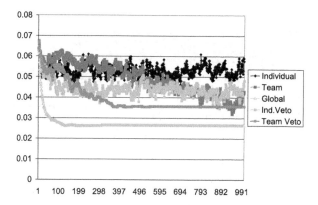

Figure 9 Veto power with partitions of two (standard deviation across 200 repetitions).

policies that are identified. Under a team reward structure, as opposed to a global reward structure, the organization tends to cycle among possible solutions. One unit initiates changes that appear attractive from its vantage point which, in turn, disrupts the performance of another unit and provides an incentive for that unit to initiate change which in turn feed-backs to the original subunit that initiated change, and so on. The presence of a veto breaks such cycling. Only a subset of proposed changes are allowed to become policy; the subset that will not disrupt the performance of the powerful sub-unit.

3.3 Decompositions, span of control and elicitation costs

Next, let us extend our model in order to introduce costs that the organization has to bear in order to induce its members to act in a given fashion. What we are trying to model here is not a principal–agent relationship in a strict sense, because we do not assume any given relationship between effort and outcome. Rather, we focus instead on *control*. The principal, the residual claimant of the organizational total payoff, wants to induce the agents to keep performing some given action or to switch to a different one. But when actions are linked by interdependencies, the control function itself cannot be entirely decomposed into independent control problems. Thus, the cognitive dimension (given by the decomposition) and the control dimension interact in some non-trivial way.

In order to explore these issues, let us refine the above model, introduce a costly control function and analyse the relationship between conflict arising from 'cognitive' factors—i.e. from incorrect decomposition of the problem—on the one hand, and conflict arising from control and incentives, on the other.

In particular, we assume that the costs of action elicitation grow with the span of control, i.e. the size of elements of the decomposition, and that they are higher when the principal wants to elicit a change in the agent's action than when he wants to elicit the

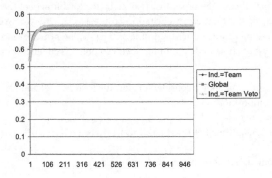

Figure 10 Veto power with perceived partitions of one and real partitions of two (average fitness across 200 repetitions).

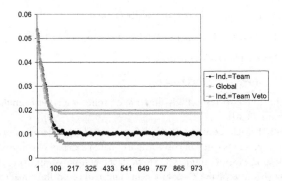

Figure 11 Veto power with perceived partitions of one and actual partitions of two (standard deviation across 200 repetitions).

same behaviour. This assumption is based on two independent premises. First, we assume that agents are naturally adverse to change. Second, we assume that the observation and elicitation of 'business as usual' can be routinized and take advantage of standard procedures and devices.

More specifically, in the following analysis we assume that elicitation costs have two components:

1. The 'business as usual component': $C_1 = c \times \text{span}^2$.
2. The 'new action component': $C_2 = c \times n\_\text{mutation}^2$.

where 'span' is the size of the blocks of the decomposition and 'n_mutation' is number of bits that have been mutated. Finally, c is a constant coefficient. Total elicitation costs, C, simply equals $C_1 + C_2$.

The principal obtains the profit that is given by the total fitness of the organization after payment of the total effort elicitation costs: $\Pi = F - C$. We assume that the principal is seeking profit (rather than fitness). That is, the principal incorporates the effect of the cost of effort in determining whether a policy is enhancing or diminishing performance.

Simulation results.   Again, we consider a landscape with $N = 20$ and generated by the following decomposition:

$$D = \{\{1,2,3,4,5\},\{6,7,8,9,10\},\{11,12,13,14,15\},\{16,17,18,19,20\}\}$$

We explore four classes of perceived decompositions:

1. *Right,* have the correct decomposition.
2. *Almost right,* use the size four decomposition:

$$\Delta = \{\{1,2,3,4,5\},\{6,7,8,9,10\},\{11,12,13,14,15\},\{16,17,18,19,20\}\}$$

3. *Wrong,* have a decomposition of correct size but biased:

$$\Delta = \{\{1,2,3,19,20\},\{4,5,6,7,8\},\{9,10,11,12,1314,15\},\{14,15,16,17,18\}\}$$

4. *Minimal,* have the finest decomposition:

$$\Delta = \{\{1\},\{2\},\{3\},\ldots,\{18\},\{19\},\{20\}\}$$

Figures 12 and 13 report respectively fitness and profit for a typical simulation with a cost coefficient $c = 0.01$.

Agents with the right decomposition perform worse both in terms of profit (indeed this might be expected because of costs proportional to the span of control) but also in terms of fitness. The former result is due to the fact that fitness-improving changes may be too costly (because of the C_2 component) and reduce profits. Smaller than right

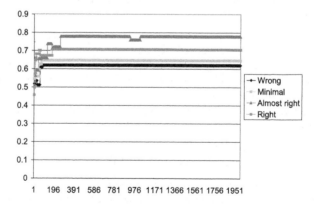

Figure 12 Agency costs (average fitness level over 200 repetitions).

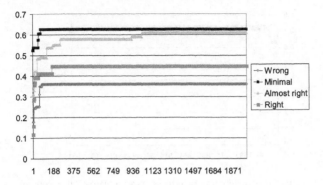

Figure 13 Agency costs (average profit value over 200 repetitions),

decompositions have higher performance both in profit and in fitness and will tend to prevail in the population. An additional disadvantage of using a large decomposition is that if they are 'wrong' the performance easily becomes extremely poor.

The virtues of a 'false' decomposition in conjunction with the challenge of motivating and monitoring action are compounded in the context of more complex problem environments. Consider the environment generated by the following decomposition of size 10:

$$D = \{\{1,2,3,4,5,6,7,8,9,10\},\{11,12,13,14,15,16,17,18,19,20\}\}$$

In this setting, we model four types of agents characterized by decompositions of different sizes, called respectively:

1. $K = 1$, with decomposition:

    $$\Delta = \{\{1\},\{2\},\{3\},\ldots,\{18\},\{19\},\{20\}$$

2. $K = 2$, with decomposition:

    $$\Delta = \{\{1,2\},\{3,4\},\ldots,\{17,18\},\{19,20\}\}$$

3. $K = 4$, with decomposition:

    $$\Delta = \{\{1,2,3,4\},\{5,6,7,8\},\{9,10,11,12\},\{13,14,15,16\},\{17,18,19,20\}\}$$

4. $K = 5$, with decomposition:

    $$\Delta = \{\{1,2,3,4,5\},\{6,7,8,9,10\},\{11,12,13,14,15\},\{16,17,18,19,20\}\}$$

Indeed, there is something of this stylized analysis which robustly carries over to the interpretation of enormously more complex real-world phenomena, that has also to do with ubiquitous dilemmas between 'explorations' and 'exploitation', in March's (1991) terms, and *together*, the dilemmas linking the efficacy of routines, the varying costs of

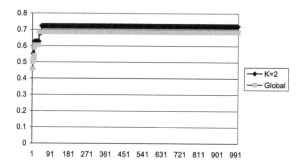

Figure 14 Interaction of cognition and control (average profit over 200 repetitions).

hierarchical controls of behaviours, the promising but costly liberties to chose and search.

To highlight the effect of the interaction between problem decompositions and problems of control, we contrast the behaviour of a system with agents that require control with that of a system with 'angels'—a set of actors that do not require such control measures. When these co-operating individuals (i.e. angels) are also perfectly knowledgeable, then we get the expected result that co-operative actors perform better than those agents that require control measures. However, if actors have the wrong cognitive representation of the problem space—i.e. they enact an incorrect partition— then non-co-operative agents may actually generate a higher level of performance. Figure 14 compares the fitness achieved by an organization in which co-operating individuals have a high dimensional representation of the environment that corresponds in partition width to the true problem representation but the elements are not correctly assigned, with agents that require control who have a 'simplistic' view of the problem space as consisting of two element partitions.

5. Conclusions

We started with a stark imagery of how discordant the major current perspectives on firm behaviours are. It is not simply that the perspectives pose contradictions; it is as if, figuratively speaking, they are from different planets. Theorists start with fundamentally different principles as to what constitutes the critical underlying elements of a theory of the firm. We have strived (i) to be able to engage issues of capabilities and incentives on a common analytical platform; and (ii) to demonstrate that there is real value to such an exercise. There are important interactions among the theoretical perspectives and treating them in a separable manners might be deeply misleading. The problem of specifying task decomposition intimately relates to the problem of incentives and to issues of power.

Notwithstanding our utterly simple assumptions, we already find a useful complementarity between the imposition of local incentives to induce 'selfish' behaviour in a problem context in which the task decomposition is ill-specified and the linkages across partitions of task decompositions. While, in such a setting, local incentives provide an impetus to search by provoking subunits to perturb each other's search process, such mutual perturbation can be excessive. Power, a factor generally absent in discussion of capabilities, turns out also to be a useful complement. Power can inhibit the endless cycling that such behaviour might engender.

Thus, factors such as incentives and power that recent capability-based writings have tended to shy away from turn out to be important sets of considerations in addressing the problem of firm behaviour from either a normative or descriptive point of view. At the same time, power and incentives are clearly not the only relevant considerations. For us, with a behavioural starting point rooted in notions of bounded rationality, the problem of capabilities is foremost a problem of search and discovery.

We are not the first to make such linkages in some fashion. Indeed, in the seminal source documents of March and Simon (1958), Cyert and March (1963), and Nelson and Winter (1982) such linkages among the problem of search, incentives and power are present. However, as we have refined our notions of capabilities and the problems of knowledge and as neoclassical economists refined the apparatus of contract theory, such linkages have largely been lost. There have been some recent calls to rebuild these linkages (cf. Coriat and Dosi, 1998). In the present work, we have not only issued such a call, but have provided a potential analytical structure with which to pursue this objective. Using recent advances in computational modelling (Marengo, 2000; Marengo *et al.*, 2000), we can provide a platform in which behaviouralists can enter the world of mechanism design (Levinthal and Warglien, 1999). The current work provides some promising initial findings that attest to the merit of such an endeavour. Perhaps more importantly, we hope that others will exploit this analytical platform and further build 'bridges' between these two 'worlds'.

Acknowledgements

We thank Nicolai Foss, Reinhard Selten and two anonymous referees for useful remarks and critiques. Luigi Marengo gratefully acknowledges financial contribution from the European Commission within the project NORMEC (SERD-2000-00316), Research Directorate, 5th framework programme, Giovanni Dosi would like to acknowledge the support received by Sant'Anna School of Advanced Studies, Pisa, and both are grateful to the National Research Council (grants CNR007B2D_002 and CNRC002AEE_005). The authors are solely responsible for the opinions expressed in this paper, which are not necessarily those of the European Union or the European Commission.

Address for correspondence

Giovanni Dosi: St Anna School of Advanced Studies, Piazza dei Martiri della Libertà 33, 56127 Pisa, Italy. Email: gdosi@sssup.it.

References

Baldwin, C. Y. and K. B. Clark (2000), *Design Rules: The Power of Modularity*. MIT Press: Cambridge, MA.

Cohen, M., R. Burkhart, G. Dosi, M. Egidi, L. Marengo, M. Warglien and S. Winter (1996), 'Routines and other recurring action patterns of organizations: contemporary research issues,' *Industrial and Corporate Change*, **5**, 653–698.

Coriat, B. and G. Dosi (1998), 'Learning how to govern and learning how to solve problems,' in A. D. Chandler, P. Hagstrom and O. Solvell (eds), *The Dynamic Firm. The Role of Technology, Strategy, Organization and Regions*. Oxford University Press: Oxford.

Cyert, R. and J. March (1963), *A Behavioral Theory of the Firm*. Prentice Hall: Englewood Cliffs, NJ.

Dosi, G. (1988), 'Sources, procedures and microeconomic effects of innovation,' *Journal of Economic Literature*, **26**, 1120–1171.

Dosi, G. (1995), 'Hierarchies, markets and power: some foundational issues on the nature of contemporary economic organization,' *Industrial and Corporate Change*, **4**, 1–19.

Dosi, G. and L. Marengo (1995), 'Toward a theory of organizational competencies,' in R. W. England (ed.), *Evolutionary Concepts in Contemporary Economics*. Michigan University Press: Ann Arbor, pp. 157–178.

Dosi, G., R. Nelson and S. Winter (eds) (2000), *The Nature and Dynamics of Organizational Capabilities*. Oxford University: Press Oxford.

Ethiraj, S. and D. Levinthal (2002), 'Modularity and innovation in complex systems,' *Academy of Management Best Papers Proceedings*.

Grossman, S. and O. Hart (1986), 'The costs and benefits of ownership: a theory of vertical and lateral integration,' *Journal of Political Economy*, **94**, 691–719.

Holmstrom, B. and J. Tirole (1989), 'The theory of firm,' in R. Schmalensee and R. Willig (eds), *Handbook of Industrial Organization*. North-Holland: Amsterdam, Vol. 1, pp. 61–133.

Kauffman, S. A. (1993), *The Origins of Order*. Oxford University Press: Oxford.

Kreps, M. D. (1996), 'Markets and hierachies and (mathematical) economic theory,' *Industrial and Corporate Change*, **5**, 561–595.

Laffont, J. J. and J. Tirole (1993), *A Theory of Incentives in Procurement and Regulation*. MIT Press: Cambridge MA.

Levinthal, D. (1997), 'Adaptation on rugged landscapes,' *Management Science*, 43, 934–950.

March, J. G. and H. A. Simon (1958), *Organizations*. Wiley: New York.

Marengo, L. (2000), 'Decentralisation and market mechanisms in collective problem-solving,' mimeo, University of Trento (revised draft 2002, LEM Sant'Anna School of Advanced Studies, Pisa, working paper).

Marengo, L., G. Dosi, P. Legrenzi and C. Pasquali (2000), 'The structure of problem-solving knowledge and the structure of organizations,' *Industrial and Corporate Change*, **9**, 757–788.

Nelson, R. R. and S. G. Winter (1982), *An Evolutionary Theory of Economic Change*. Harvard University Press: Cambridge, MA.

Page, S. E. (1996), 'Two measures of difficulty,' *Economic Theory*, **8**, 321–346.

436   G. Dosi, D. A. Levinthal and L. Marengo

Radner, R. (1986), 'The internal economy of large firms,' *Economic Journal*, **96**(Suppl.), 1–22.

Rivkin, J. and N. Siggelkow (2002), 'Choice interaction and organizational structure,' working paper, Harvard Business School, Cambridge, MA.

Simon, H. (1951), 'A formal model of the employment relationship,' *Econometrica*, **19**, 293–305.

Simon, H. (1955), 'A behavioural model of rational choice,' *Quarterly Journal of Economics*, **69**, 99–118.

Simon, H. (1969), *The Sciences of the Artificial*. MIT Press: Cambridge, MA.

[6]

Industrial and Corporate Change, Volume 15, Number 1, pp. 173–202
doi:10.1093/icc/dtj010

Technologies as problem-solving procedures and technologies as input–output relations: some perspectives on the theory of production

Giovanni Dosi and Marco Grazzi

In this work, inspired by Winter (2006), in fact of vintage 1968, we discuss the relation between three different levels of analysis of technologies, namely as (i) bodies of problem-solving knowledge, (ii) organizational procedures, and (iii) input–output relations. We begin by arguing that the "primitive" levels of investigation, "where the action is," are those which concern knowledge and organizational procedures while in most respects the I/O representation is just an ex post, derived, one. Next, we outline what we consider to be important advances in the understanding of productive knowledge and of the nature and behaviors of business organizations which to a good extent embody such a knowledge. Finally, we explore some implications of such "procedural" view of technologies in terms of input–output relations (of which standard production functions are a particular instantiation). We do that with the help of some pieces of evidence, drawing both upon incumbent literature and our own elaboration on micro longitudinal data on the Italian industry.

1. Introduction

The long-hidden essay by Sid Winter, "Toward a Neo-Schumpeterian theory of the Firm," at last published in this issue of *Industrial and Corporate Change*, raises a few fundamental challenges to economic analysis which to a good extent continues to remain challenges after more than a third of a century. They concern the nature of technologies and their relation with individual and collective knowledge; the ways economists do (and ought to) represent them; the characteristics of technological and organizational learning; and the implications of all this in terms of theory of the firm. Certainly, not bad at all for a short essay! Building on some seminal intuitions of this work, here we shall discuss where one has taken (or not taken) those ideas since, offer some evidence which largely corroborates the early hints and flag some areas of analysis which remain in need of urgent intervention.

The basic intuition, which is also the central point of departure of this essay is that a fully fledged interpretation of technologies and their dynamics–that is, technological innovation–entails three complementary levels of analysis. The *first* one pertains to the *nature of knowledge* upon which technological activities–including of course production–draws. From this angle of observation, one investigates the types of knowledge bases and skills which are called upon in, say, the transformation of pieces of iron, plastic, glass, and so on into a finished car. And dynamically, one studies the ways such a knowledge is accumulated and improved.

The conception, design, and production of whatever artifact, however, involve (often very long) sequences of cognitive and physical acts. In the example of a car, one goes from the activities of design to the development of a prototype all the way to the actual production. And, in turn, at a more detailed observation, at each step one finds a complex sequence of operations generally undertaken by different but coordinated people in association with different tools and machines. This second level of description, which we may call *procedural*, is deeply intertwined with the analysis of how business organizations actually work since big "chunks" of activities occur within single organizational entities rather than being mediated through the market.

Finally, third, precisely the same activities–seen above in terms of sequences of procedure eliciting diverse type of knowledge–may be also described in terms of the list of inputs which come, under various headings, into the production process and of what finally comes out. This *input-output* description is of course the one most familiar to economists, with all refinements on the purported relations between inputs and outputs themselves featuring in "production functions," "production possibility sets," and the like.

In all that a crucial question regards the relationships between these three levels of analysis of production activities. Winter's essay addresses precisely that question suggesting that the "primitive" levels of investigation, "where the action is," are those which concern knowledge and organizational procedures while in most respects the I/O representation is just an ex post, derived, one. Indeed, a lot of work–a good deal of which of evolutionary inspiration–has gone into the economics of knowledge and innovation, on the one hand, and into the study of organizations as problem-solving entities, on the other.

Granted that, what are the implications for the theory of production, *narrow sense*, that is in terms of sheer relations between inputs and outputs? And what does the evidence tell us about it? In the following, we shall address these issues.

In Section 2, we briefly outline what we consider to be important advances in the understanding of productive knowledge and of the nature and behaviors of business organizations which to a good extent embody such a knowledge. Next, in Section 3, we explore some implications of such "procedural" view of technologies in terms of input–output relations (of which, to repeat, standard production functions are a particular instantiation). Together we offer some pieces of evidence, drawing both upon incumbent literature and our own elaboration on micro longitudinal data on the Italian industry.

2. Technologies as (knowledge-ridden) problem-solving activities

There are a few things which we know better now as compared to the time when Sid Winter was writing his essay around 1968. They come mostly from various attempts to "open up the technological blackbox"–to use a famous expression of Nate Rosenberg– and complementary attempts to "open up the organizational blackbox."

2.1 Technological paradigms and trajectories

A variety of concepts have been put forward to define the nature of technology and technological innovation: *technological regimes, paradigms, trajectories, salients, guidepost, dominant design,* and so on. The names are not so important. More crucially, these concepts are highly overlapping in that they try to capture a few common features of technological activities and of the procedures and directions of technical change. Let us consider some of them.

The notion of *technological paradigm* which shall be for the time being our yardstick is based on a view of technology grounded on the following three fundamental ideas (see Dosi, 1982 and 1984).

First, it suggests that any satisfactory description of "what is technology" and how it changes must also embody the representation of the specific forms of knowledge on which a particular activity is based, which cannot be reduced to a set of well-defined blueprints. It primarily concerns problem-solving activities involving–to varying degrees–also tacit forms of knowledge embodied in individuals and organizations.

In this view, technology is a set of pieces of knowledge ultimately based on selected physical and chemical principles, know-how, methods, experiences of successes and failures, and also, of course, physical devices and equipment.

Second, paradigms entail specific heuristic and visions on "how to do things" and how to improve them, often shared by the community of practitioners in each particular activity (engineers, firms, technical societies, etc.), that is, they entail *collectively shared cognitive frames* (Constant, 1980).

Third, paradigms often also define basic templates of artifacts and systems (i.e., "dominant designs"),[1] which over time are progressively modified and improved. These basic artifacts can also be described in terms of some fundamental technological and economic characteristics. For example, in the case of an airplane, their

---

[1] Incidentally note that the notion of dominant design is well in tune with the general idea of technological paradigms but the latter do not necessarily imply the former. A revealing case to the point is pharmaceutical technologies which do involve specific knowledge basis, specific search heuristics, and so on–that is, the strong mark of paradigms–without however any hint of dominant design. Molecules, even when aimed at the same pathology, might have quite different structures: in that space, one is unlikely to find similarities akin those linking even a Volkswagen Beetle vintage 1937 and a Ferrari vintage 2000. Still, the notion of "paradigm" holds even in the former case in terms of underlying features of knowledge bases and search processes.

basic attributes are described not only and obviously in terms of inputs and production costs, but also on the basis of some salient technological features such as wing-load, take-off weight, speed, distance it can cover, and so on. Similar examples of technological invariances can be found, for example, in semiconductors, agricultural equipment, automobiles, and a few other micro technological studies (Sahal, 1981; Grupp, 1992; Saviotti, 1996).

What is interesting here is that technical progress often seems to display patterns and invariances in terms of some basic product characteristics. Hence, the notion of *technological trajectories* associated with the progressive realization of the innovative opportunities underlying each paradigm—which can in principle be measured in terms of the changes in the fundamental techno-economic characteristics of artifacts and production processes. The core ideas involved in this notion of trajectories are the following.

Each particular body of knowledge (each paradigm) shapes and constraints the rates and direction of technical change, in a first rough approximation, irrespectively of market inducements. In fact, technical change is partly driven by repeated attempts to cope with technological imbalances which it itself creates.[2] As a consequence, one should be able to observe regularities and invariances in the pattern of technical change which hold under different market conditions (e.g., under different relative prices) and whose disruption is mainly correlated with radical changes in knowledge bases (in paradigms).

Moreover, a rather general property, by now widely acknowledged in the innovation literature, is that learning is often *local* and *cumulative*. "Locality" means that the exploration and development of new techniques and product architectures is likely to occur in the neighborhood of the techniques and architectures already in use (Atkinson and Stiglitz, 1969; David, 1975; Antonelli, 1995). "Cumulativeness" stands for the property that current technological developments often build upon past experiences of production and innovation, proceed through sequences of specific problem solving junctures (Vincenti, 1990), and in several circumstances also lead to microeconomic serial correlations in successes and failures.

The literature on technological knowledge and technological change has offered, of course, plenty of insights also into the detailed mechanisms through which innovative search occurs, on the sources of knowledge on which it draws and on their intersectoral differences. (For critical surveys see Dosi, 1988; Freeman, 1994; and Dosi *et al.*, 2005.) For the purpose of this work, however, let us content ourselves with the basic idea that *there is a structure to technological knowledge, and dynamically to the patterns of technological innovation* which tend to be relatively invariant, linked as it is to specific routes to the solution of particular problems (e.g., going from iron oxide to steel and from steel to a steel-made combustion chamber with certain technical characteristics).

---

[2]This is akin to the notion of reverse salient (Hughes, 1983) and technological bottlenecks (Rosenberg, 1976): to illustrate, think of increasing the speed of a machine tool, which in turn demands changes in cutting materials, which leads to changes in other parts of the machine....

Together, to repeat, major changes in such knowledge structures tend to come from major discontinuities in underlying paradigms.

All we have said so far is from the angle of "technology as knowledge."

However, a good deal of "economically useful" technological knowledge is nowadays mastered by business firms, which even undertake in some developed countries a small but not negligible portion of the efforts aimed at a more speculative understandings of the physical, chemical, biological properties of our world (i.e., they also undertake "basic science")[3]. How does all that relate with the structure and behaviors of firms themselves?

2.2 Knowledge, routines, and capabilities in business organizations

Possibly one of the most exciting, far from over, intellectual enterprises developed over the last decade has involved the interbreeding between the evolutionary economics research program, (largely evolutionary inspired) technological innovation studies, and an emerging competence/capability-based theory of the firm. The roots rest in the pioneering organizational studies by Herbert Simon, James March, and colleagues (Simon 1969; March 1988; March and Simon 1993; Cyert and March 1992) and in the equally pioneering explorations of the nature and economic implications of organizational routines by Nelson and Winter (1982) [with follow-ups such as those in Cohen *et al.* (1996); Teece *et al.* (1997); Dosi *et al.* (2000b); the Special Issue of *Industrial and Corporate Change*, 2000, edited by Mie Augier and James March; Montgomery (1995); and Foss and Mahnke (2000)].

It is familiar enough to most readers that business firms "know how to do certain things"–things like building automobiles and computers–and know that with different efficacies and revealed performances. In turn, what does "organizational knowledge" mean? What are the mechanisms that govern how it is acquired, maintained, and sometimes lost? As several authors in the just cited works suggest, organizational knowledge is in fact a fundamental link between the social pool of knowledge, skills, discovery opportunities, on the one hand, and the rates, directions, economic effectiveness of their *actual* exploration, on the other.

Distinctive organizational competences/capabilities[4] bear their importance also in that they persistently shape the destiny of individual firms–in terms of, for example, profitability, growth, probability of survival–and, at least equally important, their distributions across firms shape the patterns of change of broader aggregates such as particular sectors or whole countries.

---

[3]See Rosenberg (1990) and Pavitt (1991).

[4]In the literature, the two terms have often been used quite liberally and interchangeably. In the introduction to Dosi *et al.* (2000b) and more explicitly in Dosi *et al.* (2000a) one proposes that the notion of capability ought to be confined to relatively purposeful "high level" tasks such as, for example, "building an automobile" with certain characteristics, while "competences," for sake of clarity might be confined to the ability to master specific knowledge bases (e.g., "mechanical" or "organic chemistry" competences). Clearly, such notion of competences/capabilities largely overlaps with what has come to be known as the "competence view of the firm."

"Competences" and "capabilities" build on ensembles of organizational routines. In turn, the latter (i) as thoroughly argued by Nelson and Winter (1982), embody a good part of the memory of the problem-solving repertoires of any one organization; (ii) entail complementary mechanisms of governance for potentially conflicting interests (for a more detailed discussion see Dosi and Coriat, 1988), and (iii) might well involve also some "meta-routines," apt to painstakingly assess and possibly challenge and modify "lower level" organizational practices (the more incremental R&D activities, and recurrent exercises of "strategic adjustment," are good cases to the point).

In this view, routines and other recurrent organizational practices may be interpreted as a set of problem-solving procedures in turn composed of elementary physical acts (such as moving a drawing from an office to another or boring a piece of iron on a machine tool) and elementary cognitive acts (such as doing a certain calculation).

This *procedural* view of technology is indeed quite complementary to the foregoing knowledge-centered one. One could even state that the procedural perspective simply means viewing "knowledge in action." Indeed, it is helpful to think of complex problem-solving activities–as most contemporary industrial activities in fact are–as problems of design of complex sequences of actions, rules, search heuristics,[5] drawing at each point of the sequence upon specific skills and pieces of knowledge.

2.3 *Division of labor, decompositions, complementarities*[6]

Can one "unbundle" the foregoing sequences of tasks and assess on whatever measure the effectiveness of each "elementary component"?

It turns out that the effectiveness of such "procedural systems" in most circumstances is at best only *partly-decomposable*, in that it cannot be neatly separated into the effectiveness of single acts which could then be added together into the overall effectiveness of the sequence. That is, *complementarities are endemic*. So, for example, a very effective problem-solving sequence may be that in which agent A does x, followed by B doing y, and C doing z. Conversely a sequence with A doing z might increase the overall performance if C turns to action k, but decreases it other things being equal... Hence, marginal contributions to the effectiveness of components (i.e., "acts" in problem-solving procedures and physical components in technological systems) can rapidly switch from negative to positive values and vice versa, depending on which values are assumed by other components. For instance, adding a more powerful engine could amount to decrease the performance and reliability of an aircraft (Vincenti, 1990) if other components are not simultaneously adapted. Similarly, major innovations often appears only when various elements which are already known for a long time are recombined and put together under a different frame [cf. Levinthal (1998) for a detailed account of the development of wireless

---

[5]For some example in the case of the so called Complex Product Systems cf. Dosi *et al.* (2003).

[6]For more details see Marengo and Dosi (2005).

communication]. By the same token, introducing some routines, practices or incentive schemes, which have proven superior in a given organizational context, could prove harmful in a different one where other elements are not appropriately coadapted.

Such aspects are present even in the simplest production technologies. Consider for example team production as exemplified by Alchian and Demsetz (1972): two workers lifting a heavy load. Additional individual efforts generally rise team production, but when the levels of effort applied by the two are disproportionate, this might result in the load being turned over and falling, thus sharply decreasing the output of the team itself.

In a growing literature, including works by Marengo and colleagues [cf. Marengo *et al* (2000) and Marengo and Dosi (2005)] one begins to offer explicit formal accounts of the foregoing view of technology, and dynamically, of the search thereof in terms of *combinatorics of elementary cognitive and physical components*. The formal apparatus is then put to use in terms of "comparative dynamics," studying, for example, the comparative efficiency properties of different problem-decompositions and patterns of division of labor; the outcomes and speeds of convergence of different search strategies in the problem-solving space; and the effects thereof of diverse organizational structures.

As noted in the introduction to this work, however, one still lacks any systematic link between the procedural perspective, just sketched out, which lives in the space defined by "bits of knowledge" and by the presence or absence of a particular physical and cognitive components, on the one hand, and the more mundane world of "what comes in and what goes out" the production process.

3. The (missing) links between the evolution of problem-solving knowledge and input–output relations

Let us elaborate on the illustrative example, originally put forward by Richard Nelson and Sid Winter, of *making a cake*. This involves inputs, both of the "variable" kind–flour, butter, eggs, and so on–and "fixed" ones–including spoons, pots, ovens, and so on. And, clearly, there is an output, a cake, possibly with a variable taste, caloric content, and so on.

Apparently, the input–output characterization is straightforward: a vector x of inputs for y (possibly a vector) of output(s). However, just turn the question to your grandmother: "how do I make a cake?" Suppose for a moment that the old lady answers "max price times output minus price of inputs times their quantities." Anyone would take that as ultimate evidence of old-age *dementia*. Needless to say, such an answer is also totally uninformative on how to make a cake. And so is of course the more sophisticated answer suggesting that the cake and flour, butter, sugar, and so on are related through, say, a degree-one homogeneous function! (In fact the latter statement would only further confirm the mental disorder of the poor lady. . . .)

Of course, the appropriate answer to the question on how to make a cake entails a series of procedures: ". . . mix a couple of eggs and one ounce of butter into a pound of flour. . . ." This procedural story does involve statements on quantities (the two eggs, the ounce of butter, etc.) but such quantities make sense only in relation to specific sequences of operations.[7] Moreover, note that the relation between such quantities and relative prices is at best indirect: one needs certain ingredients in order to make a cake and needs them irrespectively of their price (except perhaps "local" forms of substitution, such as margarine versus butter).

One earlier discussion of technological paradigms implies indeed that these considerations hold well beyond the example of the cake and are pertinent to the generality of production activities. Moreover, one should expect individual agents (typically firms) to develop distinct "ways of doing things," relatively persistent over time, associated with their equally persistent organizational routines. (Incidentally, recall pioneering Leibstein's "X-efficiency" which tries to capture in a somewhat blackboxed way such links between "ways-of-doing-things" and revealed efficiencies: see Leibstein 1966).

Given that, what are the implications of such properties of technologies in terms of distribution of input coefficients and their dynamics over time?

How do firm-specific combinations of routines and "pieces of knowledge" reflect into the revealed distributions of input coefficients? In order to answer the question, one requires firm-level (or plant-level) longitudinal panel data. Indeed, they have become increasingly available. And with that a few "stylized facts" have emerged.[8] They include

1. wide asymmetries in productivities, both across firms and even within them;
2. equally wide heterogeneity in relative input intensities; and,
3. high degrees of intertemporal persistence in the above properties.

We shall illustrate such "stylized facts" with the help of some evidence drawn especially from Italian firm-level data (cf. Appendix 1 for some statistical details).

However, it might be useful to start with some considerations on the notion of "productivity" itself.

3.1 Input efficiencies: a first digression on the notion of "productivity"

As well known, there are two commonly used measures of production efficiency, namely labor and total factor productivity (TFP).

It should come as no surprise (see also below) that, despite its obvious limitations, we tend to prefer a measure based on the net output [that is the "real" value added]

---

[7]In this respect it is worth mentioning the *funds-flows* theory of production which, while falling short of an explicit procedural representation of production activities, attempts to nest the use of inputs into an explicit temporal sequence flagging when the inputs themselves are used: (i.e., when the flows of their services are called upon.): cf. Georgescu-Roegen (1970) and the reappraisal and the applications in Morroni (1992).

[8]See among others Chew *et al.* (1990), Rumelt (1991), Baily *et al* (1992), Baldwin (1995), Jensen and McGuckin (1997), Power (1998), Foster *et al.* (1998), Bartelsman and Dhrymes (1998), Bartelsman *et al.* (2005), Bottazzi *et al.* (2003), and the discussions in Bartelsman and Doms (2000) and Dosi (2005) together with the earlier insights from Nelson (1981; 1991).

per employee or, even better, per worked hours. The reason for this preference lies in the dubious elements which make up conventional production functions, in turn the instrument necessary to yield the TFP measure.

It follows from our foregoing discussion that technologies essentially involve *complementarities* among inputs–so that it makes little sense to separate the "contribution" of each "factor" to the final output. Indeed, such a "decomposition" exercise makes as much sense as disentangling the separate contributions of butter, eggs, sugar, and so on to the making of a good tasting cake.

As Nelson puts it

> If factors are complements, growth is superadditive in the sense that the increase in output from growth of inputs is greater than the sum of the increases in output attributable to input growth calculated one by one holding other inputs constant at their base level in each sub-calculation (Nelson, 1981: 1053)

There is in fact a more recent literature on "superadditivity"[9] (needless to say, with little or no reference to the earlier original insights) trying to reconcile within more flexible (more "general") functional forms of production functions a notion of complementarity with the usual assumptions on micro maximization and market equilibrium (again, see also the concluding remarks below).

The bottom line in our view, however, is that one typically lives in a technological world characterized by microcoefficients which are fixed in the short term (i.e., each firm basically masters just the technique actually in use) while in the longer term techniques change essentially due to learning and technical progress. Conversely, if this is the case, it does not make much sense to distinguish changes *along* any purported production function versus changes *of* the function itself.

3.2 Asymmetries in productivity

Come as it may, an overwhelming evidence *concerning both labor productivity and TFP*, at all levels of disaggregation, suggest widespread differences in production efficiency *across firms and across plants* which tend to be *persistent over time* (cf. the evidence cited in footnote 8).

Our Italian data are well in tune with such stylized facts. Figure 1 presents the distribution in some three-digit sectors[10] of (normalized) value added (VA) per employee, that is,

$$\pi_i(t) = log\ \Pi_i(t) - \langle log\ \Pi_i(t) \rangle$$

---

[9]See Milgrom and Roberts (1990; 1995).

[10]The selection of the sector we chose to present here comes from a numerosity criterion: the top four two-digit sectors in terms of firms population in our sample and the three-digit sectors with more than 200 firms.

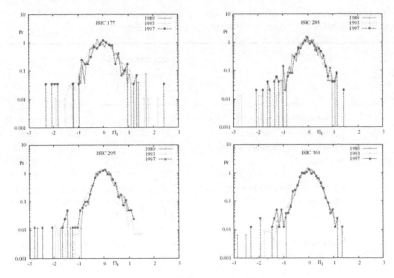

Figure 1 Distributions of labor productivity by sectors: normalized values.
Source: our elaboration of Italian (ISTAT MICRO.1) data (for the definitions of the sectors, cf.
Tables 1 and 2).

whereby,

$$\Pi_i(t) = VA_i/N_i$$

and,

$\langle log\ \Pi_i(t)\rangle \equiv$ mean (log) VA per employee (N) averaged over all firms in any particular sector, in each year.

Moreover, as shown in Table 1, such productivity differentials are quite stable over time, just with some relatively mild regression-to-the-mean tendency.[11]

The general picture is characterized by general and profound heterogeneity across firms, also with respect to capital-output ratios and relative input intensities.

First, note that not surprisingly different industrial sectors significantly differ in their mean labor productivities and capital intensities (cf. Table 2).

Second, together with the already noted asymmetries in labor productivities, one observes equally remarkable inter-firm differences in capital-output ratios (see Figure 2).

Could such differences be due primarily to some intrinsic heterogeneity *across different lines of activity* as opposed to inter-firm differences *within the* same line of activities?

---

[11]For the estimation technique see Chesher (1979).

Table 1 AR(1) coefficients for Labor Productivity in levels and first differences. Labor Productivity (Π_t) is deflated according to the sectoral output price index.

Sector		Labor Productivity		Π_t growth rates	
		SD	AR(1)	SD	AR(1)
151	Production and processing of meat	151	1.0021	0.0016	−0.3446
177	Knitted and crocheted articles	177	1.0056	0.0023	−0.2877
182	Wearing apparel and accessories	182	1.0035	0.0012	−0.3090
193	Footware	193	1.0029	0.0019	−0.3903
212	Articles of paper and paperboard	212	1.0053	0.0008	−0.3027
222	Printing and services related to printing	222	0.9962	0.0011	−0.4753
252	Plastic products	252	1.0030	0.0010	−0.3150
266	Articles of concrete, plaster, and cement	266	0.9985	0.0016	−0.4572
281	Metal products	281	1.0034	0.0012	−0.4125
285	Treatment, coating of metal and mechanical engine	285	1.0051	0.0013	−0.1846
295	Special purpose machinery	295	1.0011	0.0011	−0.3040
361	Furniture	361	0.9994	0.0001	−0.4472

Interestingly, disaggregation does *not* appear to reduce heterogeneity: as an illustration, compare the distributions on the right-hand side of Figure 2, concerning three-digit subsets of the two-digit sectors on the left-handed side.

As Griliches and Mairesse (1999) vividly put it

> We . . . thought that one could reduce heterogeneity by going down from general mixtures as "total manufacturing" to something more coherent, such as "petroleum refining" or "the manufacture of cement." But something like Mandelbrot's fractal phenomenon seems to be at work here also: the observed variability-heterogeneity does not really decline as we cut our data finer and finer. There is a sense in which different bakeries are just as much different form each others as the steel industry is from the machinery industry.

3.3 Further evidence on technological asymmetries: wage-profit frontiers

A way of appreciating the differences among the techniques mastered by each firm entails the identification of the *wage-profit frontiers* (WPF) associated with it.[12]

---

[12]Such a formal instrument was commonly used within the so called capital controversy (cf. Harcourt, 1972). On its use in order to characterize different forms of technical progress, see Schefold (1976).

Table 2 Sectoral specificities in input/output relations: mean labor productivities ($\Pi = VA/L$) and capital intensities (VA/K)

Sector	ISIC code	1989		1991		1994		1997	
		Π	VA/K	Π	VA/K	Π	VA/K	Π	VA/K
Production and processing of meat	151	4.24 (0.428)	−0.346 (0.764)	4.34 (0.551)	−0.417 (0.811)	4.33(0.429)	−0.629 (0.838)	4.36(0.513)	−0.378(1.29)
Knitted and crocheted articles	177	3.74 (0.421)	0.123 (0.805)	3.83 (0.44)	0.094 (0.829)	3.9 (0.576)	0.243 (0.946)	3.86 (0.508)	0.211 (1.16)
Wearing apparel and accessories	182	3.60 (0.502)	0.67 (0.860)	3.61 (0.547)	0.640 (0.933)	3.66 (0.542)	0.701 (0.916)	3.71 (0.581)	0.809 (1.27)
Footwear	193	3.67 (0.363)	0.455 (0.784)	3.74 (0.420)	0.547 (0.814)	3.81 (0.510)	0.622 (0.858)	3.79 (0.553)	0.793 (1.16)
Articles of paper and paperboard	212	4.30 (0.338)	−0.299 (0.658)	4.35 (0.372)	−0.401 (0.680)	4.41 (0.474)	−0.401 (0.755)	4.48 (0.454)	−0.210 (1.15)
Printing and services related to printing	222	4.44 (0.335)	0.187 (0.654)	4.49 (0.345)	0.173 (0.737)	4.47 (0.369)	0.091 (0.778)	4.32 (0.507)	0.0481 (1.21)
Plastic products	252	4.30 (0.379)	−0.307 (0.627)	4.37 (0.424)	−0.405 (0.614)	4.43 (0.535)	−0.369 (0.813)	4.40 (0.473)	−0.128 (1.03)
Articles of concrete, plaster, and cement	266	4.31 (0.417)	−0.478 (0.601)	4.34 (0.454)	−0.543 (0.682)	4.34 (0.454)	−0.441 (0.722)	4.40 (0.449)	−0.128 (0.995)
Metal products	281	4.11 (0.365)	0.225 (0.721)	4.20 (0.397)	0.136 (0.733)	4.11 (0.451)	0.0099 (0.885)	4.26 (0.436)	0.423 (1.07)
Treatment and coating of metals; general mechanical engine	285	4.08 (0.350)	−0.203 (0.698)	4.10 (0.349)	−0.326 (0.755)	4.18 (0.391)	−0.174 (0.865)	4.24 (0.435)	0.11 (1.29)
Special purpose machinery	295	4.41 (0.361)	0.343 (0.696)	4.45 (0.319)	0.262 (0.772)	4.48 (0.385)	0.253 (0.805)	4.49 (0.393)	0.456 (0.0966)
Furniture	361	4.04 (0.425)	0.0076(0.788)	4.12 (0.337)	−0.0235 (0.706)	4.13 (0.387)	−0.06 (0.784)	4.10 (0.384)	0.047 (0.0947)

Constant price log variables; standard errors in parentheses.

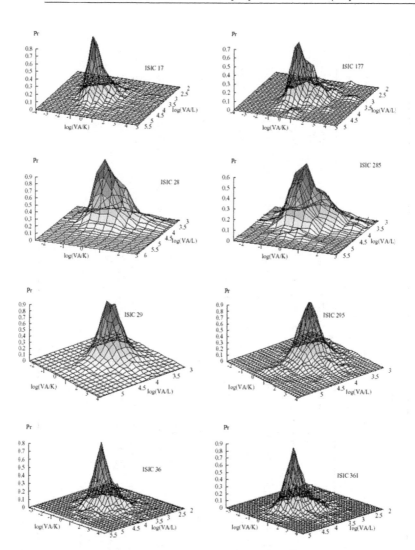

Figure 2 Labor productivities and input intensities: the microdistributions. (**Left side**) Kernel density estimate of [log(*VA/K*), log(*VA/L*)] in 1997 for four different manufacturing sectors at two digit. (**Right side**) Kernel density estimate of [log(*VA/K*), log(*VA/L*)] in the same year for some nested sectors at three digit.

Assume for simplicity homogeneous output and labor. To make it even simpler assume the absence of intermediate goods. Hence output coincide with VA. (Note, however, that if the ratios of intermediate inputs to "physical" net output were roughly constant across firms within the same activity, the simpler relation would directly apply also to the more realistic one.)

Consider the following variables: K, capital stock; r, gross return on capital; Y, output (in our simplified example = VA, the value added); w, monetary wages; Py, output price index (~deflator for VA); Y_r, deflated output; $v = K/Y$, capital-output ratio; $\tilde{w}$, real wages; L, labor input; $\Pi = Y_r/L$, labor productivity.

Thus, by definition,

$$rK + wL = Y_r P_Y$$

and rearranging,

$$r\frac{K}{Y} + \frac{wL}{P_Y Y_r} = 1$$

Then, since $K/Y = v$, $w/P_v = \tilde{w}$, and $L/Y_r = 1/\Pi$, we can rewrite it as

$$rv + \frac{\tilde{w}}{\Pi} = 1 \tag{1}$$

Equation (1) yields a linear relation between real wages and profits, given the technique. It defines *a WPF* which is the locus of income distributions compatible with it.

Just rewrite equation (1) as $\tilde{w} = \Pi(1-rv)$: clearly, for $r = 0$, $\tilde{w} = W = \Pi$ i.e., all product goes to wages while, conversely, $\tilde{w} = 0$ yields the maximum rate of profit consistent with that technique.

It is straightforward that one can always rank techniques *given a wage (or profit) rate*. Moreover, if both intercepts of a certain technique are greater than those of another, it follows that the former dominates the latter irrespectively of relative prices.

Of course, one can speculate on many combinations among different WPFs, of which the standard "production function" is just a particular case. But, what does the empirical evidence tell us? Figure 3 presents the WPFs over three quantiles (bins) ordered in terms of their y-intercept, that is, their associated labor productivities. As one can see, widespread asymmetries among firms are the norm, frequently displaying ensembles of techniques which dominate many others for the whole range of notional relative prices.[13]

Over time, as Figure 3 shows, techniques basically change by the movement "outward" of the associated WPF's, interestingly displaying both increasing labor productivities

---

[13]As a term of comparison, notice that in a standard production function world, the envelope of all *notional* WPFs would look like a hyperbola while the empirical observation at any t for identical relative prices across firms would concentrate around a prevailing WPF (plus some noise).

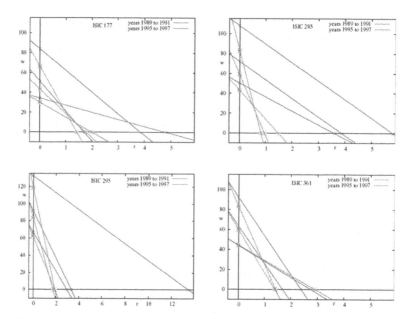

Figure 3 Wage–profit frontier. Empirical estimate for the mean values over the periods 1989–1991 and 1995–1997.

and increasing maximum attainable profit rates: hence *technical progress appears to be in many circumstances both labor–and capital–saving.*

What is the interpretation of this evidence?

In our view, an evolutionary account is quite straightforward in that it predicts persistent heterogeneity in production efficiencies (and in the degrees of innovativeness): cf. the discussions in Dosi (1988; 2005) and Freeman (1994), as the outcome of idiosyncratic capabilities (or lack of them), mistake-ridden learning and forms of path-dependent adaption. Differences in innovative abilities and efficiencies (together with differences in organizational set-ups and behaviors) we suggest make-up the distinct corporate "identities" which in turn influence those different corporate efficiencies revealed by the evidence ranging from the foregoing Italian one to that presented in the works cited above (cf. footnote 8, Winter, 1981 and 1987).

3.4   Relative input intensities and revealed efficiencies

Given the widespread heterogeneity across firms discussed so far, let us investigate whether the data display any regularity in the relationship between input intensities and productivities, in turn hinting at some underlying "production function" with the properties most often postulated by economists (e.g., decreasing returns with respect to single inputs).

In particular, recall that in the presence of a standard Cobb-Douglas, the function $Y/L = f(K/L)$ grows in K/L but has a negative second derivative. As a consequence K/Y (the capital/output ratio) should grow together with both K/L and Y/L.

Our evidence (see Figure 4) does suggest a positive correlation between VA per employee (our proxy for "net output") and K/L, which should be properly understood as an indicator of mechanization/automation of production (cf. Pasinetti (1977)). However, no correlation appears between our proxy of labor productivity and capital/output ratios, which is indeed the proper measure of "capital intensity" of production (Figure 5). Putting it another way, there are firms which use more efficiently or less efficiently *both labor and capital*. Hence, in the language of production functions, they belong to different production functions, or, in a less arcane framework, this evidence witnesses, again, that different firms master techniques which can be unambiguously ordered as more or less efficient irrespectively of input prices.

3.5 *Replication and scale*

The procedural view of technology summarized above also bears far-reaching implications in terms of *replication* and *scale*. As Szulanski and Winter (2002) put it

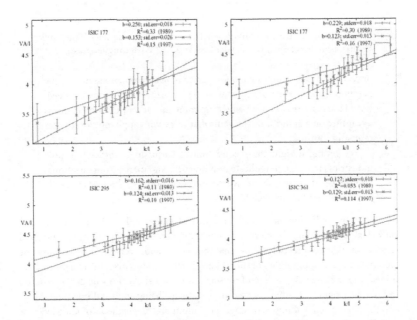

Figure 4 Labor productivities and capital/labor ratios. Bin plots and OLS estimates. Error bars display two standard errors. K and VA at constant prices.

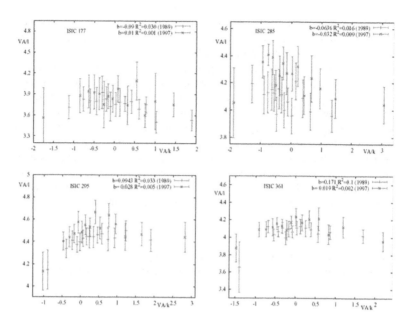

Figure 5 Labor productivities and output/capital ratios. Bin plots and values of (insignificant) OLS estimates. Error bars display two standard errors. *K* and *VA* at constant prices.

> once a business is doing a good job performing a complex activity . . . the parent organization naturally wants to replicate the initial success. Indeed, one of the main reasons for being a big company rather than a small one is to capture on a grand scale the gains that come with applying smart processes and routines.
>
> Yet getting it right the second time is surprisingly difficult. Whole industries are trying to replicate best practices and manage organizational knowledge – but even so the overwhelming majority of attempts to replicate excellence fail. (pp. 62–63)

Difficulties in replication have to do with the distributed and partly tacit character of knowledge and its "hazy frontiers" (Winter, 2005): indeed an organization (and all of its members) do not precisely know what they know, and, even less so, they know the precise domain of applicability of such a knowledge. . . . Moreover, the endemic correlations among elementary skills and routines, discussed above, impede decomposition and "credit assignment": that is, one can hardly map "being good at doing something" into the separate contributions of single operations and single pieces of knowledge. *A fortiori*, replication difficulties apply when the replicas involve "scaling up" or "scaling down."

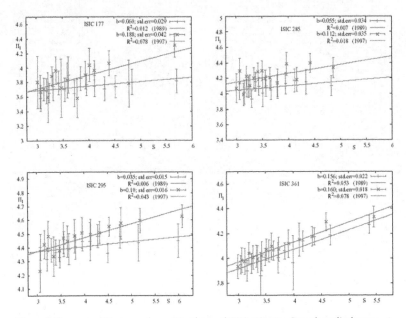

Figure 6 Size versus *VA* per employee. Bin plots and OLS estimates. Error bars display two standard errors. Size is proxied by number of employees. *VA* at constant prices.

At the end of the day, the evidence does suggest some positive correlation between firm-size, on the one hand, and labor productivity as well as degrees of mechanization of production (*K/L*), on the other, but *not* with capital intensities (approximated by capital/output ratios), (see Figures 6, 7, and 8).

Moreover, notice, first, that within each size class the inter-firm variance in labor productivities remains remarkably high.

Second, the average impact of sheer size on productivity appears to be rather low (cf. Table 3).

Third, and more importantly, the direction of causality is not at all clear: indeed it is likely to run both ways. That is, our evidence on Italian firms is consistent with the notion that *some economies of scale apply*–possibly associated with scale-biased forms of mechanization/automation of production. However, the opposite causality sign is likely to apply, too: relatively more efficient firms might be bigger because they are more efficient and not the other way round.

There are also important theoretical consequences of all this: indeed the microeconomic evidence on the hurdles of replication, together with that on the size-specificity of different techniques, make the assumptions from standard production theory of additivity and divisibility (and the derived one of convexity) hard to accept [for a germane discussion, see Winter (2005)].

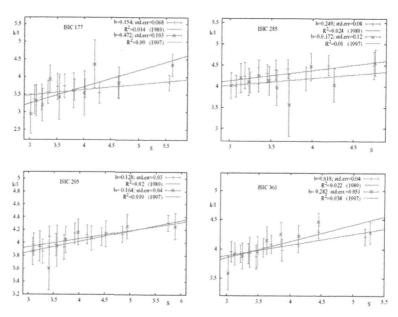

Figure 7 Relation size–capital/labor ratio. Size and labor are proxied by number of employees. Error bars display two standard errors; K at constant prices.

3.6 Aggregation and income distribution

More than forty years ago, Walters (1963) was already noting that

> after surveying the problems of aggregation one may easily doubt whether there is much point in employing such a concept as an aggregate production function. The variety of competitive and technological conditions we find in modern economies suggest that we cannot approximate the basic requirements of sensible aggregation except, perhaps, over firms in the same industry or from a narrow sections of the economy. (p. 11)

The evidence discussed above suggests indeed that one lacks the conditions of "sensible aggregation" even at the level of single industries.

Of course one can always try to reconstruct the revealed "production possibility sets" building on heterogeneous microcoefficients. By doing that, one is going to find, as shown by Hildenbrand (1981), that

> short-run efficient production functions do not enjoy the well-known properties which are frequently assumed in production theory. For example, constant returns to scale never prevail, the production functions

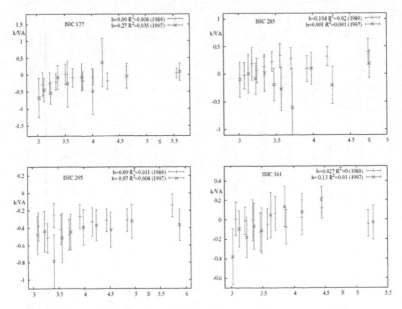

Figure 8 Size versus *K/VA*. Bin plots of size (number of employees) versus *K/VA*. Error bars display two standard errors. *K* and *VA* at constant prices.

> are never homothetic, and the elasticities of substitution are never constant. On the other hand, the competitive factor demand and product supply functions [. . .] will always have definite comparative static properties which cannot be derived from the standard theory of production (p. 1095)

Given these findings, it is remarkable how most of the discipline has stuck to a *theory* of production based on far-from-innocent assumptions concerning the access of agents to production knowledge (most often assumed to be free and identical across them) and on the nature of techniques themselves (additivity and divisibility are good cases to the point). Likewise, the economic discipline has stuck to an *empirics* of production based on a construct (the production function) mainly justified by its "nice" distributive properties (that is, relations between *income* distribution and apparent partial derivatives of output to inputs), rather than by any microevidence on the distribution and dynamics of technical coefficients.[14]

---

[14]In this context, all attempts to measure empirical distributions of microtechnical coefficients are just welcome [cf. Simar and Wilson (2000), Balk (2001) and Briec *et al.* (2004) for contributions and discussions]. In that, the less the imposed parametric structure, the less the appeal to convexity assumptions, the less the use of purported but unobservable profit-maximizing /cost-minimizing behaviors, all the better. . .

Table 3 Size versus labor productivity: OLS regressions

Sector	ISIC code	1989			1993			1997		
		α	β	R^2	α	β	R^2	α	β	R^2
Production and processing of meat	151	4.11 (0.132)	0.033 (0.032)	0.004	3.95 (0.113)	0.098 (0.028)	0.035	4.00 (0.160)	0.086 (0.04)	0.024
Knitted and crocheted articles	177	3.50 (0.117)	0.060 (0.029)	0.0117	3.16 (0.12)	0.18 (0.031)	0.06	3.143 (0.164)	0.188 (0.04)	0.078
Wearing apparel and accessories	182	2.83 (0.078)	0.192 (0.019)	0.096	2.614 (0.071)	0.2690 (0.019)	0.106	2.58 (0.091)	0.288 (0.0238)	0.141
Footwear	193	3.078 (0.089)	0.152 (0.023)	0.08	3.074 (0.094)	0.187 (0.025)	0.060	3.308 (0.140)	0.127 (0.037)	0.025
Articles of paper and paperboard	212	4.016 (0.096)	0.072 (0.023)	0.029	3.907 (0.099)	0.012 (0.024)	0.056	3.877 (0.121)	0.152 (0.03)	0.075
Printing and services related to printing	222	3.97 (0.082)	0.122 (0.0212)	0.07	3.901 (0.081)	0.154 (0.022)	0.079	3.78 (0.134)	0.014 (0.035)	0.04
Plastic products	252	4.076 (0.083)	0.057 (0.021)	0.011	3.799 (0.086)	0.154 (0.022)	0.048	3.778 (0.097)	0.15 (0.024)	0.05
Articles of concrete, plaster, and cement	266	4.35 (0.013)	−0.011 (0.034)	0.001	4.249 (0.156)	−0.004 (0.041)	0.001	3.65 (0.156)	0.181 (0.041)	0.06
Metal products	281	3.758 (0.107)	0.09 (0.028)	0.027	3.786 (0.091)	0.091 (0.024)	0.02	3.63 (0.013)	0.166 (0.037)	0.04
Treatment and coating of metals; general mechanical engine	285	3.877 (0.127)	0.055 (0.03)	0.006	3.742 (0.124)	0.099 (0.035)	0.012	3.801 (0.130)	0.11 (0.036)	0.018
Special purpose machinery	295	4.26 (0.064)	0.034 (0.015)	0.007	4.15 (0.058)	0.072 (0.014)	0.023	4.071 (0.068)	0.10 (0.017)	0.043
Furniture	361	3.44 (0.08)	0.156 (0.022)	0.05	3.382 (0.076)	0.193 (0.02)	0.068	3.48 (0.071)	0.16 (0.018)	0.078

$\Pi(=VA/L) = \alpha + \beta(VA)$. Constant price value added. Labor is proxied by the number of employees. Standard errors are in parentheses. These estimates include those presented in Figure 6.

And, in all that, it failed to recognize that the apparent good fit of the function to the data is sheer algebraic outcome of the rough constancy of aggregate distributive shares. As shown by Shaikh (1974; 1980)

> . . . when the *distribution* data (wages and profits) exhibit constant shares, there exist broad classes of *production* data (output, capital, and labor) that *can always be related to each other through a functional form which is mathematically identical to a Cobb-Douglas "production function" with "constant returns to scale," "neutral technical change" and "marginal products equal to factors rewards* (Shaikh, 1980: 92, emphasis in the original)[15]

Clearly, if one takes seriously these properties of aggregation, together with the properties of micro empirical data discussed above, one looses the easy link between purported (even if false or just tautological) "technical" aggregate relations, input prices, input demand functions, and income distribution. With that, of course, one looses also any nicely behaved "duality property." By the same token one gains the possibility of genuinely *studying* the relations between, for example, technological characteristics of firms and micro income distribution, between technological change and inputs demands, and so on, rather than simply postulating them.

4. By way of a conclusion, where do we go here?

There is certainly a *pars denstruens* to this all argument, which we have already spelled out. Basically, it boils down to the rupture of any well-behaved correspondence between technological conditions and input market properties, in turn nested into maximizing microbehaviors and collective equilibrium assumptions.

There is a *pars construens* as well.

It involves, first, the investigation of the properties of *distributions* over heterogeneous entities of variables like revealed productivities, relative input intensities, and their evolution over time.

A growing number of scholars has indeed began doing precisely what we could call *evolutionary accounting* (even if most do not call it that way!). The fundamental

---

[15]The property had already been noted by Fisher (1971), who, on the ground of a simulation exercise found a "good fit of a Cobb-Douglas" even though the true relationships were far from yielding an aggregate Cobb-Douglas: "the view that constancy of the labor's share is due to the presence of an aggregate Cobb-Douglas production function is mistaken. Causation runs the other way and the apparent success of aggregate Cobb-Douglas production functions is due to the relative constancy of labor's share" (Fisher, 1971: 306). See also Phelps-Brown (1957) and Simon and Levy (1963). For fun, we just repeated the OLS cross-sectional estimates on our three-digit sectors, alike Fisher (1971), and with no surprise we obtained excellent estimates with high significance and all R^2 above 7.

evolutionary idea is that distributions (including, of course, their means, which end-up in sectoral and macrostatistics!) change as a result of (i) *learning* by incumbent entities; (ii) *differential growth* (that is, a form of *selection*) of incumbent entities themselves; (iii) *death* (indeed, a different and more radical form of selection); and (iv) *entry* of new entities.

The basic theoretical intuition is discussed at length in Nelson and Winter (1982) [see also Iwai (1984), Dosi *et al.* (1995), and Metcalfe (1998), among others].

Empirically, favored by the growing availability of microlongitudinal panel data, at last, an emerging line of research [see Baily *et al.* (1996), Foster *et al.* (1998), Baldwin and Gu (2006), among others, and the discussion in Bartelsman and Doms (2000)] investigates the properties of decomposition of whatever mean sectoral performance variable, e.g. typically productivity of some kind, of the following form, or variations thereof:

$$\Delta\Pi_t = \sum_i s_i(t-1)\Delta\Pi_i(t) + \sum_i \Pi_i(t-1)\Delta s_i(t)$$
$$+ \sum_e s_e(t)\Pi_e(t) + \sum_f s_f(t-1)\Pi_f(t-1)$$

+some interaction terms

where Π = productivities (or, for that matter, some other performance variables), s = shares (in total output or VA or employment or total capital assets . . .), while i is an index over incumbents, e over entrants, and f over exiting entities.

Many intriguing research questions follow. To begin with, how do the distribution evolve over time? Moreover, what is the relative balance between incumbent learning and market selection? What is the role of entry? What is the relative importance of bankruptcy mechanisms? On which time scale (i) learning, (ii) inter-incumbent competition, (iii) entry, and (iv) exit exert their relative influence?

A second major research challenge concerns the *coupled dynamics* between the foregoing quantities and some underlying "idiosyncratic" covariates regarding, so to speak, the "identity cards" of individual firms–ideally revealing their *technological and organizational capabilities*. We have now quite a few surveys on innovative capabilities and innovative outputs (ranging from patent data to the EU Community Innovation Survey to many country-specific organizational surveys) but one is only beginning to exploit them.

Third, a tricky but fascinating set of questions regards precisely the mappings between *procedure-centered* and *input/output-centered* representations of technologies. Suppose to be able to develop some metrics–an exercise indeed already difficult–in the input/output space, and, also, albeit overly difficult and fuzzy, in the high dimensional "problem-solving space." Granted that, how do the respective dynamics map into each other? Do "small" changes in the knowledge/problem-solving space correspond roughly to "small" changes in input/output relations? And, if so, when does one empirically detect major discontinuities?[16] Can one detect paradigm changes also in the input/output space, *in general*, well beyond the examples given in the economics of innovation literature?

Fourth, there are propositions concerning production theory which are intuitively very reasonable–for example, "firms try to save on inputs whose prices have augmented"–while, at the same time the standard "proof" is utterly far-fetched. The "proof" of the Hotelling and Shephard lemmas invoking the envelope theorem is an archetypal example. One knows how the standard argument goes. Suppose "the firm" (i.e., all firms, on average) is in some equilibrium, that is with equilibrium input intensities, equilibrium returns, and so on. Next, suppose a shock to relative prices. Given the standard theory of production, the representative agent will adjust its optimal input combinations to the new relative prices and thereof decrease its demand of the relatively more expensive inputs. Hence the "well-behaved" notional demand curve for inputs.

Clearly this line of argument does not hold in the evolutionary worlds sketched out above. But does all this mean that the basic intuition on some negative price quantity *dynamics* does not apply? Rephrasing it in the knowledge-focused language, to what extent, *technological trajectories* of corporate and industry-wide learning can be affected by relative-price shocks?

Last but not least, fifth, a major challenge regards the possible links between microfounded analyzes of production, such as those sketched above, with more aggregate representations of technological interdependencies which try to account for input–output flows without making at the same time any binding commitment to "general equilibrium" assumptions. [Examples of such a modeling style with a "classical favor" are Pasinetti (1977), and Kurz and Salvadori (1995).]

These are just examples of a rich research agenda ultimately linking investigations at the levels of knowledge dynamics and organizational behavior with questions, more familiar to economists, addressing possible regularities in the input/output structure of the economy and its dynamics. In all this scientific enterprise, Winter's old contribution is still a fresh source of inspiration.

Acknowledgements

Support to the research by the Italian Ministry of Education and Research (MIUR, Grant 2004133370_003), the Sant' Anna School of Advanced Studies (grant E6005GD) and by *Fondazione Cesifin – Alberto Predieri*, is gratefully acknowledged. This work partly draws from Dosi *et al.* (2005), and Dosi *et al.* (2006), to which the reader is referred for more detailed discussions of the knowledge-centered view of

---

[16]A somewhat similar problem, which the authors of this article found to be a tall challenging analogy is, in biology, the mapping between genetic structures and phenotypical characters which are in fact subject to environmental selection: see Stadler *et al.* (2001).

technologies. The statistical exercises which follow would not have been possible without the precious help of the Italian Statistical Office (ISTAT) and in particular of Roberto Monducci and Andrea Mancini.

Addresses for correspondence

Giovanni Dosi, Sant' Anna School of Advanced Studies, Pisa, Italy. e-mail: gdosi@sssup.it
Marco Grazzi, The Wharton School, University of Pennsylvania. e-mail: grazzi@sssup.it

References

Alchian, A. and H. Demsetz (1972), 'Production, information costs and economic organization,' *American Economic Review*, **62**, 777–795.

Antonelli, C. (1995), *The Economics of Localized Technological Change and Industrial Dynamics*. Kluwer Publishers: Boston.

Atkinson, A. B and J. E. Stiglitz (1969), 'A new view of technological change,' *The Economic Journal*, **79**, 573–578.

Augier, M. and J. G. March (eds) (2000), 'Roots and branches of organizational economics,' *Industrial and Corporate Change*, **9**, Special Issue, 555–788.

Baily, M. N., C. Hulten and D. Campbell (1992), 'Productivity dynamics in manufacturing plants,' *Brookings Papers on Economic Activity, Microeconomics*. **4**, 187–249.

Baily, M. N., E. Bartelsman and J. C. Haltiwanger (1996), 'Downsizing and productivity growth: myth or reality,' *Small Business Economics*, **8**, 259–278.

Baldwin, R. J. (1995), *The Dynamics of Industrial Competition: A North American Perspective*. Cambridge University Press: Cambridge, MA.

Baldwin, J. R. and W. Gu (2006), 'Plant turnover and productivity growth in Canadian manufacturing,' *Industrial and Corporate Change*, **15**, forthcoming.

Balk, B. M. (2001), 'Scale efficiency and productivity change,' *Journal of Productivity Analysis*, **15**, 159–183.

Bartelsman, E. and P. J. Dhrymes (1998), 'Productivity dynamics: U.S. manufacturing plants 1972–1986,' *Journal of Productivity Analysis*, **9**, 5–34.

Bartelsman, E. and M. Doms (2000), 'Understanding productivity: lessons from longitudinal data,' *Journal of Economic Literature*, **38**, 569–594.

Bartelsman, E., J. Haltiwanger and S. Scarpetta (2004), 'Microeconomic evidence of creative destruction in industrial and developing countries,' Discussion Paper 2004–114/3, Tinbergen Institute, Amsterdam.

Bartelsman, E., S. Scarpetta and F. Schivardi (2005), 'Comparative analysis of firm demographics and survival: evidence from micro-level sources in OECD countries,' *Industrial and Corporate Change*, **14**, 365–391.

Bottazzi, G., G. Dosi, E. Cefis and A. Secchi (2003), *Invariances and Diversities in the Evolution of Manufacturing Industries*. LEM Working Paper 2003/21, Sant' Anna School of Advanced Studies, Pisa.

Bottazzi, G., M. Grazzi and A. Secchi (2005), 'Characterising the production process: a disaggregated analysis of Italian manufacturing firms,' *Rivista di Politica Economica*, I–II, 243–270.

Briec, W., K. Kerstens and P. V. Eeckaut (2004), 'Non-convex technologies, and cost functions: definitions, Duality and nonparametric tests of convexity,' *Journal of Economics*, 81, 155–192.

Chesher, A. (1979), 'Testing the law of proportionate effect,' *Journal of Industrial Economics*, 27, 403–411.

Chew, W. B., T. Bresnahan and K. B. Clarke (1990), 'Measurement, coordination, and learning in a multiplant network,' in R.S. Kaplan (ed,) *Measures of Manufacturing Excellence*, Harvard Business School Press: Cambridge, MA.

Cohen M. D., R. Burkhart, G. Dosi, M. Egidi, L. Marengo, M. Warglien and S. Winter (1996), 'Routines and other recurring action patterns of organizations: contemporary research issues,' *Industrial and Corporate Change*, 5, 653–698.

Constant, E. W. (1980), *The Origins of the Turbojet Revolution*. Johns Hopkins University Press: Baltimore, MD.

Cyert, R. M. and J. G. March (1992), *A Behavioral Theory of the Firm*, 2nd edn. Blackwell Business: Oxford.

David, P. A. (1975), *Technical Choice, Innovation and Economic Growth*. Cambridge University Press: Cambridge, MA.

Dopfer, K. (ed.) (2005), *The Evolutionary Foundations of Economics*. Cambridge University Press: Cambridge.

Dosi, G. (1982), 'Technological paradigms and technological trajectories. A suggested interpretation of the determinants and directions of technical change,' *Research Policy*, 11, 147–162.

Dosi, G. (1984), *Technical Change and Industrial Transformation*. Macmillan: London.

Dosi, G. (1988), 'Sources, procedures and microeconomic effects of innovation,' *Journal of Economic Literature*, 26, 1120–1171.

Dosi, G. (2005), *Statistical Regularities in the Evolution of Industries. A Guide through Some Evidence and Challenges for the Theory*, LEM Working Paper 2005/17, Sant' Anna School of Advanced Studies, Pisa.

Dosi, G. and B. Coriat (1998), 'Learning how to govern and learning how to solve problems. On the co-evolution of competences, conflicts and organizational routines,' in A. Chandler, P. Hagström and Ö. Sölvell (eds), *The Dynamic Firm*. Oxford University Press: Oxford and New York.

Dosi, G., O. Marsili, L. Orsenigo and R. Salvatore (1995), 'Learning, market selection and the evolution of industrial structures,' *Small Business Economics*, 7, 411–436.

Dosi, G., B. Coriat and K. Pavitt (2000a), *Competences, Capabilities and Corporate Performances: Final Report to the European Union*, Dynacom Working Paper, Sant' Anna School of Advanced Studies, Pisa.

Dosi, G., R. R. Nelson and S. Winter (2000b), *The Nature and Dynamics of Organizational Capabilities*. Oxford University Press: Oxford.

Dosi, G., M. Faillo and L. Marengo (2006), 'Organizational capabilities, patterns of knowledge accumulation and governance structures in business firms an introduction,' LEM Working Paper 2003/11, Sant' Anna School of Advanced Studies, Pisa, forthcoming in Touffut J. P. (ed.), *Organizational Innovation within Firms*. Edward Elgar: Cheltenham, UK and Brookfield, WI.

Dosi, G., M. Hobday, L. Marengo and A. Prencipe (2003), 'The economics of system integration: toward an evolutionary interpretation,' in A. Prencipe, A. Davies, M. Hobday (eds), *The Business of Systems Integration*. Oxford University Press: Oxford and New York.

Dosi, G., L. Orsenigo and M. Sylos Labini (2005), 'Technology and the economy,' in N. J. Smelser and R. Swedberg (eds), *The Handbook of Economic Sociology*, 2nd edn. Princeton University Press and Russell Sage Foundation: Princeton and New York.

Fisher, F. (1971), 'Aggregate production functions and the explanation of wages: a simulation experiment,' *Review of Economics and Statistics*, **53**, 305–325.

Foss, N. J. and V. Mahnke (2000), *Competence, Governance, and Entrepreneurship: Advances in Economic Strategy Research*. Oxford University Press: Oxford and New York.

Foster, L., J. C. Haltiwanger and C. J. Krizan (1998), 'Productivity dynamics: US manufacturing plants 1972–1986,' *Journal of Productivity Analysis*, **9**, 5–34.

Freeman, C. (1994), 'The economics of technical change: a critical survey,' *Cambridge Journal of Economics*, **18**, 1–50.

Georgescu-Roegen, N. (1970), 'The economics of production,' *American Economic Review*, Papers and Proceedings, pp. 1–9.

Griliches, Z. and J. Mairesse (1999), 'Production functions: the search for identification,' in Steiner Strøm (ed.), *Econometrics and Economic Theory in the Twentieth Century: The Ragner Frisch Centennial Symposium*. Cambridge University Press: Cambridge.

Grupp, H. (1992), *Dynamics of Science-Based Innovation*. Springer Publishers: Berlin and Heidelberg.

Harcourt, G. C. (1972), *Some Cambridge Controversies in the Theory of Capital*. Cambridge University Press: Cambridge.

Hildenbrand, W. (1981), 'Short-run production functions based on microdata,' *Econometrica*, **49**, 1095–1125.

Hughes, T. P. (1983), *Networks of Power: Electrification in Western Society 1880–1930*. Johns Hopkins University Press: Baltimore, MD.

Iwai, K. (1984), 'Schumpeterian dynamics. Parts I and II,' *Journal of Economic Behavior and Organization*, **5**, 159–190; 321–351.

Jensen, B. and H McGuckin (1997), 'Firm performance and evolution: empirical regularities in the US microdata,' *Industrial and Corporate Change*, **6**, 25–47.

Kurz, H. and N. Salvadori (1995), *Theory of Production. A Long-Period Analysis*. Cambridge University Press: Cambridge.

Leibestein, H. (1966), 'Allocative efficiency vs. X-efficiency,' *American Economic Review*, 56, 392–415.

Levinthal, D. (1998), 'The slow pace of rapid technical change. Gradualism and punctuation in technological change,' *Industrial and Corporate Change*, 7, 217–247.

March, J. G. (1988), *Decision and Organization*. Basil Blackwell: Oxford.

March, J. G. and H. Simon (1993), 'Organizations revisited,' *Industrial and Corporate Change*, 2, 299–316.

Marengo, L. and G. Dosi (2005), 'Division of labor, organizational coordination and market mechanisms in collective problem-solving,' *Journal of Economic Behavior and Organization*, 58, 303–326.

Marengo, L., G. Dosi, P. Legrenzi and C. Pasquali (2000), 'The structure of problem-solving knowledge and the structure of organizations,' *Industrial and Corporate Change*, 9, 757–788.

Metcalfe, J. S. (1998), *Evolutionary Economics and Creative Destruction*. Routledge: London.

Milgrom, P. and J. Roberts (1990), 'The economics and modern manufacturing: technology strategy, and organization,' *American Economic Review*, 80, 511–528.

Milgrom, P. and J. Roberts (1995), 'Complementarity and fit: strategy, structure and organizational change in manufacturing,' *Journal of Accounting and Economics*, 19, 178–208.

Montgomery, C. A. (ed.) (1995), *Resource-Based and Evolutionary Theories of the Firm*. Kluwer: Dordrecht.

Morroni, M. (1992), *Production Process and Technical Change*. Cambridge University Press: Cambridge.

Nell, E. J. (ed) (1980), *Growth, Profits and Property. Essays in the Revival of Political Economy*. Cambridge University Press: Cambridge.

Nelson, R. R. (1981), 'Research on productivity growth and productivity differences: dead end and new departures,' *Journal of Economic Literature*, 19, 1029–1064.

Nelson, R. R. (1991), 'Why do firm differ and how does it matter?,' *Strategic Management Journal*, 12, 61–74.

Nelson, R. R. and S. G. Winter (1982), *An Evolutionary Theory of Economic Change*, The Belknap Press of Harvard University Press: Cambridge, MA.

Pasinetti, L. L. (1977), *Lectures on the Theory of Production*. Colombia University Press and London, The Macmillan Press Ltd.: New York.

Pavitt, K. (1991), 'What makes basic research economically useful?,' *Research Policy*, 20, 109–119.

Phelps-Brown, E. H. (1957), 'The meaning of the fitted Cobb-Douglas production function,' *Quarterly Journal of Economics*, 71, 300–313.

Power, L. (1998), The missing link: Technology, investment and productivity, *The Review of Economics and Statistics*, 80, 300–315.

Rosenberg, N. (1976), *Perspectives on Technology*. Cambridge university Press: Cambridge, MA.

Rosenberg, N. (1990), 'Why do firms do basic research (with their money)?,' *Research Policy*, 19, 165–174.

Rumelt, R. P. (1991), "How much does industry matter?" *Strategic Management Journal*, **12**, 167–185.

Sahal, D. (1981), *Recent Advances in the Theory of Technological Change*. Addison-Wesley: New York.

Saviotti, P. (1996), *Technological Evolution, Variety and the Economy*. Edward Elgar: Cheltenham, UK.

Schefold, B. (1976), 'Different forms of technical progress,' *Economic Journal*, **86**, 806–819.

Shaikh, A (1974), 'Laws of production and laws of algebra. The humbug production function: a comment,' *Review of Economics and Statistics*, **56**, 115–120.

Shaikh, A (1980), 'Laws of production and laws of algebra: Humbug II,' in Nell (1980), pp. 80–95.

Simar, L. and P. Wilson (2000), 'Statistical influence in nonparametric frontier models: the state of the art,' *Journal of Productivity Analysis*, **13**, 49–78.

Simon, H. A. (1969), *Science of the Artificial*. MIT Press: Cambridge, MA.

Simon, H. A. and F. K. Levy (1963), 'A note on the Cobb-Douglas function,' *Review of Economic Studies*, **30**, 93–94.

Stadler, B. M., P. F. Stadler, G. P. Wagner and W. Fontana (2001), 'The topology of the possible: formal spaces underlying patterns of evolutionary change,' *Journal of Theoritical Biology*, **213**, 241–274.

Szulanski, G. and S. Winter (2002), 'Getting it right the second time,' *Harvard Business Review*, **80**, 62–69.

Teece, D. J., G. Pisano and A. Shuen. (1997), 'Dynamic capabilities and strategic management,' *Strategic Management Journal*, **18**, 509–533.

Vincenti, W. (1990), *What Engineers Know and How They Know it: An Analytical Study from the Aeronautical History*. The John Hopkins University Press: Baltimore, MD.

Walters, A. A. (1963), 'Production and cost functions: an econometric survey,' *Econometrica*, **31**, 1–66.

Winter, S. G. (1981), 'An essay on the theory of production,' in S. Hymans (ed.), *Economics and the World Around It*. University of Michigan Press: Ann Arbor, MI.

Winter, S. G. (1987), 'Knowledge and competences as strategic assets,' in D. Teece (ed.), *The Competitive Challenge*. Ballinger: Cambridge, MA.

Winter, S. G. (2005), 'Toward an evolutionary theory of production,' in Dopfer (ed.), *The Evolutionary Foundations of Economics*, 223–254.

Winter, S. G. (2006), 'Toward a Neo-Schumpeterian theory of the firm,' *Industrial and Corporate Change*, this issue.

Appendix 1

The elaborations on the Italian data draw upon the MICRO.1 databank developed by the Italian Statistical Office (ISTAT). MICRO.1 contains longitudinal data on a panel of several thousand Italian manufacturing firms with employment of 20 units or more over the period 1989–1997. Since the panel is open, due to entry, exit fluctuations around the 20 employees threshold and variability in response rates, we consider only the firms that are present both at the beginning and at the end of our window of observation.

In order to control for mergers, acquisitions, and divestments, we build "super-firms" which account throughout the period for the union of the entities which undertake such changes. So, for example, if two firms merged at some time, we consider them merged throughout the whole period. Conversely, if a firm is spun off from another one, we "re-merge" them starting from the separation period.

Ultimately, one ends up with a balanced panel of 8091 ("super") firms.

Note that firms above 20 employees account for just 11% of the universe of Italian manufacturing firms but they include 68% of the total employment (Bartelsman *et al.*, 2004).

PART II

DEMAND AND MARKET DYNAMICS

[7]

Demand Dynamics with Socially Evolving Preferences

Roberta Aversi[a], Giovanni Dosi[b], Giorgio Fagiolo[c], Mara Meacci[d] and Claudia Olivetti[e]

([a]Finsiel, Rome, [b]St Anna School of Advanced Studies, Pisa, Italy and IIASA, Laxenburg, Austria, [c]European University Institute, Florence, Italy, [d]Oxford University, Oxford, UK and [e]University of Pennsylvania, Philadelphia, PA, USA)

In this work we, first, identify a few stylized facts concerning microconsumption acts. Second, building on them, we develop a simple model of 'boundedly rational' consumers who endogenously evolve their preferences via both innovation and social imitation. Third, we explore some statistical properties of the demand patterns generated by the model which, despite its simplicity, are surprisingly in line with the empirical evidence. These results, we suggest, bring encouraging support to microfoundations of demand theory based on cognitive and behavioral foundations more in tune with the psychological and sociological evidence, based on heterogeneous agents who are much less 'rational' and much more social than in standard theory, and who collectively discover 'along the way' what they like within a growing universe of available commodities.

1. Introduction

In this work we begin to explore some aggregate dynamic properties of demand patterns when preferences are shaped by the cognitive structures of consumers and evolve in socially embedded fashions.

After setting the general framework of the discussion (Section 2), in Section 3 we identify some 'stylized facts' stemming from the 'state of the art' of different social disciplines such as cognitive and social psychology and marketing. We employ them as the reference points for the model developed in Section 3, analyzing the dynamics of consumption with heterogeneous, 'boundedly rational' agents which are nonetheless able to endogenously evolve their preferences, innovate and imitate the others. Finally, the statistical properties of the model are discussed in Section 4.

Industrial and Corporate Change Volume 8 Number 2 1999

2. *Consumption Acts and Demand Patterns: Some Interpretation Frameworks*

A while ago, one of the authors of this paper witnessed at a seminar the horror of most colleagues when Werner Hildenbrand, presenting some further development on his theory of demand (Hildenbrand, 1994) provocatively suggested more or less that 'preferences and choices are matters for psychiatrists and not for economists,' while the task of the latter should be primarily to establish some statistical conditions under which basic propositions of economic theory—such as downward sloping demand curves, etc.—hold in the aggregate, in presence of heterogeneous, and possibly 'irrational' consumers.

In a nutshell, the provocation highlights, first of all, a major divide cutting across the economic discipline—as well as other social sciences—namely, how seriously should one take standard utility theory (with or without its more recent refinements) and the associated 'rational' theory of decision making as the foundation of a descriptive theory of demand?[1]

Needless to say, the majority of the economic profession seems to take that type of microeconomic foundation of decisions very seriously indeed, entrenched as they are with deep ('anthropological') views on the nature of 'rationality' and self-seeking behaviors, passed through successive generations via conventional teaching tools such as 'indifference curves' and the like, and further justified by their purported role in bridging descriptive and normative analyses (welfare theorems, etc.).

However, admittedly minority views in economics (but nearly 'mainstream' in other social disciplines) claim that classic decision theory has little to offer by way of the interpretation of what people actually do and that one should turn in fact to cognitive and social psychology, sociology (and—why not?—psychiatry) in order to derive empirically sound theories of how people behave and choose the way they do.

Note that the appeal to inductive generalizations—in this perspective—does not concern solely the nature and origins of preferences [which could, as such, nicely complement rather than upset 'rational' decision-theoretic views; after all, in the latter, as reminded by Stigler and Becker (1977), '*de gustibus non est disputandum . . .*']. More profoundly, it relates to both the procedures by which decisions are taken and the interactions (possibly at a collectively level) between decisions, outcomes and preferences themselves.

First, at a procedural level, as Legrenzi *et al.* (1993, pp. 37–8) put it,

the classical theory of decision-making, whatever its status as a

---

[1] Another major problem concerns the aggregate properties of diverse demand schedules, no matter how constructed. We shall come to that below.

――――――――― *Demand Dynamics with Socially Evolving Preferences* ―――――――――

> specification of rationality, does not begin to explain the mental processes
> underlying decisions. . . . On the one hand, the theory is radically
> incomplete: it has nothing to say about when one should decide to make
> a decision, or how one should determine the range of options, or how
> one should assess the utilities of various outcomes. On the other hand,
> the theory conflicts with the evidence on how people reach decisions in
> daily life.

The literature on this subject is immense: see, among others, Slovic (1990),
Payne *et al.* (1992), Tversky and Kahneman (1986), Thaler (1992) and the
companion paper by Devetag (1999).[2] In economics, the emphasis on the
'bounds' of rationality, and the related analytical requirement, so to speak, to
'open up the cognitive black-box,' has found a good deal of inspiration in the
path-breaking work of Herbert Simon (1959, 1986, 1988). Indeed, the
empirical departures from the canonic procedures prescribed by rational
decision theory are likely to be even deeper than those envisaged by Simon, in
that human agents might not only be bound away from 'substantive' rationality, but often also display systematic biases in the procedures themselves for
judgment and choice.[3]

Moreover, as Shafir *et al.* (1993, p. 34) conclude, also on the grounds of the
cited Payne *et al.* (1992),

> in contrast to classical theory that assumes stable values and preferences,
> it appears that people often do not have well-established values, and that
> preferences are actually constructed—not merely revealed—during their
> elicitation . . .[4]

Finally, the literature on cognitive dissonance reveals another, symmetric,
source of endogeneity of preferences, namely the post-decisional adjustment
of goals in order to rationalize counter-intentional behaviors and outcomes
(Fastinger, 1956; Wicklund and Brehm, 1976; for an economic application,
see Akerlof and Dickens, 1982).

All this *lato sensu* 'cognitive' evidence suggests that, first, we should
primarily call in psychologists rather than decision-theorists in order to
explain goal formation, deliberation and choice. Second, other pieces of
evidence hint that we should call in social psychologists and sociologists, too.
More precisely, one finds widespread occurrences of social endogeneity of
preferences, including social imitation, formation of relatively homogeneous

---

[2] A rather balanced assessment of the merits and limitations of standard utility theory from an
economist's point of view is in Schoemaker (1982).

[3] Dosi *et al.* (1996) discusses some of them with an eye on their implications for evolutionary theories of
learning in economics.

[4] See also Tversky and Simonson (1993).

───────────── *Demand Dynamics with Socially Evolving Preferences* ─────────────

'lifestyles' within specific social groups, 'snob effects,' authority-induced changes in values and choices, and many others.[5] In these domains, T. Veblen is one of the outstanding early contributors of plenty of conjectures and 'appreciative theories,' notwithstanding their sometimes irritating analytical fuzziness.[6]

As already mentioned, it is worth recalling the caveat that under certain conditions the endogeneity of preferences as such does not pose any overwhelming challenge to standard decision theory. That includes those circumstances whereby (i) the timescale of preference evolution is of orders of magnitude greater than the timescale of decisions themselves (so that, for example, the 'disutility of eating pork' might have evolved over millennia, but for all practical purposes that can be taken as a given and stable preference trait of any practicing Jew or Muslim while selecting meat); (ii) preferences are not context-dependent, so that, in James March's language, they fulfil the conventional 'logic of consequences' rather than a 'logic of appropriateness' ('what is appropriate for anyone with my identity and my social role in those circumstances to do?'; cf. March, 1994); (iii) future changes in preferences are fully anticipated by forward-looking intertemporally utility maximizers (cf. Becker, 1976);[7] and (iv) the collective distributions of preferences, at each time, are not among the arguments of individual decision algorithms (i.e. 'like to do what my neighbors do,' etc.). Here and throughout, we refer to 'social endogeneity' to mean those circumstances—in our view, quite frequent indeed—whereby those conditions are violated.

The two sets of evidence—related, broadly speaking, first, to the cognitive and behavioral processes of choice, and, second, to their social embeddedness—strongly militate in favor of inductively disciplined theories of microeconomic behaviors, in general, and—as far as this work is concerned—final consumption, in particular, grounded in the relevant 'phenomenological' generalizations drawn from, for example, cognitive and social psychology, sociology, etc. It is a view certainly shared by those breeds of economists who might label themselves 'behaviorist,' 'institutionalist' and 'evolutionary'.[8]

However, even granted all that (a point by no means uncontroversial

─────

[5] A thorough discussion of a few of these issues with respect to consumption patterns is in Earl (1986). Relatedly, within an enormous literature, see also, e.g. Milgram (1974), Maital and Maital (1993), Hirschman (1965), Kuran (1987), all the way to the suggestive conjectures on the historical dynamics of social adaptation and rebellion in Moore (1978).

[6] Cf. Veblen (1899, 1919) and, later, along somewhat similar lines, Duesenberry (1949), Leibenstein (1950, 1976); see also Katona (1975, 1980).

[7] Cf. also Gary Becker (1996) who tries to derive 'endogenous' preferences from a sort of invariant 'meta-utility functions'.

[8] For quite germane developments of this argument, see Nelson and Winter (1982), Coriat and Dosi (1998), Hodgson (1988) and Earl (1986).

──────── *Demand Dynamics with Socially Evolving Preferences* ────────

among economists), why should we not leave this domain of micro-investigation to psychologists and sociologists (and psychiatrists), and limit our attention as economists to much more general, and, so to speak, 'minimal' statistical restrictions on the characteristics of the populations of, for example, consumers which are sufficient for aggregate propositions on demand patterns to hold?[9] If we understand correctly, this is the perspective under-lying the pioneering works of Trockel (1984) and especially Hildenbrand (1994), whereby one attempts to establish the requirements for aggregate shapes of demand curves as functions of prices, entirely disposing of dubious psychological constructs based on 'utilities,' etc. and explicitly overcoming the aggregation problems undermining the extrapolation of the purported behavior of single consumers to pseudo-behavioral entities like 'the representative agent'.[10]

In order to illustrate this point, let us just recall the very basics which most undergraduates learn in Economics 101.

When dealing with demand, one starts with the intuition that when prices of any one commodity are higher, demand is lower, and, conversely, when prices are lower demand is higher. Next, one easily draws on the blackboard a standard demand curve relating prices and quantities with its familiar downward slope, and that remains as one of the most profound imprints of the discipline thereafter.

But, on second thoughts, what does that demand curve mean (even in a partial equilibrium setting)? After all, at any point in time, one only observes *one* actual combination between a certain price and a certain quantity of a good or a bundle of them. Keeping to the static framework, the curve must necessarily imply some sort of counterfactual experiment, namely *what would have happened if* prices were higher or lower (holding everything else constant—including initial endowment and preferences).

In turn, that counterfactual exercise either applies at the level of the individual consumer or, alternatively, of collections of them. In the former case, the hypothetical experiment basically concerns the degrees of coherence in microeconomic preference structures. This belongs to the first domain of analysis mentioned above. So, for example, we know—from Samuelson

[9] Of course, matter would look in any case quite different in fields like marketing or applied industrial economics, but for the time being we shall confine our discussion to those more general properties of demand which one typically finds in any intermediate economics textbook.

[10] The fundamental inconsistencies of such a notion have been thoroughly discussed by Kirman (1989, 1992). One of the points, among others, is that, even admitting individual maximizers, with well-behaved utility functions, etc., aggregation does not carry over any restriction on the shape of the aggregate demand functions (i.e. the demand functions attributed to the 'representative agent') without further *ad hoc* assumptions on the nature of preferences themselves. Complementarily, on the lack of isomorphism between microbehavioral rules and aggregate dynamics of the corresponding time-series, see Lippi (1988).

─────────── *Demand Dynamics with Socially Evolving Preferences* ───────────

(1938) all the way to Varian (1982)—that 'revealed preferences,' under different consistency restrictions, may be, so to speak, 'mapped back' to an underlying (and unobservable) utility function of a maximizing consumer (cf. also Sippel, 1997). In the opposite counterfactual experiment, the focus is upon the statistical robustness of the demand curves one routinely draws— irrespective of any greater knowledge on microdecision processes. In the latter approach, one is entirely agnostic on the ways preferences are formed (and whether they obey the consistency requirements of standard decision theories); rather, distributional invariances, together with budget constraints, account for the aggregate patterns one is meant to explain.[11]

We do indeed believe that this is a highly promising route that is just beginning to be investigated. However, we also believe that the 'agnosticism' on behavioral microfoundations can go only part of the way in explaining observed 'stylized facts' on demand. First, the question why distributions of revealed preferences are what they are seems to us an interesting one in its own right. Second, one might wonder how and when those distributions change—under the influence of, for example, introduction of new products, social interactions, etc.—and what implications all this has for aggregate demand properties.

Note that both points are likely to be particularly relevant when one increases the number of empirical phenomena one tries to account for, e.g. in addition to the question of why demand schedules tend to be downward sloping, one investigates, together, the determinants of diffusion patterns of new commodities, the conditions of occurrence of Engel-type demand profiles over time, or—even more complicated—the emergence of particular 'norms of consumption' within a population of consumers or subgroups of them.

It is in these domains where we see a profound complementarity between behaviorally parsimonious statistical approaches—'à la Hildenbrand'—on the one hand, and constructive micro-theories in a 'Simonesque' and 'Veblenesque' spirit, which indeed build upon what cognitive scientists, sociologists and psychologists tell us about choices and behaviors, on the other. In order to build that bridge, of course, we must undertake the difficult task of constructing micro-founded models which respect the spirit of the behavioral findings and, at the same time, are 'abstract' enough to generate stylized statistical properties of the ensuing aggregate demand profiles. This is indeed what we shall begin to do in the following.

The basic rationale of the exercise is to show how social processes of 'preference learning' and innovation, in the presence of stochastically growing

─────

[11] An early modeling attempt to derive the sign of demand adjustments to price changes solely from budget constraints is in Sanderson (1974).

incomes, can generate patterns of demand, and also diffusion patterns of new goods, which are statistically similar to those observed empirically. We are far from claiming that, by that token, this is 'explaining' the evidence. More modestly, we take it as an 'exercise in plausibility,' whereby, notwithstanding heroic modeling assumptions, a few observed statistical properties of consumption can be constructively generated on foundations built on heterogeneous agents who are much less 'rational' and much more social than in standard theories, and who discover collectively 'along the way' what they like and what they demand within a growing universe of available commodities.

3. *Toward a Descriptive Theory of Consumption: Some Building Blocks*

It is obviously impossible to provide here any fair account of the diverse pieces of evidence on the processes leading to consumption choices; a whole book would not be enough to adequately cover the findings, which range from marketing to cognitive sciences.[12]

Here, we shall just try to abstract some properties which appear sufficiently general to be candidates for building blocks of modeling efforts.

1. *The coherence criteria prescribed by decision-theoretic models are systematically violated by empirical agents* (i.e. by most of us human beings) *even under utterly simple experimental circumstances.*

Given its inherent double nature—normative and descriptive—the standard theory of consumer behavior requires, as a bottom line of rationality, that beliefs and preferences obey some set of coherent formal rules.

However, as experimental evidence suggests, consumers tend often to act in ways that are inconsistent with standard decision-theoretic tenets in that many widely accepted *normative* principles appear indeed to be pervasively and systematically violated as *descriptive* laws of consumer behavior, both in real life and experimental setups.[13]

For instance, as far as generic decisions under uncertainty are concerned, *framing effects* often imply that actual choices not only depend on the 'objective' characteristics of the options at hand but also on the ways the choice setup is perceived and represented by the agents. In particular, *preference*

[12] See anyhow Earl (1986) for an ambitious overview and interpretation, Devetag (1999), this volume, and Robertson and Kassarjian (1991).

[13] Cf. Devetag (1999), this volume, for a thorough discussion.

reversal phenomena have been shown to systematically arise in consumer choices. Moreover, in all circumstances where agents face an alternative between certain (or apparently certain) gains and uncertain lotteries, the emergence of the so-called *certainty* (or *pseudo-certainty*) *effects* leads to the violation of basic axioms, such as *dominance* (i.e. if option A is better than B in every respect, then A should always be preferred to B), *cancellation* (i.e. the choice between two options depends upon the states in which they yield different outcomes) and *substitution*, and also dramatically challenges the *sure-thing principle* and the *independence axiom*. The very notion of *utility* as commonly depicted by the theory is also questioned by experimental evidence, as it turns out that, even though utility should be assigned to states (e.g. *levels* of wealth), agents systematically assign utility to events (e.g. *variations* of wealth) relative to a reference point (the *status quo*), and, more seriously, tend to evaluate the same objective output as a gain or a loss depending on the framing of the reference state. As a consequence, indifference curves cannot be drawn without references to current endowments (*endowment effect*). In addition, as shown, for example, by Ellsberg (1961) in his well-known paradox, the subjective probabilities which should be employed in weighting the utility of a given outcome are not generally independent of the origin of the uncertainty, so that people, when faced with ambiguity, choose as if they have assigned the 'true' probabilities to the events, making on average the wrong choice.

Even more dramatically, choices made in (nearly) *deterministic* situations often imply strong conflicts with basic assumptions of economic theory as well. For example, a large body of work has singled out situations in which consumers' choices exhibit strong discrepancies between willingness to pay and willingness to sell (even in the absence of any income effects and transaction costs) and between marginal costs and marginal benefits. Moreover, systematic evidence has been presented in favor of the statement that fixed, sunk, costs *do* indeed matter in economic decisions. Finally, consumers tend to frame their purchase decisions—and consequently their way of perceiving costs, losses and the value of money—by their *mental accounting systems*, so that, in many deterministic situations, *money illusion* and the emergence of *reference prices* are often reported.

In many respects, the foregoing systematic inconsistencies between normative prescriptions and evidence, whether formally accounted or not, should also help in establishing some loose boundary between those decision incidents where 'coherence' of some kind should be plausibly imputed to consumption acts and where it should not (with that bound being indeed quite restrictive). However, this same evidence can be taken as the starting point for the identification of relatively invariant behavioral patterns consistent with alternative theories.

2. *Consumption acts (as well as other economic behaviors) are nested into cognitive categories and 'mental models' of the actors.*

As argued at some greater length in Dosi *et al.* (1996), any theory of choice, behavior and learning in complex and changing environments is most likely bound at some point to take explicitly on board the cognitive structures by which people frame the interpretations of their experience and their expectations. And consumption activities are no exception (cf. Devetag, 1999, this volume). Works from cognitive and social psychology and artificial sciences, including Holland *et al.* (1986), Tversky and Kahneman (1986), Lakoff (1987), Johnson-Laird (1983, 1993) and Goffman (1974), are painstakingly making timid inroads into economics; and, with reference to consumption theory, Earl (1986) makes extensive use of Kelly's Personal Construct Psychology (cf. Kelly, 1955) and Steinbrunner's 'cybernetic' approach (see Steinbrunner, 1974).

Notwithstanding the enormous diversity across these cited approaches, it seems to us that what they have in common for our rudimentary purposes is the general acknowledgement of the importance of diverse and possibly evolving mental models, cognitive categories and 'frames' shaping perception and deliberation.

3. *The relationships between 'mental models', preferences and consumption behaviors are to some extent implicit and, possibly, also partly inconsistent with each other.*

The fact that 'models' provide a structure through which people 'make sense' of what they do (and, together, what they want) is likely to entail the emergence and reproduction of recognizable lifestyles (cf. Earl, 1986).

However, these structures tend to be fuzzy and ridden with inconsistencies in terms of both actual choices and mapping between the latter and perceived goals (cognitive dissonance relates precisely to this phenomenon). Conflicting preference structures and criteria for choice might precariously (and sometimes painfully) coexist within the same agent.

'Models' offer satisficing inferential machineries for choice (Legrenzi *et al.*, 1993; Johnson-Laird, 1993). However, given their 'satisficing' nature and their blurred links with (possibly conflicting) goals, first, they leave open 'reason-based' decision-procedures:

> decisions . . . are often reached by focusing on the reasons that justify the

─────────── *Demand Dynamics with Socially Evolving Preferences* ───────────

selection of one option over another. Different frames, contexts and elicitation procedures highlight different aspects of the options and bring forth different reasons and considerations that influence decisions. (Shafir *et al.*, 1993, p. 34)

This implies a sort of inseparability between preference-formation and preference-revelation (through the choices act): in a sense, preferences are constructed through the very process of deliberation. An implication, in this perspective, is that one cannot innocently separate some unequivocal objective [e.g. max $U(. , . , ...)$] from the algorithms for its implementation. Rather, mental and behavioral models are (rough) templates for the elicitation of both the choice procedures and what is to be preferred.

Second, the choice process is often guided by heuristic criteria which might not bear any rigorous mapping into any underlying coherent structure of preferences. This point finds ample support from what in various models of consumer's behavior are called noncompensatory criteria of choice (heuristics often based on hierarchical filtering procedures, 'focusing' upon salient aspects of the choice context, exercises of comparison with prototypical expectations, etc.) (cf. Earl, 1986; Devetag, 1999, and references therein).[14]

Conversely, the 'compensatory' archetype of choice is a necessary condition for maximization over convex combinations of attributes (or goods) and prices. Attempts to hold together standard decision-theoretic assumptions and the acknowledgement of some nonconvexities in the purported utility sets have been made through the so-called 'multi-attribute utility theory' (cf. Dyer *et al.*, 1992; see also Fishburn, 1974).

4.   *Habits, routines and explicit deliberative processes coexist to varying degrees as determinants of most consumption acts.*

As Olshavsky and Granbois (1979) put it (also cited in Earl, 1986):

For many purchases a decision process never occurs, not even on the first purchase. . . . Purchases can occur out of necessity; they can be derived from culturally mandated lifestyles or from interlocked purchases; they can reflect preferences acquired in early childhood; they can result from simple conformity to group norms or from imitation of others; purchases can be made exclusively on recommendations from personal or non-personal sources; they can be made on the basis of surrogates of various types; or they can even occur on a random or superficial basis. . . . Even

─────────────────────────────────────

[14] Interestingly, this literature mainly from marketing or from experimental studies has drawn relatively little attention from the scholars more directly inspired by standard economic theory: cf., for example, the otherwise thorough and balanced discussions of models and statistical evidence of Brown and Deaton (1972) and Deaton and Muellbauer (1980b).

─────────── *Demand Dynamics with Socially Evolving Preferences* ───────────

> when purchase behavior is preceded by a choice process, [the latter] is
> likely to be very limited. It typically involves the evaluation of few
> alternatives, little external search, few evaluative criteria, and simple
> evaluation models.   (Olshavsky and Granbois, 1979, pp. 98–99)

Clearly, the evidence on routinization of behavioral patterns is quite in tune
with that taken on board and theorized upon, in other domains of economic
activity, by various evolutionary approaches—cf. in particular Nelson and
Winter (1982) and Cohen *et al.* (1996). And, of course, it fits well with the
ample sociological evidence on adaptation to specific social roles.[15]

More generally:

5. *Consumption habits and routines, and, dynamically, their formation and
   acquisition, are embedded in the processes of socialization and identity-building.*

The 'social embeddedness' notion of economic behaviors is obviously near the
spirit of a lot of sociological thinking and evidence.[16] Taken seriously, that
view implies also that one should be wary of assuming any individual
preference structures (or, for that matter, individual behavioral patterns) as
sole 'primitives' of micro-founded theories of economic behaviors.

Rather, one ought to account for explicit dynamics of collective adaptation
from the start. Multiple factors support this view. Some of them underlie the
possibility of social bandwagon effects (see Leibenstein, 1976). Freely citing
from Granovetter and Soong (1986, pp. 84–5), they include interpersonal
correlations of preferences nested in (i) status seeking; (ii) consumption
externalities of whatever kind; and (iii) the revealed outcome of other people's
experiences as surrogate for one's own search.[17]

Even more profoundly, social adaptation also in consumption patterns is
likely to be part of fundamental processes of identity-building, involving
(imperfect) adaptation to the habits and norms of specific social groups. In
this respect, many of the works of Bourdieu are suggestive illustrations of how
the social context contributes to structure social behaviors and revealed
preferences (cf. Bourdieu, 1976, 1979; see also Berger and Luckman, 1967).[18]

[15] Incidentally, note that in the early works of G. Becker, one finds the possibility of explanations of
economic behaviors based on habits rather utility maximization: cf. Becker (1962).

[16] For appraisals relevant for the current discussion, see, among others, Granovetter (1985), Barron and
Hannan (1994), Hodgson (1988); see also Dosi (1995) and Coriat and Dosi (1998) on the background of
some of the ideas put forward here.

[17] Conversely, differentiation effects may emerge as well, such as 'snob' inclinations to distinguish oneself
from the revealed majority [and also more complex—'cognitively dissonant'—attitudes such as those
summarized by Marx (Groucho), unwilling to 'join any club which would accept him as a member . . .'].

[18] Straightforwardly, this point links with the previous ones on 'mental models' and 'lifestyles': in this
perspective, the evolution of the latter is dynamically coupled with a social context framing the meanings
and also the reinforcements (the 'pleasures and pains') of individual experiences.

───────── *Demand Dynamics with Socially Evolving Preferences* ─────────

Straightforwardly, this point links with the previous ones on 'mental models' and 'lifestyles'; in this perspective, the evolution of the latter is dynamically coupled with a social context framing the *meanings* and also the *reinforcements* (the 'pleasures and pains') of individual experiences.[19]

However, at least in contemporary capitalist economies, adaptation to social roles is rather imperfect, ridden with conflicts and with multiple (possibly contradictory) archetypal identities, with these archetypes themselves changing rather quickly over time.[20]

As a consequence:

6.   *Habits and routines-formation hold varying and precarious balances with search and innovation.*

Pushing it to an extreme, the idea is that a good part of the complement to one of routinized, relatively automatic and repetitive consumption patterns is not any canonically 'rational' deliberative choice, but rather some wilder process of search/experimentation, whereby also some 'utility' (whatever that means) is drawn from the very exploratory process—whether or not one subscribed to the general anthropological conjecture of Scitovsky (1992) on the intrinsic stimuli and pleasure brought about by novelty.[21] As with routines, we find here some loose analogy with the exploratory patterns of producers, which has been investigated much more in the literature on the economics of technological innovation (cf. Freeman, 1982, Nelson and Winter, 1982; Rosenberg, 1982; Dosi, 1988).

7.   *(Imperfect) social adaptation, learning—on both preferences and consumption 'technologies'—and search, all entail path-dependencies (at the very least at individual level).*

By now, it is, at last, generally acknowledged that both collective externalities and dynamic increasing returns generally involve dependence of dynamic

---

[19] Incidentally, note that the importance of the social context in determining judgements and behaviors is also revealed by *accountability effects* which can be detected in the choice process: cf. Tetlock (1985) and Dalli and Tedeschi (1997).

[20] For insightful discussions on potentially 'multiple selves' pertinent to different domains of experience, cf. Elster (1986). A subtle issue, which cannot be pursued here, is the relative 'rational' coherence of each of the purported 'selves,' however, as should be clear from the foregoing argument, we are inclined to depict a 'self' (i.e. an identity) with a good deal of internal inconsistencies in both goals and procedures in order to achieve them.

[21] With a robust body of evidence from experimental psychology supporting it, notwithstanding equally robust examples of reinforcements to social adaptation, there is certainly strong empirical grounds for the idea that, at least in a few circumstances, consumers 'experiment,' 'explore,' 'discover,' develop novel 'consumption technologies' and lifestyles, etc. (cf. Earl, 1986; Bianchi, 1997).

paths upon initial conditions (or, in richer stochastic formulations, the dependence of limit states upon early fluctuations). However, in a strange paradox, the relevance of this widespread phenomenon has been much more emphasized on the supply side of production and technological innovation (see, among others, David, 1985; Arthur, 1988; Dosi, 1997), rather than on the final demand side.

It is some paradox because on the supply side, microeconomic path-dependencies (e.g. regarding the learning patterns of individual firms) might not exert long-term collective influences insofar as selection environments (e.g. markets) remain test-beds for different innovative trial-and-errors on the grounds of unchanged selection criteria (i.e. insofar as the 'selection landscape' remains unchanged).

Conversely, on the final demand side, agent-specific and collective path-dependencies are even more likely to arise, since there is no 'selection environment' to speak of (after all, everyone agrees that, except for ethical considerations, *'de gustibus non est disputandum'*).

In its essence, the point had been already made by Duesenberry when taking issue against the assumptions that, first, 'every individual's consumption behavior is independent of that of every other individual, and [second], the consumption relations are reversible in time' (Duesenberry, 1949, p. 1).

Since then, a lot of corroborating evidence on consumer behaviors has indeed supported both of Duesenberry's counter-assumptions (cf. Earl, 1986), without, however, any appropriate acknowledgement in terms of demand theory.

8. *Micro-consumption patterns are likely to be characterized by: (a) complementarities among multiple goods within lifestyle-shaped consumption-systems; and (b) (roughly) lexicographic patterns of consumer's selection over hedonic attributes and goods.*

At least as a first cut, let us assume that (socially shaped) 'mental models' link together multiple—and, possibly, partly contradictory—goals, heuristics perceived to be appropriate to their achievement, and particular types of goods. After all, if different 'lifestyles' exist, they ought to involve discretely different maps across these sets of variables. In turn, collectively shared models and behavioral patterns are likely to involve proximate complementarities in preference structures over both hedonic attributes of goods and goods themselves. (In an illustrative caricature, one is not very likely to find

――――――――― *Demand Dynamics with Socially Evolving Preferences* ―――――――――

Ferrari drivers wearing chainstore shoes; or Mozart fanatics content to listen to music on a Walkman.)

Complementarities are, of course, enormously reinforced by 'harder' social interdependencies—like those linking patterns of spatial mobility, uses of leisure time, ownership of cars, service stations, the presence of infrastructures like highways—and so on. And, relatedly, mental models and social lifestyles add up to more mundane 'physical' hierarchies of needs in determining rough lexicographic orders of consumption priorities.

Hence, on top of rather predictable hierarchies from basic necessities (such as food) to more discretional expenditures, socially acquired norms and visions tend to drive proximate rankings over commodities, or classes of them well above the sheer physiological constraints.

This does not mean, of course, that discretionality, 'choice,' price-dependent substitution, etc., are ruled out. On the contrary, cognitive and behavioral structures can be seen as a sort of basin of attraction allowing for a good deal of stochastic fluctuations where both explicit deliberations and path-dependent influences play major roles.

However, we still maintain the hypothesis that while 'compensatory choices' might hold locally for butter versus vegetable oil, etc., broader changes in consumption patterns are largely nested into deeper, discrete, changes in cognition and socialization models (and in ways possibly independent from any change in relative prices).

To sum up: a descriptive theory of consumption, in our view, should in principle encompass relatively ordered 'models' and 'lifestyles,' routines, explicit deliberations held together with 'imperfect coherence,' all of which path-dependently evolve through both (partial) social imitation and innovation. Can one capture at least some elements of this view in a formal model? This is the question we shall try to answer in the next section.[22]

4. *The Model*

The starting point is utterly simple agents whose (lexicographic) preference structure is represented through a modified version of *genetic alghorithms* (GAs).[23]

In essence a GA is based on the reproduction and modification of information coded on strings of finite length. In an analogy with DNA coding, think of a sequentially ordered set of elements (genes in the biological

―――――――――――――――
[22] Other models which attempt to tackle at least part of the foregoing 'stylized facts' are discussed in Dosi *et al.* (1999).

[23] Much more on this is in Holland (1975) and Goldberg (1989).

———————— *Demand Dynamics with Socially Evolving Preferences* ————————

interpretations; demanded goods in this application). Each element can take two or more alternative forms (or 'alleles'): below straightforwardly it can have two states, 1 or 0, i.e. the good is either demanded or not by any one consumer.[24]

Hence, for example, the string {01010} encodes the fact that the consumer is going to demand only—reading from left to right—the second and the fourth good. GAs evolve through two operators, namely crossover and mutation.

Crossover entails a recombination over two 'parent' strings. For example, given two strings, say, {01010} and {10011}, a random draw of an integer K (in the case, $1 \leq K \leq 5$) determines, so to speak, the 'cutting point' (say, 3). In this case the recombined strings will consist of the first three alleles of the first one and the last two of the second one, {01011}, and vice versa for the second 'child': {10010}, i.e. the first three of the second 'parent' and the last two of the first one.

Mutation involves the change of state of any one random element on the sequence (from 0 to 1 or vice versa).

In the standard formulation, strings are in turn selected over time according to their relative 'fitness' as revealed by the environmental payoffs that they obtain. This will not be so in the model which follows. As already mentioned, there is no reason to think that some consumption pattern may be intrinsically 'better' than another one, and, in any case, there is no collective mechanism (thank God!!) to check it. Therefore, more technically, our strings evolve over a flat selection landscape, solely driven by crossover and mutation. The death process (of strings) in our model is only determined by the (time-lagged) effects of budget constraints ('Once upon a time, I desired to have a villa at Cap Ferrat, five servants and caviar every day . . . however, I have now forgotten all that, and I am quite content with my little apartment and meat twice a week . . .').

In the model that follows each element of the string encodes, as mentioned, one particular commodity (which might or might not be supplied at any particular time t).[25]

For our purposes here, GAs provide a simple (albeit inevitably rough) account of an evolving lexicographic order over the desired commodities, whose structure is indeed a proxy for the 'lifestyle' of the consumer.[26]

[24] For our purpose here we can neglect the element (*) of the GA alphabet, meaning 'wildcards' whose specification does not affect the overall performance of the string itself.

[25] In the latter case, of course, the corresponding value of that element will be zero for all consumers.

[26] Here and throughout, there is a major, and admittedly unresolved, ambiguity between preferences over 'attributes' versus preferences over commodities. While we share with Earl (1986), and, before, Lancaster (1971), the idea that some underlying (hedonic) attributes and not commodities themselves are the object of consumption acts, our very simple model avoids any explicit account of the 'cognitive' mappings between the former and the latter, and their evolution in the minds of consumers.

―――――――― *Demand Dynamics with Socially Evolving Preferences* ――――――――

Needless to say, the model of consumer behavior that we propose is highly stylized and 'abstract'—possibly as 'abstract' as the standard utility-based model. However, the assumptions that it incorporates are radically different from the latter in that it tries to capture (i) the social nature of preference formation; (ii) the role of individual and collective history; (iii) the formation (and change) of consumption habits; and (iv) the permanent possibility of innovation. Contrary to the canonic decision model, we assume agents with extremely limited computational capabilities, but with the possibility of 'learning their preferences' through the very process by which they select their consumption patterns.

Representation of Consumers

At any time t each consumer j is characterized by:

- $y_j(t)$, its income level (in monetary terms);
- $r_j(t)$, the income class to which it belongs (these classes endogenously change as income grow—see also below);
- $L_j^\tau(t)$, a binary string of length ℓ (with ℓ = number of actual and eventually possible goods), where each element $i \in \{1, \ldots, \ell\}$ takes the value of 1 or 0 depending on whether the corresponding good appears or not in the consumption pattern of consumer j. Note also that goods are further distinguished according to their product group g (below $g = 1, \ldots, 5$), metaphorically standing for different basic functions, so that—reading the strings from left to right—one goes from 'basic' to more 'luxury' categories of expenditures;
- $S_j^\tau(t)$, a string of length ℓ coding the actual expenditures (in monetary terms) on each good i (clearly, taking value zero for all goods which have a zero on the $L_j^\tau(t)$ string);
- $L_j^f(t)$, a binary string of length ℓ, which we call 'frustrated memory', where element $i \in \{1, \ldots, \ell\}$ takes value 1 if that good has been selected to be part of one's own consumption pattern but no purchase has yet been made due to the budget constraint. Note that whenever a purchase occurs on any i in $L_j^f(t)$, that i will start to appear as '1' on the string of actual consumption patterns $L_j^\tau(t)$, and correspondingly disappear from the 'frustrated memory' (a '1' will turn into a '0'). We shall see below how the frustrated memory emerges, as indirect outcome of innovation and social imitation; moreover, it stochastically decays as an exponential function of time (so that, '1's turn 'radioactively' into '0's as time goes by);

- $S_j^f(t)$, a string of length ℓ, listing the desired expenditures (in monetary terms) corresponding to the items which appear on the 'frustrated memory'.

This description of the consumers, together with the string $P(t)$, which is the system-level vector of unit prices $p_i(t)$ is sufficient to determine the actual quantities purchased by each j.[27]

Income Dynamics

The logs of (monetary) incomes of individual consumers are random walks with a reflecting barrier, so that:

$$y_j(t) = y_j(t-1)\left[1+\varepsilon_j(t)\right] \tag{1}$$

where $\varepsilon_j(t)$ is an i.i.d., serially uncorrelated, random variable drawn from a truncated normal $\sim N(\mu,\sigma^2)$ and truncation is such to prevent, for simplicity, negative income changes.[28]

Consumers do not save (except possibly for some residual involuntary saving, see below); hence in general income is equal to total expenditure (correspondingly, all commodities ought to be rigorously considered as 'nondurable').

Income Classes

We define $r = 20$ income classes, initially set so that the higher value of the class exceeds the lower one by some given $\eta\%$ (obviously, near the very beginning of the simulation most of the classes are going to be empty: see below on 'initial conditions'). As incomes growth, the 20 classes are endogenously redefined so that they will continue to partition the whole population in 20 groups of log-identical sizes.

[27] In the model we assume indivisibility of the first unit purchased, but divisibility over any amount above 1 (one might want to consider that as a very rough proxy of quality-related differentiation, albeit totally unspecified on the supply side, so that, for example 'one and a half unit of a commodity might be metaphorically understood as one unit plus added gadgets and optionals). We further add the convention that any commodity i which is not actually produced at t has price zero and obviously cannot be bought by any consumers.

[28] Throughout the simulations presented here we assume $\mu = 0.03$.

——————— *Demand Dynamics with Socially Evolving Preferences* ———————

Old and New Products

At the beginning of 'history' (i.e. at $t = 0$), available commodities are very few, and mainly concentrated in product group one (the metaphorical equivalent of 'basic necessities'). Hence also most elements in the strings $L_{(\cdot)}{}^\tau(\cdot)$ and $P(\cdot)$ have value zero. However, at each time point new commodities stochastically arrive, whose number is drawn from a Poisson distribution.

Given that number, each virtual i (i.e. each commodity which takes at $t - 1$ a value zero on the price vector) has a uniform probability of coming into existence. Consider all that as a simplified version of some unspecified dynamics of innovation on the supply side. Note that whenever a new commodity is born, it appears with a positive price in the $P(\cdot)$ vector. That, however, does not automatically imply that it is bought by any one consumer (see below on 'innovation'). A commodity unsold for more that t^* periods (in our simulations $t^* = 3$) becomes 'dead'.

Commodity Unit Prices

When a commodity is introduced it is associated with a random price $p_i(0)$, drawn from a uniform distribution defined on a finite support (in our simulations, $1 \leq p_i(0) \leq 100$). We experimented with two versions of price dynamics. In version 1,

$$p_i(t) = p_i^{(0)}\left[1 + v_i(t)\right] \tag{2}$$

where $v_i(t)$ is an i.i.d., serially uncorrelated, random variable drawn from a truncated normal distribution with zero mean, defined over $-1 < -a \leq v_i \leq +a$.

In version 2,

$$p_i(t) = p_i^{(0)}\left[\sum_{\tilde{\tau}} q_i(\tilde{\tau})\right]^{\alpha_i} \tag{3}$$

where $\alpha_i \leq 0$ and $q_i(t)$ stands for total quantities of the commodity sold at each t. In a nutshell, in version 1, prices are subject to uncorrelated random shocks, while in version 2, they fall as a function of cumulated sales, in a fashion similar to what is often suggested in the literature on 'learning curves' and dynamic increasing returns.

——————— *Demand Dynamics with Socially Evolving Preferences* ———————

Dynamics of Individual Consumption

At each 'period' after individual incomes have been updated, each consumer *j* faces four stochastic alternatives:

1. *Leave unchanged the consumption basket, with probability* θ_j^u. In the following we have assumed θ_j^u identical for all *j*'s and experimented with different parametrizations, ranging from 0.2 to 0.8). Under this option, all budget items are identically increased in proportion to income growth.[29]
2. *Access the 'frustrated memory' with probability* θ_j^f. In this case, all income increase is in principle devoted to the purchase of one or more items which, as mentioned, had been acquired as part of the chosen 'lifestyle' but could not be bought due to the budget constraint. (Note that despite income growth, the addition of new items to the actual consumption basket is not necessarily guaranteed: see below on 'adjustment algorithms'.)
3. *Change (part) of the consumption patterns via innovation or imitation with probability* $(1 - \theta_j^u - \theta_j^f)$. In our model, quite in tune with the evidence on innovation diffusion,[30] we have assumed that, once the consumer has stochastically 'decided' to change, the innovative option (i.e. adopt a new product) is a function of its income class, r_j.[31] The complement to one is the effort to imitate, which, we assume, is restricted to one's own income class and higher ones (if any). Imitation has clearly to do also with phenomena of social integration, formation of (partially) homogeneous lifestyles within similar social groups or, conversely, efforts to sanction upward social mobility. A rough way to capture all that is to assume that the consumer to be imitated is drawn from a Poisson-type distribution with mean 1 (for the purposes of this draw we reclassify income classes, so that we indicate with zero the class to which the consumer belongs, with 1 that immediately higher, etc.).[32]

[29] That hypothesis amounts to assuming, under this option, a homothetic demand function with unitary price elasticities of demand. It is an extreme assumption, running counter to a lot of evidence on different price- and income-elasticities of different goods. We made it just in order not to in-build any possible emergent properties of the model into the assumptions. Hence, for example, if Engel-type patterns in budget coefficients were to emerge, they ought to be solely due to the dynamics of preference evolution and not to some preimposed preference structure differently weighting different goods as incomes grow. Of course, the conclusions would hold *a fortiori* in a more realistic model that would allow for both preference evolution and 'intrinsic' propensities, e.g. to trade off 'inferior' and 'superior' goods.

[30] See, for example, Rogers (1983). Discussions of evidence and models of innovation diffusion from different angles are in Mahajar *et al.* (1989), Dosi (1991) and Stoneman (1995).

[31] We assume that the probability of innovating is distributed as an exponential function of the income classes.

[32] Since the distribution will have a truncation corresponding to the highest income class, probabilities are proportionally reassigned to the relevant income classes.

——————— *Demand Dynamics with Socially Evolving Preferences* ———————

3a. *Innovation.*   If the consumer has opted, so to speak, for the 'exploration' route, it randomly draws (within a uniform probability distribution) one of the 'new' products which have become available (see above) but are not included in its desired consumption patterns of that particular consumer.

3b. *Imitation.*   Conversely, after having selected the income class to be imitated through the above procedure, a consumer is randomly selected in that class, and, together, a random product group from g. Next, the crossover operator from GAs is applied to the substring corresponding to that product aggregate and that consumer.[33] In that way, the imitator 'borrows,' so to speak, part of the preference structure of the imitated agent, and, in a first approximation, also its budget allocation to the corresponding items (i.e. the relevant parts of the strings $L_k^\tau(t-1)$ and $S_k^\tau(t-1)$, with k being the imitated agent).[34]

Adjustment Algorithms

Given the indivisibility of the first unit of any item of consumption (cf. footnote 27) changes in the consumption patterns—no matter whether due to access to the 'frustrated memory,' innovation or imitation—do not necessarily fulfill the budget constraint. If they do, the new consumption profile will be implemented (with any possible income residual being subject again to the same stochastic allocation process described so far, i.e. between 'no change,' memory-activation, imitation, innovation). If the new consumption profile, on the contrary, violates the budget constraint, an iterated procedure of adjustment is implemented, checking whether relatively 'local' adjustments can accommodate for the new desired expenditures. The steps are the following:

(a)   check if reductions of expenditures over up to five goods within the same product group are sufficient to make up to the novel desired expenditure (under the requirement of a minimal unitary expenditure on the former);

(b)   same as sub (a) plus the reduction of desired quantities of new items to one unit each;

[33] Out of the two substrings so obtained, the imitator is assumed to retain that which has on the right-hand the preferences of the imitated consumer. (Recall that the whole string can be read from left to right as going from 'old' to 'new' products, and in terms of product aggregates, from necessities to more discretional items of expenditure.)

[34] In fact, we allow also with small probability a sort of 'involuntary innovation' to occur through the imitation process, in so far as the relevant part of the $L_k^\tau(\cdot)$ string is imperfectly copied (with a '0' instead of '1' or vice versa).

——————— *Demand Dynamics with Socially Evolving Preferences* ———————

(c) same as (b), but with the added possibility of giving up entirely up to two 'old' goods;

(d) same procedure as (a) and (b), but with the expenditure reduction applicable to the *whole consumption string* (up to a maximum of 10 items);

(e) same procedure as (c), again applied to the whole string.

We assume that the corresponding changes in consumption patterns always occur when either steps (a) or (b) generate budget-consistent schedules, while they happen only in probability in cases (c)–(e) (with the probability falling from the former to the latter).[35]

This algorithm, as simple as it is, is meant to capture the relative inertia and path-dependency of 'models of consumption' and related 'lifestyles'. Moreover, note that when only part of the new desired expenditures can be fulfilled, in the spirit of our earlier considerations on lexicographic hierarchies in consumption, the order of priorities goes 'from left to right' on the string, in terms of product groups. Whenever, after the mentioned adjustment iterations, some (or all) desired new expenditures remain unfulfilled, they transit to the 'frustrated memory'.

Initial Conditions

At time zero, we assume consumers (1000 in the following) with an identical (and low) income and identical preferences over a small number of initially available commodities (five goods, of which three are within group 1, i.e. 'necessities').[36]

One of the purposes of the model is precisely to see whether, notwithstanding these initial conditions and the quite simple dynamics described above, the model can generate as sorts of *emergent properties*[37] some of the regularities that one generally detect in the empirically observed consumption patterns.

5. *A Preliminary Look at Some Statistical Properties*

Let us begin by noting that the model endogenously generates differentiation

[35] In order to prevent nearly infinite recursions, we stipulate that whenever the income to be allocated is <5% of the total disposable income, that will be added to next period income as a sort of 'involuntary saving'.

[36] In the simulations presented below, we set the notional number of commodities which can be explored by the system at $\ell = 223$.

[37] For a detailed discussion of this notion, see Lane (1993).

———————— *Demand Dynamics with Socially Evolving Preferences* ————————

in individual consumption patterns, and, at the same time, entails processes of social imitation which prevent such diversity from exploding.

Despite totally uniform initial conditions, as incomes stochastically grow, both patterns of consumption and 'preferences' evolve in ways that are path-dependent and socially embedded. Path-dependency appears at two levels: first, the individual consumption patterns at any time depend also on the sequence of past 'preferences' and consumption acts; second, indirectly, they depend on the whole collective history of the latter. Relatedly, the social embeddedness of the dynamics is straightforward, in that preferences and revealed purchasing patterns emerge from collective mechanisms of social imitation, which represent also ordering mechanisms, possibly accounting for the relative predictability of aggregate patterns over time[38]. In the present model, almost entirely focused on the demand side, this implies that implicit dynamics on the supply side provides coevolving opportunities of innovation.[39] Given all that, an important 'exercise in plausibility' (although not a rigorous validation of the model itself) is, as mentioned in Section 2, the analysis of both qualitative and statistical properties of the patterns of consumption generated by the model, our goal being to assess the extent to which they are able to replicate actual properties of empirically observed (cross-section and time-series) expenditure patterns.[40]

Diffusion Patterns

Figure 1(a,b) depicts two quite typical diffusion profiles that the model generates, displaying the usual S-shape generally found in the empirical diffusion patterns (see e.g. Rogers, 1983; Mahajar *et al.*, 1989; Grübler and

———————————————————

[38] Incidentally, note that our model does not appear to display, under the parameterizations which we explored, those phenomena of sudden 'regime transitions' and possibly chaotic behavior predicted by the model of social imitation of Granovetter and Soong (1986). Our intuition is that this does not happen here, first, because of the higher path-dependency, and thus 'inertia' in-built in our model. Second, here consumers tend to imitate consumption bundles and not individual items, implying also a slower and more imperfect drive to social uniformity (since the imitated bundles are generally different from each other). However, it does not seem unlikely that Granovetter and Soong's properties could emerge in modified versions of this model allowing for, e.g., 'fashion' goods, faster rates of imitation on them and sampling mechanisms for the imitation with respect to the imitated population. Finally, the model allows the persistent exploration of new items of consumption—and through that, an everlasting evolution of 'lifestyles'.

[39] Note, also, that empirically testing restrictions on a purported (and unobservable) 'utility function' does not have a much different epistemological status.

[40] The simulations discussed in the following are based on 500-period runs with 1000 agents. Unless otherwise specified the results which we present hold for the whole range of parametrizations on the 'inertia' consumption patterns (i.e. the probability of sticking to the past basket composition) which we varied from 0.2 to 0.8. Similarly, they hold under both versions of price dynamics (see above).

———————————————————————— 374 ————————————————————————

———————— *Demand Dynamics with Socially Evolving Preferences* ————————

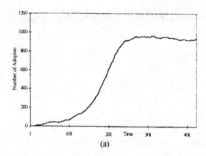
(a)

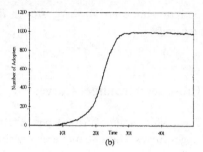
(b)

FIGURE 1. Two typical examples of diffusion patterns.

Nakicenovic, 1991). With regard to empirical data, one often finds in the literature estimates of the rate equations of the diffusion process as a (nonlinear) function of the number of potential adopters and of the total number of consumers who have already adopted the commodity in their consumption basket. A typical model is some discretization of a rate equation such as

$$\frac{dN(t)}{dt} = a\overline{N} + (b-a)N(t) - \frac{b}{N}\left[N(t)\right]^2 \tag{4}$$

where $N(t)$ stands for the total number of adopters at t, $\overline{N}$ is the number of potential adopters, the parameter a is meant to capture the 'autonomous' (i.e. in our language, 'innovation-related') adoption choices and b governs 'imitation-related' choices—nonlinearly dependent on N (cf. Mahajar *et al.*, 1989). (Note also that in our model as well as in reality, 'older' commodities may be driven out of the consumption baskets by the arrival of new ones.)

For sake of illustration, we report in Appendix 1 one of the estimates of the discrete reformulation of (4)

$$S(t) = \alpha + \beta N(t-1) + \delta\left[N(t-1)\right]^2 \tag{5}$$

where $S(t)$ is the net arrival of new adopters at t.

Notwithstanding their widespread use, however, estimates of models like (5) are ridden with serious econometric problems (see Appendix 1). Hence, we do not want to make much out of it. Let us simply state primarily as a conjecture—apparently not contradicted by the data—that 'autonomous' innovation in consumption, as well as social imitationm do not only appear in the 'microscopic' description of how agents evolve their consumption

———————— *Demand Dynamics with Socially Evolving Preferences* ————————

patterns, but seem to carry over to the 'macroscopic' description of system dynamics.

Cross-section Engel Curves

For a wide range of parameters, the model is able to generate cross-section Engel curves whose shapes are very similar to the empirically observed ones.

Recently collected evidence on the shape of the relationship between commodity expenditure and income (or total expenditure) seems to suggest that, cross-sectionally, standard linear logarithmic expenditure-share models[41] are robust in describing the observed behavior for certain classes of goods (e.g. food and, more generally, 'basics'), but should be generalized when one turns to more 'luxury' categories of expenditures (e.g. alcohol and clothing), so as to allow for nonlinearities in total expenditure.[42]

As briefly reported in Appendix 2, when expenditure shares are plotted against the log of total individual (real) expenditure (for a given, sufficiently large, t), both standard OLS and nonparametric kernel regressions show that, no matter the level of aggregation of goods into product groups, 'basics' (respectively, 'luxury') budget shares tend to be negatively (respectively, positively) correlated with log of income, as expected.

Strong evidence for nonlinearities is furthermore displayed by non-parametric kernel regressions (in line with, e.g., Banks *et al.*, 1997), suggesting the need for higher-order terms in the Engel curve relationships (see Figure A1).

Quantitative support for this conjecture is further obtained by testing convenient specifications of the general (cross-section) expenditure system:

$$w_j^g = b_{0g}(\mathbf{p}) + \sum_{b=1}^{L} b_{bg}(\mathbf{p}) g_b\left(\log m_j\right) \qquad (6)$$

where w_j^g is the budget share of consumer j for commodities belonging to group $g = 1, \ldots, 5$; $g_b(\cdot)$ are polynomials in the (log of) real consumer j's income m_j; and $\mathbf{p}$ is the price-vector (time-subscripts have been omitted for clarity). Thanks to its interesting properties, the class of expenditure systems (6) has been recently employed in both *theory-driven* and *data-driven*

[41] For example, the Almost Ideal (AI) model of Deaton and Muellbauer (1980a).

[42] Cf. Banks *et al.* (1997), Blundell and Ray (1984), Blundell *et al.* (1993), Hardle and Jerison (1990), Hildenbrand (1994) and Hausman *et al.* (1995). See, however, Bierens and Pott-Buter (1990) for a quite distinct point of view.

———————————————— 376 ————————————————

——————— *Demand Dynamics with Socially Evolving Preferences* ———————

analyses.[43] Note, first, that (6) is indeed general enough to nest, as special cases, linear expenditure models as Working-Leser (cf. Deaton, 1986; Blundell, 1988) and Deaton and Muellbauer's (1980a) Almost-Ideal demand systems, while preserving (exact nonlinear) aggregability.[44] Second, Gorman (1981) and Banks *et al.* (1997) have shown that: (i) in order to be theory-consistent, the rank of demand systems such as (6) cannot be higher than 3, i.e. $L \leq 2$; and (ii) the rank-3 conditions forces, so to speak, $g_h(\log m_j)$ to be $(\log m_j)^2$, as long as one also desires to preserve exact aggregability. As a consequence, the special case:

$$w_j^g = b_0^g(\mathbf{p}_t) + b_1^g(\mathbf{p}_t)\log m_j + b_{2,t}^g(\mathbf{p}_t)\left(\log m_j\right)^2 \qquad (7)$$

also known as QUAIDS model, turns out to be an 'as general as we can go,' theory-consistent, model (Deaton, 1981, p .3), which is, at the same time, well supported by recently collected empirical evidence.

Quite in tune with Banks *et al.* (1997), results reported in Appendix 2 (cf. Table A2) seem to suggest that, once (7) is tested against other functional specifications in a 'general-to-specific' framework, it appears as the *sole* correctly specified model explaining the cross-section relationships between individual budget shares and the log of individual (real) incomes generated by our model for a wide range of parameters. Even more importantly, the model seems to be able to simulate cross-section expenditure patterns which, independently of the level of aggregation over commodities, indirectly support Gorman's rank-3 assumption, even though individual consumption behaviors are of course designed to be at odds with those postulated by the standard utility-based model of rational choice.[45]

---

[43] At one extreme, a totally *data-driven* approach would imply fitting (either parametrically or not) statistical models to cross-section or time-series data and finding the 'preferred' ones according to a battery of econometric tests involving functional form mispecification, normality, heteroscedasticity, etc. In this case, very few restrictions are needed *ex ante*, so that, provided the model does not display any evidence for mispecification and allows for meaningful testing, it is possible to check *ex post* the plausibility of any theory of consumer behavior by performing appropriate econometric tests. On the other hand, a *theory-driven* approach prescribes that the model employed in the estimation of separate (or systems of) commodity demand functions should be consistent, generally speaking, with some theory of household expenditure behavior. Specifically, as long as this theory is the standard *utility-based model of rational choice*, one requires that (i) the functional form of demand equations to be estimated is generated by constrained maximization of a well-defined utility function; (ii) the unknown parameters involved in the estimation satisfy all derived restrictions, e.g. adding-up, homogeneity, symmetry: cf. Deaton and Muellbauer (1980b).

[44] That is, the aggregate Engel curve (i.e. weighted averages of budget shares) has the same coefficients of the individual one.

[45] This evidence, at the very least, casts some doubts on the robustness of the results obtained, among others, by Hausman *et al.* (1995) and Banks *et al.* (1997), who try to find empirical evidence agreeing with Gorman's rank-3 result.

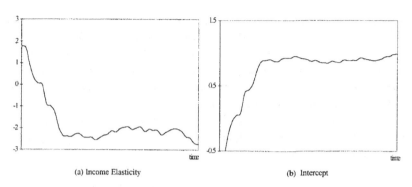

(a) Income Elasticity   (b) Intercept

FIGURE 2. Evolution over time of income elasticity and intercept for commodity group 1.

The Evolution of Income Elasticities over Time

As far as repeated cross-section analyses of individual expenditure patterns are concerned, an interesting question is whether income elasticities for different commodities groups display any meaningful intertemporal patterns. For example, recent empirical evidence (cf. Anderson and Vahid, 1997) appears to show that the (average) individual income elasticity for food-like commodities has declined over time.

This empirical finding is robustly confirmed by the data generated for group 1 commodities by our model under different parametrizations (see Figure 2). Moreover, our results also display a general tendency for increasing intercepts over time. However, this pattern of behavior is not so clear for other (less 'basic') commodity groups.

Engel-type Dynamics of Consumption Patterns and Structural Instability

As mentioned earlier, in order not to bias by construction our results, we have made the extreme (and unrealistic) hypothesis that, when consumers opt for the reproduction over time of their past consumption patterns, they do so in a way that amounts to assuming a homothetic demand with unitary price elasticity. It is interesting to check whether, despite this assumption, long-term changes in budget coefficients emerge, driven by social innovation and imitation, jointly with stochastically growing incomes.

More generally, one wants to investigate whether some stable, parameter-constant, relationship between aggregate budget shares and aggregate real income and prices would exist in simulated data, displaying Engel-type patterns of evolution in the share of different product groups.

———————— *Demand Dynamics with Socially Evolving Preferences* ————————

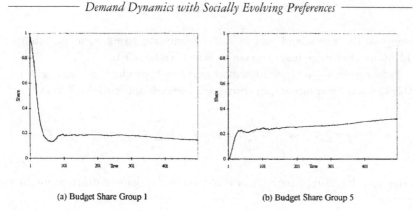

(a) Budget Share Group 1   (b) Budget Share Group 5

FIGURE 3. Budget shares time series.

An important *caveat*, however, applies. The presence of nonlinearities in log-linear cross-section Engel curves (see above) will *per se* destroy any isomorphisms between individual and aggregate functional forms; hence, it must be stressed that, even though such a stable time-series relationship would be found over subsamples, its functional specification will in general be very complicated. Moreover, additional 'aggregation errors' which are likely to be detected in the data (e.g. income distribution might not be *mean-scaled*, income-dependent heteroscedastic errors might arise), can in principle lead to aggregated, correctly specified time-series models whose functional form is so convoluted to prevent any interpretation of macro-parameters in terms of individual ones.[46]

In line with recent studies on food-like commodities, we found (see Appendix 3) that the data generated by the model are indeed characterized also by, in addition to the nonlinearities in cross-section relationships already singled out, other 'aggregation errors' [income is not mean-scaled (cf. Lewbel, 1992), and income-dependent heteroscedastic errors are detected (cf. Anderson and Vahid, 1997)].

Nevertheless, as Figure 3 shows, budget shares *do* display, remarkably, the expected long-term changes. This type of dynamics appears most evidently in the case of group 1 (a metaphorical proxy for 'basics') and group 5 (which,

---

[46] Cf. Stoker (1986), Lewbel (1992) and Anderson and Vahid (1997). If one is primarily interested in preserving some isomorphisms between aggregate (time-series) and individual (cross-section) parameters (e.g. consumption/income elasticity), so as to be able to interpret macro-estimates as micro ones in a 'representative-agent' account, many overly restrictive assumptions are essential—both on the aggregate functional form to be tested, on its dynamic specification and on the distributional properties of the involved variables. Since the available empirical evidence clearly shows that those conditions are hardly met in reality, a *data-driven* approach which does not impose any *a priori* functional forms (either at the individual or at the aggregate level) is then strongly suggested. See Deaton and Muellbauer (1980a), Deaton (1992), Tobin (1950), Stoker (1980, 1982).

──────────── *Demand Dynamics with Socially Evolving Preferences* ────────────

being on the right-hand part of the consumption string is, in probability, 'filled up' after more basic necessities have been satisfied).

More rigorously, as reported in more detail in Appendix 3, we are in general able to select (over subsamples) preferred, correctly specified, VAR models as:

$$\Delta w_t^g = \alpha_0 + \sum_{i=1}^{k} \alpha_i^g \Delta w_{t-i}^g + \sum_{j=0}^{n} \beta_j \Delta \log m_{t-j} + \sum_{h=0}^{m} \gamma_h p_{t-h} + \varepsilon_t^g, \quad g = 1,\dots,5$$

(8)

displaying Engel-type patterns of evolution in the share of different product groups.[47]

Price-coefficients, although they are negative, are not generally significant (neither in the estimates shown here nor in most other tests that we have carried out)—which is not too surprising given our extreme assumptions. What is much more interesting is the significant effect of lagged incomes, yielding Engel-type patterns which are purely an aggregate emergent property, driven by the collective exploration of new consumption opportunities, together with the progressive relaxation of budget constraints.

Moreover, in empirical time prices, one often detects evidence of important and generalized structural breaks in the patterns of consumption within and across product groups.[48] Remarkably, notwithstanding our rather rudimentary behavioral assumptions, structural instability most often emerges with respect to both commodity groups and within groups shares of individual commodities. When applying the usual tests for structural stability (Chow, CUSUM and CUSUMSQ), one generally finds (especially with regards to groups $g = 1$ and $g = 5$) significant structural change, intertwined with rather long periods of structural stability. At the risk of some overinterpretation, these patterns might suggest the easy emergence of punctuated discontinuities in historically shaped, collectively shared, 'models of consumption,' which, however, display a 'metastable' character (in the sense that they persist on timescales of orders of magnitude greater that those of the processes which generated them, but nonetheless tend to vanish with probability one as time goes on).[49]

───────────────────────────────────

[47] All simulations have been carried out under the stationary/stochastic price version. Moreover, note that to avoid singularity of regression matrices entailed by the identity between total expenditure and total income, we have chosen to model $g = 1, \dots, 4$ (the results hold irrespective of this choice). Finally, first differences are employed because of nonstationarity of the corresponding levels. See Appendix 3 for further details.

[48] On the former, cf. Combris (1992); more generally on changes in consumption patterns, cf. Houthakker (1957), Kuznets (1962), Gardes and Louvet (1986), Deaton and Muellbauer (1980b).

[49] A stimulating discussion of meta-stability notions in the domain of evolutionary models in economics is in Lane (1993). Conversely, on the recurrence and economic importance of specific social 'norms of consumption,' cf. the broad historical interpretations in Aglietta (1979) and Boyer (1986).

'Demand Laws' with Innovative Exploration and Social Adaptation

As emphasized in Section 2, a crucial question concerns the robustness of aggregate economic propositions, such as 'demand laws,' well beyond those circumstances whereby aggregate dynamics is presumed to map exactly into corresponding behavioral patterns of some purported 'representative' (most often, utility-maximizing) agent. A major advantage of a model such as that presented here is that one is bound to specify the microscopic decision algorithms, which, in our case, are clearly at odds with any assumption of both (i) statistical invariance in some 'revealed preferences,' and, at least equally important, (ii) algorithmic coherence in the choice process. Do well-established pieces of conventional economic wisdom—such as downward sloping demand schedules for individual commodities—hold in these cases too?

As mentioned in the introduction, this is precisely the question addressed by Hildenbrand (1994), in a perspective which is on purpose much more agnostic about microeconomic decision rules. Here, having constructed the data-generating process, we may also try to establish the nature of the underlying microconditions under which 'demand law' type propositions apply. As a premise, note that we have already touched on the issue, from a dynamic point of view, hinting that, for commodity aggregates, seemingly 'well-behaved' demand schedules might (often but not always) emerge out of the interactions between price changes, dynamic income effects, social imitation, relaxation of budget constraints, and so on

However, 'laws of demand,' as mentioned above, imply a major static (with respect to time) thought-experiment. That is, despite the fact that at any given time one obviously observes only one price–quantity combination, what would happen if the price of the commodity at hand were higher/ lower—holding constant all other system parameters and microdecision rules? Hildenbrand (1994) proves indeed some sufficient conditions for standard demand-law propositions (and weaker versions thereof) to hold, which carry observationally testable implications concerning the distribution of demand patterns, at any t, conditional on different income classes (cf. Appendix 4).

One of the basic ideas is that if the distribution of preferences—irrespective of how they formed (or, for that matter, of how coherent they are)—is sufficiently homogeneous across income cohorts, one can establish sufficient conditions to guarantee non-upward-sloping notional demand curves (at each t), whose fulfillment can be detected from the statistical properties of actual demand conditional on different income classes.

─────────── *Demand Dynamics with Socially Evolving Preferences* ───────────

In brief, a 'law of demand' (LD) is verified {i.e. the demand function $F_t(p)$ is strictly monotonically decreasing} if for any pair of price vectors p and p′, $p \neq p′$:

$$(p - p′) \cdot [F_t(p) - F_t(p′)] < 0$$

A weaker version is represented by the so-called Wald axiom (WA), that is

$$(p - p′) \cdot F_t(p′) \leq 0 \quad \text{implies} \quad (p - p′) \cdot F_t(p) \leq 0 \tag{9}$$

or in the strict formulation,

$$(p - p′) \cdot F_t(p′) \leq 0 \quad \text{implies} \quad (p - p′) \cdot F_t(p) < 0 \tag{10}$$

The 'law of demand' satisfies the WA but the converse is not true. The bottom line is how to establish the conditions under which the LD and the WA are verified without imposing corresponding restrictions on (unobservable) individual demand schedules. These conditions turn out to be related to various measures of dispersion of demand patterns across income cohorts (cf. Appendix 4).

In Appendix 4 we show that, indeed, under some parametrizations of our model the conditions for the WA (and also for the LD) are satisfied. Note, again, that this is another emergent property of the model which does not necessarily find any direct isomorphism into microbehavioral rules. It is also interesting to observe under which specifications of the model these properties hold. The results presented in Appendix 4 apply under the stationary-price version, with relatively high inertia in individual consumption patterns.[50] However, an admittedly preliminary exploration of different parameter values shows that the LD and WA properties tend to be lost as one increases the probability of innovating (and this is so, above some threshold, also if one correspondingly increases the probability of imitating, too).

Our conjecture is that in fact the fulfillment of the conditions for the LD and WA to hold are ultimately determined by (imperfect) social imitation, so that the distribution of notional 'preferences'—or 'desired lifestyles'—are not too different across income classes, together with the different impact that budget constraints exert on actual expenditures of consumers (so that, loosely

───────────────────────────────────────

[50] In the simulations analyzed there the probability of sticking to the past is 0.8.

speaking, with higher incomes, the 'cloud' of commodity combinations corresponding to each consumer tend to be more dispersed).[51]

However, if innovative behaviors acquire a major role in the evolution of individual consumption patterns the relative homogeneity of the distribution of 'preferences' across income classes [i.e. what Hildenbrand (1994) calls 'metonymy' of demand schedules] tends to be lost, and with that also the aggregate statistical properties sufficient for the validation of the LD and of the WA. Let us state this conjecture in a more extreme and provocative way: (i) whenever one abandons the assumptions of well-behaved micropreference functions together with rather demanding and quite *ad hoc* restrictions on their distributions, aggregate LD and/or WA properties might continue to hold as statistical collective properties (these are Hildenbrand's results); however, (ii) what basically determines these aggregate properties are ultimately phenomena of social imitations, together with budget constraints; and, relatedly, (iii) sufficiently fast processes of 'autonomous' consumer innovation might also imply the breakdown of conventional assumptions on (static) inverse relations between prices and demanded quantities.

6. *Conclusions*

In this work, building on what we consider to be some general empirical properties of consumption decisions and their evolution, we have developed a simple model which tries to capture—albeit in a very rudimentary form—phenomena like the existence of recognizably different 'lifestyles,' lexicographic orders on consumption acts, (limited) path-dependency of individual and collective consumption patterns, innovation and social imitation. It turns out that, despite its simplicity, the model generates emerging aggregate patterns of consumption with statistical properties quite in tune with empirically observed regularities, such as S-shaped diffusion of new commodities, Engel-type dynamics of budget shares, and, under quite a few microparametrizations, distributions of consumption coefficients yielding in the aggregate notional downward sloping demand curves. Of course, one can think of several improvements upon both the model and the exploration of the statistical properties of the data it generates.

Concerning the model, one can easily imagine two complementary directions. On the one hand, one might gain many insight from models

[51] Note that the two propositions are not in conflict with each other. The first one claims that 'desired lifestyles' are relatively similar across income groups (of course one assumes on that several such 'lifestyles' coexist at any *t*). The second proposition holds that as one goes from one income cohort to a higher one, the dispersion of actual consumption baskets will increase because under a relaxed budget constraint more of those desired (and cross-sectionally diverse) 'lifestyles' will be satisfied.

──────────── *Demand Dynamics with Socially Evolving Preferences* ────────────

which, paraphrasing Malerba *et al.* (1996), are more 'evidence-friendly,' in that they take on board much more detailed phenomenological specifications on, for example, cognitive processes shaping the formation of 'lifestyles' and decision rules, different characteristics of commodities, different 'consumption technologies,' etc. (For example, it is obvious that the distribution between durable versus nondurable, necessities versus discretionary items, etc. are likely to map also into different decision rules.) In the same vein, sooner or later, one will have to tackle the challenge of providing more rigorous accounts of coevolutionary processes among consumption acts, preferences and cognitive representations.[52] In the other direction, one might want to explore the properties of even more reduced form models with some hope of studying analytically some generic invariances in the ensuing statistical properties.[53] With respect to statistical follow-ups, what we have tried here are just a few and rather naive attempts to check the coherence between the properties of the data generated by the model and those observed in actual history. Ahead, there are obviously more rigorous exploration of the robustness of the results (including Monte Carlo-type exercises holding para-metrizations constant, and systematic comparisons across sample paths generated under different parametrizations and behavioral assumptions). Moreover, one may envisage—as mentioned earlier—promising interactions between analyses establishing parsimonious sufficient statistical conditions for aggregate economic propositions to hold [such as those, discussed above, proved by Hildenbrand (1994) on notional 'demand laws'] and explicitly microfounded models that might illuminate the classes of data-generating processes yielding certain aggregate statistical outcomes.

Increasing numbers of scholars are coming to appreciate the importance of nesting the interpretation of economic phenomena into microfoundations different from coherent self-seeking monads with well-behaved 'utility functions' and extraordinary calculating capabilities. In this perspective, the foregoing work is hopefully moving some modest steps forward in the direction of an evolutionary (and socially grounded) theory of demand, still to come.

---

[52] As pleaded by Devetag (1999), this volume, and, with reference to other economic domains, by Marengo and Tordjman (1996) and Dosi *et al.* (1996).

[53] In this mode, one can intuitively see fruitful overlapping with much simpler (and more elegant and analytically tractable) models of socially evolving preferences, such as Brock and Durlauf (1995). Relatedly, note that, in principle, our consumption model might be possibly be reformulated as some Markov process in some high-dimensional (or infinitely dimensional) state space.

———————— *Demand Dynamics with Socially Evolving Preferences* ————————

Acknowledgements

Marianna Vintiadis has provided a very knowledgeable assistant researchship, and Silvio Crivellini has been a uniquely valuable support in the implementation of the simulation program. Endless discussions with Luigi Marengo and Helène Tordjman have contributed to imprint the importance of cognitive representations in economic behaviors. Comments by two anonymous referees, Paul David, Peter Earl, Geoffrey Hodgson, and the participants of the Conference in Honor of Brian Loasby (Sterling, June 1997), and those of seminars at Augsburg, Siena, Strasbourg and the London School of Economics, have been very useful in shaping this version of the work. Support to the research, at various stages, by the Italian Ministry of Research (MURST, 'Progetti 40%'), the Italian National Research Council (CNR) and the International Institute of Applied Systems Analysis (IIASA), Laxenburg, Austria, is gratefully acknowledged. The usual *caveats* of course apply.

References

Aglietta, N. (1979), *A Theory of Capitalist Regulation*. New Left Books: London.

Akerlof, G. A. and W. T. Dickens (1982), 'The Economic Consequences of Cognitive Dissonance,' *American Economic Review*, 72, 307–319.

Anderson, H. M. and F. Vahid (1997), 'On the Correspondence Between Individual and Aggregate Food Consumption Functions: Evidence from the USA and the Netherlands,' *Journal of Applied Econometrics*, 12, 477–507.

Arthur, W. B. (1988), 'Competing Technologies: An Overview,' in G. Dosi, C. Freeman, R. R. Nelson, G. Silverberg and L. Soete (eds), *Technical Change and Economic Theory*. Francis Pinter: London.

Banks, J., R. W. Blundell and A. Lewbel (1997), 'Quadratic Engel Curves and Consumer Demand,' *Review of Economics and Statistics*, 79, 527–539.

Barron, J. N. and M. T. Hannan (1994), 'The Impact of Economics on Contemporary Sociology,' *Journal of Economic Literature*, 32, 1111–1146.

Becker, G. S. (1962), 'Irrational Behavior and Economic Theory,' *Journal of Political Economy*, 70, 1–13.

Becker, G. S. (1976), *The Economic Approach to Human Behavior*. University of Chicago Press: Chicago, IL.

Becker, G. S. (1996), *Accounting for Tastes*. Harvard University Press: Cambridge, MA.

Berger, P. L. and T. Luckman (1967), *The Social Construction of Reality*. Penguin: Harmondsworth.

Bianchi, M. (ed.) (1997), *The Active Consumer*. Routledge: London.

Bierens, H. J. and H. A. Pott-Buter (1990), 'Specification of Household Engel Curves by Nonparametric Regressions,' *Econometric Reviews*, 9, 123–184.

Blundell, R. W. (1988), 'Consumer Behavior: Theory and Empirical Evidence. A Survey,' *Economic Journal*, 98, 16–65.

Blundell, R. W., P. Pashardes and G. Weber (1993), 'What Do We Learn about Consumer Demand Patterns from Micro Data?,' *The American Economic Review*, 83, 570–597.

Blundell, R. W. and R. Ray (1984), 'Testing for Linear Engel Curves and Additively Separable Preferences using a New Flexible Demand System,' *Economic Journal*, 94, 800–811.

———————— *Demand Dynamics with Socially Evolving Preferences* ————————

Bourdieu, P. (1976), 'Goutes des classes et styles de vie,' *Actes de la Recherche en Sciences Sociales*, 5, 2–112.

Bourdieu, P. (1979), *La Distinction*. Minuit: Paris.

Boyer, R. (1986), *La Théorie de la Regulation*. La Decouverte: Paris.

Brock, W. A. and S. N. Durlauf (1995), 'Discrete Choice with Social Interactions. I: Theory,' SSRI Working Paper, University of Wisconsin, Madison.

Brown, A. and A. S. Deaton (1972), 'Surveys in Applied Economics: Models of Consumer Behaviour,' *Economic Journal*, 82, 1145–236.

Cohen, M., R. Burkhart, G. Dosi, M. Egidi, L. Marengo, M. Warglien, S. G. Winter and B. Coriat (1996), 'Routines and Other Recurring Action Patterns of Organisations: Contemporary Research Issues,' *Industrial and Corporate Change*, 5(3), 653–698.

Combris, P. (1992), 'Changements Structurels: le cas des consommations alimentaires en France de 1949 à 1988,' *Economie et Prevision*, 102, 221–245.

Coriat, B. and G. Dosi (1998), 'The Institutional Embeddedness of Economic Change. An Appraisal of the "Evolutionary" and "Regulationist" Research Programmes,' in K. Nielsen and E. J. Johnson (eds), *Institutions and Economic Change*. Edward Elgar: Cheltenham.

Dalli, M. and M. Tedeschi (1997), 'Individual Perception and Social Context in Consumer Decision Making: Experimental Analysis,' in R. Viale (ed.), *Cognitive Economics*. LASCOMES: Milan, Bocconi University.

David, P. A. (1985), 'Clio and the Economics of QWERTY,' *American Economic Review*, 75, 332–337.

Deaton, A. S. (ed.) (1981), *Essays in the Theory and Measurement of Consumer Behavior in Honour of Sir Richard Stone*. Cambridge University Press: New York.

Deaton, A. S. (1986), 'Demand Analysis,' in Z. Griliches and M. D. Intrilligator (eds), *Handbook of Econometrics*, Vol. III. Elsevier: Amsterdam.

Deaton, A.S. (1992), *Understanding Consumption,* Oxford, Clarendon Press.

Deaton, A. S. and J. Muellbauer (1980a), 'An Almost Ideal Demand System,' *American Economic Review*, 70, 312–326.

Deaton, A. S. and J. Muellbauer (1980b), *Economics and Consumer Behaviour.* Cambridge University Press: Cambridge.

Devetag, M. G. (1999), 'From Utilities to Mental Models: A Critical Survey on Decision Rules and Cognition in Consumer Choice,' *Industrial and Corporate Change*, 8, 289–351.

Dosi, G. (1988), 'Sources, Procedures and Microeconomic Effects of Innovation,' *Journal of Economic Literature*, 26, 126–171.

Dosi, G. (1991), 'The Research on Innovation Diffusion: An Assessment,' in A. Grubler and N. Nakicenovic (eds), *Diffusion of Technologies and Social Behavior*. Springer Verlag: New York.

Dosi, G. (1995), 'Hierarchies, Markets and Power: Some Foundational Issues on the Nature of Contemporary Economic Organisations,' *Industrial and Corporate Change*, 4, 1–19.

Dosi, G. (1997), 'Opportunities, Incentives and the Collective Patterns of Technological Change,' *Economic Journal*, 107, 1530–1547.

Dosi, G., G. Fagiolo, R. Aversi, M. Meacci and C. Olivetti (1999), 'Cognitive Processes, Social Adaptation and Innovation in Consumption Patterns: From Stylized Facts to Demand Theory,' in S. C. Dow and P. E. Earl (eds), *Economic Organizations and Economic Knowledge: Essays in Honour of Brian Loasby*. Edward Elgar: Cheltenham (forthcoming).

Dosi, G., L. Marengo and G. Fagiolo (1996), 'Learning in Evolutionary Environments,' Working Paper, WP-96–124/November, IIASA, Laxenburg.

Duesenberry, J. (1949), *Income, Savings and the Theory of Consumer Behavior.* Harvard University Press: Cambridge, MA.

———————— 386 ————————

———————— *Demand Dynamics with Socially Evolving Preferences* ————————

Dyer, J. S., P. C. Fishburn, R. E. Stuer, J. Wallius and S. Zionts (1992), 'Multiple Criteria Decision-making, Multiattribute Utility Theory: The Next Ten Years,' *Management Science*, 38, 645–655.

Earl, P. E. (1986), *Lifestyle Economics. Consumer Behaviour in a Turbulent World.* Wheatsheaf/Harvester Press: Brighton.

Ellsberg, D. (1961), 'Risk, Ambiguity and the Savage Axioms,' *Quarterly Journal of Economics*, 75, 643–669.

Elster, J. (1986), *The Multiple Self.* Cambridge University Press: Cambridge.

Fastinger, L. (1956), *A Theory of Cognitive Dissonance.* Harper and Row: New York.

Fishburn, P.C. (1974), 'Lexicographic Orders, Utilities and Decision Rules: A Survey,' *Management Science*, 20, 1442–1471.

Freeman, C. (1982), *The Economics of Industrial Innovation.* Francis Pinter: London.

Gardes, F. and Ph. Louvet (1986), *La Convergence Internationale des Structures de Consommation.* CREDOC: Paris.

Goffman, E. (1974), *Frame Analysis. An Essay on the Organisation of Experience.* Penguin: Harmondsworth.

Goldberg, D. E. (1989), *Genetic Algorithms in Search, Optimization and Machine Learning.* Addison-Wesley: Reading, MA.

Gorman, W. M. (1981), 'Some Engel Curves,' in A. S. Deaton (ed.), *Essays in the Theory and Measurement of Consumer Behavior in Honour of Sir Richard Stone.* Cambridge University Press: New York.

Granovetter, M. (1985), 'Economic Action and Social Structure: The Problem of Embeddedness,' *American Journal of Sociology*, 51, 481–510.

Granovetter, M. and R. Soong (1986), 'Threshold Models of Interpersonal Effects in Consumer Demand,' *Journal of Economic Behavior and Organization*, 7, 83–99.

Grübler, A. and N. Nakicenovic (eds) (1991), *Diffusion of Technologies and Social Behavior.* Springer Verlag: New York.

Hardle, W. and M. Jerison (1990), 'Cross Section Engel Curves Over Time,' CORE, Discussion Paper, 9016.

Hausman, J. A., W. K. Newey and J. L. Powell (1995), 'Nonlinear Errors in Variables Estimation of Some Engel Curves,' *Journal of Econometrics*, 65, 205–233.

Hildenbrand, W. (1994), *Market Demand.* Princeton University Press: Princeton, NJ.

Hirschman, A. (1965), 'Obstacles to Development: A Classification and a Quasi-vanishing Act,' *Economic Development and Cultural Change*, 13, 385–393.

Hodgson, G. M. (1988), *Economics and Institutions: A Manifesto for a Modern Institutional Economics.* Polity Press: Cambridge.

Holland, J. H. (1975), *Adaptation in Natural and Artificial Systems.* MIT Press: Cambridge, MA.

Holland, J. H., K. J. Holyoak, R. E. Nisbett and P. R. Thagard (eds) (1986), *Induction. Processes of Inference, Learning and Discovery.* MIT Press: Cambridge, MA.

Houthakker, M. S. (1957), 'An International Comparison of Household Expenditure Patterns,' *Econometrica*, 25, 532–551.

Johnson-Laird, P. N. (1983), *Mental Models.* Harvard University Press: Cambridge, MA.

Johnson-Laird, P. N. (1993), *The Computer and the Mind.* Fontana Press: London.

Katona, G. (1975), *Psychological Economics.* Elsevier: Amsterdam.

Katona, G. (1980), *Essays in Behavioral Economics.* University of Michigan Press: Ann Arbor.

Kelly, G. A. (1955), *The Psychology of Personal Constructs.* Norton: New York.

Kirman, A. P. (1989), 'The Intrinsic Limits of Modern Economic Theory: The Emperor Has No Clothes,' *Economic Journal*, 99, 126–139.

Kirman, A. P. (1992), 'Whom or What Does the Representative Individual Represent?,' *Journal of Economic Perspectives*, 6, 117–136.

───────────── *Demand Dynamics with Socially Evolving Preferences* ─────────────

Kuran, T. (1987), 'Preference Falsification, Policy Continuity and Collective Conservatism,' *Economic Journal*, 97, 642–655.

Kuznets, S. (1962), 'Quantitative Aspects of the Growth of Nations. VII: The Share and the Structure of Consumption,' *Economic Development and Cultural Change*, 10, 1–92.

Lakoff, G. (1987), *Women, Fire and Dangerous Things. What Categories Reveal About the Mind*. University of Chicago Press: Chicago.

Lancaster, K. J. (1971), *Consumer Demand. A New Approach*. Columbia University Press: New York.

Lane, D. (1993), 'Artificial Worlds in Economics,' *Journal of Evolutionary Economics*, 3, 89–107 (part I), 177–197 (part II).

Legrenzi, P., V. Girotto and P. N. Johnson-Laird (1993), 'Focussing in Reasoning and Choice,' *Cognition*, 49, 37–66.

Leibenstein, H. (1950), 'Bandwagon, Snob and Veblen Effects in the Theory of Consumer Demand,' *Quarterly Journal of Economics*, 64, 183–207.

Leibenstein, H. (1976), *Beyond Economic Man. A New Foundation For Microeconomics*. Harvard University Press: Cambridge, MA.

Lewbel, A. (1992), 'Aggregation with Log-linear Models,' *Review of Economic Studies*, 59, 635–642.

Lippi, M. (1988), 'On the Dynamics of Aggregate Macroequations: From Simple Microbehaviours to Complex Macrorelationships,' in G. Dosi, C. Freeman, R. R. Nelson, G. Silverberg and L. Soete (eds), *Technical Change and Economic Theory*. Francis Pinter: London.

Mahajar, V., E. Muller and F. M. Bass (1989), 'Dynamics of Innovation Diffusion: New Product Growth Models in Marketing,' mimeo, E. L. Cox School of Business, Southern Methodist University, Dallas, TX.

Maital, S. and S. L. Maital (eds) (1993), *Economics and Psychology*. Edward Elgar: Aldershot.

Malerba, F., R. R. Nelson, L. Orsenigo and S. Winter (1996), 'A Model of the Computer Industry,' mimeo, Bocconi University, Milan.

March, J. G. (1994), *A Primer on Decision Making. How Decisions Happen*. Free Press: New York.

Marengo, L. and H. Tordjman (1996), 'Speculation, Heterogeneity and Learning: A Model of Exchange Rate Dynamics,' *Kyklos*, 47, 407–438.

Milgram, S. (1974), *Obedience to Authority: An Experimental View*. Tavistock Institute: London.

Moore, B. M. (1978), *Injustice. The Social Bases of Obedience and Revolt*. Pantheon Books: New York.

Nelson, R. R. and S. G. Winter (1982), *An Evolutionary Theory of Economic Change* The Belknap Press of Harvard University Press: Cambridge, MA.

Olshavsky, R. W. and D. H. Granbois (1979), 'Consumer Decision-making—Fact or Fiction?,' *Journal of Consumer Research*, 6, 93–100.

Payne, J. W., T. R. Bettman and E. J. Johnson (1992), 'Behavioural Decision Research: A Constructive Process Perspective,' *Annual Review of Psychology*, 43, 87–131.

Robertson, T. S. and H. K. Kassarjian (eds) (1991), *Handbook of Consumer Behaviour*. Prentice Hall: Englewood Cliffs, NJ.

Rogers, E. M. (1983), *Diffusion of Innovation*. Free Press: New York.

Rosenberg, N. (1982), *Inside the Blackbox*. Cambridge University Press: Cambridge.

Samuelson, P. A. (1938), 'A Note on the Pure Theory of Consumer's Behavior,' *Economica*, 5, 61–71.

Sanderson, W. C. (1974), 'Does the Theory of Demand Need the Maximum Principle?,' in P. A. David and N. W. Reder (eds), *Nations and Households in Economic Growth. Essays in Honor of Moses Abramovitz*. Academic Press: New York.

Schoemaker, P. J. H. (1982), 'The Expected Utility Model: Its Variants, Purposes, Evidence and Limitations,' *Journal of Economic Literature*, 20, 529–563.

—————————— *Demand Dynamics with Socially Evolving Preferences* ——————————

Scitovsky, T. (1992), *The Joyless Economy. The Psychology of Human Satisfaction.* Oxford University Press: Oxford.

Shafir, E. B., I. Simonson and A. Tversky (1993), 'Reason-based Choice,' *Cognition*, 49, 11–36.

Simon, H. A. (1959), 'Theories of Decision-making in Economics and Behavioural Sciences,' *American Economic Review*, 49, 253–283.

Simon, H. A. (1986), 'Rationality in Psychology and Economics,' in R. M. Hogart and N. W. Reder (eds), *Rational Choice.* University of Chicago Press: Chicago, IL.

Simon, H. A. (1988), *Models of Thought.* Yale University Press: New Haven, CT.

Sippel, R. (1997), 'An Experiment on the Pure Theory of Consumer's Behavior,' *Economic Journal*, 107, 1431–1444.

Slovic, P. (1990), 'Choice,' in D. N. Osherson and E. E. Smith (eds), *An Invitation to Cognitive Science.* MIT Press: Cambridge, MA.

Steinbrunner, J. D. (1974), *The Cybernetic Theory of Decision.* Princeton University Press: Princeton, NJ.

Stigler, G. T. and G. S. Becker (1977), 'De gustibus non est disputandum,' *American Economic Review*, 67, 76–90.

Stoker, T. (1980), 'Distribution Restrictions and the Form of Aggregate Functions,' Working Paper, 1117–80, MIT Sloan School of Management.

Stoker, T. (1982), 'The Use of Cross-section Data to Characterize Macro Functions,' *Journal of the American Statistical Association*, 77, 369–380.

Stoker, T. (1986), 'Simple Tests of Distributional Effects on Macroeconomic Equations,' *Journal of Political Economy*, 94, 763–795..

Stoneman, P. (ed.) (1995), *Handbook of the Economics of Innovation and Technological Change.* Blackwell: Oxford.

Tetlock, P. E. (1985), 'Accountability: The Neglected Social Context of Judgement and Choice,' in B. M. Staw and L. Cummings (eds), *Research in Organizational Behavior.* JAI Press: Greenwich, CT.

Thaler, R. H. (1992), *The Winner's Curse. Paradoxes and Anomalies of Economic Life.* Free Press: New York.

Tobin, J. (1950), 'A Statistical Demand Function for Food in USA,' *Journal of the Royal Statistical Society, Series A*, 113, 113–141.

Trockel, W. (1984), *Market Demand: An Analysis of Large Economies with Non-convex Preferences.* Springer-Verlag: Berlin.

Tversky, A. and D. Kahneman (1986), 'Rational Choice and the Framing of Decisions,' *Journal of Business*, 59, 251–278.

Tversky, A. and I. Simonson (1993), 'Context-dependent Preferences,' *Management Science*, 39, 1179–1189.

Varian, H. R. (1982), 'The Non-parametric Approach to Demand Analysis,' *Econometrica*, 50, 945–973.

Veblen, T. (1899), *The Theory of the Leisure Class.* Random House: New York.

Veblen, T. (1919), *The Place of Science in Modern Civilization and Other Essays.* Transaction Publishing: New Brunswick, NJ.

Wicklund, R. A. and J. W. Brehm, (1976), *Perspectives on Cognitive Dissonance.* Lawrence Erlbaum: Hillsdale, NJ.

Appendix 1

The basic model of diffusion explains the variation of the number of adopters at time t, i.e. $S_t = \Delta N_t$, as a function of the lagged number of total adopters, i.e. N_{t-1}, and its square, i.e. N_{t-1}^2. However, if we consider subsamples of the

———————— *Demand Dynamics with Socially Evolving Preferences* ————————

TABLE A1

Variable	Coefficient	SE	*t*-value	HCSE	PartR^2	Instability
Constant	−3.3328	1.0740000	−3.103	0.9226700	0.0895	0.06
N_{t-1}	0.0625	0.0064673	9.670	0.0064453	0.4883	0.04
N_{t-1}^2	−0.0001	0.0000072	−8.507	0.0000076	0.4248	0.03

Variables: 3	Var. instab. test: 0.65403*	AR 1–2 $F(2,96) = 0.41165$ [0.6637]
Observations: 101	Joint instab. test: 0.935403	ARCH 1 $F(1,96) = 0.20172$ [0.6543]

$R^2 = 0.53859$	Information criteria:	Normality $\chi^2(2) = 1.4576$ [0.4825]
$F(2,98) = 57.196$ [0.0000]	SC = 2.52722;	$X_i^2\ F(3,94) = 2.2337$ [0.0894]
$\sigma = 3.35397$	HQ = 2.48099;	$X_i*X_j\ F(4,93) = 1.6595$ [0.1661]
DW = 2.14	FPE = 11.5833	RESET $F(1,97) = 3.3138$ [0.0718]
RSS = 1102.414139		

whole observation period (e.g. $t = 200, \ldots, 300$), both a graphical analysis and ADF tests on the order of integration of the above series suggest that N_t and N_t^2 are both I(2), so that S_t turns out to be I(1). It is well known that if we try to estimate a linear regression:

$$S_t = \alpha + \beta N_{t-1} + \gamma N_{t-1}^2 + \varepsilon_t \quad \text{with } \varepsilon_t \approx NI\left(0, \sigma^2\right) \quad \text{(A1.1)}$$

by computing OLS estimates of α, β, γ when the variables involved are not I(0), they no longer have standard asymptotic properties (as normality) and standard significance tests (as the *t*-statistics) are useless. Furthermore, before testing equation (A1.1) with OLS, we should test whether weak exogeneity of N_{t-1} and N_{t-1}^2 for the parameters of interest is fulfilled. Despite these serious econometric problems, we report in Table A1, as an illustration, the outcomes stemming from a crude estimation of the model (A1.1). As already stressed in the text, our principal aim is just to check whether our results match those typically found in the literature although we do not want to infer much from the following analysis.

As one can easily see, the model is well specified (apart from a very low evidence of parameter nonconstancy). The data are well fitted by the chosen linear form and, despite a very low coefficient on N_{t-1}^2, both coefficients of interest are significant with the expected sign.

The above results are also confirmed, albeit not so strongly, for a second model of diffusion, namely:

$$N_t = \alpha' + \beta' C_{t-1} + \gamma' C_{t-1}^2 + \varepsilon_t \quad \text{with } \varepsilon_t \approx NI\left(0, \sigma^2\right) \quad \text{(A1.2)}$$

—————— *Demand Dynamics with Socially Evolving Preferences* ——————

where C_{t-1} is the cumulated number of adopters up to $t-1$ and C_{t-1}^2 is its square. Typically, both C_t and C_{t-1}^2 appear to be $I(3)$ (in the same subsample) so that a crude estimate of (A1.2) displays the same difficulties.

Appendix 2

In order to try to assess the shape of cross-section Engel curves, we have first performed a descriptive analysis of the Working–Leser model:

$$w_j^g = \alpha^g + \beta_t^g \log m_j^g$$

where w_j^g is the budget share of agent j in commodity group g and m_j is total real income (expenditure) of agent j. As for aggregation in commodity groups, we considered two different setups, namely (i) goods are aggregated into the original five groups, $g = 1, \ldots, 5$; and (ii) goods are aggregated into two groups, i.e. $g = \{B,L\}$, where $B = 1 \cup 2$ stands for 'basics' and $L = 4 \cup 5$ stands for 'luxury'. For every commodity group, and for different points in time, we carried out cross-plots of w_j^g versus $(\log m_j^g)$ and we performed both para- metric (OLS) and non-parametric (Kernel) regressions.

As a general pattern (see Figure A1), one is likely to find a low correlation between budget shares and log of income. Despite that, irrespective of the aggregation setup, budget shares and log of individual incomes seem to be correlated with the expected signs [cf. panels (a) and (b) with (c) and (d)]. Moreover, quite in line with the results of Banks *et al.* (1997), nonlinearities appear throughout, suggesting the need for higher-order terms of $\log m_j^g$ in cross-section Engel curves.

We then estimated by standard OLS in both aggregation setups the alternative specifications:

$$M1: \quad w_j^g = \alpha^g + \beta_{1t}^g \log m_j^g + \beta_{2t}^g \left(\log m_j^g\right)^2 + \varepsilon_j^g$$

$$M2: \quad w_j^g = \alpha^g + \beta_t^g \log m_j^g + \varepsilon_j^g$$

Estimation results for an archetypal case [with an aggregation setup as in (ii) above] are reported in Table A2. Although the R^2s for all cross-section regressions are very low, both 'basics' and 'luxury' expenditure shares display non-linearities in the log of income. Tests for autoregressive conditional (ARCH) and income dependent heteroscedasticity (F-test, not reported) failed to find any evidence for heteroscedastic residuals. Nevertheless, functional form misspecification arises in all estimated log-linear models: both the equivalent reset F-test and LM tests—performed to assess whether the

———————————— *Demand Dynamics with Socially Evolving Preferences* ————————————

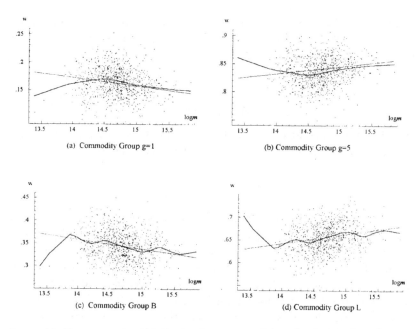

FIGURE A1. Linear regression (thin lines) and nonparametric kernel estimates of Engel curves.

variable (log $m_{j,t}$)² has been omitted—strongly reject the null hypothesis. However, once the square of the log of income is introduced into the regression, no mispecifications are reported, even though the R^2s still remain very low. Finally, further nonlinear terms appear not to be significant in explaining budget shares, as the $X_i \cdot X_j$ F-tests show (see M1 column in Table A2).

Evidence of nonlinearities in Engel curve specifications also arises from the OLS estimation of the log-linear specification:

$$\log C_{j,t}^g = \alpha_t^g + \beta_t^g \log m_{j,t} + \varepsilon_{j,t}^g, \quad \varepsilon_{j,t}^g \approx N(0,\sigma^2) \qquad (A2.1)$$

where $C_{j,t}^g$ is time-t (total) real expenditure of agent i in commodity group g = 1,2, . . .,5, $m_{j,t}$ is real income and $t \in \{200, 250, 300, \ldots, 500\}$. In Figure A2 we show an example (period $t = 500$) of the cross-plots (log $C_{j,t}^g$, log $m_{j,t}$) for each commodity group. The shape of the cross-plots is robust across time and through different levels of aggregation over commodities.

Moreover, in Table A3 we report the results of the comparison of the regression for commodity group 1 ('basics') and that for the aggregate group L (i.e. 'luxury', $g = 4 \cup 5$). Income elasticities are all significant and the R^2 are very high. However, the widespread, strong evidence for functional-form

———————— *Demand Dynamics with Socially Evolving Preferences* ————————

TABLE A2. An Example of OLS Estimation Results of Cross-section Engel Curve Regressions ($t = 500$)

	Model M1: $w_j^g = \alpha_t^g + \beta_{1t}^g \log m_j^g + \beta_{2t}^g(\log m_j^g)^2 + \varepsilon_j^g$		Model M2: $w_j^g = \alpha_t^g + \beta_{1t}^g \log m_j^g + \varepsilon_j^g$	
	Group $g = 1$	Group $L = 4 \cup 5$	Group $g = 1$	Group $L = 4 \cup 5$ +
Estimated coefficients				
Constant				
Est.	−1.8393	3.3321	0.3404	0.4421
σ	0.9944	1.2555	0.0321	0.0405
t	1.850	2.654	10.602	10.903
t-pr	0.0647	0.0081	0.0000	0.0000
$\log m_j{}^g$				
Est.	0.3562	−0.4740	−0.0144	0.0175
σ	0.1691	0.2134	0.0027	0.0034
t	2.107	−2.221	−5.291	5.0691
t-pr	0.0353	0.0266	0.0000	0.0000
$(\log m_j^g)^2$				
Est.	−0.0157	0.0209	–	–
σ	0.0072	0.0091		
t	−2.193	2.303		
t-pr	0.0285	0.0215		
Diagnostics				
R^2	0.1312	0.1303	0.1273	0.1251
F-test	16.455 [0.0000]	15.556 [0.0000]	27.995 [0.0000]	25.696 [0.0000]
σ	0.0244	0.0308	0.0245	0.0309
AR 1–2	1.331 [0.2648]	0.0787 [0.9242]	1.429 [0.2400]	0.0872 [0.9165]
ARCH 1	0.069 [0.7918]	1.8712 [0.1716]	0.117 [0.7323]	1.3868 [0.2392]
Norm. χ^2	1.372 [0.5036]	1.2526 [0.5346]	1.726 [0.4220]	0.9459 [0.6232]
X_i^2	0.076 [0.9896]	0.6426 [0.6322]	0.124 [0.8831]	0.6725 [0.5107]
RESET	0.087 [0.7677]	2.4372 [0.1188]	4.809 [0.0285]**	5.3046 [0.0215]**
X_i*X_j	0.400 [0.8484]	1.3312 [0.2485]	–	–

mispecifications (cf. the large value of the F-test for omitted variables) suggests the incluson of (at least) the square of log of income in the regressions. As to other kind of mispecifications (not reported in Table A4), one often finds evidence for non-normality.

After having introduced the additional explanatory variable $(\log m_{j,t})^2$ in the regression (A2.1), RESET tests fail to display functional form mispecifications—see Table A4. This, however, is not completely true for group 1, suggesting that, after all, the linear specification for 'basic' commodities is not completely wrong (see Banks *et al.*, 1997).

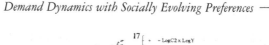

——————— *Demand Dynamics with Socially Evolving Preferences* ———————

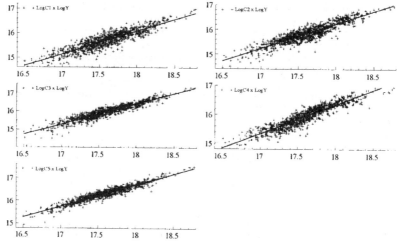

FIGURE A2. Cross-plots of log (C_g) versus log (m) at time $t = 500, g = 1, 2, \ldots, 5$.

TABLE A3. Output of the Regressions: $\log C_{j,t}{}^g = \alpha_t^g + \beta_t^g \log m_{j,t} + \varepsilon_{jt}{}^g$

	α_t^g	β_t^g	SE of β_t^g	t-value $H_0: \beta_t^g = 0$	R^2	LM test for omitted $(\log m_{jt})^2$
Commodity group 1						
$t = 200$	−0.2498	0.8293	0.3847	19.064 [0.0000]**	0.27	7.0917 [0.0079]**
$t = 250$	−0.1628	0.8446	0.0250	33.721 [0.0000]**	0.53	2.1374 [0.1441]
$t = 300$	−0.5754	0.8978	0.0162	55.316 [0.0000]**	0.75	2.2440 [0.1344]
$t = 350$	−1.0496	0.9446	0.0141	66.731 [0.0000]**	0.81	6.8328 [0.0091]**
$t = 400$	−1.0251	0.9461	0.0143	66.359 [0.0000]**	0.82	16.030 [0.0001]**
$t = 450$	−1.0058	0.9474	0.0152	62.354 [0.0000]**	0.80	8.4432 [0.0037]**
$t = 500$	−0.9558	0.9475	0.0149	63.196 [0.0000]**	0.81	3.3934 [0.0822]*
Commodity groups 4 and 5 (aggregated)						
$t = 200$	−0.4585	1.0294	0.0096	107.66 [0.0000]**	0.92	4.7358 [0.0298]*
$t = 250$	−0.4774	1.0277	0.0052	198.02 [0.0000]**	0.97	4.8723 [0.0402]*
$t = 300$	−0.3919	1.0174	0.0033	308.54 [0.0000]**	0.99	4.6806 [0.0307]*
$t = 350$	−0.3400	1.0116	0.0028	356.32 [0.0000]**	0.99	7.0823 [0.0079]**
$t = 400$	−0.3414	1.0110	0.0027	367.72 [0.0000]**	0.99	16.033 [0.0001]**
$t = 450$	−0.3041	1.0081	0.0028	362.38 [0.0000]**	0.99	17.215 [0.0000]**
$t = 500$	−0.3411	1.0098	0.0027	367.92 [0.0000]**	0.99	4.6001 [0.0318]*

The results suggest, first, that nonlinear terms (square of log of income) matter in Engel curve specifications, and, secondly, that Gorman's rank 3 assumption is satisfied by our computer-simulated data. This conjecture is further supported by jointly testing a demand system for four out of the five commodity groups (avoiding singularity of the dependent variables matrix)

———————— *Demand Dynamics with Socially Evolving Preferences* ————————

TABLE A4. Reset Test for Functional Form Specification in the Extended Regression:
$\log C_{j,t}^g = \alpha_t^g + \beta_t^g \log m_{j,t} + (\log m_{j,t})^2 + \varepsilon_{j,t}^g$

Time period	Reset test $F(1,996)$	
	Commodity group 1	Commodity groups 4 and 5 (aggregated)
200	0.37068 [0.5428]	0.29995 [0.5840]
250	0.67287 [0.4122]	0.15043 [0.6982]
300	0.00980 [0.9211]	0.00083 [0.9769]
350	5.95680 [0.0148]*	2.31770 [0.1282]
400	8.50660 [0.0036]**	2.67330 [0.1024]
450	4.76523 [0.0293]*	2.65432 [0.1035]
500	0.15582 [0.6931]	0.89528 [0.3443]

and employing χ^2 statistics to test nonlinear restrictions implied by the determinants of the matrices of estimated parameters (not reported).

Appendix 3

Concerning the estimation of time-series models relating total consumption levels (suitably disaggregated into commodity groups), aggregate income and prices, it is common practice to employ a log-linear specification so as to keep some isomorphism with the correspondent individual functional form widely employed in cross-section analyses.

However, as shown by, among others, Tobin (1950), Stoker (1986), Lewbel (1992), and Anderson and Vahid (1997), aggregation preserves the cross-section functional form purported at the individual level only if some restrictive conditions are satisfied. Among the others, three such necessary conditions for log-linearity to hold in the aggregate (and hence for macro-estimates of consumption–income elasticities to be interpreted as micro ones) are: (i) absence of nonlinear terms (in the log of individual incomes) in cross-section log-linear regressions; (ii) (cross-section) real income distributions must be mean-scaled, i.e. changes in the mean of real income distributions have to be independent of changes in its *relative* distribution;[54] (iii) the errors in the log-linear cross-section regressions must not display income-dependent heteroscedasticity.[55]

[54] More precisely, if $F(m_{h,t}; M_t, \zeta t)$ is the distribution of real income across agents h at time t (where ζt is a vector of parameters and M_t is aggregate real income), then F is 'mean scaled' if: $F(m_{h,t}|M_t, \zeta t) = M_t^{-1} \cdot G'(m_{h,t}/M_t | \zeta t)$, i.e. if changes in the parameters ζt are independent of M_t, cf. Lewbel (1992).

[55] Given the simple cross-section log-linear regression: $\log q_{h,t} = \alpha_t + \beta_t \log m_{h,t} + \varepsilon_{h,t}$, where $q_{h,t}$ is time-t real consumption of agent h, then $\varepsilon_{h,t}$ display income-dependent heteroscedasticity, if for some function κ, we have $\varepsilon_{h,t}|m_{h,t} \sim N(0, \kappa(\log m_{h,t}))$, cf Anderson and Vahid (1997).

———————— *Demand Dynamics with Socially Evolving Preferences* ————————

TABLE A5. Mean Scaling

(a) Correlation coefficients, slopes and t-tests (with related two-tail probabilities) in the linear regression between λ_{qt} and m_t^a

Quantile	Correlation coefficients	Slope	Intercept	t-test (H_0: slope $= 0$)	t-prob
0.05	−0.48434	−0.02701	0.931281	−26.4454	2.87E−30
0.10	−0.49381	−0.0233	0.95172	−29.7429	1.4E−32
0.15	−0.48586	−0.02054	0.965446	−31.2597	1.44E−33
0.20	−0.48467	−0.01792	0.975194	−31.5544	9.4E−34
0.25	−0.50168	−0.01574	0.984421	−36.3622	1.36E−36
0.30	−0.5158	−0.01339	0.990982	−40.8192	6.27E−39
0.35	−0.50572	−0.0109	0.995992	−41.6818	2.36E−39
0.40	−0.5456	−0.00887	1.003407	−54.91	5.55E−45
0.45	−0.57435	−0.00667	1.008879	−43.11	4.88E−40
0.50	−0.64344	−0.00399	1.010857	−22.0775	8.71E−27
0.55	−0.7525	−0.0013	1.014056	−6.10536	1.73E−07
0.60	0.007196	0.001201	1.01882	4.644559	2.67E−05
0.65	0.362836	0.00375	1.024419	11.36428	3.27E−15
0.70	0.356507	0.006315	1.032558	14.48989	3.75E−19
0.75	0.430486	0.009965	1.036768	19.30651	2.87E−24
0.80	0.47293	0.014504	1.038847	23.58233	4.78E−28
0.85	0.500399	0.020081	1.040037	28.57797	8.63E−32
0.90	0.517477	0.029452	1.026954	37.13548	5.12E−37
0.95	0.534887	0.043081	1.015893	48.10711	2.84E−42
1.00	0.551493	0.107345	1.002358	27.31886	6.64E−31

(b) Correlation coefficient, slope and t-test in the linear regression between m_t^a and m_t^g

	Correlation coefficient	Slope	R^2	t-test (H_0: slope $= 0$)	t-prob
Statistics	−0.6008	−1.2629E−09	0.36	−5.1553	4.7404E−06

Following Lewbel (1992), we first tested whether our model is able to generate mean-scaled cross-section real income distributions.[56] The results reported in Table A5 strongly reject mean-scaling. This is in line with the evidence reported by Lewbel (1992) about the income distribution in the US

[56] To that end, we performed two different kinds of computations. First, given a sufficiently long time-period sample T, let s_{qt} be the qth quantile of the distribution of individual real income m_t. Next, define by m_t^a and m_t^g, respectively, the arithmetic and geometric average of the time-t income distribution. Finally, let $\lambda_{qt} = s_{qt}/m_t^a$ and $\omega t = m_t^a/m_t^g$. It is easy to show that the distribution of m_t is mean-scaled if and only if λ_{qt} and m_t^a are independent over time for every q. Moreover, the condition that ω_t and m_t^a are independent over time is necessary for the distribution of m_t to be mean-scaled. In our computations, see Table A5(a), we considered $T = 10, 20, 30, \ldots, 500$ and $q = 0.05, 0.10, \ldots, 0.95$. Second, in order to test the independence over time of the pairs of time-series (λ_{qt}, m_t^a), for every q, and (m_t^a, m_t^g), we performed a t-test on the slope of the related linear regression (after having checked for mispecifications), cf. Table A5(b).

——————— *Demand Dynamics with Socially Evolving Preferences* ———————

Current Population Reports data 1947–83 and allows one to conclude that, even though a log-linear model relating consumption and income is assumed in cross-section regressions, the same specification cannot arise from aggregation. Second, we detected strong evidence of income-dependent heteroscedasticity, which is often present in simulated cross-section data both at different levels of aggregation over commodities (in particular, for 'luxury' goods) and across time (see Table A6).[57]

The foregoing evidence, in addition to that suggesting the presence of nonlinearities in cross-section log-linear models, led us to revert to a more data-driven approach, the goal being the selection of well-specified, time-series VAR (and single-equation) models relating aggregate budget shares (w_t^g) to (some functions of) real total expenditure (m_t) and commodity groups price indices (p_t^g).[58] All five budget shares, as well as real income, appear to be stochastically nonstationary in the selected sample simulation period, i.e. $t = 250, \ldots, 500$ (see also Figure 3[59]). Therefore, all subsequent analyses have been carried out on differences in budget shares and real income. We estimated—both simultaneously and separately—models of the form:

$$\Delta w_t^g = \alpha_0 + \sum_{i=1}^{k} \sum_{g'=1}^{5} \alpha_i^{g'} \Delta w_{t-i}^{g'} + \sum_{j=0}^{n} \beta_j \Delta \log m_{t-j}$$
$$+ \sum_{h=0}^{m} \gamma_h p_{t-j} + [\text{other terms}] + \varepsilon_t^g \qquad (A3.1)$$

As a general result, we get that in the equation for Δw_t^g neither lagged terms of Δw_t^g nor (contemporaneous and lagged) terms of $\Delta w_t^{g'}$, $g' \neq g$, are statistically significant (i.e. $\alpha_i^{g'} = 0$, all i and $g' \neq g$). Therefore, one can revert to a single-equation analysis, since both income and price indices are (weakly

[57] To test for income-dependent heteroscedasticity, we considered the regression: $\log q_{h,t} = \alpha_t + \beta_t \log m_{h,t} + \varepsilon_{h,t}$, and we assumed that $\varepsilon_{h,t} | m_{h,t} \sim N(0, \kappa(\log m_{h,t}))$. Then, we ran an auxiliary regression to test whether the specification: $\kappa(\log m_{h,t}) = \omega_0 + \omega_1 \log m_{h,t} + \omega_2 (\log m_{h,t})^2$ correctly explains the variance of the errors.

[58] In testing VAR specifications, one has to face two important issues. Indeed, our data are characterized by (i) endogeneity of consumption and income (i.e. total expenditure approximately equals total income); and (ii) prices and income are exogenous (independent) stochastic processes, while, of course, the series C_t^g are not, because consumption choices in our model are taken simultaneously. Therefore, one should model together the series $\{w_t^g, g = 1, \ldots, 5\}$ and assume—by (ii) above—weak (and strong) exogeneity of both prices and (log of) income. However, because of the identity between total expenditure and total income, one can only model simultaneously up to four budget shares' series so as to avoid singularity of the matrices involved in the regressions. In the following, we have chosen to model w_t^g for $g = 1, \ldots, 4$ (even though our main results hold irrespective of that choice).

[59] In the model, prices are generated by two alternative data-generating processes (stationary versus non-stationary). The results we present in this section are examples of the case in which price indices are $I(0)$.

———————— *Demand Dynamics with Socially Evolving Preferences* ————————

TABLE A6. χ^2 and F-tests for Income Dependent Heteroscedasticity (Auxiliary Regression: $\varepsilon_{b,t}^g = \omega_0 + \omega_1 \log m_{b,t} + \omega_2 (\log m_{b,t})^2 + v_{b,t}^g$)

Time	Commodity group 1		Commodity groups 4 and 5 (aggregated)	
	χ^2 (2) test	F-form $F(2,995)$	χ^2 (2) test	F-form $F(2,995)$
200	1.4007 [0.4964]	0.6978 [0.4979]	17.030 [0.0002]**	8.6190 [0.0002]**
250	0.1052 [0.9488]	0.0523 [0.9423]	14.965 [0.0006]**	7.5582 [0.0006]**
300	4.0997 [0.1288]	2.0480 [0.1295]	7.826 [0.0199]*	3.901 [0.0202]*
350	3.3612 [0.1863]	1.6778 [0.1873]	5.9344 [0.0514]*	2.9700 [0.0518]*
400	5.9352 [0.0514]*	2.9704 [0.0517]*	5.2625 [0.0720]*	2.6319 [0.0724]*
450	1.4154 [0.4928]	0.7051 [0.4943]	1.7359 [0.4198]	0.8651 [0.4213]
500	8.4578 [0.0146]*	4.2437 [0.0146]*	14.468 [0.0007]**	7.3034 [0.0007]**

and strongly) exogenous for the parameters to be estimated. Following a 'general to specific' modeling strategy, we can in general select preferred models with no mispecifications displaying Engel-type patterns of evolution in the share of different product groups. Our preferred expenditure schedules are of the form:

$$\Delta w_t^g = \alpha_0 + \sum_{i=1}^{k} \alpha_i^g \Delta w_{t-i}^g + \sum_{j=0}^{n} \beta_j \Delta \log m_{t-j}$$
$$+ \sum_{h=0}^{m} \gamma_h p_{t-j} + \varepsilon_t^g$$

(A3.2)

In Table A7, two examples of OLS estimates of (A3.2) are reported for commodity groups 1 and 5. We found significant lagged values for both $\Delta \log m_t$ and p_t very far from time t (even for the lags $t - j, j > 20$), despite our extreme modeling assumptions and the stationarity of the price-generating process.

As to the required dynamic specification, a dynamic analysis of the lag structure generally suggests that the choice of $k \approx 10$, $n \approx 20$ and $m \approx 10$ is the one which optimally trades-off the goodness of fit and correct specification. Solving for the static long-run equations allows us to get statistically significant coefficients which have the 'right' expected sign. Moreover, a Wald test for the joint significance of all the variables (excluding the constant) in the long-run solution (see Table A7) strongly rejects the null hypothesis, suggesting that in the long run (i.e. when the means of the independent variables have remained at a constant level for long enough and the dependent one has reached its long-run solution) the influences of income and prices on budget shares are similar to the empirically observed ones.

———————— *Demand Dynamics with Socially Evolving Preferences* ————————

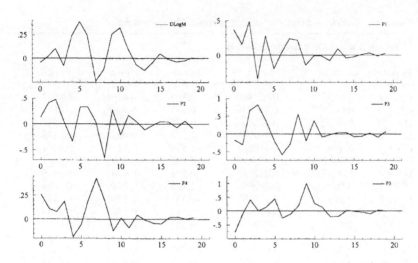

FIGURE A3. Plots of the normalized lag weights (lags $t + 1, t + 2, \ldots$ on the x-axis) for the regression:

$$\Delta w_t^g = \alpha_0 + \sum_{i=1}^{k} \alpha_i^g \Delta w_{t-i}^g + \sum_{j=0}^{n} \beta_j \Delta \log m_{t-j} + \sum_{h=0}^{m} \gamma_h p_{t-j} + \varepsilon_t^g, \quad g = 1$$

However, even after the dynamics has reached its static long-run solution, in the short-run there appear to be a sort of cycles in the response of the change of budget shares to the impulses of a change in (the log of) real income and price indexes. This can be clearly seen if we take a look at the plots of the normalized lag weights (see Figure A3 for an example concerning group 1), which give the responses of the dependent variable at time $t + 1, t + 2$, etc., when one slightly perturbs the level of an explanatory variable at time t.

Tests on other simulation results conducted on the 'version 2' of price dynamics (i.e. price falling along with 'learning curves'), not shown here, show that, while in general Engel-type patterns continue to emerge, prices (both the price index of the group in question and of the others) appear to exert a significantly greater influence of the dynamics of budget shares (up to the fifth lag, and mostly but not always with the expected sign). However, note that, again, this should be considered as an emergent property which does not bear any isomorphism with microscopic behavior: in fact, by construction, individual agents either have unit price elasticities when acting 'business-as-usual' or do not look at all at prices when imitating or innovating—except insofar as prices affect budget constraints. Indeed, what appears in the aggregate as the dynamic influence of prices upon shares rests in fact on the process by

———————— *Demand Dynamics with Socially Evolving Preferences* ————————

TABLE A7. Estimation Results for Budget Shares of Groups 1 and 5

Modelling ΔW^1 by OLS; sample: 250–491

Variable	Coefficient	SE	t-value	t-prob	PartR^2
Constant	0.014399	0.017400	0.828	0.4091	0.0041
DW1_1	0.067477	0.080796	0.835	0.4048	0.0042
DW1_2	0.072266	0.078136	0.925	0.3564	0.0052
DW1_3	−0.13778	0.079565	−1.732	0.0852	0.0178
DW1_4	−0.12425	0.078185	−1.589	0.1139	0.0151
DW1_5	0.0081782	0.079610	0.103	0.9183	0.0001
DW1_6	0.041917	0.081683	0.513	0.6085	0.0016
DW1_7	−0.093529	0.079630	−1.175	0.2419	0.0083
DW1_8	−0.11975	0.077689	−1.541	0.1251	0.0142
DW1_9	0.11576	0.076248	1.518	0.1309	0.0138
DW1_10	−0.037119	0.077013	−0.482	0.6305	0.0014
DLog m	−0.0079119	0.034163	−0.232	0.8171	0.0003
DLogm_1	0.0055317	0.034025	0.163	0.8711	0.0002
DLogm_2	0.020731	0.033492	0.619	0.5368	0.0023
DLogm_3	−0.018563	0.034391	−0.540	0.5901	0.0018
DLogm_4	0.045341	0.034535	1.313	0.1910	0.0103
DLogm_5	0.077241	0.034523	2.237	0.0266	0.0294
DLogm_6	0.039277	0.035487	1.107	0.2700	0.0074
DLogm_7	−0.051060	0.034684	−1.472	0.1429	0.0130
DLogm_8	−0.0069982	0.035748	−0.196	0.8450	0.0002
DLogm_9	0.074726	0.034452	2.169	0.0315	0.0277
DLogm_10	0.057994	0.034924	1.661	0.0987	0.0164
P1	−0.0040681	0.0022155	−1.836	0.0681	0.0200
P1_1	−0.0014405	0.0022903	−0.629	0.5303	0.0024
P1_2	−0.0049606	0.0023072	−2.150	0.0330	0.0273
P1_3	0.0038150	0.0023237	1.642	0.1025	0.0161
P1_4	−0.0037049	0.0023212	−1.596	0.1124	0.0152
P1_5	0.0012277	0.0023123	0.531	0.5962	0.0017
P1_6	−0.00018341	0.0023001	−0.080	0.9365	0.0000
P1_7	−0.0029585	0.0023352	−1.267	0.2070	0.0096
P1_8	−0.0027406	0.0024003	−1.142	0.2552	0.0078
P1_9	0.0018748	0.0023725	0.790	0.4305	0.0038
P1_10	−0.00032785	0.0023565	−0.139	0.8895	0.0001
P2	0.00085988	0.0022112	0.389	0.6979	0.0009
P2_1	0.0026362	0.0021606	1.220	0.2242	0.0089
P2_2	0.0028655	0.0022212	1.290	0.1988	0.0100
P2_3	−3.1874e−005	0.0022014	−0.014	0.9885	0.0000
P2_4	−0.0019596	0.0022060	−0.888	0.3757	0.0048
P2_5	0.0030341	0.0022523	1.347	0.1798	0.0109
P2_6	0.0025096	0.0022884	1.097	0.2744	0.0072
P2_7	−0.00037745	0.0022475	−0.168	0.8668	0.0002
P2_8	−0.0041533	0.0022574	−1.840	0.0676	0.0201
P2_9	0.0031807	0.0022966	1.385	0.1679	0.0115

———————— *Demand Dynamics with Socially Evolving Preferences* ————————

TABLE A7. *Continued*

Modelling ΔW^1 by OLS; sample: 250–491

Variable	Coefficient	SE	t-value	t-prob	PartR^2
P2_10	−0.00064465	0.0022645	−0.285	0.7762	0.0005
P3	−0.00075375	0.0021648	−0.348	0.7281	0.0007
P3_1	−0.0012626	0.0020942	−0.603	0.5474	0.0022
P3_2	0.0031266	0.0021020	1.487	0.1388	0.0132
P3_3	0.0034611	0.0021262	1.628	0.1055	0.0158
P3_4	0.00095185	0.0021348	0.446	0.6563	0.0012
P3_5	−0.0010036	0.0020987	−0.478	0.6331	0.0014
P3_6	−0.0017712	0.0020423	−0.867	0.3871	0.0045
P3_7	−0.00038312	0.0020183	−0.190	0.8497	0.0002
P3_8	0.0025405	0.0020090	1.265	0.2078	0.0096
P3_9	−0.0013308	0.0019754	−0.674	0.5015	0.0027
P3_10	0.0018484	0.0020330	0.909	0.3646	0.0050
P4	−0.0032225	0.0019425	−1.659	0.0990	0.0164
P4_1	−0.0011197	0.0019668	−0.569	0.5699	0.0020
P4_2	−0.00061173	0.0019426	−0.315	0.7532	0.0006
P4_3	−0.0026184	0.0019550	−1.339	0.1823	0.0108
P4_4	0.0019880	0.0019309	1.030	0.3047	0.0064
P4_5	0.00047779	0.0018993	0.252	0.8017	0.0004
P4_6	−0.0029956	0.0019146	−1.565	0.1196	0.0146
P4_7	−0.0054100	0.0019310	−2.802	0.0057	0.0454
P4_8	−0.0020209	0.0019950	−1.013	0.3126	0.0062
P4_9	0.0020014	0.0019600	1.021	0.3087	0.0063
P4_10	−0.0015133	0.0019722	−0.767	0.4440	0.0036
P5	0.0040710	0.0024694	1.649	0.1011	0.0162
P5_1	0.00015334	0.0025030	0.061	0.9512	0.0000
P5_2	−0.0025588	0.0024199	−1.057	0.2919	0.0067
P5_3	0.00064062	0.0023429	0.273	0.7849	0.0005
P5_4	−7.1316e−005	0.0023095	−0.031	0.9754	0.0000
P5_5	−0.0026849	0.0023655	−1.135	0.2580	0.0077
P5_6	0.0010634	0.0022633	0.470	0.6391	0.0013
P5_7	0.00091247	0.0022652	0.403	0.6876	0.0010
P5_8	−0.00093153	0.0022951	−0.406	0.6854	0.0010
P5_9	−0.0060717	0.0023336	−2.602	0.0101	0.0394
P5_10	−0.00094319	0.0024006	−0.393	0.6949	0.0009

$R^2 = 0.374521$; $F(76,165) = 1.3$ [0.0839]; $\sigma = 0.000248291$; DW = 1.98
RSS = 1.017200123E−005 for 77 variables and 242 observations

AR 1-2 $F(2,163) = 1.1594$ [0.3162]
ARCH 1 $F(1,163) = 0.32107$ [0.5717]
Normality $\chi^2(2) = 3.053$ [0.2173]
X_i^2 $F(152,12) = 0.13954$ [1.0000]
RESET $F(1,164) = 1.0579$ [0.3052]

───────────── *Demand Dynamics with Socially Evolving Preferences* ─────────────

TABLE A7. *Continued*

Solved static long-run equation (SE in parentheses)

$$\Delta W^1 = \quad +0.01193 \qquad -0.1958\Delta logm \qquad -0.01116P^1$$
$$(0.01485) \qquad\quad (0.09559) \qquad\quad (0.006759$$

$$+0.006562P^2 \qquad +0.004494P^3 \qquad -0.01247P^4$$
$$(0.005806) \qquad\quad (0.005267) \qquad\quad (0.006793)$$

$$-0.00532P^5$$
$$(0.007467)$$

Wald test on the joint significance of the regressors in the static long-run equation:
$\chi^2(6) = 12.14 \; [0.0589]*$

Modelling ΔW^5 by OLS; sample: 250–491

Variable	Coefficient	SE	t-value	t-prob	PartR^2
DW5_1	−0.082185	0.077074	−1.066	0.2878	0.0068
DW5_2	0.071646	0.076488	0.937	0.3503	0.0053
DW5_3	−0.0096307	0.077876	−0.124	0.9017	0.0001
DW5_4	0.055801	0.077361	0.721	0.4717	0.0031
DW5_5	0.033120	0.078369	0.423	0.6731	0.0011
DW5_6	−0.051880	0.076937	−0.674	0.5011	0.0027
DW5_7	−0.035467	0.076054	−0.466	0.6416	0.0013
DW5_8	0.00098872	0.076691	0.013	0.9897	0.0000
DW5_9	−0.12282	0.075094	−1.636	0.1038	0.0159
DW5_10	0.022530	0.075979	0.297	0.7672	0.0005
DLog m	0.012063	0.047117	0.256	0.7983	0.0004
DLogm_1	0.030212	0.046187	0.654	0.5139	0.0026
DLogm_2	−0.043489	0.046183	−0.942	0.3477	0.0053
DLogm_3	−0.036847	0.047890	−0.769	0.4427	0.0036
DLogm_4	0.029431	0.047730	0.617	0.5383	0.0023
DLogm_5	0.079272	0.048522	1.634	0.1042	0.0158
DLogm_6	−0.036480	0.048421	−0.753	0.4523	0.0034
DLogm_7	0.050134	0.047122	1.064	0.2889	0.0068
DLogm_8	−0.024313	0.047179	−0.515	0.6070	0.0016
DLogm_9	0.010077	0.046147	0.218	0.8274	0.0003
DLogm_10	−0.041547	0.046244	−0.898	0.3703	0.0048
P1	−0.0027548	0.0029610	−0.930	0.3535	0.0052
P1_1	0.0026985	0.0029956	0.901	0.3690	0.0049
P1_2	0.0036776	0.0030099	1.222	0.2235	0.0089
P1_3	0.0013651	0.0030325	0.450	0.6532	0.0012
P1_4	0.0011860	0.0030519	0.389	0.6981	0.0009
P1_5	−0.0055964	0.0030561	−1.831	0.0689	0.0198
P1_6	0.0025663	0.0030818	0.833	0.4062	0.0042
P1_7	0.00062041	0.0030890	0.201	0.8411	0.0002
P1_8	0.0017759	0.0031212	0.569	0.5701	0.0019
P1_9	−0.00069218	0.0031232	−0.222	0.8249	0.0003

―――――――― *Demand Dynamics with Socially Evolving Preferences* ――――――――

TABLE A7. *Continued*

Modelling ΔW^5 by OLS; sample: 250–491

Variable	Coefficient	SE	*t*-value	*t*-prob	PartR^2
P1_10	0.00086999	0.0030791	0.283	0.7779	0.0005
P2	−0.0032273	0.0030453	−1.060	0.2908	0.0067
P2_1	−0.0023747	0.0029514	−0.805	0.4222	0.0039
P2_2	0.0010171	0.0029625	0.343	0.7318	0.0007
P2_3	−0.0036754	0.0029815	−1.233	0.2194	0.0091
P2_4	0.0021103	0.0030270	0.697	0.4867	0.0029
P2_5	−0.0048765	0.0031438	−1.551	0.1228	0.0143
P2_6	1.3506e−005	0.0032066	0.004	0.9966	0.0000
P2_7	−0.0033518	0.0031482	−1.065	0.2886	0.0068
P2_8	−0.0040231	0.0031632	−1.272	0.2052	0.0097
P2_9	0.00076303	0.0031769	0.240	0.8105	0.0003
P2_10	−0.0020661	0.0030912	−0.668	0.5048	0.0027
P3	0.0015409	0.0029322	0.525	0.5999	0.0017
P3_1	0.0028598	0.0027970	1.022	0.3081	0.0063
P3_2	0.0029338	0.0027934	1.050	0.2951	0.0066
P3_3	0.0018003	0.0028435	0.633	0.5275	0.0024
P3_4	−0.0041426	0.0028621	−1.447	0.1497	0.0125
P3_5	−0.00081055	0.0028010	−0.289	0.7726	0.0005
P3_6	−0.0031370	0.0027469	−1.142	0.2551	0.0078
P3_7	−0.0016872	0.0028079	−0.601	0.5487	0.0022
P3_8	−0.0026356	0.0027974	−0.942	0.3475	0.0053
P3_9	0.0059293	0.0027877	2.127	0.0349	0.0265
P3_10	−0.0030227	0.0028883	−1.047	0.2968	0.0066
P4	−0.00096590	0.0025289	−0.382	0.7030	0.0009
P4_1	0.0020119	0.0025429	0.791	0.4300	0.0038
P4_2	0.0061854	0.0025650	2.411	0.0170	0.0338
P4_3	0.0027090	0.0026503	1.022	0.3082	0.0063
P4_4	−0.0015558	0.0026208	−0.594	0.5536	0.0021
P4_5	0.0023941	0.0026267	0.911	0.3634	0.0050
P4_6	0.0010877	0.0026446	0.411	0.6814	0.0010
P4_7	0.00078059	0.0026301	0.297	0.7670	0.0005
P4_8	0.0020296	0.0026642	0.762	0.4473	0.0035
P4_9	−0.0030548	0.0026582	−1.149	0.2521	0.0079
P4_10	0.0030617	0.0026875	1.139	0.2563	0.0078
P5	0.0012626	0.0033587	0.376	0.7075	0.0009
P5_1	−0.0030755	0.0033403	−0.921	0.3585	0.0051
P5_2	0.0032968	0.0032282	1.021	0.3086	0.0062
P5_3	−0.00097235	0.0031370	−0.310	0.7570	0.0006
P5_4	0.0029049	0.0030984	0.938	0.3498	0.0053
P5_5	−0.0044821	0.0031865	−1.407	0.1614	0.0118
P5_6	0.0011213	0.0031122	0.360	0.7191	0.0008
P5_7	0.00068764	0.0030605	0.225	0.8225	0.0003

————————— *Demand Dynamics with Socially Evolving Preferences* —————————

TABLE A7. *Continued*

Modelling ΔW^5 by OLS; sample: 250–491

Variable	Coefficient	SE	*t*-value	*t*-prob	PartR^2
P5_8	−0.0017455	0.0030233	−0.577	0.5645	0.0020
P5_9	0.00081573	0.0030821	0.265	0.7916	0.0004
P5_10	−0.00097498	0.0031339	−0.311	0.7561	0.0006

$R^2 = 0.346397$; $\sigma = 0.000343694$
DW $= 1.99$RSS $= 1.960882911E$–005 for 76 variables and 242 observations

AR 1–2 $F(2,164) = 0.077785$ [0.9252]
ARCH 1 $F(1,164) = 1.4758$ [0.2262]
Normality $\chi^2(2) = 0.9086$ [0.6349]
X_i^2 $F(152,13) = 0.085042$ [1.0000]
RESET $F(1,165) = 0.23458$ [0.6288]

Solved static long-run equation (SE in parentheses)
$\Delta W^5 = \quad +0.02551\Delta logm \quad +0.005113P^1 \quad -0.01761P^2$
$\qquad\qquad$ (0.1359) $\qquad$ (0.008066) $\qquad$ (0.007964)

$\qquad\qquad -0.0003325P^3 \quad +0.01313P^4 \quad -0.001039P^5$
$\qquad\qquad$ (0.007537) $\qquad$ (0.008583) $\qquad$ (0.0095)

Wald test on the joint significance of the regressors in the static long-run equation:
$\chi^2(6) = 20.006$ [0.0028]**

which the fall in the former helps relaxing budget constraints (a sort of dynamic version of an income effect) and that in turn makes innovation, imitation and fulfillment of 'frustrated' options easier.

Appendix 4

As already mentioned in the text, Hildenbrand (1994) establishes sufficient conditions under which the Wald Axiom and the Law of Demand hold.

Let us start with the Wald Axiom and define $\upsilon(p|x)$ as the (observable) distribution of the x-households' demand, where by x-household we mean a 'household with income x'. Each household is completely characterized by: (i) the short-run demand function f; (ii) the current level of the disposable income x. Hence, the market demand function $F(p)$ is defined as the mean of individual demand functions f with respect to the distribution μ of the space of the households' characteristics (f,x). Moreover, let the (cross-sectional) demand function $\bar{f}(p,x)$ be the mean of the individual demand functions f with

──────── *Demand Dynamics with Socially Evolving Preferences* ────────

respect to the conditional distribution $\mu \,|\, x$. Finally, let the income distribution be given by $\rho(x)$ and define $\upsilon(p) = \upsilon(p \,|\, x)\rho(x)$.

Hypothesis 1* **(increasing dispersion of x-households' demand):** The (unobservable) distribution $\widetilde{\upsilon}(x + \Delta, x, p)$ (i.e. the distribution of x-households' demand under the hypothesis that their income were $x + \Delta$) is more 'dispersed' than the distribution $\widetilde{\upsilon}(x,x,p) = \upsilon(p \,|\, x)$, all $\Delta > 0$, in the sense that the matrix

$$\widetilde{C}_{1*}(\Delta, x) = \left[\operatorname{cov}\widetilde{\upsilon}(x + \Delta, x, p) - \operatorname{cov}\upsilon(p \,|\, x)\right]$$

is positive semi-definite for all $\Delta > 0$, all x.

Hypothesis 1 (average increasing dispersion of x-households' demand): The matrix

$$\widetilde{C}_1(\Delta) = \int \left[\operatorname{cov}\widetilde{\upsilon}(x + \Delta, x, p) - \operatorname{cov}\upsilon(p \,|\, x)\right]\rho(x)\,dx$$

is positive semi-definite for all $\Delta > 0$.

Hypothesis 2 (increasing dispersion of all households' demand): For all directions υ orthogonal to the market demand $F(p)$, the unobservable distribution $\widetilde{\upsilon}(\Delta,p)$, obtained assuming that the income of every household is increased by $\Delta > 0$, is more dispersed that the (observable) distribution $\upsilon(p)$ for all $\Delta > 0$, in the sense that the matrix

$$\widetilde{C}_2(\Delta) = \left[\operatorname{cov}\widetilde{\upsilon}(\Delta, p) - \operatorname{cov}\upsilon(p)\right]$$

is positive semi-definite, all $\Delta > 0$.

Under standard assumptions on the distribution μ, Hildenbrand (1994) shows that if Hypothesis 1* (respectively Hypothesis 2) is fulfilled, then $\widetilde{f}(p,x)$ [respectively the demand function $F(p)$] satisfies the Wald Axiom. Under an additional regularity condition (see p. 86), Hypothesis 1 implies that the demand function $F(p)$ satisfies the strict version of the Wald Axiom.

Clearly, the above hypotheses are not empirically verifiable, since the distributions denoted by $\widetilde{\upsilon}$ are not observable. However, they can be easily replaced by observable proxies of them, allowing to formulate empirical counterparts of Hypotheses 1*, 1 and 2, namely:

Property 1* **(increasing dispersion of conditional demand):** The

──────── 405 ────────

———————— *Demand Dynamics with Socially Evolving Preferences* ————————

conditional distribution $\upsilon(p|x)$ is increasing in all x such that $\rho(x) > 0$, i.e. the matrix

$$C_{1*}(\Delta,x) = \left[\operatorname{cov}\upsilon(p|x+\Delta) - \operatorname{cov}\upsilon(p|x)\right]$$

is positive semi-definite for all $\Delta > 0$, all x: $\rho(x) > 0$.

Property 1 (average increasing dispersion of conditional demand): The matrix

$$C_1(\Delta) = \int\left[\operatorname{cov}\upsilon(p|x+\Delta) - \operatorname{cov}\upsilon(p|x)\right]\rho(x)dx$$

is positive semi-definite for all $\Delta > 0$.

Property 2 The Δ-shift of the distribution $\upsilon(p)$—denoted by $\upsilon(p,\Delta)$ and obtained from the (observable) distribution $\upsilon(p) = \upsilon(p|x)\rho(x)$ replacing $\rho(x)$ by $\rho(x-\Delta)$—is more dispersed than the distribution $\upsilon(p)$, all $\Delta > 0$, in the sense that the matrix

$$C_2(\Delta) = \left[\operatorname{cov}\upsilon(\rho,\Delta) - \operatorname{cov}\upsilon(p)\right]$$

is positive semi-definite for all $\Delta > 0$.

Hildenbrand (1994) shows that, if the demand behaviour of the x-households is sufficiently homogeneous (i.e. they satisfy the property called 'conditional covariance metonymy', see p. 116), Properties 1*, 1 and 2 imply the corresponding hypotheses above.

 The matrices $C_i(\Delta)$, $i = 1*, 1, 2$ involved in the above properties can be easily computed using the outcomes of our model (see Section 4). In particular, consider $g = 5$ product groups, $x = 1, \ldots, 8$ income classes (obtained by aggregating the initial 20 classes) and discrete shifts $\Delta = 1, \ldots, 7$. Note that all the following results refer to a period well down the road of our simulation histories ($t = 500$), in order to let the mechanisms of innovation, imitation, income differentiation, etc., work their way through. For convenience, the positive semi-definiteness of C_i matrices (which are 5×5) is checked by computing their five principal minors instead of their smallest eigenvalue. We report here only the results coming from a 'representative' simulation, with stationary prices and a small probability of innovation. Some preliminary Monte Carlo-type studies about the robustness of the outcomes and 'response surfaces' analyses have been carried out, with encouraging results throughout.

 In Table A8 the kind of definiteness of the matrices $C_i(\Delta,x)$, $x = 1, \ldots, 8$ and $\Delta = 1, \ldots, 7$ is reported. Apart from negative definite matrices for the

———————————————— 406 ————————————————

—————————— Demand Dynamics with Socially Evolving Preferences ——————————

TABLE A8. Definiteness of Matrices $C_{1*}(\Delta,x)$: Property 1*

Income class	$\Delta = 1$	$\Delta = 2$	$\Delta = 3$	$\Delta = 4$	$\Delta = 5$	$\Delta = 6$	$\Delta = 7$	Income distribution
1	–	–	–	–	–	–	–	0.106
2	POS	–	–	–	–	–	–	0.422
3	POS	POS	–	–	–	–	–	0.262
4	POS	POS	POS	–	–	–	–	0.141
5	POS	POS	POS	POS	–	–	–	0.055
6	?	?	POS	POS	POS	–	–	0.011
7	NEG	NEG	NEG	NEG	NEG	NEG	–	0.002
8	?	NEG	NEG	NEG	NEG	NEG	NEG	0.001

TABLE A9. Principal Minors of the matrices $C_1(\Delta)$: Property 1

Minors	$\Delta = 1$	$\Delta = 2$	$\Delta = 3$	$\Delta = 4$
1st	2.97E+11	6.08E+11	8.64E+11	6.06E+11
2nd	1.28E+21	4.46E+21	8.89E+21	3.17E+21
3rd	9.8E+30	6.81E+31	1.84E+32	3.13E+31
4th	9.53E+40	1.34E+42	5.06E+42	3.04E+41
5th	2.71E+50	6.69E+51	2.29E+52	6.09E+50

TABLE A10. The Matrix $C_2(1)$ and its Principal Minors

Matrix					Principal minors
1.72E+10	5.48E+09	5.7E+09	6.69E+09	5.17E+09	1.72E+10
5.48E+09	1.82E+09	1.89E+09	2.26E+09	1.82E+09	1.23E+18
5.7E+09	1.89E+09	2E+09	2.31E+09	1.87E+09	4.04E+25
6.69E+09	2.26E+09	2.31E+09	2.92E+09	2.35E+09	2.85E+33
5.17E+09	1.82E+09	1.87E+09	2.35E+09	1.99E+09	7.43E+40

income classes where $\rho(x) \approx 0$ (not to be considered, see Property 1*), we can conclude that the (cross-section) demand function $\tilde{f}(p,x)$ generated by the model satisfy the Wald Axiom in the weak form.

Moreover, Table A9 shows that the market demand function $F(p)$ also satisfies the Wald Axiom in the weak form, since at least for $\Delta = 1,2,3,4$ the matrices $C_1(\Delta)$ are positive definite. Finally, Table A10 reports the matrix $C_2(\Delta)$ for $\Delta = 1$ and its principal minors. Again, Property 2 and consequently

──────── *Demand Dynamics with Socially Evolving Preferences* ────────

TABLE A11. The Matrix $C_3(1)$ and its Principal Minors

Matrix					Principal minors
7.14E+10	2.86E+10	2.64E+10	2.88E+10	2.89E+10	7.14E+10
2.86E+10	1.17E+10	1.07E+10	1.17E+10	1.2E+10	1.74E+19
2.64E+10	1.07E+10	9.86E+09	1.07E+10	1.09E+10	7.34E+26
2.88E+10	1.17E+10	1.07E+10	1.18E+10	1.2E+10	1.43E+35
2.89E+10	1.2E+10	1.09E+10	1.2E+10	1.24E+10	−2.3E+43

Hypothesis 2 are satisfied, so that the market demand function $F(p)$ satisfies the Wald Axiom also in its strong form.

Let us turn now to the Law of Demand. The corresponding hypothesis involves the second moments matrices (denoted by m^2) of the distributions υ. More precisely:

Hypothesis 3 (increasing spread of household demand): The unobservable distribution $\widetilde{\upsilon}(\Delta,p)$, obtained assuming that the income of every household is increased by $\Delta > 0$, is more spread than the (observable) distribution $\upsilon(p)$ for all $\Delta > 0$, in the sense that the matrix

$$\widetilde{C}_3(\Delta) = \left[m^2 \widetilde{\upsilon}(\Delta, p) - m^2 \upsilon(p) \right]$$

is positive semi-definite for all $\Delta > 0$.

The empirical counterpart of the latter is given by:

Property 3 (average increasing spread of conditional demand): The observable distribution $\upsilon(\Delta,p)$ is more 'spread' than the distribution $\upsilon(p)$ for all $\Delta > 0$, in the sense that the matrix

$$C_3(\Delta) = \left[m^2 \upsilon(\Delta, p) - m^2 \upsilon(p) \right]$$

is positive semi-definite, all $\Delta > 0$.

Again, we computed the matrix $C_3(1)$ for our 'benchmark' simulation and it turns out to be positive definite, as the principal minors show (see Table A11). Hence, we can conclude that the market demand $F(p)$ satisfies the Law of Demand.

[8]

ELSEVIER Simulation Modelling Practice and Theory 10 (2002) 321–347

www.elsevier.com/locate/simpat

Adaptive learning and emergent coordination in minority games [☆]

G. Bottazzi [a], G. Devetag [b], G. Dosi [a,*]

[a] *S. Anna School of Advanced Studies, via G. Carducci, 40 Pisa, Italy*
[b] *Department of Management and Computer Science, University of Trento via Inama, 5-38100 Trento, Italy*

Received 1 August 2001; received in revised form 1 March 2002; accepted 22 May 2002

Abstract

This work studies the properties of a coordination game in which agents repeatedly compete to be in the population minority. The game reflects some essential features of those economic situations in which positive rewards are assigned to individuals who behave in opposition to the modal behavior in a population. In this work we model a large group of agents who repeatedly interact in the game and we investigate the extent to which the system medium and long-run efficiency properties depend upon the specification of the agents' micro-behaviors in terms of their degree of rationality, the amount of information they use in making their choices, their learning patterns and the level of heterogeneity in the population. Our results show that, first, the system long-run properties strongly depend on the particular behavioral assumptions adopted, and, second, adding noise at the individual decision level and hence increasing heterogeneity in the population substantially improve aggregate welfare, although at the expense of a longer adjustment phase. In fact, the system achieves in that way a higher level of efficiency compared to that attainable by perfectly rational and completely informed agents.
© 2002 Elsevier Science B.V. All rights reserved.

Keywords: Minority game; Coordination; Heterogeneity; Adaptive learning; Efficiency; Emergent properties

[☆] Comments on a previous drafts by Buz Brock, Nicolas Fernando Garrido, Cars Hommes, Nicolas Jonard, Sid Winter and four anonymous referees are gratefully acknowledged.

[*] Corresponding author. Address: Scuola Superiore Sant'Anna, Piazza dei Martiri della Liberta 33, 56127 Pisa, Italy. Tel.: +39-050-883326; fax: +39-050-883343/4.
E-mail address: gdosi@sssup.it (G. Dosi).

1569-190X/02/$ - see front matter © 2002 Elsevier Science B.V. All rights reserved.
PII: S1569-190X(02)00086-2

322   *G. Bottazzi et al. / Simulation Modelling Practice and Theory 10 (2002) 321–347*

1. Introduction

One of the central topics of economic analysis since its origins has concerned the properties of coordination processes amongst multiple heterogeneous agents who can take, so to speak, "opposite sides" in an interaction mechanism [1]. In turn "opposite sides" might concern e.g. entering or not a market, buying or selling, or, somewhat more metaphorically, choosing between externality-ridden locations. In the following we shall take a fresh look at such coordination issues, with the help of a simple but suggestive formal apparatus, namely "minority games".

A minority game [2,3] is a repeated game in which a group of N agents (with N odd in order to avoid ties) must choose—autonomously from each other—one out of two alternatives (say 0 and 1) at each time step. Those who happen to be in the minority win a fixed positive reward, while agents belonging to the majority obtain a null payoff. [1] Despite its apparent simplicity, the game offers quite a number of interesting features for the analysis of interaction mechanisms in which a number of agents must autonomously make decisions about activities whose payoffs depend on other agents' decisions. Restated differently, agents' choices are assumed to be taken independently and in a fully decentralized manner, while outcomes of these choices are dependent upon the distribution of choices themselves in the population: hence a basic problem of coordination.

Although traditional game theory offers simple solutions to the game in case of hypothetical, hyper-rational players, if one assumes that agents are only limitedly rational, the degree of heterogeneity in their choice behavior becomes a key feature in determining the overall degree of coordination. In fact, it is straightforward to see that if all players analyze the situation in the same way, they all will choose the same alternative and lose. Therefore, intuitively, the more heterogeneous players are, the more efficient the resulting aggregate outcome is likely to be.

Formally, the model is an N-person non-cooperative game with multiple asymmetric Nash equilibria in pure strategies, i.e., mutual best response outcomes in which agents differentiate from one another on the basis of the side chosen, and a unique symmetric equilibrium in mixed strategies, requiring that all agents pick the two sides with equal probability. In the following, we assume a large population, and we study the aggregate properties of interaction under different degrees of heterogeneity in the population and different learning procedures.

The game, in its outmost simplicity, is a stylized representation of several processes of social and economic interaction whereby agents compete for limited resources. The choice between the two sides can be interpreted as a choice between, say, entering or not a given market, undertaking or not a certain activity and in general, all those choice situations in which a positive payoff from choosing a given course of action occurs only insofar as the number of agents picking the same action does not exceed a certain threshold value. From a game-theoretic stand point, these

---

[1] For a large collection of papers concerning both the analytical and numerical explorations of the original minority game and various extensions see also http://www.unifr.ch/econophysics/.

games present a multiplicity of equilibria, which makes it natural to ask whether certain equilibria, if any, are more likely than others to emerge in the medium and long run. From the broader point of view of economics, the interesting question to address is whether and under what conditions the interaction of beliefs and behavior at the microlevel is likely to produce efficient patterns of interaction at the aggregate level.

Coordination problems of this kind had first been discussed in Schelling's seminal work on those patterns of "sorting and mixing" where order at an aggregate level finds its roots in persistent micro adjustments within heterogeneous populations [1]. In these examples, dynamics of agglomeration, congestion and separation across populations might be driven by factors such as income or race.

Another seminal contribution is the famous "El Farol" Problem devised by Brian Arthur in [4]. In this game, a number of agents must independently decide each night whether or not to attend a bar called "El Farol". Each agent receives a positive utility from attending the bar as long as this is not too crowded. Otherwise it prefers to stay at home. Arthur was especially interested in investigating if, and to what extent, aggregate coordination emerges out of a population of agents acting on the basis of the above described preferences and of experience-based, heterogeneous beliefs.

Highly similar problems have been extensively investigated within the experimental economics literature, usually going under the heading of 'market entry games' (e.g., [5–7] and references therein). In these games, a group of N players must repeatedly and autonomously decide whether or not to enter one or more markets each having a fixed capacity k, with $k < N$. It is generally assumed that entrants receive a positive profit—often declining with their number—up to a capacity threshold, beyond which the incentive to enter disappears (Non-entrants may or may not receive a fixed positive payoff from their choice). If too many people enter the market, they all suffer losses, while if too few people enter, opportunities for gain are left unexploited; therefore, aggregate efficiency is maximal when the average number of entrants equals market capacity, which corresponds to the outcome occurring at any of the games' Nash equilibria.

Several variations of the basic 'market-entry' setup have been studied experimentally; most of them involve changes in the payoff function, which in turn imply different long-run stability properties of the resulting pure strategy equilibria (for a discussion see e.g. [8]). Interestingly, the experimental evidence gathered so far appears mostly inconsistent with equilibrium predictions both at the aggregate and at the individual level, while revealing a high and persistent degree of heterogeneity among players' beliefs and behavior (see also [9–11]). Further, players' individual behavior, and consequently patterns of equilibrium selection, seem largely influenced by the choice of the particular game parameters. [2]

---

[2] Incidentally note that minority games (MG) may be considered as a sort of extreme form of entry game characterized by very unstable equilibrium configurations, i.e., configurations which can be easily disrupted by the behavior of a deviant minority.

Finally, the minority games captures some basic features of speculation on financial markets—which has been indeed the primary concern of minority-game modeling so far. A classic reference in this respect is to Keynes' "Beauty Contest" metaphor, where the payoff to an individual player does not stem from the accuracy of the appreciation of the intrinsic beauty of various contest candidates but rather from guessing the guesses of the ensemble of the other evaluators.

Strictly speaking, the beauty contest metaphor crucially involves *positive feedback* investment strategies—in the language of technical trading in finance—since the payoff is based on a majority rule, while MG fundamentally address those aspects of speculation dynamics involving activities of *arbitrage against* average market behaviors. These *negative feedback* strategies characterize agents trying to infer some— actual or imagined—structure in the history of collective interactions and, through that, trying to "beat the market"—that is, "beat the majority view"—by arbitraging against it. In the literature on chartist rules, this roughly corresponds to *contrarian strategies* (in the behavioral finance literature see e.g. [12]).

Throughout our analysis, we will tackle the following basic research question: in this class of interactions is the system's level of efficiency dependent on the specification of the agents' microbehaviors? In particular, what is the relevance of factors such as the amount of information that agents hold regarding the game history, their degree of inertia in responding to new information, their learning patterns and finally the degree of population heterogeneity in determining the overall efficiency of the resulting coordination patterns?

Here, the MG framework is taken as a bare-bone instantiation of the underlying problem of coordination of decentralized and interdependent decisions. We assume the simplest payoff function, with a fixed payoff conveyed to agents on the minority side, regardless of the size of such minority. Further, we assume perfect symmetry between the two actions available to players, so that players are totally indifferent as to which side to choose as long as they pick the 'minoritarian' one. Individual preferences, in other words, are only expressed in terms of others' behavior. Finally, the payoff asymmetry between agents belonging to the two parties prevents the possibility of pure strategy equilibria (in which agents repeatedly choose the same side). By ruling out such trivial solutions in the long run, we investigate whether stable coordination patterns emerge resting upon forms of co-evolution between individual behaviors and system dynamics.

In doing so, we explore the efficiency properties of the system under diverse hypotheses about agents' behavior in terms of (1) the amount of information they use in making their choices (i.e., the amount of 'memory' of the past outcomes they are able to retain), (2) their degree of rationality, here expressed as sensitivity to marginal information, (3) the degree of heterogeneity they exhibit at the population level. In particular, following Arthur's approach, we focus on the combined role of *inductive reasoning* and population *heterogeneity* on aggregate efficiency.

We endow our agents with inductive *strategies* in the form of prescriptions on the action to take based on the series of past aggregate outcomes (i.e., the series of winning sides at every stage), and we allow these strategies to be heterogeneous over the population and be updated over time based on diverse learning algorithms.

G. Bottazzi et al. / Simulation Modelling Practice and Theory 10 (2002) 321–347 325

We compare the long-run system performance achieved with such populations of agents with some simple 'benchmark' values represented by the case of perfectly rational and completely informed agents, with and without the addition of beliefs.

The paper is organized as follows: In Section 2 we briefly illustrate the basic features of the game, study the properties of its equilibria and introduce a notion of *adaptive strategy*. Section 3 discusses the role of heterogeneity for collective dynamics when agents choose on the basis of experience-based strategies and learn through time following a deterministic algorithm. In Section 4 we introduce a probabilistic learning model and study both the transient and limit properties of the dynamics. In particular, we analyze the *allocative* and *informational* efficiencies—which we shall define below—of the system under different degrees of rationality of the purported agents and different parameterizations of the learning rule.

2. The minority game

2.1. The baseline game-theoretic framework

The minority game is played by a group N of players, where N must be an odd number. On each period of the stage game, each player must privately and independently choose between two actions or sides, say 0 and 1. [3] The payoff π_i for players choosing side $i \in \{0, 1\}$ is the same for all N players and is equal to

$$\pi_i = \begin{cases} 1 & \text{if } n_i \leqslant (N-1)/2 \\ 0 & \text{otherwise} \end{cases} \tag{1}$$

where n_i is the number of players choosing side i. Each player is rewarded with a unitary payoff whenever the side he chooses happens to be chosen by the minority of the players, while players on the majority side get nil.

It is easy to see that the game has $\binom{N}{(N-1)/2}$ asymmetric Nash equilibria in pure strategies, in which exactly $(N-1)/2$ players choose either one of the two sides. Clearly, under pure-strategy equilibrium play, the payoffs for the two "parties" are quite different. Players belonging to the minority side are rewarded a fixed positive payoff, while those on the majority side earn nothing. The pure strategy equilibria, hence, are not strict, because players on the majority side are just indifferent between sticking to equilibrium play and deviating. The game also presents a unique symmetric mixed-strategy Nash equilibrium, in which each players selects the two sides with equal probability. [4]

The "collective" goodness of the achieved coordination can be easily measured by the average size of the winning minority. The further this size is from $(N-1)/2$, the

---

[3] Although in principle one could study the case in which players can communicate prior to making their choices, we are mainly interested in the case in which players make their decisions in an autonomous way.

[4] Of course, there are infinite asymmetric mixed-strategy equilibria.

higher is the amount of money which is, so to speak, left on the table, hence the lower the resulting aggregate welfare. Note that under mixed strategy equilibrium play, individual expected payoff is approximately equal to 0.5 on each period of the stage game, as the group payoff follows a binomial distribution with mean equal to $N/2$ and a variance of $N/4$, truncated to values lower than or equal to $(N-1)/2$. [5] The measure of variance is indeed an equivalent measure of the degree of efficiency achieved in a population: the higher the variance, the higher the magnitude of fluctuations around the mixed strategy Nash equilibrium and the corresponding aggregate welfare loss.

2.2. The behavioral foundations of the minority game: adding beliefs

Let us start by discussing the nature of the game equilibria when players choose their actions on the basis of idiosyncratic (i.e. agent-specific) beliefs about other players' future behavior based on observation of their past behavior. This perspective, which amounts to considering agents endowed with inductive rather the deductive rationality, has been adopted in the minority literature including the El Farol model [4] and it is common to multi-agent accounts of financial markets (see [13–16] and references therein). One way to model beliefs in this setting, which has traditionally been used in the previous simulation studies of the MG, is to endow players with sets of adaptive strategies, where a strategy may be defined as a function mapping a particular sequence of observed past outcomes up to a certain period into a chosen action in the next period. In the following we show indeed that an explicit account of this form of strategic behavior does not change the set of the mixed strategy Nash equilibria of the game.

Consider a group of N agents who play the MG with a payoff function [6] as from Eq. (1). The only information made available after each round is the winning side (0 or 1). We define the market information as the history h of play, i.e., a binary string specifying which side has won in each period of the stage game. We also define a parameter m as the portion of the past history h that players retain in memory. So, if $m = 3$, players' strategies will be based only on the outcomes observed in the last three rounds of the game.

An *adaptive strategy* may be defined as a prescription on the action to take on the next round of play (i.e., to choose 0 or 1) provided that a particular history (i.e., a particular sequence of m bits) has been observed up to that point. For example, in the case in which $m = 3$, an example of strategy is shown in Table 1.

---

[5] Using the Gaussian approximation to the binomial distribution one can easily obtain, for the expected payoff, the estimate $0.5 - 1/\sqrt{2N\pi}$, valid with a high level of accuracy for the values of N used in the present work.

[6] Various modifications of this payoff function have been proposed by Challet and Zhang and by de Cara et al. [17]. We stick to the original one for its simplicity and because the essential features of the model are highly insensitive to the proposed variations.

G. Bottazzi et al. / Simulation Modelling Practice and Theory 10 (2002) 321–347 327

Table 1
An example of strategy with $m = 3$

History	Action	History	Action
000	1	100	1
001	0	101	0
010	0	110	1
011	1	111	0

The history columns specify all the possible sequences of aggregate outcomes (i.e., of winning sides) in the last m periods; the action columns specify which action to choose on the next round in correspondence to each particular sequence observed. [7] Given a certain value of the parameter m, the total number of strategies that can be generated is equal to 2^{2^m}, corresponding to the 2^{2^m} ways of assigning either action to all the 2^m possible binary strings of length m.

Given the foregoing definition of strategies, we study, as a first important benchmark, the equilibria associated with the "homogenous" game where all the players have access to the full set of strategies. Moreover, rather than considering the updating of the history string h over time, generated by the successive players' choices, we begin by focusing on the static case requiring that all the strings h can appear with equal probability. [8] Under this hypothesis, despite the high number of strategies, we show that a unique mixed strategy Nash equilibrium exists by which players assign equal probability to choosing either side, 1 and 0, regardless of past history. However, given the above definition of strategy, there are actually infinite ways in which players may end up choosing sides with equal probability.

In order to clarify the analysis that follows, let us introduce some notation. A pure strategy $s \in S_l$ is a mapping $H_l \rightarrow \{0,1\}$ from the set of binary strings of length l to the set of actions. Consequently, a mixed strategy $y = \{x_\alpha, \alpha \in S_l | \sum_{\alpha \in S_l} x_\alpha = 1\}$ can be thought as a map $H_l \rightarrow [0,1]$ which associates to each binary string $h \in H_l$ the probability $y(h) = \sum_{j \in S_l} x_j j(h)$ that the action following it be 1. Let Δ_l be the 2^{2^l}-dimensional mixed strategies simplex. For what follows, it is important to notice that the actual mapping between the mixed strategies space and the space $\times^{2^l} [0,1]$ of maps from H_l to [0,1] is many to one and surjective, i.e. there are many ways of building up the same mixed strategy starting from the pure strategies set and each mixed strategy can be realized in at least one way.

Consider a population of N (odd) agents. If $\bar{y} \in \times^N \Delta_l$ is a mixed strategy profile (the vector composed by the players' mixed strategies) we denote the mixed strategy of player i as y_i and the vector of mixed strategies of all players except i as $\bar{y}_{-i}$.

---

[7] Note again that this definition of strategy differs considerably from the notion of strategy as complete plan of action used in standard game theory. Rather it represents "mental models" or "subjective beliefs" as in [4,18].

[8] This prescription is introduced for purposes of analytical tractability and stems from a symmetry consideration: there is no reason for a player to assign ex ante a greater probability to a particular history string.

328   *G. Bottazzi et al. / Simulation Modelling Practice and Theory 10 (2002) 321–347*

Let $\bar{y}(h)$ be the population probability of playing 1 following the binary string h when the mixed strategy profile is $\bar{y}$. This is

$$\bar{y}(h) = \frac{1}{N} \sum_{i=1}^{N} y_i(h) = \sum_{j \in S_i} P_j(\bar{y}) j(h) \tag{2}$$

where $P_j(\bar{y})$ is the probability of playing strategy j (the frequency with which this strategy will be played).

The payoff function in Eq. (1) defines the expected payoff of player i given the past history h and the complete mixed strategy profile $\bar{y}$:

$$U_{y_i,\bar{y}}(h) = y_i(h)(1 - \bar{y}(h)) + \bar{y}(h)(1 - y_i(h)) \tag{3}$$

We introduce a partial ordering on the strategies space Δ_l with the following:

Definition. Given a mixed strategy profile $\bar{y}$, a mixed strategy y_1 is superior to y_2 if it is $U_{y_1,\bar{y}}(h) \geqslant U_{y_2,\bar{y}}(h)$, $\forall h \in H_l$.

This definition allows one to discuss equilibria in a way similar to what is done in more canonical population games and one obtains:

Theorem. *The strategy profile $\bar{y}$ is a Nash equilibrium iff $y_i(h) = 1/2$, $\forall y_i \in \bar{y}$, $\forall h \in H_l$.*

The meaning is rather straightforward: a mixed strategy profile is a Nash equilibrium only when the players' mixed strategies assign probability one half to pick either side, 1 and 0 irrespectively of the past history, i.e. when all the players are perfectly symmetric random players. Notice, however, that the ways of realizing such a mixed strategy are infinite. Hence, the actual number of mixed strategy Nash equilibria is also infinite.

Proof. In order to demonstrate the assertion we proceed by identifying the ith player's best replies (in the sense of the definition above) to a given mixed strategy profile $\bar{y}_{-i}$ for the rest of the population. For this purpose, it is convenient to express the payoff in Eq. (3) isolating the contribution of the ith player's strategy from that of the rest of the population:

$$U_{y_i,\bar{y}_{-i}}(h) = \frac{N+1}{N} y_i(h) + \frac{N-1}{N} \bar{y}_{-i}(h) - \frac{2}{N} y_i(h)^2 - \frac{2(N-1)}{N} y_i(h) \bar{y}_{-i}(h) \tag{4}$$

and $y_i(h)$ has to be chosen in order to maximize the foregoing expression. The solution depends on the value of $\bar{y}_{-i}(h)$ and the quadratic form of Eq. (4) allows one to immediately find it. Defining

$$x(h) = \frac{N + 1 - 2(N-1)\bar{y}_{-i}(h)}{4} \tag{5}$$

the solution reads

$$
\hat{y}_i(h) = \begin{cases} 0 & x(h) \leqslant 0 \\ 1 & x(h) \geqslant 1 \\ x(h) & \text{otherwise} \end{cases} \tag{6}
$$

The same procedure can be repeated for each string h to obtain the best reply mixed strategy to $\bar{y}_{-i}(h)$. In order to obtain the set of Nash equilibria, we have to find strategies that belong to the set of mutual best replies, i.e. $\hat{y}_i(h) = \bar{y}_{-i}(h)$, $\forall h \in H_l$. Inspecting Eq. (6), it turns out that this can happen only when $0 < x(h) < 1$ and the following condition is satisfied

$$
\bar{y}_{-i}(h) = \frac{N + 1 - 2(N - 1)\bar{y}_{-i}(h)}{4} \tag{7}
$$

The solution is then $\bar{y}_{-i}(h) = 1/2$, implying $\hat{y}_i(h) = 1/2$. □

3. The minority game with heterogeneous agents

One of the interesting questions one may explore in the MG framework is whether and how the presence of heterogeneity among players' beliefs may impact on the system coordination around the Nash equilibria of the game.

In line with previous simulation studies by Challet and Zhang [2,3], one may introduce heterogeneity in the population via diversity of strategies. Given a certain value of m, each player is initially endowed with a number s of strategies which are randomly drawn from a common pool. Hence, although both m and s are identical over the population, heterogeneity arises from the random initial strategy assignments.

In the course of play, each strategy i is characterized by a value $q_i(t)$, which indicates the total number of points accumulated by that strategy at time t. Indeed, after each period of the game, all the strategies that have made a correct prediction in that period (i.e., all strategies prescribing the choice of the side which ex post resulted the winning side) are assigned one point each.

Given the initial strategy assignment and the updating rule just described, players' behavior at each round of the stage game is completely deterministic, as each agent picks, among the strategies he or she possesses, the one with the highest number of accumulated points.

Note that in such a framework, however, agents' heterogeneity is *only* introduced via the initial assignment of strategies to players and does not stem from different "personal histories". If, for example, the same strategy i is initially assigned to two different players, the value of $q_i(t)$, which determines the strength of that strategy at time t will necessarily be the same for both players, as it will only depend on the number of times that strategy has made a correct prediction whether it was actually played or not.

In order to evaluate the population performance, it is necessary to introduce a measure of *allocative efficiency* [2,3]. A natural candidate is provided by the average

330   *G. Bottazzi et al. / Simulation Modelling Practice and Theory 10 (2002) 321–347*

number of players belonging to the winning party, i.e. the average number of points earned by the whole population. [9] In accordance with the previous literature, as a measure of allocative efficiency we compute a quantity associated to the foregoing one, namely the mean squared deviation from the half population, σ. Let N be the number of agents, and $N_0(t)$ the number of agents choosing side 0 at time t, then in a repeated game of duration T the mean squared deviation is computed as

$$\sigma = \frac{1}{T} \sum_{\tau=0}^{T} \left(N_0(\tau) - \frac{N}{2} \right)^2 . \tag{8}$$

Clearly, the lower the value of σ, the higher the system efficiency.

The process can be expected to depend to some degree on the initial strategy distribution and on the initial game history, which are both generated randomly. Therefore, in order to eliminate any dependence on initial conditions from our results and to focus only on asymptotically stable states, in all the simulations presented here we applied an averaging procedure over 50 independent sample paths with randomly generated initial histories and strategy distributions.

In addition, at the beginning of each simulation the system was left to evolve for an initial "adjustment phase" of length T_0 in order to wash away any possible transient effects on the subsequent averaging procedure. The quantities so obtained can thus be considered as asymptotic properties of the system as long as T_0 and T are chosen long enough as to provide a good approximation of the limit $T \to \infty$.

The dependence of the volatility measure σ on N, m and s for the original minority game has been thoroughly investigated in the previous simulation studies and is summarized in Fig. 1 for the case $s = 2$. [10]

As noticed in [19], the type of market regime is determined, at least in first approximation, by the ratio $z = 2^m/N$: hence the curves for various N collapse if plotted in this variable. In this respect, notice that even if the actual number of possible strategies is 2^{2^m}, their relative strengths are completely defined in terms of the frequency $P(0|h_m)$ with which, over a history, a 0 follows a given m-length string h_m. And there are 2^m of such variables. So, z can be interpreted as the density of agents in the strategy space degrees-of-freedom.

As shown in Fig. 1 three different regimes of the system can be identified. First, a "random regime" occurs when z is large (the agent are sparse in the strategy space). Here the system can hardly organize and its behavior can be described as a collection of random agents choosing their side with a coin toss. In fact suppose the past history to be a given h_m and suppose there are $N_d(h_m)$ agents whose strategies prescribe different actions based on that history while there are $N_0(h_m)$ and $N_1(h_m)$ agents

---

[9] Recall from the previous section that this quantity measures the degree to which the population is close to a Nash equilibrium, whether in pure or mixed strategies.

[10] The choice to consider $s = 2$ is justified by the fact that the system exhibits the same qualitative properties for any $s \geqslant 2$, while reducing to a trivial case for $s = 1$.

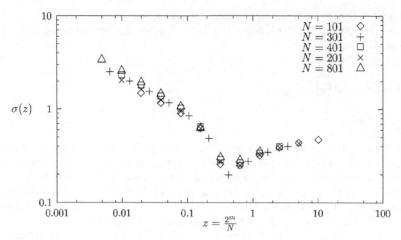

Fig. 1. The volatility $\sigma(z)$ for $s = 2$ and different values of N and m.

whose strategies prescribe the same party (we restrict ourselves to the $s = 2$ case), respectively 0 and 1. If the agents in N_d choose randomly, the variance is $\sigma(h_m) = N_d(h_m)/4 + (N_0(h_m) - N_1(h_m))^2/4$. The average over the possible h_m will then give $\sigma = N/4$. Notice that σ is shaped by two factors, namely fluctuations in the choices of agents able to choose and fluctuations in the initial distribution of strategies. Note also that the allocative efficiency in this case (as measured by σ) equals that of a population of players playing the mixed strategy Nash equilibrium defined over the two actions 0 and 1 (cf. Section 2.1).

The second regime could be called the "inefficient regime" for $z \ll 1$. Here the agents densely populate the strategy space, and their actions are strongly correlated. This correlation leads to a worsening of the overall performance due to a "crowd" effect [20]: the agents in fact are too similar to each other and they all tend to choose the same party on the basis of the available information.

The third regime for $z \sim 1$ is where coordination produces a better-than-random performance. Here the agents are differentiated enough to not yield "crowd" effects, but at the same time distributed densely enough over the space of strategies as to not produce a random-like behavior.

The early literature on the MG in fact, has mostly focused on the criticality of the value z_c where σ is minimum, suggesting that a major change in the system behavior occurs when this point is crossed [21].

More recent studies (see [22]) have shown the existence and analyzed the nature of such 'phase transition' in the large system limit (i.e., with a large number of agents) when agents' past choices are not reflected into the perceived aggregate 'signal', i.e. when the string of h past outcomes on which agents base their decisions is randomly drawn from a stationary distribution. Since we are mainly interested in studying the effects of different microbehaviors on the properties of the aggregate signal, we do not make use of such an approximation. However, as will be shown in the following sections, the "criticality" of the z_c region survives, to some extent, in our analysis.

4. Adaptive learning

4.1. The model

What happens to the system's properties when additional heterogeneity is introduced in the population? In particular, what happens when agents are endowed with a probabilistic decision rule? In order to tackle the problem, in the following we investigate changes in the dynamics and asymptotic properties of a population of agents playing the MG as a function of changes in the nature of the agents' learning models. Hence, we leave unaltered the setup previously described, and modify only the way in which agents update their strategies' relative strengths. In particular, we adopt the following probabilistic updating rule.

Recall the definition of $q_i(t)$ as the total number of points strategy i would have won if played until time t. Then each agent chooses among its strategies following the probability distribution:

$$p_i(t) = \frac{e^{\beta q_i(t)}}{\sum_j e^{\beta q_j(t)}} \tag{9}$$

where the sum on j is over all the strategies possessed by the player. Note that, in general, different players will assign different probabilities to the same strategy due to the different strategy endowments. Hence, the introduction of a probabilistic learning rule adds noise at the individual level and it also increases heterogeneity in the population.

The choice of a stochastic learning model is well supported by the available experimental evidence on adaptive behavior in games as well as by more general evidence from psychological experiments. In fact, most descriptive models of adaptive learning, whether belief based or reinforcement based, imply a probabilistic choice and updating of available actions [23,24].

The parameter β can be considered as a sort of *sensitivity of choice to marginal information*: when it is high, the agents are sensitive even to little differences in the notional score of their strategies. In the limit for $\beta \to \infty$ the usual minority game rule is recovered. On the contrary, for low values of β a great difference in the strategies' strengths is required in order to obtain significant differences in probabilities.

The model indeed bears close similarities with a discrete time replicator dynamics [25]. The connection is straightforward if one looks at the probability updating equation associated with Eq. (9):

$$p_i(t+1) = p_i(t) \frac{e^{\beta \, \delta q_i(t)}}{\sum_j p_j(t) e^{\beta \, \delta q_j(t)}} \tag{10}$$

G. Bottazzi et al. / Simulation Modelling Practice and Theory 10 (2002) 321–347   333

where $\delta q_i(t) = q_i(t+1) - q_i(t)$ are the points won by strategy i at time t. If one thinks of a continuous process $\delta q_i(t) = \dot{q}_i(t)\,\delta t$, where $\dot{q}_i(t)$ is the instantaneous "fitness" of strategy i, then the continuous time replicator dynamics equation is recovered keeping only the first terms in δt expansion:

$$\frac{\dot{p}_i(t)}{p_i(t)} = \dot{q}_i(t) - \sum_j p_j(t)\dot{q}_j(t) \tag{11}$$

4.2. Transient length

In the following we will restrict our analysis to the case $N = 101$ and $s = 2$ and we will refer to the optimal value for memory length m_o as the value of m which minimizes σ under this parameter choice.

Let us consider the problem of defining the correct values for T_0 and T in Eq. (8) above. The central question is: How long must the system be left evolving before it reaches the asymptotically stable dynamics? Fig. 2 plots the average σ value based on the "deterministic" (i.e. $\beta = +\infty$) MG as a function of the time length T over which this average is taken with a transient $T_0 = T$. As it can be seen from the graph, the values used in the literature on the MG are generally sufficient to obtain a prediction correct to few percentage points. However, two properties are worth noticing:

- The system approaches the asymptotic value from above, intuitively suggesting that the system "learns" over time to self-organize.
- For low values of m, in the "inefficient regime", and for high value of m, in the "random regime", the system reaches a stable dynamic quite fast. On the contrary, for values of m near the optimal value m_o, the system takes a much longer time to self-organize.

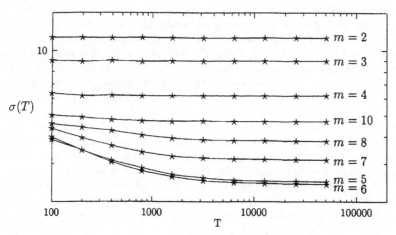

Fig. 2. The mean σ along the run length for different ms. The points are averages over a sample of 30 independent runs with $N = 101$ and $s = 2$.

334   *G. Bottazzi et al. / Simulation Modelling Practice and Theory 10 (2002) 321–347*

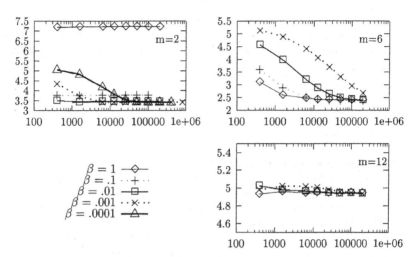

Fig. 3. σ along the run length T for different βs. The points are averages over a sample of 30 independent runs with a transient time $T_0 = T$.

Consider now the case in which the learning rule is the one described in Eq. (9), shown in Fig. 3. For high values of β this learning rule approaches the standard one, and accordingly, the transient length is similar to the one found in such cases. However, as β decreases, the length generally increases. The increase is most dramatic for values of m near the optimal value m_0, and it progressively disappears for higher values of m. The interpretation of such a result stems from the meaning of β in terms of the learning rule. Supposing non-trivial dynamics for m near m_0, the parameter β sets the time scale on which such dynamics are attained.

As an illustration, consider the following example: Let $r(t) = p_1(t)/p_2(t)$ be the ratio of the probabilities that an agent associates to its two strategies, and $\Delta q(t) = q_1(t) - q_2(t)$ the difference in their respective strengths. From Eq. (9) it follows that $r(t) = e^{\beta \Delta q(t)}$. Assuming that the difference in the two strategies' performance holds constant over time (an assumption which is generally true in the initial transient regime where agents' behavior is basically random) we obtain $\Delta q(t) \sim t$: hence, from the equality above, a given difference in probability is obtained at a time which is inversely proportional to β.

In order to estimate the time scale over which the system long-run properties are attained, we use the following procedure. Holding all the parameters and the initial conditions constant, the system volatility can be expressed as a function of both the transient phase duration, and of the time length over which it is averaged, i.e. $\sigma = \sigma(T, T_0)$. Starting from a reference time T_r,[11] we compute the mean volatility progressively doubling T and T_0, and thus obtaining a series of values $\sigma_n = \sigma(2^n T_r, 2^n T_r)$. When the relative variation $|\sigma_n - \sigma_{n-1}|/\sigma_n$ falls below a fixed threshold ϵ, we

---

[11] Note that the chosen value for T_0 is irrelevant as long as it is small compared to the typical time scale.

G. *Bottazzi et al. / Simulation Modelling Practice and Theory 10 (2002) 321–347*   335

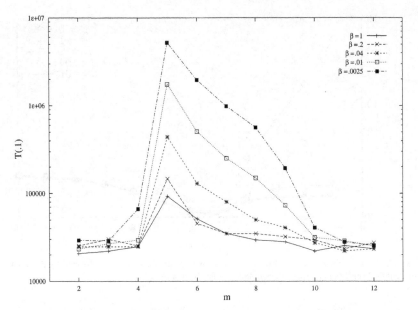

Fig. 4. A (rough) estimate of the time $\widehat{T}$ required to reach the stable asymptotic σ value with an error not greater than a given threshold (the plots are made against *m* for different values of β).

stop and take the last computed value of σ as an estimate of its asymptotic value. The corresponding time length $\widehat{T}(\epsilon)$ will be an estimate of the time implied by the system to reach this asymptotic state. As can be seen in Fig. 4 the increase in $\widehat{T}$ when β is lowered is mainly concentrated around m_o, with shapes that suggest the presence of a regime discontinuity.

4.3. Allocative efficiency

In order to analyze the asymptotic properties of $\sigma(m)$ for different βs, we use the procedure just described regarding the calculation of $\widehat{T}$, i.e. we leave the system evolve until "stability" is reached. [12] The simulation results are plotted in Fig. 5. Interestingly, when β decreases, the performance level of the system generally increases. Moreover, such increase is larger the lower the value of *m*, and it becomes negligible for $m \geqslant m_o$. The observed behavior is consistent with the idea that for high values of *m*, the system dynamics tends to be determined by the initial distribution of strategies among players, while players themselves have no opportunity to attain a higher performance by adjusting their behavior. Recall that an increasing *m* means an

---

[12] Let us emphasize that the stable state does not imply point convergence to any state but simply long-run stability of the relevant time averages (e.g., the mean volatility σ) even if the system continues to fluctuate in its limit state.

336   *G. Bottazzi et al. / Simulation Modelling Practice and Theory 10 (2002) 321–347*

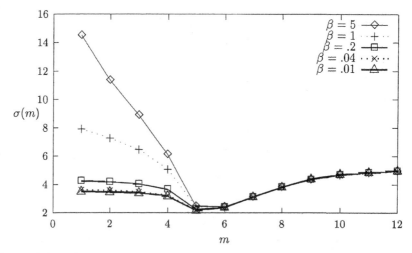

Fig. 5. Volatility σ for $s = 2$, $N = 101$ and various ms and βs. The runs are performed by doubling the time length T until the last two values obtained differ by less than 1%.

increasing number of possible strategies over which players may initially draw. For a fixed N, the "ecology" of drawn strategies becomes thinner as compared to the notionally available ones. That phenomenon, it turns out, prevents the system from self-organizing. Note that this property is quite robust and largely independent from the particular learning rule adopted. Our results, in fact, are perfectly in line with previous simulation studies in the high m region.

Conversely, for low values of m, the choice of the particular learning rule adopted does matter in terms of aggregate efficiency. In fact, when m is small, the original learning rule ($\beta = \infty$) produces a "crowd" effect (corresponding to large groups of agents choosing the same side) which, due to homogeneity in the initial strategy endowments, prevents the system from attaining a high degree of efficiency. [13] On the contrary, the introduction of a probabilistic learning rule for the strategy choice acts like a brake that dumps the amplitude of such correlated fluctuations. At the individual level, this corresponds to lower βs, i.e. to higher degrees of "inertia", as agents update their probabilities more slowly. In other words, as β decreases each agent behaves as if it was applying a sort of stochastic fictitious play approximation [27], [14] with an implicit assumption of stationarity on the distribution of other agents' choices. If the whole population shares the same β—as in the present model—the assumption is, in a way, self-fulfilling: a decrease in β makes the behavior of the population as a whole change at a slower pace. A slower probability updating at the individual level and the resulting more stable collective behavior, together, imply

---

[13] In some sense, one can interpret the "crowd" effect as a collective form of *overreaction* [26].

[14] Note that fictitious play implies that a player best responds to the observed frequency of the opponent's play.

G. Bottazzi et al. / Simulation Modelling Practice and Theory 10 (2002) 321–347   337

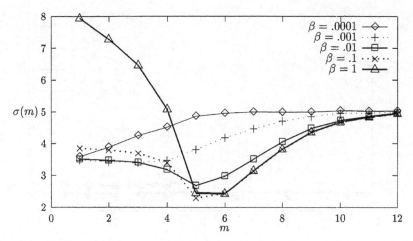

Fig. 6. The volatility σ for $s = 2$, $N = 101$ and various ms and βs. The runs are performed with a fixed time length $T = T_0 = 10,000$. When $\beta \rightarrow 0$ the system approaches a collection of randomly choosing agents.

that σ is a non-increasing function of β. In fact, if the system reaches a dynamical stability via an averaging procedure over the past outcomes, increasing the time scale over which averaging occurs cannot rule out previously attainable equilibria.

However, note that in order to capture the long-run efficiency properties of the system for low values of β it is necessary to let the population play until stability is reached, according to the procedure described above. Our results, in fact, were not captured by previous simulation studies [28]. Since the latter were all performed with a fixed time length their conclusion was that when β is small enough, the system behavior resembles the behavior of a random system. However, this finding was in fact due to both the increase in the transient length and the purely random initial dynamics which occur when β is decreased. Then, by fixing a time length, for small values of β the simulations capture throughout the adjustment phase, and the system behavior perfectly mirrors that of a collection of agents who choose at random. (Indeed our results of a fixed time simulation are plotted in Fig. 6 and are perfectly in line with the existing literature. [15])

As can be seen in Fig. 5 the performance attainable in the MG via a collective organization of agents with limited information is, in general, surprisingly high. In the following we show that the level of efficiency achieved in the double limit $\beta \rightarrow 0$ and $m \rightarrow 0$ actually equals that attainable with hypothetical perfectly informed and perfectly rational agents endowed with a greater flexibility in choice.

Consider for instance a collection of agents with the following characteristics: each agent is assigned $S = 2$ strategies, and a vector of length 2^m containing

---

[15] In other words, to discover the asymptotic properties of the system, the limits $T \rightarrow \infty$ and $\beta \rightarrow 0$ have to be performed in this order.

338   *G. Bottazzi et al. / Simulation Modelling Practice and Theory 10 (2002) 321–347*

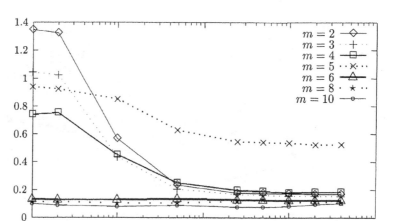

Fig. 7. Variance of the distribution of σ over a sample of 50 independent runs. As β becomes small the point $m \sim m_o$ maintains a significantly larger variance.

the probability $p(h_m)$ of playing according to its first strategy after the occurrence of the history string h_m. Moreover, for each h_m, each agent knows the values of $N_0(h_m)$, $N_1(h_m)$ and $N_d(h_m)$ indicating respectively the number of agents for which their strategies both prescribe to play 0, both to play 1, or to play differently. Assuming that the game structure and the amount of information available to agents is common knowledge and that the agents are perfectly rational, the problem completely factorizes and, for each h_m, every agent in $N_d(h_m)$ will solve the game analytically choosing $p(h_m)$ in order to minimize

$$\frac{(N_1(h_m) - N_0(h_m))}{2} - p(h_m)N_d(h_m) \tag{12}$$

i.e. making the average fraction of the population choosing a given side as near to $N/2$ as possible. This choice will produce a volatility $\sigma \sim N_d/4 = N/8$ which is roughly similar to what obtained in the simulation shown in Fig. 5 in the low m, low β region. [16] However, note that, as from Fig. 5, these fully rational, fully informed players are (on average) "beaten" by a set of "self-organizing" agents with memory $m \sim m_o$, reaching a nearly double efficiency.

A final remark concerns the variance of the distribution of σ as a function of β for various ms, as shown in Fig. 7: when β decreases the variance of σ decreases for any m. However it remains three times greater for $m = m_o$ suggesting a stronger dependence of the asymptotic performance on the initial strategy assignment which the

---

[16] We are assuming $\Delta N = N_1(h_m) - N_0(h_m) < N_d(h_m)$. Notice that for random agents $\Delta N \sim \sqrt{(N)}$ and $N_d \sim N$ and that one can neglect the $\Delta N / N_d$ terms in the solution of Eq. (12) when N is large.

system is not able to wash out. That is, significant *path-dependence effects* are present.

4.4. Informational efficiency

What we have been calling allocative efficiency basically highlights the collective ability of capturing the payoffs which the game notionally allows. A complementary issue regards the *informational efficiency* of the market process, i.e. the extent to which the future system outcomes are unpredictable, or, in other words, the absence of any arbitrage opportunities. Thus, let us analyze the informational content of the binary string H of successive winning sides. Let $p(0|h_l)$ be the probability that a 0 follows a given string h_l of all the possible 2^l strings of length l (as depicted in Fig. 8).

For the original "deterministic" MG the analysis performed in [19] leads to the identification of two regimes: a "partially efficient regime" for $m < m_0$ in which $p(0|h_l) \sim 0.5, \forall h_l$ as long as $l \leqslant m$ and in which no informational content is left for strategies with memory less or equal to the one used by the agents; and an "inefficient regime" for $m > m_0$ in which the distribution of $p(0|h_l)$ is not flat, even for $l \leqslant m$, meaning there are good strategies that might exploit the market signal to obtain differential profits. For $l > m$ both the regions show a non-trivial distribution $p(0|h_l)$ with an increasing degree of "ruggedness" as l increases. The effect of introducing some degree of behavioral randomness through the parameter β leads to the obvious effect of reducing the "ruggedness" of the distribution of $p(0|h_l)$ (see Fig. 8).

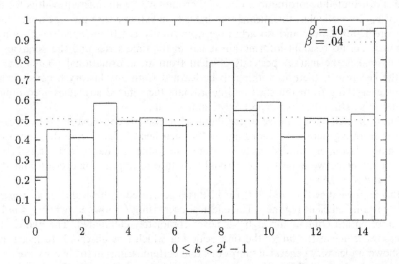

Fig. 8. Probability $p(0|h_l)$ of obtaining a 0 following a given binary string h_l in the system history for $m = 3$ and $l = m + 1 = 4$. When β is reduced the distribution "flattens" and any structure disappears.

In order to study the behavior of the system as β changes we introduce two related quantities which can be used to characterize the informational content of the time series. The first is the conditional entropy $S(l)$ defined as:

$$S(l) = -\sum_{h_l} p(h_l) \sum_{i \in \{0,1\}} p(i|h_l) \log p(i|h_l) \tag{13}$$

where the summation is intended over all the possible strings of length l and $p(h_l)$ is the frequency of a given string in the system history H. The maximum value $S(l) = 1$ is reached for a flat distribution $p(0|h_l) = 0.5$, and it corresponds to the impossibility of forecasting (in probability) the next outcome based on the previous l outcomes. The idea that the information content can be used to "exploit the market" leads to the definition of a second quantity $A(l)$:

$$A(l) = \sum_{h_l} p(h_l) \max \{p(0|h_l), p(1|h_l)\} \tag{14}$$

which is the average fraction of points won by the best strategy of memory l. This is a measure of the reward obtained by the best arbitrageur with memory l (whereas if no arbitrage opportunities are present $A(l)$ is equal to 0.5).

Before analyzing the behavior of these quantities when β is varied, let us briefly consider as a sort of ideal benchmark the properties of a population composed of perfectly rational, perfectly informed, agents with common knowledge of strategy distributions. Not surprisingly, in these circumstances the problem factorizes for each past history and the dependence on m disappears. The history produced by such a system is a random series of 0 and 1. Indeed the number of agents choosing one side is distributed according to a binomial around $N/2$ with different widths for different h_m. In particular, this means that in such an extreme case the "memory" loses any predicting power and no arbitrage opportunity is left for agents with longer memory, i.e. no residual information is left in the time series and the behavior of agents makes the market perfectly efficient from an informational point of view. In the last resort, there is nothing to be learned from any history because agents know everything from the start and coordinate their mixed strategies accordingly. Under this assumption we expect $S \sim 1$ and $A \sim 0.5$.

Short of such an ideal case where the market loses its coordinating role, because agents ex ante generate the coordination "in their heads", let us consider, for example, a population of "random agents". Here, due to the unbalance in the initial strategy endowments we expect a non-trivial structure to appear for every l, and thus $S < 1$ and $A > 0.5$.

In Fig. 9 we plot $S(l)$ and $A(l)$ for histories generated with a value of $m < m_o$, in the "partially efficient regime". The effect of decreasing β shows up when $l > m$ but the information content for high l is never completely eliminated. The market becomes less efficient the larger the time scale l at which it is observed. In fact it can be shown under very general assumptions that certain strings in the history are more frequent than others [19] and the long-range correlation that was shown to be responsible for the "crowd" effect at high β survives as a non-trivial structure in

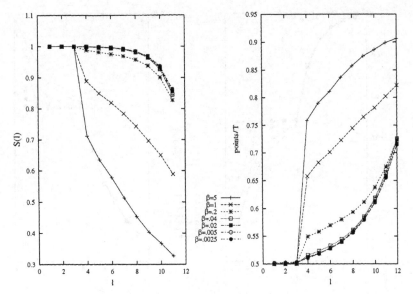

Fig. 9. Conditional entropy $S(l)$ (left) and arbitrage opportunity $A(l)$ (right) as a function of the time depth l for $m = 3 < m_o$.

$p(0|h_l)$ for high l. All this applies despite the fact that to any agent with memory $l \leqslant m$ the market appears perfectly efficient regardless of the β value.

For values of $m > m_o$, in the "inefficient regime", the effect is in some sense reversed. As can be seen in Fig. 10, the effect of decreasing β is again negligible for $l \leqslant m$ but in the limit $\beta \rightarrow 0$ the curve becomes flat for $l > m$. This last result deserves some comments: the flatness in $l \geqslant m$ means that no gain is achieved from inspecting the time series with a very long memory $l \gg m$ because no greater arbitrage opportunities are open for a longer memory agent than the best possible agent of memory m. The market can be considered to be, again, *partially efficient* in the sense that it generates an upper bound on the maximal attainable arbitrage possibilities which do not depend on the arbitrageur memory.

The particular form of the conditional entropy in Fig. 10 suggests that in the limit $\beta \rightarrow 0$ the system can be described as a Markov chain of memory m.[17] The result can be explained by noticing that when β is small only great differences in the past performances of strategies are relevant and in the limit $\beta \rightarrow 0$ only infinite differences matter. Putting it another way, the frequency of victories of the various strategies becomes constant implying the formation of a static hierarchical structure in the

---

[17] Notice that by construction, in the learning rules considered here the past is not discounted, and the agents weigh their strategies on the basis of all the game outcomes starting from the beginning of the simulation: see, however, Appendix A for an analysis of the system properties when a time decaying factor is introduced.

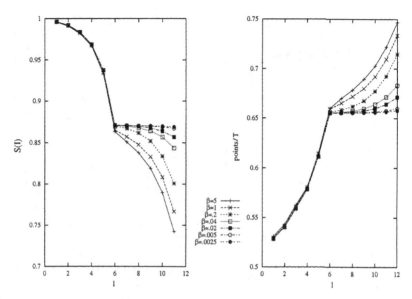

Fig. 10. Conditional entropy $S(l)$ (left) and arbitrage opportunity $A(l)$ (right) as a function of the time depth l for $m = 6 > m_0$.

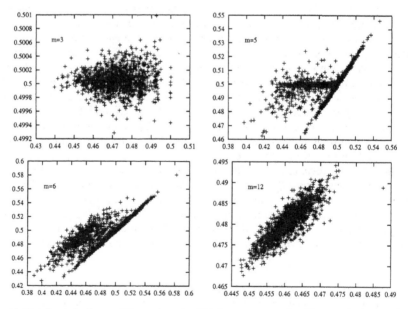

Fig. 11. Plot, for each player, of the scoring rate of his best strategy against his own winning rate for a population of 101 players over 30 independent runs with $\beta = 0.04$.

G. Bottazzi et al. / Simulation Modelling Practice and Theory 10 (2002) 321–347   343

strategy space which is ultimately responsible of the Markov character of the resulting history. The appearance of "best strategies" in $m > m_o$ region is well revealed by
the plot of the average score by the best strategy versus the average score of the
player (see Fig. 11): a correlation in fact appears between the performance of a
player and the performance of its best strategy. Moreover, in the $m \sim m_o$ region a
sub-population showing the same kind of high correlation co-exists with another
group that presents no correlation, composed of agents possessing two equally performing strategies.

Conversely, only in the low m region no strategy ends up being preferable to others and no player is bound to lose due only to its initial strategy endowment.

Notice, however, that equivalence between strategies does not necessarily imply
equivalence in the agents' performances. This is highlighted by the plot of the variances and the supports of the score distributions for different values of β and m in
Fig. 12. Interestingly, only for low m and low β does equivalence in strategy performance imply a relatively uniform distribution of performances over the population.
In the other parameter regions learning does not eliminate performance heterogeneity over the population itself. Loosely speaking, the market self-organizes over an
ecology of "mental models" and players carrying them, entailing the long-run coexistence of relative "winners" and "suckers".

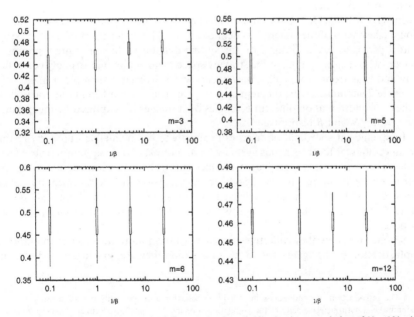

Fig. 12. Variance (□) and support (—) of the scored points distribution in a population of $N = 101$ with
$s = 2$, over 30 independent runs. Notice that while in the high β simulations the distributions are similar in
width for any m, when β is reduced the low m region emerges as the "socially optimal" one.

Table 2
System properties: a summary (A.E. and I.E. stand for Allocative and Informational Efficiency, respectively)

	Low z	High z
Low β	High A.E., high I.E.	Partial A.E., partial I.E.
High β	Low A.E., high I.E.	Partial A.E., low I.E.

5. Conclusions and outlook

One of the central question of any analysis of interaction amongst large populations of agents is whether orderly coordination and aggregate efficiency emerge as a sort of generic properties, regardless of particular behavioral assumptions. Our investigation of such an issue in the MG "framework" suggest a largely negative answer: simple variations in the agents' learning algorithms, we show, yield important modifications in the asymptotic properties of the system.

More specifically, we have shown that *less* sensitivity to marginal information, i.e., *more inertia* in the learning algorithm entails improved long-run collective performances, although at the expense of longer adjustment phases. Together, *performance asymmetries* across agents, as measured by the variance (or analogously) the support of the earnings distribution over the population, fall as inertia in the agents' behavior increases.

In general, some degrees of randomness help in improving allocative and informational efficiencies of the system—as defined above. The major effect of randomness is that it performs like a "brake" on the system dynamics, thus preventing groups of players who densely populate the strategy space from acting in a strongly correlated way and thus from producing *crowd effects* which worsen system performance. [18]

Table 2 summarizes the different system properties—i.e. different "interaction regimes"—conditional on different ecologies of strategies (as captured by the parameters $z = 2^m/N$ and β respectively).

First, efficient coordination turns out robustly to be an emergent property resting on an ecology of heterogeneous agents who do not play Nash equilibrium strategies. Indeed, one of our major conclusions, which refines over previous results in the Minority Game literature, is that aggregate efficiency—in the complementary definitions proposed above—is only achieved in correspondence of an "optimal" degree of heterogeneity, whether in the agents' decision behavior or in their underlying sets of beliefs.

Second, we show that collective efficiency is not monotonic either in the rational sophistication of the agents nor in the information they are able to access. In partic-

---

[18] The introduction of randomness in individual behavior is indeed only one of possible ways to maintain behavioral heterogeneity in the population. For instance, similar effects have been obtained in [29] by substituting the "global" evaluation of strategies on the system history H with a "personal" evaluation in which each agent uses the binary string made up of its own record of "victories". A diversification mechanism is again at work breaking the correlation among agents.

ular, we show that a population of 'inductive', heterogeneous agents with limited rationality and limited information is able to achieve a higher degree of efficiency compared to that attainable by a system of sophisticated and perfectly informed agents. Our results suggest that more rationality—as approximated here by a greater ability of the agents to track novel environmental information—may well *lower* average performances (an analogous result is obtained in a different setup in [14]).

The general sensitivity of system dynamics upon particular learning algorithms also indicates a few research tasks ahead.

One of them concerns the experimentation with cognitively less demanding learning rules. So, for example, it would be interesting to explore the properties of pure reinforcement learning whereby agents update only the strategies they play. That would also set a "zero-level" benchmark in terms of degrees of required information and cognitive abilities—somewhat at the extreme opposite to the models studied so far in the MG literature (and, somewhere in between, one might explore learning models such as that in [30]).

A complementary line of inquiry regards the analysis of behaviors and learning of human subjects under experimental settings isomorphic to the interactions formalized above.

In the last resort, all these further exercises, together with the results presented here, ought to be considered as adding some pieces of evidence to the much broader effort aimed at identifying the variables which determine a "universality class", if any, of market processes involving coordination *cum* heterogeneity, as distinguished from those characteristics which strictly depend upon specific distributions of beliefs and learning rules. Were our results confirmed in further studies, they would add strength to the conjecture that efficient coordination might not primarily stem from the adherence of populations of agents to Nash equilibrium behaviors, but rather emerge out of persistent ecologies of heterogeneous beliefs and behaviors within the population itself.

Appendix A

Many authors, especially in the experimental literature (e.g., [24]) add to the description of the learning process one more parameter, connected with the idea that agents weigh more the information they received in the recent history as compared to the one coming from far back in the past. This parameter typically takes the form of a decay factor. If $\epsilon_i(t)$ are the points scored by strategy i at time t and α $(0 < \alpha \leqslant 1)$ is the information decay factor, the updating rule for the total strength becomes

$$q_i(t+1) = \alpha q_i(t) + \epsilon_i(t) \tag{A.1}$$

with the associated updating rule for the probabilities:

$$p_i(t+1) = p_i^{\alpha}(t) \frac{e^{\beta q_i(t)}}{\sum_j p_j^{\alpha}(t) e^{\beta q_j(t)}} \tag{A.2}$$

346   *G. Bottazzi et al. / Simulation Modelling Practice and Theory 10 (2002) 321–347*

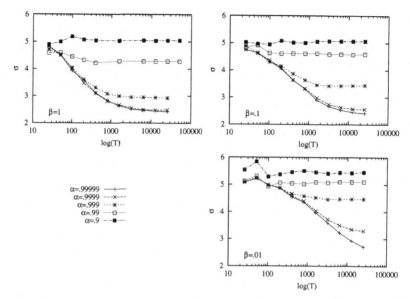

Fig. 13. σ as a function of the run length T for different values of β and α. The simulations are performed with $m = 6$ where a greater sensitivity of the transient time length to the learning parameters β and α is expected (see Section 4.2).

The effect of introducing such a "memory leakage" is twofold. First, it puts an upper limit to the maximal strength any strategy can reach, namely $1/(1 - \alpha)$. Second, in presence of no information flow, the equiprobability between strategies is steadily restored. This effect implies that if one takes the limit $\beta \to 0$ keeping the value of α constant, the system will converge to a collection of random agents. In turn, this implies that agents, loosely speaking, have to be exposed to a larger amount of information before they start behaving as a self-organized system.

The effect of introducing "forgetting" in the learning rule is easily understood: if the agents forget more rapidly than they learn they are always bounded to less efficient behavior. Indeed, as can be seen from Fig. 13, if the value of α is decreased the efficiency of the system is proportionally reduced.

References

[1] T.C. Schelling, Micromotives and Macrobehavior, W.W. Norton and Company, New York, 1978.
[2] D. Challet, Y.-C. Zhang, Emergence of cooperation and organization in an evolutionary game, Phys. A 246 (1997) 407–418.
[3] D. Challet, Y.-C. Zhang, On the minority game: analytical and numerical studies, Phys. A 256 (1998) 514–532.
[4] W.B. Arthur, Inductive reasoning and bounded rationality, Am. Econ. Rev. Papers Proc. 84 (1994) 406–412.

[5] D.J. Mayer, J. Huyck, R. Battalio, T. Soring, Histories role in coordinating decentralized allocation decision: laboratory evidence on repeated binary allocation games, J. Politic. Economy 100 (1992) 292–316.

[6] J. Ochs, The coordination problem in the decentralized markets: An experiment, Quart. J. Econ. 105 (1990) 545–559.

[7] J. Ochs, Coordination problems, in: J.H. Kagel, A.E. Roth (Eds.), Handbook of Experimental Economics, Princeton University Press, Princeton, 1995.

[8] R. Zwick, A. Rapoport, Tacit Coordination in a Decentralized Market Entry Game with Fixed Capacity, Working Paper, Hong Kong University of Science and Technology, Hong Kong, 1999.

[9] I. Erev, A. Rapoport, Coordination, "magic", and reinforcement learning in a market entry game, Games Econ. Behavior 23 (1998) 146–175.

[10] A. Rapoport, D.A. Seale, I. Erev, J.A. Sundali, Equilibrium play in large group market entry games, Mgmt. Sci. 44 (1998) 119–141.

[11] J.A. Sundali, A. Rapoport, D.A. Seale, Coordination in market entry games with symmetric players, Organizat. Behavior Human Decision Processes 64 (1995) 203–218.

[12] W.F.M. De Bondt, R.H. Thaler, Financial decision-making in markets and firms: a behavioral perspective, in: R. Jarrow, et al. (Eds.), Handbooks in OR & MS, Elsevier, Amsterdam, 1995.

[13] W.B. Arthur, J.H. Holland, B. Le Baron, R. Palmer, P. Taylor, Asset pricing under endogenous expectations in an artificial stock market, in: W.B. Arthur, S.N. Durlauf, D. Lane (Eds.), The Economy as an Evolving Complex System II, Adisson Wesley, Reading Mass, 1997.

[14] W.A. Brock, C.H. Hommes, Heterogeneous beliefs and routes to chaos in a simple asset pricing model, J. Econ. Dyn. Control 22 (1998) 1235–1274.

[15] A. Kirman, Aggregate activity and economic organization, Revue Europeenne des Sciences Sociales 38 (1999) 189–230.

[16] B. LeBaron, Agent-based computational finance: Suggested readings and early research, J. Econ. Dyn. Control 24 (2000) 679–702.

[17] M.A.R. de Cara, O. Pla, F. Guinea, Competition, efficiency and collective behaviour in the "El Farol" bar model, Eur. Phys. J. B 10 (1999) 187–191.

[18] L. Marengo, H. Tordjman, Speculation, heterogeneity and learning: a simulation model of exchange rate dynamics, Kyklos 49 (1996) 407–437.

[19] R. Savit, R. Manuca, R. Riolo, Adaptive competition, market efficiency and phase transition, Phys. Rev. Lett. 82 (10) (1998) 2203–2206.

[20] N.F. Johnson, M. Hart, P.M. Hui, Crowd effects and volatility in a competitive market, Phys. A 269 (1999) 1–8.

[21] D. Challet, M. Marsili, Phase transition and symmetry breaking in the minority game, Phys. Rev. E 60 (1999).

[22] M. Marsili, D. Challet, R. Zecchina, Exact solution of a modified El Farol's bar problem: Efficiency and the role of market impact, Phys. A 280 (2000) 522–553.

[23] C. Camerer, T. Ho, Experience weighted attraction learning in games: a unifying approach, Econometrica 67 (4) (1999) 827–874.

[24] I. Erev, A. Roth, Predicting how people play games: reinforcement learning in experimental games with unique, mixed strategy equilibria, Am. Econ. Rev. 88 (1998) 848–881.

[25] J.W. Weibull, Evolutionary Game Theory, MIT Press, Cambridge, Mass, 1995.

[26] R.H. Thaler, Advances in Behavioral Finance, Russell Sage Foundation, New York, 1993.

[27] D. Fudenberg, D.K. Levine, The Theory of Learning in Games, MIT Press, Cambridge, Mass, 1998.

[28] A. Cavagna, J.P. Garrahan, I. Giardina, D. Sherrington, A thermal model for adaptive competition in a market, Phys. Rev. Lett. 83 (21) (1999) 4429–4432.

[29] M.A.R. de Cara, O. Pla, F. Guinea, Learning, competition and cooperation in simple game, Eur. Phys. J. B 13 (2000) 413–416.

[30] D. Easley, A. Rustichini, Choice without beliefs, Econometrica 67 (1999) 1157–1184.

[9]

ELSEVIER

Journal of Mathematical Economics 41 (2005) 197–228

JOURNAL OF
Mathematical
ECONOMICS

www.elsevier.com/locate/jmateco

Institutional architectures and behavioral ecologies in the dynamics of financial markets

Giulio Bottazzi*, Giovanni Dosi, Igor Rebesco

S. Anna School of Advanced Studies, P.za Martiri della Liberta 33, Pisa, Italy

Received 8 November 2002; received in revised form 11 July 2003; accepted 16 February 2004
Available online 2 July 2004

Abstract

The paper examines the properties of financial market dynamics, under different trading protocols. We start with an empirical analysis of the statistical properties of daily data from the world's major Stock Exchanges, comparing the behavior of different market phases characterized by different trading protocols. The evidence lends support to the importance of investigating the outcome of alternative market mechanisms. Motivated by this finding, we present an agent-based model allowing the consistent treatment of agents' behavior under three different trading set-ups, namely a Walrasian auction, a batch auction and an 'order-book' mechanism. The results highlight the importance of the institutional setting in shaping the dynamics of the market but also suggest that the latter can become the outcome of a complicated interaction between the trading protocol and the ecology of traders behaviors. In particular, we show that market architectures bear a central influence upon the time series properties of market dynamics. Conversely, the revealed allocative efficiency of different market settings is strongly influenced by the trading behavior of agents.
© 2003 Elsevier B.V. All rights reserved.

Keywords: Financial market; Trading protocol; Market; Architecture

1. Introduction

In this work we explore the impact of different institutional structures governing financial market interactions upon market dynamics. Motivated also by some suggestive comparative evidence drawn from the world's largest Stock Exchanges, we compare the properties of three alternative market models, namely (i) Walrasian auctions (ii) batch auction-type markets and (iii) 'order-book'-type markets.

---

* Corresponding author. Tel.: +39 050 883343; fax: +39 050 883344.
E-mail address: bottazzi@sssup.it (G. Bottazzi).

0304-4068/$ – see front matter © 2003 Elsevier B.V. All rights reserved.
doi:10.1016/j.jmateco.2004.02.006

The roots of the investigation ramify well beyond the confines of financial markets. They concern indeed one of the most controversial questions which the economic discipline has faced since its origins, that is: What determines the relatively orderly aggregate properties – if any – and the degrees of efficiency of market exchanges? Are they mainly due to what goes on in the agents' minds, or, conversely, are they primarily the outcome of some organizing processes which market mechanisms themselves impose? And, if market mechanisms matter at all, how do they fare in terms of comparative efficiency, however defined? Ultimately, one may think of two basic interpretations (with many combinations thereof).

A *first* one emphasizes the purported equilibrating features stemming from the fine understanding that agents supposedly hold of both of their environment (possibly including the strategies of other agents) and of the means to pursue their interests. Obviously, "rational expectations" are the extreme version, but – in much milder forms – the emphasis on the equilibrating (or disequilibrating) role of agents' beliefs and behavioral rules dates back at least to Adam Smith's *Theory of Moral Sentiments*.

A *second*, nearly opposite, view focuses upon the properties of particular distributions of budget-constrained behaviors over heterogeneous, possibly 'bounded rational', populations. A prominent example is Gode and Sunder's analysis of markets populated by 'zero-intelligence' agents (Gode and Sunder, 1993, see however also the critical remarks in Cliff and Bruten, 1997).

Come as it may, institutions governing the *physics of exchanges* – including centralized versus decentralized trading mechanisms, the frequency of trading, the rules for price formation and those prescribing who is trading with whom and when – are central to this latter interpretation, but are also likely to be important parts of the former ones, except for their simplest versions. After all, market institutions also shape the information agent access, the processes of competition and selection, the mechanisms of aggregation and price formation, etc.

However, surprising as it sounds, not much work has gone into the study of the aggregate implications of different architectures of both financial and real markets[1]. As LeBaron ends his survey of agent-based models of financial markets, one of the major open issues ahead concerns the study of the properties of different trading set-ups (LeBaron, 2000, p. 698). This is also the point of departure of this work which tries to identify some distinctive properties of diverse market mechanisms.

More precisely, one begins to address two challenging questions, namely,

(i) what happens to market dynamics if one changes market interaction mechanisms, while holding constant individual characteristics (including the distribution of cognitive and behavioral patterns), and, conversely,

(ii) holding constant institutional set-ups governing information diffusion and interaction patterns, what happens as one varies the "ecology" of behavioral types of agents?

---

[1] Among the remarkable exceptions one finds the studies by Alan Kirman and collaborators: see for example, Kirman and Vignes (1991) on the fish market. Concerning financial markets, 'microstructure' studies (see Goodhart et al., 1996) certainly represent a major step in the right direction, although one still falls short of any explicit account of the dynamics of exchange.

We address these questions making use of an agent-based simulation model[2] describing heterogeneous populations of boundedly rational, budget-constrained agents trading an asset whose price is endogenously determined by market exchanges. Agents are endowed with an "adaptive" rationality on which they ground their expectations about the future price of the asset. In our model, different types of agents come to different expectations even in presence of an identical information. In turn, these expectations shape their behavior in the market. For the time being, we freeze all learning and all selection processes and we focus on the comparative properties of diverse institutional architectures, i.e. diverse trading mechanisms, nesting different populations of traders.

The spirit of the model which follows is to a large extent akin that inspiring already existing computer-simulated "artificial financial markets", such as those by Arthur et al. (1997), Beltratti and Margarita (1992), Brock and Hommes (1998), Chiaromonte et al. (1998), Farmer (2002), Hens et al. (2002), Lux and Marchesi (1999), Marengo and Tordjman (1996) and Yang (2000) (see the review in LeBaron, 2000).

Obvious common points of departure are (i) the acknowledgment of the limitations of models of market dynamics centered upon the behavior of a mythical representative agent endowed with unbiased forward-looking expectations and, conversely, (ii) the challenge of founding the theory on an explicit account of heterogeneous interactive agents.

Within such a common perspective, however, distinct families of models significantly differ in the ways they model both the agents' behavioral repertoires and the mechanisms of interaction.

In particular, regarding trading protocols, one finds three basic modeling styles and variations thereof. A first one generates temporary equilibrium prices making use of a Walrasian mechanism (see for example, Brock and Hommes, 1998). Conversely, a second *genre* summarizes collective interactions into some "law" governing price responses to excess demands entailing price dynamics in persistent disequilibrium cf. Farmer (2002). Finally, a third family of models attempts to account for explicit trading mechanisms (this family includes Lux and Marchesi, 1999; Chiaromonte and Dosi, 1998 among others). Remarkably, however, even those models taking the latter route have hardly addressed systematic comparisons of the properties of different mechanisms. In fact, in the analysis of the results of the different agent-based models of speculative trading, one finds it hard to disentangle the effects of sheer market organization from the impact of agents behaviors. To what extent are such results dependent on the assumed ecology of beliefs and to what extent are they due to the chosen trading protocols? These questions are the central tasks of the present work.

In Section 2 we present some novel evidence on the properties of daily time series under the two alternative market protocols which distinguish the opening and trading phases of major Stock Exchanges. While a few statistical 'stylized facts' hold across country and market regimes, finer properties are seemingly influenced by the latter. In Section 3 we introduce our model, describing the implementation of the different trading protocols and of the

---

[2] The software used for this work is part of the YAFiMM package, which is publicly available at http://www.sssup.it/ bottazzi. Early investigations of the model have been conducted on 'The Financial Toy Room' (FTR), a general purpose simulation environment originally developed by Francesca Chiaromonte and collaborators at the International Institute of Applied System Analysis (IIASA), Laxenburg, Austria: cf. Chiaromonte and Dosi (1998). FTR is now available at the site http://ftrsim.sssup.it.

behavior of the different agents. In Section 4 we undertake a partial analytical investigation of the model. This analysis represent a useful benchmark for the numerical investigations performed in Section 5. The simulation results robustly support the importance of specific institutional arrangements, and, together, they hint at a thread of interactions between market institutions and behavioral ecologies. Finally, in Section 6 we undertake a comparison between "artificial" and empirically observed market set-ups, highlighting encouraging qualitative analogies.

2. Generic *stylized facts* and institution-dependent phenomena

A good deal of current research on the statistical properties of financial time-series has gone, for sound reasons of scientific priority, into the identification of robust, generic properties which appear to hold across markets and temporal windows of observation. As well known, such stylized facts include fat-tailed distributions of returns; ARCH effects; auto-correlation of volumes and cross-correlation volumes/volatility (for detailed discussions, cf. Brock and de Lima, 1995; Dacorogna et al., 2001; Guillaume et al., 1997; Levy et al., 2000). Together, quite a few studies, broadly in the 'microstructure perspective', have been also devoted to the degrees to which particular market organizations contribute to parameterize the foregoing generic properties and/or yield further institution-specific phenomena (cf. among others Amihud and Mendelson, 1987; Biais et al., 1999; Madhavan, 1992; Stoll and Whaley, 1990, and the survey in Calamia, 1999).

One way of tackling the latter topics, which we share here, is by exploiting the fact that most Stock Exchanges daily undergo the transition between two diverse sets of market protocols. A first opening section is typically organized as a periodic batch auction in which orders are collected during a call period to form demand and supply schedules that are crossed to determine the unique equilibrium price (corresponding to the maximum executable volume) at which all transactions occur. This is followed by a trading section characterized by continuous double auctions in which each agent can post bid and ask prices. In turn such continuous auctions may involve (i) a special category of agents – the market makers –surrogating the auctioneer and making public either firm bid and ask prices (under the "quote-driven" system) or buy/sell intentions (under the "order-driven" system) and, (ii) an order book in which limit orders are stored waiting to be bit or taken by market ones. The trading phase terminates with a closing section yielding the fixing, i.e. the closing price computed as the average of transaction prices, weighted by respective quantities, over the last period of the trading section.

Given the significant difference in the architectures of exchanges between the opening and trading phases, their comparison might reveal precious albeit circumstantial information on their comparative properties.

So, for example, Amihud and Mendelson (1987) and Stoll and Whaley (1990) compare the open-to-open and close-to-close daily series on the NYSE highlighting higher volatility and negative autocorrelation of returns in the former.

Expanding on such a line of inquiry, here we compare the open-to-open and close-to-close daily series for "blue-chips" over periods of at least 1000 trading days taken, subject to data availability, within the window 1 January 1997 to 14 April 2002 for the Stock Exchanges of

G. Bottazzi et al. / Journal of Mathematical Economics 41 (2005) 197–228

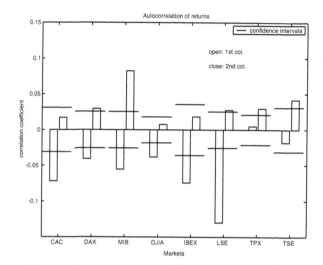

Fig. 1. The one-lag autocorrelation of returns for open-to-open and close-to-close series (confidence intervals are two standard deviations).

Paris, Frankfurt, Milan, New York, Madrid, London, Tokyo and Toronto[3]. This methodology allows one to capture differences in the ways in which different trading protocols matter.

In particular, one is interested in comparatively assessing linear predictability; autocorrelation of price returns; skewness and kurtosis in the distribution of returns themselves; cross-correlation volume/returns; ARCH effects and cross correlation returns/volatility[4].

Some properties, our evidence suggests, do not discriminate between the two market regimes. They include the presence of unit roots in price time series, the positive autocorrelation in volumes and the positive cross-correlation volumes/returns and volumes/volatility.

At the same time, two properties stand out as regime-related (see Figs. 1 and 2) :

- Opposite autocorrelation patterns (with the exception of the Tokyo Stock Exchange) occur. Open-to-open price series display a negative autocorrelation while close-to-close series entail positive autocorrelation[5];
- ARCH effects, while generally present appear to be more pronounced in opening prices (with the exception of the Italian and Japanese Stock Exchanges).

We do not have any ready interpretation of these latter phenomena. For the time being, let us just consider them as adding to the circumstantial evidence on the impact of the forms of market organization upon market dynamics. Indeed, two different market phases, associated

---

[3] Our series are simple averages over a subset of blue chips from CAC 40, DAX 30, MIB 30, DJIA 30, IBEX 35, UKX 100, TPXC 30, and TSE 35.

[4] The full analysis is not reported here but is available from the authors upon request.

[5] A priori, one should just expect a modest positive autocorrelation on the whole indexes due to the so-called "small cap effect" (cf. Brock, 1997; Campbell et al., 1997 and to the non-synchronous trading effects discussed in Fisher, 1966.)

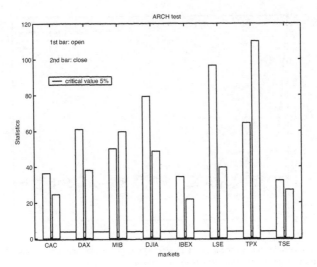

Fig. 2. Testing for ARCH effects for open-to-open and close-to-close returns.

to different trading protocols and intertwined in an appropriate order, are involved in the determination of the open-to-open and close-to-close returns. In the open-to-open case, a continuous trading phase follows the opening batch auction, while the opposite applies to the close-to-close case.

In this respect, it is equally interesting to independently analyze the dynamics over time of each market phase, considered as a proxy of a distinct trading protocol. The close-to-next-open returns can provide evidence on the behavior of the opening phase batch auction, while the analysis of the open-to-close returns witnesses for the dynamics generated by the continuous trading phase.

Some problems do however arise in the latter case with time series of returns because the trading phase is often a complex mixing of continuous trading sessions and market maker intervention (sometimes interrupted by intra-day batch auctions). They involve different trading protocols and it is impossible to disentangle their effects in the open-to-close series of returns. In order to overcome this drawback we have singled out a market segment whose continuous trading phase is characterized by a pure 'order book' protocol, namely the Stock Exchange Electronic Trading Services (SETS) of the London Stock Exchange (LSE) of which we have analyzed daily data for 73 equities over the time window 1 January 1997 to 14 April 2002. In Table 1 we report some basic statistics computed on their unweighted

Table 1

Statistics from SETS of LSE. The annual volatility is computed multiplying the daily standard deviation by $\sqrt{250}$

Returns	Skewness	Kurtosis	Absolute deviation	Annual volatility
Close-to-next-open	−2.51	37.7	0.0034	0.084
Open-to-close	0.46	8.4	0.006	0.13

G. Bottazzi et al. / Journal of Mathematical Economics 41 (2005) 197–228

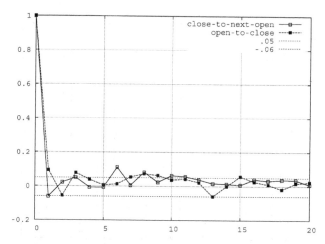

Fig. 3. Returns autocorrelogram for the the SETS index. The approximate confidence bounds (at two standard deviations) are computed using the Box–Jenkins–Reinsel method.

index. This simple analysis is sufficient to highlight the different properties of the opening phase, characterized by a batch auction protocol, as distinct from the trading phase, driven by an order book protocol.

In particular, notice that the skewness of returns is significantly negative for the close-to-open phase, whereas it is not present in open-to-close returns.

Next, consider the autocorrelogram of returns and absolute returns (i.e. the absolute values of returns themselves) as shown in Figs. 3 and 4, respectively. While the long memory effect

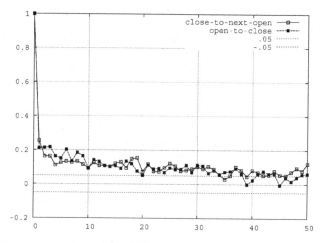

Fig. 4. Absolute returns autocorrelogram for the SETS index. The approximate confidence bounds (at two standard deviations) are computed using the Box–Jenkins–Reinsel method.

204   *G. Bottazzi et al. / Journal of Mathematical Economics 41 (2005) 197–228*

in absolute returns is present in both cases, the one-lag autocorrelation coefficient is negative for the close-to-next-open series, and positive in the opposite case.

How does one interpret such an evidence on the apparent impact of trading protocols upon market dynamics?

Clearly, one of the paramount difficulties in disentangling such a relationship bears upon the impossibility of making real world, historical, experiments changing market institutions and leaving the rest constant.

However, one way of partially overcoming such an obstacle is via laboratory experiments (for influential discussions of the role of market set-ups in experimental economics, cf. Plott and Sunder, 1988; Smith et al., 1988, among others).

Another, complementary, way is through the "thought experiments" entailed in the comparison between computer-simulated "artificial markets", diverse by construction in their market set-ups. This is what we shall do next.

3. Different market architectures and agent behaviors: an agent-based model

The present model describes the market dynamics emerging from the interaction of a population of N heterogeneous agents acting as speculative investors participating in the discrete-time trading of an asset. Traders are supposed to be boundedly rational myopic utility maximizers, whose trading behavior is only influenced by their wealth expectations one step ahead in time.

We consider a simple two asset economy comprising a riskless asset (a bond) which yields a constant interest rate $0 < R < 1$ and a risky one (an equity) which pays a constant dividend D at the end of each period t. The bond is assumed to be the numéraire of the economy and its price is fixed to 1. The price of the risky asset p_t is determined at each period by the trading activity on the market. The assumption about constant dividends implies that there is no uncertainty about fundamentals in the model: all economic uncertainty concerning future changes of the asset price is the endogenous outcome of the heterogeneous expectations of agents themselves.

While the model is in principle quite general, for tractability purposes, we stick on the behavioral side to a rather simple ecology of agents, just comprising "noise" traders and trend following chartists.

In that, our agents, unlike the noise traders in De Long et al. (1991) or the "zero intelligence" agents in Gode and Sunder (1993) do have some reaction algorithms to the dynamics of the environment, but, like them, are prevented from adaptively refining their "mental models" of the market itself. We also censor here any selective mechanism between agents' types and, relatedly, we do not undertake any comparison of the relative performances of the different trading behaviors. The purpose of this work is to investigate the effect on aggregate market dynamics of the interplay between *given* behavioral ecologies and distinct forms of market architecture.

Concerning the latter, we compare three institutional set-ups, namely,

- A *Walrasian auction* in which all agents are assumed to be able to transfer their whole demand curves to the auctioneer who, in turn, matches them in order to clear the market.

- A *batch auction* in which each agent can simultaneously post a *buy* or a *sell* order, both of *limit* and *market* types. Demand and supply schedules are then derived and crossed in order to determine the equilibrium price at which all agents exchange.
- An *order book* in which agents can post both market and limit orders that are matched following a price priority.

The next Section describes the implementation of the foregoing protocols in our model. The description of the different protocols will also clarify the kind of requirements they impose on the description of the agents behavior, that will be illustrated in Section 3.2.

3.1. The trading protocols

In each round of the *Walrasian auction* each agent $i \in \{1, \dots, N\}$ is supposed to provide the auctioneer with its complete individual demand curve $\Delta A_{i,t}(p)$, i.e. the amount of the asset ΔA that it is willing to buy ($\Delta A > 0$) or sell ($\Delta A < 0$) for each possible price p. The auctioneer then computes the aggregate excess demand $\Delta A_t(p) = \sum_i \Delta A_{i,t}(p)$ and fixes the asset price p_t at the value that clears the market: $\Delta A_t(p_t) = 0$. Notice that, in general, the individual demand functions are time-dependent as agents react to changing "market conditions". However, as long as individual demand curves are well-behaved decreasing functions, the existence and uniqueness of p_t is guaranteed.

This stylized exchange protocol provides a price fixing mechanism that forces the market to equilibrium at each iteration. Such a feature makes it an excellent analytical benchmark. At the same time, since the amount of information that the agents must provide to the auctioneer is infinite, encompassing all the possible desired positions for all the possible prices, this can hardly represent a sound approximation of any real trading mechanism wherein processing of (finite) information always entails a non-zero cost, no matter how small.

The other two trading protocols that we shall analyse are indeed based on the processing of a finite amount of information.

In the *batch auction*, at each round, each agent provides a (finite) number of "orders" that can be considered as statements concerning the conditions for its participation to the market. The following two basic instances of an order are analyzed:

Limit orders represented as ordered couples (p, q) of a price $p > 0$ and a quantity q. For "buy limit orders" ($q > 0$), the price p stands for the maximum price at which the order issuer is willing to buy the quantity q of the asset. For "sell limit orders" ($q < 0$), p is the minimum price at which the order issuer wants to sell a quantity q.

Market orders $(\cdot, q)$ express only a quantity that should be sold ("sell market orders"), if $q < 0$, or bought ("buy market orders"), if $q > 0$ at the best available price on the market (the lowest for buy orders and the highest for sell orders).

Once all the limit and market orders are collected, the auctioneer uses them to build demand and supply schedules, computing the total amount of the asset demanded and offered at a given notional price. Within this procedure, the market orders are "priced" at the price that is more likely to guarantee their fulfillment among the prices of the limit orders of the same side, that is the largest price for buy orders and the smallest for sell

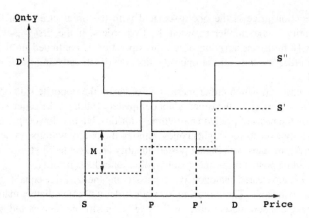

Fig. 5. An example of supply and demand schedules for a batch auction. Suppose that buy orders are all limit orders (the *DD'* line). Conversely, sell orders are composed by both limit orders (the *SS'*, dotted line) and by an amount *M* of market orders which shifts upward total supply to the line *SS''*. Correspondingly, market price shifts downward from *P'* to *P*.

orders. Their quantities are simply added to the schedules obtained with limit orders, hence shifting them vertically: see Fig. 5 for an illustration.

The crossing point between the two curves thus obtained identifies both the price p_t and the total traded quantity. The orders whose price p is consistent with p_t (i.e. buy orders with $p > p_t$ and sell orders with $p < p_t$) are totally or partially fulfilled. For this purpose the orders are considered in sequence, with higher (lower) prices and higher quantities taking priority for buy (sell) orders. This rule guarantees that market orders are the first to be fulfilled.

Notice that, when the largest buy price is less than the smaller sell price, a null total traded quantity is obtained. This event indicates that no trading can take place during this session. The price is considered fixed at the value of the previous session and the next session begins.

The two protocols presented so far are both characterized by some centralized price fixing mechanism that determines a unique price at which all the transactions take place. An alternative "physics of interaction" has to be devised in order to approximate market settings similar to a "continuous trading" phase of a stock exchanges, characterized by a steady flow of arriving orders that can be immediately executed or stored for possible delayed execution. One such protocol is an *order book* type mechanism. The term *book* comes from the list of unmatched orders which stand on the market and are "written" into a file in order to be possibly taken into consideration in future transactions.

In our implementation, during a *book* session, agents are sequentially selected at random and are requested to place a given amount of orders, both of limit and market types, to the market. The arriving orders are managed according to the following simple rules:

Limit orders are immediately executed against orders of the opposite side of the book (i.e. buy side for sell orders and sell side for buy orders) if the two prices cross each other, i.e. if the price of the buy order is not lower than the price of the sell order.

G. Bottazzi et al. / Journal of Mathematical Economics 41 (2005) 197–228   207

The execution price is the one associated with the order already in the book and the quantity is the smaller between the two orders. If the first matching does not completely fulfill the arriving order, this operation is continued until either: (i) no suitable order remains on the opposite side, or, (ii) the arriving order is completely fulfilled.

In the cases in which either there is no order on the opposite side of the book, or there is no crossing, or the order is not completely fulfilled, the order is stored in the "book" on the basis of price/quantity/time priorities. Higher (lower) priced bids (asks) have priority over lower (higher) ones. Among the orders with the same posted price (bid or ask) the ones with higher posted quantity are executed first. Among the orders with the same posted price and quantity, older ones have priority.

Market orders are treated analogously, after assigning them a price equal to the best order on the opposite side. Therefore a market buy order will immediately match the lowest ask price and a sell market order will "take" right off the highest bid price. If there are no orders on the opposite sides, a market order is stored on the book assigning it a *reference price*, i.e. it becomes a limit order with a limit price equal to the *reference price*.

The *reference price* is equal to the price of the last transaction or to the fixing price of the last trading session if no transactions have taken place yet. The fixing price of the session is the last reference price of the session.

3.2. The Agents

The implementation of the foregoing trading protocols involves the basic requirement for the agent that it should be able both to provide the auctioneer with a well-behaved demand function and, alternatively, to provide "the market" with limit/market orders. However, in order to compare market dynamics under different protocols, it is mandatory to model as much as possible agents behaviors as governed by the same rules and as shaped by the same kind of information when the different trading protocols are considered. Ultimately, this means that the way in which agents generate the orders to be posted in the batch auction and book protocols should be consistent with the demand function they transmit to the auctioneer in the Walrasian auction.

Let us thus turn to the description of how agents, in our model, build their individual demand functions and of the mechanism with which they generate, consistently with such demand functions, the orders they transmit to the market.

3.2.1. The demand function

At the beginning of each trading session, each agent constructs its individual demand function and determines the amount of wealth it would like to invest in the risky asset for any possible value of the notional transaction price p. The residual wealth is invested in the riskless asset.

For simplicity, in this Section we drop the agent index from all variables. The following procedure for the determination of individual demand functions is understood to apply to every agent $i \in \{1, \ldots, N\}$.

208   *G. Bottazzi et al. / Journal of Mathematical Economics 41 (2005) 197–228*

Let W_t be the wealth of the agent at time t and let B_t and A_t be the amount of bond and stock present in its portfolio, respectively. Denote with $x_t = A_t p_t / W_t$ the share of the agent's wealth invested in the risky asset. Then the wealth of the agent at period $t+1$ as a function of the stock return $\rho_t = p_{t+1}/p_t - 1$ reads:

$$W_{t+1} = W_t(1 + R) + x_t W_t \left(\rho_t - R + \frac{D}{p_t} \right) \tag{1}$$

The future value of the portfolio obviously depends on the future price of the stock. Let us suppose that the agent possesses some forecasting abilities concerning the future price return ρ_t, which are used to formulate expectations on its own future wealth and, consistently with these expectations, to maximize its expected utility U. We represent for convenience the expected utility of the agent by the simplest function of the expected return and variance (Brock and Hommes, 1998; Hommes, 2001; Kirman and Teyssie're, 2002)

$$U_t = E_{t-1}W_{t+1} - \tfrac{1}{2}\beta V_{t-1}W_{t+1} \tag{2}$$

where $E_{t-1}[\cdot]$ stands for the expected mean and $V_{t-1}[\cdot]$ stands for the expected variance of the distribution of return ρ_t computed at the beginning of time t, i.e. conditional on the information available at time $t-1$, and β is the "risk-aversion" parameter[6].

Using the expression for W_{t+1} in (1) one obtains

$$\begin{aligned} E_{t-1}[W_{t+1}] &= xW_t \left(E_{t-1}[\rho_t] - R + \frac{D}{p_t} \right) + W_t(1 + R) \\ V_{t-1}[W_{t+1}] &= x^2 W_t^2 V_{t-1}\rho_t \end{aligned} \tag{3}$$

The portfolio composition chosen by the agent is the one that maximizes the expression in (2). From the first order condition $dU_t/dx = 0$ and using (3) one immediately obtains

$$\Delta A_t(p_t) = -A_{t-1} + \frac{E_{t-1}[\rho_t] - R + D/p_t}{\beta V_{t-1}[\rho_t] p_t} \tag{4}$$

where A_{t-1} stands for the quantity of risky asset in the agents' portfolio at the end of the previous trading session and $\Delta A_t = A_t - A_{t-1}$ is the quantity of stock the agent is willing to trade (i.e. to buy if it is positive or to sell if it is negative) at time t conditional on the stock price p_t.

The individual demand function is inversely proportional to the risk aversion parameter β. This parameter set the "scale" of the agent's position on the market and, as we will see in the next section, basically defines the impact of the agent on the trading activity. When $\beta \ll 1$ even a relatively low uncertainty on the future asset price is sufficient to strongly decrease its attractiveness for the agent; conversely for $\beta \gg 1$ the opposite holds.

Notice that the demand function in (4) is obtained from a Constant Absolute Risk Aversion (CARA) utility function and does not explicitly contain the wealth of the agent: the desired amount of asset depends on the agent's forecast on future asset performances, but is independent from the agent's actual wealth.

---

[6] The same expression can be obtained from EUT with a negative exponential utility function $U(W) = -\exp(-\beta W)$ under the hypothesis of normally distributed returns.

G. Bottazzi et al. / Journal of Mathematical Economics 41 (2005) 197–228   209

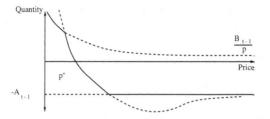

Fig. 6. An example of individual demand function for $E_{t-1}[\rho_t] < R$.

We add to (4) the restriction that agents cannot hold short positions in terms of both assets and bonds. This means that $\Delta A_t(p)$ must be not less then $-A_{t-1}$; hence if the offered quantity of asset resulting from (4) is greater then $-A_{t-1}$, it is replaced by $-A_{t-1}$. At the same time, the demanded quantity of asset at price p cannot be larger then B_{t-1}/p. The resulting demand function in general is not differentiable but does present a continuous nonincreasing behavior. Its shape depends on the sign of the difference $E_{t-1}[\rho_t] - R$: illustrations are presented in Figs. 6 and 7.

3.2.2. The generation of orders

Whatever the form of the demand function, in order to trade under both batch auction and book protocols, agents must be able to express single orders of both market and limit types. To obtain that, we use the following procedure: when an agent is required to provide an order, it picks a price at random in the neighborhood of the last asset price p_{t-1} and then decides the associated quantity on the ground of its demand function. The support of this distribution is determined by the distance between the last price of the asset p_{t-1} and the agent's individual equilibrium price p^*, i.e. the price at which its present portfolio would face no rebalancing $\Delta A_t(p^*) = 0$. The exact procedure depends on the side of the order, i.e. whether of the buy or sell type.

For a *sell order*, the order price p is obtained from

$$\log(p) = \log(p^*) + \varepsilon|\log(p_{t-1}) - \log(p^*)| \tag{5}$$

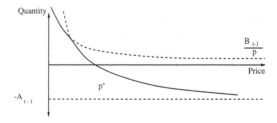

Fig. 7. An example of individual demand function for $E_{t-1}[\rho_t] > R$.

where ε is a random variable drawn from an uniform distribution on $[0, 1]$. The associated quantity is derived from the demand function $q = \Delta A_t(p)$. The quantity is negative as it should be for a sell order, since, according to (5), $p \geq p^*$ and ΔA_t is a nonincreasing function of p. If $\varepsilon < \eta$, with $\eta \in [0, 1]$ a parameter specific of the agent, the supplied order is a market order $(\cdot, \Delta A_t(p))$; otherwise it is a limit order $(p, \Delta A_t(p))$. The parameter η defines the agent propensity to submit market orders: if $\eta = 1$ all the orders are market orders while if $\eta = 0$ all the orders are of the limit type. Under this prescription market orders tend to be generated with prices nearer to p^* and, consequently, they entail smaller quantities.

Analogously, for a *buy order* the price is obtained by

$$\log(p) = \log(p^*) - \varepsilon|\log(p_{t-1}) - \log(p^*)| \tag{6}$$

where ε has the same meaning as above. Notice that a buy order can in principle be issued by agents owning no asset, i.e. $A = 0$. In this case p^* does not exist and the following rule is used instead

$$\log(p) = \log(p_{t-1}) - \varepsilon|\log(p_{t-2}) - \log(p_{t-1})| \tag{7}$$

The subsequent determination of the order quantity and the decision whether to submit a limit or a market order is undertaken following the same rules as of the sell-type decision.

Notice that, according to this whole procedure, the generated limits order $(p, \Delta A_t(p))$ are points which always lay on the agents demand function. Moreover, the requirement that agents take into consideration the last price of the asset to generate prices for their orders is consistent with the idea of maximizing the probability of the order to be fulfilled.

3.3. Agents typologies

The form of the demand function assumed in (4) is consistent with the agent budget-constraint and depends only on the parameter β, measuring the agent risk aversion, and on the agent's forecasts about future asset prices, captured by the two expectations $E_{t-1}[\rho_t]$ and $V_{t-1}[\rho_t]$.

In this paper we confine our attention to the case where the agents belong to two generic types, meant to be stylized metaphors of two different trading patterns, which we call *trend followers* and *noise traders*. Both types believe in the existence of some underlying stochastic process describing the dynamics of prices and form their expectations about the mean and variance of future returns on the ground of their distinct "visions of the world".

3.3.1. Trend followers

Trend followers assume that price dynamics follow a (geometric), almost stationary, Brownian motion and that future returns can be predicted on the base of past history using some consistent statistical estimator. More precisely, in their forecasting of return and volatility, they behave as naïve econometricians, using the exponentially weighted moving average (EWMA) of return R_{t-1}^{MA} in order to obtain the forecast for the return, and the

G. *Bottazzi et al. / Journal of Mathematical Economics 41 (2005) 197–228*   211

exponentially weighted sample variance of past returns V_{t-1}^{MA} for the prediction of variance. The EWMA estimates R_{t-1}^{MA} and V_{t-1}^{MA} are defined as follows:

$$R_{t-1}^{MA} = (1 - \lambda) \sum_{\tau=2}^{\infty} \lambda^{\tau-2} \rho_{t-\tau}$$
$$V_{t-1}^{MA} = (1 - \lambda) \sum_{\tau=2}^{\infty} \lambda^{\tau-2} [\rho_{t-\tau} - R_{t-1}^{MA}]^2 \tag{8}$$

where $\lambda \in (0, 1)$ is a measure of the length of the memory of the agent: the smaller λ, the lower the relative weight of observations far from the past. Notice that these expressions are analogous to the one proposed by the RiskMetrics^{TM} group (see Longerstaey et al., 1996), and widely applied by actual operators in their forecasting activity[7]. The estimates in (8) also admit a recursive form:

$$R_{t-1}^{MA} = \lambda R_{t-2}^{MA} + (1 - \lambda) \rho_{t-2}$$
$$V_{t-1}^{MA} = \lambda V_{t-2}^{MA} + \lambda (1 - \lambda) (\rho_{t-2} - R_{t-2}^{MA})^2. \tag{9}$$

In order to differentiate among different trend followers, we introduce a source of idiosyncratic noise affecting agents' individual forecasts. We assume that the forecasts by trend followers are noisy version of the EWMA estimator and set

$$E_{t-1}^{TF}[\rho_t] = R_{t-1}^{MA} + \varepsilon_t^{TF}$$
$$V_{t-1}^{TF}[\rho_t] = V_{t-1}^{MA} \tag{10}$$

where ε^{TF} is an i.i.d. random variable, with zero mean, independently generated for each agent at each time step.

3.3.2. Noise traders

Noise traders are assumed to have a pure-noise forecasting rule for future price returns while they follow the same rule as trend followers concerning the estimation of future variance:

$$E_{t-1}^{NT}[h(t)] = E^{NT} + \varepsilon_t^{NT}$$
$$V_{t-1}^{TF}[h(t)] = V_{t-1}^{MA} \tag{11}$$

where ε^{NT} is a random variable with the same structure of ε^{TF} and E^{NT} is a fixed parameter, different for different agents, which describes a static idiosyncratic component of noise traders forecast. The value of E^{NT} is randomly and independently generated for each agent at the beginning of the simulation and kept fixed along the whole simulation history.

Notice that, within this setting, the heterogeneity inside the population of noise traders is, in general, higher that the one among trend followers. The latter, indeed, differ only with respect to the idiosyncratic component in their return forecasts, while the former also possess different underlying (constant) estimators E^{NT}.

---

[7] The RiskMetrics^{TM} group actually proposes an EWMA estimator of the volatility, defined as the second moment of the returns distribution. The expression above represents its natural extension to the central moments.

4. A benchmark: the "large market" limit

Before comparing the different types of trading protocols it is revealing to analyze the dynamics of the market in the particular case in which prices are set via a Walrasian mechanism and no budget constraint on the agents positions is assumed, i.e. agents can take short positions in both the risky asset and the riskless bond.

In total generality, under these assumptions, it is possible to directly derive the asset pricing equation from the demand curve in (4). After some algebra, from the market clearing condition $0 = \sum_i \Delta A_{i,t}(p)$, one obtains the following quadratic equation:

$$p^2 \bar{A} - p \left\langle \frac{E_{i,t-1}[\rho_t] - R}{\beta_i V_{i,t-1}[\rho_t]} \right\rangle_i - \left\langle \frac{D}{\beta_i V_{i,t-1}[\rho_t]} \right\rangle_i = 0. \tag{12}$$

where $\bar{A} = A_{\text{TOT}}/N$ is the average number of asset units per agent, i.e. the total amount of asset over the number of agents, and $\langle \cdot \rangle_i$ denotes the average of the argument on the population of agents. The term $\bar{A}$ is positive and (12) has two real roots, of which only one positive, which we take to be the price p_t. Thus, the form of the utility function assumed in (2) generates demand schedules which in equilibrium yield unique and positive prices.

Incidentally, note that, in contrast with Brock and Hommes (1998), we obtain a non-linear price equation due to the fact that we do not assume a null total supply of asset, i.e. we do not put $\bar{A} = 0$.

If all agents expect that the price will be constant - so that they predict zero mean and zero variance for future returns - the only solution of (12) is $\bar{p} = D/R$. This outcome can be easily seen from (12) by taking the limit $E_{i,t-1}[\rho_t] \to 0$ and $V_{i,t-1}[\rho_t] \to 0$ for each i. This solution corresponds to the fixed point of the dynamics of the model, and, interestingly, it does not depend on any behavioral parameter of the agents (in fact, it is easy to show that it corresponds to the rational expectation equilibrium of the model).

Further properties can be uncovered by specifying Eq. (12) according to the behavioral restrictions, deriving from traders types described in Section 3.3 above.

Suppose that there are N^{TF} trend followers and N^{NT} noise traders operating on the market ($N^{\text{TF}} + N^{\text{NT}} = N$), characterized for simplicity by the same forecasting parameter λ. Let

$$\beta^{\text{TF}} = \left(\left\langle \frac{1}{\beta_i} \right\rangle_{i \in \text{TF}} \right)^{-1}, \quad \beta^{\text{NT}} = \left(\left\langle \frac{1}{\beta_i} \right\rangle_{i \in \text{NT}} \right)^{-1} \tag{13}$$

be the effective risk aversions of the population of trend followers and noise traders. Here $\langle \cdot \rangle_{i \in \text{TF}}$ and $\langle \cdot \rangle_{i \in \text{NT}}$ denote the average of the argument over the N^{TF} trend followers and over the N^{NT} noise traders, respectively. In (13) the effective risk aversion of a group of agents is defined as the harmonic mean of the risk aversions of the agents belonging to the group, i.e. as the inverse of their average risk tolerance.

Next define the average idiosyncratic shocks of the two groups as the average of the forecasting shocks of the agents belonging to the groups weighted with their risk tolerances, namely

$$e_t^{\text{TF}} = \beta^{\text{TF}} \left\langle \frac{\varepsilon_{i,t}^{\text{TF}}}{\beta_i} \right\rangle_{i \in \text{TF}}, \quad \bar{e}_t^{\text{NT}} = \beta^{\text{NT}} \left\langle \frac{\varepsilon_{i,t}^{\text{NT}}}{\beta_i} \right\rangle_{i \in \text{NT}} \tag{14}$$

G. Bottazzi et al. / Journal of Mathematical Economics 41 (2005) 197–228   213

while

$$\bar{E}^{NT} = \beta^{NT} \left\langle \frac{E_i^{NT}}{\beta_i} \right\rangle_{i \in NT} \tag{15}$$

is the average of the static component of the return forecasting for the noise traders population again weighted with their risk tolerances.

Substituting the explicit expressions for the return and variance forecasts given in (10) and (11) and using the above definitions, the pricing equation in (12) becomes

$$\beta \bar{A} \, V_{t-1}^{MA} \, p_t^2 - p_t \left(s^{TF}(R_{t-1}^{MA} + e_t^{TF}) - R + s^{NT}(\bar{E}^{NT} + e_t^{NT}) \right) - D = 0 \tag{16}$$

where $\beta = N/(N^{TF}/\beta^{TF} + N^{NT}/\beta^{NT})$ is the effective risk aversion of the total population and $s^i = \beta N^i/\beta^i$ with $i \in \{TF, NT\}$ are the population shares of the two groups of trend followers and noise traders, rescaled by their effective risk tolerances. Notice that the impact of one group of agents on the price of the asset is not proportional to its relative size, since it also depends on the group effective risk aversion. Even a relatively small group of agents can have a big impact on the determination of the price p_t if its effective β is low.

Using the recursive definition of the EWMA estimator in (8) and taking the positive root of (16) one straightforwardly derives the set of equations that recursively describe the dynamic of the system

$$\begin{cases} p_t = (s^{TF} R_{t-1}^{MA} + s^{TF} e_t^{TF} + s^{NT} e_t^{NT} - r \\ \qquad + \sqrt{(R_{t-1}^{MA} + s^{TF} e_t^{TF} + s^{NT} e_t^{NT} - r)^2 + 4\gamma D V_{t-1}^{MA})(2\gamma V_{t-1}^{MA})} \\ R_t^{MA} = \lambda R_{t-1}^{MA} + (1 - \lambda)\rho_{t-1} \\ V_t^{MA} = \lambda V_{t-1}^{MA} + \lambda(1 - \lambda)(\rho_{t-1} - R_{t-1}^{MA})^2 \end{cases}$$

where

$$\begin{aligned} \gamma &= \beta \bar{A} \\ r &= R - s^{NT} \bar{E}^{NT}. \end{aligned} \tag{18}$$

The system in (17) is a noisy dynamical system with two independent sources of noise, e_t^{TF} and e_t^{NT}, originating from the agents' idiosyncratic shocks on return forecasts. The deterministic skeleton of the system, where these sources of noise are removed, that is $e^{TF} \to 0$ and $e^{NT} \to 0$, corresponds, under the Central Limit Theorem, to the "large market" limit, obtained when one considers an infinite number of independent agents operating on the market.

The analysis of the deterministic skeleton of a system of the type (17) has been undertaken in Bottazzi (2002), to which we refer for the relevant proofs. For the present discussion just a few properties ought to be mentioned:

- The deterministic skeleton of system (17) possesses a single fixed point characterized by the price

$$\bar{p} = \frac{D}{r} = \frac{D}{R - s^{NT} \bar{E}^{NT}} \tag{19}$$

- The stability domain in the parameters' space of this fixed point is defined by the inequality

$$\lambda + \frac{R - s^{NT} \bar{E}^{NT}}{s^{TF}} > 1 \tag{20}$$

- The system does, in general, possess more then one attractor, and the general (i.e. not fixed point) attractor of the system is a bounded set with possibly strange character, associated with periodic, quasi-periodic or chaotic price dynamics.

Notice that the fixed point differs from the asset fundamental value D/R by a correction factor due to the aggregate impact of the noise traders' biases $\bar{E}^{NT}$. If one assumes that the static component of the noise traders' forecast rule is centered around zero – corresponding to a complete symmetry between overvaluation and undervaluation of future asset returns – the price at the fixed point reduces to the asset fundamental value.

From (20) it is also clear that the trend followers play a destabilizing role. When their number is zero ($s^{TF} \to 0$) the system fixed point is always stable, provided, of course, that the static components of noise traders' forecast errors is small enough to satisfy $E^{NT} < R/s^{NT}$.

Finally, notice that the bounded nature of the system attracting set and the intertemporal budget constraint (1) imply that, even if the total wealth of the underlying economy exponentially increases with an average rate of growth equal to the riskless return R, the shares of wealth owned by the two populations of agents follow a cyclical behavior. In the language of De Long et al. (1991), even if one group can possibly dominate the other, the survival of both groups is always guaranteed.

5. Simulation features and results

To sum up, the behavior of any generic agent in our model can be completely specified by just three parameters: its risk aversion, β; the time horizon over which it evaluates past asset performances in order to build its own forecasts about price movement, λ; and its propensity to submit market orders instead of limit orders, η (this last parameter applying only to markets characterized by a batch auction or book protocols).

As described above, there are two sources of heterogeneity in our model. A first one is static and "intrinsic" to the agents, in so far as they differ from the start in their parameters β, λ and η. A second one is dynamic and concerns idiosyncratic shocks on the estimates agents make. In the following analysis we shall use both forms of heterogeneity.

We consider a mixed population made of *noise traders* and *trend followers*. We set the memory parameter to the same value $\lambda = 0.97$ for the whole population of agents. This value sets the decay characteristic time for the impact of past price dynamics on price present dynamics at about 30 time steps. Thus, we expect the cyclical behavior of prices in our simulations to display a period ranging between 60 and 300 time steps, depending on the level of noise.

The value of β for the different agents is randomly drawn from an uniform distribution on $[10^6, 2 \times 10^6]$. This seemingly very large number is due to the fact that we normalize the total amount of asset to 1 and the dynamic depends on the parameter $\gamma = \beta \bar{A}$ (cf. 17

G. Bottazzi et al. / Journal of Mathematical Economics 41 (2005) 197–228   215

Table 2
Values of parameters used in simulation

Parameter	Value
R	0.00001
D	0.0002
λ	0.97
β	$U(10^6, 2 \times 10^6)$
ε^{TF}	$U(-0.01, 0.01)$
ε^{NT}	$U(-0.05, 0.05)$
E^{NT}	$U(-0.01, 0.01)$
Number of agents	100
Transient	10,000
Simulation length	5,000

and 18), i.e. the product of the population effective risk-aversion and the average number of asset units per agent. The support of the distribution from which the values of β are drawn is the same for the two groups of agents. This implies that the order of magnitude of the aggregate demand function of the two groups is similar and the modification of their relative sizes does not affect the effective risk-aversion of the whole population. Moreover, the impact of the two groups on the market is simply proportional to their respective sizes. We have experimented with different support for the distribution of β, from $\beta \sim 10^3$ to $\sim 10^8$: results happen to be robust to such variation.

The dynamic components of the agents' heterogeneity, ε^{TF} and ε^{NT}, are randomly and independently drawn from an uniform distribution with support $[-0.01, 0.01]$ for trend followers and $[-0.05, 0.05]$ for noise traders. The static components of noise traders forecasts E^{NT} are drawn from an uniform distribution with support $[-0.01, 0.01]$.

Finally, in order to warrant some market liquidity, we require agents to post, at the same time, a sell and a buy order within both the batch auction and the order book protocols, following the procedure outlined in Section 3.2.2.

The values of the parameters used during the simulations are summarized in Table 2.

5.1. Market dynamics and the role of noise

Before starting the systematic exploration of the properties of the model under a wide set of conditions, in terms of agent ecologies and trading protocols, it is interesting to qualitatively inspect the typical dynamics of the aggregate time series for prices and quantities generated under the parameters setting described above. In this way, one can also verify the extent to which the system in (17) is able to approximate the emerging dynamics when agents' budget constraints apply and different trading protocols are used. We perform this analysis considering a mixed population of 50 trend followers and 50 noise traders. We run two sets of simulations, allowing only for limit orders ($\eta = 0$). In a first set, the agents have parameters values as described in Table 2, except that we reduce the idiosyncratic noise on return forecasts by a factor of 10, i.e. we take $\varepsilon^{TF} \in U(-0.001, 0.001)$, $\varepsilon^{NT} \in U(-0.005, 0.005)$ and $E^{NT} \in U(-0.001, 0.001)$. In a second set we use exactly the values reported in Table 2.

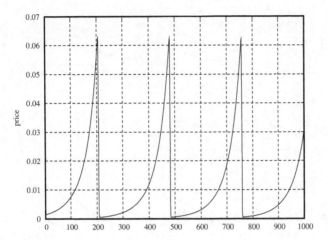

Fig. 8. Price dynamics of the deterministic skeleton of (17) with R, D and λ as in Table 2, $\beta = 1.5 \times 10^6$ and $s^{\mathrm{TF}} = s^{\mathrm{NT}} = 0.5$.

As shown in Fig. 9, in the first set of simulations, when the idiosyncratic noise components are rather low, the three protocols generate a quite similar price history. In Fig. 8 we report the price time series generated directly from the deterministic version ($e_t^{\mathrm{TF}} = e_t^{\mathrm{NT}} = 0 \forall t$) of (17) with R, D and λ set according to Table 2, with $s^{\mathrm{TF}} = s^{\mathrm{NT}} = 0.5$ and with the risk aversion parameter taking the average value considered in simulations $\beta = 1.5 \times 10^6$. As one can see, the cyclical behavior in the dynamics of (17) shown in Fig. 8 still appears in all the price series reported in Fig. 9 and the average price is roughly the same for the three protocols. The observed reduction in the support of price oscillations is due to the presence of the noise, which tends to shorten the average lifetime of the market "bubbles", i.e. the periods of steady upward trend, and, consequently, reduces the height of the price peaks. The reduction in the oscillations amplitude is more pronounced in the order-driven protocols, due to their intrinsic "noisy" nature. In fact, in the batch auction, a source of randomness is present at the level of the order generation mechanism while in the book protocol, a further source of noise derives from the random arrivals of agents orders.

The dynamics of traded quantities are also similar, with an increase in the volume volatility and a decrease in the average volume levels whenever one moves from a Walrasian mechanism to order-driven protocols. This is easily understandable, since the Walras case allows for the transaction of the entire intramarginal quantity while in the other two protocols there is a "tradable" amount of asset that remains untraded (we shall come back to this issue below when dealing with the allocative efficiency of different protocols).

In the second set of simulations, reported in Fig. 10, the picture is different. The increase in the idiosyncratic noise magnifies the dynamic differences between the three protocols. First, traded quantities and volatilities turn out to be different across market set-ups. Second, this also applies to the whole price dynamics. Now the cyclical behavior of prices appearing in Fig. 8 is clearly present only in the Walrasian protocol. Moreover, the three protocols also differ with respect to the average asset price.

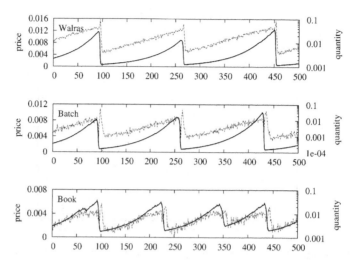

Fig. 9. Price (thicker line) and quantity dynamics under the three market protocols. The simulation is performed with 50 trend followers and 50 noise traders with parameters as reported in Table 2 except for the idiosyncratic shocks, whose support is reduced to $[-.001, .001]$ for trend followers dynamic component ε^{TF} and the static components of noise traders E^{NT}, and to $[-0.005, 0.005]$ for the dynamic components of noise traders ε^{NT}.

There is an important qualitative conclusion already stemming from this exercise. It is the idiosyncratic noise, capturing the fine intra-group heterogeneity of agents, that makes the different dynamic properties of the diverse trading protocols emerge.

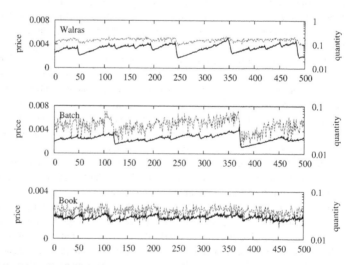

Fig. 10. Price (thicker line) and quantity dynamics under the three market protocols. The simulation is performed with 50 trend followers and 50 noise traders under the parameterization reported in Table 2.

218   G. Bottazzi et al. / Journal of Mathematical Economics 41 (2005) 197–228

With this qualitative property in mind, let us turn to a more systematic analysis of the different behavioral ecologies and their interactions with the institutional frameworks.

5.2. Different trading protocols and ecologies of behaviors

We run simulations with the parameters values as reported in Table 2 and, within every market structure, we consider the following proportions between trend followers and noise traders: 0/100, 10/90, 20/80, 30/70, 40/60, 50/50, 60/40, 70/30, 80/20, 90/10, 100/0.

Concerning the proportion of market orders, we consider different values of η (0, 0.1, 0.2, 0.3, 0.4, 0.5), homogeneous over the population. In the course of the simulations, we discovered that it was impossible to experiment with the full range of values (i.e. $\eta \in [0, 1]$): for values of η higher than 0.5 the overwhelming number of market orders generates an abnormal price volatility which eventually leads to the absence of trade for long periods of time.

In computing the statistics which follow we use the last 5000 steps of each simulation, after discarding the first 10,000 in order to carefully avoid transient effects due to initial conditions. We have in fact checked that this transient length is large enough to let the aggregate dynamics settle around the attracting set of the underlying deterministic system (17). Moreover, the chosen simulation length allows the computation of the relevant statistics on a time scale that is one order of magnitude greater than the price cycles generated by (17) when the parameters take the values from Table 2.

5.2.1. Comparative allocative efficiency

A crucial property of different market institutions regards their relative allocative efficiency, i.e. their ability to efficiently allocate resources among traders. We begin by comparing the revealed allocative efficiency of different trading protocols.

Were one to know the traders' demand functions, a natural measure of allocative efficiency under periodic auction protocols would be the aggregate surplus of buyers and sellers (see Gode and Sunder, 1997). However, since we also want to compare continuous auction market mechanisms, such a notion of aggregate surplus cannot be applied and an alternative measure has to be devised. To this purpose just take the outcome of a notional Walrasian auction as a benchmark and define a measure of "efficiency loss" L for agent i at time t as

$$L_{i,t} = 1 - \frac{1}{1 + |A_{i,t}(p_t) - A_{i,t}| p_t} \tag{21}$$

where $A_{i,t}(p_t) = A_{i,t-1} + \Delta A_{i,t}(p_t)$ is the agents' desired quantity of asset at price p_t and $A_{i,t}$ is the amount of asset that the agent possesses at the end of the trading session. This measure expresses the distance of the agent's post-trade position on the market from the optimal one, given its demand function and the prevailing asset price. The possible values of L range between 0 and 1. Indeed if the agent participation to the market led it to a market position laying on its individual demand function, this would imply $A_{i,t}(p_t) = A_{i,t}$ and consequently $L_{i,t} = 0$. Notice that this outcome is automatically guaranteed when the trading protocol is a Walrasian auction. Conversely, if the agent, at the end of the trading session, finds itself far from its individual demand curve, the difference $|A_{i,t}(p_t) - A_{i,t}|$ increases and, in the absence of budget constraints, it can become infinite, so that $L_{i,t} = 1$.

G. Bottazzi et al. / Journal of Mathematical Economics 41 (2005) 197–228   219

From expression (21) we can compute the aggregate loss of efficiency as the sum of the individual losses

$$L_t = \sum_{i=1}^{N} L_{i,t} \tag{22}$$

over the N agents. For our present purposes, this measure exhibits two advantages with respect to the aggregate surplus used by (Gode and Sunder, 1997). First, as already mentioned, it can be applied to any trading protocol, since it only uses the end-of-trade asset price and end-of-trade positions of the agents. Second, it considers both intra-marginal and extra-marginal traders. This is crucial because in an order-driven protocol a trader may find itself in an extra-marginal position due to the order it originally issued, notwithstanding the fact that it would have chosen to participate at the price at which trade actually happens to take place.

We have computed the average aggregate loss of efficiency L in the simulation experiments under both batch auction and order book protocols: the results are reported in Fig. 11. Notice, first, that the allocative efficiency is relatively insensitive to the particular ecology of agents operating on the market, while it is extremely sensitive to the parameter η that describes the share of market orders issued by the agents themselves. Interestingly, the comparative efficiency of the alternative market architectures turns out to crucially depend upon this parameter.

Under both batch and order book protocols, the loss of efficiency generally increases with η. In fact, market orders bear two conflicting influences upon allocative efficiency. On one hand, since they do not entail any constraint on transaction prices, they may yield post-trade positions which are very far from the agents' demand curves. On the other

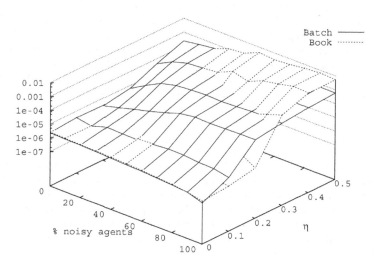

Fig. 11. The allocative efficiency of the order book and batch auction protocols for different ecologies of agents and different share of market orders.

hand, they facilitate the matching of orders and they increase market liquidity, reducing the source of efficiency loss due to involuntary exclusion from trade. The ways the two effects combine depend upon the specific architectures and affect in nonlinear ways the allocative efficiency of the market. Under the order book protocol, for low levels of η, a rise in the latter induces no or very low efficiency loss. However, for higher proportions of market orders, the probability for them to be traded against "abnormal" limit orders increases and, with that, also volatility and market inefficiency. Prices resulting from a match between a market order and an "abnormal" limit order are likely to generate market positions for issuers of the market orders which are far from their demand curves. Moreover, the ensuing "abnormal" prices tend to hinder subsequent trade. Thus, for higher levels of η, allocative inefficiency grows faster.

Conversely, in the batch auction the foregoing trade-off between liquidity and volatility disappears. Abnormal limit orders are automatically prevented from trading by the auction mechanism itself, which, at the same time "forces", so to speak, the liquidity of the market. Thus, the overwhelming effect of market orders is to loosen the control of traders upon actual trading prices. Consequently, the allocative inefficiency steadily increases with η.

5.2.2. Comparative statistical properties of market dynamics

In line with the empirical evidence discussed in Section 2, let us analyze the statistics concerning skewness, kurtosis, autocorrelation of returns and volatility clustering.

It is remarkable that the simulation results, notwithstanding the utter simplicity of the model, most often display comparative properties in tune with those of actual financial markets, both in terms of sign and even in the (rough) orders of magnitude.

We first discuss results for $\eta = 0$ (that is, only limit orders are allowed) and, next, highlight the impact of an increasing possibility to place market orders.

Consider first the skewness in the distribution of returns, shown in Fig. 12. Rather surprisingly, it is absent in the book protocol, while it is significantly negative in both the batch and Walrasian auctions. At the same time, one observes excess kurtosis in the distribution of returns for both batch and Walrasian auctions, while it is not significantly different from zero under the book mechanism (see Fig. 13). Interestingly, the foregoing properties distinguishing auctions from book form of market organizations do *not* appear to depend upon the proportions of agents types, except for the "degenerate" case wherein only noise traders are present. In this case, the distribution of returns converges to a Gaussian one.

Next, let us consider the possibility of market orders ($\eta > 0$).

The effect of an higher value of η in the skewness and kurtosis of returns is shown in Figs. 14 and 15, respectively. The increase of η does not affect these statistics both in the batch auction and in the order book, until its value attains a level of around 0.4. For higher value of η, the kurtosis starts to rapidly increase, while the market approaches the low trading and high volatility condition generated by an high number of market orders.

An interpretation of this phenomenon could be that an increasing proportion of market orders might increase the probability that extreme prices coming from limit orders are actually taken, then inducing fatter tails in the distribution of returns.

Autocorrelations of returns are shown in Table 3. They display a very short memory in both batch auctions and order book markets, qualitatively in line with empirical markets (although not in terms of orders of magnitude: our simulations yield a far too high one-step

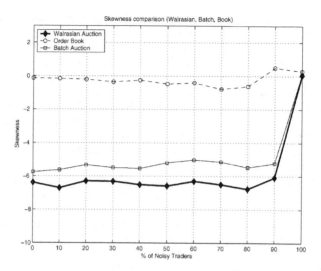

Fig. 12. Skewness of returns for the Walrasian auction, the batch auction and the order book for different proportions of agents types.

autocorrelation). Moreover it is rather striking that the one lag negative autocorrelation for the order book seems independent from both the ecology of agents and the types of order posted and is reminiscent of the negative autocorrelation in high frequency financial markets due to price bounces featured by continuous auctions (see Goodhart and Figliuoli, 1991).

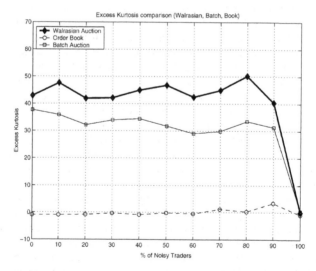

Fig. 13. Excess kurtosis of returns for the Walrasian auction, the batch auction and the order book for different proportions of agents types.

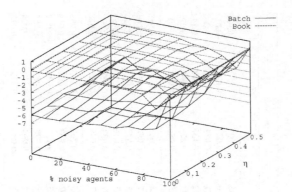

Fig. 14. Skewness of returns for the batch and the order book protocols. The statistics are computed for different agents ecologies and for different values of η.

The same does not apply to the batch auctions which are apparently very sensitive to both sources of heterogeneity. Counterintuitive as it may seem, even a small presence of market orders is sufficient to revert the first order autocorrelation.

Volatility clustering is measured here by the autocorrelation of the absolute value of returns. For the batch auction and the order book, part of the autocorrelograms are reported in Tables 4 and 5, respectively. They show a rather long memory, significant for several time lags.

Finally the ratio of absolute deviations between order books and batch auctions is around 1.4, implying a more volatile dynamics in the former (cf. Table 6). Note also that this property seems to apply irrespectively of the ecologies of agents and of the different propensities to deliver market orders (again, as long as $\eta \leq 0.4$)

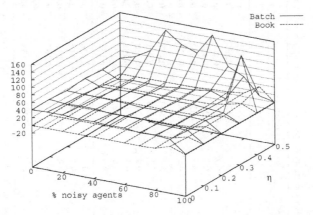

Fig. 15. Excess kurtosis of returns for the batch and the order book protocols returns. The statistics are computed for different agents ecologies and for different values of η.

Table 3
Returns autocorrelation coefficients for the batch auction and the book protocols

Noise (%)	η	Batch auction					Book				
		1	2	3	4	5	1	2	3	4	5
0	0	**0.814**	**0.491**	**0.23**	**0.084**	**0.016**	−0.218	−0.045	0.004	−0.013	−0.02
0	0.1	**0.124**	**0.235**	**0.193**	**0.12**	**0.141**	−0.337	−0.086	0.025	0.032	−0.017
0	0.2	−0.361	**0.06**	**0.061**	**0.035**	**0.132**	−0.316	−0.121	0.031	0.045	0.008
0	0.3	−0.26	−0.16	−0.056	−0.054	−0.004	−0.197	−0.142	−0.133	−0.068	0.142
0	0.4	−0.334	−0.092	−0.041	−0.046	0.025	−0.163	−0.14	−0.075	−0.064	−0.035
0	0.5	−0.443	0.016	−0.046	−0.028	0.001	−0.26	−0.115	−0.056	−0.019	−0.007
50	0	**0.802**	**0.477**	**0.219**	**0.079**	**0.014**	−0.178	0.064	0.042	0.008	−0.015
50	0.1	−0.343	0.011	−0.136	0.092	−0.064	−0.34	−0.017	0.058	−0.031	−0.001
50	0.2	−0.269	−0.212	−0.031	−0.073	0.053	−0.309	−0.055	0.07	−0.016	0.016
50	0.3	−0.317	−0.182	−0.023	0.002	0.026	−0.212	−0.045	−0.016	0.03	0.051
50	0.4	−0.342	−0.103	−0.059	−0.014	0.032	−0.289	−0.131	−0.034	−0.012	−0.002
50	0.5	−0.301	−0.132	−0.028	−0.019	−0.049	−0.29	−0.097	−0.049	−0.035	−0.028
100	0	−0.573	**0.086**	−0.027	**0.034**	−0.039	−0.759	**0.423**	−0.269	**0.167**	−0.093
100	0.1	−0.606	**0.114**	0.005	−0.035	0.03	−0.698	**0.257**	−0.067	0.001	0.019
100	0.2	−0.52	−0.011	0.038	−0.005	0.001	−0.56	−0.023	0.13	−0.039	−0.037
100	0.3	−0.594	**0.187**	−0.156	**0.148**	−0.159	−0.489	−0.101	0.093	0.033	−0.052
100	0.4	−0.292	−0.12	−0.047	−0.067	0.016	−0.441	−0.115	0.042	0.016	−0.004
100	0.5	−0.283	−0.133	−0.048	−0.042	−0.004	−0.187	−0.113	−0.09	−0.029	−0.027

The first five time lags are shown. Higher lags never yield significant correlation coefficients. Values with significance higher then 0.95 are reported in bold.

G. Bottazzi et al. / *Journal of Mathematical Economics 41 (2005) 197–228*

Table 4
Autocorrelation coefficients of absolute returns of the Batch Auction for different fractions of noise traders (in percentage) and different values of η (market order propensities)

Noise (%)	η	1	2	3	4	5	6	7	8	9	10	20	30	40	50	100
0	0	**0.8**	**0.44**	**0.17**	**0.05**	0.00	−0.02	−0.03	−0.04	−0.04	−0.04	−0.04	−0.03	−0.03	−0.03	−0.03
0	0.1	**0.35**	**0.34**	**0.26**	**0.21**	**0.19**	**0.18**	**0.15**	**0.08**	**0.04**	0.01	−0.04	−0.03	−0.04	−0.04	−0.02
0	0.2	**0.45**	**0.22**	**0.34**	**0.41**	**0.39**	**0.33**	**0.27**	**0.23**	**0.26**	**0.31**	**0.2**	**0.08**	0.00	−0.01	−0.04
0	0.3	**0.34**	**0.2**	**0.13**	**0.16**	**0.17**	**0.22**	**0.19**	**0.18**	**0.21**	**0.19**	**0.2**	**0.18**	**0.17**	**0.14**	**0.13**
0	0.4	**0.33**	**0.23**	**0.16**	**0.17**	**0.16**	**0.14**	**0.13**	**0.15**	**0.14**	**0.14**	**0.13**	**0.11**	**0.07**	**0.09**	**0.02**
0	0.5	**0.28**	**0.21**	**0.13**	**0.08**	**0.05**	**0.06**	**0.03**	**0.07**	**0.08**	**0.07**	**0.02**	**0.04**	**0.02**	**0.02**	0.00
50	0	**0.79**	**0.43**	**0.17**	**0.05**	0.00	−0.02	−0.03	−0.04	−0.04	−0.04	−0.04	−0.03	−0.03	−0.03	−0.01
50	0.1	**0.64**	**0.57**	**0.59**	**0.59**	**0.49**	**0.48**	**0.47**	**0.4**	**0.37**	**0.35**	**0.07**	−0.02	−0.03	−0.03	−0.02
50	0.2	**0.53**	**0.43**	**0.46**	**0.47**	**0.48**	**0.48**	**0.46**	**0.45**	**0.41**	**0.44**	**0.37**	**0.32**	**0.25**	**0.15**	−0.04
50	0.3	**0.39**	**0.23**	**0.22**	**0.2**	**0.23**	**0.23**	**0.24**	**0.23**	**0.22**	**0.22**	**0.15**	**0.12**	**0.03**	**0.02**	−0.01
50	0.4	**0.42**	**0.31**	**0.29**	**0.27**	**0.26**	**0.26**	**0.24**	**0.24**	**0.25**	**0.23**	**0.14**	**0.07**	**0.01**	−0.01	**0.02**
50	0.5	**0.38**	**0.24**	**0.24**	**0.23**	**0.21**	**0.22**	**0.21**	**0.17**	**0.17**	**0.15**	**0.09**	**0.04**	**0.04**	−0.01	−0.02
100	0	**0.35**	**0.04**	0.00	0.01	0.00	−0.02	−0.02	0.01	**0.02**	−0.01	**0.02**	**0.02**	−0.01	−0.01	0.00
100	0.1	**0.32**	−0.04	−0.04	−0.02	−0.01	0.00	**0.04**	**0.03**	−0.01	−0.03	0.00	−0.03	−0.02	0.00	−0.01
100	0.2	**0.29**	−0.01	0.00	0.00	**0.02**	**0.05**	**0.04**	**0.03**	**0.02**	0.01	−0.03	−0.01	0.00	0.00	0.00
100	0.3	**0.59**	**0.35**	**0.29**	**0.22**	**0.21**	**0.22**	**0.18**	**0.1**	**0.08**	**0.05**	−0.01	0.01	0.00	−0.01	0.00
100	0.4	**0.36**	**0.2**	**0.19**	**0.17**	**0.21**	**0.19**	**0.16**	**0.15**	**0.14**	**0.14**	**0.07**	**0.08**	**0.03**	**0.02**	−0.01
100	0.5	**0.33**	**0.15**	**0.12**	**0.11**	**0.12**	**0.14**	**0.15**	**0.1**	**0.09**	**0.1**	**0.03**	**0.02**	0.01	0.00	**0.02**

Values with significance higher then .95 are reported in bold.

Table 5

Autocorrelation coefficients of absolute returns of the Order Book for different fractions of noise traders (in percentage) and different values of η (market order propensities)

Noise (%)	η	1	2	3	4	5	6	7	8	9	10	20	30	40	50	100
0	0	**0.30**	−0.01	−0.02	−0.04	−0.05	−0.05	−0.03	−0.01	−0.02	−0.03	−0.02	−0.00	−0.00	**0.02**	**0.01**
0	0.1	**0.15**	−0.09	−0.02	0.03	0.01	−0.02	−0.02	0.01	−0.01	−0.01	0.01	−0.01	−0.00	−0.01	−0.00
0	0.2	**0.08**	−0.05	**0.04**	**0.07**	**0.02**	−0.02	0.01	−0.01	−0.00	−0.03	0.01	−0.00	−0.00	0.00	0.00
0	0.3	**0.46**	**0.32**	**0.45**	**0.45**	**0.46**	**0.35**	**0.47**	**0.42**	**0.43**	**0.34**	**0.29**	**0.21**	**0.17**	**0.13**	−0.02
0	0.4	**0.11**	**0.04**	**0.06**	**0.04**	**0.06**	**0.08**	**0.09**	**0.11**	**0.08**	**0.11**	**0.05**	0.01	**0.03**	**0.02**	0.00
0	0.5	**0.19**	**0.07**	**0.03**	**0.04**	0.01	0.01	**0.03**	**0.05**	**0.05**	**0.06**	**0.04**	**0.05**	**0.05**	**0.02**	**0.02**
50	0	**0.40**	**0.15**	**0.10**	**0.03**	−0.02	−0.05	−0.03	−0.05	−0.06	−0.06	−0.01	−0.02	−0.03	**0.02**	**0.01**
50	0.1	**0.18**	−0.01	**0.04**	0.01	−0.01	−0.02	−0.02	−0.01	−0.01	−0.04	0.01	−0.03	0.01	0.01	−0.01
50	0.2	**0.17**	**0.03**	**0.10**	**0.10**	**0.08**	**0.02**	**0.02**	**0.02**	**0.04**	**0.03**	−0.02	−0.02	−0.02	0.01	−0.02
50	0.3	**0.27**	**0.24**	**0.27**	**0.25**	**0.25**	**0.23**	**0.22**	**0.17**	**0.14**	**0.12**	0.01	−0.04	−0.05	−0.01	−0.00
50	0.4	**0.38**	**0.24**	**0.22**	**0.23**	**0.25**	**0.25**	**0.26**	**0.24**	**0.24**	**0.25**	**0.21**	**0.20**	**0.16**	**0.16**	**0.11**
50	0.5	**0.27**	**0.09**	**0.07**	**0.06**	**0.05**	**0.07**	**0.10**	**0.09**	**0.05**	**0.08**	**0.06**	**0.05**	**0.04**	**0.03**	**0.02**
100	0	**0.38**	−0.07	0.01	**0.02**	−0.01	−0.01	−0.00	−0.01	−0.03	−0.02	0.01	−0.03	−0.01	0.01	−0.02
100	0.1	**0.32**	−0.09	**0.04**	**0.02**	−0.01	0.00	−0.01	−0.02	−0.02	−0.02	−0.00	−0.02	0.00	−0.01	−0.02
100	0.2	**0.24**	−0.10	**0.04**	**0.03**	−0.01	**0.03**	0.01	−0.01	0.00	−0.01	**0.02**	0.01	0.01	0.01	−0.01
100	0.3	**0.22**	−0.07	**0.03**	**0.10**	**0.04**	**0.02**	0.00	0.01	**0.02**	−0.01	−0.02	0.01	−0.02	−0.01	−0.00
100	0.4	**0.31**	**0.04**	**0.08**	**0.11**	**0.10**	**0.12**	**0.07**	**0.06**	**0.12**	**0.08**	**0.02**	−0.02	−0.01	−0.01	0.00
100	0.5	**0.10**	**0.05**	**0.04**	**0.03**	**0.04**	**0.05**	**0.06**	**0.04**	**0.06**	**0.06**	**0.02**	0.00	**0.03**	0.01	0.01

Values with significance higher then .95 are reported in bold.

Table 6
Skewness, kurtosis, mean absolute deviation (MAD): a qualitative comparison between the simulated Batch Auction (BA) and Order Book (OB) and the statistical properties of LSE described in Section 2.

Statistics	BA	OB	Close-to-next-Open	Open-to-Close
Skewness	negative	absent	negative	absent
Kurtosis	high	absent	high	quite low
MAD ratio	MAD_{book}/MAD_{batch} ≈ 1.4		$MAD_{trading}/MAD_{opening}$ ≈ 1.76	

6. Conclusions

The institutional arrangements governing trading mechanisms, we have shown, bear significant influences upon price and quantity dynamics. The comparative empirical evidence assessed in this work hints at this property. And this is robustly confirmed by inter-institutional comparisons based on our multi-agent model of 'artificial' financial markets. Moreover, while each market mechanism exerts its distinct impact on market dynamics, the actual properties of the latter stem from the interactions between market set-ups and the ecologies of behaviors within the population of agents. More precisely, our results suggest that some basic dynamic properties of the time series of price, volumes and returns, like skewness, kurtosis and autocorrelation profiles, are largely shaped by the specific architectures of trading mechanisms, in ways largely independent from differences in traders ecology. The same does not apply to the allocative efficiency of different set-ups.

Interestingly, our simulation exercises suggest that the relative degrees of allocative efficiency are influenced, together, by trading protocols (e.g. batch auction versus order book mechanisms), by the forms of market participations (e.g. limit versus market orders) and, to a lesser extent, by the ecologies of traders types.

How do simulated results help in understanding the observed differences in the properties of observed market dynamics?

Of course, there is no way to match our ecologies of behaviors with empirical, unobserved ones. However, inter-institutional comparisons between simulated batch auction and order book are at least roughly isomorphic to the empirical comparison between close-to-next-open and open-to-close dynamics, respectively. As summarized in Table 6, qualitative comparisons between our "artificial" markets are well in line with the corresponding empirical ones, especially with regards to skewness and kurtosis. Moreover, our model reproduces the empirically observed volatility clustering effects, especially in the case of the batch auction, although it does track less precisely the empirical observations with respect to returns autocorrelations.

More generally, it is encouraging to notice that comparisons between time series generated by our "artificial" markets architectures qualitatively match, quite well, corresponding comparisons between empirical time series observed under different forms of market organization.

Acknowledgements

We gratefully acknowledge the support of the Italian Ministry of University and Research (project A.AMCE.E4002GD) and S. Anna School of Advanced Studies (project ERIS02BG). Among the many insightful comments which helped in shaping the present work, we would like to mention in particular those by Doyne Farmer, Thorsten Hens, Blake LeBaron, Yi-Cheng Zhang and two anonymous referees. The usual disclaimers apply.

References

Amihud, Y., Mendelson, H., 1987. Trading mechanisms and stock returns: An empirical investigation. Journal of Finance 42, 533–553.

Arthur, W.B., Holland, J.H., LeBaron, B., Palmer, R., Tayler, P., 1997. Asset pricing under endogenous expectations in an artificial stock market. In: Arthur, W.B., Durlauf, S.N., Lane, D.A. (Eds.), The Economy as an Evolving Complex System II. Addison-Wesley, Boston.

Beltratti, A., Margarita, S., 1992. Simulating an Artificial Adaptive Stock Market. Mimeo, Turin University.

Biais, B., Hillion, P., Spatt, C., 1999. Price discovery and learning during pre-opening period in the Paris Bourse. Journal of Political Economy 107, 1218–1248.

Bottazzi, G., 2002. A Simple Micro-Model of Market Dynamics, LEM Working Paper, Sant'Anna School of Advanced Studies, Pisa, forthcoming in Proceedings of the Conference WEHIA 2002. Springer-Verlag, Berlin.

Brock, W.A., 1997. Asset price behavior in complex environment. In: Arthur, W.B., Durlauf, S.N., Lane, D.A. (Eds.), The Economy as an Evolving Complex System II. Addison-Wesley, Boston.

Brock, W.A., de Lima, P., 1995. Nonlinear time series, complexity theory and finance. In: Maddala, G.S., Rao, H., Vinod, H. (Eds.), Handbook of Statistics 12: Finance. North Holland, Amsterdam.

Brock, W.A., Hommes, C.H., 1998. Heterogeneous beliefs and routes to chaos in a single asset pricing model. Journal of Economic Dynamics and Control 22, 1235–1274.

Calamia, A., 1999. Market Microstructure: Theory and Empirics, LEM Working Paper. Sant'Anna School of Advanced Studies, Pisa.

Campbell, J.Y., Lo, A.W., MacKinley, A.C., 1997. The Econometrics of Financial Markets. Princeton University Press, Princeton.

Chiaromonte, F., Dosi, G., 1998. Modeling a Decentralized Asset Market: An Introduction to Financial Toy-Room, Interim Report #98015. IIASA, Laxemburg, Austria.

Chiaromonte, F., Dosi, G., Jonard, N., 1998. A Speculative Centralized Asset Market with Adaptive Heterogenous Agents, LEM Working Paper. Sant'Anna School of Advanced Studies, Pisa.

Cliff, D., Bruten, J., 1997. Zero is not enough: On the Lower Limit of Agent Intelligence for Continuous Double Auction Markets. Hewlett-Packard Laboratories, Bristol.

Dacorogna, M.M., Gençay, R., Müller, U., Olsen, R.B., Pictet, O.P., 2001. An Introduction to High-Frequency Finance. Academic Press, New York.

De Long, J.B., Shleifer, A., Summers, L., Waldmann, R., 1991. The survival of noise traders in financial markets. Journal of Business 64, 1–20.

Farmer, J.D., 2002. Market force, ecology and evolution. Industrial and Corporate Change 11, 895–953.

Fisher, L., 1966. Some new stock-market indexes. Journal of Business 39, 191–225.

Gode, D.K., Sunder, S., 1993. Allocative efficiency of markets with zero-intelligence traders: market as a partial substitute for individual rationality. The Journal of Political Economy 101, 119–137.

Gode, D.K., Sunder, S., 1997. What makes markets allocationally efficient. Quarterly Journal of Economics 112, 603–630.

Goodhart, C., Figliuoli, L., 1991. Every minute count in financial markets. Journal of International Money and Finance 10, 23–52.

Goodhart, C., Ito, T., Payne, R., 1996. One day in June 1993: a study of the workings of Reuters D2000-2 electronic foreign exchange trading system. In: Frankel, J., Galli, G., Giovannini, A. (Eds.), The Microstructure of Foreign Exchange Markets. University of Chicago Press, Chicago.

Guillaume, D.M., Dacorogna, M.M., Daveè, R.R., Miller, U.A., Olsen, R.B., Pictet, O.V., 1997. From the Bird's Eye to the Microscope: A Survey of New Stylized Facts of the Intra-Daily Foreign Exchange Markets. Finance and Stochastics 1, 95–129.

Hens, T., Schenk-Hoppé, K.R., Stalder, M., 2002. An application of evolutionary finance to firms listed in the Swiss market index. Swiss Journal of Economics and Statistics 138, 465–488.

Hommes, C.H., 2001. Financial markets as nonlinear adaptive evolutionary systems. Quantitative Finance 1, (1) 149–167

Kirman A., Vignes, A., 1991. Price dispersion. Theoretical considerations and empirical evidence from the Marseille fish market. In: Arrow, K.J. (Eds.), Issues in Contemporary Economics. Macmillen, London.

Kirman, A., Teyssie're, G., 2002. Bubbles and Long Range Dependence in Asset Prices Volatilities. In: Hommes, C., Ramer, R., Withagen, C. (Eds.) Equilibrium, Markets and Dynamics, Essays in Honour of Claus Weddepohl. Springer-Verlag, Berlin.

LeBaron, B., 2000. Agent based computational finance: suggested readings and early research. Journal of Economic Dynamics and Control 24, 679–702.

Levy, H., Levy, M., Solomon, S., 2000. Microscopic Simulation of Financial Markets. Academic Press, New York.

Longerstaey, J., Zangariand, A., Howard, S., 1996. RiskMetrics^{TM}– Technical Document, 4th ed. Morgan Guaranty Trust Company of New York, New York.

Lux, T., Marchesi, M., 1999. Volatility Clustering in Financial Markets: A Micro-Simulation of Interacting Agents. International Journal of Theoretical and Applied Finance 3, 675–702.

Madhavan, A., 1992. Trading Mechanisms in Securities Markets. Journal of Finance 47, 607–642.

Marengo, L., Tordjman, H., 1996. Speculation, heterogeneity and learning: a simulated model of exchange rate dynamics. Kyklos 49, 407–437.

Plott, C.R., Sunder, S., 1988. Rational expectations and the aggregation of diverse information in laboratory securities markets. Econometrica 56, 1085–1118.

Smith, V.L., Suchanek, G.L., Williams, A.W., 1988. Bubbles, crashes and endogenous expectations in experimental spot asset markets. Econometrica 56, 1119–1151.

Stoll, H., Whaley, R., 1990. Stock market structure and volatility. Review of Financial Studies 3, 37–71.

Yang, J., 2001. Price-efficiency and risk sharing in two inter-dealer markets: An agent-based approach. In: Proceedings of the Workshop on Simulations of Social Agents: Architectures and Institutions. Argonne National Laboratory, Argonne (Il), pp., 52–61.

PART III

PATTERNS OF INDUSTRIAL EVOLUTION AND THEIR SPATIAL EMBEDDEDNESS

[10]

Statistical regularities in the evolution of industries: a guide through some evidence and challenges for the theory

Giovanni Dosi

Introduction

Fundamental drivers of the evolution of contemporary economies are the activities of search, discovery and economic exploitation of new products, new production processes and new organizational arrangements within and amongst business firms. Such processes ultimately entail the emergence and development of novel bodies of technological knowledge, novel 'ways of doing things' and novel organizational set-ups. Indeed the identification of the sources of change and the 'political economy' of their economic selection continues to be a major challenge for all analysts of socio-economic change. Knitted together, however, comes also the understanding of the statistical properties that such processes might possibly display. This work focuses on the latter, concerning specifically the patterns of industrial evolution. Three basic questions in particular are addressed here:

(1) Are there distinct characteristics of the micro entities (*in primis*, business firms) and their distributions which systematically persist over time?

(2) How do such characteristics within the population of competing firms affect their relative evolutionary success over time? And, in

Support to the research by the Italian Ministry of Education, University and Research (MIUR, Project 2002132413_001) is gratefully acknowledged. The work builds on ongoing exciting research collaboration with Giulio Bottazzi, Elena Cefis and Angelo Secchi: the reader will indeed notice the widespread influence of Bottazzi's analyses on this work. It benefited from insightful discussions with Bronwyn Hall, Mariana Mazzucato, Sid Winter and from several comments of the participants to the Schumpeter Conference, Milan – in particular Steven Klepper and John Sutton. A skillful research assistance has been provided by Marco Grazzi. This research would have not been possible without the precious help of the Italian Statistical Office (ISTAT) and in particular of Andrea Mancini and Roberto Monducci.

particular, what are the ultimate outcomes in terms of growth and profitability performances?

(3) Amongst the foregoing statistical properties and relations between them, which ones are invariant across industries, and, conversely, which ones depend on the technological and market characteristics of particular sectors?

Note that the answer to these questions has also major implications with respect to the empirical validation of evolutionary theories of industrial change. After all, such theories focus on the twin processes of technological and organizational learning, on the one hand, and market selection, on the other, as the central drivers of industrial change.

If this is so, one ought to be able to robustly detect also in the empirical data the marks of variables and processes which are so crucial for the theory – including, for example, the footprints of firm-specific knowledge accumulation, competition-based selection, and industry-specific *regimes* of learning. Hence the discussion of the evidence which follows can also be read as an assessment of the elements of empirical corroboration of evolutionary interpretations of economic change, together with a series of challenges which the theory still faces.

At the same time, the increasing availability of longitudinal panels of firm-level data is likely to shed new light also on old questions raised in the old 'structuralist' and 'structure–conduct–performance' perspectives in industrial economics concerning for example the relationships between firm size, industrial concentration and the ability to exercise 'monopoly power' and thus extract 'super-normal' profits.

In order to address these questions we proceed in a sort of 'inductive' manner. We start by examining some basic features of the distributions of firms sizes, growth rates and profitability (Section 5.1). Next, Section 5.2 considers some evidence on the underlying inter-firm heterogeneity – particularly with regard to technological innovativeness and productivity – and their relationships with corporate performances.

Finally, Section 5.3 recalls the basic elements of an evolutionary interpretation of the evidence. Together with important points of corroboration of such a view – including those regarding a profound heterogeneity of firms at all levels of observation – one also faces standing challenges – *in primis*, concerning the purported role of markets as effective selection devices.

Some *caveats*. Concerning the sources of evidence, while this work draws on multiple secondary sources, it heavily relies upon the data banks analysed by the research groups of which I am or have recently been part. These data regard (1) longitudinal micro-evidence on

Italian manufacturing (the MICRO.1 data from the Italian Statistical Office, ISTAT), (2) U.S. manufacturing (COMPUSTAT data), and (3) the world pharmaceutical industry (the PHID data bank organized by Fabio Pammolli at EPRIS, Florence).

Moreover, the discussion which follows largely neglects most phenomena concerning 'life cycle' properties of industries, which would require a much greater disaggregation and much longer time spans (for a through discussion on the subject, see Klepper, 1997). Neither do I address explicitly the 'stylized facts' on entry and exit dynamics (cf. the recent survey by Bartelsman, Scarpetta and Schivardi, 2005). Rather, this work is restricted to the distributions of sizes and performances of incumbents, their dynamics and their relations with their underlying technological characteristics.

5.1 Firm sizes, growth rates and profitabilities

Let me begin by considering the old and new evidence concerning industrial structures together with two common performance variables, namely corporate growth and profitabilities.

5.1.1 Size distributions

A first, extremely robust, 'stylized fact' regards the quite wide variability in firm sizes. More precisely, one observes – throughout industrial history and across all countries – right-skewed distributions of firm sizes[1]: within a large literature, see Steindl (1965), Hart and Prais (1956), Ijiri and Simon (1977), all the way to Stanley et al. (1996), Bottazzi et al. (2006), and Bottazzi and Secchi (2003b).

Here Figure 5.1 presents the distribution of Italian firms with more than twenty employees. Here, *size* is measured in terms of value added but alternative proxies such as sales and number of employees yield a very similar picture. Irrespectively of the precise form of the density function, the intuitive message is the coexistence of many relatively small firms with quite a few large and very large ones – indeed in a number much higher than one would predict on the ground of any Gaussian shape. In turn, all this militates against any naive notion of some 'optimal size' around which empirical distributions should be expected to fluctuate. Notice that, as a consequence, also any theory of production centred around invariant U-shaped cost curves, familiar in

---

[1] This property as well as few other ones that we shall discuss below apply also to *plant* distributions. However, in this essay we shall mostly focus on firms which as such may well be composed of several plants.

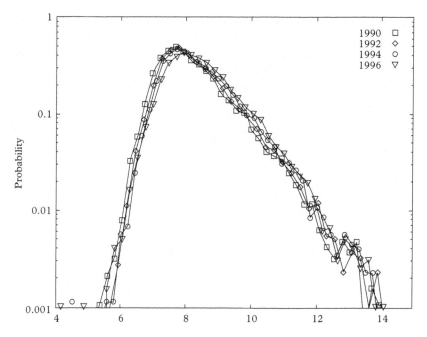

Figure 5.1   Empirical densities of log (VA_i) in different years (size measured in terms of value added). *Source* Bottazzi G., Cefis E., Dosi G., and Secchi A. (2006)

microeconomic theory, lose a lot of plausibility. Were they the rule, one ought to reasonably expect also a tendency to converge to such technologically optimal equilibrium sizes.[2]

Plausible candidates to the representation of the empirical size distributions are the log-normal, Pareto and Yule ones. Certainly, the full account of the distributions suffers from serious problems in offering also an exhaustive coverage for the smallest firms. Recent attempts to do that, such as Axtell (2001) on the population of U.S. firms, lend support to a 'power-law' distribution linking firm sizes probability densities with the size ranking of firms themselves (cf. Figure 5.2).[3]

---

[2] The literature does present interpretations which try to reconcile standard production theory with such an evidence. My personal view is that they tend to range between the implausible and the incredible – the latter including Lucas (1978), suggesting that the observed distributions are the outcome of an optimal allocation of managerial skills-.

[3] The (cumulative) probability density function of a Pareto distribution of discrete random variables is

$$(S) \; \Pr[S \geq S_i] = \left(\frac{S_0}{S_i}\right)^\alpha \quad S_i \geq S_0 \tag{5.1}$$

Statistical regularities in the evolution of industries 157

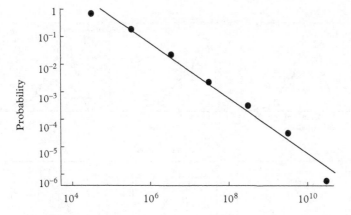

Figure 5.2 Cumulative distribution of US firms by receipts (logs, 1997 $). *Source* Axtell (2001)

The evidence discussed so far concerns *aggregate manufacturing* firm size distributions. Are these properties *robust to disaggregation?* An increasing body of finer sectoral data suggest that in fact *they are not.*

Corroborating a conjecture put forward in Dosi et al. (1995) and further explored in Marsili (2001), aggregate 'well-behaved' Pareto-type distributions may well be a *puzzling outcome of sheer aggregation* among diverse manufacturing sectors, characterized by diverse regimes of technological learning and market interactions which do *not* display Paretian size distributions. While some sectors present distributions rather similar to the aggregate ones, others are unimodal symmetric and almost log-normal and yet others are bi-modal or even multi-modal. Figures 5.3 and 5.4, taken from Bottazzi et al. (2006) on three Italian manufacturing sectors, vividly illustrate such inter-sectoral diversity.

The more recent evidence (e.g. on Italy, see Bottazzi et al. (2006)) based on extensive micro panels does robustly confirm an older "stylized fact" regarding the remarkable inter-sectoral differences in concentration ratios (cf. the thorough overview in Schmalensee (1989), and also the inter-country comparison in Pryor (1972)).

Together, however, the same evidence appear to go against the conventional wisdom according to which sectoral concentration should go together with (sectoral) average firm sizes: in fact the data analysed by Bottazzi et al. (2006) suggest the lack of any correlation whatsoever.

---

where S_0 is the smallest firm size and S_i is the size of the *i*-firm, as increasingly ranked. Under the restriction that $\alpha \cong 1$, this is known as *Zipf Law.* Note that, generally, the Pareto description is generally restricted to the upper tail of the distribution (for which one also finds more reliable data).

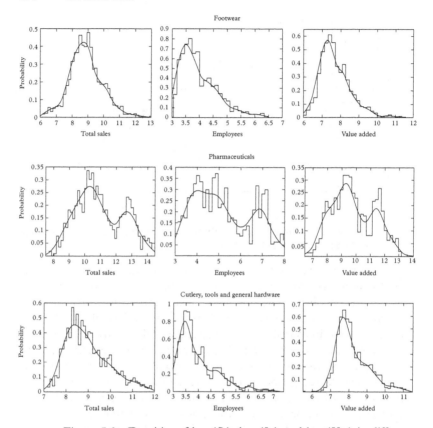

Figure 5.3   Densities of log (S_i), log (L_i) and log (Va_i) in different Italian manufacturing sectors. *Source* Bottazzi G., Cefis E., Dosi G., and Secchi A. (2006)

Finally, admittedly circumstantial evidence hints at a plausible oligopolistic core versus fringe firms separation in several sectors – indirectly supported by the mentioned bimodality of size distributions.[4]

Come as it may, *industrial structures* – in this case proxied by size distributions – are the outcomes of the growth dynamics undergone by every entity in the industrial population (jointly, of course, with birth and death processes).

What about such growth processes?

---

[4] Indeed, an important research task ahead concerns the transition probabilities between "core" and "fringe".

Statistical regularities in the evolution of industries 159

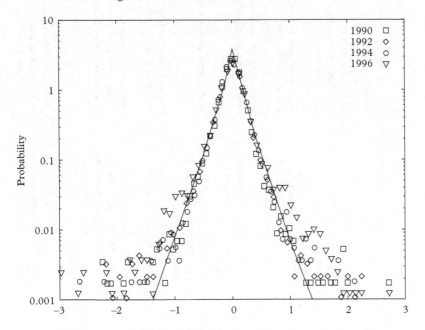

Figure 5.4 Growth-rate distributions in different years. Size measured in terms of Value added. Italian aggregate manufacturing. *Source*
Bottazzi G., Cefis E., Dosi G., and Secchi A. (2006)

5.1.2 Corporate growth rates

It is handy to start the analysis of firm growth processes by setting a
sort of 'straw man' which also happens to be a classic in the literature,
namely the so called *Gibrat Law* (cf. Gibrat (1931), Simon and
Bonini (1958), Kalecki (1945), Steindl (1965), Ijiri and Simon (1977)
and Sutton (1997)).

Let

$$s_i(t+1) = \alpha + \theta_i s_i(t) + \varepsilon_i(t) \tag{5.2}$$

where $s_i(\cdot)$ are the log sizes of firm i at times t, $t+1$ and α captures the
sector-wide (both nominal and real) components of growth.

Gibrat law in its strong form suggests that

(a) $\theta_i = 1$ for every i,
   and
(b) $\varepsilon_i(t)$ is an independent identically and normally distributed
random variable with zero mean

Table 5.1 *Selected empirical studies on Gibrat's Law*

Study	Methodology	Controls	Data	Results
Mansfield, 1962	Logarithmic specification	None	About 1,000 US firms in steel,petro leum and tires over 1916–57.	Gibrat's law fails to hold in about 50% of cases; smaller firms grow faster.
Brusco–Giovannetti–Malagoli, 1979	Logarithmic specification	None	1,250 Italian firms in ceramics, mechanical and textiles over 1966–77.	Gibrat's law fails to hold in most cases when only survived firms are included. Smaller firms grow faster.
Kumar, 1985	Logarithmic specification	Persistence	1,747 UK quoted firms in manufact. and services over 1960–76.	Smaller firms grow faster.
Hall, 1987	Growth-rate regression	Sample selection, heteroskedasticity	1,778 US manufact. firms over 1972–79 and 1976–83 (only incumbents)	Smaller firms grow faster.
Evans, 1987a and 1987b	Growth-rate regression	Sample selection, heteroskedasticity	42,339 US manufacturing firms, subdivided in 100 sectors.	Smaller firms grow faster in 89 industries out of 100.
Contint–Revellt, 1989	Growth-rate regression	Persistence	1,170 Italian firms over 1980–86 (only incumbents).	Moderate evidence that smaller firms grow faster.
Dunne–Roberts–Samuelson, 1989	Growth-rate regression with grouping procedure	None	219,754 US manufacturing plants over 1967–82 (only entrants).	Smaller firms grow faster.
Wagner, 1992	Logarithmic specification	Persistence	About 7,000 West German manufact. plants over 1978–89; (only incumbents).	Gibrat's law fails to hold, but no evidence that smaller firms grow faster.

Dunne–Hughes, 1994	Logarithmic specification	2,149 UK companies over 1980–85 (only incumbents).	Sample selection, heteroskedasticity, persistence	Smaller firms grow faster.
Mata, 1994	Growth-rate regression	3,308 Portuguese manufacturing firms over 1983–87 (only entrants).	Sample selection, heteroskedasticity	Smaller firms grow faster.
Solinas, 1995	Logarithmic specification	5,128 Italian firms over 1983–88 (only entrants).	None	Once the sample is limited to companies with at least one employee, smaller firms grow faster.
Hart–Oulton, 1996	Logarithmic specification	87,109 UK companies over 1989–93 (only incumbents).	Heteroskedasticity, persistence	Smaller firms grow faster.
Tschoegl, 1996	Logarithmic specification, growth-rate regression	66 Japanese regional banks over 1954–93 (only incumbents).	Heteroskedasticity, persistence	Moderate evidence that smaller firms grow faster.
Weiss, 1998	Logarithmic specification	43,685 Austrian farms over 1986–90 (only incumbents).	Sample selection, heteroskedasticity, persistence	Smaller firms grow faster.
Harhoff–Stahl–Woywode, 1998,	Growth-rate regression	10,902 West German firms over 1989–94 (only incumbents).	Sample selection, heteroskedasticity	Smaller firms grow faster.
Almus–Nerlinger, 1999	Logarithmic specification	39,355 West German manufacturing firms over 1989–96 (only incumbents).	Persistence	Smaller firms grow faster.

Source: Lotti F., Santarelli E., Vivarelli M. (2003), to which the reader is referred also for the full references to the mentioned works

Hypothesis (a) states the 'law of proportionate effects': growth is a *multiplicative* process independent of initial conditions. In other words, there are no systematic scale effects.

Note that were one to find $\theta_i > 1$ one ought to observe a persistent tendency toward monopoly. Conversely, $\theta_i < 1$ would be evidence corroborating regression-to-the-mean, and, indirectly, witness for some underlying 'optimal size' attractor.[5]

A good deal of evidence is summarized in Table 5.1, borrowed from Lotti, Santarelli and Vivarelli (2003).

Overall, hypothesis (a) which is indeed the object of most inquiries gets a mixed support:

(1) Most often, smaller firms – on average – grow faster (under the *caveat* that one generally considers small *surviving* firms);
(2) Otherwise, no strikingly robust relationship appears between size and average rates of growth (cf. Mansfiled (1962), Hall (1987), Kumar (1985), Bottazzi et al. (2006) and Bottazzi and Secchi (2003b), among others).
(3) The relationship between size and growth is modulated by the age of firms themselves – broadly speaking, with age exerting *negative* effects of growth rates, but *positive* effects on survival probabilities, at least after some post-infancy threshold (cf. Evans (1987a and b))[6].

Note that such pieces of evidence are easily consistent with evolutionary theories of industrial change. Indeed an evolutionary interpretation would be rather at odds with a notion of convergence to some invariant 'optimal' size, with decreasing returns above it. Conversely, it is rather agnostic on the precise specification of *non-decreasing* returns. In particular, it does not have any difficulty in accepting a world characterized by *nearly constant returns to scale*, (i.e. by values of θ_i in eq. 5.2 on average not too far from one) jointly with drivers of firm growth on average uncorrelated with size itself.

Conversely, precious clues on the basic characteristics of the processes of market competition and corporate growth are offered by the statistical properties of the 'error term' ($\varepsilon_i(t)$ in eq. 5.2). Note in this

---

[5] More rigorously, with $\theta < 1$ there exist a limit distribution with finite variance (if ϵ has a finite variance). In turn, any properly instructed economist would conjecture that such a distribution should display a good part of its mass around the 'optimal size' value. That is, intuitively even under the persistent arrival of 'disturbances' of several origins and several magnitudes, with $\theta < 1$ one may still easily conjecture some 'fundamental' driving tendency toward some underlying 'optimal structure' – whatever that means.

[6] Moreover, the relationship between size and growth appears to be influenced by the stage of development of particular industries along their life cycles: cf. Geroski and Mazzucato (2002).

Statistical regularities in the evolution of industries 163

Table 5.2 *Growth variability / firm-size relations: 'Scaling Law': σ $(g|s) \approx S^\beta$*

$\rightarrow$ *Aggregate manufacturing, U.S. data*

- Amaral et al. (1997): $\beta \approx -.2 \pm 0.03$
- Bottazzi and Secchi (2003b): $\beta \approx -0.19 \pm 0.01$

$\rightarrow$ *International pharmaceutical industry*

- Bottazzi et al. (2001): $\beta \approx -0.2 \pm 0.02$
- De Fabritiis Pammolli and Riccaboni (2003): $\beta \approx -0.17 \pm 0.05$

$\rightarrow$ *Aggregate and sectoral manufacturing, Italian data*

- Bottazzi et al. (2002): $\beta \approx .0$

respect that the absence of any structure in the growth process (as in fact argued by Geroski (2000)) would be very damaging indeed to evolutionary theories of industrial change. In fact, if one were to find corroboration to hypothesis (b) according to which – to recall – growth would be driven by a multiple, small 'atom-less' uncorrelated shocks, this would come as bad news to evolutionary interpretations whose basic building blocks comprise the twin notions of (1) persistent heterogeneity among agents, and (2) systematic processes of competitive selection among them. What properties in fact the statistics on firm growth display?

Growth variability Since the early insights from Hymer and Pashigian (1962), a quite robust (albeit not unanimous) evidence suggests that the *variance* of firms growth rates *falls* as firms sizes increase (cf. Table 5.2 for a concise summary). Interestingly, however, it falls less than proportionally.

Why is that?

An interpretation is that the variance-scale relation depends on the *diversification-size* relation. In fact, firms grow by both expanding within their incumbent lines of business and by diversifying into new ones. In turn, if market dynamics across activities are not perfectly correlated and if size goes together with an increasing number of lines of business in which a firm operates, then one should indeed expect a lower variance for bigger firm sizes.[7]

---

[7] The relationship between diversification and growth variance might also explain the absence of such a scaling in the Italian evidence (Bottazzi et al. (2002)), probably due to

In the absence of any correlation in market dynamics across lines of business and with a number of lines of business proportional to size, one should expect to see the variance fall with the square root of size (that is, to observe a coefficient β in table 5.2 of around −0.5). However, most of the evidence suggests a coefficient of around −0.2, as such suggesting either non-proportionality in the relation diversification size or correlation between markets or a mixture of both. In fact, in Bottazzi et al. (2001) and Bottazzi and Secchi (2003b), one begins to disentangle the issue on the grounds of disaggregate data on the pharmaceutical industry, showing, at least in this case, that the scaling coefficient is entirely due to a less than proportional increase in the number of markets in which firms are active as a function of their size. Moreover, Bottazzi and Secchi (2006b) offers an explanation of such diversification patterns in terms of a *branching process* which is intuitively consistent with *capability-driven patterns of diversification*. As capability-based theories of the firm would predict, the expansion into new activities builds incrementally upon the knowledge and the complementary assets accumulated within existing ones (see also the conjectures in Teece et al. (1994) on the ensuing 'coherence' in the diversification profiles).

Growth rates distributions   One of the most important pieces of evidence able to throw some light on the underlying drivers of corporate growth regards the distribution of growth rates themselves.

For convenience consider again the normalized (log) size

$$s_i = \log S_i (t) \; - <\log S(t) >$$

where $<\log S(t)>$ ($\equiv 1/N \sum_i \log S_i(t)$) is the mean log size. The variable of interest is thus the normalized growth $g_i(t) = s_i(t+1) - s_i(t)$

The evidence suggests an extremely robust stylized fact: growth rates display distributions which are *at least exponential (Laplace) or even fatter in their tails* (see Stanley et al. (1996a) and Bottazzi and Secchi (2003b) on U.S. data; Bottazzi et al. (2001) on the international pharmaceutical industry; Bottazzi, Cefis and Dosi (2002) and Bottazzi et al. (2006) on the Italian industry).

Figures 5.4 and 5.5 present some examples from Italian data.

This property holds across (1) levels of aggregation; (2) countries; (3) different measures of size (e.g. sales, employees, value added, assets),

---

low degrees of diversification of Italian firms, *as they appear in the statistics.* Anecdotal evidence suggests in fact that diversification events often entail the formation of a new legal entity (also due to fiscal reasons) rather than the development of new lines of business within the original company.

Statistical regularities in the evolution of industries   165

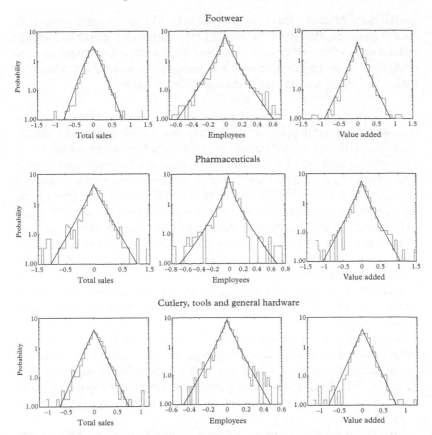

Figure 5.5   Probability densities and maximum likelihood estimation of firm growth rates *g* in three different Italian sectors. *Source* Bottazzi G., Cefis E., Dosi G., and Secchi A. (2006)

even if (4) one observes some (moderate) variations across sectors with respect to the distribution parameters.

Note that such statistical properties of growth rates are indeed good news for an evolutionary analyst. The generalized presence of fat tails in the distribution implies much more structure in the growth dynamics than generally assumed. More specifically, ubiquitous fat tails are a sign of some underlying correlating mechanism which one would rule out if growth events were normally distributed, small and independent. In Bottazzi et al. (2006) we conjecture that such mechanisms are likely to be of two types. First, the very process of competition induces correlation. Market shares must obviously add up to one: someone's gain is someone else's loss. Second, in an evolutionary world one should indeed expect 'lumpy' growth events (of both positive and negative sign) such as the introduction of new products, the construction/closure of plants and entry to and exit from particular markets.[8]

Autocorrelation in growth rates   Another piece of evidence on the structure of growth processes concerns the possible autocorrelations over time. Here the variable under study is in the first difference $g_i(t + \tau) - g_i(t)$, where, as above, the $g_i (.)$ are the (normalized) growth rates of each firm i. Begin by noting that ideally one would like to have time series long enough to describe the properties of the sample path of each firm on the grounds of the conjecture that the evolutionary pattern of each firm ought to be specific to each entity in its interactions with the population of other firms which happen to compete in that particular market in those particular times – all bearing distinctly different technological, organizational and strategic features.

Well short of that, one generally has to be content with *sectoral averages* in the differences $<g_i(t+\tau) - g_i(t)>$, under different autoregressive lags.

Interestingly, in an industry for which one has reasonable longitudinal panel data at different levels of disaggregation – namely the international drugs industry – one does find a robust autocorrelation structure. For example, firm-level growth rates exhibit a long-lasting positive autocorrelation, statistically significant up to the seventh lag (cf. Bottazzi et al. (2001)).

Broader, inevitably coarser, evidence typically on three-digit sectors (as such already aggregates of a quite large number of lines of business) like that in Bottazzi and Secchi (2003b) on U.S. manufacturing displays (1) only a relatively short autoregressive structure (typically with one-lag-only significance); and (2) a good deal of inter-sectoral variability.

At similar levels of aggregation, the Italian panel of manufacturing firms often displays average autocorrelations which are quite small (around $|.1|$), and significant if at all only at the first lag (Cf. Bottazzi et al. (2006)). Even in this case, however, the data suggest *highly heterogeneous firm-specific autocorrelation profiles* within each sector. This is confirmed by 'bootstrapping' exercises involving the comparison between the distribution of *actual* firm-specific coefficients with any

---

[8] Suggestive attempts to model increasing-return dynamics yielding the observed fat-tailed distribution are in Bottazzi and Secchi (2003a) and (2006b).

'virtual' one obtained by randomly scrambling actual growth rates over the same (but randomly drawn) firms. The two distributions turn out to be significantly different, meaning that there are *systematic but idiosyncratic differences* in autocorrelation structures, which are not captured by sectoral average autocorrelation coefficients (cf. Bottazzi, Cefis, and Dosi (2002)).[9]

5.1.3   *Profitabilities and their dynamics*

Together with corporate growth, profitability is another crucial measure of revealed corporate performances. There are three major intertwined issues here, namely (1) the revealed *inter-firm differences* in profitability proxies; (2) their persistence over time; and (3) the properties of their patterns of change.

Some due premises. I strongly believe that simpler measures are better measures because they reduce theory-driven biases. So, for example, derivations of profitability measures from purported technological relations which nobody has actually seen such as Cobb-Douglas and alike are likely to lead to blind alleys (those on this point in Dosi and Grazzi (2006)).

Given that, let me stick to the simplest possible measure of profitability, aiming at the same time at the highest possible degree of sectoral disaggregation.

Consider the variables

$$gom_i(t) = \log(GOM_i(t)) - log(GOM(t))$$
$$GOM_i(t) = VA_i(t) - W_i(t)$$

where

$$GOM_i = gross\ operating\ margins$$
$$VA_i = value\ added$$
$$W_i = total\ wage\ costs$$

and, as above, $< \ldots >$ stands for the sectoral averages.

If capital/output ratios are not too different across firms – as they should not be – the more one refines the sectoral disaggregation, then the simple *MOL* measure should not be too biased a proxy for 'true'

---

[9] Revealing complementary evidence to the same effect suggests that even growth paths, *conditioned on size*, tend to be significantly *firm-specific*: cf. Cefis, Ciccarelli, and Orsenigo (2002).

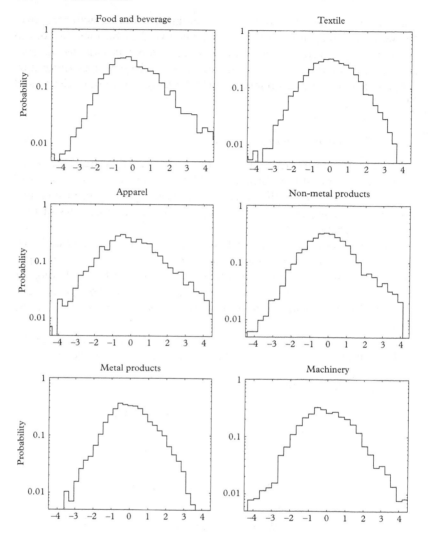

Figure 5.6   Distribution of (normalized) gross margins by sectors. *Source* Our elaboration of Italian (ISTAT MICRO.1) data: cf. text on the data description

profitabilities. Figure 5.6 offers some impressive evidence drawn from the Italian sample on inter-firm profitability asymmetries: the reader is indeed invited to appreciate the width of the support of the density distributions going well beyond, say, ten to one ratios in profitability margins between the best and the worse performers.

Given that, a crucial property regards the persistence of such differentials. After all, evidence on low persistence could simply suggest that capitalism involves daring and heroic efforts by multitudes of firms which happen to make many mistakes as well as reap huge rewards, but markets are there to help and quickly redress individual mistakes and wash away abnormal rents. It turns out that this view does not quite match the evidence.

There is indeed a wide literature on the *persistence of profitability differences across firms*: see, among others, Müller (1986) and (1990), Cubbin and Geroski (1987), Geroski and Jacquemin (1988), Goddard and Wilson (1999), Cable and Jackson (2003), Cefis (2003b), Gschwandter (2004). The Italian evidence strongly supports the persistence view.

As shown in Table 5.3, the autocorrelation over time in profit margins is extremely high in all manufacturing sectors, with just a relatively mild tendency of mean-reversion, revealed by both the negative coefficient on the first differences and the value of the autoregressive coefficient on the *levels* slightly lower than unity.

Finally note that, interestingly, the rates of change in profit margins display distributions which are again fat-tailed, at least exponential, or even fatter-tailed: see Figure 5.7, displaying the growth rates of the normalized margins, $g_{\text{gom}_i}(t) = \text{gom}_i(t+1) - \text{gom}_i(t)$. The sectors shown in the figure are chosen simply to illustrate the point that the property holds across activities that are very different in terms of technologies and forms of corporate organizations.

For the interpretation of such an evidence let me refer the reader back to the discussion of a similar evidence in the case of growth rates of companies as such. Again we find here the mark of powerful underlying correlation mechanisms which tend to induce 'coarse grained' shocks upon profitabilities.

Recalling our previous argument, consider – as a term of comparison – a process of variation in profitabilities of individual firms driven by little idiosyncratic shocks occurring all the time, independent from each other. A caricatural way of illustrating it is by depicting a multitude of producers which all survive near equilibrium (i.e. in the conventional definitions, near a zero-profit steady state), while being nonetheless continuously hit by small and uncorrelated profit opportunities (e.g. one or few unexpected or uniformed customers; some small advances on products characteristics, etc.) If such shocks are uncorrelated, again for the law of large numbers, summing up over, say, years, one should expect normally distributed changes. Not getting it as such is a revealing evidence on 'drivers of change' which are more 'lumpy' and more powerfully correlated with each other.

Table 5.3 *Autocorrelation of gross margin levels and growth rates*

	ISIC CODES	LEVELS		DIFFERENCES	
		AR(1) coefficient	Standard deviation	AR(1) coefficient	Standard deviation
Food products and beverages	15	0,9516	0,0060	−0,3424	0,0190
Textiles	17	0,9117	0,0067	−0,2953	0,0163
Wearing apparel, dressing and dyeing of fur	18	0,9328	0,0087	−0,3992	0,0254
Tanning and dressing of leather; luggage, footwear	19	0,8781	0,0144	−0,2984	0,0307
Manufacturing of woods and related products	20	0,9430	0,0115	−0,3658	0,0332
Paper and allied products	21	0,9432	0,0104	−0,2935	0,0298
Printing and publishing	22	0,9471	0,0098	−0,3917	0,0293
Chemicals and allied products	24	0,9370	0,0081	−0,3315	0,0216
Rubber and miscellaneous plastics products	25	0,9203	0,0085	−0,2917	0,0208
Other non-metallic mineral products	26	0,9430	0,0067	0,3337	0,0190
Basic metals	27	0,9149	0,0101	−0,3245	0,0248
Fabricated metal products, except machinery	28	0,9213	0,0064	−0,2957	0,0155
Industrial machinery and equipment	29	0,9207	0,0055	−0,3215	0,0137
Electrical machinery and apparatus	31	0,9649	0,0086	−0,2382	0,0265
Forniture and other N.E.C. manu-facturing industries	36	0,9210	0,0080	−0,3349	0,0185

Source: Our elaborations on Italian (ISTAT MICRO .1) data. The selected sectors are those which include more than 200 firms

Statistical regularities in the evolution of industries 171

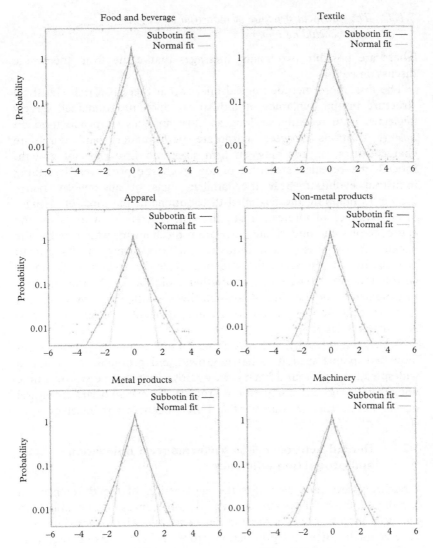

Figure 5.7 Distribution of gross margins growth rates by sectors, Italian data. Each figure displays the maximum likelihood estimates of Subbotin distributions (cf. Bottazzi and Secchi (2006a)) (The fit of a normal distribution is added just to highlight how much were fatter than the observed data are)

5.1.4   *The statistical structure of industrial evolution: some concluding remarks*

There are possibly two major messages that come from the whole discussion so far.

The *first*, more methodological one, is that there is a rich statistical structure in the dynamics of industries which has remained largely neglected until recently, as long as most analyses simply focused on *average* relations between corporate performances and corporate characteristics, or just between firm sizes and firm rates of growth. Indeed, the revealed structure of the stochastic processes describing industrial evolution bear the familiar signs of all *complex system dynamics*, including the fat-tailed distributions in the rates of changes of all variables of interest. That, in turn, is likely to witness for the existence of some underlying correlation mechanism, which makes the system (in our case, each industry) 'self-organizing' in its growth process. In most respects, the statistical evidence on industrial change corroborates the exciting conjecture that evolutionary phenomena tend to generically undergo 'non-Gaussian' lives – influenced by persistent (positive or negative) interactions amongst agents within and across relevant populations.

Second, but relatedly, the core indicators of corporate performances discussed in this section – that is growth and profitability – reveal a widespread and profound *heterogeneity* across firms that persist over time notwithstanding the competition process. Given all that, a natural question concerns the sources of such heterogeneities themselves.

5.2   Behind heterogeneous performances: innovation and production efficiency

Straightforward candidates for the explanation of the differences in corporate performances are in fact (1) differences in the ability to innovate and/or adopt innovation developed elsewhere regarding product characteristics and production processes; (2) different organizational arrangements; (3) different production efficiencies.

Needless to say, the three sets of variables are profoundly related. Technological innovations typically involve also changes in the organization of production. Different ways of searching for innovations imply distinct organizational arrangements regarding the relationships amongst different corporate tasks (e.g. R&D, production, sales). And, most obviously, technological and organizational innovations ultimately shape the degrees of efficiency in which inputs happen to generate outputs.

With that in mind, let me offer some telegraphic overview of the evidence concerning the patterns of technological innovation, on the one hand, and production efficiencies on the other. (I am forced to neglect here the role of organizational variables. In fact, *organizational capabilities* are intimately linked with the very process of technological innovation and with production efficiencies: cf. among others the discussions to which I have contributed in Dosi, Nelson and Winter (2000) and Dosi, and Marengo Faillo (2005)).

5.2.1 *Technological innovativeness*

A rich and wide literature in the field of economics of innovation does indeed suggest that firms deeply differ also in their ability to innovate: for detailed surveys and discussions, see Freeman (1994), Freeman and Soete (1997), Nelson (1981) and (1991), Pavitt (1999), Dosi, Orsenigo and Sylos Labini (2005), Dosi (1988).

(1) Innovative capabilities appear to be highly asymmetric, with a rather small number of firms in each sector responsible for a good deal of innovation output.
(2) Somewhat similar considerations apply to the *adoption* of innovations (in the form of new production inputs, machinery, etc.) revealing asymmetric capabilities of learning and 'creative adaptation' and entailing long-lasting logistic-shape profiles of diffusion.
(3) Differential degrees of innovativeness are generally persistent over time and often reveal a small 'core' of systematic innovators (together with the foregoing broad critical surveys, see more specifically Cefis (2003a and c)).
(4) Relatedly, while the arrivals of major innovations are rare events, they are not independently distributed across firms. Rather, recent evidence suggests that they tend to arrive in firm-specific "packets" of different sizes.[10]

In terms of intuitive comparisons of such evidence with the predictions of evolutionary theorizing, heterogeneity in innovative/initiative abilities is indeed a robust piece of corroborating evidence. And so is the evidence on micro-correlation of innovative events, well in tune with an evolutionary notion of few, high-capability, persistent innovators.

---

[10] On the statistical properties of the discrete innovations, *in general*, cf. Silverberg (2003) arguing for a secular Poisson-type process. However, at a much finer level of observation the firm-specific patterns of innovation are not likely to be Poisson-distributed. Rather, as one shows in Bottazzi et al. (2001) in the case of the pharmaceutical industry, few firms 'draw' relatively large 'packets' of innovations well described by Bose–Einstein (rather than Poisson) statistics.

On a much larger scale, the persistent asymmetries across countries, even within the same lines of business, cry out in favour of profound heterogeneities in learning and searching capabilities.

5.2.2   *Production efficiencies*

As well known, there are two straightforward measures of production efficiency, namely labour and total factor productivity (TFP).

It should come as no surprise at this point of the discussion that, despite its obvious limitations, I tend to prefer a measure based on the net output (that is the 'real' value added) per employee or, even better, per worked hours. The reason for this preference lies in the dubious elements which make up conventional production functions, in turn the instrument necessary to yield the TFP measure. This is not the place to discuss the issue. Suffice to mention, first, that technologies as we know them essentially involve *complementarities* among inputs – so that it makes little sense to separate the 'contribution' of each 'factor' to the final output. To paraphrase on a suggestive metaphor suggested by Dick Nelson, it makes as much sense as trying to disentangle the separate contributions of butter, sugar, eggs, and so on to the taste of a cake. (Again I am forced to refer to Dosi and Grazzi (2006) for more details.)

Second, but related, one typically lives in a technological world characterized by micro-coefficients which are fixed in the short term (i.e. each firm basically masters the technique actually in use), while in the longer term techniques change essentially because of learning and technical progress. Conversely, if this is the case, it does not make much sense to distinguish changes *along* any purported production function versus changes of the function itself.

Come as it may, an overwhelming evidence *concerning both labour productivity and TFP* and at all levels of disaggregation suggests widespread differences in production efficiency *across firms and across plants* which tend to be persistent *over time*: see, among others, Nelson (1981), Baily, Hulten and Compbell (1992), Baldwin (1995), Bartelsman and Doms (2000), Foster, Haltiwanger and Krizan (2001), Jensen and McGuckin (1997), Power (1998).

Our Italian data are well in tune with such stylised facts. Figure 5.8 presents the distribution of (normalized) value added per employee, that is

$$\pi_i(t) = \log \Pi_i(t) - <\log \Pi_i(t)>$$

whereby

$$\Pi_i(t) = \mathrm{VA}_i/N_i;$$

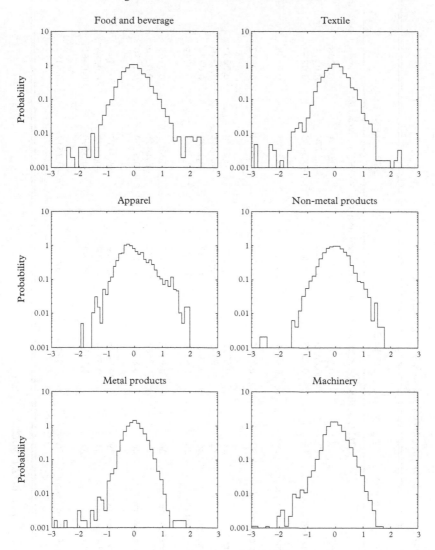

Figure 5.8 Distribution of labour productivity by sectors. *Source*: our elaboration on Italian (ISTAT MICRO.1) data

and

$<\log \Pi_i(t)> \equiv$ mean (log) value added (VA) per employee (N) averaged over all firms in any particular sector.

Moreover, as shown in Table 5.4, productivity differentials are quite stable over time with some mild regression-to-the-mean tendency.

Table 5.4 *Autocorrelation of labour productivity levels and growth rates*

(Labour productivity=VA/#employees)	ISIC CODES	LEVELS		DIFFERENCES	
		AR(1) coefficient	Standard deviation	AR(1) coefficient	Standard deviation
Food products and beverages	15	0,8619	0,0092	−0,2641	0,0208
Textiles	17	0,8699	0,0076	−0,2770	0,0171
Wearing apparel, dressing and dyeing of fur	18	0,9285	0,0087	−0,3428	0,0250
Tanning and dressing of leather; luggage, footwear	19	0,8932	0,0158	−0,3123	0,0398
Manufacturing of woods and related products	20	0,8357	0,0154	−0,3254	0,0312
Paper and allied products	21	0,8772	0,0140	−0,2348	0,0030
Printing and publishing	22	0,8391	0,0127	−0,1596	0,0319
Chemicals and allied products	24	0,7947	0,0132	−0,1883	0,0234
Rubber and miscellaneous plastics products	25	0,8920	0,0108	−0,2831	0,0244
Other non-metallic mineral products	26	0,9057	0,0077	0,3065	0,0195
Basic metals	27	0,8583	0,0135	−0,1645	0,0270
Fabricated metal products, except machinery	28	0,8572	0,0079	−0,3299	0,1580
Industrial machinery and equipment	29	0,8098	0,0079	−0,3177	0,0143
Electrical machinery and apparatus	31	0,8534	0,0119	−0,1072	0,0236
Manufacturing of other transport equipment	35	0,7518	0,0299	−0,3490	0,0481
Forniture and other N.E.C. manufacturing industries	36	0,8609	0,0093	−0,3512	0,0187

Source: Our elaborations on Italian (ISTAT MICRO .1) data

Also at the level of input efficiencies the broad picture is characterized by general and profound heterogeneity across firms.

As Griliches and Mairesse (1997) vividly put it

"we ... thought that one could reduce heterogeneity by going down from general mixtures as 'total manufacturing' to something more coherent, such as 'petroleum refining' or 'the manufacture of cement'. But something like Mandelbrot's fractal phenomenon seem to be at work here also: the observed variability – heterogeneity does not really decline as we cut our data finer and finer. There is a sense in which different bakeries are just as much different from each others as the steel industry is from the machinery industry."

For evolutionary scholars, heterogeneity in the degrees of innovativeness and production efficiencies should not come as a surprise. Indeed, this is what one ought to expect to be the outcome of idiosyncratic capabilities (or lack of them), mistake-ridden learning and forms of path-dependent adaptation. Differences in innovative abilities and efficiencies (together with differences in organizational set-ups and behaviours) ought to make up the distinct corporate 'identities' which in turn should somehow influence those corporate performances discussed in the previous section.

But do they? How? And on what time scales?

5.2.3   *Corporate capabilities, competition and performances*

Let us distinguish between profitability and growth indicators of performances.

The positive impact of innovativeness upon corporate profitabilities appears to be well documented: see Geroski, Machin and van Reenen (1993), Cefis (2004), Cefis and Ciccarelli (2005), Roberts (1999), among others; see also Kremp and Mairesse (2004) on the relationship between innovation and productivity.

Together our Italian data highlight a positive relationship between profit margins and relative labour productivities (that is, normalized with the respective sectoral means): see Figure 5.9.

At the same time, the impact of both innovativeness and production efficiency upon growth performances appears to be somewhat more controversial. Mainly North-American evidence, mostly at *plant* level, does suggest that increasing output shares in high-productivity plants and decreasing shares of output in low-productivity ones are very important drivers in the growth of average productivities, even if the process of displacement of lower efficiency plants is rather slow (cf. the evidence discussed in Baily et al. (1992) and Baldwin (1995)).

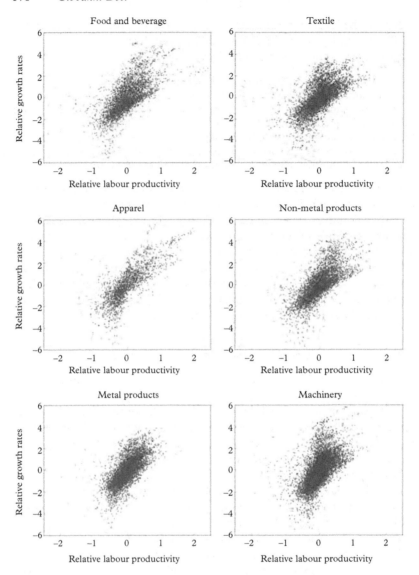

Figure 5.9   Gross margins and (normalized) labour productivity, 1989–1997. *Source*: Our elaboration on Italian (ISTAT MICRO.1) data

Statistical regularities in the evolution of industries 179

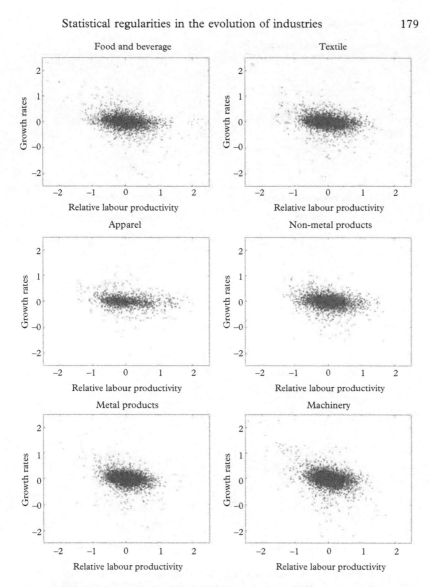

Figure 5.10 Labour productivity and growth rates (measured in terms of sales), 1989–1997. *Source*: Our elaboration on Italian (ISTAT MICRO.1) data (Growth of Value Added)

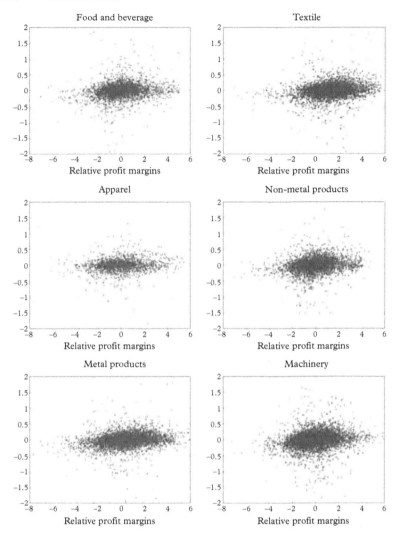

Figure 5.11   Growth rates and profit margins in different manufacturing sectors. *Source* Our elaboration on Italian (ISTAT MICRO.1) data.
(Growth of Value Added)

Firm-level data are less straightforward. For example, our Italian data
show

(1) A weak or non-existent relationship between growth however
measured (e.g. in terms of Value Added, Employment or Sales)

and relative productivities (see Figure 5.10): more efficient firms do *not* grow more;

(2) Even when some positive relation between efficiency and growth appears, this is almost exclusively due to the impact of few *outliers* (the very best and the very worst);

(3) Similarly, no systematic relation appears between (relative) profit margins and (relative) growth rates (cf. Figure 5.11).

(4) Moreover, the evidence from other data sets such as the international pharmaceutical industry shows that more innovative firms do *not* grow more (Bottazzi et al. (2001)). Rather the industry constantly displays the coexistence of heterogeneous types of firms (e.g. innovators versus imitators).

The implications of all these empirical regularities, if confirmed by the observation of other countries and other industries are far-reaching. Let us consider them from an evolutionary perspective.

5.3   Evolutionary interpretations: corroborations and challenges by way of a conclusion

How well does the whole statistical story reviewed in this essay fit with evolutionary interpretations?[*]

Certainly, the recurrent evidence at all levels of observation of *inter-firm heterogeneity* and its persistence over time is well in tune with an evolutionary notion of idiosyncratic learning, innovation (or lack of it) and adaptation.

Heterogeneous firms compete with each other and, given the prevailing input and output prices obtain different returns. Putting it in a different language, they obtain different 'quasi-rent' on conversely losses below the notional 'pure competition' profitability. At the same time, even leaving aside any entry or mortality phenomenon, surviving incumbents undergo changes in their market shares and therefore in their relative (and, of course, absolute) sizes.

In all that, the evidence increasingly reveals a rich structure in the processes of learning, competition and growth.

Various mechanisms of correlation – together with the 'sunkness' and indivisibilities of many technological events and investment

---

[*] Here, with evolutionary interpretation we mean that body of literature focusing on economic change as an evolutionary process driven by technological and organizational change which finds one of its central roots in Nelson and Winter (1982). See also Winter (1984) and for a discussion of its main building, Dosi and Winter (2002).

decisions – yield a rather structured process of change in most variable of interest – for example size, productivity, and profitability – also revealed by the 'fat-tailedness' of the respective growth rates.

At the same time, market selection – the other central tenet, together with learning, of evolutionary interpretations of economic change – do not seem to work particularly well, at least on the yearly timescale at which statistics are reported (while the available time series are not generally long enough to precisely assess what happens in the long run). Conversely, diverse degrees of efficiencies and innovativeness seem to yield primarily relatively persistent profitability differentials.

That is, contemporary markets do not appear to be too effective selectors delivering rewards and punishments according to differential efficiencies. Moreover, the absence of any strong relationship between profitability and growth militates against the 'naively Schumpeterian' (or for that matter 'classic') notion that profits feed growth (by plausibly feeding investments).

Finally, the same evidence appears to run against the conjecture, put forward in the 1960s and 1970s by the 'managerial' theories of the firm on a trade-off between profitability and growth, with 'managerialized' firms trying to maximize growth subject to a minimum profit constraint.[11]

In turn, the very fact that market selection might play less of a role than that assumed in many models of evolutionary inspiration, if confirmed, is as such an important advance in the understanding of how markets work (or do not).

More generally, the increasing availability of longitudinal panel data with an array of variables describing both the 'inner features' and the performances of individual firms begins to unveil the rich statistical structure of the processes of industrial evolution. In that, one can go a long way, I have tried to show, with little or no use of (typically unobservable) strategic variables. One has just begun. Ahead lie, first, exercises of 'evolutionary accounting' trying to disentangle the relative role of entry, market selection and incumbent learning as drivers of industrial change. Together, second, it is of paramount importance to try to condition the observed performance profiles of individual firms upon their underlying technological and organizational 'identities'.

There is indeed a whole world to be discovered resting somewhere in between the 'pure stochasticity' of a Gibrat-type framework, on the one extreme, and, the *ex post* rationalization of whatever observation in terms of sophisticated hyper-rational behaviours, on the other.

---

[11] In fact the absence of such a trade-off had been already noted by Barna (1962). Note also that this proposition is orthogonal to the finding that current growth appears to be correlated with *future* long-term profitability (cf. Geroski, Machin and Walters (1997)).

References

Amaral, L.A.N., Buldyrev S.V., Havlin, S., Salinger, M.A., Stanley, H.E., and Stanley, M.H.R. 1997. 'Scaling behavior in economics: the problem of quantifying company growth', *Physica A*, 244: 1–24

Axtell, R.L. 2001. 'Zipf distribution of U.S. firm sizes', *Science* 293: 1818–20

Baily, M.N., Hulten, C., and Campbell, D. 1992. 'Productivity dynamics in manufacturing plants', *Brookings Papers on Economic Activity. Microeconomics*, 187–267 (with comments by Bresnehan, T. and Caves, R.E.)

Baldwin, J.R. 1995. *The Dynamics of Industrial Competition*. Cambridge: Cambridge University Press

Barna, T. 1962. *Investment and Growth Policies in British Industrial Firm*. Cambridge: Cambridge University Press

Bartelsman, E. and Doms, M. 2000. 'Understanding productivity: lessons from longitudinal microdata', *Journal of Economic Literature* 38: 569–94

Bartelsman, E., Scarpetta, S., and Schivardi, F. 2005. 'Comparative analysis of firm – demographics and survival: micro level evidence for the OECD countries', *Industrial and Corporate Change* 14: 365–91

Bottazzi, G. and Secchi, A. 2003a. 'Why are distributions of firm growth rates tent-shaped?', *Economics Letters* 80: 415–20

Bottazzi, G. and Secchi, A. 2003b. 'Common properties and sectoral specificities in the dynamics of U.S. manufacturing companies', *Review of Industrial Organization* 23: 217–32

Bottazzi, G. and Secchi, A. 2005. 'Growth and diversification patters of the worldwide pharmaceutical industry', *Review of Industrial Organization* 26: 195–216

Bottazzi, G. and Secchi, A. 2006a. 'Explaining the distribution of firms growth rates', *Rand Journal of Economics*, forthcoming

Bottazzi, G. and Secchi, A. 2006b. 'Firm diversification and the Law of Proportional Effect', *Industrial and Corporate Change, forthcoming*

Bottazzi, G., Cefis, E., and Dosi, G. 2002. 'Corporate growth and industrial structure. Some evidence from the Italian manufacturing industries', *Industrial and Corporate Change* 11: 705–23

Bottazzi, G., Cefis, E., Dosi, G., and Secchi, A. 2006. 'Invariances and Diversities in the Evolution of Manufacturing Industries'. *Small Business Economics*, forthcoming

Bottazzi, G., Dosi, G., Lippi, M., Pammolli, F., and Riccaboni, M. 2001. 'Innovation and corporate growth in the evolution of the drug industry', *International Journal of Industrial Organization* 19: 1161–87

Cable, J.R. and Jackson, R.G. 2003. 'The persistence of profits in the long-run: a new approach', *American Economic Review* 93: 1075–90

Cefis, E. 2003a. 'Is there persistence in innovative activities?', *International Journal of Industrial Organization* 21: 482–515

Cefis, E. 2003b. 'Persistence in innovation and profitability', *Rivista Internazionale di Scienze Sociali* 110: 19–37

Cefis, E. 2003c. 'Is there persistence in innovative activities?', *International Journal of Industrial Organization* 21: 489–515

184   *Giovanni Dosi*

Cefis, E. 2004. *Persistent asymmetries in firm performances*. Bergamo: Department. of Economics, mimeo

Cefis, E. and Ciccarelli, M. 2005. 'Profit differentials and innovation', *Economics of innovation and new technologies* 14(1–2): 43–61

Cefis, E., Ciccarelli, M., and Orsenigo, L. 2002. 'From Gibrat's Legacy to Gibrat's Fallacy. A Bayesian Approach to Study the Growth of Firms', WP–AD 2002–19, IVIE, University of Alicante, Alicante

Cubbin, J. and Geroski, P. 1987. 'The convergence in profits in the long-run: inter-firm and inter-industry comparisons', *Journal of Industrial Economics* 35: 427–42

De Fabritiis, G., Pammolli, F., and Riccaboni, M. 2003. 'On the size and growth of business firms', *Physica A* 324: 38–44

Dosi, G. 1988. 'Sources, procedures and Microeconomic Effects of Innovation', *Journal of Economic Literature* 26: 1120–71

Dosi, G., Nelson, R., and Winter, S. (eds.) 2000. *The Nature and Dynamics of Organizational Capabilities*. Oxford/New York: Oxford University Press

Dosi, G., Marsili, O., Orsenigo, L., and Salvatore, R. 1995. 'Learning market selection and the evolution of industrial structures', *Small Business Economics* 7: 411–36

Dosi, G., Faillo, M. and Marengo, L. 2005. 'Organizational capabilities, patterns of knowledge accumulation and governance structures in business firms: an introduction', forthcoming in Touffut, J-P. (ed.), *Organizational Innovation within Firms*, Cheltenham, UK and Brookfield, U.S.: Edward Elgar, (currently available as Sant'Anna School of Advanced Studies, LEM Working Paper 2003/11)

Dosi, G. and Grazzi, M. 2006. 'Technologies at problem-solving procedures and Technologies at input-output relations: some perspectives on the theory of production', *Industrial and Corporate Change* 15: 173–202.

Dosi, G., Orsenigo, L., and Sylos Labini, M. 2005. 'Technology and the economy', in Smelser and Swedberg (eds.) *The Handbook of Economic Sociology*, 2nd edn, Princeton, NJ: Princeton University Press, Russell Sage Foundation

Dosi, G. and Winter, S. 2002. 'Interpreting economic change: evolution, structures and games', in Augier, M. and March, J. (eds.), *Choice, Change and Organizations: Essays in Memory of Richard M. Cyert*, Cheltenham: Edward Elgar.

Evans, D.S. 1987a. 'The relationship between firm growth, size and age: estimates for 100 manufacturing industries', *Journal of Industrial Economics* 35: 567–81

Evans, D.S. 1987b. 'Tests of alternative theories of firm growth', *Journal of Political Economy* 95: 657–74

Foster, L., Haltiwanger, J.C. and Krizan, C.J. 2001. 'Aggregate productivity growth: lessons from microeconomic evidence', in Dean, E., Harper, M., and Hulten, C. (eds.), *New Developments in productivity Analysis*. Chicago: Chicago University Press.

Freeman, C. 1994. 'The economics of technical change', *Cambridge Journal of Economics* 18: 463–514

Freeman, C. and Soete, L. 1997. *The Economics of Industrial Innovation.* London: Pinter, 2nd edn.

Geroski, P.A. 2000. 'The growth of firms in theory and in practice' in Foss and Mahnke (eds.), *New Directions in Economics Strategy Research,* Oxford: Oxford University Press

Geroski, P. and Jacquemin, A. 1988. 'The persistence of profits: a European comparison', *Economic Journal* 98: 357–89

Geroski, P. and Mazzucato, M. 2002. 'Learning and the sources of corporate growth', *Industrial and Corporate Change* 11: 623–44

Geroski, P., Machin, S.J., and van Reenen, J. 1993. 'The profitability of innovating firms', *Rand Journal of Economics* 24: 198–211

Geroski, P., Machin, S.J. and Walter, C.F. 1997. 'Corporate growth and profitability', *Journal of Industrial Economics* 45: 171–89

Gibrat, R. 1931. *Les inégalités économiques.* Paris: Librairie du Recueil Sirey

Goddard, J.A. and Wilson, J.O.S. 1999. 'The persistence of profit: as new empirical interpretation', *International Journal of Industrial Organization* 17: 663–87

Griliches, Z. and Mairesse, J. 1997. 'Production function: the search for identification', in Steiner Strøm (ed.), *Econometrics and Economic Theory in the Twentieth Century: the Ragner Frisch Centennial Symposium,* Cambridge: Cambridge University Press

Gschwandtner, A. 2004. *Profit persistence in the 'Very' Long Run: Evidence from Survivors and Exiters.* Vienna: University of Vienna, Department of Economics, WP 0401

Hall, B.H. 1987. 'The relationship between firm size and firm growth in the U.S. manufacturing sector', *Journal of Industrial Economics* 35: 583–606

Hart, P.E. and Prais, J.S. 1956. 'The analysis of business concentration', *Journal of the Royal Statistical Society* 119: 150–91

Hart, P.E. and Dulton, N. 1996. 'Firm size and rate of growth', *Economic Journal* 106: 1242–52

Hymer, S. and Pashigian, P. 1962. 'Firm size and rate of growth', *Journal of Political Economy* 70: 556–69

Ijiri, Y. and Simon, H.A. 1977. *Skew Distributions and the Sizes of Business Firms.* Amsterdam: North Holland

Kalecki, M. 1945. 'On the Gibrat distribution', *Econometrica* 13: 161–70

Klepper, S. 1997. 'Industry life cycles', *Industrial and Corporate Change* 6: 145–81

Kremp, E. and Mairesse, J. 2004. '*Knowledge Management, Innovation and Productivity: A Firm Level Exploration Based on French Manufacturing Data*'. Cambridge MA: NBER, WP 10237

Kumar, M.S. 1985. 'Growth, acquisition activity and firm size: evidence from the United Kingdom', *Journal of Industrial Economics* 33: 171–96

Jensen, B. and McGuckin, H. 1997. 'Firm performance and evolution: empirical regularities in the US micro data', *Industrial and Corporate Change* 6: 25–47

Lotti, F., Santarelli, E. and Vivarelli, M. 2003. 'Does Gibrat's law hold in the case of small, young, firms?', *Industrial and Corporate Change* 13: 213–35

186   *Giovanni Dosi*

Lucas, R.E. 1978. 'On the size distribution of business firms', *Bell Journal of Economics* 9: 508–23

Mansfield, E. 1962. 'Entry, Gibrat's law, innovation and the growth of firms', *American Economic Review* 52: 1023–51

Marsili, O. 2001. *The Anatomy and Evolution of Industries*. Cheltenham: Edward Elgar

Mueller, D. 1986. *Profits in the Long-Run*. Cambridge: Cambridge University Press

Mueller, D. (ed.) 1990. *The Dynamic of Company Profits. An International Comparison*. Cambridge: Cambridge University Press

Nelson, R. 1981. 'Research on productivity differences: dead ends and new departures', *Journal of Economic Literature* 19: 1029–64

Nelson, R. 1991. 'Why do firm differ and how does it matter?', *Strategic Management Journal* 12: 61–74

Nelson, R. and Winter, S. 1982. *An Evolutionary Theory of Economic Change*. Cambridge MA: The Belknap Press of Harvard University Press

Pavitt, K. 1999. *Technology, Management and Systems of Innovation*. Cheltenham: Edward Elgar

Power, L. 1998. 'The missing link: technology, investment and productivity', *Review of Economics and Statistics* 80: 300–13

Pryor, F.L. 1972. 'An international comparison of concentration ratios', *The Review of Economics and Statistics* 54: 130–40

Robert, P.W. 1999. 'Product innovation, product-market competition and persistent profitability in the U.S: pharmaceutical industry', *Strategic Management Journal* 20: 655–70

Schmalensee, R. 1989. 'Inter-industry studies of structure and performance' in Schmalensee and Willig (eds.), *Handbook of Industrial Organization*. Amsterdam: North-Holland

Silverberg, G. 2003. 'Breaking the waves: a Poisson regression approach to Schumpeterian clustering of basic innovations', *Cambridge Journal of Economics* 27(5): 671

Simon, H.A. and Bonini, C.P. 1958. 'The size distribution of American firms', *American Economic Review* 48: 607–17

Stanley, M.H.R., Amaral, L.A.N., Buldyrev S.V., Havlin, S., Leschhorn, H., Maass, P., Salinger, M.A, and Stanley, H.E. 1996a. 'Scaling behavior in the growth of companies', *Nature* 379: 804–06

Stanley, M.H.R., Buldyrev, S.V., Havlin, S., Mantegna, R., Salinger, M.A. and Stanley, H.E. 1996b. 'Zipf plots and the size distribution of firms', *Economic Letters* 49: 453–57

Steindl, J. 1965. *Random Processes and the Growth of Firms*. London: Griffin

Sutton, J. 1997. 'Gibrat's legacy', *Journal of Economic Literature* 35: 40–59

Teece, D., Rumelt, R., Dosi, G., and Winter, S. 1994. 'Understanding corporate coherence: theory and evidence', *Journal of Economic Behavior and Organization* 23: 1–30

Winter, S. 1984. 'Schumpeterian competition in alternative technological regimes', *Journal of Economic Behavior and Organization* 5: 287–320

[11]

ELSEVIER

International Journal of Industrial Organization
19 (2001) 1161–1187

International Journal of
**Industrial
Organization**

www.elsevier.com/locate/econbase

Innovation and corporate growth in the evolution of the drug industry

Giulio Bottazzi[a,*], Giovanni Dosi[a], Marco Lippi[b], Fabio Pammolli[c], Massimo Riccaboni[a]

[a]*Sant'Anna School of Advanced Studies, Pisa, Italy*
[b]*University of Rome, "La Sapienza", Rome, Italy*
[c]*Faculty of Economics R.M. Goodwin, Siena, Italy*

Abstract

This work studies the processes of growth of the worlds top 150 pharmaceutical firms, on the grounds of an original database which also allows disaggregate analysis at the level of single therapeutical classes and chemical entities. Our findings show that the industry — whose long-term evolution is driven by innovation, imitation and permanent creation of new markets — displays (i) "fat tails" in the distribution of growth shocks, present at all levels of aggregation, with (relatively rare) big "spurs of growth", (ii) a significant autocorrelation of growth rates, (iii) a fall of variance of growth rates with size entirely dependent on corporate diversification patterns, in turn plausibly shaped by the "competence scope" of each firm, and (iv) different "lifecycles" of diverse types of products, and persistent forms of heterogeneity across firms in terms of innovative output, which, however, do not not seem to affect comparative growth performances. © 2001 Elsevier Science B.V. All rights reserved.

Keywords: Innovation; Corporate growth; Drug industry; Evolution

JEL classification: L1; L6; O3

1. Introduction

This work investigates the patterns of change in the international pharmaceutical industry, in particular with respect to the industry structure and the growth

---

*Corresponding author.

processes of a large sample of incumbents, against the background of the observed patterns of innovation.

Pharmaceuticals are indeed an archetypical example of a "science-based" industry, wherein innovation — in the form of new therapeutical entities, and imitation/improvements of existing ones — is the fundamental source of competitiveness within the industry, largely shaping the dynamics of growth and decline of different firms.

As such, the industry also represents a rich domain for the analysis of the properties of microeconomic processes of growth — touching upon the dynamics of innovation arrival and imitation, the processes of inter-product and inter-firm competition, corporate diversification across markets, and the ensuing characteristics of industrial structures. These are indeed the main topics addressed in this work. In particular, we shall primarily address three (inter-related) questions, namely, first, the relationship between firm size and growth, second, and more generally, the statistical properties, both at aggregate and disaggregate (market-specific) levels, of corporate growth and, third, the relations between the latter and the process of technological innovation, imitation and market competition.

Our analysis, based on longitudinal data, disaggregated down to single product markets, allows one to characterize, at least qualitatively, the systematic forces driving the evolution of the industry, the sources of heterogeneity across firms and the nature of "technological shocks" and of competition processes. Putting it another way, one is able to investigate the statistical properties which are "emergent" from specific evolutionary dynamics of heterogenous learning and market selection.

In Section 2 we shall briefly recall some major features of the secular evolution of the drug industry. This also sets the background of the subsequent analysis, developed in Section 3, addressing (i) the size distribution of the 150 top firms operating in the seven major Western countries, (ii) the properties of "growth shocks" at both levels of firms as a whole and of disaggregated markets, and (iii) the relationship between corporate size, diversification patterns and variances in growth rates. Finally, Section 3.5 explores the process of the arrival of innovations and their impact upon corporate growth and market dynamics. Finer statistical details along a similar interpretative thread may be found in Bottazzi et al. (2000).

2. The evolution of the industry: an overview

The history of the international pharmaceutical industry, dating back to its origin in the 19th century, has already been extensively analyzed by several scholars.[1] Here, let us just mention a few major characteristics of the processes of technological learning and market competition.

---

[1] See, among others, Aftalion (1959), Arora and Gambardella (1998), Chandler (1990), Freeman (1982), Gambardella (1995), and Henderson et al. (1999).

G. Bottazzi et al. / Int. J. Ind. Organ. 19 (2001) 1161–1187   1163

Let us begin with the latter. Competition has always centered around the discovery and introduction to the market of new products, often subject to rather quick incremental improvements, as well as to imitation and generic products competition.

Notwithstanding the historically high R&D intensity of the industry, the successful introduction of major innovations, in the form of new molecules (New Chemical Entities, NCEs) with novel therapeutical properties, has always been a rather rare event. For example, Barral (1996) estimates the total number of NCEs introduced throughout the world over the period 1975–1994 to be 154. While major innovative breakthroughs arrive quite rarely, after arrival they experience extremely high rates of market growth (more on this point in Grabowski and Vernon, 1992).

NCEs, however, only capture a part of the innovative activities within the industry. In fact, pharmaceutical innovations, broadly defined, include "inventing-around" existing molecules, new combinations among them, new ways of delivery, etc.

Remarkably, the degree to which early innovators have enjoyed an advantage in later introducing major drugs within the same family has traditionally been fairly limited (see Sutton, 1998). That, together with the coexistence of several compounds or variations thereupon targeted to the same pathology, generally hinders the persistence of dominant positions in a single market (cf. also Temin, 1980). In fact, in most single markets and in the industry as a whole, one observes the (*persistent*) coexistence of two basic types of firms, mapping into distinct technological ensembles of competencies and competitive strategies. Briefly, the first group, closely corresponding to some "oligopolistic core" of the industry, undertakes what is sometimes called "pioneering R&D" (Grabowski and Vernon, 1987), generates the overwhelming majority of NCEs and, when successful, enjoys large, albeit not very long-lasting, first-mover advantages, and charges premium prices. The second group undertakes primarily "imitative R&D", generates incremental innovations and more competitively priced "me-too" drugs, and takes up licenses from the core and is present to different degrees in the "generic" markets, after patent expirations.[2]

The qualitative historical evidence hints, in fact, at a long-term "ecology" of the industry relying on the competition, but also the complementarity, between two organizational populations, whose relative sizes is shaped by diverse competencies in accessing innovative opportunities (and, to some extent, also by Intellectual Property Right regimes, influencing the span and length of legal protection for temporary monopolies on innovation). Some of the statistical properties of such an ecology will indeed be explored below.

In a nutshell, the archetypical evolutionary story concerning each "disaggre-

---

[2] The two basic types are not evenly distributed across countries. Firms belonging to the former come almost exclusively from the USA, Germany, the UK and Switzerland, while France, Italy and Japan (not included in our sample) show up primarily in the second group.

gate" market (i.e. a market aimed at one particular pathology) runs more or less as follows.

A few firms — generally from the "core" — search for NCEs with the desired properties. Some of them (a small minority) achieve the stage of clinical trials. Even among these, only very few immediately fulfill therapeutic efficacy and required safety standards. Many NCE prototypes, on the contrary, show various clinical shortcomings, which might sometimes be overcome by alterations to the original chemical structures, the introduction of compound combinations, or different ways of administering them. In some cases these changes are undertaken by the original discoverer of the compound itself, while frequently the project based on that particular NCE is abandoned — leaving potential room for the development of modified analogues by other firms. Moreover, even when the original innovator carries the project through to a marketable product, molecular modifications of prototypes often enable followers within any chemical/therapeutic trajectory to introduce drugs with equivalent (or even superior) pharmaceutical activities, side-effect profiles, patient tolerability, etc.[3]

Come as it may, when the first NCE successfully reaches the market, it generally undergoes a very rapid market diffusion (cf. the examples in Figs. 1–3 below), partly through the competitive displacement of "older" drugs — whenever they exist for that particular therapeutic application — and, even more importantly, through the creation of its own fast-growing market niche. Quite soon, however, the niche, i.e. the product market, is invaded by competing NCEs and/or "creative analogues" which curb the growth of the early monopolist. All this might happen well before the expiration of the original patent — even if the latter event generally marks another "market shock", with generic drugs and firms expanding in the market.

Note that, in the evolutionary story we have just sketched, there are two basic dynamic processes at work. The first concerns the multiplication of markets through the introduction of new families of products roughly aimed at the same therapeutic targets (either "old" targets with new methods or "new" pathologies, yet unchallenged). The second process regards competition stricto sensu amongst firms within each "micro" market. Clearly, the growth of firm size depends on both, with the timing of entry into each "micro market" being an important factor in the combination of the two effects.

Figs. 1–3 illustrate the market dynamics associated with the evolutionary patterns sketched above. Fig. 1 shows the profile of an entirely novel market, angiotensin-II antagonists, in the cardiovascular area. The new niche expands very fast allowing for the steady growth of both the first-comer and other early innovators. Here, in a sense, a fast expanding market provides "room for

---

[3] Sneader (1996) presents a detailed analysis of 244 currently employed drug prototypes, showing that, out of these, more than 1200 medical compounds have been derived.

G. Bottazzi et al. / Int. J. Ind. Organ. 19 (2001) 1161–1187   1165

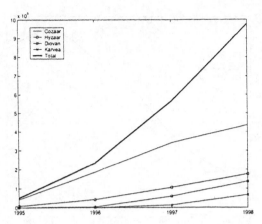

Fig. 1. Angiotensin-II antagonists: size of the market and firms/products sales, 1987–1998 (US$ millions).

everyone" — and with that, also expanding sizes (in that market) for all early incumbents. Fig. 2 illustrates the case of antiulcerants, with two families of products, namely H2 antagonists, the older product, and acid pump inhibitors, the new product, which over time crowds out the former. All this goes together with the fate of the two leading NCEs/products (Zantac and Losec, respectively), while new "innovative invaders" begin to enter the younger niche only in the late 1990s. Finally, Fig. 3 depicts a relatively "old" market, antivirals, where the first innovative mover (Zovirax), despite a steady erosion of its market share by

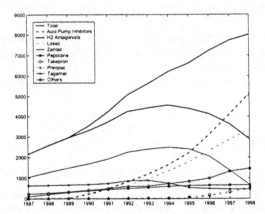

Fig. 2. Antiulcerants: acid pump inhibitors and H2 antagonists: size of the market and firms/products sales, 1987–1998 (US$ millions).

1166   *G. Bottazzi et al. / Int. J. Ind. Organ. 19 (2001) 1161–1187*

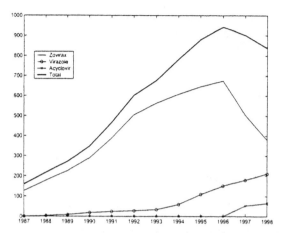

Fig. 3. Antivirals, excl. vaccines: size of the market and firms/products sales, 1987–1998 (US$ millions).

late-coming innovators and analogues, maintained its dominance until patent expiration, in 1997, by which date a swarm of generic competitors entered the market.[4]

A final set of characteristics of the evolutionary dynamics of the industry that we want to recall concerns the nature of product markets themselves. Indeed, one observes a highly skewed distribution both of product market sizes and of intra-firm distribution of sales across products. So "a few *blockbusters* dominate the product range of all major firms" (Matraves, 1999; cf. also Sutton, 1998; Bottazzi et al., 2000).[5]

In an extreme synthesis, the evolutionary patterns of the industry display:

– rare arrivals of major innovations (new chemical entities with novel therapeutical targets or pharmacological mechanisms) often associated with the emergence of new markets;
– a more steady activity of incremental innovation, development of therapeutic analogues, imitation, licensing;
– systematic forms of heterogeneity, even amongst incumbents, distinguishing a few rather persistent innovators from the rest of the organizational population;
– "hierarchically nested" competitive mechanisms[6] involving, at one level,

---

[4] Note that the decrease in the total "size" of the market after 1996 is entirely due to price reductions, with quantities still rising.

[5] In our database the three most important products of the top five firms account for more than 50% of the total sales. Matraves (1999) also suggests that only the top 30 drugs worldwide cover average R&D costs.

[6] We borrow the expression from Warglien (1995).

innovation/imitation and market share dynamics within single product groups, and, on a longer time scale, the generation of new markets and the diversification processes across them.

Given all this, what are the resulting statistical properties of the evolution of the industry, in terms of relative sizes, rates of growth, etc.? This is what we shall explore in the following.

3. Patterns of corporate growth

Let us begin by noting that the foregoing pieces of qualitative evidence suggest that the process of corporate growth is likely to display more structure than what would be predicted on the grounds of uncorrelated idiosyncratic shocks, i.e. a so-called Gibrat-type process.

In the following, in order to disentangle the actual growth patterns, after a summary description of our database (Section 3.1), we shall analyze the main properties of size distributions (Section 3.2) and growth processes (Section 3.3). Possible departures from the Gibrat hypothesis are studied by means of basic non-parametric methods. In particular, we shall study: (a) the shape of the tails in the observed growth distribution; (b) the time autocorrelation in growth profiles; and (c) the relationship between size and growth. Systematic departures from the "null" (Gibrat) hypothesis are indeed identified in all three domains of analysis.

Next, we present an interpretative framework able to account for the observed properties of growth processes, concerning in particular: (i) the relationship between size, diversification across different markets and growth variance (Section 3.4), and (ii) the effects of product innovation, entry and imitation upon the growth of markets and of the firms within them (Section 3.5).

3.1. The data set

Our statistical analysis in the following is based on the dataset PHID (Pharmaceutical Industry Database) developed at the University of Siena. It covers the top 100 companies in the seven major Western markets (USA, United Kingdom, France, Germany, Spain, Italy, Canada) with 10 to 20 years of observations (depending on the variables). In this paper we aggregate the respective figures in the different national markets and consider the resulting top 150 firms.[7] Both sales figures and market shares are available for each firm from 1987 to 1997, disaggregated up to the four-digit level of the Anatomical Therapeutic Classification scheme (ATC) in 517 microclasses.

---

[7] In consequence, firms which are "big" in one single national market but smaller at the aggregate level are neglected.

1168   *G. Bottazzi et al. / Int. J. Ind. Organ. 19 (2001) 1161–1187*

The database also contains detailed information on the sales of 7654 drugs commercialized in the US by 57 major pharmaceutical companies. The launch date is reported for 4921 of them (64.29%). Launches are evenly distributed over the last 20 years, so we are able to track the lifecycle of 1600 products over 10 years after their launch. Products are distinguished according to whether they are a New Chemical Entity (NCE), a patented innovation that is not an NCE, or an unpatented product (including both products whose patents expired before the years under observation and products licensed from other firms).

As already mentioned, this work is focused on the processes of *internal* growth. Hence, to take into account mergers and acquisitions during the period of observation, we have constructed "super firms" which correspond to the end-of-period actual entity (so, for example, if any two firms merged during the observed history, we consider them merged from the start). This procedure might bias intertemporal comparisons on actual size distributions, but it helps to highlight those changes in the distributions themselves which are due to processes of intra-market competition and inter-market diversification.[8]

Finally, when studying the relationship between innovation and growth (Section 3.5) we shall confine the analysis to the US market wherein the overwhelming majority of innovative products were first introduced.[9]

3.2. Size distributions

Let us begin with a descriptive analysis of size distributions. Let $S_i(t)$ be the sales of firm i ($i \in [1, \ldots, 150]$) at time t ($i \in [0, \ldots, 10]$). The evidence (see Bottazzi et al., 2000, for more details) shows that the ratio of the standard deviation to the mean as well as the skewness and the kurtosis are nearly constant over time. These properties imply that the "normalized size" $G_i(t) = S_i(t)/\langle S_i(t) \rangle$ (the brackets $\langle \ldots \rangle$ denote the average over all firm sizes in a given year) is stationary over time.[10] This quantity is proportional to the market share when the number of firms is constant, but provides two advantages: first, it can also be used to characterize distributions whenever the number of firms changes over time (while the shares distribution would yield a spurious shift of their means) and, second, it provides an easy way of comparing distributions with different numbers of observations.[11] In Fig. 4 we plot the distribution function for $g_i(t) = \log(G_i(t))$. The normal fit (dotted line in Fig. 4) clearly shows that the distribution possesses a fatter upper tail than a Gaussian. Think of a growth process as

---

[8] In particular, our analysis is intended, purposely, to entirely wash away the effects upon industrial concentration of acquisition processes.

[9] We choose to do this in order to avoid problems of international comparisons between different institutional and regulatory systems.

[10] For a discussion of the accuracy of this procedure, see Bottazzi et al. (2000).

[11] The analysis of G is fully equivalent to the analysis of S apart from a scale factor. A similar approach is adopted in Kalecki (1945) and Hart and Prais (1956).

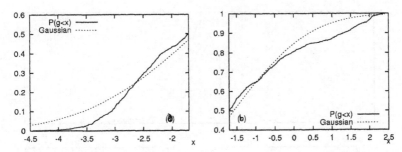

Fig. 4. Distribution function of firm sizes (lower half (a), upper half (b)). A fit with the normal distribution is also shown ($\cdot \cdot \cdot$).

$$g_i(t+1) = g_i(t) + h_i(t), \tag{1}$$

with $h_i(t)$ independent random variables. Under mild assumptions on the distribution of h, the size distribution should asymptotically tend to a Gaussian distribution.[12] We checked, however, that this trend is absent from the data (see Bottazzi et al., 2000). As such, this property may already be considered as a piece of circumstantial evidence against a simple Gibrat model. However, let us explicitly examine the properties of the growth process both at aggregate and disaggregate levels.

3.3. Corporate growth dynamics

As already mentioned, a classic benchmark in the analysis of growth processes addresses the relationship between size and growth and, in particular, possible departure from the so-called "Law of Proportionate Effect".[13] A first step is to check for possible "reversion to the mean" in our data. In order to do that we estimated the model $g_i(t+1) = \beta g_i(t) + \varepsilon_i(t)$ cross-sectionally for all the years, finding values for β statistically equal to one, thus rejecting the "reversion" hypothesis (see Appendix A for more details). Consequently, one is entitled to refer to (1) and confine the analysis to the properties of h. Fig. 5 reports the distribution for h averaged over time together with the distribution for some time

---

[12] For the Central Limit Theorem the nth normalized cumulant $\lambda_n = c_n/\sigma^n$ of the size distribution $\Sigma_{t=0}^{T} h_i(t)$ would behave as $\lambda_n \sim T^{1-n/2}$ where T are the total time steps. In particular, the third and fourth normalized cumulants, the skewness and the kurtosis, would decrease respectively as $T^{-0.5}$ and T^{-1}.

[13] The literature on the subject is vast and cannot be surveyed here: cf. Ijiri and Simon (1977) and for recent critical discussions of both the evidence and the related theoretical implications, Boeri (1989), Brock and Evans (1986), Sutton (1997) and Geroski (2000).

1170   *G. Bottazzi et al. / Int. J. Ind. Organ. 19 (2001) 1161–1187*

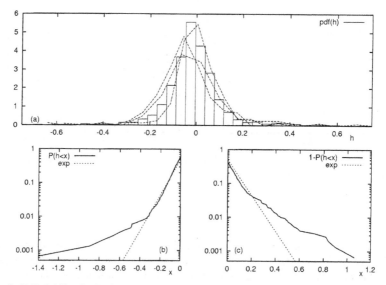

Fig. 5. (a) Probability density for growth obtained with bins (quantiles) of 100 values. The bars show the "average" distribution and the dotted lines the distributions at different time steps. (b) Distribution function for h (lower half). (c) Distribution function for h (upper half). The fit is performed with the exponential distribution.

steps ($t = 0$, 5, 10). As can be seen, differences are small, supporting the assumption, from now onward, that the distribution of h is stationary over time. However, such a distribution is highly non-Gaussian (see Fig. 5) and a fit with a symmetric exponential

$$p(h = x) = \frac{\alpha}{2} e^{-\alpha|x - m|} \tag{2}$$

provides a good description of its central part. Moreover, the distribution is asymmetric with fat tails corresponding to spurs of growth that are more frequent than those predictable on the grounds of a Gaussian noise process (see Fig. 5).

We have previously argued that the stability and the shape of the size distribution can hardly be explained using the simplest Gibrat-type model in (1) with independent increments. An interesting problem indeed concerns the identification of possible sources of "dependence" in the growth process governing this industry. The first effect to analyze is the possible autocorrelation in time of firm growth. In Fig. 6 we plot the autocorrelation coefficient of the logarithmic growth $c(t,\tau)$. The plotted line is the average $\bar{c}(\tau) = \Sigma_t^T c(t,\tau)/T$, where T is the number of

G. Bottazzi et al. / Int. J. Ind. Organ. 19 (2001) 1161–1187   1171

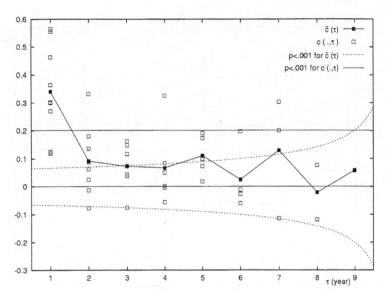

Fig. 6. Time autocorrelation of firm growth. The points are the values $c(t,\tau)$ for different times t plotted against τ. The line is the mean value $\bar{C}(\tau)$. The significance line for $P = 0.001$ (about 2.46 standard deviations) is plotted for both the single points and the average.

years covered in our database and τ is the time lag.[14] If one considers the average correlation $\bar{c}(\tau)$, contrary to the prevailing results in the literature (for a critical discussion, cf. Geroski, 2000) our data do highlight, on average, a significant ($P < 0.001$) positive autocorrelation until the second lag $\tau = 1, 2$ (while we do not dare to make any claim on longer time lags).[15]

Fig. 6 refers to the growth of firms as a whole. However, in order to fully understand corporate growth, it is necessary to investigate the persistency profiles by firms within single therapeutic categories ("sub-markets"). Indeed, this is a level of observation nearer to the actual competition process, where innovative shocks are likely to exert their effect. Let us look at the distribution function of the autocorrelation $\bar{c}_j(\tau)$ over the set of all sub-markets and plot it for different τ lags.

---

[14] The data points relative to the same lag τ but different initial time t are dispersed, partly due to the relatively small number of observations and partly for a seemingly "true" difference in the growth from time to time (indeed, there are points separated by more than three standard deviations). In any case, the hypothesis $c(t,1) = 0$ is rejected with a significance greater than 0.001 in seven over nine time steps t.

[15] Notice, however, that one should be cautious about the procedure of taking the average correlation as an estimate of a "true" (stationary) correlation, due to the high dispersion of $c(t,\tau)$ for different initial times t.

1172   *G. Bottazzi et al. / Int. J. Ind. Organ. 19 (2001) 1161–1187*

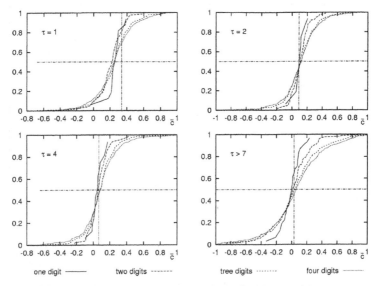

one digit ——————   two digits --------   tree digits ·········   four digits ············

Fig. 7. Distribution function of the autocorrelation coefficients $\bar{c}_j(\tau)$. Different aggregation levels and time lags τ are plotted. The vertical lines correspond to "aggregate" values at the firm level. The horizontal line is centered at 0.5.

Fig. 7 presents the results for different levels of disaggregation (one, two and three digits, according to the therapeutical classification; see above). As can be seen the distributions are similar for different disaggregation levels and, remarkably, sales aggregation at the firm level does *not* wash away autocorrelation in growth; on the contrary, for $\tau = 1$, *firm-level autocorrelations* are significantly *higher* than the average *autocorrelation* calculated at any disaggregation level (this property disappears for $\tau > 1$). Moreover, a positive average autocorrelation seems to survive for a long time even if of negligible magnitude.[16]

Interestingly, one is also able to observe important market-specific characteristics in the competitive dynamics. In fact, as shown in Bottazzi et al. (2000), the distribution of the growth correlation of the two leading firms for each sub-market is U-shaped, suggesting that different market-specific growth processes coexist within the industry, including both highly correlated and anti-correlated patterns. The inter-market heterogeneity might indeed be the effect of considering statistics over different "windows of observation" of a "technology cycle" shaping the

---

[16] We also searched for a possible dependence of the autocorrelation $\bar{c}_j(\tau)$ on the size M_j of the sub-markets themselves, but no evidence of any such dependence was found.

G. Bottazzi et al. / Int. J. Ind. Organ. 19 (2001) 1161–1187   1173

growth process in each sub-market.[17] So, for example, one might expect a positive correlation in the stages of penetration of new products and an anti-correlation associated with imitative entry and patent expirations (for an illustrative example, see Section 2).

To further investigate the growth structure we computed the 1-year transition matrices of the stochastic variable h both at the aggregate and at the three-digit sub-market levels. Having controlled the robustness of our results for different numbers of bins[18] (ranging from 20 to more than 200) without revealing remarkable variations, let us present the analysis at the highest level of resolution supported by the data. More precisely, the actual rate of variation over time of the aggregate standardized growth (h_i) and disaggregate one (h_{ij}) were uniformly divided into 50 quantiles and every firm was assigned to them in each year. Since the transition matrices of h do not change substantially over time (as well as the distribution of h itself, see Fig. 5), we analyzed jointly the 1-year transition probability matrices. Two transition matrices were computed, at the aggregate (Π_a) and at the sub-market level (Π_d):

$$[h_i(t)] = \Pi_a[h_i(t-1)], \tag{3}$$

$$[h_{ij}(t)] = \Pi_d[h_{ij}(t-1)], \tag{4}$$

where $[h_{i(j)}(t)]$ are column vectors of binned growth at time t and each row of Π_a and Π_d represents the conditional probability vector of moving through the grid. Figs. 8 and 9 show the three-dimensional plot of transition matrices Π_a and Π_d. To interpret the graphs, take any point on the $[h_{i(j)}(t-1)]$ axis and look in the direction parallel to the other axis in order to trace out the probability density describing the transition to different parts of the growth distributions (more details on discrete stochastic kernel analysis can be found in Quah, 1996). If the graphs pile up on the positive sloped diagonal this may be interpreted as evidence of high persistence and "inertia". Actually, Fig. 8, in line with our previous findings, shows a significant autocorrelation in growth rates at the aggregate firm level: more specifically, an oblique shape clearly emerges which may be fitted by a line with slope 0.38 passing through the mean values of $h_i(t)$ and $h_{ij}(t-1)$. Over time, the growth distribution converges towards its mean value where most of the observations are concentrated. However, note that the autocorrelation appears to be highly dependent on relatively rare events of sustained growth represented by the spikes in the top right quadrant of the transition matrix. Remarkably, qualitative inspection shows that the majority of these growth events corresponds to large innovation breakthroughs.

---

[17] Our statistics cannot discriminate between purely random micro-processes and more systematic competition processes observed at random times.

[18] The "bins" are the different intervals of values (quantiles) by which the data are partitioned.

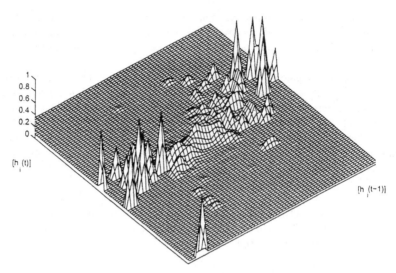

Fig. 8. Growth transition matrix at the aggregate level.

The companion Fig. 9, computed at the sub-market level, enables us to disentangle growth autocorrelation in terms of single market dynamics. Two different regimes are clearly distinguishable. The products that at time $t-1$ experienced growth above the average are sharply divided into two groups: some

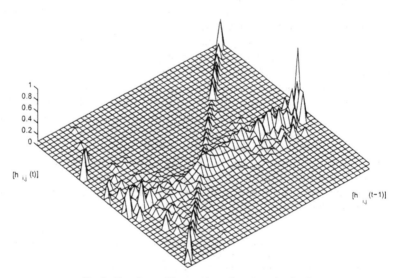

Fig. 9. Growth transition matrix at the sub-market level.

of them maintain their growth pace unchanged, while most of them subsequently drop on the mean. Conversely, the mean growth level also represents an absorptive state for slow (below the mean) growing products, but the phase transition is considerably smoother. New products burst onto the market and grow swiftly for a short period of time, then a cluster of analogue drugs enter (and possibly licensing begins also). As a result, innovative drug growth slows down. After a while, all incumbents tend to grow approximately at the same rate, even if with highly asymmetric shares in favor of the early movers.

Given the foregoing features of growth processes, at both corporate and disaggregate market levels, let us suggest some elements of an interpretation drawing upon possible forms of heterogeneity across firms, in particular with reference to diversification profiles and innovative patterns.

3.4. Size, diversification across sub-markets and Gibrat violations

The tangled and "classic" question concerning the possible dependence of the distributions of the growth rates on the initial firm size is, of course, not exhausted by the forgoing (negative) findings on correlation measures between growth and size. While the existence of correlation in a Gibrat-type test between growth and size would be sufficient to reveal dependence, the converse does not hold: dependence might just show up at higher moments of the conditional distributions. In Fig. 10 we plot the moments of the growth distribution for different size classes built considering, at each time step, all the firms with a size in a given range.

In line with a few contributions in the literature,[19] as Fig. 10 shows, no dependence of mean growth appears, and neither does dependence in auto-correlation. However, a clear pattern emerges concerning the variance of growth rates, decreasing with increasing size. Fitting the relation between growth variance and size with an exponential law:

$$\sigma(h) \sim e^{\beta g}, \tag{5}$$

we obtain a value $\beta \sim 0.2 \pm 0.02$, which is strikingly similar to the value found in other analyses of different data sets (cf. Stanley et al., 1996; Lee et al., 1998).

The rather unique possibility offered by the PHID database is to break down sales until the fourth digit of the ATC code, allowing, as mentioned, the identification of sub-markets that are "specific" enough to be considered the loci of competition among firms, and also a more accurate evaluation of the relationship between diversification, and variance of growth and size.

Were one to assume that firms are collections of independent elementary lines of business, roughly of the same size, whose number is proportional to the overall size of the firm, then the Law of Large Numbers would predict a relation between variance of aggregate growth and firm size of the form $\text{var}(h) \sim g^{0.5}$. However,

---

[19] cf. Boeri (1989), Evans (1987), Geroski (2000), Geroski et al. (1998), Hall (1987), Hymer and Pashigian (1962), Mansfield (1962) and Sutton (1997) among others.

1176   *G. Bottazzi et al. / Int. J. Ind. Organ. 19 (2001) 1161–1187*

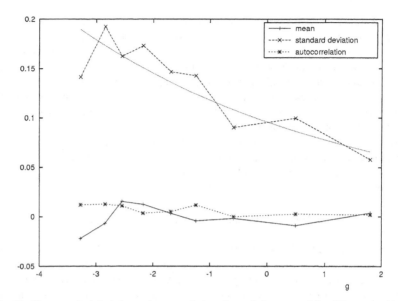

Fig. 10. Mean, standard deviation and autocorrelation of growth h computed for different size bins plotted against the average size in the bin. The exponential fit to the standard deviation (see (5)) gives a value $\beta = -0.20 \pm 0.03$.

both the existing literature and our data (see Fig. 10) show a *smaller* exponent.

In the literature, this departure from the predictions of the Law of Large Numbers is typically imputed to some interrelation between the "components" that make up each firm[20] (cf. Boeri, 1989; Stanley et al., 1996).

Conversely, as we shall do, one could relax the assumption of (unobserved) elementary components and measure the actual relationship between aggregate firm size and the number and size of its lines of business. In fact, our analysis shows that the Law of Large Numbers does explain the observed relationship between size and variance of growth if one considers as elementary lines of business the different sub-markets in which each firm operates. This result comes from two observations: first, that the correlation across sub-markets is negligible and, second, that the number of active sub-markets of a given firm increases, on average, with its size following a non-linear scaling law.

More formally, let $S_{i,j}(t)$ be the size of firm i in sub-market j at time t, and $S_i(t) = \Sigma_j S_{i,j}(t)$ its total size. The aggregate growth of each firm can be written as

$$\frac{S_i(t+1)}{S_i(t)} = \sum_j \frac{S_{i,j}(t+1)}{S_i(t)}. \tag{6}$$

---

[20] Note that imposing a simple correlation in components growth is not enough to explain the small value of γ.

G. Bottazzi et al. / Int. J. Ind. Organ. 19 (2001) 1161–1187 1177

We computed the correlation of $S_{i,j}(t + 1)/S_i(t)$ for all firms in all sub-markets, obtaining a distribution sharply centered around zero.[21] For any practical purpose, the growth in different sub-markets can then be considered uncorrelated and, therefore, the variance of the aggregate growth is the sum of the variances of growth in each sub-market.

Defining $R_{i,j}(t) = S_{i,j}(t + 1)/S_{i,j}(t)$ and $\Delta_{i,j}(t) = N_i(t) S_{i,j}(t)/S_i(t)$, where $N_i(t)$ is the number of sub-markets in which firm i operates at time t (active sub-markets), the variance of the growth of the "normalized" size G becomes

$$\text{var}_{i,t}[H_i(t)] = \text{var}_{i,t}\left[\frac{G_i(t + 1)}{G_i(t)}\right] = \sum_j \text{var}_{i,t}\left[\frac{M(t)}{M(t + 1)}R_{i,j}(t)\frac{\Delta_{i,j}(t)}{N_i(t)}\right], \qquad (7)$$

where $M(t)$ is the average (aggregate) size of the firm at time t and the ratio $M(t)/M(t + 1)$ is a normalization factor (proportional to the rate of growth of the total industry). Here, $\text{var}_{i,t}$ denotes the variance of the distribution obtained using the complete panel (all firms at all time steps).

In (7) the contribution of each sub-market factorizes in three terms, namely, first, $R_{i,j}(t)$, the actual growth of firm i in sub-market j; second, the inverse number of active markets, $1/N_i(t)$; and, third, $\Delta_{i,j}(t)/N_i(t)$, a weighting coefficient describing the "diversification asymmetry" of firm i.[22] It happens that the mean and variance of the distribution of $R_{i,j}(t)$ and $\Delta_{i,j}(t)$ obtained using different size bins do not show any clear dependence on the average size of the firms in each bin (see Bottazzi et al., 2000). Therefore, the number of active sub-markets, $N_i(t)$, must be solely responsible for the observed dependence of the variance over the aggregate size. Fitting on a log–log scale the average number of active sub-markets for each bin against the average size of the bin, one obtains a slope $\alpha = 0.39 \pm 0.02$ and an intercept $q = 6 \pm 0.12$ (see Fig. 11). The Law of Large Numbers would predict a relation between the exponent in Fig. 5 and the slope in Fig. 11 of the form $\beta = -\alpha/2$ which is in perfect agreement with our evidence.[23]

Summarizing, our evidence shows (i) that the number of sub-markets in which a firm operates increases non-linearly with firm size and (ii) that such a number fully accounts for the observed relationship between growth variance and size.

The relation provided by the Law of Large Numbers is valid as long as one considers the actual number of sub-markets a firm operates in. In order to demonstrate this statement, it was necessary to rule out two possible sources of functional dependence between aggregate growth variance and size, namely, first, the possibility that the mean and the variance of firm growth in individual

---

[21] With a standard deviation of 0.388×10^{-4} and an average deviation of 0.24×10^{-5}.

[22] This term captures the asymmetry in the contribution of each sub-market to the overall sales of the firm. If firm i at time t is symmetrically diversified over its active sub-markets, the distribution of $\Delta_{i,j}(t)$ in j is centered around 1, otherwise it is more broadly distributed.

[23] Notice that there is a weak relationship between the variance of $\Delta_{i,j}(t)$ and the aggregate size. A linear fit provides a slope of 0.09, which is, however, negligible compared to the effect of the number of active sub-markets.

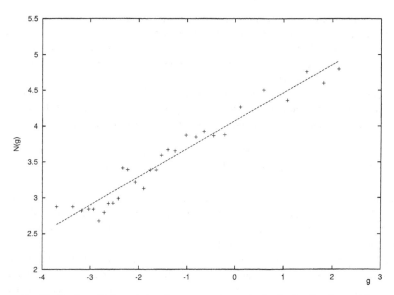

Fig. 11. Number of sub-markets a firm operates in vs. the firm's size (log–log scale).

sub-markets depend (on average) on its total size and, second, the possibility that the diversification pattern of a firm varies (on average) with its size.[24]

In turn, however, a puzzling implication of these findings (as already pointed out by Boeri, 1989) is that a large firm is more "risky" than a collection of smaller firms: a notional investor would face a lower risk by diversifying their portfolio in N (independent) firms of size S rather than betting on one single firm of size NS.

From an interpretative perspective all this militates against the hypothesis that diversification is driven by risk-minimizing considerations. Rather, the evidence may be plausibly interpreted in terms of *competence-driven* diversification processes, in the presence of knowledge spillovers across products and lines of search. In fact, as formally discussed in Bottazzi (2000), the observed diversification patterns can essentially be described by a stochastic branching process: its economic interpretation may be plausibly grounded in the incremental development of knowledge bases, driving the exploration of an expanding range of products/markets.

3.5. Innovation and growth

A major tenet of evolutionary theories of industrial dynamics is indeed the general conjecture that the processes of technological innovation and imitation are

---

[24] Both these possibilities are actually discussed in the literature as possible sources of violation of Gibrat Law (see, for instance, Hart and Prais, 1956).

G. *Bottazzi et al.* / *Int. J. Ind. Organ.* 19 (2001) 1161–1187   1179

major drivers of industrial dynamics and also of the competitive fate of individual firms.[25] How does our evidence bear on this proposition?

Let us begin by considering the process of the introduction of innovative drugs, both New Chemical Entities and patented products,[26] into the US market. Consider first the distribution of NCE launches over the population of firms throughout the 11 years of observation (1987–97). In fact, the number of NCEs that a firm introduces over a given period may be understood as one proxy for its "degree of innovativeness", and as such contributes to the possible revelation of underlying forms of heterogeneity across firms in their ability to innovate.

As a benchmark, let us model what would happen with technologically homogeneous firms. Under these circumstances, as a first approximation, one may consider the arrival of different NCEs as independent events. This means that, given a set of N NCEs introduced by a population of F firms, the probability of finding a firm which introduced exactly k NCEs is given by the binomial distribution

$$p_{M.B.}(k) = \binom{N}{k}\left(\frac{1}{F}\right)^k\left(1 - \frac{1}{F}\right)^{N-k}. \tag{8}$$

As shown in Fig. 12, this model (known as Maxwell–Boltzmann statistics) provides a poor description of the observed frequencies.

Indeed, the assumption of random independent assignments is at odds with the qualitative evidence of whole families of research projects conducted by each firm over several years, often entailing knowledge spillovers across them. Hence, one may conjecture some correlation amongst NCE arrivals due to learning effects across individual research projects. In order to check this hypothesis empirically, one should check whether the random assignments of innovations to individual firms indeed concern "packets" of NCEs rather than single products. Under the assumption of equiprobability of the packet sizes, the appropriate statistics, known in physics as the Bose–Einstein statistics (Reichl, 1980), consider the probability of finding a firm who introduced exactly k NCEs:

$$p_{B.E.}(k) = \frac{\binom{F + N - k - 2}{N - k}}{\binom{F + N - 1}{N - 1}}. \tag{9}$$

As can be seen from Fig. 12, the latter distribution provides an excellent description for low to average NCE numbers and only fails for the very large assignments. It is also interesting to note that the propensity to introduce NCEs is not monotonic in the size of the innovative firms themselves (so that, for example, the upper tail in the distribution in Fig. 12 does not feature the largest firms in the

---

[25] For theoretical arguments, cf., among others, Nelson and Winter (1982) and Dosi et al. (1995, 1997), and for qualitative historical discussions, Freeman (1982) and Pavitt (1999).

[26] Note that the former are a small subset of the latter.

1180   *G. Bottazzi et al. / Int. J. Ind. Organ. 19 (2001) 1161–1187*

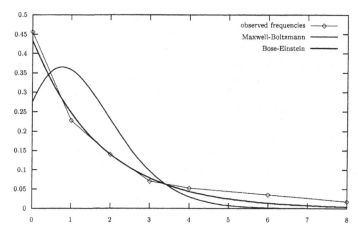

Fig. 12. Frequencies of total NCEs introduced over the firms population (*x*-axis, firms introducing 0,1, . . . ,8 NCEs; *y*-axis, frequencies thereof).

industry). This evidence hints at some underlying forms of heterogeneity in search competences and/or search orientation (e.g., biased in favor or against the quest for relatively major innovations). Together, the widespread occurrence of "clustering" in the arrivals of NCEs does suggest the importance of firm-specific learning effects across different research projects.

Given the foregoing evidence, a crucial question concerns if (and how much) the introduction of a NCE during a firm's history affects its growth performance. One can start by partitioning the set of firms depending on the number of NCEs they have introduced during the time window of observation. In Bottazzi et al. (2000) we show that no relationship appears between the number of NCEs and firm performance: indeed, "more innovative" firms do not seem to gain, on average, market shares with respect to "less innovative" firms.

As another, broader, proxy for the innovative capability, let us consider the *patent intensity* of each given firm, defined as the share of patented products present in its products portfolio.[27] Again, we observe that, first, the distribution of patent intensity on the population of firms is very heterogeneous; second, larger firms tend to show lower than average patent intensity in their product portfolios, while some of the smaller firms have a value near to unity; and, third, no systematic relationship appears between the structure of product portfolios and growth performance. Taken together, all the foregoing pieces of evidence suggest that firms embody rather idiosyncratic bundles of products, characterized by varying degrees of innovativeness, without, however, systematic effects of the "technological ID" of the firm itself upon its global growth performances (more on this in Bottazzi et al., 2000).

---

[27] Recall that patents, often based on "creative analogues", new ways of combining existing NCEs, etc. are much more frequent than NCEs.

G. Bottazzi et al. / Int. J. Ind. Organ. 19 (2001) 1161–1187 1181

Note that all this does not imply homogeneous market dynamics of the three groups of products (NCEs, patented drugs and non-patented drugs) in the four-digit sub-markets in which they compete. Let us consider $S_{i,j,k}$, the sales of product k of firm i in sub-market j, and define the "normalized" sales with respect to all other products in the same four-digit sub-market as

$$G_{i,j,k} = \frac{S_{i,j,k}}{\langle S_{i,j,k} \rangle_{i,k}}.$$ (10)

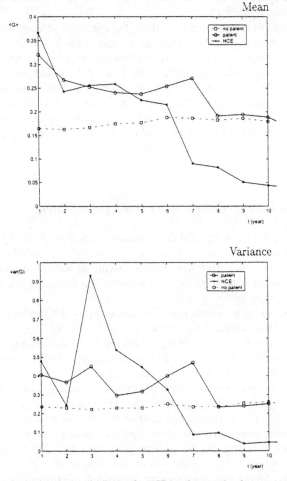

Fig. 13. Mean and variance of sales distribution for NCEs, and patented and non-patented products. At any given time we consider only sub-markets with at least 10 products. The product sales are rescaled by the average sales of the sub-market where the product is launched.

1182   *G. Bottazzi et al. / Int. J. Ind. Organ. 19 (2001) 1161–1187*

Fig. 13 reports the mean and variance of $G_{i,j,k}$ for three categories of products (i.e. NCEs, patented products and all others) as a function of the time elapsed since their introduction (so that on the *x*-axis one reads the "market age" of each product). Here, one observes a pronounced "market cycle" of NCEs which tends to "hit the market big" and decline relatively soon thereafter, with a burst in the variance (intuitively, a burst in competition with an ensuing high turbulence in market shares) early in their life cycle. The much more numerous family of patented drugs follows, on average, a "market cycle" loosely similar to NCEs, but with much less pronounced changes in both their means and variances. Finally, non-patented drugs appear to be highly stable and occupy from the start their long-term market position.

Therefore, innovation does indeed drive the evolution of each sub-market, but the competitive regime is not such as to guarantee a sustained competitive advantage and systematic above-average growth to the individual innovators either in the affected sub-markets or for the firms as a whole. Rather, one may think of some analogue to population-level mixed-strategy equilibria (here, populations of innovative vs. imitative and "old" products) which persistently coexists within sub-markets and also within single firms. Innovations continue to upset this population, but imitations, analogue developments, etc. are fast enough to curb any long-term advantage to specific products.

4. Conclusions and conjectural implications for the theory

In this work we have explored the statistical properties of the dynamics of an industry — pharmaceuticals — whose long-term evolution is fueled by innovation, imitation and the creation of new markets, trying to identify the possible links between the fundamental features of such evolutionary patterns and the quantitative evidence on corporate growth.

Here — as well as in several studies of this *genre* — a benchmark of departure was the so-called Gibrat Law. However, such a "law", as Brock (1999) emphasizes, "is useful as a rough approximation to the unconditional distribution of rates of growth of firm sizes, which is especially pertinent to illustrating the degree of accuracy of the 'Law of Proportionate Growth'; [however] it has poor power to discriminate across different plausible stochastic processes that might fit the stochastic dynamics of firm growth" (p. 432). Our data, breaking down firms' dynamics over highly disaggregated product markets, as well as complementary pieces of evidence on innovation and competitive patterns, allows us to discriminate the finer structure of the growth processes and their links with size distributions, on one hand, and innovative activities, on the other.

The evidence shows: (a) fat tails in the distribution of growth shocks, present at all levels of aggregation, with (relatively rare) large "spurs of growth"; (b) a significant autocorrelation in growth rates, again at all aggregation levels; (c) a fall

G. Bottazzi et al. / Int. J. Ind. Organ. 19 (2001) 1161–1187 1183

of the variance of growth rate with size (in line with previous findings) which, at closer inspection, is entirely dependent on diversification patterns, in turn plausibly shaped by the "competence scope" of each firm; (d) different "lifecycles" of diverse types of products (defined in terms of their degrees of innovativeness) displaying equally diverse growth profiles; and (e) a persistent form of heterogeneity across firms in terms of innovative output, which, however, does not appear to affect their comparative growth performances.

Our results, on the negative side, allow us to rule out some interpretations of the growth processes as the sum of independent events. For example, the fat-tailed growth distribution and its departure from a Gaussian distribution, even in its central part, is at odds with a "pure Gibrat process". In this respect, note that if Gibrat dynamics were a strict description of the process this should apply to all time scales (e.g., on monthly or weekly bases, etc.). But then, pushing the reasoning to the extreme, "years" should display a much more Gaussian profile — for the Central Limit Theorem — irrespective of the original distribution of events.

On the positive side, our evidence, first of all, is well in tune with the conjecture (Geroski, 2000) that the time scale of the arrival of "big" growth impulses associated with the arrival of major innovations — i.e. in the case of pharmaceuticals, New Chemical Entities — is different from the scale on which corporate growth is measured (i.e. accounting years). Such shocks are quite rare, are persistently generated by a relatively small number of innovators (indeed, a subset of the population of top incumbents considered in this work), but any one innovator is unlikely to hit the same market twice. Moreover, NCEs a few times *create new markets*.

Hence, the overall, industry-wide growth dynamics is likely to be the mixing of two different underlying evolutionary processes. The first, driven by major, rather rare, innovations, often entails the generation of new market niches (new therapeutic targets, etc.). The second ("faster") process is associated with imitation, development of analogue drugs, incremental therapeutic improvements, etc., and drives the competition process within already existing markets.

Our analysis also reveals persistent forms of heterogeneity across firms. First, the autocorrelation in firm growth, increasing with the scale of observation, does indeed hint at some significant firm-specific structure in the growth process, possibly related, we conjecture, to firm-specific organizational competences in the search for and introduction of products in different markets. Second, firms systematically differ in their innovative propensity (either when measured in terms of NCEs or of patented products).

However, the diversity in the technological profile of each firm does not appear to influence long-term growth performance. Rather, our evidence appears to support some sort of "ecology" of heterogeneous firms (and of products at different stages of their lifecycle within single firms) holding some sort of long-term evolutionary complementarity.

Further corroborations of this interpretation will also involve conditioning the observed dynamics upon finer proxies for the technological characteristics of firms and upon the "stages" of market development. We would like to consider this work as an initial exploration of links between some basic features of industrial evolution — so far analyzed empirically in a largely qualitative manner — on the one hand, and the "emergent" statistical properties of industrial structures and growth dynamics, on the other.

Acknowledgements

Support of this research by the Merck Foundation (EPRIS Program), the European Union (ESSY Project, TSER, contract No. SOE1-CT 98-1116 DGXII-SOLS) and the Italian Ministry of Universities and Research (grant 9913443984) is gratefully acknowledged. IMS International and Glaxo Wellcome Italia kindly provided the data on which our databank is partly based. Comments by Buz Brock, Paul Geroski and two anonymous referees contributed significantly to improve upon earlier versions of this paper. The usual caveats apply.

Appendix A. A linear test of the Gibrat Law

A common procedure to analyze growth processes, to which we shall adhere, is to check for departures from the so-called Gibrat Law, that is for growth patterns deviating from the proportionality of mean growth to size. The "law" may be stated in different but statistically equivalent forms.[28]

In the version proposed by Kalecki (1945) and adopted, among others, by Hart and Prais (1956) and Chesher (1979), the Gibrat linear test refers to the dynamics of the deviations of natural logarithms of firm sizes from their means ($g_{i(j)}(t) = s_{i(j)}(t) - \langle s_{i(j)}(t) \rangle$) and it is meant to provide an estimate of the divergence/convergence of the size distribution toward its mean. In that vein, one tests the model

$$g_i(t) = \beta g_i(t-1) + \varepsilon_i(t),$$ (A.1)

and one typically concludes that the Gibrat Law is satisfied if the OLS estimator of $\beta(t)$ is close to unity.

We apply this analysis on our panel, testing the model cross-sectionally for each time step. Let $\beta(t)$ be the OLS estimation of the coefficient in (A.1) at time t:

$$\beta(t) = \frac{\sigma_g(t)}{\sigma_g(t-1)} \rho_g(t),$$ (A.2)

where $\sigma_g^2(t) = \langle g_i(t)^2 \rangle$ is the variance of g at time t and $\rho_g(t) = \langle g_i(t)g_i(t-1) \rangle$ is the autocorrelation.

---

[28] Cf., among others, Mansfield (1962), Ijiri and Simon (1977), Geroski (2000) and Sutton (1997).

Table 1
Gibrat test results — aggregate level, 1-year time lag. R^2 is always greater than 0.98

t	β	ξ
1988	0.982	0.998
1989	0.991	0.989
1990	1.006	1.006
1991	1.008	0.958
1992	1.017	1.004
1993	0.997	0.982
1994	1.004	0.938
1995	1.001	0.953
1996	1.000	0.959
1997	1.005	0.978

From (A.2) it immediately follows that the variance of the size distribution decreases at time t when $\beta(t) < \rho(t) \leqslant 1$. Table 1 reports the statistics resulting from the tests carried out over the period 1987–1997. As shown, $\beta(t)$ and $\xi(t) = \sigma_g^2(t)/\sigma_g^2(t-1)$ are always very close to unity, indicating that size does not exert a significant influence on expected growth, with the variance of the size distribution remaining constant over time. In fact, given these results, one is entitled, as we did, to refer constantly to (1) and analyze the distribution of h defined there (since this analysis is fully equivalent to the analysis of errors ε of (A.1)).

Let $h_{i,j}(t) = g_{i,j}(t) - g_{i,j}(t-1)$ be the (logarithmic) growth of firm i in sub-market j. Remember that g is defined as the logarithm of the "normalized" size G.

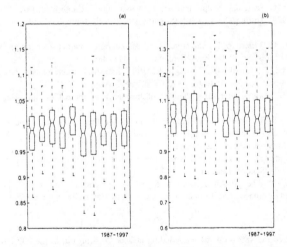

Fig. 14. Gibrat test at the three-digit sub-market level, 1 year time lag. Boxplot (a) reports the distributions of $\beta_j(t)$, while (b) depicts the distributions of $\xi_j(t)$ (cf. Eq. (A.1)).

Here, $G_{i,j}(t)$ is normalized using the size of the jth sub-market $M_j(t)$. We then test the analogue to (A.1) at the disaggregate level.[29] Fig. 14 reports the values of $\beta_j(t)$ and $\xi_j(t)$ for each sub-market j. In line with the aggregate results, the median of $\beta_j(t)$ stays quite close to unity over time, but the distribution of $\beta_j(t)$ display a remarkable degree of heterogeneity among sub-markets, ranging from 0.82 to 1.14. On the contrary, the median of the $\xi_j(t)$ distribution is constantly above unity, indicating that the variance of firm sizes in individual sub-markets increases (on average) over time.

References

Aftalion, J., 1959. History of the International Chemical Industry. University of Pennsylvania Press, Philadelphia.

Arora, A., Gambardella, A., 1998. The chemical industry: evolution of industry structure. In: Arora, A., Landau, R., Rosenberg, N. (Eds.), Chemicals and Long Run Economic Growth. Wiley, New York.

Barral, E., 1996. 20 Years of Pharmaceutical Research Results Throughout the World. Rhone Poulenc Foundation, Antony, France.

Boeri, T., 1989. Does firm size matter? Giornale degli Economisti e Annali di Economia 48, 477–495.

Bottazzi, G., Dosi, G., Lippi, M., Pammolli, L., Riccaboni, M., 2000. Processes of corporate growth in the evolution of an innovation-driven industry. The case of pharmaceuticals. LEM Working Paper, Sant'Anna School of Advanced Studies, Pisa.

Bottazzi, G., 2000. Diversification of firms and the Law of Proportionate Effect. LEM Working Paper, Sant'Anna School of Advanced Studies, Pisa.

Brock, W.A., Evans, D., 1986. The Economics of Small Businesses: Their Role and Regulation in the U.S. Economy. Holmes and Meier, New York.

Brock, W.A., 1999. Scaling in economics: a reader's guide. Industrial and Corporate Change 8, 409–446.

Chandler, A., 1990. Scale and Scope. Harvard University Press, Cambridge, MA.

Chesher, A., 1979. Testing the Law of Proportionate Effect. Journal of Industrial Economics 27, 403–411.

Dosi, G., Marsili, O., Orsenigo, L., Salvatore, R., 1995. Learning, market selection and the evolution of industrial structures. Small Business Economics 7, 411–436.

Dosi, G., Malerba, F., Marsili, O., Orsenigo, L., 1997. Industrial structures and dynamics: evidence, interpretations and puzzles. Industrial and Corporate Change 6, 3–24.

Evans, D., 1987. Tests of alternative theories of firm growth. Journal of Industrial Economics 95, 657–674.

Freeman, C., 1982. The Economics of Industrial Innovation. Francis Printer, London.

Gambardella, A., 1995. Science and Innovation. The US Pharmaceutical Industry During the 1980s. Cambridge University Press, Cambridge.

Geroski, P.A., Walters, C., Urga, G., 1998. Are differences in firm size transitory or permanent? Mimeo, London Business School, London.

Geroski, P.A., 2000. The growth of firms in theory and practice. In: Foss, N., Mahnke, V. (Eds.), Competence, Governance and Entrepreneurship. Oxford University Press, Oxford.

---

[29] We considered the 180 sub-markets including at least 20 firms out of the 302 covered by PHID. They account for 85.6% of the pharmaceutical market. Furthermore, we checked the invariance of our results considering sub-markets with different numbers of competitors.

Grabowski, H., Vernon, J., 1987. Pioneers, imitators, and generics. A simulation model of Schumpeterian competition. Quarterly Journal of Economics 102, 491–525.

Grabowski, H., Vernon, J., 1992. Brand loyalty, entry, and price competition in pharmaceuticals after the 1984 Drug Act. Journal of Law and Economics 35, 311–350.

Hart, P.E., Prais, S.J., 1956. The analysis of business concentration: a statistical approach. Journal of the Royal Statistical Society 119 (Ser. A), 150–191.

Hall, B.H., 1987. The relationship between firm size and firm growth in the US manufacturing sector. Journal of Industrial Economics 35, 583–606.

Henderson, R.M., Orsenigo, L., Pisano, G., 1999. The pharmaceutical industry and the revolution in molecular biology: interactions among scientific, institutional, and organizational change. In: Mowery, D., Nelson, R.R. (Eds.), Sources of Industrial Leadership. Cambridge University Press, Cambridge, pp. 267–311.

Hymer, S., Pashigian, P., 1962. Firm size and rate of growth. Journal of Political Economy 72, 556–569.

Ijiri, Y., Simon, H.A., 1977. Skew Distributions and the Sizes of Business Firms. North-Holland, New York.

Kalecki, M., 1945. On the Gibrat distribution. Econometrica 13, 161–170.

Lee, Y., Nunes Amaral, L.A., Canning, D., Meyer, M., Stanley, H.E., 1998. Universal features in the growth dynamics of complex organizations. Cond. Mat. 9804100.

Mansfield, D.E., 1962. Entry, Gibrat's Law, innovation, and growth of the firms. American Economic Review 52, 1024–1051.

Matraves, C., 1999. Market structure, R&D and advertising in the pharmaceutical industry. The Journal of Industrial Economics 47, 169–194.

Nelson, R.R., Winter, S.G., 1982. An Evolutionary Theory of Economic Change. The Belknap Press of Harvard University Press, Cambridge, MA.

Pavitt, K., 1999. Technology, Management and Systems of Innovation. Edward Elgar, Cheltenham.

Quah, D.T., 1996. Convergence empirics across economies with (some) capital mobility. Journal of Economic Growth 1, 95–124.

Reichl, L.E., 1980. A Modern Course in Statistical Physics. Edward Arnold, London.

Sneader, W., 1996. Drug Prototypes and their Exploitation. Wiley, New York.

Stanley, M.H.R., Nunes Amaral, L.A., Buldyrev, S.V., Havlin, S., Leschhorn, H., Maass, P., Salinger, M.A., Stanley, H.E., 1996. Scaling behavior in economics: empirical results and modelling of company growth. Nature 319, 804.

Sutton, J., 1997. Gibrat's legacy. Journal of Economic Literature 35, 40–59.

Sutton, J., 1998. Technology and Market Structure, Theory and History. MIT Press, Cambridge, MA.

Temin, P., 1980. Taking your Medicine: Drug Regulation in the United States. Harvard University Press, Cambridge, MA.

Warglien, M., 1995. Hierarchical selection and organizational adaptation. Industrial and Corporate Change 4, 161–186.

[12]

Industrial and Corporate Change, Volume 19, Number 6, pp. 1953–1996
doi:10.1093/icc/dtq063
Advance Access published November 8, 2010

Corporate performances and market selection: some comparative evidence

Giulio Bottazzi*, Giovanni Dosi**, Nadia Jacoby***, Angelo Secchi[†] and Federico Tamagni[‡]

Diverse theories of industry dynamics predict heterogeneity in production efficiency to be the driver of firms' growth, survival, and industrial change, either through a direct link between efficiency and growth, or through an indirect effect via profitabilities, as more productive firms can enjoy higher profit margins which, under imperfect capital markets, allow them to invest and grow more. Does the empirical evidence bear out such predictions? This article explores the dynamics of selection and reallocation through an investigation of the relations linking productivity, profitability and growth at the firm level. Exploiting large panels of Italian and French industrial firms, we find that heterogeneity in efficiencies primarily yields persistent profitability differentials, whereas the relationships of corporate growth with either productivity or profitability appear much weaker, if at all existent. This suggests that selection forces are much less strong than usually assumed. The results robustly apply across different industrial sectors and across the two countries.

1. Introduction

One of the most general and robust stylized facts in industrial economics, revealed by recent micro evidence on plants and firms, cross-sectionally and over time, is an

*Giulio Bottazzi, LEM-Scuola Superiore Sant'Anna, Piazza Martiri della Libertá 33, 56127, Pisa, Italy. e-mail: bottazzi@sssup.it

**Giovanni Dosi, LEM-Scuola Superiore Sant'Anna, Piazza Martiri della Libertá 33, 56127, Pisa, Italy. e-mail: gdosi@sssup.it

***Nadia Jacoby, CES - Centre d'économie de la Sorbonne, University of Paris 1 – Panthéon-Sorbonne, 106-112 Boulevard de l'Hôpital, 75647 Paris Cedex 13, Paris, France. e-mail: Nadia.Jacoby@univ-paris1.fr

[†]Angelo Secchi, Dipartimento di Scienze Economiche, Facolta' di Scienze Politiche, Università di Pisa, Via Serafini 3, 56125, Pisa, Italy. e-mail: angelo.secchi@sp.unipi.it

[‡]Federico Tamagni, LEM-Scuola Superiore Sant'Anna, Piazza Martiri della Libertá 33, 56127, Pisa, Italy. e-mail: f.tamagni@sssup.it

impressive heterogeneity, in every dimension one is able to observe. The heterogeneity in the 'identity cards' of individual entities concerns sizes, degrees of efficiency (however measured), innovativeness, organizational setups, and financial structures. This equally applies to the dynamics of all these corporate features, and it also concerns seemingly behavioral characteristics, including the propensity to expand and to invest. And, finally, it concerns revealed micro performances, e.g. profitability, growth rates, and survival probabilities.[1] Heterogeneity is ubiquitous across sectors and applies irrespectively of the degrees of statistical disaggregation of industries. It is very persistent over time in the levels of whatever micro variable one looks at, while often it is less so in the rates of change of the same variables.

Granted all that, are there some regularities that one can identify concerning the relations between the 'identities' of individual entities, plants or firms, and their revealed performances? And, more specifically, are there systematic links between some micro characteristics which are plausible candidates for the determinants of differential competitiveness, on the one hand, and revealed performances, on the other?

In fact, several models, grounded in diverse theoretical traditions, do predict heterogeneity in production efficiency and/or innovativeness to be the driver of firms' growth, survival, and industrial change. This applies, first, to the perspectives that we could call "equilibrium dynamics" including the models of Jovanovic (1982), Hopenhayn (1992), and Ericson and Pakes (1995) (see also the extensions to trade in Melitz, 2003). In Jovanovic (1982), new, entrant firms are characterized by heterogeneous efficiency. Selection results from a (passive) process of postentry Bayesian learning: those firms which discover to be efficient enough to ensure nonnegative profitability rationally choose to continue their operations and grow, while the others quit the market. The selection process is similar in Ericson and Pakes (1995), but here firms are able to undertake active learning in that they can influence their own efficiencies and profitabilities by investing in technological search whose intensity is determined via their rational technological expectations on the stochastic outcomes of search itself. Even more so, heterogeneity is the driver of differential firm growth and industrial dynamics in the models sharing an evolutionary perspective—whose formalizations include Nelson and Winter (1982), Winter (1984), Silverberg *et al.* (1988), Silverberg and Verspagen (1994), Dosi *et al.* (1995), Metcalfe (1998), Winter *et al.* (2000, 2003), and Bottazzi *et al.* (2001). In such a perspective a continuous process of out-of-equilibrium creative destruction is driven by the twin processes of idiosyncratic learning—involving changes in production techniques, output characteristics, and organizational practices—and competitive selection among persistently different firms. Such differences, in interactive market environments, influence the degrees of competitiveness and, ultimately, the degrees of 'fitness'

---

[1]Reviews, covering parts of this broad area, are in Nelson (1981), Dosi (1988, 2007), Caves (1998), Geroski (1998, 2002), Bartelsman and Doms (2000), Ahn (2001), and Dosi and Nelson (2010).

within the population of firms, determining differential growth, and survival opportunities.

One of the predictions of theory is that productivity—proxying production efficiency—ought to be positively related to profitability and firm growth, at least on average. Depending on the models, this occurs either through a direct link between efficiency and growth—as relatively more efficient firms gain market shares by setting lower prices—or through an indirect effect via profitabilities—as more productive firms can enjoy higher profit margins which in turn allow them to invest more (in presence of endemically imperfect capital markets) and eventually grow more.

The increasing availability of longitudinal micro-data allows us to address empirically how efficiency, profitability, and corporate growth relate to market selection and survival.

In this respect, a good deal of effort has gone into the decomposition of aggregate (sectoral or economy-wide) productivity growth, separating (i) idiosyncratic changes in firm/plant productivity levels—the so-called *within component*; (ii) changes in average productivity due to reallocation of output or employment shares across firms—the *between component*; and (iii) the contribution thereof due to entry into and exit from the market. Most studies, to a large extent based on plant-level data from North American countries (cf. Foster *et al.*, 2001, Baldwin and Gu, 2006, and the critical surveys in Bartelsman and Doms, 2000 and Ahn, 2001), do find evidence of a steady process of creative destruction involving significant rates of input and output reallocation even within 4-Digit industries. Moreover, the process is accompanied by a good deal of 'churning' with relatively high flows of entry and exit. Approximately a half of the new firms in all countries for which there is evidence die within the first 5 years of life (Bartelsman *et al.*, 2005). However, some of those which survive grow in their industry shares and provide a significant contribution to overall productivity growth (Baldwin, and Gu, 2006).

Within such a turbulent dynamics in industrial populations and structures, what is the role played, *stricto sensu*, by selection among the incumbents? That is, how effective are competitive interactions in reallocating resources and output shares in favor of the more efficient firms? Here the evidence is mixed. Start by noting that the between component in the decomposition of productivity changes provides only an indirect account of the relation between relative productivity levels and firms' growth. Indeed, it just measures the total sum of the changes in firms' shares weighted by their initial productivity levels. Granted that, if we take this component as a measure of the presence of selection dynamics, everything seems to suggest that the reallocation pressure due to differential productivities is at best weak or, according to some studies, even 'perverse' in that reallocation can go in favor of *less* productive plants or firms. Indeed, when the between component has the expected positive sign, idiosyncratic learning (the within term) generally offers a comparatively larger contribution to productivity growth. However, the sign is *not* always unequivocally positive. Baily *et al.* (1996) find that the contribution to productivity growth is equally split between growing and shrinking firms. In a similar vein, Baldwin and Gu (2006) conclude, on Canadian data, that "... the component that measures the effect of compositional changes arising from shifts in employment shares among continuing plants plays a negligible to moderate role in aggregate productivity growth after 1979" (pp. 438–439), such shifts appearing to be more relevant over the period 1973–1979. The evidence in Disney *et al.* (2003), on UK data, shows a *negative* between effect.[2]

The possibility for selection to be mediated via profitabilities (and differential investment rates) has been much less studied.[3] One of the few such attempts (Coad, 2007) does not find any robust association between profitabilities and subsequent growth.

In any case, beyond broad decompositions of changes in industry aggregates—as revealing as they are—the natural way forward is to explicitly analyze the statistical relations between the characteristics of individual firms (for the time being in terms of productivities) and their growth, both directly and indirectly via the relationships between productivity and profitability, and between the latter and growth. Some preliminary evidence on Italian data is presented in Bottazzi *et al.* (2002, 2008) and Dosi (2007), hinting at a quite weak power of selection forces. In the following we go much deeper into this type of analysis. In addition to contemporaneous relations, we explore longer term structures and we study their dynamics.[4] Moreover, we offer comparative analysis on Italian and French data, trying to illuminate the degrees to which the properties of the productivity–profitability–growth relationships depend on country-specific institutional characteristics or, conversely, are relatively generic features of contemporary industrial dynamics. The characteristics of available data on the two countries, covering long time spans and allowing for a fine level of sectoral aggregation, provide robustness to the results.

The article is organized as follows. In Section 2, we describe the datasets of Italian and French industrial firms. Next, in Section 3, we present intertemporal patterns of sectoral productivities, and perform nonparametric analyses of the pairwise relationships between productivity, profitability, and corporate growth, yielding an initial

---

[2]The size and even the sign of the various effects depend a good deal also on the method used. So, for example, Baldwin and Gu (2006) find, too, a negative between term in most sectors, when using the Griliches and Regev (1995) decomposition formula.

[3]An important caveat here is that one should explicitly disentangle the relation between physical productivities and the ability/willingness to charge higher margins per unit of output. One study that does it (Foster *et al.*, 2008) shows that in fact the two variables seem to move in opposite directions.

[4]Similar issues are considered through a VAR analysis in Coad *et al.* (2010) and in Coad (2010), respectively, Italian and French manufacturing data. Those works however focus on *growth rates* of productivity and profitability, providing a complementary exercise to the one we perform here.

descriptive picture about the strength of the different associations. We then turn to panel data regressions (Section 4) allowing for unobserved heterogeneity, and we estimate both short run effects and longer time relations.

2. Data and variables

This article draws upon two similar datasets, Micro.3 and EAE, reporting firm-level information for Italy and France, respectively. The Micro.3 database has been developed through a collaboration between the Italian Statistical Office (ISTAT) and members of the Laboratory of Economics and Management of Scuola Superiore Sant'Anna, Pisa. The EAE French databank is collected by the statistical department of French Ministry of Industry (SESSI) and provided by the French Statistical Office (INSEE).[5] The two databanks are open panels combining information from census and corporate annual reports about all the firms with 20 or more employees operating in any sector of activity on the national territory. We consider the period 1989–2004 for the EAE database and the period 1991–2004 for Micro.3.[6]

The study addresses manufacturing firms. As one of our major goals is to understand the strength of selection and reallocation forces operating in each market, we perform the analysis at the finest level of sectoral aggregation allowed by the data. This increases the likelihood that we compare firms which are actually competing with each other. Given the number of observations, we undertake an analysis at the level of 3-Digit industries and, among them, we restrict the attention to those sectors recording at least 100 firms in each year. Since this selection removes the transport equipment industries, where few producers are involved despite their relevance in manufacturing structure of both countries, we also report 2-Digit-level analyses for the sector 'Motor vehicles, trailers & semi-trailers'.[7]

The variables we are focusing on are productive efficiency, profitability, and growth. First, concerning the proxy for growth of the firm (labeled G in the following), our choice is consistent with the general aim of relating such dynamics with the selection and reallocation mechanisms nested in market competition. Thus, we

---

[5]Both databanks have been made available to authors under the mandatory condition of censorship of any individual information.

[6]The EAE dataset also indicates if the firms underwent any kind of structure modification such as merger, acquisition, etc. The analysis of French firms only includes firms which do not experience any such restructuring.

[7]In both datasets, firms are classified according to their sector of principal activity, on the basis of the French NAF 700 classification standards for the French data, and on the Italian ATECO 2002 ones for the Italian data. In the following, national industrial classifications are converted to the European NACE (Nomenclatures statistique des activités économiques dans la Communauté européenne) classes – Rev 1.1, with which both ATECO and NAF standards perfectly match. In turn, this substantially matches with ISIC Rev 3.1 classification.

measure firm size in terms of sales, rather than in terms of employees or assets, and G is the log difference of total sales at constant prices, in two consecutive years. Second, our proxy for profitability (henceforth P) is the ratio of gross operating margins (GOM, defined as value added minus cost of labour), divided by total sales. Third, our proxy for efficiency will be a simple labor productivity index, computed as the ratio between value added and number of employees (henceforth Π). We prefer to use this measure, instead of alternative multi-factor proxies of efficiency, to assure direct comparability of our micro productivity measures with those more aggregated ones available from national accounts. Moreover, estimates of multi-factor productivity are highly sensitive to the assumptions concerning the underlying production function (more on this point Dosi and Grazzi, 2006; Bottazzi *et al.*, 2008). In any case, the finding in Foster *et al.* (2001), that TFP and labor productivity tend to be highly correlated, supports the idea that these two measures point in the same direction.[8]

The current values of the variables are deflated with output deflators at the highest level of disaggregation. Consistent 3-Digit production price indexes are available for Italy starting in 1991, hence our choice to consider only the period 1991–2004. In the case of France, 3-Digit deflators are available only for the most recent years: thus, we opted for 2-Digit ones, covering the whole 1989–2004 panel.

3. Productivity, profitability, and corporate growth: broad picture and nonparametric analysis

Tables 1 and 2 offer an introductory picture of the sectoral tendencies followed by labor productivity in the 3-Digit industries selected for the analysis, for Italy and France, respectively (the measures are computed aggregating all the firms present in each sector in a given year).

The bird's-eye view of the data confirms the poor performance of Italian labor productivity when compared with France. In our database, the aggregate productivity of the Italian manufacturing sector grows in 4 years, from 2000 to 2004, by a mere 2%. In the same period, France sees the productivity of its manufacturing industry growing by more than 8%. Moreover, in Italy average productivity in 16 out of 41 3-Digit sectors tends to stop growing or even fall in the new millennium, while the same happens in France only in 5 out of 33 sectors. The interpretation of the sector-wide or even economy-wide factors influencing such average patterns is beyond the scope of this work. Conversely, the focus here is on the dispersion in firm-specific efficiency underlying the sectoral productivity averages and its relation with firm growth together with dispersion in profitabilities. Heterogeneity is indeed

---

[8]Also, since we focus on relatively narrowly defined industries, we do not expect large differences in capital intensity across firms.

Table 1 Italy—sectoral productivities at constant prices in selected 3-Digit industries, index numbers (2000 = 100)

NACE	SECTOR	1991	1992	1993	1994	1995	1996	1997	1998	1999	2000	2001	2002	2003	2004
151	Production, process, and preserv. of meat	114.22	125.40	116.68	110.55	101.77	108.94	105.93	115.06	105.99	100.00	99.64	111.02	112.04	108.99
155	Dairy products	100.64	105.95	99.06	97.42	96.50	91.49	95.84	97.27	104.36	100.00	101.18	110.16	110.61	108.37
158	Prod. of other food (bread, sugar, etc.)	93.14	99.59	98.36	91.08	89.12	91.49	92.28	94.34	99.48	100.00	104.52	110.38	100.02	107.35
159	Beverages (alcoholic and not)	85.51	91.41	90.85	92.73	89.84	82.47	89.06	98.52	97.67	100.00	91.34	94.89	88.91	84.81
171	Preparation and spinning of textiles	74.28	86.71	91.70	101.43	97.21	93.32	95.08	93.81	94.09	100.00	94.86	91.10	86.16	85.46
172	Textiles weaving	76.69	79.99	85.46	94.05	101.06	94.04	95.80	92.94	95.98	100.00	97.37	96.63	90.95	95.09
175	Carpets, rugs, and other textiles	76.69	80.22	86.17	91.18	95.19	92.58	95.81	96.43	94.40	100.00	96.34	94.99	93.22	91.45
177	Knitted and crocheted articles	80.89	87.93	91.82	94.71	105.37	96.91	95.87	96.00	87.89	100.00	99.26	99.01	94.84	103.11
182	Wearing apparel	75.55	81.21	85.32	89.59	99.94	99.38	95.33	98.02	93.00	100.00	105.65	107.82	103.94	110.16
193	Footwear	83.63	81.23	90.64	95.65	103.23	98.78	81.37	90.75	95.73	100.00	107.08	106.07	102.14	107.02
203	Wood products for construction	96.91	106.62	107.38	103.54	106.24	103.13	103.58	98.57	99.38	100.00	102.94	107.51	103.71	104.78
212	Articles of paper and paperboard	80.16	79.71	88.43	94.48	92.15	100.88	101.61	101.00	104.38	100.00	92.80	97.07	98.02	102.13
221	Publishing	66.43	72.22	71.10	71.71	69.03	68.51	78.84	77.81	86.32	100.00	84.59	91.46	94.91	111.72
222	Printing	109.75	113.40	110.62	108.36	99.14	99.80	92.89	98.80	98.56	100.00	104.65	100.22	101.37	103.01
241	Production of basic chemicals	65.34	74.71	75.32	96.07	125.51	99.43	99.54	106.53	97.61	100.00	85.26	88.09	83.40	89.36
243	Paints, varnishes, inks, and mastics	94.23	97.19	96.50	100.14	99.92	104.40	95.67	100.48	105.55	100.00	95.25	102.04	110.30	111.79
244	Pharma., med. chemicals, botanical prod	78.84	85.92	87.64	91.09	95.60	99.54	93.18	97.46	99.13	100.00	99.45	104.40	97.67	99.69
246	Other chemical products	80.21	89.17	96.32	102.42	105.93	122.61	112.12	113.55	112.66	100.00	96.88	99.69	90.45	100.62
251	Rubber products	102.06	106.44	113.11	119.20	110.58	99.28	102.71	100.96	103.04	100.00	97.14	102.63	97.41	103.10
252	Plastic products	90.49	95.68	100.66	103.22	102.22	105.02	99.42	99.10	103.42	100.00	97.64	103.18	100.03	98.42
263	Ceramic goods for construction	90.34	95.54	110.77	110.03	111.02	97.19	100.26	100.22	104.50	100.00	91.44	95.13	96.82	101.53
266	Concrete, plaster, and cement	84.55	86.82	78.44	79.04	85.24	89.10	87.91	90.45	94.03	100.00	103.17	110.35	107.02	104.33
267	Cutting, shaping, and finishing of stone	86.87	94.68	95.82	97.32	100.40	97.81	100.36	93.86	97.30	100.00	94.56	97.25	98.59	100.39
275	Casting of metals	79.38	77.31	79.65	88.46	96.73	92.75	94.39	94.96	97.34	100.00	92.81	101.28	95.13	96.09

(continued)

Table 1 Continued

NACE	SECTOR	1991	1992	1993	1994	1995	1996	1997	1998	1999	2000	2001	2002	2003	2004
281	Structural metal products	94.39	92.16	92.45	90.76	99.13	105.93	106.33	96.50	100.92	100.00	107.98	111.01	107.12	105.92
284	Forging, pressing, stamping of metal	83.45	89.87	88.30	95.32	106.38	100.27	96.61	97.95	101.23	100.00	103.44	107.16	98.15	91.43
285	Treatment and coating of metals	83.21	82.89	85.38	89.85	97.40	102.52	95.21	94.17	96.99	100.00	102.03	110.03	110.17	113.45
286	Cutlery, tools, and general hardware	87.93	88.48	89.71	93.71	96.35	92.91	95.43	93.78	97.04	100.00	100.03	101.76	99.26	104.49
287	Other fabricated metal products	89.05	92.89	96.31	100.07	105.38	102.91	96.91	97.38	96.12	100.00	98.25	98.68	97.04	99.53
291	Machinery for prod. and use of mech. power	81.16	88.59	91.50	99.02	101.84	98.71	92.20	90.27	95.95	100.00	98.59	107.62	102.81	109.09
292	Other general purpose machinery	90.49	93.23	94.77	99.76	103.89	107.39	98.34	97.32	97.17	100.00	100.16	101.89	102.24	104.73
294	Machine tools	84.66	79.91	80.92	87.50	94.61	95.61	94.61	97.11	87.68	100.00	99.15	93.63	84.29	91.21
295	Other special purpose machinery	86.72	86.37	94.46	99.57	105.12	96.78	98.31	92.84	94.52	100.00	99.15	94.13	93.56	97.27
297	Domestic appliances not e/where class	82.10	91.31	99.09	103.59	96.93	96.42	93.76	94.97	103.13	100.00	97.08	104.75	94.44	94.30
311	Electric motors, generators, and transform	83.15	81.84	83.81	87.05	92.03	89.62	90.54	88.90	90.25	100.00	91.91	97.52	100.71	98.38
312	Manuf. of electricity distrib, control equ	80.61	84.16	86.07	88.51	98.92	89.09	100.55	90.32	91.85	100.00	104.34	103.60	101.24	106.76
316	Electrical equipment not e/where class	99.42	101.90	100.77	111.56	105.59	99.04	100.30	99.73	100.01	100.00	101.20	102.87	103.85	108.60
343	Production of spare parts for cars	80.95	83.89	84.58	94.74	97.96	90.64	101.09	95.69	103.62	100.00	100.08	104.09	102.87	106.30
361	Furniture	88.70	90.11	93.06	94.63	97.10	90.26	91.13	94.02	96.53	100.00	99.19	95.79	90.37	91.71
362	Jewelry and related articles	80.59	78.77	78.21	79.33	84.72	92.89	88.88	100.04	106.81	100.00	102.34	100.29	102.62	105.53
366	Miscellaneous manufact. not elsewhere class	73.36	90.00	94.98	95.75	104.54	106.11	93.88	95.21	98.34	100.00	105.47	103.07	109.88	111.68
34	Motor vehicles, trailers, and semi-trailers	83.99	78.52	61.42	80.58	102.02	86.41	114.51	95.03	95.25	100.00	88.7	87.09	92.31	94.41
	Total	86.55	90.80	93.22	97.16	101.54	98.84	97.84	95.80	97.39	100.00	98.81	101.69	98.93	102.06

Table 2 France—sectoral productivities at constant prices in selected 3-Digit industries, index numbers (2000 = 100)

NACE	SECTOR	1989	1990	1991	1992	1993	1994	1995	1996	1997	1998	1999	2000	2001	2002	2003	2004
171	Preparation and spinning of textiles	86.33	79.71	88.30	93.89	92.20	103.59	90.55	88.10	94.23	90.26	88.84	100.00	89.00	94.92	97.58	105.03
172	Textiles weaving	77.99	72.18	73.66	78.36	84.00	92.05	92.00	89.35	90.23	96.99	91.90	100.00	90.45	96.83	94.90	100.19
175	Carpets, rugs, and other textiles	86.19	86.38	83.90	90.90	94.45	92.98	90.46	89.52	92.42	93.00	96.90	100.00	94.41	97.36	99.00	103.42
182	Wearing apparel	79.14	87.54	86.38	86.63	88.04	88.44	90.99	90.84	91.95	94.18	99.12	100.00	109.61	120.00	124.30	130.38
193	Footwear	81.54	87.93	90.27	88.08	89.92	91.02	91.49	90.47	94.19	95.41	100.83	100.00	101.82	105.30	103.14	98.33
204	Wooden containers	74.43	79.55	83.16	87.60	92.71	88.80	86.48	93.83	97.82	97.31	101.91	100.00	105.79	107.78	103.97	108.28
211	Pulp, paper, and paperboard	69.96	76.78	76.80	65.60	70.65	81.80	100.38	83.45	90.37	96.56	97.76	100.00	108.62	98.76	86.62	86.76
212	Articles of paper and paperboard	86.56	93.44	96.28	102.95	113.55	112.01	100.20	109.89	109.36	105.89	110.48	100.00	101.04	105.12	109.53	112.55
221	Publishing	77.31	76.81	77.16	79.44	82.47	83.54	83.77	89.28	92.57	93.82	95.56	100.00	96.54	93.68	96.95	95.93
222	Printing	96.27	98.07	98.75	100.35	99.59	101.62	101.88	95.81	97.81	97.04	99.66	100.00	95.99	98.92	99.25	102.86
241	Production of basic chemicals	60.90	61.59	68.31	72.73	75.86	82.81	91.37	86.80	90.19	91.63	102.69	100.00	93.54	78.48	76.10	76.68
244	Pharma., med. chemicals, botanical prod	69.21	74.25	76.39	79.82	82.78	95.16	105.84	107.40	112.95	99.89	98.02	100.00	102.33	103.29	101.15	99.40
245	Soap and deterg., and perfumes and toilet prep	78.60	78.72	80.17	86.54	87.08	95.22	98.06	89.21	95.75	92.89	91.25	100.00	93.29	99.05	99.95	105.76
246	Other chemical products	78.69	81.54	84.03	89.88	95.80	102.41	96.46	95.79	98.87	90.36	99.11	100.00	91.45	100.40	97.65	105.66
252	Plastic products	80.15	88.18	92.21	96.38	99.03	102.46	97.93	100.00	99.79	101.73	107.98	100.00	100.13	104.63	106.12	104.01
266	Concrete, plaster, and cement	95.30	97.40	97.15	95.00	92.57	96.05	97.07	86.27	85.41	93.02	95.09	100.00	101.66	104.44	108.11	112.79
281	Structural metal products	82.90	85.89	85.52	84.60	84.57	88.60	94.49	89.30	95.66	95.09	97.52	100.00	104.74	107.76	107.75	108.04
284	Forging, pressing, stamping of metal	89.96	97.33	99.96	103.62	103.17	106.40	101.21	98.99	101.70	99.39	101.51	100.00	98.35	100.46	101.00	101.06
286	Cutlery, tools, and general hardware	89.13	97.37	93.49	98.16	99.37	100.80	97.82	98.29	99.50	101.14	104.45	100.00	99.87	101.65	103.57	102.28
291	Machinery for prod. and use of mech. power	76.03	77.62	77.11	81.30	80.60	94.41	97.70	95.84	97.51	100.87	98.48	100.00	98.50	102.95	106.18	113.89

(continued)

Table 2 Continued

NACE	SECTOR	1989	1990	1991	1992	1993	1994	1995	1996	1997	1998	1999	2000	2001	2002	2003	2004
292	Other general purpose machinery	75.24	79.56	79.45	80.15	83.12	88.05	93.24	93.69	93.15	95.14	98.66	100.00	98.23	101.27	105.44	110.79
293	Agricultural and forestry machinery	76.79	77.99	75.26	77.67	84.74	94.57	96.80	98.65	101.30	96.63	97.85	100.00	89.76	98.15	96.78	104.57
294	Machine tools	79.32	83.45	79.39	78.41	78.42	87.10	96.74	93.51	92.85	98.48	102.18	100.00	100.88	89.50	97.18	108.66
295	Other special purpose machinery	77.25	79.33	75.63	76.72	82.11	86.97	91.87	90.27	94.24	96.76	97.21	100.00	102.08	100.37	98.54	103.14
311	Electric motors, generators, and transform	50.06	54.81	59.37	61.45	66.48	69.37	72.78	74.50	84.11	93.35	96.90	100.00	109.89	113.46	124.32	131.73
312	Manuf. of electricity distrib, control equip	67.52	71.94	75.65	80.73	100.04	89.41	92.11	93.20	96.73	98.16	104.52	100.00	99.93	104.21	106.53	115.44
331	Medical and surgical equip. orthopedic appl	58.30	60.73	65.29	70.00	76.88	78.07	79.19	80.44	88.68	92.70	97.01	100.00	104.71	113.41	124.70	134.53
332	Measuring, checking, testing, and navigat app.	50.00	54.60	57.36	56.87	64.08	69.43	72.63	69.70	75.00	79.91	86.47	100.00	96.70	100.77	109.65	114.96
333	Industrial process control equipment	56.68	61.64	65.75	64.72	69.40	73.65	81.93	78.98	79.77	88.04	94.74	100.00	107.04	109.60	108.71	116.93
361	Furniture	87.68	89.70	90.70	92.37	94.08	95.22	96.48	94.83	95.75	100.00	101.82	100.00	98.11	102.09	102.93	107.81
366	Miscellaneous manuf. not elsewhere class	85.27	87.22	80.95	87.95	94.02	95.02	97.72	100.49	106.55	98.12	98.65	100.00	107.25	113.86	108.91	118.91
34	Motor vehicles, trailers, and semi-trailers	93.30	97.56	95.81	93.67	87.58	95.21	99.47	102.48	98.35	101.32	102.67	100.00	96.46	103.25	152.49	171.41
Total		80.04	83.74	84.66	86.58	89.77	94.12	95.19	94.46	96.16	97.32	100.93	100.00	99.87	102.88	105.13	108.04

the name of the game. The ratios of the 95th to the 5th percentile of firms' productivity distributions are quite high and persistent over time. In Italy they range from 2.78 to 6.02 in 1991 and from 3.28 to 8.55 in 2004, displaying a general growing trend. The same trend is observed in France, when they range from 2.31 to 9.40 in 1991 and from 2.46 to 13.16 in 2004. Similar considerations apply to our profitability measure.[9]

Given the deep and widespread differences in productivity levels among firms belonging to the same 3-Digit sector, it is interesting to investigate how these differences relate to the observed aggregate behavior. Some hints can be obtained performing a decomposition exercise. Let $\Pi_{i,t}$ be the labor productivity of firm i in year t, computed as value added per employee, and $AP_{j,t}$ the aggregate labor productivity of sector j, defined as

$$AP_{j,t} = \sum_{i \in j} (\Pi_{i,t} \cdot s_{i,t})$$

where $s_{i,t}$ represents the share of each firm i in the sector. The annual variation of sectoral productivity can thus be decomposed as

$$\Delta AP_{j,t} = AP_{j,t} - AP_{j,t-1} = \sum_{i \in j} (\Delta \Pi_i \cdot s_{i,t-1}) + \sum_{i \in j} (\Delta s_i \cdot \Pi_{i,t-1})$$

$$+ \sum_{i \in j} (\Delta \Pi_i \cdot \Delta s_i).$$

The first term represents the *within* effect, i.e. the contribution of firm-specific productivity changes holding constant the share of the firm in the industry. The second term is the *between* effect, capturing the overall contribution due to variation in firm shares, holding initial productivities constant. Finally, the third term is an *interaction* effect, accounting for co-variations between firm productivities and shares.

We compute the percentage contribution of the three components for each sector and for each year in our database, and then average these percentages across all years and sectors. Results are reported in Table 3. Notice that sectoral productivity figures reported in previous Tables 1 and 2 are implicitly obtained by weighting productivity of each firm by employment shares.[10] However, since one of our objects of analysis will be the link between productivity and growth of sales, we also report results of the same decomposition with shares measured in terms of sales.[11] Notice also that

---

[9]Detailed, not reported for consideration of space, results are available upon request.

[10]Indeed, indicating value added with VA and employment with L, one has $AP_{j,t} = (\sum_{i \in j} VA_{i,t})/(\sum_{i \in j} L_{i,t})$ when $s_{i,t}$ is in terms of employment.

[11]The decomposition in Equation (10) still holds when $s_{i,t}$ is measured in terms of sales, but resulting sectoral productivities will obviously assume different values with respect to the case when employment shares are used.

Table 3 Decomposition of productivity growth, cross-sectoral mean contributions

	Within (%) $\sum_i(\Delta\pi_i \cdot s_{i,t})$	Between (%) $\sum_i(\Delta s_i \cdot \pi_{i,t})$	Interaction (%) $\sum_i(\Delta\pi_i \cdot \Delta s_i)$
With employment weights			
Italy	103.73	41.39	−45.12
France	121.43	63.38	−84.81
With sales weights			
Italy	152.73	−29.69	−23.04
France	89.23	11.79	−1.02

our datasets do not allow to study the contribution of entry and exit. Hence, our argument is limited to firms present in the dataset in the two consecutive years over which the variations are calculated.

The variability across sectors and across years is quite high, and results are subject to changes depending on the weights used (Appendix A presents the full set of results by industry). On average, however, idiosyncratic learning (the within component) tends to dominate upon selection effects (the between component).[12] And the apparent low effectiveness of selection dynamics is further highlighted by the impact of the covariance effects: those firms which increase more their productivities tend to undergo shrinking shares.[13]

Exercises of 'evolutionary accounting' such as those summarized in Table 3, however, just present broad tendencies, in that they sum up the different effects over all firms in an industry. Much finer interpretations can only come from the analysis of the relationships between efficiency and growth at the level of individual firms. This is precisely what we shall do in the following, in two steps. First, we directly explore the relationship between productivity and growth, the firm-level equivalent of the decomposition analysis done above. Second, by considering firm profitability, we decompose the productivity–growth interaction in two pieces, and explore the association of productivity with profit margins, on the one hand, and the relationship between profit margins and growth, on the other. All the analyses are conducted separately in the 3-Digit industries. In order to ease the presentation of results, we

---

[12]Sectoral evidence, in Appendix A, also reveals few cases displaying negative within components. It is hard to think of generalized drops in labor productivity in a sector, however. More likely candidates to an explanation are particularly noisy value added deflators—especially in sectors characterized by a lot of product differentiation.

[13]However, as suggested by an anonymous referee, this last phenomenon might not reveal so much lack of selection as such, but be the mask of restructuring processes: firms which restructure by downsizing tend to undergo both a growth in productivity and a decrease in size.

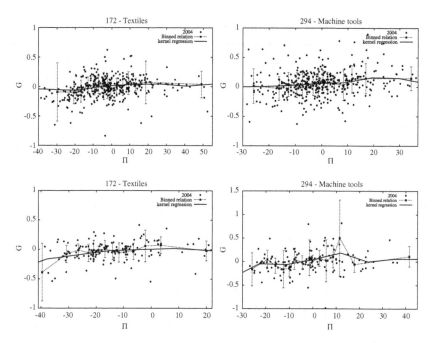

Figure 1 Productivity–growth relationship in selected 3-Digit sectors—binned statistics and kernel regression in 2004. Firm productivities are normalized with annual sectoral averages: Italy (top panel) versus France (bottom panel).

show graphs reporting estimates for 2004 on two sectors, Textiles (NACE 172) and Machine Tools (NACE 294), chosen because they are among the sectors with the highest number of observations. However, the results emerge as time- and sector invariant, suggesting that the structure of the relationships is independent from sectoral characteristics.[14]

Consider first the link between productivity (Π) and growth of sales (G), presented in Figure 1. The clouds of points represent the scatter plot of the raw data for the couples (Π_i, G_i). With dashed lines we represent binned statistics: the data are divided in equipopulated bins according to relative productivities, and the average within-bin values of Π are plotted against the average of G computed in the same bin, together with 2-standard deviation error bar. Finally, the thick lines represent kernel regressions of the conditional expectation of G given Π.[15]

---

[14]Results on other sectors and years are available from the authors upon request.

[15]Computation of binned statistics is based on 15 equipopulated bins, while kernel estimates employ an Epanenchnikov kernel function. Conclusions do not depend on these particular choices.

The evidence suggests a lack of any clear association between the variables. This applies to all sectors and to both countries. The clouds of points are quite dispersed and do not present any apparent shape. Further, notice that a flat line is a good first approximation connecting the pairs (average G, average Π) computed over the different productivity bins.[16] The impression is confirmed by the kernel estimates of the conditional expectation of G, which yield basically flat regression lines, in all of the sectors under analysis. Increasing or decreasing patterns can be considered only as a minor deviation from the general pattern, limited to the extreme parts of the productivity distribution (where kernel estimates become less reliable due to lower number of observations).

The absence of a clear positive relationship between relative productivity levels and growth testifies against the existence of any strong selection dynamics among incumbent firms. This evidence extends a similar finding on 2-Digit Italian manufacturing sectors reported in Bottazzi *et al.* (2005b), suggesting that the result does not depend on the disaggregation level. The question is whether this absence is due to the inability of firms to translate their technical advantages in internal resources, which can be in turn used for expanding their operations, or if a more abundant availability of resources does not translate automatically in an increased ability or willingness to grow. Some hints about this issue are obtained by investigating how productivity and growth relate to firm profitability. Plots in Figure 2 show results concerning the productivity–profitability relation. As before, a simple scatter plot of the raw data (Π_i, P_i) is depicted with dots, while binned statistics (within-bin average values of Π versus within-bin average of P, with 2-standard deviation error bar) are in dashed lines, and kernel estimates of the conditional expectation of P given Π are reported as a thick line. The tendency displayed by the graphs is in this case revealing of a positive association between the variables. This is a clearcut result highlighted by both binned statistics and kernel regressions, which indeed show steeper patterns as compared with the productivity–growth relations. Moreover, the relationship is steeper for those firms with relatively low values of productivity, and becomes weaker, yet still positive, as one moves toward higher productivity levels. This hints at the emergence of a peculiar nonlinearity, already noted in Bottazzi *et al.* (2008) on a different sample of Italian firms. The result is more pronounced for Italian firms, and applies to all sectors. It is then clear that, at least on average, firms with higher productivity levels are characterized by higher profit margins.

Conversely, no evident pattern emerges in the relationship between growth and profitability, shown in Figure 3. Here, the findings closely resemble what was observed for the productivity–growth relationship. The clouds of points remain much dispersed, while both binned statistics and kernel regressions allow us to

---

[16]These pairs always fall within the confidence band, suggesting that growth performance does not display any statistically significant difference in the different productivity bins.

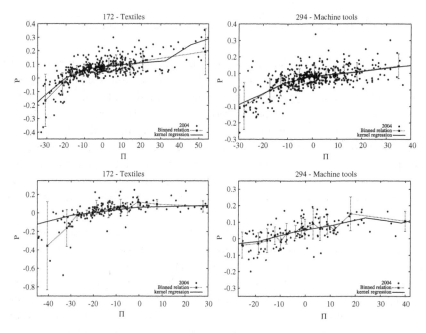

Figure 2 Productivity–profitability relationship in selected 3-Digit sectors—binned statistics and kernel regression in 2004. Firm productivity is normalized with annual sectoral averages: Italy (top panel) versus France (bottom panel).

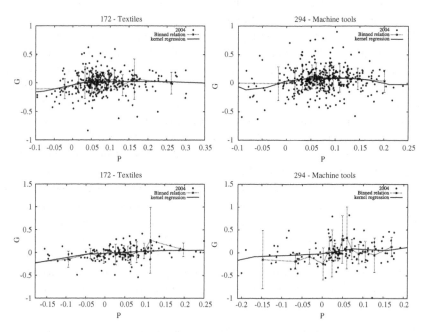

Figure 3 Profitability–growth relationship in selected 3-Digit sectors—binned statistics and kernel regression in 2004: Italy (top panel) versus France (bottom panel).

conclude that a flat line provides a good approximation of the data. Again, this applies to both countries and irrespective of the sectors considered.

Summarizing, the relations linking productivity, profitability, and growth seem considerably weaker than what one would have expected on the grounds of any simple view that market competition would lead to reallocation of production and market shares toward the more efficient and/or the more profitable firms. The productivity–profitability relationship seems indeed the only link displaying relevance in the data, whereas the relationships of growth with either productivity or profitability appear much weaker, if at all existent. The following section explores to what extent this picture survives if we control for the effect of firm-specific unobserved variables, and analyzes the unfolding of such relationships over time.

4. Panel analysis

The nonparametric exercises presented in Section 3 look at the relation between productivity, profitability, and growth by comparing the values of these variables for all the firms belonging to one sector in one particular year. In this section, we start by investigating the same contemporaneous relationships, but introduce a parametric specification that allows us to exploit the panel structure of the data to control for possibly unobserved firm-specific factors. The basic regression specification is a bivariate model of the form

$$Y_{i,t} = c + \alpha X_{i,t} + u_i + \varepsilon_{i,t}, \tag{1}$$

where Y and X represent the pair of productivity–profitability–growth measures considered in the different regressions, while the term u_i is a firm-specific constant, modeling unobserved characteristics, and $\varepsilon_{i,t}$ a standard *i.i.d.* error term. All the estimates are undertaken separately for each 3-Digit sector, adding a full set of year dummies that control for possible time effects common to all the firms in the same sector. In line with the unconditional pairwise analysis of previous section, we want to isolate the association of each variable with another, and therefore we do not augment the regressions with further explanatory variables. However, we did compare estimated effects across sectors sharing similar characteristics in terms of information and communication technologies (ICT) intensity, skill composition of the labor force, and patterns of innovation, based on standard taxonomies used in international studies (O'mahony and Van Ark, 2003).[17] The results of this comparison tell that the effects are very similar across taxonomy classes for all the investigated relationships: distribution of effects in one class do not differ from distributions of effects in another class defined by the same taxonomy. This suggests

---

[17]See Appendix B for details and precise definitions.

a minor impact of sector-specific technological and organizational characteristics on the relations under study.

Notice also that a sheer comparison of the estimated α across the different regressions is not very informative about the relative strength of the association between the pair of variables involved, since the values of α obviously depend on the scale (or unit of measurement) of the variables. The strength of association is better captured by the index

$$S_{Y,X}^2 = \left(\hat{\alpha}\frac{\sigma_X}{\sigma_Y}\right)^2, \tag{2}$$

where $\hat{\alpha}$ is the Fixed Effects estimate of the coefficient in Equation (1), while σ_X and σ_Y represent the sample standard deviation of X and Y, respectively. Thus, $S_{Y,X}^2$ yields a measure of the fraction of total explained variance which is accounted for by the variance of X. That is, it captures the explanatory power due to the economic regressor X alone, net of the contribution of annual dummies and unobserved heterogeneity. We shall compare its values with the canonical $R^2 = (1 - \frac{\sigma_\varepsilon^2}{\sigma_Y^2})$ which gives a measure of the overall explanatory power of the model, including the contribution of annual dummies and unobserved heterogeneity. However, in all our regressions the explanatory power associated with year dummies is negligible and, thus, the fraction of the R^2 which is not captured by $S_{Y,X}^2$ can be seen as a proxy for the explanatory power due to unobserved heterogeneity alone. Of course, given that the heterogeneity is assumed to be time invariant in panel models, the contribution of the u_i terms tend to be higher in specifications where the dependent Y displays higher persistence over time. Indeed, to check this, we estimated a simple AR(1) model on each variable. The average of the coefficients obtained in the different sectors considered is 1.01 in the case of productivity, for both Italy and France; average coefficients obtained in the case of profitability equal 0.94 in Italy and 0.97 in France. The average AR(1) coefficients on growth are instead significantly lower, and equal 0.19 in Italy and 0.17 in France. These results are consistent with other previous studies (see Bottazzi, et al., 2008; Coad, et al., 2010, and the works cited therein) and should be kept in mind in interpreting the following results.

We start by exploring the direct association of productivity with growth. The estimated equation is

$$G_{i,t} = c + \alpha\Pi_{i,t} + u_i + \varepsilon_{i,t}, \tag{3}$$

where productivities are again normalized with the annual sectoral averages (i.e. they are relative productivities).

Table 4 shows coefficient estimates obtained for the sample of sectors available in the two countries, as well as the associated values of $S_{Y,X}^2$ and R^2. As a general result, we observe a clearcut pattern, with positive (and significant) estimates in practically all sectors, in both countries. Notice, however, that while the productivity variable

Table 4 Contemporaneous relationship between productivity and growth—Fixed Effects estimates of Equation (3)

NACE	Sector	Italy $\hat{\alpha}$	S^2_{YX}	R^2	France $\hat{\alpha}$	S^2_{YX}	R^2
151	Production, process and preserv. of meat	0.0023[a]	0.0477	0.2185	–	–	–
155	Dairy products	0.0020[a]	0.0317	0.1490	–	–	–
158	Prod. of other food (bread, sugar, etc.)	0.0011[a]	0.0272	0.2930	–	–	–
159	Beverages (alcoholic and not)	0.0022[a]	0.1098	0.1757	–	–	–
171	Preparation and spinning of textiles	0.0045[a]	0.0936	0.2561	0.0004[a]	0.0049	0.1907
172	Textiles weaving	0.0023[a]	0.0623	0.2916	0.0003[a]	0.0046	0.2415
175	Carpets, rugs, and other textiles	0.0039[a]	0.2383	0.3585	0.0003[a]	0.0033	0.1946
177	Knitted and crocheted articles	0.0071[a]	0.2433	0.2913	–	–	–
182	Wearing apparel	0.0052[a]	0.1543	0.3269	0.0028[a]	0.0000	0.0601
193	Footwear	0.0086[a]	0.2048	0.2859	0.0100[a]	0.0000	0.1178
203	Wood products for construction	0.0066[a]	0.1564	0.2836	–	–	–
204	Wooden containers	–	–	–	0.0072[a]	0.0000	0.1429
211	Pulp, paper, and paperboard	–	–	–	0.0022[a]	0.0954	0.1354
212	Articles of paper and paperboard	0.0021[a]	0.0632	0.2412	0.0026[a]	0.0388	0.1973
221	Publishing	0.0012[a]	0.0746	0.3028	0.0005[a]	0.0640	0.2113
222	Printing	0.0027[a]	0.1063	0.3688	0.0062[a]	0.1169	0.1975
241	Production of basic chemicals	0.0006[a]	0.0158	0.1255	0.0009[a]	0.1056	0.1470
243	Paints, varnishes, inks and mastics	0.0015[a]	0.0290	0.1961	–	–	–
244	Pharma., med. chemicals, botanical prod	0.0012[a]	0.0310	0.3863	0.0004[a]	0.0570	0.2306
245	Soap and deterg and perfumes and toilet prep	–	–	–	0.0001[a]	0.0094	0.1555
246	Other chemical products	0.0023[a]	0.1166	0.3168	0.0022[a]	0.1367	0.2317
251	Rubber products	0.0026[a]	0.0532	0.2833	–	–	–
252	Plastic products	0.0032[a]	0.1200	0.2789	0.0014[a]	0.0245	0.1711
263	Ceramic goods for construction	0.0033[a]	0.1125	0.3327	–	–	–
266	Concrete, plaster, and cement	0.0025[a]	0.0851	0.3158	0.0011[a]	0.0210	0.1857
267	Cutting, shaping, and finishing of stone	0.0039[a]	0.2360	0.3045	–	–	–
275	Casting of metals	0.0051[a]	0.1436	0.2758	–	–	–
281	Structural metal products	0.0060[a]	0.1183	0.3131	0.0096[a]	0.1319	0.2179
284	Forging, pressing, stamping of metal	0.0059[a]	0.2009	0.2812	0.0080[a]	0.1942	0.2391
285	Treatment and coating of metals	0.0060[a]	0.1957	0.3556	–	–	–
286	Cutlery, tools, and general hardware	0.0054[a]	0.2267	0.2850	0.0085[a]	0.2079	0.2101

Table 4 Continued

NACE	Sector	Italy			France		
		$\hat{\alpha}$	S^2_{YX}	R^2	$\hat{\alpha}$	S^2_{YX}	R^2
287	Other fabricated metal products	0.0037[a]	0.0928	0.2719	–	–	–
291	Machinery for prod. and use of mech. power	0.0035[a]	0.0942	0.2823	0.0052[a]	0.1671	0.2203
292	Other general purpose machinery	0.0052[a]	0.1613	0.2626	0.0083[a]	0.1885	0.1961
293	Agricultural and forestry machinery	–	–	–	0.0086[a]	0.1450	0.2093
294	Machine tools	0.0062[a]	0.1525	0.3340	0.0099[a]	0.1932	0.3316
295	Other special purpose machinery	0.0061[a]	0.1553	0.2389	0.0087[a]	0.1948	0.2072
297	Domestic appliances not e/where class	0.0027[a]	0.0607	0.2552	–	–	–
311	Electric motors, generators, and transform	0.0040[a]	0.1147	0.3973	0.0097[a]	0.1518	0.2434
312	Manuf. of electricity distrib, control equip	0.0046[a]	0.1059	0.3092	0.0104[a]	0.2508	0.2728
316	Electrical equipment not e/where class	0.0050[a]	0.1771	0.2849	–	–	–
331	Medical and surgical equip, orthopedic appl	–	–	–	0.0053[a]	0.1455	0.2417
332	Measuring, checking, testing, and navigat app.	–	–	–	0.0068[a]	0.1217	0.2885
333	Industrial process control equipment	–	–	–	0.0088[a]	0.1990	0.2705
343	Production of spare parts for cars	0.0043[a]	0.0845	0.2259	–	–	–
361	Furniture	0.0057[a]	0.1331	0.2826	0.0119[a]	0.2633	0.2604
362	Jewelry and related articles	0.0047[a]	0.0870	0.2231	–	–	–
366	Miscellaneous manufact. not elsewhere class	0.0043[a]	0.1590	0.3188	0.0000[a]	0.0017	0.1649
34	Motor vehicles, trailers, and semi-trailers	0.0038[a]	0.0707	0.2470	0.0025[a]	0.1122	0.2214
	S^2_{YX} statistics	AVG	MIN	MAX	AVG	MIN	MAX
		0.1186	0.0158	0.2433	0.1268	0.0000	0.2633

Productivity is in deviation from annual sectoral average. [a]Coefficient significant at 5% confidence level.

has the expected sign, the strength of the relationship is actually very weak. The values of $S^2_{Y,X}$ reveal indeed that only a small fraction of the total explained variance measured by R^2 comes from productivity alone, while the contribution of unobserved heterogeneity is always much larger. Take sector 151 as an example. Out of about 22% of total variance explained by the model ($R^2 = 0.2185$), we observe that less than 5% is due to variation in productivity ($S^2_{Y,X} = 0.0477$): this means only a mere 1% of the growth rates' variance is accounted for by productivity. Similar patterns emerge also in the other sectors, where the contribution of productivity to the explanation of the variance in growth rates is typically less than 5% and most often less than 3%. Overall, even if industry-wide forces driving toward selection/reallocation of resources in favor of more efficient firms are present, their strength is extremely low, at least in the short term.

Let us move a step further and ask whether selection operates via profitability. We again consider the two relationships capturing the association of productivity with profitability, on the one hand, and that of profitability with growth, on the other. Results in Table 5 present the estimates of the regression model

$$P_{i,t} = c + \alpha \Pi_{i,t} + u_i + \varepsilon_{i,t}. \tag{4}$$

where productivity is again measured in relative terms.

In general the association between the two variables is positive and significant, in both countries, irrespective of the sectors. Moreover, the relationship stands out as considerably stronger as compared with the results obtained for the productivity–growth relation. The total explained variance is higher than before (cf. R^2 greater than 60 or 70% in most cases) and we also observe a significant increase in the estimates of $S^2_{Y,X}$, which display average values of about 35%, in fact greater in the vast majority of the sectors, with peaks above 60%.[18] Thus, the explanatory power of relative productivity is comparable with that stemming from firm-specific factors capturing unobserved heterogeneity: more efficient firms do tend to be more profitable.

Finally, let us consider the profitability–growth relationship. Here, the issue is whether gross profits spur growth, which we capture through the regression model

$$G_{i,t} = c + \alpha P_{i,t} + u_i + \varepsilon_{i,t}. \tag{5}$$

The estimates, reported in Table 6, provide a picture that is quite similar to that offered by the productivity–growth regressions. The estimated coefficients are positive and significant, but the values of $S^2_{Y,X}$ and R^2 are once again revealing that the relationship is almost entirely driven by the firm-specific components u_i. With R^2's in the range of 0.2–0.4, and $S^2_{Y,X}$'s on average around 0.1 (indeed lower in most

---

[18] An higher R^2 is also due to the higher persistence of the dependent variable.

Table 5 Contemporaneous relationship between productivity and profitability—Fixed Effects estimates of Equation (4)

NACE	Sector	Italy			France		
		$\hat{\alpha}$	S^2_{YX}	R^2	$\hat{\alpha}$	S^2_{YX}	R^2
151	Production, process, and preserv. of meat	0.0019[a]	0.3285	0.6392	–	–	–
155	Dairy products	0.0019[a]	0.2706	0.4214	–	–	–
158	Prod. of other food (bread, sugar, etc.)	0.0019[a]	0.4542	0.8100	–	–	–
159	Beverages (alcoholic and not)	0.0020[a]	0.3880	0.4465	–	–	–
171	Preparation and spinning of textiles	0.0033[a]	0.3358	0.7226	0.0004[a]	0.0554	0.4612
172	Textiles weaving	0.0023[a]	0.3378	0.7294	0.0002[a]	0.0269	0.5069
175	Carpets, rugs, and other textiles	0.0031[a]	0.5200	0.7122	0.0002[a]	0.0192	0.5238
177	Knitted and crocheted articles	0.0041[a]	0.3711	0.6082	–	–	–
182	Wearing apparel	0.0033[a]	0.0570	0.4543	0.0011[a]	0.1502	0.5231
193	Footwear	0.0043[a]	0.3193	0.5284	0.0035[a]	0.2313	0.6318
203	Wood products for construction	0.0045[a]	0.5588	0.6670	–	–	–
204	Wooden containers	–	–	–	0.0038[a]	0.6098	0.7159
211	Pulp, paper, and paperboard	–	–	–	0.0024[a]	0.6674	0.8393
212	Articles of paper and paperboard	0.0024[a]	0.5459	0.7218	0.0019[a]	0.2481	0.6614
221	Publishing	0.0018[a]	0.3503	0.6948	0.0001[a]	0.0482	0.6707
222	Printing	0.0026[a]	0.3479	0.6672	0.0026[a]	0.3904	0.6153
241	Production of basic chemicals	0.0006[a]	0.1053	0.5202	0.0004[a]	0.1312	0.7240
243	Paints, varnishes, inks, and mastics	0.0020[a]	0.5437	0.8200	–	–	–
244	Pharma., med. chemicals, botanical prod	0.0011[a]	0.2682	0.5029	0.0002[a]	0.0275	0.7751
245	Soap and deterg and perfumes and toilet prep	–	–	–	0.0001[a]	0.0504	0.5885
246	Other chemical products	0.0019[a]	0.3325	0.4788	0.0009[a]	0.2170	0.6271
251	Rubber products	0.0030[a]	0.4570	0.7896	–	–	–
252	Plastic products	0.0023[a]	0.3510	0.7132	0.0009[a]	0.1378	0.5832
263	Ceramic goods for construction	0.0031[a]	0.4818	0.7029	–	–	–
266	Concrete, plaster and cement	0.0007[a]	0.0584	0.6106	0.0005[a]	0.0551	0.6049
267	Cutting, shaping, and finishing of stone	0.0020[a]	0.3579	0.6700	–	–	–
275	Casting of metals	0.0025[a]	0.3003	0.6580	–	–	–
281	Structural metal products	0.0033[a]	0.3410	0.6435	0.0042[a]	0.6292	0.7275
284	Forging, pressing, stamping of metal	0.0034[a]	0.4029	0.5412	0.0040[a]	0.5303	0.7160

(continued)

1974 G. Bottazzi *et al.*

Table 5 Continued

NACE	Sector	Italy			France		
		$\hat{\alpha}$	S_{YX}^2	R^2	$\hat{\alpha}$	S_{YX}^2	R^2
285	Treatment and coating of metals	0.0040[a]	0.4132	0.6952	–	–	–
286	Cutlery, tools, and general hardware	0.0035[a]	0.3188	0.6038	0.0048[a]	0.6753	0.7034
287	Other fabricated metal products	0.0031[a]	0.4788	0.7096	–	–	–
291	Machinery for prod. and use of mech. power	0.0031[a]	0.3929	0.6945	0.0033[a]	0.5360	0.7326
292	Other general purpose machinery	0.0029[a]	0.4341	0.7503	0.0041[a]	0.6293	0.7198
293	Agricultural and forestry machinery	–	–	–	0.0044[a]	0.5913	0.7028
294	Machine tools	0.0024[a]	0.3433	0.6764	0.0048[a]	0.6061	0.7145
295	Other special purpose machinery	0.0035[a]	0.5164	0.6621	0.0049[a]	0.6817	0.7104
297	Domestic appliances not e/where class	0.0023[a]	0.4152	0.7349	–	–	–
311	Electric motors, generators, and transform	0.0029[a]	0.4990	0.7598	0.0051[a]	0.4939	0.7714
312	Manuf. of electricity distrib, control equip	0.0033[a]	0.3516	0.7454	0.0035[a]	0.4427	0.6711
316	Electrical equipment not e/where class	0.0024[a]	0.3247	0.7587	–	–	–
331	Medical and surgical equip, orthopedic appl	–	–	–	0.0031[a]	0.3913	0.6871
332	Measuring, checking, testing, and navigat app.	–	–	–	0.0030[a]	0.2919	0.6221
333	Industrial process control equipment	–	–	–	0.0037[a]	0.5462	0.6334
343	Production of spare parts for cars	0.0139[a]	0.0060	0.1296	–	–	–
361	Furniture	0.0035[a]	0.4313	0.6371	0.0056[a]	0.6517	0.7337
362	Jewelry and related articles	0.0019[a]	0.2132	0.5142	–	–	–
366	Miscellaneous manufact. not elsewhere class	0.0032[a]	0.5358	0.6848	0.0000[a]	0.0060	0.5637
34	Motor vehicles, trailers, and semi-trailers	0.0105[a]	0.0046	0.1287	0.0015[a]	0.2664	0.5716
	S_{YX}^2 statistics	AVG	MIN	MAX	AVG	MIN	MAX
		0.3471	0.0046	0.5588	0.4172	0.0060	0.6753

Productivity is in deviation from annual sectoral average. [a]Coefficient significant at 5% confidence level.

Table 6 Contemporaneous relationship between profitability and growth—Fixed Effects estimates of Equation (5)

		Italy			France		
NACE	Sector	$\hat{\alpha}$	S^2_{YX}	R^2	$\hat{\alpha}$	S^2_{YX}	R^2
151	Production, process and preserv. of meat	1.2511[a]	0.1754	0.2901	–	–	–
155	Dairy products	1.7550[a]	0.3299	0.3728	–	–	–
158	Prod. of other food (bread, sugar, etc.)	0.4858[a]	0.0364	0.3067	–	–	–
159	Beverages (alcoholic and not)	1.2601[a]	0.3196	0.3561	–	–	–
171	Preparation and spinning of textiles	0.6340[a]	0.0545	0.2449	0.7440[a]	0.0923	0.2546
172	Textiles weaving	0.5265[a]	0.0478	0.2943	1.0546[a]	0.0923	0.2890
175	Carpets, rugs, and other textiles	0.4540[a]	0.0553	0.3291	1.1378[a]	0.1048	0.2419
177	Knitted and crocheted articles	0.7578[a]	0.1472	0.3055	–	–	–
182	Wearing apparel	0.1096[a]	0.0147	0.3138	0.5653[a]	0.0757	0.2550
193	Footwear	0.8679[a]	0.1056	0.2997	1.3384[a]	0.1159	0.2207
203	Wood products for construction	0.5279[a]	0.0359	0.2892	–	–	–
204	Wooden containers	–	–	–	0.8592[a]	0.0581	0.1908
211	Pulp, paper and paperboard	–	–	–	0.1758	0.0070	0.1006
212	Articles of paper, and paperboard	0.7236[a]	0.0747	0.2582	0.5924[a]	0.0318	0.1946
221	Publishing	0.1706[a]	0.0121	0.2939	0.0429[a]	0.0068	0.1875
222	Printing	0.6643[a]	0.1376	0.3542	0.7332[a]	0.0438	0.1695
241	Production of basic chemicals	1.4128[a]	0.3470	0.3491	0.5441[a]	0.1165	0.1627
243	Paints, varnishes, inks, and mastics	0.9854[a]	0.0653	0.2206	–	–	–
244	Pharma., med. chemicals, botanical prod	1.0134[a]	0.1213	0.4519	0.3796[a]	0.0829	0.2632
245	Soap and deterg, and perfumes and toilet prep	–	–	–	0.9769[a]	0.1026	0.1872
246	Other chemical products	0.8846[a]	0.2527	0.4737	0.6959[a]	0.0873	0.2203
251	Rubber products	0.2447[a]	0.0095	0.2852	–	–	–
252	Plastic products	0.8717[a]	0.1263	0.2904	0.5802[a]	0.0285	0.1761
263	Ceramic goods for construction	0.3509[a]	0.0240	0.3070	–	–	–
266	Concrete, plaster, and cement	0.4693[a]	0.0200	0.2790	0.8573[a]	0.0627	0.2035
267	Cutting, shaping, and finishing of stone	0.5609[a]	0.0563	0.2697	–	–	–
275	Casting of metals	0.8911[a]	0.1018	0.2873	–	–	–
281	Structural metal products	0.8370[a]	0.0684	0.3142	1.1263[a]	0.0544	0.1998
284	Forging, pressing, stamping of metal	0.8923[a]	0.1239	0.2989	0.9334[a]	0.0926	0.2110

(continued)

1976 G. Bottazzi *et al.*

Table 6 Continued

NACE	Sector	Italy $\hat{\alpha}$	S^2_{YX}	R^2	France $\hat{\alpha}$	S^2_{YX}	R^2
285	Treatment and coating of metals	0.6561[a]	0.0911	0.3456	–	–	–
286	Cutlery, tools, and general hardware	0.3338[a]	0.0342	0.2474	0.6970[a]	0.0586	0.1841
287	Other fabricated metal products	0.9017[a]	0.1189	0.3106	–	–	–
291	Machinery for prod. and use of mech. power	0.8954[a]	0.1487	0.3153	0.8816[a]	0.0979	0.2170
292	Other general purpose machinery	0.8271[a]	0.0701	0.2553	1.0287[a]	0.0832	0.1678
293	Agricultural and forestry machinery	–	–	–	1.1647[a]	0.1388	0.2208
294	Machine tools	0.6543[a]	0.0382	0.2998	1.1168[a]	0.1029	0.3195
295	Other special purpose machinery	0.9698[a]	0.0828	0.2307	1.0194[a]	0.0995	0.1849
297	Domestic appliances not e/where class	0.3325[a]	0.0103	0.2403	–	–	–
311	Electric motors, generators, and transform	0.7281[a]	0.0628	0.3965	1.0876[a]	0.1020	0.2356
312	Manuf. of electricity distrib, control equip	0.4637[a]	0.0390	0.2864	0.0021	0.0000	0.2834
316	Electrical equipment not e/where class	0.7113[a]	0.0557	0.2767	–	–	–
331	Medical and surgical equip, orthopedic appl	–	–	–	0.4818[a]	0.0684	0.2292
332	Measuring, checking, testing, and navigat app.	–	–	–	0.7112[a]	0.0633	0.2672
333	Industrial process control equipment	–	–	–	0.5837[a]	0.0896	0.2598
343	Production of spare parts for cars	0.0306[a]	0.1770	0.3518	–	–	–
361	Furniture	0.6915[a]	0.0546	0.2846	1.0099[a]	0.0960	0.2312
362	Jewelry and related articles	1.5110[a]	0.1609	0.2871	–	–	–
366	Miscellaneous manufact. not elsewhere class	0.7875[a]	0.0958	0.3261	1.0989[a]	0.0921	0.2079
34	Motor vehicles, trailers, and semi-trailers	0.0307[a]	0.1375	0.3385	0.0001[a]	0.0132	0.2573

S^2_{YX} statistics		AVG	MIN	MAX	AVG	MIN	MAX
		0.1032	0.0095	0.3470	0.0699	0.0000	0.1388

[a]Coefficient significant at 5% confidence level.

sectors), the profitability variable accounts for about 5% of the variance in growth rates in most cases. The relationship is generally there, but appears to be extremely weak.

An overall reading of the findings yields conclusions which closely agree with the impression drawn from previous nonparametric investigations. The contemporaneous relations between firm growth, on the one hand, and both productivity and profitability, on the other, appear to be rather weak. This, in turn, witnesses for relatively weak selection forces at work, at least in the short term, neither through a productivity effect—efficiency spurring differential growth—nor via a profitability one—higher margins entailing greater cash flows and through that greater possibilities of expansion. Greater degrees of efficiency are indeed robustly associated with higher profitability, but the latter does not display any straightforward association with growth.

As compared with the nonparametric analysis of the previous section, panel regressions allow us to disentangle the importance of idiosyncratic, firm-specific unobserved factors. In fact, the regression modeling profitability as dependent on productivity stands out as the only case where the statistical relevance of the economic regressor is comparable with the explanatory power of unaccounted sources of micro heterogeneity. Conversely, the relevance of systematic, economically interpretable regressors is weak in both the productivity–growth and the profitability–growth relationships, where a good deal of the explained variance rests upon unobserved fixed effects.

Of course, contemporaneous relations capture linkages only over the very short run, while it is indeed reasonable that the relationships we are investigating have an essentially dynamic and structural nature. Hence, one should consider the workings of the relationships over a longer time scale, allowing for the effect of each variable on the others to take some time to emerge. In this perspective we now investigate panel estimates of the links between average values of productivity, profitability, and growth records computed over multi-year subperiods.

Indicating with s the period and with T_s the number of years spanned by each period, the time series average of the variables are defined over three periods p_1, p_2, and p_3, as follows

$$\bar{Z}_{i,s} = \frac{1}{T_s} \sum_{t \in s} Z_{i,t} \quad s \in \{p_1, p_2, p_3\} \quad Z \in \{ \Pi, P, G \}. \tag{6}$$

Then, we set $p_1 = 1992{-}1995$, $p_2 = 1996{-}1999$, and $p_3 = 2000{-}2004$ for Italian data, while $p_1 = 1990{-}1994$, $p_2 = 1995{-}1999$, and $p_3 = 2000{-}2004$ for the French data.[19]

---

[19]Previous analysis on similar database in Bottazzi *et al.* (2005a) show that a period of 4–5 years is enough to smooth out fluctuations in production structure due to structural adjustments. An alternative strategy looking at time effects would be to still consider yearly values of the variables, but include lagged regressors, experimenting with different orders of lag. However, taking

This leaves us with a panel of three periods, which can be used to replicate the same kind of analysis explored above. The baseline empirical model thus becomes

$$\bar{Y}_{i,s} = c + \alpha \bar{X}_{i,s} + u_i + \varepsilon_{i,s},\qquad(7)$$

where Y and X represent the pair of economic performance considered in each pairwise regression, and u_i is again a firm-specific constant absorbing unobserved characteristics. For consistency with previous analysis, we present Fixed Effects estimates obtained separately for each sector, also including time (period) dummies. As compared with the previous models where we take yearly values, averaging over time is likely to entail a reduction in the intertemporal variability of the variables, and thus we expect an increase in the R^2's, due to an increased explanatory power of time-invariant heterogeneity. The question is whether we can confirm the above finding of a relatively weak explanatory power of the economic regressors.

Table 7 shows results for the specification exploring the link between average productivity and average growth

$$\bar{G}_{i,s} = c + \alpha \bar{\Pi}_{i,s} + u_i + \varepsilon_{i,s}.\qquad(8)$$

The main conclusions are consistent with results drawn from contemporaneous yearly regressions. The weakness of the association between the variables is even more apparent, if one considers that the estimates of α turn out not statistically different from zero in about a half of the sectors. The expected increase in the overall explained variance (R^2 generally equals 60–70%) is entirely due to the increased explanatory power of the firm-specific constants u_i, while the contribution attributable to average productivity is negligible (cf. very small $S^2_{Y,X}$'s, equal to about 0.04 on average).

Table 8 reports results concerning the pairwise regressions between average productivity and average profitability

$$\bar{P}_{i,s} = c + \alpha \bar{\Pi}_{i,s} + u_i + \varepsilon_{i,s}.\qquad(9)$$

The estimates confirm statistical relevance of this relationship. First, estimates are significant in almost all the sectors. Second, the values of $S^2_{Y,X}$ confirm that, despite some sectoral variability, the explanatory power of productivity, net of the contribution of fixed effects and period dummies, is sizeable and ranges between around 30–60% of total variance explained by the model. The overall message is consistent with the evidence from contemporaneous yearly regressions.

Similar conclusions emerge also from Table 9, where we show the estimation results for the specification

$$\bar{G}_{i,s} = c + \alpha \bar{P}_{i,s} + u_i + \varepsilon_{i,s},\qquad(10)$$

---

multi-year averages is preferable, as it is likely to reduce possible biases due to measurement errors in yearly figures. Anyhow, we did estimate specifications with lagged regressors, but the results do not depart from the patterns stemming from the yearly contemporaneous analyses.

Table 7 Multi-year averages: productivity and growth—Fixed Effects estimates of Equation (8)

NACE	Sector	Italy			France		
		$\hat{\alpha}$	S^2_{YX}	R^2	$\hat{\alpha}$	S^2_{YX}	R^2
151	Production, process and preserv. of meat	0.0014[a]	0.0379	0.7211	–	–	–
155	Dairy products	−0.0003	0.0018	0.6144	–	–	–
158	Prod. of other food (bread, sugar, etc.)	−0.0014[a]	0.0280	0.6207	–	–	–
159	Beverages (alcoholic and not)	0.0005	0.0108	0.6031	–	–	–
171	Preparation and spinning of textiles	0.0005	0.0012	0.4750	0.0010[a]	0.0429	0.7193
172	Textiles weaving	0.0008	0.0081	0.6141	0.0008[a]	0.0244	0.8598
175	Carpets, rugs, and other textiles	0.0024[a]	0.1389	0.6029	0.0000	0.0003	0.8461
177	Knitted and crocheted articles	0.0022[a]	0.0393	0.7248	–	–	–
182	Wearing apparel	0.0021[a]	0.0325	0.7179	0.0009[a]	0.0068	0.7786
193	Footwear	0.0053[a]	0.0652	0.6343	0.0032[a]	0.0150	0.7519
203	Wood products for construction	0.0022	0.0213	0.6586	–	–	–
204	Wooden containers	–	–	–	−0.0002	0.0002	0.7713
211	Pulp, paper, and paperboard	–	–	–	−0.0001	0.0006	0.4445
212	Articles of paper and paperboard	−0.0001	0.0001	0.6265	0.0011[a]	0.0085	0.7753
221	Publishing	0.0010[a]	0.0491	0.6984	0.0004[a]	0.0535	0.7313
222	Printing	0.0026[a]	0.0667	0.6038	0.0015[a]	0.0107	0.7345
241	Production of basic chemicals	0.0003	0.0104	0.5634	0.0002	0.0104	0.7651
243	Paints, varnishes, inks, and mastics	−0.0031	0.0745	0.5441	–	–	–
244	Pharma., med. chemicals, botanical prod	0.0007[a]	0.0157	0.8952	0.0001	0.0019	0.7274
245	Soap and deterg, and perfumes and toilet prep	–	–	–	0.0000	0.0001	0.6974
246	Other chemical products	0.0002	0.0008	0.5985	0.0009[a]	0.0444	0.7232
251	Rubber products	0.0009	0.0094	0.6536	–	–	–
252	Plastic products	0.0015[a]	0.0333	0.6604	0.0002	0.0006	0.7142
263	Ceramic goods for construction	0.0030[a]	0.1226	0.6484	–	–	–
266	Concrete, plaster, and cement	0.0011[a]	0.0118	0.6197	0.0025[a]	0.1003	0.7072
267	Cutting, shaping, and finishing of stone	0.0020[a]	0.0742	0.6633	–	–	–
275	Casting of metals	0.0024[a]	0.0325	0.5464	–	–	–
281	Structural metal products	0.0024[a]	0.0213	0.7133	0.0015	0.0045	0.6871
284	Forging, pressing, stamping of metal	0.0026[a]	0.0621	0.5928	0.0029[a]	0.0379	0.6902

(continued)

Table 7 Continued

NACE	Sector	Italy $\hat{\alpha}$	S^2_{YX}	R^2	France $\hat{\alpha}$	S^2_{YX}	R^2
285	Treatment and coating of metals	0.0040[a]	0.0902	0.7124	–	–	–
286	Cutlery, tools, and general hardware	0.0002	0.0003	0.6131	0.0019[a]	0.0213	0.7240
287	Other fabricated metal products	0.0019[a]	0.0332	0.6663	–	–	–
291	Machinery for prod and use of mech. power	0.0011[a]	0.0148	0.6681	−0.0007	0.0042	0.6751
292	Other general purpose machinery	0.0024[a]	0.0521	0.6547	0.0022[a]	0.0272	0.7251
293	Agricultural and forestry machinery	–	–	–	0.0037[a]	0.0539	0.6998
294	Machine tools	0.0042[a]	0.1308	0.7345	0.0027	0.0194	0.8444
295	Other special purpose machinery	0.0018[a]	0.0180	0.6049	0.0034[a]	0.0596	0.7592
297	Domestic appliances not e/where class	−0.0009	0.0091	0.7017	–	–	–
311	Electric motors, generators and transform	0.0014	0.0160	0.7934	0.0059[a]	0.0863	0.7617
312	Manuf. of electricity distrib. control equip	0.0001	0.0001	0.7530	0.0001	0.0000	0.8215
316	Electrical equipment not e/where class	0.0043[a]	0.1525	0.6848	–	–	–
331	Medical and surgical equip, orthopedic appl	–	–	–	0.0011	0.0091	0.8189
332	Measuring, checking, testing, and navigat app.	–	–	–	0.0012	0.0039	0.8032
333	Industrial process control equipment	–	–	–	0.0047[a]	0.0832	0.8254
343	Production of spare parts for cars	0.0046[a]	0.0759	0.2681	–	–	–
361	Furniture	0.0014[a]	0.0111	0.6036	0.0025[a]	0.0206	0.8211
362	Jewelry and related articles	0.0011	0.0115	0.6238	–	–	–
366	Miscellaneous manufact. not elsewhere class	0.0010	0.0120	0.6372	0.0000	0.0007	0.7118
34	Motor vehicles, trailers, and semi-trailers	0.0039[a]	0.0592	0.3224	0.0010	0.3529	0.6997

S^2_{YX} statistics	AVG	MIN	MAX	AVG	MIN	MAX
	0.0399	0.0001	0.1525	0.0347	0.0000	0.3529

[a]Coefficient significant at 5% confidence level.

Table 8 Multi-year averages: productivity and profitability—Fixed Effects estimates of Equation (9)

NACE	Sector	Italy			France		
		$\hat{\alpha}$	S^2_{YX}	R^2	$\hat{\alpha}$	S^2_{YX}	R^2
151	Production, process, and preserv. of meat	0.0019[a]	0.3053	0.8893	–	–	–
155	Dairy products	0.0015[a]	0.2923	0.7367	–	–	–
158	Prod. of other food (bread, sugar, etc.)	0.0022[a]	0.4965	0.9243	–	–	–
159	Beverages (alcoholic and not)	0.0020[a]	0.5558	0.7913	–	–	–
171	Preparation and spinning of textiles	0.0034[a]	0.3374	0.8690	0.0004[a]	0.0262	0.6912
172	Textiles weaving	0.0024[a]	0.3268	0.8772	0.0004[a]	0.0900	0.7940
175	Carpets, rugs, and other textiles	0.0031[a]	0.4643	0.8174	0.0001[a]	0.0066	0.7600
177	Knitted and crocheted articles	0.0029[a]	0.2036	0.7825	–	–	–
182	Wearing apparel	0.0032	0.0515	0.7163	0.0009[a]	0.0546	0.8153
193	Footwear	0.0034[a]	0.1362	0.7146	0.0032[a]	0.1756	0.8210
203	Wood products for construction	0.0040[a]	0.4101	0.8417	–	–	–
204	Wooden containers	–	–	–	0.0035[a]	0.5586	0.8166
211	Pulp, paper, and paperboard	–	–	–	0.0026[a]	0.5860	0.8953
212	Articles of paper and paperboard	0.0020[a]	0.4259	0.8906	0.0028[a]	0.4408	0.8432
221	Publishing	0.0022[a]	0.4649	0.8895	0.0001[a]	0.0220	0.8771
222	Printing	0.0027[a]	0.3654	0.8331	0.0026[a]	0.6113	0.8444
241	Production of basic chemicals	0.0008[a]	0.1287	0.8820	0.0003[a]	0.0885	0.8618
243	Paints, varnishes, inks, and mastics	0.0020[a]	0.3350	0.9589	–	–	–
244	Pharma., med. chemicals, botanical prod	0.0006[a]	0.1142	0.6978	0.0001	0.0008	0.6043
245	Soap and deterg and perfumes and toilet prep	–	–	–	0.0001[a]	0.0336	0.8030
246	Other chemical products	0.0019[a]	0.4896	0.7408	0.0003[a]	0.0306	0.9035
251	Rubber products	0.0030[a]	0.4475	0.9004	–	–	–
252	Plastic products	0.0020[a]	0.2614	0.8723	0.0005[a]	0.0038	0.9740
263	Ceramic goods for construction	0.0026[a]	0.3370	0.8280	–	–	–
266	Concrete, plaster, and cement	0.0015[a]	0.1616	0.8564	0.0005[a]	0.0322	0.8499
267	Cutting, shaping, and finishing of stone	0.0015[a]	0.1808	0.8133	–	–	–
275	Casting of metals	0.0033[a]	0.4852	0.8533	–	–	–
281	Structural metal products	0.0036[a]	0.3468	0.8640	0.0040[a]	0.6322	0.8671
284	Forging, pressing, stamping, of metal	0.0032[a]	0.4178	0.7814	0.0041[a]	0.5007	0.9136

(continued)

Table 8 Continued

		Italy			France		
NACE	Sector	$\hat{\alpha}$	S_{YX}^2	R^2	$\hat{\alpha}$	S_{YX}^2	R^2
285	Treatment and coating of metals	0.0050[a]	0.6199	0.8630	–	–	–
286	Cutlery, tools, and general hardware	0.0037[a]	0.3810	0.8407	0.0051[a]	0.7388	0.8655
287	Other fabricated metal products	0.0037[a]	0.5749	0.8602	–	–	–
291	Machinery for prod. and use of mech. power	0.0040[a]	0.6019	0.8118	0.0027[a]	0.3717	0.8760
292	Other general purpose machinery	0.0026[a]	0.2514	0.9167	0.0039[a]	0.5323	0.8240
293	Agricultural and forestry machinery	–	–	–	0.0040[a]	0.4003	0.9184
294	Machine tools	0.0031[a]	0.5748	0.8658	0.0056[a]	0.1825	0.9724
295	Other special purpose machinery	0.0032[a]	0.4399	0.8565	0.0049[a]	0.6987	0.8742
297	Domestic appliances not e/where class	0.0022[a]	0.4149	0.8509	–	–	–
311	Electric motors, generators, and transform	0.0032[a]	0.6548	0.8547	0.0047[a]	0.4780	0.8877
312	Manuf. of electricity distrib, control equip	0.0037[a]	0.6102	0.9252	0.0024[a]	0.2654	0.8888
316	Electrical equipment not e/where class	0.0026[a]	0.4285	0.9064	–	–	–
331	Medical and surgical equip, orthopedic appl	–	–	–	0.0027[a]	0.1784	0.9223
332	Measuring, checking, testing, and navigat app.	–	–	–	0.0039[a]	0.3813	0.8708
333	Industrial process control equipment	–	–	–	0.0034[a]	0.4914	0.8533
343	Production of spare parts for cars	0.0204	0.0162	0.3375	–	–	–
361	Furniture	0.0028[a]	0.2652	0.8346	0.0051[a]	0.5101	0.8858
362	Jewelry and related articles	0.0031[a]	0.4965	0.7477	–	–	–
366	Miscellaneous manufact. not elsewhere class	0.0036[a]	0.5801	0.8253	0.0000	0.0044	0.7429
34	Motor vehicles, trailers, and semi-trailers	0.0169	0.0140	0.3370	0.0016[a]	0.0684	0.9985
	S_{YX}^2 statistics	AVG	MIN	MAX	AVG	MIN	MAX
		0.3639	0.0140	0.6548	0.2716	0.0008	0.7388

[a]Coefficient significant at 5% confidence level.

Table 9 Multi-year averages: profitability and growth—Fixed Effects estimates of Equation (10)

NACE	Sector	Italy $\hat{\alpha}$	S^2_{YX}	R^2	France $\hat{\alpha}$	S^2_{YX}	R^2
151	Production, process, and preserv. of meat	0.3948[a]	0.0308	0.7203	–	–	–
155	Dairy products	−0.4148[a]	0.0363	0.6239	–	–	–
158	Prod. of other food (bread, sugar, etc.)	0.2372[a]	0.0071	0.6193	–	–	–
159	Beverages (alcoholic and not)	−0.7192[a]	0.1357	0.6456	–	–	–
171	Preparation and spinning of textiles	−0.2303	0.0083	0.4756	0.2802[a]	0.0189	0.7337
172	Textiles weaving	0.3926[a]	0.0329	0.6280	0.7447[a]	0.0499	0.8593
175	Carpets, rugs, and other textiles	0.3471[a]	0.0494	0.5968	−0.0667	0.0017	0.8442
177	Knitted and crocheted articles	0.2192[a]	0.0220	0.7266	–	–	–
182	Wearing apparel	0.0394	0.0016	0.7160	0.5176[a]	0.1141	0.7844
193	Footwear	0.2886[a]	0.0116	0.6312	1.1300[a]	0.1192	0.7705
203	Wood products for construction	0.5587[a]	0.0441	0.6611	–	–	–
204	Wooden containers	–	–	–	0.5559[a]	0.0462	0.7836
211	Pulp, paper, and paperboard	–	–	–	−0.3544[a]	0.1010	0.4529
212	Articles of paper and paperboard	0.9324[a]	0.1185	0.6474	0.4375[a]	0.0249	0.7792
221	Publishing	0.2346[a]	0.0218	0.6921	0.0107	0.0046	0.7256
222	Printing	0.6338[a]	0.0645	0.6076	0.4789[a]	0.0258	0.7375
241	Production of basic chemicals	−0.0145	0.0001	0.5842	0.2872[a]	0.0666	0.7707
243	Paints, varnishes, inks, and mastics	1.4104[a]	0.0641	0.5525	–	–	–
244	Pharma., med. chemicals, botanical prod	0.1661[a]	0.0036	0.8920	−0.2391[a]	0.3285	0.8312
245	Soap and deterg and perfumes and toilet prep	–	–	–	0.6632[a]	0.0899	0.7084
246	Other chemical products	1.6332[a]	0.3780	0.7114	0.7734[a]	0.1199	0.7264
251	Rubber products	0.4371[a]	0.0413	0.6836	–	–	–
252	Plastic products	0.2268[a]	0.0106	0.6574	0.1400	0.0203	0.7107
263	Ceramic goods for construction	0.2111	0.0104	0.6237	–	–	–
266	Concrete, plaster, and cement	0.0801	0.0007	0.6338	0.3134	0.0128	0.7036
267	Cutting, shaping, and finishing of stone	0.5938[a]	0.1021	0.6833	–	–	–
275	Casting of metals	−0.0803	0.0008	0.5501	–	–	–
281	Structural metal products	0.2752[a]	0.0085	0.7121	0.6330[a]	0.0188	0.6901
284	Forging, pressing, stamping of metal	−0.2829[a]	0.0186	0.5877	0.5110[a]	0.0391	0.6916

(continued)

Table 9 Continued

NACE	Sector	Italy			France		
		$\hat{\alpha}$	S^2_{YX}	R^2	$\hat{\alpha}$	S^2_{YX}	R^2
285	Treatment and coating of metals	0.7119[a]	0.1100	0.7277	–	–	–
286	Cutlery, tools, and general hardware	0.5823[a]	0.1005	0.6463	0.3760[a]	0.0272	0.7282
287	Other fabricated metal products	0.5104[a]	0.0445	0.6714	–	–	–
291	Machinery for prod. and use of mech. power	0.4656[a]	0.0540	0.6779	−0.0646	0.0008	0.6748
292	Other general purpose machinery	0.4216[a]	0.0250	0.6529	0.2509[a]	0.0101	0.7235
293	Agricultural and forestry machinery	–	–	–	1.0035[a]	0.1595	0.7203
294	Machine tools	0.6531[a]	0.0500	0.7286	0.4937[a]	0.1253	0.8467
295	Other special purpose machinery	0.3336[a]	0.0128	0.6067	0.4594[a]	0.0418	0.7600
297	Domestic appliances not e/where class	−0.7356[a]	0.0723	0.7156	–	–	–
311	Electric motors, generators and transform	0.5501[a]	0.0387	0.8035	1.0222[a]	0.1251	0.7690
312	Manuf. of electricity distrib. control equip.	−0.0082	0.0000	0.7418	0.4016	0.3727	0.8648
316	Electrical equipment not e/where class	0.4452[a]	0.0280	0.6755	–	–	–
331	Medical and surgical equip. orthopedic appl	–	–	–	0.1021	0.0044	0.8181
332	Measuring, checking, testing, and navigat app.	–	–	–	0.4727[a]	0.0252	0.8087
333	Industrial process control equipment	–	–	–	0.4387[a]	0.1277	0.8335
343	Production of spare parts for cars	0.0760[a]	0.6714	0.7043	–	–	–
361	Furniture	0.3311[a]	0.0141	0.6055	0.4675[a]	0.0366	0.8252
362	Jewelry and related articles	0.2261	0.0079	0.6269	–	–	–
366	Miscellaneous manufact. not elsewhere class	0.5076[a]	0.0585	0.6568	0.8539[a]	0.1108	0.7386
34	Motor vehicles, trailers, and semi-trailers	0.0761[a]	0.5771	0.6951	0.0002[a]	0.0694	0.6659
	S^2_{YX} statistics	AVG	MIN	MAX	AVG	MIN	MAX
		0.0761	0.0000	0.6714	0.0718	0.0008	0.3727

[a]Coefficient significant at 5% confidence level.

concerning the relation between average growth and average profitability. The estimates tend to be positive and significant, with the fraction of sectors displaying statistical significance rising up to 2/3. Still, comparisons of $S^2_{Y,X}$ with R^2 once again highlight that the strength of the relationships is low. With few exceptions, the small values of $S^2_{Y,X}$ (about 0.08 on average) imply that profitability can hardly contribute to more than 5–10% to the overall explanatory power of the model captured by the R^2 (actually much less in most of the sectors).

Summarizing, results are quite in accordance with what we find in the case of contemporaneous estimates. The productivity–profitability link turns out to be the only one where the explanatory power of the 'systematic economic regressor' is comparable with, or even higher than, that coming from firm-specific terms. Conversely, selection mechanisms are at best weak along the productivity–growth and the profitability–growth links. Such patterns do not display striking differences between the two countries and, despite some variations, tend to apply quite generally across sectors. Moreover, as found in the case of contemporaneous yearly regression, estimates do not vary significantly if we compare the estimated effects across groups of sectors corresponding to the different classes identified by taxonomies on ICT intensity, skill composition of the labor force, and patterns of innovation.

5. A weak selective hand of market competition? Some conclusions

The micro evidence presented in this work reinforces the robust stylized fact on widespread and persistent inter-firm heterogeneity revealed by widely different degrees of efficiencies. Such evidence is also well in tune with an evolutionary notion of idiosyncratic learning, innovation (or lack of it), and adaptation. Heterogeneous firms compete with each other and, given (possibly firm- or location-specific) input and output prices, obtain different returns. Putting it in a different language, they obtain different "quasi-rent" or, conversely, losses above/below the notional "pure competition" profit rates. At the same time, market selection among firms—the other central mechanism at work, together with firm-specific learning, in evolutionary interpretations of economic change—does not seem to be particularly powerful, at least on the yearly or multi-yearly time scale at which statistics are reported (the available time series are not long enough to assess what happens in the very long run, say decades). Diverse degrees of efficiencies seem to yield primarily relatively persistent profitability differentials. That is, markets do not appear to be too effective selectors delivering rewards and punishments in terms of relative sizes or shares according to differential efficiencies. Moreover, the absence of any strong relationship between profitability and growth militates against the "naively Schumpeterian" or "classic" notion that profits feed growth (by plausibly feeding investments).

Selection amongst different variants of a technology, different vintages of equipment, different lines of production does occur, and is a major driver of industrial dynamics. However, it seems to occur, to a good extent, within firms, driven by the implementation of "better" processes of production and the abandonment of older less productive ones. Finally, the same evidence appears to run against the conjecture, put forward in the 1960s and 1970s by the managerial theories of the firm on a trade-off between profitability and growth with managerialized firms trying to maximize growth subject to a minimum profit constraint.[20]

Note that weakness of differential efficiency as direct or indirect driver of differential growth and inter-firm reallocation of resources, as we have shown, robustly applies across different industrial sectors and across countries—in our case Italy and France—characterized by quite different institutional set-ups and forms of industrial organization. In turn, the observation that market selection that winnows directly on firms may play less of a role than that assumed in many models (of heterogeneous inspiration) demands further advances in the understanding of how markets work (or do not), and of the structure of demand. Here note the following.

First, one measures efficiency—supposedly a driver of differential selection—very imperfectly: we have already mentioned, as emphasized by Foster *et al.* (2008), that one ought to disentangle the price component of value added (and thus the price effect upon competitiveness) from physical efficiency to which productivity strictly speaking refers. This applies to homogeneous products and even more so when products differ in their characteristics and performances: as this is often the case in modern industries, one ought to explicitly account for the impact of the latter upon competitiveness and revealed selection processes.

Second, but relatedly, the notion of generalized inter-industry competition is too heroic to hold. It might be more fruitful in many industries to think of different sub-market of different sizes as the locus of competition (cf. Sutton, 1998). The characteristics and size of such sub-markets offer also different constraints and opportunities for corporate growth. Ferrari and Fiat operate in different sub-markets, face different growth opportunities and do not compete with each other. However, the example is interesting also in another respect: Fiat can grow, as it actually happened, by acquiring Ferrari. But such a dynamics has little bearing on the relative initial productivities of Fiat and Ferrari.

Third, in any case, the links between efficiency (and innovation), on the one hand, and corporate growth, on the other, are likely to be profoundly mediated by large degrees of behavioral freedom, in terms, e.g. of propensities to invest, export, expand abroad, pricing strategies, and patterns of diversification. In fact, such degrees of

---

[20]In fact the absence of such a trade-off had been already noted by Barna (1962). Note also that this proposition is compatible with the finding (cf. Geroski *et al.*, 1997) that current growth appears to be correlated with future long-term profitability.

behavioral freedom can only be possible if market interactions occur over "selection landscapes" which are roughly flat over significant intervals. In turn, such a "flatness" is likely to be the consequence of various forms of market imperfections—including informational ones. Such imperfections, together with endemic satisficing behaviors, would allow firms characterized by diverse degrees of efficiency (and product qualities) to co-exist without too much competitive pressures.

The broad patterns discussed in this work need to be corroborated with evidence from other countries and on longer time periods. And, at least equally important, they have to be matched by complementary evidence on the impact of entry and exit. However, were they to hold, they would bear far-reaching implications for theory, empirical analysis, and polices. On the side of both theory and empirical investigations, much more work awaits to be done on how markets work, the nature of competitive interactions, and the dimensions over which competitive selection occurs, if any. On the policy side, a much more sobering view might have to be taken on the "magic of market competition". It could well be that policy measures aimed at *creative accumulation* of technological knowledge and equipment might be more effective in fostering progress than trying to wag the forces of *creative destruction*. Together, if proved robust, our evidence on the negligible impact of profit margins upon growth takes away a lot of plausibility from the argument that taxing profits is bad for the economy because it harms growth. Rather, corporate growth seems to be driven much more by elusive and idiosyncratic "animal spirits".

Acknowledgments

Financial support to the research that led to this article by MIUR (PROT. 2007HA3S72_003, PRIN 2007), European Commission 6th FP (Contract CIT3-CT-2005-513396, Project: DIME-Dynamics of Institutions and Markets in Europe), Fondazione Cassa di Risparmio di Livorno (Bando 2008), and Research & Strategy Office of Unicredit Group is gratefully acknowledged. The research would not have been possible without precious help from the Italian Statistical Office (ISTAT), and in particular from Roberto Monducci, Roberto Sanzo and Alessandro Zeli. Also, we gratefully acknowledge the permission to use data from the French Statistical Office (INSEE), and we would like to thank particularly Daniele Bastide at the Office of Industrial Studies and Statistics (SESSI) at the French Ministry of Industry. The work has benefited from comments on previous drafts by participants to the MFJ-RIETI-WASEDA International Conference "Organization and Performance: Understanding the Diversity of Firms," Maison Franco-Japonaise, Tokyo, November 14–15, 2008, and to the FIRB-RISC Conference "Research and entrepreneurship in the knowledge-based economy," Bocconi University, Milan, September 7–8, 2009. In particular, we wish to thank Eric Bartelsman,

Richard R. Nelson, and Reinhilde Veugelers, in addition to an anonymous referee. The usual disclaimers apply.

References

Ahn, S. (2001), 'Firm dynamics and productivity growth: a review of micro evidence from OECD countries,' *Economics Department Working Paper 297*, OECD.

Baily, M. N., E. J. Bartelsman and J. Haltiwanger (1996), 'Downsizing and productivity growth: myth or reality?' *Small Business Economics*, **8**, 259–278.

Baldwin, J. R. and W. Gu (2006), 'Plant turnover and productivity growth in Canadian manufacturing,' *Industrial and Corporate Change*, **15**, 417–465.

Barna, T. (1962), *Investment and Growth Policies in British Industrial Firms*. Cambridge University Press: Cambridge.

Bartelsman, E. J. and M. Doms (2000), 'Understanding productivity: lessons from longitudinal microdata,' *Journal of Economic Literature*, **38**, 569–594.

Bartelsman, E. J., S. Scarpetta and F. Schivardi (2005), 'Comparative analysis of firm demographics and survival: micro-level evidence for the OECD countries,' *Industrial and Corporate Change*, **14**, 365–391.

Bottazzi, G., E. Cefis and G. Dosi (2002), 'Corporate growth and industrial structure. some evidence from the italian manufacturing industry,' *Industrial and Corporate Change*, **11**, 705–723.

Bottazzi, G., G. Dosi and G. Rocchetti (2001), 'Modes of knowledge accumulation, entry regimes and patterns of industrial evolution,' *Industrial and Corporate Change*, **10**, 609–638.

Bottazzi, G., M. Grazzi and A. Secchi (2005a), 'Characterizing the production process: a disaggregated analysis of italian manufacturing firms,' *Rivista di Politica Economica*, **95**, 243–270.

Bottazzi, G., M. Grazzi and A. Secchi (2005b), 'Input output scaling relations in italian manufacturing firms,' *Physica A*, **355**, 95–102.

Bottazzi, G., A. Secchi and F. Tamagni (2008), 'Productivity, profitability and financial performance,' *Industrial and Corporate Change*, **17**, 711–751.

Caves, R. E. (1998), 'Industrial organization and new findings on the turnover and mobility of firms,' *Journal of Economic Literature*, **36**, 1947–1982.

Coad, A. (2007), 'Testing the principle of growth of the fitter: the relationship between profits and firm growth,' *Structural Change and economic dynamics*, **18**, 370–386.

Coad, A. (2010), 'Exploring the processes of firm growth: evidence from a vector autoregression,' *Industrial and Corporate Change*, **19**(6), 1677–1703.

Coad, A., R. Rao and F. Tamagni (2010), 'Growth processes of italian manufacturing firms,' *Structural Change and Economic Dynamics*, forthcoming.

Disney, R., J. Haskel and Y. Heden (2003), 'Entry, exit and establishment survival in UK manufacturing,' *Journal of Industrial Economics*, **51**, 91–112.

Dosi, G. (1988), 'Sources, procedures, and microeconomic effects of innovation,' *Journal of Economic Literature*, **26**, 1120–71.

Dosi, G. (2007), 'Statistical regularities in the evolution of industries. A guide through some evidence and challenges for the theory,' in F. Malerba and S. Brusoni (eds), *Perspectives on Innovation*. Cambridge University Press: Cambridge, UK, pp. 153–186.

Dosi, G., A. Gambardella, M. Grazzi and L. Orsenigo (2008), 'Technological revolutions and the evolution of industrial structures: assessing the impact of new technologies upon the size and boundaries of firms,' *Capitalism and Society*, **3**.

Dosi, G. and M. Grazzi (2006), 'Technologies as problem-solving procedures and technologies as input–output relations: some perspectives on the theory of production,' *Industrial and Corporate Change*, **15**, 173–202.

Dosi, G., O. Marsili, L. Orsenigo and R. Salvatore (1995), 'Learning, market selection and evolution of industrial structures,' *Small Business Economics*, **7**, 411–436.

Dosi, G. and R. R. Nelson (2010), 'Technological change and industrial dynamics as evolutionary processes,' in B. H. Hall and N. Rosenberg (eds), *Handbook of the Economics of Innovation*, Vol. 1, North Holland/Elsevier: Amsterdam, pp. 51–128.

Ericson, R. and A. Pakes (1995), 'Markov-perfect industry dynamics: a framework for empirical work,' *Review of Economic Studies*, **62**, 53–82.

Foster, L., J. Haltiwanger and C. J. Krizan (2001), 'Aggregate productivity growth: lessons from microeconomic evidence,' *in New Developments in Productivity Analysis*. University of Chicago Press: Chicago, 303–372.

Foster, L., J. Haltiwanger and C. Syverson (2008), 'Reallocation, firm turnover, and efficiency: selection on productivity or profitability?' *American Economic Review*, **98**, 394–425.

Geroski, P., S. Machin and C. F. Walters (1997), 'Corporate growth and profitability,' *Journal of Industrial Economics*, **45**, 171–189.

Geroski, P. A. (1998), 'An applied econometrician's view of large company performance,' *Review of Industrial Organization*, **13**, 271–293.

Geroski, P. A. (2002), 'The growth of firms in theory and in practice,' in N. Foss and V. Mahnke (eds), *Competence, Governance, and Entrepreneurship - Advances in Economic Strategy Research*. Oxford University Press: Oxford and New York.

Griliches, Z. and H. Regev (1995), 'Firm productivity in israeli industry 1979–1988,' *Journal of Econometrics*, **65**, 175–203.

Hopenhayn, H. (1992), 'Entry, exit and firm dynamics in long run equilibrium,' *Econometrica*, **60**, 1127–1150.

Jovanovic, B. (1982), 'Selection and the evolution of industry,' *Econometrica*, **50**, 649–670.

Marsili, O. (2001), *The Anatomy and Evolution of Industries: Technological Change and Industrial Dynamics*. Edward Elgar Publishing: Cheltenham, Northampton, MA.

Melitz, M. J. (2003), 'The impact of trade on intra-industry reallocations and aggregate industry productivity,' *Econometrica*, **71**, 1695–1725.

Metcalfe, S. J. (1998), *Evolutionary Economics and Creative Destruction.* Routledge: London.

Nelson, R. R. (1981), 'Research on productivity growth and productivity differences: dead ends and new departures,' *Journal of Economic Literature*, **19**, 1029–1064.

Nelson, R. R. and S. G. Winter (1982), *An Evolutionary Theory of Economic Change.* The Belknap Press of Harvard University Press: Cambridge, MA.

OECD (2002), *Measuring the Information Economy.* OECD Publishing.

O'Mahony, M. and B. Van Ark (2003), 'EU productivity and competitiveness: An industry perspective,' Enterprise publications, European Commission.

Pavitt, K. (1984), 'Sectoral pattern of technical change: towards a taxonomy and a theory,' *Research Policy*, **13**, 343–373.

Silverberg, G., G. Dosi and L. Orsenigo (1988), 'Innovation, diversity and diffusion: a self-organisation model,' *Economic Journal*, **98**, 1032–1054.

Silverberg, G. and B. Verspagen (1994), 'Learning, innovation and economic growth: a long-run model of industrial dynamics,' *Industrial and Corporate Change*, **3**, 199–223.

Sutton, J. (1998), *Technology and Market Structure: Theory and Evidence.* MIT Press: Cambridge, MA.

Winter, S. G. (1984), 'Schumpeterian competition under alternative technological regimes,' *Journal of Economic Behavior and Organization*, **5**, 287–320.

Winter, S. G., Y. M. Kaniovski and G. Dosi (2000), 'Modeling industrial dynamics with innovative entrants,' *Structural Change and Economic Dynamics*, **11**, 255–293.

Winter, S. G., Y. M. Kaniovski and G. Dosi (2003), 'A baseline model of industry evolution,' *Journal of Evolutionary Economics*, **13**, 355–383.

Appendix A

A.1. Sectoral productivity decomposition

For completeness, we present here results of productivity decomposition analysis broken down by each industry, pooling over time. Table A1 reports figures obtained by weighting firm-level productivities with employment shares, while in Table A2 weights are measured as shares of sales.

Appendix B

B.1. Sectoral taxonomies

Table B1 shows how the sectors included by us in the analysis are classified according to the taxonomies presented in O'Mahony and Van Ark (2003). These taxonomies try to capture in different ways the technological characteristics of sectors, and can

Table A1 Decomposition of productivity growth by sector—within, between, and interaction effects, employment weights

		Italy			France		
NACE	Sector	With.(%)	Bet.(%)	Int.(%)	With.(%)	Bet.(%)	Int.(%)
151	Production, process, and preserv. of meat	87.57	2.48	9.95	–	–	–
155	Dairy products	91.74	−22.97	31.23	–	–	–
158	Prod. of other food (bread, sugar, etc.)	96.57	80.63	−77.21	–	–	–
159	Beverages (alcoholic and not)	107.07	−14.39	7.32	–	–	–
171	Preparation and spinning of textiles	104.27	−5.86	1.59	111.16	−7.33	−3.83
172	Textiles weaving	89.82	24.01	−13.82	−52.41	3.92	148.49
175	Carpets, rugs, and other textiles	94.09	14.34	−8.43	150.35	−76.53	26.18
177	Knitted and crocheted articles	93.73	35.11	−28.85	–	–	–
182	Wearing apparel	88.81	−99.84	111.03	−234.83	672.76	−337.93
193	Footwear	180.25	−131.65	51.40	103.23	−5.14	1.91
203	Wood products for construction	75.23	43.00	−18.24	–	–	–
204	Wooden containers	–	–	–	113.98	−12.12	−1.86
211	Pulp, paper, and paperboard	–	–	–	99.33	25.75	−25.08
212	Articles of paper and paperboard	95.42	−13.17	17.75	99.76	1.65	−1.41
221	Publishing	100.59	−148.28	147.69	−85.73	−135.56	321.30
222	Printing	124.87	−7.86	−17.00	94.11	7.68	−1.79
241	Production of basic chemicals	88.86	45.73	−34.59	109.32	7.42	−16.74
243	Paints, varnishes, inks, and mastics	59.41	38.76	1.83	–	–	–
244	Pharma., med. chemicals, botanical prod	116.58	21.61	−38.19	45.18	9.42	45.40
245	Soap and deterg and perfumes and toilet prep	–	–	–	−604.58	−273.29	977.87
246	Other chemical products	113.73	−6.90	−6.84	90.23	25.11	−15.35
251	Rubber products	84.22	−7.92	23.69	–	–	–
252	Plastic products	88.79	−11.97	23.18	92.56	16.97	−9.53
263	Ceramic goods for construction	107.07	−37.45	30.38	–	–	–
266	Concrete, plaster, and cement	311.65	744.86	−956.51	154.61	38.22	−92.82
267	Cutting, shaping, and finishing of stone	−240.02	918.20	−578.19	–	–	–
275	Casting of metals	54.99	43.91	1.09	–	–	–
281	Structural metal products	103.18	−40.94	37.76	107.87	21.93	−29.80

(continued)

Table A1 Continued

NACE Sector	Italy			France		
	With.(%)	Bet.(%)	Int.(%)	With.(%)	Bet.(%)	Int.(%)
284 Forging, pressing, stamping, of metal	102.76	−14.52	11.76	117.42	−41.74	24.31
285 Treatment and coating of metals	33.38	20.57	46.05	–	–	–
286 Cutlery, tools and general hardware	69.73	153.00	−122.73	73.75	−24.33	50.57
287 Other fabricated metal products	91.26	−16.33	25.07	–	–	–
291 Machinery for prod. and use of mech. power	95.66	−34.30	38.64	100.35	11.79	−12.14
292 Other general purpose machinery	272.01	−725.11	553.10	89.83	23.51	−13.34
293 Agricultural and forestry machinery	–	–	–	109.11	8.09	−17.20
294 Machine tools	130.91	204.43	−235.34	110.11	−15.12	5.01
295 Other special purpose machinery	102.93	−20.86	17.92	94.86	2.60	2.54
297 Domestic appliances not e/where class	24.86	24.33	50.81	–	–	–
311 Electric motors, generators and transform	35.86	29.65	34.49	94.50	22.32	−16.82
312 Manuf. of electricity distrib, control equip	248.46	−18.08	−130.38	103.90	−5.85	1.96
316 Electrical equipment not e/where class	57.92	7.51	34.57	–	–	–
331 Medical and surgical equip, orthopedic appl	–	–	–	100.64	14.57	−15.21
332 Measuring, checking, testing, and navigat app.	–	–	–	111.59	−10.25	−1.35
333 Industrial process control equipment	–	–	–	−10.97	−127.31	238.28
343 Production of spare parts for cars	108.38	44.06	−52.45	–	–	–
361 Furniture	95.86	10.13	−5.99	93.01	35.11	−28.12
362 Jewelry and related articles	570.46	93.61	−564.06	–	–	–
366 Miscellaneous manufact. not elsewhere class	135.30	−0.16	−35.14	295.42	−352.35	156.92
34 Motor vehicles, trailers, and semi-trailers	120.13	6.20	−26.34	61.19	84.83	−46.02

Table A2 Decomposition of productivity growth by sector—within, between and interaction effects, sales weights

		Italy			France		
NACE	Sector	With.(%)	Bet.(%)	Int.(%)	With.(%)	Bet.(%)	Int.(%)
151	Production, process, and preserv. of meat	77.43	15.94	6.63	–	–	–
155	Dairy products	36.44	9.85	53.71	–	–	–
158	Prod. of other food (bread, sugar, etc.)	1060.56	−991.83	31.28	–	–	–
159	Beverages (alcoholic and not)	−162.35	585.59	−323.24	–	–	–
171	Preparation and spinning of textiles	−25.06	−23.14	148.19	85.28	−17.99	32.71
172	Textiles weaving	94.82	5.10	0.08	−113.76	−167.61	381.37
175	Carpets, rugs, and other textiles	112.83	−9.64	−3.19	47.33	−4.27	56.94
177	Knitted and crocheted articles	105.90	13.40	−19.30	–	–	–
182	Wearing apparel	158.47	−49.50	−8.97	116.14	−8.89	−7.25
193	Footwear	66.06	3.40	30.54	59.38	−15.68	56.30
203	Wood products for construction	145.71	−87.60	41.89	–	–	–
204	Wooden containers	–	–	–	114.88	−35.30	20.41
211	Pulp, paper and paperboard	–	–	–	97.13	1.47	1.40
212	Articles of paper, and paperboard	125.93	0.07	−26.00	94.66	−2.13	7.47
221	Publishing	126.72	−10.29	−16.43	15.16	−52.92	137.76
222	Printing	92.07	63.58	−55.65	66.72	−46.79	80.08
241	Production of basic chemicals	82.38	5.73	11.89	165.71	−37.20	−28.52
243	Paints, varnishes, inks, and mastics	93.30	−7.10	13.81	–	–	–
244	Pharma., med. chemicals, botanical prod	57.07	−8.34	51.26	57.11	50.00	−7.11
245	Soap and deterg and perfumes and toilet prep	–	–	–	55.71	15.44	28.84
246	Other chemical products	237.26	−105.70	−31.56	72.73	6.62	20.64
251	Rubber products	109.82	−10.41	0.59	–	–	–
252	Plastic products	89.78	1.28	8.95	97.31	−28.00	30.70
263	Ceramic goods for construction	37.27	−35.12	97.85	–	–	–
266	Concrete, plaster, and cement	97.12	4.76	−1.88	376.93	27.22	−304.15
267	Cutting, shaping, and finishing of stone	949.55	−366.76	−482.79	–	–	–
275	Casting of metals	69.83	−28.36	58.53	–	–	–
281	Structural metal products	708.61	378.03	−986.64	121.83	88.92	−110.75

(continued)

Table A2 Continued

NACE	Sector	Italy			France		
		With.(%)	Bet.(%)	Int.(%)	With.(%)	Bet.(%)	Int.(%)
284	Forging, pressing, stamping of metal	152.29	−44.37	−7.92	−42.07	−37.59	179.66
285	Treatment and coating of metals	18.00	−117.06	199.07	−	−	−
286	Cutlery, tools and general hardware	82.04	−24.99	42.95	126.22	1.16	−27.38
287	Other fabricated metal products	−107.86	−23.90	231.76	−	−	−
291	Machinery for prod. and use of mech. power	830.16	−761.11	30.95	41.10	21.70	37.20
292	Other general purpose machinery	−75.65	−129.13	304.79	163.26	60.25	−123.52
293	Agricultural and forestry machinery	−	−	−	65.27	5.25	29.48
294	Machine tools	125.43	3.62	−29.05	100.96	−6.21	5.25
295	Other special purpose machinery	88.12	25.64	−13.77	115.91	77.28	−93.18
297	Domestic appliances not e/where class	294.49	−96.13	−98.36	−	−	−
311	Electric motors, generators and transform	74.69	−4.12	29.42	−284.35	187.72	196.63
312	Manuf. of electricity distrib. control equip	23.92	129.93	−53.85	60.99	2.06	36.95
316	Electrical equipment not e/where class	111.00	13.33	−24.33	−	−	−
331	Medical and surgical equip, orthopedic appl	−	−	−	96.62	38.18	−34.80
332	Measuring, checking, testing, and navigat app.	−	−	−	66.97	8.96	24.07
333	Industrial process control equipment	−	−	−	38.26	−110.57	172.31
343	Production of spare parts for cars	175.34	−13.83	−61.51	−	−	−
361	Furniture	72.86	−18.22	45.36	−86.62	−62.80	249.42
362	Jewelry and related articles	37.64	33.99	28.37	−	−	−
366	Miscellaneous manufact. not elsewhere class	111.22	−22.89	11.67	79.35	20.55	0.10
34	Motor vehicles, trailers, and semi-trailers	249.57	−12.70	−136.87	−244.88	330.90	13.97

Table B1 Sectoral taxonomies for selected 3-Digit industries

		Taxonomy classes		
NACE	SECTOR	I-ICT classes	II-Skill classes	III-Pavitt classes
151	Production, process, and preserv. of meat	N-ICT	LS	SI
155	Dairy products	N-ICT	LS	SI
158	Prod. of other food (bread, sugar, etc.)	N-ICT	LS	SI
159	Beverages (alcoholic and not)	N-ICT	LS	SI
171	Preparation and spinning of textiles	N-ICT	LS	SD
172	Textiles weaving	N-ICT	LS	SD
175	Carpets, rugs, and other textiles	N-ICT	LS	SD
177	Knitted and crocheted articles	N-ICT	LS	SD
182	Wearing apparel	ICT-U	LS	SD
193	Footwear	N-ICT	LS	SD
203	Wood products for construction	N-ICT	LIS	SD
204	Wooden containers	N-ICT	LIS	SD
211	Pulp, paper, and paperboard	N-ICT	LIS	SI
212	Articles of paper and paperboard	N-ICT	LIS	SD
221	Publishing	ICT-U	LIS	SD
222	Printing	ICT-U	LIS	SD
241	Production of basic chemicals	N-ICT	HS	SI
243	Paints, varnishes, inks, and mastics	N-ICT	HS	SI
244	Pharma., med. chemicals, botanical prod	N-ICT	HS	SB
245	Soap and deterg and perfumes and toilet prep	N-ICT	HS	SI
246	Other chemical products	N-ICT	HS	SI
251	Rubber products	N-ICT	LS	SD
252	Plastic products	N-ICT	LS	SD
263	Ceramic goods for construction	N-ICT	LS	SI
266	Concrete, plaster, and cement	N-ICT	LS	SD
267	Cutting, shaping, and finishing of stone	N-ICT	LS	SD
275	Casting of metals	N-ICT	LS	SI
281	Structural metal products	N-ICT	LIS	SD
284	Forging, pressing, stamping of metal	N-ICT	LIS	SI
285	Treatment and coating of metals	N-ICT	LIS	SD
286	Cutlery, tools and general hardware	N-ICT	LIS	SD
287	Other fabricated metal products	N-ICT	LIS	SD
291	Machinery for prod. and use of mech. power	ICT-U	LIS	SS
292	Other general purpose machinery	ICT-U	LIS	SS
293	Agricultural and forestry machinery	ICT-U	LIS	SI
294	Machine tools	ICT-U	LIS	SS

(continued)

Table B1 Continued

| NACE | SECTOR | Taxonomy classes | | |
		I-ICT classes	II-Skill classes	III-Pavitt classes
295	Other special purpose machinery	ICT-U	LIS	SS
297	Domestic appliances not e/where class	ICT-U	LIS	SI
311	Electric motors, generators and transform	ICT-U	LIS	SS
312	Manuf. of electricity distrib. control equip	ICT-U	LIS	SS
316	Electrical equipment not e/where class	ICT-U	LIS	SS
331	Medical and surgical equip. orthopedic appl	ICT-P	HIS	SB
332	Measuring, checking, testing, and navigat app.	ICT-P	HIS	SB
333	Industrial process control equipment	ICT-P	HIS	SB
343	Production of spare parts for cars	N-ICT	LS	SI
361	Furniture	ICT-U	LS	SD
362	Jewelry and related articles	ICT-U	LS	SD
366	Miscellaneous manufact. not elsewhere class	ICT-U	LS	SI
34	Motor vehicles, trailers, and semi-trailers	N-ICT	LS	SI

be usefully taken as a meaningful guidance to compare estimates across sectors sharing similar characteristics. Taxonomy-I looks at the role of Information and Communication Technologies (ICT). Following OECD (2002), three types of industries are identified, based on sectoral ICT intensities in the United States (with ICT intensity defined as the share of ICT capital on total capital stock of a sector): ICT producing (ICT-P), ICT using (ICT-U), and non-ICT (N-ICT) sectors. Taxonomy-II distinguishes sectors according to the relative intensity of skilled and unskilled labor force, based on an integration of United States, UK, and Eurostat skills classifications. Four classes are defined: Low Skilled (LS), Low-Intermediate Skilled (LIS), High-Intermediate Skilled (HIS), and High Skilled (HS). Finally, Taxonomy-III considers sectoral patterns of innovation. Based on the early work of Pavitt (1984), one identifies four groups: Science Based (SB), Specialized Supplier (SS), Scale Intensive (SI), and Supplier Dominated (SD) industries. Original Pavitt's classification employed in O'Mahony and Van Ark (2003) straightforwardly applies to 2-Digit industries. Here, we extend to 3-Digit sectors drawing from Marsili (2001) and Dosi *et al.* (2008).

[13]

Modes of Knowledge Accumulation, Entry Regimes and Patterns of Industrial Evolution

Giulio Bottazzi[a], Giovanni Dosi[a] and Gaia Rocchetti[b]

([a]S. Anna School of Advanced Studies, Pisa and [b]University of Rome 'La Sapienza', Rome, Italy)

This paper explores the interplay between entry, selection and innovative learning as determinants of industrial evolution. It proposes a model aimed at capturing some essential features of learning and competition as drivers of the dynamics. Using both analytical and numerical techniques, the paper disentangles possible generic properties which robustly hold for a wide range of parameterizations. In particular, the paper identifies different generic 'evolutionary archetypes', defined by characteristic inter-actions between entry/exit regimes, learning and industrial structures.

1. Introduction

This work builds on the general conjecture, in tune with evolutionary analyses of economic change, that the primary determinants of industrial dynamics ought to be found in the underlying process of knowledge accumulation, on the one hand, and market competition among heterogenous firms, on the other.

We shall develop a model that formalizes some basic features of technological learning and competitive selection, in order to explore, first, the possible existence of evolutionary invariances, i.e. of generic properties of the process of industrial evolution that hold robustly across different learning modes and for wide range of parameters. Conversely, second, we address the properties of industrial structures and change which happen to depend on specific modes of innovative exploration, entry and market selection—i.e. on what elsewhere have been empirically identified and formalized as different *technological* and *market regimes* (cf. Winter, 1984; Dosi *et al.*, 1995; Malerba and Orsenigo, 1995; Winter *et al.*, 2000).

Industrial and Corporate Change Volume 10 Number 3 2001

——— *Knowledge Accumulation, Entry Regimes and Industrial Evolution* ———

In particular, in the following we shall compare the emergent properties of regimes characterized by: (i) different innovative opportunities, (ii) different degrees of cumulativeness in the probability of innovative success by incumbents; (ii) dynamic entry barriers, or conversely, learning advantage of potential entrants, and, finally, (iv) different rates of entry.

The following model is derived from one of those presented in Winter *et al.* (2000), but, together with other changes, it is extended to cover wider variations in learning and entry patterns. Moreover, here we shall undertake extended Monte Carlo simulations to explore the impact of different learning regimes and of within-regime parameterizations upon a few properties of industrial structure and dynamics. Proxies of the latter include productivity and output growth, cross-sectional asymmetries in productivity across firms, patterns of (net) entry and exit, and size distributions, all of which we study conditional upon diverse regimes.

In Section 2 we briefly map the background of this work with respect to both theory and available evidence. The model is presented in Section 3. Section 4 studies some analytical properties, while in Section 5 we report on a wide numerical study of the model using Monte Carlo techniques.

2. *Industrial Structures and Dynamics: Some Background on Evidence and Theories*

The empirical counterpart of this work regards the observed properties of industries persistently characterized by (i) technological learning by incumbents or entrants or both, (ii) entry of new firms, and (iii) some competitive process weeding out, at least partly, the heterogeneity in the populations of firms. Needless to say, these conditions do indeed apply to the overwhelming majority of contemporary industries.

This subject has been reviewed in greater detail elsewhere (Dosi *et al.*, 1995), together with the related 'stylized facts' (see also the Special Issues of the *International Journal of Industrial Organization*, 1995 and 2001, and of *Industrial and Corporate Change*, 1997). Here, let us just highlight a few major empirical regularities central to the analysis that follows.

First, industries typically display a skewed size distribution which turns out to be relatively stable over time, notwithstanding systematic underlying dynamics in market shares, births and deaths. *Second*, one tends to find—both cross-sectionally and longitudinally—rather robust correlations between (gross) entry and exit rates, even after controlling for industry-specific characteristics, such as scale-related entry barriers, etc. *Third*, there is no apparent impact of profitability conditions upon entry rates. [More on this highly controversial issue can be found in Geroski (1994, 1995) and Dosi and Lovallo (1997)]. *Fourth*, the modal fate of entrants is grim (Geroski, 1995) but, possibly, a few outliers turn out to be major drivers of long-term growth of productivity and output (one of the most favorable discussions of the evidence on the point is in Baldwin, 1995). *Fifth*, jointly with the foregoing cross-industry 'stylized facts', one observes equally robust interindustry differences in the values of statistics such as concentration, the age distribution of firms, and, together, in the characteristics and distributions of innovators.

How does one account for all that? Let us recall the major interpretations that address at least a subset of the foregoing empirical patterns.

Due to limitations of space, one cannot engage here in any in-depth controversy with the enormous IO literature that attempts to rationalize whatever observation by building *ex-post* corresponding Nash equilibria, often through some quite imaginative reconstructions of history, under the sole constraint of preserving the notions of forward-looking micro-rationality and collective, intertemporally consistent, equilibria. In this respect we generally agree with Sutton's point that 'explaining everything *ex-post*' largely stands for 'explaining nothing' (Sutton, 1998).

However, one cannot avoid placing our contribution *vis-à-vis* the germane literature which one could call on 'rational evolution'. Paradigmatic examples of the genre include Jovanovic (1982) and Ericson and Pakes (1995). The empirical regularities that this perspective addresses—at least qualitatively—primarily regard asymmetric size distributions and different growth/death rates as conditional on age (Jovanovic, 1982) and collective invariances in industrial structures, notwithstanding persistent dynamics on relative, micro, competitive positions (cf. Ericson and Pakes, 1995, and related works). In a nutshell, both streams of analysis of 'rational evolution' share some acknowledgment of micro-diversity and also of the paramount role of market interactions in shaping the destiny of individual firms. However, they both confine the interpretation of the evidence simply to modeling exercises that depend on the consistency between micro-rationality and collective outcomes. Indeed, they do that, in our view, at the price of violating a few 'stylized facts', such as those regarding inertial asymmetries in performances [this is especially a problem for Ericson and Pakes (1995)], 'irrational' entry process and market interactions selecting over seemingly disequilibrium micro-features. Together, as Kaniovski (2001) argues, the consistency between micro-behaviors and collective outcomes is obtained at the price of some corner-cutting mathematical assumptions that basically rule out most aggregation and strategic interdependence issues.

We must admit that it is hard for us to subscribe to such interpretations

———— *Knowledge Accumulation, Entry Regimes and Industrial Evolution* ————

of industrial dynamics as fundamentally driven by 'rational' explorations and equilibrium market tests: for example, we find it hard to swallow idiosyncratic competencies of individual firms (a very robust hypothesis, indeed) coupled with unbiased, collectively shared, expectations on their very means and variances (on the contrary a rather bizarre idea); or microtechniques entailing an infinite number of infinitesimally small firms whose aggregation nonetheless yields finite (and common-knowledge) output quantities; or commonly shared 'technological expectations' linking search efforts and outcomes.[1]

The *bounds* approach, pioneered by Sutton (1991, 1998), is much nearer and, indeed, overlaps significantly with the perspective wherein the model below finds its roots.

In an extreme synthesis, both share the epistemological commitment to relatively robust, empirically falsifiable, predictions on the characteristics of industrial structures—orthogonal to the nuances of fine tunings of individual corporate behaviors, but powerfully influenced by relatively inertial properties of industry-specific technologies and demand patterns. Moreover, both Sutton's and 'evolutionaxy' views on industrial structures and dynamics are meant to yield cross-sectional predictions as well—addressing questions such as 'Why is sector A more concentrated than sector B?' and so on—in addition to cross-industrial invariances—such as the above-mentioned generic occurrence of skewed size distributions, etc.[2]

The 'bound approach' and the 'evolutionary approach' (in the interpretation explored here), however, depart on some underlying conjectures regarding the determinants of both 'bounds' and adjustment processes.

Sutton's perspectives suggests that technological and demand-related factors make bounds on industrial structures effective via some no-arbitrage conditions—entailing corresponding Nash equilibria on industry-specific entry processes. Moreover, so far, the 'bounds approach' has almost entirely neglected learning dynamics. (But, we conjecture, developments in this direction might also uncover further areas of overlap with evolutionary interpretations.)

Conversely, the evolutionary perspective theoretically gambles on further departures from either 'rational' micro-foundations or collective equilibrium

---

[1] Of course, no theory should be asked to renounce courageous abstractions and simplifications: it is the very essence of theorizing itself. Our point is, however, that this style of interpretation displays—paraphrasing from another context Colin Camerer—a dramatically low ratio of evidence to theory (Camerer, 1995). Moreover it does not appear to display much robustness to the relaxation of the most far-fetched hypotheses (e.g. what happens if one allows out-of-equilibrium adjustments?).

[2] Different 'rational evolution' models are, of course, likely to yield different predictions on microdynamics, as Pakes and Ericson (1998) show. However, the models of this family have not, so far, shown much interest, with the exception of the latter, in exercises of *ex-ante* mapping between 'types' of industries and 'types' of industrial dynamics.

——— *Knowledge Accumulation, Entry Regimes and Industrial Evolution* ———

outcomes. Rather, it grounds its empirical predictions concerning industrial structures and dynamics upon the identification of underlying regularities, first, in *microeconomic learning processes*—of different kinds, concerning in principle technologies, organizational forms, behavioral patterns—and second, in *interaction mechanisms*—entailing also specific selection processes with heterogeneous populations of firms.

Incidentally, note that this latter perspective involves a rather radical subversion of the strategy-centered perspective of most current IO in that it identifies crucial explanatory factors of industrial organizations in the features of learning processes which are, to some extent, specific to particular bodies of knowledge and which shape the modes and rates at which individual firms, in each production activity, access notional opportunities of innovation and imitation. Indeed, it is a theme of enquiry that Dick Nelson has pioneered [among many works, see Nelson (1982), for an insightful assessment of the evidence available twenty years ago that is just now being appreciated by the economic community].

There are at least two fundamental theoretical issues here related to the foregoing *destrategizing* conjecture. In its weak form, the conjecture suggests that some basic properties of industrial structures and industrial change may be easily understood as quite generic consequences of many processes of experimentation and imperfect trial-and-error learning—without invoking any more sophisticated form of 'strategic rationality' on the part of individual agents. The strong form of the same proposition suggests that also intersectoral differences in structures and dynamics might be understood, as a first approximation, independently from detailed micro-strategies, but just with reference to intersectoral differences in the process of technological accumulation.[3]

Evolutionary theories of industrial change have indeed made significant progress in the understanding of why industrial structures are what they are and, also, the reasons for the taxonomic differences between them. Here, let us just provide an extremely concise map, confined to modeling exercises, whose major roots rest in Winter (1971) and Nelson and Winter (1982) and sub- sequent developments include Iwai (1984a,b), Winter (1984), Metcalfe (1992), Kwasnicki (1996), Silverberg and Verspagen (1994), Mazzucato (2000), Dosi *et al.* (1995), Winter *et al.* (1997, 2000), Malerba *et al.* (1999) and Marsili (2001). Within such expanding literature, however, one might

---

[3] So, as an extreme illustration, consider, say IBM, which became for a long period the dominant player in the international computer industry, due also to its systematically successful strategies. However, the foregoing conjecture suggests that, even without IBM as such, the computer industry would have followed rather similar dynamics, fundamentally shaped by the nature of collectively shared learning processes. Indeed, the results from 'history-friendly models' put forward in Malerba *et al.* (1999) corroborate the hypothesis.

possibly distinguish some sort of 'first generation' whereby the primary task was to show the consistency of the exercise and the empirical plausibility of the results—a fundamental initial task indeed.[4] A more recent 'second generation', however, attempts to derive also finer empirical predictions and it does so within two diverse but quite complementary styles of analysis.

First, 'history-friendly models' add richer, history-based, phenomenological details to the formal representation of specific industries (Malerba *et al.*, 1999). Together, one must of course demand an account for a much wider set of empirical phenomena. At the other, complementary, extreme, one begins to explore rather parsimonious 'reduced form' models, which ought, however, to be able to generate a few generic collective statistics on industry structures and dynamics, even when on purpose neglecting most historical, industry-specific, characteristics. This is what one has begun to do, together with other scholars from different quarters in Winter *et al.* (1997, 2000), and this is also the spirit of the model below. Hence, in the following, we neglect on purpose history-specific features of technological learning and market competition but try to identify, first, possible invariances in the revealed outcomes, and, together, second, possible transitions across 'evolutionary archetypes', dependent on some critical threshold values in the rates of microeconomic learning, rates of entry of new firms, entrants' size and death rules.

3. The Model

The model studied here is a close descendent of Winter *et al.* (1997, 2000), which in turn has close ancestors in Nelson and Winter (1982) and Winter (1984). Let us first provide a qualitative overview.

In the 'benchmark case' below we model an industry with a number of firms that varies throughout its history—that number being determined by stochastic entry at each 'period' and competition-driven market selection. Competition, in agreement with Nelson and Winter (1982), affects differential growth rates via investment opportunities, stemming in turn from different current gross profits. Firms that shrink below a certain minimal size 'die'. Entry rates, in probability, depend on the number of incumbents. Learning, like one of the models studied in Winter *et al.* (2000), concerns only the productivity of physical capital (and, as labor inputs are assumed to be constant, we set them to zero, without loss of generality). In terms of empirical plausibility, the assumption of solely capital-related learning is indeed a rather awkward one. However, in order to construct some relatively

---

[4] A good deal of the formal explorations in Nelson and Winter (1982) clearly focus on this target and implicitly, and so do a lot of subsequent works in the formal evolutionary tradition.

———— *Knowledge Accumulation, Entry Regimes and Industrial Evolution* ————

simple 'thought experiments' on learning, selection and growth, this is the most congenial candidate. As one finds in Winter *et al.* (2000), learning on the labor productivity dimension—which is, indeed, a more realistic assumption—generally implies that the long-term dynamics depend also on the shape of the demand function. But this introduces a further interaction term into our study: here we rather choose to focus, as a first approximation, on the supply side within a sort of 'partial disequilibrium analysis'.[5]

Moreover, in our benchmark case, both incumbents and entrants are able to stochastically learn. [In this respect, the benchmark resembles what many of us have come to call conventionally a 'Schumpeter II' industrial regime: cf. Malerba and Orsenigo (1995) and Dosi *et al.* (1995), among others.]

The model considers an industry I whose firms i are characterized at each time by a productivity $\pi_i(t)$ and a capital $k_i(t)$ evolving respectively under learning dynamics and competitive pressures. The initial conditions of the industry are given by $N(0)$ firms whose initial capital $k_i(0)$ is randomly drawn from a uniform distribution with support $(\varepsilon, \varepsilon + M_k)$. The initial (log) productivity $\log[\pi_i(0)]$ is randomly drawn from a Gaussian distribution of mean 0 and variance 1. At each time step t the following actions are performed:

1. **Exit.** The firms whose capital $k_i(t)$ is smaller that a given fraction ε of the whole industry capital leave the industry.
2. **Production** and **price determination.** Each firm assigns its total physical capital to production contributing to the total supply with $q_i(t) = \pi_i(t)k_i(t)$.

   We assume that the output price is related via a given demand function to the aggregate supply. Specifically, if $Q(t) = \Sigma_i\, q_i(t)$ we set:

$$p(t) = H(Q(t)) \tag{1}$$

   where H is in general a non-increasing function of its arguments. In order to not introduce any further assumption on the nature of the produced good and its demand characteristics, we suppose a homogeneous commodity with a demand function of the form $H(Q) = 1/Q$. In so doing we keep the total industry revenue (and gross profits) invariant, irrespective of actual output.
3. **Capital update.** If $p(t)$ is the price of output, the (gross) profit of firm i reads:

[5] A significant step forward, which we are beginning to explore, involves indeed learning on both labor and 'machine' efficiencies.

—————— *Knowledge Accumulation, Entry Regimes and Industrial Evolution* ——————

$$p(t)\ \pi_i(t)\ k_i(t) \qquad\qquad (2)$$

Assuming that the fraction of profit reinvested in production, λ, is constant over the industry, the capital of firm i is updated according to

$$k_i(t + 1) = k_i(t)(i - d) + \lambda k_i(t)\ p(t)\ \pi_i(t) \qquad\qquad (3)$$

where d is the capital depreciation rate (assumed constant) and where the expression of output in terms of capital has been substituted.

4. **Entry.** The number of entrants $n_{in}(t)$ is obtained from a Poisson distribution with mean proportional to the number of incumbent firms present in the industry, $<n_{new}> = rN(t)$. Their capital is randomly drawn from a uniform distribution ranging from $\varepsilon K(t)$ to $(\varepsilon + M_k)K(t)$, and their productivity is drawn from a lognormal distribution whose mean and variance are the actual weighted mean and variance of the logarithms of the incumbents' productivities.[6]

5. **Learning.** Each firm present in the industry (including the just entered ones) has a probability $1/2$ of facing a productivity increase

$$\log[\pi_i(t + 1)] = \log[\pi_i(t)] + \varepsilon_i$$

The extent of the increase ε_i is randomly generated from an exponential distribution with mean α (and hence variance $\alpha^2/2$).

In particular, below we shall study the effects on industry structure and dynamics of the following parameters:

- ε, the minimal allowed capital share, corresponding to the death threshold;
- M_k, the maximal initial capital share of entrants;
- α, the mean of the exponential distribution from which productivity increments are drawn;
- r, the ratio of the average number of the entrants cohort to the industry population.

These parameters, together with the parameters d and λ defined in (3) and kept constant, completely specify the model.

[6] This entry rule is meant to simulate a 'smooth' insertion of new firms in the productivity distribution of the incumbents.

———— *Knowledge Accumulation, Entry Regimes and Industrial Evolution* ————

4. *Some Analytical Properties of the Model*

In order to better understand some basic properties of the model, before tackling its full-fledged version, let us begin by studying some analytical properties of two special cases.

The closed industry without learning Consider a 'closed' industry where each firm is endowed from the beginning with a given capital productivity π_i and where no exit and entry of firms takes place. Let us analyze the long-term fate of the industry, in terms of asymptotic values of aggregate quantities, together with the role played by the aggregate demand function H.

Consider (3) and sum over the firms to obtain the evolution of the total capital

$$K(t) = \sum_{i \in I} k_i(t)$$

which reads:

$$K(t + 1) = (1 - d)K(t) + \lambda \tag{4}$$

Then, as $t \to \infty$, the capital converges exponentially toward the 'asymptotic' value $\overline{K} = \lambda/d$.

In order to simplify the recursive relations driving the industry dynamics, let us rescale individual firms' capitals by introducing the variable $x_i(t) = d/\lambda k_i(t)$, so that (3) becomes

$$x_i(t+1) = (1-d)x_i(t) + d \frac{x_i(t)\pi_i(t)}{\sum_j x_j(t)\pi_j(t)} \tag{5}$$

and the evolution of the 'rescaled' aggregate capital[7] $X(t) = \sum_i x_i(t)$ is given by

$$X(t+1) = (1-d)X(t) + d \tag{6}$$

The variables x_i remain positive and the stationary points $\overline{x}^* = (x_1^*, \ldots, x_N^*)$ of (3) satisfy the relation

$$\sum_i \pi_j x_j^* = \pi_i \quad \forall i \in N \tag{7}$$

---

[7] Notice that the rescaling of capital makes the parameter λ disappear. This parameter, when identical across firms, has indeed the sole purpose of setting the scale of the aggregate capital and can be conveniently eliminated.

——— *Knowledge Accumulation, Entry Regimes and Industrial Evolution* ———

i.e. they are the vertices of the N-dimensional simplex.[8]

In order to identify the asymptotic state of the industry, it is necessary to identify 'stable' equilibria among those defined by (7). For this purpose, let us consider the industry aggregate productivity defined as the average firm's productivity weighted with their capital shares:

$$\Pi(t) = \sum_i \pi_i(t) \frac{x_i(t)}{X(t)} \tag{8}$$

Using (5) and (6), it is straightforward to write the evolution equation for Π, which reads

$$\Delta\Pi(t) \quad = \quad \Pi(t+1) - \Pi(t)$$

$$= \quad \frac{d}{\Pi(t)\big[(1-d)X(t)+d\big]} \left(\sum_i \pi_i^2(t) \frac{x_i(t)}{X(t)} - \Pi(t)^2 \right) \tag{9}$$

The right-hand side of (5) is positive for any t and the aggregate productivity Π is a Lyapunov function for the dynamic defined by (5). We may thus conclude that for any initial condition[9] $[k_i(0), \ldots, k_N(0)]$, *the closed industry evolves towards a finite asymptotic aggregate capital and the share of this capital possessed by the most productive firm is asymptotically 1.*

Moreover, the last factor on the right-hand side of (5) is the variance of the productivity over the industry so that the rate of growth of average productivity is proportional to the 'heterogeneity' of the productivity distribution over the firms. Due to the strong similarity of (5) with a replicator dynamics, it is not surprising to see the Fisher Law (Metcalfe, 1998) at work here.

Finally, it is easy to show that with a demand function of the form $H(Q) = 1/Q^{\alpha_p}$, the previous statement is true irrespectively of the value of α_p. This means that for what concerns the qualitative behavior of the industry, the exact specification of the demand function is irrelevant. (When $\alpha_p \neq 1$, however, the limit value of the aggregate capital is a function of the best productivity in the industry.)

The closed industry with learning Next, let us show that the introduction of some generic random growth dynamics for firm productivities, i.e.

---

[8] Equation (3) is basically identical to a discrete time replicator dynamics. In the canonical definition of the latter (Weibull, 1998) the payoff of each 'type' does depend only on the shares of each 'type', while in (3) it depends also on the total population $X(t)$. This difference, however, turns out to have a negligible effect for the present analysis.

[9] Exluding, of course, the zero-measure set formed by the non-dominant simplex vertices.

——————— *Knowledge Accumulation, Entry Regimes and Industrial Evolution* ———————

'learning', in the previous closed industry model does not substantially change the final outcome for the industry itself.

Suppose that the productivity of each firm increases over time according to a stochastic growth dynamic of the form $\ln[\pi_i(t + 1)] = \ln[\pi_i(t)] + \varepsilon_i(t)$, where $\varepsilon_i(t)$ is a random variable with density function $q(\varepsilon)$ and support in $[0, +\infty)$, equal for each firm.

Let $p_t(k,\pi)$ be the probability density of finding at time t a firm with capital k and productivity π. Such a process on productivity growth together with (3) are enough to define an evolution equation for this density

$$p_{t+1}(k,\pi) = \int_0^{+\infty} dk' \int_0^{+\infty} d\pi' p_t(k',\pi') q(\pi - \pi') \delta\left[k - k'\left(1 - d + \lambda \frac{\pi'}{Q(t)} \right) \right] \quad (10)$$

where $\delta(x)$ is the Dirac delta function.

From this expression it is possible to derive the asymptotic behavior of the industry total output

$$\overline{Q}(t) \sim \sqrt{\lambda \overline{K}} e^{\sigma_\varepsilon t} \quad (11)$$

where σ_ε is the variance of the productivity growth[10] (for the detailed derivation, see Appendix).

Moreover, one can also extract the leading term (in the asymptotic expansion for high t) of the share distribution. At time t it reads

$$p_t(k) = \frac{1}{(1-d)^t} p_0 \frac{k}{(1-d)^t} \quad (12)$$

where $p_0(t)$ is the initial share distribution.

A notable property of (12) is that it shows how the competitive dynamics defined in (4) progressively 'shrink' the distribution of capital shares, scaling down all its moments. Notice also that the density function in (12) does not conserve the total capital. This is perfectly consistent with our previous finding: when $t \to +\infty$ the amount of capital possessed by any finite measure set (i.e. by a given fraction of firm population) goes to 0, while the total

---

[10] The exponential growth of $Q(t)$ is the effect of a multiplicative process on the firm's learning. If one modeled the productivity growth as an additive process, the ensuing growth in total production would be linear.

capital concentrates in the hands of a single firm (which constitute a zero measure set in the continuous description used here).

This 'closed economy with learning' basically boils down to the same asymptotic properties, in terms of industry structure, as the non-learning case. The progressive 'shrinking' of the size distribution implies that any 'exit' condition imposed on the industry in terms of an exit threshold on a firm's capital, leads, irrespectively of its value, to the formation of a monopoly.[11]

4.1 Asymptotic Values for Some Aggregate Quantities

Next, let us analyze our complete benchmark model where, together with competitive and learning dynamics, we insert an entry and exit condition for all firms, 'opening' the industry to an external flux of capital.

We start by studying the number of firms present in the industry. Due to the stochastic nature of the model, we are interested in a mean value:

$$N^* = \lim_{T \to \infty} \sum_{\tau=0}^{T} N(\tau) \tag{13}$$

First of all let us note that this value cannot diverge. This comes from the very nature of the entry and exit rules defined above: when new firms enter the industry, they do not only increase the number of previously present firms, but also contribute a positive increment to the aggregate capital. This implies that the number of firms that are likely to exit at the next time step are incremented from this entry event more than proportionally. To be a bit more rigorous, let $p_t(k)$ be the probability density of finding a firm with capital k at time t [with $k > \varepsilon K(t)$] and let $N(t)$ be the number of incumbent firms.

The average number of entrants will be $N_{in} = rN(t)$ and the average inflow of capital $K_{in} = rN(t)K(t)M_k/2$. The rise in total capital produced by the entry will shift the lower bound on 'surviving' capital and will possibly induce both incumbent and just-entered firms to leave the industry. On average, the number of exiting firms can be approximated by

$$N_{out} = N(t) \int_{\varepsilon K(t)}^{\varepsilon(K(t)+K_{in})} dk' p(k') + rN(t)\Phi\left[rN(t)\frac{\varepsilon}{M_k}\left(\varepsilon + \frac{M_k}{2}\right)\right] \tag{14}$$

where the first term is the contribution to exit coming from the incumbent

---

[11] Without exit conditions, the identity of the monopolist possessing the total mass of the shares distribution is, of course, not asymptotically fixed.

———— *Knowledge Accumulation, Entry Regimes and Industrial Evolution* ————

firms' distribution and the second is the contribution of the just-entered firms, which are uniformly distributed between $\varepsilon K(t)$ and $(\varepsilon + M_k)K(t)$. To simplify the expression, we have used a function $\Phi(x)$ defined according to:

$$\Phi(x) = \begin{cases} x & \text{for } 0 < x < 1 \\ 1 & \text{for } x > 1 \end{cases} \qquad (15)$$

The expression in (14) increases at least quadratically (when N is small). It therefore suggests that when N is small enough, entry does not immediately affect the successive exit flow, but for higher N, the entry of new firms will be followed by a higher exit effect, thus producing a total net *decrease* in the total number of firms.

We can use (14) to extract an upper bound on $N(t)$. Suppose that $N(t)$ happens to be so high that the second term on the right-hand side of (14) equals $rN(t)$. This would imply that the whole set of entrants will be pushed out from the industry by the same capital they brought in, leaving the total number of firms in the industry unchanged: there is no way to increase the total number of firms above this level. Hence we can obtain an upper bound for the number of firms by equating the second term on the right-hand side of (10) to $rN(t)$. It reads

$$N_{u.b.} = \frac{M_k}{\varepsilon(M_k + \varepsilon)r} \qquad (16)$$

This, of course, represents a gross overestimation of the actual average number of firms. Nevertheless, its existence implies that for any finite value of the entry and exit parameters the number of firms is limited.

It must be stressed, however, that the foregoing analysis is significant only for sufficiently high values of the entry coefficient r. When entry rates are low, we have to consider the actual evolution of incumbents in the industry, i.e. one has to modify the previous equation, taking into account the actual 'shrinking' in the firms' distribution described in (12).

The fact that we can define an average number of firms N^* allows us to obtain an estimate for the asymptotic average value of the total industry capital. The idea is to modify (4) in order to accommodate entry and exit dynamics. Taking into account the average values for the entrants' initial capital and the lower bound for exit flow, equation (4) can be written as:

——— *Knowledge Accumulation, Entry Regimes and Industrial Evolution* ———

$$K(t+1) = (1-d)K(t) + \lambda + N_{in}\left(\varepsilon + \frac{M_k}{2}\right)K(t) - N_{out}\varepsilon K(t) \qquad (17)$$

But (on average) $N_{in} = N_{out} = rN^*$, so that the asymptotic total capital computed from (17) reads

$$K^* = \frac{\lambda}{1 - d + 0.5rN^*M_k} \qquad (18)$$

This expression clearly suggests the existence of two phases:[12] when $rN^*{\cdot}M_k < 2d$, i.e. for small enough values of the entry ratio r and initial capital M_k, the industry is in a 'finite' phase and the aggregate capital asymptotically converges towards a finite value as in the 'closed' case—the latter being, however, a lower bound with a value $K^* = \lambda/d$. On the other hand, when $rN^*M_k > 2d$ the industry is in a 'divergent' phase and its total capital diverges exponentially[13] when $t \to +\infty$.

The approximation in (18) is, however, numerically unreliable for two reasons. First, the capital outflow due to exit is overestimated, since the capital shares possessed by exiting firms will be in general less than the threshold ε. Second, the capital inflow is overestimated, since—as we have discussed above—the net firm entry ratio can be significantly less than r.[14] This notwithstanding, the expression in (18) provides a good approximation of the numerical results below if one allows for a single parameter γ capturing the whole 'impactedness' of entry. In this spirit we have fitted the expression:

$$K^*_{fit} = \frac{\lambda}{1 - d + 0.5rN^*M_k\gamma} \qquad (19)$$

as a function of γ on our simulations results (described below). With $\gamma = 0.7131$, the standard deviation of the simulation results from the value

[12] Here and throughout, 'phase' stands for the collection of the characteristic properties of system dynamics which turn out to be qualitatively invariant within regions of the parameter's space. Hence such a notion does *not* have any bearing in terms of evolutionaty 'stages' over time.

[13] Notice that even if the only parameters that explicitly appear in (18) are those pertaining to entry rules, the other parameters could influence the asymptotic values through the value of N^*.

[14] Here it is the net firms' entry ratio *and* not the gross one (i.e. r) that matters, because only firms surviving a fall in productive cycle can contribute to the next period's aggregate capital.

——— *Knowledge Accumulation, Entry Regimes and Industrial Evolution* ———

predicted by (19) is 0.0192 (and the maximal deviation is 3.9%) despite the fact that the values involved span three orders of magnitude.[15]

Finally, concerning the behavior of the total output, in the 'finite' phase it is described by an expression like (11), with α in place of σ_ε, while in the 'exploding' phase this expression has to be corrected to take into account the exponential increase of the aggregate capital.

5. *Numerical Analysis*

Let us now present a wider exploration of the benchmark model described above, based on Monte Carlo simulations for different parameterizations.

The evolving structure of the industry is captured by various aggregate observables. Together with the total number of firms and total aggregate capital already discussed, we consider the average growth rate of the industry productivity, defined as a weighted mean of the firms' productivity

$$\pi_I(t) = \sum_i \frac{\pi_i(t) k_i(t)}{K(t)}$$

and, as a measure of industry concentration, the 'rescaled' entropy defined as

$$S_I(t) = -\frac{1}{\log N(t)} \sum_{i \in I} \frac{q_i(t)}{Q(t)} \log \frac{q_i(t)}{Q(t)} \qquad (20)$$

whose value ranges from 0 for a monopoly to 1 when shares are equal among firms. Moreover we consider both the average age of firms and the average age of firms weighted according to their market share.[16]

The previous analysis has shown how the entry and exit parameters affect both the number of firms and the aggregate capital of the industry, leading to the existence of two different 'phases' (in the meaning of footnote 12). It is thus natural to begin our numerical exploration with the analysis of how entry and exit parameters affect other relevant aspects of behavior in the industry. As we will see, the conclusions above, based on rough approximations of the entry/exit dynamics will be confirmed, at least qualitatively, by numerical simulation.

Let us start by considering the simulation results[17] shown in Figure 1 for

---

[15] This estimate is performed considering only the value associated with a finite limit in (19).

[16] The possible difference between these statistics allows us to discern, for each parameter's region, if firms who have more market share are the younger or the older ones.

[17] In this plot and in the following ones the points shown are the result of averaging over 50 independent simulations.

———— *Knowledge Accumulation, Entry Regimes and Industrial Evolution* ————

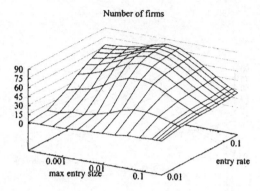

FIGURE 1. Mean number of firms N^* as a function of the rate of entry r and of the upper bound of initial capital distribution M_k.

TABLE 1. Default Values of the Model's Parameters Used in Simulations

Param.	Default	Param.	Default
ε	0.01	r	0.05
M_k	0.1	α	0.01
d	0.3	λ	0.6

different values of the rate of entry r and the maximal initial share M_k, keeping all other parameters fixed.[18] The total number of firms increases with the rate of entry, but its effect is much less pronounced at high entry rates. In this region, in fact, the dynamics described by (14) dominates and a large proportion of the just-entered firms immediately leave the industry, so that the 'net' effect of entry reaches a maximum. The effect of the maximal entry size follows the prediction of (14): when it decreases the total number of firms increases until it has values smaller than ε; then its effect tends to disappear.

Analogous conclusions can be drawn by studying simulations for different values of the rate of entry r and of the exit bound ε, shown in Figure 2. We again observe a 'saturation effect' on the entry rate, while, as expected, the number of firms increases when the exit bound is lowered.

Since the behavior of aggregate capital is accurately captured by (18) as a function of the average number of firms, we do not plot it but refer instead to the analytical expression above.

We turn next to the study of quantities for which no prediction has been made in the previous section. One of the most interesting variables is the rate

---

[18] In what follows when not otherwise specified the parameters used in the simulation have the default value given in Table 1.

——— *Knowledge Accumulation, Entry Regimes and Industrial Evolution* ———

Number of firms

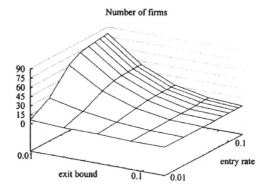

FIGURE 2. Mean number of firms N^* as a function of lower bound on capital shares ε and of the rate of entry r. The simulations are performed with $M_k = 0.04$.

Rate of growth of productivity

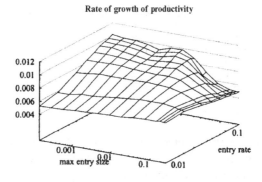

FIGURE 3. Rate of productivity growth as a function of the rate of entry r and of the upper bound of initial capital distribution M_k.

Rate of growth of productivity

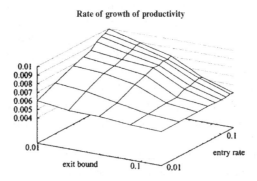

FIGURE 4. Rate of productivity growth as a function of lower bound on capital shares ε and of the rate of entry r.

——— *Knowledge Accumulation, Entry Regimes and Industrial Evolution* ———

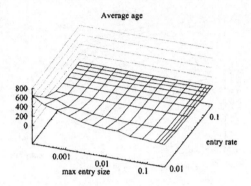

FIGURE 5. Average firms age as function of the rate of entry *r* and of the upper bound of initial capital distribution M_k.

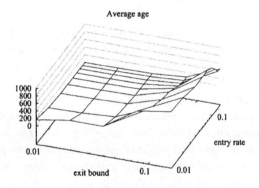

FIGURE 6. Average firms age as a function of lower bound on capital shares ε and of the rate of entry *r*.

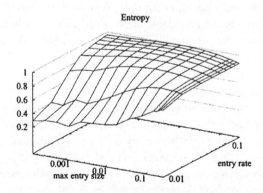

FIGURE 7. The rescaled entropy as a function of the rate of entry *r* and of the upper bound of initial capital distribution M_k.

——————— *Knowledge Accumulation, Entry Regimes and Industrial Evolution* ———————

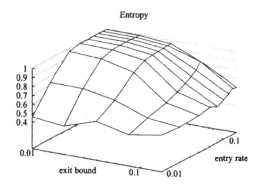

FIGURE 8. The rescaled entropy as a function of lower bound on capital shares ε and of the rate of entry *r*.

of growth of the average productivity (see Figures 3 and 4). Consider its behavior together with that of entropy (which is, to repeat, an inverse measure of concentration) shown in Figures 7 and 8, and together with measures of average age (Figures 5 and 6).

Note that we are comparing here the outcomes of different entry and exit regimes, conditional on the same notional opportunities, as expressed by the probability distribution on productivity increments, and the same ability of accessing it by incumbents and entrants. As one can see, when the entry rate is high but both the maximal initial size and the exit threshold are low, the industry is characterized by a high value of productivity growth and by small concentration, and is composed by relatively young firms. Notice than in this fast-growing region the aggregate capital remains finite.

If, however, the maximal entry capital is increased, the industry enters the divergent phase, characterized by unbounded capital, wherein the high turbulence disrupts the productivity growth process. Here, the massive entry of firms with relatively high amount of capital leads to the continuous expulsion of big shares of the incumbents' population, so disturbing the underlying learning possibilities.

On the other hand, if the entry rate is lowered and the entry threshold increased, the industry shows a more 'sedate' behavior, eventually reaching a *strong oligopolistic* structure in which entry is a rare event and only medium and big firms survive. Old incumbents, even if their productivity is almost stationary, easily survive since they are protected from their relatively big size.

To summarize, we have identified three main 'phases' that describe the behavior of our benchmark model. First, a *divergent phase* is characterized by a high turbulence and slow productivity increase. Moreover the *finite phase* can

───── *Knowledge Accumulation, Entry Regimes and Industrial Evolution* ─────

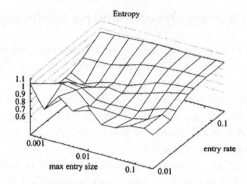

FIGURE 9. The ratio of entropy values obtained with $\alpha = 0.2$ to those obtained with $\alpha = 0.4$, as a function of the rate of entry r and of the upper bound of initial capital distribution M_k.

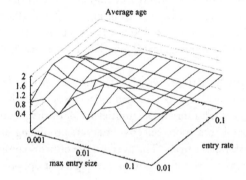

FIGURE 10. The ratio of the average age obtained with $\alpha = 0.2$ to that obtained with $\alpha = 0.4$, as a function of the rate of entry r and of the upper bound of initial capital distribution M_k.

be split into two parts, namely a *fast growing* phase, and a *strong oligopolistic* phase characterized by a nearly stagnant industry.

From a qualitative point of view, the results highlight the fundamental role of 'reasonable' rates of (small) entry as driver of the dynamics. Indeed, entry processes have to be sufficiently frequent as to foster multiple innovative searches without however being 'massive' enough as to destroy the process of adaptation and of differential growth of competing entities.

Next, let us study how the model behaves with varying degrees of opportunity that firms face concerning their potential productivity growth.

——— *Knowledge Accumulation, Entry Regimes and Industrial Evolution* ———

5.1 Changing Relative Opportunities for Incumbent Firms

Here we are interested in the effect on the aggregate industry behavior produced by a modification of the parameter α, setting the scale of the distribution from which productivity growth is drawn.

In this spirit we perform a comparison, for the range of the entry/selection parameters analyzed above, of different Monte Carlo simulations obtained varying the opportunity parameter. While its default value was 0.01, here we also consider values of 0.04 and 0.08.

A first obvious effect on the average productivity rate of growth is that the latter, as expected, scales with α. Less intuitively, we find that the effect of the parameter α on the industry behavior varies depending on the 'phase' that characterizes the industry.

The learning dynamic has indeed a negligible effect in the 'divergent' and 'oligopolistic' phases. As can be seen from Figures 9 and 10, if the entry rate and the initial share are both very high or both very low, the average age and the entropy computed remain almost invariant to changes in the opportunity parameters.

For intermediate situations, we observe that when the degree of opportunity grows, the total number of firms decreases, and the concentration increases. So, in general, more opportunities for both the incumbents and the entrants correspond to a more selective market, producing as a net effect a slight advantage for older firms. The average age of firms confirms this point: this statistic increases, even if weakly, as the degree of opportunity grows.[19]

5.2 The Benchmark versus a 'Schumpeter I' Learning Regime

In order to analyze the asymptotic properties of a regime of the 'Schumpeter I' genre, we obviously have to depart from the benchmark model and consider an industry in which incumbents cannot improve their productivity, so that they produce throughout their life with the technique implemented at birth.

An intuitive way of obtaining a model of such type, starting from the benchmark one presented above, would be simply to 'turn off' the learning process of incumbents, leaving all the other features of the model unchanged. Note, however, that this procedure does not work. If one does that, the productivity of any firm converges towards the same asymptotic value, and the variance of the productivity distribution becomes zero. In fact, in each iteration the less-productive firms are likely to disappear, while above-

---

[19] The same conclusion is confirmed by studying the ratio between average age and average weighted age, not shown due to space constraints

——— *Knowledge Accumulation, Entry Regimes and Industrial Evolution* ———

Number of firms (positive drift)

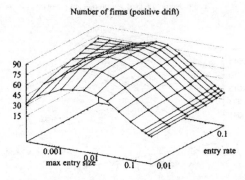

FIGURE 11. Total number of firms as a function of the rate of entry r and of the upper bound of initial capital distribution M_k for the 'Schumpeter I' model with positive drift.

Productivity rate of growth (positive drift)

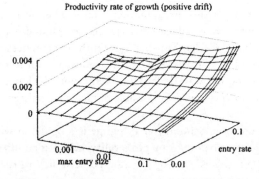

FIGURE 12. Rate of growth of productivity as a function of the rate of entry r and of the upper bound of initial capital distribution M_k for the 'Schumpeter I' model with positive drift.

Number of firms (negative drift)

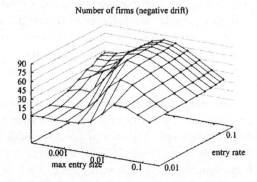

FIGURE 13. The number of firms for the 'Schumpeter I' model with negative drift. The values are plotted as function of the rate of entry r and of the upper bound of initial capital distribution M_k.

———— Knowledge Accumulation, Entry Regimes and Industrial Evolution ————

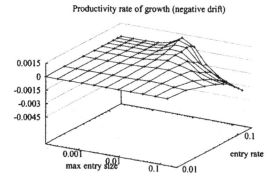

FIGURE 14. Average productivity rate of growth for the 'Schumpeter I' model with negative shift. The 'divergent' phase is characterized by a reduction in industry productivity.

average-productivity firms gain market share. Therefore, the selective mechanisms progressively reduce heterogeneity in productivity, and in the absence of a learning mechanism that constantly reintroduces diversity, the productivities of all the firms present in the industry tend toward the same value. Putting it another way, no faithful distribution of 'clones' from the in-cumbents' environments appears to be able to fuel any persistent evolutionary drive.

A richer account of a 'Schumpeter I' regime is a model in which entrants have an innovative advantage in probability, while incumbents learning remains turned off: this is done by giving a positive drift to the distribution from which entrants extract their initial productivities, with respect to the revealed productivity distribution of incumbents. In order to perform an analysis comparable with previous findings, we assign to the drift the same value of the 'opportunity' parameter α in the benchmark model (see Table 1).

As can be seen from Figure 11, the behavior of this model is very similar to the behavior of the benchmark for high values of the entry rate r. However, when this parameter is lowered, no 'oligopolistic phase' appears. The absence of such a phase is easily understood: since the relative productivity of different incumbent firms is not subject to random fluctuations, there is no advantage in having a bigger size, and even a few, small entrants are able to displace the industry core firms. These same features are reflected also in the degrees of concentration and in average age. The entropy for this model is always near to 1, implying an almost uniform distribution of market shares, while the industry average age remains lower than in the benchmark case, where the formation of the 'oligopolistic core' produces an increase in the average lifespan of incumbency.

Allowing for a drift in the entrants' productivity *vis-à-vis* the incumbents'

——— *Knowledge Accumulation, Entry Regimes and Industrial Evolution* ———

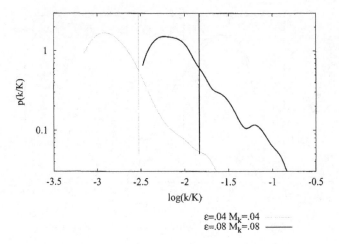

$$\varepsilon=.04 \ M_k=.04 \quad \cdots\cdots$$
$$\varepsilon=.08 \ M_k=.08 \quad ———$$

FIGURE 15. Share distribution for different parametrization of the entry process. For each curve is also shown (vertical line) the value $\varepsilon + M_k$ which provides an estimation of the core lower boundary. Simulations performed with $r = 0.04$.

distribution also changes the system behavior in the 'divergent' phase. As can be seen in Figure 12, the rate of productivity growth is less affected by an increase in initial size and entry rate than in the benchmark case, since now there is no 'learning' process inside the industry core which could be disturbed by an increase (and widening) of industry turbulence.

It is also interesting to analyze what happens if one introduces a negative drift into entrants' productivity, so that their mean productivity is less then the industry average.[20] (Notice that a dynamic in which the drift gets a negative value is more in line with what is actually found in empirical investigations.)

First of all, the negative drift provides again an implicit advantage to incumbent firms and thus restores the existence of an oligopolistic phase. When the rate of entry is low, a relatively small number of incumbents has a low probability of being perturbed by the arrival of new firms, since there is a low probability that at least one among the latter would possesses a higher productivity than the incumbents. As can be seen in Figure 13, the number of firms in the negative-drift model is very similar to the benchmark.

An interesting effect, however, emerges in relation to the divergent phase. When the turbulence of the industry is very high (with a high rate of entry) and wide (with large initial capitals), affecting also the industry core, the

[20] We model this regime setting the drift value at the same level of the positive drift case, with a reversed sign.

———— Knowledge Accumulation, Entry Regimes and Industrial Evolution ————

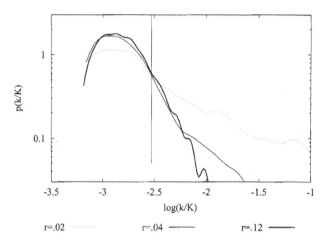

FIGURE 16. Share distribution for three different values of the entry parameter r. simulations axe performed with $\varepsilon = M_k = 0.02$. The value $\varepsilon + M_k$ is also shown.

smaller incumbents are likely to be pushed out from the industry by the 'impactness' of new firms, with bigger capital even if smaller productivity. As shown in Figure 14, the net effect is a steady *decrease* of the industry's productivity.

5.3 Size Distribution

So far, in order to succinctly describe different learning, entry and selection regimes, we have purposefully neglected a few statistics that describe distributions of characteristics across the population of firms, regarding size, productivity, age, growth, etc.

Here, due to limitations of space, let us confine ourselves to the analysis of the quantity most ubiquitously studied, namely the distribution of (the log of) firm sizes.

The structure shown by the shares distribution of our model is rather robust and it largely rests upon the variables that characterize the entry and exit dynamics.[21]

First of all it must be noted than a stationary shares distribution emerges (asymptotically) both in the 'finite' and in the 'divergent' phases discussed above. The existence of a stationary distribution is in contrast to the closed

---

[21] Instrumental to the identification of the general structure of shares distributions has been the development of a 'diffusive' continuous-time approximation of our model. For more details, see Bottazzi (2001).

models analyzed in Section 4 and comes from the 'openness' of the system, i.e. from the constant flux of firms and capital in and out of the industry.[22]

Due to the exit condition, the share distribution has support $[\varepsilon, +\infty)$. Its shape can be divided in two regions according to the entry dynamics. In the region $[\varepsilon, M_k]$ there is a constant influx of firms and their number is relatively high. Firms in this region are more likely to exit and are directly competing with the entering ones. This region constitutes the 'fringe' of the industry, the locus of higher turbulence. On the other hand, the region $[M_k, +\infty)$ is constituted of firms which have, so to speak, so far won the 'competitive struggle' by reaching higher market shares. This is the core of the industry. Here turbulence is lower and the firms in this region are more clearly ranked. Only on a longer term are they possibly displaced from their current position and eventually reduced to the fringe by more productive competitors that steadily, but relatively slowly, 'climb' the successive positions of the rank ladder.

Due to their different nature, in these two regions the distribution of the (log) shares shows a very different shape. In fact, as can be seen in Figure 15, it turns out than in the $[\varepsilon, M_k]$ region the distribution is rather flat, while it decreases linearly in $[M_k, +\infty)$. A rescaling of both the *market impactedness* M_k and of the *selection coarseness* ε has the sole effect of translating the distribution. If, however, one increases the former while keeping the latter constant, giving a higher weight to the entry dynamics, the 'flat' region is increased and consequently the industry core is reduced. Above some threshold value, the turbulence invades the entire industry and the divergent phase begins.

The effect of entry rates can be analogously interpreted. When r is high, entry has a greater impact and we expect an higher concentration of firms in the 'fringe' region. When it is low, the 'core' region is dominant and we expect longer, fatter tails in the distribution. An example of the effect obtained by varying the entry rate can be seen in Figure 16.

6. *Conclusions and Outlook*

This work has, we hope, added some novel insights into the understanding of the interplay between learning, entry and selection regimes in determining industrial structure and dynamics.

In that respect we were able to identify three quite generic 'evolutionary archetypes' or 'phases' (in the sense spelled out in Section 4) in the evolution

---

[22] Trying a comparison with 'physical' systems, we could say that the industries described in Section 4 are 'closed dissipative systems' converging toward the minimal entropic state, the monopoly, while the model with entry and exit is an 'open system' which evolves towards a stationary, out-of-equilibrium state.

——— *Knowledge Accumulation, Entry Regimes and Industrial Evolution* ———

process, *in primis* dependent on the rates and impactedness of entry, namely (i) an 'oligopolistic phase' where neither (very low) entry rates nor learning processes are able to shake the industry out of a quasi-stationary state; (ii) at the opposite extreme, a 'divergent phase', whereby massive entry is disruptive of any process of adaptation and self-organization of the industry; and (iii) in-between, what we could be tempted to call the 'healthy evolutionary phase', whereby entry is sufficient to guarantee multiple search trials by a few entrants but also a progressive competitive adaptation of the most successful incumbents. Interestingly, it is primarily in this phase that the rates and modes of learning by incumbents and entrants influence the structure of the industry and its changes.

More specifically, regarding productivity growth, a remarkable property of our model is that long-term rates are obviously influenced by the level of notional opportunities, but also, holding opportunities constant, by entry regimes. Our results robustly suggest that the most conducive regime is one where a relatively numerous population of (small) entrants steadily coexists with a 'core' of industrial incumbents. That distinction bears its implications also in terms of size distribution, with a 'fringe' region and a core region displaying Pareto-type size (market shares) distributions, well in accordance with the empirical evidence. The core–fringe distinction also matches our earlier distinction of 'oligopolistic' and 'divergent' phases of evolution, so that only the core appears in the former and only the fringe in the latter.

More generally, our investigation of some fundamental invariances in evolutionary processes has led us to disentangle some robust mechanisms of interaction between the competitive dynamics, on the one hand, and learning processes, on the other. The analysis is also amenable to exercises of a more normative flavor, investigating the 'efficiency' of different evolutionary regimes. This is a task that we are currently beginning to undertake.

Acknowledgements

Support for this work from the Italian Ministry of University and Research (MURST project no. 9913443984) and the European Union (TSER, ESSY project, contract no. SOEL-CT 98–1116 DGXII-SOLS) are gratefully acknowledged. Comments by several participants to the Essy project, in particular Stan Metcalfe, and to the Fest Conference for Richard Nelson, and by two anonymous referees have helped shape the current version of this work.

──────── *Knowledge Accumulation, Entry Regimes and Industrial Evolution* ────────

References

Baldwin, J. R. (1995), *The Dynamic of Industrial Competition*. Cambridge University Press: Cambridge.

Bottazzi, G. (2001), 'Continuous-Time Limit of a Modified WKD Model of Industry Evolution', LEM Working Paper, S. Anna School of Advanced Studies, Italy.

Camerer, C. (1995), 'Individual Decision Making,' in J. H. Kagel and A. E. Roth (eds), *The Handbook of Experimental Economics*. Princeton University Press: Princeton.

Dosi, G., O. Marsili, L. Orsenigo and R. Salvatore (1995), 'Learning, Market Selection and Evolution of Industrial Structure,' *Small Business Economics*, 7, 411–436.

Dosi, G. and S. Lovallo (1997), 'Rational Entrepreneurs or Optimistic Martyrs? Some Considerations on Technological Regimes, Corporate Entries, and the Evolutionary Role of Decision Biases,' in R. Garud, P. Nayyar and Z. Shapira (eds), *Technological Innovation: Oversights and Foresights*. Cambridge University Press: Cambridge, pp. 41–68.

Ericson, R. and A. Pakes (1995), 'Markov-perfect Industry Dynamics: a Framework for Empirical Work,' *Review of Economic Studies*, 62, 53–82.

Geroski, P. A. (1994), *Market Structure, Corporate Performance and Innovative Activity*. Oxford University Press: Oxford.

Geroski, P. A. (1995), 'What Do We Know About Entry?,' *International Journal of Industrial Organization*, 13, 421–440.

Iwai, K. (1984a), 'Schumpeterian Dynamics I: Technological Progress, Form Growth and Economic Selection,' *Journal of Economic Behavior and Organization*, 5, 159–190.

Iwai, K. (1984b), 'Schumpeterian Dynamics Part II: Technological Progress, Form Growth and Economic Selection,' *Journal of Economic Behavior and Organization*, 5, 321–351.

Jovanovic, B. (1982), ' Selection and Evolution in Industry,' *Econometrica*, 50, 649–670.

Kaniovski, Y. M. (2001), 'On a Rational Expectation Equilibrium,' Working Paper, University of Bolzano.

Kwasnicki, W. (1996), 'Innovation Regimes, Entry and market Structure,' *Journal of Evolutionary Economy*, 6, 375–409.

Malerba, F. and L. Orsenigo (1995), 'Schumpeterian Patterns of Innovation,' *Cambridge Journal of Economics*, 19, 47–65.

Malerba, F., R. Nelson, L. Orsenigo and S. Winter (1999), 'History Friendly Models of Industry Evolution: The Computer Industry,' *Industrial and Corporate Change*, 8, 3–40.

Marsili, O. (2001), *The Anatomy and Evolution of Industry*. Edward Elgar: Aldershot.

Mazzucato, M. (2000), *Firm Size, Innovation and Market Structure: The Emergence of Market Concentration and Instability*. Edward Elgar: Aldershot.

Metcalfe, S. (1998), *Evolutionary Economics and Creative Destruction*. Routledge: London.

Metcalfe, S. (1992), 'Variety, Structure and Change: an Evolutionary Perspective on the Competitive Process,' *Revue d'Economie Industrielle*, 59, 46–62.

Nelson, R. R. (1982), 'Research on Productivity Growth and Productivity Differences: Dead Ends and New Departures,' *Journal of Economic Literature*, XIX, 1029–1064.

Nelson, R. and S. Winter (1982), *An Evolutionary Theory of Economic Change*. Belknap Press of Harvard University Press: Cambridge, MA.

Pakes, A. and R. Ericson (1998), 'Empirical Implications of Alternative Models of Firm Dynamics,' *Journal of Economic Theory*, 79, 1–45.

Silverberg, G. and B. Verspagen (1994), 'Learning, Innovation and Economic Growth: a Long Run Model of Industrial Evolution,' *Industrial and Corporate Change*, 3, 199–223.

———— *Knowledge Accumulation, Entry Regimes and Industrial Evolution* ————

Sutton, J. (1991), *Sunk Costs and Market Structure.* MIT Press: Cambridge, MA.

Sutton, J. (1998), *Technology and Market Structures.* MIT Press: Cambridge, MA.

Weibull, J. W. (1995), *Evolutionary Game Theory.* MIT Press: Cambridge, MA.

Winter, S. (1971), 'Satisficing, Selection, and the Innovating Remnant,' *Quarterly Journal of Economics,* 85, 237–261.

Winter, S. (1984), 'Schumpeterian Competition Under Alternative Technological Regimes,' *Journal of Economic Behavior and Organization,* 5, 287–320.

Winter, S. G., Y. M. Kaniovski and G. Dosi (1997), 'A Baseline Model of Industry Evolution,' Interim Report IR-97-013/March, International Institute for Applied Systems Analysis, Laxemburg, Austria.

Winter S., Y. M. Kaniovski and C. Dosi (2000), 'Modeling Industrial Dynamics with Innovative Entrants,' *Structural Change and Economics Dynamics,* 11, 255–293.

Appendix: Closed Industry with Learning

Consider the evolution equation presented in (10). The associated evolution equation for the total production

$$Q(t) = \sum_{i \in I} q_i(t)$$

can be immediately obtained multiplying both sides for π and k before integrating. It reads

$$
\begin{aligned}
Q(t+1) &= \int_0^{+\infty} dk \int_0^{+\infty} d\pi \; k\pi p_{t+1}(k, \pi) \\
&= m_\varepsilon \left((1-d)\frac{K(t)}{N} + \lambda \right) + (1-d)Q(t) + \lambda \frac{M_{1,2}[p_t]}{Q(t)}
\end{aligned}
\tag{21}
$$

where $m_\varepsilon = \int dx \; x \; q(x)$ is the average productivity growth and where we have denoted the higher moments of the p density as

$$M_{i,j}[p_t] = \int_0^{+\infty} dk \int_0^{+\infty} d\pi \; k^i \pi^j p_t(k, \pi) \tag{22}$$

Since the dynamics of $k(t)$ is characterized by (4), the previous expression shows that $Q(t)$ oscillates around an equilibrium value $\overline{Q}(t)$ which grows exponentially in time. Indeed, the last term in the right-hand side of (21) provides the leading contribution and under the approximation of independence between k and π [i.e. supposing $p(k, \pi) = p_k(k)p_\pi(\pi)$] one obtains

——— *Knowledge Accumulation, Entry Regimes and Industrial Evolution* ———

$$\overline{Q}(t) \sim \sqrt{\lambda M_{1,2}[p_t]} \qquad (23)$$

which after substituting the definition in (22) gives the expression reported in (11).

In order to extract the leading term of $p_t(k,\pi)$ as $t \to +\infty$ it is useful to consider the double Laplace transform (the characteristic function) of the density, which is given by:

$$\widetilde{p}_t(l,m) = \int_0^{+\infty} dk \int_0^{+\infty} d\pi\, e^{-kl} e^{-\pi m} p_t(k,\pi) \qquad (24)$$

This function is defined and analytical in the positive real part complex half-plane. Applying the Laplace transform to both sides of (10), one obtains (after some algebra):

$$\widetilde{p}_{t+1}(l,m) = \widetilde{q}(m) \int_0^{+\infty} dk' \int_0^{+\infty} d\pi'\, e^{-k'(1-d)l} e^{-\pi'm} e^{-\frac{\lambda k'\pi'}{Q(t)}l} p_t(k',\pi') \qquad (25)$$

From (23), the coefficient of the mixed exponent in k' and π' is going to zero as $t \to +\infty$ and in order to extract the leading term it can be put equal to 1. With this approximation, the integration can be formally performed, obtaining:

$$\widetilde{p}_{t+1}(l,m) = \widetilde{q}(m)\widetilde{p}_t\big[(1-d)l,m\big] \qquad (26)$$

which can be immediately solved for the tth step density

$$\widetilde{p}_t(l,m) = \widetilde{q}(m)^t \widetilde{p}_0\big[(1-d)^t l,m\big] \qquad (27)$$

Without any lack of generality we can assume that the initial assignment of productivity is independent of the initial assignment of capital shares, and choose as initial distribution of productivities with the same distribution q so that $p_0(k,\pi) = p_0(k)q(\pi)$. The solution obtained anti-transforming (27) reads

$$p_t(k,\pi) = \int_{c_1} dl \int_{c_2} dm\, \widetilde{p}_0\big[(1-d)^t k\big]\widetilde{q}(m)^{t+1} = \frac{1}{(1-d)^t}\, p_0\, \frac{k}{(1-d)^t}\, q^{*(t+1)}(\pi)$$

$$(28)$$

where the $*$ denotes the convolution operator and c_1, c_2 are suitable contours of integration in the complex plane.

[14]

Journal of Economic Geography 7 (2007) pp. 651–672
Advance Access Published on 24 June 2007

doi:10.1093/jeg/lbm024

Modeling industrial evolution in geographical space

Giulio Bottazzi*,†, Giovanni Dosi*, Giorgio Fagiolo* and Angelo Secchi*

Abstract

In this article we study a class of evolutionary models of industrial agglomeration with local positive feedbacks, which allow for a wide set of empirically testable implications. Their roots rest in the Generalized Polya Urn framework. Here, however, we build on a birth-death process over a finite number of locations and a finite population of firms. The process of selection among production sites that are heterogeneous in their 'intrinsic attractiveness' occurs under a regime of dynamic increasing returns depending on the number of firms already present in each location. The general model is presented together with a few examples of small economies which help to illustrate the properties of the model and characterize its asymptotic behavior. Finally, we discuss a number of empirical applications of our theoretical framework. The basic model, once taken to the data, is able to empirically disentangle the relative strength of technologically specific agglomeration drivers (affecting differently firms belonging to different industrial sectors in each location) from site-specific geographical forces (horizontally acting upon all sectors in each location).

Keywords: industrial location, agglomeration, dynamic increasing returns, markov chains, polya urns
JEL classifications: C1, L6, R1
Date submitted: 23 October 2006 **Date accepted:** 15 February 2007

1. Introduction

The evolution of technologies and industries clearly occurs in 'spaces', both geographical spaces and more metaphorical ones wherein 'distances' and boundaries are shaped by institutions, networks of interaction and associated knowledge spillovers. However, while a lot of efforts has gone into the formalization of the processes of technological and economic evolution *in general* [for some overview of the progress since the seminal Nelson and Winter(1982), cf. Dosi and Winter (2002)], it is fair to say that much less progress has been made in the formal representation of the spatial nesting of such evolutionary processes and even less so in the elaboration of models yielding empirically testable formulations.[1] This is the central concern of this work.

The basic skeleton of the class of models we present is made of a simple economy composed of a finite number of distinct locations (i.e. production sites) and populated

†Corresponding author: Giulio Bottazzi, Scuola Superiore Sant'Anna, P.za Martiri della Liberta' 33, 56127 Pisa, Italy.
email <bottazzi@sssup.it>
*Laboratory of Economics and Management (LEM), Scuola Superiore Sant'Anna, Pisa, Italy.

1 Discussions of the inroads made by evolutionary ideas in the field of economic geography are in Boschma and Frenken (2006) and Martin and Sunley (2006).

by a finite number of firms. New firms enter the economy, and select a site in which to place their activities. Conversely incumbent firms from every location face some probability of leaving them (i.e. dying). New firms are randomly selected from a notionally infinite number of potential entrants and select their production sites depending on their expected benefits (most likely including expected profits). In that, note that well in tune with evolutionary interpretations of economic change, expectations do not map in any precise sense into what the economic environment will eventually deliver (hence, in general rational expectations are deemed as just a particular case out of many possible descriptions of investment processes). We assume that the benefits perceived by entrants are made up of a common component, identical across the potential population, and an individual term, which captures idiosyncratic (actual or expected) returns from locating in one particular site.

Since we are interested in investigating the effect of different degrees of 'agglomeration economies' on the ultimate distributional patters, we assume that the common term in firm preferences is composed of two elements: the intrinsic 'geographic attractiveness' of a location and an 'agglomeration' benefit. The latter is in general different for different locations and is assumed to be proportional to the number of firms already located there.

We describe the entry and exit process of firms and the ensuing evolution of the geographic distribution of economic activities as a finite Markov chain. This stochastic model does retain the basic evolutionary methodological prescription that reasonable accounts of economic phenomena—in this case evolving industrial geographies—have to be grounded into explicit *process stories* entailing micro behaviors which evolve over time and bear macro-level effects. Micro heterogeneity here fully appears even if black-boxed into the stochastic structure of the entry process, accounting for those trial-and-error behaviors and, together, those degrees of bounded rationality which are likely to underlie micro processes of exploration and adaptation. At the same time, the presence of agglomeration benefits accounts for *dynamic increasing returns* often associated with, e.g. learning-by-doing and by-using, network effects, user-producer relations and various forms of Marshallian externalities which characterize evolutionary dynamics in the socio-economic domain. In turn, such increasing returns are likely to be, at least partly, local, also in a strict geographical sense.

The foregoing ingredients suffice to account also for the interplay between *chance* and *necessity* involved in industrial evolution and its geographical unfolding. Indeed, the spatial distribution of economic activities is likely to depend on the intrinsic features of space itself—features that look very much like endowments or at least 'slow' variables, like many institutional set-ups which change on a time scale much longer than the scale over which micro decisions occur. Together, there are agglomeration forces which emerge, so to speak, along the process of agglomeration itself, with earlier locational events influencing the attractiveness of the site for future investors. In turn, such agglomeration forces might be location-specific and independent of individual sectors and technologies, or, conversely, sector-specific, applying across different locations within the same sector of activity.

The formal apparatus presented in this work is meant precisely to offer an account of the different agglomeration forces at work and together to allow the derivation of empirically testable formulations.

As compared to the incumbent literature, such a reduced form evolutionary model does share with New Economic Geography (NEG) [cf. Krugman (1991) and Fujita et al. (1999), among others] the interpretation of the observed spatial agglomeration patterns as phenomena of self-organization, driven by externalities and increasing returns of some kind. On the other hand, the two streams of interpretations tend to depart with respect to the micro-foundations (with NEG much more committed to rational decision-makers) and also with respect to the style of analysis whereby NEG searches whenever possible for closed form equilibrium solutions and most often builds explanations upon comparisons among equilibria themselves, whereas models like those presented below try to explicitly account for whatever dynamics and ask where it may lead to. Correspondingly, NEG models straightforwardly assume agglomeration phenomena as equilibrium outcomes of location decisions in monopolistically competitive markets, while no such commitment is necessarily made by models closer to an evolutionary inspiration. In fact, precisely because of such an agnosticism, evolutionary-inspired models can be usefully applied also to dynamic processes such as those concerning the development of technological externalities or the diffusion of knowledge within and across geographical sites which often *do not* involve any *market* and, even less so, any equilibrium notion.

More precisely, the models in this work find their roots into the notion of *local dynamic increasing returns* explored in Arthur (1990, 1994); Dosi et al. (1994) and Dosi and Kaniovski (1994).[2] Using the formal tool of *generalized urn schemes*, those models begin to offer a simple spatial characterization of adaptive processes of growth accounting for the presence of positive, and possibly also negative, feedbacks over ever-growing populations of firms or customers. However, a significant drawback of generalized urn schemes rests in their limited interpretative ability over small population and short time horizons. In such a framework, the initial conditions of the system (i.e. the initial number of firms present in each location), together with the sequences of stochastic realizations, characterizes the asymptotic geographical distribution of firms. The strength of such representation is precisely its ability to account for the 'power of history' to shape long-term outcomes under dynamic increasing returns of most kinds. The symmetric drawback is that such an approach hardly applies to circumstances wherein choices are somewhat reversible over time, while—together—one may easily account for small populations of agents. The representation of such alternative set-up involves repeated and reversible decisions by finite populations of agents in presence of 'local' dynamic increasing returns. This is the focus of this study, formally grounded on the analytical results presented in Bottazzi and Secchi (2007). Following this approach we consider, instead of an irreversible birth dynamics, a Markov process with finite number of firms/locations and reversability of locational choices. In this framework we are able to derive the equilibrium distribution of firms across geographical locations and to obtain empirically testable models. Next we show that, by varying the relative strength of geographical attractiveness and of agglomeration positive feedbacks, the model is able to reproduce highly different degrees of spatial concentration and different temporal dynamics. In particular, when the agglomeration benefits are absent or very low, different locations attract, on average, a share of the overall population of firms that is proportional to their intrinsic attractiveness (we shall define more precisely these notions subsequently). These shares,

---

2   In a similar spirit see also Brenner (2003).

however, tend to fluctuate in time with a relatively high volatility. Conversely, when the strength of the agglomeration benefits increases, the system moves toward more polarized distributional patterns in which a small fraction of location contains almost the entire economy. At the same time, the introduction of agglomeration benefits and the ensuing polarization of spatial distribution entails a major indeterminacy [to some extent alike that shown in Arthur(1994)]: locations which absorb the largest part of the economy are dynamically selected and history plays a fundamental role in it. However, the prominence of particular sites is not permanent. Rather, they represent sort of 'metastable' states: over the long term, new locations do emerge displacing previous ones as leading attractive poles.

The remainder of the article is organized as follows. Section 2 presents a stochastic model of multi-site location in which we disentangle the role played by the intrinsic geographic attractiveness of each site from the one due to pure agglomeration forces. Section 3 presents some small economies examples, while Section 4 studies the asymptotic behavior of our model when only entry dynamics are retained. Section 5 explores the case where all locations is characterized by the same (industry-specific) agglomeration coefficient. Finally, Section 6 discusses possible applications of the model to empirical analyses.

2. A stochastic process of multi-site location

Assume that the economy is composed of $L \geq 2$ distinct locations, labeled by integers between 1 and L, which can be thought as 'production sites' or 'industrial districts' or 'regions'. The economy is populated by N firms. Each firm locates its productive activities in a single location. Time is discrete and at each time step $t \in \{1, 2, \ldots\}$ new firms can enter the economy and incumbents can leave it. Each firm, when entering the economy, chooses to locate its production activities in the site which is expected to provide the highest benefits (which economists generally take to be the highest stream of future profits). Firms are boundedly rational and their expectations build on two terms: a common factor and an idiosyncratic component. The common factor affects the decision of any possible entrant and is meant to represent the common 'perceived' advantage of locating activities in a certain site. The idiosyncratic component captures the individual preferences of that particular firm. Firms are heterogenous with respect to their revealed preferences. This heterogeneity can be due to asymmetric information or cognitive biases, but even more plausibly, be the effect of the diverse requirements that drive the choices of different firms inside an industry.

Since for the time being we are interested only in deriving the aggregate dynamics of the system, we consider the same logarithmic utility function for all firms and model their heterogeneity through a random effect. Formally, we assume the following

Assumption 1: *Let $\mathcal{F}$ be the population of potential entrants and let $c_l \leq 0, l \in \{1, \ldots, L\}$ stand for the common benefits (to all firms) from locating an economic activity in l.*

When a new firm enters the economy, it is selected at random from $\mathcal{F}$ and chooses location l which satisfies

$$l = \arg \max_j \{\ln(c_j) + e_j | j \in \{1, \ldots, L\}\}$$

where $(e_1, \ldots, e_L)$ represents the individual preferences of the firm.[3]

Essentially, such an assumption postulates that the entry process is defined by the probability distribution $F(e)$ of individual preferences $e = (e_1, \ldots, e_L)$ on the population of potential entrants $\mathcal{F}$. The probability p_l that the next entrant chooses location l is indeed[4]

$$p_l = \text{Prob}\{\ln(c_l) + e_l \geq \ln(c_j) + e_j \forall j \neq l | c, F(e)\}.$$

The dynamical process implied by this assumption is undetermined until one provides a precise definition of the distribution F. This is generally a very difficult task as it requires to model the (private and unexpressed) preferences of the whole population of possible entrants.

However, Bottazzi and Secchi (2007) show that it is possible to significantly simplify this problem without restricting too much the generality of the approach. Indeed, by introducing a minimal degree of structure in the decision process or, alternatively, by assuming a simple but plausible structure of the economy, one can show that the entry decision is, in probability, only driven by the common components c of the variables (e.g. profits) which enter the decision process. In particular one may either interpret the entry decision in terms of the 'law of comparative judgment' (Thurstone, 1927) or, alternatively, one may assume that each location is composed by a large number of sublocations characterized by the same common expected profit c_l (but allowing different firms to posses different preferences over different sublocations). In these circumstances, it can be proved that the probability that a given location l get selected is

$$p_l = \frac{c_l}{\sum_j c_j}. \tag{2.1}$$

Notice that even if the two different interpretations of the 'choice' process start from highly different premises in terms of the information processing abilities of the agents and, together, of their abilities to specify their 'fine-grained' preferences, they do simplify our dynamical process in exactly the same way, thus adding plausibility to the assumptions underling Equation (2.1).

In order to completely specify the model, at this point one has to provide the analytic expression for the common attractiveness of a location (that is, common to all would-be entrants). To recall, our aim is to describe the spatial distribution of economic activities under different agglomeration (or anti-agglomeration) forces. We start by assuming that the locational choice of entrant firms is affected by the actual distribution of firms that they observe when they assess their would-be location. For sake of tractability, we will try to capture this effect with a simple linear relationship, assuming the following

---

3   For sake of simplicity we are neglecting here the fact that would-be entrants might have different sizes and thus also the distinction between would-be returns per unit of investment and returns per firm. In our framework it is straightforward to consider the c_l as returns to firms.

4   Notice that this is exactly the same entry process assumed in Arthur (1990).

Assumption 2: *The common expected profit c_l from locating a new activity in location l at time t is given by*

$$c_l = a_l + b_l n_l$$

where n_l represents the number of firms present in location l at the time of choice and $a_l \geq 0$, $b_l \geq 0$.

Since this is the core relation of the family of models which we are going to discuss in the following, let us spell out at some detail its empirical grounds.

Each location $l \in \{1, \ldots, L\}$ is characterized by an 'intrinsic attractiveness' parameter a_l and by an 'agglomeration' parameter b_l.

The coefficient a_l captures the perceived gains that a firm would obtain by choosing to locate its activity in l, net of any agglomeration effects. In tune with the quite 'agnostic' nature of our modeling skeleton, on purpose, we mean such a coefficient to capture an ensemble of phenomena, identified in the literature as *catalyzers* and 'exogenous' drivers of agglomeration as distinct from the drivers which are inbuilt in the location processes themselves. Hence, they include sheer geographical aspects—e.g. a harbor or a river—and also infrastructural factors which are indeed man-made but change at time-scales plausibly slower than those characterizing the entry/exit flows addressed in our model. The intrinsic attractiveness parameter covers also the 'enabling conditions' and 'catalyzer' which Bresnahan et al. (2001) identify at the root of the 'novel silicon valleys' [e.g. locally available skilled labor and knowledge spillovers from thereby universities which—as Adams (2002) shows—are geographically quite sticky].[5] If location decisions are in some way related to localized knowledge spillovers, a_l captures indeed their location-specific pull. Finally, suppose that the industry described by the foregoing relation is 'small' as compared to the whole economy of any particular location. Then, a_l may also naturally account for pecuniary and non-pecuniary externalities—ranging from market availability to relationships with suppliers and customers—which are 'endogenous' to the location as a whole, but exogenous to any particular ('small') sector of activity.

Conversely, the parameter b_l measures the strength of agglomeration economies in location l: it is the amount by which the advantages obtained by locating in l increases as a function of the number of firms already located there. The larger is the value of b_l the higher is the incentive for firms to locate as the number of firms that have already settled there increases. In a way, this is 'agglomeration in action', with relative advantages of particular locations straightforwardly stemming from the very history of location decisions. Again, multiple (possibly complementary) dynamics are captured by positive b_l. Local network externalities are an obvious example, but equally important processes include the development of 'social networks' (Sorenson, 2005), 'horizontal' and 'vertical' development of knowledge clusters (Maskell and Malmberg, 2007), 'face-to-face' coordination and learning dynamics (Storper and Venables, 2004) and locally nested processes of 'corporate filiation' along the life cycles of industries (Klepper, 2001). Needless to say, the dynamic-increasing-returns story which our modeling skeleton is meant to capture is consistent with the well-known 'Silicon Valley' example but also with the dynamics of e.g. Emilia Romagna districts in Italy

---

5   On the localized dimension of knowledge spillovers see also Jaffe et al. (1993), among others.

(Brusco, 1982) or the german production clusters in Baden-Württemberg (Herrigel, 1996).

Finally, notice that in our baseline formulation we assume linear increasing returns to the number of location events at any one site. As a first approximation, the assumption seems to us as the most unbiased benchmark. However, the model, appropriately modified, can easily account for non-linearities in agglomeration economies and also 'anti-agglomeration' factors above certain thresholds (due e.g. to congestion phenomena or increasing rents).

Concerning the exit of incumbent firms from the economy, we also take the simplest possible approach and consider the

Assumption 3: *Each firm can be randomly chosen, with equal probability, to exit the economy.*

Moreover, in the following we assume that entry rates are positive, constant and equal to exit rates. The idea behind this assumption comes from the observation that the share of firms belonging to a given sector which enter and leave a given location in a relatively short period of time (e.g. a year) is typically much larger than the net growth of industry size, so that the time-scale at which spatial reallocations occur is generally quite short.[6] Broadly in line with this piece of evidence, we keep constant the number of locations L and the number of firms N present in the industry.

2.1. Analysis of the model

In our model at each time step a firm leaves the economy according to Assumption 3 and, after such an exit, a new firm is allowed to enter the economy according to Assumption 1. Notice that the entrant may well choose a location different from the one where 'death' occurred. Thus, the process is designed to capture both the genuine formation of new firms and the reversibility of locational decisions of incumbents which might close a production unit in one site just to open up another one elsewhere. Let us summarize assumptions and results discussed earlier in the following

Proposition 2.1: *At the beginning of each time period t a firm is chosen at random among the N incumbents to exit the economy according to Assumption 3. Let $m \in \{1, \ldots, L\}$ be the location affected by this exit. After exit takes place, a new firm enters the economy. The probability p_l to choose location l conditional on the exit occurred in m, according to Assumption 2 and (2.1), is defined as*

$$p_l = \frac{a_l + b_l\left(n_{l,t-1} - \delta_{l,m}\right)}{A + \boldsymbol{b} \cdot \boldsymbol{n} - b_m}, \tag{2.2}$$

where $A = \sum_{l=1}^{L} a_l$, $\boldsymbol{b} \cdot \boldsymbol{n} = \sum_{l=1}^{L} b_l n_l$ and the Kronecker delta $\delta_{x,y}$ is 1 if $x = y$ and 0 otherwise.

---

6   For a detailed comparative cross-country overview cf. Bartelsman et al. (2005).

In (2.2) $n_{l,t-1}$ is the number of firms present in location l at the previous time step $t-1$ while Kronecker delta $\delta_{l,m}$ in (2.2) implies that it is the number of firms present in location l after exit took place that affects the probability of the entering firm to be located in l. The assumption of non-negative b_l coefficients implies non-decreasing dynamic returns and, whenever $b_l > 0$, linear increasing returns to agglomeration.

If $n_{l,t}$ is the number of firms present in location l at time t (with $\sum_{l=1}^{L} n_{l,t} = N$, $\forall t$) the occupancy vector $\boldsymbol{n}_t = (n_{1,t}, \ldots, n_{L,t})$ completely defines the state of the economy at this time. Due to the stochastic nature of the dynamics (as implied by Proposition 2.1), the only possible description of the evolution of the economy is in terms of probability of observing, at a given point in time, one particular occupancy vector among the many possible ones.

Let $\boldsymbol{a} = (a_1, \ldots, a_L)$ and $\boldsymbol{b} = (b_1, \ldots, b_L)$ be the L-tuples containing the parameters for intrinsic attractiveness and for the agglomeration strength of locations $\{1, \ldots, L\}$. The dynamics of the system described in Proposition 2.1 is equivalent [cf. Bottazzi and Secchi (2007)] to a finite Markov chain with state space

$$S_{N,L} = \{\boldsymbol{n} = (n_1, \ldots, n_L) | n_l \geq 0, \sum_{l=1}^{L} n_l = N\}.$$

If $p_t(\boldsymbol{n}; \boldsymbol{a}, \boldsymbol{b})$ is the probability that the economy is in the state $\boldsymbol{n}$ at time t, the probability that the economy is in state $\boldsymbol{n}'$ at time $t+1$ is given by

$$p_{t+1}(\boldsymbol{n}'; \boldsymbol{a}, \boldsymbol{b}) = \sum_{\boldsymbol{n} \in S_{N,L}} P(\boldsymbol{n}'|\boldsymbol{n}; \boldsymbol{a}, \boldsymbol{b}) p_t(\boldsymbol{n}; \boldsymbol{a}, \boldsymbol{b})$$

where $P(\boldsymbol{n}'|\boldsymbol{n}; \boldsymbol{a}, \boldsymbol{b})$ represents the generic element of the Markov chain transition matrix. Let $\delta_h = (0, \ldots, 0, 1, 0, \ldots, 0)$ be the unitary L-tuple with h-th component equal to 1. Then

$$P(\boldsymbol{n}'|\boldsymbol{n}; \boldsymbol{a}, \boldsymbol{b}) = \begin{cases} \frac{n_m}{N} \frac{a_l + b_l (n_l - \delta_{l,m})}{C(\boldsymbol{n}, \boldsymbol{a}, \boldsymbol{b})} & \text{if } \exists l, m \in (1, \ldots, L) \text{ s.t. } \boldsymbol{n}' = \boldsymbol{n} - \delta_m + \delta_l \\ 0 & \text{otherwise} \end{cases} \qquad (2.3)$$

where

$$C(\boldsymbol{n}, \boldsymbol{a}, \boldsymbol{b}) = A + \left(1 - \frac{1}{N}\right) \boldsymbol{b} \cdot \boldsymbol{n}. \qquad (2.4)$$

The state space of the Markov chain that describes the evolution of the model is the set of all the L-tuples of non-negative integers whose sum of elements is equal to N. Note that when the number of locations L and/or of firms N increase, the dimension of the Markov chain becomes soon very large. For instance, for $N = 50$ and $L = 10$ the state space contains more than a billion states. On the other hand, according to Proposition 2.1, at most one firm is allowed to move at each time steps. This implies that the transition matrix of the chain contains many zeros and all transitions happen between very similar states, i.e. states that differ by the location of a single firm.

Moreover, Assumption 2 allows for a location l to have zero intrinsic attractiveness ($a_l = 0$). This kind of location is peculiar because, if at some point in time it is empty, it will never be occupied again. Indeed, according to (2.2), if $a_l=0$ and $n_l=0$ the probability of location l to receive the entrant firm is $p_l=0$. One can think of this location as if it had disappeared from the economy. Since the probability that any occupied location looses a firm is always positive, one should expect that, asymptotically, all locations with zero intrinsic attractiveness become empty.[7] Consequently we assume that all the locations present attractiveness strictly greater than zero and we present a complete characterization of the 'equilibrium' condition of the present model in the following

Proposition 2.2: *The finite dimensional Markov chain described in (2.3) admits a unique stationary distribution* $\pi(\mathbf{n}; \mathbf{a}, \mathbf{b})$.

If $\mathbf{n} \in S$ *it reads*

$$\pi(\mathbf{n}; \mathbf{a}, \mathbf{b}) = \frac{N! C(\mathbf{n}, \mathbf{a}, \mathbf{b})}{Z_N(\mathbf{a}, \mathbf{b})} \prod_{l=1}^{L} \frac{1}{n_l!} \vartheta_{n_l}(a_l, b_l), \tag{2.5}$$

where

$$\vartheta_n(a, b) = b^n \frac{\Gamma(a/b + n)}{\Gamma(a/b)} = \begin{cases} \prod_{h=1}^{n} [a + b(h-1)] & n > 0 \\ 1 & n = 0 \end{cases} \tag{2.6}$$

and $Z_N(\mathbf{a}, \mathbf{b})$ *is a normalization coefficient depending on the number of firms N and on the L-tuples* $\mathbf{a}$ *and* $\mathbf{b}$.

Proof: *See Bottazzi and Secchi (2007).*   ∎

3. Examples of small economies

The analysis in general terms of the model presented in the previous section would require a good deal of technical details which are beyond the scope of the present article. Here in order to appreciate its main properties, we consider the behavior of our model in some simple instantiations.

Example 1: no positive agglomeration feedbacks

Consider the simplest case with two distinct locations, 1 and 2. In this case the state of the system is completely described by the number of firms belonging to one location. Let n be the number of firms located in 1. From (2.5) it is

$$\pi(n) = \left(A + \left(1 - \frac{1}{N}\right)(b_1 n + b_2(N-n))\right) \binom{N}{n} b_1^n \frac{\Gamma(a_1/b_1 + n)}{\Gamma(a_1/b_1)} b_2^{N-n} \frac{\Gamma(a_2/b_2 + N - n)}{\Gamma(a_2/b_2)}. \tag{3.1}$$

---

7   For a formal proof of this statement see Bottazzi and Secchi (2007).

660 • *Bottazzi et al.*

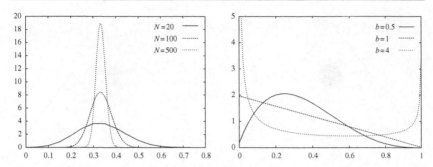

Figure 1. Two-locations model with $a_1 = 1$ and $a_2 = 2$. Left panel: probability density for the number of firms in location 1 for $b = 0$ and different values of N. Right panel: probability density for the number of firms in location 1 for $N = 100$ and different values of b.

If $b_1 = b_2 = 0$, the previous expression reduces to the binomial distribution of N independent trials with probability $p = a_1/(a_1 + a_2)$. This distribution has mean equal to Np and variance $Np(1 - p)$. Consequently, at equilibrium, location 1 is, on average, occupied by a number of firms proportional to its relative intrinsic attractiveness (cf. the discussion above), that is $n \sim a_1/A$.

The same property also applies to the general model with L distinct locations: when all the agglomeration parameters are set to zero, the average occupancy of each location is proportional to its intrinsic attractiveness.

However, the stochastic nature of the process implies that, in general, the actual number of firms observed in one location fluctuates through time. At the same time, when the number of firms increases, due to the Central Limit Theorem, the relative amplitude of these fluctuations decreases. An example is provided in Figure 1 (left panel) for the $L = 2$ case. As can be seen, when $N = 500$, the probability to observe a deviation larger then 10% from the average value of $1/3$ is extremely low.

Example 2: positive agglomeration feedbacks uniform across locations

Let us continue with the example in Figure 1, set $N = 100$ and consider different values for the agglomeration economies parameter b, keeping it equal across the two locations. As can be seen from the right panel of Figure 1, a slight increase in the value of b_1 is enough to generate a noticeable widening in the support of the distribution. Such a widening suggests a more turbulent dynamics, with larger fluctuations in the fraction of firms which occupy location 1. This phenomenon becomes stronger when the agglomeration parameter reaches a value comparable to the value of the geographic attractiveness ($b_1 \sim a_1$). In this case, the support spans the entire range $[0, 1]$ and fluctuations of any order are likely to be observed. We will briefly discuss some typical time series at the end of this Section. Here it is interesting to notice than when the parameter b further increases, the phenomenon is reversed: the set of points on which the distribution achieves relatively large values shrinks. In particular, the probability weights becomes increasingly concentrated

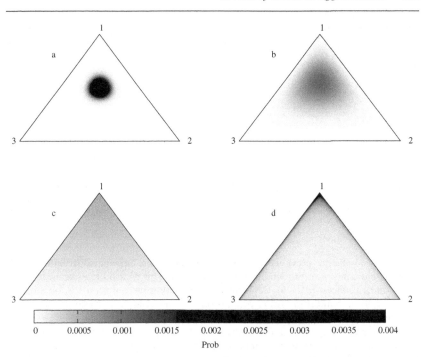

Figure 2.   Model with three locations and $N = 100$ firms. We set the geographic attractiveness as follows: $a_1 = 2$ and $a_2 = a_3 = 1$. Agglomeration parameters are set as follows: (a) $b_1 = b_2 = b_3 = 0$ (b) $b_1 = b_2 = b_3 = 0.3$ (c) $b_1 = b_2 = b_3 = 1$ (d) $b_1 = b_2 = b_3 = 2.2$.

in the two extremes, $n = 0$ and $n = 1$. The reason of this reversal is straightforward: when the agglomeration strength parameter is high, the most probable configurations are those that are associated with a highly concentrated industry. In the case of two locations and 100 firms, the occupancies displaying with the highest concentration are those near $(n_1 = 100, n_2 = 0)$ and $(n_1 = 0, n_2 = 100)$. As can be seen for the right panel of Figure 1, when $b = 4$ they are, by a large extent, the most probable ones.

The behavior described above is not restricted to the two locations case but has a general character. For instance, the same behavior is observed when three distinct locations are considered. This case is illustrated in Figure 2, where the probability of each fractional occupancy (f_1, f_2, f_3) is shown, where $f_i = n_i / N$. Of course $f_1 + f_2 + f_3 = 1$, so that these vectors all belong to the 2-dimensional unit simplex and can be represented using barycentric coordinates. In this coordinate system the triplet (f_1, f_2, f_3) is represented by a point inside the triangles of Figure 2 whose distance from vertex i is proportional to $f_j^2 + f_h^2 + f_j f_h$, where j and h stand for the other two vertices. A point inside the triangles of Figure 2 represents a possible distribution of the N firms across the three locations. The number of firms for a given locations decreases with its distance from the point.

Example 3: uniform agglomeration feedbacks with different intrinsic attractiveness

Set the geographic attractiveness of location 1, $a_1 = 2$, while the attractiveness of the other two locations is, $a_2 = a_3 = 1$. Consider the case of a homogeneous b. As can be seen in Figure 2(a), when the value of b is low, the distribution is concentrated around the center of the triangle. That is, the three locations contain roughly comparable shares of firms. Location 1 having the highest value of a, results the more attractive one, so that the probability mass is shifted toward its vertex. In this case, fluctuations are relatively modest. When b is increased, as in Figure 2(b), the picture changes: the probability is spread on a larger support. When $b = 1$, Figure 2(c), the distribution is uniform. This happens because the agglomeration strength parameter has, in each location, a value equal to the geographic attractiveness of that location.

For any $L > 0$, if $b_i = a_i$, $\forall i$, the generic expression (2.5) reduces to

$$\pi(\boldsymbol{n}) \sim \left(A + \left(1 - \frac{1}{N}\right)\boldsymbol{a} \cdot \boldsymbol{n}\right), \tag{3.2}$$

that is, it becomes proportional to an hyperplane. In terms of the fractional occupancy vector $f = (f_1, \ldots, f_L)$, the distribution (3.2) is defined over the $(L-1)$ -simplex and is sloped in such a way that its highest point (that is the point with greatest probability) is located in the vertex of the simplex associated with the most attractive location. In these circumstances when one moves away from this location the probability falls linearly: hence the distribution displays rather heavy tails. Such decay of the probability gets slower as the degrees of locational attractiveness become more similar. In particular, when all the parameter a's are equal, the distribution becomes uniform.

Example 4: agglomeration feedbacks with different intensities

In the foregoing examples we analyzed cases with identical b values only. In other terms, we assumed that the strength of agglomeration effects is equal in all locations. If one considers different values of b the picture changes. Consider the case with two locations. Assume $a_1 = 1$, $a_2 = 2$ and set $b_2 = 0$. In Figure 3 the probability distribution of the fraction of firms in location 1 is shown for different values of the parameter b_1. The left

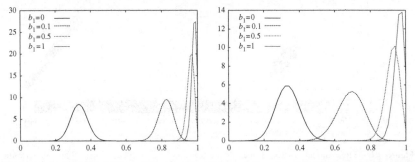

Figure 3. Probability density of the fraction of firms in location 1 for different values of b_1 with $a_1 = 1$, $a_2 = 2$ and $b_2 = 0$. The number of firms N is set equal to 100 (left panel) and 50 (right panel).

panel reports the distributions for $N=100$, and the right panel for $N=50$. As can be seen, in both cases, a small increase in the value of b_1 is enough to generate a big shift of the distribution to the right. This shift implies a larger average population for location 1. If the value of b_1 is further increased, the shape of the distribution starts to change, so that the probability of finding the large majority of firms in location 1 tends toward 1. Notice that when the number of firms is lower, the impact of the parameter b is somewhat reduced. This is not surprising, as the effective strength of the agglomeration coefficient depends on the number of firms composing the industry. Roughly speaking, the relative attractive strength is proportional to the total number of firms times the dynamic externality (Nb). An analogous example for the case of three locations is reported in Figure 4.

When local positive returns to localization are absent ($b=0$) the distribution is around the center of the simplex. Since the value of a_1 is lower, the probability weight is nearer to the $1-3$ line. A slight increase in the agglomeration strength of location 1 ($b_1 = 0.1$), is enough to move the weight toward the vertex with the same label (panel b). The shape of the distribution does not change and the effect is similar to the one obtained with an increase of the parameter a_1. If also the agglomeration strength of location 2 is increased (panel c), the weight moves toward the $1-2$ line and the shape

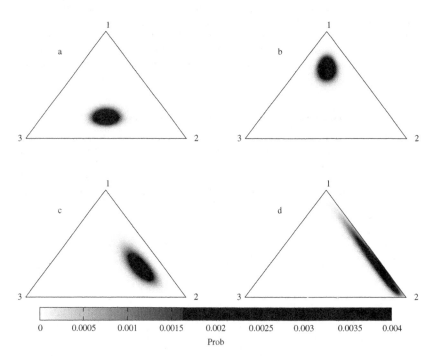

Figure 4. The model with three locations and $N=100$ firms. The geographic attractiveness parameters are $a_1=1$, $a_2=2$ and $a_3=2$. Agglomeration parameters are as follows: (a) $b_1 = 0, b_2 = 0, b_3 = 0$; (b) $b_1 = 0.1, b_2 = 0, b_3 = 0$; (c) $b_1 = 0.1, b_2 = 0.1, b_3 = 0$; (d) $b_1 = 0.5, b_2 = 0.5, b_3 = 0$.

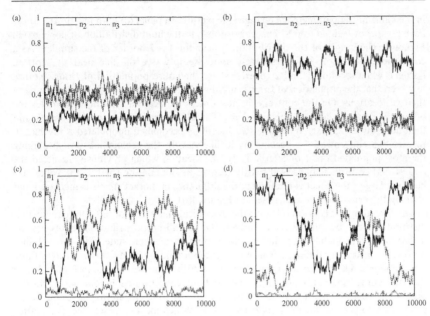

Figure 5. Temporal dynamics of the location firm shares for a model with three locations and $N = 100$ firms. The geographic attractiveness parameters are $a_1 = 1$, $a_2 = 2$ and $a_3 = 2$. Agglomeration parameters are as follows: (a) $b_1 = 0$, $b_2 = 0$, $b_3 = 0$; (b) $b_1 = 0.1$, $b_2 = 0$, $b_3 = 0$; (c) $b_1 = 0.5$, $b_2 = 0.5$, $b_3 = 0$; (d) $b_1 = 0.5$, $b_2 = 0.5$, $b_3 = 0$.

becomes more oblong. With higher values for b_1 and b_2 (panel d) the effect becomes stronger, and the probability weight is completely concentrated near the $1 - 2$ line. This implies that location 3 remains mostly empty, while the population of firms is distributed across locations 1 and 2, with a relative preference for the latter.

The differences in the shape of the limit distribution for different values of the agglomeration parameters b's we observed above do also reflect different dynamical properties of the model. As we have seen before, if one considers industries shares n_l/N, the possible occupancy vectors **n** for the L-locations case map in different points inside the $(L-1)$-simplex. When the probability weight of the limit distribution is heavily clustered around an interior point, like in Figure 1(a) or Figure 4(a), the model displays a rather stable distribution of firms, with relatively minor fluctuations around the equilibrium market shares. An example of this behavior is provided in Figure 5(a). These trajectories are obtained by simulating a model with $N = 100$ firms and three locations. The geographic attractiveness of the three locations are equal to the ones considered in Figure 4, namely $a_1 = 1$, $a_2 = a_3 = 2$. The dynamics of firm shares is reported for different values of the agglomeration parameters. The case of zero agglomeration strength—panel (a)—follows the pattern described above: the share of firms located in 2 and 3 fluctuates around 0.4, while the share of location 1 is around 0.2, reflecting the lower intrinsic attractiveness of this site. If we slightly increase b_1 we recover the dynamics of panel (b) the average fraction of location 1 increases, but the shares belonging to different locations remain rather stable in time. A further increase in the value of the parameters b changes the picture. In panel (c) both locations 1 and 2 have a value of b equal to 0.5. This corresponds to the limit distribution of panel (d) in Figure 4. The weight of the distribution is near the $1 - 2$ border of the simplex. As a consequence, location 3 is persistently almost empty (see the line near the bottom border), while location 1 and 2 (nearly) share the entire population of firms. Notice, however, that the population of firms is not distributed in time-stationary shares among the two locations. On the contrary, at any time, one location typically dominates the other and attracts a larger number of firms. This cluster can last for several periods, and then abruptly disappear. When the two locations become equipopulated a reversal in the relative concentrations become more likely, with the second location becoming the most populated one (or alternatively, the location which previously attracted the largest part of firms may as well swiftly recover its dominating role). If the value of b becomes larger, the effect is reinforced: the difference in market shares is increased and is likely to persist for a longer time: see Figure 4(d).

The foregoing analysis reveals that the dynamical characters of different equilibrium distributions can be quite diverse. In fact, the equilibrium distribution represents the unconditional probability of finding the system in a given state. This probability, however, can be very different from the average fraction of firms observed over finite time windows. The proper interpretation of a distribution like the one in Figure 2(d) is that the entire population of firms will end up concentrated in one large cluster, occupying exactly one location. Nonetheless, the three locations have the same probability to become the main industry cluster. Which location is selected, is a matter of history and chance. This highly concentrated state of the industry can last for several thousand of steps, but is only a metastable state. At some point, the sequence of random allocations can lead one of the other sites to catch up, in terms of number of firms, with the most populated location and, possibly, to overtake it. At this point, in relatively few time steps, this location may become the new cluster of the industry. Loosely speaking the time profile recalls what in biology are known as 'punctuated equilibria', with long period of relative environmental stability intertwined by relatively sudden transitions.

Just to give an idea of the time scale of the previous dynamics, consider that the typical turbulence in entry and exit dynamics in industrial sectors is around 5%. So, with a sector of 100 firms, five time steps of the simulations can be thought as representing one year of 'real' time. In the example above Figure 5(d), the metastable state in which the largest part of industry is clustered in location 1 can last for several thousand of steps. That would be equivalent to several centuries of historical time. So, even if these states are only metastable, they can be indeed considered stable for all practical purposes. Notice, however, that this relative stability is in place only for strongly 'polarized' industries: if the coefficients b are zero, or very low, then one can observe significant fluctuations also on relatively short time scales Figure 5(a).

4. Pure entry process and large industry limit

In the present section we study the asymptotic behavior of our model when we switch off the exit process and retain only the entry dynamics described in Assumption 2.1. This implies that the number of firms in the industry will increase linearly with time.

Assuming that the process starts with no firms present in the industry, if $n_l(t)$ is the number of firms present in location l at time t, one has $\sum_l n_l(t) = t$. Let $\boldsymbol{n}(t) = (n_1(t), \ldots, n_L(t))$ be the occupancy vector at time t, the probability that the next firm chooses location l is

$$p_l(\boldsymbol{n}(t)) = \frac{a_l + b_l n_l(t)}{A + \boldsymbol{b}.\boldsymbol{n}(t)}, \tag{4.1}$$

with the same notation used in Proposition 2.1. The function $p_l(\boldsymbol{x}, t)$ describes the probability that the new entrant firm locates its activity in l, given the time t in which it enters the industry and the actual occupancy of all the locations $\boldsymbol{n}$.

Consider now the conditional expected occupancy of location l at time $t+1$

$$\bar{n}_l(t+1) = E[n_l(t+1)|\boldsymbol{n}(t)].$$

It clearly depends on the previous occupancy $n_l(t)$. More precisely, it is equal to the number of firms previously present in l plus the average number of firms which entered that location at time $t+1$. This number (between zero and one) is exactly equal to the probability in (4.1). One can thus write

$$\bar{n}_l(t+1) = n_l(t) + p_l(\boldsymbol{n}(t)),$$

which in terms of the 'fractional occupancy' $\boldsymbol{x}$, where $x_l(t) = n_l/t$, reads

$$\bar{x}_l(t+1) = x_l(t) + \frac{1}{t+1}(p_l(\boldsymbol{n}(t)) - x_l(t)).$$

Substituting the definition of p_l in (4.1) and the previous equation becomes

$$\bar{x}_l(t+1) - x_l(t) = \frac{1}{t+1} \frac{1}{\frac{A}{t} + \boldsymbol{b} \cdot \boldsymbol{x}(t)} \left[\frac{1}{t}(a_l - Ax_l(t)) + \sum_{j=1}^{L} x_j(t)x_l(t)(b_l - b_j) \right]. \tag{4.2}$$

The previous expression can be used to derive some properties of the asymptotic behavior of the system.

Case 1: positive agglomeration feedbacks with different intrinsic attractiveness

First, consider the case in which at least one b is different from zero. In this case, the first term inside the square brackets vanishes, when $t \to \infty$, proportionally to t^{-1}, with respect to the second term. The same applies to the first term of the denominator in front of the square brackets. In this case, retaining only the leading terms in the asymptotic expansion one has

$$\bar{x}_l(t+1) - x_l(t) \sim \frac{1}{t+1} \frac{1}{\boldsymbol{b} \cdot \boldsymbol{x}(t)} \sum_{j=1}^{L} x_j(t)x_l(t)(b_l - b_j). \tag{4.3}$$

Notice that the coefficients a have completely disappeared from this expression and the asymptotic behavior seems completely driven by the coefficients b. In particular, if there exists a location l which possesses an agglomeration economy coefficient greater than any other location, that is $b_l > b_j, \forall j \neq l$, then, for this location, the right hand side of (4.3) is always positive, that is $E[f_l(t+1)] > f_l(t)$. This means that the expected value of the fraction of firms in l at the next time step is always *higher* than the presently realized value. This seems to suggest that, with probability one, $f_l(t) \to 1$ when $t \to \infty$.

The previous heuristic argument can be proved to be true. In Bottazzi and Secchi (2007), using formal results derived in Pemantle (1990), it is shown that for the pure entry process defined by (4.1), when the number of firms diverges, it is impossible to find finite shares of firms in two locations with different b's. In other terms, when the number of firms in the industry diverges, only two types of distributions can possibly be observed: a complete concentration in one single location, or a population of firms split across locations with the same coefficient b. Moreover, it is possible to show that only the locations with the *largest* agglomeration coefficients are populated in the limit. This finally proves our heuristic conclusion: if there exists a location whose b is larger than any other b, then, when the number of firms becomes large, the industry finds itself completely clustered in that single location. On the other hand, if there are several locations which share the highest coefficient b, a constant positive (in probability) flows of firms will be observed from the location with lower b's toward the location with higher b's. Consequently, as t increases, the industry becomes increasingly concentrated among the latter locations and, in the limit, only these locations retain a positive fraction of firms. Notice, however, that the previous analysis does not give any hint on the way in which the population of firms is distributed across these locations.[8] In fact, in tune with the original Polya model (Polya, 1931) all the shares between the most attractive locations are asymptotically attainable: history fully rules.

Case 2: no agglomeration feedbacks with different intrinsic attractiveness

In order to complete our analysis, let us consider the case in which all coefficient b's are equal to zero, that is the industry lacks any agglomeration effect in any location. Following our heuristic approach and setting $b = 0$ in (4.2) one has

$$\bar{x}_l(t+1) - x_l(t) = \frac{a_l - A x_l(t)}{A(t+1)} \tag{4.4}$$

The right hand side of (4.4) becomes zero when

$$x_l = \frac{a_l}{\sum_{j=1}^{L} a_j}, \tag{4.5}$$

so that, as expected, each location contains, asymptotically, a number of firms proportional to its intrinsic geographic attractiveness. In this case, indeed, the process retains no history: the choice of each agent is identical. At each time t, the distribution of occupancies follows a multinomial laws, with probabilities given by (4.5), so that the result follows.

To sum up, we started with a model with reversible choices and a finite population of agents, we turned off the death process—thus making location decisions irreversible—and allowed the number of firms to go to infinity. By doing that in absence of any agglomeration economies, the asymptotic picture boils down a distribution of activities

---

8   The interested reader find in Bottazzi and Secchi (2007) a discussion of the asymptotic distribution for large t is derived in analogy with a well-known Polya process.

somewhat in tune with the conventional notion of invariant 'endowment-based' comparative advantages of the different locations. Conversely under positive returns to agglomeration, the limit properties are shaped by the very location processes and their different pulling strengths. In particular, when more than one location posses the highest agglomeration force, one recovers the path dependency property typically characterizing polya urn models under increasing returns [cf. (Arthur, 1994) and (Dosi and Kaniovski, 1994)].

5. Industry-specific agglomeration economy

The model presented in Section 2 allowed for different agglomeration coefficients b in different locations. While this represents part of the whole agglomeration story, it is equally plausible to think of the agglomeration effect as a force acting inside a certain industry with a strength which does not depend from the specific location.

In our notation this means assuming a constant b across all locations. As showed in the previous section, this assumption is also suitable to describe cases in which the agglomeration economies are, to some extent, location-dependent but the size of the industry is large. In this case, only the site with the highest coefficient b's will contain a relevant number of firms so that, in discussing the empirical consequences of the model, one can assume all other sectors as having $a = b = 0$, that is remove them from the dynamics.

Let us consider different geographic attractiveness a_l for each different location l. The strength of the agglomeration economy is represented by an industry-specific parameter b, equal for all locations. If we assume, as in the previous sections, that all locations posses strictly positive intrinsic attractiveness a_l then we have the following

Proposition 5.1: *If $b_l = b \ \forall l \in \{1, \dots, L\}$ with constant $b > 0$, the stationary distribution defined in (2.5) reduces to*

$$\pi(\boldsymbol{n}; \boldsymbol{a}, b) = \frac{N!\Gamma(A/b)}{\Gamma(A/b + N)} \prod_{l=1}^{L} \frac{1}{n_l!} \frac{\Gamma(a_l/b + n_l)}{\Gamma(a_l/b)} \tag{5.1}$$

where b stands for the L-tuple of constant b's.

Proof: *See Bottazzi and Secchi (2007).* ∎

In this case locations do, in general, differ and are characterized by their specific attractiveness parameter a_l. In order to define a marginal distribution, one has to specify the parameter a of the location of interest.

Proposition 5.2: *The marginal distribution $\pi(n, a)$ of the number of firms in a location with geographic attractiveness* a *for the model in (5.1) reduces to the Polya distribution*

$$\pi(n; N, L, a, A, b) = \binom{N}{n} \frac{\Gamma(A/b)}{\Gamma(A/b + N)} \frac{\Gamma(a/b + n)}{\Gamma(a/b)} \frac{\Gamma((A - a)/b + N - n)}{\Gamma((A - a)/b)} \tag{5.2}$$

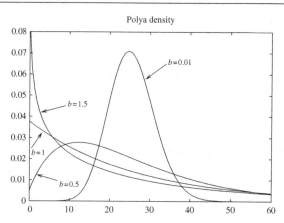

Figure 6. Polya marginal distributions (for different values of *b*). All distributions are computed for $N = 20,000$, $L = 800$ and geographic attractiveness $a = 1$.

and the average occupancy of site $l \in \{1, \ldots, L\}$ with attractiveness a_l reads

$$<n_l> = N \frac{a_l}{A} \tag{5.3}$$

Proof: *See Bottazzi and Secchi (2007).*   ∎

The marginal distribution in (5.2) depends on the total number of firms N, the total number of locations L, the two global parameters $A = \sum_{j=1}^{L} a_j$ and b and the location-specific parameters a_l. Figure 6 reports the marginal distribution (5.2) for different values of the parameter b. As we observed before, an increase in the value of b induces an apparent change in the shape of the distribution and, in particular, an increase in the size of its support again hinting at more turbulent dynamics of location.

The case is indeed interesting because it highlights the relevance for the ensuing distributions of the sheer strength of agglomeration forces, even when they apply identically in all locations.

6. Empirical issues for further research

An important feature of the family of models presented above rests in its ability to be empirically estimated on the actual locations of firms, plants and employment by sector and by site. The characterization of the stationary distribution derived in Equation (5.1) allows to go well beyond the exercises of indirect model validation generally found in the literature [for a discussion concerning NEG cf. Brakman and Garretsen (2006)].

As we have already began to do in Bottazzi et al. (2006) and Bottazzi et al. (2008) one may undertake at least four classes of empirical exercises.

First, one may statistically compare the whole shape of the empirical distribution of business plants with the theoretical one (Equation 5.1) in each given industrial sector.

This improves upon the existing empirical literature, where only synthetic agglomeration indices are derived [cf. Ellison and Glaeser (1999); Maurel and Sedillot (1999); Dumais et al. (2002); Overman and Duranton (2002); Combes and Overman (2004); Devereux et al. (2004) for exercises in a similar spirit].

Second, one may test simpler instances of our model obtained from the general one by switching off and on geographical and technological heterogeneity, thus gaining insights on their importance in determining the observed locational profiles. For example, one may start from an utterly simple specification where all agglomeration parameters are set to zero (i.e. $b_l = 0$, $\forall l$) and all locations possess the same intrinsic attractiveness ($a_l = a$, $\forall l$). This case is a sort of 'null hypothesis' benchmark whereby neither spatial specificities nor agglomeration processes play any lasting role. Nevertheless, this unrealistic specification allows to test our model against pure randomness in the vein of Ellison and Glaeser (1997, 1999) and Rysman and Greenstein (2005). Furthermore, in order to explore the relevance (or irrelevance) of geographical heterogeneity, one can consider models where locations are homogeneous and share the same geographic attractiveness $a > 0$, but agglomeration economies are now present in the form of an industry-wide agglomeration force measured by a single parameter $b > 0$. Finally, one can envisage models where one considers heterogeneous geographic attractiveness a_l for each different location l, while retaining an industry-specific agglomeration parameter b, equal for all locations. As we do in Bottazzi et al. (2008), on Italian data disaggregated by sector of activity and by location, one is able to disentangle the 'pull' of each location irrespectively of the sector of activity (call it the *urbanization effect*) from *sector-specific* agglomeration (or anti-agglomeration) forces. Hence, one is able to distinguish the 'horizontal' forces of agglomeration—stemming from e.g. inter-sectoral linkages and marshallian externalities—as distinct from sector-specific forms of localized increasing (or decreasing) returns, in turn, possibly associated with the characteristics of knowledge accumulation in each line of activity.

Third, revealing evidence is likely to come from the comparison of the distributions of agglomeration parameters across different variables. So, for example, comparisons between the location patterns of firms as compared to the location pattern of employment tell how much of the purported agglomeration forces are in fact 'internalized' within a few relatively big firms, or conversely, result in the proximity of several 'district-like' firms.

Fourth, the increasing availability of spatially tagged time-series allows an easy intertemporal application of the foregoing model asking how agglomeration patterns have changed over the years and exploring the evolution of the 'urbanization' and sector-specific forces.

7. Conclusions

In this work we have presented a family of models of evolutionary inspiration where boundedly rational heterogeneous agents decide to locate their production activities influenced by both the 'intrinsic' attractiveness of individual locations and by the number of firms already operating there, entailing the possibility of local dynamic increasing returns.

Firms enter and firms die. In fact, in the current specification, such a process keeps constant the number of incumbents but relaxations are easily possible. The Markov processes define a dynamic over a finite number of states whose limit distributions can be empirically estimated. In fact, the model allows to *empirically* address the question of how relevant are agglomeration economies driven by some form of localized positive feedbacks associated with the very history of birth and death of firms in each location. Together, it allows to empirically distinguish agglomeration forces which are, so to speak, 'horizontal', in the sense that they apply across sectors of activity within the same location and those which, on the contrary, are sector-specific.

Granted these achievements, one can think of several ways ahead. One such way is to make less rudimentary the representation of space by adding some notion of distance among sites with a related impact upon location decisions. A second development that comes to mind involves the explicit account of multiple sectors of activities with ensuing inter-sectoral spillovers. Third, an important extension involves the account not only of birth and death of firms but also of spatially nested growth [a sketch of a model along these lines is in Boschma and Frenken (2007), this volume]. However, possibly the most important step forward involves adding a *process of learning* through which firms could change their technological capabilities over time (i.e. innovation) and a process of *selection* driving the growth and death of each firm. Doing that would largely fulfill the objective of formalizing a fully fledged evolutionary model explicitly nested in space.

Acknowledgements

We gratefully acknowledge the support to the research by the European Union—STREP Project 'CO3 Common Complex Collective Phenomena in Statistical Mechanics, Society, Economics, and Biology'. Comments by Ron Boschma, Thomas Brenner, Alan Kirman, Yannis Ioannides, Ron Martin, Karl Schlag and two anonymous referees have helped along the various revisions of the work.

References

Adams, J. (2002) Comparative localization of academic and industrial spillovers. *Journal of Economic Geography*, 2: 253–278.

Arthur, W. (1990) Silicon valley locational clusters: when do increasing returns imply monopoly. *Mathematical Social Sciences*, 19: 235–231.

Arthur, W. (1994) *Increasing Returns and Path-dependency in Economics*. Ann Arbor: University of Michigan Press .

Bartelsman, E., Scarpetta, S., Schivardi, F. (2005) Comparative analysis of firm demographics and survival: evidence from micro-level sources in oecd countries. *Industrial and Corporate Change*, 14: 365–391.

Boschma, R. and Frenken, K. (2006) Why is economic geography not an evolutionary science? towards an evolutionary economic geography. *Journal of Economic Geography* 6, 273–302.

Bottazzi, G., Dosi, G., Fagiolo, G. (2006) On sectoral specificities in the geography of corporate location. In S. Breschi and F. Malerba (eds) Cluster, Networks and Innovation. Oxford: Oxford University Press.

Bottazzi, G., Dosi, G., Fagiolo, G., Secchi, A. (2008) Sectoral and geographical specificities in the spatial structure of economic activities. *Structural Change and Economics Dynamics*, forthcoming.

Bottazzi, G. and Secchi, A. (2007) Repeated choice under dynamic externalities. LEM Working Paper 2007–08. Scuola Speriore Sant'Anna.

Brakman, S. and Garretsen, H. (2006) New economic geography: closing the gap between theory and empirics. *Regional Science and Urban Economics*, 36: 569–572.

Brenner, T. (2003) An identification of local industrial clusters in germany. Papers on Economic and Evolution No. 0304. Jena, Germany: Max Planck Institute.

Bresnahan, T., Gambardella, A., Saxenian, A. (2001) Old economy inputs for new economy outcomes: clusters formation in the new sylicon valleys. *Industrial and Corporate Change*, 10: 835–860.

Brusco, S. (1982) The emilian model: productive decentralisation and social integration. *Cambridge Journal of Economics*, 6: 167–184.

Combes, P. and Overman, H. (2004) The spatial distribution of economic activities in the european union. In V. Henderson and J. Thisse (eds) Handbook of Urban and Regional Economics, vol. 4. North Holland: Amsterdam.

Devereux, M., Griffith, R., Simpson, H. (2004) The geographic distribution of production activity in britain. *Regional Science and Urban Economics*, 34: 533–564.

Dosi, G., Ermoliev, Y., Kaniovski, Y. M. (1994) Generalized urn schemes and technological dynamics. *Journal of Mathematical Economics*, 23: 1–19.

Dosi, G. and Kaniovski, Y. (1994) On 'badly behaved' dynamics. *Journal of Evolutionary Economics*, 4: 93–123.

Dosi, G. and Winter, S. (2002) Interpreting economic change: evolution, structures and games. In M. Augier and J. March (eds) The Economics of Choice, Change and Organizations: Essays in Memory of Richard M. Cyert. Cheltenham: Edward Elgar.

Dumais, G., Ellison, G., Glaeser, E. (2002) Geographic concentration as a dynamic process. *Review of Economics and Statistics*, 84: 193–204.

Ellison, G. and Glaeser, E. (1997) Geographical concentration in U.S. manufacturing industries: a dartboard approach. *Journal of Political Economy*, 105: 889–927.

Ellison, G. and Glaeser, E. (1999) The geographic concentration of industry: does natural advantage explain agglomeration? *American Economic Review*, 89: 311–316.

Frenken, K. and Boschma, R. A. (2007) A theoretical framework for evolutionary economic geography: industrial dynamics and urban growth as a branching process. *Journal of Economic Geography*, 7: 635–649.

Fujita, M., Krugman, P., Venables, A. (1999) *The Spatial Economy: Cities, Regions, and International Trade.* Cambridge: The MIT Press.

Herrigel, G. (1996) *Industrial Constructions. The Sources of German Industrial Power.* New York: Cambridge University Press.

Jaffe, A., Trajtenberg, M., Henderson, R. (1993) Geographic localization of knowledge spillovers as evidenced by patent citations. *Quarterly Journal of Economics*, 108: 577–598.

Klepper, S. (2001) Employee startups in high-tech industries. *Industrial and Corporate Change*, 10: 639–674.

Krugman, P. (1991) Increasing returns and economic geography. *Journal of Political Economy*, 99: 483–499.

Martin, R. and Sunley, P. (2006) Path dependence and regional economic evolution. *Journal of Economic Geography*, 6: 395–437.

Maskell, P. and Malmberg, A. (2007) Myopia, knowledge development and cluster evolution. *Journal of Economic Geography*, 7: 603–618.

Maurel, F. and Sedillot, B. (1999) A measure of the geographic concentration in French manufacturing industries. *Regional Science and Urban Economics*, 29: 575–604.

Nelson, R. and Winter, S. (1982) *An Evolutionary Theory of Economic Change*, Harvard: Belknap.

Overman, H. and Duranton, G. (2002) Localisation in U.K. manufacturing industries: assessing non-randomness using micro-geographic data. CEPR Discussion Paper 3379, Centre for Economic Policy Research.

Pemantle, R. (1990) Nonconvergence to unstable points in urn models and stochastic approximations. *The Annals of Probability*, 18: 698–712.

Polya, G. (1931) Sur quelques points de la theorie des probabilités. *Annals of Institute H. Poincaré*, 1: 117–161.

Rysman, M. and Greenstein, S. (2005) Testing for agglomeration and dispersion. *Economics Letters*, 86: 405–411.

Sorenson, O. (2005) Social networks and the persistence of clusters: evidence from the computer workstation industry. In S. Breschi and F. E. Malerba (eds) Clusters, Networks and Innovation. Oxford/New York: Oxford University Press.

Storper, M. and Venables, A. (2004) Buzz: face-to-face contact and the urban economy. *Journal of Economic Geography*, 4: 351–370.

[15]

Structural Change and Economic Dynamics 19 (2008) 189–202

Contents lists available at ScienceDirect

Structural Change and Economic Dynamics

journal homepage: www.elsevier.com/locate/sced

Sectoral and geographical specificities in the spatial structure of economic activities

Giulio Bottazzi [a,b,*], Giovanni Dosi [a], Giorgio Fagiolo [a], Angelo Secchi [b]

[a] Sant'Anna School of Advanced Studies, Pisa, Italy
[b] Dse, University of Pisa, Italy

ARTICLE INFO

Article history:
Received 1 October 2005
Received in revised form 1 May 2007
Accepted 1 May 2007
Available online 18 March 2008

JEL classification:
C1
L6
R1

Keywords:
Industrial location
Agglomeration
Markov chains
Dynamic increasing returns

ABSTRACT

This work explores the spatial distribution of productive activities in the Italian manufacturing industry. We propose an econometric model which tries to disentangle location-specific from sectoral drivers in the dynamic process of spatial agglomeration. The basic idea is that the former typically apply "horizontally" (i.e. across all industrial sectors), while the latter unfold in the form of non-decreasing dynamic returns to the current stock of installed business units. Three different specifications of the model are tested against Italian data on the location of manufacturing activities, studying the distribution of the number of firms and employees. Our results suggest that different locations exert different structural influences on the distribution of both variables. Moreover, a significant horizontal power of "urbanization", which makes some locations, especially metropolitan areas, more attractive irrespectively of the sector, does emerge. However, after controlling for the latter, one is still left with very significant sector-specific forms of dynamic increasing returns to agglomeration, which vary a lot across different manufacturing activities and which plausibly have to do with sectoral-specific and localized forms of knowledge accumulation and spin-offs.

© 2008 Elsevier B.V. All rights reserved.

1. Introduction

This work studies the structure of the statistical distribution of economic activities in the geographical space. In particular, we propose different econometric exercises, based on the stochastic Markov model of firm location developed in Bottazzi et al. (2007), aimed to disentangle two distinct classes of agglomeration drivers: "location-specific" drivers, which cut across different types of economic activities and "technology-specific" drivers, whose effect changes across different production sectors.

The ways economic activities are distributed over geographical space along relatively ordered patterns has been a concern for economic analysis at least since Alfred Marshall. Indeed, the first basic stylized fact of economic geography is that locational patterns, over the whole history for which we have some records throughout the world, tend to be much more clustered than any theory of comparative advantage might predict (cf. Krugman, 1991; Fujita et al., 1999, among many others).

At the same time, the evidence suggests a remarkable inter-sectoral variability in agglomeration structures. This applies across different countries such as the US, France, the UK, Germany and Italy: cf. Ellison and Glaeser (1997), Maurel and

---

* Corresponding author at: Scuola Superiore Sant'Anna, Piazza Martiri della Libertà 33, I-56127 Pisa, Italy. Tel.: +39 050 883365; fax: +39 050 883344.
  E-mail address: giulio.bottazzi@sssup.it (G. Bottazzi).

190   *G. Bottazzi et al. / Structural Change and Economic Dynamics 19 (2008) 189–202*

Sedillot (1999), Devereux et al. (2004), Overman and Duranton (2002) and Brenner (2006). That same evidence hints also at diverse degrees of "attractiveness" of different locations. So, for instance, there are several locations where business units belonging to almost all sectors are equally represented. On the contrary, in many other sites, agglomeration occurs only for business units belonging to a small number of sectors (in some cases, one or two). For example, as discussed in Bottazzi et al. (2006), in the Italian case a quite large fraction of sectors is not even represented in more than 50% of locations. Moreover, any measure of agglomeration appears to be quite stable over time, notwithstanding the great variability of agglomeration observed across locations and a turbulent underlying micro-dynamics with persistent flows of entry, exit, and variation in the relative sizes of incumbents (Dumais et al., 2002).

Taken together, the foregoing pieces of evidence suggest a general picture characterized by different drivers of agglomeration, which might be economy-wide, location-specific or sector-specific. Acknowledging the heterogeneous nature of the different agglomeration forces, in this work we investigate the relative role of location-specific mechanisms of agglomeration, independent of individual sectors and technologies *vs.* the sector-specific ones which apply across different locations within similar ensembles of production activities. The idea behind the present analyses is that cross-sectoral differences in agglomeration forces ought to be, at least partly, explained on the grounds of underlying differences in the relative importance of phenomena such as localized knowledge spillovers, inter- *vs.* intra-organizational learning, knowledge complementarities fueled by localized labor pooling, innovative explorations undertaken through spin-offs and, more generally, the birth of new firms.

The proposed econometric exercises are different specifications of the simple stochastic model developed in Bottazzi et al. (2007). This model is built upon the idea of dynamic increasing returns and shares its general structure and several hypotheses with the models explored by Arthur (1994), Dosi et al. (1994) and Dosi and Kaniovski (1994). However, in order to obtain empirically testable predictions, instead of the irreversible pure-birth dynamics characterizing those models, we consider a Markov dynamics where the reversibility of locational choices by firms entails a notion of stochastic equilibrium (i.e. invariant limit distribution). Bottazzi and Secchi (2007) show that, under rather general hypothesis about the selection mechanism characterizing a heterogeneous population of agents, this equilibrium is equivalent to the Ehrenfest–Brillouin urn-scheme (cf. Garibaldi and Penco, 2000 and Garibaldi et al., 2002). Building on this notion of dynamic equilibrium characterizing the spatial distribution of "productive units", which can be either plants or unit of employment, we obtain three different statistical models that we estimate using Italian data, disaggregated by "locational units" and by sector.

Let us illustrate the intuition behind our analysis borrowing from the "dartboard" metaphor discussed in the seminal work by Ellison and Glaeser (1997). Suppose that the economic space is a sort of dartboard where darts of different colors are thrown (i.e. economic activities belonging to different sectors are located). Here, the null hypothesis (i.e. "agglomeration does not matter") is a distribution of darts on the board solely due to random factors. In departing from pure randomness, however, one might observe systematic patterns ultimately due to three different factors. The first one has to do with the generic attractiveness (or repulsiveness) of some areas on the board: hence, one will systematically find there more (or less) darts *of all* colors than what sheer randomness would predict. That is, to trivialize, one will find "more of everything" in New York as compared to Pisa, irrespectively of any finer pattern of comparative advantage. Second, on the top of these generic locational patterns, one may observe specific patterns *distinctive of any one color* (i.e. sectoral specificities). Finally, the last concerns the different *size* of different darts (i.e. different degrees of lumpiness of single investments).

Ellison and Glaeser (1997, 1999) and Dumais et al. (2002) control for the latter, as captured by the concentration in plant size distribution, and study the importance of sector-specific agglomeration factors as compared to inter-sectoral, location-wide, ones (which they call "natural advantage" of a location).[1]

Our exercise largely shares a similar spirit, albeit with some distinct features. Indeed, we do not "wash out" any lumpiness effect. We do it partly out of necessity and partly out of choice. The constraint is that given our small spatial units (defined in terms of local labor mobility basins, typically smaller than most US counties) and our fine-grained sectoral partition, it is very hard to find the relevant sectoral/spatial breakdown of the data. At the same time, at a conceptual level, it is not entirely uncontroversial that one should take out the "size effect". In order to see this, think of, say, five entities located in one particular place which at some point merge into one. This does not mean that agglomeration has fallen, but rather that whatever forces driving agglomeration have now been internalized within a single firm. Thus, complementary information may be usefully obtained by studying, side by side, the agglomeration dynamics in terms of number of firms and of employment units.

The rest of the paper is organized as follows. After a brief description of our data, in Section 3 we present the basics of the stochastic model derived from Bottazzi et al. (2007) which constitutes the conceptual framework for the econometric specifications discussed in Section 4. In Section 5 we test these specifications against data on locational patterns of different sectors of the Italian manufacturing industry, using both firms and workers as proxy for production units. Finally, Section 6 concludes.

---

[1] Refinements and applications of this basic methodology are in Maurel and Sedillot (1999), Devereux et al. (2004) and Overman and Duranton (2002). See also the detailed reviews in Combes and Overman (2004) and Ottaviano and Thisse (2004).

G. Bottazzi et al. / Structural Change and Economic Dynamics 19 (2008) 189–202

Table 1
Descriptive statistics of the firm occupancy distribution by sector in 1996

Sector	Statistics of the occupancy distribution									
	Business units					Employees				
	Number	Mean	S.D.	Minimum	Maximum	Number	Mean	S.D.	Minimum	Maximum
15 Food products	75420	96.2	170.2	1	1854	434515	554.2	1254.2	4	20673
17 Textiles	36217	46.2	262.4	0	6675	345338	440.5	1980.5	0	38667
18 Apparel	49782	63.5	179.3	0	2297	346387	441.8	1036.4	0	9036
19 Leather products	25451	32.5	145.7	0	2311	230543	294.1	1282.1	0	17502
20 Wood processing	50662	64.6	119.0	0	1728	170294	217.2	405.6	0	3579
21 Pulp and paper	5268	6.7	26.0	0	577	85424	109.0	376.3	0	6943
22 Publishing and printing	28183	36.0	193.1	0	4162	175012	223.2	1549.3	0	35391
23 Coke, refined petroleum and nuclear fuel	825	1.1	3.1	0	45	24147	30.8	218.8	0	4496
24 Organic and Inorganic chemicals	7593	9.7	48.3	0	1197	209242	266.9	1976.7	0	51772
25 Rubber and plastic products	14626	18.7	64.7	0	1364	198401	253.1	909.3	0	17691
26 Non-metallic mineral products	30709	39.2	79.9	0	943	250824	319.9	877.7	0	17173
27 Basic metals	4034	5.1	19.5	0	353	136123	173.6	704.9	0	9843
28 Fabricated metal products	94771	120.9	323.3	2	5576	621642	792.9	2277.0	2	35873
29 Industrial machinery and equipment	42984	54.8	176.7	0	3605	554105	706.8	2447.4	0	46634
30 Office machinery	592	0.7	4.5	0	94	18609	23.7	257.4	0	6454
31 Electrical machinery	17312	22.1	91.5	0	2055	205797	262.5	1390.8	0	33261
32 Radio, TV and TLC devices	9773	12.5	48.8	0	980	103161	131.6	942.3	0	23064
33 Precision instruments	28280	36.1	142.0	0	2808	129448	165.1	834.1	0	17699
34 Motor vehicles and trailers	2261	2.9	12.8	0	297	185748	236.9	2186.6	0	57705
35 Other transport equipment	4514	5.8	17.5	0	166	100780	128.5	635.4	0	11525
36 Furniture	59627	76.1	257.8	0	4040	309911	395.3	1372.2	0	20509
37 Recycling	2061	2.6	7.5	0	105	8327	10.6	32.6	0	510

2. Data

This research draws upon the "Census of Manufacturers and Services", a database developed by the Italian Statistical Office (ISTAT) that contains observations about five millions employees and more than half a million business units (BUs).[2] Each observation identifies the location of the employees and of the business units at a given point in time (1996), as well as the industrial sector which they belong to. We consider data disaggregated according to the Italian ATECO classification (which corresponds to the NACE classification system). Among all industries, we focus on the manufacturing segment excluding, however, the sector "16—Tobacco products" which presents a too limited number of business units.

Business units and employees are classified with respect to 784 geographical locations. Each geographical location represents a "local system of labor mobility" (LSLM), that is a geographical area characterized by relatively high internal labor commuters' flows. LSLMs are periodically updated by multivariate cluster analyses employing census data about social, demographic, and economic variables (see Sforzi, 2000 for details). Table 1 reports for each sector a brief description of the occupancy distribution of employees and business units across sites.

3. A stochastic model of location with dynamic increasing returns

Consider a single-sector economy composed by a fixed number of location, L, which can be thought as production sites, and populated by a constant number, N, of heterogeneous agents representing different production units. Agents, which are assumed to be boundedly rational profit seekers, have to choose where to locate themselves among the set of available locations. The sequence of locational choices by agents is described as a stochastic process: at each time step an agent is chosen at random to die (i.e. to leave the location where it operates) and, once the exit took place, a new agent enters the economy selecting as productive location the one which maximize his expected utility. The possibility that agents posses heterogeneous preferences and beliefs is introduced by assuming that the expected return associated to different locations posses a common component and an individual, idiosyncratic, one. In turn, the common component is characterized by a constant term which describes the intrinsic "geographic attractiveness" of each locations and by a "social term" which depends on the actual distribution of agents across different locations and captures the strength of agglomeration forces. Bottazzi and Secchi (2007) show that, under rather general assumptions about agents' preferences structure, their locational choices are, in probability, driven exclusively by the common component of the expected individual return. Assuming a linear form for the social term, the new entrant chooses location $l \in \{1, \ldots, L\}$ with probability:

$$p_l \sim a_l + b_l n_{l,t-1}, \tag{3.1}$$

---

[2] Incidentally note that in the Italian case in more than 88% "business units" and "firms" coincide.

G. Bottazzi et al. / Structural Change and Economic Dynamics 19 (2008) 189–202

where $n_{l,t-1}$ is the number of agents present in that location at the end of the previous time step. The coefficient a_l represents the geographical attractiveness of location l and captures the gain that an agent on average expects by choosing to locate its activity in a given site irrespectively of the choices of other agents. This coefficient might be interpreted as controlling for intrinsic exogenous geographical factors (e.g., cost of inputs, infrastructures, etc.). Conversely, the parameter b_l represents the social term and measures the strength of agglomeration economies in a given location: it is the amount by which the advantages obtained by locating in a certain site increases as a function of the number of agents already located there due for instance to technological factors and externalities of various types. A larger value of the parameter b implies that the incentive for an agent to locate in that site increases faster with the number of agents that have already settled there.

Before we illustrate how this model can be used to build empirically testable specifications, two remarks are in order. First, notice that the new "entrant" may well choose a location different from the one where "death" occurred. Thus the model is designed to capture both genuine entry of new agents and the reversibility of locational decisions of incumbents which might exit from one site just to select another one elsewhere. Second, in this model one may refer to events of birth and death as concerning both firms (more precisely business units) and employment opportunities (i.e. the apparence and disappearance of employment units). In both cases the assumption that entry rates are positive, constant and equal to exit rates can be justified on an empirical ground. Indeed the share of firms (employees) belonging to a given sector which enter and leave a given location in a relatively short period of time (e.g. a year) is typically much larger than the net growth of industry size, so that the time-scale at which spatial reallocations occur is generally quite short.[3] Similar considerations apply to employment turnover whereby one observes quite high gross turnover even in presence of low net variations.[4]

In our model, the dynamics implied by the foregoing rules for entry and exit is equivalent to a finite Markov chain whose state space is the set of all the possible distributions of the N agents across the L locations. In particular, it can be shown (cf. Bottazzi and Secchi, 2007) that the assumptions of zero net-entry together with the reversibility of individual locational decisions and the constant impact of any single decision on the state of the system (implied by the Eq. (3.1)) guarantee that the evolution of locational choices is an ergodic process that allows for non degenerate limit distributions. Moreover, Bottazzi and Secchi (2007) show (cf. Proposition 3.4) that the process governing the evolution of the economy admits a unique long-run equilibrium (i.e. a unique invariant limit distribution) so that a probability π is assigned to each possible configuration $\boldsymbol{n} = \{n_1, \ldots, n_L\}$ where n_l is the number of agents in location l. This limit distribution $\pi(\boldsymbol{n}; \boldsymbol{a}, \boldsymbol{b})$ is analytically characterized as a function of the set of parameters of the model, the L-tuples of the geographic attractiveness $\boldsymbol{a} = (a_1, \ldots, a_L)$ and of the agglomeration strength $\boldsymbol{b} = (b_1, \ldots, b_L)$ of the L different locations. By varying the relative strength of geographical attractiveness and of agglomeration positive feedbacks this model is able to reproduce a rich variety of different patterns of spatial concentration. At one extreme, when agglomeration forces are very low, different locations attract on average a number of agents that is proportional to their geographical attractiveness, a_l. At the other hand, when agglomeration forces are very strong this model implies the emergence of highly polarized distribution, where few locations capture the great majority of agents.

To sum up, the dynamics governing the model does generate sharp empirically testable implications, in terms of the probability of finding the economy in a given state $\pi(\boldsymbol{n}; \boldsymbol{a}, \boldsymbol{b})$. Notice that this equilibrium (limit) distribution *does not* necessarily depict a long-run (limit) state associated to some 'old' or 'mature' industry. Since each entry/exit decision made by any one firm constitutes one time-step in the model, the invariant distribution describes the state of the system after a sufficient large number of spatial reallocation events have taken place (which may well imply a relatively short period of real time). Invariant distributions can then be directly compared with cross-section empirical data as far as they describe a system which is, on average, near its stochastic equilibrium state.

4. Testable instances of the model

The most general version of the model described in the previous section does contain a quite large number of free parameters. More precisely, one has to deal with two parameters for each location l: its geographic attractiveness a_l and the local strength of agglomeration b_l. In order to estimate such a model against empirical observations time series data on the number of firms in every single location would be required. Unfortunately, we do not have such information. Indeed, in the following we apply the model to a dataset, described in Section 2, which contains only one observation per location per industrial sector. This forces us to explore less general models containing a lower numbers of parameters. Consequently, in estimating our model on empirical data, we will mainly employ the marginal distribution of the number of firms in a given location. The probability to find n out to N firms in a location characterized by coefficients (a, b), $\pi(n; a, b, N, L)$, can be easily obtained from the limit distribution $\pi(\boldsymbol{n}; \boldsymbol{a}, \boldsymbol{b})$ (Bottazzi and Secchi, 2007).

---

[3] For a detailed comparative cross-country overview concerning firms turnover cf. Bartelsman et al. (2005). On the Italian case, see, e.g. Quarterly Reports by Unioncamere, "Movimprese: Dati Trimestrali sulla Nati-Mortalità delle Imprese", *Uffici Studi e Statistica Camere di Commercio*, Italy, various years, available on line at the url: http://www.starnet.unioncamere.it. Clearly the extent to which the assumption of zero net entry is realistic depends on the level of aggregation. At higher level of disaggregation one should in fact allow for (possibly endogenous) entry-exit processes with positive or negative net entry flows.

[4] On the employment turnover rates in Italy cf. Contini (2002) and more generally Davies and Haltiwanger (1999) for international comparisons.

G. Bottazzi et al. / Structural Change and Economic Dynamics 19 (2008) 189–202

In what follows we present different instances of our general model, starting with a simple (and, as we will see, utterly unrealistic) example, characterized by "homogeneous" space and constant returns to agglomeration, and progressively introducing more general models that differentiate locations and sectoral dynamics.

4.1. Model 0: homogeneous locations without agglomeration effects

Let us start with the simplest model where the agglomeration strength parameter is set to zero in any location and all locations possess the same geographic attractiveness a,

$$a_l = a > 0, \qquad b_l = 0 \quad \forall\ l.$$

This case represents as a sort of "null hypothesis" benchmark whereby neither spatial specificities nor agglomeration processes play any lasting role. In this extreme setup, firms choose locations totally at random. The limit distribution $\pi(n; a, b)$ will then be multinomial, while the probability to find n firms in any given location reduces to

$$\pi(n; a, 0, N, L) = \binom{N}{n} \left(\frac{1}{L}\right)^n \left(1 - \frac{1}{L}\right)^{N-n}, \tag{4.1}$$

that is a binomial distribution with N trials and probability $1/L$. Therefore, in a homogeneous-space model without agglomeration economies, the stationary distribution does not depend on the common geographic attractiveness a. The intuition is that since the asymptotic occupancy of a location is driven by its relative attractiveness rather than its absolute one, when the value of the common parameter a is the same, the locations are all and always equally attractive. Consequently, given the full symmetry of the model, the marginal distribution is the same for all locations.

4.2. Model 1: homogeneous locations with agglomeration effects

Next, let us consider a model where locations are homogeneous and share the same positive geographic attractiveness a, but one allows for agglomeration economies in the form of a positive and industry-wide agglomeration parameter b

$$a_l = a > 0, \qquad b_l = b > 0 \quad \forall\ l.$$

As in the Model 0 discussed above, also in this case all locations are identical with respect to the geographic attractiveness and the model is perfectly symmetric. The marginal distribution of the number of firms in a location $\pi(n)$ does not depend on the particular chosen location and can be shown (Bottazzi et al., 2007) to follow a Polya distribution

$$\pi(n; a, b, N, L) = \binom{N}{n} \frac{\Gamma(La/b)}{\Gamma(La/b + N)} \frac{\Gamma(a/b + n)}{\Gamma(a/b)} \frac{\Gamma((L-1)a/b + N - n)}{\Gamma((L-1)a/b)}. \tag{4.2}$$

where Γ is the Gamma function. In this case the marginal distribution (4.2) depends on the total number of firms N, the total number of locations L and the ratio of the two parameters a and b. As an illustration, we report in Fig. 1 the Polya distributions for different values of the parameter b. All distributions are computed according to (4.2), by setting $a = 1$ and with the same values for the parameters N and L (the latter values are chosen to be similar to the ones found in the subsequent empirical analyses). As shown, for small values of the parameter b the Polya distribution is similar to the Binomial distribution, with a positive modal value and its well-known "bell" shape. When the parameter b increases, the mode of the distribution moves

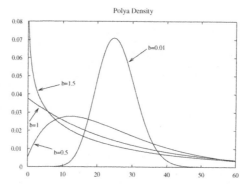

Polya Density

Fig. 1. Polya marginal distributions for different values of b. All distributions are computed for $N = 20000$, $L = 784$, and geographic attractiveness $a = 1$. Note that values for N and L are set to be similar to values empirically found in our subsequent analyses.

towards $n = 0$ and the upper tail becomes noticeably fatter. In tune with the intuition on the properties of agglomeration economies, an increase in the agglomeration strength parameter b yields a stronger "clusterization" of firms, i.e. a large number of firms in few locations (hence the fat tail), leaving, at the same time, more locations empty (hence the modal value of zero).

4.3. Model 2: heterogeneous locations with agglomeration effects

Let us now relax the assumption of homogeneity among locations and consider different geographic attractiveness a_l for each different location l. The strength of the agglomeration economy is still represented by an industry-specific parameter b, equal for all locations. In this case locations do, in general, differ and are characterized by their specific attractiveness parameter a_l. As it happens to Model 1, also in this case the marginal distribution of the number of firms in a location with geographic attractiveness a can be shown to follow a Polya distribution, given by

$$\pi(n; a, A, b, N, L) = \binom{N}{n} \frac{\Gamma(A/b)}{\Gamma(A/b+N)} \frac{\Gamma(a/b+n)}{\Gamma(a/b)} \frac{\Gamma((A-a)/b+N-n)}{\Gamma((A-a)/b)}, \tag{4.3}$$

where $A = \sum_{h=1}^{L} a_h$ (cf. Bottazzi et al., 2007). The marginal distribution in (4.3) depends, for a given location with attractiveness parameter $a_l = a$, on the total number of firms N, the total number of locations L, the global parameter b and the location-specific parameters a_l through their sum A.

5. Empirical analysis

To recall, the model presented in Section 3 describes the localization pattern of a single sector economy wherein the number of firms is kept constant and the economy is governed by a steady entry/exit process capturing both the flow of firms to and from the industry, and a reallocation process by incumbents across locations. As mentioned, the empirical flows in and out industries are quite high. Hence it is not implausible to assume that the actual observations tell us something about the underlying invariant distribution $\pi(\mathbf{n}; \mathbf{a}, \mathbf{b})$. Of course, this does not rule out the possibility that in the long-term the nature and intensity of agglomeration drivers may well change. Such longer-term modifications may be captured by corresponding changes in the a and b coefficients (eventually detectable by comparing estimates across, say, different decades). However, since our database contains information on one single year, we can only compute the occupancy value for a given location and a given sector at a given point in time. This means that neither a direct verification of the dynamic process described in Section 3 nor a maximum-likelihood estimation of the equilibrium distribution in $\pi(n; \mathbf{a}, \mathbf{b})$ are possible. We have therefore to resort to some derived statistics in order to fit our models, exploiting the rich cross-sectional information which derives from the presence of multiple sectors.

Let $n_{j,l}$ be the number of BUs in LSLM l operating in sector j, where $1 \leq j \leq 22$ and $1 \leq l \leq 784$ (cf. Section 2). Denote with $N_{.l} = \sum_j n_{j,l}$ the total number of BUs operating in location (LSLM) l and with $N_{j.} = \sum_l n_{j,l}$ the total number of BUs belonging to the jth sector.

For each sector j, we can build the occupancy frequency $f_j(n)$, counting the number of locations that contain exactly n firms operating in sector j. For instance, $f_3(0)$ is the number of locations that contain no firms of sector 3, $f_3(1)$ is the number of locations that contain exactly 1 firm operating in sector 3, and so on. The formal definition is

$$f_j(n) = \sum_{l=1}^{L} \delta_{n_{j,l}, n} \tag{5.1}$$

where $\delta_{n_{j,l}, n}$ is the Kronecker delta. From (5.1) it is obvious that[5]

$$\sum_{n=0}^{+\infty} f_j(n) = L \quad \forall j \in \{1, \dots, 22\}.$$

In Fig. 2 we show, as an example, the occupancy frequencies in four different sectors. Sectoral specificities are striking: both the shape of the distributions and the scales on the x and y axis are, indeed, very different. For instance, consider the ATECO 20 sector (wood processing): there are few locations which do not contain any firm belonging to this sector and the majority of locations contains 10–20 firms operating in it. In the case of the ATECO 28 sector (fabricated metal products) the picture changes. Here the number of empty locations is quite large, around 380, i.e. more than 50% of the total. For this sector, a location with 15 firms is a "crowded" one, and indeed $n = 15$ belongs to the upper tail of the frequency distribution. For sector 20 (wood processing), on the other hand, observing around 100 firms in a location is a quite common event. In general, a

---

[5] Note that one sets infinity as the upper bound of the summation even if, clearly, such a summation stops with the number of firms in the most populated location. For instance, if sector 3 has a location with 5000 firms and no locations with a larger occupancy, we get $f_3(5000) = 1$ and $f_3(n) = 0$, $\forall n > 5000$ so that the summation effectively stops at 5000.

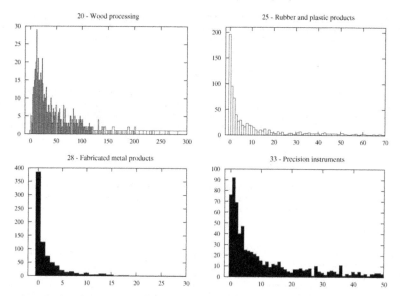

Fig. 2. Occupancy frequency in four different sectors. The largest locations have been removed in order to better focus on the behavior of the distributions near the origin.

frequency distribution with an high modal value around 0 and long tails represent a sector where the majority of firms is clustered in few places and the remaining locations are basically empty. On the contrary, a "bell-shaped" distribution is associated with a sector where the large part of the firms is evenly distributed in a relatively large number of locations.

In the rest of this section we will use the empirical occupancy frequency, defined in (5.1), to study the degree of agreement of the empirical data with the theoretical models presented in Section 4. Indeed, if $\pi(n)$ is the marginal distribution derived from a theoretical model and associated with a given sector, say j, the theoretical prediction for the occupancy frequency is $\pi(n) N_{j_*}$.

Since the support of the empirical occupancy frequency is in general large, due to the presence of few extremely populated locations and many (almost) non-populated ones, instead of using each occupancy number we consider occupancy classes (analogous to the often-used size classes) defined, for each sector, as the number of locations having a number of firms belonging to that same sector inside a given range. We define classes with ranges following a geometric progression

$$C_k = [2^k - 1, 2^{k+1} - 1), \quad k = 0, 1, 2, \ldots, \tag{5.2}$$

Table 2
Definition of the the first 12 occupancy classes

Class	Range
C_0	0
C_1	1–2
C_3	3–6
C_4	7–14
C_5	15–30
C_6	31–62
C_7	63–126
C_8	127–254
C_9	255–510
C_{10}	511–1022
C_{11}	1023–2046
C_{12}	2047–4094

and we report in Table 2 the first 12 occupancy classes as an example. The frequency of the different occupancy classes $f_j(C_h)$ for $h \in \{1, \ldots, 12\}$ can then be easily computed from (5.1). We have

$$f_j(C_h) = \sum_{n \in C_h} f_j(n),$$ (5.3)

where the sum spans over the integers belonging to each class range.

5.1. Model 0

Let us start with the simplest benchmark provided by Model 0, described in Section 4.1, where all locations are assumed to be homogeneous and the agglomeration strength is set to zero ($b = 0$). In this case no estimation procedure is necessary. Indeed, the marginal distribution only depends on the number of locations L and the number of firms N operating in the sector (see Section 4.1). For each sector j we can obtain a theoretical prediction for the class frequency directly from (4.1). One has

$$f_j^{\text{th}}(C_h) = \sum_{n \in C_h} L \pi(n; N_{j_{\cdot\cdot}}, L)$$ (5.4)

where $L = 784$ (i.e., the number of LSLM contained in our database).

Fig. 3 plots the empirical class frequency (5.3) together with the theoretical prediction (5.4) for two representative sectors. The observed agreement is basically nil and it is the same for all sectors. The theoretical frequency is proportional to the binomial distribution, and thus displays a bell-like shape with almost all the weight distributed in few central classes. This pattern, however, is never observed in empirical data. Note that this negative result is indeed an important one in that it falsifies any notion of random attribution of business units over a homogeneous space with null returns to agglomeration (see also Rysman and Greenstein, 2005).

5.2. Model 1

Next, we investigate the relevance of agglomeration economies by considering Model 1, described in Section 4.2, in which we allow for a non-zero agglomeration strength parameter $b > 0$. In this case, the marginal distribution of the model, defined in (4.2), depends on the parameters ratio a/b. This means that the model is insensitive to re-scaling, by a common factor, of both the locational geographic attractiveness a and the agglomeration strength b. Without loosing in generality, in the following analysis we set $a = 1$, and, for each sector, we estimate the best fit by varying the parameter b. For this purpose, we use the χ^2 statistics with the occupancy classes C_h as categories. For each sector, starting from the marginal distribution in (4.2), we can build the observed class frequencies $f_j(C_h)$ and also the theoretical class frequencies as

$$f_j^{\text{th}}(C_h) = \sum_{n \in C_h} N_{j_{\cdot\cdot}} \pi(n; N_{j_{\cdot\cdot}}, L, 1, A, b).$$ (5.5)

We then consider the χ^2 statistics

$$\chi_j^2(b) = \sum_h \frac{(f_j(C_h) - f_j^{\text{th}}(C_h))^2}{f_j^{\text{th}}(C_h)}$$ (5.6)

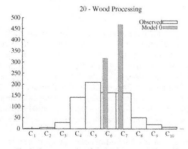
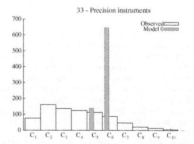

Fig. 3. Occupancy class frequencies computed on observed data (white bars) and estimated using Model 0 (gray bars).

G. Bottazzi et al. / Structural Change and Economic Dynamics 19 (2008) 189–202

Table 3
Summary statistics of estimates from Models 1 and 2, by sector (estimates are based on the *number of firms*)

Sector	# of firms		Model 1		Model 2, all sites			Model 2, no metropolis		
	All sites	No urban	b^*	AAD	β	$b^{*\,a}$	AAD	β	$b^{*\,a}$	AAD
15 Food products	75420	62751	1.17	0.0364	0.00	1.17	0.0364	0.00	0.95	0.0303
17 Textiles	36217	32043	6.05	0.0530	834.83	0.00	0.0108	0.00	6.76	0.0579
18 Apparel	49782	38137	3.42	0.0388	820.35	0.00	0.0084	0.00	2.48	0.0308
19 Leather products	25451	19791	6.57	0.0469	0.00	6.57	0.0469	0.00	5.57	0.0465
20 Wood processing	50662	42322	1.36	0.0366	652.54	0.06	0.0121	0.00	0.95	0.0342
21 Pulp and paper	5268	3794	5.63	0.0301	795.67	0.48	0.0144	0.01	3.50	0.0155
22 Publishing and printing	28183	16402	9.02	0.0785	954.12	0.51	0.0655	813.43	0.00	0.0154
23 Coke, refined petroleum and nuclear fuel	825	617	3.67	0.0111	786.78	0.46	0.0039	233.82	2.47	0.0067
24 Organic and inorganic chemicals	7593	4941	7.43	0.0525	812.40	0.29	0.0160	871.17	0.00	0.0104
25 Rubber and plastic products	14626	11324	4.49	0.0330	847.53	0.00	0.0071	854.77	0.00	0.0091
26 Non-metallic mineral products	30709	25140	1.55	0.0401	715.51	0.07	0.0058	697.11	0.08	0.0064
27 Basic metals	4034	3010	6.16	0.0297	1.42	6.16	0.0297	0.00	4.65	0.0199
28 Fabricated metal products	94771	74340	2.67	0.0465	784.81	0.00	0.0076	774.05	0.00	0.0096
29 Industrial machinery and equipment	42984	33157	3.47	0.0331	830.67	0.00	0.0065	832.34	0.00	0.0080
30 Office machinery	592	331	12.02	0.0091	0.00	12.02	0.0091	856.86	3.77	0.0039
31 Electrical machinery	17312	11906	6.44	0.0478	844.53	0.00	0.0093	849.32	0.00	0.0122
32 Radio, TV and TLC devices	9773	6546	3.53	0.0415	825.08	0.00	0.0131	0.00	2.37	0.0284
33 Precision instruments	28280	18713	4.80	0.0556	827.10	0.00	0.0134	818.89	0.00	0.0152
34 Motor vehicles and trailers	2261	1619	8.13	0.0297	961.57	0.35	0.0036	0.05	4.37	0.0076
35 Other transport equipment	4514	3500	5.43	0.0138	0.75	5.43	0.0138	0.34	5.12	0.0097
36 Furniture	59627	46460	3.26	0.0449	822.64	0.00	0.0139	0.00	3.28	0.0416
37 Recycling	2061	1568	3.19	0.0124	729.96	0.63	0.0043	1.04	2.67	0.0032

[a] Values smaller than 10^{-4} are reported as 0.0.

defined, for each sector j, as a function of the parameter b. Finally, we estimate the sector-specific optimal value b_j^* according to

$$b_j^* = \operatorname*{argmin}_{b \in R^+} \chi_j^2(b). \tag{5.7}$$

The resulting b_j^* for different sectors are reported in Table 3 together with the average absolute deviation (AAD) that represents a measure of the agreement between the empirical and the theoretical frequencies and is defined as

$$AAD_j = \frac{1}{K_j} \sum_h |f_j(C_h) - f_j^{\text{th}}(C_h)|, \tag{5.8}$$

where K_j denotes the number of classes in sector j. From Table 3, it is apparent the high degree of sectoral heterogeneity in both the strength of the agglomeration forces and in the ability of Model 1 to reproduce empirical distributions in different sectors. This is well illustrated by Fig. 4 showing, for six different sectors, the theoretical class frequencies obtained using (4.2) with the estimated value b_j^* (gray bars). Visual inspection of these plots reveals that the degree of accordance with the data dramatically improves as compared with Model 0. In particular, the agreement with empirical frequencies (white large bars) is, in general, good in the central part of the distribution while the fit remarkably worsens at the two extremes: in some sectors (for instance ATECO sectors 20, 26, 28 and 36) Model 1 largely overestimates the number of locations with few firms. In other sectors (for instance in sectors 20, 25 and 26), the model fails to capture the upper tail of the distribution, underestimating the occurrences of very "busy" sites.

5.3. Model 2

Ultimately Model 1, while significantly improving the ability to reproduce the observed patterns, seems unable to describe the tails of the empirical distributions, in particular when the latter displays both a large number of locations containing a relatively small number of firms and a few locations with an high number of firms. These tail effects cannot be replicated by varying the parameter b alone. Indeed if the value of b is large, Model 1 predicts the existence of several locations with a huge number of firms but, at the same time, predicts that all other locations are essentially empty. Conversely, a small value of b accounts for a large number of locations with few firms, but reduces the probability of finding occupancies close to zero. This difficulty can be partly tackled with Model 2, wherein different locations are allowed to have different geographic attractiveness, so that the observed clusterization of a large number of firms in a single location can be explained by the presence of a relative high geographic attractiveness, even if the sector is characterized by a mild value of the agglomeration parameter b.

The drawback of Model 2 as presented in Section 4.3, however, rests in its large number of parameters: one should specify the value of the sector-specific parameter b and the value of the parameter a for each location. Hence, one cannot hope to

G. Bottazzi et al. / Structural Change and Economic Dynamics 19 (2008) 189–202

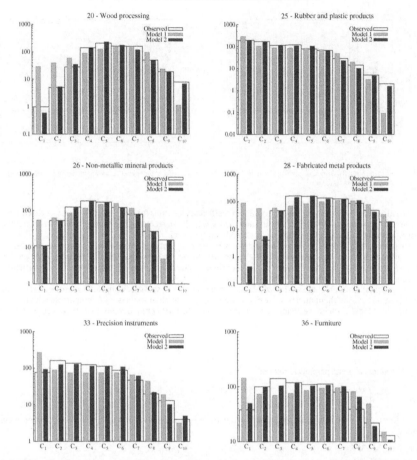

Fig. 4. Occupancy class frequencies computed on observed data (white bars) and estimated using Model 1 (gray bars) and Model 2 (black bars).

obtain the values of all these parameters from a χ^2 minimization procedure, as in (5.6), undertaken on each sector separately. Indeed, in our case the number of parameters is equal to the number of observations plus one (i.e. 785). In order to overcome this problem, we exploit the double disaggregation (by sector and by location) of our database.

First of all, let us make the following

Assumption 1 *(Urbanization effect).* The geographic attractiveness $a_{j,l}$ of location l for firms operating in sector j is proportional to the number of firms located in l belonging to all the sectors except j

$$a_{j,l} \sim \alpha_j + \beta_j \frac{N_{-j,l}}{N_{-j,\cdot}} \tag{5.9}$$

where, with the usual notation

$$N_{-j,l} = \sum_{i \neq j} n_{i,l}$$
$$N_{-j,\cdot} = \sum_{l} N_{-j,l} \, .$$

G. Bottazzi et al. / Structural Change and Economic Dynamics 19 (2008) 189–202   199

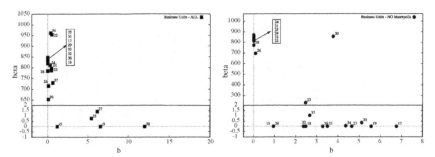

Fig. 5. Scatter plot of the b and β parameters estimated from model 2 for different sectors with(left panel) and without(right panel) the metropolitan areas (estimates are based on the *number of firms*).

As noted in Section 3, the geographic attractiveness coefficient a controls for all geographical factors that are not related with the sector under study. We can think to all such factors as both exogenous "geographical" and infrastructural ones, but also general demand-induced externalities or market proximity effects.

The linear relation in (5.9) depends on two sectoral parameters α_j and β_j. The parameter β_j represents a measure of the overall "pull" exerted by all business units from all other sectors on the locational decision of firms belonging to sector j. Parameter β_j captures what we call "urbanization effect": the overall installed base of production units in a particular location brings about a stronger attractive strength in sectors with a higher value of β.

The stationary distribution of Model 2 depends only on the ratios a_l/b so that, again, we can rescale all the parameters a and b by the same factor without affecting the distribution. In order to obtain values for b comparable with the ones found when estimating Model 1, where we assumed $a = 1$, we impose[6] the further requirement that the average value of a is 1, i.e.

$$\frac{1}{L}\sum_l a_{j,l} = 1$$

so that (5.9) reduces to a one parameter relation

$$a_{j,l} = 1 + \beta_j\left(\frac{N_{-j,l}}{N_{-j}} - \frac{1}{L}\right). \tag{5.10}$$

Substituting (5.10) in the marginal distribution (4.3) one can compute the theoretical prediction for the occupancy class frequency

$$f_j^{th}(C_h) = \sum_{n \in C_h}\sum_l \pi(n; N_{j,\cdot}, L, \beta_j, A, b). \tag{5.11}$$

Notice that in (5.11) a summation over l is required since different locations now possess different geographic attractiveness and, consequently, are characterized by different marginal distributions.

Finally, following the same approach described in the previous section, one can obtain an estimate for (b, β) as

$$(b_j^*, \beta_j^*) = \operatorname*{argmin}_{b,\beta \in R^+}\chi_j^2(b, \beta), \tag{5.12}$$

where χ^2 is defined as in Eq. (5.7).

Let us start by noting that moving from Model 1 to Model 2, one observes an unambiguous improvement of the ability of model to reproduce the empirical observations: this is clear from visual inspection of Fig. 4, where one observes a very good accordance of predicted frequencies (black bars) with the observed ones and is confirmed by the reduction in the average absolute deviation (AAD) reported in Table 3 together with the point estimates. Indeed, Model 2 seems able to overcome, at least in first approximation, the inability of the previous one to capture the tails behavior of the empirical distributions.

The distribution of estimates (b_j^*, β_j^*) is illustrated in Fig. 5 (left panel). A rather striking feature of the plot is the apparent polarization between a group of sectors which shows a nearly exclusive impact of "urbanization effect" and a second group wherein sector-specific agglomeration effects dominate. In that, the attribution of individual sectors to the two groups turns

---

[6] This assumption is made only for comparability purposes and does not affect our results in any respect.

Table 4
Summary statistics of estimates from Models 1 and 2, by sector (estimates are based on the *number of employees*)

Sector	# of employees		Model 2, all sites			Model 2, no metropolis		
	All sites	No urban	β	$b^{*\,a}$	AAD	β	$b^{*\,a}$	AAD
15 Food products	434515	357838	728.85	0.03	0.0104	0.00	1.69	0.0235
17 Textiles	345338	317929	0.00	6.45	0.0275	0.00	6.86	0.0299
18 Apparel	346387	292519	791.87	0.00	0.0102	0.00	3.19	0.0226
19 Leather products	230543	190829	398.67	4.81	0.0240	0.00	8.05	0.0250
20 Wood processing	170294	146997	0.00	1.57	0.0300	693.84	0.05	0.0122
21 Pulp and paper	85424	68215	0.00	7.72	0.0079	838.57	0.50	0.0099
22 Publishing and printing	175012	90325	680.44	2.87	0.0529	0.00	3.64	0.0288
23 Coke, refined petroleum and nuclear fuel	24147	15058	0.00	16.21	0.0117	1928.72	0.80	0.1080
24 Organic and Inorganic chemicals	209242	120570	843.29	0.31	0.0192	0.00	6.69	0.0114
25 Rubber and plastic products	198401	155614	0.00	6.07	0.0121	4.11	5.05	0.0067
26 Non-metallic mineral products	250824	216898	756.22	0.06	0.0072	1.28	3.76	0.0335
27 Basic metals	136123	108682	872.11	0.96	0.0062	1004.81	2.80	0.0146
28 Fabricated metal products	621642	502906	594.54	0.80	0.0273	0.00	2.90	0.0302
29 Industrial machinery and equipment	554105	430467	290.72	3.71	0.0223	0.00	4.58	0.0231
30 Office machinery	18609	9359	1083.65	15.05	0.0123	997.39	19.65	0.0098
31 Electrical machinery	205797	136008	821.10	0.15	0.0203	0.00	5.08	0.0122
32 Radio, TV and TLC devices	103161	53877	556.44	2.77	0.0373	0.00	6.79	0.0352
33 Precision instruments	129448	79972	660.57	0.81	0.0345	0.00	4.23	0.0365
34 Motor vehicles and trailers	185748	100842	0.00	15.09	0.0080	0.00	13.47	0.0073
35 Other transport equipment	100780	63304	0.00	11.59	0.0084	1218.21	3.79	0.0117
36 Furniture	309911	260270	0.00	4.66	0.0344	770.49	0.80	0.0487
37 Recycling	8327	6364	2.30	5.71	0.0114	144.00	5.14	0.0108

[a] Values smaller than 10^{-4} are reported as 0.0.

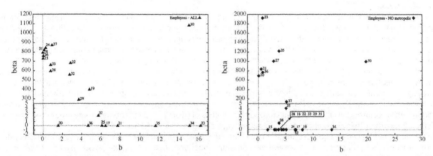

Fig. 6. Scatter plot of the b and β parameters estimated from model 2 for different sectors with(left panel) and without(right panel) the metropolitan areas (estimates are based on the *number of employees*).

out to be somewhat puzzling (for example "17—Textiles" and "18—Apparel" appear to belong, counterintuitively, to the former group). Such a puzzling evidence, in fact, may be largely the outcome of a sort of "horizontal pull" of metropolitan areas which tend to exert what we could call a *more-of-everything* effect (including more of the activities which are traditionally associated with sector-specific agglomeration phenomena, such as the mentioned Textiles and Apparel). In fact by removing the metropolitan areas[7] the picture significantly changes: cf. Fig. 5(right panel) and Table 3. When they are present, agglomeration effects tend to be mostly of a sector specific nature. Note that, even in those sectors where β is positive, urbanization tends to explain a relatively small part of the inter-site variation in locational intensities.[8]

In the previous analyses agglomeration has been measured by considering only the number of firms present in each location, and not their (relative) size. Further precious information, stemming from firm size distribution in different locations, may be obtained by estimating our model on employment data. That is, instead of using data on the number of firms belonging to any given sector that are present in each location, we can apply the model to the number of firm employees, per location and per sector. In this case agglomeration also captures the effect of increasing returns and internalization of productive activities within single firms. So, for example, in employment-based estimates the strength of agglomeration

---

[7] The Italian Statistical Office identifies 11 (out of 784 LSLM) Metropolitan areas around the cities of Bari, Bologna, Cagliari, Firenze, Genova, Milano, Napoli, Palermo, Roma, Torino, Venezia.
[8] Rough but illustrative evidence comes from the low goodness of fit of the linear relation between the share of activity of a particular sector in a given location and the share of the overall, excluded that sector, economic activity located there.

of a location with say one firm with a thousand employees is taken to be equivalent to another one with 100 firms of 10 employees each (which of course would not be the case in the previous estimation procedures).

The estimates of the (b_j^*, β_j^*) are presented in Table 4 and illustrated in Fig. 6 (left panel). Again the analysis of the universe of locations tend to be affected by the rather special agglomerative pull of metropolitan areas. If one excludes them, the picture, Fig. 6 (right panel), is relatively similar to the one stemming from firms locational patterns. Sectoral agglomeration effects seem to dominate.[9] And, of course, given the somewhat expansive notion of agglomeration, the estimates now capture also the effects of the location patterns of few but large firms (cf. for example, the sector "34—motor vehicles").

6. Conclusions

The aim of this work has been to offer rather general and empirically applicable formal tools able to assess the importance of agglomeration phenomena distinguishing between their location-wide and sector-specific drivers. Indeed, despite its simple structure, the model generates testable implications on the whole shape of the distribution of firms locational and employment choices in any given sector, a notable improvement over the majority of existing models which only provide insights on agglomeration indices (cf. for instance Ellison and Glaeser, 1997). The outcomes are quite encouraging.

First, the evidence from the locational patterns of Italian manufacturing industry adds very robust statistical support to the old claim that the spatial dimension provides structure to the distribution of production activities. Our results, indeed, strongly reject any hypothesis that observed locational patterns are explained by purely random factors for every two-digits manufacturing sectors.

Second, our model allows to disentangle the relative importance of the "pull" of particular locations from the agglomeration forces associated with each sector. The former include inter-sectoral linkages via technological and demand flows and other location-wide externalities which together compose what we have called the attractiveness of a location. We have found that such forces appear to matter in particular for metropolitan areas which tend to exert a powerful pull upon locational patterns irrespectively of the characteristics of sectors. This pull is horizontal in the sense that it tends to join together all activities.

However, when few big urban centers are excluded from the analysis the impact of horizontal agglomeration forces appears reduced so that we are able to detect also the important role played by the very history of locational decision within each sector. In several cases a form of dynamic increasing returns is observed, such that the number of production units belonging to one particular sector of production in a given point in time influences the probability that an additional unit will be located there. The strength of this effect seems to vary a good deal across sectors.

As such our findings suggest that beyond the location-wide externalities typically emphasized by the new economic geography models, the agglomeration dynamics is driven by sector specific mechanisms, plausibly related to localized forms of knowledge accumulation, spin-offs and formation of new firms. Such conclusions are indeed strengthened by the application of the model to the dynamics of employment: again, sector specific agglomeration forces appears to be powerfully at work, sometimes closely resembling the agglomeration profiles of (district-type) firms and some other time internalized within the employment strategies of relatively fewer but bigger firms.

The foregoing model can be extended in different ways. First, one might explicitly take into account interdependencies between locations and industries. In its present version, our model does not include the possibility that firms locational choices may be influenced by the choices made by firms belonging to different sectors, possibly located in neighboring regions. One might think to an extended version of the model where locations are positioned over some metric space, e.g. a two-dimensional lattice, and firms decisions (entry and exit) are somewhat correlated in space. Similarly, one might introduce urbanization economies whose advantages spill over to neighboring regions (unlike being concentrated in a given region). Second, one might try to explicitly consider the time dimension, and directly estimate the evolution predicted by the model instead of exclusively rely on the equilibrium distribution. Third, it would be interesting to obtain a testable specification of the model that considers the contemporaneous location of both business units and workers, so that a more proper account of the relative importance of agglomeration and scale economies could be derived. Finally, starting from the present analysis and the refinements suggested above, an interesting challenge might involve the development of an evolutionary inspired theoretical approach (Frenken and Boschma, 2007; Bottazzi and Dindo, 2008) which could provide a more reliable interpretative framework and make more effective economic and policy implications possible.

Acknowledgements

We gratefully acknowledge the support to the research by the Italian Ministry of Education, University, and Research (MIUR, Project EFIRB03GD), the Scuola Superiore Sant'Anna (Grant ERIS03GF), the European Commission (CO3 STREP Project, Contract No. 012410, NEST) and The University of Manchester. Part of the research that has lead to this work has been undertaken inside the activities of the DIME Network of Excellence, sponsored by the European Union. Comments by Thomas

---

[9] Also in this case the goodness of fit of the relation discussed in footnote 8 is relatively low.

Brenner, Yannis Ioannides, Karl Schlag, Alan Kirman and two anonymous referees have helped along the various revisions of the work.

References

Arthur, W., 1994. Increasing Returns and Path-dependency in Economics. University of Michigan Press, Ann Arbor.

Bartelsman, E., Scarpetta, S., Schivardi, F., 2005. Comparative analysis of firm demographics and survival: evidence from micro-level sources in oecd countries. Industrial and Corporate Change 14, 365–391.

Bottazzi, G., Dindo, P., 2008. An evolutionary model of firms location with technological externality. In: Boschma, R., Martin, R.E. (Eds.), Handbook on Evolutionary Economic Geography. Edward Elgar, Cheltenham.

Bottazzi, G., Dosi, G., Fagiolo, G., 2006. On sectoral specificities in the geography of corporate location. In: Breschi, S., Malerba, F. (Eds.), Cluster, Networks and Innovation. Oxford University Press, Oxford.

Bottazzi, G., Dosi, G., Fagiolo, G., Secchi, A., 2007. Modeling industrial evolution in geographical space. Journal of Economic Geography 7, 651–672.

Bottazzi, G., Secchi, A., 2007. Repeated choice under dynamic externalities. LEM Working Paper 2007–08. Scuola Speriore Sant'Anna.

Brenner, T., 2006. Identification of local industrial clusters in Germany. Regional Studies 40, 991–1004.

Combes, P., Overman, H., 2004. The spatial distribution of economic activities in the European union. In: Henderson, V., Thisse, J. (Eds.), In: Handbook of Urban and Regional Economics, vol. 4. North Holland, Amsterdam.

Contini, B., 2002. Osservatorio sulla mobilità del lavoro in Italia. Il Mulino, Bologna.

Davies, S., Haltiwanger, J., 1999. Gross job flows. In: Ashenfelter, O., Card, D.E. (Eds.), Handbook of Labor Economics. Elsevier, Amsterdam.

Devereux, M., Griffith, R., Simpson, H., 2004. The geographic distribution of production activity in Britain. Regional Science and Urban Economics 34, 533–564.

Dosi, G., Ermoliev, Y., Kaniovski, Yu., M., 1994. Generalized urn schemes and technological dynamics. Journal of Mathematical Economics 23, 1–19.

Dosi, G., Kaniovski, Y., 1994. On 'badly behaved' dynamics. Journal of Evolutionary Economics 4, 93–123.

Dumais, G., Ellison, G., Glaeser, E., 2002. Geographic concentration as a dynamic process. Review of Economics and Statistics 84, 193–204.

Ellison, G., Glaeser, E., 1997. Geographical concentration in U.S. manufacturing industries: a dartboard approach. Journal of Political Economy 105, 889–927.

Ellison, G., Glaeser, E., 1999. The geographic concentration of industry: Does natural advantage explain agglomeration? American Economic Review 89, 311–316.

Frenken, K., Boschma, R., 2007. A theoretical framework for economic geography: industrial dynamics and urban growth as a branching process. Journal of Economic Geography, 635–649.

Fujita, M., Krugman, P., Venables, A., 1999. The Spatial Economy: Cities, Regions, and International Trade. The MIT Press, Cambridge.

Garibaldi, U., Penco, M., 2000. Ehrenfest urn model generalized: an exact approach for market participation models. Statistica Applicata 12, 249–272.

Garibaldi, U., Penco, M., Viarengo, P., 2002. An exact physical approach for market participation models. In: Cowan, R., Jonard, N. (Eds.), Heterogeneous Agents, Interactions, and Economic Performance. Lecture Notes in Economics and Mathematical Systems. Springer-Verlag, Berlin/Heidelberg.

Krugman, P., 1991. Increasing returns and economic geography. Journal of Political Economy 99, 483–499.

Maurel, F., Sedillot, B., 1999. A measure of the geographic concentration in French manufacturing industries. Regional Science and Urban Economics 29, 575–604.

Ottaviano, G., Thisse, G., 2004. Agglomoration and economic geography. In: Henderson, V., Thisse, J. (Eds.), Handbook of Urban and Regional Economics, vol. 4. North Holland, Amsterdam.

Overman, H., Duranton, G., 2002. Localisation in U.K. manufacturing industries: assessing non-randomness using micro-geographic data. CEPR Discussion Paper 3379. Centre for Economic Policy Research.

Rysman, M., Greenstein, S., 2005. Testing for agglomeration and dispersion. Economics Letters 86, 405–411.

Sforzi, F., 2000. Local development in the experience of Italian industrial districts. In: CNR. (Ed.), Geographies of Diverse Ties. An Italian Perspective. CNR-IGU, Rome.

PART IV

ECONOMIC EVOLUTION AND THE ROLE OF HISTORY

[16]

The Grip of History and the Scope for Novelty: Some Results and Open Questions on Path Dependence in Economic Processes*

Carolina Castaldi[†‡] *and Giovanni Dosi*[‡]

Introduction

The very notion of multiple paths of socio-economic change ultimately rests on the idea that history is an essential part of the interpretation of most socio-economic phenomena one observes at any time and place. The property that *history matters* is also intimately related to that of *time irreversibility*. In the socio-economic domain and in many areas of natural sciences as well, one cannot reverse the arrow of time – even in principle, let alone in practice – and still recover invariant properties of the system under investigation. That is, in a caricature, you may get a lot of steaks out of a cow but you cannot get a cow out of a lot of steaks.

Such ideas of irreversibility and history-dependence are indeed quite intuitive and, as Paul David puts it, 'would not excite such attention nor require much explication, were it not for the extended prior investment of intellectual resources in developing economics as an ahistorical system of thought' (David 2001).[1] However, even after acknowledging that 'history matters' – and thus also that many socio-economic phenomena are *path dependent* – challenging questions still remain regarding when and in which fashions it does. In tackling path-dependent phenomena, an intrinsic difficulty rests also in the fact that in social sciences (as well as in biology) one generally observes only one of the many possible histories that some 'initial conditions' would have allowed. Moreover, is history-dependence shaped only by initial conditions, however defined? Or does it relate also to irreversible effects of particular unfolding of events? How do socio-economic structures inherited from the past shape and constrain the set of possible evolutionary paths? And finally, what are the factors, if any, which might de-lock socio-economic set-ups from the grip of their past?

In this chapter, partly drawing on other works by one of the authors (Dosi and Metcalfe 1991 and Bassanini and Dosi 2001) we discuss some of these questions.[2] In the next section we appraise the potential for path dependences and their sources at different levels of observation and within different domains. The following section presents a highly introductory overview of the different modeling tools one is utilizing in order to interpret the history-dependence of an increasing number of socio-economic phenomena. Next, in the penultimate section, we highlight some results and interpretative challenges concerning some path-dependent properties of socio-economic evolution. Finally, in the concluding section we discuss the factors underlying the tension, so to speak, between *freedom* and *necessity* in such evolutionary processes.

Sources of path dependence and irreversibilities

One indeed observes many potential causes for path dependence from the micro level all the way to system dynamics. Let us review a few of them.

For our purposes here, we refer to a broad definition of path dependence as dependence of the current realization of a socio-economic process on previous states, up to the very initial conditions.

Irreversibilities related to the decision-making of individual agents

Start by considering quite orthodox decision settings wherein agents hold invariant choice sets and preferences and are endowed with the appropriate decision algorithms. Suppose however that one of the following holds: (i) decisions are taken sequentially over time; (ii) they reflect uncertainty or imperfect information. Either of these conditions is sufficient for path dependence, in the sense that past decisions or past beliefs determine present and future decision processes.[3]

Individual learning

More generally, a powerful driver of self-reinforcing dynamics for individual agents or collections of them is any process of *learning*. If agents learn, their behaviours depend, other things being equal, also on their memory of the past, i.e. on initial conditions and on the history of their experience. This is a quite general property which holds irrespectively of the purported degrees of 'rationality' attributed to the agents themselves. So it is easily shown to hold under Bayesian learning whereby agents update expectations on some characteristics of the environment or on each other's features.[4] More so, path dependence applies under a wider class of learning processes whereby agents endogenously change also their 'models of the world', i.e. the very interpretative structures through which they process information from the environment (cf. the discussion in Dosi *et al.*, 1996). In all that, path dependence goes hand in hand with irreversibility: all agents with what they know now would not go back to yesterday's beliefs and actions even under yesterday's circumstances.

Local interactions

In many interactive circumstances one is likely to find that individual decisions are influenced by the decision of other agents, in ways that are not entirely reducible to price mechanisms.[5] One famous example concerns segregation phenomena. Suppose that an individual moves to a certain neighborhood only if at least a good proportion of his neighbors is of his same 'kind' (wealth, race, or other). If individuals are influenced by each other's decision in this fashion, homogenous neighborhoods tend to form. Hence, very rapidly, the housing configuration will lock into segregation of the different kinds of agents.[6] Similarly, another example of interdependence of preferences is provided by the way fashions, customs or conventions emerge. It suffices that individuals have some tendency to conform to the behaviour of people around them for a common behaviour to spread within the population of agents.[7]

Increasing returns

A quite general source of path dependence in allocation processes is associated with the presence of some form of *increasing returns* in production or in the adoption of technologies and products. The basic intuition is that production technologies (or collective preferences) in these circumstances entail *positive feedbacks* of some kind.

Recall for comparison the properties of *decreasing returns*, say, in production: in such a case, less input of something – for an unchanged output – means more input of something else, and, if returns *to scale* are decreasing, inputs have to rise more than proportionally with the scale of output. Conversely, under increasing returns, loosely speaking, 'one can get more with (proportionally) less' as a function of the scale of production or of the cumulated volume of production over time. In the economists' jargon increasing returns imply 'non-convex technologies'.

Non-convex production possibility sets may have different origins. They may stem from sheer physical properties of production plants. For example, in process plants output grows with the volumes of pipes, reaction equipments, etc., while capital costs tend to grow with the surfaces of the latter. Since volumes grow more than proportionally to surfaces, we have here a source of *static* increasing returns. Another example, still of 'static' kind, involves indivisibilities for some inputs (for example, minimum scale plants). The point for our purposes here is that under non-convex technologies history is generally not forgotten. The production system may take different paths (or select different equilibria) according to its very history.

The property is indeed magnified if one explictly accounts for the role of information/knowledge 'impactedness', of untraded interdependences amongst agents and of *dynamic* increasing returns.

Properties of information

The way information is distributed across different agents in a system, say a market or any other environment that provides the ground for economic interactions, together with the very properties of information, contribute to shape the consequences of economic interactions themselves.

As the seminal works of Arrow have highlighted (cf. the overview in Arrow, 1974) information is not an ordinary good which can be treated, say, like a machine tool or a pair of shoes. Shoes wear out as one uses them, while information has typically got a high up-front cost in its generation but can be used repeatedly without decay thereafter. Moreover information typically entails a non-rival use, in that it can be used indifferently by one or one million people. These properties entail decoupling of the costs of generation and the benefits of use of information. One could say that the cost of production of Pythagoras' theorem was entirely born by Pythagoras himself, while all subsequent generations benefited from it for free (except for their efforts to build their own *knowledge* enabling them to understand it).

At the same time, information (and more so knowledge[8]) might be appropriable in the sense that other agents might have significant obstacles to access it, ranging from legal protections, such as patents, all the way to sheer difficulty of fully appreciating what a particular piece of information means. This property exerts an influence opposite to the former ones in terms of incentives to profit-motivated investment in knowledge generation. Increasing returns in use and non-rivalry may produce 'under-investment' from the point of view of social usefulness, while conditions for appropriability may provide effective incentives for investment.[9] Together, path-dependent learning is influenced by the trade-off between 'exploitation' and 'exploration' (as Marcn, 1991 put it), that is between allocation of efforts to refining and exploiting what one already knows and investment in search for new potentially valuable information and knowledge (and equally important, by the belief agents hold about them).

Agglomeration economies

A number of case studies have posed the question of why specific production activities have concentrated in certain areas and not in others. The Silicon Valley and many other local industrial districts whose history is associated also with specific economic and technological activities, provide striking examples of 'agglomeration economies'. The common story starts from initial settlements and, possibly, some favorable conditions for specific activities. Then decisions to locate similar activities in the same region are re-inforced via (partly) *untraded interdependences* supported by spatial proximity. These may include stronger technological spillovers among producers (even when competitors), access to specialized labour force that tends to concentrate in the area and easier interactions with suppliers.[10]

Dynamic increasing returns

Technological innovation and diffusion are domains frequently displaying *dynamic increasing returns*, that is nonlinear and self-reinforcing processes that occur over time.[11]

The process of accumulation of technological knowledge

The processes of accumulation of technological knowledge typically display dynamic increasing returns: new knowledge cumulatively builds upon past one, and it does so in ways whereby in many circumstances yesterday's advances make today's improvements relatively easier.[12] The cumulativeness of technological learning is enhanced by the property of knowledge – as distinct from sheer information – of being partly tacit, embodied in the skills, cognitive frames and search heuristics of practitioners as well as in the collective practices of organizations.[13]

Moreover, as one of us argues elsewhere (Dosi 1982), technological innovations are often shaped and constrained by particular *technological paradigms* and proceed along equally specific *technological trajectories*. In all that, initial conditions – including the economic and institutional factors influencing the selection amongst alternative would-be paradigms – as well as possibly small seemingly 'random' events, affect which trajectories are actually explored. It is a story that one reconstructs at length in Dosi (1984) in the particular instantiation of silicon-based microelectronics, but it appears in different variants across diverse technologies.

Finally, throughout the whole process of establishment of new paradigms and the more incremental patterns of innovation thereafter, the emergence of networks of producers, suppliers, etc. together with other organizations (universities, technical societies, etc.) institutionalizes and so to speak 'solidifies' specific paths of technological learning.

The adoption of technology

Somewhat symmetrically, on the demand side of technological change, i.e. on the side of consumers and technology-users, a wide theoretical and empirical literature has emphasized the relevance of positive feedbacks: for the seminal explorations of the choice problem among alternative products that embody competing technologies, cf. Arthur (1994) and David (1985). Dynamic increasing returns and externalities appear to be at the core of the explanation of why the pool of users/consumers may select technologically inferior standards simply because that technology was the first to be chosen. Indeed, interpretations such as the foregoing ones place a good deal of path dependence weight, together with initial conditions, on 'historical accidents', i.e. more formally on small initial stochastic fluctuations that happen to determine the final outcome for the system. The story of the QWERTY typewriter keyboard is a famous one (David 1985). The keyboard was introduced in 1868. Alternative, more efficient, keyboards were brought to the market later, but did not succeed in replacing the initial one: QWERTY remained the dominant standard due to the 'lock-in' induced by the complementarity between installed base and specificities in the skills of the users.[14] Many other examples can be found when it comes to so-called 'network technologies' for which the issue of compatibility among the different components of the system is a crucial one (a discussion of some examples is in Bassanini and Dosi, 2001).

Properties of selection

Selection processes among heterogenous entities, both at the biological and economic levels, are another important source of path dependence. In the economic arena, selection occurs in multiple domains, concerning, e.g. products (and indirectly firms) on product markets; firms, directly, on financial markets; technologies, indirectly through the foregoing processes and directly via the social dynamics of inter-technology competition.[15] In fact selection processes may entail multiplicity of outcomes for the system[16] if different *traits* (or maybe, *genes*, in biology) – i.e. idiosyncratic characteristics of the composing entities of any agent – contribute in interrelated ways to the *fitness* (in biological terms) or to the *competitiveness* (in economic terms) of agents. This happens for example when there are complementarities between specific characteristics.

One way to represent the relationship between traits and fitness is in terms of *fitness landscapes*.

When the fitness contribution of every trait or gene is independent, the fitness landscape looks like a so-called *Fujiyama single-peaked landscape* (see Figure 8.1). Under the assumptions that higher fitness corresponds to evolutionary advantage in the selection process and that the biological or economic agents adapt in a fixed environment, then the system converges to the single maximum peak, whatever the rule of adaptation and whatever the initial condition.[17]

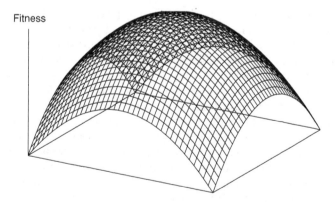

Figure 8.1 The Fujiyama single-peaked fitness landscape

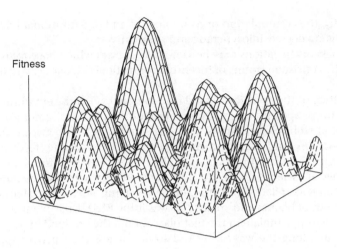

Figure 8.2   A fitness landscape with several local maxima peaks (Schwefel's function)

However, as soon as the fitness contributions of some traits depend on the contributions of other traits, i.e. *epistatic correlations* appear, then the fitness landscape becomes *rugged* and *multi-peaked*, as shown in Figure 8.2. In this case the initial positions in the landscape and the adaptation rules that underlie the movement of individual entities in the landscape together determine which (local) peaks are going to be attained by the system.[18]

The nature of corporate organizations

Organizations typically compete on a rugged landscape because of complementarities in the organizational components that contribute to their 'fitness' (or 'competitiveness'). Adaptation over rugged competitive landscapes may often yield lock-ins into different fitness peaks. And, indeed, interrelated technological and behavioural traits are likely to be a primary cause of the path-dependent reproduction of organizational arrangements (Marengo, 1996; Levinthal, 2000).

More generally, an interpretatively challenging view of economic organizations (*in primis* business firms) depicts them as *history-shaped behavioural entities*, carriers of both specific problem-solving knowledge and of specific coordination arrangements amongst multiple organizational members holding (potentially) conflicting interests.

Individual organizations carry specific ways of solving problems which are often hard to replicate also because they have a strong tacit and partly collective component. Organizational knowledge is stored to a significant extent in the organization's *routines*,[19] that is in the operating procedures and rules that firms enact while handling their problem-solving tasks.

Relatedly, the accumulation of technological and organizational knowledge is, to a good degree, idiosyncratic and cumulative.

Business organizations may be viewed as entities which *imperfectly* evolve mutually consistent norms of incentive-compatible behaviours and learning patterns.

Together, (i) the complexity (and non stationarity) of the environments in which firms operate; (ii) multiple 'epistatic correlations' amongst behavioural and technological traits; and (iii) significant lags between organizational actions and environmental performance-revealing feedbacks, all contribute to render utterly opaque the link between what firms do and the ways they are selectively rewarded in the markets where they operate. After all, 'epistatic correlations' on the problem-solving side blur straightforward attributions of blames and credits ('... was it the R&D department that delivered the wrong template in the first place, or did the production department mess it up along the way? ...'). And so do far less than perfect spectacles interpreting environmental signals ('... are we selling a lot, notwithstanding some temporary fall in profitability, precisely because we are on the winning track, or just because we badly forgot the relation between prices and costs ... ?'). In these circumstances path dependence is likely to be fueled by both behavioural ('procedural') and 'cognitive' forms of inertia.

This is also another aspect of the fundamental 'exploitation/exploration' dilemma mentioned above. Within uncertain, ill-understood, changing environments, reasonably favorable environmental feedbacks are likely to reinforce the reproduction of incumbent organizational arrangements and behaviours, irrespectively of whether they are notionally 'optimal' or not.

Institutions

In fact these latter properties are part of a more general point which applies to many other formal organizations, in addition to business firms – e.g. public agencies, trade unions, etc. – and to many institutional arrangements including ethical codes, 'habits of thoughts', etc.[20] As argued by David (1994), *institutions* are one of the fundamental *carriers of history*. They carry history in several ways. First, they carry and inertially reproduce the architectural birthmarks of their origin and tend to persist even beyond the point when the conditions which originally justified their existence, if any, cease to be there. Second, they generally contribute to structure the context wherein the processes of socialization and learning of the agents and their interactions take place. In this sense, one could say that institutions contribute to shape the very fitness landscapes for individual economic actors and their change over time. Third, at least as important, they tend to reproduce the *collective perceptions and expectations*, even when their mappings into the 'true' landscapes are fuzzy at best. At the same time, fourth, institutions also represent social technologies of coordination: as argued by Nelson and Sampat (2001), they are a source of (path dependent) opportunities for social learning.

In brief, institutions bring to bear the whole constraining weight of past history upon the possible scope of discretionary behaviours of individual agents, and relatedly, contribute to determine the set of possible worlds which collective dynamics attain, given the current structure of any socio-economic system.

Such path-dependent properties are indeed magnified by the widespread *complementarities* amongst different institutions which make up the socio-economic fabric of particular countries: cf. the evidence and interpretations put forward from different angles, including 'institutionalist' political economy (Hollingsworth and Boyer, 1997; Hall and Soskice, 2001; Streeck and Yamamura, 2001), game-theoretic inspired institutional comparisons (Aoki, 2001) and historical institutionalism (North, 1990). A thorough discussion of political institutions is in Pierson (2000) who has recently argued that politics is characterized by a prevalence of specific ('political') versions of increasing returns. The major roots are traced, among others, in the collective nature of politics (making for the political equivalent of network externalities), in the complexity of political institutions and in the possibility of using political authority to enhance asymmetries of power. All this, together with the usually short time horizon of political actors and the inertia of political institutions, makes the cost of reversing a specific course of events particularly high, and thus tends to induce widespread lock-in phenomena.

To repeat, complementarities generally induce 'rugged' selection landscapes. So, at this level of analysis, there is no unequivocal measure of any particular mode of organization of e.g. labour markets or financial markets or State/business firm relations. Revealed performances depend on the degrees of complementarity between them. But the other side of the same coin is the frequent presence of 'local maxima' in the admittedly rather metaphorical space of institutional arrangements where countries path-dependently converge.

Take an example among many and consider the institutional arrangements governing national systems of innovation and production. A recent literature has rather convincingly argued that they are major ingredients in shaping growth patterns of different countries and their specialization in international trade (Lundvall, 1992; Nelson, 1993; Archibugi *et al.*, 1999). Moreover, an enormous literature, involving sociology, political science and the political economy of growth, has powerfully emphasized the inertial and self-sustained reproduction of institutions and organizational forms as determinants of specific growth patterns of different nations, showing variegated patterns of 'catching up, falling behind and forging ahead'.[21] Still, political and institutional lock-ins are almost never complete, and what appeared to be 'stable equilibria' for a long period, may be quickly disrupted by a sequence of strongly self-reinforcing, possibly surprising, events. So, even when looking at growth performances across countries, recent history has shown the rise of new (sometimes unlikely) actors in the international economic scene as well as the decline of seemingly unlikely others.

Indeed, secular comparisons between the fates of e.g. the UK, Germany, and the USA; Russia and Japan; Argentina and Korea; etc. entail major challenges to the analysts irrespectively of their theoretical inclinations. So, e.g. while there is hardly any evidence on long-term convergence patterns in e.g. technological capabilities, labour productivities, per capita incomes, etc. equally, there is no easy story on the 'drivers of convergence/divergence' that may be mindlessly applied across different countries. 'History' – both economic and institutional – in our view, most likely matters a lot. But it does so in ways that certainly go well beyond any naive 'initial condition' hypothesis. For example, Korea in the late 40s had educational levels, (population-normalized) capital stock, etc. comparable to the poorest countries in the world and certainly of orders of magnitude worse than Argentina, but also of India. Given that, what are the differences in the socio-economic processes and in their forms of institutional embeddedness, if any, which account for such striking differences in revealed performances?

From micro behaviours to system dynamics, and back

In this section we have tried to flag out a few of the very many likely sources of history- (or, equivalently, in our jargon here, path-) dependence. Some of them straightforwardly pertain to the dynamics of individual agents and, more metaphorically, individual organizations. Conversely, other properties have to do with *system dynamics*, i.e. they concern some properties of the dynamics of *collections of interacting agents*.

The relationship between the two levels of observation however turns out to be a tricky one. Admittedly, economists still do not know a great deal about all that. Two relatively robust properties appear however to stand out.

First, system dynamics is generally shaped by the characteristics, beliefs, expectations of micro actors, even when such beliefs are evidently at odds with any reasonable account of the environment wherein agents operate. Hence, there is often ample room for 'self-fulfilling' expectations and behaviours, obviously entailing multiple *expectation-driven* equilibria or dynamic paths. A good case to the point is the wide literature on 'sunspot equilibria'.[22] The punchline is the following. Suppose some agents in the system hold the view that some 'weird' variables (e.g. sunspots or, for that matter, patterns in beauty contest winners or football scores, etc.) bear lasting influences on economic dynamics. What will happen to the dynamics of the system itself? The answer (obviously overlooking here a lot of nuances) is that the dynamics, or analogously, the equilibrium selection will most often depend upon the distribution of beliefs themselves, no matter how 'crazy' they are.

A *second* robust result concerns aggregation and the general lack of isomorphism between micro- and system-level behaviours. So, e.g. distributions of stationary ('routinized') micro rules may well engender an apparently history-dependent dynamics as a sheer result of statistical aggregation over a multiplicity of agents (Forni and Lippi, 1997). In a similar vein, seemingly 'well behaved' relations amongst aggregate variables – e.g. between prices and quantities – are shown to be the outcome of sheer aggregation over heterogenous, budget-constrained, agents (Hildenbrand 1994).

For our purposes here, these latter properties imply also that one may conceive different combinations between 'flexible', reversible, micro behaviours and powerful system-level path dependences, and vice versa (one proposes a taxonomy in Dosi and Metcalfe, 1991).

Last but not least, note that one ought to account for the importance of *macro-foundations* of micro behaviours. Collective norms, institutions, shared habits of thoughts, etc. have a paramount importance in shaping micro 'mental models', preferences and behavioural patterns: in that, all history frozen in incumbent institutions exerts its self-reproducing effects.

Theoretical representations of path-dependent processes

In the history of the economic discipline one finds lucid early accounts of path-dependent increasing returns. Adam Smith's story on the 'pin factory' is a famous one. In brief, the efficiency of pin production grows with the division of labour, the degrees of mechanization of production and the development of specialized machinery, which in turn depend on the extent of the market, which in turn grows with production efficiency.

Indeed throughout the last two centuries a few seminal contributions have addressed positive feedback processes in knowledge accumulation and economic growth.[23] (Recall also that, as already noted, increasing returns are not necessary for the occurrence of path dependence.[24]) Nonetheless, it is fair to say that increasing returns *and* path dependence have been stubbornly marginalized by the mainstream of economic theory for reasons that is impossible to discuss here.[25] At the same time, a facilitating condition for such a lamentable state of affairs has been for long time the lack of formal instruments accounting for path-dependent processes. However, things have recently changed in this latter respect.

Formal tools

A set of powerful formal results in mathematical modeling tools has provided new ways of representing both nonlinear deterministic dynamics and stochastic ones. Let us provide here a brief, very simple, overview of some helpful formal tools.

Nonlinear dynamics and chaos

Suppose one can represent system dynamics through a *transition function f* that determines the value of the variable at time $t + 1$ in relation to its value at time t:

$$x_{t+1} = f(x_t) \tag{1}$$

110   *Economics of Continuity*

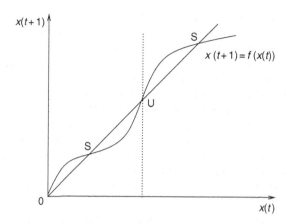

Figure 8.3   A nonlinear transition function that implies multiple steady states*
* Stable and unstable steady states are indicated with S and U, respectively.

Define a *steady state* as a point x^* for which $x^* = f(x^*)$, i.e. a point where the system settles. If the transition function is linear, there exists only one steady state (whether stable or unstable). Multiplicity of steady states occurs as soon as the transition function presents nonlinearities (an example is shown in Figure 8.3). In a deterministic setting, the steady state to which the system will eventually converge is going to be determined solely by initial conditions. An important property of this system is its full predictability. Given the initial condition and the transition function, one in principle knows the final state to which the system will get and also the exact path followed to reach it.

The growing understanding of the properties of nonlinear dynamic systems has brought new insights and tools of analysis.[26] Moreover, as widely shown in fields like physics, chemistry and molecular biology, nonlinear processes can result in 'self-organization' of systems as a far-from-equilibrium property. Highly complex behaviours can arise even with very simple transition functions, the best known example being the logistic function. Such systems however may be highly sensitive to small disturbances in initial conditions and display a multiplicity of patterns in their long-term behaviour. Arbitrarily small initial differences can result in cumulatively increasing differences in the historical trajectories *via* self-reinforcing dynamics. The best known examples are *chaotic* dynamics.

A definition of chaos rests on the sensitive dependence of the underlying dynamical systems on initial conditions, in the sense that arbitrarily small differences lead to increasingly divergent paths in the system dynamics. Hence, chaotic patterns are those whereby the path of the dynamical system is fully unpredictable in the long term, yet with a characteristic structure that differentiates it from a purely casual behaviour and allows short-term predictability.

Stochastic processes

A distinct potential source of path dependence in the dynamics relates to the impact of *ex-ante* unpredictable shocks occurring throughout the process. The property is captured by various types of stochastic models, possibly with time-dependence or state-dependence of probability distributions of shocks themselves.[27]

David (2001) provides two complementary definitions of path-dependent processes, namely:

> *A negative definition:* Processes that are non-ergodic, and thus unable to shake free of their history, are said to yield path dependent outcomes.
>
> ... *A positive definition:* A path dependent stochastic process is one whose asymptotic distribution evolves as a consequence (function of) the process' own history.

The key concept here is that of *ergodicity*. Intuitively, a process is ergodic if in the limit its underlying distribution is not affected by events happened 'along the way' (we provide a more formal definition in the Appendix). This means that in the long run, initial history does not affect the likelihood of the different possible states in which the system may end up. The opposite applies to *non-ergodicity*.

In the theory of stochastic processes, *Markov processes* provide a sort of benchmark for analysis. In a canonic Markov process, the 'transition probabilities' that define the dynamics of the system depend only on the current state of the system, regardless of the whole history of previously visited states. Think of the simple case of a 'random walk', which can be thought to describe the motion of a particle along a line. The particle can either jump up or down, with respective probabilities p and q. These transition probabilities characterize the motion from t to $t + 1$ and only look at one time step, irrespectively to the previous positions occupied by the particle.[28] Conversely, history of previous events is relevant in non-Markovian processes, which have been exploited to model path-dependent economic phenomena. We provide two illustrative examples that also relate to previously discussed sources of path dependence.

The first example concerns *Polya urn processes*.[29] Arthur *et al.* (1983) have utilized them to model increasing returns in adoption of alternative technologies when the incentive to adopt each technology depends on the number of previous adopters. The setting involves an urn containing balls of different colors. Basically, one can think of different colors as alternative technologies. Each agent draws a ball and then inserts a ball of the same color back in the urn. Then every time that a technology is chosen, the probability that the same technology is chosen at the next time step increases. One can then prove that under rather general conditions the limit state of the system is the dominance of one of the technologies. Being the limit state an absorbing one, this formally defines a process of lock-in in one techno-logical monopoly. The second example is provided by the so-called *voter model*.[30] The model entails random local interactions between agents in a finite population. The basic idea is that agents vote depending on the voting fre-quencies of their 'neighbours'. In one and two dimensional spaces, it can be proved that the system clusters into an homogenous setting where all agents vote for the same party. Local positive feedbacks represent the key for explain-ing locking in this irreversible state. At the same time, initial conditions and the particular unfolding of micro-choices determine which of the states is attained within any one 'history' (David, 2001 discusses the socio-economic importance of the model).

Understanding path dependence in economic evolution: some results and challenges

The foregoing examples of formal modeling of path-dependent economic processes ought to be taken as promising even if still rather rudimentary attempts to grasp some fundamental properties of economic dynamics. They certainly fall short of any thorough account of socio-economic evolution (compare for example the 'grand' evolutionary research program as outlined in Dosi and Winter, 2002) which in turn builds upon the seminal Nelson and Winter, 1982). However, they already offer precious insights, and together, interesting interpretative puzzles.

Degrees of history dependence and their detection

David (2001) offers the following categorization of the degree of 'historicity', i.e. of the strength of the influence of the past in economic dynamics:

> *weak history* goes so far as to recognize 'time's arrow' (the rooted sense of difference between past and present) … ;
>
> *moderate to mild history* acknowledges that instantaneous transitions between discrete states have high and possibly infinite adjustment costs, so that it would take time and a sequence of motions to attain a terminal state (family size, capital stock, reputation, educational or skill level) – whence we have the notion of a dynamic path being an object of choice;
>
> *strong history* recognizes that some dynamical systems satisfy the conditions for path dependence of outcomes, or of transition probabilities and asymptotic distributions of outcomes. (italics added)

Within the broad class of processes displaying *some* forms of history depen-dence, *how much* does history actually matter? Which one of the foregoing 'degrees of historicity' apply to which phenomena?

In order to address such questions, a major methodological issue immediately springs up. Social scientists (to repeat, as well as biologists) most often observe just one historical path. When very lucky, evolutionary biologists neatly catch – as Darwin was able to do – just some independent (on biological scales, rather short) branches of the same evolutionary process. Social scientists find it even harder to observe and compare alternative sample paths. Hence, how can one be sure that what one seemingly detects in the actual history was not the only feasible path given the system constraints?

For sure, anthropologists have a rich comparative evidence, but it is very hard to bring it to bear on the issues of path dependence discussed here. A comparatively more modest, albeit still daunting, task concerns the analysis of technological and institutional dynamics within the domain of modern, mostly 'capitalist', history. Have they been the only feasible paths given the system constraints? Or, conversely, can one think of other dynamics – notionally feasible on the grounds of initial conditions – whose exploration has been ruled out by any actual sequence of events?

Even more specifically, why have historically observed technologies been chosen? Were they 'intrinsically' better in ways increasingly transparent to the involved actors? Or, conversely, did they become dominant as a result of multiple (mistake ridden) micro decisions, piecemeal adjustments, co-emergence of institutional structures, etc. – irrespectively of the presence of notionally 'superior', relatively unexplored activities? (Of course similar questions apply to the emergence and persistence of particular institutions, forms of corporate organizations, etc.)

Competing answers to this type of questions and competing methodologies of investigation clearly fold together.

At one extreme, a style of interpretation focuses on the final outcome of whatever process, and – when faced with notional, seemingly 'better' alternatives – it tries to evaluate the 'remediability' of the *status quo*. Under high or prohibitive remediation costs and in absence of striking 'irrationalities' along the past decisions history, one next declares the absence of path dependence. This extreme view tries to justify and explain any end-state of the system as being the best possible outcome given the (perceived) constraints by imperfectly informed but fully 'rational' agents along the whole path. The view, emphatically illustrated in Liebowitz and Margolis (1990, 1995)[31] basically aims at rationalizing whatever one observes as an equilibrium and, at the same time, at attributing rational purposefulness to all actions which led to any present state.

On all that, David (2001) and Dosi (1997) coincide in the skepticism about any Panglossian interpretations of history as 'the best which could have happened', mainly 'proved' by the argument that 'rational agents' would not have allowed anything short of the optimal to happen (compared with Voltaire's *Candide* on the virtues of Divine Providence).

Conversely, a distinct perspective rather bravely tries to face the *challenge of counter-factuals* ('... what would have happened if ...'): hence it focuses on the actual thread of events, on the possible amplification mechanisms linking them, and together, on the (varying) potential leverage that individuals and collective actors retain of influencing selection amongst future evolutionary paths.

A good part of such exercises is inevitably 'qualitative', based on case studies, circumstantial comparisons across firms and countries displaying different evolutionary patterns, etc.[32] However, complementary investigations address some path-dependent properties on more quantitative grounds, concerning, e.g. real and financial time series.

A complementary task: detecting nonlinearities

Early examples of statistical tools devised for detecting forms of path dependence are those trying to detect chaos. While *chaos* can be easily obtained out of economic models, not much supporting evidence has been collected so far. Limitedly to high-frequency financial time series, there is some evidence of chaotic behaviour,[33] but there is hardly evidence for other economic series.[34] Brock *et al.* (1991) formally test for chaos in a number of economic and financial datasets. This is done by applying the 'BDS' test, presented in Brock *et al.* (1996) in order to detect low-dimensional chaos. At the same time, as Brock (1993) himself critically discusses '... chaos is a very special species of nonlinearity ...'; so that it is misleading '... to conclude that weak evidence for chaos implies weak evidence for non linearity' (p. 7).

Moreover, note that the apparent linearity/predictability/lack of path dependence on some time scale does not rule out 'deeper', possibly 'slower' path-dependent dynamics. So, for example, under conditions resembling what in biology are called 'punctuated equilibria' (Elredge and Gould 1972) phase transitions between apparent steady states might occur infrequently, rather abruptly, unpredictably triggered by particular chains of events,[35] while possibly still leaving linear structures of the time series in the (quasi) equilibrium phases.

Path dependence in economic evolution

Granted all that, how do such different degrees of path dependence show up in the 'grand' evolutionary interpretation of economic change? The latter, as outlined in much greater detail in Coriat and Dosi (1998a) and Dosi and Winter (2002), entails at the very least as fundamental building blocks:

(i) heterogenous, 'boundedly rational' but innovative agents;
(ii) increasing returns in knowledge accumulation;
(iii) collective selection mechanisms, including of course market interactions;

(iv) multiple forms of social embeddedness of the processes of adaptation, learning and selection.

The late S. Gould has reminded us (originally addressing evolution in the biological domain) that an illuminating angle to interpret evolutionary dynamics is by trying to identify what would remain unchanged if 'the tape of evolution would be run twice' (1977). It is indeed a very challenging question for social scientists too.

Needless to say, 'running the tape' all over again most likely would change the identities of who is 'winning' or 'losing'; who survives and who does not; who is getting at the top and who is getting at the bottom of the social ladder. However, this should not come as such a big surprise. After all, it is much more plausible to think of *system-level* path-*independent* or path-dependent equilibria, irrespectively of individual destinies.

Hence, what about system-level dynamics? One must sadly admit that evolutionary arguments have too often been used as *ex post* rationalizations of whatever observed phenomena: again, the general belief is that 'explaining why something exists' has too often meant showing why in some appropriately defined space 'whatever exists is a maximum of something' and this is the reason why it inevitably exists.

Quite a few applications of 'evolutionary games' to both economics and biology are dangerously near such an interpretative archetype. And so is a good deal of 'socio-biology' (a bit more of a discussion by one of us in Dosi and Winter, 2002). Admittedly, even relatively sophisticated evolutionary interpretations of economic change tend to overlook the possible history dependence of specific evolutionary paths.

Conversely, a few (mostly qualitative) analyses – already mentioned above – of the properties of national systems of production and innovation and of the 'political economy' of growth powerfully hint at underlying path dependencies. And the conjecture is indirectly corroborated by several formal results, from different theoretical fields. They include, as already mentioned, path-dependent selection amongst alternative institutional arrangements (Aoki, 2001), models of selection amongst alternative technologies, and also path dependencies in the statistical properties of growth processes of stylized industries and economies – even under unchanged initial conditions – (cf. Winter *et al.*, 2000) and Dosi and Fagiolo, 1998).

Certainly, most of the work of exploration of the possible properties of history dependence in incumbent models of economic evolution still awaits to be done. At the same time, an equally urgent task regards the development of broader interpretative frameworks explicitly addressing *hierarchically nested evolutionary processes*, allowing for e.g. (on average, slowly changing) institutions which in turn structure (on average, faster) dynamics of social adaptation, technological explorations, etc. (A fascinating template of such an exercise concerning biology is presented in Fontana, this volume.)

Selected histories might be quite 'bad': the painful acknowledgment of the distinction between interpretative and normative analyses

'Evolution' as such, both in the biological and socio-economic domains, does generally involve at least 'weak to mild' history dependence – in the foregoing definitions. However, a much trickier question regards the properties of those very evolutionary processes as judged against any normative yardsticks. Does 'evolution' entail some notion of 'progress' in some appropriately defined space?

As already mentioned, the general notion of history dependence of any socio-economic process is in principle quite separate from any normative evaluation of the 'social quality', however defined, of the outcomes which history happens to choose. As David (2001) argues in detail, one may think of quite a few circumstances easily involving multiple *neutral* equilibria or paths which turn out to be (roughly) equivalent in normative terms. On formal grounds, the original Polya urn example is a good case to the point. The whole set of reals on the interval [0, 1] happens to be fixed points satisfying the condition $f(x) = x$, where x may stand for frequencies of e.g. technologies, behaviours, strategies, organizational forms, etc. and $f(x)$ for the probabilities of their social adoption, without any distinct normative feature attached to them.

Further suggestive examples come from biology hinting at the widespread occurrence of *neutral drifts* in the genotypical space mapping into diverse but fitness-equivalent phenotypical structures.

At the same time, it equally holds that many path-dependent processes do entail the possibility of lock-in into equilibria or paths which are 'dominated' in normative terms (i.e. intuitively are 'socially worse'), as compared to other notionally 'better' ones which *could have been explored* given some initial conditions but ultimately turn out to be unreachable under reasonable switching costs at later times[36] (the argument is forcefully presented in Arthur, 1994). In this respect, a few analyses have focused so far upon rather simple cases of choices amongst technologies and social conventions, often highlighting the path-dependent properties of the underlying selection processes. However, the relevance of path-dependent selection of relatively 'bad' institutional set-ups and technologies remains a highly controversial question. One inclination is to depart from any naive notion of evolutionary dynamics leading – notwithstanding painful detours and setbacks – 'from worse to better'. In many respects such a 'progressive' view is shared by a whole spectrum of scholars, ranging from Karl Marx to contemporary neoclassical economists.[37] Empirically, as Nelson (2002) has recently suggested, it may well be that 'physical technologies' tend to often display more 'hill-climbing' features as compared to 'social' technologies, due to our relatively higher ability in the former domain to test hypotheses and codify solutions to the problems at hand. So, for example, while, electricity or antibiotics or vaccines happened to be rather uncontroversial technological advancements, one seldom finds crisp matching examples in the social domain.

Come as it may, history is full of cases of collective dynamics irreversibly leading *from better to worse*: in our view, the story of Easter Island vividly depicted in Diamond (1995), far from being an odd outlier, is indeed an archetype of common processes of transitions to worse and worse coordination equilibria. The decadence of many civilizations probably belongs to that same class of collective dynamics: institutions and microbehaviours coevolve in ways such as to yield recurrent transitions to 'worse and worse' social arrangements.

Locking and de-locking: some conclusions on the tension between freedom and necessity

It follows from our foregoing discussion that two somewhat complementary mechanisms are always at work. On the one hand, specific histories of competence-building, expectation formation, emergence of particular organizational structures, etc. together yield relatively *unique* and hence *heterogenous* micro histories.

On the other hand, broader mechanisms of alignment of individual and organizational decisions, together with convergence to dominant technologies and institutions, tend to reduce such a diversity among agents and bring about relative consistency of behaviours, practices, expectations.

More precisely, mechanisms at the heart of aggregate 'coherence' include: (i) social adaptation by individual actors; (ii) the path-dependent reproduction of a multiplicity of institutions governing interactions amongst agents; (iii) selection mechanisms (comprising of course market-selection dynamics). These processes contribute to explain locking into specific 'socio-economic paths'. But lock-ins seldom have an absolute nature: the unfolding of history, while closing more or less irremediably opportunities that were available but not seized at some past time, is also a source of new 'windows of opportunities' – using again Paul David's terminology – which allow de-locking and escaping from the past.

Let us outline some of the forces that work as potential factors of 'de-locking'.

First, a straightforward mechanism of 'de-locking' is related to *invasions*. They can be literal ones as it has often happened with past civilizations, and also more metaphorical ones, i.e. the 'contamination' with and diffusion of organizational forms, cultural traits, etc. originally developed elsewhere. Sticking just to organizational examples, think of, for example, the worldwide 'invasion' of Tayloristic principles of work organization – originally developed in the US, or more recently the diffusion of 'Japanese' management practices. *Second*, social adaptation is never complete, at least in modern societies. However, precisely the gap between social norms and prescribed roles, on the one hand, and expectations, 'mental models', identities which agents actually hold, on the other, may be an extremely powerful source of 'unlocking' dynamics: within an enormous literature, see the fascinating comparative analysis of the riots of obedience and revolt by Moore (1978), and also, from the economists' camp, the formal explorations of some implications of 'cognitive dissonance' including Akerlof and Dickens (1982) and Kuran (1987, 1991). *Third*, and relatedly, non-average ('deviant') behaviours may well entail, under certain circumstances, what natural scientists call 'symmetry breaking' and phase transitions to different collective structures (Allen 1988).

More generally, *fourth*, a fundamental role in preventing irreversible socio-economic lock-ins is played by various forms of heterogeneity among agents – in terms of e.g. technological competences, behavioural repertoires, strategies, preferences, etc.[38]

Fifth, 'de-locking' possibilities might be a byproduct of those very mechanisms which tend to induce path dependence in the first place. Indeed many organizational forms, behavioural patterns, etc. tend to be selected over multiple selection domains, possibly characterized by diverse selection criteria. So, for example, as one argues in Coriat and Dosi (1998a), organizational routines entail possibly uneasy compromises between their problem-solving efficacy and their properties in terms of governance of conflicting interests. Complementarity of functions, as discussed above, is likely to induce multiplicity of equilibria and path dependence. However, such equilibria may well be 'meta-stable', entailing the possibility of de-locking induced by increased inadequacies in some of the affected domains (i.e. over some 'selection landscapes'). A good case to the point is the increasing mismatching between formal hierarchies, incentives and actual decision powers driving toward the collapse of centrally-planned economies (Chavance 1995).

Finally, *sixth*, a major de-locking force has historically been the emergence of radical technological innovations, new knowledge bases, new sources of technological opportunities (i.e. what one calls in Dosi, 1982, new technological paradigms): on the powers of 'Unbound Prometheus' of technological change cf. the seminal works of Landes (1969), Freeman (1982) and Rosenberg (1976). Ultimately, as we have tried to argue in this chapter, human affairs always involve a tension between the tyranny of our collective past and the apparent discretionality of our wills. Admittedly, one is still rather far from getting any robust understanding even of the basic mechanisms underlying this tension. However, it is a fundamental exercise if one wants to handle the uncountable problems of collective action we continuously face and try to (imperfectly) shake free of the grip of the past and shape our future.

Appendix

Ergodicity in stochastic processes

Take the family of *Markov processes* as baseline reference for the stochastic processes of interest here. Given the set of possible states in which the system may find itself, one is in general interested in the probability distribution over the states, possibly different at different points in time. For (time invariant) Markov processes:

$$Pr\,(X_t = y | X_{t-1} = x, \cdots, X_0 = x_0) = Pr\,(X_t = y | X_{t-1} = x) = p_{x,y} \tag{2}$$

i.e. the probability of being in state x at time t conditional on all states visited in the past reduces to the probability conditional only on the state visited in the previous time $t - 1$. The probability $p_{x,y}$ is called the transition probability from state x to state y[39] and together with the distribution on the initial states, fully determines the joint (unconditional) probability distribution over the set of possible states. Moreover, one can partition the set of all possible states into *transient* and *recurrent* states depending on the probability that the stochastic process returns to the states after a first visit. A stochastic process is *ergodic* if one can obtain a probability distribution over the recurrent states that in the limit does not depend on the initial state of the system.

Non-Markovian processes do not satisfy condition (2), implying that the whole path of previously visited states is relevant in determining the probability of finding the process in a specific state at any given time.

Polya urn processes

Assume an urn of infinite capacity containing balls of two colours, say, white and black. At every draw a number c of balls of the same color as the drawn ball is added to the urn. (In the generalized urn scheme there are k different ball colours.) If c is greater or equal to one, the process entails positive feedbacks: if a color is drawn once, then the likelihood of drawing that same colour at the next time step is higher. If $c = 0$ the process reduces to independent Bernoullian draws, when c is negative the process accounts for negative feedbacks. It can be proved that when $c \geq 1$ such a process converges with probability one to the dominance of one single colour of the balls. This limit state is *absorbing*, meaning a zero probability of leaving it.[40] In the case of an urn with two colors, let X_t be the proportion of white balls in the urn at time t. Consider the case when one ball is added into the urn at time steps $t = 1, 2, \ldots$. The probability that the new ball is white is a function of the share X_t, say $f_t(X_t)$, where $f_t : [0,1] \rightarrow [0,1]$. The new ball is then black with probability $1 - f_t(X_t)$.

One can then represent the dynamics of X_t as

$$X_{t+1} = X_t + \frac{\xi_t(X_t) - X_t}{t + n} \quad \text{with } t \geq 1 \quad \text{and} \quad X_1 = \frac{n_w}{n} \tag{3}$$

where n_w is the proportion of white balls at the initial time and ξ_t are independent random variables with binary outcome defined by

$$\xi_t(X_t) = \begin{cases} 1 \text{ with prob } f_t(X_t) \\ 0 \text{ with prob } 1 - f_t(X_t) \end{cases} \tag{4}$$

$f_t(X_t)$ represents the average of $\xi_t(X_t)$. Call $\psi_t(X_t) = \xi_t - f_t(X_t)$ the difference between $\xi_t(X_t)$ and its mathematical expectation, so that $E[\psi_t(X_t)] = 0$. Then we can rewrite Eq. 3 as

$$X_{t+1} = X_t + \frac{[f_t(X_t) - X_t] + \psi_t(X_t)}{t + n} \qquad (t \geq 1)$$

Under this formulation the realization of the process at time $t + 1$ is given by the realization at time t plus a term with two components. The first component, $f_t(X_t) - X_t$, is a systematic one, the second component is the zero-mean noise $\psi_t(X_t)$. Then the limit points of the sequence X_t have to belong to an appropriately defined set of zeros of the function $f_t(x) - x$ for $x \in [0, 1]$.

The outlined case is indeed the most general one, without conditions on the continuity of the f function. For discussions and formal proofs of the limit results see Arthur *et al.* (1983), Dosi and Kaniovski (1994), Hill *et al.* (1980).

Replicator dynamics

Evolutionary theory developed in biology rests on two main elements: (i) perpetual generation of novelty; (ii) selection of 'superior' species, given heterogenous populations.

The original mathematical representation of the selection mechanism via the so-called *replicator dynamics*, is through the Fisher equation (more on economic applications in Metcalfe, 1998). Assume the existence of n types of entities in the population. Call x_i the fraction of the population of type i and call F_i its fitness. Then the Fisher equation in the linear continuous simplification reads:

$$\dot{x}_i = c x_i [F_i - \bar{F}]$$

where $\bar{F}$ is the weighted fitness average in the population:

$$\bar{F} = \sum_i x_i F_i$$

The way such a simple version of the replicator dynamics operates is such that the relative frequency of types with higher-than-average fitness grows, while the proportion of types characterized by below average fitness shrinks. If the fitness measure is constant over time, the system is bound to converge to the dominance of the fittest type. More general formulations allow for non linear interactions amongst traits which contribute to overall fitness and for changes of fitness landscapes themselves (cf. Silverberg, 1988 for a discussion of various selection models).

Notes

* This work is part of an ongoing research project involving from the start Andrea Bassanini. Support by the Sant'Anna School and by the Center for Development Research (ZEF), Bonn is gratefully acknowledged. We also wish to thank comments by Giulio Bottazzi, Uwe Cantner, Ping Chen, Paul David and Willi Semmler.
† ECIS, Eindhoven Center for Innovation Studies, Eindhoven, The Netherlands.
‡ LEM, Sant'Anna School of Advanced Studies, Pisa, Italy.

1. Indeed, it is difficult to find *purely* ahistorical representations even in mainstream economics, except from some breeds of economic theory such as rational expectations or general equilibrium theories.
2. Detailed discussions of some of the issues tackled in this chapter are in Arthur (1994), David (1988, 2001), Freeman and Louçã (2001), Hodgson (2001) and Witt (2005).
3. Of course, path dependence holds, *a fortiori*, if preferences are themselves endogenous (cf. the discussion in Aversi *et al.* (1999) and the references therein). In these circumstances past events irreversibly change the decision criteria agents apply even under an invariant choice set and invariant information from the environment.
4. Within the enormous literature, cf. Kreps and Spence (1985), Hahn (1987), Arthur and Lane (1993).
5. For interaction-based models cf. Brock and Durlauf (2001a), which reports a variety of empirical examples.
6. Cf. Schelling (1971).
7. For formal models in different perspectives cf. Föllmer (1974), Bikhachandani *et al.* (1992) and Young (1998).
8. The distinction between the two is discussed in Dosi *et al.* (1996): see also the references therein.
9. Incidentally note however that the latter investment might turn out of a socially pernicious kind, trading off relatively small private rents against huge collective losses in knowledge accumulation. The current lamentable legal arrangements on so-called Intellectual Property Rights (IPR) are an excellent case to the point (a sophisticated discussion of IPR is in Arora *et al.*, 2001), while a more sanguine but convincing illustration is presented in Coriat and Orsi, 2002).
10. The wide literature includes a variety of models and explanations that also assign different relevance to the initial conditions: see, among others, Krugman (1991a) and (1996), Arthur (1994), Fujita *et al.* (1999).
11. Cf. Dosi (1988) for a detailed discussion of the properties of technological knowledge.
12. This is not to say of course that some forms of 'decreasing returns' never endanger knowledge accumulation. Intuition suggests immediately a few historical cases where technological opportunities appear to progressively shrink. However, at a closer look, what generally happens is that increasing returns may well tend to dry out, but one is still a long way from decreasing returns setting in (that is, more formally, one is basically talking about the properties of second derivatives). This applies even in the case of all those resource-based activities such as agriculture and mining which have been for more than two centuries the menacing reference of the mainstream in the economic discipline.
13. A partly overlapping idea is that learning is typically *local*, in the sense that what agents learn tends to be 'near' what agents already know: cf. the pioneering models by Atkinson and Stiglitz (1969) and David (1975) and within the subsequent literature, Antonelli (1995), among others. All this admittedly involves a highly metaphorical notion of 'nearness', since we still fall short of any robust topology, or anything resembling it, in the space of knowledge.
14. The QWERTY story reports on initial events that may constrain long-term outcomes. In a different example, David (1992) vividly reports about the individual role played by Thomas Edison in the early battle to win dominance in electricity supply market and discusses in general the power of intentionality in determining historical paths. See also the discussion in Section 5.

15. One of the formal representations of such competitive processes is through so-called replicator dynamics: cf. Silverberg (1988), Weibull (1995), Metcalfe (1998), Young (1998), and the pioneering Winter (1971) (we offer a basic intuition in the Appendix).

16. Using the terminology that will be more formally defined in the next section, we can define this property in terms of 'multiplicity of equilibria'.

17. Even in this case, things might not be so simple. For example, the irrelevance-of-initial-conditions property may well turn out to rest on very demanding assumptions, including the presence of the 'best' combination of traits from the very start and its survival throughout the ('disequilibrium') process of adaptation/selection. For an insightful discussion cf. Winter (1975).

18. A general introduction to 'rugged landscape' formalizations is in Kauffman (1989).

19. Cf. Nelson and Winter (1982), Cohen *et al.* (1996), Coriat and Dosi (1998a), Dosi *et al.* (2000), among others.

20. More detailed discussions of the nature of 'institutions' by one of us are in Dosi (1995) and Coriat and Dosi (1998b).

21. For some stylized facts, cf. Abramovitz (1986), Dosi *et al.* (1994) and Meliciani (2001), among others.

22. The original reference is Cass and Shell (1983); for a recent survey cf. Benhabib and Farmer (1999).

23. Outstanding examples include A. Young, N. Kaldor and G. Myrdal. See the discussion in Arthur (1994), ch. 1.

24. Cf. the thorough discussions in David (1988, 1993, 2001). Moreover, in Bassanini and Dosi (2001) one shows that under certain conditions increasing returns are neither sufficient for path dependence (see also below, the final section).

25. On different facets of the epistemology of a paradigm which, for a long time, has stubbornly focused on the properties of history-independent equilibria, cf. Freeman and Louçã (2001), Hodgson (2001) and Nau and Schefold (2002).

26. Cf. Haken (1981), Prigogine (1980), Prigogine and Stengers (1984), Brock and Malliaris (1989), Rosser (1991).

27. A good deal of the formal tools can already be found in classics such as Feller (1971) and Cox and Miller (1965). However their economic application (with some significant refinements) is a more recent phenomenon.

28. An important feature is however worth mentioning: even for the simplest random walk the state at time t embodies the full memory of all shocks which drove it from its very beginning.

29. See the appendix for some formal definitions and results.

30. For details, cf. the original model Holley and Liggett (1975) and Liggett (1999).

31. For critical assessment see David (2001) and Dosi (1997).

32. An interesting exercise, involving a few respected historians is Cowley (1999).

33. For a survey of the literature on chaos in macroeconomics and finance see LeBaron (1994), and previously Kelsey (1988).

34. A more optimistic view on the pertenance of chaotic dynamics for economic phenomena is in Chen (1993, 2005).

35. An insightful germane discussion, building on the 'long waves' debate on 'economic growth' is in Freeman and Louçã (2001).

36. Formally, one can show that asymptotic switching costs may well be infinite, *under dynamic increasing returns* even from an 'inferior' to a (notionally) 'superior' technology/organizational form, etc.

37. Indeed, many economists, even among the most sophisticated ones, are inclined to read history as a painstaking process driving – notwithstanding major setbacks – toward market ('capitalist') economies: see for example Hicks (1969).
38. In fact heterogeneity of agents can help also in explaining why 'locking' might not occur: instead one might observe market sharing of different technologies or organizational forms. As shown in Bassanini (1999) and Bassanini and Dosi (2005), convergence to monopoly of a technology, an organizational form, etc. may in fact not occur even under conditions of increasing returns if the degree of heterogeneity of agents is high enough. Similarly Herrendorf *et al.* (2000) prove that heterogeneity of agents is a condition for avoiding multiple or indeterminate equilibria in GE models.
39. Here we take the transition probability to be time-invariant. One could generalize to time-dependent probabilities.
40. For an overview of the state-of-the-art in generalized urn schemes and hints on their economic applications, cf. Dosi and Kaniovski (1994).

References

Abramovitz, M. (1986) 'Catching up, forging ahead and falling behind', *Journal of Economic History*, 86, pp. 385–406.

Akerlof, G.A., Dickens, W.T. (1982) 'The economic consequences of cognitive dissonance', *American Economic Review*, 72, pp. 307–19.

Allen, P.M. (1988) *Evolution, Innovation and Economics*, in Dosi *et al.* (1988), pp. 95–119.

Antonelli, C. (1995) *The Economics of Localized Technological Change and Industrial Dynamics*, Boston: Kluwer Publishers.

Antonelli, C., Foray, D., Hall, B., Steinmuller, E. (eds) (2005) *New Frontiers in the Economics of Innovation: Essays in Honor of Paul David*, Cheltenham, UK and Northampton, MA: Edward Elgar.

Aoki, M. (2001) *Toward a Comparative Institutional Analysis*, Cambridge: MIT Press.

Archibugi, D., Howells, J., Michie, J. (eds) (1999) *Innovation Policy in a Global Economy*, Cambridge: Cambridge University Press.

Arora, A., Fosfuri, A., Gambardella, A. (2001) *Markets for Technology: The Economics of Innovation and Corporate Strategy*, Cambridge, MA: MIT Press.

Arrow, K. (1962a) 'Economic welfare and the allocation of resources for innovation', in R.R. Nelson (ed.), *The Rate and Direction of Inventive Activity*, Princeton: Princeton University Press.

Arrow, K. (1962b) 'The economic implications of learning by doing', *Review of Economic Studies*, 29, pp. 155–73.

Arrow, K. (1974) *The Limits of Organization*, New York: Norton.

Arthur, W.B. (1988) 'Competing technologies: an overview', in G. Dosi *et al.* (eds), *Technical Change and Economic Theory*, London: Pinter Publisher.

Arthur, W.B. (1994) *Increasing Returns and Path Dependence in the Economy*, Ann Arbor: University of Michigan Press.

Arthur, W.B., Ermoliev, Y.M., Kaniovski, Y.M. (1983) 'A generalized urn problem and its applications', *Kibernetika*, 19, 49–56 (republished in Arthur 1994).

Arthur, W.B., Lane, D.A. (1993) 'Information contagion', *Structural Change and Economic Dynamics*, 4, pp. 81–104 (republished in Arthur 1994).

Atkinson, A.B., Stiglitz, J.E (1969) 'A new view of technological change', *Economic Journal*, 79, pp. 573–8.

Aversi, R., Dosi, G., Fagiolo, G., Meacci, M., Olivetti, C. (1999) 'Demand dynamics with socially evolving preferences', *Industrial and Corporate Change*, 8, pp. 353–408.

Banerjee, A.V. (1992) 'A simple model of herd behavior', *Quarterly Journal of Economics*, 107, pp. 797–818.

Bassanini, A.P. (1999) *Can Science and Agents' Diversity Tie the Hands of Clio?: Technological Trajectories, History, and Growth*, mimeo, OECD, Paris.

Bassanini, A.P., Dosi, G. (2000) 'Heterogeneous agents, complementarities, and diffusion: do increasing returns imply convergence to international technological monopolies?', in D. Delli Gatti, M. Gallegati and A. Kirman (eds), *Market Structure, Aggregation and Heterogeneity*, Berlin: Springer.

Bassanini, A.P., Dosi, G. (2001) 'When and how chance and human will can twist the arms of Clio', in Garud and Karnoe (eds) (2001).

Bassanini, A.P., Dosi, G. (2005) 'Competing technologies, technological monopolies, and the rate of convergence to a stable market structure', working paper, forthcoming in Antonelli *et al.* (eds) (2005).

Benhabib, J., Farmer, R.E.A. (1999) 'Indeterminacy and sunspots in macroeconomics', in J. Taylor and M. Woodford (eds), *Handbook of Macroeconomics*, Amsterdam: Elsevier Science.

Bikhchandani, S., Hirshleifer, D., Welch, I. (1992) 'A theory of fads, fashion, custom, and cultural change as informational cascades', *Journal of Political Economy*, 100, pp. 992–1026.

Brock, W.A. (1993) 'Pathways to randomness in the economy: emergent nonlinearity and chaos in economics and finance', *Estudios Economicos*, 8, pp. 3–54.

Brock, W.A., Dechert, W.D., Scheinkman, J.A., LeBaron, B. (1996) 'A test for independence based on the correlation dimension', *Econometric Reviews*, 15, pp. 197–235.

Brock, W.A., Durlauf, S.N. (2001a) 'Interactions-based models', in J.J. Heckman and E. Leamer (eds), *Handbook of Econometrics*, Vol. 5, ch. 54, pp. 3297–380, Elsevier Science B.V.

Brock, W.A., Durlauf, S.N. (2001b) 'Discrete choice with social interaction', *The Review of Economic Studies*, 68, pp. 235–60.

Brock, W.A., Hsieh, D.A., LeBaron, B. (1991) *Nonlinear Dynamics, Chaos and Instability: Statistical Theory and Economic Evidence*, Cambridge: MIT Press.

Brock, W.A., Malliaris, A.G. (1989) *Differential Equations, Stability and Chaos in Dynamic Economics*, North-Holland.

Cass, D., Shell, K. (1983) 'Do sunspots matter?', *Journal of Political Economy*, 92, pp. 193–227.

Chavance, B. (1995) 'Hierarchical forms and coordination problems in socialist systems', *Industrial and Corporate Change*, 1, pp. 271–91.

Chen, P. (1993) 'Searching for economic chaos: a challenge to econometric practice and nonlinear tests', in R. Day and P. Chen (eds), *Nonlinear Dynamics and Evolutionary Economics*, Oxford: Oxford University Press.

Chen, P. (2005) 'Evolutionary economic dynamics: persistent business cycles, chronic excess capacity, and strategic innovation in division of labor', forthcoming in Dopfer (ed.) (2005).

Cohen, M.D., Burkhart, R., Dosi, G., Egidi, M., Marengo, L., Warglien, M., and Winter, S. (1996) 'Routines and other recurring action patterns of organizations: contemporary research issues'. *Industrial and Corporate Change*, 5, pp. 653–98.

Cooper R., John A. (1988) 'Coordinating coordination failures in Keynesian models', *Quarterly Journal of Economics*, 103, pp. 323–42.

Coriat, B., Dosi, G. (1998a) 'The institutional embeddedness of economic change: an appraisal of the "evolutionary" and the "regulationist" research programs', in K. Nielsen and B. Johnson (eds), *Institutions and Economic Change*, Cheltenham, UK: Edward Elgar.

Coriat, B., Dosi, G. (1998b) 'Learning how to govern and learning how to solve problems: on the double nature of routines as problem solving and governance devices', in A. Chandler, P. Hagstrom, O. Solvell (eds), *Dynamic Firm*, Oxford: Oxford University Press.

Coriat, B., Orsi, F. (2002) 'Establishing a new regime of intellectual property rights in the United States: origins, content, problems', *Research Policy*, 31, pp. 1491–507.

Cowley, R. (ed.) (1999) *What If*, New York: Putnam Publisher.

Cox, D.R., Miller, H.D. (1965) *The Theory of Stochastic Processes*, London and New York: Chapman and Hall.

David, P.A. (1975) *Technical Choice, Innovation and Economic Growth: Essays on American and British Experience in the Nineteenth Century*, Cambridge: Cambridge University Press.

David, P.A. (1985) 'Clio and the economics of QWERTY', *American Economic Review*, 75, pp. 332–7.

David, P.A. (1988) *Path Dependence: Putting the Past into the Future of Economics*, Stanford University, Institute for Mathematical Studies in the Social Science, Technical Report 533.

David, P.A. (1992) 'Heroes, herds and hysteresis in technological history: Thomas Edison and "The Battle of the Systems" Reconsidered', *Industrial and Corporate Change*, 1, pp. 129–81.

David, P.A. (1993) 'Path dependence and predictability in dynamic systems with local network externalities: a paradigm for historical economics', in D. Foray and C. Freeman (eds), *Technology and the Wealth of Nations*, London: Pinter Publishers.

David, P.A. (1994) 'Why are institutions the "carriers of history"?: path dependence and the evolution of conventions, organizations and institutions', *Structural Change and Economic Dynamics*, 5, pp. 205–20.

David, P.A. (2001) 'Path dependence, its critics and the quest for "historical economics" ' in P. Garrouste and S. Ioannides (eds), *Evolution and Path Dependence in Economic Ideas: Past and Present*, Cheltenham, UK: Edward Elgar.

Diamond, J. (1995) 'Easter's end', *Discover*, 16, pp. 63–9.

Dopfer, K. (ed.) (2005) *The Evolutionary Foundations of Economics*, Cambridge: Cambridge University Press.

Dosi, G. (1982) 'Technological paradigms and technological trajectories: a suggested interpretation', *Research Policy*, 11, pp. 147–62.

Dosi, G. (1984) *Technical Change and Industrial Transformation*, New York: St. Martin's Press.

Dosi, G. (1988) 'Sources, procedures and microeconomic effects of innovation', *Journal of Economic Literature*, 26, pp. 120–71.

Dosi, G. (1995) 'Hierarchies, market and power: some foundational issues on the nature of contemporary economic organization', *Industrial and Corporate Change*, 4, pp. 1–19.

Dosi, G. (1997) 'Opportunities, incentives and the collective patterns of technological change', *The Economic Journal*, 107, pp. 1530–47.

Dosi, G., Fagiolo, G. (1998) 'Exploring the unknown: on entrepreneurship, coordination and innovation-driven growth', in J. Lesourne and A. Orléan (eds), *Advances in Self-Organization and Evolutionary Economics*, Paris: Economica.

Dosi, G., Freeman, C., Fabiani, S. (1994) 'The process of economic development: introducing some stylized facts and theories on technologies, firms and institutions', *Industrial and Corporate Change*, 1, pp. 1–45.

Dosi, G., Freeman, C., Nelson, R.R., Silverberg, G., Soete, L. (eds) (1988) *Technical Change and Economic Theory*, London: Pinter Publisher.

Dosi, G., Kaniovski, Y. (1994) 'On "badly behaved dynamics:" some applications of generalized urn schemes to technological and economic change', *Journal of Evolutionary Economics*, 4, pp. 93–123.

Dosi, G., Kogut, B. (1993) 'National specificities and the context of change: the co-evolution of organization and technology', in B. Kogut (ed.), *Country competitiveness: Technology and the Organization of Work*, New York: Oxford University Press.

Dosi, G., Marengo, L., Fagiolo, G. (1996) *Learning in Evolutionary Environment*, IIASA Working Paper, WP-96-124, IIASA (International Institute for Applied Systems Analysis), Laxenburg, Austria, forthcoming in Dopfer (ed.) (2005).

Dosi, G., Metcalfe, J.S. (1991) 'On some notions of irreversibility in economics', in Saviotti, P.P., Metcalfe, J.S. (eds), *Evolutionary Theories of Economic and Technological Change*, Harwood Academic Publishers.

Dosi, G., Nelson, R.R., Winter, S.G. (eds) (2000) *The Nature and Dynamics of Organizational Capabilities*, Oxford/New York: Oxford University Press.

Dosi, G., Orsenigo, L., Sylos Labini, M. (2003) 'Technology and the Economy', forthcoming in N.J. Smelser and R. Swedberg (eds), *Handbook of Economic Sociology*, 2nd edn, Princeton University Press.

Dosi, G., Winter, S.G. (2002) 'Interpreting economic change: evolution, structures and games', in M. Augier and J. March (eds), *The Economics of Choice, Change and Organizations: Essays in Memory of Richard M. Cyert*, Cheltenham, UK: Edward Elgar.

Durlauf, S.N. (1993) 'Nonergodic economic growth', *Review of Economic Studies*, 60, pp. 349–66.

Durlauf, S.N. (1994) 'Path dependence in aggregate output', *Industrial and Corporate Change*, 1, pp. 149–72.

Eldredge, N., Gould, S.J. (1972) 'Punctuated equilibria: an alternative to phyletic gradualism' in T.J.M. Schopf (ed.), *Models in Paleobiology*, San Francisco: Freeman, Cooper and Company.

Feller, W. (1971) *An Introduction to Probability Theory and Its Applications*, New York: J. Wiley.

Föllmer, H. (1974) 'Random economies with many interacting agents', *Journal of Mathematical Economics*, 1, pp. 51–62.

Forni, M., Lippi, M. (1997) *Aggregation and the Microfoundations of Dynamic Macroeconomics*, Oxford: Oxford University Press.

Freeman, C. (1982) *The Economics of Industrial Innovation*, London: Pinter Publisher.

Freeman, C., Louçã, F. (2001) *As Time Goes By: From the Industrial Revolution to the Information Revolution*, Oxford: Oxford University Press.

Fujita, M., Krugman, P.R. and Venables, A.J. (1999) *The Spatial Economy: Cities, Regions and International Trade*, Cambridge, Mass.: MIT Press.

Garud, R., Karnoe, P. (eds) (2001) *Path Dependence and Creation*, Mahwah, NJ: Lawrence Erlbaum Associates.

Gould, S.J. (1977) *Ever Since Darwin*, New York: Norton.

Granovetter, M. (1985) 'Economic action and social structure: the problem of embeddedness', *American Journal of Sociology*, 91, pp. 481–510.

Hahn, F.H. (1987) 'Information, dynamics and equilibrium', *Scottish Journal of Political Economy*, 34, pp. 321–34.

Hall, P.A., Soskice, D. (2001) *Varieties of Capitalism: The Institutional Foundations of Comparative Advantage*, Oxford: Oxford University Press.

Haken, H. (1981) *Chaos and Order in Nature*, Berlin: Springer.

Herrendorf, B., Valentinyi, A., Waldmann, R. (2000) 'Ruling out multiplicity and indeterminacy: the role of heterogeneity', *Review of Economic Studies*, 67, pp. 295–307.

Hicks, J.R. (1969) *A Theory of Economic History*, Oxford: Oxford University Press.

Hildenbrand, W. (1994) *Market Demand: Theory and Empirical Evidence*, Princeton: Princeton University Press.

Hill, B.M., Lane, D., Sudderth, W. (1980) 'A strong law for some generalized urn processes', *Annals of Probability*, 8, pp. 214–26.

Hodgson, G.M. (2001) *How Economics Forgot History: The problem of Historical Specificity in Social Science*, London and New York: Routledge.

Hollingsworth, J.R., Boyer, R. (1997) *Contemporary Capitalism: The Embeddedness of Institutions*, Cambridge: Cambridge University Press.

Holley, R.A., Liggett, T.M. (1975) 'Ergodic theorems for weakly interacting systems and the voter model', *Annals of Probability*, 3, pp. 643–63.

Kauffman, S.A. (1989) 'Adaptation on rugged fitness landscapes', in D.L. Stein (ed.), *Lectures in the Sciences of Complexity*, 1, pp. 527–618, New York: Addison Wesley.

Kelsey, D. (1988) 'The economics of chaos or the chaos of economics', *Oxford Economic Papers*.

Kreps, D., Spence, A.M. (1985) 'Modeling the role of history in industrial organization and competition', in G.R. Feiwel (ed.), *Issues in Contemporary Microeconomics and Welfare*, London: Macmillan.

Krugman, P.R. (1991a) 'Increasing returns and economic geography', *Journal of Political Economy*, 99, 484–99.

Krugman, P.R. (1991b) *Geography and Trade*, Cambridge, MA: MIT Press.

Krugman, P.R. (1996) *The Self-Organizing Economy*, Cambridge, MA and Oxford: Blackwell Publishers.

Kuran, T. (1987) 'Preference falsification, policy continuity and collective conservatism', *Economic Journal*, 97, pp. 642–65.

Kuran, T. (1991) 'Cognitive limitations and preference evolution', *Journal of Institutional and Theoretical Economics*, 146, pp. 241–73.

Landes, D.S. (1969) *The Unbound Prometheus; Technological Change and Industrial Development in Western Europe from 1750 to the Present*, Cambridge: Cambridge University Press.

LeBaron, B. (1994) 'Chaos and nonlinear forecastability in economics and finance', *Philosophical Transactions of the Royal Society of London*, A 348, pp. 397–404.

Levinthal, D. (2000) 'Organizational capabilities in complex worlds', in Dosi *et al.* (eds) (2000).

Liebowitz, S.J., Margolis, S.E. (1990) 'The fable of the keys', *Journal of Law and Economics*, 33, pp. 1–25.

Liebowitz, S.J., Margolis, S.E. (1995) 'Path dependence, lock-in, and history', *Journal of Law, Economics, and Organization*, 11, pp. 205–26.

Liggett, T. (1999) *Stochastic Interacting Systems: Contact, Voter and Exclusion Processes*, New York: Springer-Verlag.

Lundvall, B.A. (ed.) (1992) *National Systems of Innovation. Towards a Theory of Innovation and Interactive Learning*, London: Pinter Publisher.

Marengo, L. (1996) 'Structure, competence and learning in an adaptive model of the firm', in G. Dosi and F. Malerba (eds), *Organization and Strategy in the Evolution of the Enterprise*, London: Macmillan.

Marcn, J.G. (1991) 'Exploration and exploitation in organizational learning', *Organization Science*, 2, pp. 71–87.

March, J.G., Simon, H.A. (1992) *Organizations*, 2nd edn, Oxford, UK: Blackwell.

Meliciani, V. (2001) *Technology, Trade and Growth in OECD countries*, London/New York: Routledge.

Metcalfe, J.S. (1998) *Evolutionary Economics and Creative Destruction*, London: Routledge.

Mokyr, J. (1990) *The Lever of Riches*, New York: Oxford University Press.

Moore, B.J. (1978) *Injustice: The Social Bases of Obedience and Revolt*, White Plains, NY: M.E. Sharpe.

Mowery, D., Rosenberg, N. (1998) *Paths of Innovation: Technological Change in 20th Century America*, Cambridge: Cambridge University Press.

Nau, H.H., Schefold, B. (eds) (2002) *The Historicity of Economics*, Berlin: Springer.

Nelson, R.R. (ed.) (1993) *National Innovation Systems: A Comparative Analysis*, New York: Oxford University Press.

Nelson, R.R. (2002) 'Physical and Social Technologies, and Their Evolution', working paper, Columbia University.

Nelson, R.R., Sampat, B. (2001) 'Making sense of institutions as a factor shaping economic performance', *Journal of Economic Behavior and Organization*, 44, pp. 31–54.

Nelson, R.R., Winter, S.G. (1982) *An Evolutionary Theory of Economic Change*, Cambridge, MA: Harvard University Press.

Nicolis, G., Prigogine, I. (1989) *Exploring Complexity*, New York: Freeman.

North, D.C. (1990) *Institutions, Institutional Change and Economic Performance*, Cambridge: Cambridge University Press.

Pierson, P. (2000) 'Increasing returns, path dependence, and the study of politics', *American Political Science Review*, 94, pp. 251–67.

Prigogine, I. (1980) *From Being to Becoming*, New York: Freeman.

Prigogine, I., Stengers, I. (1984) *Order Out of Chaos*, London: Heinemann.

Rosenberg, N. (1976) *Perspectives on Technology*, Cambridge: Cambridge University Press.

Rosser, J.B. (1991) *From Catastrophe to Chaos: A General Theory of Economic Discontinuities*, Boston: Kluwer.

Schelling, T.C. (1971) 'Dynamic models of segregation', *Journal of Mathematical Sociology*, 1, pp. 143–86.

Silverberg, G. (1988) 'Modeling economic dynamics and technical change: mathematical approaches to self-organization and evolution', in Dosi *et al.* (eds) (1988).

Stadler, B.M.R., Stadler, P.F., Wagner, G.P., Fontana, W. (2001) 'The topology of the possible: formal spaces underlying patterns of evolutionary change', *Journal of Theoretical Biology*, 213, pp. 241–74.

Streeck, W., Yamamura, K. (eds) (2001) *The Origins of Nonliberal Capitalism: Germany and Japan*, Ithaca, London: Cornell University Press.

Young, A.A. (1928) 'Increasing returns and economic progress', *Economic Journal*, 38, pp. 527–42.

Young, H.P. (1998) *Individual Strategy and Social Structure: An Evolutionary Theory of Institutions*, Princeton: Princeton University Press.

Weibull, J.W. (1995) *Evolutionary Game Theory*, Cambridge: MIT Press.

Winter, S.G. (1971) 'Satisficing, selection and the innovating remnant', *Quarterly Journal of Economics*, 85, pp. 237–61.

Winter, S.G. (1975) 'Optimization and evolution in the theory of the firm', in R.H. Day and T. Groves (eds), *Adaptive Economic Models*, New York: Academic Press.

Winter, S.G., Kaniovski, Y., Dosi, G. (2000) 'Modeling industrial dynamics with innovative entrants', *Structural Change and Economic Dynamics*, 11, pp. 255–93.

Witt, U. (2005) 'Path-dependence in institutional change', in Dopfer (ed.) (2005).

[17]

Competing technologies, technological monopolies and the rate of convergence to a stable market structure*

Andrea P. Bassanini and Giovanni Dosi

1 INTRODUCTION

In this chapter we address the dynamics of diffusion of different technologies competing for the same market niche.

The stylised fact at the origin of this work is the observation that a stable empirical pattern of market sharing between competing technologies with no overwhelming dominant position rarely occurs in markets with positive feedbacks.[1] For example, even in the case of operating systems, which is often quoted as a case of market sharing, Apple MacIntosh has never held a market share larger than 1/5 (a partial exception being the submarket of personal computers for educational institutions). This fact has also triggered suspicion of market inefficiencies: technological monopolies may prevail even when the survival of more than one technology may be socially optimal (Katz and Shapiro, 1986; David, 1992). Think for example of the competition between Java-based architectures and ActiveX architectures for web-based applets: given that with any of the two paradigms the standard tasks that can be performed are different, the general impression of experts is that society would benefit from the survival of both.

In turn, from the point of view of interpretation of the processes of diffusion of new products and technologies, it is acknowledged that, in many modern markets, they are characterised by increasing returns to adoption or positive feedbacks. This has partly to do with supply-side causes: the cumulation of knowledge and skills through the expansion of markets and production usually reduce the hedonic price of both production and consumption goods, thus increasing the net benefit for the user of a particular technology. The Boeing 727, for example, which has been on the jet aircraft market for years, has undergone constant modification of the design and improvement in structural soundness, wing design, payload capacity and engine efficiency as it accumulates airline adoption and hours of flight (Rosenberg, 1982; Arthur, 1989). Similar observations can be made for many helicopter designs (Saviotti and Trickett, 1992) as well as for electric power plants designs (Cowan, 1990; Islas, 1997).

Supply-side causes of this type have received some attention in the economic literature for quite a while. However, in the last 15 years a great deal of attention has been devoted also to demand-side positive feedbacks, so-called network esternalities or (more neutrally) network effects (Katz and Shapiro, 1994; Liebowitz and Margolis, 1994). For example, telecommunication devices and networks (for instance, fax machines), as a first approximation, tend not to provide any utility per se but only as a function of the number of adopters of compatible technologies with whom the communication is possible (Rohlfs, 1974; Oren and Smith, 1981; Economides, 1996). The benefits accruing to a user of a particular hardware system depend on the availability of software whose quantity and variety may depend on the size of the market if there are increasing returns in software production. This is the case of video cassette recorders (VCRs), microprocessors, hi-fi devices and in general systems made of complementary products which need not be consumed in fixed proportions (Cusumano et al., 1992; Church and Gandal, 1993; Katz and Shapiro, 1985; 1994). A similar story can be told for the provision of post-purchase service for durable goods. In automobile markets, for example, the diffusion of foreign models has often been slow because of consumers' perception of a thinner and less experienced network of repair services (Katz and Shapiro, 1985). Standardisation implies also saving out of the cost of investment in complementary capital if returns from investment are not completely appropriable: in software adoption firms can draw from a large pool of experienced users if they adopt software belonging to a widespread standard, thus *de facto* sharing the cost of training (Farrell and Saloner, 1986; Brynjolfsson and Kemerer, 1996). Moreover product information may be more easily available for more popular brands or, finally, there may be conformity or psychological bandwagon effects (Katz and Shapiro, 1985; Banerjee, 1992; Arthur and Lane, 1993; Bernheim, 1994; Brock and Durlauf, 1995).

Katz and Shapiro (1994) in their review of the literature on systems competition and dynamics of adoption under increasing returns distinguish between *technology adoption decision* and *product selection decision*.

The former refers to the choice of a potential user to place a demand in a particular market. Relevant questions in this case are the conditions for an actual market of positive size, the notional features of a 'socially optimal' market size and the conditions allowing penetration of a new (more advanced) technology into the market of an already established one (Rohlfs, 1974; Oren and Smith, 1981; Farrell and Saloner, 1985; 1986; Katz and Shapiro, 1992). For example, purchasing or not a fax or substituting a compact disc player for an analogical record player are technology adoption decisions.

Conversely product selection refers to the choice between different technological solutions which perform (approximately) the same function and are therefore close substitutes. Relevant questions here are whether the market enhances variety or standardisation, whether the emerging market structure is normatively desirable and what is the role of history in the selection of market structure (Arthur, 1983; 1989; Katz and Shapiro, 1985; 1986; David, 1985; Church and Gandal, 1993; Dosi et al., 1994). Choosing between VHS or Beta in the VCR market or between Word or Wordperfect in the word-processor market are typical examples of product selection decisions.

This work is concerned with the dynamics of product selection. To explain the stylised fact recalled above we analyse properties of a fairly general and nowadays rather standard class of models of competing technologies, originally suggested by Arthur (1983) and Arthur et al. (1983) and further explored by Arthur (1989), Cowan (1991) and Dosi et al. (1994), among others. This class of models will be presented in details in section 2.

Despite mixed results of some pioneering works on the dynamics of markets with network effects (for example, Katz and Shapiro, 1986), unbounded increasing returns are commonly called for as an explanation of the emergence of technological monopolies. Usually the argument is based on the results of the model set forth by Arthur (1989). For instance, Robin Cowan summarises it in the following way:

> If technologies operate under dynamic increasing returns (often thought of in terms of learning-by-doing or learning-by-using), then early use of one technology can create a snowballing effect by which that technology quickly becomes preferred to others and comes to dominate the market.
>
> Following Arthur, consider a market in which two types of consumers adopt technology sequentially. As a result of dynamic increasing returns arising from learning-by-using, the pay-off to adopting a technology is an increasing function of the number of times it has been adopted in the past. Important with regard to which technology is chosen next is how many times each of the technologies has been chosen in the past. Arthur shows that if the order of adopters is random (that is, the type of the next adopter is not predictable) then *with certainty one technology will claim the entire market*. (Cowan, 1990: 543, italics added)

It will be shown in the following that *this statement does not always hold*. Unbounded increasing returns to adoption are neither necessary nor sufficient to lead to the emergence of technological monopolies. As proved in the next section, strictly speaking, Arthur's result applies only when returns are linearly increasing and the degree of heterogeneity of agents is, in a sense, small. Moreover it cannot be easily generalised further: some meaningful counter-examples will be provided. More generally the emergence of technological monopolies depends on the nature of increasing returns and their relationship with the degree of heterogeneity of the population. Given a sufficiently high heterogeneity amongst economic agents, limit market sharing may occur even in the presence of unbounded increasing returns.

The bearing of our analysis, in terms of the interpretation of the empirical evidence, stems from the results presented in section 3: in essence, we suggest that the observation of the widespread emergence of monopolies is intimately related to the properties of different rates of convergence (to monopoly and to market sharing respectively) more than to the properties of limit states as such. It will be shown that a market can approach a monopoly with a higher speed than it approaches any feasible limit market shares where both technologies coexist. Following a line of reasoning put forward by Winter (1986), our argument proceeds by noticing that when convergence is too slow the external environment is likely to change before any sufficiently small neighbourhood of the limit can be attained. The result that we obtain, based on some mathematical properties of Generalised Urn schemes,[2] is general for this class of models. The empirical implication is that among markets with high rate of technological change and increasing returns to adoption, a prevalence of stable monopolies over stable market-sharing should be observed.

The applications of Arthur's result have gone far beyond the dynamics of competing technologies and typically extended to the role of history in selecting the equilibrium in any situation wherein complementarities are relevant. The analysis of industry location patterns is a case to the point (for example, Arthur, 1990; Krugman, 1991a; 1991b; Venables, 1996). As James Rauch puts it:

> In Arthur's model, firms enter the industry in sequence. Each firm chooses a location on the basis of how many firms are there at the time of entry and a random vector that gives the firm's tastes for each possible location. *If agglomeration economies are unbounded* as the number of firms increases, then as the industry grows large, *one location takes all but a finite set of firms with probability one.* (Rauch, 1993: 843–4, italics added)

The implications of our results extend to this domain of analysis as well.

The remainder of the chapter is organised as follows. Section 2 reviews standard models of competing technologies and provides counter-examples to Arthur's main result. Section 3 establishes our main results on rate of convergence to a stable market structure and builds upon that an alternative explanation for observable patterns of dynamics between competing technologies. Section 4 briefly summarises the results.

2   COMPETING TECHNOLOGIES REVISITED: ARE UNBOUNDED INCREASING RETURNS SUFFICIENT FOR THE EMERGENCE OF TECHNOLOGICAL MONOPOLIES?

The class of competing technology dynamics models that we consider shares the two basic assumptions that adopters enter the market in a sequence which is assumed to be exogenous, and that each adopter makes its adoption choice only once. More than one agent can enter the market in each period (for example, Katz and Shapiro, 1986) but in order to simplify the treatment we abstract from this complication. The simple theoretical tale that underlies these models can be summarised as follows.

Every period a new agent enters the market and chooses the technology which is considered best suited to its requirements, given its preferences, information structure and the available technologies. Preferences can be heterogeneous and a distribution of preferences in the population is given. Information and preferences determine a vector of pay-off functions (whose dimension is equal to the number of available technologies) for every type of agent. Because of positive (negative) feedbacks, such as increasing (decreasing) returns to adoption, these functions depend on the number of previous adoptions. When an agent enters the market it compares the values of these functions (given its preferences, the available information, and previous adoptions) and chooses the technology which yields the maximum perceived pay-off. Which 'type' of agent enters the market at any given time is a stochastic event whose probability depends on the distribution of types (that is, of preferences) in the population. Because of positive (negative) feedbacks, the probability of adoption of a particular technology is an increasing (decreasing) function of the number of previous adoptions of that technology.

More formally we can write a general reduced form of pay-off functions of the following type:

$$\Pi_j^i(\overrightarrow{n}(t)) = h_i(a_j^i, \overrightarrow{n}(t)),$$

where $j \in D$, D is the set of possible technologies, $i \in S$; S is the set of possible types; $\overrightarrow{n}(t)$ is a vector denoting number of adoptions for each technology at time t $(n^j(t))$ is the number of adoptions of technology j at time t); $\overrightarrow{a}_j^i$ represents the network-independent components of agent i's preferences (a_j^i identifies a baseline pay-off for agents of type i from technology j), and $h_i(\cdot)$ is an increasing (decreasing) function that can differ across agents capturing increasing (decreasing) returns to adoption. Information and expectations are incorporated in $h_i(\cdot)$. If, at time t, an agent of type *i* comes to the market, it compares the pay-off functions, choosing *A* if and only if:[3]

$$\Pi^i_A(\overrightarrow{n}(t)) = \arg \max_{j \in D}\{\Pi^i_j(\overrightarrow{n})\} \tag{2.1}$$

Equation (2.1) can be seen as describing an equilibrium reaction function. Consequently, strategic behaviours (including sponsoring activities from the suppliers of technologies) are not ruled out by the foregoing formalisation.

In the remainder of this chapter we assume that the order of agents entering the market is random, hence *i*(*t*) can be considered as an iid sequence of random variables whose distribution depends on the distribution of the population of potential adopters. Under this assumption, the dynamics of the foregoing model can be analysed in terms of generalised urn schemes.

Consider the simplest case where two technologies, say *A* and *B*, compete for a market. Let us denote *A*'s market share with *X*(*t*). Given the relationships between (a) total number of adoptions of both technologies $n(t) = t - 1 + n^A(0) + n^B(0)$, (b) the current market share *X*(*t*) of *A*, and (c) number of adoptions of one specific technology, $n^i(t)$, $i = A, B$, that is, $n^A(t) = n(t)X(t)$, the dynamics of *X*(*t*) is given by the recursive identity

$$X(t + 1) = X(t) + \frac{\xi^t(X(t)) - X(t)}{t + n^A(0) + n^B(0)}.$$

Here $\xi^t(x)$, $t \geq 1$ are random variables independent in *t* such that

$$\xi^t(x) = \begin{cases} 1 \text{ with probability} & f(t,x) \\ 0 \text{ with probability} & 1 - f(t,x) \end{cases},$$

and $\xi^t(\cdot)$ is a function of market shares dependent on the feedbacks in adoption. $f(t, x)$ equals the probability that (2.1) is true when $X(t) = x$ and is sometimes called *urn function*. Denoting $\xi^t(x) - E(\xi^t(x)) = \xi^t(x) - f(t, x)$ with $\zeta^t(x)$ we have

$$X(t + 1) = X(t) + \frac{[f(t, X(t)) - X(t)] + \zeta^t(X(t))}{t + n^A(0) + n^B(0)}. \tag{2.2}$$

Provided that there exist a limit urn function $f(\cdot)$ (defined as that function $f(\cdot)$ such that $f(t,.)$ tends to it as *t* tends to ∞) and the following condition is satisfied

$$\sum_{t \geq 1} t^{-1} \sup_{x \in [0,1] \cap R(0,1)} |f(t,x) - f(x)| < \infty, \tag{2.3}$$

where $R(0,1)$ is the set of rational numbers in $(0,1)$, limit market shares attainable with positive probability can be found by analysing the properties of the function

$$g(x) = f(x) - x = \lim_{t \to \infty} f(t,x) - x.$$

Particularly, treating $g(x)$ in the same way as the right-hand side of an ordinary differential equation, it is possible to show that the process (2.2) converges almost surely to the set of stable zeros.[4] The foregoing formal representation is employed for every result of the present chapter.

In some cases, equation (2.1) can be expressed directly in terms of shares rather than total numbers: in this case $f(.,.)$ is independent of t and (2.3) is easily verified.

The foregoing formal model can be better visualized by looking at some well-known example. Consider for instance the celebrated example of the VCR market. JVC's VHS and Sony's Beta were commercialised approximately at the same time. According to many studies (see Cusumano et al., 1992; Liebowitz and Margolis, 1994), none of the two standards has ever been perceived as unambiguously better and, despite their incompatibility, their features were more or less the same, due to the common derivation from the U-matic design. The relevant decisions were likely to be sequential. First, a consumer chooses whether or not to adopt a VCR – technology adoption decision in Katz and Shapiro's terminology. Then, once the adoption decision has been made, it devotes its mind to choose which type of VCR to purchase – product selection decision – (in general it can be expected that most of the consumers buy one single item and not both). Network effects in this market come mainly from increasing returns in design specialisation and production of VCR models (so that historically all firms specialised just in one single standard) on the supply side, and from increasing returns externalities and consequent availability of home video rental services on the demand side (Cusumano et al., 1992). Despite technical similarities between the two standards, preferences are likely to be strongly heterogeneous, due mainly to a brand-name-loyalty in consumer behaviour, which was in fact exploited (especially by JVC) through original equipment manufacturers' (OEM) agreements with firms with well-established market shares in electronic durable goods.

The size of VCR market is sufficiently large (hundreds of millions of sold units) to make it approximable by the abstract concept of an infinite capacity market. Therefore, the asymptotic dynamics of this market may be meaningfully analysed through the asymptotics of generalised urn schemes.

Many other markets display somewhat similar characteristics (for instance, spreadsheets, wordprocessors, computer keyboards, Pc hardware, automobiles and so on). In particular, in many markets product selection can be assumed to sequentially follow technology adoption decisions.[5] The fact that decisions are sequential suggests that product selection decisions might be dependent on market shares rather than on the absolute size of the network. In this case the urn scheme would be even more simplified, with the urn function independent of t.

Arthur (1983; 1989) considers a pay-off function of the following type:

$$\Pi_j^i(\overrightarrow{n}(t)) = a_j^i + r(n^j(t)),$$

where $j = A, B, i \in S$, S is the set of possible types [in the simplest case, considered also in the above quotation from Cowan (1990), $S = \{1,2\}$], and r is an increasing function (common for every agent) capturing increasing returns to adoption. If, at time t, an agent of type i comes to the market, it compares the two pay-off functions choosing A if and only if:

$$\Pi_A^i(\overrightarrow{n}(t)) \geq \Pi_B^i(\overrightarrow{n}(t)),$$

that is

$$a_A^i + r(n^A(t)) \geq a_B^i + r(n^B(t)). \tag{2.4}$$

Suppose that the selection of which type of agent enters the market at time t is the realisation of an iid random variable $i(t)$. Thus (2.2) implies that the agent coming to the market chooses A with probability

$$\mathcal{P}(A(t)) = F_0(r(n^A(t) - r(n^B(t))),$$

where $F_\theta(\cdot)$ denotes the distribution function of $\theta(t) = a_B^i(t) - a_A^i(t)$.

From these considerations Arthur's main theorem was derived:

Theorem 1 (Arthur (1989), Theorem 3)

If the improvement function r increases at least at rate $\varepsilon > 0$ as n^j increases, the adoption process converges to the dominance of a single technology, with probability one.

The proof of the theorem offered by Arthur is based on theorem 3.1 of Arthur et al. (1986). In fact it is easy to check that in this case, whatever the distribution of a_j is, the limit urn function $f(\cdot)$ is a step function defined in the following way:

$$f(x) = \begin{cases} 1 & \text{if} \quad x > 1/2 \\ F_\theta(0) & \text{if} \quad x = 1/2 \\ 0 & \text{if} \quad x < 1/2 \end{cases} \quad (2.5)$$

A generaliszed urn scheme characterised by an urn function such as (2.5) converges to $\{0,1\}$ with probability 1.[6]

However theorem 3.1 of Arthur et al. (1986) is not applicable here because condition (2.3) does not hold in this case. Actually the urn functions are defined by:

$$f_t(x) = F_\theta(r(x(t + n^w + n^b)) - r((1 - x)(t + n^w + n^b))).$$

Moreover for $t > K > 0$, t even, they are such that $f_t(0) = 0$, $f_t(1/2) = F_\theta(0)$, $f_t(1) = 1$ and they are continuous in a left neighbourhood (which depends on t) of $1/2$; therefore

$$\sup_{x \in [0,1] \cap R(0,1)} |f_t(x) - f(x)| \geq \min\{F_\theta(0), 1 - F_\theta(0)\}$$

which is constant with respect to t.[7]

Even though Arthur's proof is *wrong*, the theorem is *right* and an ad hoc proof can be constructed by showing that $n^A(t) - n^B(t)$ is a time-homogeneous Markov chain with two absorbing barriers (Bassanini, 1997, proposition 2.1, provides a complete proof along these lines). However this result strictly depends on the fact that the function $r(\cdot)$ is asymptotically linear or more than linear. Arthur's result is not generalisable to any type of unbounded increasing returns. Both in the case of increasing returns that are diminishing at the margin and in the case of heterogeneous increasing returns it is possible to find simple examples where convergence to technological monopolies is not an event with probability 1.

Let us illustrate all this by means of two straightforward counter-examples.

Example 1

Let us assume that increasing returns have the common sense property that the marginal contribution to social benefit of, say, the 100th adopters is larger than that of, say, the 100 000th and that this contribution tends asymptotically to zero; formally this means that $\frac{d}{dn^j}f(n^j) > 0$, $\frac{d^2}{dn^{j2}}f(n^j) < 0$ and $\lim_{n^j \to \infty}\frac{d}{dn^j}f(n^j) = 0$ (this class of functions has been considered by Katz and Shapiro, 1985).

Focusing on the case set forth by Robin Cowan in the above quotation, let us assume that there are only two types of agents ($i = 1, 2$) and two technologies. Recall Arthur's pay-off functions (2.4), $\Pi_j^i(\overrightarrow{n}(t)) = a_j^i + r(n^j(t))$, and assume that $r(\cdot) = s\log(\cdot)$ is a function (which is common for every agent:

s is a constant) that formalises unbounded increasing returns to adoption. Agent i chooses technology A if and only if $\Pi^i_A(\overrightarrow{n}(t)) \geq \Pi^i_B + (\overrightarrow{n}(t))$. By taking the exponential on both sides and rearranging we have:

$$\frac{X(t)}{1 - X(t)} \geq e^{s(a^i_B(t) - a^i_A(t))}. \tag{2.6}$$

The function of the attributes of agent's type which is on the right-hand side can be considered a random variable because, as discussed above, $i(t)$ is a random variable. Moreover such agent characteristics are iid because $i(t)$ is iid. Denoting the random variables on the right-hand side with $\varsigma(t)$, from (2.6) we have that the adoption process can be seen as a generalised urn scheme with urn function given by:

$$f(x) = F\varsigma,(x/(1-x)), \tag{2.7}$$

where $F\varsigma(\cdot)$ is the distribution function of $\varsigma(t)$. Because $i(t)$ takes just two values $(1, 2)$, also $\varsigma(t)$ takes just two values:

$$\varsigma(t) = \begin{cases} e^{\frac{1}{s}(a^1_B - a^1_A)} & \text{with probability} \quad \alpha \\ e^{\frac{1}{s}(a^2_B - a^2_A)} & \text{with probability} \quad 1 - \alpha \end{cases}$$

where we have assumed without loss of generality that

$$a^1_B - a^1_A \leq a^2_B - a^2_A.$$

Thus F_ς is by construction a step function with two steps:

$$F_\varsigma(y) = \begin{cases} 0 & \text{if} \quad y \leq e^{\frac{1}{s}(a^1_B - a^1_A)} \\ \alpha & \text{if} \quad e^{\frac{1}{s}(a^1_B - a^1_A)} < y \leq e^{\frac{1}{s}(a^2_B - a^2_A)} \\ 1 & \text{if} \quad y > e^{\frac{1}{s}(a^2_B - a^2_A)} \end{cases}$$

Therefore, taking into account (2.7), we have that the urn function has two steps and is defined in the following way:

$$f(x) = \begin{cases} 0 & \text{if} \quad x < \dfrac{e^{\frac{1}{s}(a^1_B - a^1_A)}}{1 + e^{\frac{1}{s}(a^1_B - a^1_A)}} \\[3mm] \alpha & \text{if} \quad \dfrac{e^{\frac{1}{s}(a^1_B - a^1_A)}}{1 + e^{\frac{1}{s}(a^1_B - a^1_A)}} < x \leq \dfrac{e^{\frac{1}{s}(a^2_B - a^2_A)}}{1 + e^{\frac{1}{s}(a^2_B - a^2_A)}} \\[3mm] 1 & \text{if} \quad x > \dfrac{e^{\frac{1}{s}(a^2_B - a^2_A)}}{1 + e^{\frac{1}{s}(a^2_B - a^2_A)}} \end{cases}$$

If the following condition is satisfied

$$\frac{e^{\frac{1}{s}(a^1_B - a^1_A)}}{1 + e^{\frac{1}{s}(a^1_B - a^1_A)}} < \alpha < \frac{e^{\frac{1}{s}(a^2_B - a^2_A)}}{1 + e^{\frac{1}{s}(a^2_B - a^2_A)}}$$

the urn function has five fixed points, three of which are down-crossing, therefore there is a set of initial conditions (that imply giving both technologies a chance to be chosen 'at the beginning of history') for which market sharing is asymptotically attainable with positive probability.[8] The above condition imply that the ratios $(e^{a_A^j})^{1/r}/(e^{a_B^j})^{1/r}$ are sufficiently different between the two types. In other words *there might be sufficient heterogeneity among agents to counterbalance the effect of increasing returns to adoption.*[9]

Example 2

Consider now pay-off functions of this type:

$$\Pi_j(\vec{n}(t)) = a_j + r_j n^j,$$

where r_j, a_j, $j = A, B$, are bounded random variables which admit density. Such functions allow agents to be heterogeneous also in terms of the degree of increasing returns which they experience. By applying (2.1), dividing pay-off functions by total number of adoptions, and rearranging we have that A is chosen if and only if:

$$X(t) \geq \frac{r_B}{r_A + r_B} + \frac{a_B - a_A}{(t + n^A(0) + n^B(0))(r_A + r_B)}. \tag{2.8}$$

Denoting the random variables on the right-hand side with $\varsigma(t)$, from (2.8) we have that the adoption process can be seen as a generalised urn scheme with urn function $f(t, x) = F_{\varsigma(t)}(x)$, where $F_{\varsigma(t)}(\cdot)$ is the distribution function of $\varsigma(t)$. Now suppose that r_A and r_B are highly correlated and both have bimodal distributions very concentrated around the two modes, in such a way that the distribution of r_A/r_B is also bimodal and very concentrated around the two modes too. Furthermore suppose that the two modes are far away from each other. To fix the ideas say that for a percentage α of the population r_A/r_B, is uniformly distributed on the interval $[1/(1-b), 1/(1-a)]$, while for a percentage $1 - \alpha$ of the population r_A/r_B is uniformly distributed on the interval $[1/(1-d), 1/(1-c)]$, with $0 < a < b < c < d$. First, let us consider the case of $a_j = 0, j = A, B$. F_ς is by construction independent of t, implying the following urn function:

$$f(x) = F_{\varsigma(t)}(x) = \begin{cases} 0 & \text{if } y \leq a \\ \alpha \frac{1}{b-a}(y-a) & \text{if } a < y \leq b \\ \alpha & \text{if } b < y \leq c \\ \alpha + (1-\alpha)[\frac{1}{d-c}(y-c)] & \text{if } c < y \leq d \\ 1 & \text{if } y > d \end{cases}$$

If $b<\alpha<c$, then there are three stable fixed point of $f(x)$ and, as stated above, it can be shown that there is a set of initial conditions (that imply giving both technologies a chance to be chosen 'at the beginning of history') for which market sharing is asymptotically attainable with positive probability. If $a_j\neq 0$ but has bounded support and admits density, then condition (2.3) applies and the same argument holds: in fact, relying on the fact that r_j, a_j are bounded it is easy to show that $\sup_{x\in[0,1]\cap R(0,1)}|f(t,x)-f(x)|<K/t$, where $K>0$ is a constant. The essential ingredient of this example is that the distribution of r_A/r_B is bimodal and very concentrated around the two modes. The argument has nothing to do with the particular (and extreme) distributional form assumed above: following the same constructive procedure adopted here it is easy to build examples with any other distributional form. The only requirement is that the two modes are sufficiently distant. In other words the only requirement is a sufficient degree of heterogeneity in the population to counterbalance the pro-standardisation effects of increasing returns to adoption.

The two examples above show that the degree of increasing returns needs to be compared to the degree of heterogeneity. Unbounded increasing returns that are diminishing fast at the margin are not sufficient to generate asymptotic survival of only one technology, provided that agents are not completely homogeneous (see also Farrell and Saloner, 1985; 1986, for early models with homogeneous agents that lead to the survival of only one technology). Even more interesting, when heterogeneity is so wide that there are agent-specific increasing returns, the emergence of technological monopolies is not guaranteed even with returns that are linearly increasing.

To summarise, the foregoing examples show that if preferences are sufficiently heterogeneous and/or increasing returns to adoption are less than asymptotically linear, then Arthur's result cannot be generalised and variety in the asymptotic distribution of technologies can be an outcome with positive probability.

From the point of view of empirical predictions, at first look, the foregoing results might sound, if anything, as a further pessimistic note on 'indeterminacy'. That is, not only 'history matters' in the sense that initial small events might determine which of the notional, technologically attainable, asymptotic states the system might 'choose': more troubling, the argument so far suggests that, further, the very distribution of the fine characteristics and preferences of the population of agents might determine the very nature of the attainable asymptotic states themselves. Short of empirically convincing restrictions on the distribution of agents (normally unobservable) characteristics, what we propose is instead an interpretation of the general occurrence of technological monopolies (*cum* increasing returns of some kind) grounded on the relative speed of convergence to the underlying (but unobservable) limit states.

3 RATE OF CONVERGENCE IN ONE-DIMENSIONAL MODELS OF COMPETING TECHNOLOGIES

In the example of the VCR market, as well as for many other markets, the possibility of predicting limit market shares depends on the feasibility of formalising the structure of the market in question in terms of a specific urn function. Heterogeneity of preferences, the degrees of increasing returns, the type of expectations, price-policies of producers, all affect the functional form of the urn function. As mentioned before, the goal of this chapter in general and of this section in particular is to provide some general asymptotic results that can be used as guidance for the interpretation of the empirical evidence on emergence of dominant designs.

Propositions 2, and 4 suffice for the task. Together they imply the relevant statements on the rate of convergence to technological monopoly or to a limit market share where both technologies coexist.[10] Furthermore the analysis that follows applies even in the absence of a clear pattern of increasing returns to adoption. In essence, in the presence of constant returns to adoption, the urn function would be completely constant but the following theorems would still hold.

As above, denote the urn function with $f(\cdot,\cdot)$; the following proposition gives a first result on the rate of convergence to 0 and 1.

Proposition 1
Let $\varepsilon > 0$ and $c < 1$ be such that eventually

$$f(t,x) < cx \quad for \ x \in (0, \varepsilon)$$

$$(f(t,x)) \geq 1 - c(1 - x) \quad for \ x \in (1 - \varepsilon, 1)). \tag{2.9}$$

Then for any $\delta \in (0, 1 - c)$ and $\tau > 0$

$$\lim_{t \to \infty} \mathcal{P}\{t^{1-c-\delta}X(t) < \tau | X(t) \to 0\} = 1$$

$$(\lim_{t \to \infty} \mathcal{P}\{t^{1-c-\delta}[1 - X(t)] < \tau | X(t) \to 1 = 1),$$

where $X(\cdot)$ stands for the random process given by (2.2).
The proposition is proved in the appendix (section 5).

A similar result can be expressed in terms of variances (L^2 − convergence):

Proposition 2

Let $\varepsilon > 0$ and $c < 1$ be such that eventually (2.9) holds. Then for any $\delta \in (0, 1 - c)$

$$\lim_{t \to \infty} t^{2(1-c)-\delta} P\{X(t) \to 0\} \int_{\{X(t) \to 0\}} X(t)^2 d\mathcal{P} = 0$$

$$(\lim_{t \to \infty} t^{2(1-c)-\delta} P\{X(t) \to 1\} \int_{\{X(t) \to 1\}} (X(t) - 1)^2 d\mathcal{P} = 0$$

The proposition is proved in the appendix (section 5).

Notice that proposition 2 states that the rate of convergence of the mean square distance from the limit market share is of the order of $1/t$ as $t \to \infty$, conditional to the fact that the process is actually converging to 0 or 1. Roughly speaking it defines the rate of convergence of mean square errors when the process converges to a technological monopoly. If the set of limit market shares that the process can reach with positive probability contains only these two points, proposition 2 implies a similar statement in terms of the unconditional mean square distance from the limit market share.

One would like to derive a counterpart of proposition 1 and 2 for the case of market sharing, whenever this can be attained with positive probability. For a differentiable $f(\cdot)$ at 0(1), (2.9) holds with c arbitrarily close to $\frac{d}{dx} f(0)(\frac{d}{dx} f(1))$. We can easily derive a similar result for a differentiable $f(\cdot)$ independent of t from the following conditional limit theorem for the generalised urn scheme.

Theorem 2 (Arthur et al., 1987)

Let $\theta \in (0,1)$ be a stable root of $f(x) - x = 0$ and $f(\cdot)$ is differentiable at θ with $\frac{d}{dx} f(\theta) < 1/2$. Then for every $y \in (-\infty, \infty)$

$$\lim_{t \to \infty} P\left\{ \sqrt{t \frac{1 - 2\frac{d}{dx} f(\theta)}{2\theta(1 - \theta)}} [X(t) - \theta] < y \mid X(t) \to \theta \right\} = \Phi(y),$$

where $\Phi(\cdot)$ stands for the Gaussian distribution function having zero mean and variance 1.

From this theorem, we can give an even better characterisation of the lowest possible convergence rate for a limit market share where both technology coexist that can be attained with positive probability. Indeed, the next proposition follows immediately:

Proposition 3
Let $\theta \in (0,1)$ *be a stable root and let*

$$[f(x) - \theta](x - \theta) > k(x - \theta)^2 \quad \text{for} \quad x \in (\theta - \varepsilon, \theta + \varepsilon), x \neq \theta$$

take place for some $\varepsilon > 0$ *and* $k < 1/2$. *Then for every* $\delta, \tau > 0$

$$\lim_{t \to \infty} \mathcal{P}\{t^{1/2 + \delta}|X(t) - \theta| < \tau|X(t) \to 0\} = 0.$$

Differentiability of the urn function at the limit point is a highly demanding restriction, as well as the fact that the urn function has to be independent of t. As said before, several actual markets can present overwhelming problems of formalisation. Consequently, it may be impossible to check these conditions, albeit intuitively there is no reason why differentiability should matter. Conversely, we can obtain a general result in terms of L^2- convergence that suffices to the task:

Proposition 4
Let $\theta \in (0,1)$ *be such that*

$$[f(t,x) - \theta](x - \theta) > k(x - \theta)^2 \quad \text{for} \quad x \in (\theta - \varepsilon, \theta + \varepsilon), x \neq \theta \quad (2.10)$$

takes place eventually for some $\varepsilon > 0$ *and* $k < 1$. *Then for every* $\delta > 0$

$$\lim_{t \to \infty} t^{2\min\{1-k, 1/2\} + \delta} \mathcal{P}\{X(t) \to \theta\} \int_{\{X(t) \to \theta\}} (X(t) - \theta)^2 d\mathcal{P} \neq 0.$$

The proposition is proved in the appendix (section 5).

Propositions 2 and 4 show that convergence to 0 and 1 can be much faster (almost of order $1/t$ as $t \to \infty$) than to an interior limit (which can be almost of order $1/\sqrt{t}$ only).[11] Here t stands for the number of adoptions to the urn. That is, we are talking about relative rates (the ideal time which is considered here is the time of product selection choices). This result is, however, stronger than it may seem at first glance. In fact it has also implications for the patterns of product selection in 'real' (empirical) time where plausibly the speed of the market share trajectory depends also on technology adoption decisions. There is much qualitative evidence and some econometric results [for example, Koski and Nijkamp, 1997) showing that technology adoption is at the very least independent of market shares if not enhanced by increasing asymmetry in their distribution. Thus a fortiori we can conclude that there is a natural tendency of this class of processes to converge faster to 0 or 1 rather than to an interior limit. The explanation is that the variance of $\zeta^t(x)$, which characterises the level of random disturbances in the process (2.2), is $f(t, x)(1 - f(t, x))$. Under condition (2.9) this value vanishes at 0 and 1 but it does not vanish at $\theta \in (0,1)$, being equal to $\theta(1 - \theta)$, under condition (2.10). Notice also that in example 1 $c = 0$ and in example 2 $c \cong 0$.

As shown in the previous section, the urn function can have any shape and there is no reason to believe that problems characterised by 0 and 1 as the only stable points are the only ones that we can expect. Therefore, in principle, an asymptotic outcome where both technologies survive should be observable with positive frequency in real markets. As discussed in the previous section the tendency to converge to market sharing or technological monopolies is an outcome induced by the relative impact of heterogeneity of preferences and increasing returns to adoption. What tendency is realised depends on which of the two prevails. Notice, however, that the prevalence of one of the two factors is not always predictable *ex ante* even for a nearly omniscient agent fully aware of all fundamentals of the economy: in the examples of the previous section both type of outcomes are possible, but which one is realised depends on the actual sequence of historical events that lead to it. In this type of models, in general, when multiple asymptotic equilibria are attainable, history plays a major role in the selection of the actual one.[12]

If asymptotic patterns were observable, the results of the previous section would imply that we should observe both stable market sharing and technological monopolies. However, for the interpretation of empirical stylised facts, the point where the process eventually would converge may be irrelevant. Indeed, the rate of change of the technological and economic environment can be sufficiently high that one can always observe diffusion dynamics well short of any meaningful neighbourhood of the limit it would have attained under forever constant external conditions. So while it is true that a convergent process should generate a long-lasting stable pattern, the time required to generate it may be too long to actually observe it: the world is likely to change well before convergence is actually attained. In a sense these changes can be viewed as resetting the game to its starting point.

On the basis of the propositions of this section we notice that convergence to technological monopolies tends to be much faster (in probabilistic terms) than to any stable market sharing where both technologies coexist, because of the intrinsic variability that market sharing carries over. Thus the empirical prediction of these results can be stated as follows: in markets with increasing returns to adoption and a high rate of technological change we expect to observe a prevalence of both unstable market sharing (persistent fluctuations in the market shares) and stable technological quasi-monopolies as compared to stable patterns of market sharing. The reason for this is that technological monopolies can be easily attained in a reasonably short time, that is, sufficiently before any significative change in the underlying basic technological paradigms takes place (Dosi, 1982).

Finally note that the observation of the frequent emergence of different monopolies in different related markets (for example, different geographical areas) does not contradict our empirical predictions. Of course, it is trivially true that, with mutually independent markets, different trajectories could emerge in different markets as if they were different realisations of the same experiment. In a related paper (Bassanini and Dosi, 1999a) we show that the foregoing results can be extended also to the case when markets are interdependent: not contrary to the intuition, it is the balance between local and global feedbacks which determines whether the system converges to the same or different monopolies in every market. However, even though at high level of aggregation a system of different local monopolies looks like a stable market sharing, it is shown there that it has the same rate-of-convergence properties of a 'univariate' system converging to a monopoly.

4   CONCLUSIONS

This Chapter has reassessed the empirical evidence on prevalence of technological monopolies over market sharing in the dynamics of competing technologies. First, we have argued that the dominant explanation in the literature, namely that unbounded increasing returns can be identified as the factor responsible for this pattern, does not always hold. Brian Arthur's results – we have shown – hold only when increasing returns to adoption are linear or more than linear and the degree of heterogeneity of agents is small. The presented counter-examples suggest that asymptotic patterns of the dynamics of competing technologies depend on the relative impact of (unbounded) increasing returns and the degree of heterogeneity of the population of adopters. Second, given all this, we propose, however, that in a market with high technological dynamism, no interesting predictions can be made by simply looking at theoretical asymptotic patterns. If convergence is too slow the environment may change before the limit can be actually approached. Conversely, developing upon some mathematical properties of Polya urns, we show that convergence to technological monopolies tends to be (in probabilistic terms) much faster than to a limit where both technologies coexist, the empirical implication being that in markets with high turnover of basic technologies, a prevalence of technological monopolies over stable market sharing is likely to be observed.

40   *Path dependence in technical change*

APPENDIX

For the purpose of exposition, to keep the notation simple, all proofs are exposed for generalised urn scheme involving time-independent urn functions. They can be easily repeated for the general case.

Proof of Proposition 1

Consider only the first case – convergence to 0. Without loss of generality we can assume that $P\{X(t) \to 0\} > 0$. Indeed the theorem, being a statement about the convergence rate to 0, does not make any sense if $X(\cdot)$ does not converge to 0.

Let $Z(\cdot)$ be a conventional urn process with cx as the urn-function and the same initial numbers of balls $n = n^w + n^b$. Then

$$EZ(t+1) \le \left(1 - \frac{1-c}{t+n}\right)EZ(t), \ t \ge 1,$$

and consequently

$$EZ(t) \le EZ(1)\Pi_{j=1}^{t-1}(1 - \tfrac{1-c}{j+n}) \le EZ(1)e^{c-1\sum_{j=1}^{t-1}\frac{1}{(n+j)}}$$

$$\le EZ(1)e^{c-1}\int_{n+1}^{n+t-1}\tfrac{1}{x}dx = EZ(1)(\tfrac{n+1}{n+t-1})^{1-c} = EZ(1)t^{c-1}[1 + o_t(1)],$$

where $o_t(1) \to 0$ as $t \to \infty$. Hence from Chebychev's inequality

$$P\{t^{1-c-\delta}Z(t) > \tau\} \to 0 \quad as \quad t \to \infty \tag{2.11}$$

for every $\delta \in (0, 1 - c)$ and $\tau > 0$.

For arbitrary $\sigma \in (0, \varepsilon)$ and $v > 0$ there is N depending on these variables such that

$$P\{\{X(t) \to 0\} \Delta \{X(s) \le \sigma, s \ge N\}\} < v$$

where $A\Delta B = (A\backslash B) \cup (B\backslash A)$. Also since $Z(t) \to 0$ with probability 1 as $t \to \infty$, we can choose this N so large that

$$P\{\{X(t) \to 0\} \Delta \{X(s) \le \sigma, Z(s) \le \sigma, s \ge N\}\} < v. \tag{2.12}$$

To prove the theorem it is enough to show that

$$P\{t^{1-c-\delta}X(t) > \tau, X(t) \to 0\} \to 0,$$

or, taking into account that v in (2.12) can be arbitrary small, that

$$P\{t^{1-c-\delta}X(t)>\tau, X(s)\leq\sigma, Z(s)\leq\sigma, s\geq N\}\to 0. \qquad (2.13)$$

However

$$P\{t^{1-c-\delta}X(t)>\tau, X(s)\leq\sigma, Z(s)\leq\sigma, s\geq N$$

$$=\sum_{y\in S_N^X} P\left\{\begin{array}{l}t^{1-c-\delta}X(t)>\tau, X(s)\leq\sigma, \\ Z(s)\leq\sigma, s\geq N\end{array}\bigg| X(N)=y\right\}$$

$$P\{X(N)=y\}, \qquad (2.14)$$

where $S_t^X = \{\frac{X(1)(n+i)}{n+t-1}, 0\leq i\leq t-1\}$ is the set of values that $X(t)$ can attain (not necessarily with positive probability). Due to lemma 2.2 of Hill et al. (1980), there exists a probability space such that $Z(\cdot)$ dominates $X(\cdot)$ on the event $Z(t)\leq\sigma$, $t\geq N$, providing that these processes start from the same point. Therefore, for any $y\in S_N^X$

$$P\{t^{1-c-\delta}X(t)>\tau, X(s)\leq\sigma, Z(s)\leq\sigma, s\geq N|X(N)=y\}$$

$$\leq P\{t^{1-c-\delta}Z(t)>\tau, X(s)\leq\sigma, Z(s)\leq\sigma, s\geq N|X(N)=y\}.$$

However for every $y\in S_N^X$

$$P\{t^{1-c-\delta}Z(t)>\tau, X(s)\leq\sigma, Z(s)\leq\sigma, s\geq N\}$$

$$\leq P\{t^{1-c-\delta}Z(t)>\tau\}\to 0$$

as $t\to\infty$ by (2.11). Thus (2.14) is a sum of a finite number – namely N – of terms each converging to zero. This completes the proof.

Proof of Proposition 2

As before, consider only the first case – convergence to 0.

Let $Z(\cdot)$ be a conventional urn process with cx as the urn-function and the same initial numbers of balls $n = n^w + n^b$. Then

$$E[Z(t+1)^2|Z(t)] = Z(t)^2$$

$$+\frac{2}{n+t}(c-1)Z(t)^2 + \frac{1}{(n+t)^2}(c-1)^2Z(t)^2$$

$$+\frac{1}{(n+t)^2}c(1-c)^2Z(t)^2$$

and

$$E[Z(t+1)^2] = \left(1 - \frac{2(1-c)}{t+n} + \frac{1-c}{(t+n)^2}\right) E[Z(t)^2], \quad t \geq 1,$$

and consequently

$$E[Z(t)^2] = E[Z(1)^2] \Pi_{j=1}^{t-1} [1 - \tfrac{2(1-c)}{j+n} + o_j(1/j)]$$

$$\leq E[Z(1)^2] e^{2(c-1)\sum_{j=1}^{t-1} \frac{1}{(n+j)}} \leq E[Z(1)^2] e^{2(c-1)\int_{n+1}^{n+t-1} \frac{1}{x} dx}$$

$$= E[Z(1)^2] (\tfrac{n+1}{n+t-1})^{2(1-c)} = E[Z(1)^2[t^{2(c-1)}][1 + o_t(1)],$$

where $t^s o_t(1/t^s) \to 0$ as $t \to \infty$. Hence:

$$t^{2(1-c-\delta)} E[Z(t)^2] \to 0 \quad as \quad t \to \infty \tag{2.15}$$

for every $\delta \in (0, 1-c)$.

For arbitrary $\sigma \in (0, \varepsilon)$ and $v > 0$ there is N depending on these variables such that

$$P\{\{X(t) \to 0\} \Delta \{X(s) \leq \sigma, s \geq N\}\} < v,$$

where $A\Delta B = (A\backslash B) \cup (B\backslash A)$. Also since $Z(t) \to 0$ with probability 1 as $t \to \infty$, we can choose this N so large that

$$P\{\{X(t) \to 0\} \Delta \{X(s) \leq \sigma, Z(s) \leq \sigma, s \geq N\}\} < v. \tag{2.16}$$

To prove the theorem it is enough to show that

$$t^{2(1-c-\delta)} \int_{\{X(t) \to 0\}} X(t)^2 d\mathcal{P} \to 0,$$

or, taking into account that v in (2.16) can be arbitrary small, that

$$t^{2(1-c-\delta)} \int_{\{X(s) \leq \sigma, Z(s) \leq \sigma, s \geq N\}} X(t)^2 d\mathcal{P} \to 0, \tag{2.17}$$

However,

$$t^{2(1-c-\delta)} \int_{\{X(s) \leq \sigma, Z(s) \leq \sigma, s \geq N\}} X(t)^2 d\mathcal{P}$$

$$= \sum_{y \in S_N^X} t^{2(1-c-\delta)} \int_{\{X(s) \leq \sigma, Z(s) \leq \sigma, s \geq N, X(N)=y\}} X(t)^2 d\mathcal{P} \tag{2.18}$$

where $S_t^X = \{\frac{X(1)(n+i)}{n+t-1}, 0 \leq i \leq t-1\}$ is the set of values that $X\{t\}$ can attain (not necessarily with positive probability). Due to lemma 2.2 of Hill et al. (1980), there exists a probability space such that $Z(\cdot)$ dominates $X(\cdot)$ on the event $Z(t) < \sigma$, $t > N$, providing that these processes start from the same point. Therefore, for any $t > N$ and $y \in S_N^X$

$$t^{2(1-c-\delta)} \int_{\{X(s) \leq \sigma,\, Z(s) \leq \sigma,\, s \geq N,\, X(N)=y\}} X(t)^2 d\mathcal{P}$$

$$\leq t^{2(1-c-\delta)} \int_{\{X(s) \leq \sigma,\, Z(s) \leq \sigma,\, s \geq N,\, X(N)=y\}} Z(t)^2 d\mathcal{P}$$

However, for every $y \in S_N^X$

$$t^{2(1-c-\delta)} \int_{\{X(s) \leq \sigma,\, Z(s) \leq \sigma,\, s \geq N,\, X(N)=y\}} Z(t)^2 d\mathcal{P}$$

$$\leq t^{2(1-c-\delta)} E[Z(t)^2] \to 0$$

as $t \to \infty$ by (2.15). Thus (2.18) is a sum of a finite number – namely N – of terms each converging to zero. This completes the proof.

Proof of Proposition 4

The proof is based on the following lemmas:[13]

Lemma 1
Let $f(.)$ be the urn function of the process $Z(t)$ such that

$$[f(x) - \theta](x - \theta) > k(x - \theta)^2$$

for some $k < 1$ and $\theta \in (0,1)$ and $f(x)[1 - f(x)] \geq \alpha > 0$. Then $\lim_{t \to \infty} d_t = \lim_{t \to \infty} E(Z(t) - \theta)^2$, where

$$d_t \geq K \begin{cases} (n+t)^{-1} & \text{if } 2(1-k) - 1 > 0 \\ (n+t)^{-1} \log(n+t) & \text{if } 2(1-k) - 1 = 0 \\ (n+t)^{-2(1-k)} & \text{if } 2(1-k) - 1 < 0 \end{cases}$$

where K is a constant term.

44   *Path dependence in technical change*

Proof

Consider the process (2.2) and write $n = n^w + n^b$, then:

$$E[(Z(t+1) - \theta)^2]X(t)] = (Z(t) - \theta)^2$$
$$+ \tfrac{2}{n+i}[f(Z(t)) - Z(t)](Z(t) - \theta) + \tfrac{1}{(n+t)^2}[f(Z(t)) - Z(t)]^2$$
$$+ \tfrac{1}{(n+t)^2}f(Z(t))[1 - f(Z(t))].$$

Setting $\Delta_t = E(Z(t) - \theta)^2$, from the assumptions of the lemma, taking into account that $f(Z(t))[1 - f(Z(t))] \geq \alpha$, and that

$$[f(Z(t)) - Z(t)](Z(t) - \theta) = [f(Z(t)) - \theta](Z(t) - \theta) - (Z(t) - \theta)^2,$$

we have

$$\Delta_{t+1} \geq \Delta_t \left[1 - \frac{2(1-k)}{n+t} \right] + \frac{\alpha}{(n+t)^2}$$

Thus

$$\Delta_{t+1} \geq \Delta_t \prod_{i=1}^{t} \left[1 - \frac{2(1-k)}{n+i} \right] + \sum_{i=1}^{t} \frac{\alpha}{(n+i)^2} \prod_{j=i+1}^{t} \left[1 - \frac{2(1-k)}{n+j} \right]$$

Since

$$\prod_{j=i+1}^{t} \left[1 - \frac{2(1-k)}{n+i} \right] = e^{-2(1-k)\sum_{j=i+1}^{t} \frac{1}{(n+j)}}(1 + \beta_{it})$$

$$\geq e^{-2(1-k)[\log(n+t-1) - \log(n+i)]}(1 + \beta_{it}) = \left(\frac{n+i}{n+t} \right)^{2(1-k)}(1 + \gamma_{it}),$$

where β_{it} and γ_{it} are small terms ($o_t(1)$) not necessarily non-negative,[14] then

$$\Delta_{t+1} \geq \Delta_t \left(\frac{n+1}{n+t} \right)^{2(1-k)}(1 + \gamma_{1t})$$

$$+ \alpha(n+t)^{-2(1-k)}\sum_{i=1}^{t}(n+i)^{-2+2(1-k)}(1 + \gamma_{it}).$$

Since, in terms of asymptotic behaviour,

$$\sum_{i=1}^{t}(n+i)^{-2+2(1-k)} \cong \begin{cases} \frac{1}{2(1-k)-1}(n+t)^{2(1-k)-1} & \text{if } 2(1-k) - 1 \neq 0 \\ \log(n+t) & \text{if } 2(1-k) - 1 = 0 \end{cases}$$

we have that

$$
\Delta_{t+1} \geq K \begin{cases} \frac{1}{2(1-k)-1}(n+t)^{-1} & \text{if } 2(1-k)-1>0 \\ (n+t)^{-1}\log(n+t) & \text{if } 2(1-k)-1=0, \\ \Delta_1(n+t)^{-2(1-k)} & \text{if } 2(1-k)-1<0 \end{cases}
$$

which implies the statement of the lemma.
   Set

$$
f(x) = \begin{cases} f(\theta-\varepsilon) & \text{if } x<\theta-\varepsilon \\ f(x) & \text{if } \theta-\varepsilon<x<\theta+\varepsilon, \\ f(\theta+\varepsilon) & \text{if } x>\theta+\varepsilon \end{cases}
$$

$$
x(t+1) = x(t) + \frac{j^t(x(t)) - x(t)}{t+n},
$$

$$
x(1) = X(1).
$$

Then, with probability $1, x(t) \to \theta$ as $t \to \infty$. Also by lemma 1,

$$
t^{2\min\{1-k,1/2\}+\delta}E[(x(t)-\theta)^2] \to 0 \quad \text{as } t \to \infty. \tag{2.19}
$$

As for proposition 2, we can ignore the case when $X(t)$ does not converge with positive probability.
   We have to show that as $t \to \infty$

$$
t^{2\min\{1-k,1/2\}+\delta} \int_{\{X(t)\to\theta\}} (X(t)-\theta)^2 d\mathcal{P} \to 0, \tag{2.20}
$$

For every $\sigma>0$ there is $t(\sigma)$ such that

$$
\mathcal{P}\{\{X(s)\to\theta\} \Delta \{|X(t)-\theta|<\varepsilon, t \geq t(\sigma)\}\} \leq \sigma.
$$

Since σ can be arbitrarily small, (2.20) holds if and only if

$$
t^{2\min\{1-k,1/2\}+\delta} \int_{\{|X(s)-\theta|<\varepsilon,s\geq t(\sigma)\}} (X(t)-\theta)^2 d\mathcal{P} \to 0,
$$

However,

$$
t^{2\min\{1-k,1/2\}+\delta} \int_{\{|X(s)-\theta|<\varepsilon,s\geq t(\sigma)\}} (X(t)-\theta)^2 d\mathcal{P}
$$

$$
= t^{2\min\{1-k1/2\}+\delta} \sum_{y \in S_{t(\sigma)}} \int_{\{|X(s)-\theta|<\varepsilon,s\geq t(\sigma), X(t(\sigma))=y\}} (X(t)-\theta)^2 d\mathcal{P},
$$

46   *Path dependence in technical change*

where $S_t = S_t = \{\frac{X(1)(n+i)}{n+t-1}, 0 \le i \le t-1\}$ is the set of values that $X(t)$ and $X(t)$ can attain (not necessarily with positive probability). Notice that for any $t > t(\sigma)$ and $y \in S_{t(\sigma)}$

$$\int_{\{|X(s)-\theta|<\varepsilon, s \ge t(\sigma), X(t(\sigma))=y\}} (X(t)-\theta)^2 d\mathscr{P}$$

$$= \int_{\{|X(s)-\theta|<\varepsilon, s \ge t(\sigma), X(t(\sigma))=y\}} (X(t)-\theta)^2 d\mathscr{P}$$

This follows from the fact that $\bar{f}(x)$ and $f(x)$ are the same for $x\,[\theta-\varepsilon, \theta+\varepsilon]$. However,

$$t^{2\min\{1-k,1/2\}+\delta} \sum_{y \in S_{t(\sigma)}} \int_{\{|X(s)-\theta|<\varepsilon, s \ge t(\sigma), X(t(\sigma))=y\}} (X(t)-\theta)^2 d\mathscr{P}$$

$$= t^{2\min\{1-k,1/2\}+\delta} \int_{\{X(t)\to\theta\}} (X(t)-\theta)^2 d\mathscr{P}$$

$$= t^{2\min\{1-k,1/2\}+\delta} E[(X(t)-\theta)^2] \to 0,$$

as $t \to \infty$ by (2.19). This completes the proof.

NOTES

*   The views expressed here cannot be ascribed to the Organisation for Economic Co-operation and Development (OECD) Secretariat or its Member Countries. We are indebted to Yuri Kaniovski for very helpful suggestions. We thank also Brian Arthur, Robin Cowan, Klaus Desmet, Judith Gebauer, Michael Horvath, Andrea Prat, Aldo Rustichini, Valter Sorana, and participants to the 3rd workshop on Economics with Heterogeneous Interacting Agents, Ancona, Italy, May 1998, and to the Conference on Economic Models of Evolutionary Dynamics and Interacting Agents, Trieste, Italy, September 1998, for their comments. Financial support from International Institute for Applied Systems Analysis (IIASA), Banca Nazionale del Lavoro (BNL), Italian Research Council (CNR), and Italian Ministry of University and Scientific Research (MURST) is gratefully acknowledged. All errors are ours.
1.   See, for example, the empirical literature on dominant designs (for a survey, cf. Tushman and Murmann, 1998).
2.   Throughout this chapter we label the generalisation of Polya urn schemes set forth by Hill et al. (1980) as generalised urn scheme. That generalisation is the most popular in economics but obviously it is not the only possible one (see, for example, Walker and Muliere, 1997).
3.   We assume that, if there is a tie, agents choose technology A. Qualitatively, breaking the tie in a different way would not make any difference.
4.   A convenient review of analytical results on generalised urn schemes can be found in Dosi et al. (1994). The reader is referred to that volume for the results that are not proved in this chapter. Particularly, $X(\cdot)$ converges almost surely, as t tends to infinity, to the set of appropriately defined zeros of the function $g(x) = f(x) - x$. However, since we are not

going to restrict ourselves to the case when $g(\cdot)$ is a continuous function, we need some standard definition concerning equations with discontinuous functions. For a function $g(\cdot)$ given on $R(0,1)$ and a point $x \in [0,1]$ set

$$a(x,g) = \inf_{\{y_k\} \subset R(0,1)} \lim \inf_{k \to \infty} g(y_k),$$

$$\bar{a}(x,g) = \sup_{\{y_k\} \subset R(0,1)} \lim \sup_{k \to \infty} g(y_k).$$

where $\{y_k\}$ is an arbitrary sequence converging to x. Then the set of zeros $A(g)$ of $g(\cdot)$ on $[0,1]$ is defined by the following relation

$$A(g) = \{x \in [0,1]: [a(x, g), \bar{a}(x, g) \ni 0\}.$$

Note that for a continuous $g(\cdot)$ this definition gives the roots of the equation $g(x)=0$ in the conventional meaning. One particular class of attainable singleton components comprises the *downcrossing* or *stable* ones, that is, the points where $f(x) - x$ changes its sign from plus to minus. More precisely, $\theta \in R(0,1)$ is said to be *stable* if there exists $\varepsilon > 0$ such that for every $\delta \in (0, \varepsilon)$

$$\inf_{\delta \leq |x - \theta| \leq c} [f(x) - x](x - \theta) < 0. \tag{*}$$

If $\theta \in R(0,1)$ is stable then $X(\cdot)$ converges to θ with positive probability for some initial combination $\vec{n}(0)$. If in addition to (*)

$$f(x) \in (0,1) \quad \text{for all} \quad x \in R(0,1),$$

then it converges with positive probability to θ for any initial combination $\vec{n}(0)$. Finally if the urn function does not have touchpoints and the set $A(g)$ with $g(x)=f(x)-x$ is composed only of singleton components then almost surely the process converges to the set of stable components.

5. For instance, in the data set of Computer Intelligence InfoCorp employed by Breuhan (1996), more than 80 per cent of the firms in the sample report using a single word-processing package.
6. See note 4 above, or Dosi et al. (1994), theorems 1 and 3.
7. To be precise Arthur (1989) quotes also Arthur et al. (1983), though there the properties are stated only as yet-to-be-proved good sense conjectures.
8. See note 4 above, or Dosi et al. (1994), theorem 2.
9. Cowan and Cowan (1998) acknowledge this role of heterogeneity, although only for models where interactions are local. They suggest that many models from other scientific disciplines can be adapted to show market-sharing survival as a result of local interaction effects, and they provide one such example, although restricted to linear returns.
10. Notice that, provided that inequalities (2.9) and (2.10) are eventually satisfied for any t, propositions 1, 2 and 4 hold even if the inequality (2.3) does not hold as may happen when agents are assumed to be forward looking.
11. If returns are constant, the result of proposition 3 and 4 simply becomes the well-known textbook result on rate of convergence of the sample mean and its variance. Bassanini and Dosi (1999b) shows that $2\min\{1-k, 1/2\}$ is also an upper bound to the rate of convergence to an interior limit, therefore proposition 4 could be written in an even stronger way, although not necessary for the task of the present chapter.
12. For a general discussion on this point see also Dosi (1997).
13. We are indebted to Yuri Kaniovski for suggesting us the line of the following proof.
14. The line of reasoning here is the same as for the proof of proposition 1 and 2.

REFERENCES

Arthur, W.B. (1983), 'On competing technologies and historical small events: the dynamics of choice under increasing returns', IIASA Working Paper WP-83-90 (reprinted in W.B. Arthur (1994) *Increasing Returns and Path-Dependence in the Economy*, Ann Arbor, MI: University of Michigan Press, 1983).

Arthur, W.B. (1989), 'Competing technologies, increasing returns and lock-in by historical events', *Economics Journal*, **99**, 116–31.

Arthur, W.B. (1990), ' "Silicon Valley" locational clusters: when do increasing returns imply monopoly?', *Mathematical Social Sciences*, **19**, 235–51.

Arthur, W.B. and D. Lane (1993), 'Information contagion', *Structural Change and Economic Dynamics*, **4**, 81–104.

Arthur, W.B. (1983), Y. Ermoliev and Y. Kaniovski, 'Generalised urn problem and its applications', *Cybernetics*, **19**, 61–71.

Arthur, W.B., Y. Ermoliev and Y. Kaniovski (1986), 'Strong laws for a class of path-dependent urn processes', *Proceedings of the International Conference on Stochastic Optimization, Lecture Notes on Control and Information Sciences*, **81**, 187–300.

Banerjee, A. (1992), 'A simple model of herd behaviour', *Quarterly Journal of Economics*, **107**, 797–817.

Bassanini, A.P. (1997), 'Localized technological change and path-dependent growth', IIASA Interim Report IR-97-086.

Bassanini, A.P. and G. Dosi (1999a), 'Heterogeneous agents, complementarities, and diffusion of technologies: do increasing returns imply convergence to international monopolies?', in D. Delli Gatti, M. Gallegati and A. Kirman (eds), *Market Structure, Aggregation and Heterogeneity*, Berlin, Springer.

Bassanini, A.P. and G. Dosi (1999b), 'Competing technologies, technological monopolies and the rate of convergence to a stable market structure', Laboratory of Economics and Management Working Paper no. 3, Sant 'Anna School of Advanced Studies.

Bernheim, B.D. (1994), 'A theory of conformity', *Journal of Political Economy*, **102**, 841–77.

Breuhan, A.L. (1996), 'Innovation and the persistence of technological lock-in', unpublished manuscript.

Brock, W.A. and S.N. Durlauf (1995), 'Discrete choice with social interactions I: theory', NBER Working Paper no. 5291.

Brynjolfsson, E. and C.F. Kemerer (1996), 'Network externalities in microcomputer software: an econometric analysis of the spreadsheet market', *Management Science*, **42**, 1627–47.

Church, J. and N. Gandal (1993), 'Complementary network externalities and technological adoption', *International Journal of Industrial Organization*, **11** 239–60.

Cowan, R. (1990), 'Nuclear power reactors: a study in technological lock-in', *Journal of Economic History*, **50**, 541–67.

Cowan, R. (1991), 'Tortoises and hares: choice among technologies of unknown merit', *Economic Journal*, **101**, 801–14.

Cowan, R., and W. Cowan (1998), 'Technological standardization with and without borders in an interacting agents model', unpublished paper.

Cusumano, M.A., Y. Milonadis and R.S. Rosenbloom (1992), 'Strategic maneuvering and mass-market dynamics: the triumph of VHS over Beta', *Business History Review*, **66**, 51–94.

David, P. (1985), 'Clio and the economics of QWERTY', *AEA Papers and Proceedings*, **75**, 332–7.

David, P. (1992), 'Heroes, herds and hysteresis in technological theory: Thomas Edison and the battle of systems reconsidered', *Industrial and Corporate Change*, **1**, 129–80.

Dosi, G. (1982), 'Technological paradigms and technological trajectories', *Research Policy*, **11**, 142–67.

Dosi, G. (1997), 'Opportunities, incentives and the collective patterns of technological change', *Economics Journal*, **107**, 1530–47.

Dosi, G., Y. Ermoliev and Y. Kaniovski (1994), 'Generalized urn schemes and technological dynamics', *Journal of Mathematical Economics*, **23**, 1–19.

Economides, N. (1996), 'The economics of networks', *International Journal of Industrial Organization*, **14**, 673–99.

Farrell, J. and G. Saloner (1985), 'Standardization, compatibility and innovation', *Rand Journal of Economics*, **16**, 70–83.

Farrell, J. and G. Saloner (1986), 'Installed base and compatibility: innovation, product preannouncements, and predation', *American Economic Review*, **76**, 940–55.

Hill, B.M., D. Lane and W. Sudderth (1980), 'A strong law for some Generalized urn processes', *Annals of Probability*, **8**, 214–26.

Islas, J. (1997), 'Getting round the lock-in in electricity generating systems: the example of the gas turbine', *Research Policy*, **26**, 49–66.

Katz, M.L. and C. Shapiro (1985), 'Network externalities, competition, and compatibility', *American Economic Review*, **75**, 424–40.

Katz, M.L. and C. Shapiro (1986), 'Technology adoption in the presence of network externalities', *Journal of Political Economy*, **94**, 822–41.

Katz, M.L. and C. Shapiro (1992), 'Product introduction with network externalities', *Journal of Industrial Economics*, **40**, 55–84.

Katz, M.L. and C. Shapiro (1994), 'Systems competition and network effects', *Journal of Economic Perspectives*, **8**, 93–115.

Koski, H. and P. Nijkamp (1997), 'The installed base effect: some empirical evidence from the microcomputer market', unpublished manuscript.

Krugman, P. (1991a), 'History vs. expectations', *Quarterly Journal of Economics*, **106**, 651–67.

Krugman, P. (1991b), *Geography and Trade*, Cambridge, MA: MIT Press.

Liebowitz, S.J. and S.E. Margolis (1994), 'Network externality: an uncommon tragedy', *Journal of Economic Perspectives*, **8**, 133–150.

Oren, S. and S. Smith (1981), 'Critical mass and tariff structure in electronic communications markets', *Bell Journal of Economics*, **12**, 467–87.

Rauch, J.E. (1993), 'Does history matter only when it matters little? The case of city-industry location', *Quarterly Journal of Economics*, **108**, 843–67.

Rohlfs, J. (1974), 'A theory of interdependent demand for a communication service', *Bell Journal of Economics*, **5**, 16–37.

Rosenberg, N. (1982), *Inside the Black Box*, Cambridge: Cambridge University Press.

Saviotti, P.P. and A. Trickett (1992), 'The evolution of helicopter technology', 1940–1986, *Economics of Innovation and New Technology*, **2**, 111–30.

Tushman, M.L. and J.P. Murmann (1998), 'Dominant designs, technology cycles, and organizational outcomes', in B. Staw and L.L. Cummings (eds), *Research in Organizational Behaviour*, **20**, Greenwich, CT: JAI Press.

Venables, A.J. (1996), 'Localization of industry and trade performance', *Oxford Review of Economic Policy*, **12** (3), 52–60.

Walker, S. and P. Muliere (1997), 'Beta-Stacy processes and a generalisation of the Polya-urn scheme', *Annals of Statistics*, **25**, 1762–80.

Winter, S.G. (1986), 'Comments on Arrow and Lucas', *Journal of Business*, **59**, S427–34.

PART V

MACROECONOMIC DYNAMICS AND DEVELOPMENT

[18]

The Process of Economic Development: Introducing Some Stylized Facts and Theories on Technologies, Firms and Institutions*

Giovanni Dosi[a], Christopher Freeman[b] and Silvia Fabiani[c]

([a]Department of Economics, University of Rome 'La Sapienza', Rome, Italy, [b]SPRU, University of Sussex, Brighton, UK and MERIT, University of Limburg, Maastricht, The Netherlands and [c]University of Cambridge, UK)

1. Introduction

This special issue of *Industrial and Corporate Change* brings together diverse streams of analysis on the determinants and characteristics of growth and development. (Here and throughout we accept the distinction between the two put forward in Nelson's article, in this volume, whereby 'growth' is that idealization of economic dynamics in which 'things simply get bigger or smaller or stay the same size', while 'in development, a lot of qualitative changes are also happening'. Needless to say, in this definition, development analyses are by no means confined to less developed countries.)

Despite the variety of the perspectives represented in this volume, most of the articles display at least two unifying themes. The first one is the emphasis on development as a multifaceted process that demands the investigation of the conditions allowing it to take off and to be self-sustained. The second theme is the importance of technological change, of firms' characteristics and behaviours and of institutions, in shaping specific development patterns.

These two themes, by themselves, set also a huge research agenda for

---

* This paper, as well as that by G. Dosi, S. Fabiani, R. Aversi and M. Meacci in this same issue of *ICC*, draws on Dosi *et al.* (1993). The list of 'stylized facts' is enriched by some drawn from K. Arrow and G. Dosi, 'A few stylized facts and puzzles for economic analysis', unpublished communication, Santa Fe Institute, Santa Fe, NM. Earlier versions containing some of these ideas as well as initial explorations of the model of Dosi–Fabiani–Aversi–Meacci's paper appear in Pasinetti and Solow (1994) and Soete and Silverberg (1994).

—————————— *The Process of Economic Development* ——————————

which the contributions that follow can only be considered as sparse elements of a much larger picture still awaiting to be drawn. Indeed, an important achievement would already be to show how the different pieces of the puzzle could in principle hold together.

Until recently, technologies, firms and institutions had all three been strikingly absent from the core of the economists' explanation of growth patterns. (Development theories followed a somewhat different course but in so far as they relied on the analytic apparatus of the economist, they, too, often referred back to variants of the standard growth model—in a shorthand, of the Solow-type.) On the contrary, the view underlying the contributions to this volume—a view held by many other scholars in different quarters of social sciences—is that the interpretation of growth and development requires a detailed understanding of how technological innovations are generated and diffused; of the incentive structure facing economic actors; of the internal organization, competences and strategies of business firms; of the institutions in which agents are embedded and which constrain and guide both microeconomic coordination and change. It seems to us that the neglect of these variables, as once Richard Nelson put it, would be like trying to write a detective story without the detective, the murder, the murderer . . .

A Test Case: The Determinants of Convergence and Divergence

A good point of departure to illustrate the tension between alternative interpretations regards the question of 'why growth rates differ'—as the famous contribution by Denison and Poullier (1967) was entitled. Certainly, economists have put a good deal of effort into answering that question. Equally, economic historians such as Landes (1969), Rosenberg (1976, 1982), Maddison (1982, 1991) and Abramovitz (1989) have devoted considerable attention to 'catching up' as well as divergence ('forging ahead' and 'falling behind') in economic development. However, the prevailing interpretation of economic growth, drawing on neoclassical models, is certainly more comfortable with 'why growth rates should be the same' or at least with convergence to a unique international pattern, rather than with divergence. Even 'new growth' theories, while attempting to account for persistent differences in growth rates, yet do not appear to be apt to handle the historical evidence concerning, e.g. the relative decline of some countries, the instability of the growth performance of the same country over different periods, the 'leap-frogging' which sometimes occurs in international economic leadership.

One of the central topics of many of the articles that follow is precisely the

—————————————————— 2 ——————————————————

———————— *The Process of Economic Development* ————————

analysis of the determinants of both convergence and divergence in the levels and rates of growth of per capita income among countries. In turn, this obviously implies a search for the underlying determinants and processes which might have generated the diverse patterns of development which we observe. Economic historians have stressed the role of technical and institutional change (or lack of it), together with broad country-specific factors such as education, geography, political events. Moreover, some of them have pointed to the importance of capital accumulation (although this remains a somewhat controversial issue) and to the dynamic interaction between trade performance and growth performance.

Conversely, the theoretical account which the orthodox economic discipline provides seems to capture only some of the elements which historians identify as the major determinants of development and very little of the 'action' which they describe. Consider, for example, technological change. Neoclassical models since the pioneering work of Solow (1956, 1957) have pointed—at least by default—to the crucial importance of technical and institutional change as expressed in a relatively large 'residual factor'. But until recently little progress was being made in the formal modeling of technical change itself. 'New growth' theory (e.g. Romer, 1986, 1990a, 1990b; Lucas, 1988; Grossman and Helpman, 1991; Aghion and Howitt, 1992) does attempt to incorporate some measures of technological innovation (despite some significant limitations in the ways technology itself is represented—which we shall discuss below). However, possibly the most striking difference between historians' and economists' interpretations is that the former heavily relies on the joint identification of variables and processes affecting development while the latter most often assumes an invariant (and indeed quite peculiar) economic 'process'—implicitly summarized by the properties of the postulated production function. As well known, the standard Solow production function, $Y(t) = A(t) \cdot F(.)$ relates output to an invariant allocation process, and to a time-drift $(A(t))$, which supposedly ought to capture all the action about which economic historians are talking. In many respects, 'new growth' theories pursue even further that analytical strategy. The thrust of most recent developments is indeed to push the drift within the production function itself, either as an externality or as the outcome of an allocative decision to the production of a particular input— 'knowledge'. While in Solow-type models one has implicitly two major explanatory headings, namely optimal allocations of inputs (the *PF*) and 'learning' (what is left out), many contemporary growth models attempt to model learning, too, as the equilibrium outcome of an optimal allocation mechanism. (Lucas (1988) is a lucid and extremist statement of this research programme.)

———————— 3 ————————

──────────── *The Process of Economic Development* ────────────

Relatedly, 'new growth' models imply also an answer to the question whether it is capital accumulation to drive knowledge growth or the other way round: the claim, in this perspective, is that the former holds, either as an explicit 'investment in knowledge' or as an externality or both.

The answer that historians and students of technological change give to the same question is much less straightforward (see Rosenberg, 1976, 1982; Freeman, 1982; Dosi, 1988; Nelson, in this volume). A lot depends on historical contingencies: sometimes it is the explicit investment in physical capital and innovative search which is the major force driving knowledge augmentation, while in other occurrences it is the progressive realization of unexpected applications of new knowledge sources which leads capital accumulation (a good example of the latter case is the transistor and the subsequent development of a microelectronics industry: more on this in Dosi, 1984; Malerba, 1985). In the last resort, most historians and innovation economists are likely to be comfortable with a 'co-evolutionary' account whereby causality dynamically runs both ways. Indeed, 'evolutionary' modes of analysis—well represented in this volume—try to capture this double link, albeit with frequent bias in favour of the Schumpeterian view that it is ultimately innovation which drives accumulation and growth.

The role of corporate organizations is no less controversial. Were one to literally believe the story presented by 'old'—and also 'new'—growth theories, one would be inclined to think that the specificities of firms' structures and strategies are just epiphenomena—'veils' covering the fundamental determinants of growth as revealed by equilibrium functions of production. Of course, the story that business historians and also a few microeconomists tell is quite at odds with this account. For example, the classic Chandlerian account of the rise of modern multidivisional corporation (Chandler, 1990) is in fact a business-centered interpretation of the reasons why one country—the USA—happened for a period to forge ahead in terms of income generating abilities. Many advances and qualifications may have been added to the Chandlerian view. Still, it seems quite misleading to attempt to explain growth processes and international growth differentials while neglecting the information and incentive structure associated with particular forms of organizational governance—as emphasized from different angles by M. Aoki, J. Stiglitz and O. Williamson, among others—or neglecting the specificities of problem-solving competences, highlighted in the evolutionary literature. Quite a few of the papers which follow in this volume tackle this tension between 'organization-free' models and 'organization-embedded' explanations of development patterns. Nelson discusses it from the point of view of a more general tension between 'formal' and 'appreciative' theorizing and argues for formal theories (of the evolutionary

──────────── 4 ────────────

———————— *The Process of Economic Development* ————————

breed) that promise to capture some of the spirit of what we know about corporate growth and industrial dynamics. Amsden and Hikino add important insights to the latter by examining the role of conglomerates in late industrializing countries. Stiglitz discusses the complementarity between *lato sensu* technological factors (such as 'local' learning and externalities) and organizational ones (including the structure of business firms and the nature of financial institutions). Silverberg and Verspagen and Dosi *et al.* present two evolutionary models where dynamics explicitly rests on the interactions among heterogeneous, continuously learning, agents. Conversely, Greenan and Guellec try to bridge some of the gap between equilibrium models and micro evidence by incorporating finer organizational specifications into a 'new growth' perspective.

The role of institutions is the last—and enormously complex—topic. It is probably where economic theory (in both neoclassical and evolutionary modes) is at its weakest. Many historians—as well as sociologists, political scientists, economic anthropologists—would put a good part of the explanatory burden of 'why growth and development patterns differ' on the particular forms of 'embeddedness' of economic behaviors into broader networks of social interactions and institutions (on the notion of embeddedness, see Granovetter (1985); on the general point cf. Zysman's article in this volume). Conversely the inclination of mainstream economists would be to claim that if institutions matter at all, their effect would simply show up in the parametrizations of some functionally invariant model that they propose. Evolutionary economists do go further, generally put forward an institutionally rich 'appreciative theory' and are ready to acknowledge the embeddedness of whatever form of learning and selection they model into specific institutional set-ups. However, modeling of institutions—as, in this volume, Zysman urges and Nelson admits—is still at a highly rudimentary stage. Relatedly, the greater the emphasis of the explanation on specific institutional arrangements, the greater of course also the importance of history in the selection of particular development trajectories (although path-dependency is likely to emerge even in absence of explicit institutional inertia: see Durlauf's article, and the discussion below).

Clearly, convergence/divergence in development patterns is only one of the numerous areas where the varying degrees of attention to technical change, organizational characteristics and institutions do make a profound difference in terms of the proposed theoretical interpretation. Indeed, to set the stage for the analyses that follow it might be useful to highlight a long, albeit by no means exhaustive, series of empirical regularities which ought to be explained by the theory (or at least the observational implications of the theory should not be in open conflict with them).

———————— 5 ————————

———————————— *The Process of Economic Development* ————————————

2. *Some Stylized Facts on Technical Change, Trade and Growth*

Divergence, Convergence and Persistent Differences

Let us start with the broad historical picture. Consider the last three centuries as the unit of observation. What is striking is indeed the explosion of diverging patterns, starting from quite similar pre-industrial levels of per capita incomes. Table 1, from Bairoch (1981) presents estimates showing that before the Industrial Revolution 'the income gap between the poorest and the richest country was certainly smaller than the ratio 1.0 to 2.0 and probably of the order of only 1.0 to 1.5' (p. 5). The dominant pattern after the industrial revolution is one with fast increasing differentiation among countries and overall divergence (see Table 2). Even in the post-World War II period, commonly regarded as an era of growing uniformity, the hypothesis of 'global' convergence (that is convergence of the whole population of countries toward increasingly similar income levels) does not find support from the evidence (De Long, 1988; Easterly *et al.*, 1991; Verspagen, 1991a, 1991b; Soete and Verspagen, 1992). Rather, one finds some—although not overwhelming—evidence of local convergence, i.e. within subsets of countries grouped according to some initial characteristics such as income levels (Durlauf and Johnson, 1992) or geographical location. Still, across-groups differences in growth performances appear to be strikingly high (clearly, convergence in the end-period levels of income ought to show up in inverse correlation between rates of growth and initial levels but the evidence does not support this proposition). For some recent regional data see Tables 3 and 4.

Fully acknowledging a 'post-selection bias' (De Long, 1988), the performance of OECD countries displays much stronger convergent characteristics. It is well known that after World War II, one observes a strong catching-up process by other OECD countries in per capita incomes and labour productivity *vis-à-vis* the USA (Maddison, 1982; Abramovitz, 1989). At least since 1870 the OECD followers have become increasingly homogeneous, in the sense that the standard deviations of their relative gaps compared to the USA have steadily fallen. However, the mean gap itself has increased until World War II and fallen thereafter (Abramovitz, 1989, Table 7.1, p. 226).

An interesting phenomenon concerns the persistence of relative growth performances over time. Historical evidence regarding specific countries seems to suggest the persistence of above/below-average growth rates at least within particular phases of development: compare for example the below-average performance of Japan, Germany and Italy. However, long-term

──────────── *The Process of Economic Development* ────────────

TABLE 1. Estimates of Pre-industrial Per Capita GNP (at 1960 US$ and Prices)

	Period	GNP per capita
Countries now developed		
Great Britain	1700	160–200
USA	1710	200–260
France	1781–1790	170–200
Russia	1860	160–200
Sweden	1860	190–230
Japan	1885	160–200
Countries now less developed		
Egypt	1887	170–210
Ghana	1891	90–150
India	1900	130–160
Iran	1900	140–220
Jamaica	1832	240–280
Mexico	1900	150–190
Philippines	1902	170–210

Source: Bairoch, 1981.

Note: It is probably safe to assume nearly stationary per capita incomes in the years which precede the estimates, so that for example the figure of Ghana 1700 should not have been significantly different from that of Ghana 1891 (if anything it could have been higher before slave trade).

Clearly, the figures should be taken as rough orders of magnitude.

TABLE 2. Estimates of Trends in Per Capita GNP (1960 US$ and Prices, 1750–1977)

Year	Developed countries		Third World		Gaps	
	(1) Total ($bn)	(2) Per capita	(3) Total ($bn)	(4) Per capita	(5) = (2)/(4)	(6) Ratio of the most developed to the least developed
1750	35	182	112	188	1.0	1.8
1800	47	198	137	188	1.1	1.8
1830	67	237	150	183	1.3	2.8
1860	118	324	159	174	1.9	4.5
1913	430	662	217	192	3.4	10.4
1950	889	1054	335	203	5.2	17.9
1960	1394	1453	514	250	5.8	20.0
1970	2386	2229	800	380	7.2	25.7
1977	2108	2737	1082	355	7.7	29.1

Source: Bairoch, 1981, pp. 7–8.

──────────── 7 ────────────

——————— *The Process of Economic Development* ———————

TABLE 3. Real GDP Growth Rates % p.a.
in Various Regions, 1965–1989

	1965–80	1980–89
East Asia*	7.3	7.9
South Asia	3.9	5.1
Africa (sub-Sahara)	4.0	2 1
Latin America	5.8	1.6

Source: World Bank, 1991.
*Including China.

TABLE 4. Real GDP Growth Rates % p.a.
Per Capita, 1965–1989

	1965–80	1980–89
East Asia*	5.0	6.3
South Asia	1.5	2.9
Africa (sub-Sahara)	1.1	−1.2
Latin America	3.5	−0.5

Source: World Bank, 1991.
*Including China.

persistence of growth rates systematically different from the mean world growth, somewhat surprisingly, does not appear to be a general characteristic of the whole set of countries: Easterly *et al.* (1991) find a rather low cross-period correlation in relative growth rates (around 0.3), with a greater instability among developing countries. Obviously, this also implies that countries which appear to catch up in one period, fall behind in another one. This is broadly confirmed by new long-term evidence on both developed and developing countries elaborated by Maddison (1991) (see Table 5).

A particularly interesting interpretative puzzle concerns the comparative performance of East Asia and Latin America, respectively.[1] It is often forgotten today that in the 1950s the prospects for growth in Latin America seemed far more favorable than in Asia. USA investment was substantial and the levels of industrialization were well above those in Asia (Table 6). Argentina was regarded as already almost 'developed' or industrialized and

---

[1] The analysis of 'East Asia' concentrates on the 'four tigers'—S Korea, Taiwan, Singapore and Hong Kong—but also occasionally refers to the so-called 'second tier' of Thailand, Malaysia, Indonesia, Philippines and to mainland China. 'Latin America' refers mainly to the largest and most industrialized countries: Brazil, Mexico, Argentina and Venezuela but occasionally also to the smaller and less developed economies or the entire continent including the Caribbean.

──────────── *The Process of Economic Development* ────────────

TABLE 5. Rates of Catching Up in the Per Capita GDP Levels relative to the USA, 1913–1989 (annual average compound rates of growth)

	1913–50	1950–89		1913–50	1950–89
Austria	−1.4	1.9	Argentina	−0.8	−1.2
Belgium	−0.8	0.9	Brazil	0.4	0.9
Denmark	−0.1	0.5	Chile	0.2	−0.6
Finland	0.3	1.6	Colombia	0.0	0.0
France	−0.4	1.2	Mexico	−0.7	0.3
Germany	−0.9	1.7	Peru	−0.2	−1.0
Italy	−0.4	1.6	Bangladesh	−1.8	−1.5
Netherlands	−0.5	0.6	China	−2.1	2.5
Norway	0.6	1.4	India	−1.8	0.1
Sweden	0.6	0.7	Indonesia	−1.8	0.7
UK	−0.6	0.3	Japan	−0.6	3.9
Australia	−0.8	0.2	Korea	−1.7	3.6
Canada	−0.1	0.8	Pakistan	−1.9	0.3
Czechoslovakia	−0.2	0.4	Taiwan	−1.1	4.1
Greece	−1.0	2.3	Thailand	−1.5	2.0
Hungary	−0.8	0.6	Côte d'Ivoire	n.a.	−0.8
Ireland	−0.8	1.0	Ghana	−0.4	−2.6
Portugal	−0.2	2.0	Kenya	n.a.	−0.2
Spain	−1.3	1.8	Morocco	n.a.	−0.6
USSR	0 7	0.6	Nigeria	n a.	−1.2
			South Africa	−0.3	−0.5
			Tanzania	n.a.	−1.1

Source: Maddison, 1991, Table 2, p. 5.

per capita incomes generally were much higher in Latin America. However, already by the 1970s, despite this lower starting point in terms of industrialization, the four tigers of East Asia were generally being bracketed with Brazil, Mexico and Venezuela as newly industrializing countries (NICs). They all enjoyed growth rates well above those of the USA and Europe for quite a long period so that catching up seemed a feasible prospect for them if not yet for the great majority of less developed countries. However, in the 1980s there was a very sharp process of differentiation between the Latin American NICs and the East Asian NICs. Whereas the East Asian countries continued their rapid growth and even accelerated it, the Latin American countries slowed down or declined (Table 3). Now the contrast was increasingly between rather sharply defined geographical regions. Whereas real per capita incomes were actually falling over the past decade in Africa and Latin America, they were rising quite fast in South Asia and very rapidly in East Asia (Table 4).

Let us summarize some general 'stylized facts' (SF) concerning the international patterns of growth.

—————————— *The Process of Economic Development* ——————————

TABLE 6. Ratio of Manufacturing to Agricultural Net Product and Net Value of Manufacturing Per Head of Population in Various Latin American and Asian Countries (1955)

	Ratio of manufacturing to agricultural net product	Net value of manufacturing per head
Argentina	1.32	145
Brazil	0.72	50
Mexico	1.00	60
Venezuela	1.43	95
Chile	1.35	75
Colombia	0.42	45
Peru	0.52	25
Thailand	0.28	10
S Korea	0.20	8
India	0 30	7
Indonesia	0.20	10
Philippines	0.32	13

Source: Maizels, 1963, p. 35.

SF1.   Economies have grown over the past two centuries probably faster than during any previous period in recorded history.

SF2.   They have grown at different and variable rates (sometimes negative for particular periods and particular countries—Argentina, a few less developed countries, USSR, etc.—or for many countries for particular periods—i.e. deep recessions).

SF3.   The long-term patterns for the whole set of countries show an increasing differentiation, highlighted by a secular increase in the variance in per capita income.

SF4.   Catching up with forging ahead has been relatively rare (Britain overtaking Holland in the 18th century; the USA, Germany and others overtaking Britain in the late 19th and 20th centuries; Japan overtaking almost everyone in the late 20th century).

SF5.   Progress in catching up has been more widespread (western–central Europe in the 19th century, Scandinavia and Italy in the 20th; East Asian countries in the late 20th century; the EEC catching up with the USA during the 1960s and 1970s).

—————————— 10 ——————————

--------- *The Process of Economic Development* ---------

SF6. Falling behind has been a rather frequent phenomenon, too (many less developed countries in the 1970s and 1980s; a few countries falling behind after a considerable 'spurt' of catching up—compare the 1950s with the 1980s in Latin America and Eastern Europe; Britain experiencing a long-term relative decline).

SF7. One can hardly identify, in general, persistent features of national growth patterns just conditional on initial performances (e.g. 'all laggard countries will tend to grow faster' or 'those that have grown faster will grow faster also in the future'). Closer inspection of particular economies or groups of them does appear to show long-term persistence (e.g. Japan or, conversely, Britain) but the causes of the phenomenon are plausibly country-specific rather than a common feature of the world economy.

Technology, Trade and Growth

The historian David Landes, in his reconstruction of the process by which the 'modern Prometheus' of innovation and entrepreneurship arose and was diffused through the industrialized world, points to the cumulative and self-propelling advance of technology as a sort of *primus inter pares* within the menu of ingredients of economic development that come under the heading of 'modernization' and include, for example, general education, mobility of finance, industrial entrepreneurship, urbanization (Landes, 1969).

Together with the Industrial Revolution came an impressive differentiation in the technological capabilities among countries, starting from a rather homogeneous distribution, at least between Europe, China and the Arab world. Findlay (1992) argues, for example, that most of the technologies involved in European voyages of discovery came from China and the Arab world but the picture dramatically changes after the Industrial Revolution.

Table 7 provides a highly impressionistic but still revealing picture of the international distribution of innovations from 1750. Although there is probably some Anglo-American bias in Streit's (1949) data, a similar pattern is revealed by long-term patenting activities (see Dosi *et al.*, 1990): innovation appears to be highly concentrated in a small group of industrialized countries (Table 8).

Of course, technological learning involves many more elements than simply inventive discovery and patenting: as discussed at length elsewhere (Freeman, 1982, 1987; Dosi, 1988) equally important activities are imitation, reverse engineering, adoption of capital-embodied innovations, learning by doing and learning by using. And, of course, most often technological change goes together with organizational innovation. Still, it is important to

---------------- *The Process of Economic Development* ----------------

TABLE 7. Major Inventions, Discoveries and Innovations by Country, 1750–1950

Period	Total	Inventions, discoveries and innovations (percentage of total)				
		Britain	France	Germany	USA	Others
1750–75	30	46.7	16.7	3.3	10.0	23.3
1776–1800	68	42.6	32.4	5.9	13.2	5.9
1801–25	95	44.2	22.1	10.5	12.6	10.5
1826–50	129	28.7	22.5	17 8	22.5	8.5
1851–75	163	17.8	20.9	23.9	25.2	12.3
1876–1900	204	14.2	17.2	19.1	37.7	11 8
1901–25	139	13.7	9.4	15.1	52.5	9.4
1926–50	113	11.5	0.9	12.4	61.9	13.3

Source: Based on Dosi *et al.*, 1990, p. 41, derived from Streit, 1949 data.

notice the significant links between innovative activities (measured in an indirect and narrow sense, i.e. in terms of patenting or R&D activities) and GDP per capita (for the time being we shall avoid any detailed argument on the direction of causality).

Let us start from some naïve statistics. Tables 9 and 10 show the correlation coefficients between per capita US patenting (levels and rates of change), R&D and per capita incomes (levels and rates of change) since 1890 for a sample of 14 OECD countries, as elaborated by Pavitt and Soete (1981). The evidence appears to suggest that the relationship between innovative activities and levels of GDP has become closer over time, and is highly significant after World War II. One can get also a rough idea on convergence and/or divergence in innovativeness and income (remember, however, that one is considering here a subset of OECD developed countries). The following patterns seem to emerge:

(i)   The relationship between levels of innovative activity and subsequent growth of output (column 3, Table 10) seems to have switched from positive to negative. Only for the first period (1890–1913) do we find a positive and significant relationship. Since 1950 and in particular for the most recent period, a negative relationship emerges, which indicates that countries at the 'innovation frontier' have been less successful than 'imitators' in terms of economic growth.

(ii) Giving further support to the previous point, 'imitation' (or catching up) defined as a negative relation between levels of GDP per capita and subsequent growth of output per capita (column 5)

---------------- 12 ----------------

──────────── *The Process of Economic Development* ────────────

TABLE 8. Patents Granted in the USA by country of origin, 1883–1986 (as a percentage of all foreign patenting)

Country	1883	1890	1900	1913	1929	1938	1950	1958	1965	1973	1979	1986
Australia	1.11	1.20	2.33	1.97	1.96	1.18	1.54	0.60	0.94	0.92	1.12	1.14
Austria	2.62	3.37	3.36	3.99	2.47	2.91	0.48	1.12	1.16	1.02	1.19	1.09
Belgium	1.59	0.86	1.35	1.28	1.30	1.23	1.07	1.14	1.50	1.23	0.98	0.74
Canada	19.94	17.63	10.54	13.22	10.25	6.35	11.16	7.99	7.00	6.20	4.56	4.01
Denmark	0.56	0.38	0.46	0.67	0.71	0.71	1.36	0.74	0.74	0.70	0.56	0.56
France	14.22	8.46	9.79	8.07	9.76	9.23	15.54	10.36	10.90	9.38	8.46	7.22
Germany	18.67	21.47	30.72	34.02	32.36	38.18	0.57	25.60	26.40	24.25	23.87	20.80
Italy	0.24	0.29	0.92	1.31	1.19	1.43	0.86	3.02	3.38	3.39	3.14	3.05
Japan	0.16	0.10	0.03	0.45	1.40	1.51	0.03	1.93	7.43	22.10	27.69	40.35
Netherlands	0.24	0.29	0.75	0.47	1.57	3.38	8.10	5.71	4.15	3.03	2.80	2.20
Norway	0.32	0.14	0.49	0.74	0.71	0.54	0.95	0.61	0.42	0.42	0.43	0.25
Sweden	0.95	1.52	1.32	2.07	3.19	3.13	6.67	4.64	4.50	3.40	3.02	2.70
Switzerland	1.75	2.66	2.27	3.11	4.46	3.72	9.73	8.80	6.97	5.79	5.40	3.70
United Kingdom	34.55	36.15	30.52	23.29	22.23	22.70	36.00	23.45	20.62	12.56	10.07	7.37
Eastern Europe including USSR	0.40	0.67	1.49	1.19	1.62	1.61	1.23	0.55	0.89	2.53	2.76	1.13
NICs	0.40	1.19	1.12	1.21	1.03	0.90	1.41	1.31	1.71	1.36	1.45	1.50
Others	3.28	3.62	2.54	2.94	3.07	1.29	3.28	2.43	1.29	1.72	2.50	2.19

Source: Dosi *et al.*, 1990, p. 43.

--------------------- *The Process of Economic Development* ---------------------

TABLE 9. Correlation Coefficients between Levels of Innovative Activity and GDP Per Capita

Year	1890	1913	1929	1950	1963	1967	1971	1977
GDP per capita with:								
US patents per capita (PT_t)	0.20	0.38	0.56*	0.63*	0.73**	0.72**	0.74**	0.88**
R&D per capita					0.79**	0.69**	0.71**	0.61*

Source: Pavitt and Soete, 1981, p. 119.
*Significant at 5% level.
**Significant at 1% level.

        emerges strongly for the periods 1890–1913, and 1950–1970. Interestingly it still appears but is statistically weaker in the period 1970–77 while the relation is positive in the 'divergence' period 1913–1950.

(iii)   With the exception of the period from 1929 to 1950, levels of GDP per capita are negatively correlated with subsequent growth in innovation activity (column 5). In other words, before World War I and after World War II, activities of innovation/creative imitation occurred at a higher rate in 'late-comers'.

(iv)   Innovative dynamism, expressed by the growth of USA patenting, always appears positively correlated with per capita GDP growth (column 4). The link is strong and significant between 1913 and 1970. Another sign that the regime of international growth has changed in the 1970s is that the relation gets weaker and loses statistical significance in the period 1970–1977.

Fagerberg (1988) expands and refines the econometric tests presented in Pavitt and Soete (1981). Using a sample of 27 countries, including Latin American and Asian countries, he tests a model where the rates of growth of GDP appear to depend on (i) international technological diffusion, (ii) domestic innovative activities, (iii) rates of investment. Fagerberg shows the importance of all three factors and also that the contribution of each of them is contingent on the degree of industrialization already achieved and is also country-specific and region-specific (for example, one identifies 'a much better performance in all respects by Asian NICs than by Latin American' economies for the period 1973 to 1983). This evidence is in many ways complementary to the findings concerning a robust correlation between investment in equipment and economic growth (De Long and Summers, 1991).

        Technical change appears to affect growth both directly and via its

———————————— *The Process of Economic Development* ————————————

TABLE 10. Correlation Coefficients between Innovative Activity and Output of OECD Countries, 1890–1977

Period	GDP growth (g)	GDP per capita growth (y)	USA patents per capita at $t = 1$ (PT$_c$)	USA patents per capita growth (pt$_c$)	GDP per capita at $t = 1$ (Y)
	1	2	3	4	5
1890–1913					
g	1.00	0.60†	0.60†	−0.22	−0.18
y		1.00	0.20	0.05	−0.66*
PT$_c$			1.00	−0.61†	0.22
pt$_c$				1.00	−0.67*
Y					1.00
1913–1929					
g	1.00	0.76*	−0.12	0.66*	−0.41
y		1.00	−1.21	0.67*	−0.62†
PT$_c$			1.00	−0.55†	0.38
pt$_c$				1.00	−0.43
Y					1.00
1929–1950					
g	1.00	0.82*	0.31	0.66*	0.37
y		1.00	0.41	0.58†	0.40
PT$_c$			1.00	0.22	0.56†
pt$_c$				1.00	0.67*
Y					1.00
1950–1970					
g	1.00	0.75*	0.38	0.89*	−0.76*
y		1.00	0.40	0.71*	−0.76*
PT$_c$			1.00	−0.48	0.63†
pt$_c$				1.00	−0 84*
Y					1.00
1970–1977					
g	1.00	0.91*	−0.67*	0.29	−0.47
y		1.00	−0.60†	0.16	−0.48
PT$_c$			1.00	−0.28	0.66*
pt$_c$				1.00	−1.16
Y					1.00

Source: Pavitt and Soete, 1981.
*Significant at the 1% level.
†Significant at the 5% level.

influences on trade flows. In his classic work on *Industrial Growth and World Trade* (1963), Alfred Maizels examined in great depth the changing patterns of world commodity trade in relation to industrialization and growth of per capita incomes. He concluded that:

> Since exports sales are also an important part of total demand for final output in most industrial countries, a change in competitive power—which

———————————— *The Process of Economic Development* ————————————

implies a change in export sales—will itself affect the rate of growth in industrial production. Thus exports interact in a dynamic way with the growth of the whole economy. There has been in fact a relatively close relationship over the past 60 years in the relative growth rates of the main industrial countries and their shares of the world export market in manufactures (p. 17).[2]

His analysis pointed to the importance of both relative export price movements and non-price factors, especially technological progress, quality, design, delivery and marketing, in the competitive process. To fall behind in design and technology may render products less saleable or even unsaleable on the world market, while a fall behind in process technology may render them uncompetitive in terms of price. More recent work (e.g. Dosi *et al.*, 1990; Amendola *et al.*, 1993) has confirmed this view of the dynamic interdependence of technical change with trade and growth performance. It shows that in most industrial sectors, 'disembodied innovations'—as proxied by patenting activity—and innovations embodied in capital investment, are the main determinants of national export performances—measured by per capita exports or shares on the world markets.

Moreover, different commodities and sectors are likely to be associated with different levels of opportunities for innovation and different income elasticities of demand. Hence, the national patterns of technological and production specialization may feed back on the long term dynamism of each economy. (The Kaldorian hypothesis of 'manufacturing as an engine of growth' as well as the possible conflict between 'static' and 'dynamic' efficiencies of particular patterns of resource allocation belong to this domain of analysis.)

In order to illustrate the coupled dynamics between technical change, exports and growth, let us compare again East Asia with Latin America. The high growth rates achieved by the East Asian countries were associated with an even more impressive achievement in export performance. All the four tigers surpassed the leading Latin American countries (Brazil and Mexico) in their share of world merchandise exports and far surpassed them in world manufacturing exports (Table 11). Manufacturing exports were growing much more rapidly than primary commodity exports in the 1980s. More generally, Maizels (1963, Chapter 3) shows that all industrializing countries had a rising ratio of manufacturing to total exports from 1899 to 1959 so that this is the continuation of a persistent long-term trend, only partly obscured by oil price movements in the 1970s. Manufacturing accounted on average for about 70% of total world merchandise exports in 1990 but, with

———————————————————————————

[2] For a recent survey on the relationship between trade and growth in developing countries, see Edwards (1993).

———————————————————— 16 ————————————————————

———————— *The Process of Economic Development* ————————

the exception of Singapore, the tigers resemble Japan in having an extremely high ratio of manufacturing exports to total exports (over 90%). Most Latin American countries on the other hand resemble China, Australia and Canada in having a relatively high ratio of non-manufacturing exports, mainly primary commodities, such as foodstuffs, minerals, non-ferrous metals and fuels. It is desirable, of course, even essential, to exploit comparative advantages in natural resources and resource-based industries but they may often have the disadvantage of relatively slower growth.

TABLE 11. Shares of Various Countries and Rates of Growth in Merchandise Exports 1980–1988

	Exports of merchandise 1989 ($bn)	Exports of manufactures 1989 ($bn)	Annual average growth of merchandise exports 1980–1988
Hong Kong	73.1	66.8	15.5
Taiwan	66.2	61.1	15.0
S Korea	62.3	57.8	17.0
China	51.6	28.3	13 0
Singapore	44.7	31.8	9 0
Thailand	20.1	11.5	12.0
Mexico	35.6	22.8	6 5
Brazil	34.4	19.9	6.5
Venezuela	13.0	2.0*	−7.5

Source: GATT, 1990.
* Estimated.

One of the major points to emerge from the analysis by Maizels of the long-term trends in world exports of manufactures was the huge change in the commodity composition. Whereas the share of textiles and clothing declined from over 40% in 1899 to about 11% in 1959, the share of machinery and transport equipment increased from 12% to 42% (Table 12). As he anticipated, the share of machinery and transport equipment increased even further, although much more slowly. The share of chemicals in value terms remained relatively stable.

The original success of Britain in growth and trade in the Industrial Revolution was of course based on the leadership in the mechanization of the textile industries and in enormous textile exports. Even at the end of the 19th century, textiles and clothing still accounted for over 50% of all British exports of manufactures, while Britain still accounted for 30% of all world exports. But machinery, transport equipment and chemicals played an increasingly important part in British growth during the 19th century and

———————— 17 ————————

———————— *The Process of Economic Development* ————————

TABLE 12. Shares of Various Commodity Groups in Total Value
of World Exports of Manufactures (%)

Commodities	1899	1929	1959	1989
Machinery	8	14	25	36
Transport equipment	4	10	17	15
Chemicals	8	9	12	13
Textiles and clothing	41	29	11	9
Metals, metal goods and other	39	38	35	27

Sources: 1899–1959, Maizels, 1963.
1989 estimated from GATT, 1990.

those countries which were overtaking Britain, especially Germany and the USA, showed an even greater concentration of exports in these new faster growing commodity groups. By 1929 machinery, transport equipment and chemicals accounted for over 70% of USA manufacturing exports and for 70% of German manufacturing exports but for only 40% of British. Britain had been the leader in railway equipment and steam engines but in electrical machinery and other types of electrical products German and USA firms forged ahead of their British competitors.

Many historical accounts (e.g. Ashby, 1969; Landes, 1969; Maddison, 1982; Freeman, 1987) point to the importance of institutional innovations in both Germany and the USA which facilitated their catching up and forging ahead of Britain. Particularly important were specialized institutions for the education of graduate engineers and the lags in engineering education and vocational training in Britain. The social innovation of the in-house industrial R&D department in the chemical and electrical industries of Germany and the USA from the 1970s onwards was also of major importance in the introduction, exploitation and diffusion of the new technologies. Britain continued to perform relatively well in the older industries and technologies but did not really catch up in the new ones until much later and in some cases not at all (Lewis, 1978).

Thus, while textiles and clothing still play an important role in the early stages of industrialization in many countries, some capability in the manufacture and export of capital goods has become increasingly important in the 20th century in the later stages of industrialization and catching up. The Asian tigers have done extremely well both in the export of clothing and of capital goods. Hong Kong was by far the largest exporter of clothing in the world in 1989, accounting for 15% of total world exports. S Korea was the third largest exporter, accounting for 10% of world exports, while China and Taiwan were respectively fourth and sixth. Together they accounted for 35%

—————————— *The Process of Economic Development* ——————————

of all world clothing exports and for 25% of textile exports. In the far larger category of machinery and transport equipment their share is of course smaller (8% of world exports in 1989) but nevertheless all four tigers figure in the top 15 world exporters and their total capital goods exports are now much larger than their total textile and clothing exports.

However, within the category of 'machinery and transport equipment' there has been an extremely important shift in the second half of the 20th century which has played a crucial role in the relative success of the East Asian countries and especially Japan. The major change in technology in this period has been the increasingly pervasive influence of information and communication technology throughout all industries and services, amounting to a change of 'techno-economic paradigm' (Perez, 1983). Just as at the close of the 19th century and the early 20th century leadership in electrical technology was critical for countries such as the USA, Germany, Switzerland and Sweden, which were catching up and forging ahead, so today it is information and communication technology. Reflecting this change, electronic capital goods, electronic components, telecommunication equipment and a wide variety of other electronic products, including instruments and durable consumer goods have now become the fastest growing category in world exports (Table 13).

As a result of its extraordinary rapid growth, this category now alone accounts for over 12% of all world exports of manufactures, i.e. much more than textiles and clothing combined and about as much as chemicals. Even so, the classification understates the influence of competence in information and communication technology, since it is not merely a question of particular categories of capital goods and consumer goods, but of a technology which affects all services as well as manufactures. It is more important to be able to use this technology in every sector of the economy than to manufacture specific products or components. Nevertheless, relative performance in world trade in this commodity group does provide a clear indication of long-term shifts in competitiveness in the fastest growing commodities. What emerges from an analysis which separates out this category in world trade is the extraordinary strength of Japan but also of the other East Asian countries and of their intra-industry trade in this category (Table 14).

The combined exports of the four tigers in 1989 were greater than those of the USA in this commodity group and nearly as large as those of Japan, although in 1980 they still had been only about half of the exports of either of those countries. No Latin American country appears at all in the first 15 exporters in this category and nor do they appear in the first 15 exporters in the entire category of 'machinery and transport equipment'. However, Brazil and Mexico do figure, along with Korea, in the subcategory of the 15 largest

———————————————— 19 ————————————————

──────────── *The Process of Economic Development* ────────────

TABLE 13. Rates of Growth of Various Categories of
Commodities in World Exports 1980–1989
(percentage annual increases)

All primary commodities	2
Of which:	
Food	3
Raw materials	4
Ores, minerals, non-ferrous metals	4
Fuels*	−5
All manufactures	8
Of which:	
Iron and steel	4
Textiles	6
Chemicals	7
Clothing	10
Machinery and transport equipment	8
Of which:	
Automotive equipment	9
Office machines and telecom equipment	13

Source: GATT, 1990.
* The negative sign reflects mainly the decline in
world oil prices

exporters of the wider group of 'machinery and transport equipment' largely
because of their strong performance in electronics. For Japan, Taiwan and
S Korea, exports of this commodity group now account for nearly a quarter of
their total merchandise exports, while for Singapore the proportion is one
third.

A synthetic appreciation of the 'dynamic quality' of export specializations
of various economic regions can be drawn from Table 15, showing the ratios
between the market shares on the OECD market between 'dynamic' and
'declining' commodities (that is, commodities with above/below average
growth of international demand). Japan and the 'Asian tigers' appear to have
the best abilities to reap the benefits from fast growing markets, while at the
opposite extreme one finds Latin American and eastern European countries.

Let us, again, summarize some stylized facts (and 'stylized processes')
concerning technology, trade and growth:

SF8.   Since the Industrial Revolution a highly skewed international distribution of innovative activities has emerged. The 'club of major innovators'
historically has been quite small, with only one major entrant in the post-war
period (Japan), and possibly another one currently emerging (Korea).

SF9.   Successful latecomers have combined heavy imports of technology

──────────── 20 ────────────

——————— *The Process of Economic Development* ———————

TABLE 14. Leading Exporters of Office Machines and Telecom Equipment 1989 (billion dollars and percentages)

| | Value | | Share in world exports | | Average annual change | Share of product in economy's merchandise | | |
| | | | | | | Exports | | Imports |
	1980	1989	1980	1989	1980–1988	1980	1989	1989
1. Japan	18.0	65.0	21.0	25.5	17.0	14.0	23.5	4.5
2. United States	17.2	47.4	20.0	18.5	12.0	8.0	13.0	13.0
3. Germany Fed. Rep.	8.5	18.3	10.0	7.0	9.5	4.5	5.5	8.5
4. United Kingdom	5.5	16.2	6.5	6.5	13.5	5.0	9.0	11.0
5. Singapore[a]	2.7	15.3	3.0	6.0	21.5	14.0	34.0	21.0
6. Rep. Korea	1.7	13.5	2.0	5.5	28.5	9.5	21.5	11.5
7. Taiwan	2.7	12.5	3.0	5.0	20.0	13.5	24.5	12.5
8. Hong Kong[b]	2.4	11.2	3.0	4.5	19.5	12.0	15.5	14.5
9. France	4.0	10.0	4.5	4.0	11.5	3.5	6.5	7.5
10. Netherlands	3.4	7.7	4.0	3.0	9.5	4.5	7.0	9.5
11. Italy	2.9	6.9	3.5	2.5	9.5	4.0	5.0	7.0
12. Malaysia	1.2	6.0	1.5	2.5	19.5	9.0	23.5	—
13. Canada	1.7	5.0	2.0	2.0	13.0	2.5	4.0	9.0
14. Ireland	0.7	4.7	1.0	2.0	23.0	9.0	22.5	—
15. Sweden	1.9	3.8	2.0	1.5	8.5	6.0	7.5	9.0
Above 15	74.5	243.5	87.5	95.5	—	—	—	—

[a] Includes re-exports. In 1989 they were valued at $3.4 billion.
[b] Includes re-exports. In 1989 they were valued at $6.6 billion.

——————— *The Process of Economic Development* ———————

TABLE 15. Dynamic Efficiency of the Regional Patterns of Specializations, 1961–1989 (Ratio of market shares in OECD imports in 'dynamic' versus 'declining' commodities)*

	Period					
	1963–1971		1971–1989		of which 1979–1989	
USA	1.22	1.22	1.63	1.39	1.72	1.60
Japan	2.45	3.52	1.64	3.15	3.40	3.34
EEC (12 members)	1.52	1.23	1.55	1.21	1.98	1.40
Eastern Europe	0.41	0.38	0.58	0.53	0.83	0.25
Central and Latin America	0.38	0.22	0.21	0.39	0.28	0.36
Four Asian tigers	1.48	2.29	2.38	2.58	3 40	3.08

Source: Elaborations by O Mandeng on the CAN databank, CEPAL, Santiago, Chile.
* 'Dynamic' commodities are those which have undergone above average growth of OECD trade (imports) over the considered period. Vice versa for 'declining' commodities. The calculations are based on three-year moving averages at current prices and exchange rates, OECD Import by Commodity data.

with strong expansion of indigenous efforts devoted to technical change. Imports of technology and autonomous innovative efforts are not alternative but complementary activities.

SF10.   The rates of investment in capital equipment are robustly correlated with economic growth (De Long and Summers, 1992).

SF11.   Within the group of major innovators one observes secular changes in the relative rankings: forging ahead tends to be associated with leadership in new technologies and competence in basic science (although not necessarily leadership in basic science). It is also associated with institutional changes in the generation and diffusion of new pervasive technologies and with the rapid expansion of education and training.

SF12.   There appear to be robust correlations between the capabilities of innovating and quickly adopting new technologies, on the one hand, and (i) export shares on the world markets, (ii) per capita incomes, (iii) rates of income growth, on the other. Circumstantial evidence also suggests that the links between technological performance and trade performance have become stronger over time. Moreover, historical evidence suggests that the sources of economic growth have changed in the 20th century, increasing even more the importance of technological and organizational change, as compared to the accumulation of 'tangible' capital.[3]

[3] According to Moses Abramovitz, '[in] the twentieth century. . . . the sources of growth were different. And the differences apply both to the proximate sources of advance—the per capita growth of

——————————— *The Process of Economic Development* ———————————

SF13.   Despite international technological diffusion, one can identify differentiated national patterns of technical change: specific national systems of innovation have been identified, based on the characteristics of the scientific and technical infrastructure, local user–producer relationships and other institutional and policy features of each country (Lundvall, 1988, 1992; Nelson, 1993).

SF14.   International differences in labor productivity quite closely correlate with differences in per capita income and, dynamically, so do labor productivity growth and income growth. Moreover, labor productivity gaps across countries generally hold at all levels of statistical disaggregation available. Conversely, there does not appear to be any systematic correlation between capital/output ratios and income per head, either across countries or over time, i.e. output per unit of capital does not exhibit any evident trend along the growth process (cf. Dosi *et al.*, 1990).

SF15.   Inter-temporal correlations of national specializations have been relatively 'sticky' (Germany in chemicals, machine tools; USA in aircraft, oil refining, electrical equipment; UK in mining machinery, aero engines, etc.) but export shares of the various countries on the world market have changed greatly.

SF16.   Although national specializations have been, in general, relatively sticky over quite long periods, catching-up and forging ahead (itself not a very frequent phenomenon) is associated with explosive export growth in products related to new technologies (including organizational innovations). So 'traditional' industries such as textile and clothing generally play an important role in early stages of industrialization. Thereafter, fast growth is linked to pervasive technologies (Perez, 1983): this has been the case of the USA, Germany and Switzerland with respect to electrical, mechanical and chemical technologies and it is now the case of Japan, Korea and Taiwan in relation to information technologies.

SF17.   Regarding factors' returns, the available evidence does not suggest any systematic correlation between profit rates and levels of development, either cross-sectionally or over time. Conversely, robust correlations exist between wage rates, levels of labor productivity and levels of per capita income.

———————————

labour, of capital and of their productivity—and to the deeper causes that governed all three' (Abramovitz, 1989, p. 1). On the different 'phases' and 'regimes of growth' see also Maddison (1991) and Boyer (1988a, 1988b). We shall briefly come back to this issue below.

——————————————————— 23 ———————————————————

──────────── *The Process of Economic Development* ────────────

Clearly, the theory counterparts of these 'stylized facts' are a long list of questions and 'puzzles' concerning, e.g. the 'causes' of growth; the processes which trigger it and, under some circumstances, make it self-sustained; the origins of persistent international differences in incomes and wages; the relationships between technical change and growth; the international diffusion of technological knowledge; the links between international trade, growth and factors' returns; and many others.

Other 'stylized facts' refer to some finer macroeconomic properties of each country.

SF18.   Irrespective of the particular long-term patterns of growth, each economy exhibits persistent fluctuations (see also Durlauf in this volume). Roughly, it exhibits some 'cycle-type' behavior (take this statement only as a loose approximation: in fact, a good deal of current time-series analysis questions precisely the decomposability between 'trend' and 'cyclical' elements).

SF19.   One typically observes co-movements in most economic aggregates (e.g. investment, inventories, employment, aggregate output).

SF20.   Involuntary unemployment of some fraction of the labor force and often also underutilization of production capacity tend to be the norm rather than the exception (as regards unemployment, this applies—even more so—to developing countries).

SF21.   Wages, at least in contemporary developed economies, tend to be relatively 'rigid', in the sense that they appear to adjust very slowly, if at all, to unbalances in the labor market.

SF22.   Somewhat similar 'rigidities' are displayed by output prices or, at least, by some of them: there is evidence that this applies in particular to manufacturing output, while fluctuations in primary commodity prices are relatively higher.

SF23.   'Markets' in reality display a relatively high variety in the ways they are organized and in the ways they function (e.g. some rely on decentralized interactions while others centralize transactions; some mainly rely on quantity adjustments and others mainly on price changes, etc.). Equally important, markets differ in their degree of international openness (compare, for example, the labor market with the market for finance) and in the institutional rules governing them.

──────────── 24 ────────────

──────────── *The Process of Economic Development* ────────────

Economic theory has started to tackle some of these properties of contemporary economies but this has mainly occurred outside the realm of growth theory (e.g. in macroeconomics, especially within the post- and new-Keynesian perspectives). Indeed, one of the most resilient acts of faith in the economic profession is that in some unspecified long-term equilibrium conditions must prevail and thus growth theory can dispose innocently of most microeconomic details leading to frictions, fluctuations, market failures, etc. This is precisely an assumption that most of the authors in this volume would challenge and would argue that, first, the short- and long-term properties of the economy might have many underlying causes in common and, second, that the determinants of specific patterns of growth should be traced back also to the characteristics of microeconomic organization (see, in this volume, Nelson; Stiglitz; Amsden and Hikino; Zysman on the second point, and Durlauf and Dosi *et al.* on the first one).

Firms and Technological Accumulation

Notwithstanding the importance of context conditions, infrastructures, national policies, firms play a central role in technological learning.

National histories of industrialization are intertwined with the strategies of growth, diversification, vertical integration/disintegration of a few major firms and many small ones, together with processes of birth and death of new firms—which in turn are specific to sectors and national institutional set-ups (see also Nelson; Stiglitz; Amsden and Hikino in this volume). In many respects, economic and technological history can be reconstructed to a good extent as business history. So, for example, the rise of German strength in chemicals has at its core the development of those firms which came together in Farben; the American path to international leadership is associated with the diffusion of 'Chandlerian' multidivisional corporations; *zaibatsus* and *chaebols* are fundamental actors in Japanese and Korean development; etc. (On the relationships between long-term technological accumulation and business organizations, see Dosi *et al.* (1992); on Korea, Amsden (1989) and Kim (1993); on Brazil, Dahlman and Frischtak (1991); and more generally on developing countries, Bell and Pavitt (1992), and Amsden and Hikino in this volume.)

Clearly, one does not always observe technological learning concentrated in few large firms: historical evidence shows that this depends both on the sectors (compare, e.g. chemicals or automobiles with textiles) and on the countries (compare Korea with Taiwan). Indeed, industrial growth is associated with quite high rates of birth and death of new firms. However, the crucial point is that national patterns of technological accumulation can be

──────────── 25 ────────────

─────────────── *The Process of Economic Development* ───────────────

traced back to the strategies and performances of—few or many—business firms. These strategies—business historians suggest—are obviously influenced by the environment and incentives which firms face but do retain a certain amount of discretionality. In turn, countries' dynamics reproduce and amplify the outcomes of such microdecisions.

In recent years a novel interest in the microeconomics of innovation has also contributed to highlight the intersectoral variety in the processes of innovation, in the sources of technical advance, in the impact that innovation exerts on industrial structure (for discussions, cf. Freeman, 1982; Rosenberg, 1976, 1982; Dosi, 1988). In a synthesis, a few stylized facts emerge:

SF24. Firms are the main locus of technological accumulation. The rates and directions at which firms learn depend on the richness of unexploited opportunities which they face and on the incentives that they perceive to do so—including of course appropriability conditions. However, at least equally important, technological learning depends on firm-specific abilities. Learning tends to be 'local' in the sense that it generally occurs in the neighborhood of those activities which the firm is already mastering.

SF25. It is increasingly acknowledged that many processes of technological and economic change involve path-dependence and dynamic increasing returns. This has to do with knowledge indivisibilities; the incremental and 'cumulative' nature of learning; standardization requirements; network externalities; interactions that are spatially 'local'; and other sources of positive feedbacks (Arthur, 1988; David, 1992).

SF26. A general feature of innovative learning is that it involves a lot of trials, a lot of errors and sometimes unexpected successes. In turn, this leads to a persistent heterogeneity among firms, revealed also by wide and persistent differences in inputs productivities, product performances, costs and profits. These asymmetries shape evolution of industrial structures by affecting market share changes, entries and exits. All industries are characterized by significant intertemporal fluctuations in the market shares of individual firms and persistently high rates of entry and mortality. Moreover, the rates of entry do not seem to be related with industry profitability or to average post-entry performance. (For a general discussion of these points, cf. Dosi *et al.*, 1993.)

SF27. Industrial structures and industrial growth present a few remarkable regularities (more on this evidence in Dosi *et al.*, 1993). A first one is a

——————— *The Process of Economic Development* ———————

relatively stable Pareto-type size distribution of firms (measured in terms of employment or sales). This applies to broad statistical aggregates such as 'manufacturing'. However, systematic departures from such a distribution emerge at a higher level of disaggregation. At the finest level of observation, that of single technologies or relatively homogeneous groups of products, one may often identify time-dependent distributions following some sort of 'technological life-cycle.'

SF28. Diffusion of innovations is never instantaneous. Factors of 'retardation' include imperfect information diffusion, agents' heterogeneity, 'vintage' effects, lack of relevant infrastructure and, possibly even more important, the time required by each firm to learn how to master new technologies and develop new skills. Indeed, the very distinction between innovation and diffusion is little more than a handy theoretical simplification: most often 'diffusion' and 'adoption' require painstaking learning and further modification of product, processes and corporate organizations.

SF29. Most innovations are industry-specific (despite the fact that a few of them exert in the longer term their impact across diverse activities via intersectoral flows of innovative commodities and production knowledge). Therefore, innovative shocks as such are an unlikely candidate for the explanation of economy-wide fluctuations. (What adds to the puzzle is that the economy-wide component appears to be relatively more important than the sectoral one even for the fluctuations of individual sectors.)

It would be a naïve epistemology to ask any theory to account for all these 'stylized facts', and others which have not been mentioned here, concerning for example the sectoral patterns of growth and decline; structural change, etc. (see Burns, 1934; Kuznets, 1972; Abramovitz, 1989; Dosi *et al.*, 1990). However, what ought to be researched are models which, while explaining one or more stylized facts, do not generate predictions which are in open conflict with the others (see Stiglitz, 1991). Just a quick look at the overwhelming number of stylized facts listed above is also a reminder of the limitations of our existing knowledge and of the intricacies of the research agenda ahead on growth and development.

Certainly, in our view, significant progress can be made if research addresses also the 'deeper processes' of development as opposed to the 'proximate sources', revealed by changes in the quantities and productivities of inputs (Abramovitz, 1989, pp. 23–29). Indeed, it is at this level of investigation that one might hope to find the sources of self-sustained growth and thus also answers to Stiglitz's provocative questions:

——————————————— 27 ———————————————

—————————————— *The Process of Economic Development* ——————————————

. . . where was the evidence of diminishing returns which that theory would have led one to expect? Could growth feed upon itself? Could there be increasing returns, so that the marginal return to investment actually increased as the economy grew? Or was there something about technical progress which meant that its pace increased as the marginal product of capital decreased? (Stiglitz, 1992, p. 1).

Here, to use the terminology of Nelson and Winter (1982) (see also Nelson in this volume), one must still draw heavily on the insights stemming from 'appreciative theories'—that is, inductive generalizations grounded in detailed historical accounts. As a sort of illustrative example on the nature of and relationship among these 'deeper processes' let us briefly compare the somewhat archetypical dynamics of East Asian and Latin American countries. (Much more detailed accounts can be found in Amsden, 1989; Gereffi and Wyman, 1990.)

3. Institutional Change and Catching Up in Technological Competence: Some International Comparisons

A general historical intuition is that economic development is intertwined with the change in the institutions supporting the generation, diffusion and exploitation of technological knowledge and with change in corporate organizations and strategies. However, none of them is a smooth and steady process. Institutions quite often survive well beyond their social usefulness (if they ever had one). Technologies sometimes improve in a relatively incremental and cumulative fashion; some other times relatively abrupt discontinuities occur, which elsewhere we have defined as 'paradigm changes' (Dosi, 1982; Freeman and Perez, 1988). In turn, a crucial factor in economic development is likely to be the complementarity and timing between institutional transformation and major technological discontinuities (Perez, 1983).

Perez and Soete (1988) have suggested that times of change in techno-economic paradigm could create especially favorable 'windows of opportunity' for catching-up countries. But these opportunities could be seized only if they had made the necessary infrastructural investments and institutional changes over a long period, so that an intensive and fruitful learning process could take place both in the new and in older technologies. The import of the technologies is very far from being a costless diffusion of perfect information. Technologies cannot be taken 'off the shelf' and simply put into use anywhere. Without infrastructural investment in education, training, R&D and other scientific and technical activities, very little can be accomplished by way of acquisition of imported technologies.

The type of institutional infrastructure which is needed varies with each

———————— *The Process of Economic Development* ————————

successive wave of technical change. It is quite obvious that the curricula of educational institutions must change with a change of techno-economic paradigm but many other changes are needed which are not so obvious but which reflect the special needs of each new technology. Even to change the curricula of education and training systems is by no means so simple as it might appear (Ashby, 1969). The acquisition of a major new technology is a very complex and widespread learning process at all levels of society, involving social as well as technical innovations. At the level of the enterprise, several (and complementary) mechanisms of learning underlie the accumulation of technological competences. In every one of these domains, the case of the four 'Asian tigers' is highly suggestive on the nature of the changes involved in successful development strategies.

First, the education of large numbers of qualified engineers and especially of electronic engineers is obviously extremely important. All the four tigers now have an output of graduate engineers per 100 000 population which is greater than that of Japan (Table 16) and also greater than most Latin American countries and OECD countries. Even where the ratio of total education expenditure to GDP is lower than in some OECD or Latin American countries, the bias in the system towards engineering and within engineering towards information technology ensures an adequate flow of these key people. As in the case of Japan, the strength of the engineering education, of vocational education and of in-house training in firms should be seen in the context of a high level of general educational attainment, best illustrated by the example of Korea (Table 17). It should also be emphasized that the achievements of the education system were certainly not the heritage of Japanese colonial rule but the result of active education policies since the achievement of independence. The same is largely true of Taiwan but there the private education sector played a larger role (Wade, 1990).

A second essential feature of catching up in new technology is the promotion of a wide range of technical and scientific activities within industry and commerce itself. While a substantial flow of graduate engineers and other well-educated people is a *sine qua non* of an active catching-up policy, their efficient deployment in productive activities is, of course, also essential. Characteristic of many Third World countries is a concentration of scientific and technical activities within government institutions. While this is necessary during the early stages of development of a science–technology basic infrastructure, competitive industries for the world market can only emerge if they develop their own in-house competence in R&D and other technical activities. Partly as a result of deliberate policy incentives the tigers now typically have half or more of their total R&D activities conducted within industry, whereas in Latin American countries, this proportion has remained

———————————— 29 ————————————

--------------------------- *The Process of Economic Development* ---------------------------

TABLE 16. Engineering, Science and Maths
Students as Percentage of Population in Various
Countries, 1987

	Engineering	Engineering, science and maths
Japan	0.34	0.40
Brazil	0.13	0.24
South Korea	0.54	0.76
Singapore	0.61	0.73
Taiwan	0.68	0.78

Source: Kim, 1993.

TABLE 17   S Korea: Science and Education Indicators (1953–1987)

	1953	1970	1987
Literacy (%)	22	89	99
Middle school (12–14 years) (%)	21	53	99
High school (15–17 years) (%)	12	29	83
College/university (%)	3	9	26
Scientists/engineers (No.)	4157	65 687	361 920
Corporate R&D laboratories (No.)	–	1	455
Researchers (No.)			
Governments RIs	–	2477	9184
Universities	–	1918	17 415
Private industry	–	925	26 104
Total	–	5320	52 783
R&D/GNP (%)	0.1	0.3	1.9

Source: Kim, 1993.

typically at 20–30% of the total or even less. The results of empirical studies in this area are clear-cut both for Third World countries and for the former communist countries of eastern Europe: it is essential to develop the competence for technology acquisition and technical innovation within the enterprises themselves. As firms progress in their learning activities this will increasingly involve in-house research and development. However, it is by no means only a question of R&D. It is also a question of a wide range of scientific and technical services (STS) which reinforce and interact with R&D and in the early stages can often substitute for it. They include design, testing, quality control, production engineering, technical information services, market research and, of course, a range of training activities (Bell, 1991).

--------------------------- 30 ---------------------------

──────────────── *The Process of Economic Development* ────────────────

They often go by different names in different firms and in different countries but what they have in common is a persistent effort to improve the quality of products, processes and services which the firm delivers, whether they are based on imported technologies or not. The respective lessons of Japanese and of east European experience are particularly relevant here. Both relied heavily on the import of technology but whereas Japanese firms were characterized by active efforts to adapt these technologies to local conditions and to improve them in many ways (Freeman, 1987), east European countries suffered from a system which gave very low priority to enterprise—level R&D and other STS—and put the main technical and design effort in institutions which were largely separated from productions, both managerially and geographically. They also suffered from a management and planning system which offered little incentive and sometimes negative incentives to product and process innovation (Gomulka, 1990).

Thirdly, the fact that technological learning in the enterprises is the most essential factor of catching up does not mean that the public, private and hybrid infrastructure is unimportant. On the contrary, as we have seen, not only does the (largely public) education system play an absolutely essential role in the whole process but other public, scientific and technical services are also crucial for success, for example technical information and abstracting services and databanks, scientific libraries, standard institutions, advisory and consultancy services, research associations of various kinds, patents offices and so forth. As Perez and Soete (1988) point out, the availability of such services is often taken for granted in the OECD countries. Without this network of supporting public and private services the cost of designing new products and processes becomes astronomical. Again, the findings of empirical research in this field are unequivocal: innovation depends on a combination of in-house experience, learning and development with a wide variety of external sources of information and advice, i.e. formal or informal networking (Freeman, 1991), hence, the importance of national infrastructure and national systems of innovation (Lundvall, 1992; Nelson, 1993).

Fourthly, technological catch up and learning also depends continuously on learning from production and marketing. It is not enough to have R&D within the firm if it does not interact with other functions. Here again Japanese experience is of exceptional importance in interpreting the divergence of East Asia and Latin America. An outstanding feature of Japanese management and firm organization has been the horizontal integration of R&D, design, production and marketing (Aoki, 1986; Freeman, 1987; Aoki and Dosi, 1992). Many observers have contrasted this with the more hierarchical, vertical structures of typical large American firms. It is American management practice, however, which has been by far the most powerful

──────────────── 31 ────────────────

—————————— *The Process of Economic Development* ——————————

influence on Latin American firms, through USA subsidiaries, through widespread management consultancy, through imitation of structures and through a hundred and one intangible and unseen but no less influential informal learning processes. In East Asia, on the other hand, the huge wave of Japanese investment, the subcontracting networks, the increasing Japanese consultancy, the engineering culture within many firms, the historical integration of marketing and production in Hong Kong and Singapore and many other informal influences have combined to produce a different pattern of managerial behavior.

Fifth, learning takes place also through investment in physical equipment, in new (and second-hand) plant and machinery. Japan is now the main source of imports of plant and equipment for the countries of East Asia. Latin American countries lag behind East Asian countries not only in patenting (and R&D activities) but also in their investment activity, which is essential for the successful diffusion of new technology. Of course, some technology is disembodied and can be acquired or transferred without specific tangible investment in physical plant and equipment but generally there is a complementary relationship between the two.

Sixth and finally, the composition of investment is fundamental, too: East Asia has forged ahead of Latin America in the 1980s especially in some of the most dynamic areas of investment such as telecommunications and computers (Table 18).

Summing up this discussion on catching up in new technology, the basis of the East Asian success and the relative failure of the Latin American countries in the 1980s lies in a combination of institutional and social changes promoted by active policies (Gereffi and Wyman, 1990; Wade, 1990) as in the earlier case of Japanese catching up (Freeman, 1987).

The earlier phase (1960s) of catch up by a variety of NICs in several continents (East Europe, Latin America, Middle East, East Asia) was based on the widespread diffusion of established American mass and flow production technology and management techniques in such industries as oil, petrochemicals, steel, automobiles, consumer durables, textiles, clothing, paper and related services. These technologies were also heavily imported into Japan herself and into the four tigers as well as western Europe in the 1950s and 1960s. The USA was the main source of both technology and capital goods.

The more recent (1980s) phase of strong divergence between Latin America and East Asia and Japan forging ahead requires an explanation in terms of comparative rates of learning and adoption in the new techno-economic paradigm based on information and communication technology; and in terms of specific patterns of organizational innovation.

————————————————————— 32 —————————————————————

—— *The Process of Economic Development* ——

TABLE 18. International Indicators of Developments in Telecommunications

Country	Telephone lines per 100 persons	Per capita sales of equipment (US$)
Brazil	6	10
Colombia	7	21
Malaysia	7	32
Korea	24	77
Singapore	34	235
UK	39	166
Japan	39	315
Former W Germany	46	306
USA	53	389

Source: KISDI, 1990.

In drawing a contrast between 'Latin America' and 'East Asia', here we have concentrated on the 'national systems' of innovation and production as a crucial factor in facilitating the acquisition and exploitation of new technologies (the two contrasting experiences are summarized in Table 19). In its broadest sense, of course, this 'national system' also involves and interacts with other features of the social and political system which have not been discussed here. (These broader, and indeed crucial aspects of each national economy are emphasized by Zysman, in this volume.) Clearly the capacity to make institutional changes in education and in infrastructural investment depends on political institutions responsive to these needs and capable of overcoming inertia, vested interests and other sources of opposition. The political systems of the East Asian countries are, in fact, extremely varied although Wade (1990) has pointed to certain common features. Following MacArthur's Land Reform in Japan, similar reforms in South Korea and the Communist Revolution in China, the opposition to social change of a traditional land-owning class has not been the major problem which it still is in many Latin American countries. In turn a more equitable distribution of income than is found in Latin America has not hindered high saving rates, while at the same time it has allowed a rapid expansion of the domestic markets (Tylecote, 1992.)

Finally, at a political level Far Eastern countries have in common with Latin America a history of quite authoritarian regimes. However, while in Latin America despotic practices have often favored the rent-seeking activities of particular industrial or agricultural interests, in the Far East public administrations have been able to make an instrumental use of varying mixtures of 'stick and carrot' policies aimed at industrial accumulation and technological learning. As Alice Amsden has shown:

─────────────── *The Process of Economic Development* ───────────────

> The State intervenes with subsidies deliberately to distort relative prices in order to stimulate economic activity. This has been true in Korea, Japan and Taiwan as it has been in Brazil, India, Turkey. In Korea, Japan and Taiwan, however, the State has exercised discipline over subsidy recipients. In exchange for subsidies, the State has imposed performance standards on private firms (Amsden, 1989, p 8).

What we have just recounted is the basic skeleton of a comparative story, whereby the strategies of different actors—e.g. states, domestic and multinational firms, etc.—determined quite diverse collective outcomes, in terms of institutional set-ups, technological capabilities and growth performances. This is mainly a process story. In fact, in our historical reconstruction, initial 'endowments' did not play any major role in explaining what happened thereafter: if anything, we are to consider the initial conditions, circa 1950, as the 'original endowments', one would have plausibly predicted a higher potential for growth in Latin American countries. For example, industrial structures were more developed, educational levels in many Latin American countries were higher, there was a higher availability of natural resources, etc.: hence, conditional on initial per capita GDPs, common economic wisdom might have forecast higher growth, at least as a 'transitional' dynamic.

TABLE 19. Divergence in National Systems of Innovation in the 1980s

East Asia	Latin America
Expanding education system with high proportion of engineering studies	Deteriorating education system with proportionately lower output of engineers
Rapid growth of scientific and technical activities at enterprise level, especially R&D	Slow growth stagnation or decline of enterprise level, R&D and other STS
Development of strong science–technology infrastructure	Weakening of science–technology infrastructure
Strong influence of Japanese models of management and networking organization	Continuing influence of outdated American management models
High levels of investment and major inflow of Japanese investment	Decline in foreign investment and generally lower levels of investment
Heavy investment in advanced telecommunications	Slow development of modern telecommunications
Strong and fast-growing electronic industries with high exports	Weak electronic industries with low exports
Growing participation in international technology networks and agreements	Low level of international networking in technology

——————————— *The Process of Economic Development* ———————————

What can be recovered of this story, as well as of the 'stylized facts' outlined in the previous section, at the more general level of the theory? We shall turn to this question in the next section.

4. 'Ingredients' and Processes of Development: 'Equilibrium' versus Evolutionary Microfoundations

In very general terms, moving from stylized evidence to theory involves the identification of both some basic 'ingredients' (or 'factors') of growth—what Abramovitz would call the 'proximate causes' of development—and some underlying processes which shape the dynamics of these 'ingredients' and link them together, hence generating the observable patterns of development—Abramovitz's 'deeper causes' (cf. Abramovitz, 1989).

In the light of the previous discussion, one would inductively identify among the relatively invariant 'ingredients' (or at least necessary conditions) of industrialization and rapid growth variables like education and infrastructures. Among the 'processes', one has discussed above, among others, institutional change influencing national accumulation of technological competences; the emergence of socioeconomic conditions and corporate strategies yielding high rates of investment in new equipment; the trajectories of technological learning by individual firms and the ways they are affected by market incentives and internal capabilities. Moreover, technological learning appears to be associated intimately with various forms of indivisibilities and dynamic increasing returns.

Finally, one may distinguish—within the historical discussion above—three major sources of change, namely processes of technological and institutional innovation that are (i) country-specific, (ii) company-specific and (iii) technology-specific, such as major changes in 'technological paradigms'. (It is with reluctance that in some of the discussion below we shall standardize on the current literature and represent them as different types of 'shocks': in fact, they are shocks which are to a great extent endogenously generated.)

Significant progress has been made in recent years toward a more satisfactory theoretical understanding of both 'ingredients' and 'processes' (although some of the novel directions of inquiry are inconsistent with each other). For the purposes of this introduction, let us just mention the following streams of analysis.

- The 'Schumpeterian' acknowledgement that a good deal of innovative exploration is endogenous to the activities of business firms has led to a variety of models whereby growth is driven by technological innovations undertaken by profit motivated agents (see, among others, Romer, 1990a,

——————————————— 35 ———————————————

───────────────── *The Process of Economic Development* ─────────────────

1990b; Grossman and Helpman, 1991; and, nearer to a Schumpeterian spirit, Aghion and Howitt, 1992; Cheng and Dinopoulos, 1992). As mentioned in the introduction to this work, the methodological thrust of 'new growth' theories has been to endogenize Solow time-dependent drift within an 'enlarged' production function: a special 'production function of knowledge' yields increasing returns to knowledge itself, while at the same time preserving implicit general equilibrium microfoundations.

- The 'impactedness' of knowledge may lead to non-linearities in the relationship between inputs and outputs and this may be captured by 'technological externalities with threshold properties' in an otherwise standard production function (Azariadis and Drazen, 1990) or by big indivisibilities and structural changes associated with development. Indeed, it is shown that dynamic externalities may imply an infinite multiplicity of equilibria and the possibility of self-sustained growth as well as of 'poverty traps' (Boldrin, 1992).

- Somewhat symmetrically to new growth theories, 'new trade' theories have incorporated some forms of increasing returns and imperfect competition into open economy models, showing, remarkably, that the welfare-enhancing properties of free trade cease to hold in general (see Grossman and Helpman, 1991; Young, 1991, among others).

- Both 'old' and 'new' growth theories do not allow for any country-specificity, except those already captured by the inputs in the production function (whether standard or 'enlarged'), and also assume instantaneous intra-country diffusion of innovation. An alternative route to the explanation of why levels and growth rates of income differ focuses, on the contrary, on national determinants of the dynamics of the 'shifts' in the production function itself. Building on an early model of Nelson and Phelps (1966), Benhabib and Spiegel (1992) interpret economically the $A(t)$ dynamics as dependent on country-specific variables such as some proxies for human capital. Note that the latter enters the production function of knowledge—'*à la* P. Romer'—and also determines the country-specific rates of diffusion of knowledge. That is, 'education' influences both the rate at which knowledge is generated and the catching up of laggard countries to frontier technologies (indeed, the model allows for 'forging ahead' and 'falling behind', as a function of relative educational levels). Benhabib and Jovanovic (1991) and Jovanovic and Lach (1991) interpret persistent international differences in growth rates (and also the time series variations) as the outcome of imperfectly correlated country-specific shocks and non-instantaneous diffusion. Rates of diffusion are assumed to be identical across countries and in Jovanovic and Lach they are calibrated on the micro USA data from Klepper and Graddy (1990). The production function

───────────────── 36 ─────────────────

———————————— *The Process of Economic Development* ————————————

itself is a Solow constant returns function. As Benhabib and Jovanovic emphasize, in these models the relation goes from knowledge to capital accumulation and not the other way round (as in new growth theories).

- It was mentioned earlier that an important finding from the economics of innovation is the distinction between relatively incremental (or 'normal') technical progress versus paradigmatic changes. That distinction is somewhat captured also in various equilibrium models of invention and growth: Jovanovic and Rob (1990) distinguish between 'intensive' and 'extensive' search; Cheng and Dinopoulos (1992) between 'breakthroughs' and 'improvements'; the work by Brezis, Krugman and Isiodon (1991), although very parsimonious on acknowledgements from the innovation literature, is in fact an equilibrium model of change in international leadership associated with changes in technological 'paradigms'. In general, the presence of both incremental and radical changes, it is shown, easily generates persistent fluctuations in aggregate time series and/or persistent international differentiation.

- Two features which most of the models reviewed so far have in common are, not surprisingly, microfoundations based on perfectly rational agents and equilibrium interactions. An immediate objection to such microfoundations is that one is bound to lose a lot of the 'action' (i.e. processes of change) on which the historical interpretation of development is grounded. We shall return to this point later on but let us just point out now that even without abandoning equilibrium and rationality *tout court*, some important insights can be gained already by relaxing the most restrictive assumptions on general equilibrium (of the Arrow–Debreu type) and on perfect foresight (note that, on the contrary, most new growth endeavors have, if anything, increased the demands on the rational abilities of their 'representative agent', e.g. the predictions of many models stand or fall with rational technological expectations).

In this regard, two directions of inquiry are worth mentioning for our purposes. A first one points to the importance of coordination failures and demand externalities that can be simply derived by the absence of Arrow–Debreu contingency markets. In that vein, Murphy *et al.* (1989) formulate an argument, familiar in development literature, on the importance of 'big-pushes' (Rosenstein–Rodan) and intersectoral demand linkages (Hirschmann) in order to switch from one growth path to another one; Durlauf, in this volume, models an economy with endogenous cyclicity due to changing intersectoral demand flows (but the argument can be in principle extended to multi-economies worlds).

A second direction studies the aggregate implications of microeconomic

—————————— *The Process of Economic Development* ——————————

behaviors based on various informational imperfections (e.g. in the market for finance) and local learning: Stiglitz (1992 and in this volume) shows that these conditions are sufficient to generate multiple growth trajectories. He also argues that the transitional dynamics between them squares with a few stylized facts of growth and catching up.

To summarize: as widely acknowledged, in recent years diverse endeavors have enriched growth theory, by bringing into the picture some forms of increasing returns, threshold effects, demand complementarities, country-specific and technology-specific shocks, and—sometimes—also a more satisfactory microeconomics based on informational asymmetries.

Still, it seems to us, progress toward a better understanding of the 'deeper sources' of growth is hindered by the obstinate adherence to equilibrium microfoundations and to the attempt by many to incorporate learning within a familiar optimal allocation mechanism by an unboundedly rational representative agent.

Indeed, the tension between dynamic phenomena—such as technical change—and the static allocative properties summarized by a Solow-type production function indirectly shows up also in the empirical estimations yielding quite weird coefficients for marginal productivities and factors' shares (see for example Durlauf and Johnson, 1992; and Behnabib and Jovanovic, 1991). One may obtain, in unconstrained estimates, negative marginal social product of capital or negative labor shares! In some respects it is like the story of Procrustes' bed in Greek mythology: if you pull the blanket to protect your head from being cut off, you uncover the feet—and the other way round.

Moreover, the quest to maintain traditional microfoundations restricts the analysis of increasing returns and non-convexities to those forms which can still be reconciled—at least in principle—with some underlying general equilibrium.

Finally, for similar reasons, firm-specific technological shocks have largely been neglected, even if they are a crucial part of the historical interpretation of development. Conversely, firm-specific learning and endogenous innovations have been a central concern of evolutionary models following the pioneering work of Nelson and Winter (see Nelson and Winter, 1982; Iwai, 1984a, 1984b; Eliasson, 1986; Metcalfe, 1988; Silverberg *et al.*, 1988; Conlisk, 1989; Chiaromonte and Dosi, 1992; and, in this volume, Dosi *et al.*; Silverberg and Verspagen).

Putting it in a somewhat extreme form, evolutionary models focus on the dynamic properties of economic systems driven by processes of learning, while neglecting—in a first approximation—optimal resource allocation

―――――――――― *The Process of Economic Development* ――――――――――

issues. That is, one focuses—loosely speaking—on the process driving the $A(t)$ dynamics of Solow's function, assuming that whatever pattern of resource allocation emerges it is, too, a highly imperfect outcome of innovation, imitation and diffusion. At least three major 'building blocks' characterize the evolutionary approach, namely (i) the microfoundations rest on boundedly rational agents; (ii) the general presumption is that interactions occur away from equilibrium; (iii) markets and other institutions perform as selection mechanisms among heterogeneous agents and technologies.

The evolutionary research programme links up, to a large extent, with the spirit of other unorthodox perspectives and, in particular, with models of Kaldorian and Goodwinian inspiration (Kaldor and Mirlees, 1962; Goodwin, 1967, 1990; Kaldor, 1985) and with the (mainly French) institutionalist approach known as the 'Regulation School' (Aglietta, 1982; Boyer, 1988a, 1988b). These approaches have in common with the evolutionary one the abandonment of standard microfoundations (implicit or explicit rational agents, market equilibria, etc.) and also an emphasis on technical change and institutional specificities as crucial explanatory variables. Evolutionary models, however, attempt to nest the dynamics on the alternative microfoundations briefly mentioned above. Conversely, e.g. Kaldorian or 'Regulation'-type models start at a higher level of generality and attempt to identify robust functional relationships among aggregate variables—for example the increasing return loop linking output growth and productivity growth known as the 'Verdoorn–Kaldor law'; or the quasi-Marxian relationship between profits, accumulation and employment in Goodwinian models. One then studies the dynamics entailed by particular aggregate relationships.[4] The 'Regulation' research project is more ambitious and aims at the analysis of the interactions among the patterns of technical change and the institutional forms of governance of the major markets (of labor, finance and goods) which make up particular regimes of growth—specific of different countries and different historical periods.[5]

If one accepts the number of 'stylized facts' that a model can account for as a criterion for judging its robustness, then unorthodox models—in our admittedly biased view—have not fared too badly. For example, in an evolutionary perspective, Nelson and Winter (1982) easily generate the macro-regularities accounted by standard neoclassical growth models (grow-

―――――――――――――――――――――――――――――

[4] A survey of the non-microfounded models is in Boldrin (1988). See also Silverberg (1988) and Day and Chen (1993). A thorough comparison between 'old', 'new' and 'Cambridge' growth models is in Bertola (1994).

[5] The notion of 'Regulation', in this approach, stands for the 'socio-economic tuning' among institutional set-ups shaping accumulation, wage formation, income distribution, demand patterns, etc.: see Boyer (1988a). For a stimulating attempt to embed this perspective into a Kaldor/Goodwin dynamics, cf. Lordon (1993).

─────────────── *The Process of Economic Development* ───────────────

ing capital/labor ratios, near constancy of distributive share) but in addition they endogenize the 'innovative' engine of growth. Moreover, the micro-structure that the model generates is in tune with some of the industrial 'stylized facts' recalled earlier (asymmetric distribution of firms sizes, persis-tent diversity in performance, endogeneity of market structures, etc.). Just to mention a few of the contributions along these lines which followed Nelson and Winter's work, Silverberg *et al.* (1988) and Metcalfe (1988) analyze the diffusion of innovation as an evolutionary process. Silverberg and Lehnert (1993) show how persistent fluctuations in aggregate income series can be generated by stochastic arrivals of capital-embedded innovations with diffusion at a pace proportional to their differential profitability. Verspagen (199 1a) shows how a non-linear interaction between the potential of imita-tion, determined by technological lags *vis-à-vis* the frontier countries, and domestic capabilities can produce either catching-up dynamics or falling behind. In this volume, Silverberg and Verspagen study the adaptive emer-gence of 'innovative routines' and their collective effect on growth dynamics; Dosi *et al.* extend evolutionary models to a multi-country setting. As regards the 'Regulation' perspective, it is yielding inspiring research into the political economy of growth, trying to bridge 'process stories' and 'institutional stories' in the interpretation of international differences in growth patterns and also of transitions and crises between different phases of development (see Boyer, 1988b; Boyer and Petit, 1990).

Some Conclusions

As this (incomplete) overview of recent theoretical developments shows, growth theories are starting to explore previously untouched domains. The 'theoretical stories' and the 'appreciative stories' told by historians have come somewhat nearer each other and new empirical phenomena have been addressed. For example, on theoretical grounds, the proposition that 'history matters' is now acknowledged even near the mainstream of economic theory—in the form of dependence of trajectories on initial conditions, multiplicity of growth paths, etc. The research on the institutional architecture of national economic systems has drawn strength—on the theory side—from asymmetric-information and transaction-cost models and—on the empirical side—from a richer understanding of how institutions and corporate organ-izations work. The appreciative evidence on technical change is slowly start-ing to percolate into modeling efforts. However, one is certainly still far from a successful account of the role of technical change, organizations and institutions in growth and development. Relatedly, only a small subset of the stylized facts discussed above finds adequate theoretical interpretations.

─────────────────── 40 ───────────────────

──────── *The Process of Economic Development* ────────

With respect to both issues, one of the aims of the collection of articles that follow is also to foster an interdisciplinary dialogue and a dialogue within the economic discipline among different theoretical approaches which—notwithstanding conflicting assumptions—have come increasingly to talk about similar things.

Acknowledgements

This research, at different stages, has benefitted from the support from the Alfred P. Sloan Foundation, through the Consortium on Competitiveness and Cooperation, University of California at Berkeley; the Italian National Research Council (CNR); the International Institution of Applied System Analysis (IIASA), Laxenburg, Austria. We gratefully acknowledge the comments by M. Abramovitz, S. Durlauf, W. Kwasnicki and the participants in the seminars at the Santa Fe Institute, Santa Fe and at CEPREMAP, Paris; D. Mandeng helped in accessing the CAN Data Bank (CEPAL, Santiago, Chile) on trade flows.

References

Abramovitz, M. (1989), *Thinking about Growth*. Cambridge University Press: Cambridge.

Aghion, P. and P. Howitt (1992), 'A Model of Growth through Creative Destruction,' in C. Freeman and D. Foray (eds), *Technology and the Wealth of Nations*. Pinter: London.

Aglietta, (1982), *Regulation and Crisis of Capitalism*. Monthly Review Press: New York

Amendola, G., G. Dosi and E Papagni (1993), 'The Dynamics of Competitiveness,' *Weltwirtschaftliches Archiv* (September).

Amsden, A. (1989), *Asia's New Giant* Oxford University Press. New York, Oxford.

Aoki, M. (1986), 'Horizontal vs Vertical Structures: The Japanese Firm in Information Structures of the Firm,' *American Economic Review*, 76, 971–983.

Aoki, M and G Dosi (1992), 'Corporate Organization, Finance and Innovation,' in V. Zamagni (ed.), *Finance and the Enterprise*. Academic Press: New York.

Arthur, B. (1988), 'Competing Technologies: An Overview,' in G. Dosi, C. Freeman, R. Nelson, G. Silverberg and L. Soete (eds), *Technical Change and Economic Theory*. Pinter: London and Columbia University Press: New York.

Ashby, E. (1969), *Technology and the Academics*. Macmillan: London.

Azariadis, C. and A. Drazen (1990), 'Threshold Externalities in Economic Development,' *Quarterly Journal of Economics*, 105, 501–526.

Bairoch, P. (1981), 'The Main Trends in National Economic Disparities since the Industrial Revolution,' in P. Bairoch and M. Levy-Loboyer, *Disparities in Economic Development since the Industrial Revolution*. Macmillan: London.

Bell, R. M. (1991), 'Science and Technology Policy Research in the 1990s: Key Issues for Developing Countries,' University of Sussex, SPRU, 25th Anniversary Conference, Brighton (July).

Bell, M. and K. Pavitt (1992), *National Capacities for Technological Accumulation: Evidence and Implications for Developing Countries*, mimeo: SPRU, University of Sussex: Brighton.

Benhabib, J. and B. Jovanovic (1991), 'Externalities and Growth Accounting,' *American Economic Review*, 81, 82–113.

──────── 41 ────────

———————————— *The Process of Economic Development* ————————————

Benhabib, J. and M. M. Spiegel (1992), *The Role of Human Capital and Political Instability in Economic Development*, mimeo: New York University: New York.

Bertola, G. (1994), 'Wages, Profits and Theories of Growth,' in L. Pasinetti and R Solow (eds), *Economic Growth and the Structure of Long-term Development*. Macmillan: London.

Boyer, R. (1988a), 'Technical Change and the Theory of Regulation,' in G Dosi, C Freeman, R. Nelson, G. Silverberg and L Soete (eds), *Technical Change and Economic Theory*. Pinter: London and Columbia University Press: New York.

Boyer, R. (1988b), 'Formalizing Growth Regimes,' in G. Dosi, C. Freeman, R. Nelson, G. Silverberg and L. Soete (eds), *Technical Change and Economic Theory*. Pinter: London and Columbia University Press: New York.

Boyer, R. and P. Petit (1990), 'Technical Change, Cumulative Causation and Growth: Accounting for the Contemporary Productivity Puzzle with Some Post-Keynesian Theories,' in *The Challenge of Economic Policy*. OECD: Paris

Boldrin, M. (1988), 'Persistent Oscillations and Chaos in Dynamic Economic Models: A Note for a Survey,' in P W. Anderson, K. F. Arrow and R Pines (eds), *The Economy as a Complex Evolving System* Addison-Wesley: New York.

Boldrin, M. (1992), 'Dynamic Externalities, Multiple Equilibria and Growth,' *Journal of Economic Theory*, 58, 198–218

Brezis, E., P. Krugman and D. Isiodon (1991), 'Leapfrogging: A Theory of Cycles in National Technological Leadership,' NBER Working Paper, n. 3886, Cambridge, MA

Burns, A. F (1934), *Production Trends in the United States since 1870*. NBER: New York

Chandler, A. D (1990), *Scale and Scope: The Dynamics of Industrial Capitalism*. Belknap Press: Cambridge, MA and London.

Cheng, L. K and E. Dinopoulos (1992), 'Schumpeterian Growth and International Business Cycles,' *American Economic Review, Papers and Proceedings*, 82, 409–414.

Chiaromonte, F. and G. Dosi (1992), 'The Microfoundation of Competitiveness and Their Macroeconomic Implications,' in C. Freeman and D Foray (eds) (1992), *Technology and the Wealth of Nations* Pinter: London.

Conlist, J. (1989), 'An Aggregate Model of Technical Change,' *Quarterly Journal of Economics*, 104, 787–821.

Dahlman, C. J. and C. R. Frischtak (1991), 'National Systems Supporting Technical Advance in Industry: The Brazilian Experience,' paper prepared for the Workshop 'National Systems Supporting Technical Advance in Industry,' Stanford University: Stanford, CA, October 1990.

David, P. (1992), 'Path Dependence and Predictability in Dynamic Systems with Local Network Externalities: A Paradigm for Historical Economics,' in C. Freeman and D. Foray (eds), *Technology and the Wealth of Nations*. Pinter: London.

Day, R. and P. Chen (eds) (1993), *Non-linear Dynamics and Evolutionary Economics*. Oxford University Press: Oxford.

De Long, B. J. (1988), 'Productivity Growth, Convergence and Welfare,' *American Economic Review*, 78, 1138–1154

De Long, B. J. and L. H. Summers (1991), 'Equipment Investment and Economic Growth,' *Quarterly Journal of Economics*, 106, 445–502.

De Long, B. J. and L. H. Summers (1992), *How Robust is the Growth–Machinery Nexus*, mimeo, Harvard University.

Denison, E. F. and J. P. Poullier (1967), *Why Growth Rates Differ*. Brookings Institution: Washington.

Dosi, G. (1982), 'Technological Paradigms and Technological Trajectories,' *Research Policy*, 11, 147–162.

Dosi, G. (1984), *Technological Change and Industrial Transfer*. Macmillan: London and St Martin's: New York.

Dosi, G. (1988), 'Sources, Procedures and Microeconomic Effects of Innovations,' *Journal of Economic Literature*, 26, 1120–1171.

———————————————————— 42 ————————————————————

——————— *The Process of Economic Development* ———————

Dosi, G , C. Freeman, S. Fabiani and R. Aversi (1993), 'On the Process of Economic Development,' *CCC Working Paper*, no. 93–2, Center for Research and Management, University of California at Berkeley. Berkeley, CA.

Dosi, G , R. Giannetti and P. A. Toninelli (eds) (1992), *Technology and Enterprise in a Historical Perspective*. Oxford University Press: Oxford.

Dosi, G., O Marsili, L. Orsenigo and R. Salvatore (1993), 'Learning, Market Selection and the Evolution of Industrial Structures,' CCC Working Paper, no. 93–99, Center for Research and Management, University of California at Berkeley: Berkeley, CA.

Dosi, G., K. Pavitt and L. Soete (1990), *The Economics of Technological Change and International Trade*. Wheatsheaf/Harvester Press: London.

Durlauf, S N. (1991), *Nonergodic Economic Growth*, mimeo, Stanford University. Stanford, CA.

Durlauf, S. N. and P. A. Johnson (1992), *Local versus Global Convergence across National Economies*, mimeo, Stanford University: Stanford, CA.

Dutt, A. K. (1992), 'The Origin of Uneven Development. The Indian Subcontinent,' *American Economic Review*, 82, 146–150.

Easterly, W., R King, R Levine and S. Rebelo (1991), 'How Do National Policies Affect Long-run Growth?,' World Bank Working Paper, WPS 794, World Bank: Washington, DC.

Edwards, S. (1993), 'Openness, Trade Liberalization and Growth in Developing Countries,' *Journal of Economic Literature*, XXXI, 1358–1393.

Eliasson, G. (1986), 'Microheterogeneity of Firms and the Stability of Industrial Growth,' in R. Day and G. Eliasson (eds), *The Dynamics of Market Economies*. North Holland: Amsterdam.

Fagerberg, I. (1988), 'Why Growth Rates Differ,' in G Dosi, C Freeman, R Nelson, G Silverberg and L Soete (eds), *Technical Change and Economic Theory*. Pinter: London and Columbia University Press. New York.

Findlay, R. (1992), 'The Roots of Divergence' Western Economic History in Comparative Perspective,' *American Economic Review*, Papers and Proceedings, 82, 158–161

Freeman, C. (1982), *The Economics of Industrial Innovation*. 2nd edition Pinter· London.

Freeman, C. (1987), *Technology Policy and Economic Performance*. Pinter: London.

Freeman, C. (1991), 'Networks of Innovators,' *Research Policy*, 20, 499–514.

Freeman, C. and C Perez (1988), 'Structural Crises of Adjustment,' in G Dosi, C Freeman, R. Nelson, G. Silverberg and L. Soete (eds), *Technical Change and Economic Theory*, Pinter. London and Columbia University Press: New York.

GATT (1990), *International Trade 1989–90*. II, GATT, Geneva.

Gereffi, G. and D L. Wyman (eds) (1990), *Manufacturing Miracles. Pathways of Industrialization in Latin America and East Asia* Princeton University Press. Princeton, NJ.

Goglio, A (1991), *'Technology Gap' Theory of International Trade: A Survey*. UNCTAD Geneva.

Gomulka, S (1990), *The Theory of Technological Change and Economic Growth*. Routledge: London and New York.

Goodwin, R M (1967), 'A New Growth Cycle,' in C H. Feinstein (ed.), *Socialism, Capitalism and Economic Growth*. Macmillan: London.

Goodwin, R. M. (1990), *Chaotic Economic Dynamics*. The Clarendon Press of Oxford University Press: Oxford.

Granovetter, M. (1985), 'Economic Action and Social Structure. A Theory of Embeddedness,' *American Journal of Sociology*, 19, 481–510.

Grossman, G. M. and E. Helpman, (1991), *Innovation and Growth. Technological Competition in the Global Economy*. MIT Press: Cambridge, MA.

Iwai, K. (1984a), 'Schumpeterian Dynamics: An Evolutionary Model of Innovation and Imitation,' *Journal of Economic Behaviour and Organization*, 5, 159–190.

Iwai, K. (1984b), 'Schumpeterian Dynamics, Part II: Technological Progress, Firm Growth and 'Economic Selection,' *Journal of Economic Behaviour and Organization*, 5, 321–351.

──────────── *The Process of Economic Development* ────────────

Jovanovic, B. and S. Lach (1991), 'The Diffusion of Technology and Inequality among Nations,' NBER Working Paper, n. 3732, Cambridge, MA

Jovanovic, B. and R. Rob (1990), 'Long Waves and Short Waves: Growth through Intensive and Extensive Search,' *Econometrica*, 58, 1391–1409.

Kaldor, N. (1985), *Economics without Equilibrium*. University College Cardiff Press: Cardiff

Kaldor, N and J A. Mirlees (1962), 'A New Model of Economic Growth,' *Review of Economic Studies*, 29, 174–192.

Kim, L. (1993), 'National System of Industrial Innovation: Dynamic of Capability Building in Korea,' in R R. Nelson (ed.), *National Systems of Innovation*. Cambridge University Press: Cambridge.

Kuznets, S. (1972), *Modern Economic Growth*. Yale University Press: New Haven, CT.

Landes, D. (1969), *The Unbounded Prometheus*. Cambridge University Press: Cambridge.

Lewis, A. (1978), *Growth and Fluctuations 1870–1913*. Allen and Unwin London.

Lordon, F. (1993), *Endogenous Structural Change and Crisis in a Multiple Time-Scales Growth Model*. Working Paper 9324, CEPREMAP: Paris.

Lucas, R. E. B. (1988), 'On the Mechanisms of Economic Development,' *Journal of Monetary Economics*, 22, 3–42.

Lundval, B. A. (1988), 'Innovation as an Interactive Process· From User–Producer Interactions to the National System of Innovation,' in G Dosi, C. Freeman, R. Nelson, G. Silverberg and L. Soete (eds), *Technical Change and Economic Theory*. Pinter: London and Columbia University Press: New York.

Lundvall, B. A. (ed.) (1992), *National Systems of Innovation—Towards a Theory of Innovation and Interactive Learning*. Pinter: London.

Maddison, A. (1982), *Phases of Capitalist Development*. Oxford University Press: Oxford.

Maddison, A. (1991), *Dynamic Forces in Capitalist Development* Oxford University Press: Oxford.

Maizels, A. (1963), *Industrial Growth and World Trade*. Cambridge University Press and NIESR: Cambridge.

Malerba, L. (1985), *The Semiconductor Business: The Economics of Rapid Growth and Decline*. Pinter: London.

Metcalfe, S. (1988), 'The Diffusion of Innovation: An Interpretative Survey,' in G. Dosi, C. Freeman, R. Nelson, G. Silverberg and L. Soete (eds), *Technical Change and Economic Theory*. Pinter: London and Columbia University Press: New York.

Murphy, K. M., A. Shleifer and R. W. Vishny (1989), 'Industrialization and the Big Push,' *Journal of Political Economy*, 97, 1003–1026.

Nelson, R. R. (ed.) (1993), *National Systems of Innovation*. Cambridge University Press: Cambridge.

Nelson, R. and E. S. Phelps (1966), 'Investment in Humans, Technological Diffusion and Economic Growth,' *American Economic Review*, 56, 69–75.

Nelson, R. and S. Winter (1982), *An Evolutionary Theory of Economic Change*. The Belknap Press of Harvard University Press: Cambridge, MA.

Pasinetti, L. and R. Solow (eds) (1994), *Economic Growth and the Structure of Long-term Development*. Macmillan: London.

Pavitt, K. and L. Soete (1981), 'International Differences in Economic Growth and the International Location of Innovation,' in H. Giersch (ed.), *Emerging Technologies: Consequences for Economic Growth, Structural Change and Employment*. JCB Mohr: Tubingen.

Perez, C. (1983), 'Structural Change and the Assimilation of New Technologies in the Economic and Social System,' *Futures*, 15, 357–375.

Perez, C. and L. Soete (1988), 'Catching Up in Technology: Entry Barriers and Windows of Opportunity,' in G. Dosi, C. Freeman, G. Silverberg and L. Soete (eds), *Technical Change and Economic Theory*. Pinter: London and Columbia University Press: New York.

Romer, P. M. (1986), 'Increasing Returns and Long-run Growth,' *Journal of Political Economy*, 94, 1001–1037.

Romer, P. M. (1987), 'A Growth Based on Increasing Returns due to Specialization,' *American Economic Review*, 77, 56–62.

─────────── *The Process of Economic Development* ───────────

Romer, P. M. (1990a), 'Are Non-convexities Important for Understanding Growth?,' *American Economic Review*, 80, 97–103.

Romer, P. M. (1990b), 'Endogenous Technological Change,' *Journal of Political Economy*, 98, 71–102.

Rosenberg, N. (1976), *Perspectives on Technology*. Cambridge University Press: Cambridge.

Rosenberg, N. (1982), *Inside the Black Box*. Cambridge University Press: Cambridge.

Silverberg, G. (1988), 'Modelling Economic Dynamics and Technical Change,' in G. Dosi, C. Freeman, R. Nelson, G. Silverberg and L. Soete (eds), *Technical Change and Economic Theory*. Pinter London and Columbia University Press: New York.

Silverberg, G., G. Dosi and L. Orsenigo (1988), 'Innovation, Diversity and Diffusion. A Self-Organization Model,' *Economic Journal*, 98, 1032–1054.

Silverberg, G. and D. Lehnert (1993), 'Long Waves and "Evolutionary Chaos" in a Simple Schumpeterian Model of Embodied Technical Change,' *Structural Change and Economic Dynamics*, 4, 9–37

Soete, L and G. Silverberg (1994), *The Economics of Growth and Technological Change. Technologies, Nations, Agents*, Edward Elgar Publishing. Cheltenham

Soete, L. and B. Verspagen (1992), 'Technology and Growth. The Complex Dynamics of Catching Up, Falling Behind and Taking Over,' paper prepared for the Conference 'Explaining Economic Growth' (April) MERIT: Maastricht.

Solow, R. (1956), A Contribution to the Theory of Economic Growth,' *Quarterly Journal of Economics*, 70, 65–94.

Solow, R (1957), 'Technical Change and the Aggregate Production Function,' *Review of Economics and Statistics*, 39, 312–320

Stiglitz, J. E. (1991), 'Alternative Approaches to Macroeconomics: Methodological Issues and the New Keynesian Economics,' NBER Working Paper, n.3580, Cambridge, MA.

Stiglitz, J. E (1992), 'Explaining Growth: Competition and Finance,' paper prepared for Villa Mondragone International Economic Seminar on 'Differences in the Rates of Growth', Rome (July) 1992.

Streit, C. K. (1949), *Union Now: A Proposal for an Atlantic Federal Union* 2nd edition. Atlantic Union. New York.

Tylecote, A. (1992), *The Long Wave in the World Economy*. Routledge. London.

Vega-Redondo, F. (1990), *Technological Change and Path-dependence: A Co-evolutionary Model on a Directed Graph*, mimeo, University of Alicante: Alicante.

Verspagen, B. (1991a), 'A New Empirical Approach to Catching Up or Falling Behind,' *Structural Change and Economic Dynamics*, 2, 359–380.

Verspagen, B. (1991b), 'Specialization, Competitiveness and Growth Rate Differentials: A Multi-sector Evolutionary Model with Neo-Keynesian Characteristics (MARK II)', MERIT Research Memorandum, 91–020, MERIT. Maastricht.

Wade, R. (1990), *Governing the Market: Economic Theory and the Role of Government in East Asian Industrialisation*. Princeton University Press: Princeton, NJ.

World Bank (1991), *World Development Report, 1991*. Oxford University Press. Oxford.

Young, A. (1991), 'Learning by Doing and the Dynamic Effects of International Trade,' *Quarterly Journal of Economics*, 106, 369–405.

[19]

Empir Econ (2009) 37:475–495
DOI 10.1007/s00181-008-0242-x

ORIGINAL PAPER

The patterns of output growth of firms and countries: Scale invariances and scale specificities

Carolina Castaldi · Giovanni Dosi

Received: 15 July 2006 / Accepted: 15 July 2008 / Published online: 20 September 2008
© Springer-Verlag 2008

Abstract   This work brings together two distinct pieces of evidence concerning, at the *macro* level, international distributions of incomes and their dynamics, and, at the *micro* level, the size distributions of firms and the properties of their growth rates. Our contribution to the literature is twofold. First, our empirical analysis provides a new look at the international distributions of incomes and growth rates by investigating more closely the relationship between the two entities and the statistical properties of the growth process. Second, we identify the statistical properties that are invariant with respect to the scale of observation (country or firm) as distinct from those that are scale specific. This exercise proposes a few major interpretative challenges regarding the correlating processes underlying the statistical evidence.

The authors wish to thank Giulio Bottazzi, Buz Brock, Alessandro Nuvolari, Bart Los, Angelo Secchi, Gerry Silverberg, Eddy Szirmai and Bart Verspagen for helpful discussions. An anonymous referee and an editor helped to substantially improve the paper. We gratefully acknowledge support from the Robert Solow Post-doctoral Fellowship of Cournot Center for Economic Studies (to C. Castaldi) and from the Italian Ministry for University and Research MIUR, prot. nr. 2002132413.001 (to G. Dosi).

C. Castaldi
Department of Innovation Studies,
Copernicus Institute for Sustainable Development and Innovation,
Utrecht University, PO Box 80115, 3508TC Utrecht, The Netherlands
e-mail: c.castaldi@geo.uu.nl

G. Dosi (✉)
LEM, Sant'Anna School of Advanced Studies,
Piazza Martiri delle Libertà 33, 56127 Pisa, Italy
e-mail: giovanni.dosi@sssup.it

G. Dosi
University of Manchester, Manchester, UK

🖄 Springer

Keywords International distribution of income · International growth rates ·
Firm growth · Scaling laws · Growth volatility · Exponential tails

JEL Classification C10 · C14 · O11

1 Introduction

A number of recent studies, including Fagiolo et al. (2008) and Maasoumi et al.
(2007), have addressed the statistical properties of the distribution of international
growth rates. The emerging evidence of non-normality of growth rates has important
implications for growth theory since it challenges all modeling exercises based on
the assumption of normally distributed growth shocks. More detailed evidence on the
statistical properties of growth rates contributes to the understanding of the possible
generating mechanisms underlying economic growth and of the processes of diffusion
of technological and demand shocks. As we argue in this paper, further insights can be
gained from the identification of those growth rates properties that are scale invariant,
from firms to countries, as distinct from those that are scale-specific.

For this purpose, our paper brings together two distinct ensembles of evidence
concerning, *first*, international distributions of growth rates in aggregate and per capita
income, and, *second*, the micro-economic evidence on the distributions of firm growth
rates. This exercise will focus on two major interpretative questions concerning:

(i) the relationships between the distributions of the size of the relevant entities
     (e.g., countries or firms) and the properties of the growth process;
(ii) the identification of the properties that appear to be invariant vis-à-vis the scale
     of observation and those that conversely are scale specific.

With respect to the first question, this work is linked to the stream of studies in
growth empirics concerning the international divergence/convergence properties of
income (for thorough reviews see Durlauf and Quah 1999; Temple 1999). We study
the properties of output growth rates and their dependence upon possible conditioning
factors including income levels and the size of the economies. To address the second
question, we compare distributions and growth processes at two levels of observation,
namely countries and firms. In particular, we apply to output growth rates some non-
parametric analyses recently used for the investigation of firm growth rates. As we
shall see, one finds striking similarities in the growth processes that hold across levels
of observation. In turn, such statistical properties hint at the ubiquitous presence of
correlating mechanisms that survive aggregation from firms to sectors to countries.

In what follows, we begin with a brief overview of the existing micro evidence on
the statistical properties of the distribution of firm sizes and growth rates (Sect. 2). In
Sect. 3 we describe the data and the variables of interest for our cross-country analysis.
Section 4 provides a reassessment of the cross-country evidence on the distribution
of levels of income. Section 5 investigates the statistical properties of the distribution
of growth shocks and their relation to the international distribution of incomes. Section 6 offers a discussion of the interpretative challenges stemming from the empirical
evidence and puts forth a few conjectures. Section 7 concludes.

 Springer

2 A review of the evidence on firm size and firm growth rates

With the purpose of bringing together two streams of literature that have rarely been connected to each other, namely those addressing the statistical properties of *firm* sizes and growth and those of *country* (income) sizes and growth, let us begin with the former level of observation.

The statistical properties of the size distribution of firms and of their growth rates have been the objects of inquiry for a longstanding stream of empirical literature dating back to the seminal contributions of Gibrat (1931), Steindl (1965), Hart and Prais (1956) and Simon and Bonini (1958). These pioneering insights and the more recent evidence (for a broad discussion cf. Marsili 2001) all indicate a generic right-skewness of the distribution of firm size, where fewer large firms co-exist with significantly more firms of smaller size. However, the overall shape of the size distributions differs when disaggregated at 3- or 4-digit level.[1]

A tricky issue is related to the properties of the upper tail of the size distribution and its 'fatness'. The evidence so far suggests that at the sectoral level such tails are generally skewed, and sometimes lognormal or Pareto-distributed.[2] Stronger evidence, however, corroborates Paretian tails only at the *aggregate* manufacturing level: indeed, this might be a puzzling property of the aggregation process itself (cf. Dosi et al. 1995 for some conjectures and some corroborating simulations).

The statistical literature on size distributions is closely linked with the studies of the statistical properties of the process of growth at the firm level. One of the longstanding issues relates to the validation of the so-called Law of Proportionate Effect [as originally presented in Gibrat (1931)].[3] This null hypothesis states that firm growth rates are realizations independent of size. Under this assumption the limit distribution of size is log-normal. The available evidence does not support any systematic dependence of growth rates on the initial size of firms. At the same time most analyses display a violation of the Gibrat hypothesis in that the *variance* of growth rates *does* depend (negatively) on size.

Moreover, recent studies including Stanley et al. (1996) and Bottazzi et al. (2007), have shifted the focus toward the analysis of the overall *distribution of firm growth rates*. The latter robustly follow a Laplacian distribution, characterized by exponential tails. This finding by itself sheds new light on the nature of the process of firm growth. Interestingly, this stylized fact holds both at the level of the whole manufacturing and at the sectoral level, independently of the degrees of statistical disaggregation. In the recent literature, the description of the properties of the distribution of growth rates has relied upon fitting a general family of distributions, the set of Subbotin densities, including the Normal and the Laplacian distributions at particular instances (cf. Bottazzi and Secchi 2003a).

---

[1] Cf. Bottazzi and Secchi (2003b) on US manufacturing data and Bottazzi et al. (2007) on Italian data.

[2] Pareto distributions yield a cumulative distribution which in a double logarithmic space displays a linear relation between probabilities and values of the variable itself (e.g., the size of firms). A different but germane formulation taking ranks rather than probabilities goes under the heading of Zipf Law.

[3] Within an extensive literature cf. Ijiri and Simon (1977), Hymer and Pashigian (1962), Hall (1987), and Evans (1987) and the discussions in Sutton (1997).

 Springer

In a nutshell, the micro statistical evidence strongly displays: (i) persistent skewed distributions in firm sizes;[4] (ii) widespread differences across sectors in the shapes of the size distribution themselves; and, at the same time, (iii) no robust relation between initial size and subsequent rates of growth (except possibly for the smallest firms); (iv) a variability in growth rates which often appears to fall with firm size; (v) robust evidence on a Laplacian distribution of firm growth rates, which appears to hold across sectors, across countries and across periods of observation.

In the next sections we will investigate whether similar properties hold true for the size and growth of countries.

3 The variables

We measure the per capita income of a country i in year t, say y_{it}, by the country's per capita GDP at constant prices and constant exchange rates. The data source are the Penn World Tables, version 6.1 (see Heston et al. 2002) for 111 countries for 1960–1996.[5]

Per capita income captures the level of economic development of a country. Instead, we call Y_{it} the aggregate income, a proxy for the actual 'size' of a national economy.

To identify country-specific properties of our variables over time, let us 'de-trend' by "washing away" any component common to all countries in a given year. For this purpose we consider 'normalized' (log) incomes as defined by:

$$s_{it} = \log(y_{it}) - \overline{\log(y_t)}$$
$$S_{it} = \log(Y_{it}) - \overline{\log(Y_t)}$$

(1)

where $\overline{\log(y_t)}$ and $\overline{\log(Y_t)}$ are the averages of $\log(y_{it})$ and $\log(y_{it})$ across countries at time t.

We calculate normalized year-by-year logarithmic growth rates as:

$$g_{it} = s_{it} - s_{i,t-1}$$
$$G_{it} = S_{it} - S_{i,t-1}$$

(2)

We refer to these last variables as the *growth shocks* of interest.[6]

4 The distribution of levels of income

We begin, somewhat symmetrically to the foregoing micro-evidence, from the distributions of the levels of per capita incomes. An insightful new set of contributions has

---

[4] Persistent inter-firm differences are also a property of relative productivities and degrees of innovativeness, as discussed in Nelson (1981), Bartelsman and Doms (2000), Marsili (2001) and Dosi (2007).

[5] See the "Appendix" for details on the construction of our balanced panel.

[6] The reader should be aware that we use the word 'shock' in tune with a common jargon of practitioners of statistics: however, the terminology does not involve any commitment to the 'exogeneity' of the event itself. In fact, 'shocks' are endogenously generated by the very process of country growth.

The patterns of output growth of firms and countries   479

recently been added to the empirics of international growth, shedding new light on the statistical distributions of income levels and their change, if any, over time (see Quah 1996, 1997; Durlauf and Quah 1999; Bianchi 1997; Jones 1997; Paap and van Dijk 1998). While it is not possible to discuss in depth the secular evidence, notice, *first*, that the *mean per capita incomes* have shown roughly exponential increases since the "Industrial Revolution" in all countries that have been able to join it, and, *second*, that the variance across countries has correspondingly exploded (for different perspectives on this see Bairoch 1981; Maddison 2001; Dosi et al. 1994). Given these long-term tendencies, the foregoing stream of analyses, largely concerning the post World War II period, finds that the distribution of income levels has been moving over the years to a bi-modal shape indicating a process of 'polarization' of countries into two groups characterized by markedly different income levels. This testifies against any prediction of a tendency towards global convergence of all countries to a common income level.

We will consider the time series available from Penn Tables version 6.1 and estimate the kernel density for the distribution of normalized income and normalized per capita income. Following the standard notation, the kernel density estimator for a sample of data $\{x_i\}_{i=1:n}$ is defined as:

$$\widehat{f}(x) = \frac{1}{nh} \sum_{i}^{n} K\left(\frac{x - x_i}{h}\right)$$ (3)

where K is the chosen kernel function and h the kernel bandwidth. This non-parametric estimation procedure depends on the choice of the kernel bandwidth. The larger the chosen bandwidth, the smoother the estimated density.

To get a graphical impression of the distributions, let us select a bandwidth with the rule of thumb proposed in Silverman (1986). The exploratory plots in Fig. 1 suggest that the estimated densities become less and less unimodal over the years. The emergence of bimodality is more evident in the case of per capita income than for total income. For per capita income, the distribution could have been already bimodal in 1960 and might have gone towards a three-humps shape after 1996. Formal multi-modality tests following the procedure introduced by Silverman (1981) and first applied to income data by Bianchi (1997), confirm the presence of bimodality starting from 1970.

Let us perform multi-modality tests on our longer time series. The Silverman test is based on kernel estimation and relies on the calculation of critical kernel bandwidths for the appearance of a given number of modes m. Call $h_c(m)$ the critical bandwidth such that for any bandwidth $h > h_c(m)$ the density displays less than m modes, while for any $h < h_c(m)$ the modes are at least $m + 1$. Any $h_c(m)$ may be used as a statistic to test the hypothesis H_0 : m modes versus H_1 : more than m modes. The actual p value of the test can be calculated via bootstrapping. When $\hat{p}_c(m) < \alpha$, where α stands for the significance level of the test, one can reject the null hypothesis that the distribution has m modes and not more. This test is known to have a bias towards being conservative, in the sense that it leads to rejection in fewer cases than other tests would. A procedure to correct this shortcoming has been proposed in Hall and York

Springer

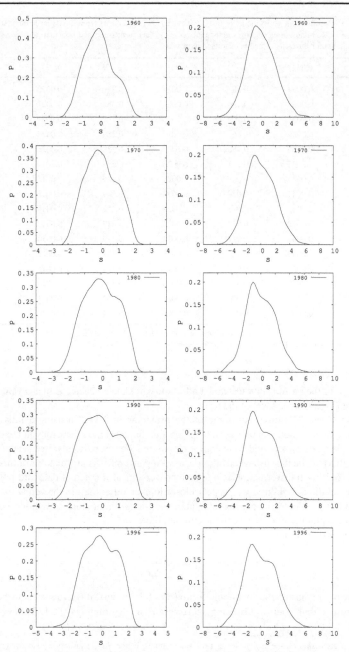

Fig. 1 Kernel estimation of the empirical density of normalized per capita income s (*left plots*) and total income S (*right plots*), different years

Table 1 Results from multi-modality tests: critical bandwidths $h_C(m)$ from Gaussian kernel estimates for $m = 1, 2, 3$ and corresponding significance scores $p_C(m)$ from smoothed bootstrap test ($B = 1{,}000$ replications) for the transformed per capita income z^*

Year	$h_C(1)$	$p_C(1)$	$h_C(2)$	$p_C(2)$	$h_C(3)$	$p_C(3)$
1960	0.0034	0.284	0.0026	0.370	0.0023	0.103
1965	0.0035	0.196	0.0026	0.352	0.0021	0.110
1966	0.0038	0.109	0.0026	0.392	0.0021	0.149
1967	0.0039	*0.061*	0.0027	0.284	0.0022	0.106
1968	0.0035	0.188	0.0028	0.239	0.0020	0.232
1969	0.0035	0.161	0.0023	0.524	0.0019	0.324
1970	0.0039	*0.049*	0.0029	0.186	0.0015	0.655
1971	0.0041	*0.024*	0.0030	0.147	0.0015	0.503
1972	0.0042	*0.015*	0.0027	0.257	0.0015	0.557
1973	0.0042	*0.014*	0.0024	0.417	0.0012	0.894
1974	0.0042	*0.011*	0.0024	0.349	0.0015	0.445
1975	0.0043	*0.003*	0.0019	0.501	0.0015	0.455
1980	0.0043	*0.005*	0.0016	0.861	0.0015	0.512
1985	0.0050	*0.000*	0.0018	0.576	0.0015	0.404
1990	0.0053	*0.000*	0.0025	0.262	0.0021	0.077
1996	0.0047	*0.011*	0.0026	0.404	0.0022	0.134

If $p_C(m) < 0.1$ the null hp that the distribution has m modes can be rejected. Scores that lead to rejection of the statistical hypothesis are highlighted in italics

(2001) for the unimodality test and it allows to calculate corrected actual p values for a given significance level of the test.[7]

Bianchi (1997) discusses some of the problems involved in using a fully non-parametric technique. In particular he points out that this kind of test may fail to detect multiple modes when modes are not well separated. For the particular instance of GDP data, this may be the case when one considers logarithmic transformations of the GDP data. The log transformation is a smoothed version of the actual data and possible modes in the distribution will appear closer to each other than in the actual data. To avoid this problem, Bianchi suggests taking non-logarithmic transformations, such as the per capita income relative to the sum of all incomes.

Let us then define:

$$z^*_{i,t} = \frac{y_{i,t}}{\sum y_{i,t}} \tag{4}$$

We report the outcome of our multi-modality Silverman tests on this specific income measure to make our results comparable with Bianchi's findings. Table 1 shows esti-

---

[7] For a discussion on the advantages and the shortcomings of the Silverman test see Henderson et al. (2007). The main shortcoming appears to be the fact that Silverman test is not nested and it may thus yield inconclusive results.

 Springer

mates for selected years and for all years in the transition phase from unimodality to a bimodality regime. We choose a significance of $\alpha = 0.1$, a reasonable level for this type of data. The results for the unimodality test include the Hall-York correction. We confirm that the assumption of bimodality can not be rejected at a 10% level, even since 1970.

Henderson et al. (2007) also discuss an alternative test, the DIP test, and find evidence for multi-modality since 1960. Their result indicates that the evidence on multi-modality depends on the test used. Still, all evidence suggests that the last decades have been characterized by multi-modality in international income levels, indicating a process of 'club convergence' (Quah 1996).

The results on bi-modality provide descriptive evidence that cannot be uncovered from regression analysis, but does not per se shed any light on the determinants of the cross-country distribution. Part of the interpretation involves the analysis of the appropriate conditioning variables that might account for the emergence of separate 'clubs' (Quah 1997). Together, important circumstantial evidence is bound to also come from the investigation of the statistical properties of growth rates.

Even superficial comparisons between firm-level and country-level distributions of 'sizes' (which should be properly understood as 'total incomes of firms or countries' and 'per capita incomes') reveal suggestive analogies concerning, at the very least, (i) the skewness of distributions; (ii) the large width of their supports; and, (iii) high persistence over time of relative rankings.

5 The statistical properties of growth shocks

The statistical properties of *country growth rates* have been investigated in a few papers including Canning et al. (1998), Lee et al. (1998) and Maasoumi et al. (2007). These properties will be analyzed by using methods proposed in the empirical literature on firm growth reviewed in Sect. 2. Using parallel methods will enable us to detect possible analogies between the two levels of observation.

5.1 Preliminary analysis

We begin by plotting the moments of the (non-normalized) growth rates $g*_{it} = log(y_{it}) - log(y_{i,t-1})$ and $G*_{it} = log(Y_{it}) - log(Y_{i,t-1})$ (Fig. 2). The evolution of the average growth rate hints at two distinct phases, possibly separated by the year 1973. This major discontinuity is well known to appear in most economic time series. Also, the years before 1973 are characterized by a somewhat higher average level of growth, with a lower mean value thereafter. The standard deviation is stable across all sample years, implying that in fact the coefficient of variation of rates is higher after 1973.

Keeping in mind these discontinuities in the overall growth patterns we study the properties of de-trended growth dynamics over the post World War II period. Following the procedure used in Canning et al. (1998), we pool together the normalized

 Springer

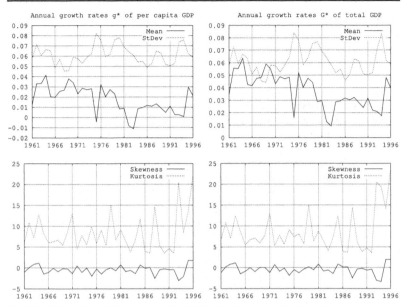

Fig. 2 Evolution in time of the moments of the distribution of non-normalized annual growth rates

observations for all years and countries and we obtain a sample of 111×36 observations, large enough to support robust statistical analysis.

As a preliminary question we ask whether higher or lower income countries are characterized on average by (relatively) higher/lower growth rates. We group countries into 40 equally populated subsets ('bins') according to the mean normalized logarithmic income s (or S) defined in Eq. 1 and calculate the mean normalized annual logarithmic growth rate g (or G) in each income class. We fit a linear relation to the observations and account for heteroskedasticity by using the White estimator (White 1980). Since the relations look like they could hide non-linearities, we also use Kernel regression, a non-parametric method, to fit the relation. Independent of the exact shape of the relation, we find a statistically significant and *positive* correlation between the average growth rates and levels of income, both the total and the per capita income (Fig. 3). Larger and more developed (i.e., with higher per capita incomes) countries are characterized, on average, by a higher growth performance.

The interpretation of the two relations offers quite different insights. When we look at per capita income data the result that richer countries display on average higher growth rates can be read as straightforward evidence for divergence and polarization of countries into two classes of 'very rich' and 'very poor' countries. Such evidence suggests the existence of some form of dynamic increasing returns in production and in the accumulation of technological knowledge. However, the plots suggest that for the highest levels of per capita income the relation is not significant or even becomes negative.

 Springer

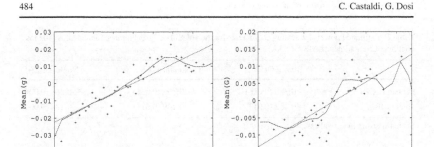

Fig. 3 The relation between income level and average growth rate for different income classes. Linear fits and fits from kernel regression are also shown. The *left plot* refers to per capita variables (linear slope = 0.0113 ± 0.0012), the right one to total income ones (linear slope = 0.0027 ± 0.0004)

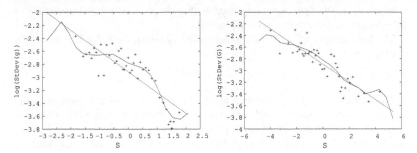

Fig. 4 The relation between the levels of income and the logarithm of the volatility of growth rates

Conversely, the positive relation between average growth rate and total domestic income hints at structural effects of the sheer size of an economy similar to 'static' economies of scale.[8]

5.2 The volatility of growth rates

Are higher income countries characterized by less volatile growth rates? Recent evidence (see, e.g., Pritchett 2000; Fiaschi and Lavezzi 2005) shows that the volatility of growth rates is much higher for developing countries than for industrialized ones. Throughout the process of development the levels of per capita GDP obviously

---

[8] Notice that the possible scale effects that we identify here do not necessarily bear any direct relation with the scale effect that has been the object of controversy among 'new growth' theorists, as discussed in Jones (1999). One of the questionable predictions by the first wave of 'new growth' models was the presence of a scale effect on the steady state growth according to which an increase in the total population, and thus, other things being equal, in the available specialized labor force, proportionally increased the long run per capita growth. In some subsequent models the impact of scale has shifted to the level of per capita income, rather than its long run growth rate. In our strictly 'inductive' analysis here we do not make any commitment to the existence of a steady state rate of growth: simply, the statistical relations between income and growth appear to suggest some forms of increasing returns.

 Springer

Table 2 Estimated power-law scaling coefficients for the volatility of growth rates: binned OLS (40 bins), nonlinear LS, nonlinear LAD

	Binned OLS	Nonlinear LS	Nonlinear LAD
Per capita GDP	−0.320 (0.036)	−0.295 (0.021)	−0.260 (0.008)
Total GDP	−0.152 (0.013)	−0.149 (0.011)	−0.134 (0.004)

Standard errors in parenthesis

increase. Together, reductions in the dispersion of growth performance may also be taken as an indication that countries move on more stable growth paths.

We again group countries by income, calculate the standard deviation of the normalized growth shocks and associate this with the central value of income in each class. Here, we uncover a negative relation between the log standard deviation of growth rates and the level of per capita (log) income (Fig. 4). In other words the volatility of growth rates scales with income as a power law.

The same scaling relation can also be studied by taking the following model as a starting point:

$$g_{it} = s_{it} - s_{i,t-1} = e^{\beta s_{i,t-1}} \epsilon_{i,t} \tag{5}$$

The scaling parameter β can then be estimated via non-linear regression, using numerical methods based on different optimization criteria, as suggested in Bottazzi et al. (2005). Depending on the underlying assumptions about the error terms ϵ_{it}: (i) non-linear LS (Least Squares) if $\epsilon_{it} \sim$ Normal; (ii) non-linear LAD (Least Absolute Deviation) if $\epsilon_t \sim$ Laplace.

Non-linear LAD estimates are the most precise (see Table 2). The assumption of Laplace, heavy-tailed, shocks considerably improves the estimation performance and is fully consistent with the results in the next section about distributional shapes.

The interesting result here is that the scaling coefficient for aggregate GDP data is much lower than that for per capita data. This may in fact tell us that a 'strong' scaling relation holds only when one considers the level of economic development, as proxied by per capita income. Growth performances are less volatile for *more developed* countries. The sheer size of an economy is relatively less relevant.

5.3 The distribution of growth rates

One way to deal with the 'size effect' on the average growth rate conditional on the degrees of development is to group countries by their level of income in three classes: Low, Medium and High per capita GDP s, and Small, Medium and Large total GDP S. This same procedure is used in Canning et al. (1998) and Lee et al. (1998), who recognize different growth distributions for countries characterized by different size in terms of total income. We further normalize the growth rates in each group and then proceed by plotting their empirical histograms.[9]

---

[9] In Figs. 7 and 8 we show only the two income classes at the extremes, since the Medium one always lies in between.

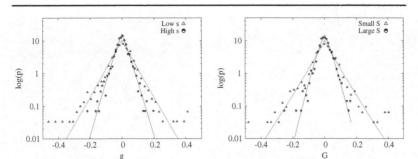

Fig. 5 The empirical distribution of growth rates of per capita income *g* (*left*) and income *G* (*right*) for two income classes

We refine the description of the properties of the distribution of growth rates by fitting on the empirical densities a general family of Subbotin distributions (cf. Bottazzi and Secchi 2003a, the original reference is Subbotin 1923).

The functional form of the Subbotin family is given by:

$$f(x) = \frac{1}{2ab^{\frac{1}{b}}\Gamma(1 + \frac{1}{b})} e^{-\frac{1}{b}\left|\frac{x-\mu}{a}\right|^{b}} \qquad (6)$$

where the parameter *a* controls the standard deviation and *b* is a parameter which determines the shape of the distribution. Note that for a value $b = 2$ the distribution turns out to be a Normal one, while for $b = 1$ the distribution is Laplacian, also known as Double Exponential. As *b* gets smaller, the tails get heavier and the peak of the density becomes more pronounced. For $b = 0$ the distribution is degenerate in the mean. We fit the family of density using a maximum likelihood procedure (for details see Bottazzi 2004).

The empirical distribution of the growth rates is quite well fitted by a Subbotin density with a *b*-parameter close to 1, hence the distribution is approximately Laplacian (Fig. 5).[10] Note that if growth residuals were Normal, the fitted curve would be a parable on a logarithmic scale. On the contrary, we find that the distribution of growth rates is markedly non-Gaussian and closer to a Laplacian density, which displays a 'tent shape' in the log scale.

Further, notice that the plots in Fig. 5 reveal a significantly different width of the distribution for low income and high income countries, as one should expect given the dependence of the dispersion of growth rates upon a country's income level shown in the previous section.

We then consider rescaled growth rates in the form of residuals from model 5, estimated with a non-linear LAD procedure. Even after eliminating any possible size effect on the dispersion of the distribution itself, the Laplacian shape of the distribution is confirmed: growth shocks are markedly not Gaussian (Fig. 6).

---

[10] The estimation is done on the normalized growth rates, thus the parameter μ of the Subbotin is always set to zero.

 Springer

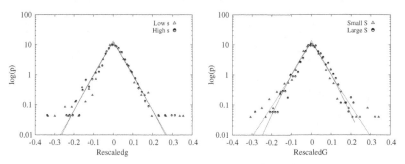

Fig. 6 The distributions of re-scaled growth rates for two income classes

Table 3 Estimated Subbotin parameters for the distributions of growth rates

Income classes	Growth rates		Rescaled growth rates	
	b	a	b	a
Per capita GDP	0.9517	0.0407	1.0448	0.0411
	(0.0277)	(0.0008)	(0.031)	(0.0008)
Total GDP	0.9313	0.0398	1.0253	0.0402
	(0.0269)	(0.0008)	(0.0310)	(0.0008)
Low per capita GDP	0.9829	0.0498	1.0015	0.0376
	(0.0498)	(0.0017)	(0.0510)	(0.0013)
High per capita GDP	1.0644	0.0296	1.1845	0.0404
	(0.0549)	(0.0010)	(0.0627)	(0.0014)
Small GDP	0.9323	0.0503	0.9431	0.0384
	(0.0467)	(0.0018)	(0.0474)	(0.0014)
Large GDP	1.1885	0.0309	1.1845	0.0414
	(0.0629)	(0.0010)	(0.0627)	(0.0014)

Standard errors are reported in parenthesis. Rescaled growth rates are obtained using LAD estimates of the scaling coefficient

The distributions for the two income classes almost coincide in the case of per capita GDP, while they still differ on the tails in the case of total GDP growth rates (cf. the estimates of both Subbotin coefficient and their standard errors as reported in Table 3, with the differences between the classes being statistically significant). The distributions differ mostly on the tails, suggesting that observations at the extremes are crucial in shaping the distributions themselves.[11] In fact, we checked also for the

---

[11] This result continues to hold also if one fits the data with distributions characterized by heavy tails. Indeed, we tried fitting the family of 'stable distributions' (which includes Cauchy and Lèvy ones) to check whether the gap between the distribution of re-scaled growth rates for the different income classes was due to an unsatisfactory fit of the Subbotin on the tails. We find that the gap between the estimated distributions for the two classes is not eliminated. Moreover, heavy tailed distributions do not provide an overall better fit to the data.

Table 4 Estimated slope coefficients for linear scaling relations of skewness and kurtosis of growth rates with respect to total and per capita GDP

	Skewness	Kurtosis
Per capita GDP	0.097 (0.140)	−1.319 (0.531)
Total GDP	0.068 (0.049)	−0.606 (0.206)

existence of scaling relations for higher moments of growth rates. Skewness positively scales with total GDP, but it does not significantly scale with per capita GDP (see the estimates of the slopes of a linear scaling in Table 4). This confirms the wider differences in the tails for GDP growth rates, where asymmetries are higher for 'larger' countries. Note that in principle this should not occur if countries were simply 'tags' for ensembles of independent and divisible activities. On the contrary, the evidence hints at the influence of the sheer size of countries on the overall distribution of negative and positive growth rates.

Conversely, kurtosis, which is a measure of the 'peakedness' of the distributions negatively scales with both per capita and total GDP, in line with the persisting gap between the two peaks of the rescaled distributions. At risk of over-theorizing, we would be tempted to suggest that there appears to be a 'dumpening effect' associated with both absolute size and levels of development. Hence, one may conjecture, the same technological and demand shock might have a much greater impact on growth of small, possibly more specialized, countries as compared to bigger/more diversified ones.

6 Interpretation

We will weave together the threads of evidence stemming from the foregoing empirical analysis and propose a few tentative interpretations and conjectures.

6.1 Candidates for an explanation of the tent-shaped distribution of country growth rates

A first robust stylized fact is that growth rates, also at the level of countries, follow a Laplacian distribution. This property holds for all subsets of countries and for different observational periods. Developed and less developed countries remarkably show the same exponential structure in their growth rates even after accounting for their different dispersion in growth performance. A first puzzle arises if we compare the invariance of this property with the evolution of the distribution of incomes. We have seen how the distribution changes over time starting from an approximately unimodal shape and acquiring later an evident bimodality for which we have provided novel evidence. How does this relate to the invariance in the distribution of growth rates?

Remarkably, the distributional invariance of GDP growth and per capita income growth rates is a statistical feature analogous to that found with respect to *corporate* growth rates. The evidence indicates Laplacian distributions of growth rates. In the industrial organization literature, a common interpretation of the growth process builds on a baseline stochastic model of growth of a given unit of observation (e.g., a firm). If the growth process proceeded as the result of the accumulation in time of independent growth shocks one would find the growth residuals to be normally distributed and, thus, only representing 'noise'. Instead, one finds quite structured processes generating growth rates, forcing one to reject the null hypothesis that growth is simply the outcome of the sum of small independent shocks. Thus, one has to search for explanations of the growth process that consider 'elementary' growth shocks as correlated with each other. Such explanations ought to account for the scale invariance of such property, since correlation mechanisms in the growth process appear at all levels of observation, from firms to sectors to countries.[12]

This scale invariant regularity is thus in need of a convincing economic explanation. Ultimately two diverse (but possibly complementary paths) seem to be available for the modeler.

(i) A known statistical result refers to the property that a mixture of a small number of Normal distributions produces fat-tailed distributions (see Lindsay 1995). Thus, a tent-shape distribution can be interpreted as a mixture of Normal distributions given an appropriate parameterization. Mixtures are in principle an appealing tool for understanding the tent-shape distribution of growth rates because one can envision mixtures of mixtures of mixtures, capturing different scales of observation. Also, one could think of relating the components of the mixture to groups of countries representing different convergence clubs (see Durlauf et al. 2001). Nevertheless, a fundamental qualification should be considered. Such a statistical exercise, as well as our 'compact' representation, both still demand an economic interpretation of the underlying processes of growth yielding either the purported distributional mixtures or, directly, a fat-tailed distributions of growth shocks.

(ii) A distinct interpretative strategy tries to explicitly interpret the observed non-Normal distributions taking into account what we know about micro-processes of growth, in particular acknowledging some basic correlating mechanisms in the processes of market competition, together with the lumpiness of major competitive events. At the micro level, the exponential tails of the distribution of firm growth rates are explained in Bottazzi and Secchi (2006a) with a minimal probabilistic model that couples a mechanism capturing some forms of increasing returns (more successful firms tend to catch more business opportunities) together with competitive forces (firms compete for market shares). We conjecture that fat-tailed distributions of growth rates might turn out to be a quite generic property of a wide class of processes of industrial evolution. One could think of elaborating on a similar multi-country model (keeping in mind the different nature of inter-firm versus inter-country competition and complementarities).

A further challenge is to show how the observed structure of micro-shocks underlies similar *macroscopic* distributions. Recent research in macroeconomics has proposed a few models where aggregate GDP fluctuations are explained by micro-shocks at

---

[12] On the sectoral evidence cf. Castaldi and Dosi (2004) and Castaldi and Sapio (2008). Both works find evidence of exponential tails for the value added growth rates of sectors at 3-digit and 4-digit level of aggregation.

firm or sector level. In these models the micro-shocks aggregate in a non-trivial way: instead of being diluted by the aggregation process, under certain circumstances they amplify and form the basis for the structure of macro-shocks. In this vein, Gabaix (2007) shows how a major part of aggregate growth shocks can be accounted for by the growth of the top 100 firms in a country. Conversely, on the theory side, Bak et al. (1993) and Durlauf (1994) model aggregate fluctuations as the outcome of the propagation of demand shocks through inter-linked sectors.

From a different perspective, Delli Gatti et al. (2005) also goes in the direction of a micro-macro bridge, by relating the Double Exponential distribution of both firm and country growth rates to the skewed distribution of firm size in a model based on the interaction among heterogenous firms. Quite overlapping evolutionary agent-based models are also good candidates within this style of modeling [see Silverberg and Verspagen (2005) for a discussion of such a literature in a perspective pioneered by Nelson and Winter (1982)]. Indeed, preliminary exercises on the grounds of the model of Dosi et al. (2006), wherein macro-dynamics are nested into heterogenous boundedly rational firms, show its ability to reproduce the tent-shape distribution of firm and country growth rates.

6.2 Scaling of the growth volatility

The other significant finding highlighted by our analysis is the existence of a negative relation between the dispersion of growth rates and the level of *per capita* income. Moreover, the volatility scales with income as a power law. The estimated coefficient for per capita data, $c = -0.32$, is much higher than the $e = -0.15$ estimated with aggregate income data. This suggests that the 'true' scaling relation does not hold for size as such, as measured by the gross product of an economy, but it characterizes in primis the level of development of a country. The structural effect of the total size of an economy plays a role, but the stability of growth performances for high income countries stands out more strongly when the income measure pertains to per capita incomes rather than the sheer size of countries.

Amaral et al. (2001) and Lee et al. (1998) propose to interpret the scaling relation by reference to a benchmark model of 'complex organizations'. The idea is to view an economic organization, i.e., a country in our specific instance, as made up of different units of identical size. Then two opposite extreme scenarios may be contemplated. If all units grew independently then the volatility of growth rates would fall as a power law with coefficient -0.5 [a result of the law of large numbers, as suggested already in Hymer and Pashigian (1962)]. Conversely, if the composing units were perfectly correlated there would be no relation between the volatility of growth shocks and size, so we would find a slope of 0.

The estimated coefficients, falling between 0 and -0.5 may be interpreted as an indicator of the overall 'complexity', or, better, the inner inter-relatedness of the economic organization under study. If we translate this into our cross-country analysis, we may consider the negative relation between the volatility of growth rates and the level of income as evidence of the importance of the internal interdependencies of any national economy. Indeed, the patterns of income generation in a country via input–

 Springer

output relations among the different sectors linked to each other may be a candidate for explaining the degree of 'internal correlation' which produces the observed stylized fact. Scaling relations clearly depend also on the number of activities (or "lines of business") within the entity under consideration (e.g., a country or a firm). Keeping this in mind, a possible explanation for the different observed scaling slopes could be the following. The degrees of economic development are likely to be correlated with the density of economic activities or, putting it another way, with the number of different economic sectors in which a country is active in. Hence, in line with the evidence, richer countries, characterized by a higher number of relevant economic activities, would display less variable growth rates, while poorer countries embodying fewer activities would be more volatile in their growth performances.[13] Yet another analogy can be made here with the micro level: as Bottazzi et al. (2001) find, the standard deviation of growth rates declines with the number of sub-markets where firms operate.[14]

7 Conclusions

The empirical evidence presented in this paper shows important statistical properties concerning invariances and specificities in the process of economic growth. The first finding is that the distributions of output growth of firms and countries are both tent-shaped. In our interpretation, the common exponential properties of growth rates mark widespread correlating mechanisms which aggregation does not dilute. We have discussed possible candidates for the explanation of this finding at the country level, including forms of increasing returns working together with the inter-sectoral propagation of technological and demand impulses.

A second finding concerns the existence of scaling relations for both to the average and the dispersion of growth rates. Such scaling relations show both invariances and specificities when compared to the corresponding relations concerning firm growth. A *caveat* to keep in mind when dealing with such scaling laws, as Brock (1999) suggests, is that, "most of them are 'unconditional objects', i.e., they only give properties of stationary distributions, e.g., 'invariant measures', and hence cannot say much about the dynamics of the stochastic process which generated them. . . . Nevertheless, if a robust scaling law appears in data, this does restrict the acceptable class of conditional predictive distributions somewhat." (p. 426).

One way to disentangle the underlying mechanisms involves, as Brock (1999) suggests, the joint consideration of scaling laws with other types of statistical evidence that may provide conditioning schemes useful to refine the evidence on the data generating process. Maasoumi et al. (2007) propose a new way of conditioning using non-parametric models that can be applied in a flexible way to growth data. We also expect that precious insights are likely to come by linking the evidence on growth with the processes of arrival of technological and organizational innovations.

---

[13] See also Harberger (1998) for a view of the growth process in line with this intuition.

[14] See also Bottazzi and Secchi (2006b) for a branching model of corporate diversification able to account for such evidence.

 Springer

Finally, this paper has discussed how the joint statistical evidence on firm and output growth provides the economic growth theorist with a number of new challenges. The ability of models to account, at the same time, for both microscopic and macroscopic patterns of growth is a crucial dimension on which to judge the validity of all economic growth models.

Appendix

The country variables used in the analysis are taken from the most recent version of the Penn World Tables (Heston et al. 2002). Version 6.1 extends the previous Version 5.6 by providing data until 1998 for most countries. The benchmark year has been changed from 1985 to 1996. We choose to perform our analysis on a balanced panel of 111 countries whose variables of interest are available for all years between 1960 and 1996. The most notable exclusions of countries from the database are for entities that have undergone some political transformation affecting the definition of their own borders, such as Germany and former-USSR. Nevertheless, the remaining sample appears to be quite representative. Table 5 provides a list of the 111 countries included in the balanced panel.

Table 5 List of countries included in our balanced panel

Code	Country	Code	Country	Code	Country
AGO	Angola	GBR	UK	NER	Niger
ARG	Argentina	GHA	Ghana	NGA	Nigeria
AUS	Australia	GIN	Guinea	NIC	Nicaragua
AUT	Austria	GMB	Gambia	NLD	The Netherlands
BDI	Burundi	GNB	Guinea-Bissau	NOR	Norway
BEL	Belgium	GNQ	Equatorial Guinea	NPL	Nepal
BEN	Benin	GRC	Greece	NZL	New Zealand
BFA	Burkina Faso	GTM	Guatemala	PAK	Pakistan
BGD	Bangladesh	GUY	Guyana	PAN	Panama
BOL	Bolivia	HKG	Hong Kong	PER	Peru
BRA	Brazil	HND	Honduras	PHL	Philippines
BRB	Barbados	HTI	Haiti	PNG	Papua New Guinea
BWA	Botswana	IDN	Indonesia	PRT	Portugal
CAF	Central African Rep.	IND	India	PRY	Paraguay
CAN	Canada	IRL	Ireland	ROM	Romania
CHE	Switzerland	IRN	Iran	RWA	Rwanda
CHL	Chile	ISL	Iceland	SEN	Senegal
CHN	China	ISR	Israel	SGP	Singapore
CIV	Cote d'Ivoire	ITA	Italy	SLV	El Salvador
CMR	Cameroon	JAM	Jamaica	SWE	Sweden
COG	Republic of Congo	JOR	Jordan	SYC	Seychelles

Table 5 continued

Code	Country	Code	Country	Code	Country
COL	Colombia	JPN	Japan	SYR	Syria
COM	Comoros	KEN	Kenya	TCD	Chad
CPV	Cape Verde	KOR	Republic of Korea	TGO	Togo
CRI	Costa Rica	LKA	Sri Lanka	THA	Thailand
CYP	Cyprus	LSO	Lesotho	TTO	Trinidad Tobago
DNK	Denmark	LUX	Luxembourg	TUR	Turkey
DOM	Dominican Republic	MAR	Morocco	TWN	Taiwan
DZA	Algeria	MDG	Madagascar	TZA	Tanzania
ECU	Ecuador	MEX	Mexico	UGA	Uganda
EGY	Egypt	MLI	Mali	URY	Uruguay
ESP	Spain	MOZ	Mozambique	USA	USA
ETH	Ethiopia	MRT	Mauritania	VEN	Venezuela
FIN	Finland	MUS	Mauritius	ZAF	South Africa
FJI	Fiji	MWI	Malawi	ZAR	Democratic Republic of Congo
FRA	France	MYS	Malaysia	ZMB	Zambia
GAB	Gabon	NAM	Namibia	ZWE	Zimbabwe

References

Amaral LAN, Gopikrishnan P, Plerou V, Stanley HE (2001) A model for the growth dynamics of economic organizations. Physica A 299:127–136

Bairoch P (1981) The main trends in national economic disparities since the industrial revolution. In: Bairoch P, Levy-Leboyer M (eds) Disparities in economic development since the industrial revolution. Macmillan, Oxford

Bak P, Chen K, Scheinkman J, Woodford M (1993) Aggregate fluctuations from independent sectoral shocks: self-organized criticality in a model of production and inventory dynamics. Ricerche Econ 47:3–30

Bartelsman EJ, Doms M (2000) Understanding productivity: lessons from longitudinal microdata. J Econ Lit 38:569–594

Bianchi M (1997) Testing for convergence: evidence from nonparametric multimodality tests. J Appl Econ 12:393–409

Bottazzi G (2004) Subbotools user's manual. http://cafim.sssup.it/~giulio/software/subbotools/doc/subbotools.pdf

Bottazzi G, Secchi A (2003a) Why are distributions of firm growth rates tent-shaped? Econ Lett 80:415–420

Bottazzi G, Secchi A (2003b) Common properties and sectoral specificities in the dynamics of US manufacturing companies. Rev Ind Organ 23:217–232

Bottazzi G, Secchi A (2006a) Explaining the distribution of firms growth rates. Rand J Econ 37:234–263

Bottazzi G, Secchi A (2006b) Gibrat's law and diversification. Ind Corp Change 15:847–875

Bottazzi G, Dosi G, Lippi M, Pammolli F, Riccaboni M (2001) Innovation and corporate growth in the evolution of the drug industry. Int J Ind Organ 19:1161–1187

Bottazzi G, Coad A, Jacoby N, Secchi A (2005) Corporate growth and industrial dynamics: evidence from French manufacturing, LEM Working Paper, Sant' Anna School, Pisa

Bottazzi G, Cefis E, Dosi G, Secchi A (2007) Invariances and diversities in the evolution of manufacturing industries. Small Bus Econ 29:137–159

Brock WA (1999) Scaling in economics: a Reader's guide. Ind Corp Change 8:409–446

Canning D, Amaral LAN, Lee Y, Meyer M, Stanley HE (1998) Scaling the volatility of GDP growth rates. Econ Lett 60:335–341

Castaldi C, Dosi G (2004) Income levels and income growth: Some new cross-country evidence and some
    interpretative puzzles. LEM Working Paper 2004-18, Sant'Anna School of Advanced Studies, Pisa
Castaldi C, Sapio S (2008) Growing like Mushrooms? Sectoral evidence from four large european econo-
    mies. J Evol Econ 18:509–527
Delli Gatti D, Di Guilmi C, Gaffeo E, Giulioni G, Gallegati M, Palestrini A (2005) A new approach to
    business fluctuations: heterogenous interacting agents, scaling laws and financial fragility. J Econ
    Behav Organ 56:489–512
Dosi G (2007) Statistical regularities in the evolution of industries. a guide through some evidence and chal-
    lenges for the theory. In: Brusoni S, Malerba F (eds) Perspectives on innovation. Cambrige University
    Press, Cambrige
Dosi G, Freeman C, Fabiani S (1994) The process of economic development: introducing some stylized
    facts and theories on technologies, firms and institutions. Ind Corp Change 3:1–45
Dosi G, Marsili O, Orsenigo L, Salvatore R (1995) Learning, market selection and the evolution of industrial
    structures. Small Bus Econ 7:1–26
Dosi G, Fagiolo G, Roventini A (2006) An evolutionary model of endogenous business cycles. Comput
    Econ 27:3–34
Durlauf SN (1994) Path dependence in aggregate output. Ind Corp Change 3:148–171
Durlauf SN, Quah D (1999) The new empirics of economic growth. In: Taylor JB, Woodford M (eds)
    Handbook of macroeconomics, vol 1A. Elsevier, North-Holland
Durlauf SN, Kourtellos A, Minkin A (2001) The local solow growth model. Eur Econ Rev 45:928–940
Evans DS (1987) The relationship between firm size, growth and age: estimates for 100 manufacturing
    industries. J Ind Econ 35:567–581
Fagiolo G, Napoletano M, Roventini A (2008) Are output growth-rate distributions fat-tailed? Some evi-
    dence from OECD countries. J Appl Econ (forthcoming)
Fiaschi D, Lavezzi AM (2005) On the determinants of growth volatility: a nonparametric approach, Working
    paper, University of Pisa
Gabaix X (2007) The Granular Origins of Aggregate Fluctuations, Working Paper. MIT Press, Cambridge
Gibrat R (1931) Les inégalités economiques. Librairie du Recueil Sirey, Paris
Hall BH (1987) The relationship between firm size and firm growth in the US manufacturing sector. J Ind
    Econ 35:583–606
Hall P, York M (2001) On the calibration of Silverman's test for multimodality. Stat Sin 11:515–536
Harberger AC (1998) A vision of the growth process. Am Econ Rev 88:1–32
Hart PE, Prais SJ (1956) The analysis of business concentration. J R Stat Soc 119:150–191
Henderson DJ, Parmeter CF, Russell RR (2007) Convergence clubs: evidence from calibrated modality
    tests. working paper, University of California, Riverside
Heston A, Summers R, Aten B (2002) Penn World Table Version 6.1, Center for International Comparisons
    at the University of Pennsylvania (CICUP), October 2002
Hymer S, Pashigian P (1962) Firm size and rate of growth. J Polit Econ 70:556–569
Ijiri Y, Simon HA (1977) Skew distributions and the size of business firms. North-Holland, Amsterdam
Jones CI (1997) On the evolution of the world income distribution. J Econo Perspect 11:19–36
Jones CI (1999) Growth: with or without scale effects. Am Econ Rev Pap Proc 89:139–144
Lee Y, Amaral LAN, Canning D, Meyer M, Stanley HE (1998) Universal features in the growth dynamics
    of complex organizations. Phys Rev Lett 81:3275–3278
Lindsay BG (1995) Mixture models: theory, geometry and applications. Institute for Mathematical Statistics,
    Hayward
Maasoumi E, Racine J, Stengos T (2007) Growth and convergence: a profile of distribution dynamics and
    mobility. J Econom 136:483–508
Maddison A (2001) The world economy: a millennial perspective. OECD, Paris
Marsili O (2001) The anatomy and evolution of industries. Edward Elgar, Cheltenham
Nelson RR (1981) Research on productivity growth and productivity differences: dead ends and new depar-
    tures. J Econ Lit 19:1029–1064
Nelson RR, Winter SG (1982) An evolutionary theory of economic change. Harvard University Press,
    Cambridge
Paap R, Dijk HKvan (1998) Distribution and mobility of wealth of nations. Eur Econ Rev 42:1269–1293
Pritchett L (2000) Understanding patterns of economic growth: searching for hills among plateaus, moun-
    tains and plains. World Bank Econ Rev 105:221–250
Quah D (1996) Twin peaks: growth and convergence in models of distribution dynamics. Econ J 106:1045–
    1055

Quah D (1997) Empirics for growth and distribution: stratification, polarization and convergence clubs. J Econ Growth 2:27–59

Silverman BW (1981) Using Kernel density estimates to investigate multi-modality. J R Stat Soc B 43:97–99

Silverman BW (1986) Density estimation for statistics and data analysis. Chapman & Hall, London

Silverberg G, Verspagen B (2005) Evolutionary theorizing on economic growth. In: Dopfer K (ed) The evolutionary principles of economics. Cambridge University Press, Cambridge

Simon HA, Bonini CP (1958) The size distribution of business firms. Am Econ Rev 48:607–617

Stanley MHR, Amaral LAN, Buldyrev SV, Havlin S, Leschhorn H, Maass P, Salinger MA, Stanley HE (1996) Scaling behavior in the growth of companies. Nature 379:804–806

Steindl J (1965) Random processes and the growth of firms. Griffin, London

Subbotin M (1923) On the law of frequency of errors. Mat Sb 31:296–301

Sutton J (1997) Gibrat's legacy. J Econ Lit 35:40–59

Temple J (1999) The new growth evidence. J Econ Lit 37:112–156

White HA (1980) A heteroskedasticity-consistent covariance matrix estimator and a direct test for heteroskedasticity. Econometrica 48:817–838

[20]

The Dynamics of International Competitiveness

Giovanni Amendola, Giovanni Dosi, and Erasmo Papagni

Contents: I. Introduction. – II. Diverse National Patterns in Innovation and Trade. – III. Technical Change, Input Prices and International Trade. – IV. Dynamic Econometric Specification. – V. Data Set. – VI. Estimation Results. – VII. Conclusions. – Appendix

I. Introduction

Shares of individual firms on the international markets change all the time. So do shares of individual countries in world exports. But, what determines these changes?

It is intuitive among business economists and corporate managers that both costs and technology play a crucial role in determining the competitiveness of individual firms. However, much more intricate questions concern the dynamics of individual countries which aggregate the performance of a high number of business units, linked with each other by a thread of economy-wide adjustment mechanism (e.g. on the input markets and via exchange rates) and possibly also by positive feedbacks (such as various externalities, collective learning, etc.).

In fact, there is a quite long tradition of aggregate estimates of the effects of changes in production costs, prices and exchange rates upon exports and imports of individual countries. Such exercises try to capture the size and speed of short-term responses of trade flows to changes in macro-economic variables. However, they typically neglect the variables affecting trade in the longer term, such as technology. Indeed, one could easily interpret such an evidence as concerning the effects of short-term disturbances around some unspecified underlying equilibrium with internationally identical production functions.

More recently, in different theoretical perspectives, a novel attention has been paid to international technological differences as determinants of trade flows. 'New Trade' theories emphasize the importance of innovative activities within imperfect-competition models of trade and growth [Grossman and Helpman, 1991]. These models,

Remark: The authors acknowledge the helpful comments and suggestions of Marco Lippi and of an anonymous referee. Usual caveats apply.

however, while powerful in analyzing the equilibrium outcomes of uneven technological activities in terms of resulting national steady states, appear to be much less suited to study the relationships between relative changes in technological activities and relative changes in trade flows by each country – both being plausibly far-from-equilibrium phenomena. For example, empirical statements concerning "... country X losing trade competitiveness because its costs are too high and its innovative performance is sluggish ..." plausibly refer to some sort of disequilibrium dynamics in both macro-economic variables and technology.

In principle, "evolutionary" approaches to technical change and trade appear to be better equipped to theoretically represent such dynamics [Dosi et al., 1990]. On the other hand, since they embody less restrictions on the dynamics that the models could generate (as compared to steady-state models), it is somewhat harder to link theoretical results and empirical (econometric) analysis.[1]

One particular feature of technological innovation, that is also crucial for econometric specification, is its inherent dynamic nature. Although widely recognized, this attribute of innovation has often been neglected by empirical studies wherein static relationships have been estimated. Even most tests on the relationship between innovation proxies and countries' exports undertaken within a "technology-gap" approach have typically used country cross-sectional data on levels or rates of change [Soete, 1981; Dosi et al., 1990; Fagerberg, 1988]. The results show robust correlations between national technological capabilities and export performances (both in terms of levels and changes). However, this type of tests fall short of a proper account of the dynamics by which technical change as well as capital accumulation and changes in input prices and exchange rates influence exports flows. Moreover, it does not allow the identification of possible country-specific effects of such dynamics. The econometric model that

---

[1] Interestingly, international trade is one of the few domains of economics where standard theory has been able to generate powerful and empirically testable predictions, which, however, have not generally been upheld by evidence, starting from the famous Leontief 'paradox' all the way to the predictions on factor price equalization. In that respect, 'New Trade' theories can be seen 'shift' in the original neoclassical research programme [Bensel and Elmslie, 1992] which certainly accommodates for new pieces of evidence but is not at all immune from the basic pitfalls of its theoretical parent. See Dosi et al. [1990] for a critical discussion of these points and also for some conjectures on the empirical prediction derivable from an alternative 'evolutionary' research programme.

we present in the following to overcome these limitations provides results which are indeed quite encouraging for a "technology-gap" interpretation of trade flows.

In Section II we start with a qualitative overview on the basic evidence on innovation and competitiveness among the major OECD countries since the late 60s. In Section III we shall present a model of technological change and international trade, whereby export shares of each country depend on that country's relative "competitiveness", determined by its dynamics in technology and input prices. Section IV discusses the econometric specification of the model. Next, we briefly present the data set in Section V. Finally, Section VI discusses the results of the estimates.

II. Diverse National Patterns in Innovation and Trade

A general overview of trade performances by OECD countries point to the existence of diverse dynamics in the relative competitiveness of each country. Table 1 reports national export shares in the late 80s as compared with the late 60s, together with some variables that a priori could be presumed to explain such different performances, namely national shares in US patenting – a proxy for innovativeness –,[2] rates of change in fixed investment and in unit labour cost denominated in a common currency.

In trade of manufactured products, Japan has strongly increased its market share (+6.8 percentage points). The huge rise of the Japanese industry in international markets has corresponded to a sharp decline of the United States share (−5.3 percentage points) and, less pronounced, of the United Kingdom (−3.4 percentage points).

These major changes in world manufactures exports have been coupled by even more impressive shifts in the international location of

---

[2] For a discussion of the merits (and limitations) of this indicator, see Pavitt [1988]. In particular, regarding the limitations of such a proxy, an important point raised by our referee relates to infra- and inter-firm transfer of technology obviously undetected by patents' counts. While we fully acknowledge the importance of that mechanism of technology acquisition – neglected in our tests here only due to data unavailability – we suggest that, nonetheless, our estimates ought not turn out biased as a result. First, it often happens that the very process of technological acquisition intertwins with in-house R&D and innovation [Pavitt, 1992]. Second, the patterns of location of MNCs is sensitive to and co-evolve with country-specific technological capabilities [Cantwell, 1989]. Third, insofar as particular countries rely systematically more than other on 'transfer' as opposed to domestically generated innovation, this should be captured in our estimates by the country-dummy variables (see below).

Table 1 – *Export, Patent Activity, Real Investment and Unit Labour Cost in Some Industrial Countries*

	Export shares[a]		Patent shares[b]		Real invest-ment, rates of growth[c] 1967–87	Unit labour cost, rates of growth[c] 1967–87
	1967/69	1985/87	1967/69	1985/87		
United States	19.90	14.58	75.76	55.14	3.68	3.40
Germany	18.39	18.36	6.80	9.68	2.98	8.24
United Kingdom	10.86	7.41	4.91	3.50	1.10	5.87
Japan	9.85	16.62	2.63	19.26	5.16	7.98
France	7.76	8.48	2.74	3.47	2.90	6.15
Italy	6.73	7.58	0.87	1.41	1.33	5.27
Canada	5.86	5.36	1.67	1.93	6.68	4.32
Belgium	5.61	4.82	0.33	0.35	0.86	3.99
Netherlands	4.08	5.02	0.91	1.09	2.85	6.17
Switzerland	3.20	2.96	1.67	1.74	3.00	8.43
Sweden	3.03	2.83	1.06	1.23	3.20	5.33
Austria	1.35	1.73	0.28	0.47	3.86	7.00
Norway	1.15	0.80	0.10	0.14	1.52	7.83
Denmark	1.08	1.34	0.19	0.26	4.40	7.20
Finland	0.92	1.25	0.06	0.31	4.49	5.84
Ireland	0.24	0.87	0.02	0.04	3.87	4.80

[a] Total exports refer to the 16 countries considered. – [b] Shares refer to patents granted in the USA. – [c] Calculated with reference to the following: initial period 1967/69; terminal period 1985/87.

Source: see Appendix.

innovative activities: Japan has strongly increased its patent share (from 2.6 per cent in 1967/1969 to 19.3 per cent in 1985/1987), as the United States share has dramatically dropped (−20.6 percentage points). The United Kingdom patenting performance has also been markedly negative.

As regards the dynamics of real investment in machinery and equipment, Japan stands out for its excellent performance (it is the second country in the ranking), while, again, the United Kingdom presents a remarkably poor performance. However, the declining trend of the United States in world trade is not accompanied by a lack of capital accumulation (the United States displays an investment rate of growth close to the country aggregate average).

Concerning unit labour costs, the paradoxical findings by Kaldor [1978] seem partly corroborated also for the period 1967/1987. As known, Kaldor found for Italy, Japan, the United Kingdom and the

United States a "perverse" relation between growth in unit labour costs and growth in export market shares over the period 1963/1975. In Table 1, at least Japan and the United States appear to conform to that "perverse relationship": Japan's large gains in market shares have not been prevented by a rather sharp growth in relative unit labour costs; the drop of the United States in world exports has occurred notwithstanding the fact that the United States has shown the lowest growth in unit labour costs.

Let us consider the performances of the other industrial countries. The Netherlands, Italy, France and Ireland are the countries that, after Japan, have gained more in world trade. Italy and France have also significantly increased their patent shares. Interestingly, Germany displays quite stable export shares, and, together, a good innovative performance (+2.9 percentage points in the patent share) and a relatively high growth of unit labour costs, mainly due to exchange rate revaluation.

The model which follows shall attempt to interpret these diverse national trade performances and, in particular, to disentangle the effects of technological change on export dynamics.

III. Technical Change, Input Prices and International Trade

A growing stream of literature, starting with early "technology-gap" and "product-cycle" models of trade [Posner, 1961; Freeman, 1963; Hufbauer, 1966; Vernon, 1966] and recently developed within both "New Trade" theories [Grossman and Helpman, 1990, 1991; Segerstrom et al., 1990; Rivera-Batiz and Romer, 1991] and "evolutionary" theories [Dosi et al., 1990], has argued that international technological differences can be a fundamental basis for trade. In particular, as discussed at length elsewhere [Dosi et al., ibid.], the nature of the innovative process generally implies diversity in the rates and direction of innovation between sectors, countries and firms. In turn, these diversities, jointly with the intrinsic uncertainty associated with innovative activities, mean also that individual firms continuously expand, shrink or die also as a function of their relative technological success.

Moreover, many innovative activities present varying degrees of cumulativeness in the process of accumulation of technological knowledge, and are partly appropriable by the innovators themselves. All this underlies also the specificities of each country in each sector with respect to their technological gaps or leads. Indeed, the existing cross-sectional evidence suggests that the relative technological capabilities of each country in each sector are a powerful determinant of the export share of that same country in that sector on the world market [Soete, 1981; Fagerberg, 1988].

Test of the form

$$X_{ij} = f(T_{ij}),$$

where X_{ij} is the export share of country i in sector j and T_{ij} is some proxy for the technological capabilities of i in j, imply a notion of absolute advantages/disadvantages.[3] That is, they attempt to explain trade flows by comparing some underlying indicator of national "strength" of each country within a particular sector, neglecting – in a first approximation – comparative-advantage mechanisms of specialization (which, as known, "explain" trade by "coupling", so to speak, inter-sectoral comparisons within the same country, jointly with some equilibrium assumption on intersectoral allocation of resources).

An interpretation of trade flows based on absolute advantages/disadvantages is clearly consistent with macroeconomic disequilibrium: for example, it does not imply any clearing on factors' and commodities' markets and, indeed, it requires an implicit assumption on some "stickiness" in the re-allocation of resources from one sector to another. More generally, it implies changes in trade and technology unpegged to some underlying equilibrium and imperfect adjustments in macroeconomic variables to continuously changing technological "fundamentals".

Of course, such adjustments – first of all, for our purposes, wages and exchange rates – occur all the time. However, on the assumption that such adjustments are only partial and that empirical data correspond to "disequilibrium" observations, it is still possible to test models of the form

$$X_{ij} = f(T_{ij}, C_{ij}),$$

where C_{ij} are some proxies for input prices or unit costs denominated in a common currency. In fact, some evidence stemming from such a specification appears to suggest that technological factors dominate in

---

[3] Here and throughout one obviously assumes that some normalization for different country sizes has been made.

the interpretation of the participation of each country to trade flows even when proxies for costs and exchange rates are accounted for [Dosi and Soete, 1983; Dosi et al., 1990].

The notion of absolute advantages/disadvantages can also be extended to the level of whole countries. Model specifications such as

$$X_i = f(T_i, C_i) \tag{1}$$

formally capture possibly disequilibrium relationships between relative technological capabilities, relative costs and export shares of each country. The economic rationale is that national export shares depend on the "competitiveness" of each country. In turn, the latter depends on country-specific patterns of innovation and imitation and on imperfect adjustments in its input prices and exchange rates.

In a first instance, one need not specify theoretically the dynamics in technology and costs (which – an "evolutionary" perspective would suggest – depend also on country-specific institutional factors). What is needed is simply to specify the selection dynamics linking "competitiveness" and shares. In fact, we assume a modified version of a Fisher-Pry selection process as the dynamic version of (1):

$$X_i(t) - X_i(t-1) = f\{[E_i(t-1) - \bar{E}(t-1)]/\bar{E}(t-1)\}, \tag{2}$$

where $E_i(\cdot)$ stands for the vector of variables affecting competitiveness (i.e. technology and costs) and $\bar{E}(\cdot)$ is the average competitiveness of the set of all considered countries.[4]

Clearly, (2) does not imply any equilibrium assumption on neither patterns of technological change nor costs: loosely speaking, it is the formal representation of ("disequilibrium") common sense statements of the type "... Britain is losing market shares because most British firms are not innovative enough ...".

In the following, we shall present an econometric specification of that basic model.

---

[4] Unlike Silverberg et al. [1988], here we use in the empirical specification unweighted averages, $\bar{E} = 1/n \sum E_i$. The selection dynamics of (2) notionally allow also for null or negative shares: in the case of inter-firm selection that can be meaningfully interpreted as the event "death" for the firm (as in Dosi et al. [1993]). But obviously countries cannot 'die' and the estimates derived from (2) ought to include a constraint for export shares to be strictly positive. However, it turns out that, as plausible, for the observed dynamics, the constraint is never binding.

IV. Dynamic Econometric Specification

As already mentioned, most of the empirical studies on the relationship between trade and technical change relies on static econometric specifications, which imply some serious shortcomings from a theoretical point of view, and, equally important, at an econometric level.

In fact, static models are generally bound to assume the existence of equilibrium relationships between variables which would occur both in the short and in the long run. Furthermore, the econometric estimation of instantaneous equations relating serially correlated variables entails some serious problems in interpreting results by usual R^2 and t statistics. As well known, this is the problem of "spurious regressions" [Granger and Newbold, 1974], which arises in models where error dynamics are not adequately accounted for. When relating variables which are in fact independent, residual errors acquire a time-series structure similar to that of the dependent variable and, in this way, they may depart from white noise features. High values of R^2 could be associated with low values of the Durbin-Watson statistic showing the existence of residual autocorrelation. In this context, interpreting high R^2 figures as usual goodness of fit measures, can be misleading. This phenomenon is quite general, although it can be especially found in regressions between variables in levels, which often are nonstationary. Granger and Newbold [1986] report some findings from studies approaching this problem by simulation methods. There, results suggest a way to minimize the probability of esimating spurious regressions, namely, taking first differences of the series. However, this procedure is not always advisable because it brings about a lack of information on long-run relationships between the levels of variables themselves.

Recent developments in the theory of cointegration [Granger, 1986], have provided some tools to detect long-run effects from regressions involving nonstationary variables. In this framework, equilibrium equations can be estimated disregarding the specification of short-run dynamics because the consistency property of estimators is preserved.[5] Although this approach is very appealing, until recently [Greenhalgh, 1990] it has been neglected in the analyses of innovation and trade.

---

[5] This result is called "super-consistency" [Stock, 1987]. However, in finite samples, cointegration "equilibrium" estimates can be biased. Banerjee et al. [1986] perform some Monte Carlo simulations of this bias in static and dynamic specifications, and suggest the use of the latter.

The approach outlined above to the analysis of international competitiveness presents even further estimation problems: the dynamics of variables is freed from any hypothesis of steady-state, while disequilibrium dynamics continuously prevail. In that context, there is no long-run equilibrium configuration of international markets since countries' shares change as a result of processes of innovation, catching-up and falling-behind. As a consequence, in dealing with an econometric analysis of this process, it should be appropriate to adopt methods geared for nonstationary time series. Unfortunately, the time series we use are too short to enable this econometric strategy. However, all the variables included in this exercise are expressed as ratios and it happens that the latter display stationary characteristics along the years considered, so allowing the use of estimators based on traditional distribution theory[6] (note that an evolutionary theory would *not* predict this to happen in general).

Another question one has to face concerns aggregation. In fact, the theory presented in the preceding paragraph strongly suggests the heterogeneity of economic agents, while, on the other hand, econometric tests are based on countries' representative equations. The link between these macro-equations and possibly simple ("boundedly rational") adaptive micro-behavioural rules which may underlie them, is formally addressed in Lippi [1988]. As shown there, usual linear macro-dynamic specifications can arise through aggregation of simple autoregressive functions, possibly micro-founded in routinized behaviours.

Let us start by considering equation (1). As it stands, it expresses an instantaneous relationship between export, technology and cost. However, the underlying dynamic process (see equation (2)) allows an immediate generalization in terms of dynamic variables. In order to use variables in ratios, we reformulate (2) as

$$X_i(t) - X_i(t-1) = f\{[E_i(t-1)/\bar{E}(t-1)] - 1\}. \tag{2b}$$

The first step is to specify the technological innovation variable in two components. One is related to innovative activities undertaken by firms with the aim of profiting from new technological knowledge. The other refers to knowledge generated through the normal productive

---

[6] Autoregressions for each variable have been performed, and the estimated parameters have been examined without finding disturbing evidence of nonstationarity.

activity such as learning by doing, and through the adoption of capital-embodied innovations:

$$T = f(P, I). \tag{3}$$

Patents, P, is the proxy we have chosen to describe the former component of technological progress, while fixed investment, I, stands for the
latter.

It is usual in econometric literature to specify dynamic equations
to account for adjustment costs, expectations etc. (see the "quasi-the-
oretical bases for dynamic models" in Hendry et al. [1984]). Here we
suggest yet another reason for dynamic econometrics, namely, positive
feedbacks and dynamic increasing returns. The former may be linked
to several cumulative mechanisms that reinforce the competitiveness
of firms on international markets – i.e. "success breeds success". These
effects are here considered by an autoregressive structure in the dependent variable X.

Dynamic increasing returns often arise in individual firms or industries along with the very process of innovative search [Dosi, 1988]
which generally draws on accumulated competences. Hence, the capabilities of firms are continuously updated and increased as their overall
activities (production, marketing, investment, R&D, etc.) proceed. A
formal picture of such a cumulative innovative process in the aggregate of all domestic firms is given by a distributed lag approximation
to (3):

$$T_t = a + \sum_{l=0}^{m} b_l P_{t-l} + \sum_{l=0}^{n} c_l I_{t-l}. \tag{4}$$

In this way, accounting for technology as in (4), a general autoregres-
sive-distributed lag (ADL) can be derived.

$$X_{it} = \sum_{l=1}^{k} \alpha_l X_{it-l} + \sum_{l=0}^{m} \beta_l P_{it-l} + \sum_{l=0}^{n} \gamma_l I_{it-l} + \sum_{l=0}^{q} \delta_l C_{it-l}$$
$$+ \lambda_i + e_{it}, \qquad i = 1, ..., N; \qquad t = 1, ..., T \tag{5}$$

where P_t, I_t, C_t are weakly exogenous variables, and are expressed as
ratios with respect to all countries aggregates; λ_i are country-fixed
effects and e_{it} is a random residual.

Equation (5) can be viewed as a dynamic generalization of (2),
wherein heterogeneity among countries is embedded in the λ_i parameters. This ADL equation focuses on short-run dynamics, while our
interest concerns mainly the evaluation of long-run relationships. The
general dynamic formulation of (5) only allows an indirect estimation

of long-run multipliers, after some calculations:

$$\Theta_P = \phi \sum_{l=0}^{m} \beta_l; \quad \Theta_I = \phi \sum_{l=0}^{n} \gamma_l; \quad \Theta_C = \phi \sum_{l=0}^{g} \delta_l,$$

where $\quad \phi = \left(1 - \sum_{l=1}^{k} \alpha_l\right)^{-1}$.

A reformulation of (5), as those proposed by Wickens and Breusch [1988], allows a direct estimation of long-run multipliers while taking account, at the same time, of short-run dynamic effects. Among several re-parameterizations of (5) examined in Wickens and Breusch [ibid.], we have chosen the following

$$X_{it} = -\phi \sum_{l=1}^{k} \alpha_l(X_{it} - X_{it-l}) + \Theta_P P_{it} - \phi \sum_{l=1}^{m} \beta_l(P_{it} - P_{it-l})$$

$$+ \Theta_I I_{it} - \phi \sum_{l=1}^{n} \gamma_l(I_{it} - I_{it-l})$$

$$+ \Theta_C C_{it} - \phi \sum_{l=1}^{g} \delta_l(C_{it} - C_{it-l}) + \phi \gamma_i + \phi e_{it}, \tag{6}$$

which can be obtained by subtracting $\left(\sum_{l=1}^{k} \alpha_l\right) X_{it}$ from each side of (5).

V. Data Set

As the theoretical framework of Section III primarily deals with trade and innovation in manufacturing, data on the variables included in this econometric exercise refer to this economic aggregate. They consist of time series from 1967 to 1987 (1966–1987 for patents) for 16 OECD countries.

In particular, the relevant variables (expressed in index numbers) are the following:

– Exports: X_{it} is the share of the export value of each country i on the country aggregate total export value (in current US dollars);
– Patents: P_{it} is the share of patents granted in the United States to country i on the total of patents granted to the country aggregate;
– Investment: I_{it} is the ratio of real investment in machinery and equipment of country i relative to that of the country aggregate (both expressed as index numbers).
– Labour costs: C_{it} is the ratio of unit labour costs of country i, denominated in a common currency, relative to the average across countries.

Details on data sources and methods can be found in the Appendix. However, some further comments on the use of patents and export indicators are in order. In equations (5) and (6), patents granted in the United States ought to approximate the innovative capabilities of each country. In this respect, these data give a somewhat biased information on the United States as compared to other countries. Obviously, data for US patents refer to their home market, so they present very high figures which would distort the meaning of P_{it}, the patent variable. We tried to overcome this problem by taking patent shares for the United States with respect to the total country aggregate, while, for other countries, the comparison is with respect to the total country aggregate less the United States. For sake of symmetry, the same formulation is used for exports.

Exports are considered in current value (US dollars), so market shares are influenced also by price movements. This specification seems consonant with the picture of the process of international competition briefly outlined above. Technological innovation influences market shares also by changing quality characteristics of products and determining the emergence of new products. Moreover, a gain in competitiveness may well imply either increasing market shares or increasing prices for unchanged market shares. As a consequence, price changes are deeply involved in this process. That is, their effects cannot be assumed to be neutral.

VI. Estimation Results

The general ADL equation as in (5) is estimated by pooled least-squares with dummy variables for country-fixed effects, and some year dummies.[7] The other dynamic specification (equation (6)) that we adopt requires instrumental variables to be estimated. In fact, Wickens and Breusch [1988] demonstrate that applying an instrumental variables estimator to a reformulated equation such as (6), with the set of instruments given by all the explanatory variables in the original equation, the same results can be obtained as estimating the original equation by OLS and then calculating the parameters of the reformulated equation.

---

[7] This estimation method is biased in dynamic models with T fixed and $N \to \infty$ [Nickell, 1981; Anderson and Cheng, 1982]. But, when T tends to infinity, least squares are asymptotically unbiased. The time series we employ, given current econometric practices, seem long enough (21 years) to allow the use of this method.

Although residuals of the reformulated equation differ from those of the original by a multiplicative constant ϕ, misspecification testing can be performed through the use of statistics that are invariant to this residual transformation. Autocorrelated error diagnostic is implemented via Ljung and Box (LB) test for five-year-lags. Estimated values of the LB statistic are far below 11.07, the critical value of χ^2 with five d.o.f., at the 5 per cent level of significance.

The most general result concerns the long-term effect of technical change – both in its "disembodies" form, as captured by patents, and "embodied" into fixed investments – upon export dynamics. Conversely, changes in wages and exchange rates appear to display only short-run effects on changes in competitiveness, which are re-absorbed in the longer term.

Table 2 presents the estimation results based on (6), showing significant long-run parameters for the technological variables. It is especially relevant the value obtained for investment. Patents also have a sizable parameter estimate, even if in the aggregate context of the present paper, they capture only parts of the innovative process in each country: for example, they underestimate the innovative contribution of those sectors where patents are not an important mechanism of appropriability. In any case, notwithstanding these caveats, our findings about the role of patents hint at the macro-economic relevance of country-specific knowledge production and knowledge appropriation.

Not surprisingly, the lag structure of the technological effects on trade is quite long. As ADL estimates, not shown here, directly based on (5) reveal, no instantaneous relationship occurs: indeed, investments start showing a positive and significant effect with a three-year lag and patents with a four-year lag. The micro-economic reasoning behind this evidence is that firms take a considerable time in embodying new knowledge in old or new products, in fully exploiting new equipment and in gathering advantage on market rivals.[8]

---

[8] This long lag structure is, most likely, one of the reasons why in the tests on the relationship between changes in bilateral net trade balances and changes in relative patenting activity, presented in Cotsomitis et al. [1991], a technology-gap hypothesis performs rather poorly. Another reason rests in the dependent variable, net balances, which especially in the short term is heavily influenced by macro-economic policies affecting import absorption. (Pushing it to the extreme, one could indeed imagine that all countries which fare badly on the export markets *due* to technology-gap factors systematically deflate and, though that mechanism improves net balances, hence yielding a spurious positive correlation between widening technological gaps and improving balances ....)

464   Weltwirtschaftliches Archiv

Table 2 – *Regression Results (Reformulated ADL equations with long-run multipliers)*

Variable	i	ii	iii	iv
$X_t - X_{t-1}$	−4.4440 (5.3342)	−3.9777 (5.7221)	−20.303 (2.0212)	−3.6767 (5.7687)
$X_t - X_{t-2}$	0.3968 (0.9600)	–	–	–
$X_t - X_{t-3}$	−0.2084 (0.6427)	–	–	–
P^*	0.1639 (1.6746)	0.1709 (1.8423)	−0.1157 (0.3158)	0.1488 (1.6391)
$P_{t-1} - P_{t-2}$	−0.1570 (0.9184)	−0.1745 (1.0727)	−0.9818 (1.1216)	−0.1216 (0.7655)
$P_{t-1} - P_{t-3}$	0.3508 (1.9248)	0.3199 (1.8893)	1.8013 (1.5372)	0.3512 (2.1041)
$P_{t-1} - P_{t-4}$	−0.3527 (2.1557)	−0.3016 (1.9739)	−0.6703 (0.9042)	−0.3076 (2.0490)
I^*	0.2612 (1.5881)	0.2985 (1.9195)	2.4281 (2.3970)	0.3171 (2.1404)
$I_{t-1} - I_{t-2}$	0.0997 (0.4166)	0.1537 (0.6777)	0.5711 (0.5169)	0.2566 (1.1427)
$I_{t-1} - I_{t-3}$	−0.4252 (2.2868)	−0.4693 (2.6470)	−1.9290 (1.7933)	−0.4893 (2.7858)
C^*	0.0065 (0.0339)	−0.1121 (0.6340)	0.2686 (0.5210)	–
$C_t - C_{t-1}$	2.1814 (4.0122)	2.0271 (4.0599)	9.7336 (1.9161)	–
$C_t - C_{t-2}$	−0.8191 (2.3301)	−0.7112 (2.2007)	−4.9614 (1.8100)	–
σ	32.122	30.621	145.172	30.240
LB(5)	3.794	4.925	3.606	6.851
DW	2.105	2.078	2.141	2.158

Note: The parameters of the variables P^*, I^*, C^* are the long-run multipliers. – Absolute values of t statistics are in parentheses. – Specification *iii* is estimated without fixed effects and with a constant whose estimated value is −97.98 (1.069). – σ is the standard error of the regression. LB(5) is the Ljung and Box statistic with 5-year lags. – The chi-square level at 5% and 5 d.o.f. is 11.07.

The opposite applies to unit labour costs denominated in a common currency. A remarkable result concerns the lack of significance for their long-run multipliers. At a first look, this contrasts with the significance of short-run parameters.[9] The whole set of estimates about labour costs shows some strong short-run effects – with alternate signs – of this variable on export shares, while the long-run impact tends to disappear.

The "instantaneous" effect of an increase in labour costs is positive – a likely consequence of market reaction lags and firms' market power. The one-year lagged effect is negative as conventional economic wisdom would suggest. On longer lags, the effect quickly fades away (indeed, ADL estimates show again a positive and significant coefficient in the second lag).

In short, changes in competitiveness related to wages and exchange rates appear to be short-run phenomena, adjusting around longer-term effects of country-specific dynamics in both investment patterns and innovative learning.

These findings shed also some light on the "Kaldor paradox". As a long-term phenomenon, it seems to be the outcome of a "spurious correlation" due to the neglect of a more fundamental dynamics in country-specific technological capabilities which influence directly trade and, in indirect ways, also changes in wages and exchange rates. Once technology is included in the model the "paradox" disappears, leaving only J-curve type effects in the short term.

Of course, this does not rule out at all the possibility of "virtuous" or "vicious" circles linking exchange rate dynamics with the incentives that firms face to innovate and rationalize production, which in turn affect trade and exchange rate. Only a model much more complex than the present one would be able to capture that feedback structure. In any case, long-term path-dependent interactions affecting our 'weakly exogenous' variables are perfectly consistent with the theory underlying our model.[10]

---

[9] An F test for the exclusion of cost variables from the ADL specification has given the value of 10.7, which means rejection of that hypothesis.

[10] This is not to say that it is easy to identify some dominant, relatively invariant, causal links. Indeed, it is a major area for future empirical research. For example, Milberg and Gray [1992] suggest that the 'overvaluation' of a currency tend to exert long-lasting *negative* effects on competitiveness and market share via an induced reduction of cash-flows and investment (in equipment, R&D, etc.). The argument is based on a behavioural model of the firm with fixed routines. However, on the grounds of very similar micro hypotheses but allowing for routines to change in response to macro-eco-

Table 3 – *Country Fixed Effects*

Country	Fixed effect	t	Country	Fixed effect	t
Ireland	31.13	4.59	Denmark	13.01	2.36
Japan	18.78	2.66	Belgium	12.47	2.55
Netherlands	15.95	2.97	Finland	12.11	2.03
Austria	15.88	2.71	Sweden	11.43	2.15
Italy	15.37	2.87	Norway	11.35	1.97
Switzerland	15.09	2.58	United Kingdom	11.18	2.12
France	14.84	2.68	United States	11.15	2.33
Germany	14.46	2.27	Canada	8.83	1.78

Further, the introduction of country fixed effects in estimated equations adds some information. The theory behind the econometric specifications rests on individual heterogeneity, in particular with respect to technological and (here unspecified) institutional variables. Moreover, since the performances of each country on international markets result from aggregation over sectors characterized by different technological opportunities, they are influenced by sectoral distributions which differ across countries. In fact, all country dummy variables have significant parameters and the F test for the exclusion of fixed effects is rejected (the estimated F statistic is 3.878).

Table 3 presents the coefficients of the countries' fixed effects. In our view, they should be interpreted as synthetic proxies for what Mistral [1983] and OECD [1991] call the "structural competitiveness" of each economy – including its forms of industrial organization, its institutions and policies – which favour or hinder the ability of domestic firms to penetrate the international markets and, thus, effectively exploit their technological capabilities.

So, for example, it is tempting to interpret the quite high coefficient of Japan with reference to the specific organizational features of Japanese companies identified by e.g. Aoki [1988] and related to the

---

nomic shocks it is possible to reach opposite conclusions: a strong currency exerts a *positive* irreversible effect by 'forcing' companies to devote more investments to innovate, rationalize, reduce organizational slack ... This, for example, is a quite diffused assessment in Italy of the decade following the entry into the EMS. Incidentally, the dominant 'hysteretic' effects of exchange rates bears implications also for long-debated questions, such as: is it 'good' or 'bad' in the long run to be exporter of primary products? Has there even been a 'Dutch disease'? What macro-economic policies are best suited for innovation and competitiveness? For some discussion see Dosi et al. [1989, 1990].

information and incentive structure that they embody. Or in the case of Ireland, one could interpret the top-ranking coefficient as the outcome of quite successful industrial policies aimed at attracting foreign investment and using the country as an export base. At the opposite extreme, the low coefficients of the United Kingdom, the United States and Canada seem to confirm that sort of "anglosaxon disease" – made of ineffective managerial practices, myopic financial institutions and policy failures – discussed at depth, for example, in Dertouzos et al. [1989].

On even more impressionistic grounds, our results show also some significant rank correlation between the values of the country intercept shown in Table 3 and the changes in export shares from the initial to the final period (1967/69 to 1985/87), possibly hinting at the specificities of each 'national system of innovation' (the Spearman rank correlation is 0.77).[11]

VII. Conclusions

At last, one can recently observe a growing awareness in the international trade literature that technological asymmetries among countries strongly affect trade performances. However, notwithstanding the appreciation of innovation as an intrinsic dynamic phenomenon, most statistical tests have been performed so far by estimating static relationships.

The econometric model presented here allowed some estimation of the short- and long-term impacts of both technological change and cost-related macro-economic adjustments on the "international competitiveness" of each country, approximated by changes in its export shares. The model – based on disequilibrium, country-specific, dynamics in learning, accumulation and macro-economic changes – accounts for export-share changes via an "evolutionary" selection process whereby heterogeneous firms and countries compete, shrink or grow as a result of their differential innovative performances and costs.

The implied notion of absolute advantages/disadvantages of each country and their country-specific dynamics is directly consistent with "technology-gap" interpretations of trade flows. And, as the results of the estimates show, technological learning and diverse rates of adop-

---

[11] More on this notion of 'national systems of innovation' in Chesnais [1987], Lundvall [1992], Nelson [1993].

tion of capital-embodied innovation do appear to shape, in the long term, the diverse trade performances of each country. However, also a strong "structural" heterogeneity among countries appears, possibly revealing the effect of some underlying institutional and organizational variables.

It is important to recall that in the historical background of the time series analyzed here one finds generalized macro shocks, such as the oil crises and country-specific events with far-reaching domestic and international consequences (among others, the Vietnam war, the formation of the European monetary system, radical changes of macro-economic policies in several countries in the 1980s, etc.). Of course, all these factors have plausibly influenced the dynamics of innovation, investment, wages and exchange rates and also modified national institutions, forms of corporate organizations, etc. (all what is succinctly captured by our country shift parameters).

What our model does is trying to identify robust 'transmission mechanisms' between the outcomes of these underlying changes, which political economy and industrial economics have extensively studied, and trade dynamics.

The normative implications are quite far-reaching. On the grounds of the evidence presented here, policies aimed at "improving competitiveness" ought to focus primarily upon the factors which influence technological learning, investment and organizational adaptation, rather than on more conventional instruments such as exchange rate adjustments.

Appendix

The variables refer to 16 industrialized countries: United States, Japan, Germany, France, United Kingdom, Italy, Canada, Austria, Belgium, Denmark, Finland, Ireland, Netherlands, Norway, Sweden, Switzerland.

Exports data in current value (US dollars) are from *OECD, Foreign Trade by Commodities*. Data on patents granted in the United States are from the *U.S. Department of Commerce, Patent and Trademark Office*. Export and patent shares have been calculated by using two country totals: the one for the United States include all 16 countries; that for the other countries does not include US data.

The investment variable has been constructed as the ratio between the index number series of investment in machinery and equipment of each country (base year: 1967) and the index number series of the country aggregate. Source: *U.N., Yearbook of Industrial Statistics*.

Investment data have been deflated by the implicit price index of investment in machinery and equipment (*OECD, Historical Statistics*).

Analogously, the labour cost variable is the ratio between the index number of unit labour costs in manufacturing at current exchange rates for each country (base year: 1967) and that for the country aggregate. Source: *OECD, Historical Statistics*. Exchange rates are effective exchange rates (MERM), given by the *IMF, International Financial Statistics* (for the years from 1970 to 1987), and obtained by our own elaborations for the years 1967–1969.

References

Anderson, Theodore W., Hsiao Cheng, "Formulation and Estimation of Dynamic Models Using Panel Data". *Journal of Econometrics*, Vol. 18, 1982, pp. 47–82.

Aoki, Masahiko, *Information, Incentives and Bargaining in the Japanese Economy*. Cambridge 1988.

Banerjee, Anindya, Juan J. Dolado, David F. Hendry, Gregor W. Smith, "Exploring Equilibrium Relationships in Econometrics Through Static Models: Some Monte Carlo Evidence". *Oxford Bulletin of Economics and Statistics*, Vol. 48, 1986, pp. 253–277.

Bensel, Terrence, Bruce T. Elmslie, "Rethinking International Trade Theory: A Methodological Appraisal". *Weltwirtschaftliches Archiv*, Vol. 128, 1992, pp. 249–265.

Cantwell, John A., *Technological Innovation and Multinational Corporations*, Oxford 1989.

Chesnais, Francois, "Internationalisation, Changement Technique Radical et Compétitivé des Systèmes Productifs Nationaux". In: J. Noisi (Ed.), *Technologie et Compétitivé Internationale*. CREDIT. Montreal 1987.

Cotsomitis, John, Chris De Bresson, Andy Kwan, "A Re-examination of the Technology Gap Theory of Trade: Some Evidence from Time Series Data for O.E.C.D. Countries". *Weltwirtschaftliches Archiv*, Vol. 127, 1991, pp. 792–799.

Dertouzos, Michael L., Richard K. Lester, Robert M. Solow, *Made in America: Regaining the Productive Edge*. Cambridge, Mass., 1989.

Dosi, Giovanni, "Sources, Procedures and Microeconomic Effects of Innovation". *The Journal of Economic Literature*, Vol. 26, 1988, pp. 1120–1171.

–, **Christopher Freeman, Silvia Fabiani,** *On the Process of Economic Development*. University of California, Center for Research in Management, CCC Discussion Paper. Berkeley, CA, 1993.

–, **Laura D'Andrea Tyson, John Zysman,** "Trade, Technologies, and Development: A Framework for Discussing Japan". In: Chalmers Johnson, Laura D'Andrea Tyson, John Zysman (Eds.), *Politics and Productivity. The Real Story of Why Japan Works*. Cambridge, Mass., 1989, pp. 3–38.

–, –, **Keith Pavitt, Luc Soete,** *The Economics of Technical Change and International Trade*. New York 1990.

–, **Luc Soete**, "Technology Gaps and Cost-Based Adjustments: Some Explorations on the Determinants of International Competitiveness". *Metroeconomica*, Vol. 35, 1983, pp. 197–222.

Fagerberg, Jan, "International Competitiveness". *The Economic Journal*, Vol. 98, 1988, pp. 355–374.

Freeman, Christopher, "The Plastics Industry: A Comparative Study of Research and Innovation". *National Institute Economic Review*, Vol. 26, 1963, pp. 22–62.

Granger, Clive W., "Developments in the Study of Cointegrated Economic Variables". *Oxford Bulletin of Economics and Statistics*, Vol. 48, 1986, pp. 213–228.

–, **Paul Newbold**, "Spurious Regressions in Econometrics". *Journal of Econometrics*, Vol. 2, 1974, pp. 111–120.

–, –, *Forecasting Economic Time Series*. II. ed. Orlando 1986.

Greenhalgh, Christine, "Innovation and Trade Performance in the United Kingdom". *The Economic Journal*, Vol. 100, 1990, pp. 105–118.

Grossman, Gene, Elhanan Helpman, "Comparative Advantage and Long-Run Growth". *The American Economic Review*, Vol. 80, 1990, pp. 796–815.

–, –, *Innovation and Growth in the Global Economy*. Cambridge, Mass., 1991.

Hendry, David F., Adrian R. Pagan, J. Denis Sargan, "Dynamic Specification". In: Zvi Griliches, M.D. Intriligator (Eds.), *Handbook of Econometrics*, Vol. II. Amsterdam 1984, pp. 1023–1100.

Hufbauer, Gary C., *Synthetic Materials and the Theory of International Trade*. London 1966.

Kaldor, Nicholas, "The Effect of Devaluations on Trade in Manufactures". In: Nicholas Kaldor (Ed.), *Further Essays on Applied Economics*. London 1978, pp. 99–118.

Lippi, Marco, "On the Dynamics of Aggregate Macroequations: From Simple Microbehaviour to Complex Macrorelationships". In: Giovanni Dosi, Christopher Freeman, Richard R. Nelson, Gerald Silverberg, Luc Soete (Eds.), *Technical Change and Economic Theory*. London 1988, pp. 170–196.

Lundvall, Bengt Äke (Ed.), *National Systems of Innovation. Toward a Theory of Innovation and Interactive Learning*. London 1992.

Milberg, William, Peter Gray, "International Competitiveness and Policy in Dynamic Industries". *Banca Nazionale del Lavoro Quarterly Review*, No. 180, 1992, pp. 59–80.

Mistral, Jacques, *Competitiveness of the Productive System and International Specialization*. OECD, DSTI/SPRU/83.31. Paris 1983.

Nelson, Richard R. (Ed.), *National Systems of Innovation*. Cambridge 1993, forthcoming.

Nickell, Stephen, "Biases in Dynamic Models with Fixed Effects". *Econometrica*, Vol. 49, 1981, pp. 1417–1426.

Organization for Economic Co-operation and Development (OECD), *Technology and the Economy – A Background Report on the TEP Programme*. Paris 1991.

Pavitt, Keith, "Uses and Abuses of Patent Statistics". In: A. Van Raan (Ed.), *Handbook of Quantitative Studies of Science and Technology*. Amsterdam 1988.

Pavitt, Keith, "Some Foundations for a Theory of the Large Innovating Firm". In: Giovanni Dosi, Renato Giannetti, Pier Angelo Toninelli (Eds.), *Technology and Enterprise in a Historical Perspective*. Oxford 1992, pp. 212–228.

Posner, Michael, "International Trade and Technical Change". *Oxford Economic Papers*, Vol. 13, 1961, pp. 323–341.

Rivera-Batiz, Luis A., Paul M. Romer, *International Trade and Endogenous Technical Change*. National Bureau of Economic Research, Working Paper No. 3594, Cambridge, Mass., 1991.

Segerstrom, Paul S., T.C.A. Anant, Elias Dinopoulos, "A Schumpeterian Model of the Product Life Cycle". *The American Economic Review*, Vol. 80, 1990, pp. 1077–1091.

Silverberg, Gerald, Giovanni Dosi, Luigi Orsenigo, "Innovation, Diversity and Diffusion: a Self-Organization Model". *The Economic Journal*, Vol. 98, 1988, pp. 1032–1054.

Soete, Luc, "A General Test of Technological Gap Trade Theory". *Weltwirtschaftliches Archiv*, Vol. 117, 1981, pp. 638–660.

Stock, James, "Asymptotic Properties of Least Squares Estimators of Cointegrating Vectors". *Econometrica*, Vol. 55, 1987, pp. 1035–1056.

Vernon, Raymond, "International Investment and International Trade in the Product Cycle". *The Quarterly Journal of Economics*, Vol. 80, 1966, pp. 190–207.

Wickens, Maurice R., Trevor S. Breusch, "Dynamic Specification, the Long-Run and the Estimation of Transformed Regression Models". *The Economic Journal*, Vol. 98, No. 390, 1988, pp. 189–205.

* * *

A b s t r a c t : The Dynamics of International Competitiveness. – This paper focuses on the determinants of international competitiveness over the seventies and eighties. The theoretical framework adopted here is based on a "technology-gap" account of trade flows. The econometric analysis relies on a dynamic model estimated by pooling time-series across countries. The short- and long-term impacts of both technical change and labour costs on trade performance are investigated. It is found that technological variables (patents and investments) play a major role in shaping dynamics of export-shares, while labour costs asymmetries among countries appear to affect trade performance only in the short term.

*

Z u s a m m e n f a s s u n g : Zur Dynamik der internationalen Wettbewerbsfähigkeit. – Dieser Aufsatz befaßt sich mit den Bestimmungsgründen der internationalen Wettbewerbsfähigkeit von Ländern in den 70er und 80er Jahren. Der theoretische Rahmen, der dabei benutzt wird, basiert auf dem Ansatz der „technologischen Lücke". Die ökonometrische Analyse stützt sich auf ein dynamisches Modell, das mit einer Kombination von Querschnitts- und Zeitreihendaten geschätzt wird. Die kurz- und langfristigen Wirkungen sowohl des technischen Wandels als auch der Lohnkosten auf die Handelsleistung werden untersucht. Dabei stellt sich heraus, daß technologische Variable (Patente und Investitionen) eine bedeutende Rolle dabei spielen, die Dynamik der Exportanteile zu gestalten, während Asymmetrien in den Lohnkosten zwischen den Ländern die Handelsleistungen nur auf kurze Sicht beeinflussen.

[21]

J Evol Econ (1995) 5: 243–268

——Journal of ——

**Evolutionary
Economics**

© Springer-Verlag 1995

Technological paradigms, patterns of learning and development: an introductory roadmap

Mario Cimoli[1] and Giovanni Dosi[2]

[1] Department of Economics, University of Venice, Ca'Foscari, Dirsodurro 3246, I-30123 Venezia, Italy
[2] Department of Economics, University of Rome, "La Sapienza", I-00100 Roma, Italy

Abstract. This paper presents an evolutionary microeconomic theory of innovation and production and discusses its implications for development theory. Using the notions of technological paradigm and trajectory, it develops an alternative view of firm behavior and learning. It is shown then how these are embedded in broader national systems of innovation which account for persistent differences in technological capacities between countries. Finally, this "bottom-up" evolutionary analysis is linked with an institutional "top-down" approach, and the potential fruitfulness of this dialogue is demonstrated.

Key words: Technological paradigms – Technological change – Theory of innovations – National systems of innovation

JEL-classification: O14-O30-O53-O54

1. Introduction

Deep relationships of some sorts between technical change and economic development are now generally acknowledged in both economic history and economic theory. Still, their nature is matter of debate concerning the precise causal links. For example, it is quite intuitive that improvements in the efficiency of techniques of production or in product performances may be a determinant or at least a binding precondition of growth in per capita incomes and consumption. But, intricate

Correspondence to: M. Cimoli

We thank the discussants and participants at the workshop on Technology and Competitiveness in Developing Countries, Venice, 26/11/93, for their useful comments.

The research leading to this work has benefited at various stages from the support of the Italian National Research Council (CNR, Progetto Strategico "Combiamento Technologico e Crescita Economica") and of the International Institute of Applied System Analysis (IIASA, Austria).

debates concern "what ultimately determines what...": e.g. is it resource accumulation that primarily fosters the exploration of novel innovative opportunities, or, conversely, does innovation drive capital accumulation?; do new technological opportunities emerge mainly from an extra-economic domain ("pure science") or are they primarily driven by economic incentives?; should one assume that the institutions supporting technical change are sufficiently adaptive to adjust to whatever underlying economic dynamics emerges from market interactions; or, conversely, are they inertial enough to shape the rates and directions of innovation and diffusion?

Clearly, these and a few other, related, questions are at the core of many controversies regarding growth patterns: for example, is convergence the dominant tendency? How does one then interpret observed phenomena of forging ahead or falling behind? Is it legitimate to exclude from the analysis at least in a first approximation the specificities of institutions and corporate organizations? Even more so, all these questions and controversies underlie the political economy of development.

Obviously, one would not do justice to these intricate questions in a single paper even if one had achieved thorough answers (that indeed one is far from having). However, there has been over at least the last two decades a flourishing of studies on the sources, mechanisms and patterns of technological innovation. And, the opening of the technological blackbox has often gone together with important insights into innovation-driven market competition. Business historians have finally achieved some cross-fertilization with (some breeds of) economic theorizing. And the institutional understanding of the socio-economic fabrics of contemporary societies starts showing fruitful complementaries with other analyses stemming from the economists quarters.

Quite a few of these contributions have been proposed by scholars who would call themselves evolutionists or institutionalists. Many, others have come within different theoretical perspectives. Still, there is a sense that these diverse streams of research show a few common threads, highlighting – to paraphrase Richard Nelson the co-evolution of technologies, corporate organizations and institutions. These threads – linking evolutionary analyses of the microeconomics of innovation all the way to (daring) generalizations on some invariant features of the process of development – are the subject of this paper. Far from being a comprehensive survey, it is rather a sort of "roadmap" with an inevitable degree of idiosyncrasy.

We start by discussing the theoretical implications of what we know about the often patterned dynamics of innovative activities at a micro level. The notions of technological paradigms, trajectories (and largely overlapping ones such as dominant designs) entail a representation of technologies centered on the cognitive and problem-solving procedures which they involve.

Another major implication of this view is in terms of theory of production. It is rather straightforward to derive some sort of non-substitution properties, in the short-term, and, also in the long-term, technological asymmetries or gaps as permanent features across firms and, even more as, across countries.

Do these micro technological properties bear consequences at broader levels of observation, i.e. whole industrial sectors and whole countries? Or, putting it another way, can one identify invariances and patterns at sectoral or national level which can be interpreted in terms of some underlying specificities in the processes of collective learning, market selection and institutional governance of both?

This is the subject of the second part of the paper, and it is also where the roadmap inevitably bifurcates into different discourses. Some will be persued in reasonable detail and while others will only be sketched out, just flagging the elements of consistency with the rest of the argument. For example, there are sound theoretical reasons and a growing empirical evidence that the observed patterns of evolution of industrial structures are the outcome of specific modes of access to innovative opportunities and market selection mechanisms. However, we shall not dwell here on this aspect of the co-evolution between technologies and production structures. Rather more attention shall be devoted to the links between micro learning and economy-wide accumulation of technological capabilities and, in particular, to the existence of specific national system of production and innovation. The argument needs to be built through several steps. First, it follows from the microeconomics of innovation that firms are central, albeit by no means unique, repositories of technological knowledge. Hence, also their specific organizational and behavioral features affect the rates and direction of learning. Second, firms characteristics are not randomly distributed across sectors and across countries. On the contrary, particular traits tend to be reinforced through their interactions with the environment in which they are imbedded. Third, broad institutional mechanisms of governance of interactions further enhance the possibility of collective lock-in into particular modes of learning. Somewhat in analogy with the earlier microeconomic analysis we shall call these patterns as national trajectories.

Far from reviewing an immense historical evidence on these issues, we shall only draw from selected examples from developed countries and, in particular, from a somewhat archetypical comparison between the experiences of Latin America and the Asian Far East.

Along this *tour de force* from micro technological studies to the political economy of development, we shall on purpose raise many more questions than we shall able to answer. The major task here is to show that they can be consistently linked together in a broadly defined evolutionary interpretation.

2. The fundamental properties of technology

Technological paradigms and trajectories

A variety of concepts have recently been put forward to define the nature of innovative activities: *technological regimes, paradigms, trajectories, salients, guideposts, dominants designs* and so on. The names are not so important (although some standardization could make the diffusion of ideas easier!). More crucially, these concepts are highly overlapping in that they try to capture a few common features of the procedures and direction of technical change (for a discussion and references, see Dosi 1988). Let us consider some of them.[1]

The notion of technological paradigms is based on a view of technology grounded on the following three fundamental ideas.

First, it suggests that any satisfactory description of "what is technology" and how it changes must also embody the representation of the specific forms of knowledge on which a particular activity is based. Putting it more emphatically, technology cannot be reduced to the standard view of a set of well-defined blueprints. Rather, it primarily concerns problem-solving activities involving – to

---

[1] In the following, we shall stick to the categories of *paradigms* and *trajectories*, but the reader who is found of other names should still recognize familiar ideas.

varying degrees – also tacit forms of knowledge embodied in individuals and organizational procedures.

Second, paradigms entail specific heuristic and visions on "how to do things" and how to improve them, often shared by the community of practitioners in each particular activity (engineers, firms, technical societies, etc.), i.e. they entail a collectively shared cognitive frames (Constant 1985).

Third, paradigms generally also define basic models of artifacts and systems, which over time are progressively modified and improved. These basic artifacts can also be described in terms of some fundamental technological and economic characteristics. For example, in the case of an airplane, these basic attributes are described not only and obviously in terms of inputs and the production costs, but also on the basis of some salient technological features such as wing-load, take-off weight, speed, distance it can cover, etc. What is interesting is that technical progress seems to display patterns and invariances in terms of these product characteristics. Similar examples of technological invariances can be found e.g. in semiconductors, agricultural equipment, automobiles and a few other micro technological studies.

The concept of *technological trajectories* is associated to the progressive realization of the innovative opportunities associated with each paradigm, which can in principle be measured in terms of the changes in the fundamental techno-economic characteristics of artifacts and the production process. The core ideas involved in this notion of trajectories are the following.[2]

First, each particular body of knowledge (i.e. each paradigm) shapes and constraints the rates and direction of technological change irrespectively of market inducements. Second, as a consequence, one should be able to observe regularities and invariances in the pattern of technical change which hold under different market conditions (e.g. under different relative prices) and whose disruption is correlated with radical changes in knowledge-bases (in paradigms). Third, technical change is partly driven by repeated attempts to cope with technological imbalances which it itself creates.[3]

A general property, by now widely acknowledged in the innovation literature, is that learning is local and cumulative. Local means that the exploration and development of new techniques is likely to occur in the neighborhood of the techniques already in use. Cumulative means that current technological development – at least at the level of individual business units – often builds upon past experiences of production and innovation, and it proceeds via sequences of specific problem-solving junctures (Vincenti 1992). Clearly, this goes very well together with the ideas of paradigmatic knowledge and the ensuing trajectories. A crucial implication, however, is that at any point in time the agents involved in a particular production activity will face little scope for substitution among techniques, if by that we mean the easy availability of blueprints different from those actually in use, which could be put efficiently into operation according to relative input prices.

---

[2] The interpretation of technical change and a number of historical examples can be found in pioneering works on economics of technical change such as those by Chris Freeman, Nathan Rosenberg, Richard Nelson, Sidney Winter, Thomas Hughes, Paul David, Joel Mokyr, Paolo Saviotti and others; see for a partial survey Dosi (1988).

[3] This is akin to the notion of reverse salients (Hughes 1992) and technological bottlenecks (Rosenberg 1976): to illustrate, think of increasing the speed of a machine tool, which in turn demands changes in cutting materials, which lead to changes in other parts of the machine...

Technological dominance, micro heterogeneity and non-substitution

The notion of paradigms contains elements of both a theory of production and theory of innovation. In short, we shall call it henceforth an evolutionary theory. Loosely speaking, we should consider such a theory at the same level of abstraction as, say, a Cobb-Douglas production function or a production possibility set. That is, all of them are theories of what are deemed to be some stylized but fundamental features of technology and, relatedly, of production process.[4]

In fact, one finds a few remarkable assumptions underlying conventional production theories. As already mentioned, technologies – at least in a first approximation – are seen as a set of blueprints describing alternative input combinations. Moreover, at any one time there must be many of them, in order to be able to interpret empirical observations as the outcome of a microeconomic process of optimal adjustment to relative prices. Information about these blueprints is generally assumed to be freely available (except those circumstances whereby they are privately appropriated via the patent system). Finally, one assumes to be able to separate the activities leading to the efficient exploitation of existing blueprints from those leading to the development of new ones (exogeneity of technical progress is its extreme version). Of course, this is only a trivialized account of a family of models that can be made much more sophisticated, by e.g. adding details on how blueprints are ordered with respect to each other (more technically, issues like continuity and convexity come under this heading). However, it still seems fair to say that the basic vision of production – also carried over in aggregate growth and development models – focuses on questions of choice among well defined techniques, generally available to all producers, who also know perfectly well what to do with all the recipes when they see them.

Well, to put it very strongly, the theory of production based on paradigms develops on nearly opposite theoretical building blocks. And indeed many of the latter yield empirically testable hypotheses.

Here, we shall argue that a paradigm-based theory of technology may perform the same interpretive tasks, at the same level of generality, and do it better, in the sense that it is more in tune with microeconomic evidence and also directly links with theories of innovation. Our theory would predict the following.

a) In general, there is at any point in time one or very few best practice techniques which dominate the others irrespectively of relative prices.
b) Different agents are characterized by persistently diverse (better and worse) techniques.
c) Over time the observed aggregate dynamics of technical coefficients in each particular activity is the joint outcome of the process of imitation/diffusion of existing best-practice techniques, of the search for new ones, and of market selection amongst heterogeneous agents.
d) Changes over time of the best practice techniques themselves highlight rather regular paths (i.e. trajectories) both in the space of input coefficients and also in the space of the core technical characteristics of outputs (see the earlier example on aircrafts).

---

[4] Few believe that a production possibility set literally exists. Many would however probably maintain that such a notion enhances the understanding of the observed technical coefficients in the economy and also how they change over time. We claim the same for the evolution theory.

A representation of production and technological activities

Let us further illustrate the previous points with a graphical example.

Start from the notion that each technical coefficient observed at the microlevel is the outcome of codified information (something resembling blueprints), but also of more tacit and firm specific forms of knowledge. Suppose that, for the sake of simplicity, we are considering here the production of an homogeneous good under constant returns to scale with two variable inputs only, x_1 and x_2.[5]

A paradigm-based theory of production predicts that, in general, in the space of unit inputs, micro coefficients are distributed somewhat as depicted in Figure 1. Suppose that at time t the coefficients are $c_1, \ldots, c_n$; where $1, \ldots, n$ are the various techniques/firms labelled in order of decreasing efficiency at time t. It is straightforward that technique/firm c_1 is unequivocally superior to the other ones no matter what relative prices are: it can produce the same unit output with less inputs of both x_1 and x_2. The same applies to the comparison between c_3 and c_n, etc....

Let us call this property *technological dominance*, and call some measure of the distribution of the coefficients across heterogeneous firms as the *degree of asymmetry* of that industry (for example, the standard deviation around the mean value C).

The first question is why doesn't firm n adopt technique $c1$? To simplify a more articulated argument (see Freeman 1982, Nelson and Winter 1982, Dosi 1988 and Dosi, Pavitt and Soete 1990), the answer is "because it does not know how to do it...". That is, even if it is informed about the existence of c_1, it might not have the capabilities of developing or using it. Remarkably, this might have little to do with the possibility for c_1 to be legally covered by a patent. The argument is much more general: precisely because technological knowledge is partly tacit, also embodied in complex organizational practices, etc., technological lags and lead may well be persistent even without legal appropriation. The opposite also holds: if the two firms have similar technological capabilities, imitation might occur very quickly, patent

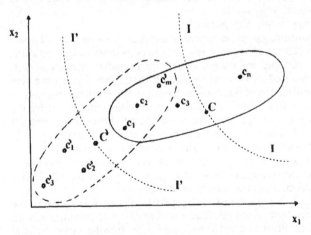

Fig. 1. Microheterogeneity and technological trajectories

---

[5] Note that fixed inputs, vintage effects and economies of scale would just strenghten the argument.

protection notwithstanding, by means of "inventing around" a patent, reverse engineering, etc. .

We are prepared to push the argument further and suggest that even if firm n were given all the blueprints of technique c_1 (or, in a more general case, also all the pieces of capital equipment associated with it), performances and thus revealed input coefficients might still widely differ. Following R. Nelson, it is easy to illustrate this by means of a gastronomical metaphor: despite readily available cooking blueprints and, indeed, also codified rules on technical procedures, unavailable in most economic representations of production ("... first heat the oven, then after around ten minutes introduce some specified mixture of flour and butter, ... etc."), one obtains systematically asymmetric outcomes in terms of widely shared standards of food quality. This applies to comparisons among individual agents and also to institutionally differentiated groups of them: for example, we are ready to bet that most eaters randomly extracted from the world population would systematically rank samples of English cooks to be "worse" than French, Chinese, Italian, Indian, ... ones, even when performing on identical recipes!!. If one accepts the metaphor, this should apply, much more so, to circumstances whereby performances result from highly complex and opaque organizational routines (Incidentally, Leibenstein's X-efficiency rest also upon this widespread phenomenon).

Suppose now that at some subsequent time t' we observe the distribution of microcoefficients $c'_3, \ldots, c'_m$. How do we interpret such a change?

The paradigm-based story would roughly be the following. At time t, all below-best-practice firms try with varying success to imitate technological leader(s). Moreover, firms change their market shares, some may die and other may enter: all this obviously changes the weights (i.e. the relative frequencies) by which techniques/firms appear. Finally, at least some of the firms try to discover new techniques, prompted by the perception of innovative opportunities, irrespectively of whether relative prices change or not (for the sake of illustration, in Figure 1, firm-3 succeeds in leapfrogging and becomes the technological leader while firm-m now embodies the marginal technique).

How do relative prices fit into this picture?

In a first approximation, no price-related substitution among firm-known blueprints occurs at all. Rather, changes in relative prices primarily affect both the direction of imitation and the innovative search by bounded-rational agents. However, the paradigm-based story would maintain that, even if relative prices change significantly, the direction of innovative search and the resulting trajectories would remain bounded within some relatively narrow paths determined by the nature of the underlying knowledge base, the physical and chemical principles it exploits, the technological systems in which a particular activity is embodied. Still more importantly, persistent shocks on relative prices, or, for that matter, on demand conditions, are likely to exert irreversible effects on the choice and relative diffusion of alternative technological paradigms, whenever such an alternative exists, and, in the long term, focus the search for new ones.

In a extreme synthesis, a paradigm-based production theory suggests as the general case, in the short term, fixed-coefficient (Leontieff-type) techniques, with respect to both individual firms and industries, the latter showing rather inertial averages over heterogeneous firms. In the longer term, we should observe quite patterned changes, often only loosely correlated with the dynamics of relative prices.

In fact, the available evidence – admittedly scattered, due also to the economists propensity to avoid disturbing questions – is consistent with these conjectures: there appear to be wide and persistent asymmetries in efficiency among firms within the same industry (cf. for a survey and discussion Nelson 1981). This applies to developed countries and, more so, to developing ones. Moreover, persistent asymmetries appear also in profitability (Geroski and Jaquemin 1988, Muller 1990). Finally, several industrial case studies highlight technology-specific regularities in the patterns of technical change hardly interpretable as direct responses to changes in relative prices and demand conditions: in this respect, the case of the semiconductors (Dosi 1984) is only an extreme example of a more general phenomenon.

Let us now expand the space over which technologies are described and include, in addition to input requirements, also the core characteristics of process and artifacts, hinted earlier: e.g. wing-load, take off weight etc. in airplanes; circuit density, processing speed in semiconductors; acceleration, fuel consumption in automobiles; etc. The conjecture is that also in this higher-dimension space, trajectories appear and that discontinuities are associated with changes in knowledge bases and search heuristics. Indeed, the evidence put forward by e.g. Devandra Sahal and, more recently, by Paolo Saviotti at Manchester University show remarkable regularities in the patterns of change within the space of core product characteristics: for example, in commercial aircrafts, one can observe a well defined trajectory leading from the DC-3 to contemporary models. (Interestingly, models which turn out to be technological or commercial failures often happen to be far from the trajectory itself).

These findings bear implications also for the economic analysis of the relationship between supply and demand dynamics. Start from a Lancasterian view of final demand (i.e., consumers demand characteristics which satisfy their "needs"). With rising incomes and heterogeneous preferences, one might have expected product variety to grow and be distributed over the whole space of characteristics. In fact, one obviously observe an enormous product variety. However, at a closer look, it appears that product innovation explore only a minor sub-set of such a space. Putting it differently, the nature of each paradigm appears to be a powerful factor binding the variety in the technical features and performances of observed products.

Technical change, international asymmetries and development

Naturally, there is an alternative interpretation of all the evidence discussed so far drawing on standard production theory. Let us consider once more Figure 1. Take for example the average technical coefficient C at time t by reading it from published industrial statistics. *Assume* by definition that C is the equilibrium technique (whereby average and best practice techniques nearly coincide). Relatedly, draw some generic *and unobservable* downward-sloped curve through C (say, in Fig. 1 the II curve) and also the observed relative price ratio. Do the same with point C' corresponding to the average values at t', and again with the subsequent average observations. Next assume a particular functional form to the unobserved curve postuled to pass through $C, C', C', \ldots$, etc. and call it the isoquant of a corresponding production function. (The same method can be applied, of course, over time or cross-sectionally). Then, run some econometric estimates based on such postulated function, using data derived from the time-series of relative prices and $C, C', \ldots$ Finally, interpret the relationship between the values of the estimated coefficients in terms of elasticities of substitution (i.e. some notional movement along the II curve, as equilibrium responses to relative price changes), and attribute the residual variance to a drift in the technological opportunity set, as represented by the movement from II to I'I', etc..

For the purpose of this argument, one can neglect whether such a drift is meant to be an exogenous time-dependent dynamics – as in Solow-type growth models –, or is in turn the outcome of some higher level production function of blueprints – as in many new growth models. In any case, if – for whatever reasons – relative prices present some intertemporal regularity and so do patterns of technological search (for example because they follow paradigm-driven trajectories), then one is likely to find a good statistical fit to the postulated model, even when no causal link actually exists between distributive shares and factor intensities. This is a well established point, convincingly argued in different perspectives by F. Fischer, R. Nelson, L. Pasinetti, A. Shaikh, H. Simon. Even if the evolutionary microdynamics described above were the true one, one could still successfully undertake the standard statistical exercise of fitting some production function. But the exercise would in fact obscure rather than illuminate the underlying links between technical change and output growth.

Take the illustration of Fig. 1 and suppose that the evidence does not refer to two distributions of micro-technical coefficients over time within the same country, but instead to two countries at the same time: after all, paraphrasing Robert Lucas, we only need informed tourists to recognize that most countries can be ranked in terms of unequivocal average technological gaps. With some additional assumptions on the nature of production function, one can still claim that C, C', etc. remain equilibrium realizations of country-specific allocation processes. Conversely, in the context of an evolutionary approach, one would suggest – as we do – that optimizing choice among technical alternatives commonly shared by all agents in the two countries have little to do with all this, and that one should rather look for an explanation of such inter-national differences within the process of accumulation of technological competence and also within the institution governing market interaction and collective learning. The contrast between (imperfect) *learning vs optimal allocation of resources* as the fundamental engine of development has indeed been repeatedly emphasized among others by Kaldor, Pasinetti and earlier by Schumpeter, but to our knowledge, no-one has yet fully explored its consequences for the theory and policy of development. Needless to say, we are dramatizing the differences. After all, learning is intertwined with the process of resource allocation. Still, it is useful to distinguish between what is assumed as having first order or second order effects.

All this has also an empirical counterpart: indeed, the economic discipline has undertaken far too few exercises at the highest available disaggregation on international comparisons among sectoral technical coefficients. Our conjecture is that, at this level, one could observe a good deal of evidence conflicting with the standard theory of production: less developed countries may well show higher utilization of all or most inputs per unit of output and perhaps even higher relative intensity of those inputs that the theory would consider more scarce (that is, some loose equivalent of what euphemistically the economic profession calls in international trade the Leontieff paradox). Conversely, an evolutionary interpretation is straightforward: unequivocal technological gaps account for generalized differences in input efficiencies. Moreover, if technical progress happens to involve also high rates of saving in physical capital and skilled-labour inputs, one may also observe less developed countries which do not only use more capital per unit of output but also more capital per unit of labour input as compared to technological leaders (Figure 1 illustrates a similar case: compare for example, techniques c'_3 and c_n).

Some important implications emerge from this approach.

First, the theory would predict persistent asymmetries among countries in the production processes which they are able to master (this of course also shows up in terms of different inputs effficiencies: see Dosi, Pavitt and Soete 1990). Thus, at any point in time, one can draw two major testable conjectures: (i) different countries might well be unequivocally ranked according to the efficiencies of their average techniques of production and, in the product space, of the (price-weighted) performance characteristics of their outputs, irrespectively of relative prices, and (ii) the absence of any significant relationship between these gaps and international differences in the capital/output ratios. Wide differences apply also to the capabilities of developing new products and to different time lags in producing them after they have been introduced into the world economy. Indeed, the international distribution of innovative capabilities regarding new products is at least as uneven as that regarding production processes. For example if one takes international patents or the number discrete innovation as a proxy for innovativeness, the evidence suggest that the club of the innovators has been restricted over the whole past century to a dozen developed countries with only one major new entry, Japan (more on the evidence in Dosi, Pavitt and Soete 1990).

Second, the process of development and industrialization are strictly linked to the inter- and intra-national diffusion of "superior" techniques. Relatedly, as already mentioned, at any point in time, there is likely to be only one or, at most, very few "best practice" techniques of production which correspond to the technological frontier. In the case of developing economies, the process of industrialization is thus closely linked with the borrowing, imitation, adaptation of established technologies from more advanced economies. These process of adoption and adaptation of technologies, in turn, are influenced by the specific capabilities of each economy.[6]

In this context, we suggest that evolutionary micro-theories are well apt to account for the processes by which technological gaps and national institutional diversities can jointly reproduce themselves over rather long spans of time. Conversely, in other circumstances, it might be precisely this institutional and technological diversity among countries which may foster catching-up (and, rarely leapfrogging) in innovative capabilities and the per capita incomes. Rigorous demonstrations of these propositions would indeed require many intermediate steps, linking the externalities and positive feedback mechanisms based on technological learning with the institutional context in which microeconomic agents are embedded, and also the economic signals they face. We shall briefly come back to this issue later on. Here let us just emphasize that systematically different rates of learning may have very little to do with "how well markets work". Rather, the incentives and opportunities which agents perceive in a particular context are themselves the result of particular histories of technologies and institutions.

The importance of the institutional dimension for evolutionary theories of production and innovation should come as no surprise, supported by a growing evidence from both micro and macro patterns of technological change. After all, at the micro level, technologies are to a fair extent incorporated in particular institutions, the firms, whose characteristics, decision rules, capabilities, and behaviors are fundamental in shaping the rates and directions of technological advance. In turn,

---

[6] Abramovitz notion of differentiated "social capabilities" is quite consistent with this view, Abramovitz (1989).

firms are embedded in rich networks of relations with each other and with other institutional actors – ranging from government agencies to universities etc...[7]

But how did particular technologies come into exist existence in the first place? Let us turn to this question.

Economic and social factors in the emergence of new paradigms

It is useful to separate the genesis of new paradigms from the processes leading to the dominance of some of them. Let us first consider the emergence of new potential paradigms; that is, the generation of notional opportunities of radical innovation involving new knowledge bases, new search heuristics, new dominant designs.

In the literature one find quite different interpretative archetypes. A first class of models entails a lot of "techno-scientific determinism": advancements in pure science determine advancements in technological opportunities which in turn determine realized technological achievements. In fact, in order to find the most naive literature along these lines one should mostly search in the archives of defunct socialist countries. There, one is likely to find plenty of examples of Engels-type vulgata on the simplest linear models from science to technology to production.

The interpretation that students of economics find in textbook production is more sophisticated although basically of the same type. It maintains the basic linear sequence from science to technological opportunities to production but it claims that science only generates those notional blueprints discussed earlier, while some optimizing microeconomic algorithm selects among them. Proper economic analysis begins indeed by stating some daring assumptions on the nature of such blueprints which maintain in principle an empirical nature albeit little empirical micro support (e.g. on continuity, convexity, etc.). From then onward, production theory is generally presented as an application of methods of constrained maximization which intends to capture the purposed behavior of the *homo economicus* facing alternative allocative choices, and most often, also the aggregate properties of industries or whole economies.

Yet more sophisticated recent modelling on new-growth, new-trade theories, while attempting to endogenize the generation of blueprints themselves, push further upstream that same notional process of optimizing allocation involving some sort of production function for the blueprints themselves. This is not the place to discuss the (rather important) achievements and the (equally important) limitations of such theories. What we simply want to emphasize is the persistence across ample streams of micro and macro literature of two basic ideas: first, the linear representation of the innovative process, running from science to technology to production; and second, the focus upon an explicit deliberation, equivalent in every respect to an allocative choice, by supposedly rational agents.

---

[7] In this co-evolutionary perspective on technologies, corporate organizations and institutions (Nelson 1994), it is straightforward to acknowledge also a bi-directional relation between market structures (as proxied by measures on the distribution of different characteristics such as firm sizes, innovative competences, ownership, persistent behavioral traits, etc.) and patterns of technological learning. Different rates of learning influence the ability of firms to survive and expand and thus affect industrial structures. Conversely any particular structure – with its associated distribution of corporate features – influences and constrains what and how fast firms are able and willing to learn. Formal applications of this general idea are in Nelson and Winter (1982), Winter (1984), Dosi, Marsili, Orsenigo and Salvatore (1993).

However, as Chris Freeman, Nathan Rosenberg, and others have convincingly shown, historical evidence rules out the general applicability of linear models of innovation. One can find plenty of counter examples. First, the lag between scientific advancements and their technological application can vary between a few months (as in case of the transistor) to centuries. Second, technological innovation may actually precede the scientific discovery of the general principle on which those very technologies work (as in the case of electric lamps). Third, scientific advancements may actually be based on the invention of new machinery and not the other way round (think of the importance of the electronic microscopes for the subsequent scientific discoveries in biology).[8]

As regards the behavioral foundations of innovative decisions, we are quite skeptical about their reduction to deliberate allocative choices. As emphasized not only by evolutionary economists by also by rational choice theorists like K. Arrow, almost by definition innovation concerns the generation of something new and at least partly unexpected. Relatedly, the genesis of exploratory ventures into novel paradigms is more the domain of institutional and organizational inquiries on the conditions fastering entrepreneurial activities rather than rational choice models.[9]

Indeed, there are good reasons to believe that one will not be able to find anything like a general theory of the emergence of new technological paradigms. However, what might be possible is a) an analysis of the necessary condition for such emergence; b) historical taxonomies and also appreciative models of the processes by which it occurs; and c) taxonomies and models of the processes of competition amongst different paradigms and their diffusion.

Regarding the first heading, one is like to find that the existence of some unexploited technological opportunities, together with the relevant knowledge base and some minimum appropriability conditions, define only the boundaries of the set of potential new paradigms: those which are actually explored within this set might crucially depend on particular organizational and social dynamics. So for example, there is good evidence that the micro e lectronics paradigm as we know it (silicon-based, etc) was shaped in its early stages by military requirements (Dosi 1984, Misa 1985). David Noble argues that the NC machine-tool paradigm – although he does not use that expression – has been influenced by power considerations regarding labour management (Noble 1984). In the history of technology one finds several examples of this kind. The general point is that various institutions (ranging from incumbent firms to government agencies), social groups and also individual agents (including, of course, individual innovators and entrepreneurs) perform as *ex ante* selectors of the avenues of research that are pursued, the techno-economic dimensions upon which research ought to focus, the knowledge base one calls upon. Thus, they ultimately select the new paradigms that are actually explored.

---

[8] See Rosenberg (1991)

[9] Of course this is not to say that the economic variables governing the incentives and penalties to entrepreneurial endeavours are irrelevant. The point is that the former tend to set only some lose incentive-compatibility constraints. Given these constraint, explanations of willingness of incumbent firms to explore new paradigms, of the rate of the birth of new start-up firms, etc. requires a much more detailed understanding of specific corporate and institutional histories. Working backward from observed outcomes to some rational expectations model does not do the trick: on the contrary, there is evidence that in many new industries, had entrants rational expectations of their future profit streams, entry would not have occurred at all! (this seems to emerge also from a research, in progress. by Don Lovallo and Giovanni Dosi).

There is a much more general theoretical story regarding the development, diffusion and competition among those (possible alternative) paradigms that are actually explored. It can be told via explicit evolutionary models (as in Nelson and Winter 1982 or in Silverberg, Dosi and Orsenigo 1988), via path-dependent stochastic models (as in Arthur 1988, Arthur, Ermoliev and Kaniovski 1987, Dosi and Kaniovski 1994 and David 1989), and also via sociological models of network development (as in Callon 1991). The basic ingredients of the story are i) some forms of dynamics increasing returns (for example in learning); ii) positive externalities in the production or the use of the technology; iii) endogenous expectation formation; iv) some market dynamics which selects ex post amongst products, and indirectly amongst technologies and firms; v) the progressive development of standards and relatively inertial institutions which embody and reproduce particular forms of knowledge and also the behavioral norms and the incentives to do so.

3. Learning and trajectories in the process of development

*Techno-ecnomic paradigms or regimes: from micro technologies
to national system of innovation*

So far, we have discussed paradigms, trajectories or equivalent concepts at a micro-technological level. A paradigm-based theory of innovation and production – we have argued – seems to be highly consistent with the evidence on the patterned and cumulative nature of technical change and also with the evidence on microeconomic heterogeneity and technological gaps. Moreover, it directly links with those theories of production which allow for dynamic increasing returns from A. Young and Kaldor to the recent and more rigorous formalizations of path-dependent models of innovation diffusion, whereby the interaction between micro decisions and some form of learning or some externalities produces irreversible technological paths and lock-in effects with respect to technologies which may well be inferior, on any welfare measure, to other notional ones, but still happen to be dominant – loosely speaking – because of the weight of their history (cf. the models by B. Arthur and P. David). However, paradigms are generally embodied in larger technological systems and in even bigger economic-wide systems of production and innovation.

The steps leading from a microeconomic theory of innovation and production to more aggregate analyses are clearly numerous and complex. A first obvious question concern the possibility of identifying relative coherence and structures also at these broader levels of observation. Indeed, historians of technology – T. Hughes, B. Gilles and P. David, among others – highlight the importance of technological systems, that is in the terminology of this paper, structured combinations of micro technological paradigms (see for example, the fascinating reconstructions of the emerging system of electrification and electrical standards in David 1992).

At an even higher level of generality, Freeman and Perez (1988) have suggested the notion of techno-economic paradigms as a synthetic definition of macro-level systems of production, innovation, governance of social relations. So, for example, they identify broad phases of modern industrial development partly isomorphic to the notion of "regimes of socio-economic Regulation" suggested by the mainly French macro institutionalists literature (see Aglietta 1976, Boyer 1988a and b).

In an extreme synthesis, both prospectives hold, first, that one can identify rather long periods of capitalist development distinguished according to their specific engines of technological dynamism and their modes of governance of the relationships amongst the major social actors (e.g. firms, workers, banks, collective political authorities etc), and, second, that the patterns of technological advancement and those of institutional change are bound to be coupled in such ways as to yield recognizable invariances for quite long times in most economic and political structures. Just to provide an example, one might roughly identify, over the three decades after WW II, across most developed economies, some "Fordist/Keynesian" regime of socio-economic "Regulation", driven by major innovative opportunities of technological innovation in electromechanic technologies, synthetic chemistry and relatively cheap exploitation of energy sources, and reproduced by some specific forms of institutional governance of industrial conflict, income distribution and aggregate demand management. Analogously, earlier in industrial history, one should be able to detect some sort of archetype of a "classical/Victorian Regime" driven in its growth by the full exploitation of textile manufacturing and light engineering mechanization, relatively competitive labour markets, politically driven efforts to expand privileged market outlets, etc. .

These general conjectures on historical phases or regimes are grounded on the importance in growth and development of specific combinations among technological systems and forms of socio-economic governance. The approach can be applied also to the analysis of the differences and similarities of development patterns in the late-industrializing countries. One has focused for example on the interplay between the modes of governance of the labour market and the pattern of technical accumulation, showing how the specificities in labour market institutions originate virtuous or vicious circles of development in different historical periods.[10]

As an intermediate step toward the identification of national socio-economic regimes let us consider the anatomy and development of particular systems of innovation and production at national level, embodying distinctive mechanisms and directions of learning, and grounded in the micro theory of production and innovation sketched above.

Even if micro paradigms present considerable invariances across countries, the ways various paradigms are combined in broader technological systems and, more so, in national systems of production and innovation highlight – we suggest – a considerable variety, shaped by country-specific institutions, policies and social factors. The hypothesis here is that evolutionary microfoundations are a fruitful starting point for a theory showing how technological gaps and national institutional diversities can jointly reproduce themselves over rather long spans of time in ways that are easily compatible with the patterns of incentives and opportunities facing individual agents, even when they turn out to be profoundly suboptimal from a collective point of view.

In order to detail this hypothesis, however, one requires to analysis of the composing elements and properties of these national systems which in the recent literature have been referred to with a variety of largely overlapping concepts, such as global technological capability of each country, national innovation systems, national technological capabilities and national systems of production.[11]

In our view, the major building blocks in an evolutionary account of the specificities of national systems of production and innovation are following.

---

[10] See Aboites (1988) Boyer (1993), Cetrangolo (1988a), (1988b), Cimoli (1988), (1990), Coriat and Saboia (1987).
[11] See Cimoli and Dosi (1988), (1990), Chesnais (1993), Ernest and O'Connor (1989), Lall (1984), (1987), (1992), Lundvall (1992), Nelson (1993), Zysman (1994).

First, there is the idea that firms are a crucial (although not exclusive) repositories of knowledge, to a large extent embodied in their operational routines, and modified through time by their higher level rules of behaviors and strategies (such as their search behaviors and their decisions concerning vertical integration and horizontal diversification, etc.).

Second, firms themselves are nested in networks of linkages with other firms and also with other non-profit organizations (such as public agencies etc.). These networks, or lack of them, enhance or limit the opportunities facing each firm to improve their problem-solving capabilities.

Third, national systems entail also a broader notion of embeddedness of microeconomic behaviors into a set of social relationships, rules and political constraints (Granovetter 1985). Even at a properly micro level, the momentum associated with single technological trajectories is itself a largely social concept: "it points... to the organizations and people committed by various interests to the system, to manufacturing corporations, research and development laboratories, investment banking houses, educational institutions and regulatory bodies" (Misa 1991: p. 15). And, in turn, these interests and institutions are sustained by the increasing-return and local nature of most learning activities. Even more so, at a system-level, the evolutionary interpretation presented here is consistent and indeed complementary with institutional approaches building on the observation that markets do not exist or operate apart from the rules and institutions that establish them and that "the institutional structure of the economy creates a distinct pattern of constraints and incentives", which defines the interests of the actors as well as shaping and channeling their behaviours (Zysman 1994: pp. 1–2).[12]

Paradigms, routines, organizations

A locus classicus in the analysis of the profound intertwining between technological learning and organizational change is certainly Alfred Chandler's reconstruction of the origins of the modern multi-divisional (the M-form) corporation and its ensuing effects on the American competitive leadership over several decades (Chandler (1990), (1992a) and (1993)). And, as Chandler himself has recently argued, there are strict links between story and evolutionary theories (Chandler (1992b). While it is not possible to enter into the richness of the Chandlerian analysis here, let us just recall one of the main messages:

> [...] it was the institutionalizing of the learning involved in product and process development that gave established managerial firms advantages over start-ups in the commercialization of technological innovations. Development remained a simple process involving a wide variety of usually highly product-specific skills, experience and information. It required a close interaction between functional specialists, such as designers, engineers, production managers, marketers and managers [...]. Such individuals had to coordinate their activities, particularly during the scale-up processes and the initial introduction of the new products on the market [...]. Existing firms with established core lines had retained earnings as a source of inexpensive capital and often had specialized organizational and technical competence not available to new entrepreneurial firms (Chandler 1993: p. 37).

---

[12] Note incidentally that the second building block – i.e. networks, etc. – in so far as it is equivalent to an externality or to some economy-wide mechanism for the generation of knowledge, is also captured in a highly simplified form by the new growth theories. (More on the general spirit of the latter in Romer 1994a and b). Conversely the first and third are distinctive of evolutionary/institutionalist analyses. These represent also a major point linkage between evolutionary theories, organizational economics and business history.

As thoroughly argued by Chandler himself, this organizational dynamics can be interpreted as an evolutionary story of competence accumulation and development of specific organizational routines (Chandler (1992b)).

Did seemingly superior organizational forms spread evenly throughout the world?

Indeed, the Chandlerian enterprise diffused, albeit rather slowing, in other OECD countries (Chandler 1990, Kogut 1992). However, the development of organizational forms, strategies and control methods have differed from nation to nation, because of the difference between national environments (Chandler 1992a: p. 283). Moreover, the diffusion of the archetypical M-form corporation has been limited to around half a dozen already developed countries (and even in countries like Italy, it involved very few companies, if any). Similar differences can be found in the processes of international diffusion of American principles of work organization – e.g. Taylorism and Fordism – (for an analysis of the Japanese case, see Coriat 1990). For the purposes of this work, it is precisely these differences and the diverse learning patterns which they entail that constitute our primary interest.

So, for example, a growing literature identifies some of the roots of the specificities of the German, the Japanese or the Italian systems of production into their early corporate histories which carried over their influence up to the contemporary form of organization and learning (see Chandler 1990, Coriat 1990, Kogut 1993, Dursleifer and Kocka 1993, Dosi, Giannetti and Toninelli 1992).

Even more so, one observes quite different organizational initial conditions, different organizational histories, and together, different patterns of learning across developing countries. Let us consider them at some detail.

During the last three decades, developing countries have shown increased technological dynamics associated with a subsequent development of their industrial structures, thus some significant technological progress did indeed occur in the NIEs and some of them also became exporters of technology.[13]

The evolutionary path of technological learning are related to both the capacity to acquire technologies (capital goods, know how etc) and the capability to absorb these technologies and adopt them to the local conditions. In these respects, one has now a good deal of microeconomic/micro technological evidence highlighting the mechanisms which stimulate and limit endogenous learning in the NIEs.[14]

Without doing any justice to the richness of these contributions, they seem to suggest the existence of some characteristics in the paths of technological learning at the firm level (see also Cimoli 1990 and Cimoli and Dosi 1988). In particular, one might be able to identify some relatively invariant sequences in the learning processes, conditional on the initial organizational characteristics of the firms and the sectors of principal activity.

A first set of regularities regards the varying combinations between acquisition of outside technologies and endogenous learning.[15] As well know, the transfer of technology to developing economies is a common source for the subsequent

---

[13] See Lall (1982), Teitel (1984) and Teubal (1984).

[14] See, among others, Bell (1982), Dahlman-Westphal (1982), Hobday (1984), Herbert-Copley (1990), Justman-Teubal (1991), Katz (1983), (1984a), (1984b), (1986) and (1987), Teubal (1987), Pack and Westphal (1986).

[15] The technology flows to developing economies show a rapid expansion in the 1960s and 1970s; during the 1980s this process decreased its intensity (UNCTAD 1991). During the whole period the Asian countries show an increasing role as the major recipient of foreign direct investment and capital goods. The flow of capital goods to Latin American countries remain stable during this period.

development of learning capabilities at the firm and sectoral levels. Possibly with too extreme an emphasis, Amsden and Hikino identify the ability to acquire foreign technology as a central characteristic,

> [...] of late industrialization at the core of which is borrowing technology that has already been developed by firms in more advanced countries. Whereas a driving force behind the First and Second Industrial Revolutions was the innovation of radically new products and processes, no major technological breakthrough has been associated with late-industrializing economies. The imperative to learn from others, and then realize lower costs, higher productivity, and better quality in mid-tech industries by means of incremental improvements, has given otherwise diverse 20th century industrializers a common set of properties (Amsden and Hikino 1993: p. 37).[16]

At a general level, learning patterns can be taxonomized according to the relative importance of the corporate activities involved,[17] namely a) the acquisition of an existing technology associated with the paradigm prevailing in the developed world, b) its adaptation and modification in the local environment and c) the creation of new innovation capabilities with respect to products and processes.

The importance of the three often follows a temporal sequence. Already the modification of the adopted technology implies learning of new production skills which grows through the adaptation of this capabilities to local specificities. Note, however, that there is no inevitability in the learning-by-doing process which, on the contrary, requires adequate organization conditions, both within each firm and each environment. Interestingly, the initial characteristics of corporate organizations appear to exert a strong influence on subsequent dynamics. For example, evidence on the last four decades (1950–1990) concerning Latin American countries (Argentina, Brazil, Colombia, Mexico and Venezuela) indicate that the evolutionary sequence of organizational and technological learning can be distinguished among four types of firms, taxonomized mainly in terms of the nature of ownership: subsidiaries of MNCs, family firms, large domestic firms and public firms.[18]

The family firm appears to be characterized by a high "propensity to self-sufficiency and self-financing" and the "mechanical ability of an individual", which frequently stems from immigrant entrepreneurs.[19] The technology acquired is related to the technical background of the entrepreneur and the initial phase is characterized by the adoption of a discontinuous mode of production.[20] At the

---

[16] Although we share their view on the curent importance of technological assimilation of outside technologies, one should not underestimate the degree to which this occured also in the past experiences of late-coming industrialization and catching-up, for example in the case of the USA or Continental Europe vis-a-vis Britain.

[17] On a similar point Teitel (1987).

[18] Information on the different phases ofthe technological accumulation of firms has been taken from the case studies of the IDB, ECLA and UNDP programmes and from the overviews of the research findings in Katz (1983), (1984a), (1984b), (1986) and (1987), Berlinski, Nosier, Sandoval and Turkieh (1982), Teitel (1984) and (1987), Teubal (1987).

[19] See Katz (1983).

[20] Two alternative modes of production namely, *continuous* and *discontinuous*, appear to be relevant for the analysis of learning patterns. Continuous methods imply 1) specialization of production along precise product lines; 2) production planning for each line of business; 3) relatively high scale economies; 4) relatively low flexibility in product design and rates of throughput. Conversely, discontinuous methods involve 1) low standardization of production; 2) low economies of scale; 3) the organization of production into multi-product "shops"; 4) general purpose, low cost machinery. It is remarkable that in many Latin American examples, (but not in Far Eastern ones) at least until the 1980s, incremental learning appeared to be more successful in discontinuous batch-production as compared to continuous and mass-production activities (such as chemicals, many consumer durables, etc.).

beginning, production is characterized by low economies of scale (also as a consequence of the limitations of the domestic market and the difficulties in exploiting
export possibilities).

A sort of ideal learning trajectory for a South American family-stablised firm
that is technologically progressive (which is not by any means a general characteristic of the whole population) would run more or less as follows. First, the effort is
concentrated on product design activities (most likely due to the incentive provided
in the past by import substitution policies), and increasingly, on quality improvements and product differentiation.

Next, attention is focused also on process engineering, the organization of
production and the exploitation of some economies of scale, until (in some empirically not too frequent cases) highly mechanized production is achieved. And, along
the process, it might happen (again, not too often) that the organization is developed
beyond the original family hierarchy and "managerialized".

The story concerning subsidiaries of foreign firms emerges from the set of cases
studies cited earlier is quite different. The bulk of competences and technologies
derives from the parent company and learning mainly concern the adaptation to the
local environment, adjustments in product mixes and re-scaling of production lines.
In some cases, this holds throughout the history of the subsidiary, while in others an
autonomous capability in product and process design is developed. (Note also that
in Latin American foreign subsidiaries tend to be concentrated in mass production
activities like vehicles, consumer durables, food processing, etc.).

State-owned firms display yet another archetypical learning story. First, they
have been concentrated in sectors that have tended to be considered "strategic" and
often happened to be continuous process industries such as bulk materials, steel,
basic petrochemicals, in addition – in some countries – to aerospace and military
production. Second, the strategies have generally be dictated also by political
considerations. Third, learning has often started via agreements with international
suppliers of equipment. In the "healthy" scenario – which is not the rule – international technology transfer agreement became more sophisticated, involving
adaptation of plants and technologies to local circumstances, while the emphasis
was kept on personnel training and learning by using. Finally, autonomous
capabilities of plant upgrading and process engineering were sometimes developed.

As regards large domestic firms, it is hard to trace any modal patterns. Scanning
through the case studies, they sometime appear to follow patterns not too different
from the family firms, in other cases they seem to perform like East Asian business
groups (see below), and yet in others learning appears to be much more directed
toward he exploitation of political rents and financial opportunities rather than
technological accumulation.

It is interesting to compare these sketchy Latin American "corporate trajectories" with other experiences, such as the Korean one.[21] To make a long and
variegated story very short, in Korea it seems that the major actors in technological
learning have been large business groups – *the chaebols* – which have been able at
a very early stage of development to internalize the skills for the selection among
technologies acquired from abroad, their efficient use and adaptation, and, not
much later, have been able to grow impressive engineering capabilities.

---

[21] As discussed at greater depth in Amsden (1989), Amseden and Hikino (1993 and 1994), Enos and
Park (1988), Bell and Pavitt (1993), Lall (1992), Kim, Westphal and Dahlman (1985).

Conversely, the Taiwanese organizational learning has rested much more in large networks of small and medium firms very open to the international markets and often developing production capabilities which complement those of first world companies (Dahlman and Sananikone 1990, Ernest and O'Connor 1989).

This impressionistic list of stylized organizational patterns of learning could be of course very lengthy. For our purposes, it should be understood only as an illustration of the multiplicity of evolutionary paths that organizational learning can take. The fundamental point here is that the rates and directions of learning are not at all independent from the ways corporate organizations emerge, change, develop particular problem-solving, capabilities, diversify, etc. It is the core co-evolutionary view emphasized by Nelson (1994).

The analysis in term of paradigms, trajectories, technological asymmetries, etc. outlined in the first part of this paper is the most abstract level of description of production pattern and technical change, whereby the "primitives" of the analysis itself are entities like "bits of knowledge" and the outcomes of their implementation in the spaces of production process and output characteristics. However, knowledge is to a large extent embodied, reproduced and augmented within specific organizations. Thus, a lot of the action is reflected in the behaviours, evolution and learning of these organizations – in primis, business firms. At this level, evolutionary analyses match and cross-fertilize with investigations on organizational dynamics, industrial demography and business history.

Inter-sectoral networks and production capacity

Of course the multiple business histories of learning and organizational change (or lack of them) in each country, as mentioned earlier, is nested into flows of commodities and knowledge across different sectors and different institutional actors. At this level, can one identify some broad regularities in the processes of system-construction.

It is useful to maintain the distinction emphasized by Bell and Pavitt (1993) (which indeed bears some Listian flavour!) between the development of a "production capacity" and of "technological capabilities". Production capacity concerns the stocks of resources, the nature of capital-embodied technologies, labour skills, product and input specification and the organizational routines in use. Technological capabilities rest on the knowledge and resources requested for the generation and management of technical change.

These seem to be some patterns, albeit rather loose, in the development of a national production capacity. For example, practically every country starts with manufacturing of clothing and textile, possibly natural resource processing, and moves on – if it does – to more complex and knowledge intensive activities. However, the tricky question is whether there are some activities which hold a special status in the construction of a national system of production and innovation, also due to the property that having a production capacity in them makes it easier, other things being equal, to develop technological capabilities. The conjecture is quite old (and goes back at least to List, Ferrier and Hamilton) and is present in contemporary notions such those of fili re or Dahmen's "development blocks", but it might gain strength on the grounds of the evolutionary microeconomics outlined above.[22]

---

[22] Classic contributions of the importance of intersectoral linkages are Dahmen (1971) and Hirschman (1992).

Whenever one abandons a view of development exclusively shaped by endowments, the degrees of perfection of market signals, and the like, but focuses on the conditions for technological/organizational learning, then it also becomes easier to appreciate the diversity of the sources in learning opportunities and their different economic potentials.

In fact, there is a good circumstantial evidence from contemporary as well as previous late-industrializing countries (such as, in their days, the USA, Germany, the Scandinavian countries, Japan, etc.). Suggesting that there are technologies whose domains of application are so wide and their role has been so crucial that the pattern of technical change of each country depends to a large degree on the national capabilities in mastering production/imitation/innovation in a set of crucial knowledge areas (e.g. in the past, mechanical engineering, electricity and electrical devices, and nowadays, also information technologies). Moreover, the linkages among production activities embody structured hierarchies whereby the most dynamic technological paradigms play a fundamental role as sources of technological skills, problem-solving opportunities and productivity improvements.[23] Thus, these core technologies shape the overall absolute advantages/disadvantages of each country. In other words, the pattern of technical change of each country in these technologies does not average out with the technological capabilities in other activities but are complementary to them. These core technologies often also imply basic infrastructures and networks common to a wide range of activities (such as, for example, the electricity grid, the road system, telecommunications and more recently the information network). Many pieces of empirical evidence strongly convey the idea that a proper technological dynamism in developing countries is impossible without major structural changes and a sequential construction of a widening manufacturing sector involving also indigenous skills in a set of "core" technologies.

We do not at all suggest that there is any invariant sequence of industrial sectors which account for the upgrading of national technological capabilities.[24] However, one might still be able to identify some rough sequences in the predominant modes of technological learning. In this respect, the taxonomy of the sectoral patterns of acquisition of innovative knowledge suggested by Pavitt (1984) is a good – albeit somewhat theoretically fuzzy – point of departure. As known, Pavitt distinguishes four groups of industrial sectors, namely (i) *supplier dominated* – where innovations mainly enter as exogenously generated changes in capital and intermediate good, and where learning is primarily associated with adoption and production skills; (ii) *specialized suppliers* – providing equipment and instruments to the industrial system, and relying in their innovative activities on both formal (more or less scientific) knowledge and more tacit one based also on the user-producer relationships; (iii) *scale-intensive sectors* – whose innovative abilities draw, jointly, on the development adoption of innovative equipment, on the design of complex products, on the exploitation of some scale economies, and on the ability of mastering complex organizations; (iv) *science-based sectors* – whose innovative opportunities link more directly with advances in basic research.

---

[23] See Rosenberg (1976), and, for contemporary late comers, Chudnovsky, Nagao and Jacobsson (1984) and Fransman (1986).

[24] Indeed, any detailed comparison of the sectoral composition of output of e.g. USA, Germany, Japan, France, Italy between 1850 and 1950, or Korea, Brazil, Taiwan, and Singapore between 1950 and 1990 – we conjecture – would show enough dispersion.

The important issue here is whether one may use that taxonomy in order to detect some patterns over the development process. The emergence of manufacturing sector is generally characterized by an initial stage where supplier-dominated sectors dominate accompanied by the emergence of specialized suppliers. The process of technical change in these sectors is characterized by a sequential development of various forms of tacit and incremental learning related to the transfer and acquisition of foreign technology. These learning activities are mainly related to the use of equipment, development of engineering skills in machine-transformation, adaptation of existing machines and final products to specific environmental conditions.

The emergence of "scale-intensive" industries entails further forms of learning related to the development and use of capital equipment. Moreover, unlike the supplier-dominated sectors, technological efforts are also focused on (i) the development of technological synergies between production and use of innovations, often internalized via horizontal and vertical integration; (ii) the exploitation of static and dynamic economies of scale; (iii) the establishment of formal institutions undertaking search (typically, corporate R&D laboratories), and complementary to informal learning and diffusion of technological knowledge.

Sectoral learning patterns are clearly nested into broader ("macro") conditions such as those defining the educational system. For example, in "supplier-dominated" and "specialized supplier" sectors, a significant role is played by the levels of literacy and skills of the workforce, and the skills and technical competence of engineers and designers in the mechanical and (increasingly) electronics fields. In scale-intensive sectors, the existence of managers capable of efficiently running complex organizations is also likely be important. In science based sectors, the quality of higher education and research capabilities is obviously relevant.

Moreover, sectoral learning patterns and overall national capabilities are dynamically coupled via input-output flows, knowledge-spillovers, complementarities and context-specific externalities.[25] Together, they contribute to shape the organizational and technological context within which each economic activity takes place. In a sense, they set the opportunities and constraints facing each individual process of production and innovation – including the availability of complementary skills, information on intermediate inputs and capital goods, and demand stimuli to improve particular products.

This links straightforwardly with the analyses focusing on structural change and development (here within a vast literature, contributions that come immediately to mind range from Hirschman to Rosenstein Rodan, Gerschenkron, Prebisch – notwithstanding his sometimes extremist interpretations -, Lowe, Kuznets, Chenery, Sirquin among others). Certanly, the dynamics of development also rest upon major structural transformations which entail a changing importance of different branches of economic activity as generators of both technological/organizational innovations and demand impulses. So, for example, in this interpretative framework, it does not sound so outragions to conjecture that the "quality" (in terms of

---

[25] An obvious question concerns the unit of analysis to which these externalities and system effect apply. Why shouldn't international trade compensate for spatially circumscribed specificities? What is unique of a nation distinguishing it from a geographical region, or a firm, or a group of individuals? Far from any intent to reduce the importance of other levels of description (e.g. regional dynamics), we maintain that nations are also specified by particular modes of institutional governance which extent make them diverse auto-reproducing entities.

technological opportunities and demand elasticities) of any one structure of production and export is bound to influence the relative ability of a country to absorve its labour supply, meet its foreign balance constraints, grow in its per capita income… At this level of analysis, one empirically finds, for example, that Latin American countries have increasingly biased their structure of production, in the 1980s, in favour of resource-based sectors, while East Asian NICs have move toward scale-intensive and science-base sectors. Obviously, in some ideal General Equilibrium world, all this is just an irrelevant epiphenomenon. Conversely, under the micro-foundation sketched above, there might be reasons to worry (even if naive technologically deterministic conclusions should be obviously discussed). Indeed, some fundamental trade-off between "static allocative efficiency" and "dynamic efficiency" of any one pattern of production might plausibly emerge (more on all this in Dosi, Pavitt and Soete 1990 and Dosi, Tyson and Zysman 1989).

Moreover, the specificities of each system of production interact with those of each national system of innovation – as throughly analyzed in Nelson (1993) – and tend to yield recognizeable national patterns or trajectories shaped by the institutions supporting technical advances and reproduced through time also by processes of lock-in into particular knowledge bases, corporate organizations and sectoral specialization.

4. From micro technological paradigms to national systems of production and innovation: some tentative conclusions and many research avenues

The third major element, mentioned earlier linking microeconomic learning with national patterns of development was the embeddedness of the thread of incentives, constraints, forms of corporate organization into the broader institutional framework of the political economy of each country. It is beyond the scope of this paper to discuss that issue at any satisfactory detail. For our purposes, let us just mention that the micro- and meso-economic theoretical building blocks sketched above and drawn from an evolutionary perspective are in principle consistent with broader institutionalist analyses of national systems of production, innovation and governance of socio-economic relations. Indeed, one can see multiple links which one is only beginning to explore. For example, an evolutionary perspective is quite at ease with the idea that markets are themselves "social constructs" which – depending on their rules and organizing principles – shape microbehaviours and adjustment mechanisms. The emphasis on patterned and local learning, and bounded rationaly assumptions, go well together with the view of political economists and sociologists of development according to which a major ingredient of development is the process of change in social norms, expectations and forms of collective organization. The patterns of *socio-economic Regulation* (Boyer 1988a and 1988b) can be in principle microfounded into underlying evolutionary processes of self-organization, learning and selection. In fact, there seem to be a large domain where more "bottom-up" evolutionary theories and more "top-down" institutional analyses can develop a fruitful dialogue.

Notions like those of technological trajectories, path-dependencies, organizational competences, self-organization, learning and selection dynamics – and many others stemming from evolutionary investigations – are becoming part of the tool-kit of many social disciplines. As regards more specifically development issue, they start becoming building blocks which might provide firmer grounds to the broad intuitions of an earlier generation of development theorists – from Myrdal to Hirschman, from Rosenstein-Rodan to Gerschenkron... In this respect our *tour de force* from technological paradigms to national systems should just be considered as a tentative roadmap over still largely unexplored terrains.

References

Aboites J (1988) Regimen de acumulacion, relacion salarial y crisis en mexico. Paper presented at the Conference on the Theory of Regulation, Barcelona, June 1988

Abramovitz M (1989) Thinking about growth, Cambridge University Press, Cambridge

Aglietta M (1976) Regulation et crises du capitalisme. Calmann-Levy, Paris

Amsden A (1989) Asia's next giant: South Korea and the last industrialization. Oxford University Press, New York and Oxford

Amsden A, Hikino T (1993) Staying behind, stumbling back, sneaking up, soaring ahead: late industrialization in historical perspective. In: Baumol W, Nelson R, Wolff E (eds) International convergence of productivity with some evidence from history. Oxford University Press, Oxford

Amsden A, Hikino T (1994) Project execution capability, organizational know-how, and conglomerate corporate growth in late industrialization. Industr Corp Change 3, 111–147

Arthur B (1988) Competing technologies. In: Dosi G, Freeman C, Nelson R, Soete L (eds) Technical change and economic theory. Frances Pinter, London

Arthur B, Ermoliev Y, Kaniovski Y (1987) Path dependent proccesses and the emergence of macro structure. Eur J Operat Res 30: 294–303

Bell M (1982) Technical change in infant industry: a review of empirical evidences. SPRU, Sussex, mimeo

Bell M, Pavitt (1993) Technological accumulation and industrial growth: contrasts between developed and developing countries. Industrial and Corporate change, 2, 157–210

Berlinski J, Nogueira da Cruz H, Sandoval D, Turkieh M (1982) Basic issues emerging from recent research on technological behavior of selected Latin American metalworking plants. CEPAL Working Paper n. 56

Boyer R (1988a) Technical change and the theory of regulation. In: Dosi et al. (1988)

Boyer R (1988b) Formalizing growth regimes within a regulation approach. In: Dosi et al (1988)

Boyer R (1993) Do labour institutions matter for economic development? Paper presented at the Workshop on Labour Institutions and Economic Development in Asia, Bali, February 4–6, 1992

Callon M (1991) Technological development and adoption networks. Conference on Constructive Technology Assessment, Twente, The Netherlands, 1991

Cetrangolo O (1988a) Import substitution and industrialization policy in Argentina under Peron. IDS, Sussex, mimeo

Cetrangolo O (1988b) State and industrial development in Argentina. MPHIL thesis, IDS, Sussex

Chandler AD (1990) Scale and scope: the dynamics of industrial capitalism. Hardvard University Press, Cambridge, Mass

Chandler AD (1992a) Corporate strategy, structure and control methods in the United States during the 20th century. Industr Corp Change 1: 263–284

Chandler AD (1992b) Organizational capabilities and the economic history of the industrial enterprise. J Econ Perspect 6: 79–100

Chandler AD (1992) Learning and technological change: the perspective from business history. In: Thomson (1993)

Chudnovsky D, Nagao D, Jacobsson S (1984) Capital goods production in the Third world: an economic study of technical acquisition. Frances Pinter, London

Cimoli M (1988) Industrial structures, technical change and the modes of regulation in the labour market. The case of Latin American countries. DRC discussion paper n. 60, SPRU, University of Sussex, Sussex

Cimoli M (1990) Technology, international trade and development: a north south perspective. PhD. Thesis, Unversity of Sussex, Sussex

Cimoli M, Dosi G (1988) Technology and development some implications of recent advances in the economics of innovation for the process of development. In: Wad A (ed) Science, technology and development: a critical perspective, Westview Press, Boulder, Col

Cimoli M, Dosi G (1990) The characteristics of technology and the development process: some introductory notes. In: Chatterji M (ed) Technology transfer in the less developing countries. Macmillan, London

Coriat B (1990) Penser l'envers. Paris, Bourgeois

Coriat B, Saboia J (1987) Regime d'accumulation et rapport salarial au Bresil (des années 1950 aux années 1980). University of Paris VII, mimeo

Constant E (1985) The turbojet revolution. Johns Hopkins University Press, Baltimore

David PA (1989) Path-dependence: putting the past into the future of economics. Discussion paper, Stanford University, Stanford

David P (1992) Heros, herds and hysteresis in technological history: Thomas Edison and the battle of the system reconsidered. Indust Corp Change 1: 129–180

Dahlman C, Westphal (1982) Technological effort in industrial development: a survey. In: Stewart F, James J (eds) The economics of new technology in developing countries. Frances Pinter, London

Dahlman C, Sananikone O (1990) Technological strategy in Taiwan: exploiting foreign linkages and developing local capabilities. Discussion paper

Dahmen E (1971) Entrepreneurial activity and the development of Swedish industry, 1919–1939. Irwin, Homewood, III

Dosi G (1984) Technical change and industrial transformation. Macmillan, London

Dosi G (1988) Sources, procedures and microeconomic effects of innovation. J Econ Lit 26: 1120–1171

Dosi G, Freeman C, Nelson R, Silverberg G, Soete L (1988) Technical change and economic theory (eds) Frances Pinter, London

Dosi G, Giannetti R, Toninelli PA (1993) Technology and entreprise in a historical perspective. The Clarendon Press of Oxford University, Oxford

Dosi G, Kaniovski Y (1984) On "badly behaved" dynamics. Some applications of generalized urn schemes to technological and economic change. J Evol Econ 4: 93–123

Dosi G, Pavitt K, Soete L (1990) The economics of technical change and international trade. Harvester Wheatsheaf Press, London

Dosi G, Tyson L, Zysman J (1989) Trade, technologies, and development: framework for discussing Japan. In: Johnson C, Tyson L, Zysman J (eds) Politics and productivity. Ballinger Publishing, New York

Durleifer B, Kocka J (1993) The impact of the pre-industrial heritage. Reconsiderations on the German patterns of corporate development in the late 19th and early 20th century. Industr Corp Change 2

Enos J, Park W (1988) The adoption and diffusion of imported technology: the case of Korea. Croom Helm, London

Ernest D, O'Connor D (1989) Technology and global competition. OCDE, Paris

Fransman M (1986) Technology and Economic Development, Wheatsheaf Brighton

Fransman M, King K (1984) Technological capability in the Third World. Macmillan, London

Freeman C (1982) The economics of industrial innovation 2nd edn. Frances Pinter, London

Freeman C, Perez C (1988) Structural crises of adjustment: business cycles and investment behavior. In: Dosi et al (1988)

Geroski P, Jacquemin A (1988) The persistence of profits: a European comparison. Econ J 98: 375–389

Granovetter M (1985) Economic action and social structure: the problem of embeddedness. Am J Sociol 91: 481–510

Guerrieri P (1993) International competitiveness, trade integration and technological interdependence in major Latin American countries. Presented at the 9x Convegno Scientifico, 30 Sept.–1 Oct. Milano

Herbert-Copley B (1990) Technical change in Latin American manufacturing firms: review and synthesis. World Devel 18: 1457–1469

Hirschman AO (1992) Linkages in economic development. In: Rival views of market society and other recent essays. Harvard University Press, Cambridge, Mass

Hobday H (1984) The Brazilian telecommunications industry: accumulation of microelectronic technology in the manufacturing and service sectors. Report prepared for Unido, Brighton, SPRU, Sussex

Justmann M, Teubal M (1991) A structuralist perspective on the role of technology in economic development. World Devel 19: 1167–1183

Katz J (1983) Technological change in the Latin American metalworking industry. CEPAL Rev. 19: 85–143

Katz J (1984a) Domestic technological innovations and dynamic comparative advantage. J Devel Econ 16: 13–38

Katz J (1984b) Technological innovation, industrial organisation and comparative advantages of Latin American metalworking industries. In: Fransman M, King K (1984) Technological capability in the Third World, Macmillan, London.

Katz J (1986): Desarrollo y crisis de la capacidad technologica Latinoamericana. CEPAL, Buenos Aires

Katz J (1987) Technology generation in Latin American manufacturing industries. Macmillan Press, London

Kim L, Dahlman C (1992) Technology policy for industrialization. An integrative framework and Korea's experience. Res Pol 21: 437–452

Kogut B (1992) National organizing principles of work and the dominance of the American multinational corporation. Industr Corp Change 1: 285–326

Kogut B (1993) Country competitiveness, Oxford University Press, Oxford

Lall S (1981) Developing countries in the international economy. Macmillan, London

Lall S (1982) Developing countries as exporters of technology. A first look at the Indian experience. Macmillan, London

Lall S (1984) India's technological capacity: effects of trade, industrial science and technology policies. In: Fransman M, King K (eds) Technological capability in the Third World. Macmillan, London

Lall S (1992) Technological capabilities and industrialization. World Devel 20: 165–186

Lundvall B (1992) National systems of innovation: towards a theory of innovation and interactive learning. Pinter Publishers, London

Misa TJ (1985) Military needs, commercial realities, and the development of the transistor, 1948–1958. In: Smith MR, Military enterprise and technological change. MIT Press, Cambridge, Mass

Misa TJ (1991) Constructive technology assessment: cases, concepts, conceptualization. Presented at the Conference on Constructive Technology Assessment, Twente, The Netherlands, Sept. 1991

Muller DC (1990) The dynamics of company profits. Cambridge University Press, Cambridge

Nelson R (1981) Research on productivity growth and productivity differences: dead ends and departures. J Econ Lit 19: 1029–1064

Nelson R (ed) (1993) National systems of innovation. Oxford University Press, Oxford

Nelson R, Winter S (1982) An evolutionary theory of economic change. Harvard University Press, Cambridge, Mass

Noble D (1984) Forces of production, Knopf, New York

Pack H, Westphal L (1986) Industrial strategy and technological change: theory versus reality. J Devel Econ 22: 87–128

Pavitt K (1984) Sectoral patterns of technological change: towards a taxonomy and a theory. Res Pol 13: 343–375

Romer P (1994a) New goods, old theory, and the welfare cost of trade restrictions. J of Devel Econ 43: 5–38

Romer P (1994b) The origins of endogenous growth. J Econ Perspect 8: 3–22

Rosenberg N (1976) Perspectives on technology. Cambridge University Press, Cambridge

Rosenberg N (1990) Why do firms do basic research (with their own money)? Res Pol. 19: 165–174

Rosenberg N (1991) Critical issues in science policy research. Sci Publ Pol 18: 12–18

Silverberg G, Dosi G, Orsenigo L (1988) Innovation, diversity and diffusion: self-organization model. Econ J 1032–1054

Teitel S (1981) Towards an understanding of technical change in semi-industrial countries. Res Pol 10: 127–147

Teitel S (1984) Technology creation in semi-industrial economies. J Devel Econ 16: 39–61
Teitel S (1987) Towards conceptualisation of technological development as an evolutionary process. In: Dunning J, Mikoto U (eds) Structural change, economic interdipendence and world development. Macmillan, London
Teubal M (1984) The role of technological learning in the exports of manufactured goods: the caseof selected capital goods in Brazil. World Devel 12: 349–865
Teubal M (1987) Innovation and development: a review of some work at the IDB/ECLA/UNDP programme. In: Katz J (ed) Technology generation in Latin American manufacturing industries. Macmillan Press, London
Thomson R (1993) Learning and technical change. Macmillan, London
UNCTAD (1989) Impact of technological change on patterns of international trade. Report by UNCTAD secretariat, Geneva
UNCTAD (1991) Transfer and development of technology in a changing world environment: the challenges of the 1990s. Report by UNCTAD secretariat, Geneva
Winter S (1982) An essay on the theory of production. In: Hymans SH (ed) Economic and the world around it. University of Michigan Press, Ann Arbor
Winter S (1984) Schumpeterian competition under alternative technological regimes. J Econ Behav Organiz 5: 287–320
Zysman J (1994) How institutions create historically rooted trajectories of growth. Industr Corp Change 3: 243–283

[22]

National Specificities and the Context of Change: The Coevolution of Organization and Technology

GIOVANNI DOSI
BRUCE KOGUT

The chapters in this book present a wide range of evidence that the organizing of work varies considerably among countries. Country variations are historically persistent; in the language of Midler and Charue (Chap. 9), they have the characteristic of "irreversibility." The challenge posed by these studies is to understand to what extent the historical persistence in the variation of national organizing principles explains the long-term differentials in the income and growth of countries.

Whereas differences in organizing principles among countries tend to persist for long periods of time, economic leadership has proven to be historically cyclical. To a large extent, the chapters in this book are a discussion of the relative decline of the United States and the organizing principles of mass production, and the rise of Japan and Germany that are advancing on the strengths of quality production. The historical record suggests a cycle of divergence in the performance of countries due to the introduction of new organizing heuristics, followed by a gradual convergence due to the diffusion of these heuristics across borders (Boyer 1988; Kogut 1991).

What we are currently witnessing is a period of divergence resulting from the expansion of new techniques of organization in a few countries. These new techniques do not spring up uniformly from the soil of a nation. Rather, as the chapters by Midler and Charue (Chap. 9) and Kern and Schumann (Chap. 5) show, there is substantial variation within a country. Certain sectors, such as machine-tools or autos, may lead in advance of other industries. The study by Fruin and Nishiguchi (Chap. 12) suggests that many new practices in Japan are still in development and that their diffusion across sectors, and even within the lead automobile industry, is still very much in progress. Despite the discussion in the chapters by Webster

(Chap. 8), Jürgens (Chap. 6), and Dunning (Chap. 11) on the diffusion of Japanese techniques, the impression left by these studies is that the adoption of flexible work roles and subcontracting systems is substantially slower in the United States, the United Kingdom, France, and, perhaps to a lesser extent, Germany.

One way to understand national patterns in organizing is to identify, along the lines of Herrigel (Chap. 1), Lincoln (Chap. 3), and Westney (Chap. 2), the roles that larger institutions play inside a country. Since schools, technical training facilities, unions, and government agencies are regional and national institutions, they generate what Dimaggio and Powell (1983) have labelled "isomorphic pressures" that drive firms toward adopting similar practices. Firms in the same country draw, for example, from a pool of workers who have been trained in similar educational institutions and whose responsibilities and rights are defined under a common body of law.

It is the absence of international institutions, on the other hand, that accounts for why these pressures do not act similarly on firms located in different countries. Unions do not effectively span borders. Though the education of white-collar workers has been influenced by an international ideology of business education (witness the diffusion of American business schools among countries), workers are, by and large, trained in uniquely different educational systems.

If there is a factor that cuts across countries, it is the role played by competition in international markets. The reason why national variations in the organizing of work become important at particular historical junctions is because international competition is, at these times, driven by technological and organizational innovations that have not diffused across the borders of countries. International competition causes not only a fundamental challenge to firms losing market share, but to the very educational, labor, and legal institutions prevailing among countries.

The force of international competition drives the nature of adjustment to four distinct, though not exclusive, outcomes. The first is that a country with inferior practices may simply withdraw from the world market; autarkic policies, such as raising tariffs or forbidding trade, are historically quite significant. Indeed, the current era of relatively free flows of international trade and investment is the exception, but the longevity of this political order is clearly in question.

Second, the inferiority of organizing practices, which is revealed in relative productivity rates, is compensated by lower wages. According to numerous recent estimates, wage rates in the United States relative to Japan and Germany have rapidly deteriorated since the 1980s. Whittaker's description (Chap. 7) of the inability of British firms to match the Japanese practice of using a single employee for the integration of programming and operating tasks subtly suggests that lower efficiency is offset by the significantly lower wage rates in the United Kingdom.

Third, the analysis by Sorge and Maurice of the machine-tool industry in France and Germany (Chap. 4) shows that adjustment may also occur through market differentiation. Over time, French producers lost market share to both Japanese and German firms, with the surviving French firms focusing on specialized markets. Even with the expansion of mass produced automobiles in the first half of this century, there remained many producers of cars who specialized in low volume, customized production. Whether this outcome generates similar levels of income and wealth across countries is problematic, but it would seem to be an unlikely event.

The fourth mechanism of adjustment is the international diffusion and adoption of best practices. Many of the chapters in this book are analyses of the process by which new principles of organization are adopted. The composition of these practices, as the divergent cases of Japan and Germany suggest, need not be the same, but the direction of development should reflect a basic convergence in the design of tasks and organizing principles.

A comparison of these alternatives would certainly imply, from an economic perspective, that the fourth outcome of adopting a variant on new organizing principles would be the most appealing. Yet, the historical record, as outlined for Taylorism in the chapter by Kogut and Parkinson (Chap. 10), indicates that convergence is slow and only approximate. Moreover, the degree of convergence varies substantially by country.

These considerations raise a few fundamental questions. Can one identify a unifying and historical logic that shapes the development of distinct national technological and organizational trajectories? If different organizational features of firms matter in terms of national economic performance, why should particular countries "lock-in" within seemingly "inferior" organizational forms? The first question is a more general way of investigating why certain countries display historically bounded leadership. The second directs attention to why such leadership appears to be cyclical; convergence is not rapid, but economic leadership is also not enduring.

The kind of unified explanation required to address these diverse observations should provide an account of (1) the coevolution of firm-specific and country-specific technological and organizational capabilities, and (2) the implications for economic performance regarding trade, investment, and growth. To be historically realistic, this explanation must provide an argument by which firms and countries reproduce over time particular technological and organizing characteristics, even when these characteristics are inferior, in terms of efficiency, to existing forms of best practice.

Though these are large questions, there has been considerable agreement that their answers require a formulation sensitive to historical events, social institutions, and the cumulative growth of knowledge specific to firms and countries. No existing theory is near the full realization of the task of combining these elements to explain why firms and countries reproduce over time particular organizational and technological characteristics. But we can suggest, as a way of commenting on the contributions to this book, an outline of what such a theory would look like.

Coevolution of Organization and Technology

There are, in our view, three central elements to the sort of story of the coevolution of organization and technology we would like to develop regarding country cycles in economic leadership. These elements are expressions, in the language of Campbell (1969), of the three fundamental social processes of variation, retention, and

selection (see also Aldrich 1979). The first element is that major innovations evolve
at particular periods of time that alter, fundamentally, the way work is organized
in specific locations. The second element is that firms and organizations retain new
knowledge in the form of institutionalized rules and heuristics of search and decision. Because new knowledge builds on old knowledge embedded in institutionalized patterns of social action, innovations evolve and diffuse in a cumulative manner, with incremental learning being a driving factor in growth. Finally, these new
practices must be in some sense selected by the environment; governments may
subsidize their use, or consumers may favor the derived goods for reasons of price
and quality (Nelson and Winter 1982; Dosi 1982, 1988; Silverberg, Dosi, and
Orsenigo 1988).

The consequence of these three processes is that economic change is spatially
and temporally bounded and is evolutionary. There are many ways to explore these
issues, from historical and social analysis to more formal models. Yet, the underlying ideas are the same. The economic and social history shows that change tends
to be ordered, complex, and irreversible. There are, in effect, self-organizing forces
capable of generating multiple but finite number of historical outcomes.

Let us take a concrete example. The decision to organize a factory by mass production has several immediate effects. First, it is a destruction of the existing knowledge on how to organize a factory by alternative methods; a return to the old organization cannot instantaneously recover previous levels of productivity. Second,
the knowledge gained in organizing a mass production system in one factory may
suggest the application of similar methods (that is, problem-solving heuristics) to
other factories or activities. Some of these activities may be quite distant from a
manufacturing facility; witness the growth of mass production in higher educational systems. Third, the change in organization makes it more attractive to
develop new capital equipment and technologies to facilitate mass production.
Some of the new capital equipment may be bought from outside of the firm.

Technology and organization tend to coevolve with each other. Adam Smith
noted this relationship when he attributed the organizing principle of the division
of labor as linked to the invention of specialized machinery (Smith 1970, p. 112).
Over time, the reciprocal effect of technology and organizing principles on each
other creates what Hughes (1983) has called a technological system in which the
efficiency of individual parts and firms depend on the whole.

To continue the example, the diffusion of mass production is, in principle, the
ordered replication of a method of organization that progressively diffuses in an
economy. This process of diffusion is self-reinforcing due to the accumulation of
learning on how to do such mass production in better ways and due to the coevolution of technologies. As long as the social environment favors the relative growth
of mass production, these techniques, once they have begun to expand, will diffuse
either by the elimination of, or their imitation by, firms using older techniques.

This process of coevolution of technology and organization is described by a
variant on the schema used in sociobiology (Durham 1991, pp. 182, 186). Initially,
there are a finite number of types of technologies and ways by which work is organized that approximate the role played by genes in biological evolution.[1] By the
tendency of firms to search locally for new ways of doing things that are similar to

current practice, these technologies and organizing principles may be incrementally and interactively adapted and changed. Simultaneously, the technological and organizational attributes of a firm are subject to selection pressures. The joint process of learning and selection generates, in turn, a new frequency of technologies and organizing principles.

There are two important complications in this process by which new techniques of production and technology coevolve within an economy. The first is that the evolution of a new heuristic is characterized initially by increasing benefit. Eventually, however, declining gains from further development sets in. The early decades of mass production showed considerable investment in exploring new methods, but as the most fertile ground for incremental innovation is explored and exhausted, the benefits of further search decline.

Second, the new techniques will not fully diffuse in an environment. A residual demand may persist for products built on alternative systems. But also the heterogeneity in social institutions will maintain a heterogeneity in organization; factories in the American south differed substantially from the factories in Philadelphia and Boston regions where Taylorism was first introduced.

Nevertheless, competition within a fairly homogeneous national environment favors over time the expansion of particular techniques. From the perspective of history, these techniques are unlikely to be the "best." By the accident of war or social conflict, one technique may have been initially favored, which, due to learning and coevolutionary economies, locked a country into a particular and irreversible developmental path.[2] In all European countries, the demand of military production in World War I was a major impetus toward the introduction of principles of standardization of work. This change caused an irreversible departure from the old system in many of these countries. The impact of the war on the organization of work varied by nation.

Of course, these abstract statements do not do justice to the institutional richness of the social process of change and development. The decision to introduce mass production is itself embedded in a wider social context. Many suggestions (e.g., Lazonick 1990) have been made for the leadership of the United States in the development of systems of standardization and mass production, from the scarcity of labor and the task of training immigrant workers, to the pull of a mass market for the new household and construction goods to build the new frontier. As suggested by Kogut and Parkinson (Chap. 10), the absence of an embedded craft and guild tradition certainly abetted the diffusion of Taylorist ideas in the United States, while these very traditions slowed the adoption of work changes in the United Kingdom.

In this sense, coevolution takes on a wider meaning than just the positive externalities between certain kinds of organization and technologies. Rather, coevolution also tends to promote the mutual expansion of complementary social institutions.[3] A system of mass production and standardization of work encourages the development of labor unions concerned about job definitions and rules by which workers are laid off in cyclical downswings. Social institutions tend to coalesce around the principles by which work and human activities are organized.

These issues are old, but unsettled, themes in organizational theory. Webster's description of the incompatibility of the new technology with the existing organization (Chap. 8) shares many concerns of social-technical theory. The sociotechnical concept was initially worked out in the course of several field studies conducted by the Tavistock Institute in the British coal mining industry. For example, the classic study by Trist and Bamforth (1951) found that the introduction of a new kind of mining technology required a change in organization that conflicted with social and psychological norms. Technology cannot simply determine the organization, it was found, because its implementation is conditioned by the prevailing social system.

Since that basic study, there has been a bounty of research on the relationship of technology and organization. The findings have tended to fall into four camps: the primacy of technology (e.g., Woodward 1965); bureaucratic processes associated with size (Pugh, Hickson, and Hinings 1969); the contingency of the environment (Lawrence and Lorsch 1967; Pennings 1992; Sorge and Maurice, Chap. 4); and strategy (Child 1972). Yet, it is fair to say that despite the considerable research, the search for the factors that determine a mapping of a specific technology to a specific organizational structure has proved elusive.

Consider the chapters in this volume. Lincoln (Chap. 3) details how American and Japanese firms, after controlling for technology, differ in their practices by which decisions are reached and authority is exercised. Sorge and Maurice (Chap. 4) describe at length different organizing modes for German and French machine-tool firms. Midler and Charue (Chap. 9) found that even within the same country, two firms evolved different organizational structures by which to adopt flexible manufacturing methods.

The difficulty of identifying a connection between technology and organization is surprising, for common sense suggests that such a relationship should exist. It cannot be expected, for example, that the processing of high-speed steel could be carried out by the factory organization of the nineteenth century. Chandler (1977), in particular, has strenuously argued that the economies of speed demanded the development of new organizational capabilities at the turn of the century.

One way to reconcile common sense with the confusing findings on the relationship between technology and organization is to think of the problem as identifying a correspondence between sets as opposed to between elements. The study by Whittaker (Chap. 7), as noted earlier, showed that the introduction of computer controlled numerical machinery in Japan changed the task responsibilities of the operator to include programming. In the United Kingdom, the lower skill level of the operator ruled out this design; instead, an engineer was assigned the task of programming. These two solutions differ substantially, and there is no unique matching of the technology of flexible manufacturing to a single organizational design.

Still, there clearly is a set-to-set correspondence in organizing principles and technology. The chapters by Whittaker, Webster, and Midler and Charue (Chaps. 7, 8, and 9) provide careful documentation that organizational practices were altered by the introduction of new technologies. As Jürgens shows in his chapter (Chap. 6), throughout the world's auto industry, several new and fundamental practices, such as multiple manning of machinery, are being adopted, but with large differences in adaptation. The history of industrial relations, firm strategy, and social context strongly conditions the nature of the relationship of technology and organization, but this relationship must still conform to the broad technical constraints discovered in implementation.

Specificities in national principles of organization are sensitive, consequently, to the coincidence of unique historical events and the prevailing social order. In a broad sense, the coevolution of technologies and organization are constrained to reveal a pattern of convergence among countries. International competition, among other forces, motivates countries toward adopting the apparent best practices by which technology and organization are structured. Yet, the specific structures revealed over time are tempered by the national contexts and initial conditions.

Costs of Change

To complete the analysis of why coevolution carries significant implications for the economic performance of countries, it is essential to examine why these country-specific principles of organizing may be reproduced despite the selective pressures of international competition. The difficulty with the question is not the lack but, rather, the plethora of answers. The challenge to the existing economic and political order, the inability to identify the need for change, or the noncomprehension of the changes required are all viable candidates for explaining why new practices are not quickly diffused across the borders of a country.

Despite this embarrassment of riches, the condition of being locked into inferior practices even when better practices are identified can be explained in terms of three kinds of three factors that influence costs: switching, learning, and hysteretic. We abstract from two important considerations. First, the process by which organizations and institutions in one country come to make comparisons between the existing order and new ways of organizing differs substantially from this stylized description of these three factors that determine a condition of "lock-in." Second, these costs are not the same for all actors in a country; entrenched powers (e.g., incumbent firms or organized labor) may attach a greater cost to switching to a new system than might start-up companies or workers entering the labor force.[4]

In Figure 13.1, these three kinds of costs are described. There are two distinct ways of organizing activities, A and B. In each case, B is revealed as a less costly way of accomplishing a given task.

Figure 13.1*A* depicts the simple case where the costs of switching between organizing principles A and B are greater than the benefits. An obvious example is the continued use of a nonmetric system of measurement in the United States. The incremental benefits of using a metric system are offset by the large costs of changing all the existing standards and measurements.

One of the most complex considerations is that the desirability of switching increases with the number of institutions and firms who find it advantageous to adopt the metric system. The dependence of any one firm in a larger technological system means that the costs of switching vary depending on the decisions of other actors in the country. Overcoming the effects of history requires a collective choice.

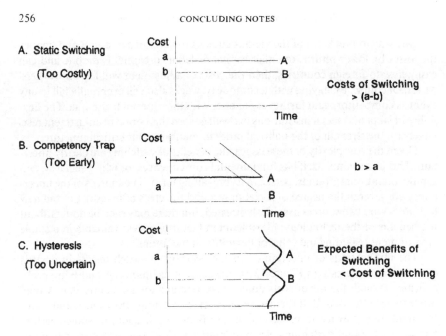

Figure 13.1 Three cases of lock-in. A and B represent technologies; a and b represent the current cost of using a given technology.

For this reason, switching to a new technique is not simply a decision for the firm, but rather, is a question of the organization of the national industrial system.

In Figure 13.1*B*, the effect of history is seen to result in a competency trap; learning to be good at an inferior technique has advanced so far as to make switching to better organizing principles unattractive. Even though technique B is better than A, a country has built up a cumulative experience in using the latter technique. To switch to B means that it must scrap the value of this gained learning. At the same time, it will be forced to begin the learning process again. A static comparison shows that the costs of producing with B are greater than those with A.

It is easy to conclude that the decision to stay with A is myopic. With proper foresight, it should be clear that with new learning, technique B is superior. The actual calculation is complicated by such factors as the discount rate (i.e., how important is the future relative to the present) and the usefulness of technique B to new endeavors.

A more complicated consideration is that a firm and country may be locked into a vicious circle. If a firm switches to technique B, it will incur losses if it faces international competitors that have already gained experience using these organizing principles and are operating at lower costs. The ability to sustain these losses is a question of whether a country and its resident firms have access to the necessary capital funding. With insufficient funding, the firm may be unable to switch to the better technique, or, if it does switch, it may become bankrupt. In the meantime, its competitors will be in a virtuous cycle by enjoying decreasing costs with further experience in the superior technique.

One way to break out of the vicious circle is to adopt technique B and finance the losses by lower returns to either capital or labor. If capital is mobile and can easily flow to foreign countries, then the costs of adjustment will fall on workers' wages. Of course, by staying with technique A, wages also will eventually fall in any event as competitors gain further experience with the superior technique. The flexibility in labor and social institutions that will govern this period of adjustment rests largely on the strength of the political order in managing this critical juncture.

Given the complexity of these issues, the benefits of switching are clearly uncertain. This uncertainty itself has fundamental consequences for why a social system should, on rational grounds, persist in its prevailing form. The sources of the uncertainty are several; the degree of social unrest and the costs of investing in the new technology are two sources previously stressed. But there may even be doubts about the benefits of the technology. Flexible manufacturing is less valuable in a stable environment regarding the value of flexibility in the future.

The implications of uncertainty on the decision to switch results in what is described as hysteresis. In Figure 13.1C the costs of techniques A and B are probabilistic. Though the mean costs differ, there remains the possibility that A may prove to be better than B. If there were no costs to switching, then a firm and country could simply switch from technique A to B, and back again. As shown earlier, one-time (or static) switching costs may render such change economically unattractive. These static costs understate, however, the unattractiveness of switching once uncertainty has been considered. Since costs are incurred and since the future best technique is uncertain, switching will not occur as frequently. After all, it may be adviseable to switch back in the near future. The effect of uncertainty is to increase the perceived dynamic (i.e., over-time) costs of switching compared to the static costs described in Figure 13.2A. Only a large disparity in the benefits of A and B will induce a switch.

The impact of uncertainty, therefore, is to heighten the persistence of history. It is easy to underestimate the importance of hysteresis. And yet rather small degrees of uncertainty over the future benefits can result in a substantial tendency toward inertia (see, e.g., Dixit 1989, and Kogut and Kulatilaka 1992). In retrospect, it is obvious to conclude that one way of doing something is superior to another. At prevailing prices of petroleum, the era of gas guzzling autos is clearly at an end, but the volatility in oil prices in the 1970s rendered such forecasting more hazardous. The costs of scrapping decades of experience in the production of large car manufacture and of investment in new plants and tooling for fuel efficient cars have proven to be astronomical. Small amounts of uncertainty over the direction of future demand can have a powerful influence on sustaining current capabilities and methods of organization.

Some Theoretical and Normative Conclusions

There is a troubling conclusion to this consideration of the costs of switching to new practices. No matter what choice a country makes, a fall in wages relative to foreign wages would appear to be avoidable. If best practices are not adopted, lower wages is a permanent state; if a decision is made to switch, the costs incurred during the transition period would require a reduction in relative wages by which to amortize the adjustment investment. However, even in the case where a country initially persists in its old practices, the desirability of switching would increase over time if the new practices should reveal greater dynamism and learning economies.

The implications of these observations is that country cycles in economic leadership are tied to the arrival of innovations in a lagging country and the high costs of the leader country to switch to the new practices. As per the argument advanced by Kogut and Parkinson (Chap. 10), the costs of adopting new innovations should be higher for new organizing principles (e.g., subcontracting systems) than for new technologies. Contrary to the belief that the decline of the United States derives from a fall in the *appropriability* of American technologies, we would suggest that this decline is linked to the diffusion of American organizing practices to other countries; at the same time, new and better practices are being introduced and worked out in other countries. But whereas the consequences of diffusion and the introduction of rival organizing principles force a decline in relative American wages, the historical process over the past century has generated substantial levels of wealth and capital accumulation by U.S. residents and corporations.

A reasonable deduction from this argument is that, in general, national specificities in organizing principles are only short-term phenomena without any long-lasting consequences on performance. Indeed, the long-term irrelevance of organizational forms can be argued from quite different theoretical points of view. Take, for example, an extreme version of a transaction-cost model of corporate organization. This model would suggest that observed institutional set-ups are the organizational responses to the requirement of efficient governance of exchanges. Hence, any observed international difference in the typical modes of organizing transactions would be primarily attributed to lags and leads in diffusion of more efficient forms of organization (assuming transaction costs to be similar across countries). In the long term, an extreme version of a transaction-cost theory of organization would suggest a convergence in institutional structures as determined by the differential efficiency of various organizational modes. There is some point where the fall in relative wages in the United States is sufficient to justify the costs of adopting better practices.

While this explanation is plausible, it need not be compelling if we are to take historical and institutional context seriously. We suggest that national specificities persist because the micro rules that generate differences in country performances are poorly understood and are difficult to change.[5] Better practices are not easily adopted because decision makers do not identify and calibrate the full set of opportunities. As suggested by many of the contributions to this book, an efficient governance approach fails to recognize the strong inertial forces that cause social institutions to be reproduced over time. Environments are complex and nonstationary, so that an understanding of the causal links between alternative organizational forms and outcomes is very opaque. The mapping between information, actions, and outcomes is, at best, imprecise, and undertaken on the grounds of available decision heuristics and untested expectations. It is not that firms and policymakers do not make choices, but, rather, that their choices are made in reference to a limited understanding of opportunities.

The variations in the micro rules that prevail in a society can generate significant differences in the macro performance of an economy. In this respect, Aoki's comparison between two "ideal" types—the "Japanese firm" and the "American firm"—is a good example: different internal governance structures affect learning and performance, despite identical economic opportunities (Aoki 1988). In an exploratory attempt to model and simulate the relationship between behavioral norms and patterns of growth, Chiaromonte, Dosi, and Orsenigo (1992) have shown how economic dynamics widely differ when simple alterations are made to behavioral rules (e.g., how adjustment occurs in labor markets), even when other system parameters, such as technological opportunities, are left unchanged.

It would follow from this discussion that the influence of history on restricting an economy's ability to transform itself radically can only be overcome by changing the expectations that inform the choices of firms, workers, and institutions. These expectations, or what can be called "notional" possibilities, concern the identity of available technologies and organizing heuristics (i.e., micro rules).[6] Because of the dependency of parts on the whole, however, these expectations consist also of anticipations regarding what other actors in the system will decide.

Several of the chapters in this volume comment directly on the process by which explicit public policies have influenced the notional set of technological and organizational opportunities. Herrigel (Chap. 1), in particular, describes the success of the government and public institutions of Baden Württemberg in providing institutional support by which new practices were diffused in the region. Similarly, Sorge and Maurice (Chap. 4) find French government policies to have been far less successful than the German in reorienting the machine-tool industry toward more flexible manufacturing technologies.

Kern and Schumann (Chap. 5) suggest a far more subtle dynamic in their study. The German economy, as argued by their original studies, was at a crossroad in the late 1960s. Rising wages threatened the export viability of mass production, and the importation of competing goods, when not prohibited by quotas or tariffs, rose in a number of sectors. Indeed, one would have been hard pressed to predict the high performance of the German economy in the 1980s in the context of the high unemployment of the 1970s. But what eventually caused a few sectors in the German economy to switch to new practices stressing flexibility and worker autonomy was the combination of a highly trained work force *and* the severe restraints on German firms to cut wages or to move production outside of the country. In other words, German firms were forced to search for new practices because the wage constraints ruled out persisting with traditional work methods.

Is there a lesson, then, in the ability of German firms to adapt to the pressures of international competition? Herrigel (Chap. 1) intimates that leaders have the capacity to lead by changing the notional possibilities understood by workers and managers. Kern and Schumann (Chap. 5) suggest that, by placing severe constraints on management and by empowering workers at the workplace, firms are forced to invest in searching and implementing new methods of organizing. Better practices evolve, they appear to suggest, when the attractiveness of short-term adjustment by cutting wages is eliminated.

But the complexity of the interdependence of institutional elements makes it difficult to extrapolate from one country's experience. Would raising minimum wages in the United States also evoke a similar response given high heterogeneity in labor training and skills? Should restrictions on outward flows of direct investment also be required, or should laws require the representation of labor on boards of directors and the formation of work councils?

These are difficult questions to address, and this difficulty is, in fact, the clue to the answers. The causality between action and outcome is highly dependent on the institutional context. National specificities in organization persist because knowledge of the causal relationships between practice and performance is gained only incrementally. The chapters in this book, by and large, agree that the direction of change is toward greater worker autonomy and reliance on skilled employees. Within this broad notion of convergence, there remains considerable play for the persistence in the variations of national principles by which work is organized.

Notes

1. There has been a growing literature in sociobiology on how to analyze culture in ways analogous to genes. See the discussion in Winter (1990) who identifies the genetic analogue with methods of organization.

2. For a discussion of historical accident and lock-in, see David (1985) and Arthur (1988).

3. This meaning is closer to the original use of coevolution in biology as the coadaptation of two species. The growth of the school stressing the population dynamics of genes, best known through the popular writings of Richard Dawkins, is closer to our discussion of the evolution of techniques. See Durham (1991, 166n.).

4. These concerns raise important issues of public choice and property rights. For applications to understanding cycles in country leadership, see Olson (1982) and North (1981).

5. See the discussion in Kogut (1990) on why practices may be more difficult to identify and adopt across borders.

6. See Dosi (1982, 1988) for a discussion.

References

Aldrich, Howard. 1979. *Organizations and Environments.* Englewood Cliffs, N.J.: Prentice Hall.

Aoki, M. 1988. *Information, Incentives and Bargaining in the Japanese Economy.* Cambridge, U.K.: Cambridge University Press

Arthur, Brian. 1988. "Competing Technologies: An Overview," in G. Dosi, C. Freeman, R. Nelson, G. Silverberg, and L. Soete, eds., *Technical Change and Economic Theory,* pp. 590–607. London and New York: Printer Publishers.

Boyer, Robert. 1988. "Technical Change and the Theory of 'Regulation'," in G. Dosi, C. Freeman, R. Nelson, G. Silverberg, and L. Soete, eds., *Technical Change and Economic Theory,* pp. 67–94. London and New York: Printer Publishers.

Campbell, Donald T. 1969. "Variation and Selective Retention in Socio-Cultural Evolution," *General Systems* 14:69–85.

Chandler, Alfred. 1977. *The Visible Hand: The Managerial Revolution in American Business.* Cambridge, Mass.: Harvard University Press.

Chiaramonte, Francesca, Giovanni Dosi, and Luigi Orsenigo. 1992. "Innovative Learning and Institutions in the Process of Development: On the Microfoundations of Growth Regimes," in R. Thompson, ed., *Learning and Technological Change,* London: Macmillan.

Child, John. 1972. "Organization Structure, Environment and Performance: The Role of Strategic Choice," *Sociology* **6**:2–22.

David, Paul. 1985. "Clio and the Economics of QWERTY," *American Economic Review* **75**:332–37.

Dimaggio, Paul, and Walter Powell. 1983. "The Iron Cage Revisited: Institutional Isomorphism and Collective Rationality in Organizational Fields," *American Sociological Review* **48**:147–60.

Dixit, Avinash. 1989. "Entry and Exit Decisions Under Uncertainty," *Journal of Political Economy* **97**:620–38.

Dosi, Giovanni. 1982. "Technological Paradigms and Technological Trajectories: A Suggested Interpretation of the Determinants and Directions of Technical Change," *Research Policy* **11**:147–63.

Dosi, Giovanni. 1988. "Sources, Procedures, and Microeconomic Effects of Innovation," *Journal of Economic Literature* **26**:1120–71.

Durham, William. 1991. *Coevolution. Geneses, Culture, and Human Diversity,* Stanford, Calif.: Stanford University Press.

Hughes, Thomas. 1983. *Networks of Power: Electrification in Western Society. 1880–1930,* Baltimore: John Hopkins University Press.

Kogut, B. 1990. "The Permeability of Borders and the Speed of Learning Among Countries," in *Globalization of Firms and the Competitiveness of Nations,* Crawford Lecture. Lund, Sweden: University of Lund.

Kogut, Bruce. 1991. "Country Capabilities and the Permeability of Borders," *Strategic Management Journal* **12**:33–47.

Kogut, Bruce, and Nalin Kulatilaka. 1993 (forthcoming). "Operating Flexibility, Global Manufacturing, and the Benefits of a Multinational Network," *Management Science.*

Lawrence, Paul, and Jay Lorsch. 1967. *Organization and Environment: Managing Differentiation and Integration.* Boston: Division of Research, Graduate School of Business and Administration, Harvard University.

Lazonick, William. 1990. *Competitive Advantage on the Shop Floor.* Cambridge, Mass: Harvard University Press.

Nelson, Richard, and Sidney Winter. 1982. *An Evolutionary Theory of Economic Change.* Cambridge, Mass.:: Belknap Press.

North, Douglass C. 1981. *Structure and Change in Economic History.* New York: W. W. Norton.

Olson, Mancur. 1982. *The Rise and Decline of Nations: Economic Growth, Stagflation, and Social Ridigities.* New Haven, Conn.: Yale University Press.

Pennings, Johannes. 1992. *Structural Contingency Theory: A Reappraisal,* vol. 14, Research in Organizational Behavior. San Francisco: JAI Press.

Pugh, Derek, David Hickson, and Robert Hinings. 1969. "The Context of Organizational Structures," *Administrative Science Quarterly* **14**:91–114.

Silverberg, Gerald, Giovanni Dosi, and Luigi Orsenigo. 1988. "Innovation, Diversity, and Diffusion: A Self-Organizing Model," *Economic Journal* **98**:1032–54.

Smith, Adam. 1970. *The Wealth of Nations.* Harmondsworth, Middlesex, U.K.: Penguin.

Trist, Eric, and Kenneth Bamforth. 1951. "Some Social and Psychological Consequences of
    the Longwall Method of Coal-getting," *Human Relations* **4**:6–38.
Winter, Sidney. 1990. "Survival, Selection, and Inheritance in Evolutionary Theories of
    Organization," in *Organizational Evolution: New Directions,* J. Singh, ed, pp. 269–
    297. Newbury Park, Calif.: Sage.
Woodward, Joan. 1965. *Industrial Organization: Behavior and Control.* London: Oxford
    University Press.

[23]

Institutions and Policies Shaping Industrial Development: An Introductory Note

Mario Cimoli, Giovanni Dosi, Richard Nelson, and Joseph E. Stiglitz

There are two complementary ways to introduce the analysis of the institutions and policies shaping industrial development.

First, one may just build on the simple empirical observation that no example can be found in history of a process of development nested in an environment even vaguely resembling the institution-free tale of economic interactions that one finds in a good deal of contemporary economic theory. On the contrary, all historical experiences of sustained economic growth—starting at least from the English Industrial Revolution—find their enabling conditions in a rich set of complementary institutions, shared behavioral norms, and public policies. Indeed, the paramount importance of institutions and social norms appears to be a rather universal property of every form of collective organization we are aware of. Moreover, much more narrowly, discretionary public policies have been major ingredients of national development strategies, especially in catching-up countries, throughout the history of modern capitalism: see the contributions by Mazzoleni and Nelson, Perez, and Di Maio to this book, together with the historical experiences analyzed in the different country chapters.

Conversely, from a symmetric perspective, there are extremely sound theoretical reasons supporting the notion that institutions and policies always matter in all processes of technological learning and economic coordination and change.

Here we focus on the latter issue and outline some theoretical foundations for institution-building and policies.

Mario Cimoli, Giovanni Dosi, Richard Nelson, and Joseph E. Stiglitz

A misleading point of departure: *market failures*

Conventionally, one would start from the very general question, when are public policies required from the point of view of the theory? And, as known, the standard answer would be, when there are market failures of some kind. However, albeit quite common, the 'market failure' language tends to be quite misleading in that, in order to evaluate the necessity and efficacy of any policy, it takes as a yardstick those conditions under which standard normative ('welfare') theorems hold. The problem with such a framework is not that market failures are not relevant. Quite the contrary: the problem is that hardly any empirical set-up bears a significant resemblance with the 'yardstick'—in terms of, for example, market completeness, perfectness of competition, knowledge possessed by economic agents, stationarity of technologies and preferences, rationality in decision-making, and so on (the list is indeed very long!). In a profound sense, when judged with standard canons, the whole world can be seen as a huge market failure!

Indeed, this is implicitly recognized in any serious policy discussion, where the argument about policy almost never is about whether the situation at hand is actually optimal, but rather about whether the problems with the incumbent institutional set-up are sufficiently severe to warrant active policy measures. In all that, most often the demand for 'proofs of failures' mainly plays as a device to put the burden of the evidence away from the believers in the dogma that in general 'more market is always better than less'.

Much nearer the empirical realities of markets and non-market institutions which govern production, exchanges, and economic coordination in modern economies, in the following we shall discuss issues of both (i) the boundaries between market and non-market forms of economic organization, and (ii) the embeddedness of markets themselves into complementary non-market institutions.

A rather universal role of institutions: the determination of the boundaries between non-market and market interactions

Which types of social activities are subject to (i) decentralized production and (ii) money-mediated exchanges, and which ones are not? There is an impressive range from the economically banal to the morally outrageous. Strategic goods? Pharmaceuticals? Natural monopolies? Public utilities? Education? Childcare? Retirement benefits? Health care? Human organs? Blood? Husbands and wives? Political votes? Children? Court rulings?

In another work one of the authors (Nelson, 2005) discusses precisely the *governance structure* of a few goods and services wherein their provision has often relied, in part or entirely, on non-market mechanisms.

Clearly the question of the determination of market boundaries applies to both developed and developing countries but is particularly crucial in emerging and ex-centrally planned economies where the boundaries between market and non-market institutions still have to be clearly defined. Far from the fury of market fundamentalism, our basic view there is that non-market institutions (ranging from public agencies to professional associations, from trade unions to community structures) are at the core of the very constitution of the whole socio-economic fabric. Their role goes well beyond the enforcement of property rights. Rather, they offer the main governance structure in many activities where market exchanges are socially inappropriate or simply ineffective. At the same time, they shape and constrain the behavior of economic agents toward competitors, customers, suppliers, employees, government officials, and so on. In that, they are also instrumental in curbing the 'self-destruction perils' for market economies flagged long ago by Polanyi (1957) and Hirschman (1982).

Moreover, notice that even when one encounters a prevailing 'market form' of governance, the latter is embedded in a rich thread of non-market institutions.

Pharmaceuticals is a very good case in point. Here in all countries with an effective, for-profit pharmaceutical industry, one finds government programs that support biomedical research, generally at universities and public labs. Together, the university parts of these programs are associated also with scientific training for people who, after finishing their education, go on to work in pharmaceutical companies. Moreover, in virtually all countries, public funds and programs play a major role in the procurement of pharmaceuticals. And, finally, in virtually all countries there are various forms of regulation of pharmaceuticals which go well beyond textbook guarantees of property rights and integrity of exchanges.

Or consider aircraft and airline services. In all countries that have major aircraft production, government funds play a significant role in R&D. And in most countries both the airports and the traffic control system are not only funded but run by government agencies. Even in the simple case of trucking and the use of automobiles, the public sector plays a major role: it builds and maintains roads, regulates safety and inspects vehicles, while a large part of the police is traffic police....

Indeed, even when the conditions which allow markets to work reasonably well are fulfilled—in terms of distribution of information, norms of interaction, etc.—we propose that their role should be evaluated not only in terms of allocative efficiency (whatever that means in ever-changing economies) but also as environments which continuously allow the experimentation of new products, new techniques of production, new organizational forms. In this perspective, markets, when they work, operate as (imperfect) mechanisms of selection. Also at this level, the ways the institutional architecture organizes the interactions amongst economic agents, and the ways policies regulate behaviors and forms of competition are of paramount importance.

21

Mario Cimoli, Giovanni Dosi, Richard Nelson, and Joseph E. Stiglitz

The case of the generation, adoption, and economic exploitation of new scientific and technological knowledge

While the importance of institutions and policies is ubiquitous in all processes of economic coordination and change, this is particularly so with respect to the generation and use of information and knowledge. As we have known since the early works of Nelson (1959) and Arrow (1962), they are in many respects similar to a 'public good' in that the use of information is (i) non-rival (the fact that one uses it does not prevent others from using it too); and (ii) non-excludable (were it not for institutional provisions such as patent-based monopoly rights of exploitation). Moreover, the generation of information is subject to: (i) sunk, upfront costs of production, and basically zero cost of reproduction; and (ii) if anything, there are increasing returns to its use, in the sense that the more we use it the easier it is, and, dynamically, the higher is the likelihood of learning and producing ourselves better, novel, in some sense innovative further pieces of information.

One should note that these very properties of information intrinsically entail phenomena of market failures, to use the jargon just criticized above (also in that marginal prices are of no guidance to efficient market allocation, and equilibria might even fail to exist).

Further insights may be gained by distinguishing between sheer information and knowledge. Knowledge includes (i) the pre-existing cognitive categories which allow information to be interpreted and put to use; (ii) search and problem-solving heuristics irreducible to well-defined algorithms.

All forms of knowledge have a significant tacit aspect, highly complementary to codified information, which makes them person- or organization-embodied and rather sticky in their transmission. Indeed, this is one of the fundamental reasons why technological catching-up by developing countries remains a challenging task even in an era of globalization and free-information flows.

It happens that all processes of generation of new scientific and technological knowledge, as well as of technological imitation and adaptation, involve a rich variety of complementary actors, often including business firms, together with public training and research institutions, communities of practice, technical societies, and trade unions, among others.

In a fundamental sense, institutions and policies addressing technological learning have to do with the construction of *national systems of production and innovation*.

In fact, the process of catch-up involves innovation in an essential way. The innovating activities that drive the process of course differ from the innovating that is the focus of a good deal of research and technological learning in advanced economies. The new technologies, and new practices more generally, that are being taken on board, while new to the country catching up, generally are well established in countries at the frontier. And much of the innovation

22

that is required is organizational and institutional. But what is going on in catch-up most certainly is innovation in the sense that there is a break from past familiar practices, considerable uncertainty about how to make the new practice work effectively, a need for sophisticated learning by doing and by using, and a high risk of failure, as well as a major potential payoff from success.

Together, the dynamics of industrialization rest upon major structural transformations which entail a changing importance of different branches of economic activity as generators of both technological and organizational innovations. The recent literature on innovation highlights the diversity in the sources of learning opportunities and the complementarities between them (Dosi, 1988a; Cimoli and Dosi, 1995; Mowery and Nelson, 1999). In fact in each epoch there appear to be technologies whose domains of application are so wide and their role so crucial that the pattern of technical change of each country depends to a large extent on the national capabilities in mastering production/imitation/innovation in such crucial knowledge areas (e.g. in the past, mechanical engineering, electricity and electrical devices, and nowadays also information technologies). Moreover, the linkages among production activities often embody structured hierarchies whereby the most dynamic technological paradigms play a fundamental role as sources of technological skills, problem-solving opportunities, and productivity improvements. Thus, these core technologies shape the overall absolute advantages/disadvantages of each country. The patterns of technical change of each country in these technologies do not average out with the technological capabilities in other activities but are complementary to them. These core technologies often also imply the construction of basic infrastructures and networks common to a wide range of activities (such as, for example, the electricity grid, the road system, telecommunication information networks). Historical evidence strongly supports the view that self-sustained technological dynamism in catching-up countries is hardly possible without a progressive construction of a widening manufacturing sector involving also indigenous skills in a set of 'core' technologies.

Complementarities, incentives, and coordination hurdles

So far, we have addressed some basic motivations underlying the policies and the institutions affecting primarily the mechanism of knowledge accumulation. But what about coordination problems, stemming in the first instance from the very interrelatedness among multiple heterogeneous agents?

Of course, the distinction is not as clear as that: 'coordination' involves also demand (Keynesian) feedbacks, and requires reasonable degrees of incentive compatibility among agents as well as coordination in learning processes. The fundamental coordination issues here are that of matching between decentralized behaviors and between distributed diverse pieces of knowledge: the radically

23

Mario Cimoli, Giovanni Dosi, Richard Nelson, and Joseph E. Stiglitz

different outcomes that such processes might entail depending crucially on the institutions in which they are nested.

Interestingly, the basics are quite clear to some founding figures of development economics as a discipline (including Nurske, Gerschenkron, Rosenstein-Rodan, Hirschman, and Prebisch).

Consider the following remarks by Nurske (1953):

in our present context it seems to me that the main point is to recognize how a frontal attack of this sort—a wave of capital investments in a number of different industries—can economically succeed while any particular industry may be blocked or discouraged by the limitation of the pre existing market. Where any single enterprise might appear quite inauspicious and impracticable, a wide range of projects in different industries may succeed because they will all support each other, in the sense that the people engaged in each project, now working with more real capital per head and with greater efficiency in terms of output per man-hour, will provide an enlarged market for the products of the new enterprises in other industries. In this way the market difficulty, and the drag it imposes on individual incentives to invest, is removed or at any rate alleviated by means of a dynamic expansion of the market thorough investment carried out in a number of different industries.

And by Gerschenkron (1962):

industrialization process begins only if the industrialization movement can proceed, as it were, along a broad front, starting simultaneously along many lines of economic activities. This is partly the result of existence of complementarity and indivisibilities in economic process. Railroads cannot be built unless coal mines are opened up at the same time; building half a railroad will not do if an inland center is to be connected with a port city. Fruits of industrial progress in certain lines are received as external economies by other branches of industry whose progress in turn accords benefit to the former. In viewing the economic history of Europe in the nineteenth century, the impression is very strong that only when industrial development could commence on a large scale did the tension between the preindustrialization conditions and the benefits expected from industrialization become sufficiently strong to overcome the existing obstacles and to liberate the forces that made for industrial policies.

Similar insights are behind Rosenstein-Rodan's *big push* theory (Rosenstein-Rodan, 1943; cf. also the contemporary revisitation in Murphy, Shleifer, and Vishny, 1989): as discussed in Hoff and Stiglitz (2001), a crucial feature on which the relevance of big push models rest is diffused externalities, where the interaction effects occur through system wide variables such as aggregate demand, industrial demand for inputs, or search costs.

These are all domains where appropriate mixes of policies may and do help— as historical experiences have shown—to 'delock' from the past and foster novel developmental trajectories. It has been so in the past, and, as we shall argue next, there is little reason to believe that it will be radically different in the future, notwithstanding so-called globalization.

24

Indeed, institutions can be seen as the social technologies (Nelson and Sampat, 2001) mastering externalities and matching/mismatching patterns between innovative activities, underlying incentives structures, investment, saving propensities, labor training, and socially distributed skills. In turn, the institutions governing such externalities and complementarities do so also governing interaction rules among agents, shaping their beliefs and the information they may access, their ethos and behavioral rules (for a more detailed discussion, see Hoff and Stiglitz, 2001).

The institutional development of technological capabilities, organizations, and incentive structures: a co-evolutionary dynamic

A fundamental element in countries that successfully caught up with the leaders during the nineteenth and twentieth centuries was active government support of the catch-up process, involving various forms of protection and direct and indirect subsidy. The guiding policy argument has been the need of domestic industry, in the industries of the day judged critical in the development process, for some protection from advanced firms in the leading nations. Alexander Hamilton's argument (1791) for infant industry protection in the new United States was virtually identical to that put forth decades later by Friederich List (1841) regarding Germany's needs. Gershenkron's (1962) famous essay documents the policies and new institutions used in Continental Europe to enable catch-up with Britain. The same story also fits well with the case of Japan, and of Korea and Taiwan somewhat later. In many countries these policies engendered not successful catch-up but a protected inefficient home industry. However, they also were the hallmark during the twentieth century of all the countries that have achieved their goals of catching up. We need to learn more about the circumstances under which infant industry protection leads to a strong indigenous industry, and the conditions under which it is self defeating, and indeed several contributions to this book shed new light on the issue.

These policies obviously angered companies in the leading countries, and their governments, particularly if the supported industry not only supplied its home market but began to invade the world market. While the case made after World War II for free trade was mostly concerned with eliminating protection and subsidy among the rich countries, and at that time there was sympathy for the argument that some infant industry protection was often useful in developing countries, the more recent international treaties that have been made increasingly have been used against import protection and subsidy in countries seeking to catch up from far behind.

Our belief is that Hamilton and List were and continue to be right that successful catch-up in industries where international trade is considerable requires some kind of infant industry protection or other means of support.

Mario Cimoli, Giovanni Dosi, Richard Nelson, and Joseph E. Stiglitz

Moreover, during the nineteenth and early twentieth centuries, many developing countries operated with intellectual property rights regimes which did not restrict seriously the ability of their companies in effect to copy technologies used in the advanced countries. There are many examples where licensing agreements were involved, but we believe that for the most part these were vehicles through which technology transfer was effected for a fee or other considerations, rather than instances of aggressive protection of intellectual property by the company in the advanced country.

As with infant industry protection and subsidy, conflicts tended to emerge largely when the catching-up company began to encroach onto world markets, or even to export to the home market of the company with the patent rights. Increasing instances of this clearly were a major factor in inducing the treaty on Trade-Related Aspects of Intellectual Property Rights. But this treaty makes vulnerable to prosecution not just companies in developing countries that are exporting, but also companies that stay in their home markets.

More generally, what are the different domains of policy intervention and how do they map into different policy measures and related institutions?

Table 2.1 summarizes an exploratory taxonomy.

In the last resort, policies and other activities of institutional engineering affect together (i) the technological capabilities of individual and corporate organizations, and the rate at which they actually learn; (ii) the economic signals that they face (including of course profitability signals and perceived opportunity costs); (iii) the ways they interact with each other and with non-market institutions (e.g. public agencies, development banks, training and research entities, etc.).

It happens that all major developed countries present indeed relatively high degrees of intervention—whether consciously conceived as industrial policies or not—that affect all the above variables. And this applies, even more so, to the period when today's developed countries were catching up with the international leader. What primarily differentiate the various countries are the instruments, the institutional arrangements, and the philosophy of intervention.

In another work, one of the authors considers the case of Japanese policies, especially in relation to electronic technologies, after WWII, as a paradigmatic example of catching-up policies (Dosi, 1984).

Interestingly, Japan appears to have acted comprehensively upon all the variables categorized in our taxonomy. A heavy discretionary intervention upon the structure of signals (also involving formal and informal protection against imports and foreign investments) recreated the 'vacuum environment' that is generally enjoyed only by the technological leader(s). However, this was matched by a pattern of fierce oligopolistic rivalry between Japanese companies and a heavy export orientation which fostered technological dynamism and prevented any exploitation of protection simply in terms of collusive monopolistic pricing.

26

Institutions and Policies

Table 2.1. Some classification of the variables and processes which institutions and policies act upon (in general and with particular reference to technological learning)

Domains of policy intervention	Policy measures	Related institutions
(i) Opportunities of scientific and technological innovation	Science policies, graduate education, "frontier" technological projects	Research universities, public research centers, medical institutes, space and military agencies, etc.
(ii) Socially distributed learning and technological capabilities	Broader education and training policies	From primary education to polytechnics, to US-type "land-grant colleges", etc.
(iii) Targeted Industrial Support Measures, affecting e.g. types of firms, etc.—*in primis* the structure, ownership, modes of governance of business firms (e.g. domestic vs. foreign, family vs. publicly owned companies, etc.)	From the formation of state-owned firms to their privatization, from "national champions" policies to policies affecting MNCs' investments; all the way to the legislation affecting corporate governance	State-owned holdings, public merchant banks, public "venture capitalist", public utilities
(iv) The capabilities of economic agents (in the first instance business firms) in terms of the technological knowledge they embody, the effectiveness and speed with which they search for new technological and organizational advances, etc.	cf. especially points (ii), (iii) and also R&D policies; policies affecting the adoption of new equipment, etc.	
(v) The economic signals and incentives profit-motivated agents face (including actual and expected prices and profit rates, appropriability conditions for innovations, entry barriers, etc.)	Price regulations; tariffs and quotas in international trade; Intellectual Property Rights regimes, etc.	Related regulatory agencies, agencies governing research and production subsidies, trade controlling entities, agencies granting and controlling IPRs
(vi) Selection mechanisms (overlapping with the above)	Policies and legislation affecting anti-trust and competition; entry and bankruptcy; allocation of finance; markets for corporate ownership; etc.	Anti-trust authorities, institutions governing bankruptcy procedures, etc.
(vii) Patterns of distribution of information and of interaction amongst different types of agents (e.g. customers, suppliers, banks, shareholders, managers, workers, etc.)	Governance of labor markets, product markets, bank–industry relationships, etc. all the way to collectively shared arrangements for within-firms information-sharing mobility and control; forms of cooperation and competition amongst rival firms, etc. (cf. for example the historical differences between Japanese vs. Anglo-Saxon forms of Industrial governance)	Basically, all of the above

27

Mario Cimoli, Giovanni Dosi, Richard Nelson, and Joseph E. Stiglitz

It is tempting to compare the Japanese experience—notwithstanding, recent, mostly macroeconomic difficulties—with others, on average less successful, such as the European ones, which heavily relied upon a single instrument, financial transfers (especially R&D subsidies and transfers on capital account), leaving to the endogenous working of the international market both the determination of the patterns of signals and the response capabilities of individual firms. Certainly, there are country-specific features of the Japanese example which are hardly transferable. However, that case, in its striking outcome, points at a general possibility of reshaping the patterns of comparative advantages as they emerge from the endogenous evolution of the international markets.

The comparison between the experience of Far Eastern countries and Latin American ones is equally revealing (cf. Amsden, 1989 and 2001; Wade, 1990; Kim and Nelson, 2000; Dosi, Freeman, and Fabiani, 1994; among others).

In a nutshell, Korea—as well as other Far Eastern economies—has been able to 'twist around' absolute and relative prices and channel the resources stemming from 'static' comparative advantages toward the development of activities characterized by higher learning opportunities and demand elasticities (Amsden, 1989).[1] And they did that in ways which penalized rent-seeking behaviors by private firms. In fact, the major actors in technological learning have been large business groups—the chaebols—which were able at a very early stage of development to internalize skills for the selection of technologies acquired from abroad, their efficient use and their adaptation and, not much later, were able to grow impressive engineering capabilities (cf. Nelson, 1993).

This process has been further supported by a set of institutions and networks for improving human resources (Amsden, 1989). All this sharply contrasts with the Latin American experience, where the arrangement between the State and the private sector has often been more indulgent over inefficiencies and rent-accumulation, and less attentive to the accumulation of socially diffused technological capabilities and skills.

Ultimately, success or failure appears to depend on the combinations of different institutional arrangements and policies, in so far as they affect learning processes by individuals and organizations, on the one hand, and selection processes (including of course market competition), on the other.

Certainly, the historical experience shows a great variety of country- and sector-specific combinations between the types of policies illustrated above. Some subtle regularities nonetheless emerge.

First, a regularity, holding from nineteenth-century Europe and the US all the way to contemporary times, is the centrality of public agencies, such as universities, and public policies in the generation and establishment of new technological paradigms.

Second, and relatedly, incentives are often not enough. A crucial role of policies is to affect the capabilities of the actors, especially in the case of new technological paradigms, but also in all cases of catching-up whereby no reasonable incentive structure might be sufficient to motivate private actors to surmount big technological lags.

Third, market discipline is helpful in so far as it weeds out the low performers and rewards the high performers within particular populations of firms. However, nothing guarantees that too high selective shocks will not wipe out those entire populations, thus also eliminating any future learning possibility.

Fourth, policies—especially those aimed at catching-up—generally face the need to balance measures aimed at capability building (and also at protecting the 'infant learner') with mechanisms curbing inertia and rent-seeking. For example, the latter are indeed one of the major elements missing in the old Latin American experience of import substitution while the former are what is lacking under many more recent liberalization policies.

Fifth, historically, a successful catching-up effort in terms of per capita income and wages has always been accompanied by catching-up in the new and most dynamic technological paradigms, irrespective of the initial patterns of comparative advantages, specialization, and market-generated signals. Our conjecture is that, *ceteris paribus*, the structural need for policies affecting *also* the patterns of economic signals (including relative prices and relative profitabilities) as they emerge from the international market will be greater, the higher the distance of any one country from the technological frontier. This is what Amsden (1989) has provocatively called policies of deliberately 'getting the prices wrong'. Conversely, endogenous market mechanisms tend to behave in a virtuous manner for those countries that happen to be on the frontier, especially in the newest/most promising technologies. This is broadly confirmed by historical experience: unconditional free trade often happened to be advocated and fully exploited only by the technologically and politically leading countries.

On some fundamental trade-offs facing institutions and policies in learning economies

In a world characterized by technical change (both continuous change along defined technological trajectories and discontinuous, related to the emergence of new technological paradigms), technological lags and leads shape the patterns of intersectoral and interproduct profitability signals and, thus, also the patterns of microeconomic allocation of resources. The latter, however, may affect the long-term macroeconomic dynamism of each country, in terms of both rates of growth of income consistent with the foreign balance constraint and of technological innovativeness. In the last resort, this happens because the effects of a multiplicity of signals (related to profitability, long-term demand growth, and technological opportunities) upon microeconomic processes of

Mario Cimoli, Giovanni Dosi, Richard Nelson, and Joseph E. Stiglitz

adjustments are likely to be *asymmetric*. In another work one of the authors elaborates on this point distinguishing between the notion of (i) allocative efficiency; (ii) innovative (Schumpeterian) efficiency; and (iii) growth efficiency of particular patterns of production (Dosi, Pavitt, and Soete, 1990). There we argue that, especially in countries far from the technological frontier, patterns of allocation of resources which are 'efficient' on the grounds of the incumbent distribution of technological capabilities and relative prices might well entail negative long-term effects in terms of demand elasticities of the goods one country will be able to produce (the 'growth efficiency') and of the innovative potential associated with that (the criterion of 'innovative efficiency'). Whenever trade-offs between different notions of efficiency arise, sub-optimal or perverse macroeconomic outcomes may emerge. Since the *future* pattern of technological advantages/disadvantages is also related to the *present* allocative patterns, we can see at work here dynamic processes which Kaldor termed as *circular causation*: economic signals related to intersectoral profitabilities—which lead in a straightforward manner to comparative advantages and relative specializations—certainly control and check the allocative efficiency of the various productive employments, but may also play a more ambiguous or even perverse role in relation to long-term macroeconomic trends.

Note that these possible trade-offs have little to do with the informational efficiency of market processes (even if, of course, various forms of informational asymmetries are likely to make things worse). Rather it is the general condition of an economic system that technological opportunities vary across products and across sectors. Moreover, within each technology and each sector the technological capabilities of each firm and each country are associated with the actual process of production and innovation in the area. Thus, the mechanisms regarding resource allocation *today* affect also where technical skills will be accumulated, (possibly) innovation undertaken, economies of scale reaped, and so on. However, the potential for these effects differs widely between technologies and sectors. This is another aspect of the irreversibility of economic processes: present allocative choices influence the direction and rate of the future evolution of technological coefficients. Whenever we abandon the idea of technology as a set of blueprints and conceive technical progress as a joint product with manufacturing, it is possible to imagine an economic system which is dynamically better off than otherwise (in terms of productivity, innovativeness, etc.), if it evolves in disequilibrium vis-à-vis conditions of allocative efficiency.

It is rather easy to see how such trade-offs between allocative efficiency and innovative efficiency can emerge. The patterns of specialization (with their properties of allocative efficiency) are determined, for each country, by the relative size of the sector-specific technology gaps (or leads) (more in Dosi, Pavitt, and Soete, 1990). Whenever the gap is highest in the most dynamic technologies (i.e. those characterized by the highest technological opportunities), allocative efficiency will conflict directly with innovative efficiency. We would suggest that the likelihood of such trade-offs between the two notions of efficiency is proportional to the distance of each country from the technological frontier in the newest, most dynamic, and most pervasive technologies.[2]

A similar argument applies to the trade-offs between allocative and growth efficiency: ultimately countries may well end up by 'efficiently' specializing in the production of commodities which a relatively small or even decreasing number of world consumers wants to buy thus tightening their ability to grow consistently with some foreign balance constraint.[3]

Under conditions of non-decreasing (often increasing) returns, there is no straightforward way in which markets can relate the varying growth and innovative efficiencies of the various commodities to relative profitability signals for the microeconomic agents.[4]

This defines also a fundamental domain for policies.

A detailed understanding of, and intervention on, patterns of signals, rules of allocative responses, and forms of institutional organization of the 'economic machine' are particularly important in those phases of transition from a technological regime (based on old technological paradigms) to a new one. These historical periods define a new set of opportunities and threats for each country: the patterns of international generation and diffusion of technologies become more fluid as do, consequently, the international trade flows and the relative levels of per capita income.

The contemporary economy—we believe—is undergoing such a change. In the process, comparative advantages become the self-fulfilling prophecy of a successful set of institutional actions and private strategies: *ex post*, technological and economic success makes 'optimal' from the point of view of the economist what *ex ante* is a political dream.

Some tricky operational questions

That having been acknowledged, interesting lessons are likely to come from the detailed comparison of the outcomes of different combinations of institutional arrangements and policy measures as historically observed.

For example, (i) what lessons can be drawn from the comparison between 'import substitution' versus 'export promotion' philosophies? (ii) how does capital accumulation complement technological learning? (iii) what is precisely the importance of the financial sector and its relationship with industrial activities? (iv) how do strategies of technological acquisition based on MNCs' investment compare with others relying on the growth of domestic firms? (v) what are the most effective policy devices aimed at curbing rent-seeking behaviors which often emerge as a by-product of the efforts to foster learning by domestic firms? (vi) what is the role of public research institutions in the process of catching-up? (vii) how is the latter affected by different IPR regimes?

31

Mario Cimoli, Giovanni Dosi, Richard Nelson, and Joseph E. Stiglitz

and (viii) how do macroeconomic policies influence microeconomic behaviors and adjustment processes especially with regard to technological and organizational learning?

Indeed several of these questions—crucial to the understanding of the effectiveness of different policy combinations—are addressed by various contributions to this book.

However, possibly the trickiest question of all concerns the extent to which the lessons from the past can be useful under the current regime of international economic relations.

Policies in a globalized world: the new challenges

Our argument so far, we believe, applies to the generality of the processes of catching-up and industrialization, notwithstanding their obvious historical variety. But what are the specific lessons which can be drawn from the most recent phase of international development?

In fact, the last couple of decades of globalization have gone hand-in-hand with powerful efforts to impose a policy regime grounded in rather extreme forms of economic orthodoxy, which in the case of developing countries has gone under the name of 'Washington Consensus'. Of that, Latin America has been an exemplar victim.

Trade liberalization, leading eventually to free trade, was a key part of such a 'consensus'—sometimes imposed indeed at gunpoint. The emphasis on trade liberalization was natural: the Latin American countries, it was claimed, had stagnated behind protectionist barriers. Import substitution according to the same view had proved a highly ineffective strategy for development. In many countries industries were producing products with negative value added, and innovation was stifled. The usual argument—that protectionism itself stifled innovation—was indeed somewhat confused. Governments could have created competition among domestic firms, which would have provided incentives to import new technologies. It was the failure to create competition internally, more than protection from abroad, that was the cause of the stagnation. Of course, competition from abroad would have provided an important challenge for domestic firms. But it is possible that in the one-sided race, domestic firms would have dropped out of the competition rather than enter the fray. Consumers might have benefited, but the effects on growth may have been more ambiguous. In fact, the subsequent experience materialized all the worries in these respects. Trade liberalization may create competition, but it does not do so automatically. If trade liberalization occurs in an economy with a monopoly importer, the rents may simply be transferred from the government to the monopolist, with little decrease in prices. Trade liberalization is thus neither necessary nor sufficient for creating a competitive and innovative economy.

32

At least as important as creating competition in the previously sheltered import-competing sector of the economy is promoting competition on the export side. The success of the East Asian economies is a powerful example of this point. By allowing each country to take advantage of its competitive strength, trade increases wages and expands consumption opportunities. For the last few decades in the case of Far Eastern countries trade has been doing just that.

Moreover, as the comparison between different experiences in Latin America and in the Far East shows, a free-trade shock does not automatically trigger any increase in the accumulation of knowledge and innovative capabilities. On the contrary, in a world characterized by multiple forms of localized increasing returns (both localized in terms of technologies and in spatial terms), greater integration may well lead to phenomena of increasing differentiation with self-reinforcement and lock-in of particular production activities, specialization patterns, technological capabilities (or lack of them): compare the discussion above. Putting it another way, it is easy to show that a world which becomes, at some level, increasingly integrated—but not (even roughly) identical in initial conditions, institutions, technological capabilities, mechanisms of economic interaction, etc.—might be subject to various forms of 'local' virtuous or vicious circles, *even more so than in the past.*

Finally, the impact of greater integration is likely to depend on the modes through which it is implemented. The experience of many Latin American countries is a good case in point. When macro (globalizing) shocks suddenly induced higher selection upon domestic firms, massive mortality of firms did often entail an apparent reduction of the productivity gap vis-à-vis the international frontier. But this happens to come together—at least in Latin America—with striking increases in both unemployment rates (i.e. transitions of parts of the labor force from low productivity to zero productivity states) and with tightening foreign-balance constraints to growth, in turn the joint outcome of relatively low elasticities of exports to world growth and high elasticities of imports to domestic growth (cf. Cimoli and Correa, 2005).

Certainly both the recent changes in international—political and economic—relations and the ongoing 'ICT revolution' are reshaping the opportunities and constraints facing policy making and institutional engineering, but by no means have decreased their importance. On the contrary, they demand new forms of governance which one is only beginning to explore.

So, for example, on the technological side, the characteristics of productive knowledge have nowadays changed as compared to, say, the electromechanical paradigms within which countries like Germany and the USA caught up and overtook England nearly one century ago, and they might be also partly different from the type of knowledge—a good deal centered on 'first generation' ICT—through which, more recently, Korea and Taiwan approached the technological frontier. In turn, with changes in the type of knowledge countries need to accumulate and improve upon, often come also changes in the most

Mario Cimoli, Giovanni Dosi, Richard Nelson, and Joseph E. Stiglitz

appropriate policy packages concerning, for example, the type of education offered; the support to national incumbent firms versus MNCs versus new entrants; the role of public training and research centers. Indeed, many of the contributions to this book tackle these issues.

Major changes have come also in the regime of international trade and property right protection, associated with WTO, TRIPS, and several bilateral agreements. The new regime, first, has implied a reduction in the degrees of freedom developing countries can enjoy in their trade policies, while, to repeat, all catching-up countries in the preceding waves of industrialization could exploit a large menu of quotas, tariffs, and other forms of non-tariff barriers. Second, it involves a much more aggressive international policing of intellectual property rights and, thus, other things being equal, more difficulties in imitating and 'inventing around' existing products and production processes—again, activities which have been at the core of the first phases of industrialization, from the US to Switzerland, to Japan, to Korea ....

Hence, a fundamental policy question concerns the degrees of freedom left for discretionary public interventions supporting in different ways specific technologies, sectors, and firms. How stringent are the new international constraints? Note that the answer here is likely to vary from sector to sector and from technology to technology. And it is likely to depend also on the distance of any country from the international technological frontier. For example, many African and some Latin American countries might not be directly affected by a tightening in the IPR regimes, having little capabilities to imitate to begin with (although they might still be badly affected by being forced to buy e.g. drugs or software at ridiculous prices from first-world MNCs rather than from more advanced but still 'imitating' countries). Conversely, tighter IPR regimes may well represent a major hindrance to more advanced catching-up countries.

Given that, how easy is it to play around with existing rules? That is, putting it the other way round, how urgent is it to reform the incumbent international trade and IPR regimes from a pro-development perspective?

On all these issues, it is time to build a 'new consensus' prominently featuring the exploration of forms of institutional governance which in developing countries also foster knowledge accumulation and render its efficient economic exploitation consistent with the multiple interests of profit-motivated agents. Such a consensus, we shall repeatedly argue, is going to be based on a pragmatic view of markets whereby the latter sometimes work in a developmental sense, sometimes do not, and even when they do work, their effectiveness cannot be separated from the contribution of supporting institutions and policies. And, last but not least, it must be a consensus sensitive to issues of equity and of access to the sharing of the benefits from growth stemming from technological and organizational learning.

The contributions to this book, from different angles, indeed move us in this direction.

Notes

1. On the 'perverse' importance of rent-seeking in the development process, cf. Khan (2000a, 2000b).
2. Somewhat similar conclusions on the crucial importance of the distance from the international technological frontier in terms of required mix of policy measures can be drawn also on the grounds of 'neo-Schumpeterian' models of growth: cf. Aghion and Howitt (2005).
3. In Dosi, Pavitt, and Soete (1990) and Cimoli (1988) one argues this proposition on the ground of a model nesting a Kaldor–Thirlwall growth dynamic onto diverse technology gaps at the commodity level. A similar proposition however can be shown to hold under more conventional assumptions: see Rodrik (2005).
4. If the same argument is put in a language more familiar to the economist, the widespread possibility of trade-offs between allocative, Schumpeterian, and growth efficiencies arises from the fact that the general case is one of non-convexity of production and consumption possibility sets and dynamic increasing returns and path-dependencies of technological advances. On the point, within a growing literature, see the complementary arguments of Atkinson and Stigliltz (1969), David (1988), Arthur (1994), Dosi, Pavitt, and Soete (1990), Krugman (1996), Antonelli (1995), Cimoli (1988), Castaldi and Dosi (2006).

References

Aghion P. and S. Durlauf (eds.) (2005), *Handbook of Economic Growth*, Elsevier, Amsterdam.

—— and P. Howitt (2005), 'Appropriate Growth Policy: A Unifying Framework,' The 2005 Joseph Schumpeter Lecture, Presented to the European Economic Association Congress, Amsterdam (August 25).

Amsden A. (1989), *Asia's Next Giant: South Korea and Late Industrialization*, Oxford University Press, New York.

—— (2001), *The Rise of 'the Rest': Challenges to the West from Late-Industrializing Economies*, Oxford University Press, Oxford.

Antonelli C. (1995), *The Economics of Localized Technological Change and Industrial Dynamics*, Kluwer Publishers, Boston.

Arrow K. (1962), 'Economic Welfare and the Allocation of Resources for Invention' in R. Nelson (ed.) *The Rate and Direction of Inventive Activity*, Princeton University Press, Princeton.

Arthur W.B. (1994), *Increasing Returns and Path Dependence in the Economy*, University of Michigan Press, Ann Arbor.

Atkinson A., and J. Stiglitz (1969), 'A New View of Technological Change,' *Economic Journal*, 79: 573–8.

Castaldi C., M. Cimoli, N. Correa, and G. Dosi (2004), 'Technological Learning, Policy Regimes and Growth in a "Globalized" Economy: General Patterns and the Latin American Experience,' LEM Working Paper 2004/01, Sant'Anna School of Advanced Studies, Pisa.

—— and G. Dosi (2006), 'The Grip of History and the Scope for Novelty: Some Results and Open Questions on Path Dependence in Economic Processes' in A. Wimmer and R. Kössler (eds.) *Understanding Change*, Palgrave Macmillan, 99–128.

Mario Cimoli, Giovanni Dosi, Richard Nelson, and Joseph E. Stiglitz

Cimoli M. (1988), 'Technological Gaps and Institutional Asymmetries in a North–South Model with a Continuum of Goods,' *Metroeconomica*, 39: 245–74.

—— and G. Dosi (1995), 'Technological Paradigms, Patterns of Learning and Development. An Introductory Roadmap,' *Journal of Evolutionary Economics*, 5: 243–68.

—— and N. Correa (2005), 'Trade Openness and Technological Gaps in Latin America: A "Low Growth" Trap' in J. A. Ocampo (ed.) *Beyond Reforms, Structural Dynamics and Macroeconomic Vulnerability*, Stanford Economics and Finance, Palo Alto.

David P.A. (1988), 'Path Dependence: Putting the Past into the Future of Economics,' Technical Report 533, Stanford University, Institute for Mathematical Studies in the Social Science.

Dosi G. (1984), *Technical Change and Industrial Transformation*, Macmillan, London and St. Martin Press, New York.

—— (1988), 'Institutions and Markets in a Dynamic World,' *The Manchester School of Economic and Social Studies*, 56: 119–46.

—— (1988a), 'Sources, Procedures and Microeconomic Effects of Innovation,' *Journal of Economic Literature*, 26(3): 1120–71.

—— K. Pavitt, and L. Soete (1990), *The Economics of Technical Change and International Trade*, Harvester Wheatsheaf, London, New York University Press, New York.

—— C. Freeman, and S. Fabiani (1994), 'The Process of Economic Development: Introducing Some Stylized Facts and Theories on Technologies, Firms and Institutions,' *Industrial and Corporate Change*, 3: 1–45.

Freeman C. (1982), *The Economics of Industrial Innovation*, 2nd edn., Francis Pinter, London.

—— (2004), 'Technological Infrastructures and International Competitiveness,' *Industrial and Corporate Change*, 541–69.

Gerschenkron A. (1962), *Economic Backwardness in Historical Perspective*, Harvard University Press, Cambridge, MA.

Greenwald B. and J. Stiglitz (1986), 'Externalities in Economics with Imperfect Information and Incomplete Markets,' *Quarterly Journal of Economics*, 101: 229–64.

Hamilton A., (1791), 'Report on the Subject of Manufactures' in H.C. Syrett et al. (1966) *The Papers of Alexander Hamilton: Vol. X*. Columbia University Press, New York.

Hausmann R., J. Hwang, and D. Rodrick (2005), 'What You Export Matters,' CID Working Paper No. 123, Center for International Development, Harvard University, Cambridge, MA.

Hirschman A.O. (1958), *The Strategy of Economic Development*, Yale University Press, New Haven.

—— (1982), 'Rival Interpretations of Market Society: Civilizing, Destructive, or Feeble?' *Journal of Economic Literature*, 20: 1463–84.

Hoff K. (1996), 'Market Failures and the Distribution of Wealth: A Perspective from the Economics of Information,' *Politics and Society*, 24: 411–32.

—— and J. Stiglitz (2001), 'Modern Economic Theory and Development' in Meier and Stiglitz (2001).

Khan, M. (ed.) (2000a), 'Rents, Efficiency and Growth' in *Rents, Rent-Seeking and Economic Development: Theory and Evidence in Asia*, Cambridge University Press, Cambridge.

—— (ed.) (2000b), 'Rent-Seeking as Process' in *Rents, Rent-Seeking and Economic Development: Theory and Evidence in Asia*, Cambridge University Press, Cambridge.

Krugman, P.R. (1996), *The Self-Organizing Economy*, Blackwell Publishers, Cambridge, MA/Oxford.

Lall S. (2000), 'Selective Industrial and Trade Policies in Developing Countries: Theoretical and Empirical Issues,' QEH Working Paper Series 48, University of Oxford, Oxford.

Landes D. (1969), *The Unbound Prometheus*, Cambridge University Press, Cambridge.

List F. (1841), *The National System of Political Economy*, trans. S.S. Lloyd. Longmans, Green and Co., London.

Meier G. and J. Stiglitz (eds.) (2001), *Frontiers of Development Economics*, Oxford University Press, Oxford/New York.

Mowery D. and R.R. Nelson (1999), *Sources of Industrial Leadership: Studies of Seven Industries*, Cambridge University Press, Cambridge.

Murphy K., A. Shleifer, and R.W. Vishny (1989), 'Industrialization and the Big Push,' *Journal of Political Economy*, 97: 1003–26.

Nelson R.R. (1959), 'The Simple Economics of Basic Scientific Research,' *Journal of Political Economy*, 67: 297–306.

—— (1982), *Government and Technical Progress*, Pergamon Press, New York.

Nelson R.R. (1993) *National Innovation Systems: A Comparative Analysis*. Oxford University Press, New York.

—— (1994), 'The Co-Evolution of Technology, Industrial Structure and Supporting Institutions,' *Industrial and Corporate Change*, 3: 47–64.

—— and B. Sampat (2001), 'Making Sense of Institutions as a Factor Shaping Economic Performance,' *Journal of Economic Behavior & Organization*, 44: 31–54.

—— (2004), 'Economic Development from the Perspective of the Evolutionary Theory,' Columbia University, New York, mimeo.

—— (ed.) (2005), *The Limits of Market Organization*, Russell Sage Foundation, New York.

Nurske R. (1953), *Problems of Capital Formation in Underdeveloped Countries*, Oxford University Press, New York.

Ocampo J.A. (ed.) (2005), *Beyond Reforms, Structural Dynamics and Macroeconomic Vulnerability*, Stanford University Press, Palo Alto.

—— (2005), 'The Quest for Dynamic Efficiency: Structural Dynamics and Economic growth in Developing Countries' in Ocampo (2005).

Polanyi K. (1957), *The Great Transformation*, Beacon Press, Boston.

Rodrik D. (1995), 'Trade and Industrial Policy Reform' in J. Behrman and T.N. Srinivasan (eds.) *Handbook of Development Economics, Vol. III*. North Holland, Amsterdam.

—— (ed.) (2003), *In Search of Prosperity: Analytic Narratives on Economic Growth*, Princeton University Press, Princeton.

—— (2005), 'Growth Strategies' in P. Aghion and S. Durlauf (2005).

Rosenberg N. (1976), *Perspective on Technology*, Cambridge University Press, Cambridge.

—— (1982), *Inside the Blackbox*, Cambridge University Press, Cambridge.

Rosenstein-Rodan P. (1943), 'Problems of Industrialization of Eastern and Southeastern Europe,' *Economic Journal*, 53: 210–11.

Stiglitz J.E. (1994), *Whither Socialism?* MIT Press, Cambridge, MA.

—— (1996), 'Some Lesson from the East Asian Miracle,' *World Bank Research Observer*, 11: 151–77.

Mario Cimoli, Giovanni Dosi, Richard Nelson, and Joseph E. Stiglitz

Stiglitz J. E. (2001), 'More Instruments and Broader Goals Moving toward the Post-Washington Consensus' in H. Chang (ed.) *The Rebel Within*, Wimbledon Publishing Company, London. (Originally presented as the 1998 WIDER Annual Lecture, Helsinki, January).

Veblen T. (1915), *Imperial Germany and Industrial Revolution*, Macmillan, London.

Wade R. (1990), *Governing the Market: Economic Theory and the Role of Government in East Asian Industrialization*, Princeton University Press, Princeton.

[24]

Advances in Complex Systems, Vol. 7, No. 2 (2004) 157–186
© World Scientific Publishing Company

MATCHING, BARGAINING, AND WAGE SETTING IN AN EVOLUTIONARY MODEL OF LABOR MARKET AND OUTPUT DYNAMICS

G. FAGIOLO

L.E.M., Sant'Anna School of Advanced Studies, Pisa, Italy
giorgio.fagiolo@sssup.it

G. DOSI

L.E.M., Sant'Anna School of Advanced Studies, Pisa, Italy
gdosi@sssup.it

R. GABRIELE

L.E.M., Sant'Anna School of Advanced Studies, Pisa, Italy

and

D.I.S.A., University of Trento, Trento, Italy
rgabriel@cs.unitn.it

Received 30 September 2003
Revised 20 April 2004

In this paper, we present an agent-based, evolutionary, model of output- and labor-market dynamics. Firms produce a homogeneous, perishable good under constant returns to scale using labor only. Labor productivities are firm-specific and change stochastically due to technical progress. The key feature of the model resides in an explicit microfoundation of the processes of: (i) matching between firms and workers, (ii) job search, (iii) wage setting, (iv) endogenous formation of aggregate demand, and (v) endogenous price formation. Moreover, we allow for a competitive process entailing selection of firms on the basis of their revealed competitiveness. Simulations show that the model is able to robustly reproduce Beveridge, Wage and Okun curves under quite broad behavioral and institutional settings. The system generates endogenously an Okun coefficient greater than one even if individual firms employ production functions exhibiting constant returns to labor. Monte Carlo simulations also indicate that statistically detectable shifts in Okun and Beveridge curves emerge as the result of changes in institutional, behavioral, and technological parameters. Finally, the model generates sharp predictions about how system parameters affect aggregate performance (i.e. average GDP growth) and its volatility.

Keywords: Labor markets; dynamics; aggregate regularities; Beveridge curve; Okun curve; wage curve; matching models.

1. Introduction

In the last decades, the issue of microfoundations of macroeconomic dynamics has played a central role in the economic profession (cf. Ref. 16 for a discussion).

Theoretical explanations of observed aggregate regularities have at least begun to employ formal frameworks where macroeconomic outcomes are interpreted as the result of the interactions of individual firms, workers, consumers, etc.

Traditionally, efforts of microfounding macroeconomic dynamics have been grounded upon a hyper-rational, maximizing, "representative agent", thus avoiding by construction the challenges posed by aggregation of heterogeneous agents [24].

Despite the fact that their high formal sophistication, the degrees of success of these models is, at best, mixed. In particular, they turn out to be unable to *jointly* account for multiple empirically observed "stylized facts." For example, as far as labor market dynamics is concerned, existing literature seems to completely lack a joint explanation of the most important aggregate regularities concerning: (i) the process through which firms and workers meet in the labor market; (ii) how this matching process affects wage setting and (un)employment dynamics; (iii) the extent to which unemployment and output interact over the business cycle.[a]

More specifically, existing (standard) microfoundations of labor market dynamics seem to have failed in jointly explaining three crucial stylized facts that one can typically observe in the data, namely: (a) the Beveridge curve, which predicts a negative relationship between rates of vacancies and rates of unemployment; (b) the Phillips (respectively, Wage) curve, suggesting that changes in wage rates (respectively, levels of wage rates) are negatively related to unemployment rates; (c) the Okun curve, which posits a more than proportional increase in real GDP for every one percentage point reduction in the unemployment rate.

In this paper, we propose an alternative, evolutionary-based, approach to the microfoundation of labor-market and output dynamics.[b] In the model we present in the following, the economy is populated by boundedly-rational firms and workers. Firms produce a homogeneous, perishable good under constant returns to scale using labor as the sole input of production. Workers are skill-homogeneous and buy the good spending all their wages. Labor productivities are firm-specific and change stochastically due to technical progress. Both firms and workers hold expectations about desired wages they want to offer and get, and they are able to adaptively revise their expectations on the basis of observed market dynamics.

A key feature of the model resides in an explicit microfoundation of the processes of: (i) matching between firms and workers; (ii) job search; (iii) wage setting; (iv) endogenous formation of aggregate demand; (v) endogenous price formation. Moreover, in the spirit of evolutionary-based approaches, we allow for selection (e.g. exit) of firms on the basis of their revealed competitiveness (as measured by last-period profits). Since firms interact both in the labor market and in the product

---

[a]For a quite exhaustive overview of the state-of-the-art of both theoretical and empirical labor market literature, cf. Refs. 3, 4 and 36.

[b]More on the general *Weltanschauung* of the evolutionary approach is in Refs. 15 and 17. The model we present has large overlappings with the "Agent-Based Computational Economics" (ACE) approach [1, 18, 40], as well as with self-organization models of labor markets pioneered by Lesourne [28].

market, their revealed competitiveness is affected not only by their production decisions, but also by their hiring and wage-setting behaviors.

Macroeconomic dynamics is generated in the model via aggregation of individual behaviors. Statistical properties exhibited by aggregate variables might then be interpreted as emergent properties grounded on persistent micro disequilibria. Consequently, even when some equilibrium relationship exists between aggregate variables (e.g. inflows and outflows from unemployment), the economy might persistently depart from it and follow some disequilibrium path. The observed stable relations amongst those same aggregate variables might emerge out of turbulent, disequilibrium, microeconomic interactions.

Computer simulations show that the model is able to robustly and jointly reproduce Beveridge, Wage and Okun curves over sufficiently large regions of the parameter space. Moreover, the system endogenously generates (absolute values of) Okun coefficients larger than one even if production at the individual level does not enjoy increasing returns to labor. Monte Carlo simulations also indicate that statistically detectable shifts in Okun and Beveridge curves emerge as the result of changes in institutional, behavioral, and technological parameters. Finally, the model generates quite sharp predictions about how system parameters affect aggregate performance (i.e. average GDP growth) and its volatility.

Our results lend support to a disequilibrium foundation of aggregate regularities: despite the fact that the economy always departs from equilibrium (if any), aggregate regularities emerge as the outcome of decentralized interactions, adaptive behavioral adjustments, and imperfect coordination.

The paper is organized as follows. In Sec. 2 we briefly survey empirical findings about aggregate regularities in labor market dynamics and we discuss how mainstream economic theory has been trying to provide explanations of such stylized facts. In Sec. 3, we introduce the model. Sections 4 and 5 present the results of simulation exercises. Finally, in Sec. 6 we draw some concluding remarks.

2. Labor Market Dynamics: Empirical Findings and Theoretical Explanations

When dealing with the interplay between labor market and output dynamics, three aggregate stylized facts stand out.

First, the Beveridge curve (BC) postulates a negative relationship (over time) between the rate of unemployment u and the rate of vacancies v, where rates are defined in terms of total employment.[c] The intuition is simple: if an economy experiments higher level of vacancies — in turn plausibly corresponding to a higher level of aggregate demand — it is easier for workers to find a job. Thus, one should also

---

[c]Observation of reliable proxies for actual vacancies entails many empirical problems, especially in Europe, see Ref. 39. For instance, one is typically bounded to observe only *ex-ante* vacancies (i.e. job openings). *Ex-post* vacancies (i.e. unfilled job openings) are much more affected by frictions than *ex-ante* ones and thus should be in principle preferred as object of analysis.

observe a lower level of unemployment. Movements along the curve should be typically induced by the business cycle, while the position of the BC in the (u, v) space is typically related to the degree of "frictions" in the market and, more generally, to its institutional setting. The closer the curve to the axes, the lower — *ceteris paribus* — market "frictions," cf. Ref. 29.

As far as co-movements between unemployment and wages are concerned, a second and complementary empirical regularity is the famous Phillips curve (i.e. negative relationship between *changes* of the wage rate and the unemployment rate); or the alternative Wage curve [8], which characterizes economies with a negative relationship between *levels* of the wage rate and the unemployment rate [7, 14, 20]. Empirical studies [8, 13] show that in homogeneous areas, WC is in general valid, while PC is not.[d] This empirical evidence seems to robustly hold across regions, countries, etc. but also among different institutional setups [9, 10]. The interpretation of a WC is quite controversial and bears some important theoretical implications. For instance, the competitive equilibrium framework cannot be invoked to account for WC emergence. In fact, a competitive labor market with all its canonical features would lead to a *positive* correlation between the unemployment rate and the wage rate. Climbing up a downward demand for labor schedule — i.e. raising wages — would indeed induce higher levels of unemployment, as the unmet supply of labor would grow.

A third fundamental aggregate regularity is the Okun curve (OC), which characterizes the interplay between labor markets and economic activity [30,31]. Inspection of aggregate data typically shows that a decrease of one percentage point in the unemployment rate is associated — *ceteris paribus* — with a growth rate of GDP of about two to three percentage points (according to original Okun estimations). The standard interpretation runs in terms of under-utilization of labor resources with respect to full employment, carrying a more-than-proportional effect on economic activity [5, 37].

Mainstream economic theory has been trying to explain the foregoing aggregate regularities in the familiar *equilibrium-cum-rationality* framework, building the explanation on the shoulder of hyper-rational, maximizing, representative worker and firm. Hence, any aggregate regularity is interpreted as the equilibrium outcome of some maximizing exercises carried out by such agents.

A paradigmatic example of such modeling strategy can be found within the theoretical literature aimed at micro-founding and explaining the BC [6, 36]. In these models, all search and matching, which in reality is an inherently dynamic process, is described in a static setting by means of a deterministic (aggregate)

---

[d]As the WC pertains to homogeneous data cells, one cannot "see it" in rough data. Panel data estimation must be performed in order to control for variables such as personal characteristics of workers, labor market institutions, "fixed" effects allowing to discriminate among sectors or regions, etc.

matching function, whose functional form and parametric assumptions tautologically imply a BC. The latter is treated as a static (long-run) equilibrium locus in the unemployment-vacancy space. Furthermore, one typically requires that all flows in and out of unemployment must always compensate.[e] Needless to say, this is at odds with any empirical observation.

Moreover, in order to get the desired results, many over-simplifying assumptions are required. First, the environment must be strictly stationary, ruling out any form of technological and organizational change, as well as any type of endogenous selection amongst firms and workers. Second, the presence of a hyper-rational, representative individual rules out the possibility of accounting for any form of heterogeneity across firms and workers. More than that: it excludes the very possibility of analyzing any *interaction* process among agents (cf. Ref. 25 for a discussion). Third, as a consequence, one is prevented from studying the dynamic outcomes of multiple (reversible) decisions of hiring, firing, quitting, and searching which unfold over time.

Similar critiques also apply to the purported micro-foundations of Wage and Okun curves.[f] Therefore, despite the existence of some competing, although not entirely persuasive, interpretations of each of the three aggregate regularities *taken in isolation*, the economic literature witnesses a dramatic lack of theories attempting to *jointly explain* Beveridge, Okun and Wage curves.

In the following, we begin to explore a radically different path and study the properties of a model where the most stringent assumptions of standard formalizations are abandoned and we explicitly account for the processes of out-of-equilibrium interactions among heterogeneous agents. We will try to provide an explicit microfoundation — within an evolutionary framework — of labor market dynamics regarding the processes governing e.g. job opening, job search, matching, bargaining, and wage setting.

Notice that the bottom line of the exercises belonging to the "pure equilibrium" *genre* is that they turn out to be unable, almost by construction, to account for involuntary unemployment or even endogenous changes in the "equilibrium" rates of unemployment.

It must be noticed that important advances, incrementally departing from the standard model, have nevertheless tried to incorporate agents' informational limitations, in order to account for phenomena such as endogenous fluctuations in aggregate activity and persistent involuntary unemployment (see e.g. the seminal works by Refs. 34 and 35).

In addition, some contributions have attempted to introduce "endogenous matching" mechanisms to describe the (Walrasian) decentralized process governing

---

[e]On the contrary, the model we present below allows the economy to evolve on a permanent disequilibrium path.
[f]Cf. Refs. 19 and 22 for a thorough discussion on this and related points.

the meetings between firms and workers in the labor market.[g] This is certainly a point our model takes on board in its full importance, and it does so through an explicit account of the (disequilibrium) unfolding of the interaction process.

In this respect, our model has three important antecedents in the labor market literature. First, the out-of-equilibrium, interaction-based, perspective that we pursue is a distinctive feature of "self-organization" labor market models.[h] Second, the ACE model in Ref. 41 also assumes many heterogenous, interacting agents, characterized by "internal states" and behavioral rules, who exchange information in the market. Third, Ref. 1 extends the ACE model of fluctuations and growth proposed in Ref. 2 to allow for unemployment dynamics.[i]

Notwithstanding many overlappings with "self-organization" and ACE formalizations, our model proposes advances, *vis-à-vis* the state of the art in this area, at least at four levels. First, it accounts for the co-evolutionary dynamics between the labor market and the product market. More specifically, we try to nest labor market interactions in what one could call a "general disequilibrium" framework with endogenous aggregate demand. This feature allows us to study also market properties associated with an endogenous business cycle. Second, we explicitly model (as endogenous processes) job opening, matching, wage bargaining, and wage setting. Third, we allow for technical progress and the ensuing macroeconomic growth. Fourth, in the analysis of the results we go beyond an "exercise in plausibility" and we explicitly compare the statistical properties of the simulated environments with empirically observed ones, specifically with respect to the emergence of Beveridge, Wage, and Okun curves.

3. The Model

Consider an economy composed of F firms and N workers.[j] Time is discrete: $t = 0, 1, 2, \ldots$ and there is a homogeneous, perishable good g whose price is $p_t > 0$. In each period, a firm $i \in \{1, \ldots, F\}$ produces q_{it} units of good g using labor as the sole input under a constant returns to scale (CRTS) regime:

$$q_{it} = \alpha_{it} n_{it}, \tag{1}$$

where α_{it} is the current labor productivity of firm i and n_{it} is the number of workers hired at t by firm i. Workers are homogeneous as far as their skills are concerned.

---

[g]See Refs. 11, 12, 23, 27, 32 and 38.

[h]Cf. Refs. 26 and 28. Self-organizing processes are discussed in Ref. 42.

[i]Similarly to our model, co-evolution between product and labor market dynamics is explicitly taken into account and simulations allow to reproduce (albeit in some benchmark parameterizations) Okun curves. However, matching and wage bargaining are not incorporated in the model as endogenous processes. Therefore, no implications about wage and Phillips curves can be derived from simulation exercises.

[j]Notice that the higher the ratio between the number of workers and the number of firms (N/F), the more economic activity is concentrated (i.e. a larger work force size must be employed in a smaller number of firms). Therefore, the higher N/F, the smaller the overall frictions in the hiring process.

If the firm offers a contractual wage w_{it} to each worker, current profits are computed as

$$\pi_{it} = p_t q_{it} - w_{it} n_{it} = (p_t \alpha_{it-1} - w_{it}) n_{it}. \tag{2}$$

Contractual wages offered by firms to workers are the result of both a matching and a bargaining process. We assume that any firm i has at time t a "satisficing" wage w_{it}^s it wants to offer to any worker. Similarly, any worker $j \in \{1, \ldots, N\}$ has at time t a "satisficing" wage w_{jt}^s which he wants to get from firms. Moreover, any worker j can only accept contractual wages if they are greater or equal to their *reservation wage* w_j^R, which we assume to be constant over time for simplicity.

We start by studying an economy where jobs last only one period. Hence, workers must search for a new job in any period. Job openings are equal to labor demand and, at the same time, to "ex-ante" vacancies. However, workers can be unemployed and firms might not satisfy their labor demand.

Let us turn now to a brief description of the flow of events in a generic time-period. We then move to a detailed account of each event separately.

3.1. *Dynamics*

Given the state of the system at the end of any time period $t - 1$, the timing of events occurring in any time period t runs as follows.

(i) Firms decide how many jobs they want to open in period t.

(ii) Workers search for a firm posting at least one job opening and queue up.

(iii) Job matching and bargaining occur: firms look in their queues and start bargaining with workers who have queued up (if any) to decide whether to hire them or not.

(iv) After hiring, production takes place according to Eq. (1). Aggregate supply and demand are then formed simply by aggregating individual supplies and demands. Subsequently, a "pseudo-Walrasian" price setting occurs.[k] We assume that the price of good g at t is given by

$$p_t Q_t = W_t, \tag{3}$$

where $Q_t = \sum_{i=1}^{F} q_{it}$ is aggregate (real) output and $W_t = \sum_{j=1}^{N} w_{jt}$ is total wages. Thus, total wages equals aggregate demand, as we assume that workers spend all their income to eat good g in any time period. Then, firms make profits:

$$\pi_{it} = (p_t \alpha_{it-1} - w_{it}) n_{it}. \tag{4}$$

(v) Given profits, firms undergo a selection process: those making negative profits ($\pi_{it} < 0$) exit and are replaced by entrants, which, as a first approximation, are simply "average" firms (see below).

---

[k]We employ the simplifying assumption of an aggregate price setting mechanism to initially avoid any additional market frictions coming from e.g. a decentralized price setting procedure.

(vi) Firms and workers update their satisficing wages (w^s_{it-1} and w^s_{jt-1}).

(vii) Finally, technological progress (if any) takes place. We assume that in each period labor productivity may increase at rates which are exogenous but firm-specific (see below).

3.2. *Job openings*

At the beginning of period t, each firm creates a queue of job openings. Since in reality only *ex-ante* vacancies (i.e. new job positions) can be empirically observed, we will employ throughout the term job openings as a synonym of (ex-ante) vacancies. "Ex-post" vacancies will be computed as the number of unfilled job-openings.

Let us then call v_{it} the number of new positions opened by firm i at time t. As far as the firm's decision about how many vacancies to open is concerned, we experiment with two alternative "behavioral" scenarios.

In the first one, a firm simply observes current (i.e. time $t - 1$) price, quantity produced and the contractual wage offered, and sets vacancies v_{it} as

$$v_{it} = \bar{v}_{it-1} = \left\lceil \frac{p_{t-1}q_{it-1}}{w_{it-1}} \right\rceil, \tag{5}$$

that is, it creates a queue with a number of open slots equal to the "ceiling" of (i.e. the smallest integer larger than) the ratio between revenues and contractual wage offered in the last period. We call this job opening scenario the "**Wild Market Archetype**," in that no history-inherited institution or behavioral feature is built into the model.

In the second "behavioral" scenario (which we shall call the "**Weak Path-Dependence**" scenario), we introduce some rather mild path-dependence into the vacancy setting. We suppose that: (a) jobs opened by any firm at time t are a non-decreasing function of last-experienced profits growth rate, and (b) cannot exceed $\bar{v}_{it-1}$. More formally:

$$v_{it} = \min\{\bar{v}_{it-1}, v^*_{it}\}, \tag{6}$$

and

$$v^*_{it} = \begin{cases} \lceil v_{it-1}(1 + |X|) \rceil, & \text{if } \dfrac{\Delta \pi_{it-1}}{\pi_{it-1}} \geq 0, \\[2mm] \lceil v_{it-1}(1 - |X|) \rceil, & \text{if } \dfrac{\Delta \pi_{it-1}}{\pi_{it-1}} < 0, \end{cases} \tag{7}$$

where X is an i.i.d. random variable, normally distributed with mean zero and variance $\sigma^2_v > 0$, and $\lceil x \rceil$ denotes the ceiling of x. Notice that the higher σ_v, the more firms react to any given profits growth rate by enlarging or shrinking their current queue size. Hence, a *higher* σ_v implies *higher* sensitivity to market signals. Notice that, in both scenarios, firms always open at least one vacancy in each period.

3.3. *Job search*

Similarly to job opening, we consider two "behavioral" scenarios for the job search procedure employed by workers to find a firm that has just opened new job positions. In the first one, called "**No Search Inertia**," each worker j simply visits any firm i in the market with a probability proportional to the last contractual wage w_{it-1} it offered. If the selected firm has places still available in the queue, the worker gets in and demands a wage equal to the "satisficing" one, i.e. w_{jt-1}^s.

In the second scenario, which we label "**Search Inertia**," we introduce some stickiness (loyalty) in firm visiting. If worker j was employed by firm i in period $t-1$, he visits first firm i. If i still has places available in the queue, the worker gets in and demands w_{jt-1}^s. Otherwise, the worker employs the random rule above ("No Search Inertia") to select among the remaining $F - 1$ firms.

In both scenarios, a worker becomes unemployed if he chooses a firm who has already filled all available slots in the queue.[1]

3.4. *Job matching and bargaining*

After workers have queued up, firms start exploring workers wage demands to match them with their *desiderata*. Suppose that, at time t, firm i observes $0 < m_{it} \leq N$ workers in the queue. Then, it will compute the average wage demanded by those workers:

$$\bar{w}_{it} = \frac{1}{m_{it}} \sum_{h=1}^{m_{it}} w_{j_h t-1}^s, \tag{8}$$

where j_h are the labels of workers in i's queue. Next, it sets the contractual wage for period t as a linear combination of $\bar{w}_{it}$ and the satisficing wage w_{it-1}^s. Thus:

$$w_{it} = \beta w_{it-1}^s + (1 - \beta)\bar{w}_{it}, \tag{9}$$

where $\beta \in [0, 1]$ is an institutional parameter governing firms' strength in wage bargaining. A higher β implies a higher strength on the side of the firm in wage setting. If $\beta = 0$, firms just set contractual wage as the average of wages demanded by workers in the queue. If $\beta = 1$, firms do not take into account at all workers' *desiderata*.

---

[1]It must be noted that both job search scenarios only depict benchmark worlds and can be considered as starting points in our analysis. They indeed embody somewhat extreme assumptions about search costs and interaction structures. For instance, in the "No Search Inertia" scenario, workers' search costs are assumed to be negligible for the first visited firm, while they become infinite if workers visit more than one firm. Moreover, in the "Search Inertia" one, employed workers only recall their last employers. Alternative formulations of our basic model that we want to explore in the future include allowing for: (i) search costs which smoothly increase with the number of visited firms, and (ii) and the possibility for a worker to build through time networks of "preferred" firms to guide his search.

Once the firm has set the contractual wage at which it is willing to hire workers in the queue, any worker j in the queue will accept the job only if w_{it} exceeds the reservation wage w_j^R.

As soon as a worker j accepts the job, he temporarily changes his satisficing wage to keep up with the new (actual) wage earned, i.e. $w_{jt-1}^s = w_{it}$. Similarly, a firm who has filled at least a job opening will replace w_{it-1}^s with w_{it}.[m]

Given the number of workers n_{it} hired by each firm, production, as well as price setting and profits determination occur as explained above. *Ex-post* firm i's vacancies are defined as $\tilde{v}_{it} = m_{it} - n_{it}$.

3.5. *Selection, exit, and entry*

Suppose that — given the new contractual wage, price p_t, and current productivity α_{it-1} — firm j faces negative profits, i.e. $p_t\alpha_{it-1} < w_{it}$. Then selection pressure makes firm j exit the market.

Each exiting firm is replaced by a new firm which starts out with the average "characteristics" of those firms still in the market at t (i.e. those making non-negative profits).[n] Notice that this entry-exit process allows to keep an invariant number of F firms in the economy at each t.

3.6. *Satisficing wages updating*

Surviving firms, as well as the N workers, will then have the opportunity to revise their satisficing wage according to their perceptions about the outcome of market dynamics.

- **Firms**: We assume that each firm has an invariant desired ratio of filled to opened jobs $\rho_i \in (0, 1]$, which it compares to the current ratio:

$$r_{it} = \frac{n_{it}}{v_{it}}. \tag{10}$$

If firm i hired too few workers (as compared to the number of job positions it has decided to open), then it might want to increase the wages it is willing to offer to workers. Otherwise, it might want to decrease it. We capture this simple rule by positing that

$$w_{it}^s = \begin{cases} w_{it-1}^s(1 + |Y|), & \text{if } r_{it} < \rho_i, \\ w_{it-1}^s(1 - |Y|), & \text{if } r_{it} \geq \rho_i, \end{cases} \tag{11}$$

where Y is an i.i.d. random variable distributed as a standard normal. Notice that w_{it-1}^s is equal to w_{it} (i.e. contractual wage just offered) if the firm has hired at least one worker.

---

[m]The new values of satisficing wages will then be employed in the updating process. Since satisficing wage can be interpreted as (myopic) expectations, satisficing wage updating plays in the model the role of expectation formation process.
[n]All results we present in the next section are robust to alternative assumptions concerning entry and exit.

- **Workers**: If worker j remains unemployed after matching and bargaining, he might want to reduce his satisficing wage (without violating the reservation wage threshold). Otherwise, he might want to demand a higher wage during the next bargaining session. We then assume that

$$w_{jt}^s = \begin{cases} \max\{w_j^R, w_{jt-1}^s(1-|Y|)\}, & \text{if } j \text{ unemployed}, \\ w_{jt-1}^s(1+|Y|), & \text{if } j \text{ employed}, \end{cases} \tag{12}$$

where Y is an i.i.d. random variable distributed as a standard normal. Again, $w_{jt-1}^s = w_{jt}$ if j has been just hired.

3.7. Technological progress

The last major ingredient of the model regards labor productivity dynamics. Here, we experiment with two "technological scenarios." In the first one ("**No Technological Progress**"), we study a system where labor productivity does not change through time (i.e. $\alpha_{it} = \alpha_i$, $\forall i$).[o] In the second scenario ("**Technological Progress**"), we allow for an exogenous, albeit firm-specific, dynamics of labor productivities. We start with initially homogeneous labor coefficients ($\alpha_{i0} = \alpha$) and we let them grow stochastically over time according to the following multiplicative process:

$$\alpha_{it} = \alpha_{it-1}(1+Z), \tag{13}$$

where Z, conditionally on $Z > 0$, is an i.i.d. normally distributed random variable with mean 0 and variance $\sigma_Z^2 \geq 0$.[p] The latter governs the opportunity setting in the economy. The larger σ_Z, the more likely firms draw large productivity improvements. Notice that if we let $\sigma_Z = 0$, we recover the "**No Technological Progress**" scenario.[q]

3.8. Initial conditions, micro- and macro-dynamics

The foregoing model, as mentioned, genuinely belongs to an evolutionary/ACE approach. Given its behavioral, bottom-up, perspective, one must resort to computer simulations to explore the behavior of the system.[r]

The dynamics of the system depends on four sets of factors. First, we distinguish behavioral (e.g. concerning job opening and job search) and technological scenarios. We call such discrete institutional and technological regimes "system setups".

---

[o]Labor productivity may in turn be either homogeneous across firms ($\alpha_i = \alpha$) or not.
[p]Hence, there is a probability 0.5 to draw a neutral labor productivity shock ($Z = 0$), while positive shocks are distributed as the positive half of a $N(0,1)$.
[q]Technological progress, despite its firm-specific nature, is essentially exogenous. An alternative modeling strategy which we want to pursue in the future is to allow labor coefficients to change in a path-dependent way. For instance, one could assume that each α_{it} is positively affected by: (i) past labor productivities of the firm where a new employed worker comes from, and/or (ii) the number of time-periods a given worker has spent working in the same firm i.
[r]Simulation code is written in C++ and is available from the authors upon request.

Table 1.   System parameters.

Parameter	Range	Meaning
N/F	R_{++}	Concentration of economic activity (number of workers/number of firms)
σ_v	R_{++}	Sensitivity to market signals in vacancy settings (only in a Weak Path-Dependence Scenario)
β	$[0, 1]$	Labor-market institutional parameter governing the strength of firms in wage-setting
σ_Z	R_+	Technological parameter tuning the availability of opportunities in the system ($= 0$ means no technological progress)

Second, a choice of system parameters $(F/N, \sigma_v, \beta, \sigma_Z)$ is required (see Table 1). Third, one should explore the would-be importance of different initial conditions.[s] Since simulations show that the latter do not dramatically affect the long-run properties of aggregate variables, we typically define a "canonical" set of initial conditions. All results presented below refer to this benchmark choice. Finally, individual updating by firms and workers induces a stochastic dynamics on micro-variables (e.g. contractual wages, desired production, desired employment, etc.). By aggregating these individual variables over firms and workers, one can study the properties of macro-dynamics for the variables of interest.

We will focus on unemployment:

$$U_t = N - \sum_{i=1}^{F} n_{it}, \tag{14}$$

total wages:

$$W_t = \sum_{j=1}^{N} w_{jt}, \tag{15}$$

and (real) GDP:

$$Q_t = \sum_{i=1}^{F} q_{it}, \tag{16}$$

as well as its growth rate:

$$h_t = \Delta \log(Q_t). \tag{17}$$

4. Simulation Results: Some Qualitative Evidence

In this section, we firstly run simulation experiments in order to identify general setups and parameters choices under which the model is able to *jointly* replicate the three aggregate regularities characterizing labor markets dynamics and

---

[s]In the model this implies defining initial values $(n_{i0}, \alpha_{i0}, w_{i0}^s, w_{i0})_{i=1}^{F}$ for firms and $(w_{j0}^s)_{j=1}^{N}$ for workers. Moreover, an initial price p_0, and some distributions for desired ratios $(\rho_i)_{i=1}^{F}$ and reservation wages $(w_j^R)_{j=1}^{N}$ have to be chosen.

economic activity discussed in Sec. 2. In the following section, we shall perform Monte Carlo exercises aimed at understanding how statistical properties of labor-market dynamics and economic activity change across different parameterizations and setups.

All simulation exercises we present in the paper refer to (and compare) four basic "system setup." Each "system setup" is characterized by a choice for behavioral/ institutional assumptions (i.e. job opening and workers' job search) and a choice for the technological scenario (with or without technological change).

We experiment with the following two combinations of behavioral/institutional assumptions: (i) Walrasian Archetype (WA): We employ the "Wild Market Archetype" scenario as far as job opening is concerned and the "No Search Inertia" scenario for workers' job search; (ii) Institutionally-Shaped Environment (ISE): Firms open new job positions within a "Weak Path-Dependence" scenario, while workers search for a firm under the "Search Inertia" scenario.

Note that in the WA world, there is no path-dependence in job openings, nor in job search. Workers visit firms at random, while the latter open a number of new positions in each period without being influenced by past experienced profits. Conversely, in the ISE workers and firms face some path-dependence in job opening and job searching, as firms adjust job openings according to last profits growth and workers visit first the last firm in which they were employed.

Each of the two foregoing behavioral choices is then associated to a technological scenario (with or without technological change) to get the four basic "system setups" under analysis.[t]

We start by qualitatively investigating the emergence of Beveridge, Wage, and Okun curves in an economy characterized by the "Walrasian Archetype," i.e. a world where agents decide myopically and do not carry over past information. The system does not allow to recover any aggregate, statistically significant, negative relationship between vacancy and unemployment rates. Simulations show that the Beveridge curve fails to emerge for a quite large region of the system parameters $(F/N, \beta, \sigma_Z)$ space, cf. Figs. 1 and 2 for an example.

Conversely, both Wage and Okun curves robustly emerge regardless of whether technological progress is shut down or not. Notice that if $\sigma_Z = 0$, the economy works as a dynamic allocation device trying to match in a decentralized and imperfect way individual labor demand and supply *for given resources*. It is then easy to see that both Okun and Wage relationships are a consequence (and not an emergent property) of the joint assumptions of quasi-Walrasian price-setting and constant returns to scale. Indeed, from (1) and (3), one gets: $W_t = -p_t U_t + p_t(N - N_t + \sum_i \alpha_i n_{it})$ and $Q_t = -U_t + (N - N_t + \sum_i \alpha_i n_{it})$. Thus, both curves are somewhat implied by the assumptions.

---

[t]In all exercises that follow, we set the econometric sample size $T = 1000$. This time span is sufficient to allow for convergence of the recursive moments for all variables under study.

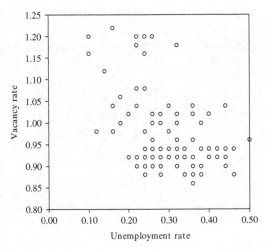

Fig. 1.   Vacancy versus unemployment rate in a "Walrasian Archetype" economy **without** technological progress. Parameters: $N/F = 5$, $\beta = 0.5$.

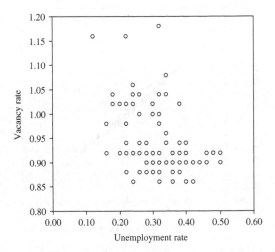

Fig. 2.   Vacancy versus unemployment rate in a "Walrasian Archetype" economy **with** technological progress. Parameters: $N/F = 5$, $\beta = 0.5$, $\sigma_Z = 0.1$.

If, on the contrary, technological progress occurs in a WA scenario, there is no apparent reasons to expect both OC and WC to robustly emerge. Yet, as simulations show, they both characterize system dynamics for a large region of the parameter space, even if no path-dependent behavior drives the economy (cf. Figs. 3 and 4).

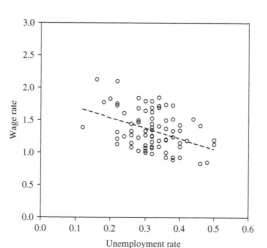

Fig. 3.   Emergence of Wage curve in a "Walrasian Archetype" economy only **with** technological progress. Parameters: $N/F = 5$, $\beta = 0.5$, $\sigma_Z = 0.1$.

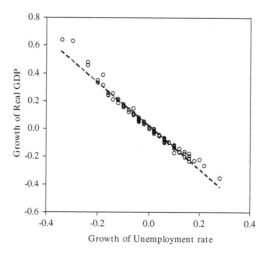

Fig. 4.   Emergence of Okun curve in a "Walrasian Archetype" economy only **with** technological progress. Parameters: $N/F = 5$, $\beta = 0.5$, $\sigma_Z = 0.1$.

Consider now an "Institutionally-Shaped Environment." Then, irrespective of the technological regime, the model is able to robustly generate Beveridge curves with statistically significant (negative) slopes: see for illustration Figs. 5 and 6. Furthermore, when technological progress is present, both Wage and Okun curves still characterize macro-dynamics as robust, emergent, properties of the system, cf. Figs. 7 and 8.

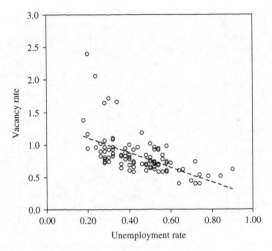

Fig. 5.   Emergence of Beveridge curve in a "Institutionally-Shaped" environment **without** technological progress. Parameters: $N/F = 5$, $\beta = 0.5$.

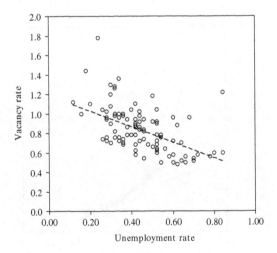

Fig. 6.   Emergence of Beveridge curve in a "Institutionally-Shaped" environment **with** technological progress. Parameters: $N/F = 5$, $\beta = 0.5$, $\sigma_Z = 0.1$.

5. Monte Carlo Experiments

The set of qualitative results presented in the last section suggest that some path-dependence seems to be a necessary condition for a Beveridge relationship. Moreover, a standard Okun curve seems to be in place even when technological progress persistently boosts available production capacity. Finally, despite

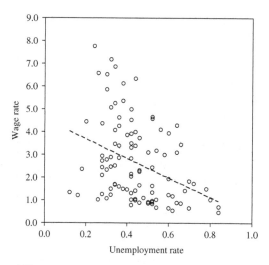

Fig. 7.   Emergence of Wage curve in a "Institutionally-Shaped" environment **with** technological progress. Parameters: $N/F = 5$, $\beta = 0.5$, $\sigma_Z = 0.1$.

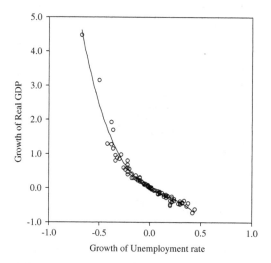

Fig. 8.   Emergence of Okun curve in a "Institutionally-Shaped" environment **with** technological progress. Parameters: $N/F = 5$, $\beta = 0.5$, $\sigma_Z = 0.1$.

persistent heterogeneity arising endogenously from labor productivity dynamics, Phillips-curve type of regularities are typically rejected by the simulated data in favor of a Wage curve relationship.

To check whether these qualitative results are robust to changes in system parameters, we turn now to a more detailed Monte Carlo analysis. We discuss two sets of exercises. First, we ask whether the three regularities we are interested in, robustly emerge in each of the four main "setups" under study. To this end, we generate M independent (Monte Carlo) simulations for each choice of relevant parameters over a sufficiently fine grid. We then study the moments of the distributions of the statistics of interest. We focus in particular on test statistics for the significance of coefficients in Beveridge and Okun regressions, the magnitude of Okun coefficient, as well as test statistics discriminating between Wage and Phillips curves.

Second, we will perform some simple "comparative dynamics" exercises to investigate what happens to emergent regularities when one tunes system parameters within each "setup". We are particularly interested in detecting shifts (if any) in the Beveridge curve and changes in Okun coefficients. Once again, we will discuss the outcome of Monte Carlo statistics coming from independent time-series simulation runs for any given parametrization.[u]

5.1. *Emergence of aggregate regularities: Robustness tests*

To begin with, consider the emergence of Beveridge curves. Consider, for any setup under analysis, a given parametrization. Following existing empirical literature, we computed, for each of M independent simulated time-series, estimates (and R^2) for the simple time-series regression:

$$u_t = b_0 + b_1 v_t + \epsilon_t, \tag{18}$$

where ϵ_t is white-noise, u_t is the unemployment rate, and v_t is the vacancy rate (both defined as activity rates). We then computed Monte Carlo statistics (e.g. average) of estimates $\hat{b}_1$ and goodness-of-fit R^2, together with the percentage of rejections for the test $b_1 = 0$ (i.e. a proxy for the likelihood of BC emergence, in case of a negative estimate). By repeating this exercise as parameters change within a given system setup (WA versus ISE), one is able to investigate Beveridge curves emergence, how large their slopes are, and how good the correspondent linear fit on average is.[v]

Notice first that, in a WA, the likelihood of the emergence of a BC is quite low. As Fig. 9 shows, the percentage of rejections of H_0: $b_1 = 0$ is almost always below 50% as we tune firms' strength in wage bargaining (β) and technological opportunities (σ_Z). Accordingly, the estimated slope does not change dramatically across the parameter space, ranging from -0.938 to -0.263 (not shown). In particular, technological progress seems to favor BC emergence: the higher σ_Z, the larger the percentage of rejections and the better the fit of the correspondent regression (cf. Fig. 10). To see why this happens, recall that a stronger technological boost induces firms to open more vacancies, which the system seems to be able to more easily fill.

---

[u]All Monte Carlo experiments are undertaken using a Monte Carlo sample size $M = 100$. Initial conditions are always kept fixed (see above).

[v]Standard errors of estimates, as well as Monte Carlo (across simulations) standard deviations of all statistics of interest appear to be very small. Therefore, we do not report confidence intervals here.

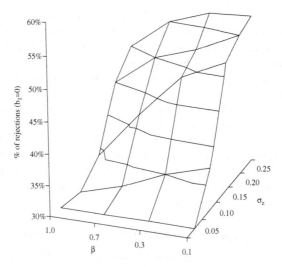

Fig. 9.   Percentage of rejections of H_0: $b_1 = 0$ for the Beveridge Regression $u_t = b_0 + b_1 v_t + \epsilon_t$ in a "Walrasian Archetype" as firms' strength in wage-setting (β) and technological opportunities (σ_Z) change ($N/F = 5$).

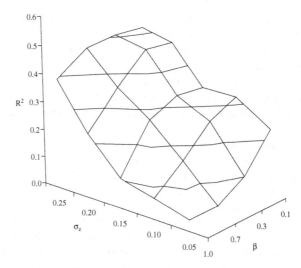

Fig. 10.   Goodness of fit (R^2) of Beveridge Regression $u_t = b_0 + b_1 v_t + \epsilon_t$ in a "Walrasian Archetype" as firms' strength in wage-setting (β) and technological opportunities (σ_Z) change ($N/F = 5$).

When technology is strong enough, a lower β also appears to favor the emergence of a BC, even if this effect turns out to be milder than the technological one.

If, on the contrary, the economy is characterized by an "institutionally-shaped environment," the percentage of rejections is almost always close to 100% across the entire $(\sigma_v, \sigma_Z, \beta)$ space and the average estimated slope is negative (not shown). Thus, unlike in a WA economy, the presence of some frictions and path-dependence in the institutional and behavioral settings allows a BC to robustly emerge. Here, firms' bargaining strength (β) appears to have a strong impact on the goodness of fit. In fact, when β is low $(\beta = 0.1)$, the linear fit turns out to better describe the vacancy-unemployment relationship (cf. Fig. 11) than in the case when firms' bargaining strength is high $(\beta = 1.0)$; see Fig. 12. In this latter case, however, a higher sensitivity to market signals (σ_v) favors the emergence of well-shaped BC. Indeed, in presence of technical progress, a larger σ_v allows firms to turn higher profits in a higher number of vacancies, which are more easily filled when firms are stronger in the wage-bargaining process.

While the Beveridge curve tends to robustly emerge only in an "institutionally-shaped" economy, simulations show that a Wage curve always characterizes our system in all four setups. In particular, statistical tests aimed at discriminating between a Phillips and a Wage world, show that the latter is almost always preferred. Following Ref. 13, we perform the lagged regression:

$$\Delta \log \tilde{W}_t = g_t + a_1 \log u_t + a_2 \log u_{t-1} + \Delta e_t, \tag{19}$$

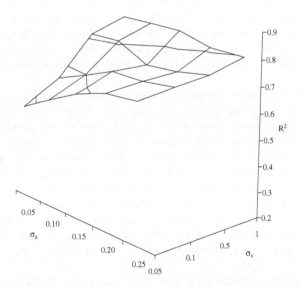

Fig. 11.   Goodness of fit (R^2) of Beveridge Regression $u_t = b_0 + b_1 v_t + \epsilon_t$ in a "Institutionally-shaped Environment" characterized by a low firms' strength in wage-setting $(\beta = 0.1)$ as firms' sensitivity to market signals (σ_v) and technological opportunities (σ_Z) change $(N/F = 5)$.

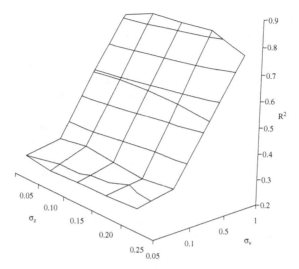

Fig. 12.   Goodness of fit (R^2) of Beveridge Regression $u_t = b_0 + b_1 v_t + \epsilon_t$ in a "Institutionally-Shaped Environment" characterized by a high firms' strength in wage-setting ($\beta = 1.0$) as firms' sensitivity to market signals (σ_v) and technological opportunities (σ_Z) change ($N/F = 5$).

where $\tilde{W}_t$ is the wage rate, u_t is the unemployment rate, g_t is a time trend, and first-differencing is taken to avoid serial correlation in e_t. As Ref. 13 shows, the Wage curve hypothesis implies $a_1 = -a_2$ (together with $a_1 < 0$), while the Phillips curve hypothesis requires $a_2 = 0$. Table 2 reports Monte Carlo testing exercises in our four setups for a benchmark parametrization.[w] Notice that the percentage of rejections of a Phillips world is quite high, while we tend not to reject the hypothesis that wage levels are negatively correlated with unemployment rates in almost all simulations.

The R^2 is very high in all setups. This might be an expected result when $\sigma_Z = 0$, because without technological progress a Wage curve follows from price-setting and constant returns. However, when $\sigma_Z > 0$ the goodness-of-fit remains high (and standard errors very low). Our model seems to allow for well-behaved Wage curves also when technological progress induces persistent heterogeneity in labor productivity dynamics. Furthermore, a quite general and robust result (see also below) concerns the effect of technological progress upon the slope of the curve. As discussed above, the latter is expected to be around -1.0 when $\sigma_Z = 0$, but nothing can in principle be said about the expected slope when $\sigma_Z > 0$. Our results suggest that, even when technological progress is present, the Wage curve robustly emerges. Indeed, wage rates become even more responsive to unemployment than in the $\sigma_Z = 0$ case.

---

[w] As far as the emergence of Okun and Wage curves are concerned, one does not detect any statistically significant differences in percentage of rejections when parameters change across different system setups. See below for some considerations on shifts of Beveridge and Okun curves across different parameterizations.

Table 2.   Emergence of the Wage curve in alternative setups.

	Setups			
	WA		ISE	
	$\sigma_Z = 0$	$\sigma_Z > 0$	$\sigma_Z = 0$	$\sigma_Z > 0$
MC average of $\hat{a}_1$	−0.814	−1.643	−1.019	−2.329
	(0.025)	(0.093)	(0.072)	(0.225)
MC average of $\hat{a}_2$	0.781	1.520	0.977	2.134
	(0.019)	(0.083)	(0.020)	(0.169)
R^2	0.985	0.906	0.978	0.914
	(0.003)	(0.023)	(0.017)	(0.026)
% of rejections (H_0: $a_2 = 0$) at 5%	100%	99%	99%	100%
% of rejections (H_0: $a_1 = -a_2$) at 5%	10%	5%	5%	1%

Note: WA = "Walrasian Archetype." ISE = "Institutionally-Shaped Environment." Functional form tested: $\Delta \log \hat{W}_t = g_t + a_1 \log u_t + a_2 \log u_{t-1} + \Delta e_t$. Rejecting Phillips curve hypothesis means rejecting H'_o: $a_2 = 0$. Rejecting Wage curve hypothesis means rejecting H'_o: $a_1 = -a_2$. Monte Carlo Standard Errors in parentheses. Monte Carlo sample size $M = 100$. Benchmark parametrization: $N/F = 5$, $\beta = 0.5$, $\sigma_Z = 0.1$ (when > 0), $\sigma_v = 0.1$ (under ISE).

Table 3.   Emergence of the Okun curve in alternative setups.

	Setups			
	WA		ISE	
	$\sigma_Z = 0$	$\sigma_Z > 0$	$\sigma_Z = 0$	$\sigma_Z > 0$
MC average of $\hat{c}_1$	−2.064	−2.196	−2.635	−3.072
	(0.042)	(0.047)	(0.068)	(0.063)
R^2	0.939	0.925	0.928	0.936
	(0.026)	(0.060)	(0.064)	(0.025)
Max of tail prob. distrib. for H_0: $c_1 = 0$	0.000	0.001	0.000	0.001
% of rejections (H_0: $c_1 = 0$) at 5%	100%	99%	100%	99%

Note: WA = "Walrasian Archetype." ISE = "Institutionally-Shaped Environment." Estimation of $\Delta \log(Q_t) = c_0 + c_1 \Delta \log(u_t) + \epsilon_t$. Monte Carlo Standard Errors in parentheses. Monte Carlo sample size $M = 100$. Benchmark parametrization: $N/F = 5$, $\beta = 0.5$, $\sigma_Z = 0.1$ (when > 0), $\sigma_v = 0.1$ (under ISE).

Alike the Wage curve, the Okun curve, too, turns out to be a robust outcome of our labor market dynamics. Evidence of this effect simply appears by linearly regressing GDP growth rates against changes in the rates of unemployment:

$$\Delta \log(Q_t) = c_0 + c_1 \Delta \log(u_t) + \epsilon_t. \tag{20}$$

We computed Monte Carlo estimates of the Okun coefficient c_1 and we tested for H_0: $c_1 = 0$ (i.e. the emergence of an Okun curve — as long as $c_1 < 0$), see Table 3 for an example. Our economy allows for an Okun relationship in all settings, especially when technological progress is present. Again, this might be considered as a not-too-surprising result when $\sigma_Z = 0$, but it becomes a truly emergent property when technological progress fuels the economy.

The absolute value of the Okun coefficient is larger than one (and indeed close to empirical estimates [5]), implying some emergent aggregate dynamic increasing returns to labor. The effect becomes stronger when an ISE is assumed: Monte Carlo averages of the Okun coefficient range from -2.196 to -3.072.

Notice that one did not assume any increasing returns regime at the individual firm level. In fact, firms produce using constant returns production functions; see (1). Moreover, no Phillips curve relationships are in place: our economy typically displays a negative relationship between unemployment rates and wage *levels*. This suggests that aggregation of imperfect and persistently heterogeneous behaviors leads to macro-economic dynamic properties that were not present at the individual level. Therefore, aggregate dynamic increasing returns emerge as the outcome of aggregation of dynamic, interdependent, microeconomic patterns [21].

5.2. *Some comparative dynamics Monte Carlo exercises*

We turn now to a comparative dynamics Monte Carlo investigation of the effect of system parameters on emergent aggregate regularities. We focus on the "institutionally-shaped" setup, wherein the economy robustly exhibits well-behaved Beveridge, Wage, and Okun curves, and we study what happens under alternative parameter settings. In particular we compare parameter setups characterized by:

(i) low versus high N/F ratio (i.e. degrees of concentration of economic activity);
(ii) low versus high σ_v (i.e. sensitivity to market signals in the way firms set their vacancies);
(iii) low versus high β (i.e. firms' bargaining strength in wage setting);
(iv) low versus high σ_Z (technological opportunities).

We *first* ask whether a higher sensitivity to market signals in vacancy setting induce detectable shifts in aggregate regularities. As Table 4 shows, the smaller σ_v is, the stronger the revealed increasing dynamic returns: GDP growth becomes more

Table 4.   Shifts in the Okun coefficient in an "Institutionally-Shaped Environment" under alternative parameter settings.

	ISE setup			
	$\sigma_v = 1.0$ (HSMS)		$\sigma_v = 0.2$ (LSMS)	
	$\sigma_Z = 0$	$\sigma_Z > 0$	$\sigma_Z = 0$	$\sigma_Z > 0$
MC average of $\hat{c}_1$	-2.700	-2.960	-2.900	-3.270
	(0.082)	(0.085)	(0.064)	(0.060)
R^2	0.928	0.936	0.939	0.925
	(0.064)	(0.025)	(0.026)	(0.060)
Max of tail prob. distrib. for H_0: $c_1 = 0$	0.001	0.001	0.000	0.001
% of rejections (H_0: $c_1 = 0$) at 5%	100%	99%	100%	99%

Note: HSMS: High Sensitivity to Market Signals. LSMS: Low Sensitivity to Market Signals. Estimation of $\Delta \log(Q_t) = c_0 + c_1 \Delta \log(u_t) + \epsilon_t$. Monte Carlo Standard Errors in parentheses. Monte Carlo sample size $M = 100$. Benchmark parametrization: $N/F = 5$, $\beta = 0.5$, $\sigma_Z = 0.1$.

responsive to unemployment growth and the Okun curve becomes steeper. Notice that σ_v can also be interpreted as an inverse measure of path-dependence in firms' vacancy setting. The smaller σ_v is, the more firms tend to stick to last-period job openings. Therefore, a *smaller* path-dependence implies a steeper Okun relation.

Analogously, we investigate the impact on the BC of simultaneously increasing N/F (i.e. increasing N for a given F) and σ_v (i.e. firms' "sensitivity to market signals"). Notice that a higher concentration allows firms — *ceteris paribus* — to more easily fill their vacancies. Similarly, the higher σ_v, the more firms are able to react to aggregate conditions and correspondingly adjust vacancies. Therefore, one might be tempted to interpret economies characterized by high values for both N/F and σ_v as "low friction" worlds, and expect the BC curve to lie closer to the axes. Notice, however, that in our model an "indirect" effect is also present. If labor demand is very low (e.g. because the economy is in a recession), then the unemployment rate might be high irrespective of the value of N/F. Moreover, if σ_v is high, firms will fire more workers during downswings, thus inducing a sort of "accelerator" effect on the recession. Hence, the consequences on the BC of assuming a larger market concentration and a higher sensitivity to market signals are *ex-ante* ambiguous: if the "indirect" effects dominate, we should observe various combinations between shifts to the right and "business-cycle" movements along the curve.

Notwithstanding all that, Monte Carlo simulations show that the model is able to reproduce the predicted shifts in the BC. We observe (cf. Table 5) that as N/F

Table 5.   Shifts in the Beveridge curve in an "Institutionally-Shaped Environment" under alternative parameter settings.

	Parameter settings			
N/F	50	20	10	5
σ_v	1.0	0.6	0.2	0.1
MC mean of $\hat{b}_0$	0.684	0.689	0.691	0.692
	(0.018)	(0.024)	(0.043)	(0.043)
MC mean of $\sigma(\hat{b}_0)$	0.020	0.027	0.040	0.033
	(0.002)	(0.002)	(0.004)	(0.004)
Max of MC tail prob. distr. for H_0: $b_0 = 0$	0.001	0.000	0.001	0.001
% of rejections for H_0: $b_0 = 0$	99%	100%	98%	99%
MC mean of $\hat{b}_1$	-0.679	-0.631	-0.535	-0.413
	(0.030)	(0.043)	(0.071)	(0.077)
MC Mean of $\sigma(\hat{b}_1)$	0.031	0.044	0.065	0.056
	(0.003)	(0.004)	(0.006)	(0.007)
Max of MC tail prob. distr. for H_0: $b_1 = 0$	0.000	0.001	0.002	0.001
% of rejections for H_0: $b_1 = 0$	100%	99%	98%	99%
MC mean of R^2	0.816	0.677	0.408	0.410
	(0.038)	(0.045)	(0.064)	(0.062)

Note: Setups: (i) Concentration of economic activity N/F; (ii) sensitivity to market signals σ_v. Estimation of $u_t = b_0 + b_1 v_t + \epsilon_t$. Monte Carlo Standard Errors in parentheses. Monte Carlo sample size $M = 100$. Benchmark parametrization: $\beta = 0.5$. No technical progress is assumed to focus on BC shifts for given resources.

and σ_v both increase in a ISE economy, Monte Carlo averages of estimated intercepts stay constant, while the BC becomes, on average, steeper (and thus closer to
the origin). A steeper BC implies that firms adaptively learn to open less vacancies
and to adjust their filled-to-open vacancy ratios in response to market signals.

Second, we explore what happens to (within-simulation) average and standard
deviation of GDP growth time-series[x] when both σ_v and firms' bargaining strength
β are allowed to vary. Recall that the higher β, the less firms take into account
workers satisficing wages when they decide their contractual wage. Figures 13 and 14
show Monte Carlo means of average and standard deviation of GDP growth rates.
We find that the *higher* firms' bargaining strength, the *smaller* both average growth
rates and their variability. Thus, allowing for some bargaining power on the workers'
side implies better aggregate performance, but also more fluctuations. Furthermore,
if firms are *less* responsive to market signals (e.g. they employ a path-dependent
vacancy setting rule), the economy enjoys persistently higher average growth rates
and persistently smaller fluctuations.

Finally, we assess the consequences of "fueling" the economy with higher technological opportunities (i.e. higher σ_Z) for different levels of β (and setting σ_v
to an intermediate level). While a higher σ_Z implies higher average growth rates
in all parameter settings (Fig. 15), a stronger bargaining power for workers still

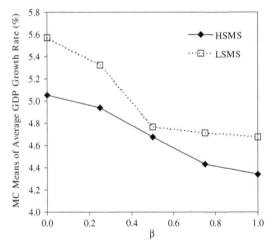

Fig. 13.   Monte Carlo Means of (within-simulation) Average Real GDP Growth Rates as a function of firms strength in wage bargaining (β). LSMS versus HSMS: Low ($\sigma_v = 0.1$) versus High
($\sigma_v = 1.0$) sensitivity to market signals in vacancy setting. "Institutionally-Shaped" Environment.
Parameters: $N/F = 5$, $\sigma_Z = 0.1$.

---

[x]That is, we compute average and standard deviation of GDP growth rates within a simulation
$\{h_t, t = 1, \ldots, T\}$, $h_t = \Delta \log Q_t$.

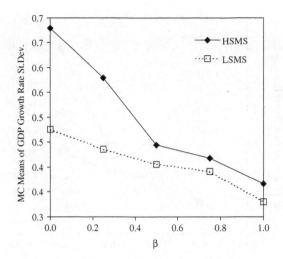

Fig. 14. Monte Carlo Means of (within-simulation) Standard Deviation of Real GDP Growth Rates as a function of firms strength in wage bargaining (β). LSMS versus HSMS: Low ($\sigma_v = 0.1$) versus High ($\sigma_v = 1.0$) sensitivity to market signals in vacancy setting. "Institutionally-Shaped" Environment. Parameters: $N/F = 5$, $\sigma_Z = 0.1$.

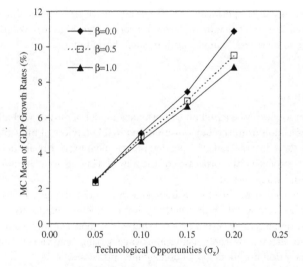

Fig. 15. Monte Carlo Means of (within-simulation) Average Real GDP Growth Rates as a function of technological opportunities (σ_Z) and firms strength in wage bargaining (β). "Institutionally-Shaped" Environment. Parameters: $N/F = 5$, $\sigma_v = 0.1$.

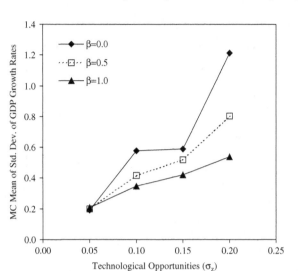

Fig. 16.   Monte Carlo Means of (within-simulation) Standard Deviation of Real GDP Growth Rates as a function of technological opportunities (σ_Z) and firms strength in wage bargaining (β). "Institutionally-Shaped" Environment. Parameters: $N/F = 5$, $\sigma_v = 0.1$.

implies better aggregate performances. Together, more technological opportunities also entail a higher volatility in the growth process (see Fig. 16). Volatility can be weakened if one increases firm strength in wage bargaining.

6. Conclusions

In this paper, we have presented an evolutionary model of output and labor market dynamics describing from the bottom-up individual behaviors of multiple firms and workers and their interactions. In particular, we have explicitly modeled from an agent-based perspective the processes of vacancy setting, as well as matching, wage bargaining, and wage setting.

We assume that firms produce a homogeneous, perishable good under constant returns to labor, enjoy labor productivity improvements thanks to technological progress, and undergo a selection process shaped by their revealed competitiveness (which is also affected by their hiring and wage-setting behaviors). Both demand and price formation are modeled as endogenous processes.

The interplay between labor and output markets allows one to appreciate the relationships between the business cycle and unemployment. Such an interplay provides a joint, evolutionary, interpretation of some of the most important aggregate stylized facts in labor market dynamics and the business cycle, such as the Beveridge curve, the Wage curve, and the Okun curve.

Simulations show that Beveridge, Wage and Okun curves can be jointly generated by our model as emergent properties under quite broad behavioral and institutional settings. Moreover, the emergent Okun curves exhibit aggregate dynamic increasing returns notwithstanding firms employing linear production functions.

Monte Carlo simulations also indicate that statistically detectable shifts in Okun and Beveridge curves emerge as the result of changes in institutional, behavioral, and technological parameters. For example, a higher concentration of market activity (i.e. a higher number of workers per firm) and a higher sensitivity to market signals in firms' vacancy setting rules imply Beveridge curves which lie closer to the axes.

Finally, the model generates quite sharp predictions about how the average aggregate performance (and volatility) of the system changes in alternative behavioral, institutional, and technological setups. For example, we find that the *higher* firms' bargaining strength, the *smaller* both average growth rates and their variability. Furthermore, if firms are *less* responsive to market signals, the economy enjoys persistently higher average growth rates and persistently smaller fluctuations. Similarly, higher technological opportunities imply higher average growth rates but more volatile growth rate time-series. Volatility can, however, be weakened if one increases firms strength in wage bargaining.

Acknowledgment

The authors thanks Uwe Cantner, Herbert Dawid, Peter Flaschel, Alan Kirman, Willi Semmler, Mauro Sylos Labini, Matteo Richiardi, Leigh Tesfatsion, two anonymous referees, and the participants of the conference "Wild@Ace: Workshop on Industry and Labor Dynamics. An Agent-based Computational Economics approach," Laboratorio Revelli, Turin, October 3–4, 2003, for valuable comments and suggestions.

References

[1] Aoki, M., A new model of output fluctuation: Ultrametrics, Beveridge curve and Okun's law, Economics online papers, No. 234, UCLA, 2003.

[2] Aoki, M. and Yoshikawa, H., A simple quantity adjustment model of economic fluctuations and growth, in *Heterogeneous Agents, Interaction and Economic Performance*, (eds.) Cowan, R. and Jonard, N. (Springer, Berlin, 2003).

[3] Ashenfelter, O. and Card, D. (eds.), *Handbook of Labor Economics,* Vol. 3 (Elsevier Science, Amsterdam, 1999).

[4] Ashenfelter, O. and Layard, R. (eds.), *Handbook of Labor Economics*, Vol. 2 (Elsevier Science, Amsterdam, 1986).

[5] Attfield, C. and Silverstone, B., Okun's coefficient: A comment, *The Review of Econ. and Stat.* **79**, 326–329 (1997).

[6] Blanchard, O. and Diamond, P., The Beveridge curve, *Brooking Papers on Econ. Activities* **1**, 1–76 (1989).

[7] Blanchard, O. and Katz, L., What we know and do not know about the natural rate of unemployment, *J. Econ. Perspectives* **11**, 57–72 (1997).

[8] Blanchflower, D. and Oswald, A., *The Wage Curve* (The MIT Press Cambridge, Massachussetts, 1994).

[9] Bleakley, H. and Fuhrer, J., Shifts in the Beveridge curve, job matching, and labor market dynamics, *New England Econ. Rev.* **2**, 3–19 (1997).

[10] Borsch-Supan, A., Panel data analysis of the beveridge curve: Is there a macroeconomic relation between the rate of unemployment and vacancy rate?, *Economica* **58**, 279–297 (1991).

[11] Burdett, K., Shi, S. and Wright, R., Pricing and matching with frictions, *J. Political Econ.* **109**, 1060–1085 (2001).

[12] Cao, M. and Shi, S., Coordination, matching and wages, *Canadian J. Econ.* **33**, 1009–1033 (2000).

[13] Card, D., The Wage curve: A review, *J. Econ. Lit.* **33**, 785–799 (1995).

[14] Card, D. and Hyslop, D., Does inflation grease the wheels of the labor market, working paper 5538, NBER (1996).

[15] Dosi, G. and Nelson, R., An introduction to evolutionary theories in economics, *J. Evolutionary Econ.* **4**, 153–172 (1994).

[16] Dosi, G. and Orsenigo, L., Macrodynamics and microfoundations: An evolutionary perspective, in *The Economics of Technology*, ed. Granstrand, O. (North Holland, Amsterdam, 1994).

[17] Dosi, G. and Winter, S., Interpreting economic change: Evolution, structures and games, in *The Economics of Choice, Change, and Organizations*, eds. Augier, M. and March, J. (Edward Elgar Publishers, Cheltenham, 2002).

[18] Epstein, J. and Axtell, R., *Growing Artificial Societies: Social Science from the Bottom-Up* (MIT Press, Washington D.C., 1996).

[19] Fagiolo, G., Dosi, G. and Gabriele, R., Towards an evolutionary interpretation of aggregate labor market regularities, working paper, LEM-WP 2004-02, Sant'Anna School of Advanced Studies, Laboratory of Economics and Management, 2004.

[20] Flaschel, P., Kauermann, G. and Semmler, W., Testing Wage and Price Phillips curves for the United States, unpublished manuscript, Bielefeld University, Faculty of Economics, 2003.

[21] Forni, M. and Lippi, M., *Aggregation and the Microfoundations of Dynamic Macroeconomics* (Clarendon Press, Oxford, 1997).

[22] Hahn, F. and Solow, R., *A Critical Essay on Modern Macroeconomic Theory* (The MIT Press, Cambridge, MA, 1997).

[23] Julien, B., Kennes, J. and King, I., Bidding for labor, *Rev. Econ. Dynamics* **3**, 619–649 (2000).

[24] Kirman, A., Whom or what does the representative individual represent?, *J. Econ. Perspectives* **6**, 117–136 (1992).

[25] Kirman, A., The economy as an interactive system, in *The Economy as an Evolving Complex System II*, eds. Arthur, W., Durlauf, S. and Lane, D. (Santa Fe Institute, Santa Fe and Addison-Wesley, Reading, MA, 1997).

[26] Laffond, G. and Lesourne, J., The genesis of expectations and of sunspot equilibria, *J. Evolutionary Econ.* **2**, 211–231 (2000).

[27] Lagos, R., An alternative approach to search frictions, *J. Political Econ.* **108**, 851–872 (2000).

[28] Lesourne, J., *The Economics of Order and Disorder* (Clarendon Press, Oxford, 1992).

[29] Nickell, S., Nunziata, L., Ochell, W. and Quintini, G., The Beveridge curve, unemployment and wages in the OECD from 1960s to 1990s, working paper No. 502, CEPR, London, U.K., 2001.

[30] Okun, A., Potential GDP: Its measurement and significance, *Proc. Busisness and Econ. Stat.*, 1962, pp. 98–103.

[31] Okun, A., *The Political Economy of Prosperity* (The Brookings Institution, Washington D.C., 1970).

[32] Peters, M., Ex ante price offers in matching games non-steady states, *Econometrica*, **59**, 1425–1454 (1991).

[33] Petrongolo, B. and Pissarides, C., Looking into the black box: A survey on the matching function, *J. Econ. Lit.* **39**, 390–431 (2001).

[34] Phelps, E., *Structural Slumps* (Harvard University Press Cambridge, 1994).

[35] Phelps, E. and Winter, S., Optimal price policy under atomistic competition, in *Microeconomic Foundations of Employment and Inflation Theory*, eds. Phelps, E., Archibald, G. and Alchian, A. (Norton, New York, 1970).

[36] Pissarides, C., *Equilibrium Unemployment Theory* (Blackwell, Oxford, 2000).

[37] Prachowny, M., Okun's law: Theoretical foundations and revised estimates, *The Rev. Econ. Stat.* **75**, 331–336 (1993).

[38] Smith, T. and Zenou, Y., A discrete-time stochastic model of job matching, *Econ. Dynamics* **6**, 54–79 (2003).

[39] Solow, R., What is labour-market flexibility? What is it good for?, *Proc. British Academy*, Vol. 97, 1998, pp. 189–211.

[40] Tesfatsion, L., How economists can get a life, in *The Economy as an Evolving Complex System II*, eds. Arthur, W., Durlauf, S and Lane, D. (Santa Fe Institute, Santa Fe and Addison-Wesley, Reading, MA, 1997).

[41] Tesfatsion, L., Structure, behavior, and market power in an evolutionary labor market with adaptive search, *J. Econ. Dynamics and Control*, **25**, 419–457 (2001).

[42] Witt, U., Coordination of individual economic activities as an evolving process of self-organization, *Economie Appliquée* **37**, 569–595 (1985).

[25]

Journal of Economic Dynamics & Control 34 (2010) 1748–1767

Contents lists available at ScienceDirect

Journal of Economic Dynamics & Control

journal homepage: www.elsevier.com/locate/jedc

ELSEVIER

Schumpeter meeting Keynes: A policy-friendly model of endogenous growth and business cycles

Giovanni Dosi [a,b,*], Giorgio Fagiolo [a], Andrea Roventini [c,a]

[a] Laboratory of Economics and Management, Sant'Anna School of Advanced Studies, Pisa, Italy
[b] MIoIR, University of Manchester, UK
[c] Department of Economics, University of Verona, Italy

ARTICLE INFO

Available online 23 June 2010

JEL classification:
E32
E6
O3
O4

Keywords:
Endogenous growth
Business cycles
Growth policies
Business cycle policies
Evolutionary economics
Agent-based computational economics
Empirical validation

ABSTRACT

This paper studies an agent-based model that bridges Keynesian theories of demand-generation and Schumpeterian theories of technology-fueled economic growth. We employ the model to investigate the properties of macroeconomic dynamics and the impact of public polices on supply, demand and the "fundamentals" of the economy. We find profound complementarities between factors influencing aggregate demand and drivers of technological change that affect both "short-run" fluctuations and long-term growth patterns. From a normative point of view, simulations show a corresponding complementarity between "Keynesian" and "Schumpeterian" policies in sustaining long-run growth paths characterized by milder fluctuations and relatively lower unemployment levels. The matching or mismatching between innovative exploration of new technologies and the conditions of demand generation appear to suggest the presence of two distinct "regimes" of growth (or absence thereof) characterized by different short-run fluctuations and unemployment levels.

© 2010 Elsevier B.V. All rights reserved.

---

1. Introduction

This work studies an agent-based model (ABM) of endogenous growth and business cycles and explores its properties under different public policies impacting on supply, demand, and the "fundamentals" of the economy.

The model addresses three major, interrelated, questions. First, it investigates the processes by which technological innovations affect macro-variables such as unemployment rates and, in the longer term, growth rates. In the current macroeconomic jargon, we explicitly model a firm-specific, *endogenous generation of supply shocks*, their diffusion and the ways they ultimately drive macro-aggregates. Together with this "Schumpeterian" question, second, we ask how such endogenous changes in the "fundamentals" of the economy interact with demand conditions. This is a basic "Keynesian" question. How does aggregate demand modulates the diffusion and the macro-impact of technological innovations? And, conversely, how does it affect, if at all, the amount of search and the degree of exploitation of innovation opportunities themselves? Third, we explore long-term effects of demand conditions. Is the long-term growth just driven by changes in the technological "fundamentals"? Or, can variations in aggregate demand influence future dynamics? And, ultimately, can one identify multiple growth paths whose selection depends on demand and institutional conditions—determining, e.g. fiscal policies.

---

* Corresponding author at: Sant'Anna School of Advanced Studies, Piazza Martiri della Libertà 33, I-56127 Pisa, Italy. Tel.: +39 050 883326; fax: +39 050 883344.
E-mail addresses: gdosi@sssup.it (G. Dosi), giorgio.fagiolo@sssup.it (G. Fagiolo), andrea.roventini@univr.it (A. Roventini).

0165-1889/$ - see front matter © 2010 Elsevier B.V. All rights reserved.
doi:10.1016/j.jedc.2010.06.018

G. Dosi et al. / *Journal of Economic Dynamics & Control 34 (2010) 1748–1767*   1749

In the analysis that follows, we extend the model presented in Dosi et al. (2006a, 2008), which we use also as a sort of "policy laboratory" where both business-cycle and growth effects of alternative public interventions may be evaluated under different techno-economic scenarios. In that, the model allows to experiment with an ensemble of policies, related to the structural features of the economy (concerning, e.g., technology, industry structure and competition) on the one hand, and to demand macro-management, on the other.

Historically, a major divide has emerged in macroeconomics theories. Long-run approaches have traditionally dealt with growth issues in a strict sense, trying to account for (broken-linear or stochastic) trends present in macro time series, while leaving to "short-run" models the task of explaining economic fluctuations around the trend. An early example is the way the IS-LM interpretation of Keynes (Hicks, 1937) and the models rooted in Solow (1956) found their division of labor addressing business cycles and growth, respectively.[1]

Since then, the balance has been shifting over time. At one extreme, the "new classical economics" has boldly claimed the irrelevance of any "Keynesian" feature of the economy. New Keynesian models have defended the turf of "non-fundamental" fluctuations most often on the grounds of informational and behavioral frictions (an insightful overview is in Blanchard, 2009), with just a minority holding the view that such "imperfections" are in fact structural, long-term characteristics of the economy (see Akerlof and Yellen, 1985; Greenwald and Stiglitz, 1993a, b; Akerlof, 2002, 2007, among them). Lacking a better name, let us call the latter *Hard New Keynesians*, HNK henceforth.

More recently, the new neoclassical synthesis between real business cycle (RBC) and a major breed of New Keynesian models has refined the interactions and the territorial divisions between "fundamental dynamics" and higher frequency, "non-fundamental" shocks within the dynamic stochastic general-equilibrium (DSGE) theoretical family (cf. the classic Woodford, 2003; Galí and Gertler, 2007). In fact, DSGE models feature a core with an RBC engine to which one may easily add sticky prices, imperfect competition, monetary-policy (Taylor-like) rules, and whatever can be imaginatively squeezed into the underlying "structural model".[2] Indeed, there is hardly any Schumpeter in terms of endogenous innovation in DSGE models.

From a quite different angle, endogenous growth models, notwithstanding very different features (from Romer, 1990 to Aghion and Howitt, 1992 and Dinopoulos and Segerstrom, 1999), possess an implicit or explicit Schumpeterian engine: innovation and thus the dynamics in the "technological fundamentals" of the economy is endogenous. At the same time, "non-fundamental" (e.g. demand-related) fluctuations do not appear in this family of models. Refinements, such as Aghion and Howitt (1998),[3] do entail *equilibrium fluctuations* wherein Keynesian features do not play any role.[4]

Somewhat similarly, evolutionary models, as pioneered by Nelson and Winter (1982), are driven by a Schumpeterian core with endogenous innovation, but do largely neglect too any demand-related driver of macroeconomic activity.[5]

The model which follows, shares evolutionary roots, but in tune with HNK insights (cf. for example Stiglitz, 1994) tries to explore the feedbacks between the factors influencing aggregate demand and those driving technological change. By doing that we begin to offer a unified framework jointly accounting for long-term dynamics and higher frequencies fluctuations.

The model is certainly *post-Walrasian* (Colander, 2006; Colander et al., 2008) meaning that it goes beyond the purported Walrasian foundations squeezed into the representative-agent assumption nested in DSGE models and the general commitment to market clearing. In that, well in tune with the growing literature on *agent-based computational economics* (ACE; see Tesfatsion and Judd, 2006; LeBaron and Tesfatsion, 2008), the model meets Solow's (2008) plea for microheterogeneity: a multiplicity of agents interact without any ex ante commitment to the reciprocal consistency of their actions.[6]

Furthermore, the model—alike most evolutionary ABMs—is "structural" in the sense that it explicitly builds on a representation of what agents do, how they adjust, etc. In that, it is as far as the DSGE perspective from "old Keynesian" models studying the relations amongst aggregate variables without any explicit microfoundation. At the same time, our commitment is to "phenomenologically" describe microbehaviors as close as one can get to available microevidence. Akerlof's (2002) advocacy of a "behavioral microeconomics", we believe, builds on that notion. In fact, this is our first fundamental disciplining device. A second, complementary one involves the ability of the model jointly to account for an ensemble of stylized facts regarding both "micro/meso" aggregates such as indicators of industrial structures (e.g. firm size distributions, productivity dispersions, firm growth rates) together with macro statistical properties (including rates of output growth, output volatility, unemployment rates, etc.).

---

[1] For an interesting reconstruction of the econometric counterpart of such a divide in the 1930s and 1940s debate, see Louca (2001).

[2] As Blanchard (2009, p. 26) puts it, "To caricature only slightly: a macroeconomic article today follows strict, haiku-like, rules: it starts from a general equilibrium structure, in which individuals maximize the expected present value of utility, firms maximize their value, and markets clear. Then, it introduces a twist, be it an imperfection or the closing of a particular set of markets, and works out the general equilibrium implications. It then performs a numerical simulation, based on calibration, showing that the model performs well. It ends with a welfare assessment."

[3] See also Aghion et al. (2010), Aghion and Marinescu (2007) and Aghion et al. (2008).

[4] Ironically, given the lack of stability of "new growth" trajectories, "Keynesianism" could show its full force. We shall go back to this point below.

[5] See, however, the exceptions of Dosi et al. (1994) and Fagiolo and Dosi (2003). Cf. Dawid (2006) for an exhaustive review of ABMs of innovation and technological change.

[6] For germane ABMs with both some Keynesian and Schumpeterian elements see Verspagen (2002), Ciarli et al. (2008), Saviotti and Pyka (2008), and the discussion in Silverberg and Verspagen (2005).

1750   *G. Dosi et al. / Journal of Economic Dynamics & Control 34 (2010) 1748–1767*

Our work shares many ingredients with (and in many ways is complementary to) the research project carried on within the European project EURACE (http://www.eurace.org), which features a large-scale ABM aiming at capturing the main characteristics of the European economy and addressing European-policy analyses (Deissenberg et al., 2008; Dawid et al., 2008). Unlike EURACE models, however, we keep the scale of the system relatively small, in line with traditional macroeconomic ABMs with little overall calibration exercises, albeit with attention to empirically sound microrules and interaction mechanisms.

The model below describes an economy composed of firms, consumers/workers and a public sector. Firms belong to two industries. In the first one, firms perform R&D and produce heterogeneous machine tools. Firms in the second industry invest in new machines and produce a homogenous consumption good. Consumers sell their labor to firms in both sectors and fully consume the income they receive. The government levies taxes on workers' wages and firms' profits and it provides unemployed workers with a fraction of the market wage.

As customary in evolutionary/ACE perspectives, the policy framework studied here is explored via computer simulations. To overcome the well-known problems related to sensitivity to the choice of parameters, possibly arising in ABMs,[7] we look for policy implications that: (i) are robust to reasonable changes in the parameters of the model; (ii) refer to model setups and parametrizations wherein the output of the model is empirically validated (i.e., simulated microeconomic and macroeconomic data possess statistical properties similar to those empirically observed in reality). We consider this as a value added of our study, as very often in the literature policy experiments are performed without imposing any ex ante empirical-validation requirement on the model (Fukac and Pagan, 2006; Canova, 2008; Fagiolo and Roventini, forthcoming). Policy configurations are captured by different "control" parameters and different institutional, market or industry setups. The impact of different policies is then quantitatively assessed in terms of ensuing aggregates such as average output growth, output volatility, average unemployment, etc. One of the main insights stemming from our extensive policy-simulation exercises is a vindication of a strong complementarity between Schumpeterian policies addressing innovative activities and Keynesian demand-management policies. Both types of policies seem to be necessary to put the economy into a long-run sustained growth path. Schumpeterian policies *potentially* foster economic growth, but they do not appear to be able alone to yield sustained long-run growth. In a broad parameter region, "fundamental" (endogenously generated) changes in technology are unable to fully propagate in terms of demand generation and ultimately output growth. By the same token, demand shocks (in the simplest case, induced by government fiscal policies) bear persistent effects upon output *levels, rates of growth*, and *rates of innovations*. In that, Keynesian policies not only have a strong impact on output volatility and unemployment, but seem to be also a necessary condition for long-run economic growth.

In fact, our results suggest that the matching or mismatching between innovative exploration of new technologies and the conditions of demand generation appear to yield two distinct "regimes" of growth (or absence thereof), also characterized by different short-run fluctuations and unemployment levels. Even when Keynesian policies allow for a sustained growth, their tuning affects the amplitude of fluctuations and the long-term levels of unemployment and output. Symmetrically, fluctuations and unemployment rates are also affected by "Schumpeterian policies", holding constant macro-demand management rules.

The rest of the paper is organized as follows. Section 2 describes the model. In Section 3 we perform empirical validation checks and in Section 4 we present results of policy exercises. Finally, Section 5 concludes and discusses future extensions.

2. The model

As already mentioned, our simple economy is composed of a machine-producing sector made of F_1 firms (denoted by the subscript i), a consumption-good sector made of F_2 firms (denoted by the subscript j), L^S consumers/workers, and a public sector. Capital-good firms invest in R&D and produce heterogeneous machines. Consumption-good firms combine machine tools bought by capital-good firms and labor in order to produce a final product for consumers. The public sector levies taxes on firms' profits and pay unemployment benefits. Innovations are clearly endogenous to our economy. It is the uncertain outcome of the search efforts of the producers of capital equipment and exerts its impact throughout the economy via both the lowering of the production costs of such equipment and its diffusion in the "downstream" consumption-good sector. Before accurately describing the model, we briefly provide the timeline of events occurring in each time step.

2.1. The timeline of events

In any given time period (t), the following microeconomic decisions take place in sequential order:

1. Machine-tool firms perform R&D trying to discover new products and more efficient production techniques and to imitate the technology and the products of their competitors.

---

[7] See Fagiolo et al. (2007) for a discussion; more on that in Section 3. The potential for policy exercises in ABMs is discussed in the special issue on "Agent-Based Models for Economic Policy Design" of the Journal of Economic Behavior and Organization, 2008 (vol. 67, no. 2), edited by Herbert Dawid and Giorgio Fagiolo.

G. Dosi et al. / Journal of Economic Dynamics & Control 34 (2010) 1748–1767   1751

2. Capital-good firms advertise their machines with consumption-good producers.
3. Consumption-good firms decide how much to produce and invest. If investment is positive, consumption-good firms choose their supplier and send their orders.
4. In both industries firms hire workers according to their production plans and start producing.
5. Imperfectly competitive consumption-good market opens. The market shares of firms evolve according to their price competitiveness.
6. Entry and exit take places. In both sectors firms with near zero market shares and negative net liquid assets are eschewed from the two industries and replaced by new firms.
7. Machines ordered at the beginning of the period are delivered and become part of the capital stock at time $t+1$.

At the end of each time step, aggregate variables (e.g. GDP, investment, employment) are computed, summing over the corresponding microeconomic variables.

Let us now turn to a more detailed description of the model and of the agents' behaviors, which—to repeat—we try to keep as close as we can to what we know they actually do as distinct from what they ought to do under more perfect informational circumstances.

2.2. The capital-good industry

The technology of a capital-good firms is (A_i^τ, B_i^τ), where the former coefficient stands for the labor productivity of the machine-tool manufactured by i for the consumption-good industry (a rough measure of producer quality), while the latter coefficient is the labor productivity of the production technique employed by firm i itself. The positive integer τ denotes the current technology vintage. Given the monetary wage w, the unit cost of production of capital-good firms is

$$c_i(t) = \frac{w(t)}{B_i^\tau}. \tag{1}$$

With a fixed mark-up ($\mu_1 > 0$) pricing rule,[8] prices (p_i) are defined as

$$p_i(t) = (1 + \mu_1)c_i(t). \tag{2}$$

The unit labor cost of production in the consumption-good sector associated with each machine of vintage τ, produced by firm i is

$$c(A_i^\tau, t) = \frac{w(t)}{A_i^\tau}.$$

Firms in the capital-good industry "adaptively" strive to increase their market shares and their profits trying to improve their technology both via innovation and imitation. Both are costly processes: firms invest in R&D a fraction of their past sales (S_i):

$$RD_i(t) = vS_i(t-1), \tag{3}$$

with $0 < v < 1$. R&D expenditures are employed to hire researchers paying the market wage $w(t)$.[9] Firms split their R&D efforts between innovation (IN) and imitation (IM) according to the parameter $\xi \in [0,1]$[10]:

$$IN_i(t) = \xi RD_i(t),$$

$$IM_i(t) = (1 - \xi)RD_i(t).$$

We model innovation as a two steps process. The first one determines whether a firm obtains or not an access to innovation—irrespectively of whether it is ultimately a success or a failure—through a draw from a Bernoulli distribution, whose parameter $\theta_i^{in}(t)$ is given by

$$\theta_i^{in}(t) = 1 - e^{-\zeta_1 IN_i(t)}, \tag{4}$$

with $0 < \zeta_1 \leq 1$. Note that according to (4), there are some scale-related returns to R&D investment: access to innovative discoveries is more likely if a firm puts more resources into R&D. If a firm innovates, it may draw a new machine embodying technology (A_i^{in}, B_i^{in}) according to

$$A_i^{in}(t) = A_i(t)(1 + x_i^A(t))$$

$$B_i^{in}(t) = B_i(t)(1 + x_i^B(t)),$$

---

[8] Survey data evidence summarized in Fabiani et al. (2006) show that European firms mostly set prices according to mark-up rules.
[9] In the following, we assume all capital-producing firms to be identical in their R&D propensity. This is not too far from reality: R&D intensities are largely sector specific and associated with the *sector-wide* nature of innovative opportunities and modes of innovative search (more in Pavitt, 1984; Dosi, 1988; Klevorick et al., 1995).
[10] Firms on the technological frontier, lacking anyone to imitate, obviously invest all their R&D budget in the search for innovations.

1752   G. Dosi et al. / Journal of Economic Dynamics & Control 34 (2010) 1748–1767

where x_i^A and x_i^B are two independent draws from a Beta(α_1, β_1) distribution over the support $[\underline{x}_1, \bar{x}_1]$ with $\underline{x}_1$ belonging to the interval $[-1,0]$ and $\bar{x}_1$ to $[0,1]$. Note that the notional possibilities of technological advance—i.e. *technological opportunities*—are captured by the support of the Beta distribution and by its shape. So, for example, with low opportunities the largest probability density falls over "failed" innovations—that is potential capital goods which are "worse" in terms of costs and performances than those already produced by the searching firm. Conversely, under a condition of rich opportunities, innovations which dominate incumbent technologies will be drawn with high probability. As we shall show below, a crucial role of "Schumpeterian" technology policies is precisely that of influencing opportunities and microcapabilities.

Alike innovation search, imitation follows a two steps procedure. The possibilities of accessing imitation come from sampling a Bernoulli($\theta_i^{im}(t)$):

$$\theta_i^{im}(t) = 1 - e^{-\zeta_2 IM_i(t)}, \tag{5}$$

with $0 < \zeta_2 \leq 1$. Firms accessing the second stage are able to copy the technology of one of the competitors (A_i^{im}, B_i^{im}). We assume that firms are more likely to imitate competitors with similar technologies and we use a Euclidean metric to compute the technological distance between every pair of firms to weight imitation probabilities.

All firms which draw a potential innovation or imitation have to put it on production or keep producing the incumbent generation of machines. Comparing the technology competing for adoption, firms choose to manufacture the machine characterized by the best tradeoff between price and efficiency. More specifically, knowing that consumption-good firms invest following a payback period routine (see Section 2.3), capital-good firms select the machine to produce according to the following rule:

$$\min[p_i^h(t) + bc^h(A_i^h, t)], \quad h = \tau, in, im, \tag{6}$$

where b is a positive payback period parameter (see Eq. (10)). Once the type of machine is chosen, we capture the imperfect information pervading the market assuming that each firm sends a "brochure" with the price and the productivity of its offered machines to both its historical (HC_i) clients and to a random sample of potential new customers (NC_i), whose size is proportional to HC_i (i.e., $NC_i(t) = \gamma HC_i(t)$, with $0 < \gamma < 1$).

2.3. The consumption-good industry

Consumption-good firms produce a homogenous goods using capital (i.e. their stock of machines) and labor under constant returns to scale. Firms plan their production (Q_j) according to adaptive demand expectations (D_j^e):

$$D_j^e(t) = f(D_j(t-1), D_j(t-2), \ldots, D_j(t-h)), \tag{7}$$

where $D_j(t-1)$ is the demand actually faced by firm j at time $t-1$ (h positive integer).[11] The desired level of production (Q_j^d) depends on the expected demand as well as on the desired inventories (N_j^d) and the actual stock of inventories (N_j):

$$Q_j^d(t) = D_j^e(t) + N_j^d(t) - N_j(t-1), \tag{8}$$

with $N_j^d(t) = \iota D_j^e(t)$, $\iota \in [0,1]$. The output of consumption-good firms is constrained by their capital stock (K_j). If the desired capital stock (K_j^d)—computed as a function of the desired level of production—is higher than the current capital stock, firms invest (EI_j^d) in order to expand their production capacity[12]:

$$EI_j^d(t) = K_j^d(t) - K_j(t). \tag{9}$$

The capital stock of each firm is obviously composed of heterogenous vintages of machines with different productivity. We define $\Xi_j(t)$ as the set of all vintages of machine-tools belonging to firm j at time t. Firms scrap machines following a payback period routine. Through that, technical change and equipment prices influence the replacement decisions of consumption-good firms.[13] More specifically, firm j replaces machine $A_i^\tau \in \Xi_j(t)$ according to its technology obsolescence as well as the price of new machines:

$$RS_j(t) = \left\{ A_i^\tau \in \Xi_j(t) : \frac{p^*(t)}{c(A_{i,\tau}, t) - c^*(t)} \leq b \right\}, \tag{10}$$

where p^* and c^* are the price and unit cost of production upon the new machines. Firms compute their replacement investment summing up the number of old machine-tools satisfying Eq. (10).[14]

---

[11] For maximum simplicity, here we use the rule $D_j^e(t) = D_j(t-1)$. In Dosi et al. (2006a) we check the robustness of the simulation results employing more sophisticated expectation-formation rules. We found that increasing the computational capabilities of firms does not significantly change either the average growth rates or the stability of the economy. These properties still hold in the model presented here.

[12] We assume that in any give period firm capital growth rates cannot exceed a fixed maximum threshold consistent with the maximum capital growth rates found in the empirical literature on firm investment patterns (e.g. Doms and Dunne, 1998).

[13] This in line with a large body of empirical analyses (e.g. Feldstein and Foot, 1971; Eisner, 1972; Goolsbee, 1998) showing that replacement investment is typically not proportional to the capital stock.

[14] Moreover, they also scrap the machines older than η periods (with η being a positive integer).

G. Dosi et al. / Journal of Economic Dynamics & Control 34 (2010) 1748–1767   1753

Consumption-good firms choose their capital-good supplier comparing the price and productivity of the currently manufactured machine-tools they are aware of. As we mentioned above (cf. Section 2.2) the capital-good market is systematically characterized by imperfect information. This implies that consumption-good firms compare "brochures" describing the characteristics of machines only from a subset of equipment suppliers. Firms then choose the machines with the lowest price and unit cost of production (i.e., $p_i(t) + bc(A_i^\tau, t)$) and send their orders to the correspondingly machine manufacturer. Machine production is a time-consuming process: capital-good firms deliver the ordered machine-tools at the end of the period.[15] Gross investment of each firm (I_j) is the sum of expansion and replacement investment. Pooling the investment of all consumption-good firms one gets aggregate investment (I).

Consumption-good firms have to finance their investments as well as their production, as they advance worker wages. In line with a growing number of theoretical and empirical papers (e.g. Stiglitz and Weiss, 1992; Greenwald and Stiglitz, 1993a; Hubbard, 1998) we assume imperfect capital markets. This implies that the financial structure of firms matters (external funds are more expensive than internal ones) and firms may be credit rationed. More specifically, consumption-good firms finance production using their stock of liquid assets (NW_j). If liquid assets do not fully cover production costs, firms borrow the remaining part paying an interest rate r up to a maximum debt/sales ratio of Λ. Only firms that are not production-rationed can try to fulfill their investment plans employing their residual stock of liquid assets first and then their residual borrowing capacity.[16]

Given their current stock of machines, consumption-good firms compute average productivity (π_j) and unit cost of production (c_j). Prices are set applying a variable markup (μ_j) on unit costs of production:

$$p_j(t) = (1 + \mu_j(t))c_j(t).\tag{11}$$

Markup variations are regulated by the evolution of firm market shares (f_j)[17]:

$$\mu_j(t) = \mu_j(t-1)\left(1 + \upsilon\frac{f_j(t-1) - f_j(t-2)}{f_j(t-2)}\right),$$

with $0 \leq \upsilon \leq 1$.

The consumption-good market too is characterized by imperfect information (antecedents in the same spirits are Phelps and Winter, 1970; Klemperer, 1987; Farrel and Shapiro, 1988; see also the empirical literature on consumers' imperfect price knowledge surveyed in Rotemberg, 2008). This implies that consumers do not instantaneously switch to products made by more competitive firms. However, prices are clearly one of the key determinants of firms' *competitiveness* (E_j). The other component is the level of unfilled demand (l_j) inherited from the previous period:

$$E_j(t) = -\omega_1 p_j(t) - \omega_2 l_j(t),\tag{12}$$

where $\omega_{1,2}$ are positive parameters.[18] Weighting the competitiveness of each consumption-good firm by its past market share (f_j), one can compute the *average competitiveness* of the consumption-good sector:

$$\bar{E}(t) = \sum_{j=1}^{F_2} E_j(t) f_j(t-1).$$

Such variable represents also a moving *selection criterion* driving, other things being equal, expansion, contraction and extinction within the population of firms. We parsimoniously model this market setup letting firm market shares evolve according to a "quasi" replicator dynamics (for antecedents in the evolutionary camp cf. Silverberg et al., 1988; Metcalfe, 1994a):

$$f_j(t) = f_j(t-1)\left(1 + \chi\frac{E_j(t) - \bar{E}(t)}{\bar{E}(t)}\right),\tag{13}$$

with $\chi > 0$.[19]

The profits (Π_j) of each consumption-good firm reads

$$\Pi_j(t) = S_j(t) - c_j(t)Q_j(t) - rDeb_j(t),$$

---

[15] Among the empirical literature investigating the presence of gestation-lag effects in firm investment expenditures see e.g. Del Boca et al. (2008).

[16] If investment plans cannot be fully realized, firms give priority to capital stock expansion, as compared to the substitution of old machines.

[17] This is close to the spirit of "customer market" models originated by the seminal work of Phelps and Winter (1970). See also Klemperer (1995) for a survey and the exploration of some important macro-implications by Greenwald and Stiglitz (2003).

[18] Recall that consumption-good firms fix production according to their demand expectations, which may differ from actual demand. If the firm produced too much, the inventories pile up, whereas if its production is lower than demand plus inventories, its competitiveness is accordingly reduced.

[19] Strictly speaking, a canonic replicator dynamics evolves on the unit simplex with all entities having positive shares. Eq. (13) allows shares to become virtually negative. In that case, the firm is declared dead and market shares are accordingly re-calculated. This is what we mean by a "quasi-replicator" dynamics. Note that an advantage of such formulation is that it determines at the same time changes in market shares and extinction events.

1754   *G. Dosi et al. / Journal of Economic Dynamics & Control 34 (2010) 1748–1767*

where $S_j(t) = p_j(t)D_j(t)$ and *Deb* denotes the stock of debt. The investment choices of each firm and its profits determine the evolution of its stock of liquid assets (NW_j):

$$NW_j(t) = NW_j(t-1) + \Pi_j(t) - cI_j(t),$$

where cI_j is the amount of internal funds employed by firm j to finance investment.

2.4. Schumpeterian exit and entry dynamics

At the end of each period we let firms with (quasi) zero market shares or negative net assets die and we allow a new breed of firms to enter the markets. We keep the number of firms fixed, hence any dead firm is replaced by a new one.

In line with the empirical literature on firm entry (Caves, 1998; Bartelsman et al., 2005), we assume that entrants are on average smaller than incumbents, with the stock of capital of new consumption-good firms and the stock of liquid assets of entrants in both sectors being a fraction of the average stocks of the incumbents.[20] Concerning the technology of entrants, new consumption-good firms select amongst the newest vintages of machines, according to the "brochure mechanism" described above. The process- and product-related knowledge of new capital-good firms is drawn from a Beta distribution, whose shape and support is shifted and "twisted" according to whether entrants enjoy an advantage or a disadvantage vis-à-vis incumbents.[21] In fact, the distribution of opportunities for entrants vs. incumbents is a crucial characteristics of different sectoral *technological regimes* and plays a role somewhat akin to the distance from the technological frontier of entrants discussed in Aghion and Howitt (2007).

2.5. The labor market

The labor market is certainly not Walrasian: real-wage does not clear the market and involuntary unemployment as well as labor rationing are the rules rather than the exceptions. The aggregate labor demand (L^D) is computed summing up the labor demand of capital- and consumption-good firms. The aggregate supply (L^S) is exogenous and inelastic. Hence aggregate employment (L) is the minimum between L^D and L^S.

The wage rate is determined by institutional and market factors, with both indexation mechanisms upon consumption prices and average productivity, on the one hand, and, adjustments to unemployment rates, on the others:

$$w(t) = w(t-1) + \left(1 + \psi_1 \frac{\Delta \overline{AB}(t)}{\overline{AB}(t-1)} + \psi_2 \frac{\Delta cpi(t)}{cpi(t-1)} + \psi_3 \frac{\Delta U(t)}{U(t-1)}\right), \tag{14}$$

where $\overline{AB}$ is the average labor productivity, *cpi* is the consumer price index, and U is the unemployment rate. Various institutional regimes for the labor market can be designed changing the system parameters $\psi_{1,2,3}$.[22]

2.6. Consumption, taxes, and public expenditures

An otherwise black boxed public sector levies taxes on firm profits and worker wages or on profits only and pays to unemployed workers a subsidy (w^u), that is a fraction of the current market wage (i.e., $w^u(t) = \varphi w(t)$, with $\varphi \in (0,1)$). In fact, taxes and subsidies are the fiscal leverages that contribute to the aggregate demand management regimes (we shall explore this issue in more detail below). Note that a "zero tax, zero subsidy" scenario is our benchmark for a *pure Schumpeterian regime* of institutional governance.

Aggregate consumption (C) is computed by summing up over the income of both employed and unemployed workers:

$$C(t) = w(t)L^D(t) + w^u(L^S - L^D(t)). \tag{15}$$

The model satisfies the standard national account identities: the sum of value added of capital- and consumption goods firms (Y) equals their aggregate production since in our simplified economy there are no intermediate goods, and that in turn coincides with the sum of aggregate consumption, investment and change in inventories (ΔN):

$$\sum_{i=1}^{F_1} Q_i(t) + \sum_{j=1}^{F_2} Q_j(t) = Y(t) \equiv C(t) + I(t) + \Delta N(t).$$

The dynamics generated at the micro-level by decisions of a multiplicity of heterogenous, adaptive agents and by their interaction mechanisms is the explicit microfoundation of the dynamics for all aggregate variables of interest (e.g. output, investment, employment, etc.). However, as the model amply demonstrates, the aggregate properties of the economy do

---

[20] The stock of capital of a new consumption-good firm is obtained multiplying the average stock of capital of the incumbents by a random draw from a Uniform distribution with support $[\phi_1, \phi_2]$, $0 < \phi_1, < \phi_2 \leq 1$. In the same manner, the stock of liquid assets of an entrant is computed multiplying the average stock of liquid assets of the incumbents of the sector by a random variable distributed according to a Uniform with support $[\phi_3, \phi_4]$, $0 < \phi_3, < \phi_4 \leq 1$.

[21] More precisely, the technology of capital-good firms is obtained applying a coefficient extracted from a Beta(α_2, β_2) distribution to the endogenously evolving technology frontier ($A^{max}(t), B^{max}(t)$), where $A^{max}(t)$ and $B^{max}(t)$ are the best technology available to incumbents.

[22] For more detailed modelizations of the labor market in a evolutionary/ACE framework see e.g. Tesfatsion (2000), Fagiolo et al. (2004), and Neugart (2008).

G. Dosi et al. / *Journal of Economic Dynamics & Control 34 (2010) 1748–1767*   1755

Table 1
Benchmark parameters.

Description	Symbol	Value
Number of firms in capital-good industry	F_1	50
Number of firms in consumption-good industry	F_2	200
R&D investment propensity	ν	0.04
R&D allocation to innovative search	ξ	0.50
Firm search capabilities parameters	$\zeta_{1,2}$	0.30
Beta distribution parameters (innovation process)	(α_1,β_1)	(3,3)
Beta distribution support (innovation process)	$[\underline{x}_1,\bar{x}_1]$	$[-0.15,0.15]$
New-customer sample parameter	γ	0.50
Capital-good firm mark-up rule	μ_1	0.04
Desired inventories	ι	0.10
Payback period	b	3
"Physical" scrapping age	η	20
Mark-up coefficient	υ	0.04
Competitiveness weights	$\omega_{1,2}$	1
Replicator dynamics coefficient	χ	1
Maximum debt/sales ratio	Λ	2
Interest rate	r	0.01
Uniform distribution supports (consumption-good entrant capital)	$[\phi_1,\phi_2]$	[0.10,0.90]
Uniform distribution supports (entrant stock of liquid assets)	$[\phi_3,\phi_4]$	[0.10,0.90]
Beta distribution parameters (capital-good entrants technology)	(α_2,β_2)	(2,4)
Wage setting $\Delta\overline{AB}$ weight	ψ_1	1
Wage setting Δcpi weight	ψ_2	0
Wage setting ΔU weight	ψ_3	0
Tax rate	tr	0.10
Unemployment subsidy rate	φ	0.40

not bears any apparent isomorphism with those microadjustment rules outlined above. And a fundamental consequence is also that any "representative agent" compression of microheterogeneity is likely to offer a distorted account of both what agents do and of the collective outcomes of their actions—indeed, well in tune with the arguments of Kirman (1992) and Solow (2008).

3. Empirical validation

The foregoing model does not allow for analytical, closed-form solutions. This general ABM distinctive feature stems from the non-linearities present in agent decision rules and their interaction patterns, and it forces us to run computer simulations to analyze the properties of the stochastic processes governing the coevolution of micro- and macro-variables.[23] In what follows, we therefore perform extensive Monte-Carlo analyses to wash away across-simulation variability. Consequently, all results below refer to across-run averages over 100 replications and their standard-error bands.[24]

Let us start from a sort of "benchmark" setup for which the model is empirically validated, i.e. it is studied in its ability to replicate a wide spectrum of microeconomic and macroeconomic stylized facts. Initial conditions and parameters of the benchmark setup are presented in Table 1.

As it should be clear from the forgoing presentation of the model, it embodies both a *Schumpeterian engine* and a *Keynesian* one. The former rests in the generation of innovations by an ensemble of equipment producers which expensively search and endogenously differentiate in the technology they are able to master. The Keynesian engine has two parts: a direct one—through fiscal policies—and an indirect one—via investment decisions and workers' consumption. Hence, the benchmark model appropriately embodies all such Schumpeterian and Keynesian features.

Next we tune so to speak "up" and "down" the key policy variables (e.g. tax rates and unemployment benefits) and we experiment with different conditions affecting the access to and exploitation of new technological opportunities (e.g. the patent regime, anti-trust policies).

---

[23] Some methodological issues concerning the exploration of the properties of evolutionary/ACE models are discussed in e.g. Lane (1993), Pyka and Fagiolo (2007), Fagiolo et al. (2007), and Fagiolo and Roventini (forthcoming).

[24] Preliminary exercises confirm that, for the majority of statistics under study, Monte-Carlo distributions are sufficiently symmetric and unimodal to justify the use of across-run averages as meaningful synthetic indicators.

1756   *G. Dosi et al. / Journal of Economic Dynamics & Control 34 (2010) 1748–1767*

Let us first explore the ability of the model to reproduce the major stylized facts regarding both the properties of macroeconomic aggregates and the underlying distribution of micro characteristics (more on both in the direct antecedents to this model: cf. Dosi et al., 2006a, 2008).

Growth and fluctuations. The model robustly generates endogenous self-sustained growth patterns characterized by the presence of persistent fluctuations (cf. Fig. 1). At business cycle frequencies, bandpass-filtered output, investment and consumption series (Bpf, cf. Baxter and King, 1999) display the familiar "roller-coaster" dynamics (see Fig. 2) observed in

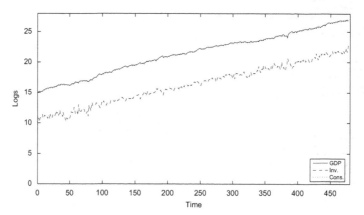

Fig. 1. Level of output, investment, and consumption (logs).

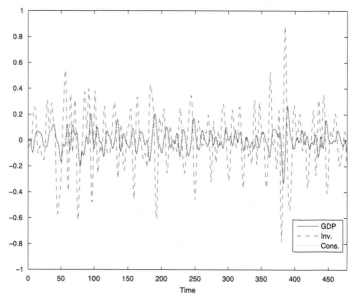

Fig. 2. Bandpass-filtered output, investment, and consumption.

G. Dosi et al. / Journal of Economic Dynamics & Control 34 (2010) 1748–1767

Table 2
Output, investment, and consumption statistics.

	Output	Consumption	Investment
Avg. growth rate	0.0254	0.0252	0.0275
	(0.0002)	(0.0002)	(0.0004)
Dickey–Fuller test (logs)	6.7714	9.4807	0.2106
	(0.0684)	(0.0957)	(0.0633)
Dickey–Fuller test (Bpf)	−6.2564*	−5.8910*	−6.8640*
	(0.0409)	(0.0447)	(0.0905)
Std. dev. (Bpf)	0.0809	0.0679	0.4685
	(0.0007)	(0.0005)	(0.0266)
Rel. std. dev. (output)	1	0.8389	5.7880

Bpf: bandpass-filtered (6,32,12) series. Monte-Carlo simulation standard errors in parentheses. (*): Significant at 5%.

Table 3
Correlation structure.

Series (Bpf)	Output (Bpf)								
	$t-4$	$t-3$	$t-2$	$t-1$	t	$t+1$	$t+2$	$t+3$	$t+4$
Output	−0.1022	0.1769	0.5478	0.8704	1	0.8704	0.5478	0.1769	−0.1022
	(0.0090)	(0.0080)	(0.0048)	(0.0014)	(0)	(0.0014)	(0.0048)	(0.0080)	(0.0090)
Consumption	−0.1206	0.0980	0.4256	0.7563	0.9527	0.9248	0.6848	0.3394	0.0250
	(0.0123)	(0.0129)	(0.0106)	(0.0062)	(0.0017)	(0.0018)	(0.0038)	(0.0058)	(0.0072)
Investment	−0.2638	−0.3123	−0.2646	−0.0864	0.1844	0.4473	0.5950	0.5757	0.4206
	(0.0102)	(0.0137)	(0.0182)	(0.0210)	(0.0206)	(0.0175)	(0.0139)	(0.0123)	(0.0129)
Net investment	−0.0838	0.0392	0.2195	0.4010	0.5114	0.5037	0.3850	0.2105	0.0494
	(0.0122)	(0.0167)	(0.0216)	(0.0235)	(0.0211)	(0.0153)	(0.0103)	(0.0112)	(0.0138)
Ch. in invent.	0.0072	0.1184	0.2349	0.2948	0.2573	0.1331	−0.0199	−0.1319	−0.1640
	(0.0081)	(0.0070)	(0.0060)	(0.0072)	(0.0090)	(0.0098)	(0.0097)	(0.0085)	(0.0067)
Employment	−0.3240	−0.1901	0.0796	0.4083	0.6692	0.7559	0.6451	0.4067	0.1555
	(0.0087)	(0.0123)	(0.0151)	(0.0160)	(0.0149)	(0.0120)	(0.0084)	(0.0069)	(0.0082)
Unempl. rate	0.3357	0.2084	−0.0596	−0.3923	−0.6607	−0.7550	−0.6489	−0.4112	−0.1583
	(0.0083)	(0.0118)	(0.0147)	(0.0158)	(0.0148)	(0.0120)	(0.0084)	(0.0070)	(0.0082)
Productivity	0.1180	0.3084	0.5316	0.7108	0.7672	0.6656	0.4378	0.1664	−0.0609
	(0.0097)	(0.0088)	(0.0092)	(0.0093)	(0.0076)	(0.0067)	(0.0097)	(0.0126)	(0.0128)
Price	0.2558	0.3181	0.2702	0.0916	−0.1645	−0.3950	−0.5067	−0.4688	−0.3249
	(0.0167)	(0.0218)	(0.0235)	(0.0216)	(0.0198)	(0.0212)	(0.0225)	(0.0210)	(0.0176)
Inflation	−0.1070	0.0841	0.3110	0.4456	0.4021	0.1966	−0.0628	−0.2478	−0.2900
	(0.0151)	(0.0135)	(0.0175)	(0.0226)	(0.0228)	(0.0188)	(0.0154)	(0.0146)	(0.0131)
Mark-up	0.2183	0.1599	0.0411	−0.0988	−0.2040	−0.2361	−0.1968	−0.1226	−0.0580
	(0.0118)	(0.0088)	(0.0128)	(0.0184)	(0.0213)	(0.0206)	(0.0174)	(0.0135)	(0.0107)

Bpf: bandpass-filtered (6,32,12) series. Monte-Carlo simulation standard errors in parentheses.

real data (e.g. Stock and Watson, 1999; Napoletano et al., 2006). Moreover, in tune with the empirical evidence, both consumption and investment appear to be procyclical variables with the latter series being also more volatile than GDP.

Output, consumption and investment display strictly positive average growth rates[25] (cf. Table 2) and, according to Dickey–Fuller tests, they seem to exhibit a unit root. After detrending the series with a bandpass filter, we compute standard deviations and cross-correlations between output and the other series. In line with the empirical literature on business cycles (cf. Stock and Watson, 1999), also in our model investment is more volatile than output, whereas consumption is less volatile; consumption, investment, change in inventories, and employment are procyclical; unemployment is countercyclical (cf. Table 3).[26]

---

[25] The average growth rate of variable X (e.g. GDP) is simply defined as

$$\overline{GR}_X = \frac{\log X(T) - \log X(0)}{T+1},$$

where $T=600$ is the econometric sample size. This value for T is a quite conservative choice, as the first iterative moments of growth statistics converge to a stable behavior well before such a time horizon. This means that the model reaches a relatively (meta) stable behavior quite soon after simulations start. Our experiment show that choosing larger values for T does not alter the main economic implications of the paper.

[26] Consumption and net investment are also coincident variables matching yet another empirical regularity on business cycles. Changes in inventories are instead slightly lagging.

1758   *G. Dosi et al. / Journal of Economic Dynamics & Control 34 (2010) 1748–1767*

Table 4
Growth-rate distributions, estimation of exponential-power parameters.

Series	b	Std. dev.	a	Std. dev.	m	Std. dev.
Capital-good	0.5285	0.0024	0.4410	0.0189	−0.0089	0.0002
Consumption-good	0.4249	0.0051	0.0289	0.0037	0.0225	0.0001
Output	1.4673	0.0122	0.0775	0.0004	−0.0027	0.0003

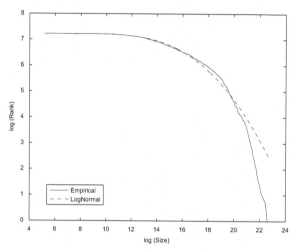

Fig. 3. Pooled (year-standardized) capital-good firm sales distributions. Log rank vs. log size plots.

The model is also able to match the business-cycle properties concerning productivity, price, inflation and markups (see Table 3): productivity is procyclical, prices are countercyclical and leading; inflation is procyclical and lagging; markups are countercyclical (for the empirics and discussion cf. Stock and Watson, 1999; Rotemberg and Woodford, 1999).

Finally, the aggregate growth rates of output display fat-tailed distributions well in tune with the empirical evidence (cf. Table 4; see Castaldi and Dosi, 2009; Fagiolo et al., 2008). Informally, this means that both in our model and in reality relatively big "spurs of growth" and recessions occur much more frequently than it would be predicted on the grounds of normally distributed shocks (see also below on firm growth patterns).

Distributions of microeconomics characteristics. Together with the ability of the model to account for a rich ensemble of macro-phenomena, how does it fare in its matching with the evidence on the ubiquitous microheterogeneity? Let us consider the regularities concerning firm-size and growth-rate distributions, firm-productivity dynamics and firm-investment patterns which are generated by the model.

To begin with, well in tune with the empirical evidence (Dosi, 2007), rank-size plots and normality tests suggest that cross-section firm (log) size distributions are skewed and not log-normal (see Figs. 3 and 4 and Table 5). Moreover, the estimation of the shape parameters of exponential-power (Subbotin) distributions[27] shows that pooled firm growth-rate distributions are "tent-shaped" with tails fatter than the Gaussian benchmark (see Table 4 and, for a comparison with the empirical evidence and some interpretation, see Bottazzi and Secchi, 2003, 2006).

Turning to firm productivity, again in line with the empirical evidence (cf. the surveys in Bartelsman and Doms, 2000; Dosi, 2007), firms strikingly differ in terms of labor productivity (cf. standard deviations of labor productivity across firms

---

[27] We estimate a distribution of the form:

$$f(x; b, a, m) = \frac{1}{2ab^{1/b}\Gamma(1 + \frac{1}{b})} e^{-(1/b)|(x-m)/a|^b}.$$

In a Subbotin distribution one parameter—b, in Table 4—governs the fatness of the tails. The Normal distribution is recovered when b=2, the fatter Laplace distribution when b=1.

G. Dosi et al. / Journal of Economic Dynamics & Control 34 (2010) 1748–1767   1759

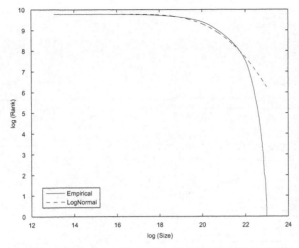

Fig. 4. Pooled (year-standardized) consumption-good firm sales distributions. Log rank vs. log size plots.

Table 5
Log-size distributions, normality tests.

Industry	Jarque–Bera		Lilliefors		Anderson–Darling	
	Stat.	p-Value	Stat.	p-Value	Stat.	p-Value
Capital-good	20.7982	0	0.0464	0	4.4282	0
Consumption-good	3129.7817	0	0.0670	0	191.0805	0

plotted in Fig. 5), productivity differentials persist over time (cf. firm productivity autocorrelations reported in Table 6)[28] and productivity growth rates are Laplace distributed (i.e. again, the distribution exhibits fat tails).

Finally, we have analyzed firm investment patterns. The model is indeed able to generate as an emergent property investment lumpiness (Doms and Dunne, 1998; Caballero, 1999). Indeed, in each time step, consumption-good firms with "near" zero investment coexist with firms experiencing investment spikes (see Fig. 6 and relate it to Gourio and Kashyap, 2007).

4. Policy experiments: tuning Schumpeterian and Keynesian regimes

The model, we have seen, is empirically quite robust in that it accounts, *together*, for a large number of empirical regularities. It certainly passes a much higher "testing hurdle", as Solow (2008) puts it, than simply reproducing "a few of the low moments of observed time series: ratios of variances or correlation coefficients, for instance" (p. 245) as most current models content themselves with. Encouraged by that empirical performance of the model, let us experiment with different structural conditions (e.g. concerning the nature of innovative opportunities) and policy regimes, and study their impact on output growth rates, volatility and rates of unemployment.[29]

---

[28] In the last 200 periods of the simulations, we consider the autocorrelation of firms that survived for at least 20 periods and we compute the industry average.

[29] Interestingly, most other statistical regularities concerning the structure of the economy (e.g. size distributions, fatness of firms growth rates, etc.) appear to hold across an ample parameter range, under positive technological progress, even when policies undergo the changes we study in the following.

1760 *G. Dosi et al. / Journal of Economic Dynamics & Control 34 (2010) 1748–1767*

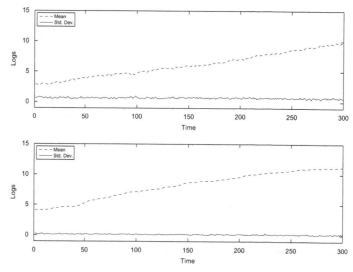

Fig. 5. Firms' productivity moments (logs). First panel: capital-good firms. Second panel: consumption-good firms.

Table 6
Average autocorrelation of productivity.

Industry	$t-1$	$t-2$
Capital-good	0.5433	0.3700
	(0.1821)	(0.2140)
Consumption-good	0.5974	0.3465
	(0.2407)	(0.2535)

Standard deviations in parentheses.

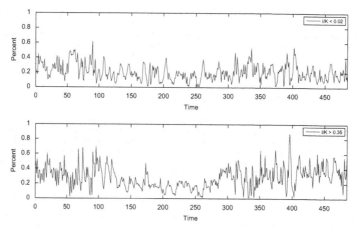

Fig. 6. Investment lumpiness. First panel: share of firms with (near) zero investment; second panel: share of firms with investment spikes.

G. Dosi et al. / Journal of Economic Dynamics & Control 34 (2010) 1748–1767   1761

Table 7
Schumpeterian regime technological and industrial policy experiments.

Experiment	Description	Avg. GDP growth rate	GDP std. dev. (Bpf)	Avg. unemployment
0	Benchmark scenario	0.0254 (0.0002)	0.0809 (0.0007)	0.1072 (0.0050)
1.1	Low technological opportunities	0.0195 (0.0001)	0.0794 (0.0008)	0.1357 (0.0050)
1.2	High technological opportunities	0.0315 (0.0002)	0.0828 (0.0007)	0.1025 (0.0051)
2.1	Low search capabilities	0.0231 (0.0002)	0.0825 (0.0008)	0.1176 (0.0059)
2.2	High search capabilities	0.0268 (0.0002)	0.0775 (0.0008)	0.1031 (0.0048)
3.1	No imitation	0.0254 (0.0002)	0.0693 (0.0008)	0.1049 (0.0059)
3.2	Patent (length only)	0.0242 (0.0002)	0.0761 (0.0008)	0.1132 (0.0060)
3.3	Patent (breadth, too)	0.0163 (0.0001)	0.0631 (0.0007)	0.1329 (0.0067)
4.1	Low entrant expected productivity	0.0183 (0.0003)	0.0798 (0.0012)	0.1402 (0.0084)
4.2	Higher entrant expected productivity	0.0376 (0.0002)	0.0697 (0.0006)	0.0853 (0.0047)
5.1	Weak antitrust	0.0265 (0.0002)	0.0698 (0.0006)	0.1036 (0.0043)
5.2	Strong antitrust	0.0273 (0.0001)	0.0508 (0.0005)	0.0837 (0.0036)
6	Schumpeter-only, no fiscal policy	0.0110 (0.0018)	1.5511 (0.0427)	0.7855 (0.0274)

Bpf: bandpass-filtered (6,32,12) series. Monte-Carlo simulations standard errors in parentheses.

4.1. Alternative innovation and competition regimes

Consider first the Schumpeterian side of the economy, holding the "Keynesian engine" constant as compared with the benchmark scenario[30]: Table 7 summarizes the results. Let us start by turning off endogenous technological opportunities. In this case, the model collapses onto a barebone 2-sector Solow (1956) model in steady state, with fixed coefficients and zero growth (absent demographic changes).

Opportunities and search capabilities. What happens if one changes the opportunities of technological innovation and the ability to search for them? Experiment 1 (Table 7) explores such a case. As compared to the benchmark, we shift rightward and leftward the mass of the Beta distribution governing new technological draws (i.e. the parameters α_1 and β_1, cf. Section 2.2). Note that the support of the distribution remains unchanged, so that one could informally state that the *notional* possibilities of drift in the technological frontier remain unchanged, too. However, the "pool" of opportunities agents actually face get either richer or more rarefied. We find that higher opportunities have a positive impact on the long-term rate of growth, reduce average unemployment and slightly increase GDP volatility (a mark of Schumpeterian "gales of creative destruction"?).

Somewhat similarly, higher search capabilities approximated by the possibilities of accessing "innovations"—no matter if failed or successful ones—(cf. the $\zeta_{1,2}$ parameters in Eqs. (4) and (5)) positively influence the rates of growth and lower unemployment. Together, business cycle fluctuations are dampened possibly because a population of "more competent" firms entails lower degrees of technological asymmetries across them and indeed also lower degrees of "creative destruction". See experiment 2, Table 7.

Note that such role of innovative opportunities and search capabilities is in principle equivalent to that black-boxed into the more aggregate notions of "human capital" (Nelson and Phelps, 1966; Benhabib and Spiegel, 1994) and of "appropriate institutions" (Acemoglu et al., 2006).[31]

Appropriability conditions. In many current models with a (neo) Schumpeterian engine, appropriability conditions play a key role via their assumptions on the forward looking rationality of the agent(s) investing into uncertain innovative search: the degrees of monopoly appropriation of the economic benefits from successful search parametrize the equilibrium

---

[30] The full list of parameters under different policy scenarios is available from the authors on request.

[31] In fact, given the increasing availability of microdata one can start thinking of disaggregated empirical proxies for our variables. The issue is, however, well beyond the scope of this work.

1762   G. Dosi et al. / Journal of Economic Dynamics & Control 34 (2010) 1748–1767

Table 8
Keynesian regime fiscal policy experiments.

Tax rate	Unemployment subsidy (in % of wages)	Avg. GDP growth rate	GDP std. dev. (Bpf)	Avg. unemployment
0	0	0.0035	1.5865	0.8868
		(0.0012)	(0.0319)	(0.0201)
0.05	0.20	0.0254	0.1539	0.1952
		(0.0002)	(0.0025)	(0.0086)
0.10	0.40	0.0252	0.0809	0.1072
		(0.0002)	(0.0007)	(0.0050)
0.15	0.60	0.0251	0.0630	0.0846
		(0.0002)	(0.0005)	(0.0034)
0.20	0.80	0.0254	0.0584	0.0602
		(0.0002)	(0.0006)	(0.0027)
0.25	1	0.0252	0.0564	0.0551
		(0.0002)	(0.0005)	(0.0023)

Bpf: bandpass-filtered (6,32,12) series. Monte-Carlo simulations standard errors in parentheses.

relation between investment in R&D and rates of innovation. In this model, we took a much more behavioral route and assumed a fixed propensity to invest in R&D—again, quite in tune with the evidence displaying relatively sticky and sectoral specific propensities. Granted that, how do changes in appropriability conditions affect aggregate dynamics?

We first studied an extreme condition (albeit rather common in the theoretical literature), turning off the possibility of imitation, and assuming that all R&D is invested in innovative search. Interestingly (and admittedly to the surprise of the authors) we basically find no differences vis-à-vis the benchmark scenario: compare experiment 3.1 with experiment 0, Table 7.

Let us then try to mimic the effect of a patent system. Under a "length only" patent scenario, the innovative technology cannot be imitated for a given number of periods determined by the patent length (cf. experiment 3.2, Table 7). Such patenting possibility is *detrimental to long-run growth* and also augments the average rate of unemployment. The negative aggregate impact of the patent system is reinforced if each firm cannot innovate in some neighborhood of the other firms' technologies—i.e. in the presence of a patent breadth: see experiment 3.3, Table 7.[32]

Entry and competition policies. Important dimensions of distinct Schumpeterian regimes of innovation regard, first, the advantages/disadvantages that entrants face vis-à-vis incumbents and, second, the market conditions placing economic rewards and punishments upon heterogenous competitors.

The first theme cuts across the evolutionary and neo-Schumpeterian literature and sometimes is dramatized as a "Schumpeterian Mark I" vs. a "Schumpeterian Mark II" scenarios, meaning systematic innovative advantages for entrepreneurial entrants vs. cumulative advantages of incumbents (cf. Malerba and Orsenigo, 1995; Dosi et al., 1995). In our model, technological entry barriers (or advantages) are captured by the probability distribution over the "technological draws" of entrants. Again, we hold constant the support over which the economy (i.e. every firm thereof) may draw innovative advances, conditional on the technology at any t. In this case we do it for the sake of consistency: results, even more so, apply if different regimes are also allowed to entail different probability supports. Let us first tune the Beta distribution parameters α_2 and β_2 (cf. Section 2.4). Our results are broadly in line with the evidence discussed in Aghion and Howitt (2007): *other things being equal*, the easiness of entry and competence of entrants bears a positive impact upon long-term growth, mitigates business cycles fluctuations and reduces average unemployment. See experiments 4.1 and 4.2, Table 7. However, the *ceteris paribus* condition is equally important: the same aggregate growth patterns can be proved to be equally guaranteed by competent cumulative learning of incumbents (see, above, the exercises on search capabilities).

What about competitive conditions? We introduce antitrust policies by forbidding capital-good firms to exceed a given market share (75% in experiment 5.1 and 50% in experiment 5.2, Table 7): the outcome is a lower unemployment rate, smaller business cycle fluctuations and also higher GDP growth (on this point see also Fogel et al., 2008). Note that such a property have little to do with any static "welfare gains"—which our model does not explicitly contemplates—but rather with the multiplicity of producers, and thus of innovative search avenues, which antitrust policies safeguard.[33]

---

[32] On purpose, we did not introduce any feedback between changes in IPR regimes and propensities to search. As discussed in Dosi et al. (2006b), such a link is absent in all historical evidence on the effects of changes in patenting regimes and both investment in R&D and innovative intensity.

[33] The thrust of our results on policies affecting entry, competition, and variety preservation are indeed broadly in tune with the advocacy for "evolutionary technology policies" in Metcalfe (1994b), while it runs against the so-called "Schumpeterian hypothesis" according to which degrees of industrial concentration should be conducive to higher rates of innovation.

G. Dosi et al. / Journal of Economic Dynamics & Control 34 (2010) 1748–1767   1763

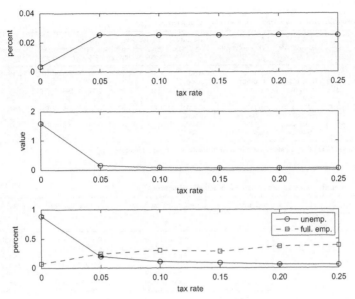

Fig. 7. Fiscal policy experiments. First panel: average output growth rate. Second panel: bandpass-filtered output standard deviation. Third panel: average unemployment rate (unemp.) and full-employment frequency (full emp.). In such policy experiments, the unemployment subsidy rate (φ) is four times the tax rate.

4.2. The Keynesian engine, or is Schumpeter enough?

So far we have explored the effects of different means of "Schumpeterian" policies and organizational setups over the long term (i.e. over the rate of growth of the economy) and on unemployment rates and output volatilities. We did find significant effects both on the long and short terms. However, to repeat, such results are conditional on a "Keynesian machine" well in place. What happens if we switch that off? Remarkably, the system dramatically slows down in terms of rates of growth, unemployment shoots up to utterly unrealistic levels and volatility increases. Note that it does so even if we consider a regime with simultaneously "high opportunities" and "high search capabilities" (experiment 6, Table 7). So for example, for the *same richness of innovative opportunities*, the long-term rate of growth falls to around a third (compare experiments 6 and 1.2).

Let us further explore the role of fiscal policies over both the short- and long-term properties of the economy. Consider the experiments presented in Table 8. We begin with eschewing the public sector from the economy by setting both tax rate and unemployment benefits to zero while keeping the benchmark Schumpeterian characteristics in place. In such a scenario, the economy experiments wilder fluctuations and higher unemployment rates in the short-run, but also an output growth in the long-run not far from nil. Countercyclical Keynesian policies, as in the common wisdom, act indeed like a parachute during recessions, sustaining consumption and, indirectly, investment on the demand side. However, they also bear *long-term effects* on the supply side: in particular on the rates of growth of productivity and output. Such a vicious feedback loop goes from low output to low investment in R&D, low rates of innovation (cf. Eq. (3)) similar to that pointed out by Stiglitz (1994).[34] In fact, in the latter as well as in our model, the system may be "trapped" into a low growth trajectories which cannot be unlocked from by a "Schumpeterian jumpstart". Indeed, as we have seen above (experiment 6, Table 7) Schumpeterian policies alone are not able to sustain high growth patterns and, even less so, mild business cycle fluctuations and low unemployment.

Let us then allow for Keynesian demand macro-management policies and repeatedly increase both the tax and the unemployment benefit rates. Tuning up fiscal demand management does delock the economy from the "bad" trajectory

---

[34] On the negative links between macroeconomic volatility, R&D investment, and long-run economic growth in presence of financial market imperfections, see also Aghion et al. (2008, 2010).

Table 9
Robustness of simulation results to alternative labor-market institutional regimes.

Parameters			Avg. GDP growth rate	Avg. unemployment	GDP std. dev. (bpf)	Rel. std. dev.		Cons. Corr.			Net Inv. Corr.		
ψ_1	ψ_2	ψ_3				Cons.	Inv.	$t-1$	t	$t+1$	$t-1$	t	$t+1$
1	0	0	0.0252 (0.0002)	0.1072 (0.0050)	0.0809 (0.0007)	0.84	5.79	0.76	0.95	0.92	0.40	0.51	0.50
1	0.75	0	0.0249 (0.0002)	0.1167 (0.0059)	0.0766 (0.0063)	0.82	6.83	0.79	0.96	0.91	0.49	0.57	0.52
1	0	−0.90	0.0251 (0.0002)	0.1207 (0.0049)	0.0761 (0.0062)	0.81	6.57	0.80	0.96	0.91	0.54	0.61	0.54
1	0.75	−0.90	0.0246 (0.0002)	0.1155 (0.0056)	0.0743 (0.0061)	0.82	5.87	0.80	0.96	0.91	0.53	0.62	0.56

Bpf: bandpass-filtered (6,32,12) series. Monte-Carlo simulations standard errors in parentheses.

Table 10
Robustness of policy experiments to alternative labor-market institutional regimes.

Parameters			Experiment	Avg. GDP growth rate	GDP std. dev. (bpf)	Avg. unemployment
ψ_1	ψ_2	ψ_3				
1	0.75	0	1.1	0.0198 (0.0002)	0.0776 (0.0062)	0.1384 (0.0051)
			1.2	0.0319 (0.0002)	0.0769 (0.0065)	0.0847 (0.0053)
			3.1	0.0250 (0.0002)	0.0729 (0.0064)	0.1051 (0.0060)
			3.3	0.0164 (0.0002)	0.0592 (0.0019)	0.1374 (0.0072)
			6	0.0033 (0.0014)	1.2743 (0.0285)	0.8836 (0.0222)
			$tax = 0,\ \phi = 0$	−0.0008 (0.0009)	1.2694 (0.0244)	0.9495 (0.0153)
			$tax = 0.2,\ \phi = 0.8$	0.0253 (0.0002)	0.0561 (0.0046)	0.0599 (0.0029)
1	0	−0.9	1.1	0.0196 (0.0002)	0.0743 (0.0059)	0.1341 (0.0050)
			1.2	0.0313 (0.0002)	0.0737 (0.0062)	0.0987 (0.0063)
			3.1	0.0252 (0.0002)	0.0627 (0.0053)	0.1025 (0.0062)
			3.3	0.0165 (0.0002)	0.0627 (0.0053)	0.1260 (0.0072)
			6	0.0134 (0.0018)	1.6084 (0.0899)	0.7627 (0.0254)
			$tax = 0,\ \phi = 0$	0.0032 (0.0012)	1.5863 (0.0890)	0.8857 (0.0197)
			$tax = 0.2,\ \phi = 0.8$	0.0249 (0.0002)	0.0547 (0.0046)	0.0673 (0.0030)
1	0.75	−0.9	1.1	0.0193 (0.0002)	0.0740 (0.0059)	0.1454 (0.0062)
			1.2	0.0312 (0.0002)	0.0742 (0.0063)	0.0993 (0.0053)
			3.1	0.0251 (0.0002)	0.0638 (0.0053)	0.1100 (0.0062)
			3.3	0.0165 (0.0002)	0.0593 (0.0047)	0.1366 (0.0071)
			6	0.0050 (0.0016)	1.2703 (0.0561)	0.8760 (0.0265)
			$tax = 0,\ \phi = 0$	0.0001 (0.0010)	1.2236 (0.0292)	0.9322 (0.0197)
			$tax = 0.2,\ \phi = 0.8$	0.0246 (0.0002)	0.0539 (0.0047)	0.0631 (0.0031)

Bpf: bandpass-filtered (6,32,12) series. Monte-Carlo simulations standard errors in parentheses.

and brings it to the "good" (high growth) one, which also our benchmark scenario happens to belong (cf. Table 8 and Fig. 7). If one further increases the size of fiscal measures, average output growth rates do not change as compared to the benchmark scenario, but output volatility and unemployment significantly fall, and the economy spends more time in full employment (cf. again Table 8 and Fig. 7).[35]

Finally, we check the robustness of Keynesian properties of the system to alternative institutional regimes governing the labor market captured by the parameters affecting the wage rate (cf. Eq. (14)). In particular, we allow wages to move as a (negative) function of the unemployment rate. Under these "classical" circumstances, wages may fall during recessions, inducing price cuts, which in turn may increase output, supposedly weakening the case for Keynesian fiscal policies. In fact, the simulation exercises presented in Table 9 suggest that, other things being equal, the dynamics of the systems are largely independent of how wages are determined. Moreover, the impact of different policy measures—including fiscal policies—does not seem to substantially change under different labor-market institutional regimes (cf. Table 10). This supports both our previous results about the importance of the "Keynesian engine" as a necessary ingredient of sustained

---

[35] On the long-run growth-enhancing effects of countercyclical macroeconomic policies, see the empirical evidence provided by Aghion and Marinescu (2007).

G. Dosi et al. / Journal of Economic Dynamics & Control 34 (2010) 1748–1767 1765

long-run growth and Keynes (1936) own insights about the irrelevance at best of wage cuts in order to reduce unemployment.

5. Concluding remarks

In this work we have studied the properties of an agent-based model that robustly reproduces a wide ensemble of macro-stylized facts and distributions of micro characteristics.

The model entails the explicit account of search and investment decisions by populations of firms that are heterogeneous in the technologies which they master and, possibly, in their decision rules. Aggregate macro properties are emergent from the thread of interactions among economic agents, without any ex ante consistency requirements amongst their expectations and their actions. In that sense, the model may be considered an exercise in *general disequilibrium analysis*. Firms in the model endogenously generate new technologies—embodied in new types of "machines"—via expensive and mistake-ridden processes of search. Inventions then diffuse via the adoption decisions of machine users. Hence, agents generate micro technological shocks and, together, micro demand shocks which propagate through the economy.

In this respect, an important feature of the model is that it bridges Schumpeterian theories of technology-driven economic growth with Keynesian theories of demand generation.

A central question that we address in the work is whether the "Schumpeterian engine" by itself is able to maintain the economy on a high-growth/near full-employment path. Broadly speaking, the answer is negative. Such an endogenous innovation engine is able to do that only in the presence of a "Keynesian" demand-generating engine, which in the present model takes the form of public fiscal policies.

Our results also throw deep doubts on the traditional dichotomy between variables impacting the long-run (typically, technology-related changes) and variables with a short-term effect (traditional demand-related variables). On the contrary, technological innovations appear to exert their effects at all frequencies. Conversely, Keynesian demand-management policies do not only contribute to reduce output volatility and unemployment rates, but also for a large parameter region, they affect also long-run growth rates insofar as they contribute to "delock" the economy from the stagnant growth trajectory which is indeed one of the possible emergent meta-stable states.

The model appears to be a quite broad and flexible platform apt to perform a long list of experiments, few of which have been presented above, studying the outcomes of different policies and different institutional setups. An obvious direction of development ought to address an explicit account of credit and financial markets (a somewhat germane attempt in this direction is in Delli Gatti et al., 2005, broadly along Stiglitzian lines). This is also a natural step in order to also analyze the real impact of monetary policies.

Another line of inquiry involves the comparison between alternative institutional specifications of the ways technologies are accessed and the ways markets work, somewhat along the lines of the "variety of capitalism" approach (Soskice and Hall, 2001). More generally, we view this as an example of a broader research program whereby explicit behavioral microfoundations nest the exploration of the relations between innovative dynamics, demand generation, and policies affecting both.

Finally, one could think to extend the model specification in order to take on board the possibility that agents respond to the state of the system by endogenously adapting their behavioral rules. In fact, as it happens in the majority of ABMs, agents in our model employ behavioral rules that remain fixed throughout the observed econometric sample size, in terms of both their parameters and functional specification. For example, adaptation of rules may be introduced in the model by endogeneizing some parameters currently governing agents behaviors and make them sensible to macroeconomic variables and the institutional framework. This may allow one to study the effectiveness of policy measures in the presence of agents that actively respond to their introduction and tuning.

Acknowledgments

Thanks to Bruno Amable, Mario Cimoli, Herbert Dawid, Andrea Ginzburg, Paola Giuri, Jean-Olivier Herault, Eckhard Hein, David Lane, Stan Metcalfe, Andreas Pyka, Pier Paolo Saviotti, Bob Solow, Bart Verspagen, and an anonymous referee for their comments and suggestions. Thanks also to the participants to the 12th International Joseph A. Schumpeter Society conference, Rio de Janeiro, Brazil; the 14th International Conference on Computing in Economics and Finance, Paris, France; the 12th conference of the Research Network Macroeconomics and Macroeconomic Policies on "Macroeconomic Policies on Shaky Foundations—Whither Mainstream Economics?", Berlin, Germany; the "Economics of Innovative Change" summer school organized by the Max Planck Institute and the Friedrich Schiller University, Jena, Germany; the "Agent-Based Models in Economic Policy Advice" workshop in Mannheim, Germany; and the seminars held at Oxford University, and Paris I, France. Previous versions of the paper have also benefited from comments received during the 5th International Globelics conference, Saratov, Russia; "The Economics of Technology Policy" conference at Monte Verità, Ascona, Switzerland; the 5th International EMAEE conference, Manchester, U.K.; the Brisbane Club Meeting, Pollenzo, Italy; and the "Institutional and Social Dynamics of Growth and Distribution" conference, Lucca, Italy. The research that has led to this work has been supported by the EU FP6 STREP Project "CO3 Common Complex Collective Phenomena in Statistical

1766   *G. Dosi et al. / Journal of Economic Dynamics & Control 34 (2010) 1748–1767*

Mechanics, Society, Economics, and Biology" and by the European Union NoE DIME. G.D. and G.F. gratefully acknowledge financial support from PRIN Projects (Italian Ministry of University). All usual disclaimers apply.

References

Acemoglu, D., Aghion, P., Zilibotti, F., 2006. Distance to frontier, selection, and economic growth. Journal of the European Economic Association 4, 37–74.

Aghion, P., Angeletos, M., Banerjee, A., Manova, K., 2010. Volatility and growth: credit constraints and the composition of investment. Journal of Monetary Economics 57, 246–265.

Aghion, P., Askenazy, P., Berman, N., Cette, G., Eymard, L., 2008. Credit constraints and the cyclicality of r&d investment: evidence from France. Working Paper 2008-26, Paris School of Economics.

Aghion, P., Howitt, P., 1992. A model of growth through creative destruction. Econometrica 60, 323–351.

Aghion, P., Howitt, P., 1998. Endogenous Growth. MIT Press, Cambridge.

Aghion, P., Howitt, P., 2007. Appropriate growth policy: a unifying framework. Journal of the European Economic Association 4, 269–314.

Aghion, P., Marinescu, I., 2007. Cyclical budgetary policy and economic growth: What do we learn from oecd panel data? NBER Macroeconomics Annual 2007, vol. 22; 2007, pp. 251–278.

Akerlof, G.A., 2002. Behavioral macroeconomics and macroeconomic behavior. American Economic Review 92, 411–433.

Akerlof, G.A., 2007. The missing motivation in macroeconomics. American Economic Review 97, 5–36.

Akerlof, G.A., Yellen, J.L., 1985. A near-rational model of the business cycles, with wage and price inertia. Quarterly Journal of Economics 100, 823–838.

Bartelsman, E., Doms, M., 2000. Understanding productivity: lessons from longitudinal microdata. Journal of Economic Literature 38, 569–594.

Bartelsman, E., Scarpetta, S., Schivardi, F., 2005. Comparative analysis of firm demographics and survival: evidence from micro-level sources in oecd countries. Industrial and Corporate Change 14, 365–391.

Baxter, M., King, R., 1999. Measuring business cycle: approximate band-pass filter for economic time series. The Review of Economics and Statistics 81, 575–593.

Benhabib, J., Spiegel, M., 1994. The role of human capital in economic development: evidence from aggregate cross-country data. Journal of Monetary Economics 34, 143–173.

Blanchard, O., 2009. The state of macro. Annual Review of Economics 1, 209–228.

Bottazzi, G., Secchi, A., 2003. Common properties and sectoral specificities in the dynamics of U.S. manufacturing firms. Review of Industrial Organization 23, 217–232.

Bottazzi, G., Secchi, A., 2006. Explaining the distribution of firm growth rates. RAND Journal of Economics 37, 235–256.

Caballero, R.J., 1999. Aggregate investment. In: Taylor, J., Woodford, M. (Eds.), Handbook of Macroeconomics. Elsevier Science, Amsterdam.

Canova, F., 2008. How much structure in empirical models? In: Mills, T., Patterson, K. (Eds.), Palgrave Handbook of Econometrics, vol. 2. Applied Econometrics. Palgrave Macmillan.

Castaldi, C., Dosi, G., 2009. The patterns of output growth of firms and countries: scale invariances and scale specificities. Empirical Economics 37, 475–495.

Caves, R., 1998. Industrial organization and new findings on the turnover and mobility of firms. Journal of Economic Literature 36, 1947–1982.

Ciarli, T., Lorentz, A., Savona, M., Valente, M., 2008. Structural change of production and consumption: a micro to macro approach to economic growth and income distribution. LEM Papers Series 2008/08, Laboratory of Economics and Management (LEM), Sant'Anna School of Advanced Studies, Pisa, Italy.

Colander, D. (Ed.), 2006. Post Walrasian Macroeconomics. Cambridge University Press, Cambridge.

Colander, D., Howitt, P., Kirman, A.P., Leijonhufvud, A., Mehrling, P., 2008. Beyond dsge models: toward an empirically based macroeconomics. American Economic Review 98, 236–240.

Dawid, H., 2006. Agent-based models of innovation and technological change. In: Tesfatsion, L., Judd, K. (Eds.), Handbook of Computational Economics II. North-Holland, Amsterdam.

Dawid, H., Gemkow, S., Harting, P., Kabus, K., Neugart, M., Wersching, K., 2008. Skills, innovation, and growth: an agent-based policy analysis. Journal of Economics and Statistics 228, 251–275.

Deissenberg, C., van der Hoog, S., Dawid, H., 2008. Eurace: a massively parallel agent-based model of the European economy. Applied Mathematics and Computation 204, 541–552.

Del Boca, A., Galeotti, M., Himmelberg, C.P., Rota, P., 2008. Investment and time to plan and build: a comparison of structures vs. equipment in a panel of Italian firms. Journal of the European Economic Association 6, 864–889.

Delli Gatti, D., Di Guilmi, C., Gaffeo, E., Giulioni, G., Gallegati, M., Palestrini, A., 2005. A new approach to business fluctuations: heterogeneous interacting agents, scaling laws and financial fragility. Journal of Economic Behavior and Organization 56, 489–512.

Dinopoulos, E., Segerstrom, P., 1999. A schumpeterian model of protection and relative wages. American Economic Review 89, 450–472.

Doms, M., Dunne, T., 1998. Capital adjustment patterns in manufacturing plants. Review Economic Dynamics 1, 409–429.

Dosi, G., 1988. Sources, procedures and microeconomic effects of innovation. Journal of Economic Literature 26, 126–171.

Dosi, G., 2007. Statistical regularities in the evolution of industries. A guide through some evidence and challenges for the theory. In: Malerba, F., Brusoni, S. (Eds.), Perspectives on Innovation. Cambridge University Press, Cambridge, MA.

Dosi, G., Fabiani, S., Aversi, R., Meacci, M., 1994. The dynamics of international differentiation: a multi-country evolutionary model. Industrial and Corporate Change 3, 225–242.

Dosi, G., Fagiolo, G., Roventini, A., 2006a. An evolutionary model of endogenous business cycles. Computational Economics 27, 3–34.

Dosi, G., Marengo, L., Pasquali, C., 2006b. How much should society fuel the greed of innovators? On the relations between appropriability, opportunities and rates of innovation. Research Policy 35, 1110–1121.

Dosi, G., Fagiolo, G., Roventini, A., 2008. The microfoundations of business cycles: an evolutionary, multi-agent model. Journal of Evolutionary Economics 18, 413–432.

Dosi, G., Marsili, O., Orsenigo, L., Salvatore, R., 1995. Learning, market selection and the evolution of industrial structures. Small Business Economics 7, 411–436.

Eisner, R., 1972. Components of capital expenditures: replacement and modernization versus expansion. The Review of Economics and Statistics 54, 297–305.

Fabiani, S., Druant, M., Hernando, I., Kwapil, C., Landau, B., Loupias, C., Martins, F., Mathä, T., Sabbatini, R., Stahl, H., Stokman, A., 2006. What firms' surveys tell us about price-setting behavior in the euro area. International Journal of Central Banking 2, 3–47.

Fagiolo, G., Dosi, G., 2003. Exploitation, exploration and innovation in a model of endogenous growth with locally interacting agents. Structural Change and Economic Dynamics 14, 237–273.

Fagiolo, G., Dosi, G., Gabriele, R., 2004. Matching, bargaining, and wage setting in an evolutionary model of labor market and output dynamics. Advances in Complex Systems 14, 237–273.

Fagiolo, G., Moneta, A., Windrum, P., 2007. A critical guide to empirical validation of agent-based models in economics: methodologies, procedures, and open problems. Computational Economics 30, 195–226.

Fagiolo, G., Napoletano, M., Roventini, A., 2008. Are output growth-rate distributions fat-tailed? Some evidence from oecd countries. Journal of Applied Econometrics 23, 639–669.

Fagiolo, G., Roventini, A. On the scientific status of economic policy: a tale of alternative paradigms. Knowledge Engineering Review, forthcoming.

Farrel, J., Shapiro, C., 1988. Dynamic competition with switching costs. RAND Journal of Economics 19, 123–137.

G. Dosi et al. / Journal of Economic Dynamics & Control 34 (2010) 1748–1767

Feldstein, M., Foot, D., 1971. The other half of gross investment: replacement and modernization expenditures. The Review of Economics and Statistics 53, 49–58.

Fogel, K., Morck, R., Yeung, B., 2008. Big business stability and economic growth: Is what's good for General Motors good for America? Journal of Financial Economics 89, 83–108.

Fukac, M., Pagan, A., 2006. Issues in adopting dsge models for use in the policy process. Working Paper 10/2006, CAMA.

Galí, J., Gertler, M., 2007. Macroeconomic modelling for monetary policy evaluation. Journal of Economic Perspectives 21, 25–46.

Goolsbee, A., 1998. The business cycle, financial performance, and the retirement of capital goods. Review of Economic Dynamics 1, 474–496.

Gourio, F., Kashyap, A.K., 2007. Investment spikes: new facts and a general equilibrium exploration. Journal of Monetary Economics 54, 1–22.

Greenwald, B., Stiglitz, J., 1993a. Financial market imperfections and business cycles. Quarterly Journal of Economics 108, 77–114.

Greenwald, B., Stiglitz, J., 1993b. New and old Keynesians. Journal of Economic Perspectives 7, 23–44.

Greenwald, B., Stiglitz, J., 2003. Macroeconomic fluctuations in an economy of phelps-winter markets. In: Aghion, P., Frydman, R., Stiglitz, J., Woodford, M. (Eds.), Knowledge, Information, and Expectations in Modern Macroeconomics: In Honor of Edmund S. Phelps. Princeton University Press, Princeton, NJ.

Hicks, J.R., 1937. Mr. Keynes and the "Classics": a suggested interpretation. Econometrica 5, 147–159.

Hubbard, G.R., 1998. Capital-market imperfections and investment. Journal of Economic Literature 36, 193–225.

Keynes, J.M., 1936. The General Theory of Employment, Interest, and Money. Prometheus Books, New York.

Kirman, A.P., 1992. Whom or what does the representative individual represent? Journal of Economic Perspectives 6, 117–136

Klemperer, P.D., 1987. Markets with customer switching costs. Quarterly Journal of Economics 102, 375–394.

Klemperer, P.D., 1995. Competition when consumers have switching costs: an overview with applications to industrial organization, macroeconomics and international trade. Review of Economic Studies 62, 515–539.

Klevorick, A.K., Levin, R., Nelson, R.R., Winter, S.G., 1995. On the sources and significance of interindustry differences in technological opportunities. Research Policy 24, 185–205.

Lane, D.A., 1993. Artificial worlds and economics, part i and ii. Journal of Evolutionary Economics 3 89–107 and 177–197.

LeBaron, B., Tesfatsion, L., 2008. Modeling macroeconomies as open-ended dynamic systems of interacting agents. American Economic Review 98, 246–250.

Louca, F., 2001. Intriguing pendula: founding metaphors in the analysis of economic fluctuations. Cambridge Journal of Economics 25, 25–55.

Malerba, F., Orsenigo, L., 1995. Schumpeterian patterns of innovation. Cambridge Journal of Economics 19, 47–65.

Metcalfe, J.S., 1994a. Competition, fisher's principle and increasing returns to selection. Journal of Evolutionary Economics 4 (327–346).

Metcalfe, J.S., 1994b. Evolutionary economics and technology policy. The Economic Journal 104, 932–944.

Napoletano, M., Roventini, A., Sapio, S., 2006. Are business cycles all alike? A bandpass filter analysis of the Italian and us cycles. Rivista Italiana degli Economisti 1, 87–118.

Nelson, R.R., Phelps, E.S., 1966. Investment in humans, technological diffusion, and economic growth. American Economic Review 61, 69–75.

Nelson, R.R., Winter, S.G., 1982. An Evolutionary Theory of Economic Change. The Belknap Press of Harvard University Press, Cambridge.

Neugart, M., 2008. Labor market policy evaluation with ace. Journal of Economic Behavior and Organization 67, 418–430.

Pavitt, K., 1984. Sectoral patterns of technical change: towards a taxonomy and a theory. Research Policy 13, 343–373.

Phelps, E.S., Winter, S.G., 1970. Optimal price policy under atomistic competition. In: Phelps, E.S. (Ed.), Microeconomic Foundations of Employment and Inflation Theory. Nortonm, New York.

Pyka, A., Fagiolo, G., 2007. Agent-based modelling: a methodology for neo-schumpeterian economics. In: Hanusch, H., Pyka, A. (Eds.), The Elgar Companion to Neo-Schumpeterian Economics. Edward Elgar Publishers, Cheltenham.

Romer, P., 1990. Endogenous technical change. Journal of Political Economy 98, 71–102.

Rotemberg, J., 2008. Behavioral aspects of price setting, and their policy implications. Working Paper 13754, NBER.

Rotemberg, J., Woodford, M., 1999. The cyclical behavior of prices and costs. In: Taylor, J., Woodford, M. (Eds.), Handbook of Macroeconomics. Elsevier Science, Amsterdam.

Saviotti, P., Pyka, A., 2008. Product variety, competition and economic growth. Journal of Evolutionary Economics 18, 323–347.

Silverberg, G., Dosi, G., Orsenigo, L., 1988. Innovation, diversity and diffusion: a self-organization model. The Economic Journal 98, 1032–1054.

Silverberg, G., Verspagen, B., 2005. Evolutionary theorizing on economic growth. In: Dopfer, K. (Ed.), Evolutionary Principles of Economics. Cambridge University Press, Cambridge.

Solow, R.M., 1956. A contribution to the theory of economic growth. Quarterly Journal of Economics 70, 65–94.

Solow, R.M., 2008. The state of macroeconomics. Journal of Economic Perspectives 22, 243–246.

Soskice, D., Hall, P. (Eds.), 2001. Varieties of Capitalism: the Institutional Foundations of Comparative Advantage. Oxford University Press, Oxford.

Stiglitz, J., 1994. Endogenous growth and cycles. In: Shionoya, Y., Perlman, M. (Eds.), Innovation in Technology, Industries, and Institutions. Studies in Schumpeterian Perspectives. Ann Arbor, The University of Michigan Press.

Stiglitz, J., Weiss, A., 1992. Credit rationing in markets with imperfect information. American Economic Review 71, 393–410.

Stock, J., Watson, M., 1999. Business cycle fluctuations in U.S. macroeconomic time series. In: Taylor, J., Woodford, M. (Eds.), Handbook of Macroeconomics. Elsevier Science, Amsterdam.

Tesfatsion, L., 2000. Structure, behavior, and market power in an evolutionary labor market with adaptive search. Journal of Economic Dynamics & Control 25, 419–457.

Tesfatsion, L., Judd, K. (Eds.), 2006. Handbook of Computational Economics II: Agent-Based Computational Economics. North-Holland, Amsterdam.

Verspagen, B., 2002. Evolutionary macroeconomics: a synthesis between neo-schumpeterian and post-keynesian lines of thought. The Electronic Journal of Evolutionary Modeling and Economic Dynamics 1007 〈http://www.e-jemed.org/1007/index.php〉.

Woodford, M., 2003. Interest and Prices: Foundations of a Theory of Monetary Policy. Princeton University Press, Princeton, NJ.